State
and
Metropolitan Area
Data Book
2017

State
and
Metropolitan Area
Data Book
2017

SECOND EDITION

Edited by Deirdre A. Gaquin
and Mary Meghan Ryan

Lanham, MD

Published by Bernan Press
An imprint of
The Rowman & Littlefield Publishing Group, Inc.
4501 Forbes Boulevard, Lanham, MD 20706
www.rowman.com
800-462-6420

ISBN: 978-1-59888-920-8
e-ISBN: 978-1-59888-921-5

Manufactured in the United States of America.

CONTENTS

Preface ix

Guide to Tabular Presentation xi

Major Federal Data Contacts xiii

PART A—STATES 1

A-1   Area and Population 3
A-2   Population, by Age Group and Sex 4
A-3   Population, by Race and Hispanic Origin 6
A-4   Population by Residence 9
A-5   Households 10
A-6   Marital Status, 2015 11
A-7   Residence One Year Ago, People Obtaining Legal Permanent Resident Status,
       and Language Spoken at Home, Selected Years 12
A-8   Place of Birth, 2015 13
A-9   Live Births and Birth Rates 14
A-10   Births and Birth Rates, by Race and Hispanic Origin and Fertility Rate, 2015 15
A-11   Deaths and Death Rates, by Race and Hispanic Origin 16
A-12   Age-Adjusted Death Rates, by Cause, 2015 18
A-13   Marriages and Divorces 19
A-14   Health Care Services, Physicians, and Nurses 20
A-15   Employment in Health Care Occupations and Type of Health Insurance 21
A-16   Health Indicators: Health Risks 23
A-17   Health Indicators: Health Conditions and Preventive Measures 24
A-18   People With and Without Health Insurance Coverage 25
A-19   Public and Private School Fall Enrollment 26
A-20   Public Elementary and Secondary Schools—Finances and Teachers 27
A-21   Public High School Graduates and Educational Attainment 28
A-22   Institutions of Higher Education 29
A-23   Violent Crimes and Crime Rates 30
A-24   Property Crimes and Crime Rates 31
A-25   Juvenile Arrests, Child Abuse Cases, and Correctional Population 32
A-26   State and Local Justice Employment and Expenditures, 2012 33
A-27   Civilian Labor Force and Employment 34
A-28   Civilian Labor Force and Unemployment 35
A-29   Employed Civilians, by Occupation, May 2016 36
A-30   Private Industry Employment and Wages, 2015 38
A-31   Average Annual Employment by Industry and Wages 39
A-32   Union Membership 42
A-33   Median Income of Households in 2015 Inflation-Adjusted Dollars and Distribution
       by Income Level 43

A-34   Family Income and Families and Individuals Below Poverty, 2015 44
A-35   Housing—Units and Characteristics, 2015 45
A-36   Owner- and Renter-Occupied Units—Value and Gross Rent, 2015 46
A-37   Home Ownership and Vacancy Rates 47
A-38   Cost of Living Indicators—Housing, Public University, Energy Expenditures,
        and Motor Fuels Taxes..48
A-39   Personal Income by State 50
A-40   Personal Income per Capita 52
A-41   Earnings by Industry, 2015.......................................54
A-42   Gross Domestic Product per State 56
A-43   Science and Engineering Indicators...................................57
A-44   Employment Establishment Changes by Firm Size and State, 2010–2011 58
A-45   Employer Firms and Nonemployer Establishments 59
A-46   Private Nonfarm Establishments, Employment, and Payroll 60
A-47   Foreign Direct Investment in the United States and U.S. Exports....................61
A-48   Farms and Farm Earnings 62
A-49   Farm Finances and Income 63
A-50   Farm Income and Wealth Statistics 64
A-51   Natural Resource Industries and Minerals 65
A-52   Agricultural Census 66
A-53   Utilities 68
A-54   Energy Consumption 69
A-55   Energy Expenditures 70
A-56   Construction 71
A-57   Manufactures 72
A-58   Manufactures Summary and Export-Related Shipments and Employment.................73
A-59   Major Manufacturing Sectors, 2015 74
A-60   Information Industries...76
A-61   Wholesale and Retail Trade 77
A-62   Retail Trade Earnings, 2015.......................................78
A-63   Transportation and Commuting 80
A-64   Motor Vehicle and Motorcycle Registrations, Bridges, and Drivers Licenses 81
A-65   Traffic Fatalities and Seat Belt Use 82
A-66   Communications..83
A-67   Financial Activities..84
A-68   Professional and Business Services and Education and Health Services 85
A-69   Leisure and Hospitality Services 86
A-70   Travel and Tourism Indicators 87
A-71   Government 88
A-72   State Government Employment and Finances..............................89
A-73   State Government Tax Collections, 2015 90
A-74   Federal Government 91
A-75   Federal Individual Income Tax Returns and Federal Real Estate 92
A-76   Social Security, Food Stamps, and School Lunch Programs 93
A-77   Social Insurance Programs and Workers' Compensation 94
A-78   Government Transfer Payments to Individuals 95
A-79   Medicare, Medicaid, and Children's Health Insurance Program 96
A-80   Department of Defense and Veterans 97
A-81   Elections 98
A-82   Composition of Congress and Public Officials 100

PART B—METROPOLITAN AREAS **101**

B-1   Area and Population 103
B-2   Components of Population Change 110
B-3   Population by Age, Race, and Hispanic Origin. 117
B-4   Migration and Commuting, 2015 124
B-5   Population and Household Characteristics 2015 131
B-6   Enrollment, Teachers, and Educational Attainment 138
B-7   Median Income, Household Income Distribution, and Poverty Status, 2015 144
B-8   Health Insurance, Medicare, Social Security and Supplemental Security Income 150
B-9   Housing Units and Building Permits 157
B-10 Housing Units, 2015 163
B-11 Personal Income and Earnings by Place of Work. 169
B-12 Employees and Earnings by Selected Major Industries, 2015. 175
B-13 Civilian Labor Force 181
B-14 Banking, Government Employment, and Private Business Establishments and Employment . . . 187

PART C—METROPOLITAN AREAS WITH COMPONENT COUNTIES (METROPOLITAN COUNTIES) **193**

C-1   Population and Population Characteristics 195
C-2   Population Characteristics and Housing Units. 216
C-3   Personal Income and Earnings by Industry 237
C-4   Labor Force and Private Business Establishments and Employment 260

PART D—MICROPOLITAN AREAS **281**

D-1   Population and Personal Income 283

APPENDIXES **299**

A   Source Notes and Explanations 301
B   Limitations of the Data and Methodology 371
C   Geographic Concepts 383
D   Guide to State Statistical Abstracts and State Information 437

INDEX **445**

PREFACE

This is the second edition of the *State and Metropolitan Area Data Book* (SMADB) produced by Bernan Press. The U.S. Census Bureau terminated its Statistical Compendia program in 2011. The Statistical Compendia program included the *Statistical Abstract of the United States* and its supplemental local area products—the *State and Metropolitan Area Data Book* and the *County and City Data Book* (CCDB). The Census Bureau published seven editions of SMADB, periodically since 1979, and 14 editions of CCDB, periodically since 1944. Since 1992, Bernan Press has produced 24 editions of *County and City Extra*, a comprehensive volume that combines some of the features of both SMADB and CCDB, and six editions of *Places, Towns, and Townships,* a companion volume with details about cities and towns not included in either CCDB or *County and City Extra.* Bernan continues to publish annual editions of *County and City Extra* that include most of the content of the former CCDB, plus many additional features. *County and City Extra* includes sections of state and metropolitan area data, but the *State and Metropolitan Area Data Book* includes a wider selection of state data, a table of data for micropolitan areas, and several tables that include the component counties of the metropolitan and micropolitan areas.

The SMADB is a convenient summary of statistics on the social and economic structure of the states, metropolitan areas, and micropolitan areas in the United States. It is designed to serve as a statistical reference and guide to other data publications and sources. The latter function is served by the source citations in Appendix A, "Source Notes and Explanations." This volume includes data from a variety of statistical publications and electronic sources, including nonprofit organizations, private businesses, as well as the majority of the federal statistical agencies. Publications and Internet sites listed as sources usually contain additional detail and more comprehensive discussions of definitions and concepts than can be presented here. Data not available in printed publications issued by the contributing agency but obtained from websites are identified in the source notes. More information on the subjects covered in this publication is generally made available by its source, including additional methodological information about how the data are collected or produced.

Changes in this edition

All data have been updated to the most recent available year. All population and housing data have been updated based on the 2010 census. Detailed social and economic characteristics have been updated and expanded using the 1-year estimates from the American Community Survey, including information on health insurance, household type, migration, and commuting.

The results of the 2016 presidential election are included.

States. Data are presented for the United States, the 50 states, and the District of Columbia. There are 1,362 data items presented for these areas in Tables A-1 through A-82. The states and the District of Columbia are presented in alphabetical order under the U.S. total.

Metropolitan areas and metropolitan divisions. Data are presented for the 382 metropolitan areas and 31 metropolitan divisions defined as of July 2015. There are 162 data items presented for these areas in Tables B-1 through B-14.

Metropolitan areas and metropolitan divisions with their component counties. Data are presented for 50 data items in Tables C-1 through C-4. The 1167 counties and county equivalents are presented under their respective metropolitan area or metropolitan division.

Micropolitan areas with their component counties. Table D-1 includes 12 data items for 551 micropolitan areas and their 658 component counties.

Appendixes. Appendix A provides information on source notes and explanations for the data items in Tables A through D. Appendix B presents a brief introduction to central concepts of statistics and provides the methodological approach of principal sources. Appendix C presents a discussion of the geographic concepts relevant to this volume, as well as the current definitions for metropolitan areas. Appendix D offers a bibliography of the latest state specific abstracts published since 1999. For additional information on data presented, please consult the source publications available in local libraries, write to the agency indicated in the source notes, or visit the Internet site listed.

Statistics for the nation. Extensive data at the national level can be found in the *ProQuest Statistical Abstract of the United States 2017,* co-published with Bernan Press.

Statistics for counties and cities. Data for counties and cities may be found in Bernan's annual *County and City Extra*—the 25th edition is scheduled to publish in the fall—and *Places, Towns, and Townships* most recently published in 2016.

GUIDE TO TABULAR PRESENTATION

Example of Table Structure:

Table A-20.   Public Elementary and Secondary Schools—Finances and Teachers

Geographic area	Total enrollment 2013–2014 (thousands)[1]	Revenues, 2013–2014 (millions of dollars)			
		Total	Source		
			Local	State	Federal
United States.............................	50,017	623,209	280,507	288,196	54,505
Alabama......................................	746	7,397	2,493	4,066	839
Alaska	131	2,677	530	1,836	312
Arizona.......................................	1,102	9,594	4,174	4,217	1,204
Arkansas.....................................	490	5,134	1,876	2,665	592
California....................................	6,313	69,343	23,107	39,293	6,943

[1]Enrollment represents the total count of pupils that are enrolled on or about October 1st of the survey year. These data are from the National Public Education Financial Survey.

Unit indicators show the specified quantities in which data items are presented. They are used for two primary reasons. Sometimes data are not available in absolute form. Other times, we round the numbers in order to save space to show more data, as in the case above.

If no unit indicator is shown, data presented are in absolute form (see Table B-1 for an example). When needed, unit indicators are found in the column or spanner headings for the data items as shown above.

Footnotes below the bottom rule of table pages give information relating to specific data items or figures within the table.

Further information on individual tables can be found in Appendix A, located in the back of the book.

Examples of Unit Indicator Interpretation table example:

Geographic area	Year	Item	Unit indicator	Number shown	Multiplier
United States.............................	2013–2014	Total enrollment	(thousands)	50,017	1,000
United States.............................	2013–2014	Revenues	(million dollars)	623,209	1,000,000

To determine the figure, it is necessary to multiply the number shown by the unit indicator.

Total enrollment, 2013–2014 = 50,017 * 1,000 or 50,017,000

Total revenues, 2013–2014 = 623,209 * 1,000,000 or 623,209,000,000

In many tables, details will not add to the totals shown because of rounding.

EXPLANATION OF SYMBOLS AND TERMS

The following symbols, used in the tables throughout this book, are explained in condensed form in footnotes on the tables where they appear.

0   Represents zero or rounds to zero.

D   Figure withheld to avoid disclosure pertaining to a specific individual or organization; or does not meet statistical standards for reliability of derived figure.

NA   Data not available.

X   Figure not applicable because column heading and stub line make entry impossible, absurd, or meaningless.

The following terms are also used throughout this publication:

Averages. An average is a single number or value that is often used to represent the "typical value" of a group of numbers. It is regarded as a measure of "location" or "central tendency" of a group of numbers.

The *arithmetic* mean is the type of average used most frequently. It is derived by summing the individual item values of a particular group and dividing the total by the number of items. The arithmetic mean is often referred to simply as the "mean" or "average."

The *median* of a group of numbers is the middle number or value when each item in the group is arranged according to size (lowest to highest or vice versa); it generally has the same number of items above it as well as below it. If there is an even number of items in the group, the median is taken to be the average of the two middle numbers.

Rates. A rate is a quantity or amount of an item measured in relation to a specified number of units of another item. For example, unemployment rate is the number of unemployed people per 100 people in the civilian labor force. Examples of other rates found in this publication include birth rate, which is the number of births per 1,000 population; infant death rate, the number of infant deaths per 1,000 live births; and crime rate, which is the number of serious offenses per 100,000 population.

A *per capita* figure represents a specific type of rate computed for every person in a specified group (or population). It is derived by taking the total for a data item (such as income, taxes, or retail sales) and dividing it by the number of people in the specified population.

Ranks. Various data items in Tables A—States, and Tables B—Metropolitan Areas, of this publication are ranked from highest to lowest with a rank of 1 representing the highest rank. In both tables, when areas share the same rank, the next-lower rank is omitted.

In Table A, only the 50 states are ranked; the District of Columbia is not included in the state rankings. In Table B, only 366 metropolitan statistical areas (MSAs) are ranked. Not ranked are the 29 metropolitan divisions, which make up 11 metropolitan statistical areas. Areas not ranked are indicated by an "X" in the data cell.

Index numbers. An index number is a measure of difference or change, usually expressed as a percentage, relating one quantity (the variable) of a specified kind to another quantity of the same kind. Index numbers are widely used to express changes in prices over periods of time but may also be used to express differences between related subjects for a single point in time.

To compute a price index, a base year or period is selected. The base year price (of the commodity or service) is then designated as the base or reference price to which the prices for other years or periods are related. Many price indexes use the year 2000 as the base year; in tables, this is shown as "2000 = 100." A method of expressing the price relationship is: the price of a set of one or more items for a related year (e.g., 1990) divided by the price of the same set of items for the base year (e.g., 2000). The result multiplied by 100 provides the index number. When 100 is subtracted from the index number, the result equals the percentage change in price from the base year.

Current and constant dollars. Statistics in some tables are expressed in both current and constant dollars (for example, see Table A-40). Current dollar figures reflect actual prices or costs prevailing during the specified year(s). Constant dollar figures are estimates representing an effort to remove the effects of price changes from statistical series reported in dollar terms. In general, constant dollar series are derived by dividing current dollar estimates by the appropriate price index for the appropriate period (for example, the Consumer Price Index). The result is a series as it would presumably exist if prices were the same throughout, as in the base year; in other words, as if the dollar had constant purchasing power. Any changes in this constant dollar series would reflect only changes in real volume of output, income, expenditures, or other measure.

MAJOR FEDERAL DATA CONTACTS

To help *State and Metropolitan Area Data Book* users find more data and information about statistical publications, we are including this list of contacts for federal agencies with major statistical programs. The intent is to give a single, first-contact point-of-entry for users of statistics. These agencies will provide general information on their statistical programs and publications, as well as specific information on how to order their publications. We are also including the Internet addresses for many of these agencies. These URLs were current in May 2017.

Executive Office of the President

Office of Management and Budget
Administrator
Office of Information and Regulatory Affairs
Office of Management and Budget
725 17th Street, NW
Washington, DC 20503
Information: 202-395-3080
https://www.whitehouse.gov/omb

Department of Agriculture

Economic Research Service
U.S. Department of Agriculture
1400 Independence Ave., SW
Washington, DC 20250
Information: 202-720-2791
https://www.ers.usda.gov/

National Agriculture Statistics Service
USDA-NASS
1400 Independence Ave., SW
Washington, DC 20250
Information: 202-720-2791 or 800-727-9540
https://www.nass.usda.gov/

Department of Commerce

U.S. Census Bureau
Customer Services Branch
U.S. Census Bureau
4600 Silver Hill Road
Washington, DC 20233
Information and publications: 1-800-923-8282
https://www.census.gov/

Department of Commerce—*Continued*

Bureau of Economic Analysis
1441 L Street, NW
Washington DC 20230
Information and publications: 202-606-9900
https://www.bea.gov/

International Trade Administration
1401 Constitution Ave., NW
Washington, DC 20230
Information: 1-800-872-8723
http://trade.gov/

National Oceanic and Atmospheric Administration
National Oceanic and Atmospheric Administration
Central Library
U.S. Department of Commerce
1315 East-West Highway
SSMC3, 2nd Floor
Silver Spring, MD 20910
Library: 301-713-2600 x.0157
https://www.lib.noaa.gov/

Department of Defense

Department of Defense
Office of Public Communication
1400 Defense Pentagon
Washington, DC 20301-1400
Information: 703-571-3343
https://www.defense.gov/

Department of Education

National Library of Education
U.S. Department of Education
400 Maryland Avenue, SW
Washington, DC 20202
Education information and statistics: 1-800-872-5327
Education publications: 1-877-433-7827
https://www.ed.gov/

Department of Energy

Energy Information Administration
National Energy Information Center
1000 Independence Ave., SW
Washington, DC 20585
Information and publications: 202-586-8800
https://www.eia.gov/

Department of Health and Human Services

Health Resources and Services Administration HRSA
Information Center
P.O. Box 2910
Merrifield, VA 22116
Information Center: 1-888-275-4772
http://www.hrsa.gov/

Substance Abuse and Mental Health Services Administration
1 Coke Cherry Road
Rockville, MD 20857
Information: 240-276-2130
Publications: 1-877-726-4727
https://www.samhsa.gov/

Centers for Disease Control and Prevention
Public Inquiries/MASO
1600 Clifton Road
Atlanta, GA 30333
Public inquires: 1-800-232-4636
https://www.cdc.gov/

Centers for Medicare and Medicaid Services (CMS)
U.S. Department of Health and Human Services
7500 Security Boulevard
Baltimore, MD 21244
Information: 1-877-267-2323
https://www.cms.gov/

National Center for Health Statistics
3311 Toledo Road
Hyattsville, MD 20782
Information: 1-800-232-4636
https://www.cdc.gov/nchs/

Department of Homeland Security

Office of Public Affairs
245 Murray Lane, SW
Washington, DC 20528
Information and publications: 202-282-8010
https://www.dhs.gov/

Department of Housing and Urban Development

Office of the Assistant Secretary for Community Planning and Development
451 7th St., SW
Washington, DC 20410
Information: 202-708-0006
Publications: 1-800-767-7468
https://portal.hud.gov/hudportal/HUD

Department of the Interior

U.S. Geological Survey
USGS National Center
12201 Sunrise Valley Drive
Reston, VA 20192
Information and Publications: 1-888-275-8747
https://minerals.usgs.gov/

Department of Justice

Bureau of Justice Statistics
Statistics Division
810 7th Street, NW
Washington, DC 20531
Information and publications: 202-307-0765
https://www.bjs.gov/

National Criminal Justice Reference Service
P.O. Box 6000
Rockville, MD 20849-6000
Publications: 1-800-851-3420
https://www.ncjrs.gov/

Federal Bureau of Investigation
J. Edgar Hoover Building
935 Pennsylvania Ave., NW
Washington, DC 20535-0001
Information: 202-324-3000
https://www.fbi.gov/

Department of Labor

Bureau of Labor Statistics
Office of Publications and Special Studies Services
Bureau of Labor Statistics
Postal Square Building
2 Massachusetts Ave., NE
Washington, DC 20212-0001
Information and publications: 202-691-5200
https://www.bls.gov/

Department of Labor—*Continued*

Employment and Training Administration
U.S. Department of Labor
Francis Perkins Building
200 Constitution Ave., NW
Washington, DC 20210
Information and publications: 1-877-872-5627
https://www.doleta.gov/

Department of Transportation

Federal Aviation Administration
800 Independence Ave., SW
Washington, DC 20591
Information and publications: 1-866-835-5322
https://www.faa.gov/

Bureau of Transportation Statistics
1200 New Jersey Avenue, SE
Washington, DC 20590
Products and statistical information: 1-800-853-1351
https://www.bts.gov/

Federal Highway Administration
Office of Public Affairs
U.S. Department of Transportation
1200 New Jersey Avenue, SE
Washington, DC 20590
Information: 202-366-0660
https://www.fhwa.dot.gov/

National Highway Traffic Safety Administration
Office of Public & Consumer Affairs
1200 New Jersey Avenue, SE,
West Building Washington, DC 20590
Information and publications: 1-888-327-4236
https://www.nhtsa.gov/

Department of the Treasury

Internal Revenue Service
Statistics of Income Division
Internal Revenue Service
P.O. Box 2608
Washington, DC 20013-2608
Information and publications: 202-874-0410
https://www.irs.gov/uac/tax-stats

Department of Veterans Affairs

Department of Veterans Affairs
Office of Public Affairs
810 Vermont Ave., NW
Washington, DC 20420
Information: 202-461-7600
https://www.va.gov/

Independent Agencies

Administrative Office of the U.S. Courts
Office of Public Affairs
1 Columbus Circle, NE
Washington, DC 20544
Information: 202-502-2600
http://www.uscourts.gov/

Board of Governors of the Federal Reserve System
Division of Research and Statistics
Federal Reserve System
20th & Constitution Avenue, NW
Washington, DC 20551
Information: 202-452-3000
Publications: 202-452-3245
https://www.federalreserve.gov/

Environmental Protection Agency
Ariel Rios Building
1200 Pennsylvania Ave., NW
Washington, DC 20460
Publications: 1-800-490-9198
https://www.epa.gov/

National Science Foundation
Office of Legislation and Public Affairs
National Science Foundation
4201 Wilson Boulevard
Arlington, VA 22230
Information: 703-292-5111
https://www.nsf.gov/

Securities and Exchange Commission
Office of Public Affairs
Securities and Exchange Commission
100 F Street, NE
Washington, DC 20549
Information: 202-551-4120
Publications: 202-551-4040
https://www.sec.gov/

Social Security Administration
Office of Public Inquiries
6401 Security Boulevard
Baltimore, MD 21235
Information and Publications: 1-800-772-1213
https://www.ssa.gov/

PART A

STATES

Page

3	Area and Population
4	Population, by Age Group and Sex
6	Population, by Race and Hispanic Origin
9	Population by Residence
10	Households
11	Marital Status, 2015
12	Residence One Year Ago, People Obtaining Legal Permanent Resident Status, and Language Spoken at Home, Selected Years
13	Place of Birth, 2015
14	Live Births and Birth Rates
15	Births and Birth Rates, by Race and Hispanic Origin and Fertility Rate, 2015
16	Deaths and Death Rates, by Race and Hispanic Origin
18	Age-Adjusted Death Rates, by Cause, 2015
19	Marriages and Divorces
20	Health Care Services, Physicians, and Nurses
21	Employment in Health Care Occupations and Type of Health Insurance
23	Health Indicators: Health Risks
24	Health Indicators: Health Conditions and Preventive Measures
25	People With and Without Health Insurance Coverage
26	Public and Private School Fall Enrollment
27	Public Elementary and Secondary Schools—Finances and Teachers
28	Public High School Graduates and Educational Attainment
29	Institutions of Higher Education
30	Violent Crimes and Crime Rates
31	Property Crimes and Crime Rates
32	Juvenile Arrests, Child Abuse Cases, and Correctional Population
33	State and Local Justice Employment and Expenditures, 2012
34	Civilian Labor Force and Employment
35	Civilian Labor Force and Unemployment
36	Employed Civilians, by Occupation, May 2016
38	Private Industry Employment and Wages, 2015
39	Average Annual Employment by Industry and Wages
42	Union Membership
43	Median Income of Households in 2015 Inflation-Adjusted Dollars and Distribution by Income Level
44	Family Income and Families and Individuals Below Poverty: 2015
45	Housing—Units and Characteristics: 2015

46	Owner- and Renter-Occupied Units—Value and Gross Rent, 2015
47	Home Ownership and Vacancy Rates
48	Cost of Living Indicators—Housing, Public University, Energy Expenditures, and Motor Fuels Taxes
50	Personal Income by State
52	Personal Income per Capita
54	Earnings by Industry, 2015
56	Gross Domestic Product per State
57	Science and Engineering Indicators
58	Employment Establishment Changes by Firm Size and State, 2010–2011
59	Employer Firms and Nonemployer Establishments
60	Private Nonfarm Establishments, Employment, and Payroll
61	Foreign Direct Investment in the United States and U.S. Exports
62	Farms and Farm Earnings
63	Farm Finances and Income
64	Farm Income and Wealth Statistics
65	Natural Resource Industries and Minerals
66	Agricultural Census
68	Utilities
69	Energy Consumption
70	Energy Expenditures
71	Construction
72	Manufactures
73	Manufactures Summary and Export-Related Shipments and Employment
74	Major Manufacturing Sectors, 2015
76	Information Industries
77	Wholesale and Retail Trade
78	Retail Trade Earnings, 2015
80	Transportation and Commuting
81	Motor Vehicle and Motorcycle Registrations, Bridges, and Drivers Licenses
82	Traffic Fatalities and Seat Belt Use
83	Communications
84	Financial Activities
85	Professional and Business Services and Education and Health Services
86	Leisure and Hospitality Services
87	Travel and Tourism Indicators
88	Government
89	State Government Employment and Finances
90	State Government Tax Collections: 2015
91	Federal Government
92	Federal Individual Income Tax Returns and Federal Real Estate
93	Social Security, Food Stamps, and School Lunch Programs
94	Social Insurance Programs and Workers' Compensation
95	Government Transfer Payments to Individuals
96	Medicare, Medicaid, and Children's Health Insurance Program
97	Department of Defense and Veterans
98	Elections
100	Composition of Congress and Public Officials

Table A-1. Area and Population

Geographic area	Land Area, 2010 (sq. mi.) Total	Rank	Population 2015[1] (thousands)	2010[1] (thousands)	2000[1] (thousands)	Rank 2015	2010	2000	Per square mile of land area[2] 2015	2010	2000	Number, 2010–2015 (thousands) Net change total[3]	Net international migration	Net domestic migration	Percent change 2010–2015	2000–2010
United States	3,531,905	X	321,419	308,758	281,425	X	X	X	91.0	87.4	79.7	12,660.7	5,334.9	-	4.1	9.7
Alabama	50,645	28	4,859	4,780	4,447	24	23	23	95.9	94.4	87.8	78.9	27.3	2.0	1.6	7.5
Alaska	570,641	1	738	710	627	48	47	48	1.3	1.2	1.1	28.2	12.1	-22.3	4.0	13.3
Arizona	113,594	6	6,828	6,392	5,131	14	16	20	60.1	56.3	45.2	435.8	77.5	160.3	6.8	24.6
Arkansas	52,035	27	2,978	2,916	2,673	33	32	33	57.2	56.0	51.4	62.2	17.8	0.2	2.1	9.1
California	155,779	3	39,145	37,255	33,872	1	1	1	251.3	239.1	217.4	1,890.3	835.0	-266.1	5.1	10.0
Colorado	103,642	8	5,457	5,029	4,302	22	22	24	52.6	48.5	41.5	427.3	59.3	192.3	8.5	16.9
Connecticut	4,842	48	3,591	3,574	3,406	29	29	29	741.6	738.1	703.3	16.8	88.2	-104.5	0.5	4.9
Delaware	1,949	49	946	898	784	45	45	45	485.5	460.8	402.1	48.0	13.7	18.0	5.3	14.6
District of Columbia ..	61	X	672	602	572	X	X	X	11,011.1	9,857.0	9,370.3	70.5	20.8	25.6	11.7	5.2
Florida	53,625	26	20,271	18,805	15,983	3	4	4	378.0	350.7	298.0	1,466.6	610.5	650.7	7.8	17.6
Georgia	57,513	21	10,215	9,689	8,187	8	9	10	177.6	168.5	142.3	526.2	135.0	82.5	5.4	18.3
Hawaii	6,423	47	1,432	1,360	1,212	40	40	42	222.9	211.8	188.6	71.3	46.8	-18.4	5.2	12.3
Idaho	82,643	11	1,655	1,568	1,294	39	39	39	20.0	19.0	15.7	87.3	9.7	19.8	5.6	21.2
Illinois	55,519	24	12,860	12,832	12,420	5	5	5	231.6	231.1	223.7	28.4	170.4	-426.0	0.2	3.3
Indiana	35,826	38	6,620	6,484	6,081	16	15	14	184.8	181.0	169.7	135.5	57.5	-47.3	2.1	6.6
Iowa	55,857	23	3,124	3,047	2,926	30	30	30	55.9	54.5	52.4	77.0	29.3	-7.2	2.5	4.1
Kansas	81,759	13	2,912	2,853	2,689	34	33	32	35.6	34.9	32.9	58.5	33.8	-52.6	2.1	6.1
Kentucky	39,486	37	4,425	4,339	4,042	26	26	25	112.1	109.9	102.4	85.7	34.5	-12.3	2.0	7.3
Louisiana	43,204	33	4,671	4,533	4,469	25	25	22	108.1	104.9	103.4	137.2	39.5	-10.6	3.0	1.4
Maine	30,843	39	1,329	1,328	1,275	42	41	40	43.1	43.1	41.3	1.0	7.0	-4.1	0.1	4.2
Maryland	9,707	42	6,006	5,774	5,297	19	19	19	618.8	594.8	545.6	232.6	148.5	-56.1	4.0	9.0
Massachusetts	7,800	45	6,794	6,548	6,349	15	14	13	871.1	839.5	814.0	246.6	202.4	-46.9	3.8	3.1
Michigan	56,539	22	9,923	9,884	9,938	10	8	8	175.5	174.8	175.8	38.4	111.1	-191.1	0.4	-0.6
Minnesota	79,627	14	5,490	5,304	4,919	21	21	21	68.9	66.6	61.8	185.7	72.4	-36.7	3.5	7.8
Mississippi	46,923	31	2,992	2,968	2,845	32	31	31	63.8	63.3	60.6	24.2	13.0	-38.5	0.8	4.3
Missouri	68,742	18	6,084	5,989	5,597	18	18	17	88.5	87.1	81.4	94.7	47.4	-51.8	1.6	7.0
Montana	145,546	4	1,033	989	902	44	44	44	7.1	6.8	6.2	43.5	3.7	22.8	4.4	9.7
Nebraska	76,824	15	1,896	1,826	1,711	37	38	38	24.7	23.8	22.3	69.8	21.9	-7.7	3.8	6.7
Nevada	109,781	7	2,891	2,701	1,998	35	35	35	26.3	24.6	18.2	190.2	41.9	69.2	7.0	35.1
New Hampshire	8,953	44	1,331	1,316	1,236	41	42	41	148.6	147.0	138.0	14.1	10.4	-5.5	1.1	6.5
New Jersey	7,354	46	8,958	8,792	8,414	11	11	9	1,218.1	1,195.5	1,144.2	166.1	270.3	-269.2	1.9	4.5
New Mexico	121,298	5	2,085	2,059	1,819	36	36	36	17.2	17.0	15.0	25.9	15.9	-43.0	1.3	13.2
New York	47,126	30	19,796	19,378	18,977	4	3	3	420.1	411.2	402.7	417.7	630.8	-653.1	2.2	2.1
North Carolina	48,618	29	10,043	9,536	8,046	9	10	11	206.6	196.1	165.6	507.1	116.9	180.2	5.3	18.5
North Dakota	69,001	17	757	673	642	47	48	47	11.0	9.7	9.3	84.3	8.1	53.0	12.5	4.7
Ohio	40,861	35	11,613	11,537	11,353	7	7	7	284.2	282.3	277.8	76.7	95.4	-153.3	0.7	1.6
Oklahoma	68,595	19	3,911	3,752	3,451	28	28	27	57.0	54.7	50.3	159.7	33.4	43.5	4.3	8.7
Oregon	95,988	10	4,029	3,831	3,421	27	27	28	42.0	39.9	35.6	197.9	36.3	93.4	5.2	12.0
Pennsylvania	44,743	32	12,803	12,703	12,281	6	6	6	286.1	283.9	274.5	99.6	164.5	-132.1	0.8	3.4
Rhode Island	1,034	50	1,056	1,053	1,048	43	43	43	1,021.8	1,018.5	1,014.0	3.4	22.3	-25.7	0.3	0.4
South Carolina	30,061	40	4,896	4,625	4,012	23	24	26	162.9	153.9	133.5	270.7	32.0	159.0	5.9	15.3
South Dakota	75,811	16	858	814	755	46	46	46	11.3	10.7	10.0	44.3	7.9	10.3	5.4	7.9
Tennessee	41,235	34	6,600	6,346	5,689	17	17	16	160.1	153.9	138.0	254.0	49.5	104.9	4.0	11.5
Texas	261,232	2	27,469	25,146	20,852	2	2	2	105.2	96.3	79.8	2,323.0	463.4	736.5	9.2	20.6
Utah	82,170	12	2,996	2,764	2,233	31	34	34	36.5	33.6	27.2	232.0	29.3	14.6	8.4	23.8
Vermont	9,217	43	626	626	609	49	49	49	67.9	67.9	66.1	0.3	4.1	-6.5	0.0	2.8
Virginia	39,490	36	8,383	8,001	7,079	12	12	12	212.3	202.6	179.2	381.9	182.4	-17.4	4.8	13.0
Washington	66,456	20	7,170	6,725	5,894	13	13	15	107.9	101.2	88.7	445.8	127.1	124.3	6.6	14.1
West Virginia	24,038	41	1,844	1,853	1,808	38	37	37	76.7	77.1	75.2	-8.9	6.3	-8.2	-0.5	2.5
Wisconsin	54,158	25	5,771	5,687	5,364	20	20	18	106.6	105.0	99.0	84.0	38.0	-52.2	1.5	6.0
Wyoming	97,093	9	586	564	494	50	50	50	6.0	5.8	5.1	22.3	2.9	3.1	4.0	14.1

X. = Not applicable.

[1]The 2015 population is estimated as of July 1, 2015. The April 1, 2010 and April 1, 2000 Population Estimates bases reflect modifications to the Census 2000 and 2010 population as documented in the Count Question Resolution program and geographic program revisions.

[2]People per square mile was calculated on the basis of land area data from the 2010 census.

[3]The estimated components of population change will not sum to the numerical population change due to the process of controlling to national totals.

Table A-2. Population, by Age Group and Sex

Geographic area	Total	Population by age, 2015[1] (thousands)									
		Under 5 years	5 to 17 years	18 to 24 years	25 to 34 years	35 to 44 years	45 to 54 years	55 to 64 years	65 to 74 years	75 to 84 years	85 years and over
United States	321,419	19,907	53,738	31,220	44,137	40,590	43,188	40,878	27,551	13,923	6,287
Alabama	4,859	293	811	469	633	602	649	638	450	228	85
Alaska	738	55	131	81	120	90	94	94	49	18	6
Arizona........................	6,828	429	1,194	672	914	842	844	814	653	336	131
Arkansas	2,978	191	514	284	389	366	382	375	277	144	56
California.....................	39,145	2,509	6,612	3,935	5,836	5,188	5,247	4,630	2,977	1,504	708
Colorado	5,457	336	921	531	823	734	714	686	434	194	84
Connecticut.................	3,591	188	576	352	442	431	538	497	315	162	90
Delaware	946	56	149	88	126	111	129	128	95	46	19
District of Columbia	672	43	75	82	152	96	77	70	44	21	11
Florida.........................	20,271	1,101	3,004	1,759	2,614	2,448	2,749	2,654	2,181	1,221	540
Georgia	10,215	660	1,844	1,017	1,402	1,371	1,407	1,209	805	364	136
Hawaii	1,432	92	218	136	216	177	176	179	133	65	38
Idaho...........................	1,655	113	320	156	218	203	199	204	146	70	28
Illinois.........................	12,860	784	2,175	1,236	1,774	1,670	1,746	1,645	1,039	533	259
Indiana........................	6,620	419	1,160	666	851	823	879	856	557	282	128
Iowa............................	3,124	197	532	322	392	366	399	413	270	153	79
Kansas	2,912	197	522	304	387	346	361	367	235	127	65
Kentucky	4,425	277	734	424	568	559	604	586	399	197	77
Louisiana	4,671	311	804	456	676	571	603	598	386	191	76
Maine..........................	1,329	65	192	111	155	153	196	209	146	72	32
Maryland......................	6,006	369	979	554	837	768	868	782	498	239	113
Massachusetts.............	6,794	367	1,021	701	944	834	978	905	589	298	159
Michigan......................	9,923	572	1,636	987	1,223	1,175	1,374	1,384	907	451	213
Minnesota....................	5,490	351	934	506	747	674	744	728	452	236	118
Mississippi...................	2,992	193	534	303	393	368	384	378	258	131	50
Missouri.......................	6,084	374	1,017	587	807	733	805	805	543	285	127
Montana.......................	1,033	62	165	101	131	117	128	151	105	51	22
Nebraska.....................	1,896	131	340	193	253	229	234	239	152	84	42
Nevada........................	2,891	177	493	253	418	386	389	354	264	118	40
New Hampshire............	1,331	65	199	129	156	155	206	202	130	60	29
New Jersey	8,958	530	1,469	793	1,155	1,164	1,324	1,180	753	393	197
New Mexico	2,085	135	362	205	280	244	258	271	195	97	39
New York......................	19,796	1,184	3,026	1,942	2,880	2,496	2,759	2,544	1,660	871	433
North Carolina..............	10,043	605	1,686	988	1,309	1,296	1,372	1,271	905	436	175
North Dakota................	757	53	121	95	113	85	88	94	57	33	18
Ohio............................	11,613	693	1,935	1,085	1,487	1,397	1,577	1,595	1,045	545	253
Oklahoma.....................	3,911	268	693	390	540	476	484	484	332	175	69
Oregon........................	4,029	231	632	364	557	524	515	545	395	181	84
Pennsylvania................	12,803	715	1,975	1,205	1,663	1,499	1,774	1,792	1,197	649	334
Rhode Island................	1,056	55	156	115	142	124	150	145	93	48	28
South Carolina	4,896	290	802	477	641	597	650	644	489	223	82
South Dakota	858	61	150	85	112	97	105	114	73	40	21
Tennessee	6,600	402	1,095	627	872	837	895	855	608	295	114
Texas..........................	27,469	1,984	5,228	2,772	4,012	3,694	3,503	3,052	1,923	927	374
Utah............................	2,996	251	662	340	442	399	310	284	182	91	36
Vermont.......................	626	30	90	68	72	71	89	97	65	30	14
Virginia........................	8,383	515	1,355	823	1,184	1,089	1,167	1,061	708	338	143
Washington..................	7,170	448	1,164	666	1,053	928	946	929	623	282	131
West Virginia................	1,844	103	276	166	219	227	248	269	197	100	39
Wisconsin....................	5,771	340	955	563	727	690	800	795	508	265	129
Wyoming	586	38	101	57	83	71	71	81	51	24	10

[1]As of July 1 for 2015. As of April 1 for decennial census years 2010 and 2000. All years include Armed Forces stationed in area.

Table A-2. Population, by Age Group and Sex—*Continued*

Geographic area	Population under 18 years old (thousands)[1]			Population 65 years and over (thousands)[1]			Percentage of population, by age[1]						Males per 100 females 2015[1]
							Under 18 years			65 years and over			
	2015	2010	2000[2]	2015	2010	2000[2]	2015	2010	2000[2]	2015	2010	2000[2]	
United States	73,645	74,181	72,294	47,761	40,268	34,992	22.9	24.0	25.7	14.9	13.0	12.4	97.0
Alabama	1,103	1,132	1,123	764	658	580	22.7	23.7	25.3	15.7	13.8	13.0	93.9
Alaska	186	187	191	73	55	36	25.2	26.4	30.4	9.9	7.7	5.7	111.3
Arizona	1,623	1,629	1,367	1,120	882	668	23.8	25.5	26.6	16.4	13.8	13.0	98.7
Arkansas	705	711	680	477	420	374	23.7	24.4	25.4	16.0	14.4	14.0	96.5
California....................	9,121	9,295	9,250	5,189	4,247	3,596	23.3	25.0	27.3	13.3	11.4	10.6	98.7
Colorado	1,257	1,226	1,101	712	550	416	23.0	24.4	25.6	13.0	10.9	9.7	101.1
Connecticut.................	764	817	842	567	507	470	21.3	22.9	24.7	15.8	14.2	13.8	95.2
Delaware	204	206	195	161	129	102	21.6	22.9	24.8	17.0	14.4	13.0	93.8
District of Columbia	118	101	115	77	69	70	17.6	16.8	20.1	11.5	11.4	12.2	90.1
Florida.......................	4,105	4,002	3,646	3,942	3,260	2,808	20.3	21.3	22.8	19.4	17.3	17.6	95.5
Georgia	2,504	2,492	2,169	1,305	1,032	785	24.5	25.7	26.5	12.8	10.7	9.6	95.1
Hawaii........................	311	304	296	237	195	161	21.7	22.3	24.4	16.5	14.3	13.3	102.7
Idaho.........................	433	429	369	243	195	146	26.2	27.4	28.5	14.7	12.4	11.3	100.3
Illinois.......................	2,959	3,129	3,245	1,830	1,609	1,500	23.0	24.4	26.1	14.2	12.5	12.1	96.5
Indiana.......................	1,579	1,608	1,574	966	841	753	23.9	24.8	25.9	14.6	13.0	12.4	97.1
Iowa..........................	729	728	734	503	453	436	23.3	23.9	25.1	16.1	14.9	14.9	98.7
Kansas.......................	720	727	713	426	376	356	24.7	25.5	26.5	14.6	13.2	13.3	99.7
Kentucky	1,012	1,023	995	673	578	505	22.9	23.6	24.6	15.2	13.3	12.5	97.0
Louisiana	1,115	1,118	1,220	653	558	517	23.9	24.7	27.3	14.0	12.3	11.6	95.7
Maine.........................	256	275	301	251	211	183	19.3	20.7	23.6	18.8	15.9	14.4	96.0
Maryland.....................	1,348	1,353	1,356	850	708	599	22.4	23.4	25.6	14.1	12.3	11.3	94.0
Massachusetts..............	1,387	1,419	1,500	1,045	903	860	20.4	21.7	23.6	15.4	13.8	13.5	94.2
Michigan.....................	2,207	2,344	2,596	1,571	1,362	1,219	22.2	23.7	26.1	15.8	13.8	12.3	96.7
Minnesota	1,284	1,284	1,287	806	683	594	23.4	24.2	26.2	14.7	12.9	12.1	98.9
Mississippi..................	727	756	775	440	380	344	24.3	25.5	27.3	14.7	12.8	12.1	94.2
Missouri......................	1,391	1,425	1,428	955	838	755	22.9	23.8	25.5	15.7	14.0	13.5	96.3
Montana......................	226	224	230	178	147	121	21.9	22.6	25.5	17.2	14.8	13.4	101.1
Nebraska	470	459	450	279	247	232	24.8	25.1	26.3	14.7	13.5	13.6	99.4
Nevada	669	665	512	422	324	219	23.1	24.6	25.6	14.6	12.0	11.0	100.7
New Hampshire.............	264	287	310	219	178	148	19.8	21.8	25.0	16.5	13.5	12.0	97.7
New Jersey	1,999	2,065	2,088	1,344	1,186	1,113	22.3	23.5	24.8	15.0	13.5	13.2	95.3
New Mexico	497	519	509	330	272	212	23.8	25.2	28.0	15.8	13.2	11.7	98.3
New York....................	4,211	4,325	4,690	2,964	2,618	2,448	21.3	22.3	24.7	15.0	13.5	12.9	94.4
North Carolina.............	2,291	2,282	1,964	1,517	1,234	969	22.8	23.9	24.4	15.1	12.9	12.0	95.0
North Dakota...............	174	150	161	107	97	94	23.0	22.3	25.0	14.2	14.5	14.7	105.6
Ohio..........................	2,628	2,731	2,888	1,843	1,622	1,508	22.6	23.7	25.4	15.9	14.1	13.3	95.9
Oklahoma....................	961	930	892	576	507	456	24.6	24.8	25.9	14.7	13.5	13.2	98.1
Oregon.......................	863	866	847	661	534	438	21.4	22.6	24.7	16.4	13.9	12.8	97.9
Pennsylvania................	2,690	2,792	2,922	2,180	1,959	1,919	21.0	22.0	23.8	17.0	15.4	15.6	95.8
Rhode Island...............	211	224	248	170	152	152	20.0	21.3	23.6	16.1	14.4	14.5	94.0
South Carolina	1,092	1,080	1,010	795	632	485	22.3	23.4	25.2	16.2	13.7	12.1	94.5
South Dakota	211	203	203	134	117	108	24.6	24.9	26.8	15.7	14.3	14.3	101.3
Tennessee	1,498	1,496	1,399	1,017	853	703	22.7	23.6	24.6	15.4	13.4	12.4	95.1
Texas.........................	7,212	6,866	5,887	3,225	2,602	2,073	26.3	27.3	28.2	11.7	10.3	9.9	98.6
Utah..........................	912	871	719	308	249	190	30.5	31.5	32.2	10.3	9.0	8.5	101.2
Vermont......................	120	129	148	110	91	78	19.2	20.7	24.2	17.6	14.6	12.7	97.2
Virginia......................	1,870	1,854	1,738	1,188	977	792	22.3	23.2	24.6	14.2	12.2	11.2	96.9
Washington..................	1,612	1,581	1,514	1,036	828	662	22.5	23.5	25.7	14.4	12.3	11.2	100.0
West Virginia...............	380	387	402	336	297	277	20.6	20.9	22.3	18.2	16.0	15.3	97.6
Wisconsin....................	1,295	1,339	1,369	902	777	703	22.4	23.6	25.5	15.6	13.7	13.1	98.8
Wyoming	139	135	129	85	70	58	23.7	24.0	26.1	14.5	12.4	11.7	104.1

[1]As of July 1 for 2015. As of April 1 for decennial census years 2010 and 2000. All years include Armed Forces stationed in area.
[2]The April 1, 2000 population does not reflect modifications to the Census 2000 population as documented in the Count Question Resolution program and geographic program revisions.

Table A-3. Population, by Race and Hispanic Origin

Geographic area	All races (thousands)[1]		White alone (thousands)[1]		Black or African Amerian alone (thousands)[1]		American Indian and Alaska Native alone (thousands)[1]		Asian alone (thousands)[1]		Native Hawaiian and Other Pacific Islander alone (thousands)[1]	
	2015[2]	2010[3]	2015[2]	2010[3]	2015[2]	2010[3]	2015[2]	2010[3]	2015[2]	2010[3]	2015[2]	2010[3]
United States	321,419	308,758	247,785	241,945	42,633	40,254	4,011	3,740	17,982	15,160	760	675
Alabama	4,859	4,780	3,375	3,363	1,301	1,259	34	33	67	55	5	5
Alaska	738	710	491	484	29	24	110	106	46	39	10	8
Arizona......................	6,828	6,392	5,698	5,419	330	281	363	335	231	188	18	16
Arkansas	2,978	2,916	2,368	2,342	466	454	29	26	47	38	9	7
California...................	39,145	37,255	28,535	27,637	2,553	2,487	648	622	5,737	5,038	197	181
Colorado	5,457	5,029	4,777	4,451	245	215	87	78	177	145	11	8
Connecticut................	3,591	3,574	2,903	2,951	418	392	19	17	166	141	4	3
Delaware	946	898	666	646	212	196	6	6	37	29	1	1
District of Columbia	672	602	296	251	325	310	4	3	28	22	1	1
Florida.......................	20,271	18,805	15,748	14,811	3,409	3,080	101	89	577	474	23	19
Georgia	10,215	9,689	6,296	6,146	3,240	2,994	51	49	409	323	12	10
Hawaii	1,432	1,360	383	349	37	22	6	5	533	532	142	138
Idaho.........................	1,655	1,568	1,545	1,476	14	11	29	26	25	20	3	3
Illinois.......................	12,860	12,832	9,940	10,031	1,888	1,903	75	74	707	604	8	7
Indiana......................	6,620	6,484	5,682	5,639	637	604	27	24	142	106	4	4
Iowa..........................	3,124	3,047	2,866	2,840	110	92	16	14	74	54	3	2
Kansas	2,912	2,853	2,523	2,501	183	173	35	33	85	70	3	3
Kentucky	4,425	4,339	3,898	3,864	366	343	13	12	64	50	4	3
Louisiana	4,671	4,533	2,954	2,903	1,517	1,463	36	33	86	72	3	3
Maine	1,329	1,328	1,262	1,270	19	16	9	9	16	14	0	0
Maryland....................	6,006	5,774	3,582	3,541	1,830	1,732	34	31	392	327	6	5
Massachusetts............	6,794	6,548	5,580	5,525	574	504	33	30	446	360	7	6
Michigan	9,923	9,884	7,909	7,950	1,410	1,416	72	68	298	243	4	3
Minnesota	5,490	5,304	4,686	4,623	329	281	73	67	268	218	4	3
Mississippi.................	2,992	2,968	1,780	1,790	1,125	1,104	18	17	32	26	2	2
Missouri.....................	6,084	5,989	5,069	5,038	719	700	33	31	121	100	9	7
Montana.....................	1,033	989	922	892	6	4	68	63	9	6	1	1
Nebraska	1,896	1,826	1,690	1,649	94	86	26	23	44	33	2	2
Nevada	2,891	2,701	2,188	2,107	268	231	48	43	247	203	22	19
New Hampshire............	1,331	1,316	1,250	1,248	20	16	4	4	35	29	1	1
New Jersey	8,958	8,792	6,507	6,547	1,330	1,282	54	50	869	746	9	8
New Mexico	2,085	2,059	1,721	1,721	53	49	219	209	36	31	3	3
New York....................	19,796	19,378	13,874	13,902	3,491	3,378	191	183	1,734	1,482	27	24
North Carolina.............	10,043	9,536	7,155	6,898	2,223	2,088	156	148	284	216	12	10
North Dakota...............	757	673	670	609	18	8	41	37	11	7	1	0
Ohio..........................	11,613	11,537	9,605	9,665	1,477	1,427	32	30	245	197	6	5
Oklahoma...................	3,911	3,752	2,926	2,852	304	284	356	336	86	67	7	5
Oregon	4,029	3,831	3,530	3,403	84	74	72	67	177	145	18	15
Pennsylvania..............	12,803	12,703	10,574	10,664	1,497	1,432	45	40	435	358	9	7
Rhode Island...............	1,056	1,053	895	911	83	75	10	9	38	32	2	2
South Carolina	4,896	4,625	3,348	3,164	1,353	1,303	26	25	78	61	5	4
South Dakota	858	814	734	707	16	11	77	73	12	8	1	1
Tennessee..................	6,600	6,346	5,199	5,056	1,130	1,068	29	26	117	94	6	5
Texas........................	27,469	25,146	21,889	20,390	3,444	3,071	280	251	1,300	1,000	38	31
Utah..........................	2,996	2,764	2,732	2,547	40	34	46	41	75	58	30	26
Vermont.....................	626	626	593	599	8	6	2	2	10	8	0	0
Virginia......................	8,383	8,001	5,886	5,725	1,654	1,579	45	42	546	449	10	8
Washington.................	7,170	6,725	5,757	5,535	295	252	136	123	603	492	53	44
West Virginia...............	1,844	1,853	1,726	1,747	67	64	4	4	16	13	1	0
Wisconsin	5,771	5,687	5,058	5,037	381	367	65	60	160	132	3	3
Wyoming	586	564	543	529	8	5	16	14	6	5	1	1

Z = Less than 500 or .05 percent.
[1]Due to the complexities associated with the production of detailed characteristics' estimates at the state levels of geography may not necessarily sum to estimates at higher levels or geography.
[2]Population estimate as of July 1, 2015.
[3]Population estimates for 2010 are for the base estimates and reflect changes to the Census 2010 population from the Count Question Resolution program and geographic program revisions.

Table A-3. Population, by Race and Hispanic Origin—*Continued*

Geographic area	Two or more races (thousands)[1]		Hispanic or Latino origin (thousands)[1,4]		Non-Hispanic White alone (thousands)[1]		Percentage of total, 2015							
	2015[2]	2010[3]	2015[2]	2010[3]	2015[2]	2010[3]	White alone	Black or African American alone	American Indian and Alaska Native alone	Asian alone	Native Hawaiian and Other Pacific Islander alone	Two or more races	Hispanic or Latino origin	Non-Hispanic White alone
United States	8,248	6,984	56,593	50,479	197,971	197,326	77.1	13.3	1.2	5.6	0.2	2.6	17.6	61.6
Alabama......................	78	64	203	186	3,205	3,208	69.5	26.8	0.7	1.4	0.1	1.6	4.2	66.0
Alaska	53	49	52	39	454	456	66.5	3.9	14.9	6.2	1.4	7.2	7.0	61.5
Arizona......................	187	153	2,098	1,895	3,810	3,705	83.5	4.8	5.3	3.4	0.3	2.7	30.7	55.8
Arkansas....................	59	49	214	186	2,176	2,176	79.5	15.6	1.0	1.6	0.3	2.0	7.2	73.1
California....................	1,475	1,289	15,185	14,014	14,882	15,029	72.9	6.5	1.7	14.7	0.5	3.8	38.8	38.0
Colorado....................	161	132	1,164	1,039	3,747	3,529	87.5	4.5	1.6	3.2	0.2	3.0	21.3	68.7
Connecticut................	80	70	554	479	2,448	2,557	80.8	11.6	0.5	4.6	0.1	2.2	15.4	68.2
Delaware....................	24	20	85	73	598	588	70.4	22.4	0.6	3.9	0.1	2.5	9.0	63.2
District of Columbia	18	14	71	55	243	210	44.0	48.4	0.6	4.2	0.1	2.7	10.6	36.2
Florida.......................	414	332	4,964	4,224	11,209	10,927	77.7	16.8	0.5	2.8	0.1	2.0	24.5	55.3
Georgia	206	166	955	854	5,501	5,428	61.6	31.7	0.5	4.0	0.1	2.0	9.3	53.9
Hawaii.......................	329	314	149	121	328	311	26.7	2.6	0.4	37.2	9.9	23.0	10.4	22.9
Idaho........................	39	32	202	176	1,365	1,318	93.4	0.8	1.8	1.5	0.2	2.4	12.2	82.5
Illinois.......................	241	211	2,175	2,028	7,957	8,183	77.3	14.7	0.6	5.5	0.1	1.9	16.9	61.9
Indiana......................	129	108	442	390	5,293	5,295	85.8	9.6	0.4	2.1	0.1	1.9	6.7	80.0
Iowa.........................	55	45	179	152	2,708	2,704	91.7	3.5	0.5	2.4	0.1	1.8	5.7	86.7
Kansas......................	83	73	337	300	2,224	2,234	86.6	6.3	1.2	2.9	0.1	2.9	11.6	76.4
Kentucky....................	80	67	152	133	3,768	3,750	88.1	8.3	0.3	1.4	0.1	1.8	3.4	85.2
Louisiana	74	60	233	193	2,761	2,741	63.2	32.5	0.8	1.8	0.1	1.6	5.0	59.1
Maine........................	22	19	21	17	1,244	1,256	95.0	1.4	0.7	1.2	0.0	1.7	1.6	93.6
Maryland....................	163	138	572	471	3,126	3,166	59.6	30.5	0.6	6.5	0.1	2.7	9.5	52.0
Massachusetts.............	154	123	759	628	4,997	5,037	82.1	8.4	0.5	6.6	0.1	2.3	11.2	73.6
Michigan....................	230	203	486	436	7,498	7,580	79.7	14.2	0.7	3.0	0.0	2.3	4.9	75.6
Minnesota	131	111	284	250	4,447	4,411	85.4	6.0	1.3	4.9	0.1	2.4	5.2	81.0
Mississippi.................	36	30	92	81	1,706	1,724	59.5	37.6	0.6	1.1	0.1	1.2	3.1	57.0
Missouri.....................	132	112	248	212	4,858	4,856	83.3	11.8	0.5	2.0	0.1	2.2	4.1	79.8
Montana.....................	27	23	37	29	894	869	89.3	0.6	6.6	0.9	0.1	2.6	3.6	86.5
Nebraska....................	39	32	197	167	1,517	1,502	89.1	5.0	1.4	2.3	0.1	2.1	10.4	80.0
Nevada......................	119	97	813	717	1,467	1,467	75.7	9.3	1.7	8.5	0.8	4.1	28.1	50.7
New Hampshire............	22	19	46	37	1,211	1,217	93.9	1.5	0.3	2.6	0.1	1.7	3.5	91.0
New Jersey	189	160	1,762	1,555	5,038	5,238	72.6	14.8	0.6	9.7	0.1	2.1	19.7	56.2
New Mexico	52	46	1,001	953	802	838	82.5	2.5	10.5	1.7	0.1	2.5	48.0	38.5
New York....................	480	410	3,727	3,417	11,092	11,345	70.1	17.6	1.0	8.8	0.1	2.4	18.8	56.0
North Carolina.............	212	175	917	800	6,404	6,236	71.2	22.1	1.6	2.8	0.1	2.1	9.1	63.8
North Dakota...............	16	11	27	13	649	598	88.5	2.4	5.4	1.5	0.1	2.1	3.6	85.7
Ohio.........................	249	213	415	355	9,266	9,373	82.7	12.7	0.3	2.1	0.1	2.1	3.6	79.8
Oklahoma...................	233	207	396	332	2,602	2,579	74.8	7.8	9.1	2.2	0.2	6.0	10.1	66.5
Oregon......................	148	127	512	450	3,086	3,012	87.6	2.1	1.8	4.4	0.4	3.7	12.7	76.6
Pennsylvania...............	242	202	872	720	9,909	10,109	82.6	11.7	0.4	3.4	0.1	1.9	6.8	77.4
Rhode Island...............	28	25	152	131	781	811	84.8	7.9	0.9	3.6	0.2	2.7	14.4	74.0
South Carolina	86	68	268	236	3,125	2,968	68.4	27.6	0.5	1.6	0.1	1.8	5.5	63.8
South Dakota	19	16	31	22	711	690	85.5	1.9	9.0	1.4	0.1	2.2	3.6	82.9
Tennessee	118	96	341	290	4,909	4,807	78.8	17.1	0.4	1.8	0.1	1.8	5.2	74.4
Texas........................	517	402	10,670	9,461	11,822	11,429	79.7	12.5	1.0	4.7	0.1	1.9	38.8	43.0
Utah.........................	72	58	411	358	2,367	2,226	91.2	1.3	1.5	2.5	1.0	2.4	13.7	79.0
Vermont.....................	12	10	12	9	584	591	94.7	1.3	0.3	1.6	0.0	1.9	1.9	93.3
Virginia......................	241	197	755	632	5,257	5,199	70.2	19.7	0.5	6.5	0.1	2.9	9.0	62.7
Washington.................	326	279	886	756	5,005	4,889	80.3	4.1	1.9	8.4	0.7	4.5	12.4	69.8
West Virginia...............	30	25	28	22	1,703	1,728	93.6	3.6	0.2	0.9	0.1	1.6	1.5	92.4
Wisconsin	105	89	382	336	4,725	4,743	87.6	6.6	1.1	2.8	0.1	1.8	6.6	81.9
Wyoming	12	10	58	50	492	485	92.7	1.4	2.7	1.0	0.2	2.0	9.9	84.0

Z = Less than 500 or .05 percent.

[1]Due to the complexities associated with the production of detailed characteristics' estimates at the state levels of geography may not necessarily sum to estimates at higher levels or geography.

[2]Population estimate as of July 1, 2015.

[3]Population estimates for 2010 are for the base estimates and reflect changes to the Census 2010 population from the Count Question Resolution program and geographic program revisions.

[4]Hispanic origin is considered an ethnicity and not a race; Hispanics may be any race.

Table A-3. Population, by Race and Hispanic Origin—*Continued*

Geographic area	Percentage change, 2010–2015								
	All races	White alone	Black or African American alone	American Indian and Alaska Native alone	Asian alone	Native Hawaiian and Other Pacific Islander alone	Two or more races	Hispanic or Latino origin	Non-Hispanic White alone
United States	4.1	2.4	5.9	7.3	18.6	12.7	18.1	12.1	0.3
Alabama......................	1.6	0.3	3.3	3.3	21.6	-2.7	20.7	9.5	-0.1
Alaska........................	4.0	1.5	17.9	3.1	18.8	25.5	7.8	32.0	-0.5
Arizona.......................	6.8	5.2	17.6	8.3	22.8	12.7	22.1	10.7	2.8
Arkansas.....................	2.1	1.1	2.7	12.0	25.0	31.0	21.0	15.0	0.0
California....................	5.1	3.3	2.7	4.2	13.9	8.4	14.4	8.4	
Colorado	8.5	7.3	14.1	10.8	22.1	25.0	21.4	12.1	6.2
Connecticut................	0.5	-1.6	6.6	14.3	18.4	12.9	14.3	15.6	-4.3
Delaware....................	5.3	3.2	7.9	4.4	26.0	25.5	19.8	16.5	1.8
District of Columbia	11.7	17.9	4.6	14.9	30.4	38.1	26.4	29.9	15.5
Florida........................	7.8	6.3	10.7	13.4	21.6	21.6	24.5	17.5	2.6
Georgia	5.4	2.4	8.2	5.7	26.5	16.9	23.8	11.9	1.4
Hawaii........................	5.2	9.7	66.5	30.5	0.3	2.9	4.9	23.1	5.4
Idaho.........................	5.6	4.7	27.2	11.8	22.8	21.4	21.2	15.1	3.5
Illinois.......................	0.2	-0.9	-0.8	2.2	17.0	11.8	14.2	7.3	-2.8
Indiana.......................	2.1	0.8	5.4	8.8	34.3	17.5	19.8	13.4	0.0
Iowa..........................	2.5	0.9	19.8	15.4	35.6	32.7	22.9	17.8	0.1
Kansas.......................	2.1	0.9	5.5	5.3	21.5	15.2	13.4	12.2	-0.4
Kentucky....................	2.0	0.9	6.9	7.5	27.5	15.7	19.7	14.6	0.5
Louisiana	3.0	1.8	3.7	7.9	19.5	21.0	23.9	20.8	0.7
Maine.........................	0.1	-0.6	18.5	4.8	18.8	26.8	14.6	23.6	-0.9
Maryland.....................	4.0	1.1	5.7	9.4	20.0	20.2	18.2	21.6	-1.3
Massachusetts.............	3.8	1.0	13.8	9.4	24.0	14.9	25.8	21.0	-0.8
Michigan	0.4	-0.5	-0.4	4.6	22.5	16.1	13.3	11.4	-1.1
Minnesota	3.5	1.3	17.0	8.6	23.1	20.6	17.2	13.6	0.8
Mississippi..................	0.8	-0.6	1.9	5.8	20.0	7.4	21.7	12.4	
Missouri.....................	1.6	0.6	2.6	9.5	21.1	23.4	17.7	16.5	0.0
Montana	4.4	3.4	48.3	7.0	34.5	25.6	18.9	30.2	2.8
Nebraska....................	3.8	2.4	9.2	13.1	33.5	13.4	21.9	17.9	1.0
Nevada.......................	7.0	3.9	15.9	10.8	21.4	13.3	22.1	13.5	0.0
New Hampshire............	1.1	0.1	21.1	10.1	20.4	20.1	15.7	24.3	-0.5
New Jersey	1.9	-0.6	3.7	7.8	16.4	19.0	18.7	13.3	-3.8
New Mexico	1.3	0.0	9.0	5.0	15.0	11.3	13.0	5.0	-4.4
New York....................	2.2	-0.2	3.3	4.1	17.0	11.6	17.1	9.1	-2.2
North Carolina.............	5.3	3.7	6.4	5.8	31.6	20.2	21.3	14.6	2.7
North Dakota...............	12.5	10.1	123.0	11.8	50.2	86.5	43.2	99.1	8.5
Ohio..........................	0.7	-0.6	3.5	7.3	24.4	15.3	16.5	16.9	-1.1
Oklahoma...................	4.3	2.6	6.9	6.0	27.8	25.5	12.5	19.4	0.9
Oregon.......................	5.2	3.7	12.4	8.3	22.4	20.6	16.7	13.7	2.5
Pennsylvania...............	0.8	-0.8	4.6	14.1	21.5	23.6	20.1	21.2	-2.0
Rhode Island...............	0.3	-1.7	10.6	11.1	19.2	17.5	12.9	16.4	-3.7
South Carolina	5.9	5.8	3.9	7.1	27.3	15.7	26.3	13.9	5.3
South Dakota	5.4	3.9	49.6	5.4	51.9	28.0	20.6	41.1	3.1
Tennessee	4.0	2.8	5.8	12.3	24.8	18.3	22.9	17.4	2.1
Texas.........................	9.2	7.4	12.2	11.6	29.9	22.3	28.5	12.8	3.4
Utah..........................	8.4	7.3	18.6	13.0	29.3	15.9	24.5	14.7	6.3
Vermont.....................	0.0	-0.9	26.1	3.2	27.4	37.7	14.8	25.2	-1.2
Virginia......................	4.8	2.8	4.7	9.5	21.6	19.2	22.2	19.5	1.1
Washington.................	6.6	4.0	16.9	10.9	22.7	22.3	16.9	17.3	2.4
West Virginia..............	-0.5	-1.2	5.1	12.2	23.0	12.6	18.0	24.9	-1.4
Wisconsin	1.5	0.4	3.9	8.3	21.1	17.1	18.2	13.6	-0.4
Wyoming	4.0	2.7	61.3	9.0	30.6	29.8	23.3	15.9	1.6

Table A-4. Population by Residence

Geographic area	Inside core-based statistical area (metropolitan and micropolitan area population)[1] (thousands)					Outside core-based statistical area[1] (thousands)				Urban population[3]			
										Number (thousands)		Percent of total population	
	2015	2010	2000[2]	Percent of total 2015	Percent change, 2010–2015	2015	2010	2000[2]	Percent change, 2010–2015	2010	2000	2010	2000
United States	303,026	290,139	263,072	94.3	4.4	18,393	18,619	18,346	-1.2	249,253	222,361	80.7	79.0
Alabama	4,412	4,319	3,970	90.8	2.2	447	461	477	-3.2	2,822	2,466	59.0	55.4
Alaska	546	523	447	73.9	4.3	193	187	180	2.9	469	411	66.0	65.6
Arizona	6,727	6,292	5,033	98.5	6.9	101	100	98	0.7	5,741	4,524	89.8	88.2
Arkansas	2,439	2,361	2,109	81.9	3.3	539	555	565	-2.8	1,638	1,404	56.2	52.5
California	38,876	36,978	33,611	99.3	5.1	269	277	261	-2.9	35,374	31,990	95.0	94.4
Colorado	5,152	4,723	4,005	94.4	9.1	305	306	297	-0.4	4,333	3,633	86.2	84.4
Connecticut	3,591	3,574	3,406	100.0	0.5	0	0	0	0.0	3,145	2,988	88.0	87.7
Delaware	946	898	784	100.0	5.3	0	0	0	0.0	748	628	83.3	80.1
District of Columbia	672	602	572	100.0	11.7	0	0	0	0.0	602	572	100.0	100.0
Florida	19,925	18,454	15,675	98.3	8.0	347	350	308		17,140	14,270	91.2	89.3
Georgia	9,429	8,899	7,469	92.3	6.0	786	790	718	-0.5	7,272	5,864	75.1	71.6
Hawaii	1,432	1,360	1,211	100.0	5.2	0	0	0	0.0	1,250	1,108	91.9	91.5
Idaho	1,517	1,428	1,159	91.7	6.2	138	140	135	-1.3	1,106	859	70.6	66.4
Illinois	12,252	12,207	11,779	95.3	0.4	608	624	641	-2.6	11,354	10,910	88.5	87.8
Indiana	6,159	6,018	5,618	93.0	2.4	460	466	463	-1.3	4,697	4,304	72.4	70.8
Iowa	2,391	2,300	2,149	76.5	4.0	733	747	777	-1.9	1,950	1,787	64.0	61.1
Kansas	2,518	2,449	2,259	86.5	2.8	393	404	430	-2.7	2,117	1,921	74.2	71.4
Kentucky	3,469	3,366	3,071	78.4	3.1	956	973	971	-1.8	2,533	2,254	58.4	55.8
Louisiana	4,343	4,198	4,125	93.0	3.5	328	335	344	-2.3	3,318	3,246	73.2	72.6
Maine	906	898	853	68.2	0.9	423	430	422	-1.7	514	513	38.7	40.2
Maryland	5,925	5,690	5,218	98.6	4.1	82	83	79	-1.9	5,034	4,559	87.2	86.1
Massachusetts	6,783	6,538	6,340	99.8	3.8	11	10	10	7.4	6,022	5,801	92.0	91.4
Michigan	9,258	9,204	9,242	93.3	0.6	664	680	697	-2.4	7,370	7,419	74.6	74.6
Minnesota	4,977	4,784	4,394	90.7	4.0	512	520	525	-1.5	3,886	3,490	73.3	70.9
Mississippi	2,348	2,310	2,183	78.5	1.7	644	658	661	-2.2	1,464	1,367	49.3	48.1
Missouri	5,252	5,144	4,777	86.3	2.1	832	845	820	-1.6	4,218	3,883	70.4	69.4
Montana	674	639	559	65.3	5.5	359	350	343	2.3	553	488	55.9	54.1
Nebraska	1,556	1,480	1,342	82.0	5.1	341	347	369	-1.7	1,336	1,194	73.1	69.8
Nevada	2,858	2,667	1,966	98.9	7.2	33	33	32	-2.3	2,544	1,829	94.2	91.5
New Hampshire	1,283	1,269	1,192	96.4	1.2	47	48	44	-1.1	794	732	60.3	59.2
New Jersey	8,958	8,792	8,415	100.0	1.9	0	0	0	0.0	8,324	7,939	94.7	94.4
New Mexico	2,012	1,981	1,737	96.5	1.6	73	78	82	-6.6	1,594	1,364	77.4	75.0
New York	19,402	18,972	18,572	98.0	2.3	394	406	405	-2.9	17,028	16,603	87.9	87.5
North Carolina	9,407	8,890	7,446	93.7	5.8	635	645	600	-1.5	6,302	4,849	66.1	60.3
North Dakota	557	485	440	73.5	14.8	200	188	202	6.7	403	359	59.9	55.9
Ohio	11,162	11,079	10,902	96.1	0.7	452	458	451	-1.3	8,990	8,782	77.9	77.4
Oklahoma	3,368	3,204	2,915	86.1	5.1	544	548	535	-0.8	2,485	2,255	66.2	65.4
Oregon	3,931	3,733	3,326	97.6	5.3	98	98	96	0.3	3,104	2,694	81.0	78.7
Pennsylvania	12,423	12,315	11,898	97.0	0.9	380	388	382	-2.1	9,991	9,464	78.7	77.1
Rhode Island	1,056	1,053	1,048	100.0	0.3	0	0	0	0.0	955	953	90.7	90.9
South Carolina	4,589	4,306	3,692	93.7	6.6	307	320	320	-4.1	3,068	2,427	66.3	60.5
South Dakota	641	599	531	74.6	6.9	218	215	224	1.3	461	391	56.7	51.8
Tennessee	5,971	5,713	5,082	90.5	4.5	630	633	607	-0.5	4,213	3,620	66.4	63.6
Texas	26,088	23,779	19,536	95.0	9.7	1,381	1,368	1,315	1.0	21,298	17,204	84.7	82.5
Utah	2,851	2,623	2,108	95.2	8.7	145	141	126	2.7	2,504	1,970	90.6	88.2
Vermont	463	461	449	73.9	0.2	164	164	159	-0.5	243	232	38.9	38.1
Virginia	7,600	7,210	6,313	90.7	5.4	783	791	759		6,037	5,170	75.5	73.0
Washington	7,016	6,572	5,751	97.8	6.8	154	152	144	1.3	5,652	4,831	84.0	82.0
West Virginia	1,440	1,439	1,391	78.1	0.1	404	414	417	-2.4	903	833	48.7	46.1
Wisconsin	5,050	4,958	4,650	87.5	1.8	722	729	714		3,990	3,664	70.2	68.3
Wyoming	425	405	352	72.6	5.0	161	159	142	1.4	365	321	64.8	65.0

Note. 0 = zero or rounds to 0.
[1] Covers metropolitan statistical areas, metropolitan divisions, and micropolitan statistical areas as defined by the Office of Management and Budget as of 2015. For information, see OMB Bulletin 15-01 at <https://obamawhitehouse.archives.gov/sites/default/files/omb/bulletins/2015/15-01.pdf>.
[2] The April 1, 2010 and April 1, 2000, Population Estimates bases reflect modifications to the decennial census population as documented in the Count Question Resolution program and geographic program revisions.
[3] Resident population.

Table A-5. Households

Geographic area	Total households (thousands) 2015	Total households (thousands) 2010	Family households Total¹ — Family households, total	Family households Total¹ — With own children under 18 years	Married couple families Total	Married couple families With own children under 18 years	Female householder, no husband present Total	Female householder, no husband present With own children under 18 years	Nonfamily households Total	Householder living alone Total	Householder living alone 65 years and over	Households with one or more people— under 18 years	Households with one or more people— 65 years and over	People per household 2015	People per household 2010
United States	118,208	116,716	65.6	27.9	48.0	18.8	12.8	6.8	34.4	27.9	10.5	31.4	28.1	2.65	2.58
Alabama	1,846	1,884	65.7	26.4	46.8	16.6	14.7	7.9	34.3	29.9	11.5	30.6	29.2	2.57	2.48
Alaska	250	258	65.5	31.2	48.1	20.3	11.3	7.3	34.5	26.7	6.5	34.4	20.1	2.84	2.65
Arizona	2,463	2,381	64.9	27.0	46.8	17.3	12.5	6.9	35.1	27.6	10.5	30.9	30.8	2.71	2.63
Arkansas	1,145	1,147	66.5	27.2	49.0	18.0	13.1	6.9	33.5	28.4	11.6	31.3	29.3	2.53	2.47
California	12,896	12,577	68.5	30.8	49.2	21.6	13.3	6.6	31.5	24.0	9.1	35.0	27.9	2.97	2.90
Colorado	2,075	1,973	64.2	28.8	50.0	21.0	9.7	5.5	35.8	27.2	8.8	31.7	24.0	2.57	2.49
Connecticut	1,344	1,371	65.2	27.2	48.2	18.5	12.7	6.9	34.8	28.5	11.4	29.8	29.0	2.59	2.52
Delaware	353	342	66.8	25.8	48.3	16.4	13.8	7.3	33.2	26.6	10.9	29.8	31.4	2.61	2.55
District of Columbia	282	267	44.4	19.3	25.5	9.9	15.1	7.8	55.6	42.0	10.2	22.7	20.4	2.24	2.11
Florida	7,463	7,421	64.4	23.9	46.2	15.0	13.4	6.7	35.6	28.9	12.6	27.3	35.2	2.66	2.48
Georgia	3,656	3,586	67.5	30.0	47.9	19.5	15.0	8.2	32.5	26.9	8.7	34.3	25.0	2.72	2.63
Hawaii	446	455	69.4	25.8	52.1	19.6	11.7	4.2	30.6	23.4	9.4	31.6	34.8	3.11	2.89
Idaho	597	579	67.0	29.3	53.7	21.2	9.4	5.8	33.0	27.2	10.1	32.3	27.8	2.72	2.66
Illinois	4,795	4,837	64.6	28.1	47.7	19.4	12.5	6.7	35.4	29.4	10.9	31.2	26.9	2.62	2.59
Indiana	2,515	2,502	65.0	27.9	48.3	18.5	12.0	6.9	35.0	29.1	10.8	31.3	26.8	2.56	2.52
Iowa	1,247	1,222	63.9	27.3	50.4	18.9	9.2	5.8	36.1	29.1	11.3	29.4	27.6	2.42	2.41
Kansas	1,112	1,112	64.8	29.2	50.4	20.5	9.9	6.1	35.2	29.5	10.8	31.7	26.5	2.55	2.49
Kentucky	1,716	1,720	66.0	26.6	48.3	17.5	12.7	6.7	34.0	28.5	10.5	30.7	27.7	2.50	2.45
Louisiana	1,738	1,728	63.8	27.2	43.0	16.0	15.9	8.7	36.2	30.7	10.8	31.3	26.8	2.61	2.55
Maine	545	557	62.9	23.2	48.5	14.7	9.8	5.8	37.1	29.6	13.1	25.5	32.2	2.37	2.32
Maryland	2,178	2,156	66.8	28.9	47.9	19.7	14.0	6.9	33.2	27.0	10.0	33.0	27.4	2.69	2.61
Massachusetts	2,560	2,547	63.0	26.7	46.4	18.5	12.5	6.6	37.0	28.8	11.5	29.3	28.6	2.56	2.48
Michigan	3,859	3,873	64.3	26.0	47.2	17.1	12.3	6.7	35.7	29.5	11.1	29.0	28.7	2.51	2.49
Minnesota	2,147	2,087	64.5	28.6	50.8	20.2	9.2	5.9	35.5	28.4	10.5	30.5	25.8	2.49	2.48
Mississippi	1,104	1,116	67.3	27.9	43.9	15.9	18.2	9.7	32.7	28.4	11.1	33.4	28.7	2.62	2.58
Missouri	2,374	2,376	64.0	26.7	47.9	17.8	11.8	6.6	36.0	29.7	11.3	29.8	28.1	2.49	2.45
Montana	415	410	61.0	24.1	48.9	17.1	8.4	4.8	39.0	31.5	11.7	26.3	29.8	2.42	2.35
Nebraska	744	721	63.1	28.8	49.6	20.7	9.5	5.9	36.9	30.0	11.1	31.3	26.2	2.48	2.46
Nevada	1,042	1,006	63.3	27.1	43.8	16.9	13.4	7.2	36.7	28.7	9.8	30.5	28.1	2.74	2.65
New Hampshire	518	519	66.0	24.9	52.0	17.7	10.0	5.3	34.0	26.2	10.1	27.3	28.8	2.49	2.46
New Jersey	3,188	3,214	69.2	30.3	51.2	21.8	13.1	6.6	30.8	25.9	10.9	33.2	29.4	2.75	2.68
New Mexico	762	791	63.7	26.1	44.9	16.0	13.1	7.2	36.3	30.6	11.8	29.8	30.4	2.68	2.55
New York	7,234	7,318	63.1	26.5	43.6	17.4	14.5	7.0	36.9	30.1	11.5	29.8	29.0	2.66	2.57
North Carolina	3,844	3,745	65.2	27.5	47.6	18.2	13.2	7.1	34.8	28.8	10.4	31.0	27.6	2.55	2.48
North Dakota	313	281	60.0	26.3	47.9	18.7	7.8	5.0	40.0	30.4	10.6	28.2	23.7	2.33	2.30
Ohio	4,607	4,603	63.4	26.4	46.1	17.0	12.8	7.2	36.6	30.3	11.5	29.6	28.2	2.45	2.44
Oklahoma	1,466	1,460	66.1	28.5	48.7	18.7	12.2	7.0	33.9	28.0	10.9	32.5	27.5	2.59	2.49
Oregon	1,553	1,519	63.0	25.5	48.3	17.5	10.3	5.9	37.0	27.9	11.1	28.3	29.8	2.54	2.47
Pennsylvania	4,956	5,019	64.7	25.3	47.8	16.8	12.3	6.4	35.3	29.2	12.2	28.2	30.6	2.50	2.45
Rhode Island	407	414	61.4	25.8	42.9	16.0	14.0	7.8	38.6	31.8	12.9	28.7	29.5	2.49	2.44
South Carolina	1,858	1,801	65.7	25.6	46.7	16.1	14.6	7.5	34.3	28.9	10.7	29.6	29.8	2.56	2.49
South Dakota	339	322	63.9	27.8	50.2	19.0	9.5	6.2	36.1	29.6	11.4	30.2	26.9	2.43	2.42
Tennessee	2,530	2,494	66.2	26.7	47.9	17.3	13.6	7.1	33.8	28.0	10.5	30.8	28.4	2.55	2.48
Texas	9,421	8,923	69.2	32.7	50.0	22.2	14.0	8.0	30.8	25.3	8.0	37.0	23.7	2.85	2.75
Utah	931	878	74.5	37.2	60.7	29.9	9.5	5.2	25.5	19.8	7.2	41.1	22.7	3.17	3.10
Vermont	255	256	59.8	23.0	48.5	16.5	7.9	4.5	40.2	30.3	12.8	25.3	30.5	2.36	2.34
Virginia	3,107	3,056	66.1	28.4	49.9	20.0	11.9	6.4	33.9	27.1	9.9	31.8	26.9	2.62	2.54
Washington	2,729	2,620	64.5	27.9	50.0	19.8	10.0	5.7	35.5	27.0	9.7	30.7	26.6	2.58	2.51
West Virginia	735	764	64.3	23.5	47.8	15.3	11.5	5.8	35.7	30.3	12.9	27.5	32.5	2.44	2.36
Wisconsin	2,320	2,280	63.4	26.7	49.0	18.2	9.8	5.9	36.6	29.1	11.1	29.0	27.1	2.42	2.43
Wyoming	229	227	63.5	27.8	51.2	19.9	7.2	4.5	36.5	29.9	10.9	30.1	25.6	2.50	2.42

¹Total includes male householder with no wife present (not shown separately).

Table A-6.   Marital Status, 2015

Geographic area	Males 15 years and over						Females 15 years and over					
	Total (thousands)	Percentage					Total (thousands)	Percentage				
		Never married	Now married, except separated[1]	Separated[2]	Widowed	Divorced		Never married	Now married, except separated[1]	Separated[2]	Widowed	Divorced
United States	127,013	36.7	49.2	1.7	2.6	9.7	133,402	30.5	45.9	2.3	8.9	12.3
Alabama	1,886	34.1	49.0	2.1	3.0	11.8	2,061	28.5	44.4	2.9	10.8	13.4
Alaska	308	40.4	46.2	1.7	1.8	10.0	274	30.5	48.2	2.3	5.7	13.3
Arizona	2,702	37.4	47.3	1.4	2.6	11.4	2,780	29.8	45.4	2.0	8.6	14.2
Arkansas	1,163	30.7	52.0	1.9	3.1	12.3	1,228	24.3	48.4	2.3	11.0	14.0
California	15,577	40.6	47.5	1.8	2.1	8.0	16,000	33.6	45.0	2.6	7.8	11.0
Colorado	2,206	35.5	50.8	1.3	2.1	10.4	2,200	27.9	50.4	1.6	6.4	13.7
Connecticut	1,435	38.2	49.2	1.1	2.5	8.9	1,537	32.6	44.9	1.6	8.7	12.3
Delaware	372	36.6	49.3	1.3	3.1	9.7	404	31.3	44.8	2.1	9.3	12.5
District of Columbia	268	57.4	31.1	2.3	2.2	7.1	302	53.6	27.1	2.1	6.8	10.4
Florida	8,168	35.4	47.7	2.1	3.2	11.6	8,722	28.5	43.4	2.7	10.7	14.8
Georgia	3,917	36.7	49.1	1.9	2.4	9.8	4,222	31.8	44.7	2.5	8.4	12.7
Hawaii	590	37.7	50.1	1.3	2.7	8.3	578	29.3	48.5	1.5	9.9	10.8
Idaho	643	31.3	54.4	1.4	2.2	10.7	652	25.5	52.4	1.4	7.5	13.2
Illinois	5,064	38.3	49.2	1.4	2.5	8.5	5,349	32.8	45.6	1.9	8.8	10.8
Indiana	2,587	34.5	49.9	1.2	2.7	11.7	2,728	28.6	46.8	1.5	9.3	13.9
Iowa	1,240	32.7	53.3	1.0	2.7	10.2	1,278	26.5	50.9	1.5	9.7	11.4
Kansas	1,145	33.6	52.1	1.1	2.6	10.6	1,168	26.5	50.5	1.6	9.3	12.1
Kentucky	1,747	31.6	50.4	1.8	3.1	13.1	1,842	25.6	48.0	2.5	10.0	13.9
Louisiana	1,807	38.7	44.9	2.1	3.3	11.0	1,934	32.7	41.2	3.0	10.2	12.9
Maine	544	32.0	51.4	1.1	2.8	12.7	578	25.6	48.0	1.3	10.0	15.2
Maryland	2,341	37.6	49.5	2.0	2.3	8.6	2,550	33.0	44.4	2.5	8.6	11.5
Massachusetts	2,717	40.4	47.8	1.3	2.4	8.1	2,942	34.5	43.6	2.1	8.6	11.2
Michigan	3,954	36.6	49.0	1.2	2.7	10.5	4,163	30.7	46.3	1.4	9.1	12.5
Minnesota	2,182	34.9	52.6	1.0	2.4	9.1	2,239	28.7	51.1	1.2	7.8	11.3
Mississippi	1,143	37.3	46.0	2.7	3.0	10.9	1,245	32.0	41.9	3.0	10.6	12.4
Missouri	2,396	33.5	50.6	1.6	2.9	11.4	2,536	27.8	47.1	2.0	9.9	13.3
Montana	424	33.3	50.6	1.2	3.2	11.7	421	25.0	50.7	1.1	8.9	14.2
Nebraska	741	34.4	52.2	1.1	2.4	9.9	761	26.9	51.3	1.6	8.9	11.4
Nevada	1,164	37.1	45.2	2.2	2.7	12.7	1,169	29.5	44.0	2.6	8.2	15.7
New Hampshire	549	33.4	52.2	0.9	2.6	11.0	569	26.4	50.1	1.3	8.4	13.8
New Jersey	3,536	37.8	51.2	1.6	2.6	6.8	3,778	31.7	46.7	2.1	9.5	10.1
New Mexico	822	37.4	46.3	1.5	3.0	11.9	847	30.9	43.7	2.1	9.0	14.3
New York	7,832	41.7	46.5	2.0	2.5	7.3	8,480	36.3	41.6	3.0	8.8	10.4
North Carolina	3,924	34.7	50.4	2.5	2.7	9.7	4,223	29.0	46.1	3.1	9.4	12.4
North Dakota	315	36.9	51.2	0.9	2.0	9.0	297	27.7	51.9	1.0	9.2	10.2
Ohio	4,578	35.2	49.1	1.6	2.9	11.2	4,874	29.2	46.1	1.9	9.7	13.0
Oklahoma	1,527	32.2	50.6	1.8	3.3	12.0	1,582	24.9	48.5	2.1	9.9	14.5
Oregon	1,630	34.7	49.7	1.6	2.4	11.5	1,687	27.4	47.6	2.0	8.1	14.9
Pennsylvania	5,131	36.9	49.4	2.0	3.0	8.8	5,459	30.8	45.8	2.4	10.3	10.6
Rhode Island	423	40.1	46.5	1.3	2.5	9.5	460	34.1	40.9	2.1	9.6	13.3
South Carolina	1,925	35.6	48.7	2.6	2.9	10.1	2,070	29.8	44.5	3.6	10.2	11.9
South Dakota	341	34.3	52.1	1.1	2.8	9.8	342	26.5	52.0	1.3	9.2	11.0
Tennessee	2,586	33.0	50.6	1.8	2.8	11.8	2,777	27.4	46.6	2.5	9.8	13.7
Texas	10,558	36.0	50.3	2.1	2.2	9.4	10,888	29.6	47.3	3.0	7.9	12.2
Utah	1,112	33.2	55.7	1.4	1.7	8.0	1,116	26.7	54.9	1.7	5.9	10.7
Vermont	258	35.1	49.9	0.9	2.5	11.6	271	28.5	47.9	1.2	8.5	13.9
Virginia	3,331	35.3	51.2	2.2	2.5	8.8	3,496	29.6	47.2	2.8	8.4	12.0
Washington	2,900	34.9	51.0	1.3	2.2	10.7	2,929	27.6	49.6	1.8	7.4	13.5
West Virginia	751	31.3	49.6	1.4	3.7	14.0	781	24.5	47.9	1.8	11.8	13.9
Wisconsin	2,321	35.4	51.4	0.9	2.5	9.8	2,383	28.9	49.5	1.3	8.7	11.5
Wyoming	235	30.9	53.5	1.1	2.5	12.0	233	25.2	52.5	1.6	8.5	12.2

[1]Includes people whose current marriage has not ended through widowhood, divorce, or separation (regardless of previous marital history). The category may also include couples who live together or people in common-law marriages, if they consider this category the most appropriate.
[2]Includes people legally separated or otherwise absent from their spouse because of marital discord. Those without a final divorce decree are classified as "separated." This category also includes people who have been deserted or who have parted because they no longer want to live together but who have not obtained a divorce.

Table A-7. Residence One Year Ago, People Obtaining Legal Permanent Resident Status, and Language Spoken at Home, Selected Years

Geographic area	Residence 1 year ago, 2015 — Population 1 year old and over (thousands)	Percentage of population who lived in same house 1 year ago	People obtaining lawful permanent resident status[1] — Total 2015	Total 2010	Total 2005	Leading countries of birth, 2015 — Mexico	China	India	Phillippines	Cuba	Dominican Republic	Vietnam	Language spoken at home, population 5 years old and over in the United States, 2015 — All languages other than English — Total (thousands)	Percentage of population	Spanish (thousands)
United States	317,636	85.3	1,051,031	1,042,625	1,122,257	158,619	74,558	64,116	56,478	54,396	50,610	30,832	64,716	21.5	40,046
Alabama.......................	4,802	85.7	3,928	3,740	4,200	640	245	321	239	49	31	190	233	5.1	150
Alaska.........................	728	80.1	1,572	1,703	1,524	101	63	11	580	8	109	19	110	16.2	27
Arizona.......................	6,748	82.0	17,997	18,243	18,986	8,277	502	789	870	408	80	480	1,733	27.1	1,317
Arkansas.....................	2,938	83.1	2,814	2,684	2,698	882	114	226	214	4	7	120	202	7.3	145
California.....................	38,675	86.5	209,568	208,446	232,014	55,166	25,030	12,925	19,633	445	189	10,618	16,326	44.6	10,646
Colorado	5,393	81.7	12,661	12,489	11,975	3,485	535	498	347	64	24	454	881	17.2	623
Connecticut..................	3,555	87.5	11,102	12,222	15,334	281	449	966	294	52	889	162	762	22.4	401
Delaware.....................	936	85.6	2,168	2,198	2,991	213	199	316	97	6	78	23	117	13.1	64
District of Columbia	663	79.2	2,976	2,897	2,457	59	198	47	72	12	90	31	110	17.4	56
Florida.........................	20,068	83.9	118,873	107,276	122,915	4,073	2,028	1,972	2,819	43,075	3,646	1,349	5,553	29.0	4,091
Georgia	10,089	84.2	25,919	24,833	31,527	3,327	1,226	2,519	703	302	342	1,284	1,338	14.0	769
Hawaii.........................	1,414	85.3	6,513	7,037	6,480	100	487	25	3,805	5	6	194	349	26.1	32
Idaho..........................	1,635	81.6	2,531	2,556	2,768	753	124	45	101	11	7	40	158	10.2	117
Illinois.........................	12,706	86.8	40,482	37,909	52,415	9,274	2,337	4,745	2,461	132	111	577	2,780	23.0	1,634
Indiana........................	6,541	84.5	8,554	8,539	6,913	1,522	489	803	402	56	81	164	522	8.4	283
Iowa...........................	3,081	84.3	5,047	4,245	4,535	862	288	252	197	24	8	225	225	7.7	117
Kansas........................	2,876	83.7	5,419	5,501	4,512	1,523	259	330	313	105	14	214	319	11.8	208
Kentucky	4,373	84.8	5,647	4,930	5,265	448	249	282	186	839	15	109	220	5.3	109
Louisiana	4,612	86.9	4,696	4,397	3,776	468	310	185	291	197	143	446	356	8.2	154
Maine..........................	1,317	85.6	1,464	1,349	1,907	27	81	28	67	D	10	41	77	6.1	11
Maryland......................	5,934	85.6	22,627	26,450	22,868	423	1,318	1,391	1,120	47	465	397	1,045	18.5	443
Massachusetts..............	6,726	87.6	28,535	31,069	34,232	248	2,388	1,694	328	66	4,036	939	1,476	23.0	550
Michigan......................	9,811	85.6	18,049	18,579	23,591	1,305	738	1,653	519	151	146	362	886	9.5	274
Minnesota....................	5,420	85.2	14,737	12,408	15,449	1,268	540	891	364	24	45	448	588	11.5	194
Mississippi...................	2,959	86.3	1,587	1,709	1,829	271	152	159	139	16	31	117	109	3.9	68
Missouri.......................	6,016	84.1	6,731	7,151	8,742	749	448	494	397	167	45	285	342	6.0	149
Montana.......................	1,020	83.9	519	457	589	40	38	12	81	D	D	11	41	4.2	14
Nebraska.....................	1,869	84.0	5,234	4,400	2,996	1,004	117	141	107	289	9	200	196	11.1	131
Nevada........................	2,859	80.1	11,053	10,803	9,823	2,577	649	192	1,893	1,296	63	199	820	30.2	576
New Hampshire.............	1,318	86.1	2,159	2,556	3,298	46	121	212	83	9	188	51	99	7.8	26
New Jersey	8,854	90.2	49,801	56,920	56,176	1,051	2,058	7,258	2,245	950	7,810	426	2,596	30.8	1,342
New Mexico	2,060	85.8	3,626	3,528	3,513	2,074	93	113	207	123	7	94	669	34.3	531
New York.....................	19,570	89.5	130,010	147,999	136,815	2,202	16,449	4,319	2,870	583	23,588	483	5,747	30.9	2,833
North Carolina..............	9,928	84.4	18,495	16,112	16,710	2,680	987	1,529	674	320	403	683	1,083	11.5	714
North Dakota................	745	81.6	1,600	1,058	864	53	58	45	102	7	5	27	42	5.9	11
Ohio...........................	11,482	84.7	16,050	13,585	16,892	746	957	1,637	674	57	192	280	759	6.9	246
Oklahoma....................	3,865	82.9	4,880	4,627	4,702	1,483	192	204	248	55	19	327	369	10.1	261
Oregon........................	3,986	82.2	8,655	7,997	9,623	2,217	646	377	409	146	22	533	573	15.1	348
Pennsylvania................	12,662	87.7	24,969	24,130	28,902	878	2,049	2,382	590	246	2,707	916	1,314	10.9	554
Rhode Island................	1,045	86.2	3,610	4,027	3,852	57	146	60	80	4	1,246	15	222	22.2	120
South Carolina	4,840	84.8	4,417	4,401	5,028	629	263	369	302	39	62	150	311	6.8	198
South Dakota	848	82.8	1,265	987	881	77	42	24	57	7	5	18	53	6.6	16
Tennessee	6,522	84.9	8,833	8,156	8,960	1,108	433	629	618	207	55	242	428	6.9	241
Texas..........................	27,093	83.9	99,727	87,750	95,951	36,684	3,368	6,084	3,349	3,398	449	4,057	9,027	35.4	7,521
Utah...........................	2,947	82.6	6,883	6,085	5,082	1,916	308	184	190	30	37	215	408	14.8	280
Vermont.......................	620	85.9	792	867	1,042	14	53	33	15	D	D	20	36	6.1	7
Virginia........................	8,284	83.9	27,622	28,607	27,095	810	1,302	2,011	1,515	139	257	969	1,252	15.9	553
Washington..................	7,089	81.5	24,765	22,283	26,480	2,986	2,602	2,011	1,926	60	37	1,448	1,296	19.3	586
West Virginia................	1,824	88.3	786	729	847	46	62	58	62	0	13	39	45	2.6	19
Wisconsin	5,708	85.7	6,655	6,189	7,907	1,253	501	617	260	27	67	113	471	8.7	253
Wyoming	579	82.0	539	452	321	163	53	11	60	0	5	12	41	7.5	30

0 = zero.

D = Figure withheld to avoid disclosure pertaining to a specific organization or individual.

[1]People obtaining legal permanent resident status—Based on U.S. application Citizenship and Immigration Services (USCIS)-based case management systems that compile information supplied by aliens on the forms they are required to submit when applying for a legal status; for information, see Internet site www.dhs.gov/yearbook-immigration-statistics.

Table A-8. Place of Birth, 2015

Geographic area	Total population (thousands)	Percentage			Foreign born											
													Percentage			
												Born in				
		Born in state of residence	Born in different state	Foreign born	Total (thousands)	Not a citizen	Entered the U.S. in 2000 or later	Europe	Asia					Latin America		
									Total	China	India	Philippines	Vietnam	Total	Mexico	El Salvador
United States	321,419	58.5	26.5	13.5	43,290	52.2	15.6	11.1	30.6	6.2	5.5	4.6	3.0	51.1	26.9	3.1
Alabama	4,859	70.1	25.7	3.5	170	63.7	20.7	12.2	28.1	4.4	5.0	3.0	2.6	51.8	31.5	1.5
Alaska	738	41.8	48.1	7.9	59	44.7	17.8	15.4	55.9	2.6	2.2	35.5	2.5	18.0	7.1	0.9
Arizona	6,828	39.2	45.9	13.4	914	58.4	14.6	9.0	20.2	3.1	4.1	2.9	2.3	62.9	56.6	0.8
Arkansas	2,978	61.7	32.7	4.8	143	66.9	16.3	6.9	24.3	3.6	6.8	1.5	2.9	61.3	38.7	11.6
California	39,145	54.8	16.6	27.3	10,688	50.3	11.2	6.4	38.6	8.5	4.5	8.1	4.8	51.2	40.0	4.0
Colorado	5,157	42.7	45.9	9.8	537	61.3	15.2	13.4	23.2	3.9	4.1	1.8	3.3	54.4	44.1	1.8
Connecticut	3,591	55.3	26.6	14.5	520	51.2	17.0	25.6	24.3	4.9	7.1	2.1	0.8	42.9	5.1	1.0
Delaware	946	45.6	43.8	9.3	88	54.8	19.1	9.6	35.7	6.2	14.8	3.7	2.0	41.3	18.2	0.2
District of Columbia	672	35.8	48.1	14.1	95	56.2	26.3	18.1	23.1	4.7	4.4	2.3	1.8	40.3	3.5	13.4
Florida	20,271	35.9	40.3	20.2	4,086	46.3	16.9	9.3	10.9	1.5	2.0	2.1	1.2	75.1	6.9	1.0
Georgia	10,215	54.9	33.8	10.0	1,024	58.1	16.4	8.9	28.6	3.6	8.4	1.3	3.4	50.1	25.3	2.9
Hawaii	1,432	53.0	25.9	17.7	253	42.2	15.3	4.9	80.0	10.7	0.7	47.1	3.5	5.7	2.8	0.1
Idaho	1,655	48.0	45.4	5.7	94	61.9	18.7	15.6	19.9	4.3	1.1	3.2	1.3	55.8	50.0	0.7
Illinois	12,860	67.2	17.5	14.2	1,826	51.8	13.0	20.0	29.2	5.1	8.4	4.9	1.1	45.7	37.6	0.6
Indiana	6,620	68.4	26.0	4.9	321	61.7	21.6	11.9	33.7	8.5	8.2	3.1	1.8	45.4	32.1	2.7
Iowa	3,124	71.1	23.6	4.8	149	62.6	25.4	12.9	35.8	8.2	6.4	2.5	3.8	39.3	29.2	3.0
Kansas	2,912	58.6	33.5	7.1	206	62.5	21.0	7.8	31.1	4.5	6.9	2.7	5.7	51.7	41.0	1.9
Kentucky	4,425	69.6	26.2	3.6	157	63.0	28.3	15.1	35.6	5.0	6.8	4.4	1.8	37.7	20.0	1.3
Louisiana	4,671	78.3	17.1	4.0	186	59.1	21.9	9.7	32.4	4.6	4.0	2.3	13.0	52.7	14.2	2.8
Maine	1,329	64.1	31.6	3.4	45	42.8	19.3	24.0	30.0	4.9	3.7	4.7	2.1	10.2	2.3	0.5
Maryland	6,006	47.2	36.1	15.2	912	50.9	17.5	9.3	33.4	6.1	7.0	4.0	2.3	39.3	4.5	13.2
Massachusetts	6,794	61.6	19.4	16.1	1,096	47.7	19.7	21.2	30.3	10.1	6.0	1.2	3.5	35.8	1.5	3.3
Michigan	9,923	76.6	16.1	6.6	652	47.5	20.8	20.6	50.7	6.8	9.9	2.7	2.1	18.6	12.2	0.3
Minnesota	5,490	67.7	23.2	8.3	457	50.8	23.5	10.5	38.8	5.0	6.7	1.7	4.4	25.1	14.7	1.5
Mississippi	2,992	71.5	25.4	2.4	72	66.6	21.8	11.0	28.7	4.3	6.8	4.1	6.4	51.5	35.4	2.2
Missouri	6,084	66.1	29.1	4.0	243	55.6	23.5	16.2	39.5	7.7	9.3	4.0	4.6	31.1	18.6	1.7
Montana	1,033	54.3	42.9	2.1	21	46.7	-	22.8	25.9	5.1	0.5	4.5	1.4	21.7	12.9	0.4
Nebraska	1,896	64.9	27.4	6.8	128	62.3	23.9	6.5	28.0	4.2	5.9	1.8	4.4	55.0	39.7	2.5
Nevada	2,891	25.8	53.1	19.3	558	53.2	11.7	7.9	30.1	4.1	2.0	14.3	1.3	56.2	40.4	4.8
New Hampshire	1,331	42.1	50.8	6.0	80	43.1	17.6	25.4	34.5	5.2	10.7	2.8	2.1	20.9	1.2	0.6
New Jersey	8,958	52.6	23.1	22.1	1,977	44.8	14.8	15.4	33.4	4.7	12.7	4.5	0.9	44.8	6.0	2.3
New Mexico	2,085	53.3	36.1	9.4	197	63.7	13.7	7.5	11.7	2.3	1.3	1.5	1.9	76.9	70.8	1.1
New York	19,796	63.1	11.5	22.9	4,530	44.8	14.9	16.3	29.3	10.4	3.8	2.1	0.6	48.6	5.2	2.6
North Carolina	10,043	57.1	33.8	7.9	795	62.6	17.0	11.1	26.4	3.9	7.8	2.0	2.8	53.6	30.2	3.8
North Dakota	757	63.7	31.7	3.8	29	56.1	-	21.5	33.2	4.4	4.7	10.1	1.9	15.2	3.1	0.2
Ohio	11,613	75.2	19.6	4.3	504	49.3	25.8	22.3	42.0	8.6	11.2	2.5	2.2	19.3	9.0	0.9
Oklahoma	3,911	60.6	32.3	6.0	235	66.7	19.7	6.1	27.1	3.9	3.5	2.4	6.4	60.1	48.7	1.9
Oregon	4,029	45.9	43.1	9.9	397	57.7	15.2	13.8	32.1	7.0	3.9	2.8	5.7	44.8	37.2	1.6
Pennsylvania	12,803	72.9	18.9	6.5	837	47.4	21.8	20.9	40.2	8.8	10.7	2.5	4.2	28.7	6.8	0.6
Rhode Island	1,056	56.6	27.5	13.5	142	45.6	16.9	21.9	19.1	5.4	3.6	1.7	0.9	43.8	1.8	1.7
South Carolina	4,896	57.7	36.5	4.8	233	60.5	18.1	15.8	25.1	4.8	4.9	4.4	2.2	51.0	28.1	1.6
South Dakota	858	64.9	31.3	3.2	28	62.6	-	17.5	38.6	4.8	2.2	6.2	0.9	20.2	11.7	1.6
Tennessee	6,600	60.1	34.0	5.0	332	63.6	22.7	9.7	30.0	3.6	6.0	3.2	2.3	44.7	27.0	2.6
Texas	27,469	59.7	21.9	17.0	4,671	64.2	16.3	4.1	21.1	3.0	5.1	2.1	3.6	68.7	54.9	4.3
Utah	2,996	62.3	28.6	8.2	244	60.9	14.7	9.3	20.0	3.0	2.6	2.9	2.2	60.5	42.3	3.4
Vermont	626	49.9	44.5	4.5	28	45.3	-	32.3	29.0	5.1	0.2	0.3	1.8	10.8	3.7	0.0
Virginia	8,383	49.5	36.5	12.2	1,019	49.0	18.2	10.1	42.0	5.0	8.0	5.1	4.6	35.8	5.7	10.3
Washington	7,170	47.3	37.1	13.7	980	53.2	17.5	15.4	42.4	8.7	6.5	7.1	5.0	30.9	24.5	1.5
West Virginia	1,844	69.7	28.2	1.6	30	47.7	27.0	26.0	43.3	9.5	8.7	4.7	3.8	22.0	4.1	0.5
Wisconsin	5,771	71.4	23.0	4.8	279	54.6	17.4	15.7	36.1	5.9	7.1	2.6	0.8	41.1	32.7	0.4
Wyoming	586	40.7	54.9	3.8	22	61.4	-	12.4	18.9	3.1	0.8	5.8	2.4	58.8	48.9	3.3

Table A-9.   Live Births and Birth Rates

Geographic area	Total			Rate[1]			Percentage with low birth weight[2]			Rate[3] for teenage mothers[4]			Percentage to unmarried women		
	2015	2010	2000	2015	2010	2000	2011	2010	2000	2015	2010	2000	2015	2010	2000
United States	3,978,497	3,999,386	4,058,814	12.4	13.0	14.4	8.1	8.1	7.6	22.3	34.2	48.5	40.3	40.8	33.2
Alabama	59,657	60,050	63,299	12.3	12.6	14.2	9.9	10.3	9.7	30.1	43.6	62.9	43.9	41.9	34.3
Alaska	11,282	11,471	9,974	15.3	16.2	15.9	6.0	5.7	5.6	29.3	38.3	42.4	36.1	37.6	33.0
Arizona	85,351	87,477	85,273	12.5	13.7	16.6	7.0	7.1	7.0	26.3	41.9	69.1	45.5	44.9	39.3
Arkansas	38,886	38,540	37,783	13.1	13.2	14.1	9.1	8.8	8.6	38.0	52.5	68.5	45.0	45.3	35.7
California	491,748	510,198	531,959	12.6	13.7	15.7	6.8	6.8	6.2	19.0	31.5	48.5	38.8	40.5	32.7
Colorado	66,581	66,355	65,438	12.2	13.2	15.2	8.7	8.8	8.4	19.3	33.4	49.2	22.7	23.9	25.0
Connecticut..................	35,746	37,708	43,026	10.0	10.6	12.6	7.7	8.0	7.4	10.1	18.7	31.9	37.5	37.4	29.3
Delaware	11,166	11,364	11,051	11.8	12.7	14.1	8.4	8.9	8.6	18.1	30.5	51.6	46.3	47.4	37.9
District of Columbia	9,578	9,165	7,666	14.2	15.2	13.4	10.5	10.2	11.9	25.6	45.4	80.7	49.3	54.8	60.3
Florida	224,269	214,590	204,125	11.1	11.4	12.8	8.7	8.7	8.0	20.8	32.0	52.6	47.8	47.5	38.2
Georgia	131,404	133,947	132,644	12.9	13.8	16.2	9.4	9.7	8.6	25.6	41.4	64.2	45.2	45.8	37.0
Hawaii.........................	18,420	18,988	17,551	12.9	14.0	14.5	8.2	8.3	7.5	20.6	32.5	45.1	37.1	37.8	32.2
Idaho..........................	22,827	23,198	20,366	13.8	14.8	15.7	6.1	6.8	6.7	22.5	33.0	43.1	27.7	26.5	21.6
Illinois........................	158,116	165,200	185,036	12.3	12.9	14.9	8.2	8.3	7.9	21.1	33.0	49.5	40.4	40.5	34.5
Indiana........................	84,040	83,940	87,699	12.7	12.9	14.4	8.1	8.0	7.4	26.0	37.3	50.3	43.3	43.0	34.7
Iowa...........................	39,482	38,719	38,266	12.6	12.7	13.1	6.5	7.0	6.1	18.6	28.6	34.7	35.3	34.2	28.0
Kansas........................	39,154	40,649	39,666	13.4	14.2	14.8	7.2	7.1	6.9	25.5	39.3	45.3	36.0	37.8	29.0
Kentucky	55,971	55,784	56,029	12.6	12.9	13.9	9.1	9.0	8.2	32.4	46.2	55.3	41.6	41.2	31.0
Louisiana	64,692	62,379	67,898	13.9	13.8	15.2	10.9	10.7	10.3	34.1	47.7	62.1	52.9	53.3	45.6
Maine..........................	12,607	12,970	13,603	9.5	9.8	10.7	6.7	6.3	6.0	15.4	21.4	28.7	40.5	41.2	31.0
Maryland......................	73,616	73,801	74,316	12.3	12.8	14.0	8.9	8.8	8.6	17.0	27.3	41.6	40.1	41.9	34.6
Massachusetts.............	71,492	72,865	81,614	10.5	11.1	12.9	7.6	7.7	7.1	9.4	17.2	27.1	33.4	34.7	26.5
Michigan......................	113,312	114,531	136,171	11.4	11.6	13.7	8.3	8.4	7.9	19.4	30.1	39.2	41.9	41.8	33.3
Minnesota....................	69,834	68,610	67,604	12.7	12.9	13.7	6.4	6.4	6.1	13.7	22.5	29.6	32.2	33.2	25.8
Mississippi...................	38,394	40,036	44,075	12.8	13.5	15.5	11.8	12.1	10.7	34.8	55.0	72.0	53.5	54.8	46.0
Missouri......................	75,061	76,759	76,463	12.3	12.8	13.7	7.9	8.2	7.8	25.0	37.1	48.8	40.4	40.2	34.6
Montana......................	12,583	12,060	10,957	12.2	12.2	12.1	7.2	7.5	6.2	25.3	35.0	35.8	36.3	36.4	30.8
Nebraska.....................	26,679	25,918	24,646	14.1	14.2	14.4	6.6	7.1	6.8	22.0	31.1	37.2	32.9	33.6	27.2
Nevada........................	36,298	35,934	30,829	12.6	13.3	15.4	8.2	8.3	7.2	27.6	38.6	62.2	46.7	44.3	36.4
New Hampshire............	12,433	12,874	14,609	9.3	9.8	11.8	7.1	6.9	6.3	10.9	15.7	23.4	34.2	33.2	24.7
New Jersey	103,127	106,922	115,632	11.5	12.2	13.7	8.5	8.2	7.7	12.1	20.1	31.7	35.1	35.4	28.9
New Mexico	25,816	27,850	27,223	12.4	13.5	15.0	8.8	8.7	8.0	34.6	53.0	66.2	52.1	52.3	45.6
New York	237,274	244,375	258,737	12.0	12.6	13.6	8.1	8.2	7.7	14.6	22.7	35.6	39.5	41.7	36.6
North Carolina..............	120,843	122,350	120,311	12.0	12.8	14.9	9.0	9.1	8.8	23.6	38.3	59.9	41.0	42.0	33.3
North Dakota................	11,314	9,104	7,676	14.9	13.5	12.0	6.7	6.7	6.4	22.2	28.8	28.2	31.6	32.7	28.3
Ohio...........................	139,264	139,128	155,472	12.0	12.1	13.7	8.6	8.6	7.9	23.2	34.1	45.6	43.3	43.8	34.6
Oklahoma....................	53,122	53,238	49,782	13.6	14.2	14.4	8.5	8.4	7.5	34.8	50.4	60.1	41.8	41.8	34.3
Oregon........................	45,655	45,540	45,804	11.3	11.9	13.4	6.1	6.3	5.6	19.0	28.2	43.2	36.0	35.7	30.1
Pennsylvania	141,047	143,321	146,281	11.0	11.3	11.9	8.2	8.3	7.7	17.7	27.0	35.2	41.2	41.5	32.7
Rhode Island................	10,993	11,177	12,505	10.4	10.6	11.9	7.4	7.7	7.2	14.3	22.3	38.4	45.1	45.0	35.5
South Carolina	58,139	58,342	56,114	11.9	12.6	14.0	9.9	9.9	9.7	26.2	42.6	60.6	46.5	47.6	39.8
South Dakota	12,336	11,811	10,345	14.4	14.5	13.7	6.3	6.8	6.2	26.4	34.9	37.2	37.2	37.6	33.5
Tennessee	81,685	79,495	79,611	12.4	12.5	14.0	9.0	9.0	9.2	30.5	43.2	61.5	43.9	44.1	34.5
Texas..........................	403,618	386,118	363,414	14.7	15.4	17.4	8.5	8.4	7.4	34.6	52.2	69.2	41.5	42.4	30.5
Utah...........................	50,778	52,258	47,353	16.9	18.9	21.2	6.9	7.0	6.6	17.6	27.9	40.0	18.8	19.2	17.3
Vermont......................	5,903	6,223	6,500	9.4	9.9	10.7	6.7	6.1	6.1	11.6	17.9	24.1	40.2	39.2	28.1
Virginia.......................	103,303	103,002	98,938	12.3	12.9	14.0	8.0	8.2	7.9	17.1	27.4	40.8	34.4	35.5	29.9
Washington..................	88,990	86,539	81,036	12.4	12.9	13.7	6.1	6.3	5.6	17.6	26.7	38.2	32.1	33.0	28.2
West Virginia...............	19,805	20,470	20,865	10.7	11.0	11.5	9.6	9.2	8.3	31.9	44.8	46.4	43.8	43.9	31.7
Wisconsin	67,041	68,487	69,326	11.6	12.0	12.9	7.2	7.0	6.5	16.2	26.2	34.5	37.5	36.7	29.3
Wyoming	7,765	7,556	6,253	13.2	13.4	12.7	8.1	9.0	8.3	29.2	39.0	40.8	33.9	34.0	28.8

[1] Birth rates are per 1,000 total population, estimated as of July 1.
[2] Less than 2,500 grams (5 pounds, 8 ounces).
[3] Per 1,000 estimated population in age group.
[4] Defined as mothers who are 15 to 19 years of age.

Table A-10. Births and Birth Rates, by Race and Hispanic Origin and Fertility Rate, 2015

Geographic area	Births								Percentage with low birth weights[3]			
	All Races[1]	White Total	White Non-Hispanic	Black Total	Black Non-Hispanic	American Indian or Alaska Native	Asian or Pacific Islander	Hispanic[2]	All races[1]	White non-Hispanic	Black non-Hispanic	Hispanic[2]
United States	3,978,497	3,012,855	2,130,279	640,079	589,047	44,299	281,264	924,048	8.1	6.9	13.3	7.2
Alabama......................	59,657	39,845	35,826	18,429	18,261	190	1,193	4,295	10.4	8.1	15.9	7.1
Alaska........................	11,282	7,244	6,543	509	423	2,415	1,114	810	5.8	5.2	8.7	6.4
Arizona.......................	85,351	71,422	36,976	5,095	4,582	5,316	3,518	35,247	7.2	6.6	12.2	7.0
Arkansas.....................	38,886	29,532	25,714	7,767	7,589	353	1,234	4,008	9.2	7.7	15.4	6.7
California.....................	491,748	377,423	141,592	30,546	27,035	3,510	80,269	234,237	6.8	5.9	11.5	6.5
Colorado.....................	66,581	58,756	40,878	4,049	3,453	803	2,973	18,139	9.0	8.5	13.2	8.9
Connecticut.................	35,746	28,164	20,395	4,988	4,439	97	2,497	8,275	7.9	6.5	12.7	8.5
Delaware.....................	11,166	7,341	5,959	3,134	2,986	16	675	1,532	9.3	7.7	13.2	8.7
District of Columbia	9,578	4,061	2,976	5,002	4,802	16	499	1,327	10.0	7.0	13.2	6.6
Florida........................	224,269	162,594	102,549	53,699	49,609	373	7,603	64,078	8.6	7.1	13.2	7.3
Georgia......................	131,404	76,904	60,328	47,734	45,461	298	6,468	17,836	9.5	7.1	13.8	6.9
Hawaii........................	18,420	6,322	4,803	620	579	35	11,443	2,775	8.3	5.8	11.1	8.4
Idaho.........................	22,827	21,618	18,087	287	240	406	516	3,645	6.6	6.4	11.3	6.9
Illinois.......................	158,116	119,630	85,424	28,059	27,160	205	10,222	33,902	8.3	6.8	13.7	7.1
Indiana.......................	84,040	70,741	63,472	10,656	10,343	120	2,523	7,634	8.0	7.4	12.4	7.1
Iowa..........................	39,482	35,279	32,028	2,597	2,503	242	1,364	3,418	6.7	6.5	10.1	6.4
Kansas.......................	39,154	34,251	28,236	3,090	2,912	330	1,483	6,300	6.8	6.5	11.6	5.9
Kentucky.....................	55,971	49,061	46,344	5,507	5,269	88	1,315	3,000	8.7	8.2	13.9	6.5
Louisiana	64,692	37,801	34,047	25,001	24,064	392	1,498	4,826	10.6	8.0	15.0	7.2
Maine.........................	12,607	11,805	11,563	473	463	143	186	251	6.9	6.8	10.2	
Maryland.....................	73,616	42,471	32,412	25,017	23,626	279	5,849	11,750	8.6	6.7	11.8	7.2
Massachusetts..............	71,492	55,350	43,651	9,288	7,019	141	6,713	13,015	7.5	6.5	10.6	8.3
Michigan.....................	113,312	85,838	78,960	22,394	21,822	786	4,294	7,431	8.5	7.0	14.3	7.5
Minnesota...................	69,834	54,407	49,673	8,353	8,030	1,415	5,659	4,852	6.4	5.8	9.4	6.0
Mississippi..................	38,394	20,730	19,635	16,846	16,419	259	559	1,613	11.4	7.8	16.5	5.6
Missouri......................	75,061	60,913	57,092	11,660	11,304	359	2,129	4,042	8.3	7.2	14.4	7.2
Montana......................	12,583	10,768	10,270	103	89	1,560	152	573	7.1	6.8	*	7.3
Nebraska.....................	26,679	23,126	19,201	2,009	1,872	557	987	4,249	7.1	6.5	13.6	6.8
Nevada.......................	36,298	27,648	14,937	4,803	4,455	510	3,337	13,225	8.5	7.8	13.6	7.3
New Hampshire..............	12,433	11,600	10,928	280	237	26	527	638	6.9	6.7	9.7	6.9
New Jersey	103,127	72,400	47,425	18,363	14,880	172	12,192	27,919	8.1	6.8	12.2	7.7
New Mexico	25,816	21,183	7,157	664	472	3,452	517	14,431	8.7	8.5	14.0	8.9
New York.....................	237,274	163,871	114,643	46,109	36,392	738	26,556	55,796	7.8	6.4	12.0	7.8
North Carolina...............	120,843	81,154	67,122	31,864	28,866	1,964	5,861	18,091	9.1	7.5	14.4	6.9
North Dakota.................	11,314	9,345	8,796	640	573	985	344	580	6.2	6.0	7.2	7.2
Ohio..........................	139,264	109,566	103,586	25,078	23,739	253	4,367	6,974	8.5	7.3	13.9	7.7
Oklahoma....................	53,122	40,143	33,293	5,293	4,995	5,924	1,762	7,406	7.9	7.3	13.5	7.3
Oregon.......................	45,655	40,484	32,147	1,463	1,335	813	2,895	8,518	6.4	6.0	9.4	6.7
Pennsylvania................	141,047	109,595	97,845	24,100	20,160	391	6,961	14,950	8.2	6.9	13.2	8.7
Rhode Island.................	10,993	8,824	6,702	1,392	952	138	639	2,622	7.6	6.9	10.9	7.8
South Carolina	58,139	38,056	33,927	18,577	17,801	217	1,289	4,942	9.5	7.3	14.5	6.4
South Dakota	12,336	9,504	9,063	344	328	2,166	322	559	6.1	5.8	*	5.5
Tennessee...................	81,685	61,814	55,420	17,507	16,792	211	2,153	7,264	9.2	7.8	14.7	6.8
Texas.........................	403,618	327,429	140,553	53,144	49,662	1,270	21,775	191,157	8.2	7.1	13.1	7.7
Utah..........................	50,778	47,381	38,473	823	644	699	1,875	7,876	7.0	6.6	9.3	8.3
Vermont......................	5,903	5,554	5,370	149	131	25	175	139	6.6	6.3	*	
Virginia......................	103,303	71,485	59,244	23,029	21,777	254	8,535	13,930	7.9	6.6	12.2	6.4
Washington..................	88,990	71,041	55,352	5,302	4,619	2,036	10,611	16,073	6.4	5.8	9.8	6.1
West Virginia................	19,805	18,814	18,442	738	698	28	225	331	9.6	9.4	13.6	7.9
Wisconsin....................	67,041	55,350	49,024	7,386	7,098	1,029	3,276	6,604	7.3	6.2	14.6	6.7
Wyoming	7,765	7,217	6,196	119	87	294	135	963	8.6	8.1	*	9.5

*Figure does not meet standards of reliability or precision, based on fewer than 20 births.
[1]Includes other races not shown separately.
[2]People of Hispanic origin may be of any race. Births by Hispanic origin of mother.
[3]Less than 2,500 grams (5 pounds, 8 ounces).

Table A-11. Deaths and Death Rates, by Race and Hispanic Origin

Geographic area	All races				Infant deaths, 2015[2]					
	Number (thousands)		Crude rate per 1,000 population[1]		Number			Mortality rate[2,3]		
	2015	2010	2015	2010	All races	White	Black	All races	White	Black
United States	2,713	2,468	8.4	8.0	23,455	14,834	7,289	5.9	5	10.6
Alabama......................	52	48	10.7	10.1	495	211	279	8.5	5.8	14
Alaska......................	4	4	5.8	5.2	78	38	D	6.9	5.3	D
Arizona.....................	54	47	8.0	7.3	469	343	67	5.4	4.9	10.2
Arkansas	32	29	10.6	9.9	293	190	96	7.8	6.7	11.9
California....................	259	234	6.6	6.3	2,169	1,605	296	4.3	4.2	7.1
Colorado	36	31	6.7	6.3	309	248	44	4.6	4.3	9.2
Connecticut.................	31	29	8.5	8.0	200	130	62	5.5	4.7	9.5
Delaware....................	9	8	9.1	8.6	100	54	44	9.1	7.5	13.8
District of Columbia	5	5	7.2	7.8	82	D	67	9	D	16.6
Florida.......................	192	174	9.5	9.2	1,400	769	590	6.3	4.8	11.4
Georgia	80	71	7.8	7.4	1,024	424	580	7.9	5.7	11.6
Hawaii.......................	11	10	7.7	7.1	108	31	D	5.7	5.1	D
Idaho........................	13	11	7.9	7.3	106	104	D	4.7	5	D
Illinois.......................	107	100	8.3	7.8	953	566	351	6.1	4.8	12.7
Indiana......................	63	57	9.5	8.8	611	456	140	7.3	6.6	11.8
Iowa.........................	30	28	9.5	9.1	166	142	21	4.2	4	8.1
Kansas......................	27	25	9.2	8.6	232	185	37	6	5.7	9
Kentucky....................	47	42	10.5	9.7	375	319	53	6.7	6.7	8.2
Louisiana	44	41	9.4	9.0	498	203	287	7.9	5.5	11.9
Maine........................	14	13	10.9	9.6	83	76	D	6.5	6.3	D
Maryland....................	47	43	7.9	7.5	490	190	272	6.7	4.6	10.6
Massachusetts.............	58	53	8.5	8.0	309	228	65	4.2	4	7.1
Michigan....................	95	88	9.6	8.9	744	440	286	6.5	5.2	12.2
Minnesota	43	39	7.8	7.3	360	227	95	5.1	4	13.8
Mississippi.................	32	29	10.6	9.8	356	132	215	9.3	6.7	12.1
Missouri.....................	60	55	9.8	9.2	490	331	149	6.6	5.5	12.2
Montana.....................	10	9	9.6	8.9	75	53	D	6	5	D
Nebraska....................	17	15	8.8	8.3	153	124	D	5.8	5.4	D
Nevada......................	23	20	7.9	7.3	190	116	54	5.3	4.3	11.3
New Hampshire............	12	10	9.0	7.7	52	50	D	4.1	4.2	D
New Jersey	72	69	8.1	7.9	487	280	182	4.7	3.9	9.1
New Mexico	18	16	8.5	7.7	131	100	D	5	4.8	D
New York....................	154	146	7.8	7.6	1,087	660	363	4.6	4.2	6.4
North Carolina.............	89	79	8.9	8.3	884	477	369	7.3	5.9	11.2
North Dakota...............	6	6	8.2	8.8	81	59	D	7.3	6.2	D
Ohio.........................	118	109	10.2	9.4	1,005	625	366	7.2	5.7	14.5
Oklahoma...................	39	37	10.1	9.7	386	236	71	7.2	6.2	10.2
Oregon	36	32	8.9	8.3	232	192	23	5	4.8	11.6
Pennsylvania...............	133	125	10.4	9.8	862	566	275	6.1	5.1	11.7
Rhode Island...............	10	10	9.6	9.1	62	42	D	5.6	4.8	D
South Carolina	47	42	9.6	9.0	405	186	213	7	5.1	10.7
South Dakota	8	7	9.0	8.7	90	55	D	7.2	5.5	D
Tennessee	67	60	10.1	9.4	570	373	187	7.1	6.2	10.2
Texas........................	190	167	6.9	6.6	2,308	1,672	574	5.8	5.2	10.2
Utah.........................	17	15	5.8	5.3	257	234	D	5.1	5.1	D
Vermont.....................	6	5	9.5	8.6	27	25	D	4.5	4.4	D
Virginia......................	66	59	7.8	7.4	612	319	259	6	4.7	10.1
Washington.................	55	48	7.6	7.2	432	326	54	4.8	4.6	8
West Virginia...............	23	21	12.3	11.5	142	128	D	6.9	6.7	D
Wisconsin	51	47	8.9	8.3	386	242	113	5.8	4.3	15.8
Wyoming....................	5	4	8.2	7.9	39	37	D	5.1	5.3	D

⁰ = zero or rounds to zero.
D = Data withheld to avoid disclosure or does not meet statistical standards for reliability.
[1]Estimated resident population as of July 1.
[2]Infants are considered under 1 year of age.
[3]Per 1,000 live births. Infant deaths are based on decedent. Live births are based on races of mother.

Table A-11. Deaths and Death Rates, by Race and Hispanic Origin—*Continued*

	Deaths by race, 2015									
	Number					Crude rate per 1,000 population[1]				
Geographic area	White	Black	American Indian	Asian or Pacific Islander	Hispanic	White	Black	American Indian	Asian or Pacific Islander	Hispanic
United States	2,306,861	320,072	19,016	66,681	179,457	9.2	7.1	4.2	3.3	3.2
Alabama......................	39,929	11,789	106	85	335	11.7	8.9	2.8	1.1	1.6
Alaska........................	2,967	142	1,022	185	94	5.7	3.8	8.2	3.0	1.8
Arizona.......................	49,421	1,842	2,314	722	7,028	8.5	4.9	6.0	2.6	3.3
Arkansas.....................	27,438	3,940	65	174	262	11.4	8.2	2.0	2.9	1.2
California....................	211,108	20,131	1,963	26,004	47,551	7.2	7.1	2.5	4.1	3.1
Colorado	34,111	1,422	274	542	4,256	7.0	5.0	2.7	2.6	3.7
Connecticut.................	27,880	2,328	30	297	1,555	9.5	5.2	1.3	1.7	2.8
Delaware	7,014	1,474	D	76	151	10.4	6.6	D	1.9	1.8
District of Columbia	1,068	3,741	D	58	125	3.5	11.2	D	1.8	1.8
Florida........................	167,790	21,758	277	1,912	23,470	10.5	6.2	2.5	2.9	4.7
Georgia......................	57,170	21,686	68	1,018	1,370	8.9	6.5	1.2	2.3	1.4
Hawaii........................	3,212	128	D	7,702	532	7.2	2.6	D	8.3	3.6
Idaho.........................	12,765	26	148	87	416	8.1	1.3	4.4	2.7	2.1
Illinois........................	88,381	16,400	63	2,028	5,019	8.8	8.4	0.7	2.7	2.3
Indiana.......................	57,409	4,982	47	275	944	10.0	7.3	1.5	1.8	2.1
Iowa..........................	28,884	520	57	139	273	10.0	4.0	3.2	1.7	1.5
Kansas	24,769	1,409	278	208	812	9.7	6.7	6.5	2.2	2.4
Kentucky	43,498	2,923	25	118	249	11.0	7.4	1.8	1.6	1.6
Louisiana	30,027	13,298	120	271	622	10.0	8.6	3.1	2.8	2.7
Maine.........................	14,300	60	80	39	33	11.2	2.5	7.3	2.1	1.6
Maryland.....................	32,599	13,433	75	1,140	908	8.9	7.1	1.9	2.7	1.6
Massachusetts.............	54,044	2,618	61	1,083	1,824	9.5	4.2	1.6	2.3	2.4
Michigan.....................	80,926	13,003	547	664	1,624	10.1	8.7	6.1	2.0	3.3
Minnesota...................	40,217	1,330	586	667	454	8.5	3.6	7.0	2.3	1.6
Mississippi..................	21,729	9,832	110	112	120	12.1	8.6	5.9	3.1	1.3
Missouri......................	53,231	6,190	117	333	534	10.4	8.1	2.7	2.3	2.2
Montana......................	9,211	40	656	35	126	9.8	4.0	8.8	3.3	3.4
Nebraska....................	15,946	588	114	92	377	9.3	5.5	3.9	1.8	1.9
Nevada.......................	19,543	1,939	211	1,186	1,961	8.7	6.5	3.8	4.0	2.4
New Hampshire............	11,866	59	D	54	68	9.4	2.4	D	1.4	1.5
New Jersey	60,520	9,706	48	1,997	5,108	9.2	7.0	0.8	2.2	2.9
New Mexico	15,731	330	1,497	127	6,079	9.0	5.2	6.5	2.9	6.1
New York....................	126,187	21,796	278	5,367	13,006	9.0	5.9	1.2	2.9	3.5
North Carolina.............	69,455	18,139	896	643	1,223	9.6	7.9	5.4	2.0	1.3
North Dakota...............	5,851	47	306	D	50	8.6	2.2	6.9	D	1.9
Ohio..........................	104,499	12,998	79	612	1,019	10.7	8.2	1.9	2.3	2.5
Oklahoma....................	33,530	2,547	3,074	271	844	11.0	7.3	7.5	2.7	2.1
Oregon.......................	34,112	520	404	669	893	9.4	4.8	4.6	3.1	1.7
Pennsylvania...............	119,080	12,312	84	1,122	2,418	11.1	7.8	1.6	2.4	2.8
Rhode Island...............	9,668	341	46	108	337	10.6	3.6	4.0	2.6	2.2
South Carolina.............	34,868	12,027	80	223	443	10.3	8.7	2.8	2.5	1.7
South Dakota	6,976	47	680	28	48	9.4	2.4	8.3	2.1	1.5
Tennessee	57,162	9,048	58	302	514	10.9	7.7	1.8	2.3	1.5
Texas.........................	162,679	23,359	314	3,302	39,648	7.3	6.6	1.0	2.3	3.7
Utah..........................	16,694	114	190	336	909	6.0	2.2	3.6	2.9	2.2
Vermont......................	5,859	23	D	27	25	9.7	2.2	D	2.4	2.2
Virginia.......................	51,298	12,774	110	1,395	1,157	8.5	7.4	2.2	2.3	1.5
Washington.................	49,714	1,654	859	2,368	1,658	8.4	4.5	5.3	3.3	1.9
West Virginia...............	22,007	706	D	31	51	12.6	9.2	D	1.8	1.8
Wisconsin	47,912	2,521	423	408	723	9.4	6.1	5.8	2.4	1.9
Wyoming	4,606	32	120	20	211	8.4	3.0	6.9	2.7	3.6

Table A-12.   Age-Adjusted Death Rates, by Cause, 2015

Geographic area	Age-adjusted rates, 2015[1]										
	All causes	Diseases of the heart	Malignant neoplasms	Chronic lower respiratory diseases	Accidents	Cerebro-vascular diseases	Alzheimer's disease	Diabetes mellitus	Influenza and pneumonia	Nephritis, nephrotic syndrome, and nephrosis	Intentional self-harm (suicide)
United States	733.1	168.5	158.5	41.6	43.2	37.6	29.4	21.3	15.2	13.4	13.3
Alabama......................	924.5	229.7	175.6	56.4	50.9	52.2	41.8	21.7	19.5	18.4	14.9
Alaska.........................	747.4	154.1	159.8	37.7	57.9	36.8	16.7	23.9	8.4	9.9	26.9
Arizona.......................	671.8	138.8	141.3	43.8	49.2	30.7	35.8	25.3	9.5	5.6	18.2
Arkansas.....................	901.7	223.2	185.4	62.4	49.6	46.8	41.5	24.7	20.0	19.8	19.1
California....................	621.6	145.6	142.8	33.1	30.6	36.2	35.7	21.2	14.8	8.6	10.3
Colorado	665.0	128.4	134.4	47.8	49.7	34.9	31.3	15.9	12.4	8.5	19.5
Connecticut.................	656.1	147.8	146.2	29.7	44.8	28.5	19.0	13.9	13.6	12.1	9.9
Delaware	741.5	165.2	165.6	42.5	46.0	39.4	22.6	18.1	16.1	14.5	12.6
District of Columbia	748.6	187.6	167.5	23.4	40.2	38.3	19.2	25.8	16.2	9.9	4.9
Florida........................	662.9	149.8	150.6	38.4	46.2	37.1	21.8	18.6	8.9	10.8	14.4
Georgia	808.1	180.3	163.0	46.8	43.2	45.3	42.4	21.4	15.5	19.1	12.7
Hawaii........................	588.2	135.6	135.3	17.3	32.2	38.2	19.5	14.5	27.4	10.8	13.6
Idaho..........................	727.8	156.4	153.6	46.3	44.7	36.3	31.6	22.1	12.4	8.7	22.1
Illinois........................	728.3	171.5	167.6	38.2	35.8	38.4	24.4	19.2	15.7	17.3	10.3
Indiana.......................	834.0	182.3	176.3	55.4	47.7	39.2	33.1	26.9	13.9	18.9	14.4
Iowa...........................	724.6	160.9	164.1	49.1	42.1	33.2	29.9	26.7	14.2	8	13.9
Kansas	774.1	158.5	164.6	49.7	47.2	38.6	23.5	20.2	18.9	16.8	16.3
Kentucky	924.7	197.8	195.9	64.3	66.0	40.8	34.9	28.2	19.3	19.7	17.1
Louisiana	874.2	212.1	180.2	43.2	54.7	46.0	42.5	23.5	15.3	23.2	15.2
Maine.........................	783.5	157.3	178.0	53.6	53.8	32.6	28.4	21.9	17.6	11.4	16.0
Maryland.....................	705.7	169.3	155.0	30.7	29.7	37.8	16.4	18.3	17.7	12.4	8.8
Massachusetts	684.8	138.5	152.9	33.0	44.0	28.4	20.2	16.7	17.1	14.3	8.9
Michigan.....................	784.4	198.9	168.0	47.5	43.9	37.6	30.1	22.5	15.2	15.6	13.8
Minnesota	653.8	116.6	153.1	36.4	42.0	33.5	26.0	18.6	10.9	9.7	13.2
Mississippi	963.7	240.5	188.4	57.1	59.8	52.7	44.1	32.4	24.0	21.9	14.0
Missouri......................	816.9	197.9	173.4	52.8	50.9	40.8	28.7	19.7	17.9	19.9	17.1
Montana......................	762.7	155.7	156.9	50.2	56.3	33.8	20.7	24.5	13.7	9.3	25.3
Nebraska.....................	739.2	154.5	157.8	52.2	38.9	33.4	24.8	24.8	16.9	11.2	11.7
Nevada.......................	757.2	200.9	157.2	54.1	45.4	37.0	32.9	13.4	21.3	10.5	18.4
New Hampshire.............	720.6	149.0	161.3	41.9	59.0	26.9	25.5	17.9	16.1	11.4	16.5
New Jersey	666.0	166.7	150.8	29.6	33.7	31.1	19.8	17.9	12.5	14.4	8.3
New Mexico	741.5	142.4	143.3	44.8	67.2	32.5	19.9	24.9	13.6	12.9	23.8
New York.....................	644.0	181.6	148.4	29.9	30.2	26.0	12.6	17.1	20.0	9.3	7.9
North Carolina..............	789.9	162.4	164.7	45.5	47.9	44.7	34.8	23.6	18.7	16	13.4
North Dakota................	696.8	142.4	152.9	40.0	44.1	33.3	36.7	22.6	17.7	12.5	17.5
Ohio...........................	828.4	191.7	175.1	49.6	55.9	40.7	31.1	25.2	16.6	14.5	13.9
Oklahoma....................	904.3	234.0	184.3	65.8	60.1	43.0	34.7	32.4	16.5	14.2	20.3
Oregon........................	722.3	136.1	160.2	42.4	44.5	37.5	33.0	22.9	9.0	8.2	17.8
Pennsylvania................	768.3	177.8	167.2	38.1	52.0	38.8	21.0	22.1	15.9	16.8	14.0
Rhode Island................	721.9	160.4	163.1	36.9	53.1	27.1	28.8	20.2	16.2	9.8	11.2
South Carolina	840.0	177.8	166.7	49.9	54.0	46.7	46.2	23.3	15.3	15.5	14.9
South Dakota	715.4	150.9	154.0	45.3	49.5	33.2	34.8	26.3	18.2	7.4	20.4
Tennessee	886.4	207.3	180.5	54.9	56.4	46.0	43.4	23.5	23.3	14.4	15.7
Texas.........................	744.9	171.7	149.1	41.3	37.4	42.7	38.2	21.2	13.0	16.1	12.5
Utah...........................	712.1	152.9	125.2	33.9	45.6	38.4	40.7	24.6	15.7	15.6	22.4
Vermont......................	714.7	152.5	165.3	42.4	48.4	36.4	35.1	19.8	10.1	4.5	14.8
Virginia.......................	721.6	154.1	159.5	37.1	39.6	38.0	25.6	21.9	15.7	16.1	12.7
Washington..................	687.4	137.6	156.4	39.7	41.9	34.2	44.4	22.4	10.6	5.9	15.4
West Virginia................	943.4	191.3	190.4	64.6	77.9	43.8	30.0	31.6	21.2	20.4	17.5
Wisconsin....................	715.9	156.0	159.3	39.3	49.3	35.6	27.5	19.4	14.2	13.7	14.7
Wyoming	748.3	159.4	139.4	57.1	65.8	31.4	24.2	20.8	16.0	13.3	28.0

[1]Causes of death classified according to tenth revision of International Classification of Diseases. Rates per 100,000 population; age-adjusted rates per 100,000 U.S. standard population as of 2000. Rates for the United States and each state are based on populations estimated as of July 1, 2015.

Table A-13. Marriages and Divorces

Geographic area	Marriages[1] Rates per 1,000 population[3]			Divorces[2] Rates per 1,000 population[3]			Marital history, 2015 Median age at first marriage		Total population age 15 and over	Percent Ever married	Married within the past year	Divorced within the past year	Married two or more times
	2015	2010	2000	2015	2010	2000	Men	Women					
United States[4]	6.9	6.8	8.2	3.1	3.6	4.0	29.7	27.8	260,415,152	66.5	1.8	0.8	16.3
Alabama......................	7.4	8.2	10.1	3.9	4.4	5.5	28.4	26.9	3,947,204	68.8	1.7	1.0	21.8
Alaska........................	7.4	8.0	8.9	4.1	4.7	3.9	28.0	26.2	582,619	64.3	2.8	1.0	18.1
Arizona.......................	5.9	5.9	7.5	3.6	3.5	4.6	29.7	27.3	5,481,996	66.5	1.8	0.9	18.9
Arkansas.....................	10.0	10.8	15.4	4.8	5.7	6.4	27.2	25.7	2,390,981	72.6	2.0	1.2	25.4
California[5]..................	6.2	5.8	5.8	---	---	---	30.6	28.7	31,576,740	62.9	1.8	0.7	12.3
Colorado	6.8	6.9	8.3	3.7	4.3	4.7	29.3	27.4	4,406,120	68.3	2.0	0.0	17.0
Connecticut..................	5.3	5.6	5.7	3.1	2.9	3.3	30.6	29.2	2,971,949	64.7	1.4	0.7	12.3
Delaware	5.7	5.2	6.5	3.1	3.5	3.9	29.8	28.5	776,531	66.2	1.8	0.6	16.9
District of Columbia	8.2	7.6	4.9	2.8	2.8	3.2	30.7	30.6	569,946	44.6	2.4	0.8	6.9
Florida	8.2	7.3	8.9	4.0	4.4	5.1	30.4	28.4	16,889,179	68.2	1.7	0.8	20.1
Georgia	6.2	7.3	6.8	---	---	3.3	28.8	27.5	8,139,039	65.8	2.0	0.9	18.4
Hawaii.........................	15.9	17.6	20.6	---	---	3.9	28.9	28.2	1,168,301	66.5	2.4	0.6	12.1
Idaho..........................	8.2	8.8	10.8	4.1	5.2	5.5	26.8	25.3	1,294,692	71.6	2.2	1.1	22.5
Illinois........................	5.9	5.7	6.9	2.2	2.6	3.2	30.3	28.7	10,412,828	64.5	1.6	0.7	13.2
Indiana........................	6.9	6.3	7.9	---	---	---	28.9	26.7	5,314,761	68.6	1.8	1.0	19.8
Iowa...........................	6.3	6.9	6.9	1.2	2.4	3.3	28.2	26.4	2,518,654	70.4	2.0	0.8	16.6
Kansas........................	5.9	6.4	8.3	2.8	3.7	3.6	27.6	25.9	2,312,560	70.0	1.9	1.0	18.8
Kentucky.....................	7.2	7.4	9.8	3.7	4.5	5.1	28.0	26.2	3,588,805	71.4	2.1	1.1	21.9
Louisiana.....................	6.8	6.9	9.1	2.8	---	---	29.3	27.4	3,740,919	64.4	1.8	0.8	17.5
Maine..........................	7.6	7.1	8.8	3.4	4.2	5.0	29.6	27.2	1,121,207	71.3	1.6	0.9	20.0
Maryland......................	6.2	5.7	7.5	2.6	2.8	3.3	30.5	29.0	4,890,571	64.8	1.6	0.7	14.0
Massachusetts.............	5.5	5.6	5.8	2.6	2.5	2.5	31.0	29.9	5,658,173	62.7	1.5	0.7	10.8
Michigan	6.0	5.5	6.7	3.0	3.5	3.9	30.1	27.9	8,116,804	66.4	1.5	0.8	16.5
Minnesota....................	5.6	5.3	6.8	---	---	3.2	29.2	27.3	4,420,760	68.3	1.7	0.7	13.0
Mississippi...................	7.0	4.9	6.9	3.4	4.3	5.0	28.6	27.0	2,388,147	65.4	1.7	0.9	19.7
Missouri......................	6.2	6.5	7.8	3.2	3.9	4.5	28.3	26.4	4,931,458	69.5	1.8	0.9	20.2
Montana......................	8.0	7.4	7.3	3.4	3.9	4.2	28.7	27.2	844,438	70.9	1.8	0.8	21.0
Nebraska.....................	6.4	6.6	7.6	3.2	3.6	3.7	28.6	26.8	1,501,794	69.4	1.8	0.9	16.0
Nevada........................	31.0	38.3	72.2	4.6	5.9	9.9	29.7	27.9	2,332,895	66.7	2.0	1.2	20.6
New Hampshire.............	6.9	7.3	9.4	3.3	3.8	4.8	30.5	28.3	1,117,604	70.1	1.5	0.7	17.3
New Jersey	5.6	5.1	6.0	2.8	3.0	3.0	30.6	29.2	7,313,818	65.4	1.4	0.6	10.6
New Mexico..................	6.2	7.7	8.0	3.3	4.0	5.1	28.3	27.6	1,668,989	65.9	1.8	0.9	17.6
New York.....................	7.1	6.5	7.1	2.7	2.9	3.0	31.0	29.7	16,312,417	61.1	1.5	0.6	10.4
North Carolina..............	7.0	6.6	8.2	3.1	3.8	4.5	29.1	27.3	8,146,843	68.3	1.9	0.8	18.2
North Dakota................	6.2	6.5	7.2	2.8	3.1	3.4	27.4	25.4	611,660	67.6	2.2	0.8	12.6
Ohio	5.9	5.8	7.8	3.1	3.4	4.2	29.5	27.7	9,451,449	67.9	1.6	0.9	17.8
Oklahoma....................	7.4	7.2	---	4.4	5.2	---	27.6	25.7	3,108,452	71.5	2.1	1.2	23.9
Oregon........................	6.9	6.5	7.6	3.4	4.0	4.8	30.2	27.9	3,316,989	69.0	1.8	0.9	20.4
Pennsylvania................	5.7	5.3	6.0	2.6	2.7	3.1	30.1	28.6	10,589,716	66.2	1.6	0.7	13.7
Rhode Island................	6.4	5.8	7.6	3.0	3.2	2.9	30.7	30.1	882,671	63.0	1.4	0.5	12.5
South Carolina	7.5	7.4	10.6	2.8	3.1	3.8	29.3	27.7	3,994,825	67.4	1.8	0.9	18.6
South Dakota	7.2	7.3	9.4	2.6	3.4	3.5	26.4	26.2	682,834	69.6	2.0	0.7	15.1
Tennessee	8.5	8.8	15.5	3.7	4.2	5.9	28.3	26.4	5,363,257	69.9	1.9	0.9	22.1
Texas..........................	7.2	7.1	9.4	2.6	3.3	4.0	28.6	26.6	21,446,565	67.3	2.1	0.9	17.5
Utah...........................	8.1	8.5	10.8	3.6	3.7	4.3	26.4	24.3	2,228,373	70.1	2.7	0.9	16.6
Vermont.......................	8.1	9.3	10.0	3.1	3.8	4.1	30.6	29.4	529,124	68.3	1.6	0.8	16.4
Virginia........................	7.0	6.8	8.8	3.3	3.8	4.3	29.4	27.6	6,826,858	67.6	1.9	0.8	16.4
Washington..................	6.2	6.0	6.9	3.4	4.2	4.6	29.2	26.9	5,828,814	68.8	2.0	0.9	18.2
West Virginia................	6.6	6.7	8.7	4.0	5.1	5.1	29.4	26.8	1,531,879	72.2	1.8	1.1	21.3
Wisconsin....................	5.6	5.3	6.7	2.6	3.0	3.2	29.4	27.4	4,703,887	67.9	1.6	0.7	14.3
Wyoming	7.3	7.6	10.0	4.1	5.1	5.8	27.5	26.1	468,057	72.0	2.3	1.3	22.5

[1]Data are accounts of marriages performed, except as noted.
[2]Includes annulments.
[3]Based on provisional counts of marriages by state occurrence; total population residing in area; population enumerated as of April 1 for 2000 and 2010 and estimated as of July 1 for 2015.
[4]U.S. total divorce rates are based solely on the combined counts and populations for reporting states and the District of Columbia.
[5]Marriage data include nonlicensed marriages registered.

Table A-14.   Health Care Services, Physicians, and Nurses

Geographic area	Health care services and social assistance, 2014[1] (NAICS 62)									Physicians,[2] 2016		Nurses,[2] 2016	
	Establishments				Employees				Annual payroll (NAICS 62) (millions of dollars)				
	Total (NAICS 62)	Ambulatory Healthcare Services (NAICS 621)	Hospitals (NAICS 622)	Nursing and residential care facilities (NAICS 623)	Total (NAICS 62)	Ambulatory Healthcare Services (NAICS 621)	Hospitals (NAICS 622)	Nursing and residential care facilities (NAICS 623)		Number	Rate per 100,000 population[3]	Number	Rate per 100,000 population[3]
United States[5]	855,253	589,906	7,072	85,090	18,861,973	6,721,047	5,775,571	3,437,002	860,378	625,930	194	2,857,220	884.2
Alabama........................	10,313	7,365	125	900	236,675	84,237	83,166	43,668	10,457	8,280	170	47,440	975.5
Alaska..........................	2,506	1,586	30	378	47,152	16,668	14,417	4,429	2,669	1,300	175	5,570	750.8
Arizona.........................	17,397	13,059	122	1,878	325,753	125,930	96,347	52,171	15,307	11,020	159	52,610	759.0
Arkansas......................	7,536	5,161	100	602	170,306	49,838	56,206	32,655	6,759	5,450	182	23,380	782.4
California.....................	106,503	78,874	542	9,250	1,818,568	732,154	525,199	277,006	99,154	59,040	150	274,650	699.7
Colorado......................	15,355	11,536	115	943	279,544	111,598	80,945	45,023	13,298	9,480	171	47,590	858.9
Connecticut..................	10,504	7,014	47	1,250	276,251	90,478	68,284	67,273	12,914	10,350	289	32,930	920.7
Delaware......................	2,544	1,696	17	232	64,183	23,086	20,102	11,069	3,293	2,460	258	11,320	1,189.0
District of Columbia	2,084	1,191	16	155	66,564	17,764	27,148	7,345	3,809	5,430	797	10,320	1,515.0
Florida........................	57,662	45,512	368	3,674	1,026,665	418,666	302,588	189,435	48,082	39,810	193	174,710	847.6
Georgia	23,660	17,393	197	1,794	462,968	175,029	159,534	64,777	21,214	18,450	179	73,330	711.2
Hawaii.........................	3,629	2,770	26	163	68,461	26,361	22,041	8,130	3,456	1,120	78	11,300	791.0
Idaho..........................	5,017	3,493	56	435	87,810	29,188	29,859	15,030	3,403	960	57	12,330	732.6
Illinois........................	33,454	24,294	236	2,821	787,928	276,453	244,042	143,467	34,857	24,720	193	121,670	950.4
Indiana.......................	15,414	10,056	170	1,999	403,393	130,663	132,054	86,291	16,554	14,710	222	63,870	962.9
Iowa...........................	8,219	4,867	137	1,292	216,134	53,523	67,254	57,739	8,358	5,550	177	32,370	1,032.6
Kansas........................	7,809	4,789	150	1,119	195,155	59,699	57,452	45,318	7,734	4,920	169	27,130	933.2
Kentucky	12,703	7,620	140	1,070	247,078	79,099	86,323	47,145	10,278	7,900	178	45,500	1,025.5
Louisiana....................	11,968	8,361	246	996	287,898	92,831	101,840	45,079	11,519	6,000	128	44,780	956.5
Maine.........................	4,732	2,499	49	937	107,476	31,130	34,591	24,560	4,634	2,040	153	14,190	1,065.7
Maryland.....................	16,155	11,469	77	1,772	360,751	121,713	106,334	75,977	17,144	16,150	268	53,330	886.4
Massachusetts.............	18,581	11,294	137	2,738	607,944	182,159	188,854	114,248	30,290	22,710	333	85,140	1,249.9
Michigan	26,380	18,422	212	3,492	D	D	D	D	D	21,560	217	92,670	933.4
Minnesota...................	15,838	8,053	149	3,731	444,786	133,777	110,418	110,696	18,071	8,490	154	61,830	1,120.1
Mississippi..................	6,140	4,211	110	409	163,145	45,199	72,476	23,573	7,070	3,820	128	28,590	956.6
Missouri......................	25,902	10,556	171	1,738	404,916	118,079	134,451	79,741	16,392	4,320	71	67,920	1,114.7
Montana......................	3,529	2,057	69	406	68,523	19,706	24,954	12,152	2,804	1,590	153	9,800	940.0
Nebraska.....................	5,412	3,435	106	465	124,250	34,640	41,839	28,326	5,275	4,060	213	21,240	1,113.7
Nevada........................	6,593	5,227	62	411	108,667	45,041	34,216	12,790	5,251	2,580	88	20,250	688.8
New Hampshire.............	3,613	2,316	34	314	88,007	30,056	28,464	14,997	4,303	3,660	274	13,260	993.4
New Jersey	27,089	20,641	123	1,996	561,829	230,006	151,630	97,612	26,704	22,570	252	79,400	887.7
New Mexico	4,953	3,393	66	387	115,814	38,888	34,595	15,219	4,811	3,350	161	16,200	778.5
New York.....................	56,985	39,228	266	5,519	1,459,585	515,097	429,598	248,050	69,887	59,070	299	180,730	915.3
North Carolina..............	23,053	15,153	157	2,612	560,309	192,271	183,330	103,838	24,056	18,940	187	99,050	976.2
North Dakota................	1,972	1,092	47	256	59,713	13,671	21,109	15,525	2,718	1,240	164	8,710	1,149.1
Ohio	28,595	19,120	250	3,436	821,510	268,390	270,415	169,240	35,195	28,880	249	128,030	1,102.3
Oklahoma....................	10,712	7,258	160	1,098	216,386	69,138	71,223	41,754	8,805	7,950	203	27,660	705.0
Oregon........................	12,959	7,899	69	2,456	227,540	82,711	59,863	50,016	10,859	9,030	221	35,220	860.4
Pennsylvania................	36,534	24,318	301	4,033	973,465	330,471	276,641	212,520	42,562	28,580	224	139,480	1,091.0
Rhode Island................	3,229	2,071	18	486	86,190	26,864	24,821	21,354	3,760	3,260	309	12,150	1,150.1
South Carolina	9,931	6,969	106	988	221,357	73,013	77,665	41,715	9,405	9,550	193	41,800	842.6
South Dakota	2,306	1,297	62	313	65,356	13,750	30,033	13,528	3,001	1,560	180	12,130	1,401.6
Tennessee	15,180	10,828	172	1,404	391,560	139,655	136,026	70,072	17,655	10,250	154	60,080	903.3
Texas..........................	63,935	48,041	689	4,475	1,411,362	613,074	393,531	196,897	60,181	43,070	155	207,810	745.8
Utah	7,550	5,884	59	530	128,811	52,145	39,569	24,347	5,308	5,000	164	21,470	703.7
Vermont......................	2,090	1,218	16	201	46,691	16,792	14,159	7,683	1,979	2,460	394	5,850	936.6
Virginia.......................	19,205	13,687	124	1,554	427,084	160,684	124,521	73,955	19,837	17,210	205	63,820	758.7
Washington..................	20,039	13,067	114	2,457	384,476	144,977	109,958	66,285	19,039	10,750	148	55,350	759.5
West Virginia................	4,911	3,032	72	687	132,829	35,999	51,196	23,109	5,208	2,990	163	20,880	1,140.3
Wisconsin	14,963	8,311	150	2,703	388,018	128,782	107,737	81,124	16,955	11,280	195	55,410	958.9
Wyoming......................	1,910	1,223	35	135	31,867	9,069	11,340	6,059	1,410	1,010	173	4,970	848.8

Data User Notice posted on July 21, 2016: Census Bureau staff identified a processing error that affects selected data from the 2014 County Business Patterns (CBP). As a result, they have suppressed 2014 employment and payroll totals in the Health Care and Social Assistance sector (Sector 62) for the following geographies: U.S.; Michigan; Battle Creek, MI metro area; Calhoun County, MI; and the 3rd congressional district of Michigan. This processing error did not affect other sectors. While suppressed values can be derived by subtraction, they do not recommend using the derived values in any analyses. The Census Bureau plans to release revised statistics at a later date.
[1] Data for 2014 are based on the 2012 North American Industry Classification System (NAICS).
[2] As of May. Physicians include the following Medical Doctors included in the Occupational Employment Statistics: Anesthesiologists, Family and General Practitioners, Internists, General, Obstetricians and Gynecologists, Pediatricians, General, Psychiatrists, Surgeons, and Physicians and Surgeons, All Other. Nurses include Registered Nurses.
[3] Based on U.S. Census Bureau estimates as of July 1, 2016.

Table A-15.   Employment in Health Care Occupations and Type of Health Insurance

Geographic area	Employment in Health Care Occupations, 2015								
	Physicians and surgeons	Therapists	Registered nurses	Other nurses	Other diagnosing and treating practitioners	Health technologists and technicians	Nursing, psychiatric and home health aides	Occupational and physical therapist assistants and aides	Other healthcare supprt occupations
United States	889,398	781,054	3,066,554	164,123	992,994	2,861,697	2,065,790	106,261	1,415,964
Alabama........................	9,928	9,676	53,983	4,481	15,187	47,327	24,440	1,796	17,011
Alaska	1,600	1,894	5,723	373	3,879	6,276	4,089	143	2,180
Arizona........................	16,775	14,410	55,560	2,591	19,637	56,145	24,267	2,990	33,074
Arkansas	6,714	6,916	27,417	1,165	7,442	32,115	22,027	1,059	12,008
California.......................	96,851	75,511	299,822	9,900	111,974	270,510	149,724	8,174	193,648
Colorado	14,051	16,939	49,477	2,493	22,332	42,457	26,461	835	28,769
Connecticut..................	12,807	9,626	41,673	2,441	14,405	34,796	29,410	900	15,750
Delaware......................	2,616	2,862	11,184	664	3,588	8,612	6,509	369	5,142
District of Columbia	3,145	1,301	1,731	176	1,151	3,046	3,185	325	1,952
Florida.........................	52,965	45,317	191,487	10,418	56,695	183,325	130,790	8,674	88,589
Georgia	21,557	19,127	87,588	5,182	28,592	81,407	49,123	2,748	37,822
Hawaii.........................	4,312	2,555	12,983	221	3,839	9,427	4,815	268	7,782
Idaho...........................	3,951	5,206	15,377	768	4,054	16,070	9,745	513	7,819
Illinois.........................	35,688	33,891	130,632	5,056	41,228	108,952	81,348	5,183	52,921
Indiana........................	13,981	14,698	73,486	3,075	17,782	61,244	37,323	3,439	27,460
Iowa............................	7,804	7,277	34,498	1,382	10,681	28,578	25,376	1,108	13,918
Kansas	8,765	7,265	34,155	2,328	9,814	28,626	23,340	1,647	11,060
Kentucky	12,046	12,196	46,406	2,270	13,034	44,461	23,523	1,813	17,735
Louisiana	10,911	9,541	44,907	2,451	14,054	53,704	31,564	1,225	16,176
Maine..........................	4,395	5,122	16,135	1,371	4,287	13,227	11,369	387	7,514
Maryland......................	21,624	15,387	62,279	3,375	21,952	51,863	40,089	1,914	27,623
Massachusetts..............	31,578	22,610	84,432	5,606	24,608	63,316	56,938	2,017	32,228
Michigan	27,580	24,460	100,080	3,690	29,305	91,236	72,794	4,682	49,450
Minnesota	17,670	14,702	68,798	3,783	20,986	57,970	45,788	2,088	25,374
Mississippi...................	4,175	8,767	32,161	3,861	6,835	30,566	17,588	1,228	8,797
Missouri.......................	17,180	15,414	62,839	3,833	15,237	64,779	48,231	2,277	26,680
Montana.......................	2,385	2,633	9,540	927	4,321	8,903	6,244	147	4,117
Nebraska......................	4,774	4,957	21,546	793	7,578	19,284	15,692	589	8,912
Nevada........................	5,276	3,642	18,985	639	6,697	18,849	8,588	472	13,744
New Hampshire.............	4,532	5,684	18,783	1,003	5,091	14,352	10,279	564	6,065
New Jersey	30,902	26,812	89,860	3,029	28,151	77,037	58,807	2,504	40,751
New Mexico	4,698	5,192	13,981	813	6,541	17,803	12,074	856	10,572
New York......................	75,940	58,017	191,455	9,957	66,423	170,877	241,020	6,511	79,039
North Carolina..............	25,717	20,913	97,478	6,171	33,374	90,981	74,257	2,169	41,560
North Dakota................	2,214	1,838	9,881	343	3,597	6,490	7,157	291	3,107
Ohio............................	35,422	29,419	131,124	7,002	34,155	124,482	97,058	5,061	48,884
Oklahoma.....................	7,976	7,363	34,144	1,236	9,085	37,723	25,118	1,664	17,124
Oregon........................	12,756	9,407	33,143	3,236	15,275	34,455	17,425	1,651	25,653
Pennsylvania................	44,214	43,839	141,347	8,207	43,987	139,800	103,405	4,888	60,736
Rhode Island................	4,204	4,458	11,836	496	2,740	10,347	11,803	582	5,957
South Carolina	10,377	11,002	47,476	2,701	13,214	48,667	29,688	1,464	17,480
South Dakota	1,614	2,252	11,044	624	2,528	8,607	7,722	132	4,495
Tennessee	16,713	15,398	63,018	6,170	20,024	71,487	33,907	2,356	20,878
Texas..........................	60,750	60,971	224,360	12,571	75,759	229,355	149,071	7,401	116,903
Utah............................	6,694	6,484	23,548	860	9,885	19,113	12,288	844	12,801
Vermont.......................	3,097	2,192	6,833	336	1,984	6,220	3,776	336	2,170
Virginia........................	25,287	19,900	71,267	4,516	25,779	77,717	43,066	3,250	31,690
Washington..................	23,014	13,782	57,882	4,315	26,276	53,319	32,214	2,072	39,618
West Virginia................	4,852	3,019	21,792	1,787	5,983	23,964	15,145	548	6,331
Wisconsin....................	14,128	17,161	67,708	3,263	19,609	58,322	47,332	2,021	27,624
Wyoming	1,193	2,049	3,710	174	2,360	3,508	2,798	86	1,271

Table A-15.　Employment in Health Care Occupations and Type of Health Insurance—*Continued*

Geographic area	Total civilian noninstitutional population	Persons with no health insurance Number	Persons with no health insurance Percent	Persons with private health insurance (percent) Any type of private health insurance	Employer-based health insurance	Direct-purchase health insurance	TRICARE/ military health coverage	Persons with public coverage (percent) Any type of public coverage	Medicare coverage	Medicaid/ means tested coverage	VA health care
United States	316,450,569	29,757,544	9.4	67.5	54.4	13.8	2.7	34.7	16.7	20.5	2.2
Alabama.....................	4,781,070	484,271	10.1	66.9	53.2	14.2	4.3	36.6	19.4	20.1	2.9
Alaska........................	713,082	105,966	14.9	67.0	54.6	9.0	10.1	28.7	10.8	18.2	3.7
Arizona......................	6,719,354	727,976	10.8	62.8	48.9	14.2	3.3	38.5	18.2	22.2	2.9
Arkansas....................	2,924,307	277,547	9.5	61.3	46.7	14.8	3.3	42.1	19.8	25.5	3.5
California...................	38,649,621	3,317,265	8.6	62.5	50.6	12.6	1.8	38.0	14.5	26.6	1.5
Colorado....................	5,367,335	432,622	8.1	70.4	54.9	14.9	4.1	32.0	14.3	19.1	2.3
Connecticut................	3,537,983	210,522	6	71.9	60.7	12.9	1.2	33.5	16.7	19.6	1.5
Delaware....................	931,203	54,498	5.9	71.3	60.5	11.5	3.6	37.4	19.2	20.6	1.9
District of Columbia	660,682	24,980	3.8	70.5	58.7	14.2	1.7	35.0	12.5	25.9	1.4
Florida.......................	19,960,169	2,661,549	13.3	61.8	44.3	17.2	3.6	37.3	21.2	19.0	3.0
Georgia	10,024,056	1,388,400	13.9	65.3	52.3	12.8	3.9	30.9	14.8	18.0	2.3
Hawaii........................	1,375,062	54,531	4	76.5	63.1	11.7	9.0	33.5	17.4	17.8	2.3
Idaho.........................	1,632,247	180,345	11	69.6	51.2	18.8	3.0	32.4	16.8	17.4	3.0
Illinois.......................	12,679,860	900,289	7.1	69.8	58.0	13.5	1.2	33.8	15.4	20.3	1.7
Indiana.......................	6,520,267	627,761	9.6	70.5	58.7	13.4	1.5	31.8	16.7	16.8	2.2
Iowa..........................	3,080,411	154,970	5	76.2	60.4	17.9	1.7	33.6	17.4	18.4	2.7
Kansas.......................	2,850,159	260,508	9.1	74.8	58.2	17.3	3.7	28.5	16.1	13.9	2.5
Kentucky....................	4,342,711	261,468	6	65.0	53.3	12.5	2.9	42.1	19.0	26.2	2.7
Louisiana	4,567,431	545,631	11.9	62.5	50.2	12.6	2.8	36.3	16.8	22.6	2.3
Maine.........................	1,314,849	110,508	8.4	68.8	53.4	15.5	3.2	37.4	21.9	20.1	3.4
Maryland....................	5,908,522	389,199	6.6	74.1	62.6	12.7	3.7	31.5	15.3	17.9	1.8
Massachusetts............	6,718,090	189,273	2.8	73.4	63.0	13.0	1.1	36.6	16.5	23.6	1.5
Michigan....................	9,810,800	596,642	6.1	71.0	59.9	13.3	1.2	38.1	18.6	22.5	2.0
Minnesota..................	5,431,894	245,108	4.5	76.4	61.1	17.1	1.4	32.5	15.8	18.2	2.5
Mississippi.................	2,927,568	371,585	12.7	58.7	45.3	13.1	3.7	39.9	18.5	25.6	2.5
Missouri.....................	5,969,392	583,108	9.8	71.0	56.8	15.1	2.6	31.1	18.1	14.9	2.7
Montana.....................	1,017,458	118,509	11.6	69.7	50.1	19.7	3.5	33.0	19.2	14.9	3.8
Nebraska....................	1,866,488	153,789	8.2	76.4	58.9	18.3	3.1	27.3	15.9	12.8	2.8
Nevada.......................	2,855,974	350,684	12.3	64.5	52.7	11.4	3.6	33.5	16.3	18.6	3.1
New Hampshire............	1,314,249	83,388	6.3	77.4	64.9	13.9	2.4	29.8	18.2	12.8	2.6
New Jersey	8,850,415	771,196	8.7	71.3	61.6	11.5	0.9	30.9	16.0	17.4	1.0
New Mexico	2,050,178	224,031	10.9	54.6	43.1	10.7	4.3	46.6	18.4	31.1	3.0
New York....................	19,556,452	1,380,548	7.1	65.9	55.7	12.2	0.9	38.4	16.4	25.8	1.4
North Carolina............	9,855,612	1,102,787	11.2	66.8	50.1	16.1	4.6	34.2	17.7	18.8	2.6
North Dakota..............	740,547	57,451	7.8	80.6	60.7	21.1	3.9	24.1	15.4	9.9	2.7
Ohio..........................	11,442,029	746,276	6.5	69.7	59.7	11.6	1.6	36.6	17.8	20.7	2.4
Oklahoma...................	3,830,329	532,509	13.9	64.7	50.9	13.7	3.9	33.7	17.6	17.5	3.3
Oregon......................	3,991,133	280,263	7	67.0	51.9	16.4	2.1	40.3	18.3	24.0	3.2
Pennsylvania..............	12,599,417	801,927	6.4	73.5	59.5	16.0	1.3	34.7	18.9	18.5	2.1
Rhode Island...............	1,041,268	59,410	5.7	70.5	57.3	14.6	2.1	36.8	17.8	22.2	2.1
South Carolina	4,801,301	523,228	10.9	66.0	51.8	14.0	4.6	36.5	19.1	19.6	3.1
South Dakota	841,363	85,915	10.2	72.7	53.3	19.2	4.0	30.3	17.1	14.4	3.7
Tennessee	6,496,300	667,417	10.3	65.8	51.9	14.4	3.4	35.9	18.2	20.2	2.7
Texas.........................	26,990,435	4,615,225	17.1	62.3	50.8	11.6	3.0	29.0	13.1	17.5	2.1
Utah..........................	2,971,003	311,341	10.5	77.3	63.8	14.2	2.2	21.3	11.3	11.1	1.5
Vermont.....................	620,107	23,676	3.8	68.4	55.6	13.9	2.2	42.1	20.1	25.9	2.7
Virginia......................	8,162,517	746,293	9.1	76.1	59.4	15.1	8.0	27.2	15.9	12.0	2.7
Washington................	7,066,812	467,967	6.6	71.1	56.4	14.6	4.2	35.1	16.2	20.8	2.6
West Virginia..............	1,815,505	108,082	6	63.4	53.8	10.6	2.2	46.2	22.2	26.8	3.6
Wisconsin	5,698,995	322,616	5.7	75.0	61.8	14.9	1.4	32.5	17.3	17.4	2.4
Wyoming	576,557	66,494	11.5	74.1	58.1	16.5	3.4	26.4	15.5	12.0	3.2

Table A-16. Health Indicators: Health Risks

Geographic area	Adult Smoking (2014)	Youth Smoking (2015)	Adult Physical Activity (2013)	Youth Physical Activity (2015)	Adult Nutrition (2013)	Youth Nutrition (2015)	Adult Binge Drinking (2014)	Youth Binge Drinking (2015)	Observed Seat Belt Use (2014)	Youth Seat Belt Use (2015)	Youth Marijuana Use (2015)
United States[7]	18.1	10.8	50.5	51.4	23.1	14.8	16.0	17.7	87.0	93.9	21.7
Alabama	21.1	14.0	45.4	58.7	25.8	10.2	12.0	16.1	95.7	90.9	17.3
Alaska	19.9	11.1	55.3	55.8	19.2	14.2	20.2	12.5	88.4	90.6	19.0
Arizona	16.5	10.1	51.9	53.6	23.8	14.7	14.9	19.0	87.2	90.5	23.3
Arkansas	24.7	15.7	41.2	56.7	28.0	13.4	13.3	16.3	74.4	89.6	17.8
California	12.8	7.7	56.3	51.9	17.3	15.9	15.6	15.1	97.1	96.4	22.9
Colorado	15.7	--	60.4	--	19.1	--	17.5	--	82.4	--	--
Connecticut	15.4	10.3	50.9	54.7	22.2	12.8	15.9	14.0	85.1	91.7	20.4
Delaware	19.9	9.9	49.7	56.7	28.9	--	15.7	14.8	91.9	93.7	23.3
District of Columbia	16.4	--	57.7	69.5	20.9	12.1	24.9	8.3	93.2	--	28.7
Florida	17.6	9.9	50.2	58.1	20.8	15.5	15.0	15.3	88.8	91.5	21.5
Georgia	17.4	--	50.8	--	23.7	--	14.2	--	97.3	--	--
Hawaii	14.1	9.7	60.2	61.9	23.1	--	19.7	13.4	93.5	--	19.4
Idaho	15.9	9.7	53.9	46.9	20.4	11.3	14.8	15.6	80.2	94.3	17.0
Illinois	16.5	10.1	52.4	50.4	24.0	12.7	20.2	15.9	94.1	93.7	18.7
Indiana	22.9	11.2	44.1	53.5	26.9	9.8	14.8	17.4	90.2	94.1	16.4
Iowa	18.5	--	47.0	--	26.8	--	21.4	--	92.8	--	--
Kansas	18.1	--	49.1	--	22.9	--	15.8	--	85.7	--	--
Kentucky	26.2	16.9	46.0	63.0	24.9	11.1	12.7	17.7	86.1	90.9	17.2
Louisiana	24.0	--	45.2	--	32.7	--	16.0	--	84.1	--	--
Maine	19.3	11.2	53.6	58.8	17.7	--	17.0	11.7	85.0	93.7	19.9
Maryland	14.6	8.7	48.6	63.1	22.0	13.4	15.4	13.1	92.1	--	18.8
Massachusetts	14.7	7.7	54.5	54.8	20.1	12.0	17.4	17.7	76.6	--	24.5
Michigan	21.2	10.0	53.1	54.0	24.8	9.8	18.9	12.5	93.3	93.4	19.3
Minnesota	16.3	--	52.7	--	23.6	--	19.5	--	94.7	--	--
Mississippi	17.0	15.2	37.4	65.8	30.6	12.4	12.8	15.3	78.3	88.9	19.7
Missouri	23.0	11.0	48.7	54.3	24.3	10.5	15.1	19.5	78.8	91.9	16.3
Montana	20.6	13.1	57.8	46.0	20.5	13.3	18.9	20.7	74.0	90.5	19.5
Nebraska	19.9	13.3	50.1	47.2	23.3	13.2	20.3	14.3	79.0	88.7	13.7
Nevada	17.3	7.5	53.6	49.4	20.8	13.8	16.0	15.8	94.0	93.8	19.3
New Hampshire	17.5	9.3	55.4	53.1	16.8	--	16.8	16.8	70.4	91.8	22.2
New Jersey	15.1	--	50.5	--	21.4	--	15.8	--	87.6	--	--
New Mexico	19.1	11.4	55.0	47.8	21.5	16.4	13.7	14.6	92.1	94.0	25.3
New York	14.4	8.8	47.3	58.2	22.0	--	15.0	15.6	90.6	--	19.3
North Carolina	19.1	13.1	48.6	56.6	22.4	12.5	13.6	13.9	90.6	93.5	22.3
North Dakota	19.9	11.7	45.3	48.7	27.4	11.1	24.0	17.6	81.0	91.5	15.2
Ohio	21.0	--	49.5	--	26.3	--	18.1	--	85.0	--	--
Oklahoma	21.1	13.1	43.9	46.0	25.3	12.1	12.9	16.5	86.3	94.3	17.5
Oregon	17.0	--	64.1	--	16.3	--	16.6	--	97.8	--	--
Pennsylvania	19.9	12.9	47.8	54.4	24.7	10.7	16.7	15.4	83.6	89.1	18.2
Rhode Island	16.3	4.8	49.1	56.3	21.3	12.0	18.4	12.8	87.4	94.1	23.6
South Carolina	21.5	9.6	49.1	57.7	26.8	9.1	14.1	11.5	90.0	94.7	17.8
South Dakota	18.6	10.1	53.7	52.6	24.5	11.9	17.4	14.3	68.9	85.4	12.4
Tennessee	24.2	11.5	37.7	57.3	24.3	9.7	10.6	--	87.7	92.7	--
Texas	14.5	--	42.1	--	21.5	--	16.3	--	90.7	--	--
Utah	9.7	--	55.3	--	20.4	--	11.4	--	83.4	--	--
Vermont	16.4	10.8	58.8	54.2	16.5	18.1	17.9	16.0	84.1	--	22.4
Virginia	19.5	8.2	51.9	54.8	21.4	13.8	15.2	11.0	77.3	93.7	16.2
Washington	15.3	--	56.3	--	18.2	--	17.1	--	94.5	--	--
West Virginia	26.7	18.8	47.6	55.1	24.2	12.9	9.6	19.8	87.8	88.8	16.5
Wisconsin	17.4	--	53.4	--	25.8	--	22.1	--	84.7	--	--
Wyoming	19.5	15.7	54.2	49.3	20.1	13.9	17.2	19.7	79.2	89.3	18.3

Note: See Appendix A. Source Notes and Explanations for meanings of all indicators.

Table A-17.　Health Indicators: Health Conditions and Preventive Measures

Geographic area	Health Conditions							Preventive measures		
	HIV Diagnosis Rate (2014)	Adult Obesity (2014)	Youth Obesity (2015)	Diagnosed Diabetes (2014)	Diagnosed High Cholesterol (2013)	Diagnosed Hypertension (2013)	Medicated Hypertension (2013)	Colorectal Cancer Screening (2014)	Influenza Vaccination Coverage (2014)	Child Vaccination Coverage (2014)
United States	16.5	29.5	13.9	9.1	38.4	31.4	78.1	68.8	47.1	71.6
Alabama......................	17.2	33.5	16.1	11.8	44.4	40.4	82.7	67.6	45.8	76.9
Alaska.........................	6.8	29.7	14.0	7.6	38.6	29.8	61.3	64.3	44.0	67.3
Arizona.......................	14.3	28.9	10.9	9.1	39.7	30.7	70.6	68.1	41.6	66.1
Arkansas.....................	13.8	35.9	18.0	11.5	42.4	38.7	79.1	64.6	50.5	66.0
California.....................	17.2	24.7	13.9	9.9	37.7	28.7	70.7	66.6	44.2	77.9
Colorado.....................	9.0	21.3	--	6.9	34.8	26.3	69.2	69.3	49.0	72.8
Connecticut.................	10.0	26.3	12.3	8.0	37.8	31.3	76.0	76.1	52.8	73.0
Delaware	16.8	30.7	15.8	9.7	40.6	35.6	82.9	76.6	53.3	74.5
District of Columbia	66.9	21.7	15.1	9.1	34.0	28.4	73.6	70.3	46.7	71.1
Florida.........................	31.3	26.2	12.3	9.4	40.3	34.6	79.4	69.9	39.2	72.7
Georgia	27.0	30.5	--	11.0	38.1	35.1	77.7	69.8	44.1	74.0
Hawaii.........................	9.2	22.1	12.9	8.9	35.0	28.5	78.8	65.7	52.0	73.7
Idaho..........................	2.0	28.9	11.1	7.0	38.4	29.4	71.9	66.4	42.2	65.9
Illinois	16.1	29.3	12.6	9.4	36.6	30.1	77.6	65.1	41.9	68.3
Indiana.......................	9.0	32.7	13.6	9.7	39.8	33.5	79.7	65.0	44.7	66.3
Iowa...........................	4.0	30.9	--	8.3	41.1	31.4	78.1	71.1	53.8	71.3
Kansas........................	5.8	31.3	--	9.5	38.1	31.3	78.5	67.8	48.0	76.5
Kentucky.....................	9.9	31.6	18.5	11.3	43.2	39.1	81.3	69.6	48.3	72.3
Louisiana	36.6	34.9	--	10.4	40.7	39.9	80.8	66.4	44.7	73.2
Maine.........................	5.2	28.2	13.3	7.8	39.7	33.3	79.6	78.1	49.5	84.7
Maryland.....................	27.7	29.6	11.5	9.2	37.0	32.8	80.4	73.0	52.1	74.4
Massachusetts.............	12.8	23.3	11.0	8.8	36.5	29.4	75.8	77.9	54.9	75.4
Michigan.....................	10.0	30.7	14.3	9.0	40.6	34.6	75.7	74.6	44.3	65.0
Minnesota...................	7.0	27.6	--	7.5	33.6	27.0	77.0	74.4	51.9	70.5
Mississippi..................	21.0	35.5	18.9	11.9	41.9	40.2	82.9	62.9	44.9	70.7
Missouri......................	9.9	30.2	13.1	10.0	38.8	32.1	82.9	66.7	49.1	70.0
Montana......................	1.9	26.4	10.3	7.6	35.7	29.3	73.5	66.8	44.4	67.1
Nebraska.....................	6.1	30.2	13.0	8.4	37.4	30.3	78.5	67.6	54.0	80.2
Nevada........................	19.6	27.7	12.2	8.8	38.6	30.6	73.6	63.0	39.7	67.7
New Hampshire............	3.6	27.4	12.2	7.8	36.7	30.1	76.8	77.8	52.1	80.4
New Jersey	20.4	26.9	--	8.6	39.2	31.1	78.0	67.7	46.8	67.2
New Mexico	8.2	28.4	15.6	10.4	36.8	29.5	74.0	63.0	49.6	75.9
New York.....................	22.8	27.0	13.1	9.2	39.1	31.6	77.8	70.7	48.6	70.7
North Carolina.............	17.0	29.7	16.4	9.8	41.0	35.5	78.4	73.2	52.4	80.8
North Dakota...............	4.0	32.2	14.0	8.0	36.5	29.7	79.3	65.3	51.0	71.3
Ohio	10.3	32.6	--	10.3	37.5	33.5	79.4	67.6	46.1	68.1
Oklahoma....................	10.5	33.0	17.3	10.9	41.2	37.5	79.0	62.3	49.1	73.3
Oregon........................	7.3	27.9	--	8.0	37.0	31.8	71.2	70.6	44.3	65.3
Pennsylvania...............	12.2	30.2	14.0	9.6	38.5	33.7	80.5	69.6	50.3	78.6
Rhode Island...............	11.2	27.0	12.0	8.3	38.7	33.8	79.3	77.8	58.7	75.6
South Carolina	20.7	32.1	16.3	10.7	42.6	38.4	80.7	71.3	48.3	72.6
South Dakota	4.1	29.8	14.7	8.2	36.6	30.7	80.6	69.7	59.6	76.3
Tennessee	14.7	31.2	18.6	11.7	38.7	38.8	83.9	68.8	48.8	71.9
Texas..........................	22.1	31.9	--	10.8	37.7	31.2	76.8	63.5	50.1	64.0
Utah...........................	5.3	25.7	--	7.7	33.4	24.2	67.9	74.2	46.9	70.8
Vermont......................	3.5	24.8	12.4	6.9	35.2	31.1	72.6	75.3	49.9	71.8
Virginia.......................	14.1	28.5	13.0	9.0	38.6	32.5	79.3	72.0	51.8	73.7
Washington..................	7.7	27.3	--	8.2	36.7	30.4	68.5	71.8	49.5	67.4
West Virginia...............	6.1	35.7	17.9	12.0	42.9	41.0	80.6	66.0	51.1	63.4
Wisconsin	4.8	31.2	--	8.0	36.3	32.3	77.2	75.9	44.1	70.9
Wyoming	2.4	29.5	11.0	7.8	35.0	28.7	74.5	61.8	40.4	64.0

Note: See Appendix A. Source Notes and Explanations for meanings of all indicators.

Table A-18. People With and Without Health Insurance Coverage

| | All People | | | | | | | | | Children under 18 years old | | | | | |
| | Total people covered (thousands) | | | Number not covered (thousands) | | | Percentage of people not covered | | | Number not covered (thousands) | | | Percentage of children not covered | | |
Geographic area	2015	2012	2008	2015	2012	2008	2015	2012	2008	2015	2012	2008	2015	2012	2008
United States	286,693	263,282	255,068	29,758	45,615	43,503	9.4	14.8	14.6	3,534	5,264	6,879	4.8	7.2	9.3
Alabama......................	4,297	4,109	3,966	484	632	609	10.1	13.3	13.3	34	46	85	3.1	4.1	7.6
Alaska	607	564	533	106	145	126	14.9	20.5	19.1	20	26	21	10.6	13.9	11.6
Arizona.......................	5,991	5,313	5,249	728	1,131	1,154	10.8	17.6	18.0	134	214	258	8.3	13.2	15.1
Arkansas	2,647	2,420	2,322	278	476	480	9.5	16.4	17.1	35	42	57	4.9	5.9	8.1
California....................	35,332	30,815	29,921	3,317	6,710	6,239	8.6	17.9	17.3	302	730	931	3.3	7.9	10.0
Colorado	4,935	4,344	4,042	433	751	812	8.1	14.7	16.7	52	109	166	4.2	8.8	13.8
Connecticut.................	3,327	3,213	3,138	211	322	302	6.0	9.1	8.8	25	30	37	3.3	3.8	4.6
Delaware	877	823	771	54	80	85	5.9	8.8	10.0	6	7	15	3.0	3.5	7.5
Distict of Columbia.......	636	585	536	25	37	44	3.8	5.9	7.6	2	2	4	1.5	1.7	3.6
Florida........................	17,299	15,195	14,356	2,662	3,816	3,639	13.3	20.1	20.2	284	436	668	6.9	10.9	16.7
Georgia	8,636	7,927	7,748	1,388	1,792	1,725	13.9	18.4	18.2	166	220	278	6.7	8.8	11.0
Hawaii	1,321	1,249	1,156	55	92	80	4.0	6.9	6.5	5	10	10	1.6	3.5	3.4
Idaho	1,452	1,321	1,241	180	255	257	11.0	16.2	17.2	25	36	52	5.8	8.5	12.7
Illinois	11,780	11,076	11,134	900	1,622	1,575	7.1	12.8	12.4	75	101	165	2.5	3.3	5.2
Indiana.......................	5,893	5,517	5,432	628	920	839	9.6	14.3	13.4	106	134	152	6.7	8.4	9.6
Iowa...........................	2,925	2,775	2,696	155	254	256	5.0	8.4	8.7	26	29	36	3.5	4.0	5.1
Kansas	2,590	2,470	2,426	261	356	313	9.1	12.6	11.4	37	48	52	5.1	6.6	7.4
Kentucky	4,081	3,697	3,637	261	595	551	6.0	13.9	13.2	43	56	65	4.2	5.5	6.5
Louisiana	4,022	3,739	3,580	546	760	733	11.9	16.9	17.0	40	59	80	3.6	5.3	7.2
Maine.........................	1,204	1,181	1,164	111	135	135	8.4	10.2	10.4	14	12	18	5.7	4.6	6.6
Maryland.....................	5,519	5,191	4,934	389	598	595	6.6	10.3	10.8	52	51	67	3.9	3.8	5.0
Massachusetts.............	6,529	6,313	6,150	189	254	249	2.8	3.9	3.9	16	20	24	1.1	1.4	1.7
Michigan.....................	9,214	8,658	8,785	597	1,114	1,081	6.1	11.4	11.0	68	90	114	3.1	4.0	4.8
Minnesota...................	5,187	4,895	4,717	245	425	433	4.5	8.0	8.4	39	68	72	3.1	5.4	5.8
Mississippi..................	2,556	2,421	2,381	372	498	486	12.7	17.0	17.0	29	55	89	4.0	7.3	11.6
Missouri......................	5,386	5,107	5,075	583	801	720	9.8	13.6	12.4	80	98	96	5.7	7.0	6.8
Montana......................	899	811	784	119	178	166	11.6	18.0	17.5	17	24	29	7.6	11.1	13.0
Nebraska....................	1,713	1,621	1,561	154	206	189	8.2	11.3	10.8	25	28	30	5.3	6.0	6.8
Nevada.......................	2,505	2,121	2,036	351	603	532	12.3	22.2	20.7	50	110	130	7.6	16.6	19.4
New Hampshire............	1,231	1,167	1,163	83	139	136	6.3	10.6	10.5	7	11	14	2.7	4.0	4.9
New Jersey	8,079	7,644	7,532	771	1,113	1,025	8.7	12.7	12.0	75	103	137	3.7	5.1	6.7
New Mexico	1,826	1,674	1,548	224	378	404	10.9	18.4	20.7	22	41	67	4.5	8.0	13.3
New York.....................	18,176	17,214	17,012	1,381	2,103	2,194	7.1	10.9	11.4	104	168	232	2.5	3.9	5.3
North Carolina.............	8,753	7,970	7,613	1,103	1,582	1,391	11.2	16.6	15.5	99	173	211	4.4	7.6	9.4
North Dakota................	683	616	561	57	69	63	7.8	10.0	10.0	13	11	10	7.9	6.9	7.1
Ohio...........................	10,696	10,068	10,014	746	1,304	1,282	6.5	11.5	11.3	115	141	185	4.4	5.3	6.8
Oklahoma....................	3,298	3,048	2,886	533	685	664	13.9	18.4	18.7	71	94	112	7.4	10.1	12.4
Oregon.......................	3,711	3,284	3,153	280	576	593	7.0	14.9	15.8	31	55	105	3.6	6.4	12.1
Pennsylvania................	11,797	11,335	11,106	802	1,225	1,103	6.4	9.8	9.0	111	139	159	4.1	5.1	5.8
Rhode Island...............	982	920	926	59	115	105	5.7	11.1	10.2	7	10	12	3.4	4.5	5.2
South Carolina	4,278	3,845	3,643	523	778	731	10.9	16.8	16.7	44	89	125	4.1	8.3	11.7
South Dakota	755	722	696	86	94	87	10.2	11.5	11.1	14	12	16	6.7	5.8	8.1
Tennessee	5,829	5,473	5,323	667	882	790	10.3	13.9	12.9	62	85	96	4.2	5.7	6.5
Texas.........................	22,375	19,822	18,263	4,615	5,762	5,564	17.1	22.5	23.4	682	863	1,138	9.5	12.4	17.0
Utah...........................	2,660	2,420	2,300	311	409	405	10.5	14.5	15.0	65	90	108	7.2	10.1	12.7
Vermont......................	596	580	561	24	40	54	3.8	6.5	8.8	1	3	5	1.0	2.8	3.7
Virginia.......................	7,416	6,974	6,649	746	1,000	871	9.1	12.5	11.6	91	104	133	4.9	5.6	7.3
Washington..................	6,599	5,848	5,622	468	945	807	6.6	13.9	12.5	43	91	117	2.6	5.8	7.6
West Virginia................	1,707	1,563	1,523	108	264	265	6.0	14.4	14.8	11	15	24	2.8	3.9	6.2
Wisconsin	5,376	5,146	5,051	323	506	489	5.7	9.0	8.8	46	62	63	3.6	4.7	4.8
Wyoming	510	480	452	66	87	72	11.5	15.4	13.7	11	13	11	7.8	9.3	8.6

Table A-19.   Public and Private School Fall Enrollment

Geographic area	Total enrollment (public and private) 2015 — 3 to 4 years of age — Total enrollment (thousands)	Percentage enrolled[1]	Percentage enrolled in public school[2]	5 to 17 years of age — Total enrollment (thousands)	Public (thousands)	Private (thousands)	Percentage enrolled in public school[2]	Public school enrollment — Total enrollment (thousands) 2014–2015	2009–2010	2004–2005	Pre-kindergarten through grade 8 (thousands) 2014–2015	2009–2010	2004–2005	Grades 9 through 12 (thousands) 2014–2015	2009–2010	2004–2005
United States	3,860	47.6	58.2	52,117	46,506	5,611	89.2	50,313	49,361	48,795	35,282	34,291	33,962	14,891	14,862	14,496
Alabama	52	44.3	54.0	792	701	91	88.5	744	749	730	523	529	522	221	219	208
Alaska	8	35.4	62.9	123	110	13	89.4	131	132	133	93	91	92	38	41	41
Arizona........................	66	37.3	61.2	1,145	1,066	80	93.1	1,112	1,078	1,043	780	760	718	332	317	321
Arkansas.....................	38	49.6	68.4	493	455	38	92.3	491	481	463	349	344	328	142	136	135
California.....................	504	48.9	59.4	6,458	5,910	549	91.5	6,312	6,263	6,442	4,356	4,260	4,472	1,950	1,997	1,915
Colorado	70	51.9	65.4	888	812	76	91.4	889	832	766	634	591	541	255	241	225
Connecticut.................	50	64.0	56.1	564	509	56	90.2	543	564	577	375	390	404	168	174	173
Delaware.....................	11	46.8	54.9	143	126	18	88.1	134	127	119	95	88	84	39	39	35
District of Columbia	12	74.6	81.2	72	59	13	81.9	81	69	77	62	51	54	18	18	18
Florida........................																
	231	51.1	54.0	2,901	2,556	345	88.1	2,757	2,635	2,639	1,934	1,851	1,858	823	784	782
Georgia	132	50.9	63.4	1,794	1,621	173	90.4	1,744	1,668	1,553	1,243	1,195	1,118	502	473	435
Hawaii.........................	16	45.1	36.5	209	166	43	79.4	182	180	183	131	127	129	51	53	54
Idaho..........................	14	30.4	46.2	303	274	30	90.4	291	276	256	205	195	178	85	82	78
Illinois........................	182	55.2	60.7	2,119	1,884	235	88.9	2,050	2,104	2,098	1,429	1,464	1,483	621	640	614
Indiana........................	66	39.0	49.1	1,112	970	141	87.2	1,046	1,047	1,021	729	731	720	316	316	301
Iowa...........................	37	47.9	71.4	520	465	55	89.4	505	492	478	359	341	324	146	151	154
Kansas........................	36	44.8	64.2	507	455	52	89.7	497	474	469	351	330	311	140	140	144
Kentucky......................	45	39.8	67.5	711	632	79	88.9	689	680	675	491	484	482	197	196	187
Louisiana.....................	64	50.3	70.9	784	651	133	83.0	717	691	724	522	510	534	195	181	191
Maine..........................	10	35.2	52.0	186	166	20	89.2	182	189	199	126	129	136	56	61	63
Maryland......................	79	51.8	48.2	950	812	138	85.5	875	848	866	620	582	597	254	267	268
Massachusetts..............	90	59.0	50.4	995	889	106	89.3	956	957	976	666	666	682	289	291	293
Michigan......................	108	46.3	65.6	1,589	1,431	157	90.1	1,538	1,649	1,751	1,049	1,105	1,180	485	530	525
Minnesota....................	64	44.5	60.0	901	803	98	89.1	857	837	839	594	565	558	263	272	280
Mississippi...................	41	52.1	69.0	522	456	65	87.4	491	492	495	348	347	353	135	138	129
Missouri.......................	65	44.9	56.2	979	846	133	86.4	918	918	905	649	638	629	269	280	277
Montana.......................	9	42.0	56.2	156	141	15	90.4	145	142	147	103	98	98	42	44	48
Nebraska.....................	22	41.6	56.3	330	285	44	86.4	313	295	286	223	207	195	90	89	91
Nevada........................	25	34.3	68.3	476	439	37	92.2	459	429	400	324	305	288	135	123	111
New Hampshire.............	14	54.7	48.3	193	170	23	88.1	185	197	207	126	133	140	59	64	67
New Jersey	142	64.6	53.6	1,435	1,250	185	87.1	1,401	1,396	1,393	940	932	932	402	413	400
New Mexico	25	46.1	76.9	353	327	26	92.6	340	334	326	241	235	228	99	99	98
New York......................	282	57.6	57.8	2,947	2,546	402	86.4	2,741	2,766	2,836	1,866	1,792	1,891	827	858	841
North Carolina..............	98	42.1	54.7	1,624	1,463	162	90.1	1,549	1,483	1,386	1,092	1,053	986	455	430	400
North Dakota................	7	36.0	59.9	112	101	11	90.2	107	95	101	76	65	67	30	30	33
Ohio...........................	128	44.9	58.3	1,870	1,603	267	85.7	1,725	1,764	1,840	1,205	1,225	1,267	520	539	573
Oklahoma....................	50	45.5	78.2	680	630	50	92.6	689	655	629	503	476	450	184	177	175
Oregon........................	44	45.4	45.2	606	537	69	88.6	601	583	553	422	404	376	180	178	175
Pennsylvania................	135	46.1	46.4	1,900	1,609	291	84.7	1,743	1,786	1,828	1,194	1,199	1,232	549	584	590
Rhode Island................	9	44.6	45.1	151	132	19	87.4	142	145	156	99	98	107	43	47	49
South Carolina	54	45.8	57.8	777	697	80	89.7	757	723	704	540	512	504	217	211	199
South Dakota	9	35.8	61.3	143	128	15	89.5	133	124	123	96	86	84	37	38	39
Tennessee....................	61	37.5	56.8	1,049	922	127	87.9	995	973	941	707	687	656	288	286	270
Texas..........................	351	43.4	62.2	5,088	4,714	374	92.6	5,234	4,850	4,405	3,783	3,520	3,184	1,450	1,330	1,221
Utah...........................	43	42.9	53.5	643	601	42	93.5	636	572	504	457	413	355	179	158	148
Vermont.......................	5	46.7	61.4	87	78	9	89.7	87	91	98	61	62	66	26	29	32
Virginia........................	98	47.2	42.7	1,314	1,162	152	88.4	1,280	1,245	1,205	898	864	840	383	381	365
Washington...................	77	42.0	45.9	1,126	1,002	124	89.0	1,074	1,035	1,020	740	705	695	333	330	325
West Virginia.................	14	33.8	73.9	269	252	17	93.7	280	283	280	200	200	198	81	82	83
Wisconsin....................	60	43.8	64.3	930	804	126	86.5	871	872	865	607	593	578	265	279	287
Wyoming	7	43.5	69.5	96	88	8	91.7	94	88	85	67	62	57	27	26	27

[1] As a percentage of all 3 and 4 year olds, including those not enrolled.
[2] As a percentage of those enrolled.

Table A-20.   Public Elementary and Secondary Schools—Finances and Teachers

Geographic area	Total enrollment 2013–2014 (thousands)[1]	Revenues, 2013–2014 (millions of dollars) Source — Total	Local	State	Federal	Expenditures Total (millions of dollars)[2]	Per capita (dollars)[3]	Current expenditures Elementary and secondary schools (millions of dollars)	Average per pupil Amount (dollars)	Rank	Full-time equivalent teachers (thousands) Total	Elementary	Secondary	Pupil-teacher ratio, 2014–2015[5]
United States	50,017	623,209	280,507	288,196	54,505	625,016	1,962.0	553,501	11,066		3,132.4	1,743.2	1,203.3	
Alabama......................	746	7,397	2,493	4,066	839	7,591	1,567.4	6,743	9,036	39	42.7	22.7	20.1	17.4
Alaska........................	131	2,677	530	1,836	312	2,736	3,714.3	2,418	18,466	4	7.8	4.3	3.5	16.9
Arizona.......................	1,102	9,594	4,174	4,217	1,204	9,453	1,406.8	8,221	7,457	49	48.1	33.3	14.9	23.1
Arkansas	490	5,134	1,876	2,665	592	5,363	1,807.6	4,778	9,752	32	35.4	18.6	14.3	13.9
California....................	6,313	69,343	23,107	39,293	6,943	70,428	1,820.7	61,051	9,671	33	267.7	180.1	85.1	23.6
Colorado.....................	877	9,241	4,522	4,028	691	9,373	1,752.1	7,924	9,036	40	51.4	29.5	21.9	17.3
Connecticut..................	546	11,018	6,132	4,419	467	11,064	3,080.2	10,050	18,401	5	42.1	26.6	15.2	12.9
Delaware.....................	132	1,970	621	1,169	180	2,075	2,219.4	1,816	13,793	13	9.6	4.9	4.8	13.9
District of Columbia	78	2,169	1,962	(X)	207	2,186	3,316.6	1,608	20,577	1	6.6	4.8	1.7	12.3
Florida........................	2,721	25,897	12,254	10,461	3,182	27,178	1,366.5	24,364	8,955	42	180.4	77.1	66.3	15.3
Georgia.......................	1,724	17,888	8,112	7,918	1,858	17,815	1,766.1	15,922	9,236	38	111.5	51.9	43.3	15.7
Hawaii........................	187	2,697	55	2,355	287	2,504	1,768.0	2,317	12,400	16	11.7	6.4	5.2	15.6
Idaho.........................	296	2,183	539	1,398	246	2,165	1,325.3	1,950	6,577	50	15.6	7.4	8.2	18.6
Illinois.......................	2,065	27,240	17,849	7,089	2,303	30,501	2,370.4	27,290	13,213	15	132.5	91.7	40.7	15.5
Indiana.......................	1,047	12,059	4,300	6,764	994	11,235	1,703.5	9,841	9,396	37	56.5	29.6	26.9	18.5
Iowa..........................	503	6,216	2,491	3,253	472	6,312	2,030.8	5,355	10,647	27	35.7	25.0	10.7	14.2
Kansas.......................	496	6,065	2,202	3,299	564	6,115	2,109.2	5,083	10,240	29	37.7	19.2	18.5	13.2
Kentucky.....................	677	7,137	2,416	3,885	836	7,244	1,641.5	6,375	9,411	35	41.6	24.7	9.9	16.6
Louisiana	711	8,734	3,604	3,794	1,335	8,632	1,857.1	7,721	10,853	25	46.3	26.9	11.9	15.5
Maine.........................	184	2,671	1,414	1,068	189	2,601	1,954.4	2,441	13,267	14	14.9	10.4	4.6	12.2
Maryland.....................	866	13,847	6,919	6,110	818	13,684	2,293.1	12,314	14,217	11	59.2	35.9	23.3	14.8
Massachusetts...............	956	16,812	9,310	6,597	906	16,174	2,396.2	15,183	15,886	8	71.9	47.1	24.7	13.3
Michigan.....................	1,549	18,884	5,898	11,212	1,774	18,614	1,877.2	16,494	10,649	26	85.0	35.2	33.4	18.1
Minnesota....................	851	11,590	2,804	8,091	695	11,618	2,130.6	9,724	11,427	20	55.7	30.1	24.0	15.4
Mississippi...................	493	4,430	1,521	2,244	665	4,383	1,464.6	4,071	8,265	47	32.3	15.3	13.1	15.2
Missouri......................	918	10,450	6,122	3,405	923	10,582	1,745.9	9,126	9,938	31	67.4	35.0	32.3	13.6
Montana......................	144	1,723	686	833	205	1,732	1,692.9	1,577	10,941	24	10.2	7.1	3.1	14.1
Nebraska.....................	308	3,931	2,338	1,283	310	4,062	2,159.2	3,654	11,877	18	23.0	14.5	8.5	13.6
Nevada.......................	452	4,342	2,379	1,560	402	4,099	1,446.7	3,739	8,275	46	21.7	10.5	8.0	21.2
New Hampshire...............	186	2,946	1,778	1,005	162	2,856	2,149.1	2,720	14,601	10	14.8	10.0	4.8	12.5
New Jersey	1,370	27,364	15,067	11,122	1,175	27,357	3,065.3	25,734	18,780	3	115.1	61.0	38.2	12.2
New Mexico	339	3,780	628	2,645	506	3,728	1,789.6	3,190	9,403	36	22.4	10.0	8.4	15.2
New York.....................	2,733	60,861	32,610	24,927	3,324	60,121	3,048.9	55,081	20,156	2	203.8	103.5	91.7	13.5
North Carolina................	1,531	13,123	3,374	8,154	1,596	13,311	1,339.9	12,685	8,287	45	99.3	69.3	29.2	15.6
North Dakota.................	104	1,502	457	889	156	1,518	2,051.2	1,251	12,032	17	9.0	5.9	3.1	11.8
Ohio..........................	1,724	23,494	11,201	10,407	1,887	22,276	1,921.2	19,714	11,434	19	106.5	50.2	47.3	16.2
Oklahoma....................	682	6,081	2,364	3,007	709	6,220	1,604.1	5,451	7,995	48	42.1	23.5	18.6	16.4
Oregon.......................	567	6,623	2,687	3,393	543	6,283	1,583.2	5,647	9,959	30	27.9	19.6	8.3	21.6
Pennsylvania.................	1,755	28,106	15,790	10,382	1,934	27,471	2,147.7	24,265	13,824	12	122.0	58.5	53.3	14.3
Rhode Island.................	142	2,387	1,243	947	197	2,401	2,276.9	2,183	15,372	9	9.5	5.2	4.3	15.0
South Carolina	746	8,641	3,700	4,093	848	8,449	1,749.9	7,164	9,608	34	49.5	34.7	14.8	15.3
South Dakota	131	1,351	741	419	191	1,364	1,599.8	1,183	9,036	40	9.6	6.2	2.5	13.8
Tennessee	994	9,324	3,903	4,321	1,100	9,469	1,446.8	8,607	8,662	43	65.3	44.7	18.7	15.2
Texas.........................	5,154	53,377	25,377	22,128	5,873	53,516	1,986.1	44,331	8,602	44	342.3	171.8	141.7	15.3
Utah..........................	625	4,906	1,799	2,673	434	4,963	1,687.0	4,094	6,546	51	27.4	13.6	11.2	23.2
Vermont......................	89	1,706	70	1,533	104	1,685	2,687.3	1,602	18,066	6	8.3	3.2	2.9	10.6
Virginia.......................	1,274	15,049	8,056	5,985	1,009	15,225	1,830.5	13,955	10,955	23	90.0	41.9	48.1	14.2
Washington...................	1,059	12,932	4,069	7,833	1,030	12,853	1,822.0	10,912	10,305	28	59.6	41.9	15.6	18.0
West Virginia.................	281	3,562	1,129	2,075	358	3,559	1,925.4	3,195	11,371	21	20.0	9.4	10.6	14.0
Wisconsin....................	874	10,981	5,144	4,981	856	11,111	1,929.5	9,920	11,345	22	58.4	29.5	28.5	14.9
Wyoming.....................	92	1,772	694	965	113	1,765	3,023.5	1,467	15,903	7	7.6	4.1	3.5	12.4

Survey, Census, or Data Collection Method: Based on U.S. Census Bureau, Public School Finance Data, see www.census.gov/govs/school/data_collection.html.
(X) = Not applicable.
[1]Enrollment represents the total count of pupils that are enrolled on or about October 1st of the survey year. These data are from the National Public Education Financial Survey.
[2]Includes interest on school debt and other current expenditures not shown separately.
[3]Based on U.S. Census Bureau estimated resident population as of July 1, 2014.
[4]Schools classified by type of organization rather than by grade-group; elementary includes kindergarten; total includes ungraded teachers.
[5]Pupils that are enrolled on or about October 1st of the survey year.

Table A-21. Public High School Graduates and Educational Attainment

Geographic area	Public high school graduates (thousands)[1]			Averaged freshman graduation rate, 2013	Population 25 years and over (thousands)	Educational attainment, 2015					
						Percentage of people 25 years and over, by highest level completed					
	2015 projected	2010	2005			Not a high school graduate	High school graduate	Some college, but no degree	Associate's degree	Bachelor's degree	Advanced degree[2]
United States	3,136.9	3,128.0	2,799.3	81.9	216,447	12.9	27.6	20.7	8.2	19.0	11.6
Alabama......................	44.6	43.2	37.5	74.2	3,282	15.1	31.0	21.6	8.1	15.4	8.8
Alaska	7.4	8.2	6.9	79.9	470	7.4	27.3	27.5	8.1	18.7	11.0
Arizona......................	64.1	61.1	59.5	76.5	4,537	13.9	24.5	25.5	8.4	17.4	10.3
Arkansas...................	29.9	28.3	26.6	80.1	1,988	14.6	34.1	22.7	6.8	14.0	7.8
California...................	414.8	405.0	355.2	83.6	26,085	17.8	20.8	21.5	7.6	20.3	12.0
Colorado....................	51.6	49.3	44.5	83.3	3,672	8.8	21.7	22.0	8.2	24.8	14.5
Connecticut................	36.2	34.5	35.5	87.4	2,475	9.8	27.4	16.9	7.6	21.7	16.7
Delaware...................	7.9	8.1	6.9	77.0	653	11.1	29.8	20.1	8.1	18.0	12.9
District of Columbia	3.3	3.6	2.8	77.7	473	10.2	17.4	12.7	3.0	23.8	32.9
Florida......................	162.4	156.1	133.3	75.8	14,394	12.4	29.2	20.4	9.6	18.2	10.2
Georgia	95.4	91.6	70.8	70.5	6,684	13.9	28.1	20.7	7.4	18.6	11.3
Hawaii......................	10.9	11.0	10.8	78.0	986	9.1	27.1	21.6	10.7	20.8	10.6
Idaho........................	17.9	17.8	15.8	82.1	1,066	10.0	27.5	27.0	9.6	17.8	8.2
Illinois......................	134.3	139.0	123.6	82.7	8,662	11.4	26.7	20.8	8.1	20.3	12.7
Indiana......................	66.0	64.6	55.4	81.0	4,364	11.8	34.3	20.6	8.3	16.0	9.0
Iowa.........................	32.6	34.5	33.5	89.4	2,075	8.3	32.1	21.4	11.4	18.2	8.7
Kansas......................	31.5	31.6	30.4	88.4	1,888	9.7	26.5	23.6	8.4	20.4	11.4
Kentucky...................	41.4	42.7	38.4	83.1	2,989	14.9	33.5	20.4	7.9	13.6	9.7
Louisiana	36.9	36.6	36.0	72.7	3,095	15.4	34.1	21.1	6.1	15.2	8.0
Maine.......................	12.6	14.1	13.1	87.5	961	8.3	32.7	19.2	9.7	19.5	10.6
Maryland...................	56.8	59.1	54.2	85.6	4,102	10.4	25.1	19.2	6.5	21.1	17.7
Massachusetts............	64.4	64.5	59.7	88.4	4,707	9.8	25.2	15.9	7.7	23.1	18.4
Michigan...................	101.1	110.7	101.6	78.3	6,728	9.9	29.4	23.7	9.2	17.0	10.8
Minnesota..................	56.4	59.7	58.4	91.0	3,701	7.2	25.4	21.5	11.2	22.9	11.8
Mississippi.................	26.2	25.5	23.5	68.4	1,952	16.5	31.0	22.4	9.2	13.0	7.9
Missouri....................	60.6	64.0	57.8	86.6	4,097	11.1	31.0	22.4	7.7	17.3	10.6
Montana....................	9.4	10.1	10.3	84.7	706	6.5	31.5	22.8	8.6	20.4	10.2
Nebraska...................	21.0	19.4	19.9	93.3	1,233	9.0	26.9	23.8	10.1	19.8	10.4
Nevada.....................	21.8	21.0	15.7	67.5	1,968	14.4	27.9	26.0	8.1	15.5	8.1
New Hampshire............	13.5	15.0	13.8	87.3	937	6.9	28.5	19.2	9.7	21.9	13.7
New Jersey	95.0	96.2	86.5	89.1	6,166	10.9	28.5	16.6	6.4	23.3	14.3
New Mexico	19.4	18.6	17.4	71.6	1,378	15.4	26.8	23.6	7.7	14.4	12.1
New York...................	178.7	183.8	153.2	78.5	13,641	14.0	26.5	16.0	8.5	20.0	15.0
North Carolina.............	96.9	88.7	75.0	80.5	6,763	13.4	26.4	21.5	9.2	18.9	10.6
North Dakota..............	6.9	7.2	7.6	91.4	492	7.5	27.6	22.7	13.1	21.5	7.7
Ohio........................	116.4	123.4	116.7	84.9	7,896	10.3	33.7	20.6	8.6	16.8	10.0
Oklahoma..................	37.6	38.5	36.2	79.4	2,558	12.7	31.6	23.7	7.4	16.5	8.1
Oregon	34.6	34.7	32.6	76.8	2,804	10.0	23.4	25.8	8.8	20.2	12.0
Pennsylvania..............	118.9	131.2	124.8	88.4	8,896	10.3	35.7	16.0	8.3	18.1	11.6
Rhode Island...............	9.7	9.9	9.9	79.0	730	12.3	28.0	18.5	8.5	19.3	13.4
South Carolina	41.4	40.4	33.4	74.2	3,320	13.7	29.4	20.7	9.4	17.3	9.5
South Dakota	8.0	8.2	8.6	83.8	563	8.9	31.2	21.3	11.1	19.6	7.9
Tennessee	59.5	62.4	48.0	82.4	4,473	13.9	33.1	20.5	6.7	16.1	9.6
Texas.......................	308.5	280.9	239.7	83.6	17,473	17.6	25.3	21.8	6.9	18.7	9.7
Utah........................	33.4	31.5	30.3	81.6	1,742	8.5	24.2	26.3	9.2	21.1	10.7
Vermont....................	6.4	7.2	7.2	89.3	439	8.3	29.0	17.1	8.6	22.3	14.6
Virginia.....................	82.5	81.5	73.7	84.8	5,685	11.1	24.6	19.8	7.5	21.3	15.7
Washington................	66.5	66.0	61.1	80.4	4,889	9.2	23.1	24.0	9.6	21.7	12.5
West Virginia..............	17.3	17.7	17.1	81.5	1,300	14.0	40.7	18.8	6.9	11.7	7.9
Wisconsin..................	60.6	64.7	63.2	93.0	3,919	8.6	31.2	21.3	10.5	18.9	9.4
Wyoming	5.6	5.7	5.6	82.5	389	7.8	28.8	26.3	10.9	17.3	9.0

[1]For school year ending in year shown.
[2]Graduate or professional degree.

Table A-22. Institutions of Higher Education

Geographic area	Fall enrollment in degree-granting institutions (thousands)[1]									Degrees conferred from degree-granting institutions, 2013–2014[2]					
	Total			Public			Private			Public		Private nonprofit		Private for-profit	
	2011	2006	2000	2011	2006	2000	2011	2006	2000	Total	Percent Bachelor's	Total	Percent Bachelor's	Total	Percent Bachelor's
United States	20,994	17,759	15,312	15,110	13,180	11,753	5,884	4,579	3,560	2,414,582	49.1	1,011,814	53.8	378,837	36.7
Alabama......................	319	258	234	261	231	207	58	28	27	42,893	52.7	4,677	73.2	8,881	39.1
Alaska........................	35	30	28	32	29	27	3	1	1	3,960	46.8	162	48.8	483	20.5
Arizona......................	797	567	342	366	331	285	431	236	58	53,237	48.3	2,944	27.4	79,678	43.6
Arkansas....................	179	147	115	159	131	102	21	16	13	26,457	47.9	3,386	77.8	376	48.9
California....................	2,686	2,435	2,257	2,179	2,048	1,928	507	387	329	274,278	48.6	85,442	44.7	62,340	44.6
Colorado	366	308	264	269	232	218	97	76	46	42,055	58.0	9,306	42.6	14,080	35.8
Connecticut................	202	177	161	126	112	101	75	64	60	20,995	53.7	18,024	53.2	1,397	60.1
Delaware....................	57	51	44	41	38	34	16	13	10	7,354	58.5	4,419	45.6	41	53.7
District of Columbia	90	110	73	5	6	5	85	104	67	866	47.3	22,934	36.6	1,212	37.5
Florida.......................	1,144	886	708	803	652	557	340	234	151	161,072	41.0	46,450	48.6	29,004	29.1
Georgia......................	565	435	346	429	346	272	137	89	74	62,806	56.6	17,557	58.3	8,862	34.1
Hawaii........................	79	67	60	60	50	45	19	17	16	10,494	42.0	3,347	64.3	1,103	32.2
Idaho.........................	90	78	66	66	59	54	24	19	12	11,813	54.9	6,103	66.6	502	30.9
Illinois.......................	893	831	744	577	553	534	316	278	210	84,099	40.1	61,941	49.4	19,557	54.5
Indiana.......................	458	368	314	340	272	240	118	96	74	55,529	55.9	21,969	67.8	5,112	20
Iowa..........................	372	239	189	178	151	135	194	88	54	29,131	42.9	14,311	72.1	12,386	42.9
Kansas	217	193	180	186	171	160	30	23	20	31,294	48.8	6,676	60.7	2,950	32.8
Kentucky....................	294	249	188	233	204	152	60	45	36	34,903	49.0	8,605	52.9	3,914	15.8
Louisiana....................	266	224	224	225	193	189	41	32	35	31,275	60.1	6,733	49.5	1,614	25.3
Maine.........................	72	66	58	50	48	41	22	18	18	7,866	52.8	4,862	66.5	504	17.1
Maryland.....................	380	319	274	314	261	224	66	59	50	52,964	47.4	14,725	43.9	1,530	39
Massachusetts.............	509	452	421	227	192	183	282	259	238	38,624	51.1	77,272	49.8	1,295	36.1
Michigan.....................	686	634	568	555	512	468	131	123	100	94,036	48.1	22,900	56.6	1,688	40.3
Minnesota...................	458	376	293	274	244	219	184	132	75	45,757	46.4	18,000	62.3	21,280	18.7
Mississippi..................	179	151	137	161	137	125	18	15	12	28,474	42.2	3,998	56.2	515	1.4
Missouri......................	457	377	321	261	218	202	196	159	120	42,695	50.3	38,067	48.3	3,927	24
Montana......................	54	48	42	49	43	37	5	5	5	8,976	58.4	986	73.5	0	0
Nebraska....................	143	125	112	107	94	89	36	30	24	17,255	51.7	8,681	62.4	678	22.3
Nevada.......................	121	112	88	105	102	83	16	10	5	13,616	51.1	1,029	25.2	2,237	38.4
New Hampshire............	77	71	62	43	42	36	34	29	26	8,709	59.4	8,826	53.3	691	37.2
New Jersey	444	386	336	359	308	267	84	77	69	62,439	48.4	17,600	56.6	1,945	42.9
New Mexico	158	132	111	147	122	101	11	10	9	19,649	41.2	318	35.8	1,807	51.6
New York....................	1,318	1,160	1,043	732	636	583	586	525	460	134,715	45.8	140,804	49.2	14,491	27
North Carolina.............	585	496	405	471	406	329	114	90	75	77,512	47.7	24,171	61	3,534	24.9
North Dakota...............	56	50	40	49	43	36	7	7	4	9,233	58.8	1,289	53.1	345	17.1
Ohio..........................	735	620	550	543	453	411	192	167	138	89,363	51.3	33,686	63.5	7,641	13.6
Oklahoma....................	230	206	178	197	178	154	33	28	24	34,271	48.4	5,706	66.2	1,556	18.4
Oregon.......................	259	198	183	215	160	155	44	38	28	34,662	49.6	10,456	48.6	1,475	32.1
Pennsylvania...............	788	707	610	428	388	339	360	319	270	80,563	59.8	77,209	55.3	10,236	18
Rhode Island...............	85	82	75	43	40	38	41	41	37	6,922	59.5	11,684	62.8	0	0
South Carolina.............	260	212	186	208	176	156	52	36	30	33,353	52.9	7,119	77.5	3,508	33.9
South Dakota	56	49	43	44	38	35	12	11	8	7,993	54.1	1,576	68.7	534	50.6
Tennessee..................	350	291	264	242	205	203	108	85	61	38,444	54.3	20,359	59.9	3,956	26.8
Texas.........................	1,564	1,253	1,034	1,367	1,094	897	197	159	137	204,772	46.7	33,337	60.6	8,903	32.4
Utah..........................	264	202	164	179	148	123	85	54	41	30,698	49.8	21,124	65.7	2,471	27.8
Vermont......................	45	41	35	27	24	20	18	17	15	4,960	67.6	4,996	56.2	140	44.3
Virginia......................	588	456	382	414	358	314	175	98	68	69,384	51.6	28,834	53.9	11,960	37.3
Washington.................	373	348	321	317	297	274	56	51	47	60,162	40.4	11,509	64.2	1,749	45.5
West Virginia...............	162	101	88	96	87	76	67	14	12	16,088	58.3	1,708	68.4	11,458	43.4
Wisconsin	377	340	307	297	272	250	80	68	57	46,675	57.9	13,979	67.7	3,030	27.8
Wyoming	38	35	30	36	33	29	2	2	1	5,576	36.0	18	27.8	261	0

[1]Degree-granting institutions grant associate's or higher degrees and participate in Title IV federal financial aid programs.
[2]Totals include Associate's, Bachelor's, Master's, Ph.D., Ed.D., and comparable degrees at the doctoral level. Also includes most degrees formerly classified as first-professional, such as M.D., D.D.S., and law degrees conferred.

Table A-23. Violent Crimes and Crime Rates

Geographic area	Number[1]				Rate (per 100,000)[2] 2015					Total		
	2015	2010	2005	2000	Total	Murder[3]	Rape[4]	Robbery	Aggravated assault	2010	2005	2000
United States	1,197,704	1,251,248	1,390,745	1,425,486	372.6	4.9	38.6	101.9	237.8	404.5	469.0	506.5
Alabama	22,952	18,056	19,678	21,620	472.4	7.2	42.0	94.9	328.3	377.8	431.7	486.2
Alaska	5,392	4,537	4,194	3,554	730.2	8.0	122.0	103.1	497.1	638.8	631.9	566.9
Arizona.......................	28,012	26,085	30,478	27,281	410.2	4.5	45.5	93.1	267.1	408.1	513.2	531.7
Arkansas	15,526	14,735	14,659	11,904	521.3	6.1	64.8	70.4	380.0	505.3	527.5	445.3
California.....................	166,883	164,133	190,178	210,531	426.3	4.8	32.7	135.0	253.8	440.6	526.3	621.6
Colorado	17,515	16,133	18,498	14,367	321.0	3.2	59.7	60.9	197.2	320.8	396.5	334.0
Connecticut..................	7,845	10,057	9,635	11,058	218.5	3.3	21.5	80.5	113.1	281.4	274.5	324.7
Delaware	4,720	5,575	5,332	5,363	499.0	6.7	36.0	130.6	325.7	620.9	632.1	684.4
District of Columbia[5]	8,531	8,004	8,032	8,626	1,269.1	24.1	73.5	556.7	614.8	1,330.2	1,459.0	1,507.9
Florida........................	93,626	101,969	125,957	129,777	461.9	5.1	37.3	104.3	315.2	542.4	708.0	812.0
Georgia[6]	38,643	39,072	40,725	41,319	378.3	6.0	31.6	119.9	220.8	403.3	448.9	504.7
Hawaii........................	4,201	3,574	3,253	2,954	293.4	1.3	39.2	84.0	168.9	262.7	255.1	243.8
Idaho.........................	3,568	3,465	3,670	3,267	215.6	1.9	41.9	11.6	160.1	221.0	256.8	252.5
Illinois.......................	49,354	55,835	70,392	81,567	383.8	5.8	37.5	115.9	224.6	435.2	551.5	656.8
Indiana[7]......................	25,653	20,389	20,302	21,230	387.5	5.6	36.3	107.4	238.2	314.5	323.7	349.1
Iowa..........................	8,936	8,333	8,642	7,796	286.1	2.3	37.0	33.5	213.2	273.5	291.3	266.4
Kansas	11,353	10,531	10,634	10,470	389.9	4.4	55.5	62.4	267.6	369.1	387.4	389.4
Kentucky	9,676	10,528	11,134	11,903	218.7	4.7	33.7	74.7	105.5	242.6	266.8	294.5
Louisiana	25,208	24,886	26,889	30,440	539.7	10.3	36.9	118.8	373.7	549.0	594.4	681.1
Maine[7]........................	1,729	1,621	1,483	1,397	130.1	1.7	35.7	23.4	69.3	122.0	112.2	109.6
Maryland......................	27,462	31,620	39,369	41,663	457.2	8.6	27.7	164.2	256.7	547.7	703.0	786.6
Massachusetts..............	26,562	30,553	29,237	30,230	390.9	1.9	30.5	77.8	280.7	466.6	456.9	476.1
Michigan......................	41,231	48,460	55,877	55,159	415.5	5.8	65.0	78.6	266.2	490.3	552.1	555.0
Minnesota....................	13,319	12,515	15,243	13,813	242.6	2.4	42.3	68.7	129.2	236.0	297.0	280.8
Mississippi[7].................	8,254	8,003	8,131	10,267	275.8	8.7	40.2	76.7	150.3	269.7	278.4	360.9
Missouri......................	30,261	27,252	30,477	27,419	497.4	8.3	42.0	104.8	342.4	455.0	525.4	490.0
Montana......................	3,611	2,693	2,634	2,171	349.6	3.5	53.0	20.3	272.8	272.2	281.5	240.6
Nebraska[7]....................	5,212	5,104	5,048	5,606	274.9	3.3	46.0	52.4	173.1	279.5	287.0	327.6
Nevada	20,118	17,841	14,654	10,474	695.9	6.2	58.4	217.5	413.9	660.6	606.8	524.2
New Hampshire.............	2,652	2,198	1,729	2,167	199.3	1.1	47.1	35.2	116.0	167.0	132.0	175.4
New Jersey	22,879	27,055	30,919	32,298	255.4	4.1	15.3	108.6	127.4	307.7	354.7	383.8
New Mexico[6]	13,681	12,126	13,541	13,786	656.1	5.6	80.2	119.2	451.2	588.9	702.2	757.9
New York[7]...................	75,165	75,977	85,839	105,111	379.7	3.1	30.7	120.9	225.0	392.1	445.8	553.9
North Carolina..............	34,852	34,653	40,650	40,051	347.0	5.1	26.7	87.9	227.3	363.4	468.1	497.6
North Dakota................	1,812	1,513	625	523	239.4	2.8	45.6	19.6	171.5	225.0	98.2	81.4
Ohio[7].........................	33,898	36,366	40,273	37,935	291.9	4.3	44.3	108.1	135.1	315.2	351.3	334.1
Oklahoma.....................	16,506	17,987	18,044	17,177	422.0	6.0	47.3	76.8	291.9	479.5	508.6	497.8
Oregon[7]......................	10,468	9,655	10,444	12,000	259.8	2.5	39.5	53.3	164.6	252.0	286.8	350.7
Pennsylvania................	40,339	46,514	52,761	51,584	315.1	5.1	33.6	101.6	174.8	366.2	424.5	420.0
Rhode Island[7]...............	2,562	2,701	2,703	3,121	242.5	2.7	43.5	52.6	143.7	256.6	251.2	297.7
South Carolina	24,700	27,648	32,384	32,293	504.5	8.1	46.9	80.3	369.1	597.7	761.1	804.9
South Dakota	3,289	2,186	1,363	1,259	383.1	3.7	57.7	25.2	296.6	268.5	175.7	166.8
Tennessee	40,400	38,921	44,891	40,233	612.1	6.2	40.5	113.2	452.2	613.3	752.8	707.2
Texas.........................	113,227	113,231	121,091	113,653	412.2	4.8	44.6	116.3	246.6	450.3	529.7	545.1
Utah[7].........................	7,071	5,879	5,612	5,711	236.0	1.8	54.9	44.3	135.1	212.7	227.2	255.7
Vermont......................	739	815	746	691	118.0	1.6	21.7	16.1	78.6	130.2	119.7	113.5
Virginia.......................	16,399	17,087	21,400	19,943	195.6	4.6	27.9	53.0	110.2	213.6	282.8	281.7
Washington[7].................	20,394	21,101	21,745	21,788	284.4	2.9	37.7	76.0	167.8	313.8	345.8	369.7
West Virginia................	6,231	5,830	4,957	5,723	337.9	3.8	36.4	41.2	256.4	314.6	272.8	316.5
Wisconsin[7]..................	17,647	14,142	13,371	12,700	305.8	4.2	30.8	90.7	180.1	248.7	241.5	236.8
Wyoming......................	1,302	1,104	1,172	1,316	222.1	2.7	29.5	10.1	179.8	195.9	230.1	266.5

[1]The violent crime figures include the offenses of murder, rape (revised definition for 2015, legacy definition for earlier years), robbery, and aggravated assault.
[2]Populations are U.S. Census Bureau estimates as of July 1 for each year 2000 and 2010, which are decennial counts.
[3]Includes nonnegligent manslaughter.
[4]The figures shown in the rape (revised definition) column were estimated using the revised Uniform Crime Reporting (UCR) definition of rape.
[5]Includes offenses reported by the Metro Transit Police and the Arson Investigation Unit of the District of Columbia Fire and Emergency Medical Services.
[6]This state's agencies submitted rape data according to the legacy UCR definition of rape.
[7]Agencies within this state submitted rape data according to both the revised UCR definition of rape and the legacy UCR definition of rape.

Table A-24.   Property Crimes and Crime Rates

| Geographic area | Number[1] | | | | Rate (per 100,000)[2] | | | | | | |
| | 2015 | 2010 | 2005 | 2000 | 2015 | | | | Total | | |
					Total	Burglary	Larceny	Motor vehicle theft	2015	2010	2005
United States[3,4,5]	7,993,631	9,112,625	10,166,159	10,181,462	2,487.0	491.4	1,775.4	220.2	2,945.9	3,429.8	3,618.3
Alabama[5]	144,746	168,828	177,393	180,539	2,978.9	725.6	2,040.7	212.7	3,528.0	3,892.1	4,059.7
Alaska	20,806	20,259	23,975	23,087	2,817.6	475.5	2,065.1	277.1	2,836.8	3,612.5	3,682.5
Arizona	207,107	226,802	287,345	271,811	3,033.2	555.9	2,231.5	245.8	3,536.5	4,838.0	5,297.8
Arkansas	96,836	103,820	112,775	98,115	3,251.5	760.2	2,297.5	193.8	3,553.5	4,057.9	3,670.0
California	1,024,914	981,939	1,200,531	1,056,183	2,618.3	504.3	1,677.1	436.8	2,629.9	3,322.6	3,118.2
Colorado	144,136	135,001	188,449	156,937	2,641.5	429.8	1,918.5	293.2	2,674.5	4,039.5	3,648.6
Connecticut	65,066	78,259	89,794	99,033	1,812.0	280.0	1,355.5	176.5	2,188.8	2,558.0	2,908.0
Delaware	25,455	31,078	26,245	29,727	2,691.0	504.6	2,061.6	124.9	3,453.9	3,111.4	3,793.6
District of Columbia[4]	31,435	28,802	26,133	33,000	4,676.2	442.0	3,748.7	485.5	4,761.4	4,747.0	5,768.6
Florida	570,270	669,035	712,998	780,377	2,813.2	539.0	2,073.6	200.6	3,551.4	4,007.9	4,882.7
Georgia	308,723	353,449	378,534	347,630	3,022.3	649.8	2,113.3	259.2	3,639.2	4,172.3	4,246.4
Hawaii	54,346	45,667	61,115	60,033	3,796.2	458.0	2,934.5	403.7	3,349.6	4,792.6	4,955.1
Idaho	28,858	31,436	38,556	37,961	1,743.8	370.0	1,260.7	113.1	2,000.9	2,697.9	2,933.7
Illinois	255,729	349,064	393,148	450,748	1,988.6	361.1	1,490.2	137.3	2,718.1	3,080.3	3,629.4
Indiana	171,847	199,274	216,778	206,905	2,596.0	519.8	1,872.0	204.2	3,070.2	3,456.3	3,402.8
Iowa	63,957	68,740	84,056	86,834	2,047.3	476.7	1,431.6	139.0	2,253.6	2,833.7	2,967.3
Kansas	79,199	89,109	103,941	108,057	2,720.1	527.6	1,953.5	238.9	3,116.6	3,787.0	4,019.4
Kentucky	96,362	111,170	105,608	107,723	2,177.6	503.0	1,498.7	175.9	2,557.3	2,530.5	2,665.2
Louisiana	156,629	165,667	166,611	211,904	3,353.4	759.0	2,385.8	208.6	3,644.8	3,683.1	4,741.7
Maine	24,327	32,900	31,889	32,003	1,830.0	352.4	1,416.4	61.2	2,478.6	2,413.1	2,510.2
Maryland	139,048	173,309	198,483	213,422	2,315.0	427.5	1,668.5	218.9	2,995.5	3,544.1	4,029.5
Massachusetts	114,871	154,496	151,241	161,901	1,690.7	322.2	1,249.7	118.8	2,356.8	2,363.6	2,550.0
Michigan	187,101	271,501	312,843	353,297	1,885.6	403.5	1,323.2	158.9	2,748.8	3,091.1	3,554.9
Minnesota	121,984	136,431	158,301	157,798	2,222.1	351.6	1,725.2	145.4	2,569.0	3,084.1	3,207.6
Mississippi	84,790	88,596	95,231	103,644	2,833.6	828.8	1,863.0	141.8	2,983.0	3,260.1	3,643.5
Missouri	173,642	200,858	227,809	225,919	2,854.2	559.0	2,015.8	279.4	3,350.0	3,927.5	4,037.7
Montana	27,100	NA	29,407	29,707	2,623.6	371.6	2,017.9	234.1	NA	3,142.9	3,292.7
Nebraska	42,495	48,827	60,207	64,479	2,241.1	338.7	1,691.4	211.0	2,667.9	3,423.2	3,767.9
Nevada	77,137	75,004	102,424	74,823	2,668.3	773.5	1,502.2	392.7	2,773.5	4,241.5	3,744.4
New Hampshire	23,229	29,230	23,532	27,901	1,745.7	260.6	1,418.2	67.0	2,219.8	1,796.4	2,257.8
New Jersey	145,701	183,042	203,391	233,637	1,626.5	312.1	1,182.9	131.5	2,080.1	2,333.0	2,776.6
New Mexico	77,094	70,776	79,995	86,605	3,697.4	819.4	2,469.1	408.9	3,425.9	4,148.3	4,761.0
New York	317,529	379,710	405,990	483,078	1,604.0	223.7	1,303.0	77.4	1,957.8	2,108.5	2,545.7
North Carolina	276,183	329,202	353,855	355,921	2,750.1	745.2	1,871.1	133.8	3,443.5	4,075.1	4,421.8
North Dakota	16,020	12,010	12,595	14,171	2,116.5	395.9	1,511.4	209.1	1,780.2	1,978.2	2,206.6
Ohio	300,525	376,836	419,899	420,939	2,587.7	596.7	1,842.6	148.4	3,266.1	3,662.7	3,707.7
Oklahoma	112,878	129,464	143,406	140,125	2,885.9	726.2	1,892.5	267.2	3,443.0	4,042.0	4,060.8
Oregon	118,719	116,657	160,199	153,780	2,946.6	455.1	2,229.7	261.8	3,039.3	4,399.8	4,494.7
Pennsylvania	232,085	276,366	300,444	316,274	1,812.8	309.8	1,408.2	94.8	2,173.1	2,417.2	2,575.3
Rhode Island	20,043	26,959	29,260	33,323	1,897.5	373.7	1,392.3	131.5	2,561.4	2,718.9	3,178.7
South Carolina	161,245	181,098	184,646	177,189	3,293.3	705.7	2,322.7	264.9	3,905.4	4,339.4	4,416.5
South Dakota	16,680	15,188	13,784	16,252	1,943.0	344.8	1,459.8	138.4	1,859.9	1,776.4	2,153.0
Tennessee	193,796	232,855	254,948	237,985	2,936.2	655.2	2,086.0	195.0	3,662.7	4,275.5	4,183.0
Texas	777,739	951,246	990,293	919,658	2,831.3	557.2	2,028.5	245.7	3,766.8	4,332.0	4,410.4
Utah	89,278	88,316	95,546	94,247	2,980.0	416.2	2,273.2	290.6	3,182.0	3,868.9	4,220.3
Vermont	8,806	14,160	14,210	17,494	1,406.6	314.4	1,063.8	28.4	2,262.3	2,280.7	2,873.4
Virginia	156,470	187,403	199,644	194,405	1,866.5	254.6	1,515.2	96.8	2,335.5	2,638.2	2,746.4
Washington	248,369	249,426	307,661	279,144	3,463.8	711.2	2,378.0	374.7	3,699.1	4,893.0	4,736.0
West Virginia	37,251	41,301	47,696	41,344	2,020.0	497.3	1,401.3	121.4	2,227.2	2,625.2	2,286.3
Wisconsin	113,924	142,781	147,275	159,424	1,974.0	338.8	1,444.8	190.3	2,508.6	2,660.2	2,972.3
Wyoming	11,151	13,869	16,070	14,969	1,902.6	300.6	1,500.9	101.0	2,456.6	3,155.3	3,031.5

[1]Property crimes include burglary, larceny-theft, and motor vehicle theft.
[2]Populations are U.S. Census Bureau estimates as of July 1 for each year except 2000 and 2010, which are decennial census counts.
[3]The crime figures have been adjusted.
[4]Includes offenses reported by the police at the National Zoo and by Metro transit Police.
[5]Because of changes in the state's reporting practices, figures are not comparable to previous years' data.

Table A-25.   Juvenile Arrests, Child Abuse Cases, and Correctional Population

Geographic area	Juvenile arrests, 2015			Child abuse and neglect cases reported and investigated, 2015				Estimated number and rate of persons supervised by U.S. adult correctional system by correctional status, 2014					
								Total correctional population[7]		Community supervision		Incarcerated	
	Total arrests[1]	Violent crime arrests[2]	Property crime arrests[3]	Number of reports[4]	Number of children who received an investigation or alternative response[5]	Number of victims[6]	First-time victims rate per 1,000 children	Number on probation or parole[8]	Correctional supervision rate[9]	Number on probation or parole[8]	Community supervision rate[9]	Number in prison or local jail[10]	Incarceration rate[9]
United States	771,064	43,775	180,437	2,236,837	3,358,347	683,487	6.9	6,814,600	2,760	4,708,100	1,910	2,188,000	890
Alabama......................	5,468	397	1,634	21,722	30,647	8,466	6.3	104,900	2,790	61,400	1,640	45,800	1,220
Alaska.......................	2,021	176	589	7,600	10,795	2,898	10.6	14,600	2,650	9,300	1,690	5,300	960
Arizona......................	21,510	618	4,691	43,961	76,581	11,955	6.1	133,600	2,590	80,700	1,570	54,800	1,060
Arkansas....................	8,163	409	2,158	33,251	58,072	9,204	10.7	69,100	3,050	49,300	2,170	23,100	1,020
California....................	67,884	7,207	15,085	235,297	375,972	72,000	6.7	589,600	1,980	382,600	1,280	207,100	690
Colorado....................	24,566	636	5,446	29,219	38,376	10,100	5.9	119,800	2,890	89,100	2,150	31,500	760
Connecticut................	7,098	360	1,666	17,434	21,750	6,970	6.4	62,300	2,200	45,600	1,610	16,600	590
Delaware	3,906	383	818	7,121	13,994	1,538	6.1	23,300	3,170	16,300	2,220	7,000	950
District of Columbia	NA	NA	NA	5,735	11,867	1,348	8.2	11,900	2,180	11,400	2,070	1,600	300
Florida.......................	62,148	4,256	18,745	160,733	281,040	43,775	5.1	382,600	2,390	231,600	1,450	153,600	960
Georgia	22,701	1,036	6,065	82,050	163,134	26,952	8.7	579,600	7,580	491,800	6,430	91,000	1,190
Hawaii.......................	3,321	173	859	2,108	3,695	1,506	3.8	28,300	2,540	22,500	2,010	5,900	530
Idaho........................	7,396	151	1,557	8,525	12,233	1,623	3.0	48,600	4,010	37,700	3,110	11,000	910
Illinois.......................	13,627	1,118	3,324	66,866	125,098	29,993	7.4	219,000	2,210	151,800	1,530	67,200	680
Indiana......................	14,282	755	3,503	107,223	139,168	26,397	12.3	175,200	3,480	128,100	2,540	47,100	940
Iowa.........................	10,662	545	3,155	23,672	28,970	7,877	7.5	46,500	1,940	35,500	1,490	12,700	530
Kansas......................	4,959	192	1,278	23,666	27,565	1,992	2.5	37,400	1,710	20,400	930	17,000	780
Kentucky	6,232	336	1,881	55,209	74,170	18,897	13.1	103,600	3,040	70,800	2,080	33,500	980
Louisiana	10,775	558	2,514	25,364	36,382	12,631	8.7	113,600	3,200	70,600	1,990	49,100	1,380
Maine........................	3,477	54	857	8,785	12,641	3,372	8.8	10,100	940	6,600	610	4,100	380
Maryland....................	15,175	1,427	3,951	20,623	30,927	6,790	3.6	109,700	2,360	91,100	1,960	31,100	670
Massachusetts	7,281	886	1,323	46,116	75,688	31,089	13.0	90,300	1,680	70,200	1,310	20,300	380
Michigan....................	17,223	1,151	4,677	93,646	147,431	34,729	7.7	256,700	3,330	199,000	2,580	59,400	770
Minnesota	21,941	992	5,224	24,262	30,481	5,120	3.4	120,500	2,870	104,300	2,490	16,200	390
Mississippi.................	3,654	63	927	24,612	34,069	8,730	10.7	69,700	3,070	44,300	1,950	25,400	1,120
Missouri.....................	19,941	974	4,729	66,121	73,523	5,699	3.5	109,500	2,340	65,800	1,400	43,700	930
Montana.....................	3,693	75	795	8,695	12,669	1,868	6.7	14,500	1,810	9,700	1,210	5,500	680
Nebraska	6,290	79	1,404	12,192	23,190	3,483	5.5	22,500	1,580	14,000	990	8,500	600
Nevada......................	9,379	953	2,033	15,900	28,277	4,953	4.6	37,500	1,710	18,000	820	19,600	890
New Hampshire............	3,421	59	441	9,005	11,266	745	2.3	11,200	1,050	6,300	590	4,900	460
New Jersey	16,348	1,298	2,887	57,180	74,546	9,689	3.8	164,500	2,370	130,800	1,880	35,200	510
New Mexico	5,179	242	1,255	21,798	28,223	8,701	13.2	32,500	2,050	18,100	1,140	14,400	910
New York....................	21,248	1,765	5,985	156,994	206,453	66,676	9.6	222,100	1,430	149,100	960	77,500	500
North Carolina.............	19,724	1,207	5,815	69,213	123,436	7,857	2.4	153,600	2,000	99,300	1,290	54,300	710
North Dakota...............	3,659	58	646	3,790	6,437	1,760	7.7	9,300	1,610	6,200	1,070	3,200	550
Ohio..........................	22,220	657	4,416	79,215	101,836	23,006	6.1	326,300	3,630	256,200	2,850	71,200	790
Oklahoma...................	10,129	447	2,847	36,941	57,141	14,449	11.9	69,600	2,370	31,100	1,060	38,400	1,310
Oregon......................	8,164	225	1,852	28,037	39,009	10,428	8.1	82,700	2,640	61,900	1,980	20,900	670
Pennsylvania..............	48,337	2,747	6,289	36,223	35,580	3,855	-	360,800	3,570	281,400	2,780	85,200	840
Rhode Island...............	2,373	94	433	6,649	8,429	3,183	10.5	25,100	2,970	24,100	2,850	3,400	400
South Carolina	12,374	497	3,361	26,114	50,417	14,856	10.5	71,900	1,910	40,000	1,060	31,900	850
South Dakota	4,982	61	856	2,560	4,235	1,073	4.1	14,500	2,240	9,400	1,460	5,100	800
Tennessee	24,113	1,596	4,807	74,669	93,154	11,362	6.3	119,900	2,360	76,400	1,500	46,900	920
Texas........................	68,279	3,743	18,754	183,696	267,880	63,781	7.1	699,300	3,490	496,900	2,480	219,100	1,090
Utah.........................	14,984	273	3,463	20,680	25,523	9,569	7.5	25,700	1,250	15,300	740	12,600	620
Vermont.....................	614	36	104	4,676	5,102	921	6.5	8,400	1,670	6,800	1,340	2,000	390
Virginia.....................	17,151	603	3,574	32,395	60,607	6,112	-	115,300	1,780	56,700	880	58,600	900
Washington.................	14,882	893	4,198	38,810	45,338	5,894	1.9	133,000	2,420	104,000	1,890	30,900	560
West Virginia..............	1,178	55	202	20,988	45,407	4,857	10.8	19,600	1,330	9,900	680	9,900	670
Wisconsin	43,693	1,146	6,769	28,647	36,330	4,840	3.2	97,300	2,180	64,500	1,440	34,600	770
Wyoming	3,239	46	552	3,206	5,632	968	5.9	9,700	2,180	5,900	1,330	3,800	850

NA = Not available.

[1]Number of arrests. If an individual was arrested more than once, each arrest is counted. Does not include traffic arrests. The rape figures in this table are aggregate totals of the data submitted based on both the legacy and revised Uniform Crime Reporting definitions. Drunkenness is considered a crime in some states; therefore, the figures vary from state to state.

[2]Violent crime includes murder or nonnegligent manslaughter, forcible rape, robbery, and aggravated assault.

[3]Property crimes include burglary, larceny-theft, motor vehicle theft, and arson.

[4]This number includes the screened-in referrals in 2015.

[5]The number of "Children subject of an investigation" is based on the "Unique count," counting a child once, regardless of the number of reports concerning that child, that received a CPS response in the year shown.

[6]Victims are defined as children for whom the State determined at least one maltreatment was substantiated or indicated; and a disposition of "substantiated," "indicated," or "alternative response victim" was assigned for a child in a specific report.

[7]Excludes an estimated 81,700 prisoners held in local jails; 23,500 probationers in prisons; 24,600 probationers in local jails; 21,800 parolees in local jails; 11,600 parolees in prisons; and 12,900 parolees on probation.

[8]Excludes an estimated 12,900 parolees on probation.

[9]Rates were computed using estimates of the U.S. resident population of persons age 18 or older within jurisdiction.

[10]Excludes an estimated 81,700 prisoners held in local jails.

Table A-26.   State and Local Justice Employment and Expenditures, 2012

Geographic area	Number of employees				Total expenditures (in milions)			
	Total justice system	Police protection	Judicial and legal	Corrections	Total justice system	Police protection	Judicial and legal	Corrections
United States	2,131,946	991,260	429,223	711,463	212,307	96,893	43,157	72,256
Alabama......................	28,998	15,139	5,189	8,670	2,277	1,156	402	719
Alaska	5,715	2,062	1,620	2,033	902	321	264	316
Arizona......................	46,432	19,735	10,658	16,039	4,580	2,072	963	1,545
Arkansas	20,262	8,905	3,439	7,918	1,350	587	205	558
California...................	235,864	104,338	44,286	87,240	37,257	14,843	8,723	13,691
Colorado	33,812	15,283	7,508	11,021	3,561	1,592	725	1,244
Connecticut................	23,098	10,891	5,329	6,878	2,516	1,116	716	685
Delaware	7,324	2,543	1,886	2,895	750	304	163	282
District of Columbia	7,796	4,386	2,139	1,271	912	564	108	241
Florida........................	141,658	67,808	31,418	42,432	13,532	7,317	2,156	4,059
Georgia	71,568	28,410	15,274	27,884	5,767	2,424	1,060	2,283
Hawaii........................	9,202	3,859	3,072	2,271	853	389	267	198
Idaho.........................	10,136	4,210	2,120	3,806	896	400	191	305
Illinois	88,840	51,536	15,747	21,557	8,151	4,600	1,492	2,060
Indiana.......................	37,826	16,962	8,030	12,834	2,579	1,150	470	959
Iowa..........................	15,680	7,715	3,165	4,800	1,548	689	336	523
Kansas	20,230	9,552	4,104	6,574	1,526	738	307	481
Kentucky	26,386	10,535	7,403	8,448	1,928	680	510	739
Louisiana	40,054	18,651	8,192	13,211	3,582	1,552	742	1,288
Maine.........................	6,370	3,368	995	2,007	532	246	93	194
Maryland.....................	43,923	19,189	8,696	16,038	4,683	2,140	793	1,750
Massachusetts.............	43,274	27,646	9,487	6,141	4,113	2,136	920	1,056
Michigan	54,298	23,945	10,868	19,485	5,726	2,356	1,138	2,232
Minnesota	32,446	16,784	6,278	9,384	3,109	1,633	612	863
Mississippi..................	19,438	10,353	3,387	5,698	1,467	662	247	558
Missouri......................	43,618	19,326	8,721	15,571	3,012	1,680	470	862
Montana.....................	6,410	2,709	1,811	1,890	660	275	147	238
Nebraska....................	11,877	5,251	2,139	4,487	933	405	166	362
Nevada......................	18,807	8,659	3,714	6,434	2,262	1,099	458	705
New Hampshire............	7,757	4,407	1,418	1,932	646	352	111	183
New Jersey	73,455	37,323	21,007	15,125	6,855	3,324	1,456	2,075
New Mexico	16,091	6,212	3,783	6,096	1,565	648	316	602
New York....................	182,856	90,771	34,116	57,969	19,380	9,273	4,335	5,772
North Carolina.............	62,698	28,986	8,130	25,582	5,513	2,852	769	1,892
North Dakota...............	4,100	1,670	1,017	1,413	397	172	82	143
Ohio	75,590	34,114	20,233	21,243	6,743	3,217	1,707	1,819
Oklahoma...................	23,199	11,696	4,776	6,727	1,935	928	352	655
Oregon	22,903	9,275	4,894	8,734	2,811	1,150	591	1,070
Pennsylvania...............	89,962	39,008	18,394	32,560	8,325	3,245	1,777	3,303
Rhode Island...............	6,299	3,451	1,278	1,570	680	354	127	199
South Carolina	31,173	14,375	4,915	11,883	2,020	1,055	289	676
South Dakota	4,783	2,125	1,025	1,633	412	169	78	165
Tennessee	41,259	21,231	7,666	12,362	3,326	1,664	613	1,049
Texas.........................	174,102	75,618	28,269	70,215	14,546	6,457	2,615	5,473
Utah..........................	16,063	7,491	3,207	5,365	1,534	658	358	518
Vermont	3,609	1,756	744	1,109	372	177	69	126
Virginia.......................	53,445	22,497	9,280	21,668	4,827	2,083	856	1,888
Washington.................	37,164	15,179	8,377	13,608	4,033	1,626	847	1,559
West Virginia...............	10,643	4,272	2,823	3,548	929	364	231	334
Wisconsin	38,217	17,979	6,121	14,117	3,944	1,779	620	1,545
Wyoming	5,236	2,074	1,075	2,087	552	220	118	214

Table A-27.   Civilian Labor Force and Employment

Geographic area	Civilian noninstitutionalized population 16 years and over[1] (thousands)				Civilian labor force[1,2] (thousands)				Employed (thousands)			
	2015	2010	2005	2000	2015	2010	2005	2000	2015	2010	2005	2000
United States	250,801	237,830	226,082	212,577	157,130	153,889	149,320	142,583	148,834	139,064	141,730	136,891
Alabama......................	3,800	3,690	3,477	3,378	2,152	2,196	2,146	2,133	2,021	1,965	2,050	2,036
Alaska........................	542	519	480	436	363	362	345	320	339	333	321	299
Arizona......................	5,267	4,897	4,465	3,849	3,165	3,090	2,883	2,510	2,974	2,769	2,748	2,411
Arkansas....................	2,298	2,233	2,113	2,026	1,333	1,353	1,346	1,258	1,265	1,242	1,275	1,205
California....................	30,379	28,543	26,762	25,116	18,893	18,336	17,530	16,868	17,723	16,092	16,583	16,033
Colorado....................	4,234	3,871	3,548	3,265	2,834	2,724	2,564	2,360	2,723	2,486	2,435	2,294
Connecticut.................	2,868	2,799	2,677	2,595	1,891	1,912	1,797	1,764	1,782	1,737	1,709	1,722
Delaware....................	748	701	645	597	467	434	432	414	445	398	414	398
District of Columbia	552	503	467	458	387	346	316	310	360	314	295	293
Florida.......................	16,291	14,946	13,895	12,489	9,619	9,212	8,721	7,857	9,098	8,194	8,399	7,566
Georgia......................	7,774	7,324	6,748	6,094	4,787	4,697	4,586	4,222	4,502	4,202	4,341	4,072
Hawaii.......................	1,088	1,030	951	901	675	647	627	606	651	602	609	580
Idaho........................	1,247	1,166	1,056	951	797	761	732	660	763	693	702	629
Illinois.......................	10,035	9,905	9,611	9,347	6,507	6,625	6,398	6,493	6,121	5,937	6,034	6,211
Indiana......................	5,118	4,963	4,753	4,601	3,272	3,175	3,205	3,126	3,114	2,846	3,030	3,029
Iowa.........................	2,432	2,358	2,275	2,233	1,703	1,678	1,630	1,590	1,638	1,577	1,560	1,549
Kansas......................	2,203	2,149	2,067	2,001	1,489	1,501	1,466	1,407	1,427	1,395	1,392	1,356
Kentucky	3,441	3,350	3,207	3,086	1,966	2,054	2,000	1,966	1,862	1,845	1,882	1,884
Louisiana...................	3,570	3,438	3,290	3,290	2,161	2,086	2,069	2,037	2,024	1,920	1,921	1,929
Maine........................	1,092	1,073	1,043	994	683	695	697	678	653	639	663	655
Maryland....................	4,704	4,489	4,254	3,994	3,147	3,074	2,925	2,804	2,987	2,838	2,803	2,703
Massachusetts.............	5,492	5,252	5,064	4,929	3,580	3,480	3,384	3,330	3,406	3,191	3,220	3,240
Michigan....................	7,870	7,739	7,737	7,517	4,757	4,799	5,083	5,163	4,500	4,194	4,739	4,976
Minnesota..................	4,283	4,116	3,929	3,731	2,976	2,939	2,880	2,813	2,865	2,721	2,763	2,724
Mississippi.................	2,279	2,228	2,143	2,096	1,270	1,307	1,317	1,319	1,189	1,171	1,219	1,248
Missouri....................	4,736	4,629	4,435	4,236	3,097	3,056	3,009	2,960	2,942	2,764	2,847	2,854
Montana....................	816	777	728	687	520	501	486	467	498	464	465	444
Nebraska...................	1,443	1,387	1,324	1,284	1,008	993	973	945	978	947	936	918
Nevada......................	2,249	2,062	1,819	1,523	1,415	1,359	1,224	1,067	1,318	1,175	1,174	1,022
New Hampshire............	1,083	1,056	1,019	950	743	738	726	688	718	695	700	670
New Jersey	7,068	6,864	6,631	6,440	4,531	4,555	4,392	4,282	4,268	4,121	4,195	4,124
New Mexico	1,604	1,560	1,437	1,342	924	936	918	846	863	860	871	804
New York....................	15,788	15,386	15,008	14,547	9,591	9,595	9,461	9,134	9,085	8,770	8,987	8,719
North Carolina.............	7,786	7,287	6,571	6,115	4,768	4,617	4,317	4,138	4,494	4,116	4,091	3,986
North Dakota...............	581	521	492	485	414	378	356	343	403	364	344	332
Ohio.........................	9,115	8,971	8,820	8,623	5,692	5,847	5,890	5,787	5,413	5,247	5,541	5,557
Oklahoma...................	2,970	2,832	2,658	2,580	1,834	1,768	1,703	1,661	1,753	1,648	1,627	1,610
Oregon......................	3,221	3,034	2,824	2,643	1,978	1,984	1,846	1,819	1,867	1,773	1,732	1,726
Pennsylvania...............	10,220	10,049	9,702	9,486	6,426	6,381	6,251	6,107	6,085	5,841	5,941	5,855
Rhode Island...............	855	842	837	813	554	567	566	544	520	503	537	521
South Carolina	3,822	3,565	3,234	3,027	2,270	2,156	2,069	1,994	2,135	1,915	1,929	1,919
South Dakota	651	619	590	562	451	441	431	409	437	419	414	399
Tennessee..................	5,162	4,926	4,610	4,358	3,071	3,091	2,905	2,843	2,899	2,792	2,743	2,733
Texas........................	20,479	18,569	16,623	15,201	13,044	12,242	11,124	10,374	12,463	11,245	10,523	9,929
Utah.........................	2,148	1,971	1,778	1,583	1,466	1,356	1,272	1,142	1,413	1,250	1,221	1,104
Vermont.....................	515	508	495	474	345	359	351	331	333	337	339	322
Virginia......................	6,497	6,146	5,706	5,305	4,212	4,158	3,897	3,606	4,024	3,860	3,758	3,523
Washington.................	5,616	5,246	4,817	4,466	3,546	3,511	3,264	3,059	3,346	3,161	3,082	2,901
West Virginia...............	1,478	1,476	1,435	1,430	783	811	791	809	730	741	751	765
Wisconsin	4,551	4,436	4,285	4,086	3,095	3,082	3,021	2,973	2,954	2,814	2,878	2,868
Wyoming....................	452	431	390	373	305	303	277	267	292	284	267	256

[1]Annual averages of monthly figures.
[2]Civilian labor force includes all persons in the civilian noninstitutional population classified as either employed or unemployed.

Table A-28. Civilian Labor Force and Unemployment

Geographic area	Civilian labor force participation, 2015[1,2,3]	Employment/ population ratio, 2015[3,4]	Unemployment[1]							
			Total (thousands)				Rate[5]			
			2015	2010	2005	2000	2015	2010	2005	2000
United States	62.7	59.3	8,296	14,825	7,591	5,692	5.3	9.6	5.1	4.0
Alabama.........................	56.6	53.2	132	231	96	98	6.1	10.5	4.5	4.6
Alaska	66.9	62.6	23	28	24	20	6.4	7.9	6.9	6.4
Arizona.........................	60.1	56.5	191	320	135	99	6.0	10.4	4.7	4.0
Arkansas.......................	58.0	55.1	67	111	70	54	5.1	8.2	5.2	4.3
California........................	62.2	58.3	1,170	2,244	947	835	6.2	12.2	5.4	4.9
Colorado	66.9	64.3	111	238	129	65	3.9	8.7	5.0	2.8
Connecticut...................	65.9	62.1	108	174	88	42	5.7	9.1	4.9	2.4
Delaware.......................	62.5	59.5	23	37	18	15	4.8	8.4	4.1	3.7
District of Columbia	70.1	65.3	27	33	20	17	6.9	9.4	6.4	5.6
Florida..........................	59.0	55.8	521	1,018	322	291	5.4	11.1	3.7	3.7
Georgia	61.6	57.9	285	495	245	151	6.0	10.5	5.3	3.6
Hawaii..........................	62.0	59.8	24	45	18	26	3.6	6.9	2.9	4.2
Idaho............................	63.9	61.2	34	68	29	31	4.2	9.0	4.0	4.7
Illinois..........................	64.8	61.0	386	688	364	282	5.9	10.4	5.7	4.3
Indiana.........................	63.9	60.8	158	330	175	97	4.8	10.4	5.5	3.1
Iowa.............................	70.0	67.3	65	101	70	42	3.8	6.0	4.3	2.6
Kansas	67.6	64.8	62	106	74	50	4.2	7.1	5.0	3.6
Kentucky	57.1	54.1	104	210	118	82	5.3	10.2	5.9	4.2
Louisiana	60.5	56.7	137	166	148	108	6.3	8.0	7.2	5.3
Maine...........................	62.5	59.8	30	57	34	23	4.4	8.1	4.9	3.4
Maryland.......................	66.9	63.5	161	235	121	100	5.1	7.7	4.1	3.6
Massachusetts..............	65.2	62.0	174	289	164	90	4.9	8.3	4.8	2.7
Michigan.......................	60.5	57.2	257	605	344	186	5.4	12.6	6.8	3.6
Minnesota.....................	69.5	66.9	111	218	117	89	3.7	7.4	4.1	3.2
Mississippi....................	55.7	52.2	81	136	99	71	6.4	10.4	7.5	5.4
Missouri........................	65.4	62.1	155	293	162	106	5.0	9.6	5.4	3.6
Montana........................	63.7	61.1	22	37	21	23	4.2	7.3	4.4	5.0
Nebraska.......................	69.9	67.7	31	46	37	27	3.0	4.6	3.8	2.8
Nevada.........................	62.9	58.6	96	184	50	45	6.8	13.5	4.1	4.2
New Hampshire.............	68.6	66.2	25	43	26	18	3.4	5.8	3.6	2.7
New Jersey	64.1	60.4	263	434	197	158	5.8	9.5	4.5	3.7
New Mexico	57.6	53.8	61	76	47	42	6.6	8.1	5.1	4.9
New York.......................	60.7	57.5	507	826	474	415	5.3	8.6	5.0	4.5
North Carolina..............	61.2	57.7	274	501	226	152	5.8	10.9	5.2	3.7
North Dakota.................	71.3	69.3	12	14	12	10	2.8	3.8	3.4	3.0
Ohio.............................	62.4	59.4	279	600	349	231	4.9	10.3	5.9	4.0
Oklahoma......................	61.7	59.0	80	120	76	50	4.4	6.8	4.5	3.0
Oregon	61.4	58.0	111	211	114	93	5.6	10.6	6.2	5.1
Pennsylvania.................	62.9	59.5	341	540	311	252	5.3	8.5	5.0	4.1
Rhode Island.................	64.8	60.9	33	63	29	22	6.0	11.2	5.0	4.1
South Carolina	59.4	55.8	136	241	139	75	6.0	11.2	6.7	3.8
South Dakota	69.2	67.1	14	22	16	10	3.1	5.0	3.8	2.5
Tennessee	59.5	56.2	172	299	161	110	5.6	9.7	5.6	3.9
Texas............................	63.7	60.9	581	997	601	445	4.5	8.1	5.4	4.3
Utah.............................	68.2	65.8	53	106	52	38	3.6	7.8	4.1	3.3
Vermont........................	67.1	64.7	12	22	12	9	3.6	6.1	3.5	2.8
Virginia.........................	64.8	61.9	188	297	139	83	4.5	7.1	3.6	2.3
Washington...................	63.1	59.6	200	351	181	158	5.6	10.0	5.6	5.2
West Virginia.................	53.0	49.4	53	70	40	44	6.8	8.7	5.1	5.5
Wisconsin.....................	68.0	64.9	141	267	143	105	4.6	8.7	4.7	3.5
Wyoming	67.6	64.7	13	20	10	10	4.2	6.4	3.6	3.9

[1] Annual averages of monthly figures.
[2] Percent of each specified group which is classified as either employed or unemployed.
[3] Preliminary data.
[4] Percent of civilian noninstitutionalized population classified as employed.
[5] Percent unemployed of the civilian labor force.

Table A-29. Employed Civilians, by Occupation, May 2016

(Numbers in thousands.)

Geographic area	Total[1]	Management occupations	Business and financial occupations	Computer and mathematical sciences	Architecture and engineering occupations	Life, physical, and social science occupations	Community and social service occupations	Legal occupations	Education, training, and library	Arts, design, entertainment, sports, and media	Health care practitioner and technical	Health care support
United States	140,400	7,091	7,281	4,165	2,499	1,153	2,019	1,076	8,636	1,903	8,319	4,043
Alabama......................	1,913	70	72	39	2	9	18	10	103	17	129	51
Alaska	324	17	14	5	0	6	7	2	21	3	17	8
Arizona......................	2,653	149	138	93	3	19	42	19	139	31	152	65
Arkansas....................	1,191	60	48	24	1	6	14	6	74	8	77	36
California....................	15,967	920	938	580	29	178	234	124	990	317	799	351
Colorado....................	2,508	110	169	104	3	30	35	20	145	39	136	63
Connecticut.................	1,666	117	92	49	3	13	35	14	125	25	102	49
Delaware....................	441	18	28	16	1	5	7	5	25	4	30	13
District of Columbia	702	86	103	41	2	25	12	39	34	36	31	12
Florida.......................	8,222	276	441	194	6	38	85	84	418	97	513	236
Georgia.....................	4,214	240	228	138	4	22	45	29	261	51	236	99
Hawaii.......................	632	36	26	9	**	7	11	4	43	9	31	19
Idaho........................	663	37	25	14	1	10	12	4	41	9	36	18
Illinois.......................	5,904	426	323	177	9	35	77	45	373	69	342	167
Indiana......................	2,991	143	118	56	4	20	35	15	160	31	186	78
Iowa.........................	1,535	86	67	33	2	12	21	7	102	18	85	43
Kansas......................	1,374	66	66	37	1	9	17	7	89	17	81	43
Kentucky....................	1,870	84	68	30	2	10	26	10	104	16	128	50
Louisiana...................	1,922	82	69	21	2	12	25	13	108	17	131	55
Maine........................	596	34	24	12	1	4	11	3	39	8	41	21
Maryland....................	2,641	152	163	124	5	42	43	25	169	30	170	75
Massachusetts.............	3,460	269	199	143	7	49	82	29	236	51	240	109
Michigan....................	4,212	196	194	105	10	31	57	26	237	57	268	135
Minnesota..................	2,810	168	164	98	4	24	53	19	165	37	174	85
Mississippi.................	1,117	55	31	11	1	6	14	6	75	8	78	32
Missouri....................	2,758	125	135	82	2	18	42	18	161	36	184	81
Montana....................	455	15	19	7	0	7	10	4	28	6	29	12
Nebraska...................	968	45	49	28	1	7	15	5	58	11	60	26
Nevada......................	1,271	60	44	18	1	8	12	8	54	20	56	24
New Hampshire............	645	37	28	19	1	4	8	3	44	8	39	18
New Jersey	3,955	205	227	141	4	37	62	32	307	43	223	151
New Mexico	805	39	35	15	2	11	13	6	52	9	47	26
New York....................	9,098	472	523	245	7	68	176	108	692	206	529	364
North Carolina.............	4,231	180	208	125	4	34	50	22	266	41	266	153
North Dakota...............	425	20	17	7	0	3	6	2	23	5	25	13
Ohio.........................	5,338	240	261	140	7	35	77	31	318	60	361	200
Oklahoma..................	1,587	89	67	30	2	10	26	12	93	15	98	47
Oregon......................	1,791	111	84	51	4	21	36	12	104	28	99	48
Pennsylvania...............	5,747	227	276	155	6	46	109	43	338	59	386	190
Rhode Island...............	475	21	25	14	0	3	9	4	33	6	31	21
South Carolina	1,980	88	75	38	3	9	25	13	114	18	120	55
South Dakota	418	12	19	8	0	4	7	2	24	6	30	11
Tennessee	2,893	165	110	51	3	15	31	14	151	29	195	76
Texas........................	11,745	456	564	350	11	82	112	83	739	126	646	313
Utah.........................	1,375	83	70	45	2	12	18	9	85	20	67	32
Vermont....................	305	12	15	7	0	3	9	2	27	6	19	7
Virginia......................	3,761	171	262	199	4	32	54	36	240	50	204	90
Washington.................	3,067	154	192	149	4	33	43	20	182	47	158	77
West Virginia...............	697	28	22	11	0	6	11	6	41	5	59	22
Wisconsin..................	2,805	130	134	75	4	20	40	14	165	34	163	69
Wyoming	276	11	8	3	0	4	4	2	20	3	14	7

(D) = Data withheld to avoid disclosure or does not meet statistical standards.

[1]Due to separate processing and weighting procedures, totals for the United States differ from the results obtained by aggregating the totals for the states.

Table A-29.   Employed Civilians, by Occupation, May 2016—*Continued*

(Numbers in thousands.)

Geographic area	Protective services	Food preparation and serving related	Building and grounds cleaning and maintenance	Personal care and services	Sales and related	Office and administrative support	Farming, fishing, and forestry	Construction and extraction	Installation, maintenance, and repairs	Production	Transportation and material moving
United States	3,386	12,982	4,426	4,515	14,537	22,026	464	5,585	5,457	9,106	9,732
Alabama.....................	42	168	59	46	218	284	6	74	92	214	149
Alaska......................	8	28	11	13	26	52	1	22	17	12	24
Arizona.....................	81	255	79	94	295	458	14	107	107	111	157
Arkansas...................	25	105	35	35	127	175	6	46	52	116	104
California...................	374	1,506	479	497	1,604	2,499	215	602	509	871	1,051
Colorado...................	56	245	83	83	291	360	5	130	97	103	140
Connecticut...............	37	135	57	66	162	263	1	50	52	97	91
Delaware...................	10	41	15	15	48	74	1	14	17	19	30
District of Columbia	29	56	22	16	27	81	0	14	9	5	14
Florida......................	233	908	323	238	1,061	1,442	22	355	347	310	501
Georgia.....................	104	396	114	90	458	654	10	139	176	304	357
Hawaii......................	21	81	35	20	62	91	1	34	24	16	42
Idaho.......................	13	59	23	23	69	102	6	36	29	42	42
Illinois......................	153	502	169	163	579	916	7	175	208	434	473
Indiana.....................	59	283	89	78	288	417	4	113	134	379	259
Iowa........................	22	134	47	49	150	221	5	69	68	156	120
Kansas.....................	28	120	41	45	135	224	4	58	58	113	93
Kentucky...................	38	176	51	54	179	282	4	70	83	204	176
Louisiana	56	191	58	72	214	276	4	117	98	118	154
Maine.......................	12	55	21	25	59	92	2	26	26	37	37
Maryland...................	72	218	85	78	265	408	3	116	101	80	164
Massachusetts............	80	292	106	123	322	500	2	118	101	155	179
Michigan...................	73	380	124	122	426	624	5	130	167	445	274
Minnesota..................	43	237	83	129	276	404	4	99	96	221	178
Mississippi.................	33	105	37	33	115	161	5	42	51	109	94
Missouri....................	60	264	85	98	282	448	5	102	115	197	184
Montana....................	8	50	20	15	51	71	2	28	22	17	28
Nebraska...................	15	82	28	27	102	156	4	43	39	77	80
Nevada.....................	41	181	73	74	139	198	1	64	48	43	93
New Hampshire............	11	57	22	21	82	107	1	21	25	45	34
New Jersey	108	300	127	113	409	654	5	119	135	176	330
New Mexico	25	82	27	40	79	123	3	49	33	26	45
New York...................	294	735	319	371	931	1,500	3	329	299	335	485
North Carolina.............	103	412	131	108	455	630	9	147	175	345	308
North Dakota...............	7	35	15	16	40	60	2	36	23	23	40
Ohio	117	507	160	126	509	815	4	181	210	495	398
Oklahoma..................	37	158	45	42	164	253	3	83	75	109	103
Oregon.....................	33	171	55	69	182	266	14	73	62	113	120
Pennsylvania..............	126	498	172	226	564	944	6	218	228	394	442
Rhode Island..............	12	50	16	12	46	76	0	16	16	30	25
South Carolina	47	196	69	52	219	298	4	74	90	195	143
South Dakota..............	6	41	17	14	47	65	2	22	16	32	30
Tennessee	67	265	81	73	287	471	4	91	127	268	276
Texas.......................	297	1,138	332	392	1,258	2,009	19	580	500	673	838
Utah........................	23	109	43	39	140	244	1	80	55	89	85
Vermont....................	5	27	11	13	30	41	1	15	13	20	17
Virginia.....................	103	330	127	127	397	547	7	157	149	175	230
Washington................	62	283	87	94	302	436	19	140	118	183	211
West Virginia..............	16	65	23	24	69	110	1	40	37	40	54
Wisconsin..................	54	243	81	114	268	410	5	98	108	322	207
Wyoming	6	25	12	8	25	36	1	28	17	13	24

(D) = Data withheld to avoid disclosure or does not meet statistical standards.
[1]Due to separate processing and weighting procedures, totals for the United States differ from the results obtained by aggregating the totals for the States.

Table A-30.   Private Industry Employment and Wages, 2015

Geographic area	Annual establishments	Average annual employment	Totral annual wages (in millions)	Annual average weekly wage	Annual wages per employee	Rank on annual wages per employee
United States	9,522,775	139,491,699	7,384,948	1,018	52,942	(X)
Alabama............................	119,251	1,890,340	83,691	851	44,273	36
Alaska...............................	22,217	331,681	18,161	1,053	54,755	10
Arizona..............................	148,593	2,609,770	125,094	922	47,933	23
Arkansas...........................	87,922	1,177,884	48,169	786	40,895	47
California...........................	1,416,493	16,295,204	1,005,383	1,187	61,698	6
Colorado	186,114	2,494,450	135,155	1,042	54,182	13
Connecticut.......................	115,612	1,662,825	108,966	1,260	65,530	4
Delaware	30,883	433,748	23,419	1,038	53,991	14
District of Columbia	37,997	743,596	65,555	1,695	88,159	1
Florida...............................	642,518	8,039,635	371,910	890	46,260	29
Georgia	288,777	4,151,011	205,685	953	49,551	21
Hawaii...............................	39,077	637,854	29,927	902	46,919	25
Idaho.................................	56,029	664,792	25,832	747	38,857	50
Illinois...............................	403,205	5,848,451	327,449	1,077	55,989	9
Indiana..............................	159,303	2,941,991	129,163	844	43,903	39
Iowa..................................	100,264	1,530,234	67,476	848	44,095	38
Kansas..............................	86,786	1,367,329	59,995	844	43,878	40
Kentucky	122,322	1,835,550	79,598	834	43,365	41
Louisiana	125,264	1,930,688	88,673	883	45,928	30
Maine................................	50,769	595,889	24,903	804	41,791	45
Maryland............................	168,788	2,591,189	148,154	1,100	57,176	7
Massachusetts...................	237,928	3,428,020	228,622	1,283	66,692	3
Michigan	238,969	4,161,641	208,346	963	50,063	20
Minnesota..........................	160,615	2,776,684	148,627	1,029	53,527	15
Mississippi........................	71,761	1,114,379	41,948	724	37,642	51
Missouri............................	191,647	2,715,579	123,736	876	45,565	32
Montana............................	45,032	448,688	17,973	770	40,056	49
Nebraska...........................	70,816	959,176	41,105	824	42,854	42
Nevada..............................	78,902	1,244,635	56,928	880	45,739	31
New Hampshire..................	50,660	636,806	33,466	1,011	52,553	16
New Jersey	259,277	3,889,975	242,597	1,199	62,365	5
New Mexico	56,911	806,762	34,332	818	42,555	43
New York...........................	627,270	9,014,385	608,659	1,298	67,521	2
North Carolina...................	266,421	4,161,654	193,642	895	46,530	27
North Dakota.....................	32,140	437,072	22,158	975	50,696	18
Ohio..................................	290,876	5,257,971	247,894	907	47,146	24
Oklahoma..........................	108,626	1,594,011	70,624	852	44,306	35
Oregon..............................	141,395	1,787,398	86,381	929	48,328	22
Pennsylvania......................	349,719	5,691,613	297,029	1,004	52,187	17
Rhode Island......................	36,347	469,981	23,805	974	50,651	19
South Carolina	122,383	1,949,881	81,899	808	42,002	44
South Dakota	32,486	416,020	16,716	773	40,181	48
Tennessee	150,237	2,820,198	131,821	899	46,742	26
Texas................................	639,721	11,655,919	632,693	1,044	54,281	11
Utah..................................	93,169	1,340,591	59,413	852	44,318	34
Vermont.............................	24,624	307,058	13,582	851	44,234	37
Virginia..............................	254,270	3,735,713	202,759	1,044	54,276	12
Washington........................	239,221	3,122,749	176,938	1,090	56,661	8
West Virginia......................	50,156	696,195	29,050	802	41,727	46
Wisconsin..........................	166,922	2,794,170	126,758	872	45,365	33
Wyoming	26,097	282,667	13,089	891	46,306	28

(X) = Not applicable.

Table A-31. Average Annual Employment by Industry and Wages

	Private industry employment, 2015[1]											
		Goods-producing				Service-providing						
Geography area	Total, all industries	Total	Natural resources and mining	Construction	Manufacturing	Total	Trade, transportation, and utlities	Information	Financial activities	Professional and business services	Education and health services	Leisure and hospitality	Other services
United States	118,307,717	20,716,645	2,001,103	6,423,866	12,291,676	97,591,072	26,670,095	2,754,109	7,828,679	19,607,372	21,080,792	15,100,935	4,308,880
Alabama......................	1,532,167	358,232	18,710	81,684	257,838	1,173,935	374,565	21,506	92,650	228,598	221,705	189,991	44,921
Alaska........................	255,274	49,941	18,239	17,662	14,041	205,333	65,670	6,309	11,792	29,964	46,326	34,925	9,998
Arizona......................	2,224,536	321,974	37,784	127,012	157,178	1,902,561	500,730	44,800	189,875	395,543	391,960	297,600	69,475
Arkansas...................	978,732	222,763	18,669	49,218	154,876	755,969	248,050	13,313	48,239	138,688	171,979	111,689	24,010
California...................	13,916,502	2,458,065	447,430	726,339	1,284,296	11,458,437	2,901,707	482,179	793,399	2,481,930	2,381,936	1,815,830	511,726
Colorado....................	2,097,611	335,593	46,174	148,604	140,816	1,762,017	441,743	70,602	153,261	398,420	309,056	312,338	75,172
Connecticut...............	1,428,395	222,321	5,444	57,920	158,957	1,206,074	296,561	32,352	128,023	216,675	319,053	151,172	61,685
Delaware....................	371,748	49,308	1,523	20,753	27,033	322,439	80,063	4,714	46,598	59,878	70,913	48,610	11,663
District of Columbia	506,774	15,615	X	14,521	1,094	491,159	31,669	16,998	26,594	160,814	111,174	72,474	67,374
Florida.......................	7,005,903	854,075	80,292	431,403	342,380	6,151,828	1,676,816	136,039	530,690	1,222,504	1,184,807	1,132,088	262,174
Georgia	3,513,397	570,825	30,074	165,335	375,416	2,942,572	894,846	106,657	224,737	635,843	516,158	445,087	101,091
Hawaii........................	514,827	55,425	6,686	34,664	14,075	459,403	119,707	8,692	27,294	83,542	80,103	114,508	25,353
Idaho.........................	551,238	124,417	26,677	36,151	61,589	426,821	133,142	9,161	28,875	79,188	92,081	67,817	16,542
Illinois.......................	5,060,798	820,390	27,118	213,245	580,027	4,240,408	1,180,450	100,769	363,811	922,125	886,367	577,238	201,521
Indiana......................	2,551,010	667,274	21,270	127,103	518,900	1,883,736	576,010	33,585	128,185	330,038	430,087	300,977	84,846
Iowa..........................	1,294,792	315,910	21,523	78,220	216,167	978,883	311,486	24,929	105,644	138,571	213,518	139,829	44,908
Kansas......................	1,124,352	242,596	20,358	60,994	161,244	881,756	259,595	20,960	73,744	179,038	189,503	125,823	33,093
Kentucky....................	1,539,903	339,001	21,936	75,720	241,345	1,200,903	382,367	25,165	91,367	215,065	252,387	187,823	46,271
Louisiana	1,620,672	338,928	54,569	140,578	143,782	1,281,744	389,625	26,608	87,601	213,409	288,394	228,239	47,427
Maine........................	500,906	83,688	6,549	26,519	50,620	417,219	119,026	7,572	28,986	64,449	114,953	64,039	17,745
Maryland....................	2,105,913	264,635	6,454	154,424	103,757	1,841,278	458,016	38,352	138,906	430,527	418,340	267,493	89,645
Massachusetts...........	3,001,359	396,475	8,399	138,991	249,084	2,604,884	566,520	88,120	211,424	536,475	736,630	350,901	114,813
Michigan....................	3,610,636	769,815	36,338	147,828	585,649	2,840,821	767,327	56,384	192,338	636,494	634,106	412,541	133,336
Minnesota..................	2,402,503	459,800	27,416	115,091	317,292	1,942,703	519,315	51,650	178,084	357,763	487,935	259,521	88,435
Mississippi................	878,389	205,663	17,905	46,004	141,754	672,726	223,449	13,601	42,863	104,888	136,987	129,087	21,852
Missouri....................	2,300,643	392,040	16,302	114,411	261,328	1,908,603	532,756	49,898	157,166	370,146	431,302	292,540	74,796
Montana.....................	365,786	58,595	13,020	26,462	19,113	307,191	91,408	6,359	20,640	40,286	68,555	62,611	17,207
Nebraska...................	799,388	161,015	14,794	48,935	97,286	638,373	194,024	17,524	64,046	116,809	132,346	88,423	25,201
Nevada......................	1,095,750	128,996	16,691	70,199	42,106	966,753	237,722	13,860	57,806	166,844	119,021	340,741	30,335
New Hampshire............	552,285	93,970	2,540	24,235	67,195	458,314	137,825	12,250	35,288	76,639	107,469	68,470	20,143
New Jersey	3,317,218	396,097	13,046	147,024	236,027	2,921,122	842,252	73,695	232,462	643,103	615,631	356,932	132,175
New Mexico	626,624	108,208	36,924	43,496	27,788	518,416	137,516	12,685	32,029	99,903	122,447	93,378	20,457
New York....................	7,648,846	842,546	30,304	359,692	452,550	6,806,300	1,558,751	264,798	697,158	1,260,422	1,737,941	892,937	357,681
North Carolina.............	3,474,750	682,421	32,017	189,375	461,030	2,792,329	794,347	75,926	213,180	589,487	555,258	459,140	104,991
North Dakota...............	367,138	87,104	27,637	34,046	25,420	280,035	101,606	6,605	23,579	36,089	59,133	40,427	12,596
Ohio	4,552,282	916,030	29,718	200,338	685,975	3,636,251	1,005,786	71,605	275,847	715,827	873,700	539,182	153,092
Oklahoma...................	1,270,090	278,696	64,439	77,340	136,916	991,394	305,231	21,078	77,270	185,490	205,522	161,436	35,367
Oregon......................	1,509,012	318,812	50,864	82,494	185,455	1,190,200	332,232	33,088	81,091	228,004	251,400	191,300	72,855
Pennsylvania..............	5,015,915	859,990	57,198	235,324	567,468	4,155,925	1,111,314	84,903	316,726	777,663	1,125,931	545,424	193,963
Rhode Island...............	411,058	59,105	953	17,007	41,145	351,953	75,885	8,613	30,661	63,578	99,247	56,224	17,704
South Carolina	1,607,203	334,809	12,021	86,933	235,855	1,272,394	383,416	27,012	94,979	262,374	215,100	238,821	50,694
South Dakota..............	344,080	71,010	6,215	22,201	42,593	273,070	86,552	5,884	29,160	30,672	63,951	46,137	10,713
Tennessee	2,414,236	456,472	11,296	112,795	332,381	1,957,764	598,901	43,448	140,966	393,041	401,245	307,821	72,073
Texas........................	9,845,769	1,891,467	329,887	683,641	877,939	7,954,302	2,370,913	200,735	705,611	1,595,531	1,515,400	1,241,135	320,598
Utah..........................	1,122,545	223,364	15,812	84,679	122,873	899,181	260,939	33,204	79,027	192,290	166,354	133,616	33,647
Vermont.....................	254,099	49,905	3,831	15,177	30,897	204,193	55,305	4,630	11,708	27,420	60,106	36,072	8,952
Virginia......................	3,043,782	436,694	19,684	184,358	232,652	2,607,088	647,248	69,505	184,987	697,794	478,617	384,750	134,593
Washington................	2,589,020	555,209	104,797	162,859	287,553	2,033,811	575,858	113,643	139,643	379,936	427,193	305,403	92,111
West Virginia..............	559,172	106,957	26,900	32,406	47,652	452,215	132,875	9,625	24,885	67,070	122,456	74,581	20,539
Wisconsin	2,416,695	604,934	30,221	109,201	465,512	1,811,762	527,640	48,751	146,661	312,031	413,046	269,664	83,625
Wyoming	215,998	59,474	26,459	23,256	9,759	156,524	53,338	3,771	11,125	18,494	25,965	36,132	7,699

[1]All estimates of labor and earnings provided by the Bureau of Labor Statistics (BLS) are based on the 2012 North American Industry Classification System (NAICS). National total may differ from sum of state total due to rounding. Annual employment data are the average employment by industry for the calendar year.

Table A-31. Average Annual Employment by Industry and Wages—*Continued*

Geography area	Public administration			Annual wages per employee, 2015[1]				
					Goods-producing			
	Federal	State	Local	Total, all industries	Total	Natural resources and mining	Construction	Manufacturing
United States	1,505,532	1,787,498	3,949,499	52,876	61,478	58,461	57,009	64,305
Alabama.....................	32,198	30,958	60,589	43,380	52,458	53,940	48,744	53,526
Alaska........................	9,696	16,776	15,124	54,026	89,062	128,751	81,317	47,248
Arizona......................	31,783	38,286	80,670	47,492	60,067	46,051	49,388	72,067
Arkansas....................	8,263	22,264	25,271	40,621	44,796	48,100	44,145	44,605
California...................	133,647	200,278	479,042	61,281	68,862	36,510	62,257	83,868
Colorado....................	31,412	25,708	86,399	54,518	64,455	87,586	55,347	66,483
Connecticut................	4,905	27,228	26,317	66,289	75,228	36,553	64,244	80,555
Delaware....................	2,402	11,570	X	54,009	59,457	36,152	55,136	64,087
District of Columbia......	170,111	22,492	X	81,402	65,863	X	63,603	95,869
Florida.......................	62,876	101,834	272,211	45,562	49,012	30,747	45,785	57,361
Georgia......................	61,275	43,974	128,404	50,234	54,134	37,696	52,947	55,974
Hawaii........................	14,401	17,484	9,940	44,393	59,634	38,175	70,595	42,834
Idaho.........................	8,034	12,647	22,545	38,710	46,798	36,058	39,992	55,444
Illinois.......................	33,559	53,503	173,080	56,308	67,521	49,316	67,763	68,283
Indiana......................	18,690	28,877	79,016	44,121	57,622	46,478	53,742	59,029
Iowa..........................	5,991	15,175	45,611	43,532	54,560	39,624	54,965	55,901
Kansas.......................	11,974	17,464	52,426	44,729	53,273	45,960	50,918	55,087
Kentucky....................	17,606	28,382	45,551	43,201	55,530	55,893	51,661	56,711
Louisiana...................	14,306	26,343	56,320	46,297	67,117	85,272	57,786	69,350
Maine........................	4,232	10,522	12,238	41,293	50,102	38,290	45,727	53,922
Maryland....................	112,979	50,707	78,557	54,777	64,757	39,565	60,028	73,363
Massachusetts............	17,752	53,417	65,355	67,303	80,224	56,092	71,063	86,149
Michigan....................	21,884	36,118	111,193	49,776	62,303	37,355	57,316	65,110
Minnesota..................	11,247	29,380	87,486	53,947	61,747	45,363	61,519	63,245
Mississippi.................	11,931	16,994	38,612	36,902	46,291	46,208	46,260	46,312
Missouri.....................	25,169	42,213	54,386	46,003	55,141	40,438	54,433	56,368
Montana.....................	8,491	10,613	17,903	39,014	51,751	66,414	47,829	47,193
Nebraska....................	8,192	13,056	29,097	42,352	46,333	39,539	47,402	46,828
Nevada.......................	8,538	16,285	34,897	44,532	57,979	84,046	53,250	55,530
New Hampshire............	3,280	8,841	18,130	53,138	63,677	40,054	57,273	66,879
New Jersey	22,094	48,232	129,704	61,992	72,246	35,287	67,676	77,136
New Mexico	17,549	14,434	28,105	41,225	52,882	60,534	43,533	57,349
New York....................	46,525	113,424	323,068	68,798	65,447	37,734	67,592	65,598
North Carolina.............	31,444	65,563	142,141	46,519	53,086	34,706	47,690	56,578
North Dakota...............	4,704	4,589	12,917	51,579	69,573	92,176	64,960	51,179
Ohio	40,450	45,893	124,697	46,582	57,390	49,069	55,887	58,190
Oklahoma...................	31,496	32,609	49,034	44,504	61,054	91,275	48,731	53,792
Oregon.......................	9,234	26,441	44,213	47,785	57,455	33,484	53,622	65,734
Pennsylvania..............	50,474	49,293	135,391	51,853	59,837	61,374	60,158	59,549
Rhode Island...............	5,917	8,371	9,003	48,740	55,772	37,907	56,730	55,790
South Carolina	15,619	39,507	57,556	41,335	53,685	37,313	47,994	56,617
South Dakota	4,273	5,185	17,083	40,157	44,861	40,451	44,995	45,434
Tennessee	18,469	35,941	84,033	46,968	55,845	42,126	52,841	57,331
Texas........................	101,613	102,503	236,444	55,191	74,651	108,744	60,538	72,829
Utah..........................	24,869	18,428	32,156	44,360	52,104	62,679	46,522	54,590
Vermont.....................	3,973	6,659	X	43,349	51,678	35,958	46,919	55,965
Virginia......................	117,778	42,347	86,589	53,844	54,547	44,330	51,560	57,778
Washington................	25,900	43,788	89,011	56,539	60,472	29,261	56,919	73,859
West Virginia..............	13,596	17,075	18,151	40,932	60,066	75,603	53,397	55,831
Wisconsin	8,991	29,504	98,389	45,230	54,782	36,541	57,241	55,389
Wyoming....................	3,741	8,325	11,772	45,788	66,989	82,527	51,068	62,803

X = Not applicable.

[1] All estimates of labor and earnings provided by the Bureau of Labor Statistics (BLS) are based on the 2012 North American Industry Classification System (NAICS). National total may differ from sum of state total due to rounding. Annual employment data are the average employment by industry for the calendar year.

Table A-31. Average Annual Employment by Industry and Wages—*Continued*

| Geography area | Annual wages per employee, 2015[1] | | | | | | | | Public administration | | |
| | Service-providing | | | | | | | | | | |
	Total	Trade, transportation, and utlities	Information	Financial activities	Professional and business services	Education and health services	Leisure and hospitality	Other services	Federal	State	Local
United States	51,050	44,321	95,098	87,915	69,270	47,383	21,807	35,116	86,676	56,039	52,611
Alabama......................	40,609	38,856	55,893	63,920	50,813	44,571	15,546	34,357	86,912	45,505	38,822
Alaska........................	45,504	44,544	64,508	54,675	63,146	49,027	23,141	38,115	84,243	58,050	48,629
Arizona.......................	45,364	43,067	65,823	65,288	52,979	48,426	21,798	33,816	79,480	47,877	55,165
Arkansas.....................	39,390	38,591	53,737	53,281	55,041	39,845	15,021	31,486	69,268	42,205	32,684
California.....................	59,655	49,298	145,627	95,853	83,052	48,669	26,946	36,446	86,829	70,756	75,498
Colorado.....................	52,625	46,030	94,154	77,317	73,552	47,150	22,809	37,475	84,246	56,962	52,356
Connecticut.................	64,641	49,274	99,271	150,652	86,344	52,567	21,899	32,683	84,855	75,035	67,768
Delaware.....................	53,176	40,427	63,781	86,800	76,613	51,626	19,260	32,520	73,692	50,759	X
District of Columbia......	81,896	53,363	121,663	133,746	108,225	60,614	36,831	85,760	110,163	79,137	X
Florida........................	45,084	41,448	73,696	68,611	55,803	48,205	23,909	33,302	82,464	40,134	54,068
Georgia	49,477	46,675	85,687	76,585	61,886	48,805	18,957	33,907	77,781	41,612	38,939
Hawaii........................	42,555	40,694	63,703	60,583	49,249	49,786	30,598	33,471	85,607	57,115	72,452
Idaho.........................	36,352	36,908	46,969	50,308	45,298	39,533	15,264	27,541	69,756	45,834	39,490
Illinois........................	54,139	48,022	80,676	99,410	71,287	47,294	21,874	39,592	86,011	73,398	56,893
Indiana.......................	39,338	38,760	56,024	59,900	46,795	44,281	17,145	30,260	75,148	42,341	38,106
Iowa..........................	39,974	37,417	52,966	68,128	48,779	40,714	15,307	30,371	66,919	61,148	40,992
Kansas	42,378	39,557	60,731	63,151	58,236	40,827	15,419	32,177	72,748	43,828	36,472
Kentucky	39,721	39,434	49,080	60,779	45,680	45,669	16,225	30,525	66,497	41,995	37,216
Louisiana	40,792	41,229	51,362	57,688	54,668	41,227	20,054	34,693	75,391	51,334	40,971
Maine.........................	39,526	34,689	47,707	61,570	51,863	44,121	19,272	30,700	72,181	45,054	39,440
Maryland.....................	53,342	44,211	84,234	86,407	73,992	51,608	21,586	39,226	102,712	54,268	55,757
Massachusetts.............	65,336	48,138	108,052	130,649	96,906	55,717	24,747	35,397	85,506	75,421	67,881
Michigan.....................	46,381	43,481	66,521	65,765	63,081	46,941	18,354	30,949	86,789	59,344	46,117
Minnesota...................	52,101	46,196	72,178	88,646	74,811	47,353	19,626	31,081	73,819	59,697	48,332
Mississippi..................	34,031	34,319	43,971	49,049	,40,792	39,481	16,637	31,584	68,697	40,525	30,262
Missouri......................	44,126	39,469	72,373	65,490	60,959	43,297	19,629	30,858	69,942	37,626	41,885
Montana......................	36,585	36,722	48,500	52,997	48,427	43,194	17,367	27,334	67,381	49,213	39,127
Nebraska....................	41,348	36,755	58,009	59,778	57,463	42,503	15,159	29,408	70,280	45,799	38,047
Nevada.......................	42,738	40,243	61,617	61,076	55,347	51,578	31,978	35,023	73,557	53,055	67,185
New Hampshire............	50,978	44,939	82,776	86,750	70,374	52,253	19,754	35,394	89,392	51,331	44,890
New Jersey	60,601	52,081	103,267	106,765	85,516	50,935	23,991	33,841	93,605	74,585	61,980
New Mexico	38,792	35,569	50,709	52,958	57,976	39,647	17,185	30,726	78,089	52,205	41,575
New York....................	69,212	48,414	115,324	176,589	89,622	50,008	29,981	38,037	85,415	72,268	57,589
North Carolina.............	44,915	40,112	76,576	78,010	58,718	44,745	18,233	31,233	73,534	45,205	40,714
North Dakota...............	45,981	49,140	59,885	58,629	58,239	48,708	17,421	33,278	68,296	53,911	42,156
Ohio	43,859	41,093	64,862	65,906	60,025	43,616	17,862	29,871	82,824	59,574	47,323
Oklahoma...................	39,851	40,124	54,748	53,622	49,716	42,932	17,111	32,699	71,137	42,843	42,290
Oregon.......................	45,195	40,413	73,565	63,536	64,617	48,257	19,553	29,655	73,844	59,387	58,889
Pennsylvania...............	50,201	42,671	73,689	81,638	73,501	48,922	19,749	31,360	77,457	62,728	48,751
Rhode Island...............	47,559	40,801	69,655	82,396	66,011	46,493	20,454	31,234	89,532	72,607	64,231
South Carolina	38,085	37,321	57,097	56,200	46,564	43,828	16,949	31,114	74,043	39,050	37,497
South Dakota	38,934	37,042	45,847	53,505	51,000	46,834	15,565	29,690	66,284	46,299	33,326
Tennessee	44,898	42,808	62,768	68,462	54,152	49,169	21,108	32,690	79,609	46,389	38,881
Texas.........................	50,563	49,537	79,820	75,931	68,545	45,481	20,222	36,054	82,192	49,139	53,918
Utah..........................	42,436	40,256	67,497	62,746	52,782	40,769	18,002	32,985	68,700	47,993	38,973
Vermont......................	41,313	38,196	56,258	64,723	59,643	43,539	21,066	32,733	76,001	57,649	X
Virginia.......................	53,726	40,584	95,307	77,424	81,959	46,630	19,148	41,114	100,248	46,485	51,143
Washington..................	55,465	48,994	150,438	72,604	71,864	46,754	22,018	36,410	80,967	59,029	66,562
West Virginia...............	36,406	35,983	51,353	47,185	45,280	41,964	16,698	28,320	75,579	39,712	30,928
Wisconsin...................	42,040	38,237	67,745	65,331	55,109	45,695	16,069	27,134	69,570	54,489	40,920
Wyoming	37,733	40,615	45,471	53,494	50,357	41,653	18,945	35,822	65,619	55,990	40,847

X = Not applicable.
[1]All estimates of labor and earnings provided by the Bureau of Labor Statistics (BLS) are based on the 2012 North American Industry Classification System (NAICS). National total may differ from sum of state total due to rounding. Annual employment data are the average employment by industry for the calendar year.

Table A-32.   Union Membership

(Numbers in thousands.)

Geographic area	2015					2014				
	Total employed	Member of unions[1]		Represented by unions[2]		Total employed	Members of unions[1]		Represented by unions[2]	
		Total	Percent of employed	Total	Percent of employed		Total	Percent of employed	Total	Percent of employed
United States	133,743	14,795	11.1	16,441	12.3	131,431	14,576	11.1	16,152	12.3
Alabama[3]......................	1,863	190	10.2	204	11.0	1,887	204	10.8	228	12.1
Alaska	304	60	19.6	66	21.7	307	70	22.8	75	24.4
Arizona[3]......................	2,661	138	5.2	163	6.1	2,593	138	5.3	173	6.7
Arkansas[3]...................	1,155	58	5.1	74	6.4	1,108	52	4.7	60	5.4
California......................	15,657	2,486	15.9	2,689	17.2	15,135	2,472	16.3	2,652	17.5
Colorado......................	2,310	194	8.4	215	9.3	2,328	221	9.5	250	10.7
Connecticut..................	1,587	269	17.0	277	17.4	1,564	231	14.8	245	15.7
Delaware	412	38	9.2	43	10.4	384	38	9.9	43	11.3
District of Columbia	334	35	10.4	40	12.1	325	28	8.6	35	10.7
Florida[3]......................	7,994	546	6.8	671	8.4	8,042	455	5.7	561	7.0
Georgia[3].....................	4,016	162	4.0	206	5.1	3,926	170	4.3	193	4.9
Hawaii	583	119	20.4	126	21.7	572	124	21.8	131	22.9
Idaho[3]........................	679	46	6.8	50	7.3	641	34	5.3	43	6.7
Illinois.........................	5,566	847	15.2	892	16.0	5,500	831	15.1	880	16.0
Indiana[3]......................	2,828	283	10.0	319	11.3	2,802	299	10.7	335	12.0
Iowa[3]..........................	1,435	138	9.6	174	12.2	1,459	156	10.7	184	12.6
Kansas[3]......................	1,255	110	8.7	136	10.8	1,287	95	7.4	116	9.0
Kentucky......................	1,705	187	11.0	207	12.1	1,714	189	11.0	219	12.8
Louisiana[3]...................	1,847	107	5.8	126	6.8	1,834	96	5.2	118	6.4
Maine..........................	549	64	11.6	75	13.6	566	62	11.0	71	12.5
Maryland......................	2,757	287	10.4	337	12.2	2,612	310	11.9	347	13.3
Massachusetts..............	3,103	402	12.9	441	14.2	3,036	415	13.7	445	14.7
Michigan[3]....................	4,083	621	15.2	672	16.5	4,028	585	14.5	631	15.7
Minnesota....................	2,565	363	14.2	385	15.0	2,538	360	14.2	380	15.0
Mississippi[3].................	1,103	60	5.4	75	6.8	1,028	38	3.7	46	4.5
Missouri.......................	2,615	230	8.8	257	9.8	2,559	214	8.4	249	9.7
Montana.......................	427	52	12.2	59	13.9	414	52	12.7	57	13.8
Nebraska[3]...................	882	68	7.7	80	9.0	877	64	7.3	79	9.0
Nevada[3]......................	1,232	177	14.3	203	16.5	1,173	169	14.4	192	16.4
New Hampshire.............	641	62	9.7	73	11.4	626	62	9.9	72	11.5
New Jersey	3,880	596	15.4	644	16.6	3,860	635	16.5	664	17.2
New Mexico	782	49	6.2	61	7.9	763	43	5.7	56	7.4
New York......................	8,249	2,038	24.7	2,141	26.0	8,060	1,980	24.6	2,081	25.8
North Carolina[3]............	4,089	123	3.0	167	4.1	3,936	76	1.9	126	3.2
North Dakota[3]..............	352	19	5.4	24	6.8	353	18	5.0	24	6.9
Ohio............................	4,914	606	12.3	670	13.6	4,958	615	12.4	688	13.9
Oklahoma[3]..................	1,567	88	5.6	116	7.4	1,465	89	6.0	106	7.2
Oregon.........................	1,586	235	14.8	256	16.2	1,554	243	15.6	264	17.0
Pennsylvania.................	5,601	747	13.3	804	14.4	5,525	703	12.7	754	13.7
Rhode Island.................	483	68	14.2	72	14.9	453	68	15.1	72	15.8
South Carolina[3]............	1,960	41	2.1	57	2.9	1,884	41	2.2	61	3.2
South Dakota[3].............	382	22	5.9	26	6.9	363	18	4.9	22	6.0
Tennessee[3]..................	2,693	146	5.4	175	6.5	2,514	127	5.0	141	5.6
Texas[3]........................	11,177	503	4.5	626	5.6	11,205	543	4.8	700	6.2
Utah[3]..........................	1,274	50	3.9	67	5.2	1,236	46	3.7	57	4.6
Vermont.......................	284	36	12.6	42	14.7	286	32	11.1	37	13.1
Virginia[3]......................	3,736	202	5.4	258	6.9	3,665	179	4.9	228	6.2
Washington...................	2,977	500	16.8	536	18.0	2,914	491	16.8	536	18.4
West Virginia.................	665	83	12.4	91	13.7	687	73	10.6	80	11.6
Wisconsin.....................	2,682	223	8.3	253	9.4	2,626	306	11.7	327	12.5
Wyoming[3]....................	261	19	7.1	22	8.2	255	17	6.7	19	7.5

[1]Members are employed workers who are union members.
[2]Data refers to both union members and workers who report no union affiliation but whose jobs are covered by a union or employee association contract.
[3]Right-to-work state.

Table A-33. Median Income of Households in 2015 Inflation-Adjusted Dollars and Distribution by Income Level

Geographic area	Median household income (in 2015 inflation adjusted dollars)	Total number of households (thousands)	Percentage of households by income level (in 2015 inflation-adjusted dollars)									
			Under $10,000	$10,000–$14,999	$15,000–$24,999	$25,000–$34,999	$35,000–$49,999	$50,000–$74,999	$75,000–$99,999	$100,000–$149,999	$150,000–$199,999	$200,000 and over
United States	55,775	118,208	6.9	5.0	10.2	9.8	13.2	17.8	12.2	13.6	5.5	5.8
Alabama......................	44,765	1,846	9.5	6.9	12.7	11.3	13.8	17.8	10.7	10.5	3.6	3.1
Alaska	73,355	250	3.9	3.2	6.8	7.6	11.8	17.7	15.0	18.8	8.5	6.7
Arizona......................	51,492	2,463	7.6	4.8	10.8	10.7	14.5	18.8	12.0	12.1	4.5	4.2
Arkansas....................	41,995	1,145	9.1	7.1	13.4	12.6	15.0	17.7	10.4	9.3	2.5	3.0
California....................	64,500	12,896	5.5	4.8	9.1	8.6	11.7	16.4	12.2	15.3	7.5	8.9
Colorado....................	63,909	2,075	5.3	3.7	8.3	8.6	13.2	18.3	13.4	16.1	6.6	6.6
Connecticut................	71,346	1,344	5.7	3.9	8.0	7.2	11.3	15.9	12.5	17.0	8.2	10.3
Delaware	61,255	353	5.4	3.3	9.3	9.2	13.2	18.8	14.9	14.4	6.3	5.2
District of Columbia	75,628	282	8.6	4.4	7.3	7.1	9.3	12.9	11.1	16.0	8.7	14.7
Florida.......................	49,426	7,463	7.4	5.2	11.8	11.3	14.8	18.5	11.4	11.1	4.2	4.4
Georgia	51,244	3,656	8.0	5.5	10.8	10.3	14.0	18.2	11.5	12.4	4.7	4.6
Hawaii.......................	73,486	446	5.3	3.2	6.8	6.8	10.9	17.8	14.5	18.8	8.5	7.4
Idaho........................	48,275	597	7.3	5.5	11.8	12.1	14.9	18.9	12.0	11.7	3.2	2.7
Illinois.......................	59,588	4,795	6.8	4.3	9.8	9.1	12.6	17.5	12.7	14.7	6.1	6.4
Indiana......................	50,532	2,515	6.7	5.0	11.2	11.3	15.3	19.3	12.5	11.9	3.6	3.3
Iowa.........................	54,736	1,247	5.9	5.1	10.1	10.2	14.1	20.4	13.9	13.1	3.9	3.3
Kansas	53,906	1,112	6.5	4.7	10.1	10.0	14.6	19.4	12.6	13.9	4.2	4.2
Kentucky	45,215	1,716	9.2	6.6	12.3	11.4	14.6	18.1	11.1	10.3	3.3	2.9
Louisiana	45,727	1,738	10.3	6.5	12.8	10.6	12.9	16.3	10.9	11.6	4.3	3.6
Maine........................	51,494	545	6.6	6.1	11.6	10.6	13.5	19.6	13.1	11.7	4.1	3.1
Maryland....................	75,847	2,178	4.9	3.1	6.5	7.2	10.5	17.1	13.4	18.0	9.5	9.6
Massachusetts............	70,628	2,560	6.0	4.9	8.0	7.6	10.2	15.7	12.1	17.2	8.3	10.0
Michigan....................	51,084	3,859	7.7	5.1	11.0	10.6	14.4	18.7	12.0	12.2	4.4	3.9
Minnesota	63,488	2,147	4.8	4.0	8.9	8.5	12.9	18.9	14.0	15.9	6.4	5.7
Mississippi..................	40,593	1,104	11.5	6.9	14.3	11.6	14.3	16.6	10.8	9.4	2.5	2.1
Missouri.....................	50,238	2,374	7.0	5.6	11.3	11.1	14.7	18.7	12.0	12.0	3.9	3.6
Montana.....................	49,509	415	7.2	5.6	12.1	11.1	14.4	19.7	11.8	11.5	3.2	3.5
Nebraska....................	54,996	744	5.7	4.9	10.4	10.2	14.1	19.3	13.2	13.9	4.4	3.9
Nevada......................	52,431	1,042	6.4	4.6	10.3	11.1	14.9	19.1	13.1	12.4	4.3	3.8
New Hampshire............	70,303	518	4.0	3.4	8.3	7.5	11.9	17.8	14.6	17.4	7.8	7.3
New Jersey	72,222	3,188	5.7	3.6	8.2	7.7	10.5	15.6	12.2	17.0	8.7	10.9
New Mexico	45,382	762	9.8	6.4	12.8	11.3	13.7	17.1	11.0	11.0	3.9	3.0
New York....................	60,850	7,234	7.8	5.0	9.5	8.6	11.4	16.3	11.8	14.7	6.9	8.1
North Carolina.............	47,830	3,844	7.4	6.1	11.9	11.5	14.7	17.8	11.4	11.2	3.9	4.0
North Dakota...............	60,557	313	5.5	5.0	8.8	9.4	13.9	17.1	13.4	15.9	5.9	5.1
Ohio	51,075	4,607	7.6	5.3	11.0	10.7	14.1	18.5	12.2	12.4	4.3	3.7
Oklahoma...................	48,568	1,466	7.7	5.7	12.0	10.9	14.8	18.9	11.6	11.2	3.7	3.5
Oregon......................	54,148	1,553	6.8	4.9	10.4	10.6	13.6	18.8	12.6	13.1	4.6	4.7
Pennsylvania...............	55,702	4,956	6.7	4.9	10.3	9.9	13.3	18.4	12.8	13.5	5.2	5.1
Rhode Island...............	58,073	407	8.0	5.6	9.3	8.8	12.1	16.5	13.1	14.8	6.2	5.6
South Carolina	47,238	1,858	8.2	6.2	11.9	11.2	14.6	18.7	11.7	10.7	3.5	3.2
South Dakota	53,017	339	6.1	5.5	10.2	10.6	14.9	19.7	14.2	12.0	3.4	3.6
Tennessee	47,275	2,530	8.0	6.0	12.1	11.4	14.9	18.5	11.1	10.8	3.5	3.7
Texas........................	55,653	9,421	6.6	4.7	10.3	10.1	13.5	18.0	12.0	13.5	5.4	6.0
Utah	62,912	931	4.5	3.5	7.7	9.1	13.6	20.8	15.0	15.4	5.7	4.7
Vermont.....................	56,990	255	4.9	5.3	11.0	9.2	13.1	19.3	14.2	14.1	4.7	4.2
Virginia......................	66,262	3,107	5.8	3.8	8.1	8.3	12.0	17.4	12.8	16.0	7.4	8.4
Washington.................	64,129	2,729	5.7	3.8	8.0	8.7	12.8	18.2	13.8	15.8	6.5	6.8
West Virginia...............	42,019	735	9.7	6.6	13.8	11.8	15.6	17.3	10.8	9.5	2.6	2.2
Wisconsin	55,638	2,320	5.4	4.7	10.3	10.3	14.0	19.9	14.0	13.6	4.2	3.7
Wyoming	60,214	229	4.7	4.5	9.6	9.5	13.4	18.8	14.4	17.1	4.7	3.4

Table A-34.   Family Income and Families and Individuals Below Poverty, 2015

Geographic area	Median family income (in 2015 inflation-adjusted dollars)	Total number of families (thousands)	Under $25,000	$25,000– $49,999	$50,000– $74,999	$75,000– $99,999	$100,000– $199,999	$200,000 and over	Families below poverty Number	Families below poverty Percent	Individuals below poverty Number	Individuals below poverty Percent	Children below poverty Number	Children below poverty Percent
United States	68,260	77,531	14.7	21.1	18.6	14.2	23.9	7.5	8,233	10.6	46,153	14.7	15,000	20.7
Alabama	57,160	1,214	19.5	23.7	20.2	13.5	19.0	4.3	167	13.7	876	18.5	291	26.6
Alaska	86,376	164	8.9	16.6	17.7	14.8	33.3	8.6	12	7.0	75	10.3	28	15.2
Arizona	61,042	1,598	16.1	23.9	20.2	13.7	20.7	5.3	199	12.5	1,159	17.4	394	24.7
Arkansas	52,449	761	19.8	27.4	20.1	13.0	15.7	4.0	105	13.7	551	19.1	188	27.2
California	73,581	8,836	14.8	19.5	16.5	13.0	25.7	10.6	999	11.3	5,892	15.3	1,902	21.2
Colorado	78,384	1,332	10.5	18.6	18.1	15.2	28.6	8.9	101	7.6	614	11.5	183	14.7
Connecticut	91,388	876	10.5	15.1	15.1	13.5	31.7	14.2	65	7.4	367	10.5	109	14.5
Delaware	74,931	235	12.5	18.8	18.7	16.7	26.7	6.5	20	8.7	114	12.4	39	19.4
District of Columbia	94,846	125	17.2	15.0	10.3	9.4	25.6	22.6	17	14.0	111	17.3	30	25.6
Florida	59,339	4,807	17.1	24.9	19.7	13.4	19.2	5.8	541	11.3	3,117	15.7	932	23.1
Georgia	61,250	2,466	17.8	22.8	18.9	13.1	21.4	6.0	322	13.0	1,695	17.0	603	24.5
Hawaii	83,823	309	8.9	15.5	18.5	15.7	32.4	8.9	21	6.9	148	10.6	43	14.2
Idaho	60,081	400	15.2	25.2	21.7	14.8	19.6	3.4	44	10.9	246	15.1	76	17.8
Illinois	73,884	3,099	13.4	19.4	17.9	14.5	26.3	8.6	304	9.8	1,703	13.6	559	19.1
Indiana	63,165	1,634	14.1	23.5	21.1	15.7	20.8	4.6	166	10.2	933	14.5	323	20.9
Iowa	69,382	797	11.4	21.0	22.3	17.5	23.3	4.5	61	7.7	367	12.2	106	14.8
Kansas	69,401	721	12.2	21.3	20.9	15.8	24.0	5.8	61	8.4	369	13.0	122	17.2
Kentucky	56,187	1,132	19.5	24.6	20.0	13.8	18.1	3.9	158	14.0	794	18.5	256	25.9
Louisiana	58,964	1,109	20.5	22.4	18.0	13.2	20.9	5.0	163	14.7	890	19.6	313	28.4
Maine	64,651	343	14.1	21.8	22.4	16.2	21.2	4.2	31	8.9	173	13.4	43	17.4
Maryland	91,567	1,455	9.2	15.0	16.2	14.2	33.0	12.5	98	6.7	571	9.7	175	13.2
Massachusetts	90,590	1,613	11.3	15.1	15.1	13.3	31.5	13.6	128	7.9	752	11.5	203	14.8
Michigan	63,893	2,480	15.3	22.6	20.2	14.6	22.0	5.3	276	11.1	1,530	15.8	486	22.4
Minnesota	79,893	1,384	9.4	18.0	19.1	16.6	29.1	7.8	87	6.3	546	10.2	165	13.1
Mississippi	50,069	743	24.2	25.8	18.8	13.0	15.6	2.7	126	17.0	637	22.0	224	31.3
Missouri	62,989	1,519	14.6	23.6	20.8	14.9	21.2	5.0	155	10.2	875	14.8	276	20.2
Montana	64,061	253	13.9	23.2	22.0	15.6	20.4	4.8	23	9.3	147	14.6	43	19.4
Nebraska	71,039	470	11.7	20.2	20.9	16.4	25.2	5.5	40	8.5	231	12.6	78	16.8
Nevada	63,206	659	15.3	23.1	20.5	15.3	20.9	4.9	72	10.9	418	14.7	137	20.9
New Hampshire............	85,873	341	8.4	15.6	17.5	16.9	32.0	9.5	17	5.0	106	8.2	28	10.7
New Jersey	90,245	2,206	11.1	15.8	14.9	13.1	31.1	14.1	178	8.1	946	10.8	308	15.6
New Mexico	56,207	485	20.3	24.4	19.0	13.5	19.0	4.0	72	14.8	418	20.4	141	28.6
New York	73,854	4,561	15.3	18.6	16.7	13.1	26.3	10.1	529	11.6	2,970	15.4	910	22.0
North Carolina..............	60,074	2,506	17.2	24.3	19.4	13.9	19.8	5.4	295	11.8	1,608	16.4	530	23.5
North Dakota................	79,642	188	10.4	18.1	18.1	16.8	29.5	7.1	13	6.9	80	11.0	20	12.1
Ohio	65,176	2,922	15.1	22.1	20.2	15.0	22.5	5.2	314	10.7	1,674	14.8	550	21.3
Oklahoma.....................	60,215	970	16.8	24.0	20.9	14.1	19.5	4.7	114	11.7	611	16.1	209	22.2
Oregon	66,287	978	14.1	22.3	20.0	14.8	22.8	6.1	97	9.9	607	15.4	171	20.3
Pennsylvania................	70,194	3,204	13.0	20.9	19.6	15.3	24.3	6.9	290	9.1	1,630	13.2	513	19.4
Rhode Island................	76,623	250	13.6	18.8	16.3	15.8	27.8	7.6	25	10.1	141	13.9	41	19.4
South Carolina	59,282	1,221	17.6	24.1	20.7	14.4	19.0	4.4	148	12.1	791	16.6	256	24.0
South Dakota	67,643	217	12.8	21.5	21.2	18.2	21.1	5.2	18	8.3	114	13.7	37	18.1
Tennessee..................	57,830	1,676	17.5	25.3	20.3	13.5	18.5	4.9	207	12.3	1,078	16.7	355	24.2
Texas	65,316	6,521	16.2	22.1	18.1	13.2	22.8	7.5	798	12.2	4,256	15.9	1,637	23.0
Utah	71,594	693	10.5	20.3	21.7	17.0	24.7	5.7	57	8.3	332	11.3	116	12.9
Vermont.....................	75,595	152	11.0	18.5	20.0	18.2	26.4	6.0	9	5.8	61	10.2	15	13.3
Virginia.....................	80,403	2,055	11.1	18.3	17.5	14.2	28.0	11.1	160	7.8	909	11.2	273	14.8
Washington..................	76,954	1,761	10.6	18.9	18.8	15.5	27.2	8.9	139	7.9	858	12.2	246	15.5
West Virginia................	53,463	472	20.1	26.6	20.2	13.9	16.3	3.0	64	13.5	322	17.9	94	25.2
Wisconsin	70,870	1,470	11.4	20.8	21.2	17.4	24.2	5.1	116	7.9	678	12.1	207	16.4
Wyoming	75,540	145	10.0	18.7	20.9	18.3	28.2	4.0	10	6.7	63	11.1	18	13.2

Table A-35.   Housing—Units and Characteristics, 2015

Geographic area	Total housing units (thousands)	Units in structure (percent) 1-unit detached	Units in structure (percent) 1-unit attached	Units in structure (percent) Mobile home	Year built (percent) 2010 or later	Year built (percent) 1990 to 2009	Year built (percent) Before 1950	Total units (thousands)	Vehicles available (percent) None	Vehicles available (percent) 1	Vehicles available (percent) 2	Vehicles available (percent) 3 or more	House heating fuel (percent) Utility gas	House heating fuel (percent) Electricity
United States	134,794	61.4	5.8	6.3	3.0	28.5	18.1	118,208	8.9	33.5	37.2	20.3	48.2	38.2
Alabama......................	2,218	68.8	1.6	12.9	4.1	33.8	9.7	1,846	6.6	33.4	36.6	23.4	27.5	64.5
Alaska........................	309	61.8	7.3	5.1	3.0	30.8	3.0	250	10.3	30.1	38.2	21.4	49.1	13.1
Arizona......................	2,929	63.2	4.9	10.6	3.1	45.3	3.0	2,463	6.9	37.0	38.1	18.0	32.6	60.5
Arkansas....................	1,348	69.3	1.7	12.3	4.3	35.8	9.1	1,145	6.4	34.1	38.1	21.3	39.3	49.4
California....................	13,988	57.7	7.0	3.8	1.9	22.4	15.5	12,896	7.5	31.7	37.2	23.6	64.0	26.6
Colorado	2,309	62.7	7.0	4.1	3.0	35.3	10.5	2,075	5.2	30.2	40.0	24.6	69.3	22.7
Connecticut.................	1,496	58.7	5.2	0.8	1.4	14.8	29.3	1,344	9.2	32.3	38.3	20.2	35.1	16.0
Delaware	422	59.5	13.9	8.6	4.0	35.2	12.9	353	6.8	34.3	38.3	20.6	41.2	32.6
District of Columbia	310	12.1	25.0	0.0	3.8	11.8	47.5	282	36.2	43.7	16.4	3.7	54.7	40.3
Florida........................	9,210	53.8	6.1	9.1	3.0	37.5	4.3	7,463	6.8	41.0	38.0	14.2	4.4	92.5
Georgia	4,182	65.9	3.8	9.1	3.1	43.0	6.9	3,656	6.9	33.6	38.1	21.3	39.8	54.1
Hawaii........................	532	52.2	9.4	0.3	2.8	28.2	6.9	446	8.2	33.5	36.4	21.9	1.8	28.3
Idaho.........................	692	72.9	3.1	9.0	4.2	40.8	12.3	597	3.6	29.2	39.3	27.9	51.4	33.7
Illinois.......................	5,318	58.5	5.8	2.5	1.5	22.2	28.4	4,795	10.8	35.4	36.1	17.7	78.5	15.6
Indiana.......................	2,841	72.3	3.6	5.0	2.6	27.7	23.5	2,515	6.9	33.0	38.1	22.0	60.3	28.9
Iowa..........................	1,369	72.9	3.8	3.8	3.4	22.3	31.5	1,247	5.9	29.7	39.4	25.0	60.8	22.7
Kansas	1,254	72.6	4.3	4.6	3.0	24.8	22.8	1,112	5.6	30.2	39.5	24.7	65.8	23.9
Kentucky	1,957	66.8	2.4	12.4	3.1	32.1	14.8	1,716	7.5	33.8	37.9	20.9	37.5	51.9
Louisiana....................	2,025	65.0	2.6	13.0	4.5	28.4	11.3	1,738	8.7	37.1	37.6	16.6	34.5	62.2
Maine.........................	729	70.2	2.2	8.3	1.8	24.4	30.4	545	8.0	34.3	39.4	18.3	6.9	6.4
Maryland.....................	2,434	51.1	21.3	1.4	3.1	26.4	17.2	2,178	9.3	32.1	37.3	21.3	44.5	40.6
Massachusetts.............	2,846	51.7	5.5	0.9	1.8	14.8	39.4	2,560	12.7	35.8	36.3	15.3	51.0	15.8
Michigan.....................	4,550	72.3	4.5	5.1	1.5	23.1	23.1	3,859	8.0	34.3	38.6	19.0	76.7	9.2
Minnesota...................	2,397	67.0	7.5	3.4	2.5	28.3	21.1	2,147	6.8	30.3	40.1	22.7	66.1	17.1
Mississippi..................	1,301	69.4	1.2	14.5	3.4	35.2	8.1	1,104	7.0	33.4	37.0	22.7	30.6	55.6
Missouri.....................	2,747	70.5	3.3	6.0	2.7	28.7	18.7	2,374	7.1	33.1	38.4	21.4	51.1	35.4
Montana.....................	494	68.7	3.3	11.7	3.6	29.0	19.0	415	5.4	27.8	38.4	28.3	54.1	23.7
Nebraska....................	821	72.5	3.7	3.5	3.2	23.8	26.1	744	5.4	30.6	38.6	25.3	59.1	30.2
Nevada......................	1,210	59.0	4.7	5.4	3.2	57.4	2.2	1,042	7.7	37.1	36.3	18.9	59.8	34.7
New Hampshire............	623	63.1	5.6	5.6	1.9	23.1	24.4	518	5.0	30.5	42.3	22.2	20.0	8.9
New Jersey	3,594	53.0	9.5	1.0	2.0	18.9	25.9	3,188	11.7	34.7	36.0	17.6	75.2	12.1
New Mexico	915	63.7	3.6	17.0	2.5	35.1	8.8	762	6.4	33.2	37.1	23.4	66.6	17.7
New York....................	8,207	41.6	4.9	2.3	1.5	12.8	41.1	7,234	29.2	33.1	25.9	11.7	58.1	11.2
North Carolina.............	4,491	64.6	3.9	13.3	4.2	40.4	9.0	3,844	6.4	32.5	38.2	23.0	24.3	62.6
North Dakota...............	363	57.8	5.0	7.6	8.0	25.7	18.4	313	4.9	29.4	38.3	27.4	41.8	39.4
Ohio..........................	5,157	68.4	4.5	3.7	1.7	21.8	26.5	4,607	8.4	33.8	37.3	20.5	66.0	23.3
Oklahoma...................	1,712	72.9	1.9	9.3	4.0	26.1	13.5	1,466	5.6	32.5	39.7	22.2	52.6	37.9
Oregon.......................	1,719	63.4	4.3	8.1	2.7	31.7	16.8	1,553	8.2	32.4	37.3	22.1	38.4	49.9
Pennsylvania...............	5,603	57.0	18.7	4.0	1.7	17.7	34.6	4,956	11.1	34.1	36.5	18.3	51.4	22.3
Rhode Island...............	463	54.0	3.6	1.1	1.2	13.7	38.7	407	10.4	37.5	35.8	16.3	53.0	10.6
South Carolina	2,210	62.8	3.1	16.4	4.4	39.4	7.7	1,858	6.9	33.2	38.3	21.5	22.1	71.2
South Dakota	380	68.3	3.9	9.1	4.4	28.5	23.0	339	5.3	27.3	37.2	30.3	47.7	30.0
Tennessee	2,892	68.8	2.8	9.4	3.8	35.0	11.0	2,530	6.3	32.3	38.4	23.0	32.6	60.6
Texas........................	10,588	65.0	2.6	7.2	6.2	36.4	7.1	9,421	5.6	33.8	39.9	20.7	36.0	59.8
Utah..........................	1,038	68.2	6.0	3.9	5.4	39.5	11.1	931	4.2	25.2	41.9	28.7	83.9	11.9
Vermont.....................	327	66.6	3.8	6.8	1.6	21.7	30.0	255	7.3	34.2	39.8	18.7	17.8	4.9
Virginia......................	3,469	61.5	10.7	5.1	3.5	31.6	12.1	3,107	6.2	31.0	38.0	24.8	33.1	54.3
Washington.................	2,992	63.5	3.8	6.6	4.0	33.6	15.5	2,729	6.7	30.4	38.3	24.6	34.7	55.1
West Virginia...............	886	70.4	2.4	14.6	2.2	25.2	24.4	735	9.2	35.6	36.8	18.5	41.7	43.5
Wisconsin	2,657	66.5	4.3	3.5	2.2	26.5	25.5	2,320	6.9	31.9	40.2	21.0	65.3	15.6
Wyoming	269	64.7	4.7	13.8	4.4	29.0	16.2	229	3.2	27.8	37.6	31.4	59.2	23.4

Table A-36.   Owner- and Renter-Occupied Units—Value and Gross Rent, 2015

| | Owner-occupied units | | | | | | | | | Renter-occupied units | | | | | |
| | | | Value—percent distribution | | | | Housing units with a mortgage | | | | | Gross rent—percent distribution | | | |
Geographic Area	Total units (thousands)	Median value	Less than $100,000	$100,000–$199,999	$200,000–$499,000	$500,000 and over	Total (thousands)	Median selected monthly owner costs (dollars)	Monthly owner costs 30 percent or more of household income	Total units (thousands)	Median gross rent (dollars)	Less than $500	$500–$1,499	$1,500 or more	Gross rent 30 percent or more of household income (percent of rental units paying rent)
United States	74,507	194,500	21.5	29.8	36.1	12.4	47,141	1,477	29.6	43,702	959	11.0	70.7	18.3	50.6
Alabama......................	1,254	134,100	36.7	34.7	24.7	3.8	713	1,124	25.2	593	729	20.7	75.8	3.5	49.7
Alaska........................	160	259,600	12.2	18.9	61.0	7.9	104	1,817	28.0	90	1,163	6.5	66.5	27.1	47.7
Arizona.......................	1,525	194,300	19.4	32.4	39.9	8.4	979	1,319	30.1	938	933	7.5	81.6	10.9	48.8
Arkansas....................	746	120,700	40.2	36.9	19.6	3.3	409	1,029	24.8	399	695	20.9	76.8	2.3	47.6
California....................	6,911	449,100	5.9	9.0	41.9	43.2	4,918	2,123	39.5	5,986	1,311	5.5	56.0	38.5	55.8
Colorado.....................	1,323	283,800	8.1	19.4	56.6	16.0	954	1,558	27.6	752	1,111	7.1	69.8	23.1	50.5
Connecticut.................	889	270,900	5.4	24.8	53.4	16.5	617	2,020	33.3	455	1,108	10.8	65.8	23.3	52.5
Delaware....................	250	240,200	10.4	26.7	55.7	7.2	163	1,506	30.8	103	1,049	8.6	78.0	13.4	48.5
District of Columbia	113	551,300	2.3	4.5	38.3	54.8	86	2,312	26.6	169	1,417	10.7	43.1	46.2	48.4
Florida........................	4,760	179,800	23.8	31.4	36.0	8.9	2,720	1,394	35.6	2,703	1,046	6.2	75.4	18.4	57.0
Georgia	2,261	159,300	26.8	36.4	30.3	6.5	1,496	1,299	28.1	1,395	909	10.0	80.9	9.2	49.9
Hawaii........................	252	566,900	2.2	5.3	34.3	58.2	166	2,248	40.0	194	1,500	5.7	44.3	50.0	56.6
Idaho.........................	412	176,300	16.1	42.9	36.3	4.7	269	1,170	29.0	185	770	14.9	81.5	3.6	47.1
Illinois.......................	3,130	180,300	22.3	32.9	36.4	8.4	2,013	1,588	29.2	1,665	936	11.5	72.7	15.8	49.2
Indiana.......................	1,715	131,000	34.3	41.3	21.5	3.0	1,137	1,089	21.1	800	758	14.7	81.3	3.9	47.8
Iowa..........................	881	136,100	33.2	40.1	23.9	2.8	527	1,170	20.0	366	718	19.9	75.2	4.9	43.8
Kansas.......................	738	141,200	34.0	36.5	26.1	3.3	444	1,279	21.3	373	782	16.5	77.6	5.9	42.5
Kentucky	1,138	130,000	36.4	38.6	21.9	3.2	659	1,089	23.9	578	702	21.0	75.0	4.0	45.9
Louisiana	1,122	155,600	30.1	36.4	29.4	4.2	588	1,219	26.0	616	800	16.4	77.1	6.5	54.1
Maine.........................	387	180,300	20.9	35.8	37.9	5.6	241	1,340	29.8	158	792	20.3	73.8	5.9	49.2
Maryland.....................	1,436	299,800	6.5	18.3	56.4	18.8	1,061	1,909	29.6	742	1,278	7.9	57.2	34.9	50.5
Massachusetts.............	1,580	352,100	3.3	12.5	58.9	25.3	1,105	2,048	32.6	980	1,164	14.7	55.6	29.7	51.3
Michigan.....................	2,717	137,500	34.9	36.1	25.5	3.6	1,649	1,220	25.1	1,141	803	13.7	79.8	6.5	50.0
Minnesota...................	1,523	200,000	14.4	35.6	43.5	6.5	1,011	1,459	23.2	624	888	14.6	73.2	12.2	46.5
Mississippi..................	744	112,700	44.4	34.1	19.4	2.0	369	1,083	30.3	360	724	19.8	77.5	2.8	52.7
Missouri......................	1,570	147,800	29.9	39.0	27.0	4.0	979	1,200	23.7	804	763	16.2	78.5	5.3	45.8
Montana......................	276	209,500	18.0	29.0	44.6	8.4	157	1,316	29.6	138	763	20.3	74.4	5.4	45.4
Nebraska....................	490	141,600	29.0	43.2	25.0	2.9	303	1,269	20.5	254	750	17.4	77.4	5.2	43.0
Nevada.......................	563	221,400	12.8	30.4	48.9	7.9	384	1,396	30.0	479	980	4.5	82.3	13.2	49.5
New Hampshire.............	367	244,500	9.0	26.0	57.5	7.6	246	1,828	29.6	151	1,017	9.8	75.9	14.2	46.4
New Jersey..................	2,009	322,600	5.4	16.4	56.7	21.6	1,356	2,349	39.4	1,179	1,214	8.1	63.3	28.6	53.8
New Mexico	514	164,100	26.4	36.3	31.6	5.6	287	1,214	31.3	248	783	15.5	78.6	5.8	50.4
New York.....................	3,839	293,500	15.5	21.5	37.9	25.1	2,384	2,009	36.1	3,395	1,173	11.7	56.7	31.5	53.6
North Carolina.............	2,455	160,100	25.8	37.2	31.1	5.9	1,566	1,234	27.5	1,389	827	12.7	80.3	7.1	49.3
North Dakota...............	193	180,900	24.0	32.1	40.2	3.8	101	1,297	16.4	120	775	16.5	75.2	8.3	39.2
Ohio..........................	3,013	136,400	33.2	39.8	24.0	2.9	1,919	1,228	23.8	1,594	746	16.7	79.1	4.2	46.7
Oklahoma....................	958	126,800	38.2	37.2	21.6	3.0	532	1,159	24.7	508	759	15.8	79.6	4.6	44.9
Oregon.......................	949	264,100	10.1	21.6	55.5	12.7	627	1,534	32.0	604	943	9.1	77.6	13.3	51.4
Pennsylvania...............	3,406	170,600	24.2	34.9	34.9	6.0	2,063	1,414	27.3	1,550	868	14.0	75.1	10.9	49.1
Rhode Island...............	241	241,000	4.6	31.1	54.0	10.3	167	1,730	31.9	167	938	17.7	71.8	10.4	48.2
South Carolina	1,266	148,600	30.9	36.1	27.0	6.1	743	1,168	28.2	592	819	13.6	78.4	8.0	49.6
South Dakota..............	231	152,800	29.0	38.7	28.7	3.7	127	1,225	21.8	108	675	25.1	71.7	3.2	40.8
Tennessee	1,665	150,600	28.9	38.6	27.4	5.1	992	1,167	26.5	865	785	16.5	77.4	6.1	48.4
Texas.........................	5,753	152,000	30.0	35.2	28.6	6.1	3,334	1,453	26.9	3,669	932	8.1	79.1	12.8	47.6
Utah..........................	641	234,600	6.6	31.5	53.6	8.3	451	1,408	24.2	290	925	9.1	79.9	11.0	44.4
Vermont......................	180	223,700	11.6	31.0	49.5	8.0	113	1,530	34.7	75	923	14.2	73.0	12.9	50.5
Virginia......................	2,020	257,900	11.9	24.8	45.3	18.1	1,398	1,692	28.2	1,087	1,144	8.5	62.5	29.0	49.5
Washington.................	1,703	284,000	8.1	20.4	52.8	18.8	1,170	1,704	29.6	1,025	1,080	8.6	68.3	23.1	48.0
West Virginia...............	531	112,100	44.8	34.1	19.1	2.0	247	972	21.2	203	675	23.6	73.2	3.2	47.5
Wisconsin...................	1,549	168,300	19.6	42.1	34.3	4.1	1,004	1,359	24.6	770	792	13.0	81.7	5.3	45.9
Wyoming	156	212,500	15.6	29.8	47.7	6.8	91	1,364	23.2	73	815	10.9	79.6	9.5	40.6

Table A-37. Home Ownership and Vacancy Rates

Geographic area	Homeownership rate[1]					Homeowner vacancy rates[2]					Rental vacancy rates[3]				
	2015	2014	2013	2012	2011	2015	2014	2013	2012	2011	2015	2014	2013	2012	2011
United States	63.7	64.5	65.1	65.4	66.1	1.8	1.9	2.0	2.0	2.5	7.1	7.6	8.3	8.7	9.5
Alabama......................	70.0	72.1	72.7	71.9	72.9	2.7	2.5	2.0	2.1	2.8	14.9	14.0	11.8	11.1	14.2
Alaska........................	62.3	64.9	64.6	63.7	64.4	1.9	2.2	1.7	1.4	1.3	6.8	6.8	5.3	4.7	5.8
Arizona......................	61.7	63.5	65.1	65.3	66.0	2.1	2.7	2.4	2.4	3.2	7.7	9.5	10.8	11.4	12.4
Arkansas....................	67.1	65.4	65.4	66.0	67.6	2.7	3.3	3.0	3.3	3.0	11.3	14.7	13.2	10.6	12.6
California....................	54.3	54.2	54.3	54.5	55.3	1.2	1.1	1.2	1.6	2.1	4.1	4.5	5.1	5.2	6.1
Colorado....................	63.6	65.0	64.4	65.3	65.9	1.1	1.2	1.4	1.7	2.4	5.3	4.9	6.8	5.8	7.4
Connecticut................	66.5	67.4	68.5	68.8	70.6	1.9	1.4	1.8	1.7	2.2	6.3	5.8	7.7	7.4	9.5
Delaware....................	73.3	74.3	74.1	73.4	74.2	1.8	1.8	2.4	2.1	2.7	6.4	7.4	8.6	9.3	11.2
District of Columbia	40.4	41.5	44.6	45.0	44.8	1.6	1.6	1.9	1.9	1.4	5.4	6.5	7.7	7.8	8.4
Florida........................	64.8	64.9	66.1	67.0	69.0	2.4	2.5	2.4	2.2	3.3	8.0	10.1	10.3	13.1	14.9
Georgia	62.9	62.9	64.2	64.3	66.2	2.6	2.8	2.5	2.7	3.6	8.0	9.7	10.6	9.9	10.0
Hawaii........................	59.3	58.4	57.3	57.2	55.4	1.5	1.6	1.8	2.3	2.2	8.7	8.3	10.1	10.2	9.4
Idaho.........................	70.0	69.6	71.5	73.0	72.4	1.4	2.4	1.6	2.2	3.8	5.8	6.1	6.4	7.1	8.9
Illinois........................	65.4	66.4	67.2	66.8	68.4	2.2	2.3	2.7	2.8	3.4	7.5	9.2	9.6	9.5	10.2
Indiana.......................	69.4	70.1	71.7	72.1	72.1	2.1	2.3	2.4	2.1	2.6	9.2	10.8	13.1	12.5	13.0
Iowa...........................	68.8	69.4	69.8	70.2	71.2	0.8	2.0	1.8	2.3	2.4	5.7	5.7	6.4	6.3	7.2
Kansas.......................	64.9	64.7	63.5	63.2	65.4	1.6	2.2	1.6	2.0	2.1	12.0	8.8	10.0	8.0	8.7
Kentucky....................	67.9	67.6	67.5	68.7	69.1	1.9	2.4	2.0	2.0	2.2	7.7	6.5	8.8	7.2	10.5
Louisiana	63.3	65.3	67.8	68.7	70.1	2.2	2.1	2.3	1.9	1.7	10.0	8.4	8.8	12.6	11.7
Maine.........................	69.9	71.0	73.5	74.1	73.9	2.3	1.8	1.9	1.9	2.2	4.4	5.1	5.5	5.3	6.1
Maryland.....................	67.1	66.2	66.9	68.5	69.7	2.0	1.4	1.8	1.9	2.7	8.1	7.5	8.6	9.3	10.1
Massachusetts.............	60.5	63.0	65.3	65.8	65.3	1.4	1.3	1.7	1.6	1.6	4.2	5.6	7.3	6.5	5.8
Michigan.....................	74.6	73.8	73.9	74.8	74.1	1.5	1.5	2.1	1.6	2.4	7.4	8.2	9.8	11.9	13.2
Minnesota...................	70.1	71.4	73.4	72.0	71.3	1.0	1.4	1.1	1.7	2.0	4.9	5.6	6.6	5.9	7.3
Mississippi..................	70.7	73.2	74.2	74.2	74.8	2.0	2.4	2.3	1.7	1.7	10.4	11.1	13.6	11.0	14.5
Missouri.....................	68.5	70.5	71.3	70.8	71.1	2.9	1.9	3.0	2.4	2.2	9.1	9.9	11.0	10.4	10.8
Montana.....................	66.4	66.9	67.4	67.8	68.4	1.7	1.6	1.5	1.6	1.6	3.9	4.0	5.2	5.9	4.9
Nebraska....................	68.1	66.7	68.2	69.3	68.9	1.1	1.3	1.4	1.3	2.1	5.9	5.5	6.5	7.5	8.1
Nevada.......................	54.8	56.0	56.0	55.7	56.2	2.3	2.6	3.0	3.4	3.6	8.0	9.7	13.1	11.9	11.0
New Hampshire............	71.6	72.2	74.1	74.8	74.1	1.8	1.8	2.1	2.0	1.9	5.7	5.6	6.4	7.2	7.5
New Jersey	64.0	65.2	64.9	66.6	66.4	1.6	1.6	2.2	2.1	2.1	5.5	6.2	7.8	11.2	8.8
New Mexico	66.5	66.3	67.3	66.8	69.1	2.8	2.1	2.5	2.1	1.4	10.3	10.8	9.6	7.0	7.4
New York....................	51.5	52.9	53.0	53.6	53.6	2.0	1.7	1.7	2.0	2.7	5.1	4.9	5.7	5.5	6.5
North Carolina.............	65.2	66.4	67.3	67.2	68.3	2.6	2.2	2.6	2.4	2.5	9.8	8.1	9.6	11.2	11.3
North Dakota...............	61.8	64.5	68.0	66.2	68.3	1.7	0.9	1.1	1.4	1.5	9.6	8.6	8.2	6.9	9.8
Ohio	66.4	67.3	67.9	67.9	68.9	1.8	1.6	1.9	1.7	2.8	7.8	7.4	8.2	9.3	10.5
Oklahoma...................	67.4	69.3	69.9	68.8	69.4	1.8	1.9	2.3	2.3	2.6	8.3	11.4	10.4	9.5	10.1
Oregon.......................	61.1	62.8	64.2	66.1	66.4	1.5	1.8	1.9	2.2	2.1	4.6	4.1	3.9	4.9	4.0
Pennsylvania...............	69.6	69.7	71.5	71.0	71.1	2.2	2.2	1.8	1.7	2.0	7.2	8.7	10.0	9.1	8.6
Rhode Island...............	58.9	61.8	61.5	62.1	63.4	1.9	1.5	1.3	1.8	2.3	4.4	6.7	6.1	6.8	7.9
South Carolina	67.1	72.9	72.4	71.5	74.2	2.1	2.7	2.6	2.1	3.3	8.9	12.0	11.2	9.7	11.6
South Dakota	70.1	69.2	67.8	69.2	69.3	1.1	1.2	1.1	1.0	1.8	6.4	8.3	7.4	8.9	9.2
Tennessee	66.5	66.7	66.8	67.9	69.3	2.4	2.3	2.0	2.6	2.8	7.5	8.5	8.9	11.6	12.0
Texas.........................	61.9	62.2	63.3	64.3	64.3	1.5	1.5	2.0	2.0	1.8	9.6	9.5	10.1	10.4	12.3
Utah...........................	69.9	70.9	70.9	71.1	71.4	1.1	1.5	1.4	1.3	1.9	5.1	8.6	6.7	7.7	6.4
Vermont......................	71.8	73.5	73.0	73.4	74.6	2.0	1.9	1.7	1.6	1.7	4.5	5.0	5.7	4.2	4.2
Virginia.......................	67.1	68.7	68.1	67.8	67.9	1.6	1.7	2.0	1.9	2.2	6.6	7.4	7.3	9.5	9.9
Washington.................	62.6	63.6	62.7	63.5	64.2	1.2	1.6	1.5	2.0	2.3	4.6	4.9	4.5	5.9	6.0
West Virginia...............	74.9	75.6	76.8	75.8	78.7	1.8	2.2	1.8	2.0	2.4	8.3	9.1	10.6	8.1	7.9
Wisconsin...................	66.6	67.8	68.5	67.5	68.5	1.2	1.7	1.3	1.5	2.1	5.3	4.6	6.3	6.3	6.6
Wyoming	69.9	70.8	70.5	70.3	71.1	1.3	1.6	1.6	1.4	1.3	9.8	8.0	7.6	5.4	6.5

[1]Proportion of owner households to occupied households.
[2]Proportion of the homeowner inventory that is vacant for sale.
[3]Proportion of the rental inventory that is vacant for rent.

Table A-38. Cost of Living Indicators—Housing, Public University, Energy Expenditures, and Motor Fuels Taxes

	Housing price indexes (All-transactions index)[1]				Average undergraduate tuition and fees and room and board rates charged for full-time students in degree-granting postsecondary institutions						Public 2-year, tuition and required fees[3]		
					Public 4-year institutions, in-state[2]								
					2014–2015				2013–2014				
Geographic area	2015	2010	2005	2000	Total	Tuition and required fees	Room	Board	Total	Tuition and required fees	In-state, 2014–2015	Out-of-state, 2014–2015	In-state, 2013–2014
United States	518.6	482.1	534.8	380.4	18,632	8,543	5,677	4,412	18,100	8,312	2,955	7,122	2,882
Alabama	332.8	341.0	324.5	272.8	17,859	8,871	5,012	3,976	17,245	8,503	4,120	8,096	4,108
Alaska	448.1	410.2	369.1	262.7	16,814	6,356	6,298	4,160	15,693	6,141	3,340	3,340	4,652
Arizona	495.6	407.9	566.5	339.8	19,839	9,775	6,422	3,641	19,781	9,906	2,025	8,086	1,949
Arkansas	354.7	346.4	339.4	274.7	15,320	7,261	4,534	3,526	14,651	6,894	2,973	4,781	2,812
California	974.4	780.9	1,109.5	556.1	21,749	9,008	7,110	5,630	21,280	8,903	1,244	6,731	1,233
Colorado	670.5	546.5	565.1	463.0	19,710	8,722	5,554	5,434	18,977	8,228	3,347	8,769	3,160
Connecticut	537.1	572.8	632.4	411.7	22,435	10,535	6,416	5,483	21,638	10,128	3,869	11,561	3,824
Delaware	471.6	488.7	508.9	321.6	23,161	11,492	7,008	4,661	22,682	11,278	3,530	8,282	3,380
District of Columbia	1,227.4	954.2	925.5	458.6	...	5,251	...	...	7,255	7,255	...	...	...
Florida	422.2	357.4	504.3	274.7	14,677	4,456	5,905	4,316	14,369	4,423	2,383	8,862	2,513
Georgia	341.2	331.2	365.1	300.4	16,522	6,753	5,910	3,860	16,060	6,614	3,177	7,769	2,926
Hawaii	860.9	729.5	748.2	400.2	19,131	8,831	5,208	5,092	18,023	8,216	2,800	7,646	2,608
Idaho	421.6	390.3	397.6	300.2	13,644	6,834	3,189	3,621	13,817	6,315	3,023	7,336	2,963
Illinois	408.5	416.6	468.9	351.8	23,792	13,084	6,146	4,561	23,093	12,520	3,499	9,871	3,306
Indiana	358.5	346.9	357.6	316.0	18,393	8,633	5,157	4,603	18,249	8,443	4,055	7,932	3,605
Iowa	378.3	357.9	347.3	290.4	16,708	7,858	4,297	4,554	16,533	7,839	4,355	5,548	4,253
Kansas	351.8	337.8	329.4	276.2	15,584	7,726	3,903	3,956	14,633	7,387	3,015	4,197	2,890
Kentucky	402.4	390.3	380.8	319.6	17,530	9,189	4,404	3,936	17,280	8,715	3,650	12,478	3,487
Louisiana	428.8	403.4	358.5	288.4	16,045	7,296	5,227	3,523	15,238	6,585	3,502	6,659	3,178
Maine	524.7	524.7	559.7	363.8	18,914	9,166	4,687	5,062	19,121	9,368	3,663	6,455	3,545
Maryland	594.8	590.6	654.6	366.0	19,375	8,482	6,151	4,741	18,879	8,320	3,668	8,841	3,550
Massachusetts	802.2	751.3	879.8	553.8	22,214	10,900	6,888	4,426	21,814	10,702	4,333	9,742	4,216
Michigan	388.4	341.8	460.1	392.9	20,843	11,507	4,617	4,720	20,412	11,295	3,062	6,323	2,922
Minnesota	491.5	468.0	547.7	384.1	18,726	10,400	4,575	3,752	18,387	10,355	5,327	5,960	5,387
Mississippi	304.1	302.5	286.8	244.4	15,710	6,880	4,975	3,855	14,411	6,612	2,518	4,676	2,409
Missouri	373.9	369.5	383.1	302.6	17,143	8,065	5,324	3,754	16,785	7,998	2,890	5,514	2,850
Montana	601.7	553.7	502.6	360.4	14,448	6,378	3,713	4,357	14,081	6,323	3,215	8,923	3,202
Nebraska	397.0	360.5	358.9	305.4	16,199	7,223	4,784	4,193	15,635	7,081	2,743	3,743	2,670
Nevada	472.0	368.9	656.4	351.8	15,138	5,016	5,301	4,822	16,034	5,029	2,700	9,345	2,700
New Hampshire...........	557.6	547.9	639.1	398.3	25,821	14,538	6,435	4,848	25,245	14,469	6,979	15,202	7,230
New Jersey	658.7	675.6	741.8	434.1	24,825	12,541	7,542	4,741	24,243	12,266	3,982	6,926	3,929
New Mexico	448.9	465.9	436.7	332.0	14,778	6,003	4,557	4,217	14,103	5,973	1,475	4,636	1,443
New York...................	610.1	602.3	631.5	398.8	20,549	7,272	8,582	4,695	19,754	6,892	4,711	8,344	4,507
North Carolina.............	402.9	400.8	386.3	328.2	15,771	6,658	5,136	3,977	15,195	6,578	2,355	8,269	2,304
North Dakota...............	487.5	368.4	317.1	246.3	14,217	7,050	2,846	4,320	13,711	6,824	4,283	8,441	3,978
Ohio	336.0	332.5	367.1	318.7	20,537	9,631	5,932	4,974	19,997	9,443	3,610	7,512	3,544
Oklahoma	381.1	354.5	324.0	267.4	14,147	6,345	4,352	3,451	13,493	6,043	3,244	7,940	3,062
Oregon	699.7	611.7	623.0	444.2	19,654	8,891	6,296	4,467	19,152	8,616	4,023	7,552	3,935
Pennsylvania..............	455.6	454.2	442.9	313.5	23,519	13,171	6,120	4,228	22,575	12,607	4,589	11,732	4,352
Rhode Island..............	626.2	638.4	785.9	417.8	22,030	10,868	6,953	4,209	21,761	10,809	3,950	10,582	3,944
South Carolina	385.2	379.5	370.3	304.2	20,354	11,448	5,448	3,459	19,502	11,066	4,061	8,537	3,928
South Dakota	441.7	399.4	367.4	297.7	14,983	7,744	3,522	3,718	14,429	7,735	5,014	4,886	4,800
Tennessee	390.4	370.2	355.3	301.3	17,147	8,495	4,700	3,951	16,263	7,958	3,820	14,859	3,637
Texas	410.7	347.2	316.7	268.8	16,872	7,870	4,733	4,269	16,209	7,476	1,948	5,398	1,898
Utah	561.1	500.2	466.0	399.6	12,970	5,942	3,032	3,996	12,800	5,656	3,469	11,011	3,342
Vermont	538.9	538.6	514.4	339.8	24,986	14,495	6,623	3,869	24,071	13,952	5,886	11,622	5,668
Virginia.....................	541.6	529.7	553.9	336.3	20,941	11,057	5,530	4,354	19,845	10,531	4,318	9,019	4,095
Washington................	782.2	711.5	711.2	505.0	18,863	8,299	5,515	5,049	19,282	8,766	3,992	6,887	4,026
West Virginia..............	294.1	285.6	281.7	227.1	15,644	6,420	4,938	4,285	14,834	5,998	3,628	8,215	3,403
Wisconsin	416.4	421.3	443.1	339.6	15,938	8,441	4,422	3,075	15,720	8,406	4,323	7,220	4,233
Wyoming	536.0	495.2	422.8	299.7	13,457	3,968	4,160	5,329	12,949	3,756	2,694	6,658	2,579

. . . = Not applicable.

[1] The housing price indexes reflect fluctuation from a base of 100. 100 represents the average price of a sample of local single-family homes in 1991. The indexes represent the change in value as of the end of the year shown.

[2] Costs include in-state tuition, required fees, and room and board.

[3] Costs include in-state tuition and required fees only and do not include room or board.

[4] Expenditures are in nominal dollars and include taxes where data are available. Population enumerated as of April 1 for 2000; estimated as of July 1 for all other years.

[5] As of January 1 of the year shown. States vary in taxation of food and in local/state taxation practices. See the source for details.

Table A-38. Cost of Living Indicators—Housing, Public University, Energy Expenditures, and Motor Fuels Taxes—*Continued*

Geographic area	Energy expenditures, 2014 (dollars)[4]			Tax rates on motor fuel, 2015[5]			
	Expenditures (millions of dollars)	Energy expenditures per person	Energy expenditures as percent of current-dollar GDP	Gasoline	Diesel	Liquefied Petroleum Gas	Gasohol
United States	1,394,974	4,374	8.0	18.4	24.4	13.6	18.4
Alabama......................	24,146	4,982	12.0	18.0	19.0	0.0	18.0
Alaska........................	6,891	9,349	12.2	8.0	8.0	0.0	8.0
Arizona......................	22,610	3,360	7.9	18.0	26.0	0.0	18.0
Arkansas....................	13,885	4,680	11.6	21.5	22.5	16.5	21.5
California...................	137,720	3,550	6.0	30.0	13.0	6.0	30.0
Colorado....................	19,994	3,733	6.5	22.0	20.5	5.0	22.0
Connecticut................	15,483	4,307	6.2	25.0	54.5	0.0	25.0
Delaware....................	3,848	4,112	6.1	23.0	22.0	22.0	23.0
District of Columbia							
Florida.......................	2,320	3,516	2.0	23.5	23.5	0.0	23.5
	66,414	3,336	7.9	17.3	17.3	0.0	17.3
Georgia	39,728	3,935	8.4	26.0	29.0	26.0	26.0
Hawaii	7,379	5,195	9.7	17.0	17.0	5.2	16.0
Idaho.........................	6,980	4,270	11.0	32.0	32.0	23.2	32.0
Illinois.......................	51,550	4,002	7.0	19.0	21.5	19.0	19.0
Indiana......................	34,152	5,176	10.7	18.0	16.0	0.0	18.0
Iowa..........................	18,022	5,796	10.6	30.8	32.5	30.0	29.3
Kansas.......................	14,646	5,046	10.1	24.0	26.0	23.0	24.0
Kentucky	22,467	5,092	12.0	24.6	21.6	24.6	24.6
Louisiana	45,400	9,765	18.0	20.0	20.0	16.0	20.0
Maine.........................	7,558	5,681	13.9	30.0	31.2	0.0	23.0
Maryland....................	22,951	3,841	6.6	32.1	32.9	0.0	0.0
Massachusetts.............	27,574	4,082	6.1	24.0	24.0	24.0	24.0
Michigan	40,740	4,108	9.1	19.0	15.0	15.0	0.0
Minnesota	25,312	4,638	8.0	28.5	28.5	21.4	28.5
Mississippi.................	15,948	5,328	15.2	18.4	18.4	17.0	18.4
Missouri.....................	26,719	4,406	9.5	17.0	17.0	17.0	17.0
Montana.....................	5,527	5,402	12.5	27.8	28.5	5.2	27.8
Nebraska....................	10,330	5,486	9.3	26.1	26.1	26.1	26.1
Nevada	10,513	3,704	7.8	24.0	27.0	22.0	24.0
New Hampshire............	6,361	4,790	9.0	23.8	23.8	22.2	18.0
New Jersey	39,117	4,376	7.1	10.5	13.5	5.3	10.5
New Mexico	9,020	4,325	9.8	17.0	21.0	12.0	17.0
New York....................	68,056	3,446	4.9	25.9	24.1	8.1	25.9
North Carolina.............	37,283	3,751	7.7	36.3	36.3	27.1	35.3
North Dakota...............	8,210	11,094	14.7	23.0	23.0	23.0	23.0
Ohio	51,386	4,431	8.9	28.0	28.0	28.0	28.0
Oklahoma...................	20,497	5,283	11.2	17.0	14.0	17.0	17.0
Oregon	14,866	3,744	7.0	30.0	30.0	23.1	30.0
Pennsylvania...............	55,666	4,351	8.5	50.5	64.2	37.2	50.5
Rhode Island...............	4,204	3,985	7.7	33.0	33.0	33.0	33.0
South Carolina	21,876	5,648	11.6	16.0	16.0	16.0	16.0
South Dakota	4,819	4,530	10.4	30.0	30.0	20.0	16.0
Tennessee	29,615	4,523	10.0	20.0	17.0	14.0	20.0
Texas.........................	162,556	6,025	9.9	20.0	20.0	15.0	20.0
Utah..........................	10,755	3,653	7.7	24.5	24.5	24.5	24.5
Vermont.....................	3,275	5,225	11.2	19.2	31.0	0.0	0.0
Virginia......................	33,980	4,080	7.3	16.2	20.2	16.2	16.2
Washington.................	25,804	3,653	6.1	44.5	44.5	44.5	44.5
West Virginia...............	8,756	4,736	11.8	34.6	34.6	2.1	34.6
Wisconsin	26,448	4,592	9.1	30.9	30.9	22.6	30.9
Wyoming	5,841	9,997	13.3	24.0	24.0	24.0	24.0

Table A-39. Personal Income by State

Geographic area	Personal income, current dollars (billion dollars)										
	2015	2014	2013	2012	2011	2010	2009	2008	2007	2006	2005
United States	15,464	14,802	14,069	13,904	13,233	12,460	12,079	12,493	11,995	11,381	10,610
Alabama.......................	185	179	173	171	167	161	156	158	152	145	136
Alaska........................	41	40	38	38	37	35	33	33	30	28	26
Arizona.......................	267	256	242	236	226	215	214	224	221	209	189
Arkansas.....................	114	112	106	107	99	93	91	92	88	83	78
California.....................	2,104	1,978	1,862	1,839	1,727	1,617	1,561	1,617	1,584	1,525	1,416
Colorado.....................	278	267	247	234	220	202	198	209	202	189	176
Connecticut.................	247	240	231	234	229	222	215	217	204	191	176
Delaware.....................	45	42	41	40	40	37	37	37	36	36	33
District of Columbia	49	46	43	42	41	37	36	36	35	33	31
Florida........................	901	853	799	793	773	728	691	735	731	704	647
Georgia	412	392	371	365	360	337	331	336	332	317	297
Hawaii.........................	69	66	63	62	59	57	56	56	53	51	47
Idaho..........................	64	61	58	55	53	50	49	51	49	46	42
Illinois........................	647	625	601	588	562	535	525	553	537	507	475
Indiana........................	278	267	257	254	243	228	220	226	215	207	195
Iowa...........................	143	138	134	131	125	116	113	117	110	103	97
Kansas........................	137	135	133	129	122	112	111	116	105	98	89
Kentucky......................	171	164	157	156	151	144	139	141	134	128	121
Louisiana	201	194	186	184	175	169	163	168	157	143	135
Maine..........................	57	55	53	53	52	50	49	49	47	45	43
Maryland......................	336	323	312	314	304	289	280	281	268	258	242
Massachusetts..............	425	403	384	381	365	348	335	338	324	310	287
Michigan......................	425	406	388	383	369	348	336	355	347	338	330
Minnesota....................	279	268	256	254	239	224	215	226	215	203	193
Mississippi...................	104	102	100	98	95	91	88	90	86	81	77
Missouri......................	257	249	241	240	229	220	217	221	209	199	188
Montana......................	43	42	40	40	38	35	34	35	33	30	28
Nebraska.....................	92	91	86	85	83	74	71	72	68	63	60
Nevada........................	121	115	109	108	103	100	97	103	104	101	94
New Hampshire.............	74	71	68	68	65	62	60	61	59	57	53
New Jersey	537	516	494	491	474	452	443	456	439	419	392
New Mexico	79	76	72	74	72	68	66	67	63	60	56
New York.....................	1,161	1,119	1,072	1,054	991	934	906	928	908	849	793
North Carolina..............	409	391	372	376	352	338	339	352	328	304	281
North Dakota................	42	43	40	39	33	29	27	27	24	21	20
Ohio...........................	506	489	471	465	448	420	411	422	408	392	373
Oklahoma....................	178	175	164	157	146	135	130	142	128	122	110
Oregon........................	176	166	155	152	145	137	135	140	133	127	117
Pennsylvania................	637	614	589	586	561	534	515	529	506	476	451
Rhode Island................	53	51	49	49	47	45	43	44	43	42	39
South Carolina	188	178	168	166	158	149	145	149	142	133	124
South Dakota	41	39	38	38	37	34	32	33	31	28	26
Tennessee	278	263	252	250	240	227	218	221	211	201	188
Texas..........................	1,290	1,234	1,149	1,126	1,047	957	910	961	873	818	747
Utah...........................	118	111	105	102	95	88	86	90	86	79	71
Vermont......................	30	30	29	28	27	26	25	25	24	23	22
Virginia.......................	436	417	401	404	386	364	351	358	345	327	306
Washington..................	372	356	333	326	302	285	279	294	279	257	236
West Virginia................	68	66	64	65	63	59	58	58	54	52	48
Wisconsin....................	265	256	245	244	233	220	215	219	211	202	190
Wyoming	33	33	31	30	28	26	24	27	24	23	20

Table A-39. Personal Income by State—*Continued*

Geographic area	Disposable personal income, current dollars (billion dollars)										
	2015	2014	2013	2012	2011	2010	2009	2008	2007	2006	2005
United States	13,527	13,016	12,393	12,395	11,782	11,222	10,928	10,986	10,504	10,026	9,398
Alabama.....................	167	162	157	156	152	148	143	142	137	130	123
Alaska	38	37	35	35	34	32	30	30	27	25	24
Arizona.....................	240	231	218	215	205	198	198	202	197	186	169
Arkansas	102	101	96	97	90	85	83	83	79	75	71
California...................	1,797	1,701	1,608	1,614	1,519	1,439	1,399	1,404	1,368	1,327	1,238
Colorado	241	233	216	207	194	180	178	182	175	166	156
Connecticut...............	206	202	194	201	197	195	189	183	170	160	149
Delaware	40	38	36	36	35	33	33	33	32	31	29
District of Columbia	42	39	37	36	35	33	31	31	29	28	26
Florida......................	800	763	717	720	704	670	637	661	652	628	578
Georgia	364	349	331	329	324	305	301	298	293	281	265
Hawaii	62	59	56	56	54	52	51	50	47	45	42
Idaho........................	57	55	52	50	48	46	45	46	44	41	38
Illinois	560	544	523	517	495	480	473	483	468	446	420
Indiana.....................	248	240	231	230	219	207	201	201	191	185	175
Iowa.........................	128	124	120	118	113	105	104	105	98	93	88
Kansas	123	121	119	117	110	102	101	103	93	87	79
Kentucky...................	153	147	141	141	136	131	127	126	120	115	109
Louisiana	181	176	168	168	160	156	150	150	141	130	124
Maine	51	49	47	48	47	45	45	44	42	41	39
Maryland...................	290	280	271	276	267	256	248	243	230	223	210
Massachusetts............	357	340	325	330	315	305	296	288	273	265	247
Michigan...................	376	361	345	343	332	317	308	316	309	302	296
Minnesota	240	232	222	223	209	199	192	196	186	177	169
Mississippi.................	95	94	91	91	87	84	82	82	78	74	71
Missouri....................	228	222	215	217	206	201	198	196	186	178	169
Montana....................	38	37	36	36	34	32	31	31	29	27	25
Nebraska...................	82	81	77	77	75	68	65	65	61	56	54
Nevada.....................	108	103	97	98	94	91	89	93	93	89	83
New Hampshire...........	67	64	62	63	59	57	56	55	53	52	48
New Jersey	461	446	427	431	414	400	394	391	375	363	341
New Mexico	72	69	66	68	66	63	61	61	57	54	50
New York...................	965	936	899	902	842	804	785	769	751	712	675
North Carolina............	363	349	332	339	316	307	309	314	290	270	250
North Dakota..............	37	38	36	35	30	27	24	24	21	19	19
Ohio	448	435	418	416	401	379	373	374	359	346	330
Oklahoma..................	161	159	149	142	132	124	119	128	114	110	99
Oregon.....................	153	145	136	135	128	123	121	123	117	111	103
Pennsylvania..............	561	543	522	524	500	481	466	466	445	421	401
Rhode Island..............	47	45	43	44	42	41	39	39	38	37	35
South Carolina	169	161	152	152	144	137	134	134	127	119	111
South Dakota	37	36	34	35	34	31	30	30	28	25	24
Tennessee	254	242	232	232	222	212	205	202	192	183	173
Texas........................	1,152	1,107	1,033	1,023	950	879	840	858	784	737	678
Utah.........................	104	99	93	91	86	80	78	81	75	70	63
Vermont	27	27	26	26	25	23	23	23	22	21	19
Virginia.....................	380	365	351	358	340	325	314	312	301	286	268
Washington................	331	318	299	297	273	261	257	265	250	231	214
West Virginia..............	61	60	58	59	57	54	53	52	49	47	44
Wisconsin	234	227	217	218	208	198	195	193	186	178	168
Wyoming	29	29	27	27	25	23	22	23	21	20	18

Table A-40. Personal Income per Capita

Geographic area	Personal income per capita										
	2015	2014	2013	2012	2011	2010	2009	2008	2007	2006	2005
United States	48,112	46,414	44,462	44,267	42,453	40,277	39,376	41,082	39,821	38,144	35,904
Alabama......................	38,030	36,930	35,770	35,481	34,699	33,699	32,685	33,430	32,581	31,315	29,802
Alaska........................	56,147	54,582	51,416	52,638	51,405	48,614	46,834	47,791	43,723	40,845	38,876
Arizona......................	39,156	38,006	36,524	36,046	34,912	33,559	33,746	35,717	35,751	34,705	32,288
Arkansas....................	38,252	37,582	35,993	36,164	33,791	31,794	31,372	32,141	30,972	29,308	27,952
California....................	53,741	50,988	48,471	48,312	45,820	43,315	42,224	44,162	43,692	42,334	39,521
Colorado....................	50,899	49,768	46,792	45,073	42,946	39,929	39,838	42,663	41,996	40,143	38,025
Connecticut................	68,704	66,716	64,110	65,036	63,852	62,129	60,428	61,232	57,919	54,191	50,226
Delaware....................	47,633	45,284	43,838	43,566	43,713	41,089	41,317	41,832	41,834	41,343	39,469
District of Columbia	73,302	70,379	66,502	66,594	65,776	61,866	59,998	62,103	60,325	57,025	53,870
Florida.......................	44,429	42,868	40,771	40,983	40,476	38,624	37,065	39,655	39,788	38,738	36,268
Georgia	40,306	38,835	37,147	36,852	36,666	34,643	34,361	35,306	35,516	34,665	33,266
Hawaii	48,288	46,466	44,567	44,402	42,861	41,722	41,473	42,073	40,441	38,648	36,528
Idaho.........................	38,392	37,153	35,703	34,691	33,296	31,727	31,436	33,031	32,580	31,357	29,311
Illinois.......................	50,295	48,508	46,610	45,638	43,718	41,699	40,994	43,358	42,265	40,124	37,648
Indiana......................	41,940	40,460	39,140	38,813	37,257	35,080	34,084	35,139	33,717	32,747	31,077
Iowa..........................	45,902	44,421	43,185	42,576	40,855	37,946	37,365	38,787	36,681	34,434	32,609
Kansas......................	47,161	46,393	45,838	44,795	42,515	39,206	39,204	41,179	37,865	35,353	32,268
Kentucky....................	38,588	37,059	35,601	35,594	34,495	33,031	32,304	32,966	31,583	30,440	29,013
Louisiana	42,947	41,811	40,094	40,017	38,148	37,226	36,284	37,796	35,776	33,276	29,422
Maine........................	42,799	41,240	39,679	39,791	38,934	37,529	36,952	36,998	35,558	34,302	32,669
Maryland....................	55,972	54,036	52,623	53,331	52,084	49,882	48,845	49,428	47,365	45,832	43,302
Massachusetts	62,603	59,603	57,165	57,194	55,233	53,058	51,412	52,283	50,417	48,307	44,842
Michigan....................	42,812	40,940	39,208	38,700	37,398	35,204	33,966	35,644	34,691	33,638	32,813
Minnesota	50,871	49,133	47,235	47,212	44,621	42,121	40,739	42,980	41,258	39,407	37,775
Mississippi.................	34,771	34,139	33,321	32,912	31,758	30,569	29,801	30,563	29,237	27,711	26,574
Missouri.....................	42,300	41,107	39,847	39,851	38,117	36,733	36,425	37,289	35,562	34,144	32,430
Montana.....................	41,809	40,599	39,505	39,822	37,784	35,457	34,318	35,448	33,803	31,809	29,765
Nebraska....................	48,544	48,321	45,858	46,060	44,864	40,518	39,226	40,248	38,082	35,512	34,130
Nevada......................	41,889	40,490	38,885	39,178	37,979	36,818	36,280	38,815	40,137	39,930	38,637
New Hampshire...........	55,905	53,629	51,609	51,826	49,562	47,154	45,742	46,365	45,199	43,763	40,922
New Jersey	59,949	57,728	55,464	55,281	53,573	51,329	50,567	52,330	50,570	48,360	45,354
New Mexico	37,938	36,656	34,724	35,410	34,729	33,109	32,523	33,447	31,703	30,364	28,755
New York....................	58,670	56,683	54,447	53,739	50,778	48,151	46,916	48,296	47,467	44,448	41,457
North Carolina.............	40,759	39,365	37,798	38,596	36,474	35,331	35,840	37,810	36,013	34,112	32,238
North Dakota..............	55,950	57,900	55,687	56,174	48,600	43,660	40,134	41,213	36,325	32,801	31,521
Ohio	43,566	42,155	40,679	40,266	38,814	36,355	35,610	36,681	35,488	34,148	32,523
Oklahoma...................	45,573	45,117	42,673	41,092	38,455	35,911	34,920	38,744	35,133	34,019	31,062
Oregon......................	43,783	41,690	39,498	39,105	37,387	35,692	35,409	37,149	35,858	34,721	32,421
Pennsylvania..............	49,745	47,955	46,113	45,867	44,018	42,002	40,696	41,932	40,302	38,060	36,247
Rhode Island..............	50,018	48,023	46,323	46,182	44,341	42,748	40,936	41,977	40,912	39,106	36,927
South Carolina	38,302	36,860	35,287	35,244	33,803	32,161	31,635	32,877	31,956	30,577	28,958
South Dakota	47,881	45,966	44,612	45,030	44,634	41,064	39,524	41,311	38,729	35,203	33,772
Tennessee	42,094	40,233	38,806	38,771	37,452	35,653	34,635	35,322	34,117	32,950	31,439
Texas........................	46,947	45,755	43,355	43,148	40,812	37,892	36,695	39,534	36,630	35,008	32,793
Utah..........................	39,308	37,644	36,045	35,538	33,702	31,682	31,619	33,932	32,965	31,154	28,759
Vermont	48,587	47,144	45,593	44,892	43,435	40,915	40,221	40,847	38,866	36,944	34,668
Virginia......................	52,052	50,105	48,460	49,294	47,544	45,340	44,232	45,707	44,554	42,654	40,319
Washington................	51,898	50,357	47,778	47,324	44,197	42,195	41,844	44,794	43,192	40,357	37,759
West Virginia..............	36,758	35,778	34,651	34,814	34,000	32,082	31,412	31,273	29,323	28,406	26,593
Wisconsin	45,914	44,406	42,722	42,536	40,749	38,598	38,012	38,873	37,573	36,133	34,173
Wyoming	56,081	56,004	52,677	52,739	49,478	45,449	43,549	48,541	44,719	43,208	38,232

Table A-40.   Personal Income per Capita—*Continued*

Geographic area	Disposable personal income per capita										
	2015	2014	2013	2012	2011	2010	2009	2008	2007	2006	2005
United States	42,085	40,815	39,165	39,460	37,796	36,275	35,624	36,128	34,869	33,600	31,803
Alabama........................	34,377	33,513	32,429	32,395	31,565	30,936	30,069	30,049	29,213	28,137	26,984
Alaska	50,979	49,733	46,822	48,456	47,130	44,863	43,303	43,189	39,623	37,265	35,654
Arizona.........................	35,168	34,276	32,924	32,752	31,656	30,842	31,172	32,169	31,866	30,919	28,864
Arkansas	34,367	33,930	32,496	32,947	30,707	29,131	28,756	28,896	27,849	26,527	25,373
California.......................	45,902	43,851	41,859	42,401	40,282	38,534	37,847	38,368	37,747	36,841	34,550
Colorado	44,232	43,561	41,071	39,824	37,859	35,619	35,814	37,281	36,508	35,143	33,590
Connecticut...................	57,418	56,141	53,921	55,899	54,967	54,342	53,176	51,629	48,106	45,580	42,426
Delaware.......................	42,239	40,212	38,881	38,888	38,966	37,018	37,328	36,832	36,705	36,388	34,739
District of Columbia	62,209	59,860	56,540	57,154	56,871	54,184	52,413	52,861	50,910	48,842	46,174
Florida..........................	39,480	38,317	36,583	37,180	36,826	35,524	34,171	35,685	35,495	34,565	32,376
Georgia	35,664	34,524	33,078	33,157	33,004	31,436	31,306	31,359	31,370	30,728	29,673
Hawaii..........................	43,114	41,686	40,029	40,315	38,912	38,218	37,923	37,620	35,942	34,385	32,560
Idaho...........................	34,556	33,574	32,296	31,586	30,346	29,174	28,940	29,685	28,969	27,893	26,279
Illinois..........................	43,529	42,208	40,587	40,129	38,505	37,402	36,971	37,929	36,893	35,290	33,336
Indiana.........................	37,512	36,350	35,155	35,122	33,568	31,914	31,135	31,344	29,899	29,213	27,823
Iowa.............................	40,938	39,801	38,672	38,321	36,867	34,559	34,152	34,805	32,802	31,023	29,544
Kansas	42,103	41,589	41,115	40,410	38,231	35,516	35,694	36,587	33,444	31,421	28,829
Kentucky	34,481	33,240	31,965	32,218	31,137	30,054	29,476	29,439	28,163	27,283	26,016
Louisiana	38,702	37,778	36,235	36,446	34,920	34,278	33,346	33,906	32,179	30,217	27,057
Maine...........................	38,299	37,062	35,596	35,993	35,168	34,232	33,751	33,103	31,748	30,721	29,338
Maryland.......................	48,239	46,812	45,626	46,807	45,611	44,189	43,323	42,787	40,634	39,651	37,594
Massachusetts	52,524	50,328	48,489	49,509	47,585	46,514	45,439	44,544	42,508	41,397	38,572
Michigan	37,870	36,417	34,849	34,729	33,648	32,045	31,098	31,756	30,853	30,083	29,425
Minnesota	43,710	42,484	40,890	41,489	39,166	37,446	36,404	37,330	35,789	34,356	33,090
Mississippi....................	31,813	31,354	30,575	30,378	29,353	28,245	27,728	27,925	26,806	25,383	24,585
Missouri........................	37,521	36,673	35,610	35,958	34,350	33,459	33,241	33,126	31,580	30,506	29,127
Montana	36,888	36,028	35,293	35,877	34,173	32,387	31,304	31,685	30,040	28,485	26,813
Nebraska......................	43,084	43,235	41,094	41,593	40,727	36,927	35,911	36,050	33,932	31,781	30,816
Nevada.........................	37,500	36,410	34,808	35,575	34,579	33,727	33,251	34,869	35,635	35,444	34,283
New Hampshire..............	50,153	48,307	46,652	47,339	45,034	43,313	42,221	41,687	40,503	39,479	37,048
New Jersey	51,506	49,906	47,927	48,559	46,805	45,454	44,947	44,886	43,204	41,893	39,454
New Mexico	34,396	33,317	31,548	32,510	31,833	30,581	29,916	30,325	28,499	27,378	26,125
New York.......................	48,750	47,373	45,669	46,001	43,131	41,431	40,656	40,051	39,261	37,278	35,276
North Carolina...............	36,146	35,078	33,697	34,811	32,737	32,084	32,701	33,745	31,822	30,272	28,746
North Dakota.................	49,334	51,302	49,336	50,214	43,592	39,835	36,826	37,093	32,799	29,766	28,889
Ohio.............................	38,568	37,481	36,161	36,032	34,700	32,821	32,315	32,453	31,230	30,155	28,810
Oklahoma.....................	41,094	40,857	38,613	37,292	34,821	32,957	32,064	34,758	31,374	30,515	28,024
Oregon.........................	38,076	36,419	34,533	34,681	33,095	31,990	31,894	32,572	31,474	30,301	28,383
Pennsylvania.................	43,792	42,404	40,833	41,017	39,231	37,819	36,776	36,971	35,419	33,670	32,242
Rhode Island.................	44,151	42,568	41,146	41,512	39,630	38,758	37,202	37,198	36,083	34,657	32,849
South Carolina	34,471	33,290	31,826	32,113	30,762	29,540	29,119	29,642	28,567	27,406	26,092
South Dakota	43,360	41,788	40,730	41,393	41,273	38,302	36,965	37,919	35,472	32,268	31,243
Tennessee	38,450	36,892	35,661	35,910	34,678	33,295	32,448	32,393	31,054	30,072	28,923
Texas...........................	41,924	41,038	38,991	39,197	37,012	34,808	33,873	35,287	32,915	31,542	29,752
Utah.............................	34,875	33,535	32,165	31,985	30,441	28,857	28,773	30,284	29,052	27,574	25,633
Vermont........................	43,383	42,282	40,991	40,738	39,282	37,448	36,892	36,501	34,536	33,006	31,134
Virginia.........................	45,339	43,848	42,448	43,678	41,908	40,436	39,593	39,884	38,853	37,288	35,389
Washington...................	46,217	45,086	42,942	43,013	40,047	38,746	38,620	40,408	38,626	36,321	34,216
West Virginia.................	33,068	32,273	31,316	31,670	30,729	29,325	28,747	28,080	26,456	25,767	24,163
Wisconsin	40,565	39,426	37,830	38,042	36,392	34,825	34,352	34,290	33,149	31,927	30,367
Wyoming	49,755	49,861	46,812	46,904	44,819	41,302	39,962	42,752	39,014	37,916	34,187

Table A-41.   Earnings by Industry, 2015

Geographic area	Private earnings[1] (millions dollars)								
	Mining, quarrying, and oil and gas extraction (NAICS 21)	Utilities (2012, NAICS 22)	Construction (2012, NAICS 23)	Manufacturing (2012, NAICS 31–33)	Wholesale trade (2012, NAICS 42)	Retail trade (2012, NAICS 44–45)	Transportation and warehousing (2012, NAICS 48–49)	Information (2012, NAICS 51)	Finance and insurance (2012, NAICS 52)
United States	166,300	86,279	640,255	1,056,023	560,140	656,599	398,984	372,156	750,651
Alabama.......................	713	1,856	7,080	17,527	5,779	7,982	3,835	1,539	6,506
Alaska........................	2,813	374	2,357	975	507	1,690	1,853	571	652
Arizona.......................	1,541	1,625	9,472	14,323	9,068	13,874	5,770	4,213	13,176
Arkansas.....................	648	919	4,041	9,316	3,872	5,008	3,653	1,016	2,889
California.....................	5,608	10,492	77,407	139,691	68,608	86,232	43,262	96,781	79,071
Colorado.....................	10,274	1,388	14,428	12,481	10,188	10,777	9,491	7,459	12,045
Connecticut..................	-4	3,086	8,679	19,535	7,337	9,158	3,641	4,094	23,506
Delaware	(D)	324	1,966	2,284	1,218	2,003	935	431	4,723
District of Columbia	-48	314	1,346	192	711	933	503	2,509	3,127
Florida........................	186	3,449	31,152	26,373	30,829	42,966	19,581	15,836	37,432
Georgia	560	2,657	15,391	27,921	20,493	19,046	14,838	15,118	18,663
Hawaii........................	39	555	3,772	891	1,341	3,022	1,956	740	1,443
Idaho..........................	499	365	2,991	4,757	2,069	3,798	1,379	600	1,753
Illinois........................	1,234	4,144	23,179	52,993	30,695	25,093	22,030	10,511	38,952
Indiana.......................	636	1,866	11,582	41,187	9,782	12,105	8,330	2,666	8,842
Iowa...........................	160	803	7,414	17,341	5,361	5,916	4,109	1,750	8,505
Kansas.......................	2,328	846	5,426	13,673	5,161	5,440	3,658	2,146	5,721
Kentucky.....................	1,193	758	6,819	17,631	5,714	7,064	6,587	1,702	6,350
Louisiana	10,691	1,038	12,397	13,285	6,137	9,052	6,769	1,843	5,156
Maine.........................	16	185	2,660	3,585	1,546	2,921	982	484	2,053
Maryland.....................	118	1,773	14,986	9,709	8,457	12,019	5,588	6,508	12,545
Massachusetts.............	404	1,931	18,055	26,834	14,102	14,880	5,921	11,685	30,895
Michigan.....................	1,038	2,963	15,028	48,123	15,917	17,290	8,430	5,156	13,852
Minnesota	744	1,862	12,258	26,831	12,931	11,333	6,744	4,981	17,052
Mississippi..................	1,199	832	4,054	8,696	2,514	5,122	2,532	809	2,522
Missouri......................	346	1,582	10,392	20,484	11,063	11,619	6,938	4,836	12,443
Montana......................	1,172	378	2,470	1,194	1,263	2,287	1,244	423	1,220
Nebraska.....................	118	461	4,448	6,904	4,107	3,751	5,894	1,336	4,622
Nevada	1,577	641	5,359	2,999	3,034	5,704	3,887	1,342	3,157
New Hampshire.............	39	313	3,560	5,701	3,124	4,012	736	1,395	3,496
New Jersey	183	3,436	19,745	26,169	25,303	20,984	12,960	10,650	28,070
New Mexico	3,007	506	3,092	1,551	1,481	3,560	1,565	865	1,766
New York.....................	1,231	6,146	39,029	39,746	37,423	43,886	20,021	44,186	133,751
North Carolina..............	181	1,936	16,994	33,983	15,814	18,189	8,298	7,565	18,534
North Dakota................	3,077	507	3,472	1,864	2,304	2,176	2,295	498	1,408
Ohio	1,979	2,661	19,967	54,536	20,613	21,528	14,702	6,405	20,923
Oklahoma....................	13,859	1,637	7,767	10,458	4,844	7,253	14,222	1,889	4,403
Oregon........................	123	624	7,527	15,588	6,465	8,320	3,954	3,410	5,591
Pennsylvania................	4,563	3,621	25,604	44,853	21,818	24,509	18,378	23,158	26,726
Rhode Island................	(D)	150	1,946	3,085	1,680	2,221	653	790	2,898
South Carolina.............	105	1,575	7,310	17,801	5,731	8,627	3,699	2,150	6,559
South Dakota...............	73	230	1,980	3,338	1,664	2,253	873	496	2,428
Tennessee	354	449	12,574	24,475	10,495	14,091	10,642	3,554	10,380
Texas.........................	83,695	7,274	75,126	89,523	60,967	57,617	44,831	19,876	59,293
Utah	943	592	6,868	9,066	4,310	7,009	3,657	2,918	5,709
Vermont......................	50	264	1,536	2,202	708	1,491	401	347	830
Virginia.......................	238	1,558	16,746	18,023	10,642	15,749	8,694	7,872	15,307
Washington..................	577	626	16,905	27,591	12,295	19,483	8,367	19,801	10,357
West Virginia................	2,726	629	2,897	3,422	1,557	2,936	1,530	735	1,281
Wisconsin	349	1,759	11,032	34,425	10,108	11,383	6,517	4,271	11,603
Wyoming	3,138	318	1,967	891	991	1,239	1,650	239	468

[1]All data estimates are in current dollars (not adjusted for inflation).
(D) = Data withheld to avoid disclosure or does not meet statistical standards, but the estimates for this item are included in the total.

Table A-41. Earnings by Industry, 2015—*Continued*

Geographic area	Private earnings[1] (million dollars)									Government and government enterprises		
	Real estate and rental and leasing (2012, NAICS 53)	Professional, scientific, and technical services (2012, NAICS 54)	Management of companies and enterprises (2012, NAICS 55)	Administrative and support and waste management and remediation services (2012, NAICS 56)	Educational services (2012, NAICS 61)	Health care and social assistance (2012, NAICS 62)	Arts, entertainment, and recreation (2012, NAICS 71)	Accommodation and food services (2012, NAICS 72)	Other services (except public administration) (2012, NAICS 81)	Federal, civilian	Military	State and local
United States	255,913	1,124,817	297,255	450,698	186,814	1,211,843	129,129	369,235	406,464	315,571	131,358	1,387,378
Alabama	1,696	9,925	1,482	4,376	1,065	13,784	490	3,703	5,260	6,043	1,706	17,597
Alaska	535	1,814	335	889	153	3,364	188	1,126	964	1,659	2,038	5,965
Arizona......................	4,887	14,256	3,266	11,412	3,073	22,423	2,166	7,074	6,679	5,731	2,017	22,845
Arkansas....................	1,312	3,553	4,138	2,471	628	8,890	264	2,140	2,773	1,928	753	10,118
California....................	49,896	191,647	34,061	54,940	23,082	142,057	26,945	51,429	55,442	27,753	14,702	215,903
Colorado	4,148	25,511	5,979	8,112	2,288	18,258	3,052	7,165	7,430	5,831	3,971	22,622
Connecticut.................	3,729	15,151	5,894	5,774	4,694	18,135	1,595	3,778	5,066	1,895	768	19,165
Delaware	1,299	4,115	665	1,343	374	4,539	333	1,048	998	567	430	4,285
District of Columbia	1,165	21,950	676	2,937	3,701	5,205	655	2,693	7,545	30,127	1,357	4,339
Florida.......................	12,497	52,987	11,900	30,499	8,145	69,538	10,717	26,758	25,063	14,282	6,874	62,758
Georgia	5,784	30,183	8,179	15,166	4,705	29,914	2,231	9,838	10,309	10,421	6,825	33,051
Hawaii	1,539	2,791	904	2,323	759	4,879	564	4,459	1,975	3,554	4,988	6,768
Idaho.........................	745	3,137	525	1,743	445	5,027	270	1,255	1,407	1,180	440	5,512
Illinois.......................	11,995	55,664	13,972	21,489	9,833	48,532	5,314	14,901	18,702	8,683	2,344	56,451
Indiana.......................	8,207	10,986	3,721	7,751	2,933	24,297	2,125	5,650	7,716	3,687	688	20,640
Iowa..........................	1,413	4,654	1,877	2,865	1,366	10,337	541	2,618	3,559	1,572	355	14,491
Kansas.......................	2,780	6,932	3,289	3,958	866	10,540	516	2,680	3,120	2,350	2,676	12,304
Kentucky....................	1,741	6,626	2,241	4,735	1,124	14,411	606	4,211	4,377	3,339	3,708	16,099
Louisiana	2,859	10,089	2,255	5,187	1,911	16,111	1,330	5,456	5,379	2,952	2,135	17,481
Maine........................	493	2,558	835	1,466	755	6,090	378	1,540	1,374	1,494	373	5,001
Maryland....................	7,778	31,096	3,409	9,398	4,782	25,412	2,688	6,452	8,383	24,130	3,988	27,887
Massachusetts	4,823	48,813	10,267	10,952	12,524	43,097	4,696	9,389	9,768	5,207	842	34,569
Michigan	7,075	31,485	7,954	13,301	3,434	36,227	2,147	8,498	10,802	5,539	670	35,012
Minnesota	4,341	17,887	10,897	6,542	2,913	26,439	2,057	5,089	7,171	3,168	620	23,645
Mississippi..................	893	2,981	1,032	2,423	722	7,453	282	2,718	2,757	2,422	1,423	11,085
Missouri.....................	3,431	16,245	7,755	7,171	3,157	22,749	2,580	5,803	7,272	5,567	1,889	21,861
Montana.....................	684	1,879	185	813	200	3,921	369	1,273	1,107	1,227	396	4,050
Nebraska....................	1,035	4,007	2,578	2,321	745	7,259	387	1,662	2,274	1,571	795	8,638
Nevada......................	1,396	5,701	3,009	3,957	600	7,794	1,605	13,822	2,876	1,818	1,188	11,012
New Hampshire.............	816	4,617	835	2,145	1,412	6,064	620	1,655	1,888	832	155	5,475
New Jersey	8,919	44,156	14,453	16,528	5,494	39,968	3,222	9,357	11,634	5,589	1,165	48,613
New Mexico	818	5,450	308	1,919	462	6,154	439	2,185	1,829	3,030	1,225	9,684
New York....................	22,572	103,565	24,251	29,948	25,168	94,152	14,793	24,996	29,029	12,645	3,092	129,336
North Carolina..............	5,381	24,031	10,391	12,988	4,760	29,923	3,075	10,188	10,776	6,803	10,230	38,843
North Dakota...............	942	1,600	507	720	139	3,538	108	869	1,056	833	689	3,725
Ohio..........................	5,426	26,853	17,400	15,963	4,979	47,865	3,780	10,802	13,242	8,195	1,635	46,452
Oklahoma...................	2,141	6,636	1,747	4,727	908	12,182	710	3,809	4,158	4,582	2,171	15,708
Oregon......................	2,239	9,739	5,986	4,725	1,673	15,866	1,185	4,792	4,785	2,840	423	17,305
Pennsylvania...............	8,257	42,952	18,617	14,642	14,087	61,835	4,773	11,422	15,918	10,032	1,368	48,811
Rhode Island...............	612	2,674	1,799	1,331	1,387	5,083	470	1,252	1,257	1,200	466	4,399
South Carolina	2,698	8,983	1,493	7,081	1,355	11,846	871	5,586	5,201	3,157	3,555	19,088
South Dakota	509	1,288	534	573	280	4,026	160	948	1,035	992	401	3,341
Tennessee	4,499	14,875	4,079	10,241	2,743	33,001	3,881	7,247	8,437	5,469	761	22,020
Texas........................	20,933	91,911	16,180	44,927	9,057	87,581	6,470	32,163	34,084	21,045	12,504	102,592
Utah..........................	2,382	8,132	1,847	3,720	1,842	7,611	825	2,545	4,144	3,361	710	11,399
Vermont.....................	246	1,629	216	623	643	2,951	198	915	791	697	137	3,003
Virginia......................	5,503	53,226	10,280	13,832	3,929	27,437	2,118	8,615	12,334	25,037	12,703	34,635
Washington.................	6,836	23,420	5,302	9,869	2,437	26,623	2,373	8,101	8,524	7,822	5,873	35,959
West Virginia...............	604	2,467	539	1,494	314	6,624	228	1,660	1,551	2,425	273	6,222
Wisconsin...................	2,756	11,016	7,119	5,959	2,683	23,312	1,655	5,001	6,610	2,633	526	25,285
Wyoming	648	974	89	427	85	1,519	84	894	635	660	337	4,326

Table A-42. Gross Domestic Product per State

Geographic area	Current dollars						Chained (2009 dollars)					
	2015	2014	2013	2012	2011	2010	2015	2014	2013	2012	2011	2010
United States	17,919,651	17,277,548	16,576,808	16,041,243	15,406,002	14,859,772	16,088,249	15,691,181	15,348,044	15,126,281	14,833,679	14,628,165
Alabama.....................	199,656	194,421	190,095	185,878	180,665	174,710	178,566	177,010	176,850	175,420	173,760	171,861
Alaska	52,747	58,253	59,762	60,890	58,759	54,134	49,353	49,653	51,323	53,719	51,004	49,671
Arizona......................	290,903	280,166	270,642	264,693	254,192	245,668	261,350	257,663	253,904	252,545	247,414	243,101
Arkansas	118,907	117,854	114,379	109,226	107,287	102,951	107,986	107,482	106,036	103,170	103,312	101,309
California....................	2,481,348	2,350,807	2,223,958	2,131,199	2,036,297	1,965,886	2,225,413	2,143,167	2,064,596	2,013,611	1,962,926	1,936,487
Colorado....................	313,748	304,943	286,751	272,799	262,719	253,374	286,789	277,952	265,804	257,622	252,256	248,667
Connecticut................	252,930	245,160	240,750	239,462	234,233	234,528	225,507	223,899	224,724	228,212	228,454	232,357
Delaware	68,724	65,419	60,943	60,628	59,937	57,471	60,335	58,742	56,037	57,013	57,919	56,541
District of Columbia	122,146	116,446	111,901	109,685	107,738	103,831	107,515	105,205	103,508	103,733	103,539	101,689
Florida.......................	888,087	833,369	793,089	764,136	741,455	735,098	794,998	764,656	743,137	729,372	723,317	727,658
Georgia	497,944	473,562	452,696	439,058	424,126	412,485	444,908	433,463	422,958	418,312	413,457	408,248
Hawaii	80,376	76,588	74,653	72,532	70,017	68,225	71,501	69,894	69,705	68,913	67,971	67,403
Idaho........................	65,549	63,050	60,969	58,105	56,744	55,258	58,676	57,135	56,117	54,411	54,288	54,389
Illinois	776,882	745,810	722,736	711,370	679,776	653,476	690,187	677,667	670,031	671,493	658,411	645,983
Indiana......................	336,053	324,901	311,332	299,996	291,570	282,259	298,666	294,438	288,323	281,540	280,588	279,068
Iowa.........................	174,030	169,661	162,814	158,246	148,843	141,697	154,734	152,813	148,883	147,665	142,603	139,979
Kansas	149,641	147,493	143,459	140,964	136,884	128,542	134,321	133,302	131,532	131,320	130,493	126,485
Kentucky	193,274	186,344	181,440	177,046	171,835	165,974	171,979	169,572	168,601	166,852	165,712	163,417
Louisiana	239,305	242,785	235,949	241,378	236,248	232,596	208,255	206,285	203,431	209,373	209,151	220,884
Maine	57,297	55,250	53,219	52,580	51,490	51,456	51,087	50,524	49,689	50,106	50,180	50,921
Maryland....................	365,356	349,605	338,806	332,500	324,830	313,952	328,103	321,539	318,255	318,146	316,774	310,702
Massachusetts............	484,943	455,979	441,042	434,098	417,283	402,652	434,957	419,154	414,075	415,832	408,409	399,239
Michigan....................	468,334	447,961	430,538	416,701	399,437	385,021	420,729	414,186	406,631	400,063	392,653	382,885
Minnesota	328,340	316,578	304,358	292,920	282,397	269,937	294,032	288,676	282,031	275,859	272,105	266,346
Mississippi.................	105,819	103,828	102,726	101,351	96,968	95,810	94,271	93,805	94,658	94,880	92,821	94,124
Missouri	294,491	282,874	276,645	266,245	257,225	255,865	262,479	257,987	257,410	252,620	250,034	253,059
Montana....................	45,237	44,448	43,230	42,349	41,187	38,375	40,332	39,560	39,027	38,737	38,458	37,380
Nebraska...................	113,282	111,297	106,735	101,973	99,935	92,231	100,068	99,194	96,327	93,957	94,619	90,713
Nevada.....................	139,724	133,784	128,321	125,440	124,445	121,713	124,669	122,659	120,136	119,411	121,118	120,537
New Hampshire............	73,867	71,153	68,533	66,948	65,214	64,159	66,747	65,804	64,619	64,278	63,952	63,721
New Jersey	567,738	543,787	531,666	514,662	493,343	489,130	507,588	497,708	496,688	489,453	480,101	484,410
New Mexico	93,339	94,731	91,234	90,146	89,261	86,079	86,592	85,119	83,063	83,547	83,457	83,203
New York....................	1,433,531	1,382,933	1,334,930	1,301,041	1,229,743	1,204,688	1,254,859	1,243,065	1,232,755	1,231,862	1,194,300	1,188,749
North Carolina.............	495,402	473,471	454,063	438,350	427,974	416,008	438,673	430,020	421,861	415,761	417,143	412,377
North Dakota..............	55,860	59,308	54,982	52,493	42,164	36,202	50,925	52,309	49,005	47,816	39,117	35,200
Ohio	610,928	591,333	565,256	550,299	528,567	498,989	547,100	537,684	524,119	518,583	510,190	492,419
Oklahoma..................	185,981	194,466	185,103	174,305	163,868	149,913	176,174	172,438	165,962	159,785	151,302	144,003
Oregon......................	217,629	203,606	197,470	196,973	199,929	191,120	201,484	192,119	189,645	192,598	198,298	190,371
Pennsylvania..............	709,762	685,420	661,348	637,896	615,411	596,662	647,041	629,369	618,471	607,172	597,346	589,684
Rhode Island..............	56,052	53,898	52,274	50,997	49,716	49,351	50,082	49,367	48,896	48,631	48,424	48,803
South Carolina	201,005	190,773	181,374	174,567	170,193	164,106	179,298	174,880	170,048	166,858	166,389	162,840
South Dakota	47,244	45,588	44,668	43,056	42,253	38,176	41,022	39,972	39,694	39,189	39,548	37,228
Tennessee	315,857	299,158	288,114	278,298	263,175	252,478	281,481	274,039	269,543	265,211	257,138	250,261
Texas........................	1,630,082	1,627,865	1,532,855	1,437,893	1,344,733	1,243,398	1,509,819	1,440,273	1,373,914	1,310,522	1,240,117	1,197,006
Utah	147,503	140,296	133,264	128,018	124,031	117,714	130,885	126,526	122,676	119,739	118,254	115,177
Vermont.....................	30,038	29,259	28,599	28,195	27,676	26,633	26,996	26,890	26,827	26,963	27,027	26,398
Virginia......................	481,084	460,151	449,502	441,144	429,174	420,862	432,061	423,576	422,530	422,269	419,724	416,903
Washington.................	445,413	423,795	404,540	388,922	370,149	359,694	398,504	386,871	376,464	368,474	358,185	355,228
West Virginia...............	74,321	74,148	72,120	70,969	70,945	67,255	67,895	66,987	66,296	65,925	66,935	65,581
Wisconsin	302,076	291,754	279,996	272,420	262,463	252,875	270,636	267,637	261,810	259,863	256,396	251,086
Wyoming	39,864	42,021	40,979	40,201	41,499	39,103	35,981	36,016	35,421	35,054	36,326	36,469

(X) = Not applicable.
[1]Per capita personal income (or disposable personal income) is total (disposable) personal income divided by total midyear population.
[2]Constant dollar estimates are computed using the national implicit price deflator for personal consumption expenditures from the Bureau of Economic Analysis. Any regional differences in the rate of inflation are not reflected in these constant dollar estimates.

Table A-43.   Science and Engineering Indicators

Geographic area	Employment 2006–2010[1]			Science & Engineering doctorates awarded, 2014[2]		R&D obligations, 2014 ($ millions)[3]	Total R&D performance, 2014 ($ millions)	State R&D expenditures, 2015 ($ thousands)
	Engineers	Life and physical scientists	Computer specialists	Number	Rank			
United States	2,269,000	776,935	3,569,860	40,588	(X)	110,914	451,631	(X)
Alabama	36,580	7,490	37,370	491	25	4,484	4,616	24,487
Alaska	6,500	3,900	5,059	44	52	137	289	11,258
Arizona........................	51,905	9,315	69,980	644	21	1,606	6,936	14,942
Arkansas	11,360	4,365	18,285	161	40	191	636	16,643
California....................	324,605	108,730	480,745	4,984	1	15,799	114,845	500,072
Colorado	53,190	16,285	91,255	757	18	3,611	6,775	16,321
Connecticut.................	32,445	11,805	51,620	564	23	2,287	10,219	55,817
Delaware	5,735	4,720	10,220	174	38	130	2,732	2,200
District of Columbia	2,575	3,145	13,400	386	29	3,980	3,935	3,216
Florida........................	99,690	24,340	162,295	1,683	7	2,448	9,009	191,599
Georgia	55,840	18,800	111,930	1,130	11	1,253	6,881	10,053
Hawaii	7,345	3,100	10,575	128	44	326	639	11,521
Idaho..........................	12,150	5,620	13,725	103	46	598	2,130	12,936
Illinois........................	86,855	28,240	162,780	1,759	6	2,369	15,964	30,817
Indiana	48,825	15,430	50,635	1,088	13	771	7,343	9,987
Iowa...........................	20,155	7,730	30,304	545	24	512	3,003	11,278
Kansas	22,175	6,325	29,385	350	32	187	2,510	5,469
Kentucky	21,885	6,035	28,420	356	30	297	1,717	17,256
Louisiana	27,695	9,825	19,970	440	26	285	1,120	32,175
Maine.........................	8,304	3,500	10,785	62	50	131	596	12,610
Maryland.....................	54,915	32,455	138,360	1,066	14	16,890	20,211	24,853
Massachusetts.............	65,295	38,400	119,985	2,197	4	6,269	27,945	22,665
Michigan	110,605	19,635	90,940	1,458	8	1,853	19,764	12,676
Minnesota	46,035	15,795	83,320	1,000	15	947	8,244	21,456
Mississippi..................	13,340	4,670	12,500	258	36	590	1,125	781
Missouri......................	31,645	14,220	62,485	645	20	1,039	7,957	9,806
Montana	4,863	4,085	6,510	85	49	171	464	10,363
Nebraska.....................	8,985	4,565	21,370	260	35	234	1,094	5,475
Nevada	14,235	4,275	17,185	140	42	510	817	3,107
New Hampshire............	16,845	3,530	23,480	160	41	336	2,424	1,607
New Jersey	61,275	31,785	154,755	834	16	1,968	15,370	33,756
New Mexico	18,340	7,875	17,620	229	37	3,714	5,816	52,303
New York.....................	99,870	38,540	203,455	3,125	2	4,581	20,820	365,552
North Carolina..............	55,380	24,890	96,870	1,327	10	1,881	11,343	34,002
North Dakota................	3,870	2,490	5,795	123	45	80	523	9,612
Ohio	86,670	24,445	117,575	1,418	9	2,454	12,005	94,299
Oklahoma....................	21,670	7,210	28,860	353	31	317	1,113	29,953
Oregon........................	30,745	11,150	44,480	343	33	602	7,279	31,990
Pennsylvania................	87,450	38,900	137,595	1,884	5	3,695	14,898	75,024
Rhode Island................	8,090	2,850	12,080	263	34	555	1,298	2,595
South Carolina	33,410	7,560	31,720	410	27	476	2,034	27,419
South Dakota	4,064	2,065	6,530	93	47	69	271	4,212
Tennessee	37,105	11,230	46,810	620	22	2,023	4,245	3,829
Texas..........................	190,865	54,080	269,395	2,919	3	4,678	22,467	185,094
Utah	20,634	6,550	36,105	410	27	1,222	3,669	38,168
Vermont......................	5,534	1,428	7,420	62	50	116	422	2,199
Virginia.......................	72,870	19,795	178,450	1,117	12	7,652	10,489	43,616
Washington..................	71,475	22,295	115,340	737	19	3,565	18,987	36,919
West Virginia...............	7,790	3,785	9,635	134	43	208	604	11,482
Wisconsin....................	45,250	15,160	61,595	815	17	701	5,789	14,518
Wyoming	4,085	2,545	2,960	89	48	46	123	5,161

(X) = Not available.

[1]The employment data represent the state of residence; technicians are included.

[2]Does not include health fields. Data are classified by the state where the doctorate holder resides.

[3]Research and Development. National totals may include data for outlying areas, offices abroad, and/or undistributed funds and may differ from the sum of state totals.

Table A-44.   Employment Establishment Changes by Firm Size and State, 2010–2011

State	Establishments in 2010			Establishment Births			Establishment Deaths			Net Change		
	Total	< 500	500+	Total	< 500	500+	Total	< 500	500+	Total	< 500	500+
United States	6,634,115	5,492,126	1,141,989	650,029	561,200	88,829	688,184	606,443	81,741	-38,155	-45,243	7,088
Alabama	92,457	73,624	18,833	7,433	6,280	1,153	9,053	7,713	1,340	-1,620	-1,433	-187
Alaska	17,036	14,461	2,575	1,739	1,449	290	1,646	1,496	150	93	-47	140
Arizona........................	116,685	91,969	24,716	13,278	11,162	2,116	14,678	12,527	2,151	-1,400	-1,365	-35
Arkansas	59,809	49,106	10,703	5,202	4,440	762	5,829	5,136	693	-627	-696	69
California.....................	753,449	639,416	114,033	81,677	72,350	9,327	82,925	74,573	8,352	-1,248	-2,223	975
Colorado	131,759	110,229	21,530	15,141	13,233	1,908	15,814	14,025	1,789	-673	-792	119
Connecticut.................	81,127	67,509	13,618	6,413	5,405	1,008	7,580	6,563	1,017	-1,167	-1,158	-9
Delaware	21,727	17,147	4,580	2,090	1,648	442	2,245	1,816	429	-155	-168	13
District of Columbia	19,867	15,052	4,815	1,901	1,330	571	1,819	1,302	517	82	28	54
Florida.........................	429,374	356,458	72,916	56,394	50,412	5,982	55,673	49,898	5,775	721	514	207
Georgia	193,908	154,866	39,042	20,332	17,293	3,039	22,250	19,366	2,884	-1,918	-2,073	155
Hawaii.........................	29,466	24,685	4,781	2,396	1,964	432	2,758	2,386	372	-362	-422	60
Idaho...........................	38,216	33,104	5,112	3,713	3,353	360	4,791	4,407	384	-1,078	-1,054	-24
Illinois.........................	277,251	230,619	46,632	26,517	23,007	3,510	27,617	24,400	3,217	-1,100	-1,393	293
Indiana........................	132,424	106,486	25,938	10,854	9,015	1,839	12,171	10,539	1,632	-1,317	-1,524	207
Iowa............................	73,421	61,921	11,500	5,381	4,635	746	6,007	5,283	724	-626	-648	22
Kansas	67,992	56,612	11,380	5,634	4,666	968	6,413	5,689	724	-779	-1,023	244
Kentucky	83,293	66,457	16,836	6,852	5,788	1,064	7,728	6,807	921	-876	-1,019	143
Louisiana	95,586	78,551	17,035	8,259	6,871	1,388	8,645	7,625	1,020	-386	-754	368
Maine..........................	35,323	30,645	4,678	3,092	2,734	358	3,612	3,270	342	-520	-536	16
Maryland......................	121,269	99,893	21,376	11,238	9,142	2,096	12,299	10,600	1,699	-1,061	-1,458	397
Massachusetts.............	152,382	126,829	25,553	13,139	11,131	2,008	13,528	11,759	1,769	-389	-628	239
Michigan......................	194,989	162,162	32,827	17,608	15,272	2,336	18,649	16,466	2,183	-1,041	-1,194	153
Minnesota	127,461	107,462	19,999	11,321	9,874	1,447	11,821	10,582	1,239	-500	-708	208
Mississippi..................	55,114	44,348	10,766	4,616	3,838	778	5,093	4,465	628	-477	-627	150
Missouri.......................	135,512	111,284	24,228	12,566	10,848	1,718	14,691	13,232	1,459	-2,125	-2,384	259
Montana.......................	31,269	27,846	3,423	2,951	2,709	242	3,467	3,228	239	-516	-519	3
Nebraska......................	47,001	39,750	7,251	3,868	3,285	583	4,142	3,646	496	-274	-361	87
Nevada	52,008	41,381	10,627	6,551	5,681	870	6,799	6,026	773	-248	-345	97
New Hampshire.............	33,905	28,388	5,517	2,782	2,354	428	3,250	2,851	399	-468	-497	29
New Jersey	203,906	174,469	29,437	20,432	18,010	2,422	22,162	19,777	2,385	-1,730	-1,767	37
New Mexico	40,320	33,016	7,304	3,726	3,109	617	4,127	3,647	480	-401	-538	137
New York......................	458,663	401,767	56,896	49,755	44,764	4,991	47,937	43,465	4,472	1,818	1,299	519
North Carolina..............	197,032	159,014	38,018	18,497	15,756	2,741	21,008	18,342	2,666	-2,511	-2,586	75
North Dakota................	19,510	17,007	2,503	1,892	1,640	252	1,582	1,423	159	310	217	93
Ohio	231,674	184,211	47,463	17,917	14,753	3,164	20,610	16,935	3,675	-2,693	-2,182	-511
Oklahoma....................	82,447	68,345	14,102	7,301	6,381	920	7,825	7,052	773	-524	-671	147
Oregon........................	96,253	82,496	13,757	9,377	8,418	959	10,147	9,218	929	-770	-800	30
Pennsylvania................	272,046	222,542	49,504	22,035	18,170	3,865	22,929	19,591	3,338	-894	-1,421	527
Rhode Island................	25,265	21,691	3,574	2,232	1,907	325	2,513	2,225	288	-281	-318	37
South Carolina.............	93,323	74,379	18,944	8,285	7,048	1,237	9,816	8,604	1,212	-1,531	-1,556	25
South Dakota	23,067	20,465	2,602	1,867	1,697	170	2,036	1,896	140	-169	-199	30
Tennessee	121,983	94,972	27,011	10,390	8,708	1,682	12,243	10,322	1,921	-1,853	-1,614	-239
Texas..........................	476,969	379,063	97,906	50,157	42,448	7,709	48,773	42,139	6,634	1,384	309	1,075
Utah............................	59,468	49,925	9,543	7,195	6,479	716	7,317	6,645	672	-122	-166	44
Vermont.......................	19,044	16,959	2,085	1,537	1,399	138	1,844	1,674	170	-307	-275	-32
Virginia........................	175,246	140,313	34,933	16,909	13,643	3,266	18,120	15,323	2,797	-1,211	-1,680	469
Washington..................	156,440	132,876	23,564	15,730	13,866	1,864	18,268	16,428	1,840	-2,538	-2,562	24
West Virginia................	35,917	28,781	7,136	2,700	2,175	525	3,158	2,731	427	-458	-556	98
Wisconsin	126,560	105,914	20,646	9,332	8,053	1,279	11,011	9,728	1,283	-1,679	-1,675	-4
Wyoming	17,902	15,661	2,241	1,825	1,607	218	1,765	1,602	163	60	5	55

Notes: Longitudinal data for establishments active (payroll) in the first quarter of the year. (Establishments with no employment in the first quarter were excluded.)

Table A-45. Employer Firms and Nonemployer Establishments

Geographic area	Firms (thousands)		By employment-size of enterprise, 2012		Employment, 2012 (thousands)		By employment-size of enterprise		Annual payroll, 2012 (million dollars)		By employment-size of enterprise		Nonemployer establishments[1] Number (thousands)		Receipts (millions)	
	2012	2010	Fewer than 20 employees	Fewer than 500 employees	Total	Fewer than 20 employees	Fewer than 500 employees	Total	Fewer than 20 employees	Fewer than 500 employees			2014	2010	2014	2010
United States	5,726.2	5,734.5	5,130.3	5,707.9	115,938	20,409	56,063	5,414,256	753,326	2,267,536			23,836.9	22,110.6	1,115,921	950,814
Alabama......................	73.7	75.5	62.1	71.3	1,586	275	764	61,285	8,716	26,700			318.1	320.6	13,067	12,111
Alaska.........................	16.7	16.5	14.5	16.1	258	57	138	13,986	2,650	6,638			55.8	53.3	2,660	2,412
Arizona.......................	101.2	102.2	86.8	98.3	2,134	332	955	90,839	12,016	35,353			438.4	396.0	19,883	16,864
Arkansas....................	50.4	51.1	43.0	48.7	979	180	477	35,634	5,348	14,799			196.6	192.0	8,269	7,499
California....................	701.9	690.5	624.7	696.2	12,953	2,423	6,472	700,102	104,087	296,673			3,117.6	2,814.4	162,457	138,315
Colorado	126.5	125.8	111.4	123.4	2,036	392	992	97,691	14,937	40,929			468.7	426.4	22,481	18,688
Connecticut................	71.6	72.7	60.9	69.5	1,464	258	720	84,562	11,347	35,091			269.8	255.8	15,820	14,243
Delaware	19.1	19.7	15.3	17.7	364	62	168	18,315	2,356	7,090			59.1	53.9	3,532	2,792
District of Columbia	17.1	16.9	12.4	15.8	483	56	229	33,864	3,745	14,437			55.0	46.0	2,677	2,230
Florida........................	409.4	400.8	372.8	405.0	6,932	1,255	3,000	280,305	44,317	111,708			1,948.4	1,686.1	84,607	68,162
Georgia	168.6	170.2	146.1	164.7	3,391	554	1,501	149,291	19,362	56,597			849.0	771.2	33,493	28,043
Hawaii........................	24.9	25.4	21.0	24.0	492	89	258	19,079	3,155	9,244			102.5	92.1	4,858	4,066
Idaho..........................	36.0	36.7	31.3	34.8	494	118	278	17,605	3,525	8,639			118.9	112.3	5,070	4,269
Illinois........................	253.1	253.6	219.9	248.7	5,120	837	2,417	255,694	33,561	106,325			955.2	903.0	41,275	35,305
Indiana.......................	109.1	111.0	92.1	106.1	2,513	399	1,174	99,677	12,397	40,758			399.2	380.1	16,106	13,839
Iowa...........................	62.7	63.4	53.5	60.9	1,294	222	638	48,946	6,667	21,944			205.9	201.4	9,021	7,607
Kansas.......................	58.2	59.2	48.9	56.1	1,134	204	595	56,039	6,562	21,124			193.9	183.6	8,603	7,326
Kentucky	67.9	69.6	57.1	65.5	1,481	247	687	56,039	7,371	22,735			277.7	272.5	11,596	10,454
Louisiana	80.9	81.3	68.1	78.7	1,644	300	892	68,864	10,168	33,343			357.8	340.6	15,879	14,084
Maine.........................	33.1	33.8	28.9	32.1	487	108	279	18,486	3,504	9,565			111.8	110.4	4,922	4,477
Maryland....................	107.3	108.2	91.2	104.6	2,152	377	1,091	105,889	15,269	48,752			473.5	424.2	20,213	17,833
Massachusetts.............	138.4	137.4	119.0	135.4	3,036	489	1,404	173,247	21,577	69,431			502.3	472.5	26,791	23,388
Michigan	172.1	174.3	149.4	169.1	3,468	624	1,756	152,248	22,014	68,293			696.7	679.8	29,278	25,659
Minnesota	117.1	117.7	100.5	114.5	2,481	390	1,187	116,324	13,944	46,165			394.7	381.8	17,982	15,550
Mississippi..................	44.7	45.8	37.9	43.1	896	165	430	30,897	4,688	13,386			209.3	196.2	8,307	7,299
Missouri......................	113.7	117.8	97.4	110.8	2,320	393	1,109	95,331	12,457	39,051			397.7	390.2	17,198	15,298
Montana.....................	31.4	31.4	27.9	30.6	344	103	232	11,886	3,019	7,293			86.2	83.7	3,852	3,324
Nebraska....................	42.0	42.0	35.8	40.6	818	144	391	31,736	4,347	13,292			129.5	123.9	5,597	4,653
Nevada.......................	47.4	47.4	39.7	45.3	1,015	152	414	40,127	5,988	15,908			199.5	177.2	10,288	8,796
New Hampshire............	30.5	31.0	25.7	29.3	549	108	284	24,055	4,177	11,796			103.3	102.8	5,762	5,164
New Jersey	192.7	193.7	169.4	189.5	3,440	657	1,736	189,911	27,186	79,670			653.3	604.7	37,998	32,500
New Mexico	35.0	35.7	29.3	33.5	603	123	329	22,380	3,945	11,216			121.3	120.5	4,828	4,434
New York.....................	450.2	444.9	404.4	445.9	7,557	1,468	3,859	451,847	61,318	188,267			1,674.3	1,575.8	84,227	71,776
North Carolina.............	167.1	168.9	144.9	163.6	3,352	583	1,556	137,929	18,815	53,931			706.5	640.7	28,823	24,682
North Dakota...............	19.5	18.2	16.2	18.7	331	67	194	14,705	2,383	7,535			53.6	47.8	2,847	2,021
Ohio...........................	186.9	190.2	158.2	183.1	4,548	707	2,124	191,070	23,458	77,255			757.8	730.4	32,875	28,739
Oklahoma...................	72.0	72.0	61.8	70.0	1,305	252	694	53,518	8,291	24,975			275.0	263.0	13,180	11,313
Oregon.......................	87.7	88.0	76.7	85.6	1,364	307	757	58,478	9,710	27,194			269.9	258.8	12,598	11,019
Pennsylvania...............	229.4	231.2	197.0	225.4	5,169	851	2,445	231,750	29,200	94,202			799.7	762.4	38,649	34,263
Rhode Island...............	24.0	24.6	20.3	23.0	403	81	222	17,287	2,976	8,681			75.2	71.9	3,382	3,113
South Carolina	77.6	78.9	66.4	75.2	1,549	275	729	56,666	8,340	23,536			319.0	295.6	13,344	11,400
South Dakota	21.5	21.6	18.3	20.7	337	75	199	11,769	2,193	6,351			63.4	60.2	2,992	2,376
Tennessee	96.3	98.0	80.7	93.3	2,344	356	1,024	96,088	12,034	38,228			487.3	465.5	22,034	19,008
Texas.........................	404.1	394.4	349.1	398.6	9,351	1,463	4,276	446,679	56,759	176,711			2,150.7	1,934.5	107,537	85,935
Utah...........................	58.6	57.7	50.5	56.6	1,071	185	504	43,318	6,094	18,684			209.6	192.0	9,598	8,005
Vermont......................	18.2	18.6	15.7	17.5	265	62	156	9,541	2,030	5,635			60.2	59.9	2,536	2,304
Virginia.......................	147.9	149.3	127.2	144.6	3,089	525	1,453	150,556	19,725	63,186			560.6	510.3	24,548	21,157
Washington.................	143.1	144.4	126.1	140.3	2,362	492	1,230	122,692	17,812	51,380			430.7	405.3	21,011	18,134
West Virginia...............	28.6	29.6	23.9	27.4	580	109	298	21,205	2,992	9,318			89.0	90.1	3,391	3,153
Wisconsin...................	108.4	110.4	91.6	105.9	2,389	396	1,210	99,666	12,681	43,458			340.0	331.7	15,613	13,829
Wyoming	17.8	17.6	15.4	17.1	214	61	134	9,589	2,114	5,061			47.6	45.6	2,367	1,901

[1]Nonemployer business defined as a firm with no payroll or paid employees.

Table A-46.   Private Nonfarm Establishments, Employment, and Payroll

Geographic area	Establishments[1]							Employment[1,2] (thousands)						Annual payroll[1] (billion dollars)	
	2014	2010	Net change, 2010–2014	By employment-size class of establishment, 2014				2014	2010	By employment-size class of establishment, 2014				2014	2010
				Under 20	20 to 99	100 to 499	500 or more			Under 20	20 to 99	100 to 499	500 or more		
United States	7,563,085	7,396,628	166,457	6,491,954	890,701	160,987	19,443	121,080	111,970	29,379	35,494	30,460	25,747	5,940	4,941
Alabama......................	97,714	99,251	-1,537	82,819	12,486	2,137	272	1,604	1,568	415	490	411	289	64	57
Alaska	20,752	19,985	767	18,318	2,034	362	38	267	255	79	80	72	36	15	13
Arizona.......................	134,434	131,849	2,585	114,237	16,832	2,971	394	2,241	2,065	517	671	558	495	97	84
Arkansas	64,670	65,158	-488	55,450	7,791	1,264	165	992	965	265	306	247	175	38	34
California....................	889,646	849,875	39,771	766,472	103,404	17,668	2,102	13,839	12,536	3,352	4,130	3,286	3,070	797	636
Colorado	158,064	151,973	6,091	138,318	16,635	2,798	313	2,181	1,955	567	654	528	433	112	89
Connecticut................	88,555	89,234	-679	75,406	10,839	2,105	205	1,485	1,437	358	426	392	310	88	80
Delaware	24,312	24,290	22	3,099	2,896	501	77	392	359	93	114	96	89	21	17
District of Columbia	22,210	21,502	708	18,057	3,309	757	87	495	463	88	136	150	120	37	31
Florida.......................	519,875	491,150	28,725	460,340	49,286	9,140	1,109	7,442	6,627	1,806	1,972	1,694	1,969	313	253
Georgia	220,605	217,099	3,506	188,766	26,326	4,909	604	3,551	3,315	834	1,050	923	744	164	138
Hawaii........................	31,801	31,939	-138	27,063	4,007	639	92	519	479	131	165	123	101	21	18
Idaho..........................	43,816	43,450	366	38,885	4,259	595	77	530	488	170	163	109	88	20	16
Illinois........................	316,120	314,171	1,949	271,240	36,661	7,268	951	5,312	4,980	1,181	1,477	1,376	1,279	273	236
Indiana.......................	143,826	145,019	-1,193	120,825	18,908	3,621	472	2,603	2,400	598	762	683	560	107	90
Iowa...........................	80,466	80,801	-335	68,845	9,705	1,703	213	1,316	1,253	327	383	337	269	53	45
Kansas	74,055	74,301	-246	63,113	9,121	1,641	180	1,178	1,127	298	362	311	207	50	43
Kentucky	91,418	90,771	647	77,546	11,442	2,166	264	1,535	1,457	377	452	417	290	60	52
Louisiana	104,976	103,365	1,611	88,577	13,814	2,330	255	1,718	1,600	436	551	432	298	77	62
Maine.........................	40,369	40,571	-202	35,693	3,987	631	58	493	481	154	155	118	66	20	17
Maryland.....................	136,501	134,579	1,922	115,657	17,448	3,089	307	2,217	2,076	533	702	571	410	114	98
Massachusetts............	173,575	169,790	3,785	147,679	21,073	4,316	507	3,087	2,929	686	849	817	735	185	158
Michigan.....................	218,282	219,119	-837	186,579	26,263	4,842	598	3,620	3,288	882	1,047	921	769	166	139
Minnesota	147,483	145,464	2,019	125,329	18,118	3,600	436	2,566	2,358	569	727	689	581	126	106
Mississippi.................	58,541	59,300	-759	50,350	6,955	1,095	141	912	882	249	273	214	175	33	29
Missouri.....................	153,945	149,903	4,042	132,334	18,133	3,091	387	2,405	2,293	587	718	594	506	104	89
Montana......................	36,791	36,011	780	33,174	3,217	374	26	364	338	138	123	67	36	13	11
Nebraska	52,991	51,886	1,105	45,625	6,213	1,026	127	851	769	209	241	200	201	35	28
Nevada.......................	61,625	59,207	2,418	52,804	7,276	1,328	217	1,090	1,003	241	287	252	310	44	38
New Hampshire............	37,396	37,452	-56	32,161	4,394	768	73	563	563	153	172	145	94	27	24
New Jersey	230,600	228,937	1,663	200,250	24,948	4,843	559	3,527	3,367	864	1,000	916	746	203	179
New Mexico	43,748	44,221	-473	37,648	5,241	798	61	603	600	182	203	150	68	24	21
New York....................	536,890	519,504	17,386	473,300	52,466	9,679	1,445	7,858	7,266	1,932	2,088	1,876	1,963	493	418
North Carolina.............	219,897	218,104	1,793	187,503	27,344	4,515	535	3,560	3,235	872	1,095	856	738	155	125
North Dakota...............	24,698	21,832	2,866	21,019	3,128	512	39	361	295	98	125	97	40	17	11
Ohio...........................	250,535	253,491	-2,956	208,943	34,065	6,769	758	4,637	4,352	1,053	1,370	1,268	946	204	175
Oklahoma...................	92,430	90,050	2,380	79,176	11,264	1,800	190	1,360	1,241	366	441	339	215	58	46
Oregon.......................	109,875	107,397	2,478	96,021	11,828	1,841	185	1,444	1,351	442	457	341	204	66	54
Pennsylvania...............	298,297	297,023	1,274	252,301	37,938	7,187	871	5,255	4,976	1,217	1,523	1,371	1,144	249	212
Rhode Island...............	28,132	28,521	-389	24,269	3,237	564	62	422	399	109	128	102	83	20	17
South Carolina	102,297	102,045	252	87,371	12,539	2,132	255	1,617	1,503	417	493	406	301	62	53
South Dakota	26,198	25,622	576	22,906	2,828	424	40	348	329	104	111	82	50	13	11
Tennessee	131,504	131,582	-78	109,699	17,872	3,522	411	2,453	2,264	554	713	673	513	104	88
Texas.........................	557,721	522,146	35,575	467,933	74,174	13,957	1,657	9,920	8,785	2,238	2,969	2,663	2,050	501	387
Utah...........................	73,375	68,820	4,555	63,536	8,196	1,444	199	1,148	1,021	271	323	279	276	48	38
Vermont......................	21,041	21,451	-410	18,687	2,022	294	38	261	264	83	78	53	47	10	9
Virginia......................	195,639	193,042	2,597	166,025	24,870	4,247	497	3,161	2,998	778	992	810	581	159	139
Washington.................	179,012	175,914	3,098	156,371	19,113	3,191	337	2,529	2,327	694	754	591	490	141	111
West Virginia...............	37,354	38,676	-1,322	31,946	4,590	733	85	575	560	166	180	140	90	22	19
Wisconsin	138,221	139,554	-1,333	115,936	18,278	3,557	450	2,450	2,321	563	737	671	479	107	91
Wyoming	20,807	20,231	576	18,614	1,928	243	22	220	205	81	72	46	20	10	8

[1]Data provided by County Business Patterns is based on the North American Industry Classification System (NAICS). Data for 2005 is based on NAICS 2002. Data for 2010 is based on NAICS 2007.
[2]Employment is measured in March.

Table A-47.   Foreign Direct Investment in the United States and U.S. Exports

Geographic area	U.S. Foreign Majority-owned Affiliates[1] Number of affiliates with assets, sales, or net income greater than $20 million in 2013[4]	Employment of affiliates[5] (thousands) 2012	2013	2014	U.S. exports[2] (million dollars) 2015 Total exports	Rank	Percent change 2010–2015	2010	U.S. agriculture exports[3] (million dollars) 2015	2010	2005
United States	4,811	5,889.0	6,181.4	6,370.9	1,504,914	X	17.7	1,278,115	133,052	115,820	63,182
Alabama	578	84.8	91.7	92.7	19,370	23	24.9	15,505	1,237	1,154	803
Alaska	158	15.1	16.5	17.5	4,675	39	12.6	4,152	17	12	10
Arizona	776	84.5	86.8	88.6	22,563	19	44.2	15,652	3,110	3,180	661
Arkansas	459	42.4	44.8	46.4	5,874	35	13.9	5,156	3,110	3,180	1,925
California.....................	2,082	618.2	647.2	665.0	165,367	2	15.4	143,269	22,547	15,456	9,735
Colorado	812	83.7	87.9	90.8	7,978	33	19.6	6,670	1,613	1,511	825
Connecticut.................	733	102.9	101.0	99.4	15,256	25	-4.8	16,033	244	215	153
Delaware	359	27.6	26.2	28.3	5,403	37	8.8	4,965	252	241	140
District of Columbia	321	24.2	23.2	24.0	1,089	51	-27.4	1,501	X	X	X
Florida........................	1,230	251.7	262.7	266.5	53,844	6	-2.5	55,227	3,540	2,981	2,119
Georgia	1,131	196.0	210.6	217.5	38,548	11	34.3	28,704	2,888	2,650	1,579
Hawaii	282	33.7	34.6	37.0	1,896	47	176.7	685	384	312	187.112
Idaho..........................	335	15.3	16.1	16.1	4,296	40	-16.6	5,150	1,877	1,483	810
Illinois........................	1,391	279.2	293.0	292.6	63,402	5	27.4	49,767	7,999	7,392	3,637
Indiana.......................	814	158.3	161.2	170.8	33,653	12	17.4	28,670	4,564	4,270	1,874.133
Iowa...........................	443	52.9	55.4	55.8	13,114	28	20.4	10,895	9,971	9,287	4,342
Kansas	525	60.5	71.3	70.6	10,686	30	7.6	9,927	4,143	4,633	2,179
Kentucky	649	94.8	101.9	107.5	28,053	17	45.2	19,320	2,117	1,525	1,313
Louisiana	527	61.7	72.4	74.3	49,183	9	19.0	41,348	1,528	1,524	776
Maine.........................	344	33.9	31.9	32.5	2,724	45	-13.5	3,148	261	241	132
Maryland.....................	729	104.8	101.6	103.8	10,030	31	-1.4	10,168	647	562	314
Massachusetts.............	939	195.3	203.6	216.0	25,206	18	-4.0	26,256	176	200	122
Michigan.....................	1,006	192.1	209.0	217.1	53,171	7	19.5	44,504	2,802	2,345	1,140
Minnesota	741	101.3	103.0	106.1	19,988	22	5.6	18,929	6,281	6,080	2,693
Mississippi..................	401	35.8	34.2	34.0	10,786	29	30.5	8,267	1,867	1,796	1,091
Missouri......................	685	89.9	100.6	104.3	13,617	26	5.4	12,920	3,605	3,472	1,680
Montana......................	232	8.2	7.5	6.9	1,386	49	-2.5	1,422	1,199	1,072	628
Nebraska	336	28.0	30.8	32.5	6,556	34	13.0	5,804	6,385	5,283	2,456
Nevada	527	41.0	44.5	45.8	8,658	32	46.5	5,911	138	111	62
New Hampshire............	462	40.1	41.4	42.5	4,007	41	-8.3	4,368	82	66	38
New Jersey	1,113	228.6	235.2	244.8	32,076	14	-0.2	32,156	505	401	294
New Mexico	329	20.5	22.4	22.4	3,772	43	141.5	1,562	756	687	372
New York.....................	1,626	409.3	416.8	428.0	80,060	4	18.3	67,686	1,467	1,226	577
North Carolina..............	1,004	207.5	232.0	242.7	30,018	16	21.0	24,817	3,542	3,396	2,104
North Dakota...............	215	15.5	14.6	13.4	3,863	42	53.2	2,522	4,068	3,784	1,735
Ohio...........................	1,109	229.4	243.6	253.0	50,694	8	22.3	41,437	3,641	3,390	1,644
Oklahoma....................	505	46.8	48.7	49.7	5,258	38	-1.9	5,360	1,523	1,542	998
Oregon........................	631	47.8	50.7	52.8	20,084	21	13.6	17,683	1,881	1,353	1,006
Pennsylvania................	1,075	279.6	287.6	299.7	39,403	10	13.1	34,826	2,040	1,610	849
Rhode Island...............	323	28.5	28.9	29.7	2,125	46	9.2	1,946	35	32	20
South Carolina	694	118.5	128.7	131.9	30,861	15	51.9	20,316	793.5	813.7	486.1
South Dakota	217	10.5	12.9	13.0	1,405	48	11.2	1,263	3,719.9	2,968.6	1,428.4
Tennessee	788	129.3	135.5	139.4	32,431	13	25.1	25,924	1,464.3	1,241.3	778.6
Texas..........................	1,641	492.4	522.2	544.8	251,087	1	21.5	206,643	6,063.9	6,341.3	3,689.9
Utah...........................	497	35.5	37.1	38.0	13,282	27	-2.1	13,572	420.1	323.6	201.2
Vermont......................	201	12.1	10.9	11.6	3,176	44	-27.4	4,376	196.0	140.4	60.0
Virginia.......................	818	155.9	171.3	175.8	18,137	24	6.1	17,090	1,052.7	882.5	576.0
Washington..................	866	98.8	103.6	105.6	86,353	3	62.2	53,244	3,794.2	2,801.3	1,603.8
West Virginia...............	317	31.4	28.1	29.0	5,722	36	-11.0	6,427	143.1	115.6	62.5
Wisconsin	674	84.8	87.3	90.0	22,445	20	13.5	19,783	2,777.7	2,412.0	1,162.0
Wyoming.....................	175	9.5	9.0	8.4	1,174	50	19.4	983	313.3	237.8	111.2

X = Not applicable.
[1]For calendar year. U.S. business enterprises that are more than 50 percent owned by foreign direct investors.
[2]For calendar year. National total includes Puerto Rico and US Virgin Islands. Foreign Trade Zone shipments are included in the U.S. total and distributed among individual states and territories. Unreported and estimated shipments are included in national totals.
[3]For calendar year. The U.S. totals include unallocated exports not included in states.
[4]National total includes data for territories as well as unspecified data (aircraft, railroad rolling stock, satellites, undersea cable, and trucks engaged in interstate transportation) and will differ from sum of state totals.
[5]National total includes data for territories and will differ from sum of state totals.

Table A-48.   Farms and Farm Earnings

| Geographic Area | Farms (USDA)[1] (as of June 1) | | | | | | | | | | | | Farm earnings (BEA)[2] (million dollars) | | | |
| | Number (thousands) | | | | Land in farms (million acres) | | | | Average acreage per farm | | | | | | | |
	2015	2012	2010	2005	2015	2012	2010	2005	2015	2012	2010	2005	2015	2012	2010	2005
United States	2,068.0	2,170.0	2,200.9	2,101.0	912.0	914.0	920.0	933.4	441	421	418	444	87,200	94,357	66,926	72,166
Alabama....................	43.2	46.5	48.5	43.5	8.9	8.9	9.0	8.6	206	190	186	198	1,628	873	851	1,693
Alaska......................	0.8	0.7	0.7	0.6	0.8	0.9	0.9	0.9	1,092	1,294	1,294	1,406	16	17	10	14
Arizona....................	19.5	15.5	15.5	10.1	26.0	26.1	26.1	26.2	1,333	1,684	1,684	2,594	1,324	838	538	995
Arkansas..................	43.5	47.8	49.3	47.0	13.8	13.5	13.7	14.4	317	282	278	306	1,750	1,468	778	1,878
California..................	77.4	80.5	81.7	76.5	25.4	25.4	25.4	26.4	328	316	311	345	17,606	15,953	12,433	12,294
Colorado..................	34.2	36.3	36.1	30.5	31.7	31.3	31.2	30.7	927	862	864	1,007	1,401	1,153	911	1,132
Connecticut..............	6.0	4.9	4.9	4.2	0.4	0.4	0.4	0.4	73	82	82	86	162	172	140	190
Delaware..................	2.5	2.5	2.5	2.3	0.5	0.5	0.5	0.5	200	196	198	226	359	297	260	292
District of Columbia	(X)	(X)	(X)	(X)	(X)	(X)	(X)	(X)	(X)	(X)	(X)	(X)	(X)	(X)	(X)	(X)
Florida......................	47.3	47.5	47.5	42.5	9.5	9.3	9.3	10.0	200	195	195	235	3,096	2,540	2,578	2,701
Georgia....................	41.0	47.0	47.4	49.0	9.4	10.4	10.3	10.5	229	221	217	214	2,476	2,643	1,565	2,469
Hawaii......................	7.0	7.5	7.5	5.5	1.1	1.1	1.1	1.3	160	148	148	236	283	244	175	262
Idaho.......................	24.4	24.5	25.7	25.0	11.8	11.4	11.4	11.8	484	465	444	472	2,283	2,147	1,528	1,202
Illinois.....................	73.4	74.3	76.0	72.5	26.8	26.6	26.7	27.3	365	358	351	377	452	3,210	2,683	1,731
Indiana.....................	57.7	60.0	62.0	59.0	14.7	14.7	14.8	15.0	255	245	239	254	1,314	2,320	1,581	1,332
Iowa........................	87.5	92.2	92.4	89.0	30.5	30.7	30.8	31.6	349	333	333	355	5,922	6,795	3,833	3,852
Kansas.....................	60.4	65.5	65.5	64.5	46.0	46.0	46.2	47.2	762	702	705	732	2,433	3,113	2,438	1,931
Kentucky..................	76.4	85.5	85.7	84.0	13.0	14.0	14.0	13.8	170	164	163	164	829	926	377	1,577
Louisiana	26.9	29.0	30.0	26.8	7.8	8.0	8.1	7.8	288	274	268	291	622	1,128	635	681
Maine......................	8.2	8.1	8.1	7.1	1.5	1.4	1.4	1.4	177 166	167	167	193	129	191	179	173
Maryland..................	12.2	12.8	12.8	12.1	2.0	2.1	2.1	2.0		160	160	169	341	584	310	392
Massachusetts............	7.8	7.7	7.7	6.1	0.5	0.5	0.5	0.5	67	68	68	85	143	193	131	125
Michigan..................	51.5	54.7	54.9	53.0	10.0	9.9	10.0	10.1	193	181	182	191	1,605	1,713	1,490	1,054
Minnesota.................	73.6	79.4	81.0	79.6	25.9	26.8	26.9	27.5	352	338	332	345	3,598	6,235	3,288	2,997
Mississippi................	36.7	42.3	42.4	42.2	10.8	11.2	11.2	11.1	294	264	263	262	1,128	1,301	922	1,768
Missouri...................	97.1	106.0	108.0	105.0	28.3	29.0	29.1	30.1	291	274	269	287	722	1,515	1,301	1,406
Montana....................	27.5	28.6	29.4	28.0	59.7	58.8	60.8	60.1	2,171	2,056	2,068	2,146	733	743	542	594
Nebraska...................	48.7	46.7	47.2	48.0	45.2	45.5	45.6	45.7	928	974	966	952	4,893	4,643	3,221	2,877
Nevada.....................	4.2	3.0	3.1	3.0	6.0	5.8	5.9	6.3	1,417	1,980	1,903	2,100	140	106	133	135
New Hampshire............	4.4	4.2	4.2	3.4	0.5	0.5	0.5	0.5	107	113	113	132	48	57	28	50
New Jersey	9.1	10.2	10.3	9.8	0.7	0.7	0.7	0.8	79	72	71	81	338	405	331	340
New Mexico	24.7	23.8	21.0	17.5	43.2	43.9	43.2	44.5	1,749	1,845	2,057	2,543	796	979	781	883
New York...................	35.5	36.0	36.3	35.6	7.2	7.0	7.0	7.6	203	194	193	212	1,212	1,594	1,326	1,072
North Carolina.............	48.8	50.0	52.4	50.0	8.3	8.5	8.6	8.9	170	170	164	178	3,426	3,026	2,474	3,169
North Dakota..............	30.0	31.6	31.9	30.3	39.2	39.6	39.6	39.4	1,307	1,253	1,241	1,300	387	3,837	2,291	1,190
Ohio........................	74.4	73.4	74.7	76.5	14.0	13.6	13.7	14.3	188	185	183	187	1,204	1,952	1,607	1,076
Oklahoma..................	78.0	85.5	86.5	83.0	34.2	34.8	35.2	33.7	438	407	407	406	2,043	1,849	846	1,321
Oregon.....................	34.6	38.1	38.8	40.0	16.4	16.5	16.4	17.1	474	433	423	428	1,798	1,454	953	1,251
Pennsylvania..............	57.9	62.1	63.2	58.2	7.7	7.7	7.8	7.7	133	124	123	132	1,573	1,834	1,181	1,389
Rhode Island..............	1.2	1.2	1.2	0.9	0.1	0.1	0.1	0.1	56	57	57	71	19	19	15	24
South Carolina	24.4	26.7	27.0	24.3	5.0	4.8	4.9	4.8	205	180	181	199	156	515	407	646
South Dakota	31.3	31.0	31.8	31.4	43.3	43.7	43.7	43.7	1,383	1,408	1,374	1,392	1,855	2,599	1,750	1,608
Tennessee.................	67.3	76.0	78.3	84.0	10.9	10.8	10.9	11.6	162	142	139	138	342	513	179	543
Texas.......................	242.0	244.7	247.5	230.0	130.0	128.0	130.4	129.8	537	523	527	564	6,323	3,398	3,321	5,018
Utah........................	18.1	16.4	16.6	15.2	11.0	11.1	11.1	11.6	608	677	669	763	469	276	189	270
Vermont....................	7.3	7.0	7.0	6.3	1.3	1.2	1.2	1.3	171	174	174	198	128	182	124	202
Virginia....................	45.0	46.2	47.3	47.0	8.1	8.1	8.1	8.5	180	174	170	181	330	584	260	589
Washington...............	36.0	39.3	39.5	34.5	14.7	14.8	14.8	15.1	408	377	375	438	4,504	3,440	2,536	1,868
West Virginia..............	20.9	22.1	23.0	20.8	3.6	3.6	3.7	3.6	172	164	159	173	-31	-21	-55	11
Wisconsin..................	68.9	76.8	78.0	76.5	14.4	15.0	15.2	15.4	209	195	195	201	2,633	2,709	1,473	1,669
Wyoming	11.6	10.8	11.0	9.2	30.4	30.2	30.2	34.4	2,621	2,796	2,745	3,739	255	95	81	232

(X) = Not applicable.
[1] U.S. Department of Agriculture.
[2] Bureau of Economic Analysis. The estimates of earnings for 2000–2006 are based on the 2002 North American Industry Classification System (NAICS). The estimates for 2007 forward are based on the 2007 NAICS. All numbers provided are in current dollars (not adjusted for inflation).

Table A-49. Farm Finances and Income

Geographic Area	Value of agricultural sector productions[1] (million dollars)						Net farm income[2] (million dollars)					
	2015	2014	2013	2012	2011	2010	2015	2014	2013	2012	2011	2010
United States	428,890	473,288	472,810	439,161	409,965	344,102	80,875	92,594	123,726	96,456	113,534	77,093
Alabama.....................	6,481	7,234	6,926	6,069	5,594	5,296	1,601	1,743	1,894	920	578	1,099
Alaska	48	51	44	46	42	39	-6	-10	-10	-7	-10	-12
Arizona......................	4,441	4,592	4,651	4,236	5,053	3,912	1,109	713	1,133	824	1,360	582
Arkansas	9,726	10,808	11,349	9,733	8,943	8,461	1,303	2,121	2,611	1,223	902	922
California...................	50,244	58,662	54,273	50,216	46,449	40,684	14,631	18,186	17,283	16,094	15,657	10,883
Colorado	8,583	8,801	8,311	8,130	8,252	6,818	1,500	1,143	1,339	1,339	1,837	1,233
Connecticut................	714	735	799	795	723	700	100	44	175	190	227	211
Delaware	1,437	1,671	1,516	1,381	1,287	1,250	408	583	525	369	378	396
District of Columbia												
Florida.......................	9,097	9,297	8,927	9,467	8,736	8,497	3,014	2,172	2,198	2,913	2,344	2,407
Georgia	10,410	10,829	10,093	10,828	9,312	8,314	2,529	2,323	2,703	3,106	1,005	1,792
Hawaii	867	885	888	926	926	821	151	67	132	189	337	250
Idaho.........................	8,294	9,291	8,640	8,461	8,050	6,313	1,868	2,006	2,046	1,954	2,242	1,289
Illinois	17,424	21,082	25,381	19,521	21,011	15,562	-87	2,772	8,206	3,348	5,426	2,622
Indiana	11,558	13,700	16,066	12,546	12,152	9,831	1,248	2,835	5,503	2,807	3,390	2,026
Iowa..........................	31,402	35,654	35,229	32,564	31,390	23,612	5,590	5,242	8,338	6,628	9,549	4,047
Kansas	18,146	18,263	18,737	18,877	16,808	14,640	1,757	2,494	5,915	3,026	5,162	3,257
Kentucky	7,110	7,446	8,017	6,187	5,684	4,788	1,665	1,750	2,966	1,150	1,518	859
Louisiana	3,591	4,154	4,527	4,383	3,732	3,372	594	859	1,579	1,382	1,080	967
Maine........................	848	902	915	915	854	832	160	155	238	262	318	343
Maryland....................	2,662	2,950	2,991	2,854	2,498	2,231	508	623	889	747	750	580
Massachusetts.............	593	636	734	754	729	691	3	-23	137	188	243	209
Michigan....................	8,904	9,412	9,686	9,107	8,894	6,946	767	668	1,835	1,172	3,031	1,609
Minnesota..................	19,938	22,151	23,263	23,022	18,758	15,975	3,421	3,282	5,620	6,403	4,821	3,818
Mississippi.................	6,182	6,957	7,433	6,647	6,077	5,705	847	1,542	2,080	1,181	618	1,022
Missouri.....................	11,047	12,878	12,765	11,028	10,523	8,843	1,353	3,472	3,327	1,762	3,055	2,208
Montana.....................	4,744	5,101	5,068	4,754	4,302	3,677	958	680	1,240	1,002	1,243	1,001
Nebraska....................	25,073	26,448	26,554	24,949	23,092	17,445	4,885	5,823	7,455	4,898	7,492	3,683
Nevada......................	831	978	790	774	797	635	126	170	68	80	238	139
New Hampshire............	321	325	321	311	291	273	63	44	74	72	77	73
New Jersey	1,270	1,309	1,312	1,350	1,382	1,265	268	172	291	365	471	371
New Mexico	3,373	3,999	3,480	3,886	4,005	3,343	789	1,130	923	1,035	1,229	925
New York....................	5,934	7,043	6,678	6,258	5,952	5,247	1,000	1,691	1,851	1,538	2,067	1,498
North Carolina.............	12,754	14,569	13,994	13,234	11,830	10,610	2,924	3,858	3,427	3,259	2,515	3,050
North Dakota..............	9,186	9,958	10,693	12,021	8,498	7,556	185	326	1,915	3,511	2,297	2,384
Ohio..........................	10,562	11,296	12,525	11,089	10,678	8,314	1,167	1,730	3,244	1,864	3,586	2,120
Oklahoma...................	8,449	9,836	8,235	7,827	7,425	6,489	2,166	2,755	1,857	1,969	1,904	1,323
Oregon......................	5,601	5,922	5,673	5,347	5,480	4,359	1,214	765	1,002	901	906	235
Pennsylvania..............	8,717	9,925	9,035	8,794	7,902	6,958	1,895	2,658	2,377	2,179	2,329	1,638
Rhode Island..............	105	103	102	101	107	106	28	12	22	24	38	40
South Carolina	2,757	3,170	3,356	3,267	3,002	2,829	105	238	740	544	467	653
South Dakota	11,126	12,131	12,924	11,395	10,948	7,962	2,067	2,134	3,713	2,706	4,538	2,137
Tennessee	4,582	4,885	5,101	4,485	4,343	3,764	730	693	1,414	866	1,175	790
Texas.........................	28,567	29,539	28,548	26,593	25,087	22,456	6,512	4,224	5,495	3,592	4,575	4,667
Utah..........................	2,311	2,554	2,315	1,975	1,991	1,523	586	551	541	366	484	223
Vermont.....................	941	1,120	1,003	951	924	796	197	320	285	253	335	229
Virginia......................	4,615	4,989	4,760	4,678	4,297	3,731	716	763	1,011	953	1,251	836
Washington.................	11,483	11,082	10,728	10,653	9,997	8,382	3,289	1,960	2,564	2,371	3,397	1,979
West Virginia...............	976	1,022	969	939	829	724	75	56	116	78	179	111
Wisconsin...................	12,822	14,729	13,806	12,964	12,373	10,112	2,549	2,765	3,163	2,632	3,573	2,166
Wyoming	2,043	2,212	2,077	1,878	1,956	1,416	351	317	271	148	552	205

(X) = Not applicable.
[1]The sum of the value of crop production, the value of livestock production, and revenues from services and forestry.
[2]Represents the value of agricultural sector production plus net government transactions (such as direct government payments) minus capital consumption, employee compensation, net rent received by nonoperator landlords, and interest payments.

Table A-50. Farm Income and Wealth Statistics

Geographic area	Direct government payments, 2015		Value of crop production, 2015 (in thousands)		Value of animals and products production, 2015 (in thousands)		Net farm income, 2015	
	Amount (in thousands)	Share of U.S. direct government payments	Amount (in thousands)	Share of U.S. direct government payments	Amount (in thousands)	Share of U.S. direct government payments	Amount (in thousands)	Share of U.S. net farm income
United States	10,804,486	(X)	182,814,777	(X)	194,557,011	(X)	80,875,497	(X)
Alabama......................	96,556	0.9	1,019,439	0.6	4,586,903	2.4	1,600,665	2.0
Alaska	11,301	0.1	27,480	0.0	7,410	0.0	-6,275	0.0
Arizona.......................	43,516	0.4	2,283,142	1.2	1,823,663	0.9	1,109,211	1.4
Arkansas....................	379,345	3.5	3,231,893	1.8	5,344,077	2.7	1,303,306	1.6
California....................	235,434	2.2	34,564,862	18.9	12,096,759	6.2	14,630,664	18.1
Colorado....................	218,644	2.0	2,152,855	1.2	5,500,991	2.8	1,499,619	1.9
Connecticut................	5,204	0.0	378,106	0.2	198,464	0.1	99,744	0.1
Delaware....................	8,440	0.1	258,356	0.1	1,021,387	0.5	407,567	0.5
District of Columbia	(X)	(X)	(X)	(X)	(X)	(X)	(X)	(X)
Florida.......................	68,912	0.6	6,137,907	3.4	2,296,913	1.2	3,013,681	3.7
Georgia......................	305,483	2.8	2,938,406	1.6	6,139,264	3.2	2,528,714	3.1
Hawaii	24,841	0.2	511,041	0.3	189,897	0.1	151,345	0.2
Idaho.........................	86,249	0.8	2,924,533	1.6	4,753,120	2.4	1,868,434	2.3
Illinois.......................	417,077	3.9	12,700,410	6.9	2,680,574	1.4	-87,423	-0.1
Indiana......................	220,742	2.0	5,894,548	3.2	4,292,893	2.2	1,248,411	1.5
Iowa..........................	1,408,333	13.0	13,125,891	7.2	14,742,920	7.6	5,589,655	6.9
Kansas......................	531,766	4.9	6,056,793	3.3	10,551,539	5.4	1,756,690	2.2
Kentucky....................	127,707	1.2	2,448,703	1.3	3,523,265	1.8	1,665,206	2.1
Louisiana	175,667	1.6	1,863,470	1.0	1,260,148	0.6	593,883	0.7
Maine........................	12,369	0.1	391,894	0.2	349,821	0.2	159,830	0.2
Maryland....................	26,786	0.2	831,646	0.5	1,379,588	0.7	507,951	0.6
Massachusetts.............	4,306	0.0	288,394	0.2	129,158	0.1	2,604	0.0
Michigan....................	187,155	1.7	4,278,940	2.3	3,483,313	1.8	766,851	0.9
Minnesota	976,584	9.0	9,359,125	5.1	7,858,145	4.0	3,421,287	4.2
Mississippi.................	174,356	1.6	1,906,092	1.0	3,379,397	1.7	846,990	1.0
Missouri.....................	209,237	1.9	3,893,820	2.1	5,210,683	2.7	1,352,946	1.7
Montana.....................	131,273	1.2	1,835,005	1.0	2,152,403	1.1	957,695	1.2
Nebraska....................	795,198	7.4	9,372,849	5.1	14,268,152	7.3	4,885,044	6.0
Nevada......................	36,609	0.3	172,823	0.1	548,735	0.3	126,285	0.2
New Hampshire............	7,001	0.1	110,230	0.1	149,658	0.1	63,111	0.1
New Jersey	8,498	0.1	881,130	0.5	156,122	0.1	267,637	0.3
New Mexico	80,312	0.7	698,866	0.4	2,408,986	1.2	788,738	1.0
New York....................	70,421	0.7	1,860,006	1.0	3,415,173	1.8	1,000,417	1.2
North Carolina.............	91,137	0.8	3,338,250	1.8	7,988,633	4.1	2,923,643	3.6
North Dakota...............	363,039	3.4	6,205,371	3.4	1,466,397	0.8	185,470	0.2
Ohio..........................	305,915	2.8	4,740,315	2.6	4,146,292	2.1	1,166,503	1.4
Oklahoma...................	534,310	4.9	1,308,870	0.7	6,301,436	3.2	2,166,468	2.7
Oregon......................	144,569	1.3	3,138,328	1.7	1,804,879	0.9	1,213,548	1.5
Pennsylvania...............	63,709	0.6	2,436,689	1.3	5,051,401	2.6	1,894,724	2.3
Rhode Island...............	4,013	0.0	50,587	0.0	30,898	0.0	27,528	0.0
South Carolina.............	63,037	0.6	786,834	0.4	1,480,586	0.8	105,459	0.1
South Dakota	425,790	3.9	5,363,814	2.9	4,337,602	2.2	2,066,840	2.6
Tennessee	63,799	0.6	1,977,136	1.1	1,721,543	0.9	729,825	0.9
Texas........................	944,830	8.7	6,454,669	3.5	16,603,898	8.5	6,511,763	8.1
Utah	51,978	0.5	449,820	0.2	1,629,710	0.8	586,174	0.7
Vermont.....................	10,272	0.1	182,018	0.1	643,032	0.3	196,715	0.2
Virginia......................	62,031	0.6	1,141,197	0.6	2,595,595	1.3	716,424	0.9
Washington.................	207,741	1.9	7,167,108	3.9	2,950,058	1.5	3,288,887	4.1
West Virginia...............	17,390	0.2	135,171	0.1	628,604	0.3	74,920	0.1
Wisconsin	305,627	2.8	3,184,913	1.7	7,880,980	4.1	2,548,653	3.2
Wyoming	59,971	0.6	355,033	0.2	1,395,942	0.7	351,474	0.4

(X) = Not applicable.

Table A-51. Natural Resource Industries and Minerals

Geographic Area	Natural resource industries (Includes Agriculture, forestry, fishing, and hunting [NAICS 11] and Mining quarrying, and oil and gas extraction NAICS 21)[1]						Value of nonfuel mineral production (million dollars)			Mineral fuels, 2015		
	Establishments		Number of employees[2]		Annual payroll (million dollars)					Crude oil production (millions of barrels)[3]	Natural gas production (millions of cubic feet)[4]	Coal production[5] (thousands of short tons)
	2014	2010	2014	2010	2014	2010	2016	2010	2005			
United States	51,598	48,783	915,334	737,637	76,827	51,428	74,600	64,000	55,400	3,437	28,752,935	896,941
Alabama......................	1,037	1,080	13,414	13,226	758	676	1,370	1,010	1,130	10	168,249	13,191
Alaska........................	618	541	13,755	11,984	1,740	1,260	3,090	3,240	1,500	176	343,534	1,177
Arizona.......................	428	431	13,350	11,699	949	697	5,550	6,700	4,350	0	95	6,805
Arkansas....................	1,053	1,076	12,639	13,345	791	707	959	630	597	6	1,010,274	91
California....................	2,700	2,679	53,604	46,848	3,440	2,822	3,520	2,710	4,290	201	231,060	X
Colorado	1,690	1,572	32,434	25,203	3,618	2,239	1,510	1,930	1,750	126	1,704,836	18,879
Connecticut.................	146	149	2,191	1,240	241	100	352	141	161	(X)	0	X
Delaware....................	55	54	281	224	18	8	20	13	20	(X)	0	X
District of Columbia	7	6	0	0	0	0	0	(X)	(X)	(X)	0	X
Florida.......................	1,265	1,248	13,394	17,382	572	633	3,260	2,080	2,910	2	499	X
Georgia......................	1,124	1,162	12,470	12,477	612	524	1,790	1,500	1,770	(X)	0	X
Hawaii........................	37	50	295	494	14	16	133	112	125	(X)	0	X
Idaho..........................	573	580	5,997	5,748	365	268	654	1,200	896	(X)	0	X
Illinois........................	892	887	11,109	9,883	783	609	1,720	910	1,210	10	2,080	56,101
Indiana.......................	549	561	7,477	7,794	495	447	1,010	837	894	2	7,250	34,295
Iowa..........................	543	462	4,637	3,558	254	180	644	542	659	(X)	0	X
Kansas.......................	1,296	1,201	11,942	9,860	714	509	623	1,040	873	45	285,236	199
Kentucky....................	743	882	17,312	23,048	1,157	1,434	525	742	782	3	85,775	61,425
Louisiana	2,311	2,195	61,737	53,794	5,102	3,735	530	492	397	63	1,776,800	3,439
Maine........................	857	807	3,308	3,575	148	138	102	114	141	(X)	0	X
Maryland.....................	265	271	2,365	2,220	108	99	310	438	580	(X)	27	1,922
Massachusetts..............	415	442	1,919	2,100	113	115	405	194	250	(X)	0	X
Michigan	883	887	9,436	8,329	561	451	2,830	1,960	1,740	6	107,634	X
Minnesota..................	669	615	8,703	7,568	669	528	3,270	3,860	2,190	(X)	0	X
Mississippi.................	1,053	1,028	10,680	9,507	680	474	220	183	221	25	58,207	3,143
Missouri.....................	536	506	5,039	4,773	265	228	2,490	2,140	1,860	0	1	138
Montana.....................	775	712	8,663	7,085	726	485	925	1,120	847	29	57,421	41,864
Nebraska....................	317	296	2,304	1,893	125	93	196	181	115	3	477	X
Nevada......................	260	281	13,879	10,922	1,255	1,018	7,650	7,550	3,890	0	3	X
New Hampshire............	187	184	904	764	50	35	131	100	88	(X)	0	X
New Jersey	283	307	2,288	2,976	133	121	333	232	356	(X)	0	X
New Mexico	875	773	22,082	15,064	1,794	1,087	1,460	1,010	1,150	147	1,244,811	19,679
New York....................	885	909	6,509	7,146	376	358	1,770	1,290	1,290	0	17,829	X
North Carolina..............	996	967	7,904	7,218	342	277	1,170	908	862	(X)	0	X
North Dakota...............	698	399	26,192	8,825	2,685	746	132	88	35	429	471,504	28,802
Ohio..........................	1,006	1,001	12,253	10,376	847	543	1,270	1,080	1,210	26	1,014,848	17,041
Oklahoma....................	3,419	2,972	59,857	41,956	5,514	3,343	777	646	616	158	2,499,599	780
Oregon.......................	1,446	1,396	13,248	13,173	555	457	507	292	439	(X)	848	X
Pennsylvania...............	1,642	1,553	34,625	25,714	2,910	1,757	1,830	1,530	1,560	7	4,812,983	50,031
Rhode Island................	59	66	284	242	18	12	72	34	35	(X)	0	X
South Carolina	578	606	4,817	5,276	207	199	823	440	659	(X)	0	X
South Dakota	201	193	1,557	1,414	86	69	363	298	217	2	14,531	X
Tennessee	438	453	5,190	4,641	239	205	1,210	814	771	0	4,276	897
Texas.........................	9,934	8,591	258,588	169,074	27,190	15,352	4,830	2,560	2,710	1,264	7,880,530	35,918
Utah..........................	603	537	11,826	9,874	922	663	2,490	4,420	2,800	37	423,300	14,419
Vermont......................	187	175	874	434	46	14	137	119	98	(X)	0	X
Virginia......................	942	963	13,619	12,459	812	732	1,230	952	1,150	0	127,584	13,914
Washington..................	1,605	1,580	15,602	14,715	820	694	965	665	638	(X)	0	X
West Virginia................	896	910	30,037	30,960	2,263	2,115	425	230	209	8	1,318,822	95,633
Wisconsin	688	652	5,997	5,176	363	273	1,730	651	570	(X)	0	X
Wyoming	933	935	26,514	23,790	2,379	1,848	2,530	1,860	1,300	86	1,793,716	375,773

(X) = Not applicable.

[1] Includes Agriculture, forestry, fishing, and hunting (NAICS 11), and Mining, quarrying, and oil and gas extraction (NAICS 21). Data provided by County Business Patterns is based on the North American Industry Classification System (NAICS). Data for 2010 is based on NAICS 2007. Data for 2005 is based on NAICS 2002, adjusted to match 2007.

[2] Covers full- and part-time employees who are on the payroll in the pay period including March 12.

[3] U.S. totals include offshore production.

[4] Excludes nonhydrocarbon gases. U.S. total includes natural gas extracted from the Gulf of Mexico that is not distributed to states. The national total will therefore differ from the sum of state totals.

[5] Includes both surface and underground mines. U.S. total includes refuse recovery not distributed by state.

Table A-52. Agricultural Census

Geographic area	Number of farms (thousands)		Land in farm (millions of acres)		Average size of farm (acres)		Value of land and buildings (million dollars)		Market value of agricultural products sold 2012 (million dollars)	
	2012	2007	2,012	2007	2012	2007	2012	2007	Products sold	Average per farm
United States	2,109.3	2,204.8	914.5	922.1	434	418	2,268,537	1,744,295	394,644	187,097
Alabama......................	43.2	48.8	8.9	9.0	206	185	23,666	20,704	5,571	128,894
Alaska........................	0.8	0.7	0.8	0.9	1,094	1,285	519	345	59	77,329
Arizona......................	20.0	15.6	26.2	26.1	1,312	1,670	16,886	19,545	3,732	186,559
Arkansas....................	45.1	49.3	13.8	13.9	306	281	36,416	32,506	9,776	216,897
California...................	77.9	81.0	25.6	25.4	328	313	160,525	162,533	42,627	547,510
Colorado....................	36.2	37.1	31.9	31.6	881	853	40,821	33,058	7,781	215,060
Connecticut................	6.0	4.9	0.4	0.4	73	83	4,838	5,138	551	92,123
Delaware....................	2.5	2.5	0.5	0.5	208	200	4,153	5,279	1,274	519,794
District of Columbia......	(X)	(X)	(X)	(X)	(X)	(X)	(X)	(X)	(X)	(X)
Florida.......................	47.7	47.5	9.5	9.2	200	195	49,662	52,054	7,702	161,322
Georgia	42.3	47.8	9.6	10.2	228	212	29,676	31,636	9,255	219,020
Hawaii	7.0	7.5	1.1	1.1	161	149	10,229	8,621	661	94,478
Idaho.........................	24.8	25.3	11.8	11.5	474	454	26,130	22,675	7,801	314,372
Illinois.......................	75.1	76.9	26.9	26.8	359	348	169,830	101,538	17,187	228,895
Indiana......................	58.7	60.9	14.7	14.8	251	242	78,817	52,937	11,211	191,001
Iowa..........................	88.6	92.9	30.6	30.7	345	331	195,641	104,187	30,822	347,728
Kansas.......................	61.8	65.5	46.1	46.3	747	707	75,280	42,205	18,461	298,845
Kentucky....................	77.1	85.3	13.0	14.0	169	164	39,459	37,533	5,067	65,755
Louisiana	28.1	30.1	7.9	8.1	281	269	20,176	16,687	3,809	135,600
Maine........................	8.2	8.1	1.5	1.3	178	166	3,356	2,968	763	93,364
Maryland....................	12.3	12.8	2.0	2.1	166	160	14,073	14,432	2,271	185,329
Massachusetts.............	7.8	7.7	0.5	0.5	68	67	5,460	6,377	492	63,470
Michigan....................	52.2	56.0	9.9	10.0	191	179	39,988	34,200	8,678	166,265
Minnesota	74.5	81.0	26.0	26.9	349	332	109,879	69,165	21,280	285,479
Mississippi.................	38.1	42.0	10.9	11.5	287	273	24,848	21,418	6,441	169,162
Missouri.....................	99.2	107.8	28.3	29.0	285	269	78,885	63,237	9,165	92,415
Montana.....................	28.0	29.5	59.8	61.4	2,134	2,079	46,901	47,568	4,230	151,031
Nebraska....................	50.0	47.7	45.3	45.5	907	953	107,896	52,693	23,069	461,661
Nevada......................	4.1	3.1	5.9	5.9	1,429	1,873	5,480	3,597	764	184,710
New Hampshire............	4.4	4.2	0.5	0.5	108	113	1,975	2,326	191	43,477
New Jersey	9.1	10.3	0.7	0.7	79	71	9,147	11,255	1,007	111,006
New Mexico	24.7	20.9	43.2	43.2	1,748	2,066	18,669	14,569	2,550	103,157
New York....................	35.5	36.4	7.2	7.2	202	197	18,678	16,322	5,415	152,380
North Carolina.............	50.2	52.9	8.4	8.5	168	160	36,506	34,715	12,588	250,670
North Dakota...............	31.0	32.0	39.3	39.7	1,268	1,241	56,002	30,597	10,951	353,693
Ohio	75.5	75.9	14.0	14.0	185	184	67,533	49,244	10,064	133,366
Oklahoma...................	80.2	86.6	34.4	35.1	428	405	46,049	40,582	7,130	88,848
Oregon......................	35.4	38.6	16.3	16.4	460	425	30,676	31,002	4,884	137,805
Pennsylvania...............	59.3	63.2	7.7	7.8	130	124	41,796	37,290	7,401	124,783
Rhode Island...............	1.2	1.2	0.1	0.1	56	56	977	1,141	60	47,990
South Carolina	25.3	25.9	5.0	4.9	197	189	14,819	13,973	3,040	120,323
South Dakota	32.0	31.2	43.3	43.7	1,352	1,401	72,968	39,127	10,170	317,929
Tennessee	68.1	79.3	10.9	11.0	160	138	38,749	37,057	3,611	53,064
Texas........................	248.8	247.4	130.2	130.4	523	527	218,109	165,573	25,376	101,988
Utah..........................	18.0	16.7	11.0	11.1	609	664	16,024	13,858	1,816	100,746
Vermont.....................	7.3	7.0	1.3	1.2	171	177	4,011	3,581	776	105,765
Virginia......................	46.0	47.4	8.3	8.1	180	171	35,752	34,141	3,753	81,540
Washington.................	37.2	39.3	14.7	15.0	396	381	33,906	29,822	9,121	244,859
West Virginia...............	21.5	23.6	3.6	3.7	168	157	8,884	8,820	807	37,544
Wisconsin	69.8	78.5	14.6	15.2	209	194	57,167	48,994	11,744	168,370
Wyoming	11.7	11.1	30.4	30.2	2,587	2,726	20,646	15,471	1,689	143,952

(X) = Not applicable.

Table A-52. Agricultural Census—Continued

Geographic area	Total number of farm operators, 2012	Farms by value of sales, 2012						Cropland (thousand acres), 2012
		Less than $2,500	$2,500–$9,999	$10,000–$24,999	$25,000–$49,999	$50,000–$99,999	$100,000 or more	
United States	3,233,358	788,310	405,667	244,954	152,873	129,366	388,133	389,690
Alabama........................	64,054	18,253	10,373	5,573	2,662	1,510	4,852	2,759
Alaska	1,230	238	202	140	55	40	87	84
Arizona........................	33,613	12,616	3,321	1,503	672	442	1,451	1,151
Arkansas	69,704	15,268	9,952	6,788	3,529	2,028	7,506	7,931
California......................	126,099	19,986	13,454	10,137	7,043	6,679	20,558	9,592
Colorado	59,269	16,597	5,954	3,525	2,368	2,103	5,633	10,650
Connecticut.................	9,880	2,652	1,529	743	352	243	458	151
Delaware	3,855	585	282	240	188	135	1,021	439
District of Columbia	(X)	(X)	(X)	(X)	(X)	(X)	(X)	
Florida.........................	74,539.0	21,263.0	10,105	5,686	2,998	2,464	5,224	2,744
Georgia	61,859	18,372	8,090	4,704	2,232	1,552	7,307	4,191
Hawaii	10,874	2,130	1,960	1,397	684	323	506	174
Idaho	40,590	8,969	4,854	2,537	1,842	1,518	5,096	5,793
Illinois	109,123	25,025	9,116	5,908	4,563	5,666	24,809	23,753
Indiana	89,818	20,283	10,063	5,681	4,101	4,254	14,313	12,591
Iowa	131,535	25,049	7,941	6,041	5,775	7,470	36,361	26,256
Kansas	92,892	18,459	8,693	7,047	6,147	5,662	15,765	28,503
Kentucky	114,210	29,963	18,968	11,453	6,458	3,882	6,340	6,336
Louisiana	41,592	12,750	6,074	3,262	1,632	1,087	3,288	4,276
Maine	13,406	3,279	2,067	1,081	589	379	778	477
Maryland......................	19,469	4,798	2,173	1,226	993	545	2,521	1,396
Massachusetts.............	12,595	3,663	1,555	861	486	432	758	161
Michigan	80,304	20,331	8,912	5,946	3,986	3,623	9,396	7,669
Minnesota	111,311	21,188	8,599	6,022	5,630	8,112	24,991	21,597
Mississippi..................	55,568	17,620	7,890	4,332	2,288	1,226	4,720	5,076
Missouri.......................	152,817	33,002	19,726	15,841	10,822	7,365	12,415	15,259
Montana	45,246	10,170	3,735	2,531	2,053	2,178	7,341	17,022
Nebraska.....................	75,855	10,648	5,074	3,998	3,711	5,071	21,467	21,597
Nevada........................	6,880	1,410	989	396	226	241	875	757
New Hampshire............	7,300	2,115	1,109	494	253	156	264	98
New Jersey	14,574	3,808	1,988	1,032	600	524	1,119	457
New Mexico	37,981	13,609	5,077	2,172	1,064	1,058	1,741	1,977
New York.....................	57,022	11,169	6,895	4,937	2,825	2,586	7,125	4,217
North Carolina.............	73,846	19,294	12,198	5,579	2,870	1,946	8,331	4,745
North Dakota................	45,015	10,447	2,251	1,816	1,817	2,074	12,556	27,147
Ohio	115,743	25,198	14,525	8,497	6,154	5,764	15,324	10,749
Oklahoma....................	121,603	29,794	17,712	12,437	7,070	5,198	8,034	11,279
Oregon	59,237	14,260	8,564	4,011	2,217	1,741	4,646	4,690
Pennsylvania...............	92,341	19,621	11,146	7,801	4,883	4,044	11,814	4,546
Rhode Island................	2,055	451	348	179	68	89	108	23
South Carolina	37,060	13,133	5,301	2,608	1,211	852	2,161	1,967
South Dakota	48,987	7,945	3,262	2,527	2,281	2,946	13,028	19,147
Tennessee	101,603	30,632	16,868	9,699	4,624	2,067	4,160	5,330
Texas...........................	375,888	112,775	62,105	31,781	15,505	9,154	17,489	29,148
Utah	28,844	7,200	4,123	2,180	1,424	1,117	1,983	1,646
Vermont	12,257	2,597	1,761	904	554	413	1,109	488
Virginia........................	69,990	17,103	11,499	6,940	3,837	2,220	4,431	2,991
Washington..................	60,912	16,900	7,626	3,398	1,843	1,380	6,102	7,527
West Virginia...............	32,178	8,861	7,197	2,956	1,108	505	862	804
Wisconsin	111,080	22,531	10,747	7,246	5,705	6,379	17,146	9,911
Wyoming	19,655	4,300	1,714	1,161	875	923	2,763	2,419

(X) = Not applicable.

Table A-53.   Utilities

| Geographic area | Utilities[1] (NAICS 22) | | | | | | Public water systems, 2012[3] | | | |
| | Establishments | | Number of employees | | Annual payroll[2] (million dollars) | | Number of systems | | | |
	2014	2010	2014	2010	2014	2010	Total	Community[4]	Non-transient, non-community[5]	Transient, non-community[6]
United States	17,962	17,600	637,840	638,058	61,581	55,396	152,143	50,452	17,594	84,097
Alabama.......................	436	417	(D)	16,546	(D)	1,241	583	514	22	47
Alaska	100	91	2,085	1,988	194	155	1,446	413	237	796
Arizona.......................	256	265	12,265	(D)	1,203	(D)	1,518	751	198	569
Arkansas.....................	328	344	7,478	7,362	616	518	1,071	694	34	343
California.....................	1,213	1,117	(D)	(D)	(D)	(D)	7,623	2,948	1,476	3,199
Colorado......................	388	385	(D)	8,837	825	713	1,979	874	168	937
Connecticut.................	139	169	(D)	(D)	(D)	1,163	2,491	502	540	1,449
Delaware.....................	55	46	2,375	2,632	245	250	499	214	91	194
District of Columbia	49	45	(D)	(D)	(D)	(D)	7	5	2	0
Florida........................	738	585	26,665	26,859	2,539	2,113	5,370	1,646	805	2,919
Georgia.......................	597	598	23,042	25,127	2,002	1,879	2,387	1,756	176	455
Hawaii........................	60	53	3,648	3,163	348	253	135	117	15	3
Idaho..........................	204	192	(D)	2,887	(D)	206	1,971	736	232	1,003
Illinois........................	492	483	28,412	28,851	2,847	2,722	5,429	1,737	424	3,268
Indiana.......................	509	626	14,853	16,176	1,340	1,234	4,073	787	587	2,699
Iowa...........................	271	271	7,964	(D)	640	(D)	1,827	1,090	132	605
Kansas........................	232	197	7,117	6,502	611	513	997	876	41	80
Kentucky.....................	329	341	8,301	8,310	697	663	439	387	17	35
Louisiana	506	537	(D)	(D)	(D)	(D)	1,342	992	142	208
Maine.........................	98	96	2,121	2,311	171	153	1,895	376	370	1,149
Maryland.....................	138	139	9,687	10,494	1,069	1,123	3,332	467	545	2,320
Massachusetts.............	276	281	12,366	12,861	1,273	1,319	8,529	2,319	718	5,492
Michigan	382	396	21,823	(D)	2,381	1,942	10,743	1,384	1,293	8,066
Minnesota	335	295	(D)	(D)	(D)	(D)	6,820	967	480	5,373
Mississippi..................	593	596	9,908	9,338	732	639	1,201	1,061	76	64
Missouri......................	364	357	15,724	16,665	1,471	1,355	2,746	1,424	217	1,105
Montana......................	209	200	3,007	2,972	257	231	2,170	727	284	1,159
Nebraska.....................	119	105	(D)	(D)	(D)	(D)	1,337	600	143	594
Nevada	130	120	(D)	(D)	(D)	(D)	590	200	136	254
New Hampshire............	128	113	3,110	3,492	310	298	2,479	699	455	1,325
New Jersey	384	375	20,650	18,018	2,433	1,823	3,709	582	738	2,389
New Mexico	226	231	4,623	5,017	380	379	1,083	572	134	377
New York.....................	616	613	39,642	42,155	3,918	3,811	8,529	2,319	718	5,492
North Carolina.............	562	472	19,494	19,636	1,818	1,726	5,668	2,009	362	3,297
North Dakota................	139	113	(D)	(D)	312	(D)	432	324	12	96
Ohio...........................	630	696	24,334	(D)	2,331	(D)	4,561	1,209	669	2,683
Oklahoma....................	369	353	8,240	7,850	678	583	1,675	1,066	102	507
Oregon........................	279	291	7,833	7,395	721	614	2,494	882	321	1,291
Pennsylvania...............	798	783	29,456	31,133	3,088	2,956	8,460	1,954	1,177	5,329
Rhode Island................	41	31	1,066	1,136	104	99				
South Carolina	352	329	12,123	11,831	1,047	892	1,400	583	107	710
South Dakota	160	154	2,246	2,198	181	138	642	458	20	164
Tennessee	146	150	3,236	3,536	216	218	850	472	35	343
Texas..........................	1,995	1,911	52,851	47,548	4,818	3,995	6,920	4,645	874	1,401
Utah...........................	216	218	(D)	4,633	(D)	380	1,029	475	70	484
Vermont.......................	58	59	(D)	2,067	181	182	1,403	418	252	733
Virginia.......................	331	360	14,403	15,050	1,512	1,430	2,714	1,121	517	1,076
Washington..................	300	302	(D)	8,291	(D)	686	4,371	2,266	359	1,746
West Virginia................	236	254	6,271	6,444	590	467	915	464	83	368
Wisconsin....................	313	317	14,369	13,484	1,332	1,168	11,470	1,055	891	9,524
Wyoming	137	128	(D)	2,492	(D)	196	789	315	97	377

0 = Represents or rounds to zero.
(D) = Data withheld to avoid disclosure or does not meet statistical standards.
NA = Not available.
[1]Data provided by County Business Patterns is based on the North American Industry Classification System (NAICS). Data for 2014 is based on NAICS 2012. Data for 2010 is based on NAICS 2007. Utilities data is for private use and excludes government employees, railroad employees, self-employed persons, and so on.
[2]National payroll figures include undisclosed data found at the State level and will therefore differ from the sum of the state totals.
[3]As of October. Covers public drinking water systems that provide water for human consumption through pipes and other constructed conveyances to at least 15 service connections or serve an average of at least 25 persons for at least 60 days a year. National totals differ from the sum of the state figures because national totals include water systems for Tribes and Territories.
[4]Includes any public water system that supplies water to the same population year-round.
[5]Includes any public water system that regularly supplies water to at least 25 of the same people at least six months per year but not year-round.
[6]Includes any public water system that provides water in a place, such as a gas station or a campground, where people do not remain for long periods of time and is open at least 60 days per year.

Table A-54. Energy Consumption

Geographic area	Total Primary Energy Consumption[1]		End-use sector, 2014[3] (trillion Btu)				Selected source, 2014 (trillion Btu)		
	2014 (trillion Btu)	Per capita[2] (million Btu)	Residential	Commercial	Industrial[1]	Transportation	Petroleum (millions of barrels)[4]	Natural gas (billion cu ft)[5]	Coal (million short tons)
United States	98,385	309	21,525	18,148	31,668	27,044	6,974	26,695	918
Alabama......................	1,958	404	379	262	848	469	98	636	27
Alaska	603	818	48	63	329	163	42	329	1
Arizona......................	1,423	211	386	338	234	464	97	307	23
Arkansas....................	1,114	376	247	183	406	279	63	268	20
California....................	7,620	196	1,397	1,418	1,856	2,948	630	2,352	2
Colorado	1,477	276	355	282	429	411	91	479	18
Connecticut.................	750	209	249	191	83	227	61	236	1
Delaware	274	293	67	57	87	63	19	101	0
District of Columbia	179	271	39	112	7	21	4	34	0
Florida.......................	4,122	207	1,199	974	468	1,480	304	1,221	24
Georgia	2,851	282	743	549	770	790	166	652	24
Hawaii	281	198	37	39	64	141	42	3	1
Idaho.........................	520	318	120	87	178	135	31	92	0
Illinois.......................	4,042	314	1,030	820	1,225	967	231	1,094	56
Indiana......................	2,932	444	582	390	1,327	632	147	713	55
Iowa..........................	1,542	496	253	213	767	309	88	330	23
Kansas	1,132	390	240	215	378	300	68	284	18
Kentucky	1,771	401	393	264	663	450	113	254	40
Louisiana	4,279	921	349	268	3,024	638	431	1,518	13
Maine	411	309	91	63	127	130	37	61	0
Maryland.....................	1,401	234	442	424	115	420	93	207	8
Massachusetts.............	1,438	213	449	394	162	432	108	420	1
Michigan	2,882	291	788	625	747	722	168	861	32
Minnesota	1,912	350	431	369	663	449	116	474	18
Mississippi	1,156	386	218	162	398	378	82	428	7
Missouri.....................	1,904	314	560	428	363	552	121	297	44
Montana.....................	403	394	87	78	125	113	32	77	11
Nebraska....................	864	459	163	141	358	202	46	173	16
Nevada	660	233	154	120	179	207	45	251	4
New Hampshire............	310	234	97	71	42	100	31	57	1
New Jersey	2,340	262	612	622	246	861	187	766	1
New Mexico	679	326	117	125	229	208	46	247	12
New York....................	3,743	190	1,124	1,135	391	1,094	250	1,345	3
North Carolina.............	2,555	257	722	577	541	715	160	453	20
North Dakota...............	640	865	78	82	334	146	44	85	29
Ohio..........................	3,810	329	946	709	1,225	929	215	1,000	44
Oklahoma...................	1,680	433	325	266	606	483	103	640	19
Oregon......................	987	249	247	189	247	304	64	220	2
Pennsylvania...............	3,902	305	972	653	1,375	903	231	1,201	47
Rhode Island...............	204	194	66	52	25	62	17	89	0
South Carolina	1,632	338	377	268	543	444	95	230	12
South Dakota	392	459	73	64	157	98	22	81	2
Tennessee	2,195	335	562	434	591	607	131	304	20
Texas........................	12,899	478	1,709	1,639	6,289	3,262	1,275	4,096	103
Utah	798	271	159	157	236	246	53	243	16
Vermont.....................	140	223	44	27	21	48	16	11	0
Virginia......................	2,430	292	642	616	452	720	155	420	12
Washington.................	2,012	285	482	376	567	587	132	307	5
West Virginia...............	753	407	178	112	293	170	36	151	34
Wisconsin	1,869	324	450	381	592	446	108	463	23
Wyoming	536	917	48	62	307	119	32	136	28

0 = Represents zero or rounds to zero.

(Z) = Less than .05 trillion Btu.

[1] U.S. total energy and U.S. industrial sector include 60.8 trillion Btu of net imports of coal coke that is not allocated to the states. U.S. total includes energy losses and co-products from the production of fuel ethanol which is not allocated to State figures.

[2] Based on estimated resident population as of July 1.

[3] End-use sector data include electricity sales and associated electrical system energy losses.

[4] Includes fuel ethanol blended into motor gasoline.

[5] Includes supplemental gaseous fuels.

Table A-55.   Energy Expenditures

Geographic area	Total expenditures, 2014[1,2,3] (million dollars)	Per capita[4] (dollars)	End-use sector, 2014[3] (million dollars)				Selected source, 2014 (million dollars)		
			Residential	Commercial	Industrial[2]	Transportation	Petroleum	Natural gas[5]	Coal
United States	1,394,974	4,374	264,610	190,934	246,625	692,805	863,909	174,019	45,119
Alabama......................	24,147	4,982	4,535	2,943	5,006	11,662	13,078	3,521	1,677
Alaska........................	6,891	9,349	764	885	1,099	4,143	5,537	481	89
Arizona.......................	22,610	3,360	4,564	3,469	2,363	12,214	13,753	2,156	945
Arkansas.....................	13,885	4,680	2,352	1,486	2,961	7,086	8,539	1,849	821
California.....................	137,720	3,550	20,016	21,589	16,276	79,839	86,002	16,128	135
Colorado.....................	19,994	3,733	3,751	2,672	2,792	10,780	12,388	2,686	684
Connecticut..................	15,483	4,307	5,120	2,892	1,101	6,371	9,041	2,162	39
Delaware.....................	3,849	4,112	957	634	569	1,689	2,092	753	32
District of Columbia......	2,320	3,517	473	1,270	100	478	553	411	*
Florida........................	66,414	3,336	14,493	10,462	4,308	37,151	40,058	7,468	1,858
Georgia	39,728	3,935	8,952	5,690	5,373	19,713	21,955	4,963	1,521
Hawaii........................	7,379	5,195	1,039	1,279	1,315	3,747	5,417	117	45
Idaho..........................	6,980	4,270	1,139	699	1,407	3,735	4,515	609	24
Illinois........................	51,550	4,002	10,719	7,153	9,011	24,668	29,290	9,088	2,155
Indiana.......................	34,152	5,176	5,781	3,414	8,548	16,410	18,850	5,266	3,514
Iowa...........................	18,022	5,796	2,900	2,016	5,046	8,060	11,483	2,579	723
Kansas........................	14,646	5,046	2,671	1,999	2,434	7,542	8,945	1,755	569
Kentucky......................	22,467	5,092	3,776	2,289	4,552	11,851	14,309	1,762	2,178
Louisiana	45,400	9,766	3,564	2,603	25,136	14,097	33,806	5,792	627
Maine.........................	7,558	5,681	1,836	1,092	1,031	3,598	5,347	623	11
Maryland.....................	22,951	3,841	5,752	4,435	1,363	11,401	13,422	2,151	595
Massachusetts.............	27,574	4,082	8,023	5,637	2,256	11,658	15,569	4,599	129
Michigan.....................	40,740	4,108	9,413	6,305	6,075	18,947	22,700	6,994	1,735
Minnesota...................	25,312	4,638	5,028	3,572	4,782	11,930	15,168	3,647	643
Mississippi..................	15,949	5,328	2,647	1,858	2,543	8,901	10,071	2,129	383
Missouri......................	26,719	4,406	5,631	3,616	3,028	14,444	16,449	2,632	1,578
Montana......................	5,528	5,402	900	708	838	3,082	3,850	528	322
Nebraska.....................	10,330	5,486	1,613	1,137	2,194	5,386	6,517	1,125	396
Nevada.......................	10,513	3,704	2,028	1,198	1,806	5,481	6,307	1,639	203
New Hampshire............	6,361	4,790	1,940	1,112	527	2,783	4,328	543	64
New Jersey	39,117	4,376	7,882	7,425	2,555	21,255	24,037	6,047	121
New Mexico	9,020	4,325	1,334	1,202	1,123	5,360	6,171	975	812
New York.....................	68,056	3,446	20,020	16,362	3,845	27,830	35,001	11,638	218
North Carolina..............	37,283	3,751	8,242	5,243	4,534	19,265	22,335	3,500	1,805
North Dakota................	8,210	11,094	798	792	3,009	3,611	5,945	363	866
Ohio	51,386	4,431	10,790	6,433	8,868	25,296	29,520	7,438	2,568
Oklahoma....................	20,497	5,283	3,268	2,191	3,671	11,366	13,053	3,454	680
Oregon........................	14,866	3,744	2,677	1,763	1,924	8,502	9,426	1,498	87
Pennsylvania...............	55,666	4,351	13,630	6,553	10,873	24,610	32,754	8,819	3,006
Rhode Island................	4,204	3,985	1,323	843	385	1,652	2,475	855	0
South Carolina	21,876	4,530	4,420	2,597	3,558	11,300	12,586	1,596	1,115
South Dakota	4,819	5,648	774	548	940	2,557	3,156	549	72
Tennessee	29,615	4,523	5,494	4,184	4,188	15,750	17,831	2,233	1,128
Texas..........................	162,556	6,025	19,964	13,547	54,864	74,181	117,944	16,884	3,214
Utah...........................	10,755	3,653	1,602	1,363	1,466	6,324	7,162	1,348	726
Vermont......................	3,275	5,225	995	543	358	1,380	2,286	113	0
Virginia.......................	33,980	4,080	7,088	4,926	3,361	18,604	21,127	3,280	962
Washington..................	25,804	3,653	4,308	3,107	2,636	15,754	17,219	2,158	200
West Virginia................	8,756	4,736	1,651	930	2,144	4,032	5,363	678	2,031
Wisconsin	26,448	4,592	5,475	3,688	4,776	12,510	15,161	3,981	1,019
Wyoming......................	5,841	9,997	501	581	1,934	2,826	4,019	456	798

0 = Represents zero or amounts to zero.
[1]Total expenditures are the sum of purchases for each source (including retail electricity sales) less electric power sector purchases of fuel.
[2]Includes sources not shown separately, such as electricity imports and exports and coal coke net imports ($347 million in 2007), which are not included in the States.
[3]Excludes expenditures on energy sources such as hydroelectric, geothermal, wind, photovoltaic, or solar thermal. Also excluded are expenditures for reported amounts of energy consumed by the energy industry for production, transportation, and processing operations.
[4]Based on estimated resident population as of July 1.
[5]Includes fuel ethanol blended into motor gasoline.

Table A-56.   Construction

Geographic area	Nonfarm employment (BLS)[1]			Earnings (BEA)[2] (million dollars)			Establishments			Total units (thousands)		Valuation (thousands of dollars)	
	2015	2010	2005	2015	2010	2005	2014	2010	Net Change	2015	2014	2015	2014
United States	6,461	5,518	7,336	640,255	474,346	549,383	667,099	682,684	-15,585	1,182,582	1,052,124	223,611,322	194,349,703
Alabama.....................	81.6	87.2	105.5	7,080	6,608	6,517	7,282	8,235	-953	14,054	13,507	2,416,774	2,231,582
Alaska	17.6	16.6	19.1	2,357	2,219	1,865	2,511	2,461	50	1,298	1,387	324,596	324,925
Arizona......................	127.9	111.5	219.4	9,472	7,825	13,260	11,438	12,091	-653	28,910	26,997	6,985,714	5,666,004
Arkansas...................	49.2	48.7	54.7	4,041	3,629	3,441	5,130	5,539	-409	8,500	7,966	1,380,106	1,326,777
California...................	731.8	559.8	905.3	77,407	54,469	82,120	67,545	66,999	546	98,188	83,657	22,637,174	18,743,512
Colorado	148.8	115.1	160.0	14,428	8,453	11,553	16,388	16,747	-359	31,871	28,698	7,532,619	6,481,914
Connecticut................	57.9	50.0	65.9	8,679	7,142	8,202	7,845	8,187	-342	6,077	5,329	1,282,308	1,148,276
Delaware	20.8	19.3	28.0	1,966	1,444	(D)	2,172	2,375	-203	5,221	5,194	641,676	615,472
District of Columbia	14.6	10.6	12.6	1,346	898	(D)	449	421	28	4,956	4,189	495,021	374,396
Florida.......................	432.4	350.8	637.5	31,152	25,799	38,547	46,585	45,041	1,544	109,924	84,084	23,439,129	19,550,711
Georgia	166.5	149.7	208.8	15,391	11,509	14,898	16,367	17,482	-1,115	45,549	39,673	7,955,101	6,588,773
Hawaii.......................	35.0	28.9	33.4	3,772	3,021	3,018	2,735	2,738	-3	5,422	3,066	1,582,395	1,011,786
Idaho........................	38.2	31.3	45.0	2,991	1,983	2,748	5,958	6,358	-400	9,954	8,805	1,934,066	1,657,417
Illinois	213.6	198.3	268.5	23,179	18,533	23,045	28,286	29,175	-889	19,571	20,602	4,136,596	4,215,395
Indiana......................	127.1	115.7	148.2	11,582	9,065	10,159	12,971	13,756	-785	18,483	17,813	3,737,044	3,222,095
Iowa.........................	78.2	61.6	71.4	7,414	5,036	4,890	8,461	8,609	-148	12,097	10,353	2,243,252	1,924,541
Kansas......................	61.0	54.1	62.4	5,426	4,319	4,020	6,920	7,064	-144	8,644	7,467	1,646,377	1,418,497
Kentucky....................	75.8	67.9	84.2	6,819	5,084	5,563	7,139	7,770	-631	10,566	9,421	1,467,802	1,298,994
Louisiana	140.6	121.5	118.8	12,397	10,292	6,833	7,876	8,441	-565	13,830	15,337	2,777,014	2,905,856
Maine........................	26.5	24.4	30.7	2,660	2,483	2,453	4,729	5,023	-294	3,699	3,249	683,014	614,414
Maryland....................	154.3	143.4	183.6	14,986	12,561	13,542	13,883	14,516	-633	17,057	16,332	3,080,620	2,889,379
Massachusetts.............	139.1	107.1	139.5	18,055	12,512	14,493	17,308	16,844	464	17,424	14,467	3,850,521	3,297,662
Michigan....................	148.3	121.6	189.5	15,028	9,794	14,716	18,341	18,895	-554	18,226	15,836	3,850,470	3,302,480
Minnesota..................	115.2	87.6	129.4	12,258	7,919	10,218	16,124	16,368	-244	19,545	17,010	4,135,089	3,682,598
Mississippi.................	46.0	49.5	52.2	4,054	3,827	3,227	3,807	4,389	-582	6,845	6,955	1,317,315	1,045,466
Missouri.....................	114.4	106.2	143.1	10,392	8,864	10,140	12,966	13,846	-880	18,344	16,314	3,146,410	2,724,091
Montana.....................	26.5	22.6	27.6	2,470	1,805	1,788	5,087	5,111	-24	4,826	3,889	827,389	647,761
Nebraska....................	49.0	41.7	46.5	4,448	4,180	2,930	6,138	5,810	328	8,096	7,690	1,317,315	1,221,773
Nevada......................	70.2	59.3	134.7	5,359	6,371	9,323	4,629	5,003	-374	14,083	13,016	2,141,757	1,754,597
New Hampshire............	24.2	21.4	29.4	3,560	2,824	3,338	3,835	4,059	-224	3,763	3,405	736,931	654,019
New Jersey	148.4	129.5	169.1	19,745	13,725	16,661	20,933	20,865	68	30,560	28,155	4,051,996	4,069,959
New Mexico	43.5	43.6	54.4	3,092	2,856	2,872	4,291	4,738	-447	4,599	4,799	872,141	881,907
New York....................	361.3	306.6	325.3	39,029	30,271	26,396	46,446	45,293	1,153	74,611	36,280	10,826,337	5,583,832
North Carolina.............	189.3	176.5	231.1	16,994	11,850	14,568	21,086	23,107	-2,021	54,757	49,913	9,707,931	8,619,904
North Dakota..............	34.7	21.6	17.5	3,472	1,790	1,070	3,087	2,570	517	6,256	12,646	953,024	1,673,572
Ohio..........................	200.5	168.8	232.9	19,967	13,831	16,876	19,603	20,620	-1,017	20,047	19,965	3,982,890	3,772,530
Oklahoma...................	77.4	67.0	66.1	7,767	5,885	4,416	8,198	8,086	112	11,545	14,238	2,216,234	2,472,378
Oregon......................	83.3	67.6	90.9	7,527	5,217	6,447	11,361	11,797	-436	17,510	16,649	3,591,958	3,244,293
Pennsylvania...............	235.4	214.9	255.7	25,604	20,103	21,127	26,209	26,835	-626	22,854	25,108	4,406,389	4,723,113
Rhode Island...............	17.0	15.9	21.8	1,946	1,685	1,869	2,953	3,091	-138	998	952	211,614	195,030
South Carolina	87.0	79.4	116.9	7,310	5,128	6,279	8,880	9,688	-808	31,030	27,551	6,242,696	5,428,946
South Dakota	22.2	20.1	21.0	1,980	1,459	1,270	3,268	3,158	110	4,482	4,738	740,741	691,430
Tennessee	112.7	100.7	121.1	12,574	8,971	9,621	9,279	10,025	-746	32,219	28,263	5,596,464	4,641,361
Texas........................	683.8	564.4	567.1	75,126	48,362	40,643	40,525	39,321	1,204	175,443	170,132	29,086,961	26,962,225
Utah.........................	84.8	65.0	81.5	6,868	4,240	4,381	8,597	8,822	-225	18,297	17,518	3,851,184	3,362,686
Vermont.....................	15.1	13.5	16.9	1,536	1,407	1,355	2,647	2,784	-137	1,998	1,547	333,954	282,006
Virginia.....................	184.8	183.1	243.6	16,744	13,159	17,392	19,137	20,779	-1,642	28,469	28,693	4,724,305	4,656,865
Washington.................	173.2	140.7	177.4	16,905	11,426	13,181	20,473	21,027	-554	40,374	33,905	8,518,859	7,017,179
West Virginia..............	32.5	32.8	36.8	2,897	2,563	2,238	3,230	3,659	-429	2,814	2,686	417,183	399,711
Wisconsin	109.4	94.6	127.5	11,032	8,184	9,752	13,379	14,325	-946	16,793	14,741	3,078,382	2,617,773
Wyoming....................	23.3	22.3	20.7	1,967	1,768	1,222	2,612	2,741	-129	1,903	1,937	607,666	511,829

(D) = Data withheld to avoid disclosure or does not meet statistical standards.

[1] All estimates of labor and earnings provided by BLS are based on the 2012 North American Industry Classification System (NAICS). Figure includes logging and mining with construction for Delaware, the District of Columbia, Hawaii, Maryland, Nebraska, South Dakota, and Tennessee.

[2] Bureau of Economic Analysis. The estimates of earnings for 2005 are based on the 2002 North American Industry Classification System (NAICS). The estimates for 2010 forward are based on the 2007 NAICS. The estimates for 2015 are based in the 2012 North American Industry Classification System (NAICS). All dollars estimates are in current dollars and not adjusted for inflation.

[3] Data based on 20,100 places in the United States having building permits systems; see Source in Appendix A for details.

Table A-57.   Manufactures

Geographic area	Nonfarm employment in manufacturing (BLS)[1] (thousands)			Earnings (BEA)[2] (million dollars)			Establishments[3] 2014		Average hourly earnings of production workers[1,4] (dollars)		Value of shipments[5] (million dollars)		
	2015	2010	2005	2015	2010	2005	Total	Net change 2010–2014	2015	2010	2015	2010	2005
United States	12,336	11,528	14,227	1,056,023	878,463	927,983	292,543	-7,439	19.91	18.61	5,546,998	4,916,647	4,735,384
Alabama	258	236	299	17,527	14,530	15,429	4,179	-223	18.79	15.71	129,827	104,183	87,841
Alaska	14	13	13	975	721	659	529	4	22.58	20.44	5,807	7,274	6,571
Arizona	158	148	182	14,323	12,151	12,393	4,224	-132	17.95	17.00	52,940	48,257	43,234
Arkansas	155	160	202	9,316	8,264	9,077	2,615	-159	16.19	13.87	59,267	54,532	58,188
California	1,302	1,249	1,508	139,691	115,689	116,955	38,293	-644	21.36	18.96	511,912	457,716	434,238
Colorado	141	124	148	12,481	9,667	10,441	4,958	149	26.54	22.04	52,722	44,573	37,420
Connecticut	157	163	193	19,535	24,209	16,619	4,198	-275	25.68	23.75	57,995	51,410	46,549
Delaware	26	26	33	2,284	1,940	3,269	592	-9	17.25	16.53	18,674	21,055	23,362
District of Columbia	1	1	2	192	137	37	98	9	NA	NA	316	216	261
Florida	343	309	416	26,373	21,771	24,015	12,912	296	20.03	19.42	107,033	88,149	91,573
Georgia	379	345	450	27,921	22,677	24,952	7,351	-332	18.02	16.64	167,762	131,815	143,960
Hawaii	14	13	15	891	729	761	760	-84	20.14	18.58	5,904	6,424	6,407
Idaho	62	53	64	4,757	3,455	3,522	1,753	-4	22.18	20.70	20,421	21,740	18,232
Illinois	581	561	688	52,993	44,195	46,342	13,531	-679	19.78	16.92	258,510	240,920	231,332
Indiana	518	446	570	41,187	31,878	36,065	8,036	-186	18.91	18.50	250,419	207,530	199,872
Iowa	216	201	229	17,341	12,702	13,541	3,542	-54	19.03	16.73	117,584	89,232	86,427
Kansas	161	158	179	13,673	11,101	10,676	2,831	-124	18.87	18.85	88,193	77,479	62,064
Kentucky	241	209	262	17,631	13,677	15,411	3,755	-23	20.33	18.94	133,362	105,553	106,365
Louisiana	144	138	152	13,285	11,606	10,553	3,255	-2	22.07	21.31	174,288	202,307	163,163
Maine	51	51	61	3,585	3,342	3,433	1,645	15	20.89	20.18	15,909	15,158	14,918
Maryland	105	115	140	9,709	9,901	9,931	3,001	-190	18.85	20.05	40,223	39,932	39,774
Massachusetts	249	252	305	26,834	24,766	24,655	6,654	-253	21.80	20.51	83,616	78,157	80,702
Michigan	588	466	667	48,123	36,528	50,221	12,361	-17	20.80	21.76	264,609	195,079	222,075
Minnesota	318	293	347	26,831	20,982	22,579	7,275	-102	20.22	18.87	119,852	107,280	97,999
Mississippi	142	136	178	8,696	7,309	8,235	2,167	-189	18.30	14.83	58,500	54,168	49,661
Missouri	261	246	312	20,484	16,774	18,820	5,946	-276	19.62	18.46	121,666	101,134	107,661
Montana	19	17	20	1,194	955	950	1,251	41	18.01	17.10	9,722	9,587	7,949
Nebraska	97	92	101	6,904	5,146	5,019	1,795	-50	17.73	16.13	56,703	44,806	38,258
Nevada	42	38	48	2,999	2,482	2,814	1,750	46	17.48	15.51	16,216	13,742	12,281
New Hampshire	67	66	80	5,701	5,177	5,285	1,806	-88	19.74	17.81	20,288	18,606	16,872
New Jersey	239	252	328	26,169	25,776	26,698	7,537	-551	20.03	18.86	96,575	98,261	103,236
New Mexico	28	29	36	1,551	1,893	2,013	1,350	-50	16.56	15.76	13,627	21,197	26,748
New York	455	457	579	39,746	35,705	38,793	16,076	-857	19.40	18.39	150,850	150,027	154,682
North Carolina	462	432	565	33,983	29,277	32,068	8,721	-242	16.98	15.85	214,445	177,658	186,665
North Dakota	26	23	26	1,864	1,248	1,251	762	24	19.96	15.93	13,827	10,308	8,978
Ohio	687	621	812	54,536	43,902	51,782	14,208	-521	19.85	18.66	325,674	263,667	278,577
Oklahoma	137	123	145	10,458	8,625	9,075	3,554	-71	18.47	14.33	63,408	60,004	55,096
Oregon	186	164	204	15,588	12,311	12,895	5,314	33	19.67	17.60	58,405	55,061	61,770
Pennsylvania	568	560	679	44,853	39,795	43,018	13,684	-483	18.95	16.88	224,894	219,949	214,876
Rhode Island	41	40	55	3,085	2,699	3,144	1,432	-122	17.69	14.71	11,907	10,813	11,548
South Carolina	236	207	260	17,801	13,367	14,224	3,770	-196	18.86	16.52	112,930	81,894	87,499
South Dakota	43	37	40	3,338	1,938	2,182	1,028	21	18.01	15.28	17,106	13,180	10,361
Tennessee	333	299	409	24,475	20,129	23,450	5,632	-329	17.48	15.33	144,722	124,090	137,388
Texas	879	817	901	89,523	67,623	65,279	19,681	88	21.67	14.49	566,356	560,696	463,953
Utah	124	111	118	9,066	7,228	6,276	3,201	51	19.06	18.46	48,646	45,720	33,572
Vermont	31	31	37	2,202	2,130	2,189	989	3	18.93	16.63	8,579	10,203	10,686
Virginia	234	231	296	18,023	15,649	17,194	4,986	-327	19.97	19.11	101,654	92,512	88,966
Washington	292	258	273	27,591	21,797	19,744	6,929	-121	25.52	23.48	144,903	103,983	93,099
West Virginia	48	49	62	3,422	3,230	3,687	1,204	-95	19.19	18.11	24,595	21,873	21,573
Wisconsin	467	431	505	34,425	29,070	29,820	8,858	-175	19.32	18.10	175,958	149,622	144,244
Wyoming	10	9	10	891	605	541	564	16	21.58	20.49	7,702	7,913	6,660

NA = Not available.
[1]All estimates of labor and earnings provided by the Bureau of Labor Statistics (BLS) are based on the 2007 North American Industry Classification System (NAICS). Earning estimates are in current dollars and not adjusted for inflation.
[2]Bureau of Economic Analysis. The estimates of earnings for 2000–2006 are based on the 2002 North American Industry Classificataion System. The estimates for 2007 forward are based on the 2007 NAICS. All dollars estimates are in current dollars and not adjusted for inflation.
[3]2,010 data for establishments are based on the 2007 North American Industry Classification System (NAICS); 2005 data are based on the 2002 NAICS.
[4]Data for average hourly earnings of production workers are provided in current dollars and not adjusted for inflation. United States totals differ from the sum of the state figures because of differing benchmarks among states and differing industrial and geographic stratification.
[5]Includes extensive and unmeasurable duplication from shipments between establishments in the same industry classification.

Table A-58. Manufactures Summary and Export-Related Shipments and Employment

| Geographic area | Manufactures summary, 2014 (2012, NAICS 31–33) | | | | | | | | | | Export-related, 2009[4,5] | | | |
| | All employees[1] | | | | Production workers[1] | | | Value added by manufactures[2] | | Value of shipments[3] (million dollars) | Export related shipments (million dollars) | Export related manufacturing employment (thousands) | Export related as a percentage of all manufacturers | |
	Number	Percentage change, 2010–2014	Payroll Total (million dollars)	Payroll Per employee (dollar)	Total	Hours (million)	Wages (million dollars)	Total (million dollars)	Per production worker (dollar)				Shipments	Employment
United States	11,424,251	5.2	639,911	56,013	7,807,966	15,969	360,741	2,430,098	311,233	5,546,998	1,327,600	2,536.7	24.1	23.8
Alabama......................	243,899	6.5	12,114	49,669	175,803	367	7,733	45,183	257,010	129,827	32,665	54.1	28.9	25.3
Alaska........................	12,846	1.0	557	43,369	10,384	21	412	(D)	(D)	5,807	1,643	3.4	19.7	30.6
Arizona......................	140,517	2.3	8,915	63,447	81,624	165	3,837	27,667	338,956	52,940	14,204	34.7	28.4	27.4
Arkansas....................	153,715	-0.9	6,627	43,110	120,359	244	4,731	25,468	211,596	59,267	9,413	20.6	15.7	14.1
California....................	1,149,707	0.5	73,089	63,572	715,682	1,448	33,570	253,830	354,668	511,912	112,870	280.4	22.7	25.2
Colorado....................	120,963	7.0	6,789	56,126	78,058	159	3,658	25,974	332,754	52,722	10,199	26.5	20.7	24.0
Connecticut................	151,363	-0.8	11,124	73,495	90,995	186	4,738	35,105	385,790	57,995	14,857	42.3	28.6	27.4
Delaware....................	25,665	-9.9	1,487	57,924	17,710	36	804	6,029	340,429	18,674	2,978	5.7	14.4	21.0
District of Columbia	940	-33.1	50	52,903	725	2	30	(D)	(D)	316	5	(D)	2.6	(D)
Florida........................	290,647	6.9	15,263	52,514	179,700	363	7,735	56,974	317,052	107,033	18,240	46.7	19.8	18.3
Georgia	352,455	7.8	17,123	48,581	261,909	535	10,845	68,622	262,007	167,762	34,066	66.8	23.6	21.3
Hawaii........................	11,958	-3.7	508	42,518	7,446	15	335	(D)	(D)	5,904	1,002	0.5	13.0	4.7
Idaho.........................	55,281	6.6	2,948	53,332	39,433	79	1,810	8,588	217,789	20,421	6,082	8.7	26.6	18.0
Illinois........................	544,488	2.6	31,569	57,980	378,812	779	17,290	108,600	286,686	258,510	71,238	143.8	25.9	26.9
Indiana.......................	475,831	13.4	25,408	53,396	357,123	739	16,619	105,755	296,131	250,419	56,355	105.8	24.3	24.7
Iowa...........................	209,256	7.0	10,631	50,806	150,367	305	6,516	48,847	324,853	117,584	21,740	47.0	21.3	24.5
Kansas.......................	164,749	4.5	8,787	53,338	114,603	233	5,453	34,517	301,190	88,193	17,775	37.4	21.1	24.8
Kentucky....................	226,808	11.7	11,567	50,997	176,085	362	8,428	46,416	263,601	133,362	27,024	47.4	22.7	23.5
Louisiana	129,832	3.9	8,686	66,900	86,549	184	5,150	49,642	573,570	174,288	55,310	26.8	20.5	21.5
Maine.........................	48,760	-3.4	2,463	50,510	35,202	71	1,677	7,689	218,420	15,909	2,647	8.2	16.7	17.1
Maryland....................	96,939	-7.3	6,081	62,726	57,995	116	2,742	22,019	379,670	40,223	5,403	13.8	12.9	13.2
Massachusetts.............	221,793	-2.2	15,249	68,753	133,171	270	6,698	45,709	343,237	83,616	26,758	69.3	33.2	30.9
Michigan	538,840	21.0	30,098	55,856	392,523	822	19,340	103,492	263,659	264,609	64,708	141.6	29.3	30.7
Minnesota	298,024	3.9	16,777	56,295	194,883	394	8,751	55,699	285,808	119,852	22,916	65.1	18.9	22.4
Mississippi	140,188	0.5	6,297	44,918	102,042	207	4,191	21,572	211,402	58,500	14,387	17.4	23.8	13.6
Missouri.....................	248,347	3.8	13,292	53,521	184,297	364	8,884	54,050	293,278	121,666	25,121	49.5	23.3	21.5
Montana.....................	17,579	11.0	796	45,276	11,140	22	512	3,402	305,382	9,722	2,457	3.1	21.0	23.5
Nebraska....................	93,135	4.8	4,254	45,679	71,525	148	2,954	19,289	269,687	56,703	7,545	14.3	14.3	15.9
Nevada......................	41,572	5.6	2,184	52,533	27,043	54	1,273	8,249	305,038	16,216	2,775	6.7	18.6	17.4
New Hampshire............	66,151	-2.9	4,236	64,029	39,619	80	1,808	11,015	278,024	20,288	5,079	18.1	25.8	25.7
New Jersey	221,901	-5.6	14,263	64,278	142,865	292	6,822	47,702	333,892	96,575	23,329	47.4	21.7	20.2
New Mexico	26,449	-5.1	1,372	51,874	15,645	31	731	5,639	360,440	13,627	5,977	4.8	20.9	18.8
New York.....................	423,971	-2.4	23,088	54,455	266,560	536	12,223	78,528	294,598	150,850	39,277	101.3	25.9	24.2
North Carolina............	408,132	2.1	19,610	48,048	303,986	615	12,181	107,969	355,179	214,445	39,308	79.8	19.6	20.6
North Dakota...............	24,862	13.0	1,169	47,033	18,495	37	752	5,019	271,344	13,827	1,909	3.0	14.2	13.9
Ohio...........................	642,967	7.3	35,296	54,895	465,631	961	21,825	130,628	280,540	325,674	77,466	165.4	26.5	27.6
Oklahoma...................	136,360	14.4	6,972	51,129	94,702	193	4,269	24,953	263,489	63,408	10,661	24.5	15.3	19.5
Oregon.......................	161,572	12.5	9,290	57,499	107,624	219	5,107	27,579	256,252	58,405	12,706	28.5	21.3	22.0
Pennsylvania..............	548,672	1.1	29,804	54,319	368,455	753	17,203	108,333	294,021	224,894	45,564	100.8	19.2	19.0
Rhode Island...............	39,275	-3.3	2,184	55,601	25,152	51	1,172	5,925	235,586	11,907	2,519	6.1	22.5	16.9
South Carolina	219,826	7.6	11,445	52,066	162,736	340	7,471	45,054	276,856	112,930	31,082	58.2	34.3	29.9
South Dakota..............	44,065	12.7	1,982	44,982	32,238	66	1,267	7,479	231,979	17,106	2,511	6.6	15.5	17.1
Tennessee	308,546	7.5	15,704	50,896	223,968	458	9,745	63,708	284,452	144,722	31,900	63.2	24.1	22.8
Texas.........................	807,515	10.5	49,428	61,210	513,403	1,067	25,072	219,272	427,096	566,356	195,395	183	29.1	26.1
Utah...........................	114,537	7.1	6,262	54,671	73,957	149	3,424	22,739	307,466	48,646	11,893	20	23.4	19.9
Vermont......................	29,823	-3.2	1,574	52,761	18,646	37	827	4,134	221,702	8,579	2,276	5.8	21.6	20.7
Virginia......................	232,965	-0.7	12,841	55,118	164,875	334	7,523	57,468	348,555	101,654	20,747	45.1	21.9	20.3
Washington................	257,814	17.0	16,117	62,515	165,678	340	8,975	69,611	420,159	144,903	45,006	89.4	39.1	38.8
West Virginia..............	49,589	-4.7	2,732	55,095	31,340	64	1,599	11,536	368,093	24,595	6,225	10.2	26.0	20.6
Wisconsin	443,111	8.3	23,166	52,279	312,467	639	13,595	80,759	258,456	175,958	33,027	86.4	20.2	20.2
Wyoming....................	10,051	3.1	645	64,210	6,734	14	425	2,809	417,204	7,702	1,359	1.6	15.5	19.0

(D) = Data withheld to avoid disclosure or does not meet statistical standards.
NA = Not available.
[1]Includes employment and payroll at administrative offices and auxiliary units. All employees represents the average of production workers plus all other employees for the payroll period ended nearest the 12th of March. Production workers represents the average of the employment for the payroll periods ended nearest the 12th of March, May, August, and November.
[2]Adjusted value added; takes into account (a) value added by merchandising operations (that is, difference between the sales value and cost of merchandise sold without further manufacture, processing, or assembly), plus (b) net change in finished goods and work-in-process inventories between beginning and end of year.
[3]Includes extensive and unmeasurable duplication from shipments between establishments in the same industry classification.
[4]Exports includes both "direct" exports (exports manufactured in the United States and consumed in foreign markets) and "indirect" exports (intermediate goods and services required to manufacture export goods).
[5]Preliminary data.

Table A-59.   Major Manufacturing Sectors, 2015

Geographic area	Food manufacturing[1] (2012 NAICS 311)				Fabricated metal products[1] (2012 NAICS 332)			
	Employment				Employment			
	Total	Percent of total manufacturing	Percent change, 2014–2015	Value of shipments (million dollars)	Total	Percent of total manufacturing	Percent change, 2014–2015	Value of shipments (million dollars)
United States	1,389,119	12.4	1.5	775,591	1,371,985	12.3	-0.2	349,958
Alabama......................	29,946	12.8	-2.4	11,024	22,887	9.8	0.1	5,858
Alaska........................	9,224	72.1	-3.2	2,530	496	3.9	1.6	127
Arizona.......................	10,167	7.6	5.1	7,088	19,351	15	3	4,419
Arkansas....................	43,120	28.7	1.2	17,180	13,393	8.9	-0.8	4,682
California....................	151,282	13.5	1.2	78,151	124,493	11.1	-0.5	28,295
Colorado....................	17,727	14.8	0.6	11,296	14,340	12.0	-0.4	3,761
Connecticut................	6,249	4.0	7.3	2,938	28,189	18.0	3.2	7,085
Delaware....................	8,664	33.4	6.2	3,450	1,892	7.3	3.1	388
District of Columbia......	D	D	D	69	30	2.6	-21.1	5
Florida.......................	25,512	10	2	14,351	28,310	11	2	6,473
Georgia......................	58,843	17.0	5.7	28,915	26,228	7.6	4.1	7,427
Hawaii........................	4,888	42.9	-2.7	1,395	425	3.7	4.4	104
Idaho.........................	15,062	28.2	-2.2	8,316	5,293	9.9	4.4	1,187
Illinois........................	72,603	13.4	3.9	43,597	86,839	16	-0	22,670
Indiana.......................	34,639	7.3	7.1	22,863	57,591	12.2	2.4	16,767
Iowa..........................	49,318	23.8	2.7	39,682	19,459	9.4	0.9	4,912
Kansas.......................	27,703	17.3	2.1	24,480	16,365	10.2	-0.9	3,748
Kentucky....................	26,193	11.5	0.4	13,197	21,274	9.4	4.2	5,417
Louisiana	13,009	10.7	-14.5	8,567	19,505	16.1	-9.9	4,649
Maine........................	4,639	9.7	-4.3	1,655	4,636	9.7	-1.1	1,205
Maryland.....................	13,752	14.6	4.7	8,137	7,962	8.5	0.2	1,867
Massachusetts.............	18,888	8.3	-0.5	8,061	29,163	12.9	1.1	8,832
Michigan.....................	28,930	5.3	3.8	16,797	77,015	14.1	4.1	18,253
Minnesota...................	44,315	15.2	-1.3	27,166	37,635	12.9	2.9	9,838
Mississippi..................	20,666	15.9	-0.5	6,271	10,479	8.1	-4.9	2,946
Missouri.....................	38,239	15.4	3.1	23,650	29,442	11.9	-1.8	6,630
Montana.....................	1,733	10.8	-2.3	1,133	2,035	12.7	19.6	405
Nebraska....................	33,765	36.1	-0.1	31,201	8,517	9.1	1.2	2,231
Nevada.......................	4,658	11.7	9.1	2,282	5,022	12.6	0.8	1,053
New Hampshire............	2,936	4.5	5.5	1,581	11,536	17.5	-3.6	2,610
New Jersey	28,621	12.7	4.3	12,906	21,426	9.5	-0.6	4,748
New Mexico	4,350	18.5	-1.0	3,079	2,224	9.5	-4.4	438
New York.....................	41,399	10.4	-1.6	20,080	49,380	12.4	0.5	11,324
North Carolina..............	49,574	12.2	0.7	21,854	32,806	8.0	-2.1	9,504
North Dakota...............	4,855	19.9	3.2	4,208	1,919	7.9	3.9	448
Ohio..........................	51,760	8.0	4.4	32,244	99,869	15.4	-0.2	29,287
Oklahoma...................	16,401	12.8	2.0	7,863	24,471	19.1	-4.8	7,292
Oregon.......................	21,806	13.9	-0.4	9,057	15,016	9.6	-1.9	3,250
Pennsylvania...............	64,381	12.1	2.7	34,742	78,850	14.8	0.6	18,775
Rhode Island...............	2,523	6.7	0.2	612	9,274	24.7	4.7	2,157
South Carolina	17,173	7.8	0.0	7,165	22,190	10.1	1.7	6,816
South Dakota	9,118	20.8	3.3	4,886	4,015	9.2	-1.0	914
Tennessee	35,581	11.8	2.6	20,090	35,987	11.9	2.7	9,348
Texas.........................	79,238	10.6	-2.3	45,433	117,660	15.8	-8.2	30,770
Utah..........................	14,991	13.6	1.6	8,942	11,393	10.4	3.7	2,817
Vermont......................	3,823	13.9	-12.9	2,394	2,191	8.0	-0.9	401
Virginia.......................	28,338	12.3	5.1	13,958	17,467	7.6	0.5	5,118
Washington..................	34,295	13.7	0.0	14,400	21,396	8.6	0.0	5,134
West Virginia...............	NA	NA	NA	NA	5,337	12.1	-5.9	1,695
Wisconsin	64,554	14.8	3.4	43,696	68,171	15.6	2.8	15,525
Wyoming	516	5.6	-6.4	225	1,145	12.4	-8.8	352

NA = Not available.
D = Data withheld to avoid disclosure or does not meet statistical standards.
[1]Data may not be available for all NAICS industries or geographies.

Table A-59. Major Manufacturing Sectors, 2015—*Continued*

Geographic area	Computer and electronic products[1] (2012 NAICS 334)				Transportation equipment[1] (2012 NAICS 336)			
	Employment			Value of shipments (million dollars)	Employment			Value of shipments (million dollars)
	Total	Percent of total manufacturing	Percent change, 2014–2015		Total	Percent of total manufacturing	Percent change, 2014–2015	
United States	773,527	6.9	-0.7	300,494	1,465,471	13.1	3.0	948,208
Alabama.....................	7,915	3.4	-9.3	2,529	53,460	22.9	3.6	49,965
Alaska	D	D	D	D	363	2.8	-5.2	91
Arizona......................	20,291	15	-10	9,097	23,710	18	-4	12,919
Arkansas	2,450	1.6	-0.7	611	14,014	9.3	-0.9	6,918
California...................	155,805	13.9	0.0	65,575	112,356	10.0	1.9	46,198
Colorado	13,676	11.4	0.8	4,734	9,967	8.3	43.7	3,591
Connecticut................	14,220	9.1	-1.4	5,162	47,441	30.3	-5.3	21,924
Delaware	1,874	7.2	1.5	668	444	1.7	13.0	121
District of Columbia	NA	NA	NA	NA	NA	NA	NA	NA
Florida.......................	32,591	12	-7	11,618	27,862	10	4	8,722
Georgia	5,883	1.7	0.9	1,794	46,102	13.3	-0.2	32,881
Hawaii	52	0.5	18.2	0	689	6.1	-12.6	200
Idaho.........................	9,344	17.5	19.3	2,168	2,186	4.1	5.6	592
Illinois.......................	25,550	5	0	9,405	53,401	10	5	31,308
Indiana......................	13,461	2.8	-5.8	5,642	118,707	25	2	79,171
Iowa..........................	12,231	5.9	2.4	3,827	14,527	7.0	7.9	4,774
Kansas	6,902	4.3	1.8	1,623	39,762	24.8	-2.6	21,513
Kentucky....................	2,244	1.0	-7.1	1,083	58,228	25.6	6.3	50,010
Louisiana	1,075	0.9	42.0	252	11,911	9.8	-5.8	2,998
Maine........................	2,536	5.3	-18.5	1,252	9,034	19.0	5.7	2,667
Maryland....................	15,769	16.7	1.2	6,603	5,069	5.4	-4.8	1,880
Massachusetts............	48,529	21.4	0.1	22,349	7,958	3.5	0.3	2,553
Michigan	12,502	2.3	-1.9	3,414	155,496	28.5	5.8	123,789
Minnesota	34,623	11.9	1.6	11,640	12,837	4.4	8.8	7,337
Mississippi.................	1,867	1.4	0.3	319	24,642	18.9	-0.3	11,075
Missouri	6,057	2.4	-6.4	2,586	42,362	17.1	15.8	32,132
Montana	D	D	D	D	690	4.3	10.9	189
Nebraska....................	4,156	4.4	7.9	1,036	8,041	8.6	4.0	2,562
Nevada......................	3,941	9.9	-0.4	2,241	734	1.8	0.8	306
New Hampshire...........	12,229	19	-1	4,099	3,261	5	5	801
New Jersey	20,568	9.2	-2.9	6,617	3,637	1.6	10.0	991
New Mexico	4,176	17.8	-5.2	1,848	493	2.1	-7.5	126
New York....................	41,159	10.3	2.2	14,102	19,498	4.9	-8.5	9,219
North Carolina.............	16,359	4.0	-0.5	6,792	30,858	7.6	7.0	25,928
North Dakota...............	1,468	6.0	-7.4	459	2,043	8.4	8.6	519
Ohio	22,218	3.4	-2.2	7,354	115,612	18	6	90,441
Oklahoma...................	4,081	3.2	3.8	1,199	11,450	8.9	-5.2	5,283
Oregon	24,244	15.5	-1.6	12,454	9,980	6.4	5.0	3,574
Pennsylvania...............	27,901	5.3	-2.3	10,117	35,194	6.6	2.4	22,282
Rhode Island...............	2,956	7.9	-1.5	863	970	2.6	-18.0	285
South Carolina	4,255	1.9	3.2	2,544	34,109	15.5	-1.2	28,078
South Dakota	2,080	4.7	-16.7	460	2,928	6.7	-10.9	894
Tennessee	7,126	2.4	20.7	2,950	51,149	16.9	11.7	34,639
Texas........................	58,085	7.8	-1.4	26,364	77,005	10	4	62,110
Utah	13,690	12.4	2.8	4,607	9,817	9	7	4,039
Vermont.....................	4,629	16.9	-10.4	1,623	1,722	6.3	-2.9	412
Virginia......................	10,699	4.6	2.8	3,308	43,810	19.0	3.0	14,209
Washington.................	18,712	7.5	6.5	6,453	79,188	31.7	-2.5	71,660
West Virginia...............	828	1.9	-2.5	180	5,608	12.7	6.1	4,528
Wisconsin	20,017	4.6	-4.4	8,734	25,029	5.7	-1.9	9,755
Wyoming	292	3.2	1.0	67	119	1.3	-7.0	47

NA = Not available.
D = Data withheld to avoid disclosure or does not meet statistical standards.
[1]Data may not be available for all NAICS industries or geographies.

Table A-60. Information Industries

| | Information industries (2007, NAICS 51) | | | | | | | | | | | | | | |
| | Nonfarm Employment (BLS)[1] (thousands) | | | Earnings (BEA)[2] (million dollars) | | | Establishments[3] | | | | | | | | |
Geographic area	2015	2010	2005	2015	2010	2005	Total, 2014	Publishing, 2014	Motion Picture/ Sound Recording, 2014	Broadcasting, except Internet 2014	Tele-communications, 2014	Data Processing, hosting and related, 2014	Other Informa-tion services, 2014	Total, 2010	Net change, 2010–2014
United States	2,750.0	2,707.0	3,061.0	372,156	289,926	269,864	138,347	27,086	25,417	9,609	50,435	13,903	11,897	135,431	2,916
Alabama......................	21.4	24.0	29.2	1,539	1,557	1,892	1,520	287	128	187	752	108	58	1,587	-67
Alaska........................	6.3	6.5	7.0	571	384	476	413	52	40	63	220	21	17	385	28
Arizona......................	44.6	36.6	44.8	4,213	2,909	2,857	2,111	471	291	160	768	265	156	2,060	51
Arkansas....................	13.5	15.3	19.3	1,016	1,194	2,068	987	193	99	118	457	74	46	1,052	-65
California....................	486.3	429.4	473.7	96,781	53,047	48,089	22,148	3,551	8,318	1,021	5,185	2,098	1,975	20,287	1,861
Colorado....................	70.7	72.0	76.9	7,459	7,303	7,193	3,102	733	420	187	1,077	413	272	2,940	162
Connecticut................	32.4	31.7	38.1	4,094	3,357	3,179	1,721	398	238	123	577	185	200	1,649	72
Delaware....................	4.7	6.0	6.7	431	512	454	499	81	53	26	207	69	63	402	97
District of Columbia	17.2	18.7	22.6	2,509	2,308	2,663	715	166	104	79	169	68	129	726	-11
Florida.......................	136.6	137.1	164.6	15,836	13,688	13,720	8,063	1,534	1,371	553	3,076	835	694	7,806	257
Georgia	111.5	98.0	108.5	15,118	15,131	18,597	4,053	771	655	343	1,586	448	250	4,064	-11
Hawaii.......................	8.7	9.8	10.8	740	723	673	501	95	86	53	189	57	21	543	-42
Idaho........................	9.3	9.6	10.3	600	578	511	645	157	75	61	232	69	51	702	-57
Illinois......................	101.0	101.8	118.2	10,511	8,983	9,463	5,426	1,123	812	351	2,137	581	422	5,535	-109
Indiana......................	33.6	35.6	40.3	2,666	2,473	2,404	2,128	404	286	178	942	238	80	2,297	-169
Iowa.........................	24.4	28.7	33.0	1,750	1,768	1,731	1,477	393	158	143	629	106	48	1,585	-108
Kansas......................	21.1	26.8	38.7	2,146	1,345	1,737	1,335	290	117	124	602	118	84	1,437	-102
Kentucky	22.7	24.7	28.3	1,702	2,364	1,564	1,512	289	155	201	662	131	74	1,487	25
Louisiana	26.4	24.7	29.1	1,843	1,570	1,619	1,406	241	174	134	682	108	67	1,393	13
Maine........................	7.7	8.7	11.2	484	559	616	766	176	91	61	254	58	126	719	47
Maryland....................	38.6	44.0	50.5	6,508	8,169	5,745	2,538	481	336	145	1,053	337	186	2,417	121
Massachusetts.............	88.2	85.0	86.9	11,685	9,887	8,523	3,712	952	426	205	1,307	454	368	3,492	220
Michigan....................	56.6	54.8	64.9	5,156	4,428	4,768	3,765	641	444	248	1,422	337	673	3,451	314
Minnesota	51.3	54.1	59.1	4,981	4,367	4,325	2,607	712	412	195	832	280	176	2,568	39
Mississippi.................	12.7	12.3	14.3	809	687	715	938	155	49	119	524	52	39	918	20
Missouri....................	54.3	60.1	63.8	4,836	4,792	4,657	2,405	489	292	192	1,080	227	125	2,537	-132
Montana.....................	6.4	7.3	7.8	423	410	363	653	153	96	71	264	46	23	575	78
Nebraska....................	18.3	17.5	20.5	1,336	1,095	1,243	895	234	96	92	336	96	41	934	-39
Nevada......................	13.9	12.5	14.7	1,342	1,275	1,305	1,246	266	211	80	400	152	137	1,119	127
New Hampshire............	12.5	11.4	12.7	1,395	1,146	1,118	743	209	67	46	280	83	58	723	20
New Jersey	74.4	79.2	97.1	10,650	9,020	9,104	3,733	723	506	105	1,621	492	286	3,841	-108
New Mexico	12.7	14.4	14.7	865	851	789	753	150	103	91	302	61	46	791	-38
New York....................	264.9	253.1	273.4	44,186	33,921	27,914	11,506	1,958	3,361	636	3,098	854	1,599	11,014	492
North Carolina.............	76.2	68.3	71.4	7,565	5,531	6,297	3,469	713	462	259	1,464	361	210	3,576	-107
North Dakota...............	6.6	7.3	7.6	498	468	394	343	106	36	76	89	22	14	352	-9
Ohio.........................	71.6	77.6	89.9	6,405	8,726	5,989	3,797	730	448	311	1,728	404	176	4,055	-258
Oklahoma...................	21.2	24.3	30.2	1,889	1,620	1,776	1,435	282	163	120	679	117	74	1,543	-108
Oregon......................	32.9	31.7	33.3	3,410	2,684	2,334	1,974	532	312	131	638	193	168	1,977	-3
Pennsylvania...............	84.9	93.3	109.5	23,158	20,158	13,718	5,102	859	522	328	2,239	461	693	5,010	92
Rhode Island...............	8.6	10.0	10.8	790	825	881	476	97	64	33	177	50	55	415	61
South Carolina	26.9	25.9	27.0	2,150	1,950	1,608	1,356	269	135	121	658	101	72	1,393	-37
South Dakota	5.9	6.5	6.8	496	369	346	454	139	60	61	144	34	16	419	35
Tennessee	44.4	45.0	49.4	3,554	2,545	2,566	2,391	412	529	261	877	202	110	2,421	-30
Texas........................	200.7	195.7	223.1	19,876	17,063	15,527	9,102	1,688	1,062	684	4,005	984	679	8,911	191
Utah.........................	34.6	29.3	32.0	2,918	2,098	1,968	1,421	312	294	62	399	207	147	1,375	46
Vermont.....................	4.7	5.4	6.2	347	367	336	481	115	68	48	131	35	84	484	-3
Virginia......................	69.6	76.0	92.7	7,872	8,060	9,727	3,911	779	377	245	1,636	559	315	3,819	92
Washington.................	114.0	103.0	94.7	19,801	11,475	10,429	3,386	853	470	170	1,118	408	367	3,199	187
West Virginia...............	9.7	10.3	11.7	735	651	637	648	105	43	82	361	36	21	747	-99
Wisconsin	48.9	46.7	49.7	4,271	3,316	3,080	2,200	508	258	185	984	181	84	2,399	-199
Wyoming....................	3.8	3.9	4.3	239	216	177	379	59	44	41	186	27	22	300	79

[1]All employment estimates provided by the Bureau of Labor Statistics are based on the 2012 North American Industry Classification System (NAICS).

[2]The estimates of earnings provided by the Bureau of Economic Analysis for 2005 are based on the 2002 North American Industry Classification System (NAICS). The estimates for 2010 forward are based on the 2007 NAICS. The estimates for 2015 are based on the 2012 North American Industry Classification System. All dollar estimates are in current dollars (not adjusted for inflation.)

[3]Data provided by County Business Patterns is based on the North American Industry Classification System (NAICS). Data for 2015 is based on NAICS 2012. Data for 2010 is based on NAICS 2007.

Table A-61. Wholesale and Retail Trade

Geographic area	Wholesale and retail nonfarm employment[1] (thousands)			Wholesale trade — Earnings (BEA)[2] (million dollars)			Wholesale trade — Establishments (NAICS 42)		Retail trade — Earnings (BEA)[2] (million dollars)			Retail trade — Establishments (NAICS 44 and 45)	
	2015	2010	2005	2015	2010	2005	2014	Net change, 2010–2014	2015	2010	2005	2014	Net change, 2010–2014
United States	21,460	19,893	21,044	560,140	448,112	413,603	416,593	1,985	656,599	544,299	540,198	1,065,368	2,616
Alabama......................	305	295	315	5,779	5,109	4,852	5,348	13	7,982	7,038	7,126	18,029	455
Alaska........................	44	42	42	507	441	397	745	2	1,690	1,553	1,477	2,496	19
Arizona.......................	415	387	407	9,068	7,862	7,189	6,607	103	13,874	11,080	11,605	17,944	49
Arkansas....................	187	176	179	3,872	3,200	2,749	3,439	53	5,008	4,143	3,754	10,866	140
California....................	2,376	2,162	2,333	68,608	53,682	50,804	59,379	1,356	86,232	70,040	79,036	107,469	-1,204
Colorado....................	366	328	339	10,188	7,948	6,788	7,206	66	10,777	8,895	8,454	18,643	122
Connecticut.................	247	241	259	7,337	6,408	6,108	4,324	-94	9,158	8,022	8,420	12,542	398
Delaware	65	62	68	1,218	1,166	1,167	1,083	60	2,003	1,739	1,764	3,627	27
District of Columbia	27	23	22	711	558	458	452	39	933	748	665	1,740	22
Florida........................	1,416	1,247	1,349	30,829	24,147	23,483	31,443	1,231	42,966	33,784	35,068	73,200	-2,573
Georgia	700	635	675	20,493	16,595	15,923	13,058	-67	19,046	14,827	14,889	33,666	54
Hawaii........................	89	84	87	1,341	1,093	1,031	1,674	-75	3,022	2,558	2,633	4,639	55
Idaho..........................	112	100	102	2,069	1,572	1,384	2,050	31	3,798	3,039	2,668	5,818	92
Illinois........................	916	874	929	30,695	24,888	23,048	18,893	-301	25,093	21,239	21,082	39,252	1,418
Indiana.......................	444	418	453	9,782	7,978	7,372	7,684	-87	12,105	9,968	9,724	21,431	645
Iowa...........................	248	239	247	5,361	4,431	3,827	4,914	113	5,916	5,332	4,885	11,828	515
Kansas.......................	209	198	208	5,161	4,436	3,716	4,497	65	5,440	4,864	4,418	10,391	336
Kentucky.....................	284	272	287	5,714	4,651	4,484	4,315	31	7,064	6,351	6,118	15,223	356
Louisiana	306	288	293	6,137	5,181	4,487	5,482	-54	9,052	7,797	6,921	16,596	91
Maine	102	100	107	1,546	1,309	1,270	1,575	-16	2,921	2,765	2,869	6,304	209
Maryland.....................	377	362	392	8,457	7,462	7,156	5,678	-83	12,019	10,377	10,807	18,171	185
Massachusetts.............	477	461	488	14,102	12,740	11,162	7,875	-286	14,880	13,326	13,412	24,136	276
Michigan.....................	637	597	677	15,917	12,480	12,298	11,234	-277	17,290	14,668	15,566	34,686	331
Minnesota...................	426	400	432	12,931	10,849	9,758	8,152	-97	11,333	9,414	9,343	18,993	554
Mississippi..................	173	167	174	2,514	2,142	1,961	2,788	-41	5,122	4,305	4,011	11,555	189
Missouri......................	432	415	438	11,063	8,655	7,986	7,789	-151	11,619	10,462	9,866	21,228	571
Montana......................	76	70	72	1,263	913	809	1,580	125	2,287	2,279	1,807	4,757	182
Nebraska....................	152	145	148	4,107	3,072	2,387	3,162	138	3,751	3,282	3,019	7,240	177
Nevada.......................	178	159	168	3,034	2,505	2,657	2,984	126	5,704	4,823	5,152	8,512	-428
New Hampshire............	123	118	125	3,124	2,331	2,239	1,847	-18	4,012	5,166	4,587	6,044	122
New Jersey	676	645	703	25,303	21,279	20,079	14,236	-635	20,984	18,150	18,525	31,685	723
New Mexico	115	111	116	1,481	1,398	1,286	1,855	-102	3,560	3,209	3,063	6,557	256
New York.....................	1,288	1,200	1,231	37,423	29,348	28,405	32,438	-537	43,886	36,173	32,867	78,763	-2,000
North Carolina.............	663	599	612	15,814	12,091	11,130	11,674	23	18,189	15,069	14,316	34,246	93
North Dakota...............	78	65	61	2,304	1,438	1,000	1,705	205	2,176	1,463	1,195	3,242	-43
Ohio	806	767	847	20,613	16,428	15,470	14,217	-93	21,528	18,809	19,154	36,260	775
Oklahoma...................	243	223	225	4,844	2,459	3,264	4,699	105	7,253	6,059	5,189	13,237	-273
Oregon	276	250	267	6,465	6,158	5,668	5,345	-160	8,320	6,955	6,739	13,994	-159
Pennsylvania................	856	844	892	21,818	18,351	16,999	14,832	-245	24,509	22,379	22,911	43,598	832
Rhode Island...............	65	62	69	1,680	1,303	1,177	1,337	-72	2,221	2,035	1,998	3,744	142
South Carolina	313	287	299	5,731	4,429	4,087	4,975	76	8,627	7,222	7,213	17,567	141
South Dakota	74	68	67	1,664	1,143	990	1,522	116	2,253	1,784	1,516	3,866	107
Tennessee	446	424	455	10,495	8,463	8,201	6,858	-81	14,091	11,421	11,496	22,533	280
Texas.........................	1,880	1,623	1,578	60,967	44,586	37,198	33,235	1,709	57,617	43,435	37,994	79,814	-3,027
Utah...........................	208	182	179	4,310	3,418	2,738	3,743	221	7,009	5,128	4,421	9,224	-408
Vermont......................	47	47	51	708	635	599	813	-52	1,491	1,326	1,353	3,400	257
Virginia.......................	527	508	536	10,642	9,227	8,511	7,204	-211	15,749	13,127	13,605	27,059	688
Washington.................	487	428	438	12,295	9,906	8,518	9,288	-94	19,483	13,373	12,396	21,586	184
West Virginia...............	109	110	114	1,557	1,450	1,278	1,530	-22	2,936	2,713	2,583	6,214	343
Wisconsin	427	406	435	10,108	8,134	7,626	6,985	-89	11,383	9,493	9,602	19,143	448
Wyoming	40	38	38	991	664	429	845	18	1,239	1,087	917	2,610	116

[1]All estimates of labor provided by the Bureau of Labor Statistics (BLS) are based on the 2007 North American Industry Classification System (NAICS). Includes Wholesale trade (NAICS 42) and Retail trade (NAICS 44).
[2]Bureau of Economic Analysis. The estimates of earnings for 2000–2006 are based on the 2002 North American Industry Classification System (NAICS). The estimates for 2007 forward are based on the 2007 NAICS. All dollars estimates are in current dollars and not adjusted for inflation.

Table A-62.   Retail Trade Earnings, 2015

Geographic area	Total retail trade (million dollars)	Food services and drinking places (2012, NAICS 722) (million dollars)	Motor vehicle and parts dealers (2012, NAICS 441) Earnings (million dollars)	Percentage of all retail	Furniture and Home furnishings (2012, NAICS 442) Earnings (million dollars)	Percentage of all retail	Electronics and appliances (2012, NAICS 443) (million dollars) Earnings (million dollars)	Percentage of all retail	Building material and garden equipment and supplies dealers (2012, NAICS 444) (million dollars) Earnings (million dollars)	Percentage of all retail	Food and beverage stores (2012, NAICS 445) (million dollars) Earnings (million dollars)	Percentage of all retail	Health and personal care (2012, NAICS 446) (million dollars) Earnings (million dollars)	Percentage of all retail
United States	656,599	286,275	126,732	19.3	22,132	3.4	29,998	4.6	52,624	8.0	102,207	15.6	50,951	7.8
Alabama........................	7,982	3,217	1,743	21.8	237	3.0	293	3.7	743	9.3	861	10.8	824	10.3
Alaska	1,690	740	267	15.8	42	2.5	34	2.0	188	11.1	243	14.4	67	4.0
Arizona........................	13,874	5,435	2,888	20.8	616	4.4	602	4.3	926	6.7	2,019	14.5	936	6.7
Arkansas.....................	5,008	1,866	1,148	22.9	136	2.7	165	3.3	381	7.6	574	11.5	395	7.9
California.....................	86,232	40,952	13,620	15.8	2,824	3.3	5,040	5.8	5,594	6.5	16,128	18.7	6,174	7.2
Colorado	10,777	5,503	2,390	22.2	469	4.4	441	4.1	903	8.4	1,808	16.8	636	5.9
Connecticut..................	9,158	3,175	1,515	16.5	364	4.0	337	3.7	735	8.0	1,823	19.9	658	7.2
Delaware......................	2,003	909	453	22.6	89	4.4	104	5.2	198	9.9	324	16.2	161	8.0
District of Columbia	933	1,734	9	1.0	37	3.9	30	3.2	84	9.0	264	28.2	138	14.7
Florida.........................	42,966	19,568	9,326	21.7	1,832	4.3	2,241	5.2	3,351	7.8	6,448	15.0	3,713	8.6
Georgia........................	19,046	8,321	3,850	20.2	786	4.1	1,231	6.5	1,535	8.1	2,581	13.6	1,358	7.1
Hawaii..........................	3,022	2,112	434	14.4	76	2.5	78	2.6	189	6.2	538	17.8	234	7.8
Idaho...........................	3,798	997	751	19.8	102	2.7	134	3.5	303	8.0	822	21.7	150	3.9
Illinois.........................	25,093	11,920	4,503	17.9	813	3.2	1,646	6.6	1,757	7.0	4,532	18.1	2,272	9.1
Indiana........................	12,105	4,892	2,312	19.1	354	2.9	442	3.6	1,206	10.0	1,382	11.4	988	8.2
Iowa............................	5,916	1,945	1,266	21.4	166	2.8	238	4.0	592	10.0	1,005	17.0	366	6.2
Kansas.........................	5,440	2,323	1,072	19.7	229	4.2	293	5.4	471	8.7	870	16.0	396	7.3
Kentucky......................	7,064	3,619	1,453	20.6	179	2.5	278	3.9	720	10.2	918	13.0	729	10.3
Louisiana.....................	9,052	4,004	1,769	19.5	257	2.8	303	3.3	950	10.5	1,299	14.4	853	9.4
Maine...........................	2,921	1,100	557	19.1	65	2.2	93	3.2	307	10.5	552	18.9	184	6.3
Maryland.......................	12,019	5,344	2,388	19.9	458	3.8	524	4.4	1,105	9.2	2,523	21.0	821	6.8
Massachusetts..............	14,880	7,543	2,620	17.6	491	3.3	459	3.1	1,239	8.3	3,152	21.2	1,257	8.4
Michigan......................	17,290	6,799	3,825	22.1	557	3.2	774	4.5	1,739	10.1	2,229	12.9	1,607	9.3
Minnesota....................	11,333	4,282	2,025	17.9	427	3.8	498	4.4	1,092	9.6	1,408	12.4	864	7.6
Mississippi...................	5,122	1,809	1,082	21.1	125	2.4	133	2.6	472	9.2	537	10.5	613	12.0
Missouri.......................	11,619	4,813	2,284	19.7	337	2.9	391	3.4	1,074	9.2	1,417	12.2	900	7.7
Montana.......................	2,287	859	446	19.5	81	3.5	67	2.9	248	10.9	339	14.8	92	4.0
Nebraska......................	3,751	1,432	785	20.9	167	4.5	130	3.5	371	9.9	546	14.6	305	8.1
Nevada.........................	5,704	3,269	1,202	21.1	165	2.9	216	3.8	337	5.9	806	14.1	372	6.5
New Hampshire.............	4,012	1,286	872	21.7	113	2.8	272	6.8	407	10.1	570	14.2	193	4.8
New Jersey	20,984	6,846	3,418	16.3	693	3.3	1,171	5.6	1,567	7.5	4,112	19.6	1,784	8.5
New Mexico..................	3,560	1,730	829	23.3	81	2.3	106	3.0	294	8.2	483	13.6	214	6.0
New York......................	43,886	20,129	5,462	12.4	1,383	3.2	2,152	4.9	2,832	6.5	7,376	16.8	4,559	10.4
North Carolina..............	18,189	8,712	4,244	23.3	636	3.5	750	4.1	1,614	8.9	2,373	13.0	1,505	8.3
North Dakota................	2,176	648	435	20.0	76	3.5	92	4.2	244	11.2	209	9.6	121	5.5
Ohio............................	21,528	9,519	4,552	21.1	614	2.9	818	3.8	1,970	9.2	3,052	14.2	1,663	7.7
Oklahoma.....................	7,253	3,372	1,632	22.5	301	4.2	256	3.5	690	9.5	929	12.8	561	7.7
Oregon.........................	8,320	3,877	1,597	19.2	293	3.5	330	4.0	683	8.2	1,497	18.0	403	4.8
Pennsylvania................	24,509	9,371	4,783	19.5	662	2.7	770	3.1	1,918	7.8	4,244	17.3	2,068	8.4
Rhode Island................	2,221	1,085	345	15.5	53	2.4	69	3.1	163	7.3	414	18.7	273	12.3
South Carolina	8,627	4,242	1,816	21.0	264	3.1	316	3.7	827	9.6	1,286	14.9	698	8.1
South Dakota	2,253	607	475	21.1	59	2.6	79	3.5	222	9.9	231	10.3	82	3.6
Tennessee....................	14,091	5,824	3,094	22.0	443	3.1	645	4.6	1,230	8.7	1,794	12.7	1,182	8.4
Texas...........................	57,617	26,763	14,362	24.9	2,123	3.7	2,560	4.4	4,285	7.4	7,832	13.6	3,974	6.9
Utah	7,009	1,895	1,417	20.2	261	3.7	352	5.0	512	7.3	720	10.3	550	7.9
Vermont.......................	1,491	497	297	19.9	43	2.9	38	2.5	153	10.2	295	19.8	93	6.2
Virginia........................	15,749	7,065	3,346	21.2	651	4.1	731	4.6	1,283	8.1	2,348	14.9	1,054	6.7
Washington...................	19,483	6,687	2,788	14.3	506	2.6	747	3.8	1,336	6.9	2,353	12.1	838	4.3
West Virginia................	2,936	1,146	600	20.4	70	2.4	102	3.5	297	10.1	351	12.0	314	10.7
Wisconsin	11,383	4,029	2,105	18.5	299	2.6	385	3.4	1,157	10.2	1,621	14.2	716	6.3
Wyoming	1,239	461	281	22.7	29	2.3	41	3.3	129	10.4	167	13.5	43	3.5

Table A-62. Retail Trade Earnings, 2015—*Continued*

Geographic area	Gasoline stations (2012, NAICS 447) (million dollars)		Clothing and clothing accessories (2012, NAICS 448) (million dollars)		Sporting goods, hobby, book, music stores (2012, NAICS 451)		General merchandise stores (2012, NAICS 452) (million dollars)		Miscellaneous stores (2012, NAICS 453)		Non-store retailers (2012, NAICS 454)	
	Earnings (million dollars)	Percentage of all retail	Earnings (million dollars)	Percentage of all retail	Earnings (million dollars)	Percentage of all retail	Earnings (million dollars)	Percentage of all retail	Earnings (million dollars)	Percentage of all retail	Earnings (million dollars)	Percentage of all retail
United States	35,591	5.4	41,134	6.3	19,219	2.9	91,305	13.9	38,278	5.8	46,428	7.1
Alabama....................	555	7.0	344	4.3	248	3.1	1,618	20.3	331	4.1	185	2.3
Alaska	70	4.1	68	4.0	78	4.6	399	23.6	132	7.8	103	6.1
Arizona.....................	560	4.0	784	5.7	308	2.2	1,909	13.8	1,033	7.4	1,293	9.3
Arkansas...................	342	6.8	205	4.1	141	2.8	1,157	23.1	239	4.8	126	2.5
California..................	5,243	6.1	6,226	7.2	2,568	3.0	10,288	11.9	5,783	6.7	6,744	7.8
Colorado...................	465	4.3	525	4.9	515	4.8	1,474	13.7	608	5.6	544	5.0
Connecticut...............	396	4.3	703	7.7	247	2.7	795	8.7	464	5.1	1,121	12.2
Delaware	67	3.4	125	6.2	51	2.6	251	12.5	87	4.3	93	4.6
District of Columbia	18	1.9	101	10.9	36	3.9	106	11.3	62	6.6	50	5.3
Florida......................	1,522	3.5	3,063	7.1	1,054	2.5	5,975	13.9	2,124	4.9	2,317	5.4
Georgia	1,107	5.8	1,011	5.3	525	2.8	3,050	16.0	1,025	5.4	986	5.2
Hawaii	68	2.2	379	12.6	108	3.6	487	16.1	365	12.1	67	2.2
Idaho........................	189	5.0	102	2.7	139	3.7	516	13.6	200	5.3	388	10.2
Illinois	1,073	4.3	1,467	5.8	679	2.7	3,745	14.9	1,239	4.9	1,369	5.5
Indiana.....................	558	4.6	1,057	8.7	308	2.5	1,889	15.6	650	5.4	961	7.9
Iowa........................	480	8.1	217	3.7	179	3.0	885	15.0	308	5.2	215	3.6
Kansas.....................	316	5.8	221	4.1	193	3.5	852	15.7	300	5.5	229	4.2
Kentucky...................	432	6.1	278	3.9	188	2.7	1,299	18.4	339	4.8	250	3.5
Louisiana	819	9.0	416	4.6	225	2.5	1,515	16.7	500	5.5	147	1.6
Maine.......................	203	7.0	126	4.3	88	3.0	348	11.9	126	4.3	272	9.3
Maryland...................	680	5.7	697	5.8	314	2.6	1,491	12.4	626	5.2	391	3.2
Massachusetts...........	560	3.8	1,070	7.2	500	3.4	1,429	9.6	782	5.3	1,321	8.9
Michigan...................	641	3.7	806	4.7	536	3.1	2,921	16.9	986	5.7	670	3.9
Minnesota.................	709	6.3	550	4.9	349	3.1	1,661	14.7	652	5.8	1,097	9.7
Mississippi................	529	10.3	226	4.4	108	2.1	1,002	19.6	182	3.6	113	2.2
Missouri....................	876	7.5	576	5.0	318	2.7	1,892	16.3	574	4.9	981	8.4
Montana....................	158	6.9	69	3.0	99	4.3	344	15.0	274	12.0	70	3.0
Nebraska...................	273	7.3	145	3.9	110	2.9	551	14.7	146	3.9	221	5.9
Nevada.....................	222	3.9	642	11.2	124	2.2	850	14.9	328	5.8	438	7.7
New Hampshire...........	153	3.8	195	4.9	167	4.2	419	10.5	222	5.5	429	10.7
New Jersey	771	3.7	1,748	8.3	1,006	4.8	2,209	10.5	1,059	5.0	1,448	6.9
New Mexico	263	7.4	177	5.0	85	2.4	649	18.2	262	7.3	118	3.3
New York...................	1,921	4.4	5,058	11.5	1,107	2.5	4,483	10.2	4,190	9.5	3,364	7.7
North Carolina............	1,161	6.4	917	5.0	437	2.4	2,957	16.3	853	4.7	742	4.1
North Dakota..............	223	10.3	72	3.3	70	3.2	275	12.6	245	11.3	114	5.2
Ohio.........................	1,044	4.9	1,301	6.0	676	3.1	3,065	14.2	1,149	5.3	1,624	7.5
Oklahoma..................	708	9.8	276	3.8	170	2.3	1,187	16.4	384	5.3	158	2.2
Oregon.....................	369	4.4	511	6.1	341	4.1	1,347	16.2	461	5.5	489	5.9
Pennsylvania..............	1,154	4.7	1,452	5.9	734	3.0	3,063	12.5	1,137	4.6	2,524	10.3
Rhode Island..............	222	10.0	123	5.6	45	2.0	275	12.4	98	4.4	140	6.3
South Carolina	545	6.3	507	5.9	219	2.5	1,528	17.7	395	4.6	226	2.6
South Dakota	183	8.1	70	3.1	63	2.8	265	11.8	327	14.5	196	8.7
Tennessee	964	6.8	664	4.7	377	2.7	2,082	14.8	926	6.6	690	4.9
Texas.......................	3,510	6.1	3,550	6.2	1,537	2.7	8,213	14.3	3,138	5.4	2,533	4.4
Utah	281	4.0	301	4.3	424	6.1	879	12.5	277	3.9	1,034	14.7
Vermont	98	6.6	75	5.0	58	3.9	91	6.1	97	6.5	153	10.2
Virginia.....................	1,002	6.4	768	4.9	409	2.6	2,512	16.0	850	5.4	795	5.0
Washington................	653	3.4	599	3.1	505	2.6	2,574	13.2	1,024	5.3	5,559	28.5
West Virginia..............	272	9.3	105	3.6	76	2.6	549	18.7	129	4.4	70	2.4
Wisconsin	808	7.1	423	3.7	337	3.0	1,799	15.8	527	4.6	1,205	10.6
Wyoming	156	12.6	41	3.3	38	3.1	187	15.1	66	5.3	59	4.8

Table A-63.   Transportation and Commuting

Geographic area	Transportation and warehousing (NAICS 48–49)							Workers 16 years and over, 2015				Vehicle miles of travel, 2015 (billions)	Railroad shipments[5] 2012 (thousand tons)	Waterborne shipments[6]	
	Nonfarm employment (BLS)[1] (thousands)		Earnings (BEA)[2] (million dollars)		Establishments[3]			Total workers (thousands)	Percentage of workers who		Mean travel time to work (minutes)					
							Net change 2010–2014		Drove alone to work	Used public transportation[4]				2013	2012
	2015	2010	2015	2010	2014	2010									
United States	4,871.2	4,190.7	398,984	290,671	220,565	208,474	12,091	148,324	76.6	5.2	26.4	3,095	1,764,078	2,274,778	2,306,770
Alabama	58.9	52.2	3,835	3,326	2,893	2,874	19	2,012	85.5	0.3	24.6	67	38,161	69,394	69,539
Alaska	19.6	18.8	1,853	1,588	1,141	1,113	28	363	67.9	1.5	19.2	5	5,561	41,599	41,041
Arizona	79.1	68.5	5,770	4,427	3,206	3,065	141	2,900	77.1	2.1	25.1	65	3,281	NA	NA
Arkansas	NA	NA	3,653	2,923	2,362	2,412	-50	1,253	82.6	0.5	22.1	35	14,493	17,409.0	16,430
California.....................	497.6	407.9	43,262	31,304	22,057	20,876	1,181	17,634	73.9	5.2	28.9	336	59,066	226,174	220,836
Colorado	71.6	61.7	9,491	4,062	3,621	3,340	281	2,740	76.5	3.0	25.4	50	30,647	NA	NA
Connecticut..................	44.4	38.7	3,641	2,513	1,620	1,641	-21	1,773	78.4	4.9	26.4	32	1,271	11,368	10,645
Delaware	NA	NA	935	620	640	652	-12	441	81.4	2.7	26.0	10	842	13,936.0	15,794
District of Columbia	NA	NA	503	388	160	182	-22	358	33.6	35.8	29.8	4	37	128	113
Florida........................	244.3	204.5	19,581	13,538	13,870	12,538	1,332	8,880	79.7	2.2	27.0	207	43,721	93,925	91,501
Georgia	185.7	160.0	14,838	10,949	6,262	5,831	431	4,555	79.6	2.3	28.0	118	31,841	35,216	36,879
Hawaii.........................	27.1	23.3	1,956	1,361	867	856	11	705	67.4	7.0	27.4	10	NA	23,180	24,932
Idaho...........................	20.4	18.0	1,379	1,012	1,731	1,602	129	735	77.1	0.8	20.5	17	7,081	825	868
Illinois.........................	260.8	228.3	22,030	16,806	14,439	12,151	2,288	6,095	73.6	9.3	28.8	105	115,899	92,015	106,399
Indiana........................	126.2	110.3	8,330	6,702	5,143	5,016	127	3,064	83.1	1.1	23.3	79	54,154	64,922	68,322
Iowa............................	60.1	53.8	4,109	3,230	3,537	3,620	-83	1,575	81.0	1.4	19.0	33	46,269	7,861	10,327
Kansas........................	49.7	45.6	3,658	2,709	2,518	2,615	-97	1,414	82.6	0.6	19.0	31	17,913	391	346
Kentucky......................	96.7	83.1	6,587	5,234	2,843	2,951	-108	1,899	82.1	1.1	23.3	49	59,158	100,232	94,688
Louisiana	79.2	69.0	6,769	5,964	3,929	3,819	110	2,014	82.8	1.5	25.3	48	29,344	501,077	510,788
Maine	16.5	15.0	982	866	1,218	1,217	1	636	79.7	0.6	24.0	15	2,126	14,078	15,127
Maryland......................	77.2	65.9	5,588	4,254	3,396	3,307	89	3,001	73.8	9.0	32.6	58	5,815	40,669	45,268
Massachusetts	82.1	72.2	5,921	4,682	3,626	3,565	61	3,451	70.2	10.6	29.7	59	2,829	18,866	17,298
Michigan......................	114.7	94.1	8,430	6,476	5,880	5,482	398	4,420	82.8	1.3	24.4	98	21,874	58,222	57,547
Minnesota	86.2	77.1	6,744	5,207	4,599	4,549	50	2,861	78.1	3.6	23.4	57	90,337	41,466	42,872
Mississippi...................	44.7	39.2	2,532	2,070	2,048	2,077	-29	1,194	85.4	0.3	24.3	40	7,699	48,582	48,592
Missouri.......................	94.0	85.1	6,938	5,485	4,537	4,704	-167	2,853	81.8	1.6	23.6	72	16,716	36,979	34,066
Montana.......................	15.2	12.5	1,244	870	1,395	1,309	86	484	74.5	0.8	18.0	12	38,320	NA	NA
Nebraska......................	53.5	49.7	5,894	3,508	2,351	2,302	49	974	82.0	0.8	18.4	20	27,027	9	22
Nevada........................	56.8	46.5	3,887	2,837	1,497	1,392	105	1,315	77.8	3.7	24.2	26	2,075	NA	NA
New Hampshire.............	13.3	12.0	736	665	798	811	-13	696	81.1	0.9	27.6	13	321	2,679	2,419
New Jersey	163.1	148.8	12,960	10,928	7,240	6,697	543	4,285	71.8	11.6	31.3	75	11,789	145,991	152,685
New Mexico	NA	NA	1,565	1,139	1,390	1,283	107	877	81.4	0.9	21.7	27	12,068	NA	NA
New York......................	246.7	224.1	20,021	15,816	12,618	11,985	633	9,276	52.7	28.6	33.1	127	7,439	38,706	38,875
North Carolina..............	120	102.6	8,298	6,238	5,509	5,342	167	4,525	81.4	1.1	24.3	112	10,362	11,632.0	11,028
North Dakota................	22.8	12.6	2,295	936	1,709	1,175	534	404	82.0	0.4	16.6	10	49,480	NA	NA
Ohio............................	188	160.5	14,702	11,106	7,075	7,029	46	5,381	83.2	1.8	23.4	114	66,191	93,749	90,569
Oklahoma.....................	51.9	43.4	14,222	2,748	2,686	2,596	90	1,740	82.5	0.4	21.4	48	18,299	6,777.0	6,116
Oregon........................	54.5	47.6	3,954	3,043	2,997	2,936	61	1,840	71.2	4.8	23.6	36	10,187	30,259	30,758
Pennsylvania................	241.3	209.8	18,378	13,134	8,403	7,907	496	5,978	76.3	5.7	26.8	101	51,550	73,546	70,431
Rhode Island................	10.3	9.2	653	561	605	640	-35	510	79.0	2.9	24.7	8	49	9,072	7,567
South Carolina	60.2	47.1	3,699	2,618	2,526	2,474	52	2,145	83.0	0.5	24.2	52	12,114	18,916.0	19,539
South Dakota	NA	NA	873	649	1,170	1,134	36	431	80.6	0.8	16.9	9	14,276		
Tennessee	153.4	128.2	10,642	8,212	4,095	4,161	-66	2,954	83.9	0.8	24.8	77	15,695	34,755	34,076
Texas..........................	458	370.9	44,831	34,469	18,244	15,745	2,499	12,557	80.8	1.5	26.3	258	92,892	492,659	485,884
Utah............................	51.4	43.2	3,657	2,512	2,248	2,051	197	1,395	75.8	2.7	21.3	30	15,775	NA	NA
Vermont.......................	6.7	6.8	401	364	501	496	5	320	76.9	1.3	23.0	7	659	0.0	0.0
Virginia........................	116.3	102.1	8,694	6,683	4,858	4,779	79	4,116	77.5	4.7	28.2	83	32,231	83,834	79,821
Washington...................	96.6	83.8	8,367	6,513	5,010	4,847	163	3,371	72.4	6.2	27.1	60	21,892	112,212	115,598
West Virginia................	NA	NA	1,530	1,299	1,212	1,249	-37	722	82.7	1.1	25.5	20	92,328	62,629	64,984
Wisconsin	94.2	91.1	6,517	5,211	5,263	5,189	74	2,912	81.2	1.9	22.0	62	20,625	34,225	31,634
Wyoming......................	13.1	11.5	1,650	914	1,022	890	132	289	77.3	2.2	19.0	10	434,299	NA	NA

NA = Not available.
0 = Represents zero or rounds to zero.
[1]All estimates of labor provided by the Bureau of Labor Statistics (BLS) are based on the 2007 North American Industry. Classification System (NAICS). United States totals differ from the sum of the state figures because of differing benchmarks among states and differing industrial and geographic stratification.
[2]Bureau of Economic Analysis. The estimates of earnings for 2000–2006 are based on the 2002 North American Industry Classification System (NAICS). The estimates for 2007 forward are based on the 2007 NAICS. All dollars estimates are in current dollars and not adjusted for inflation.
[3]Data for establishments in 2010 based on the 2007 North American Industry Classification System (NAICS); 2005 data are based on the 2002 NAICS.
[4]Excludes taxicab.
[5]Rail shipments of all commodities originating in state.
[6]Includes domestic and foreign shipments terminating and originating in state and intrastate shipments. National and state totals exclude duplication. National total includes Guam, the Virgin Islands, the Pacific Islands, Puerto Rico, other territories, and trans-shipments.

Table A-64. Motor Vehicle and Motorcycle Registrations, Bridges, and Drivers Licenses

Geographic area	Motor vehicle registrations Total¹ Number (thousands) 2015	2010	Automobile² (thousands) 2015	2010	Trucks³ (thousands) 2015	2010	Motorcycle registrations⁴ 2015	2010	Highway Vehicle-Miles Traveled⁵ 2013	2008	Bridges, 2016 Total	Good condition	Fair condition	Poor condition	Drivers licenses⁶ (thousands) 2015	2010
United States	263,610	242,061	112,864	130,892	141,256	110,322	8,601	8,010	2,988,323	2,973,509	614,387	291,412	274,306	48,559	218,084	210,115
Alabama..................	5,400	4,654	2,278	2,212	3,001	2,433	115	123	65,046	59,303	16,098	7,040	8,338	720	3,907	3,806
Alaska	815	710	193	228	586	479	32	30	4,848	4,865	1,488	644	702	141	533	515
Arizona...................	5,631	4,320	2,333	2,201	3,116	2,114	161	137	60,586	61,628	8,154	4,931	3,042	181	4,979	4,444
Arkansas................	2,772	2,073	948	945	1,721	1,120	92	76	33,493	33,163	12,871	6,984	5,291	596	2,120	2,078
California................	29,424	31,014	14,464	17,978	14,038	12,981	829	760	329,534	327,286	25,431	16,788	7,439	1,204	25,533	23,753
Colorado	5,005	4,180	1,822	1,891	2,979	2,280	191	111	46,968	47,860	8,682	3,861	4,364	455	3,975	3,779
Connecticut............	2,842	3,082	1,386	1,986	1,357	1,085	87	66	30,941	31,737	4,214	1,250	2,628	336	2,567	2,935
Delaware	964	799	438	434	494	363	28	27	9,308	8,976	877	267	567	43	743	695
District of Columbia	323	212	201	160	113	49	4	2	3,527	3,611	245	67	169	9	456	385
Florida....................	16,105	14,373	7,735	7,295	7,737	7,025	573	601	192,702	198,616	12,313	8,534	3,545	233	14,263	13,950
Georgia	8,138	7,702	3,524	3,739	4,371	3,939	200	197	109,355	109,057	14,835	7,021	7,275	539	6,906	6,508
Hawaii....................	1,242	904	523	450	683	449	34	55	10,099	10,278	1,132	436	634	62	910	909
Idaho......................	1,854	1,325	626	541	1,159	780	66	53	15,980	15,251	4,445	1,218	2,867	360	1,135	1,070
Illinois....................	10,595	10,079	4,775	5,773	5,439	4,287	346	350	105,297	106,079	26,704	13,815	10,732	2,157	8,462	8,374
Indiana...................	6,045	5,698	2,336	2,986	3,464	2,679	223	205	78,311	70,973	19,245	7,876	9,902	1,464	4,468	5,550
Iowa.......................	3,637	3,313	1,326	1,691	2,112	1,615	190	187	31,641	30,713	24,184	9,182	10,300	4,671	2,224	2,167
Kansas...................	2,635	2,436	992	880	1,543	1,552	96	87	30,208	29,727	25,013	13,890	9,664	1,458	2,029	2,033
Kentucky................	4,152	3,589	1,714	1,890	2,317	1,684	111	72	46,996	47,534	14,265	5,471	7,733	1,059	3,021	2,950
Louisiana	3,901	4,086	1,439	1,917	2,320	2,146	114	69	47,758	45,091	12,915	6,647	4,730	1,534	3,357	3,134
Maine.....................	1,104	1,054	420	519	625	531	55	56	14,129	14,559	2,450	774	1,337	339	1,020	1,020
Maryland.................	4,135	4,557	1,994	2,591	2,002	1,954	126	80	56,688	55,023	5,321	1,782	3,242	297	4,186	3,918
Massachusetts...........	5,070	5,334	2,374	3,145	2,516	2,177	168	159	56,311	54,505	5,171	1,409	3,294	468	5,041	4,593
Michigan.................	8,294	9,286	3,377	5,136	4,651	4,122	257	281	95,132	101,825	11,156	4,674	5,274	1,202	7,104	7,083
Minnesota...............	5,281	4,848	2,080	2,459	2,934	2,370	249	255	56,974	57,995	13,355	8,431	4,144	776	3,351	3,281
Mississippi..............	2,069	2,016	847	1,144	1,185	863	28	28	38,758	43,711	17,068	11,104	4,480	1,479	1,988	1,928
Missouri.................	5,624	5,153	2,273	2,579	3,116	2,564	218	109	69,458	68,273	24,468	11,009	11,335	2,124	4,213	4,246
Montana..................	1,645	926	436	352	1,007	572	197	126	12,033	10,812	5,276	1,841	3,066	369	781	744
Nebraska................	1,981	1,802	733	773	1,189	1,022	56	52	19,322	19,170	15,334	7,899	5,945	1,478	1,394	1,352
Nevada...................	2,316	1,362	1,018	690	1,221	669	75	67	24,649	20,780	1,933	981	925	27	1,836	1,691
New Hampshire...........	1,296	1,203	535	619	684	582	74	80	12,903	13,040	2,486	1,321	916	249	1,075	1,037
New Jersey	5,939	6,628	2,919	3,972	2,843	2,632	152	328	74,530	73,629	6,730	1,882	4,280	568	6,179	5,953
New Mexico	1,823	1,612	668	703	1,086	906	63	53	25,086	26,279	3,973	1,511	2,212	250	1,468	1,406
New York................	10,639	10,255	4,869	7,950	5,385	2,236	355	348	129,737	134,085	17,462	6,215	9,342	1,884	11,690	11,286
North Carolina..........	7,929	5,743	3,439	3,282	4,269	2,427	189	134	105,213	101,712	18,099	7,764	8,564	1,764	7,161	6,537
North Dakota............	891	736	247	341	602	392	39	34	10,100	7,820	4,400	2,323	1,567	509	545	483
Ohio.......................	10,557	9,801	4,739	5,615	5,377	4,139	405	384	112,767	108,302	28,284	15,957	10,445	1,882	7,923	7,963
Oklahoma................	2,989	3,357	1,157	1,582	1,700	1,756	129	126	47,999	48,499	23,053	10,900	9,273	2,877	2,622	2,349
Oregon...................	3,607	3,050	1,433	1,489	2,030	1,546	128	108	33,706	33,468	8,118	3,063	4,655	398	2,809	2,770
Pennsylvania............	10,599	9,991	4,680	5,682	5,470	4,275	393	412	98,628	107,848	22,791	6,539	11,821	4,430	8,943	8,737
Rhode Island...........	875	782	447	479	394	302	32	33	7,775	8,187	772	128	452	192	745	748
South Carolina..........	4,163	3,661	1,784	2,031	2,245	1,611	116	107	48,986	49,597	9,358	4,256	4,276	826	3,684	3,337
South Dakota............	1,082	926	329	407	655	517	96	66	9,122	8,986	5,849	1,879	2,915	1,055	656	602
Tennessee...............	5,612	5,114	2,318	2,734	3,101	2,358	166	163	71,067	69,469	20,123	9,990	9,207	924	4,621	4,418
Texas.....................	21,865	17,194	8,451	8,331	12,960	8,766	387	432	244,525	235,382	53,488	28,168	24,667	653	15,880	15,158
Utah.......................	2,229	2,655	919	1,317	1,225	1,336	79	59	27,005	25,974	3,039	1,760	1,191	88	1,914	1,660
Vermont..................	655	567	253	293	370	272	31	29	7,116	7,312	2,766	1,458	1,225	83	549	513
Virginia...................	7,239	6,149	3,270	3,510	3,743	2,623	193	74	80,767	82,278	13,892	4,857	8,154	881	5,820	5,402
Washington..............	6,725	4,683	2,841	2,600	3,626	2,071	236	218	57,211	55,558	8,178	4,337	3,477	364	5,516	5,106
West Virginia..............	1,613	1,436	566	703	985	730	59	49	19,232	20,774	7,217	2,641	3,353	1,222	1,167	1,206
Wisconsin	5,467	4,968	2,189	2,461	2,938	2,491	325	323	59,486	57,462	14,230	7,413	5,725	1,092	4,195	4,133
Wyoming	815	663	207	210	576	450	31	31	9,309	9,447	3,128	780	2,029	319	422	419

¹Automobiles, trucks, and buses (excludes motorcycles). Excludes vehicles owned by military services.
²Includes private and commercially owned (including taxis). Excludes publicly owned.
³Includes private, commercial, and publicly owned trucks.
⁴Includes private and commercially owned. Excludes publicly owned.
⁵Travel for the rural minor collector and rural/urban local functional systems is estimated by the states based on a model or other means and provided to the FHWA on a summary basis. Travel for all other systems are estimated from State-provided data in the Highway Performance Monitoring System.
⁶Include restricted drivers and graduated driver license.

Table A-65. Traffic Fatalities and Seat Belt Use

Geographic area	Traffic fatalities[1] Number 2014	2010	2005	Fatality rate[2] 2014	2010	2005	Traffic fatalities in alcohol involved crashes, 2014[3] Total	Percent of all persons killed in crashes	By highest driver BAC in crash[4] Low alcohol: BAC 0.01 to 0.07	Alcohol impaired driving fatalities: BAC 0.08 or more	Rate of seat belt use[5] 2014	2010	2007
United States	32,675	32,999	43,510	1.08	1.11	1.46	11,731	35.9	1,764	9,967	87.0	85.0	82.0
Alabama......................	820	862	1,148	1.25	1.34	1.92	312	38.0	48	264	95.7	91.4	82.3
Alaska........................	73	56	73	1.50	1.17	1.45	28	38.4	6	22	88.4	86.8	82.4
Arizona.......................	770	759	1,179	1.23	1.27	1.97	247	32.1	48	199	87.2	81.8	80.9
Arkansas....................	466	571	654	1.37	1.70	2.05	162	34.8	27	135	74.4	78.3	69.9
California....................	3,074	2,720	4,333	0.92	0.84	1.32	1,053	34.3	171	882	97.1	96.2	94.6
Colorado	488	450	606	1.00	0.96	1.26	186	38.1	26	160	82.4	82.9	81.1
Connecticut................	248	320	278	0.80	1.02	0.88	114	46.0	17	97	85.1	88.2	85.8
Delaware....................	121	101	133	1.26	1.13	1.40	52	43.0	3	49	91.9	90.7	86.6
District of Columbia	23	24	48	0.65	0.67	1.29	6	26.1	1	5	93.2	92.3	87.1
Florida........................	2,494	2,444	3,518	1.24	1.25	1.75	807	32.4	122	685	88.8	87.4	79.1
Georgia	1,164	1,247	1,729	1.04	1.12	1.52	325	27.9	47	278	97.3	89.6	89.0
Hawaii........................	95	113	140	0.93	1.13	1.39	35	36.8	3	32	93.5	97.6	97.6
Idaho..........................	186	209	275	1.15	1.32	1.85	60	32.3	7	53	80.2	77.9	78.5
Illinois........................	924	927	1,363	0.88	0.88	1.27	369	39.9	52	317	94.1	92.6	90.1
Indiana.......................	746	754	938	0.94	1.00	1.31	239	32.0	34	205	90.2	92.4	87.9
Iowa...........................	321	390	450	1.02	1.24	1.45	105	32.7	12	93	92.8	93.1	91.3
Kansas.......................	385	431	428	1.25	1.44	1.44	121	31.4	18	103	85.7	81.8	75.0
Kentucky....................	672	760	985	1.40	1.58	2.08	197	29.3	26	171	86.1	80.3	71.8
Louisiana...................	737	721	963	1.53	1.59	2.14	301	40.8	48	253	84.1	75.9	75.2
Maine.........................	131	161	169	0.92	1.11	1.13	50	38.2	6	44	85.0	82.0	79.8
Maryland.....................	442	496	614	0.78	0.88	1.09	154	34.8	24	130	92.1	94.7	93.1
Massachusetts.............	328	347	441	0.57	0.64	0.80	154	47.0	21	133	76.6	73.7	68.7
Michigan.....................	901	942	1,129	0.93	0.97	1.09	266	29.5	51	215	93.3	95.2	93.7
Minnesota...................	361	411	559	0.63	0.73	0.98	121	33.5	15	106	94.7	92.3	87.8
Mississippi..................	607	641	931	1.54	1.61	2.32	207	34.1	29	178	78.3	81.0	71.8
Missouri.....................	766	821	1,257	1.08	1.16	1.83	250	32.6	46	204	78.8	76.0	77.2
Montana.....................	192	189	251	1.58	1.69	2.26	86	44.8	13	73	74.0	78.9	79.6
Nebraska....................	225	190	276	1.15	0.98	1.43	77	34.2	17	60	79.0	84.1	78.7
Nevada......................	290	257	427	1.15	1.16	2.06	113	39.0	20	93	94.0	93.2	92.2
New Hampshire............	95	128	166	0.73	0.98	1.24	34	35.8	4	30	70.4	72.2	63.8
New Jersey	556	556	747	0.74	0.76	1.01	201	36.2	38	163	87.6	93.7	91.4
New Mexico................	383	349	488	1.51	1.38	2.04	144	37.6	28	116	92.1	89.8	91.5
New York....................	1,039	1,201	1,434	0.80	0.92	1.03	379	36.5	62	317	90.6	89.8	83.5
North Carolina.............	1,284	1,320	1,547	1.19	1.29	1.53	427	33.3	49	378	90.6	89.7	88.8
North Dakota...............	135	105	123	1.28	1.27	1.62	66	48.9	11	55	81.0	74.8	82.2
Ohio...........................	1,006	1,080	1,321	0.89	0.97	1.20	356	35.4	46	310	85.0	83.8	81.6
Oklahoma...................	669	668	803	1.40	1.40	1.71	181	27.1	27	154	86.3	85.9	83.1
Oregon.......................	357	317	487	1.03	0.94	1.38	125	35.0	25	100	97.8	97.0	95.3
Pennsylvania...............	1,195	1,324	1,616	1.20	1.32	1.50	396	33.1	51	345	83.6	86.0	86.7
Rhode Island...............	52	67	87	0.68	0.81	1.05	19	36.5	1	18	87.4	78.0	79.1
South Carolina	824	809	1,094	1.65	1.65	2.21	330	40.0	51	279	90.0	85.4	74.5
South Dakota	136	140	186	1.47	1.58	2.22	53	39.0	7	46	68.9	74.5	73.0
Tennessee	962	1,032	1,270	1.33	1.47	1.79	312	32.4	45	267	87.7	87.1	80.2
Texas.........................	3,538	3,023	3,536	1.46	1.29	1.50	670	18.9	224	446	90.7	93.8	91.8
Utah...........................	256	253	282	0.93	0.95	1.12	63	24.6	7	56	83.4	89.0	86.8
Vermont......................	44	71	73	0.62	0.98	0.95	14	31.8	5	9	84.1	85.2	87.1
Virginia.......................	703	740	947	0.87	0.9	1.18	256	36.4	42	214	77.3	80.5	79.9
Washington.................	462	460	649	0.8	0.8	1.17	168	36.4	34	134	94.5	97.6	96.4
West Virginia...............	272	315	374	1.42	1.64	1.82	96	35.3	12	84	87.8	82.1	89.6
Wisconsin...................	507	572	815	0.84	0.96	1.36	203	40.0	37	166	84.7	79.2	75.3
Wyoming	150	155	170	1.59	1.66	1.88	53	35.3	5	48	79.2	78.9	72.2

NA = Not available.

[1] Traffic fatalities pertain to a police-reported crash involving a motor vehicle in transport on a trafficway in which at least one person dies within 30 days of the crash. Data include fatalities in crashes in which there was no driver or motorcycle rider present at the scene.

[2] Deaths per 100 million vehicle miles traveled.

[3] Data represents all fatalities (both operators and passengers) in which the operator of the crash had a BAC of .01 or above.

[4] BAC stands for blood alcohol concentration and is measured in grams per deciliter (g/dl).

[5] Seat belt use pertains to both drivers and passengers in front seat.

Table A-66. Communications

Geographic area	Mobile wireless telephone subscribers[1] (thousands)			Total number of pay phones by state (as of March 31)		Internet use, 2012 (thousands)						End-user Telecommunications revenue, 2013 (million dollars)
						Individual lives in household with Internet use		Individual accesses the Internet from some location		Individual accesses the Internet from home		
	2013	2012	2010	2014	2008	Number	Percent	Number	Percent	Number	Percent	
United States	310,698	304,838	285,118	152,716	700,826	235,721	79.3	222,038	74.7	205,500	69.1	187,693
Alabama......................	4,555	4,549	4,328	1,155	6,212	559	83.1	551	81.9	502	74.6	2,704
Alaska........................	660	649	608	491	3,630	3,278	72.0	3,025	66.5	2,746	60.3	450
Arizona......................	6,007	5,774	5,285	3,695	13,980	4,579	73.7	4,321	69.5	3,872	62.3	3,543
Arkansas....................	2,852	2,963	2,673	734	3,128	2,086	74.8	1,954	70.1	1,805	64.7	1,622
California....................	36,446	35,616	33,839	25,846	96,328	29,195	81.3	26,393	73.5	24,609	68.5	21,854
Colorado	5,062	4,878	4,687	2,235	8,224	4,185	85.7	3,967	81.2	3,725	76.3	3,178
Connecticut.................	3,499	3,418	3,230	694	5,432	2,885	84.0	2,728	79.5	2,594	75.6	2,376
Delaware	897	903	851	200	2,416	680	78.2	640	73.5	601	69.0	617
District of Columbia	1,381	1,400	1,249	344	3,956	468	77.5	475	78.8	420	69.6	1,008
Florida.......................	18,985	18,369	17,251	6,871	34,412	15,003	81.5	14,025	76.2	13,190	71.7	11,620
Georgia......................	9,959	10,054	9,063	2,056	14,817	7,419	79.2	7,167	76.5	6,585	70.3	5,958
Hawaii	1,389	1,339	1,252	4,203	5,703	1,093	85.0	969	75.4	919	71.5	880
Idaho.........................	1,402	1,363	1,277	712	2,299	1,319	86.8	1,233	81.2	1,162	76.5	837
Illinois.......................	12,835	12,859	12,057	5,570	22,959	10,086	82.7	9,567	78.5	8,973	73.6	7,791
Indiana......................	5,946	5,786	5,410	2,141	11,441	4,852	77.7	4,776	76.4	4,317	69.1	3,485
Iowa..........................	2,782	2,777	2,535	983	4,627	2,352	80.2	2,233	76.1	2,083	71.0	1,727
Kansas.......................	2,840	2,696	2,560	705	3,675	2,190	80.7	2,137	78.8	1,940	71.5	1,589
Kentucky....................	4,041	3,976	3,726	1,766	7,526	3,060	74.4	2,955	71.9	2,680	65.2	2,398
Louisiana	4,755	4,898	4,340	775	6,121	2,926	67.7	2,860	66.2	2,530	58.5	2,676
Maine........................	1,202	1,204	1,124	318	3,410	1,073	84.2	1,025	80.5	959	75.3	820
Maryland....................	5,857	6,116	5,560	1,724	17,808	4,681	83.6	4,538	81.0	4,212	75.2	3,940
Massachusetts..............	6,928	6,703	6,316	3,008	21,442	5,446	86.0	5,020	79.3	4,809	76.0	4,383
Michigan	10,109	9,598	8,861	1,993	14,520	7,626	80.8	7,383	78.2	6,800	72.0	5,553
Minnesota...................	5,286	5,154	4,704	1,688	7,997	4,497	87.4	4,254	82.6	4,045	78.6	3,272
Mississippi..................	2,685	2,656	2,440	326	4,093	1,814	64.8	1,854	66.2	1,570	56.0	1,498
Missouri.....................	5,748	5,668	5,309	1,345	8,160	4,302	75.4	4,257	74.6	3,806	66.7	3,455
Montana.....................	903	888	846	586	1,954	753	78.3	744	77.4	663	69.0	596
Nebraska....................	1,738	1,675	1,523	1,744	4,646	1,320	76.1	1,317	75.9	1,170	67.4	1,139
Nevada......................	2,716	2,611	2,453	2,063	7,772	2,108	82.8	1,975	77.5	1,861	73.1	1,612
New Hampshire............	1,211	1,225	1,170	350	3,648	1,109	87.7	1,056	83.5	1,006	79.5	804
New Jersey	8,732	9,015	8,601	4,516	36,832	7,057	83.7	6,588	78.2	6,206	73.6	5,946
New Mexico	1,804	1,737	1,689	654	4,614	1,470	73.9	1,351	67.9	1,217	61.2	1,078
New York....................	21,444	20,715	19,504	28,025	94,876	15,116	81.0	13,705	73.4	12,900	69.1	12,883
North Carolina.............	9,021	8,985	8,526	3,289	17,905	7,088	77.7	6,669	73.1	6,130	67.2	5,647
North Dakota...............	702	683	623	205	705	548	84.0	531	81.4	499	76.6	445
Ohio..........................	12,198	11,549	10,511	4,194	19,335	8,277	75.6	7,864	71.9	7,223	66.0	6,732
Oklahoma...................	3,676	3,940	3,188	788	5,886	2,712	74.8	2,516	69.4	2,280	62.9	2,158
Oregon	3,601	3,519	3,340	1,859	8,251	3,274	87.9	3,056	82.1	2,892	77.7	2,147
Pennsylvania...............	12,318	11,956	11,424	7,424	35,204	9,860	80.8	9,296	76.2	8,760	71.8	8,093
Rhode Island...............	977	1,032	920	341	3,281	828	82.2	760	75.5	724	71.9	638
South Carolina	4,447	4,325	3,935	1,035	8,513	3,289	73.7	3,207	71.9	2,852	63.9	2,702
South Dakota	756	750	728	256	1,476	614	78.3	592	75.5	542	69.1	502
Tennessee	6,596	6,484	6,193	1,369	9,706	4,545	74.3	4,223	69.1	3,954	64.6	3,788
Texas........................	25,481	24,553	23,030	11,844	44,816	17,731	72.6	16,638	68.1	14,960	61.2	13,836
Utah..........................	2,489	2,409	2,251	901	3,897	2,265	85.2	2,157	81.2	2,018	76.0	1,464
Vermont.....................	521	518	485	213	1,664	5,923	77.2	5,784	75.4	5,303	69.2	411
Virginia......................	7,966	7,900	7,595	2,090	22,463	519	85.7	496	82.0	468	77.3	5,251
Washington.................	6,547	6,424	6,022	3,182	14,999	5,524	85.1	5,249	80.9	4,942	76.1	3,904
West Virginia...............	1,536	1,598	1,500	2,355	5,736	1,248	70.6	1,130	64.0	1,037	58.7	1,127
Wisconsin	5,229	5,037	4,730	1,584	6,951	4,437	80.7	4,388	79.8	4,036	73.4	3,252
Wyoming	551	545	526	271	1,380	450	82.9	436	80.5	403	74.4	346

[1]As of December. All facilities-based wireless carriers are required to report, and to use the area codes of telephone numbers provided to subscribers to determine subscriber counts by state.

Table A-67.　Financial Activities

| Geographic area | Financial activities[1] | | | | | | | | FDIC-insured financial institutions[2] | | | | | |
| | Nonfarm employment (BLS)[3] (thousands) | | | Earnings (BEA) (million dollars) | | | Establishments[4] | | Number of institutions[5] | | Number of offices | | Deposits (billion dollars) | |
	2015	2010	2005	2015[3]	2010[3]	2005[6]	2014	Net change 2010–2014	2016	2010	2016	2010	2016	2010
United States	8,197.0	7,695.0	8,123.0	1,006,564	807,445	752,834	838,027	17,206	7,589	9,106	91,445	97,954	11,197.8	7,621.9
Alabama......................	98.3	92.0	95.4	8,202	6,533	6,238	11,170	-5	166	173	1,520	1,578	97.1	82.1
Alaska	12.5	12.2	12.1	1,187	1,280	875	1,676	70	7	8	127	133	12.1	8.9
Arizona......................	176.3	167.6	193.8	18,064	11,093	13,324	17,753	348	66	81	1,248	1,381	114.7	86.1
Arkansas....................	51.4	48.8	49.9	4,201	3,110	2,885	7,213	-57	127	146	1,354	1,483	60.8	50.9
California....................	920.0	759.7	801.3	128,967	114,048	106,433	100,949	5,187	226	324	6,996	7,176	1,269.6	845.7
Colorado....................	158.5	144.3	159.0	16,193	7,959	12,394	19,881	755	141	190	1,519	1,662	125.3	91.2
Connecticut................	142.3	135.2	130.1	27,234	33,067	22,355	9,245	-326	62	68	1,212	1,296	129.2	95.8
Delaware....................	45.2	42.7	46.6	6,022	5,059	5,198	3,126	24	41	39	270	274	354.9	290.3
District of Columbia	30.2	26.9	29.8	4,291	2,275	3,585	2,169	16	32	33	229	244	46.0	27.4
Florida.......................	539.8	478.0	534.1	49,929	31,435	40,763	63,651	4,134	241	339	5,286	5,666	540.6	409.9
													0.0	0.0
Georgia	237.3	218.5	234.3	24,447	15,818	19,645	25,599	307	237	321	2,440	2,758	225.3	180.9
Hawaii.......................	29.3	26.9	28.1	2,982	2,453	2,343	3,387	5	12	12	276	284	40.7	28.3
Idaho........................	29.7	29.2	33.3	2,497	1,853	1,742	4,992	37	32	35	507	541	23.2	18.7
Illinois.......................	409.6	371.6	380.7	50,947	33,649	38,987	34,501	-329	540	665	4,505	4,942	473.5	361.8
Indiana......................	138.8	130.9	131.0	17,049	14,682	9,427	15,632	105	155	186	2,129	2,400	118.9	98.4
Iowa.........................	98.3	101.3	105.7	9,918	8,314	6,656	8,917	108	331	381	1,551	1,621	80.5	66.5
Kansas......................	70.6	72.2	80.6	8,502	6,969	4,155	9,029	107	314	367	1,464	1,561	70.4	60.0
Kentucky....................	85.7	85.7	92.1	8,091	6,204	5,596	9,989	-8	190	227	1,689	1,827	76.5	68.9
Louisiana	98.4	91.4	93.3	8,015	6,678	5,738	12,501	527	143	164	1,554	1,650	102.1	82.8
Maine........................	33.7	30.6	30.6	2,546	2,440	2,092	3,487	-43	31	33	486	511	26.8	27.6
													0.0	0.0
Maryland....................	158.8	144.4	147.9	20,323	16,766	15,736	13,829	115	100	134	1,594	1,804	136.3	112.8
Massachusetts.............	226.9	215.1	220.0	35,718	36,616	26,301	16,244	441	169	191	2,192	2,217	356.6	205.2
Michigan....................	216.1	188.1	207.2	20,927	17,232	17,275	20,656	-566	136	165	2,709	3,008	200.4	155.7
Minnesota	173.0	162.0	172.6	21,393	15,050	15,384	15,838	264	372	444	1,737	1,842	222.1	129.7
Mississippi.................	45.8	44.5	43.7	3,415	2,486	2,450	7,054	-88	98	105	1,160	1,209	50.6	45.1
Missouri.....................	163.4	162.2	166.8	15,873	14,718	10,183	16,897	-92	336	386	2,345	2,436	166.0	129.0
Montana.....................	21.4	21.2	23.7	1,904	1,481	1,310	3,797	72	63	78	384	392	22.3	17.5
Nebraska....................	64.5	68.9	71.9	5,656	4,553	3,872	6,358	181	202	242	1,074	1,092	63.1	43.0
Nevada......................	64.3	52.9	60.1	4,553	3,146	5,027	8,194	341	48	50	503	550	204.4	183.5
New Hampshire............	39.4	35.1	36.0	4,312	3,678	3,085	3,343	96	42	40	429	433	31.9	26.4
													0.0	0.0
New Jersey	279.7	251.6	247.1	36,990	34,866	30,115	20,704	-367	139	170	3,051	3,338	314.0	246.5
New Mexico	34.9	33.0	33.3	2,584	2,138	1,995	5,107	65	58	65	487	514	30.8	25.8
New York....................	712.6	669.2	705.3	156,323	130,792	114,583	59,977	245	212	242	5,175	5,479	1,534.4	854.8
North Carolina.............	198.4	199.9	219.2	23,914	22,598	17,469	23,703	337	93	129	2,481	2,779	347.4	207.4
North Dakota...............	18.8	20.6	24.4	2,350	1,579	1,001	2,797	284	87	100	429	444	26.1	17.6
Ohio.........................	308.5	276.7	293.4	26,349	21,268	20,628	27,055	-320	232	268	3,776	4,015	323.7	226.4
Oklahoma...................	79.9	78.1	79.5	6,544	5,668	4,535	10,865	330	228	264	1,350	1,411	83.7	69.0
Oregon......................	102.1	93.2	94.8	7,830	5,945	6,353	11,685	103	51	59	1,026	1,124	71.2	53.7
Pennsylvania...............	335.7	310.9	316.2	34,983	24,244	27,381	27,128	19	208	257	4,297	4,719	365.9	285.8
Rhode Island...............	34.3	30.7	33.1	3,510	2,854	2,644	2,426	-46	22	25	262	259	28.8	39.8
													0.0	0.0
South Carolina	92.5	91.9	97.4	9,257	6,705	5,966	12,050	-5	86	107	1,287	1,458	79.0	70.3
South Dakota	28.5	28.9	29.7	2,937	2,974	1,464	2,983	156	84	93	470	487	454.3	107.4
Tennessee	143.3	137.1	148.0	14,878	12,022	10,519	15,472	27	207	229	2,154	2,298	138.4	114.7
Texas........................	609.5	625.4	718.3	80,226	54,959	46,104	67,851	3,882	541	679	6,682	6,965	769.1	499.2
Utah.........................	67.5	68.0	78.7	8,091	4,796	4,504	9,868	705	57	74	553	602	555.9	271.9
Vermont.....................	13.2	12.2	12.0	1,076	1,038	903	1,723	36	23	23	243	266	12.6	10.6
Virginia......................	192.5	179.1	197.7	20,810	17,462	18,047	20,425	224	136	153	2,478	2,684	287.2	214.3
Washington.................	157.8	138.1	147.6	17,193	9,834	14,679	19,831	101	87	111	1,757	1,891	143.1	109.2
West Virginia...............	30.0	28.6	27.9	1,885	1,799	1,428	3,499	-84	76	85	646	664	31.5	28.8
Wisconsin	154.5	152.2	151.2	14,359	12,074	10,779	13,617	-304	257	299	2,128	2,351	143.5	126.7
Wyoming....................	10.8	10.8	11.1	1,116	1,182	688	2,184	92	45	47	224	235	15.5	12.0

[1] Includes Finance and Insurance (NAICS 52) and Real Estate and Rental and Leasing (NAICS 53).
[2] Includes insured U.S. branches of foreign banks. As of June 30.
[3] Based on the 2012 North American Industry Classification System (NAICS).
[4] 2014 data for establishments are based on the 2012 North American Industry Classification System (NAICS); 2010 data are based on the 2007 NAICS.
[5] Includes commercial banks, savings institutions, and insured U.S. branches of foreign banks. As of June 30.
[6] Based on the 2002 North American Industry Classification System (NAICS).

Table A-68. Professional and Business Services and Education and Health Services

| | Professional and business services[1] | | | | | | | | | Education and health services[2] | | | | | | | | |
| | Nonfarm employment (BLS)[3] | | | Earnings (BEA)[4] (million dollars) | | | Establishments | | | Nonfarm employment (BLS)[3] | | | Earnings (BEA)[4] (million dollars) | | | Establishments | | |
Geographic area	2015	2010	2005	2015	2010	2005	2014	2010	Net change, 2010–2014	2015	2010	2005	2015	2010	2005	2014	2010	Net change, 2010–2014
United States	19,633	16,728	16,954	1,872,770	1,414,278	1,186,828	1,334,738	1,284,153	50,585	22,029	19,975	17,676	1,398,657	1,159,238	883,745	954,630	902,972	51,658
Alabama	229	210	210	15,783	13,662	10,846	14,096	14,067	29	227	214	199	14,849	12,499	9,996	11,156	11,073	83
Alaska	30	28	25	3,038	2,577	1,799	3,231	3,175	56	48	43	37	3,517	2,791	2,092	2,767	2,478	289
Arizona	398	341	367	28,933	22,664	19,922	26,112	25,374	738	397	345	278	25,496	21,330	14,540	19,477	18,307	1,170
Arkansas	139	119	111	10,162	7,517	5,992	9,520	9,423	97	175	166	146	9,518	7,953	6,243	8,183	8,006	177
California	2,481	2,073	2,160	280,649	204,818	173,376	168,487	159,144	9,343	2,455	2,127	1,837	165,139	128,319	97,252	120,077	112,953	7,124
Colorado	398	331	319	39,602	29,614	23,812	34,679	32,874	1,805	314	265	225	20,547	16,407	12,229	17,847	16,700	1,147
Connecticut	219	194	204	26,820	19,949	18,506	15,288	15,435	-147	327	307	273	22,829	20,331	15,711	11,909	11,553	356
Delaware	61	55	63	6,124	4,625	3,987	4,990	5,126	-136	76	65	56	4,913	3,895	2,950	2,840	2,760	80
District of Columbia	162	148	148	25,563	20,631	16,267	6,682	6,292	390	131	108	92	8,906	7,026	5,410	2,629	2,671	-42
Florida	1,223	1,006	1,100	95,386	72,080	69,278	111,297	103,692	7,605	1,200	1,071	960	77,684	63,940	48,369	64,266	60,038	4,228
Georgia	633	523	534	53,528	42,583	33,488	42,403	41,307	1,096	540	476	419	34,619	28,167	21,444	26,610	24,746	1,864
Hawaii	84	72	74	6,018	4,733	4,067	5,368	5,429	-61	82	75	70	5,638	4,689	3,660	4,143	4,030	113
Idaho	82	75	78	5,405	4,654	4,076	6,870	6,614	256	98	84	68	5,472	4,337	3,167	5,481	5,143	338
Illinois	923	794	819	91,125	71,955	62,704	58,250	57,382	868	899	831	745	58,365	50,529	38,961	37,709	36,141	1,568
Indiana	331	276	275	22,459	16,947	14,423	20,910	20,926	-16	451	420	378	27,230	22,646	17,642	17,027	16,671	356
Iowa	139	122	113	9,396	6,983	5,451	10,366	10,297	69	226	214	195	11,703	10,018	8,092	9,009	8,758	251
Kansas	179	152	136	14,179	9,441	6,581	11,378	11,233	145	194	180	164	11,405	9,598	7,461	8,531	8,451	80
Kentucky	218	181	175	13,602	10,674	8,766	12,911	12,782	129	264	254	238	15,535	13,170	10,777	13,597	11,834	1,763
Louisiana	214	193	187	17,531	14,276	10,400	17,541	16,704	837	305	271	246	18,021	15,011	10,991	13,163	12,975	188
Maine	65	57	51	4,859	3,827	3,037	5,773	5,676	97	123	119	112	6,845	6,056	4,908	5,220	5,261	-41
Maryland	431	388	389	43,903	35,897	28,995	29,850	28,700	1,150	450	408	358	30,193	25,166	19,526	18,236	17,535	701
Massachusetts	536	464	461	70,032	51,749	42,447	33,085	32,205	880	762	688	604	55,621	45,366	33,091	21,594	20,771	823
Michigan	637	524	604	52,740	38,221	41,202	34,827	34,708	119	652	612	576	39,661	35,039	28,664	28,759	28,400	359
Minnesota	367	321	312	35,327	27,588	22,633	25,218	24,553	665	508	458	391	29,352	24,595	18,418	17,741	16,519	1,222
Mississippi	106	92	88	6,436	5,358	4,248	7,261	7,320	-59	138	131	120	8,175	7,332	5,579	6,749	6,674	75
Missouri	369	318	318	31,171	24,779	21,938	22,299	21,844	455	448	416	371	25,905	22,013	17,203	27,484	17,642	9,842
Montana	40	39	35	2,878	2,259	1,670	5,509	5,347	162	72	64	56	4,121	3,342	2,476	3,908	3,723	185
Nebraska	116	101	98	8,905	6,638	5,292	7,507	7,384	123	150	141	127	8,005	6,771	5,425	5,964	5,713	251
Nevada	167	136	146	12,668	10,079	9,542	13,220	12,775	445	121	102	85	8,394	6,770	4,902	7,296	6,852	444
New Hampshire............	77	64	59	7,597	5,726	4,845	6,306	6,320	-14	118	112	98	7,476	6,521	4,898	4,221	4,167	54
New Jersey	650	591	595	75,137	56,976	48,714	45,207	44,536	671	660	601	558	45,462	39,206	30,939	30,776	29,598	1,178
New Mexico	100	100	93	7,676	7,229	5,256	6,782	6,860	-78	133	120	105	6,616	5,738	4,322	5,527	5,447	80
New York....................	1,267	1,099	1,082	157,763	112,356	104,254	90,728	86,697	4,031	1,891	1,680	1,529	119,319	100,860	78,719	64,927	63,220	1,707
North Carolina.............	589	485	449	47,411	34,361	27,260	37,475	35,726	1,749	574	537	469	34,683	29,376	21,846	25,724	25,309	415
North Dakota...............	36	28	27	2,826	1,639	1,159	3,038	2,579	459	60	55	49	3,676	2,735	2,032	2,126	1,980	146
Ohio	716	626	644	60,215	45,998	40,084	39,564	39,917	-353	906	841	762	52,844	44,923	36,069	31,625	31,030	595
Oklahoma	184	172	174	13,110	11,039	8,065	14,781	14,275	506	232	222	201	13,090	10,775	8,308	11,445	11,285	160
Oregon	229	189	190	20,450	13,257	11,332	18,178	17,523	655	258	229	199	17,539	13,776	10,606	14,497	13,591	906
Pennsylvania...............	780	690	661	76,211	60,334	48,217	47,342	46,684	658	1,191	1,128	1,024	75,923	64,568	50,182	40,280	39,477	803
Rhode Island...............	64	53	55	5,804	4,448	3,808	4,887	4,885	2	106	101	95	6,470	5,805	4,617	3,647	3,671	-24
South Carolina	263	216	206	17,557	13,109	10,548	16,184	15,732	452	235	210	180	13,200	10,743	8,064	11,091	10,781	310
South Dakota	31	28	25	2,396	1,731	1,242	3,134	3,031	103	69	65	57	4,307	3,442	2,707	2,537	2,529	8
Tennessee	393	304	313	29,196	22,883	17,067	19,237	18,858	379	415	376	333	35,744	28,199	19,833	16,505	16,059	446
Texas.........................	1,598	1,281	1,165	153,018	106,339	80,597	98,431	89,234	9,197	1,579	1,381	1,185	96,638	77,260	55,296	70,495	64,826	5,669
Utah	195	152	146	13,700	9,346	7,337	14,350	13,082	1,268	183	155	129	9,454	7,455	5,341	8,594	7,718	876
Vermont	28	23	22	2,467	1,851	1,464	3,285	3,338	-53	64	59	54	3,594	3,045	2,420	2,477	2,495	-18
Virginia	702	650	606	77,338	65,377	48,480	42,463	40,413	2,050	514	463	397	31,366	26,348	19,269	22,193	20,663	1,530
Washington	389	326	316	38,592	30,481	23,390	31,123	29,891	1,232	449	425	362	29,060	23,446	17,287	22,748	21,596	1,152
West Virginia...............	67	61	59	4,500	3,609	2,990	4,621	4,671	-50	129	121	113	6,938	5,955	4,783	5,177	5,187	-10
Wisconsin	315	274	266	24,094	18,117	15,282	19,363	19,045	318	436	408	380	25,995	22,515	17,996	16,551	15,995	556
Wyoming	19	17	16	1,490	1,297	694	3,331	3,068	263	27	26	22	1,604	1,441	1,035	2,095	1,970	125

[1]Professional, scientific and technical services; management of companies and enterprises; administrative and support and waste management and remediation services.
[2]Education services; health care and social assistance.
[3]Bureau of Labor Statistics.
[4]Bureau of Economic Analysis.

Table A-69.   Leisure and Hospitality Services

Geographic area	Leisure and hospitality employees (BLS)[1] (includes Arts, Entertainment, and Recreation and Accommodations and Food Services) (thousands)			Arts, entertainment, and recreation services						Accommodations and food services					
				Earnings (BEA)[2] (million dollars)			Establishments			Earnings (BEA)[2] (million dollars)			Establishments[3]		
	2015	2010	2005	2015	2010	2005	2014	2010	Net change, 2010–2014	2015	2010	2005	2014	2010	Net change, 2010–2014
United States	15,160	13,049	12,816	129,129	96,758	86,132	129,839	123,151	6,688	369,235	267,796	243,966	679,296	643,960	35,336
Alabama	190	168	165	490	339	382	1,096	1,105	-9	3,703	2,717	2,385	8,395	8,123	272
Alaska	35	32	31	188	143	130	548	548	0	1,126	925	782	2,120	1,993	127
Arizona.......................	299	254	254	2,166	1,381	1,576	1,801	1,695	106	7,074	5,474	5,466	11,955	11,438	517
Arkansas	112	99	94	264	218	176	805	809	-4	2,140	1,637	1,394	5,454	5,290	164
California.....................	1,830	1,501	1,475	26,945	20,449	20,411	22,627	20,205	2,422	51,429	33,794	32,483	81,819	75,463	6,356
Colorado.....................	313	263	258	3,052	1,712	1,698	2,649	2,417	232	7,165	5,015	5,031	13,094	12,207	887
Connecticut.................	151	134	130	1,595	1,348	1,391	1,665	1,607	58	3,778	3,298	2,794	8,454	8,004	450
Delaware	49	44	42	333	362	254	429	410	19	1,048	756	776	2,000	1,910	90
District of Columbia	73	60	54	655	667	650	320	309	11	2,693	1,941	1,642	2,506	2,264	242
Florida........................	1,134	932	951	10,717	8,249	6,462	7,930	7,462	468	26,758	20,569	18,522	38,280	35,543	2,737
Georgia.......................	448	374	372	2,231	1,718	1,504	2,928	2,696	232	9,838	7,149	6,780	19,409	18,567	842
Hawaii........................	115	100	106	564	441	375	534	494	40	4,459	3,248	3,845	3,579	3,483	96
Idaho..........................	68	58	57	270	213	168	742	737	5	1,255	923	791	3,543	3,512	31
Illinois........................	578	515	512	5,314	3,672	3,289	4,616	4,450	166	14,901	11,329	8,958	27,571	26,879	692
Indiana.......................	301	273	277	2,125	1,481	1,614	2,079	2,140	-61	5,650	4,054	3,866	13,143	12,718	425
Iowa...........................	141	130	131	541	530	281	1,463	1,457	6	2,618	1,833	1,678	6,970	6,918	52
Kansas.......................	126	113	112	516	264	314	1,030	1,018	12	2,680	2,035	1,917	5,985	5,898	87
Kentucky.....................	188	167	165	606	490	469	1,277	1,274	3	4,211	3,135	2,828	7,858	7,517	341
Louisiana....................	228	194	198	1,330	1,102	1,224	1,408	1,390	18	5,456	4,163	3,317	9,276	8,657	619
Maine.........................	64	60	59	378	299	275	865	876	-11	1,540	1,118	1,063	4,099	3,960	139
Maryland.....................	268	230	226	2,688	1,353	1,149	2,064	2,037	27	6,452	5,152	4,606	11,516	10,986	530
Massachusetts.............	351	308	293	4,696	2,799	2,400	3,250	3,050	200	9,389	6,869	6,154	17,269	16,437	832
Michigan	414	378	406	2,147	2,076	2,402	3,374	3,520	-146	8,498	6,076	5,992	19,656	19,449	207
Minnesota	260	235	242	2,057	1,397	1,086	2,823	2,679	144	5,089	3,750	3,543	11,395	11,165	230
Mississippi..................	129	118	123	282	338	382	666	668	-2	2,718	2,379	2,325	5,371	4,956	415
Missouri......................	293	272	273	2,580	1,940	1,773	2,101	2,111	-10	5,803	4,567	4,090	12,483	12,313	170
Montana......................	63	56	55	369	284	241	1,169	1,150	19	1,273	879	776	3,471	3,391	80
Nebraska.....................	89	81	79	387	276	243	874	855	19	1,662	1,212	1,071	4,424	4,243	181
Nevada.......................	341	309	327	1,605	1,456	1,667	1,398	1,224	174	13,822	11,317	11,587	6,145	5,733	412
New Hampshire............	69	62	63	620	536	644	762	721	41	1,655	1,276	1,157	3,642	3,538	104
New Jersey	360	334	333	3,222	2,244	2,205	3,526	3,418	108	9,357	7,648	7,510	20,590	19,543	1,047
New Mexico	93	84	84	439	385	383	684	654	30	2,185	1,747	1,489	4,189	4,089	100
New York.....................	898	736	671	14,793	12,123	8,242	12,181	11,378	803	24,996	17,745	15,060	51,682	47,433	4,249
North Carolina..............	461	393	363	3,075	2,278	1,913	3,576	3,391	185	10,188	6,492	5,568	19,923	19,120	803
North Dakota................	41	34	31	108	79	67	441	421	20	869	541	429	2,040	1,833	207
Ohio...........................	539	475	500	3,780	3,236	2,953	3,761	3,860	-99	10,802	7,587	7,155	23,800	23,143	657
Oklahoma....................	162	139	132	710	462	380	1,081	1,074	7	3,809	3,244	2,712	7,617	7,131	486
Oregon........................	192	162	159	1,185	703	757	1,758	1,639	119	4,792	3,112	2,879	10,831	10,319	512
Pennsylvania................	545	501	485	4,773	3,762	2,648	4,552	4,508	44	11,422	8,873	8,091	28,371	27,683	688
Rhode Island................	56	50	50	470	334	325	533	543	-10	1,252	941	901	3,039	2,945	94
South Carolina	239	208	203	871	511	511	1,572	1,546	26	5,586	3,661	3,226	10,007	9,532	475
South Dakota	46	43	42	160	144	121	683	666	17	948	599	590	2,406	2,359	47
Tennessee	308	262	262	3,881	2,679	2,322	2,391	2,282	109	7,247	5,053	4,740	12,238	11,689	549
Texas..........................	1,242	1,008	907	6,470	4,001	3,191	6,703	6,101	602	32,163	21,800	17,806	50,755	46,045	4,710
Utah............................	134	111	104	825	542	403	1,048	863	185	2,545	1,836	1,522	5,359	4,851	508
Vermont......................	36	32	33	198	160	151	459	436	23	915	675	652	1,945	1,896	49
Virginia.......................	386	341	329	2,118	1,886	1,762	2,898	2,739	159	8,615	6,751	5,997	17,344	16,219	1,125
Washington..................	310	267	264	2,373	2,004	1,653	2,860	2,696	164	8,101	5,338	4,901	16,505	16,039	466
West Virginia................	75	72	69	228	302	235	770	689	81	1,660	1,250	1,086	3,639	3,682	-43
Wisconsin....................	271	251	255	1,655	1,318	1,217	2,641	2,716	-75	5,001	3,631	3,483	14,325	14,130	195
Wyoming	36	33	32	84	72	62	428	417	11	894	679	549	1,809	1,724	85

[1]All estimates of labor and earnings provided by Bureau of Labor Statistics (BLS) are based on the 2007 North American Industry Classific System.
[2]Bureau of Economic Analysis. The estimates of earnings for 2000–2006 are based on the 2002 North American Industry Classification System (NAICS). The estimates for 2007 forward are based on the 2007 NAICS. All dollars estimates are in current dollars and not adjusted for inflation.
[3]Data provided by County Business Patterns is based on the North American Industry Classification System (NAICS). Data for 2005 is based on NAICS 2002. Data for 2010 is based on NAICS 2007.

Table A-70. Travel and Tourism Indicators

Geographic area	Tourists and Business Travelers, 2015		National parks[3]						Acreage, 2015
	Visa waiver[1]	Other[2]	Visits						
			2015	2014	2013	2012	2011	2010	
United States	22,419,941	46,605,955	307,247,252	292,800,082	273,630,895	282,765,682	276,626,130	279,337,864	84,617,508
Alabama......................	54,840	64,318	792,447	753,178	749,857	717,724	755,264	781,550	22,737
Alaska	66,080	53,831	2,664,293	2,684,693	2,585,980	2,412,524	2,333,919	2,274,843	54,653,820
Arizona.......................	132,198	1,439,910	11,729,985	10,747,219	10,103,264	9,979,972	10,134,892	10,546,150	2,947,312
Arkansas....................	15,464	84,016	3,282,634	3,132,898	2,776,183	2,727,454	2,879,494	3,125,664	104,976
California....................	3,187,496	6,553,238	38,366,824	37,363,392	35,575,100	35,991,200	35,448,424	34,915,676	8,146,657
Colorado	182,823	341,195	7,077,287	6,031,874	5,393,745	5,811,546	5,819,069	5,635,307	737,810
Connecticut.................	80,168	106,905	47,220	34,082	22,862	21,465	22,415	19,313	7,782
Delaware....................	14,328	20,709	–	–	–	–	–	–	904
District of Columbia	187,677	209,320	41,801,278		34,202,516	34,286,073	30,579,692	33,140,005	8,625
Florida........................	3,100,583	6,713,838	10,639,976	10,667,459	10,282,814	10,366,613	10,580,858	9,222,981	2,638,642
Georgia	239,366	389,820	7,527,855	7,491,109	7,046,578	7,350,309	7,167,680	6,776,556	63,357
Hawaii	2,028,292	658,320	5,439,034	5,213,817	4,902,696	5,119,035	4,784,285	4,493,123	369,320
Idaho..........................	16,539	18,549	601,777	553,739	614,412	553,554	601,668	530,977	518,224
Illinois	466,631	767,944	233,299	218,132	209,405	295,464	296,214	354,125	116
Indiana.......................	56,298	95,435	1,887,762	1,778,385	1,935,295	2,148,903	2,094,529	2,395,485	15,573
Iowa...........................	18,269	35,837	209,055	216,898	199,993	207,352	216,830	222,295	2,713
Kansas	16,385	58,842	115,903	98,591	91,930	101,752	90,383	100,361	11,635
Kentucky	28,322	43,403	1,760,944	1,828,192	1,604,722	1,717,853	1,666,505	1,797,894	95,942
Louisiana	101,918	189,638	494,688	510,522	624,047	625,913	577,755	496,329	23,545
Maine.........................	32,644	30,473	2,823,741	2,574,717	2,265,631	2,431,052	2,374,645	2,504,208	91,884
Maryland.....................	109,988	206,143	6,443,376	6,815,195	6,615,152	6,658,643	6,064,410	3,541,570	74,728
Massachusetts.............	499,014	513,779	9,399,919	9,850,586	9,678,050	10,487,447	10,231,394	9,913,501	59,125
Michigan	185,781	330,956	2,386,613	1,993,139	1,989,195	2,192,477	1,961,506	1,796,006	718,148
Minnesota...................	76,564	141,796	840,008	811,616	658,330	601,274	572,795	540,195	301,330
Mississippi..................	10,514	21,101	6,359,646	6,557,120	6,784,616	6,449,713	6,990,401	6,588,026	118,549
Missouri......................	39,731	87,152	3,247,219	3,385,772	3,888,912	4,171,826	3,913,220	4,140,544	83,476
Montana......................	25,480	19,452	4,967,752	4,590,398	4,281,517	4,451,755	4,061,967	4,584,011	1,274,331
Nebraska....................	190,311	266,704	291,235	254,198	257,903	304,046	276,058	290,323	66,570
Nevada.......................	803,227	1,658,582	5,589,972	5,314,681	4,851,429	4,808,929	4,888,963	5,399,439	801,162
New Hampshire.............	29,485	22,838	39,242	37,785	37,837	33,663	32,695	30,941	21,189
New Jersey	383,663	606,510	4,205,734	4,389,637	5,028,646	4,885,202	5,357,781	5,858,443	99,328
New Mexico	17,000	280,377	1,714,677	1,602,114	1,512,529	1,502,808	1,491,144	1,657,550	480,069
New York.....................	3,957,599	3,077,761	16,328,212	16,141,397	10,986,810	12,633,278	16,206,130	17,506,353	97,004
North Carolina..............	119,017	188,687	17,834,699	16,710,759	16,138,182	17,706,032	17,191,874	17,093,464	407,092
North Dakota................	11,191	15,942	605,015	581,851	572,474	669,242	591,668	659,927	72,568
Ohio...........................	97,809	161,867	2,624,146	2,470,177	2,404,918	2,611,158	2,417,080	2,738,275	34,545
Oklahoma....................	16,729	77,895	1,266,172	1,165,269	1,108,103	1,497,654	1,223,134	1,266,189	10,241
Oregon........................	92,913	121,884	1,154,108	1,033,254	969,051	875,271	839,614	888,358	203,385
Pennsylvania...............	191,286	240,571	9,935,361	9,005,244	9,137,524	8,768,869	8,526,173	8,970,475	115,368
Rhode Island................	20,131	26,435	60,505	51,523	48,677	51,944	50,909	51,559	331
South Carolina	54,679	81,289	1,519,259	1,519,746	1,516,151	1,566,756	1,589,650	1,529,172	32,348
South Dakota	6,053	7,948	4,397,785	3,861,090	3,915,730	3,950,666	3,807,375	4,199,267	296,544
Tennessee	71,429	125,797	8,773,891	8,470,460	8,090,143	8,414,094	7,767,864	7,898,557	386,926
Texas..........................	545,495	4,035,452	5,044,926	4,680,387	3,482,052	3,939,160	4,211,655	5,495,156	1,248,150
Utah...........................	62,642	99,426	11,889,390	10,551,040	8,981,447	9,503,304	9,281,567	8,975,525	2,117,683
Vermont......................	29,127	15,668	35,003	39,086	34,112	32,403	29,049	31,209	23,237
Virginia.......................	153,828	260,688	23,249,802	22,870,531	22,024,385	23,398,517	23,459,706	22,708,338	364,453
Washington..................	444,797	563,652	7,674,514	7,652,073	7,347,284	7,529,549	7,419,258	7,281,785	1,967,532
West Virginia................	4,989	7,323	1,603,753	1,541,805	1,499,112	1,543,425	1,477,886	1,811,722	92,736
Wisconsin	53,108	82,476	544,223	625,850	320,027	273,933	312,905	251,145	133,760
Wyoming	11,286	10,393	7,250,657	6,387,455	6,079,578	6,194,752	5,955,778	6,307,997	2,396,424

– = Not applicable.
[1] Includes GB, GMB, GT, GMT, WB, and WT admissions.
[2] Includes B1, B2 and a limited number of Border Crossing Card (BCC) admissions.
[3] For year ending June 30. Data are shown as reported by state park directors. In some states, park agency has under its control forests, fish and wildlife areas, and/or other areas. In other states agency is responsible for state parks only. Includes overnight visitors.

Table A-71.   Government

Geographic area	Government employees (BLS)[1] (thousands)			Government earnings (BEA)[2] (million dollars)			Federal tax collections, 2015[3] (million dollars)	State tax collections (million dollars)			
	2015	2010	2005	2015	2010	2005		2015	2014	2013	2012
United States	22,029	22,490	21,804	1,834,307	1,699,969	1,385,240	3,302,677	916,488	874,957	855,384	796,918
Alabama......................	377	387	363	25,346	24,988	20,003	25,070	9,755	9,297	9,271	9,049
Alaska	82	85	81	9,662	8,532	6,792	5,718	864	3,393	5,133	7,049
Arizona......................	410	416	403	30,593	28,808	23,302	42,631	14,082	13,424	13,797	12,996
Arkansas...................	213	218	204	12,799	12,147	9,857	32,509	9,190	8,917	8,587	8,288
California....................	2,463	2,448	2,420	258,357	227,509	188,360	405,851	151,173	138,132	133,184	115,179
Colorado	417	394	363	32,424	28,727	23,019	47,211	12,811	11,755	11,255	10,263
Connecticut................	239	247	246	21,828	20,051	17,496	59,175	16,232	15,938	16,046	15,481
Delaware	65	64	60	5,282	4,936	4,112	22,641	3,514	3,176	3,346	3,280
District of Columbia	238	247	234	35,823	33,484	25,101	25,584	7,087	6,416	6,232.763	X
Florida.......................	1,082	1,112	1,081	83,913	81,203	68,996	177,389	37,218	36,336	35,432	32,997
Georgia	679	699	667	50,296	49,380	40,406	86,447	19,724	18,618	17,932	16,715
Hawaii.......................	126	125	120	15,311	13,426	10,543	8,221	6,486	6,053	6,111	5,516
Idaho........................	119	119	115	7,132	6,720	5,733	9,785	3,975	3,669	3,578	3,374
Illinois......................	829	854	846	67,478	64,506	54,251	158,042	39,283	39,923	38,729	36,258
Indiana......................	427	437	426	25,016	23,887	20,858	57,973	17,400	16,847	16,881	16,289
Iowa.........................	256	253	245	16,419	14,807	11,632	23,969	9,189	8,573	8,682	7,932
Kansas......................	257	262	251	17,329	15,842	12,286	27,019	7,884	7,334	7,616	7,418
Kentucky...................	319	317	301	23,145	23,140	17,634	32,708	11,598	11,104	10,875	10,619
Louisiana	327	366	374	22,568	24,108	19,640	42,628	9,719	9,695	9,224	8,994
Maine........................	100	104	105	6,868	6,485	5,630	7,464	4,064	3,847	3,884	3,777
Maryland....................	503	502	466	56,005	50,310	39,044	63,937	19,850	18,929	18,118	17,095
Massachusetts.............	451	439	425	40,619	34,267	28,143	108,049	27,012	25,237	23,901	22,821
Michigan....................	594	636	674	41,222	42,522	38,540	77,948	26,957	25,101	24,936	23,920
Minnesota..................	419	417	415	27,432	25,016	21,301	106,928	24,439	23,246	22,896	20,561
Mississippi.................	244	249	241	14,930	14,346	12,090	11,469	7,907	7,575	7,403	6,953
Missouri.....................	434	448	429	29,317	28,652	23,495	64,113	11,956	11,241	11,139	10,802
Montana.....................	90	92	86	5,673	5,209	4,250	5,805	2,843	2,656	2,645	2,459
Nebraska...................	171	170	161	11,004	10,064	8,155	25,104	5,087	4,888	4,719	4,367
Nevada......................	155	154	143	14,017	13,383	10,302	18,450	7,533	7,143	7,027	6,775
New Hampshire............	90	96	91	6,462	6,282	4,824	11,315	2,488	2,286	2,353	2,205
New Jersey	614	642	643	55,367	52,473	44,915	153,918	31,568	29,679	29,077	27,456
New Mexico	191	200	201	13,939	13,390	11,778	8,970	6,009	5,757	5,391	5,471
New York....................	1,438	1,511	1,489	145,073	134,380	109,007	269,717	78,243	76,979	73,667	71,546
North Carolina.............	720	721	671	55,876	53,502	41,073	78,736	25,062	23,470	23,818	22,715
North Dakota...............	81	80	75	5,247	4,382	3,360	7,711	5,740	6,120	5,299	4,146
Ohio	771	786	800	56,281	53,849	46,165	140,981	28,297	27,021	27,242	25,928
Oklahoma...................	351	349	321	22,460	20,901	16,014	33,942	9,407	9,103	8,893	8,824
Oregon......................	301	300	285	20,569	18,374	15,222	31,219	10,575	9,680	9,161	8,728
Pennsylvania...............	705	771	754	60,211	57,982	48,332	136,109	36,110	34,193	33,966	32,950
Rhode Island..............	60	62	65	6,065	5,752	4,932	14,373	3,197	2,974	2,932	2,868
South Carolina	360	355	336	25,800	23,006	18,633	24,086	9,633	9,004	8,735	8,063
South Dakota	78	79	75	4,734	4,354	3,518	7,732	1,674	1,608	1,534	1,522
Tennessee..................	425	431	410	28,250	25,336	21,615	62,709	12,698	11,806	11,728	11,380
Texas........................	1,885	1,891	1,712	136,142	121,278	90,901	279,904	55,086	55,147	51,801	47,991
Utah.........................	233	218	202	15,469	13,966	11,183	20,179	6,703	6,312	6,294	5,810
Vermont.....................	56	55	53	3,837	3,387	2,858	4,495	3,043	2,963	2,850	2,731
Virginia......................	711	707	662	72,375	66,875	52,958	80,243	20,537	18,930	19,187	18,145
Washington.................	562	550	527	49,654	44,570	34,611	73,334	20,644	19,448	18,787	17,625
West Virginia...............	153	153	143	8,919	8,447	7,011	7,374	5,566	5,387	5,390	5,286
Wisconsin...................	409	420	415	28,443	26,503	22,104	51,749	17,019	16,365	16,514	15,995
Wyoming	71	71	65	5,323	4,524	3,255	5,284	2,356	2,263	2,186	2,305

[1]All estimates of labor and earnings provided by BLS are based on the 2007 North American Industry Classification System (NAICS). Government employment covers only civilian employees; military personnel are excluded. Employees of the Central Intelligence Agency, the National Security Agency, the National Imagery and Mapping Agency, and the Defense Intelligence Agency also are excluded.

[2]The estimates of earnings provided by the Bureau of Economic Analysis (BEA) for 2000–2006 are based on the 2002 North American Industry Classification System (NAICS). The estimates for 2010 and 2012 are based on the 2007 NAICS. All dollar estimates are in current dollars (not adjusted for inflation). Includes Government enterprises.

[3]Excludes excise taxes collected by the Customs Service and the Alcohol and Tobacco Tax and Trade Bureau.

Table A-72. State Government Employment and Finances

Geographic area	Employment (full-time equivalent) Number (thousands) 2015	2012	Revenue (million dollars) Total 2014	2012	Revenue General, 2014 Total¹	Intergovernmental from federal government	Taxes	Expenditures (million dollars) Total 2014	2012	Expenditures General, 2014 Total¹	Intergovernmental	Direct Education	Direct Public welfare	Direct Highway
United States	4,342	4,315	2,360,070	1,905,807	1,739,018	551,274	865,752	2,036,419	1,981,198	1,727,289	496,871	609,503	544,647	115,405
Alabama....................	89	89	28,280	28,970	22,948	8,135	9,294	28,128	27,687	24,502	6,474	10,367	6,619	1,685
Alaska......................	26	27	12,871	14,983	10,436	2,810	3,393	12,920	11,729	11,427	2,059	2,769	2,169	1,244
Arizona....................	79	77	39,053	32,134	29,350	10,951	13,084	33,231	31,888	29,094	7,448	9,714	9,081	1,758
Arkansas..................	63	64	23,417	18,443	18,058	6,097	8,937	20,410	19,618	18,558	5,199	7,611	5,713	1,373
California..................	404	398	353,368	250,971	230,742	63,517	138,070	284,556	269,055	234,831	91,869	79,813	83,486	12,632
Colorado	81	74	34,388	25,688	24,739	7,278	11,755	30,649	28,238	25,202	6,750	10,079	6,715	1,645
Connecticut	64	61	31,292	27,328	25,845	6,365	15,938	29,308	28,370	24,176	4,899	7,226	7,233	1,064
Delaware	26	27	9,298	7,949	7,605	2,102	3,176	8,787	8,316	7,978	1,391	2,842	2,142	531
District of Columbia	(X)	(X)	(X)	(X)	(X)	(X)	(X)	(X)	(X)	(X)	(X)	(X)	(X)	(X)
Florida.....................	179	181	104,128	83,670	76,827	25,802	35,384	83,274	79,482	74,477	18,708	25,076	24,368	6,596
Georgia	128	130	54,207	40,644	39,007	14,612	18,629	45,452	44,751	39,049	10,558	17,402	11,742	2,300
Hawaii	58	57	15,056	10,601	11,304	2,811	6,033	12,379	11,566	11,045	256	3,276	2,583	414
Idaho.......................	23	23	10,511	8,308	7,436	2,531	3,672	8,449	8,301	7,329	2,015	2,647	2,226	667
Illinois	124	130	90,168	68,902	66,637	18,227	39,183	77,319	72,622	63,380	16,924	17,696	21,228	5,259
Indiana	88	88	39,529	35,960	33,260	11,056	16,847	35,990	35,835	33,018	9,315	14,603	10,593	2,418
Iowa........................	50	48	25,197	21,080	18,889	6,219	8,272	21,214	20,408	18,598	4,964	6,729	5,538	1,807
Kansas	50	48	19,013	16,144	15,391	3,976	7,334	16,920	16,747	15,076	4,108	6,095	3,789	1,189
Kentucky	86	85	31,508	25,684	25,268	9,769	11,104	29,938	29,349	25,711	4,649	9,253	8,349	2,501
Louisiana	74	79	33,276	26,894	25,352	10,215	9,695	31,804	31,679	27,488	6,053	8,593	8,081	1,523
Maine.......................	21	21	10,529	8,418	8,193	3,028	3,847	9,258	9,128	8,233	1,285	2,087	3,362	583
Maryland..................	88	87	44,700	36,104	36,281	11,038	18,929	41,309	41,139	36,037	8,734	11,985	10,834	2,186
Massachusetts............	102	95	61,747	49,237	49,046	14,166	25,236	58,305	56,685	48,306	9,812	13,477	16,656	2,231
Michigan	142	147	68,884	63,986	54,834	17,930	24,804	63,862	61,727	55,288	19,779	23,549	15,680	2,628
Minnesota	82	80	50,419	38,554	37,646	9,838	23,129	41,845	38,613	36,499	12,621	14,696	12,442	2,763
Mississippi................	57	58	23,347	18,765	17,576	7,378	7,575	20,013	20,051	17,273	4,920	5,507	5,809	1,364
Missouri...................	88	87	38,508	31,066	26,677	10,395	11,241	30,454	31,103	26,150	5,785	9,129	8,069	1,435
Montana...................	21	20	8,939	6,572	5,977	2,342	2,656	7,219	7,063	6,211	1,382	1,920	1,502	734
Nebraska..................	32	32	12,112	9,815	9,779	3,095	4,877	10,046	9,526	9,353	2,202	3,412	2,639	742
Nevada....................	28	27	19,049	14,318	11,480	3,021	7,143	13,217	13,477	10,780	4,169	4,460	2,720	495
New Hampshire............	19	19	8,262	7,150	5,913	1,853	2,283	7,345	7,424	6,124	1,269	2,038	1,760	512
New Jersey	141	146	65,658	57,582	56,559	16,049	29,679	69,081	68,122	53,518	12,104	17,087	15,923	3,607
New Mexico	46	45	20,421	15,265	15,591	5,558	5,757	17,721	17,059	15,494	4,605	5,501	4,224	710
New York...................	243	237	205,790	179,605	146,853	49,114	76,979	178,325	181,226	144,433	58,135	41,599	54,150	4,746
North Carolina.............	140	150	61,749	56,469	46,909	15,643	23,397	51,113	53,624	45,117	13,173	19,054	12,722	3,753
North Dakota..............	19	19	9,966	7,773	8,850	1,534	6,120	7,486	6,315	6,815	2,262	2,124	1,059	1,347
Ohio........................	138	137	96,425	72,471	62,101	22,350	27,021	79,239	76,524	61,618	16,648	21,480	21,477	3,755
Oklahoma.................	69	65	28,534	23,248	21,441	7,410	9,103	23,378	22,599	20,127	4,279	7,553	6,523	1,888
Oregon....................	67	66	37,665	25,088	24,356	8,791	9,684	29,414	26,862	24,146	6,007	7,895	8,024	1,313
Pennsylvania..............	163	162	89,538	78,467	70,355	21,869	34,193	86,986	87,340	72,881	18,836	22,858	24,369	6,867
Rhode Island..............	18	19	8,996	7,987	7,117	2,510	2,966	8,334	8,326	6,845	1,198	2,026	2,538	339
South Carolina	80	79	31,871	26,132	23,076	7,640	8,933	28,904	27,668	23,683	5,581	8,702	6,658	1,101
South Dakota	14	14	6,124	4,352	4,162	1,574	1,608	4,521	4,424	4,039	746	1,278	986	615
Tennessee	78	80	31,291	30,836	26,493	10,645	11,806	30,519	31,498	28,083	7,222	10,115	10,922	1,640
Texas.......................	304	301	160,134	130,720	121,679	40,561	55,261	130,574	125,953	114,644	29,192	50,420	32,834	8,711
Utah........................	55	53	19,414	15,601	14,974	4,211	6,312	17,040	17,109	15,147	3,266	7,026	3,147	828
Vermont....................	15	14	6,545	6,349	5,772	1,943	2,963	6,303	5,959	5,865	1,571	2,482	1,671	474
Virginia....................	127	126	53,731	43,138	41,469	10,028	18,949	48,188	46,760	40,465	11,793	14,825	10,218	4,284
Washington................	122	121	55,072	40,666	38,296	11,475	19,448	47,971	45,501	40,465	10,439	16,189	9,771	3,023
West Virginia..............	40	40	15,382	13,247	12,247	4,350	5,380	13,241	13,223	11,678	2,414	4,285	3,719	1,119
Wisconsin	74	71	47,260	35,881	32,441	9,256	16,411	38,583	37,753	33,236	9,890	11,195	9,791	2,487
Wyoming	13	14	7,451	6,599	5,780	2,208	2,263	5,895	5,774	5,066	1,913	1,763	792	522

(X) = Not applicable.
¹Includes categories not shown separately.

Table A-73. State Government Tax Collections, 2015

				State government tax collections, 2015[1]									
					Sales and gross receipts (million dollars)								
							Selective sales taxes						
Geographic area	Total[2] (million dollars)	Percent change, 2014–2015	Property taxes (million dollars)	Total	General sales and gross receipts	Total	Alcoholic beverages	Amusements	Insurance premiums	Motor fuels	Public utilities	Tobacco products	Other selective sales
United States	916,488	4.7	17,555	431,256	286,154	145,101	6,431	7,304	19,150	42,525	13,626	17,742	38,201
Alabama	9,755	4.9	337	4,936	2,464	2,472	192	0	312	560	735	116	555
Alaska	864	-74.5	128	256	X	256	40	9	66	42	4	66	29
Arizona.....................	14,082	4.9	883	8,246	6,466	1,780	71	1	467	754	23	314	151
Arkansas	9,190	3.1	1,088	4,410	3,182	1,228	53	47	191	462	0	225	247
California...................	151,173	9.4	2,316	52,347	38,465	13,883	357	0	2,445	5,711	627	832	3,896
Colorado	12,811	9.0	X	4,789	2,818	1,971	41	110	258	668	11	197	685
Connecticut................	16,232	1.8	X	6,562	4,083	2,479	62	308	189	482	290	358	784
Delaware	3,514	10.6	X	499	X	499	21	0	94	117	57	103	107
District of Columbia	7,087	10.5	2,252	1,747	1,310	437	6	X	106	26	202	31	64
Florida......................	37,218	2	0	30,336	21,801	8,535	459	198	690	2,482	2,689	1,193	817
Georgia	19,724	5.9	862	7,556	5,257	2,299	184	X	420	1,026	0	215	454
Hawaii.......................	6,486	7.1	X	4,082	2,993	1,089	50	0	151	93	163	130	502
Idaho........................	3,975	8.3	X	1,941	1,464	477	9	0	84	259	2	48	71
Illinois......................	39,283	-1.6	61	16,103	8,951	7,152	283	747	380	1,293	1,676	862	1,905
Indiana......................	17,400	3.3	9	10,591	7,280	3,312	46	619	221	832	239	439	914
Iowa.........................	9,189	7.2	2	4,269	3,041	1,228	23	288	110	542	6	223	33
Kansas	7,884	7.5	659	3,978	3,053	925	133	0	212	439	0	96	44
Kentucky	11,598	4.5	563	5,450	3,267	2,183	132	0	146	850	64	242	745
Louisiana	9,719	0.2	57	5,308	2,927	2,381	57	714	438	606	9	138	413
Maine........................	4,064	5.6	37	1,999	1,280	719	18	52	98	244	33	137	134
Maryland....................	19,850	4.9	738	8,299	4,410	3,889	31	416	445	923	136	391	1,545
Massachusetts.............	27,012	7.0	5	8,274	5,804	2,470	81	4	368	756	24	647	589
Michigan	26,957	7.4	1,963	13,124	9,212	3,913	145	111	323	1,010	28	960	1,331
Minnesota	24,439	5.1	839	9,953	5,484	4,470	85	49	438	885	0	652	2,360
Mississippi..................	7,907	4.4	26	4,874	3,423	1,451	42	131	299	428	2	148	400
Missouri.....................	11,956	6.4	30	5,084	3,380	1,704	36	366	377	695	0	99	130
Montana.....................	2,843	7.1	268	603	X	603	34	60	97	227	47	85	53
Nebraska....................	5,087	4.1	0	2,316	1,788	528	30	6	31	328	57	64	12
Nevada......................	7,533	5.5	242	6,039	4,081	1,958	44	953	294	304	24	117	223
New Hampshire.............	2,488	8.8	405	970	X	970	12	0	108	147	64	236	402
New Jersey	31,568	6.4	5	12,952	9,146	3,806	139	206	648	536	964	716	598
New Mexico	6,009	4.4	109	2,996	2,256	740	46	72	122	240	28	80	150
New York....................	78,243	1.6	X	23,970	13,104	10,865	251	1	1,431	1,648	873	1,307	5,335
North Carolina..............	25,062	6.8	X	10,713	6,863	3,850	360	2	530	1,924	-22	276	780
North Dakota...............	5,740	-6.2	4	1,939	1,389	550	9	4	58	232	45	36	164
Ohio.........................	28,297	4.7	X	17,214	11,900	5,314	101	270	545	1,908	1,114	810	561
Oklahoma...................	9,407	3.3	X	4,136	2,682	1,454	117	21	326	455	49	314	171
Oregon......................	10,575	9.2	20	1,499	X	1,499	18	0	62	525	83	266	542
Pennsylvania...............	36,110	5.6	42	18,370	9,865	8,505	359	1,408	793	2,732	1,268	978	957
Rhode Island...............	3,197	7.5	2	1,621	960	661	20	0	95	86	105	138	216
South Carolina	9,633	7.0	26	4,892	3,569	1,323	167	43	248	546	28	25	265
South Dakota	1,674	4.1	X	1,373	971	402	17	9	83	148	3	61	80
Tennessee..................	12,698	7.5	X	9,196	6,547	2,649	160	0	810	858	8	264	550
Texas........................	55,086	-0.1	X	47,654	33,664	13,990	1,148	31	1,987	3,462	655	1,492	5,209
Utah.........................	6,703	6.2	X	2,767	1,883	884	51	0	119	377	25	116	195
Vermont.....................	3,043	2.7	1,036	1,026	367	660	25	0	58	86	18	77	396
Virginia......................	20,537	8.5	33	6,495	3,793	2,702	257	0	451	756	131	178	929
Washington.................	20,644	6.2	2,018	16,241	12,518	3,723	331	0	556	1,248	483	474	629
West Virginia...............	5,566	3.3	7	2,619	1,293	1,326	18	47	156	434	152	102	415
Wisconsin	17,019	4.0	165	7,647	4,892	2,755	58	0	184	1,015	396	641	461
Wyoming	2,356	4.1	319	995	811	184	2	0	30	119	3	25	3

0 = Represents zero or rounds to zero.
(X) = Not applicable.
[1]The tax revenue data pertain to state fiscal years that end on June 30 in all but four states (NY, TX, AL, MI). Amounts shown for these four states reflect the different timing of their respective fiscal years, which were the 12-month periods ending on March 31 for New York, August 31 for Texas, and September 30 for Alabama and Michigan.
[2]Includes items not shown separately

Table A-74. Federal Government

| Geographic area | Total federal full time and part-time employment in thosands (BEA) | | | | | | Federal earnings (BEA) (million dollars) | | | | | |
| | Civilian | | | Military | | | Civilian | | | Military | | |
	2015	2010	2005	2015	2010	2005	2015	2010	2005	2015	2010	2005
United States	2,811.0	3,035.0	2,790.0	1,955.0	2,100.0	2,026.0	315,571	294,408	231,641	131,358	144,314	111,706
Alabama	53.1	58.5	51.6	29.5	32.8	36.9	6,043	5,755	4,297	1,706	2,045	1,836
Alaska	15.0	17.6	17.0	26.0	27.0	24.1	1,659	1,681	1,400	2,038	2,063	1,488
Arizona......................	54.7	60.0	51.9	32.3	34.9	34.1	5,731	5,276	4,072	2,017	2,288	1,858
Arkansas...................	20.3	22.9	20.9	16.8	18.1	20.9	1,928	1,869	1,584	753	925	881
California...................	245.2	269.1	250.9	204.1	223.8	223.5	27,753	25,978	20,753	14,702	16,264	12,363
Colorado	53.5	56.3	52.8	53.6	54.0	44.1	5,831	5,429	4,430	3,971	3,973	2,672
Connecticut................	17.8	19.7	20.0	13.7	14.7	14.8	1,895	1,800	1,534	768	904	752
Delaware	5.7	6.2	5.4	8.6	8.7	8.4	567	515	383	430	468	395
District of Columbia	193.9	206.2	188.8	14.4	19.7	22.8	30,127	27,979	20,495	1,357	1,908	1,704
Florida........................	134.3	142.5	129.1	94.0	99.0	101.6	14,282	12,825	10,288	6,874	7,202	6,116
Georgia	99.0	107.8	94.3	94.6	103.5	95.0	10,421	10,043	7,679	6,825	7,529	5,606
Hawaii........................	33.1	34.9	31.4	58.3	56.2	53.0	3,554	3,245	2,459	4,988	4,709	3,439
Idaho.........................	12.6	13.7	13.1	8.8	9.9	9.6	1,180	1,115	957	440	532	454
Illinois.......................	80.0	92.0	89.3	42.4	47.8	47.0	8,683	8,689	7,306	2,344	2,934	2,411
Indiana......................	36.7	42.3	36.5	20.9	22.2	20.5	3,687	3,545	2,801	688	905	737
Iowa..........................	17.6	19.2	18.2	11.7	13.0	13.7	1,572	1,517	1,260	355	513	477
Kansas......................	25.0	28.5	25.9	34.9	37.1	27.9	2,350	2,316	1,895	2,676	2,822	1,590
Kentucky	36.6	42.5	37.4	48.0	58.1	49.2	3,339	3,336	2,650	3,708	4,436	2,956
Louisiana	30.2	33.7	34.1	36.7	41.0	39.3	2,952	2,920	2,632	2,135	2,498	2,002
Maine........................	14.5	15.4	13.9	6.9	7.8	9.6	1,494	1,356	1,118	373	482	489
Maryland....................	173.2	172.0	157.6	50.3	46.4	47.0	24,130	21,255	15,822	3,988	3,585	2,905
Massachusetts............	46.0	51.1	50.4	19.7	20.5	19.7	5,207	4,998	4,303	842	1,013	856
Michigan	51.5	57.5	55.0	17.9	20.7	20.8	5,539	5,154	4,214	670	916	781
Minnesota..................	31.6	34.7	33.4	20.0	20.9	23.5	3,168	2,992	2,596	620	846	819
Mississippi.................	25.3	27.3	25.7	27.5	31.2	31.3	2,422	2,280	1,935	1,423	1,764	1,559
Missouri.....................	57.5	63.3	58.0	35.5	38.1	36.3	5,567	5,438	4,300	1,889	2,185	1,676
Montana.....................	13.1	14.9	13.5	7.9	8.1	8.2	1,227	1,186	996	396	428	384
Nebraska...................	16.7	17.4	16.4	12.5	13.4	14.0	1,571	1,420	1,173	795	847	791
Nevada......................	18.5	18.7	17.0	17.9	17.0	13.9	1,818	1,596	1,325	1,188	1,141	789
New Hampshire............	7.5	8.0	7.9	4.6	4.7	4.0	832	751	658	155	192	140
New Jersey	49.3	60.5	61.8	25.2	25.5	24.6	5,589	5,951	5,230	1,165	1,307	1,116
New Mexico	29.2	33.7	30.1	16.9	17.1	16.3	3,030	3,053	2,361	1,225	1,194	953
New York....................	115.1	132.8	129.0	56.8	60.2	56.2	12,645	12,214	10,125	3,092	3,585	2,660
North Carolina.............	70.4	72.1	61.9	128.7	144.9	126.3	6,803	5,948	4,545	10,230	11,291	7,362
North Dakota...............	9.2	10.2	10.1	11.4	11.7	11.8	833	782	647	689	696	618
Ohio..........................	76.6	84.8	77.5	35.7	35.8	36.3	8,195	7,850	6,392	1,635	1,859	1,662
Oklahoma...................	47.0	50.5	46.0	33.6	39.6	36.7	4,582	4,368	3,513	2,171	2,639	2,024
Oregon......................	27.8	30.6	29.7	11.7	12.3	12.7	2,840	2,742	2,343	423	539	477
Pennsylvania...............	96.1	109.8	106.2	35.8	36.6	40.5	10,032	9,915	8,398	1,368	1,676	1,574
Rhode Island...............	10.5	10.7	10.0	7.0	7.3	7.8	1,200	1,102	878	466	513	429
South Carolina.............	32.9	34.4	28.8	53.4	54.5	53.4	3,157	2,798	2,134	3,555	3,589	2,792
South Dakota	11.1	12.0	11.2	7.9	8.8	8.1	992	930	768	401	466	375
Tennessee	49.6	52.9	49.4	21.7	23.6	22.5	5,469	4,869	3,939	761	1,069	875
Texas........................	195.1	210.4	181.3	172.4	183.6	161.2	21,045	19,345	14,441	12,504	13,176	9,553
Utah..........................	35.0	38.0	35.3	16.2	16.9	17.6	3,361	3,100	2,593	710	861	779
Vermont.....................	6.8	6.8	6.1	4.4	4.3	4.0	697	580	462	137	171	139
Virginia......................	196.5	191.2	169.3	139.5	152.4	163.4	25,037	22,130	15,682	12,703	13,677	11,481
Washington.................	73.3	75.7	69.8	76.0	81.7	77.9	7,822	7,155	5,513	5,873	6,217	4,618
West Virginia...............	23.3	24.5	22.0	8.8	10.0	9.9	2,425	2,220	1,738	273	419	358
Wisconsin...................	28.9	31.6	29.3	15.9	16.7	17.7	2,633	2,469	2,099	526	687	629
Wyoming	7.4	8.1	7.5	6.0	6.3	6.1	660	626	527	337	366	307

Table A-75. Federal Individual Income Tax Returns and Federal Real Estate

Geographic area	Federal individual income tax returns										Federal buildings, 2015 (million square feet)		Federal Lands, 2015[4]
	Number of returns[1] (thousands)		Adjusted gross income[2] (million dollars)		Adjusted gross income per return (dollars)		Income tax[3] (thousands of dollars)		Deductions, 2014 (million dollars)				Total, owned or leased (acres)
	2014	2010	2014	2010	2014	2010	2014	2010	Total itemized deductions	Mortgage interest paid	Owned	Leased	
United States[5]	147,767	144,002	9,706,026	8,090,663	65,685	56,184	1,362,033	1,002,111	1,198,897	279,075	2,521	283.1	49,601,819
Alabama....................	2,047	2,102	107,937	98,932	52,741	47,060	12,482	10,778	11,610	2,849	51	4.0	282,211
Alaska......................	361	374	24,272	21,508	67,212	57,544	3,400	2,754	1,632	640	40	1.5	2,298,236
Arizona.....................	2,846	2,719	161,929	135,801	56,903	49,952	20,340	15,144	19,207	5,582	51	4.3	4,628,488
Arkansas..................	1,223	1,224	65,054	55,981	53,186	45,723	7,700	5,720	6,687	1,307	22	1.4	780,210
California..................	17,411	16,684	1,287,368	1,026,911	73,938	61,551	191,985	133,458	209,200	52,163	269	20.0	4,813,512
Colorado...................	2,553	2,370	179,601	142,647	70,342	60,190	25,613	17,803	20,545	6,538	52	7.0	895,043
Connecticut...............	1,749	1,728	164,111	145,642	93,806	84,305	28,528	22,652	23,774	4,698	13	1.0	12,629
Delaware	444	428	27,516	23,888	61,998	55,844	3,456	2,699	3,310	1,028	6	0.4	12,479
District of Columbia	337	323	29,797	23,964	88,430	74,223	5,060	3,703	4,398	963	72	24.6	4,383
Florida......................	9,399	9,631	570,293	467,521	60,676	48,542	85,599	59,914	55,953	13,342	103	11.9	916,783
			253,488										
Georgia	4,378	4,590	253,488	216,008	57,899	47,065	32,437	24,703	35,266	8,226	112	10.3	1,011,373
Hawaii......................	682	653	39,689	33,362	58,209	51,062	4,601	3,502	5,114	1,795	47	1.7	429,370
Idaho.......................	702	663	36,997	29,569	52,703	44,580	4,160	2,937	4,566	1,174	16	1.8	1,093,903
Illinois.....................	6,131	6,044	424,189	362,262	69,186	59,939	61,541	46,803	52,267	11,474	61	5.8	236,325
Indiana.....................	3,079	2,982	166,638	143,180	54,125	48,022	19,758	15,191	15,318	3,583	27	2.8	354,557
Iowa........................	1,446	1,400	86,097	72,095	59,559	51,499	10,185	7,572	9,227	1,780	15	1.9	254,665
Kansas.....................	1,336	1,307	83,260	70,710	62,299	54,096	10,881	8,025	8,269	1,661	30	2.9	680,445
Kentucky	1,892	1,856	98,332	86,693	51,977	46,698	11,120	8,893	10,654	2,384	43	3.0	827,711
Louisiana	2,008	1,991	115,571	98,239	57,560	49,344	15,366	11,668	10,853	2,370	38	3.6	443,783
Maine.......................	638	625	34,160	29,966	53,519	47,941	3,801	3,047	3,943	951	10	0.9	385,973
Maryland...................	2,936	2,787	213,549	189,301	72,746	67,914	29,001	23,632	36,928	9,492	113	20.4	216,905
Massachusetts.............	3,344	3,203	285,581	233,487	85,408	72,893	46,056	33,218	35,894	8,613	31	2.7	69,962
Michigan...................	4,685	4,607	266,767	227,557	56,937	49,396	34,063	25,396	27,267	6,402	24	5.0	165,791
Minnesota.................	2,688	2,561	184,514	152,396	68,649	59,505	24,677	18,219	23,985	5,778	19	2.3	101,830
Mississippi................	1,243	1,283	57,992	53,325	46,639	41,547	6,143	5,592	6,385	1,225	40	2.3	564,739
Missouri....................	2,767	2,689	156,728	135,415	56,634	50,361	19,645	15,114	16,977	3,733	45	10.8	598,864
Montana....................	492	475	27,178	21,570	55,240	45,425	3,280	2,258	3,158	759	14	2.3	525,487
Nebraska...................	889	854	54,867	45,209	61,711	52,934	6,882	4,952	5,908	1,086	14	1.5	187,737
Nevada.....................	1,322	1,264	77,643	66,772	58,745	52,829	10,828	8,423	8,799	2,289	26	2.1	5,418,573
New Hampshire............	685	664	47,607	41,350	69,498	62,281	6,586	5,047	4,963	1,442	4	0.6	24,671
New Jersey	4,343	4,286	353,248	308,540	81,344	71,995	55,345	43,545	54,261	11,460	39	4.8	94,593
New Mexico	912	913	46,265	41,429	50,743	45,377	5,367	4,388	4,634	1,286	54	3.3	6,803,462
New York...................	9,524	9,272	754,932	628,370	79,268	67,770	124,315	91,175	117,372	17,291	82	8.6	201,814
North Carolina.............	4,381	4,203	247,012	207,775	56,385	49,438	30,071	22,165	30,399	7,590	88	4.8	661,173
North Dakota...............	371	330	27,237	18,586	73,499	56,241	4,148	2,266	1,559	334	15	1.1	628,688
Ohio........................	5,560	5,437	313,150	267,042	56,322	49,112	38,827	29,269	31,809	6,999	62	5.4	172,158
Oklahoma..................	1,640	1,590	97,489	79,531	59,450	50,007	12,508	8,856	10,504	1,835	50	5.3	1,113,278
Oregon.....................	1,827	1,743	109,311	88,462	59,845	50,744	13,186	9,325	16,775	4,210	20	2.8	379,492
Pennsylvania...............	6,169	6,130	388,883	339,678	63,037	55,413	52,742	41,103	41,940	9,863	70	9.6	237,439
Rhode Island...............	522	509	32,512	28,279	62,296	55,548	4,285	3,344	4,155	1,047	11	0.6	3,135
South Carolina	2,124	2,052	111,386	94,103	52,434	45,863	12,681	9,463	13,258	3,324	50	2.2	512,685
South Dakota	411	394	24,939	19,818	60,690	50,327	3,340	2,278	1,723	363	15	0.9	553,501
Tennessee	2,928	2,847	161,050	136,096	54,997	47,810	20,608	15,292	13,404	3,562	48	3.2	483,932
Texas.......................	11,992	10,996	806,504	620,581	67,253	56,439	120,886	80,302	70,349	15,407	167	22.8	2,276,885
Utah........................	1,222	1,135	74,268	58,858	60,792	51,875	8,614	5,769	10,975	2,846	28	2.9	3,376,514
Vermont....................	323	318	18,588	15,678	57,573	49,315	2,204	1,677	2,112	483	3	1.2	32,284
Virginia....................	3,872	3,729	279,346	245,073	72,151	65,713	38,435	31,185	38,243	11,579	151	28.4	739,443
Washington................	3,343	3,169	244,056	190,783	73,010	60,201	34,989	23,868	25,782	8,539	78	5.4	1,701,670
West Virginia...............	783	783	39,462	35,604	50,401	45,457	4,394	3,639	2,922	686	22	2.6	158,665
Wisconsin	2,811	2,742	167,540	143,792	59,596	52,447	20,708	15,934	20,139	4,279	20	2.6	108,052
Wyoming...................	280	276	21,658	17,685	77,370	63,975	3,292	2,284	1,881	418	13	0.8	1,034,023

[1] Includes returns constructed by Internal Revenue Service for certain self-employment tax returns.
[2] Less deficit.
[3] Includes additional tax for tax preferences, self-employment tax, tax from investment credit recapture, and other income-related taxes. Total is before earned income credit.
[4] Federal real property is defined as any real property owned, leased, or otherwise managed by the federal government, within the United States, and improvements of federal lands. Federal real property shall exclude: interest in real property assets that have been disposed of for public benefit purposes pursuant to section 484 of title 40, United States Code, and are now held in private ownership; land easements or rights-of-way held by the federal government; public domain land (including lands withdrawn for military purposes) or land reserved or dedicated for national forest, national park, or national wildlife refuge purposes except for improvements on those lands; land held in trust or restricted fee status for individual Indians or Indian tribes; and land and interests in land that are withheld from the scope of this order by agency heads for reasons of national security, foreign policy, or public safety.
[5] For federal individual income tax returns, the states will not sum to U.S. totals. Totals include returns filed from Army Post Office and Fleet Post Office addresses by members of the armed forces stationed overseas; returns by other U.S. citizens abroad; and returns filed by residents of Puerto Rico with income from sources outside of Puerto Rico or with income earned as U.S. government employees.

Table A-76.   Social Security, Food Stamps, and School Lunch Programs

Geographic area	Social security benefits						Supplemental Nutrition Assistance Program (year ending September 30, 2016)					National school lunch program			
	Recipients Dec 31[1] (thousands)				Total monthly benefits, 2014 (million dollars)				Costs			Participants (thousands)		Federal cost[2] (million dollars)	
	Total		Retired workers and dependents		Total	Retired workers and dependents[1]	Number of households	Number of participants	Total (in thousands)	Per household	Per person				
	2014	2011	2014	2011								2012	2016	2012	2016
United States	57,499	53,972	40,913	37,536	70,561	51,144	21,351,627	43,493,149	$5,485,709	$256.92	$126.13	31,252	30,059	11,422	13,414
Alabama....................	1,096	1,037	631	677	1,276	823	387,152	830,742	$101,096	$261.13	$121.69	563	526	204	241
Alaska......................	89	82	59	64	103	75	35,622	84,825	$15,014	$421.49	$177.00	54	52	32	38
Arizona....................	1,207	1,105	849	906	1,518	1,151	428,968	964,979	$117,663	$274.29	$121.93	662	641	266	305
Arkansas..................	673	647	399	425	761	504	175,096	399,538	$44,284	$252.92	$110.84	349	317	129	150
California..................	5,539	5,130	3,804	4,151	6,701	4,972	2,054,322	4,252,654	$586,318	$285.41	$137.87	3,355	3,253	1,495	1,649
Colorado..................	795	721	552	591	978	729	222,565	467,426	$59,145	$265.74	$126.53	390	377	130	149
Connecticut..............	655	630	469	497	886	686	241,837	424,431	$56,280	$232.72	$132.60	297	281	92	109
Delaware..................	192	177	135	142	254	192	71,942	149,158	$18,484	$256.92	$123.92	96	99	32	42
District of Columbia	80	76	52	55	90	65	74,268	132,308	$17,278	$232.65	$130.59	48	54	21	29
Florida.....................	4,223	3,894	2,978	3,170	5,191	3,934	1,737,092	3,287,446	$410,273	$236.18	$124.80	1,654	1,704	688	905
Georgia....................	1,677	1,524	1,079	1,145	2,006	1,414	775,905	1,688,832	$214,634	$276.62	$127.09	1,287	1,225	480	582
Hawaii.....................	252	234	190	202	311	250	87,542	173,669	$39,522	$451.47	$227.57	114	107	44	49
Idaho.......................	306	279	208	223	365	270	76,145	176,217	$20,042	$263.21	$113.73	170	157	55	60
Illinois.....................	2,155	2,065	1,464	1,570	2,707	1,993	998,672	1,931,575	$252,960	$253.30	$130.96	1,142	1,084	437	509
Indiana....................	1,286	1,220	837	891	1,627	1,164	313,106	710,738	$84,224	$268.99	$118.50	801	791	262	299
Iowa........................	616	592	431	458	758	573	177,813	378,478	$42,165	$237.13	$111.41	396	382	103	124
Kansas....................	522	499	354	376	654	484	111,844	246,179	$27,731	$247.94	$112.65	362	343	108	119
Kentucky..................	954	914	537	581	1,082	680	299,554	657,389	$81,585	$272.35	$124.10	550	529	189	244
Louisiana.................	854	809	471	525	945	586	476,315	1,042,876	$193,335	$405.90	$185.39	589	548	214	251
Maine......................	325	307	210	223	369	259	95,890	183,299	$20,337	$212.08	$110.95	107	99	36	38
Maryland..................	936	873	648	687	1,203	899	375,724	720,566	$86,366	$229.87	$119.86	434	446	156	195
Massachusetts..........	1,224	1,161	807	860	1,517	1,094	446,793	771,436	$97,572	$218.38	$126.48	534	532	170	214
Michigan..................	2,122	2,017	1,363	1,463	2,737	1,939	775,869	1,434,550	$174,531	$224.95	$121.66	908	824	314	338
Minnesota................	965	905	681	722	1,221	931	226,349	465,211	$50,236	$221.94	$107.99	627	616	160	190
Mississippi...............	641	610	371	396	715	465	251,995	555,278	$63,809	$253.22	$114.91	639	599	212	240
Missouri...................	1,246	1,188	796	846	1,488	1,043	354,012	770,944	$92,189	$260.41	$119.58	87	83	27	32
Montana...................	213	198	148	158	249	187	56,294	119,863	$14,136	$251.12	$117.94	251	242	70	81
Nebraska..................	326	313	227	241	398	300	79,376	177,912	$20,375	$256.69	$114.52	219	222	90	109
Nevada....................	476	425	339	358	588	445	223,933	441,986	$52,147	$232.87	$117.98	105	86	26	27
New Hampshire..........	284	263	190	201	363	267	46,874	95,393	$9,860	$210.36	$103.37				
New Jersey	1,568	1,500	1,101	1,173	2,135	1,621	427,292	857,779	$98,530	$230.59	$114.87	729	696	248	287
New Mexico..............	400	371	258	279	453	322	223,364	480,493	$58,885	$263.63	$122.55	228	219	94	109
New York..................	3,483	3,337	2,346	2,523	4,422	3,256	1,625,747	2,950,208	$403,708	$248.32	$136.84	1,796	1,678	665	783
North Carolina...........	1,949	1,808	1,299	1,364	2,376	1,724	703,039	1,470,079	$179,734	$255.65	$122.26	943	893	370	424
North Dakota.............	124	121	85	92	145	107	25,408	54,622	$6,612	$260.22	$121.05	85	91	20	25
Ohio	2,268	2,166	1,446	1,564	2,726	1,909	776,792	1,564,498	$194,164	$249.96	$124.11	1,114	1,014	370	420
Oklahoma.................	750	717	473	506	878	610	279,369	621,462	$75,206	$269.20	$121.01	446	446	162	192
Oregon.....................	798	735	561	598	991	746	405,793	712,084	$85,728	$211.26	$120.39	307	303	111	131
Pennsylvania.............	2,723	2,618	1,815	1,937	3,433	2,496	951,638	1,858,232	$225,601	$237.07	$121.41	1,128	1,029	346	428
Rhode Island.............	216	207	145	152	267	195	100,592	168,973	$22,329	$221.98	$132.15	80	78	30	35
South Carolina	1,041	956	683	720	1,273	911	347,845	746,646	$91,552	$263.20	$122.62	493	478	194	229
South Dakota.............	165	156	117	125	192	147	42,033	95,655	$11,958	$284.49	$125.01	107	108	29	34
Tennessee................	1,372	1,288	860	916	1,633	1,134	528,745	1,083,880	$135,795	$256.83	$125.29	687	672	248	305
Texas.......................	3,842	3,552	2,424	2,660	4,503	3,147	1,629,883	3,864,686	$453,843	$278.45	$117.43	3,374	3,377	1,337	1,586
Utah........................	366	335	245	267	450	330	85,075	214,505	$24,589	$289.03	$114.63	349	334	100	113
Vermont...................	141	132	95	101	171	126	42,390	78,034	$9,600	$226.46	$123.02	54	48	16	18
Virginia....................	1,416	1,319	951	1,014	1,759	1,288	380,868	811,949	$95,600	$251.01	$117.74	749	702	227	265
Washington...............	1,230	1,127	845	907	1,572	1,171	528,419	952,711	$115,825	$219.19	$121.57	540	521	195	223
West Virginia.............	465	451	259	287	545	340	174,961	351,391	$40,352	$230.64	$114.84	201	193	67	86
Wisconsin	1,153	1,086	803	848	1,455	1,096	350,962	712,582	$75,249	$214.41	$105.60	596	527	172	194
Wyoming..................	101	94	71	75	126	95	14,277	33,806	$3,991	$279.53	$118.05	57	51	15	17

[1]Includes special benefits for persons age 72 and over not insured under regular or transitional provisions of Social Security Act.
[2]Includes cash payments and commodity costs.

Table A-77. Social Insurance Programs and Workers' Compensation

Geographic area	Supplemental security income Recipients (SSI)[1]		Temporary assistance for Needy Families (TANF) Average number of recipients		State unemployment insurance[2]							
					Beneficiaries, first payments (thousands)		Average weekly benefits		Extended benefits, first payments (thousands)		Extended benefits paid[3] (million dollars)	
	2014	2013	2016	2015	2015	2010	2015	2010	2015	2010	2015	2010
United States	8,161	8,143	2,730,783	3,073,219	6,501,251	10,726,566	328.65	299.31	47	2,293	-32	9,015
Alabama......................	175	177	25,772	31,774	65,204	140,350	215.94	205.80	0	21	-0	63
Alaska........................	12	13	8,142	8,471	26,792	34,516	266.30	239.37	0	13	-0	38
Arizona......................	119	118	20,512	24,869	82,567	178,856	222.61	214.03	0	38	-0	125
Arkansas....................	111	113	8,501	10,855	57,641	103,428	303.14	278.10	0	0	-0	-0
California....................	1,146	1,144	992,952	1,114,580	1,012,256	1,523,765	306.37	301.45	7	307	-4	1,576
Colorado	73	72	43,317	45,174	92,374	153,222	389.86	346.53	0	33	0	169
Connecticut................	63	62	22,548	26,274	120,404	174,314	356.20	327.37	0	78	2	227
Delaware....................	17	17	12,014	12,789	16,493	27,466	252.81	247.37	0	5	-0	18
District of Columbia	27	27	13,634	15,670	21,295	28,355	297.74	298.92	0	6	0	29
Florida.......................	561	548	79,040	84,148	194,170	521,763	235.35	230.89	0	129	-2	451
Georgia......................	256	253	24,830	25,853	165,308	299,963	275.69	273.22	0	70	-1	237
Hawaii.......................	24	24	18,066	21,735	22,974	41,236	441.54	416.32	0	0	0	0
Idaho.........................	30	30	2,801	2,735	30,082	75,050	298.13	255.47	0	8	-0	21
Illinois.......................	276	279	34,881	41,886	326,431	475,822	339.23	316.69	0	86	-1	417
Indiana......................	128	127	15,951	17,743	97,213	222,391	258.69	295.00	0	44	0	196
Iowa..........................	51	50	25,960	28,565	92,606	125,564	368.95	321.39	0	0	-0	0
Kansas.......................	49	49	12,150	14,384	59,694	91,193	364.66	326.27	0	14	0	80
Kentucky....................	189	191	44,682	50,185	59,899	134,738	305.78	288.80	0	18	-17	96
Louisiana	181	182	13,359	11,859	57,062	107,389	214.95	208.90	0	0	-0	153
Maine.........................	38	37	8,503	10,109	30,004	47,540	299.84	274.00	0	6	-0	22
Maryland....................	118	117	52,738	46,480	107,255	154,725	328.69	315.80	0	0	-0	2
Massachusetts.............	189	188	58,912	67,345	189,738	270,133	452.77	391.80	0	45	-0	316
Michigan....................	275	275	41,016	52,225	242,223	387,386	286.90	296.62	0	134	-1	402
Minnesota	94	94	45,000	43,155	122,686	184,752	409.14	355.96	0	69	-0	132
Mississippi..................	126	126	11,777	13,972	36,346	79,533	203.11	189.99	0	0	0	0
Missouri.....................	143	142	38,473	59,066	103,654	189,210	247.30	244.16	0	25	-0	85
Montana.....................	18	19	7,653	7,113	24,082	34,424	314.47	271.83	0	2	0	2
Nebraska....................	28	27	10,718	10,622	23,732	54,022	300.18	251.86	0	0	0	0
Nevada......................	50	48	24,980	28,802	71,275	128,499	320.56	317.88	0	36	0	107
New Hampshire............	20	20	4,784	5,732	17,437	42,319	303.54	272.24	0	8	0	0
New Jersey	176	175	41,756	56,865	294,169	385,201	410.17	397.41	0	97	-2	607
New Mexico	64	64	29,364	31,120	33,423	53,745	320.89	315.76	2	17	-0	101
New York....................	654	657	244,480	256,741	459,372	666,359	316.83	306.61	1	174	-3	797
North Carolina.............	235	234	28,682	23,920	108,235	378,791	235.81	298.46	1	143	-0	8
North Dakota...............	8	8	2,707	2,917	27,636	17,569	498.47	310.43	0	0	0	0
Ohio..........................	313	311	107,761	113,806	196,409	308,311	341.82	296.59	2	77	-0	321
Oklahoma...................	97	98	16,036	15,802	59,805	76,334	368.67	276.19	0	0	0	0
Oregon.......................	85	83	38,000	46,128	94,121	199,506	348.18	289.70	0	62	-0	294
Pennsylvania...............	371	376	144,087	162,233	391,726	587,347	376.30	338.23	17	93	0	416
Rhode Island...............	33	33	9,542	29,733	31,551	48,750	333.52	380.40	0	15	-0	76
South Carolina.............	118	118	21,013	23,572	56,329	149,306	252.34	236.41	0	25	-0	96
South Dakota...............	15	15	6,015	5,935	5,932	13,014	302.04	251.12	0	0	0	0
Tennessee	184	184	68,975	87,101	94,077	193,834	225.63	223.44	0	58	-0	141
Texas.........................	666	666	64,233	70,524	482,925	544,794	225.63	223.44	1	139	-1	568
Utah..........................	31	31	8,617	9,018	37,992	74,936	369.65	315.61	0	0	0	0
Vermont.....................	15	15	5,622	5,969	16,928	29,008	328.51	296.67	0	2	-0	4
Virginia......................	155	153	46,180	51,341	85,956	177,577	299.28	288.48	0	27	-0	69
Washington.................	151	150	67,034	75,739	162,883	263,691	416.77	383.95	0	50	-0	314
West Virginia...............	78	79	14,843	16,139	51,734	58,082	300.67	255.12	0	5	-0	21
Wisconsin	118	117	41,243	53,771	152,641	324,879	295.97	274.94	16	47	-0	143
Wyoming....................	7	7	927	675	16,092	22,368	401.65	337.05	0	0	0	0

[1]Data cover federal SSI payments and/or federally administered state supplementation. National figures include data not distributed by state.
[2]Includes unemployment compensation for state and local government employees where covered by state law. National totals include data for territories.
[3]Extended benefits are paid during an extended benefit period to claimants following exhaustion of their rights to regular benefits.

Table A-78.   Government Transfer Payments to Individuals

Geographic area	Total government transfer payments (million dollars) 2015 Total	Percent change, 2010–2015	Per capita[1] (dollars)	2010	2005	Program area 2015 (million dollars) Retirement and disability insurance benefits	Medical payments	Income maintenance benefits	Unemployment insurance benefits	Veterans benefits	Federal education and training assistance payments[2]	Other[3]
United States	2,678,606	15.2	8,347	2,324,655	1,516,700	909,191	1,195,026	268,869	32,490	89,828	63,589	45,952
Alabama	42,899	13.1	8,838	37,940	24,845	16,335	16,553	4,709	231	2,104	1,150	700
Alaska	6,609	24.9	8,959	5,290	3,391	1,313	2,395	843	95	322	64	1,409
Arizona	56,304	16.5	8,259	48,316	28,737	19,220	24,275	4,910	351	2,089	3,268	622
Arkansas	27,309	15.7	9,171	23,612	15,413	9,762	11,867	2,518	270	1,146	800	265
California.....................	323,786	21.3	8,303	266,868	169,602	91,111	158,738	35,918	5,274	8,452	8,879	6,408
Colorado	36,881	24.9	6,769	29,528	17,532	12,827	16,171	2,939	519	1,908	880	381
Connecticut.................	31,690	9.1	8,840	29,046	18,947	10,953	15,028	2,600	617	559	623	493
Delaware	9,007	24.7	9,540	7,221	4,519	3,215	4,145	689	83	245	310	104
District of Columbia	6,256	14.7	9,333	5,455	3,584	1,152	3,615	987	56	120	151	27
Florida........................	180,329	18.9	8,907	151,603	98,517	65,293	75,549	17,262	639	6,764	4,009	6,143
					0							
Georgia	72,940	17.9	7,151	61,888	38,555	25,630	27,592	9,337	445	3,680	1,959	1,958
Hawaii	10,872	17.4	7,628	9,259	5,702	3,855	4,382	1,301	144	583	196	85
Idaho	11,812	15.3	7,147	10,241	6,175	4,788	4,443	1,019	127	471	272	310
Illinois	99,401	6.6	7,742	93,214	61,752	34,462	43,385	11,079	1,790	2,067	2,455	1,212
Indiana.......................	54,532	15.3	8,246	47,305	30,565	20,744	22,990	4,943	362	1,411	1,743	828
Iowa	24,677	13.7	7,904	21,708	14,248	9,564	10,389	1,969	402	675	747	220
Kansas	21,256	10.9	7,313	19,173	12,682	8,439	8,519	1,894	260	758	413	307
Kentucky	42,201	19.2	9,538	35,403	23,187	14,193	19,556	4,125	319	1,393	1,287	318
Louisiana	40,818	18.3	8,743	34,495	27,709	12,319	19,433	4,552	262	1,381	1,076	723
Maine.........................	12,833	13.2	9,653	11,334	8,155	4,644	5,638	1,005	129	574	209	331
					0							
Maryland.....................	46,673	19.2	7,785	39,171	25,945	15,468	21,648	4,397	670	1,654	914	543
Massachusetts.............	63,029	12.2	9,290	56,171	39,076	18,933	32,159	5,985	1,425	1,387	945	656
Michigan	91,438	10.6	9,220	82,674	52,451	34,419	39,974	8,419	924	2,221	1,944	1,259
Minnesota	44,234	13.3	8,068	39,027	24,110	15,437	20,177	3,950	741	1,306	1,119	246
Mississippi..................	27,334	13.6	9,144	24,061	17,437	9,136	12,138	3,236	131	904	636	471
Missouri......................	51,659	13.3	8,502	45,605	30,946	18,967	22,713	4,303	394	1,862	1,098	934
Montana......................	8,088	14.6	7,836	7,058	4,536	3,345	3,048	624	120	372	167	175
Nebraska.....................	13,452	13.4	7,103	11,866	8,269	5,267	5,324	1,143	94	624	303	264
Nevada	20,713	23.0	7,182	16,838	9,595	7,410	8,480	2,069	384	940	454	305
New Hampshire............	10,726	17.5	8,064	9,132	5,928	4,525	4,403	628	89	380	249	150
					0							
New Jersey	76,221	7.8	8,530	70,689	45,731	27,327	33,879	6,841	2,000	1,284	1,645	1,182
New Mexico	19,088	20.3	9,175	15,867	9,705	5,797	8,978	2,126	183	874	414	235
New York	201,039	10.2	10,181	182,438	130,233	57,256	106,012	22,096	2,315	3,015	3,960	1,868
North Carolina..............	82,122	16.4	8,183	70,555	44,562	29,768	33,410	8,474	316	3,971	1,659	2,223
North Dakota................	5,326	17.1	7,038	4,547	3,143	2,120	2,116	427	115	197	91	89
Ohio	101,930	12.3	8,783	90,740	62,413	35,996	47,095	9,668	948	2,553	2,058	955
Oklahoma....................	31,253	12.9	7,998	27,678	18,305	11,360	12,522	3,033	351	1,996	705	391
Oregon	35,702	21.8	8,871	29,301	17,752	12,782	15,740	3,245	554	1,456	645	354
Pennsylvania................	122,229	10.1	9,555	111,011	76,110	43,910	55,936	10,894	2,229	2,830	1,991	1,533
Rhode Island...............	10,670	11.9	10,107	9,534	6,551	3,475	5,001	1,135	166	268	248	139
					0							
South Carolina	42,679	17.5	8,719	36,325	22,881	16,157	16,652	4,232	204	2,209	1,340	766
South Dakota	6,088	13.2	7,096	5,377	3,575	2,426	2,354	545	31	272	134	132
Tennessee	57,156	13.4	8,666	50,417	32,780	20,728	24,090	6,215	320	2,348	1,215	723
Texas.........................	190,023	19.9	6,928	158,496	97,429	57,952	84,667	21,580	2,835	8,964	3,920	3,790
Utah	16,014	16.3	5,355	13,771	8,094	5,939	5,704	1,836	177	576	672	418
Vermont	6,349	18.7	10,140	5,347	3,403	2,127	3,003	586	71	157	163	99
Virginia.......................	59,304	20.0	7,087	49,402	31,463	22,376	22,763	5,294	404	3,697	1,531	1,326
Washington..................	56,395	12.5	7,876	50,142	29,992	21,709	21,830	5,347	1,023	2,578	1,564	691
West Virginia................	19,118	13.6	10,384	16,833	11,765	7,269	8,133	1,714	245	766	418	150
Wisconsin	46,005	9.4	7,976	42,037	26,311	18,182	18,920	3,988	567	1,287	811	928
Wyoming	4,138	13.5	7,056	3,647	2,387	1,812	1,494	240	89	177	81	111

[1] Based on estimated resident population as of July 1.

[2] Consists largely of federal fellowship payments (National Science Foundation fellowships and traineeships, subsistence payments to state maritime academy cadets, and other federal fellowships), interest subsidy on higher education loans, Pell grants, Job Corps payments, education exchange payments, and state education assistance.

[3] Consists largely of Bureau of Indian Affairs payments, Alaska Permanent Fund dividend payments, compensation of survivors of public safety officers, compensation of victims of crime, disaster relief payments, compensation for Japanese internment, the American Recovery and Reinvestment Act of 2009, funded Federal Additional Compensation for unemployment, COBRA premium reduction, and the Economic Recovery lump sum payment; and other special payments to individuals.

Table A-79. Medicare, Medicaid, and Children's Health Insurance Program

| Geographic area | Medicare enrollment (thousands) | | | Number of Children Ever-Enrolled in Medicaid and CHIP | | | | | | Total Medicaid and CHIP Enrollment, December 2016 preliminary | Medicaid and CHIP Child Enrollment as a percent of total Enrollment, December 2016 preliminary |
| | | | | CHIP | | Medicaid | | CHIP and Medicaid | | | |
	2014	2010	2005	2014	2015	2014	2015	2014	2015		
United States	52,882	46,585	41,536	8,099,448	8,397,651	36,024,318	36,833,664	44,123,766	45,231,315	74,165,854	50.49
Alabama......................	947	845	755	105,491	133,043	637,750	658,242	743,241	791,285	883,070	70.81
Alaska	80	66	52	9,661	10,182	86,571	87,537	96,232	97,719	173,321	48.16
Arizona.......................	1,093	930	794	54,361	38,811	952,532	942,546	1,006,893	981,357	1,739,041	
Arkansas....................	585	531	472	100,112	112,071	406,178	364,822	506,290	476,893	948,181	47.61
California....................	5,483	4,757	4,201	1,717,572	1,912,128	4,641,655	4,888,674	6,359,227	6,800,802	11,901,083	42.25
Colorado	755	625	522	125,471	86,133	467,969	502,210	593,440	588,343	1,375,041	45.77
Connecticut................	621	568	525	20,095	24,884	336,763	365,676	356,858	390,560	761,310	40.05
Delaware....................	175	149	128	18,650	16,379	100,944	100,258	119,594	116,637	241,664	43.51
District of Columbia	87	78	73	7,085	10,676	91,149	89,210	98,234	99,886	264,849	
Florida........................	3,888	3,375	3,046	423,351	428,094	2,286,649	2,264,344	2,710,000	2,692,438	4,337,514	59.71
Georgia......................	1,469	1,236	1,039	261,861	230,815	1,241,254	1,341,668	1,503,115	1,572,483	1,723,548	70.21
Hawaii........................	237	206	182	30,505	27,239	143,557	143,075	174,062	170,314	345,724	41.84
Idaho..........................	271	230	192	30,615	34,513	189,768	202,190	220,383	236,703	299,005	73
Illinois........................	2,030	1,839	1,691	295,948	330,571	1,617,273	1,540,694	1,913,221	1,871,265	3,099,444	46.49
Indiana.......................	1,125	1,006	905	89,563	100,560	672,150	689,672	761,713	790,232	1,498,978	51.68
Iowa...........................	561	517	490	83,411	82,657	320,595	334,419	404,006	417,076	622,071	48.73
Kansas.......................	478	433	402	73,574	77,139	232,761	250,084	306,335	327,223	408,885	69.72
Kentucky....................	847	760	678	84,882	86,976	513,002	525,516	597,884	612,492	1,230,475	45.59
Louisiana	774	687	610	136,263	135,614	663,291	685,163	799,554	820,777	1,415,385	53.97
Maine.........................	300	265	235	27,461	22,310	179,170	166,871	206,631	189,181	267,657	42.09
Maryland....................	906	785	695	137,192	142,327	514,576	532,090	651,768	674,417	1,265,867	46.95
Massachusetts............	1,192	1,061	971	126,513	168,941	546,703	568,446	673,216	737,387	1,661,951	39.88
Michigan....................	1,856	1,651	1,483	104,127	119,699	1,174,170	1,139,982	1,278,297	1,259,681	2,297,344	40.63
Minnesota	888	786	698	3,590	3,835	538,792	599,730	542,382	603,565	1,026,547	49.41
Mississippi.................	550	497	454	80,575	87,105	452,565	447,883	533,140	534,988	675,657	67.84
Missouri.....................	1,114	1,004	912	86,920	78,344	545,611	579,019	632,531	657,363	976,256	65.05
Montana.....................	195	170	148	49,671	45,261	89,932	94,546	139,603	139,807	243,320	50.43
Nebraska....................	306	279	261	56,476	62,218	158,162	165,181	214,638	227,399	237,567	66.24
Nevada	434	357	297	45,870	61,908	297,738	352,510	343,608	414,418	623,574	47.88
New Hampshire...........	259	223	192	16,523	16,651	94,153	94,488	110,676	111,139	187,129	49.88
New Jersey	1,466	1,327	1,227	211,371	215,191	709,144	755,476	920,515	970,667	1,761,395	47.65
New Mexico	361	313	267	16,037	17,195	384,924	398,864	400,961	416,059	775,020	46.42
New York....................	3,287	2,988	2,776	604,566	630,732	2,193,421	2,293,708	2,797,987	2,924,440	6,390,438	38.4
North Carolina............	1,719	1,490	1,277	236,893	234,654	1,167,377	1,145,975	1,404,270	1,380,629	2,025,016	69.4
North Dakota..............	117	109	104	5,032	4,955	54,076	61,525	59,108	66,480	84,587	46.07
Ohio	2,111	1,901	1,754	136,169	181,100	1,340,636	1,363,329	1,476,805	1,544,429	2,971,319	41.8
Oklahoma...................	666	603	541	164,831	190,858	533,859	519,694	698,690	710,552	804,355	65.41
Oregon.......................	727	621	540	109,085	121,869	431,109	487,013	540,194	608,882	966,178	41.58
Pennsylvania..............	2,493	2,283	2,132	258,455	294,342	1,313,820	1,241,249	1,572,275	1,535,591	2,918,260	47.35
Rhode Island..............	200	183	172	22,136	31,324	98,689	99,712	120,825	131,036	294,264	39.42
South Carolina	909	774	651	79,740	98,336	608,415	619,859	688,155	718,195	996,551	63.05
South Dakota..............	152	137	125	14,829	16,216	80,758	80,764	95,587	96,980	119,956	69
Tennessee..................	1,206	1,058	922	112,826	106,215	775,480	819,456	888,306	925,671	1,631,305	
Texas.........................	3,517	3,001	2,545	1,191,938	1,049,623	3,500,116	3,535,755	4,692,054[4]	4,585,378	4,768,961	73.71
Utah...........................	333	283	237	65,485	55,285	250,990	254,776	316,475	310,061	304,468	70.55
Vermont......................	128	112	96	5,953	4,766	73,537	74,718	79,490	79,484	167,130	38.23
Virginia......................	1,312	1,141	993	186,513	189,366	656,094	675,868	842,607	865,234	977,452	66.57
Washington................	1,146	972	821	42,881	46,037	761,055	787,486	803,936	833,523	1,810,889	46.33
West Virginia..............	412	382	355	40,864	48,278	290,037	297,450	330,901	345,728	567,064	39.91
Wisconsin	1,024	911	826	183,115	168,576	551,807	546,579	734,922	715,155	1,037,863	47.26
Wyoming	92	80	71	7,340	5,649	55,591	57,662	62,931	63,311	61,925	62.18

Table A-80. Department of Defense and Veterans

	Department of Defense												Number of veterans[6] (thousands)	
	Personnel[1]						Defense spending, 2014[4] (million dollars)							
	Total			2016										
Geographic area	2016	2005	2000	Active duty military[2]	Civilian[3]	Reserve and National Guard	State share of total U.S. defense spending (percent)	Defense spending as share of GDP (percent)	Defense spending per resident	Payroll[5] ($ billions)	Contracts ($ billions)	Ranking by total defense spending	2015	2010
United States	2,594,182	2,847,783	2,791,331	1,116,124	700,944	777,114	(X)	2.4	$1,312	135.8	$282.7	(X)	21,479	23,032
Alabama.....................	51,316	61,943	63,333	8,383	23,601	19,332	2.7	5.9	2,363	3.1	8.4	10	412	424
Alaska........................	28,484	28,733	25,986	18,833	5,015	4,636	0.8	5.7	4,576	1.8	1.6	31	73	74
Arizona......................	40,890	50,624	48,126	17,420	8,896	14,574	2.7	4.0	1,659	1.9	9.2	11	528	541
Arkansas....................	18,288	26,960	25,015	3,688	3,366	11,234	0.3	1.1	469	0.7	0.7	42	248	257
California...................	243,053	295,517	263,173	124,841	61,860	56,352	12.5	2.3	1,353	14.6	37.9	2	1,802	1,943
Colorado	58,882	60,211	61,230	34,165	11,553	13,164	2.2	3.0	1,717	3.3	5.9	16	409	405
Connecticut................	13,543	17,617	17,712	4,419	2,531	6,593	2.4	3.9	2,758	0.7	9.2	14	207	231
Delaware	9,747	10,595	10,941	3,287	1,417	5,043	0.2	1.1	771	0.4	0.3	45	77	33
District of Columbia	26,895	37,335	35,171	9,752	13,025	4,118	1.6	5.8	9,924	2.3	4.2	21	29	80
Florida.......................	120,425	134,621	127,677	54,232	30,772	35,421	4.3	2.2	898	6.5	11.4	5	1,558	1,588
Georgia	118,537	138,753	133,663	58,836	33,140	26,561	2.9	2.6	1,208	6.3	5.9	8	752	778
Hawaii.......................	65,746	70,208	62,111	37,788	18,800	9,158	1.8	9.9	5,352	5.6	2.0	18	120	117
Idaho.........................	9,532	12,630	12,489	2,776	1,500	5,256	0.2	1.0	386	0.4	0.3	47	132	139
Illinois.......................	53,295	73,180	84,045	16,619	12,596	24,080	1.3	0.8	431	2.2	3.3	23	706	804
Indiana......................	30,615	32,896	36,929	950	10,796	18,869	1.1	1.4	674	1.1	3.3	25	469	517
Iowa..........................	12,361	16,837	18,556	253	1,451	10,657	0.3	0.8	450	0.3	1.1	40	228	248
Kansas......................	38,265	36,523	37,255	20,774	6,864	10,627	0.8	2.4	1,190	2.1	1.4	30	218	233
Kentucky...................	49,234	63,579	60,709	26,750	9,886	12,598	2.2	4.9	2,048	3.0	6.0	17	328	348
Louisiana	40,208	47,209	50,968	14,978	5,930	19,300	0.9	1.4	786	1.8	1.9	28	326	326
Maine.........................	12,586	14,270	14,918	1,044	7,660	3,882	0.6	4.4	1,855	0.6	1.9	35	125	135
Maryland....................	90,861	84,264	87,002	28,703	44,153	18,005	4.7	5.7	3,287	6.9	12.7	4	430	464
Massachusetts............	25,028	27,878	33,039	3,560	6,396	15,072	2.9	2.7	1,793	1.0	11.1	9	368	416
Michigan....................	26,526	32,824	36,976	2,146	9,253	15,127	0.9	0.8	367	1.1	2.5	29	641	719
Minnesota..................	21,407	28,686	25,948	629	2,330	18,448	0.9	1.2	679	0.5	3.2	27	361	387
Mississippi.................	34,293	39,252	42,834	9,309	8,813	16,171	1.3	5.1	1,833	1.5	4.0	24	219	231
Missouri.....................	41,324	51,245	53,743	14,353	7,530	19,441	2.6	3.9	1,809	1.6	9.4	12	488	522
Montana.....................	8,802	10,854	10,654	3,174	1,254	4,374	0.1	1.1	502	0.3	0.2	49	99	104
Nebraska....................	16,244	19,515	20,120	5,887	4,113	6,244	0.3	1.2	742	0.8	0.6	41	141	145
Nevada......................	20,041	18,221	16,118	10,235	2,408	7,398	0.5	1.6	754	0.9	1.2	37	225	233
New Hampshire............	5,719	6,521	6,809	727	982	4,010	0.3	2.1	1,094	0.2	1.2	39	111	118
New Jersey	34,803	41,135	44,016	7,351	10,118	17,334	1.6	1.2	740	1.6	5.0	20	413	476
New Mexico	23,206	24,516	26,303	11,670	6,402	5,134	0.8	3.5	1,555	1.3	2.0	33	170	174
New York....................	60,364	77,295	79,443	20,846	10,986	28,532	2.3	0.7	487	2.7	6.9	15	863	984
North Carolina.............	140,080	148,014	137,176	96,531	21,632	21,917	2.4	2.1	1,012	7.1	3.0	13	774	777
North Dakota...............	12,973	14,516	14,474	7,010	1,684	4,279	0.2	1.2	1,034	0.6	0.2	44	57	57
Ohio..........................	59,635	64,979	71,679	6,607	25,648	27,380	1.7	1.2	617	2.8	4.3	19	848	943
Oklahoma...................	56,040	62,850	66,529	18,665	23,958	13,417	1.0	2.3	1,105	2.7	1.6	26	336	347
Oregon......................	14,197	17,605	18,447	1,502	2,982	9,713	0.3	0.5	290	0.4	0.7	43	326	340
Pennsylvania..............	56,722	72,405	78,642	2,597	23,667	30,458	3.4	2.2	1,112	2.5	11.8	6	917	1,036
Rhode Island...............	12,087	12,282	13,683	3,037	4,705	4,345	0.5	3.8	1,948	0.8	1.3	38	70	76
South Carolina	60,729	68,752	73,865	32,602	10,155	17,972	1.5	3.3	1,262	2.7	3.4	22	418	422
South Dakota	9,189	10,083	10,451	3,211	1,355	4,623	0.2	1.4	805	0.3	0.4	46	72	76
Tennessee	26,718	31,751	37,243	2,150	6,066	18,502	0.6	0.8	361	1.0	1.4	36	504	534
Texas........................	211,680	225,990	228,790	110,560	47,491	53,629	9.5	2.5	1,468	10.6	29.0	3	1,675	1,690
Utah	31,029	34,554	31,556	4,086	15,209	11,734	0.8	2.3	1,122	1.5	1.8	32	151	154
Vermont.....................	4,219	4,919	5,509	121	465	3,633	0.1	1.0	462	0.1	0.2	51	48	52
Virginia......................	208,262	243,871	198,095	90,095	93,854	24,313	13.1	11.8	6,567	16.6	38.0	1	783	828
Washington.................	94,634	98,534	84,071	44,397	31,365	18,872	3.0	3.1	1,793	5.8	6.8	7	598	617
West Virginia..............	9,969	12,756	13,937	206	1,759	8,004	0.1	0.7	292	0.3	0.2	48	166	180
Wisconsin	17,677	23,571	26,331	939	2,502	14,236	0.7	1.0	532	0.5	2.6	34	406	437
Wyoming	6,762	7,904	7,841	2,938	1,050	2,774	0.1	0.9	682	0.3	0.1	50	50	56

[1] As of September 30.

[2] Military personnel include active duty personnel based ashore or afloat. Excluded are personnel temporarily shore-based in a transient status. Before 2005, active duty military strength data for U.S. Navy and Marine Corps service members were only enumerated for those who were shore-based; members who were not shore-based (afloat) did have their payroll included in the payroll outlay figures for their home port. Beginning with 2005 Service members in afloat status are included in the strength counts of their homeport locations. Reserve and National Guard personnel called to active duty under Title 10, United States Code 12,304, are not included in the active duty military personnel counts.

[3] Civilian personnel includes United States citizens and foreign national direct hire civilians subject to Office of Management and Budget (OMB) ceiling controls and civilian personnel involved in civil functions in the United States. Excludes indirect-hire civilians and those direct-hire civilians not subject to OMB ceiling controls.

[4] For year ending September 30.

[5] Includes the gross earnings of civilian, active duty military personnel, reserve and national guard, and retired military for services rendered to the government and for cash allowances for benefits. Excludes employer's share of employee benefits, accrued military retirement benefits and most permanent change of stations costs.

[6] Includes only those veterans living as of September of the stated year. Veterans serving in more than one period of service are counted only once in the total. Veterans are considered any civilian honorably discharged from active duty, other than for training only without service-connected disability.

Table A-81.   Elections

| Geographic area | Voting-age population[1] (thousands) | | Percent of voting-age population casting votes for President | | Electoral votes cast for President[2] | | Popular vote for President 2016 | | |
| | | | | | | | Total[3] (thousands) | Percent of total | |
	2016	2012	2016	2012	2016	2012		Democratic	Republican
United States	249,485	240,186	54.8	53.8	R-306	D-232	136,787	48.0	45.8
Alabama......................	3,766	3,698	56.4	56.1	R-9	R-9	2,123	34.4	62.1
Alaska	555	544	57.5	55.2	R-3	R-3	319	36.6	51.3
Arizona.......................	5,300	4,932	48.6	46.6	R-11	R-11	2,573	45.1	48.7
Arkansas	2,283	2,238	49.5	47.8	R-6	R-6	1,131	33.7	60.6
California....................	30,157	28,801	47.0	45.3	D-55	D-55	14,182	61.7	31.6
Colorado	4,279	3,956	65.0	64.9	D-9	D-9	2,780	48.2	43.3
Connecticut.................	2,823	2,797	58.3	55.7	D-7	D-7	1,645	54.6	40.9
Delaware	748	712	59.1	58.1	D-3	D-3	442	53.4	41.9
District of Columbia	560	523	55.8	56.2	D-3	D-3	313	90.5	4.1
Florida........................	16,466	15,315	57.2	55.3	R-29	D-29	9,420	47.8	49.0
Georgia	7,799	7,430	52.8	52.5	R-16	R-16	4,115	45.6	50.8
Hawaii........................	1,121	1,089	39.1	40.1	D-4	D-4	438	61.0	29.4
Idaho..........................	1,246	1,169	55.4	55.8	R-4	R-4	690	27.5	59.3
Illinois........................	9,875	9,811	56.1	53.4	D-20	D-20	5,536	55.8	38.8
Indiana.......................	5,058	4,946	54.1	53.1	R-11	R-11	2,735	37.8	56.9
Iowa...........................	2,404	2,351	65.1	67.3	R-6	D-6	1,566	41.8	51.2
Kansas	2,192	2,162	54.0	53.7	R-6	R-6	1,184	36.1	56.7
Kentucky	3,426	3,362	56.2	53.5	R-8	R-8	1,924	32.7	62.5
Louisiana	3,568	3,484	56.9	57.2	R-8	R-8	2,029	38.4	58.1
Maine.........................	1,077	1,063	71.7	68.2	D-3	D-4	772	46.3	43.5
Maryland.....................	4,668	4,541	59.6	59.6	D-10	D-10	2,781	60.3	33.9
Massachusetts.............	5,434	5,245	62.2	60.7	D-11	D-11	3,379	59.1	32.3
Michigan	7,737	7,616	62.0	62.1	R-16	D-16	4,799	47.3	47.5
Minnesota	4,232	4,103	69.6	71.6	D-10	D-10	2,945	46.4	44.9
Mississippi..................	2,267	2,240	53.3	57.4	R-6	R-6	1,209	40.1	57.9
Missouri......................	4,706	4,619	59.7	59.7	R-10	R-10	2,809	38.1	56.8
Montana......................	815	783	60.7	61.8	R-3	R-3	495	35.9	56.5
Nebraska....................	1,434	1,392	58.9	57.1	R-5	R-5	844	33.7	58.7
Nevada.......................	2,263	2,095	49.7	48.4	D-6	D-6	1,125	47.9	45.5
New Hampshire............	1,074 0	1,046	69.3	68.0	D-4	D-4	744	46.8	46.5
New Jersey	6,960	6,838	55.7	53.2	D-14	D-14	3,874	55.5	41.4
New Mexico	1,590	1,571	50.2	49.9	D-5	D-5	798	48.3	40.0
New York.....................	15,565	15,307	50.1	46.5	D-29	D-29	7,802	56.1	32.4
North Carolina.............	7,848	7,466	60.4	60.3	R-15	R-15	4,742	46.2	49.8
North Dakota...............	582	545	59.2	59.3	R-3	R-3	344	27.2	63.0
Ohio...........................	9,002	8,881	61.1	62.8	R-18	D-18	5,496	43.6	51.7
Oklahoma....................	2,962	2,877	49.1	46.4	R-7	R-7	1,453	28.9	65.3
Oregon.......................	3,225	3,039	62.1	58.9	D-7	D-7	2,001	50.1	39.1
Pennsylvania...............	10,109	10,024	60.5	57.3	R-20	D-20	6,115	47.9	48.6
Rhode Island...............	848	834	54.7	53.5	D-4	D-4	464	54.4	38.9
South Carolina	3,863	3,644	54.4	53.9	R-9	R-9	2,103	40.7	54.9
South Dakota	652	629	56.7	57.8	R-3	R-3	370	31.7	61.5
Tennessee	5,149	4,962	48.7	49.5	R-11	R-11	2,508	34.7	60.7
Texas.........................	20,568	19,074	43.6	41.9	R-38	R-38	8,969	43.2	52.2
Utah...........................	2,129	1,967	53.1	51.7	R-6	R-6	1,131	27.5	45.5
Vermont......................	506	502	63.3	59.6	D-3	D-3	320	55.7	29.8
Virginia.......................	6,542	6,329	60.9	60.9	D-13	D-13	3,983	49.8	44.4
Washington..................	5,659	5,312	58.6	58.8	D-12	D-12	3,317	52.5	36.8
West Virginia...............	1,456	1,471	49.0	45.6	R-5	R-5	713	26.5	68.6
Wisconsin....................	4,491	4,409	66.3	69.7	R-10	D-10	2,976	46.5	47.2
Wyoming	447	441	57.9	56.9	R-3	R-3	259	21.6	67.4

[1]Estimated population for those 18 years and over as of July 1 for the listed year. Includes armed forces stationed in each state, aliens, and institutionalized population.
[2]By major political party. D = Democratic, R = Republican.
[3]Includes other parties not shown separately.

Table A-81. Elections—Continued

Geographic area	Popular vote for President 2012 Total[3] (thousands)	Percent of total Democratic	Percent of total Republican	Votes cast for U.S. Senators 2016 Total[3] (thousands)	Percent of total Democratic	Percent of total Republican	2014 Total[3] (thousands)	Percent of total Democratic	Percent of total Republican
United States	129,140	50.9	47.0	96,867	53.0	42.2	43,975	43.9	51.4
Alabama......................	2,074	38.4	60.5	2,087	35.9	64.0	818	0.0	97.3
Alaska.........................	300	40.8	54.8	311	11.6	44.4	282	45.8	48.0
Arizona.......................	2,299	44.6	53.7	2,531	40.7	53.7	(X)	(X)	(X)
Arkansas.....................	1,069	36.9	60.6	1,108	36.2	59.8	848	39.4	56.5
California.....................	13,039	60.2	37.1	12,244	100.0	0.0	(X)	(X)	(X)
Colorado.....................	2,570	51.5	46.1	2,743	50.0	44.3	2,041	46.3	48.2
Connecticut.................	1,558	58.1	40.7	1,596	57.7	34.6	(X)	(X)	(X)
Delaware	414	58.6	40.0	(X)	(X)	(X)	234	55.8	42.2
District of Columbia	294	90.9	7.3	(X)	(X)	(X)	(X)	(X)	(X)
Florida........................	8,474	50.0	49.1	9,302	44.3	52.0	(X)	(X)	(X)
Georgia	3,898	45.5	53.3	3,899	41.0	54.8	2,568	45.2	52.9
Hawaii	437	70.1	27.7	438	70.1	21.2	(X)	(X)	(X)
Idaho..........................	652	32.6	64.5	679	27.7	66.1	437	34.7	65.3
Illinois........................	5,242	57.6	40.7	5,492	54.9	39.8	3,604	53.5	42.7
Indiana.......................	2,625	43.9	54.1	2,733	42.4	52.1	(X)	(X)	(X)
Iowa...........................	1,582	52.0	46.2	1,541	35.7	60.1	1,130	43.8	52.1
Kansas.......................	1,160	38.0	59.7	1,178	32.2	62.2	866	0.0	53.1
Kentucky	1,797	37.8	60.5	1,903	42.7	57.3	1,436	40.7	56.2
Louisiana	1,994	40.6	57.8	1,997	35.3	62.1	1,523	38.1	61.0
Maine.........................	725	55.4	40.3	(X)	(X)	(X)	617	30.8	67.0
Maryland.....................	2,707	62.0	35.9	2,726	60.9	35.7	(X)	(X)	(X)
Massachusetts.............	3,184	60.3	37.3	(X)	(X)	(X)	2,187	59.0	36.2
Michigan.....................	4,731	54.2	44.7	(X)	(X)	(X)	3,122	54.6	41.3
Minnesota...................	2,937	52.7	45.0	(X)	(X)	(X)	1,982	53.2	42.9
Mississippi..................	1,286	43.8	55.3	(X)	(X)	(X)	632	37.9	59.9
Missouri......................	2,757	44.4	53.8	2,803	46.4	49.2	(X)	(X)	(X)
Montana......................	484	41.7	55.4	(X)	(X)	(X)	370	40.1	57.8
Nebraska.....................	794	38.0	59.8	(X)	(X)	(X)	540	31.5	64.3
Nevada.......................	1,015	52.4	45.7	1,108	47.1	44.7	(X)	(X)	(X)
New Hampshire............	711	52.0	46.4	739	48.0	47.8	488	51.5	48.2
New Jersey	3,638	58.3	40.6	(X)	(X)	41.4	1,870	55.8	42.3
New Mexico	784	53.0	42.8	(X)	(X)	40.0	516	55.6	44.4
New York.....................	7,117	60.8	31.2	7,801	61.3	32.4	(X)	(X)	(X)
North Carolina..............	4,505	48.4	50.4	4,691	45.4	49.8	2,915	47.3	48.8
North Dakota................	323	38.7	58.3	343	17.0	63.0	(X)	(X)	(X)
Ohio...........................	5,581	50.7	47.7	5,374	37.2	51.7	(X)	(X)	(X)
Oklahoma....................	1,335	33.2	66.8	1,448	24.6	67.7	821	28.5	68.0
Oregon.......................	1,789	54.2	42.1	1,952	56.6	33.3	1,462	55.7	36.9
Pennsylvania...............	5,742	52.1	46.7	6,052	47.3	48.8	(X)	(X)	(X)
Rhode Island...............	446	62.7	35.2	(X)	(X)	(X)	317	70.6	29.2
South Carolina	1,964	44.1	54.6	2,050	34.4	60.6	1,240	36.8	54.3
South Dakota	364	39.9	57.9	370	28.2	71.8	279	29.5	50.4
Tennessee	2,459	39.1	59.5	(X)	(X)	(X)	1,374	31.9	61.9
Texas.........................	7,994	41.4	57.2	(X)	(X)	(X)	4,648	34.4	61.6
Utah...........................	1,017	24.7	72.8	1,116	27.1	68.1	(X)	(X)	(X)
Vermont......................	299	66.6	31.0	320	60.0	32.3	(X)	(X)	(X)
Virginia.......................	3,854	51.2	47.3	(X)	(X)	(X)	2,184	49.1	48.3
Washington..................	3,126	56.2	41.3	3,243	59.0	41.0	(X)	(X)	(X)
West Virginia................	670	35.5	62.3	(X)	(X)	(X)	454	34.5	62.1
Wisconsin	3,071	52.8	45.9	2,949	46.8	50.2	(X)	(X)	(X)
Wyoming.....................	251	27.6	68.2	(X)	(X)	(X)	171	17.2	71.0

(X) = Not applicable.
[3]Includes other parties not shown separately.

Table A-82.   Composition of Congress and Public Officials

| Geographic area | Votes cast for U.S. Representatives[1] 2016 | | | Composition of 115th Congress, 2017[2] | | | | Composition of 114th Congress, 2015[3] | | | |
| | Total[5] | Percentage of total | | Senate[4] | | House of Representatives | | Senate | | House of Representatives | |
		Democratic	Republican	Democratic	Republican	Democratic	Republican	Democratic	Republican	Democratic	Republican
United States	129,833,250	47.3	48.3	46	52	193	237	44	54	187	247
Alabama...........................	1,889,685	32.9	64.7	0	2	1	6	0	2	1	6
Alaska.............................	308,198	36.0	50.3	0	2	0	1	0	2	0	1
Arizona...........................	2,412,064	42.9	52.4	0	2	4	5	0	2	4	5
Arkansas.........................	1,068,577	10.4	71.2	0	2	0	4	0	2	0	4
California.........................	13,414,018	64.3	34.9	2	0	38	14	2	0	38	14
Colorado	2,701,438	46.8	47.7	1	1	3	4	1	1	3	4
Connecticut.....................	1,575,183	58.2	35.4	2	0	5	0	2	0	5	0
Delaware	420,617	55.5	41.0	2	0	1	0	2	0	1	0
District of Columbia	X	X	X	X	X	X	X	X	X	X	X
Florida.............................	8,837,426	45.1	53.6	1	1	11	16	1	1	10	17
Georgia	3,772,862	39.7	60.2	0	2	4	9	0	2	4	10
Hawaii	437,664	72.3	19.6	2	0	2	0	2	0	2	0
Idaho...............................	681,594	30.7	65.7	0	2	0	2	0	2	0	2
Illinois.............................	5,241,767	53.6	45.7	2	0	11	7	1	1	10	8
Indiana............................	2,658,367	39.6	54.3	1	1	2	7	1	1	2	7
Iowa................................	1,515,555	44.5	53.7	0	2	1	3	0	2	1	3
Kansas............................	1,173,736	27.1	59.1	0	2	0	3	0	2	0	4
Kentucky	1,765,376	29.3	70.7	0	2	1	5	0	2	1	5
Louisiana	1,749,021	30.3	67.3	0	2	1	5	0	2	1	5
Maine	771,828	50.1	46.3	0	1	1	1	0	1	1	1
Maryland..........................	2,707,745	60.4	35.5	2	0	7	1	2	0	7	1
Massachusetts	3,378,801	69.4	13.4	2	0	9	0	2	0	9	0
Michigan..........................	4,670,905	47.0	48.0	2	0	5	9	2	0	5	9
Minnesota........................	2,860,389	50.2	46.7	2	0	5	3	2	0	5	3
Mississippi.......................	1,182,273	38.1	57.6	0	2	1	3	0	2	1	3
Missouri...........................	2,750,079	37.9	58.2	1	1	2	6	1	1	2	6
Montana...........................	507,831	40.5	56.2	1	1	0	0	1	1	0	1
Nebraska..........................	788,266	28.0	70.7	0	2	0	3	0	2	1	2
Nevada............................	1,078,497	47.1	46.2	1	1	3	1	1	1	1	3
New Hampshire.................	716,493	47.0	44.1	2	0	2	0	1	1	1	1
New Jersey	3,463,311	52.6	44.5	2	0	7	5	2	0	6	6
New Mexico	780,126	56.0	44.0	2	0	2	1	2	0	2	1
New York..........................	7,800,361	53.9	27.4	2	0	18	9	2	0	18	9
North Carolina..................	4,598,458	46.6	53.2	0	2	3	10	0	2	3	10
North Dakota....................	338,459	23.7	69.1	1	1	0	1	1	1	0	1
Ohio................................	5,218,355	41.3	57.4	1	1	4	12	1	1	4	12
Oklahoma........................	1,133,244	26.9	69.0	0	2	0	5	0	2	0	5
Oregon............................	1,911,865	53.7	38.2	2	0	4	1	2	0	4	1
Pennsylvania....................	5,743,978	45.7	53.9	1	1	5	13	1	1	5	13
Rhode Island....................	431,519	61.1	32.8	2	0	2	0	2	0	2	0
South Carolina	2,011,746	38.2	58.5	0	2	1	5	0	2	1	6
South Dakota	369,973	35.9	64.1	0	2	0	1	0	2	0	1
Tennessee	2,391,061	34.1	62.5	0	2	2	7	0	2	2	7
Texas...............................	8,528,526	37.1	57.2	0	2	11	25	0	2	11	25
Utah................................	1,114,144	32.0	63.8	0	2	0	4	0	2	0	4
Vermont...........................	320,467	82.5	0.0	1	0	1	0	1	0	1	0
Virginia............................	3,781,568	49.2	48.7	2	0	4	7	2	0	3	8
Washington......................	3,141,035	55.3	44.7	2	0	6	4	2	0	6	4
West Virginia....................	686,349	32.7	64.8	1	1	0	3	1	1	0	3
Wisconsin........................	2,773,662	49.8	45.8	1	1	3	5	1	1	3	5
Wyoming	258,788	29.2	60.3	0	2	0	1	0	2	0	1

X = not applicable.

[1] In each state, totals represent the sum of votes cast in each Congressional District or votes cast for Representative at Large in states where only one member is elected. In all years there are numerous districts within the state where either the Republican or Democratic party had no candidate. In some states the Republican and Democratic vote includes votes cast for the party candidate by endorsing parties.

[2] As of April 3, 2017.

[3] As of December 5, 2016.

[4] Vermont and Maine each had one had one Independent senator.

[5] Includes votes cast for minor parties not shown separately.

Page

103   Area and Population
110   Components of Population Change
117   Population by Age, Race, and Hispanic Origin
124   Migration and Commuting, 2015
131   Population and Household Characteristics 2015
138   Enrollment, Teachers, and Educational Attainment
144   Median Income, Household Income Distribution, and Poverty Status: 2015
150   Health Insurance, Medicare, Social Security and Supplemental Security Income
157   Housing Units and Building Permits
163   Housing Units: 2015
169   Personal Income and Earnings by Place of Work
175   Employees and Earnings by Selected Major Industries: 2015
181   Civilian Labor Force
187   Banking, Government Employment, and Private Business Establishments and Employment

Table B-1.   Area and Population

Metropolitan statistical area and division	Area, 2016 (square miles) Total	Land	2015 Estimate (July 1)	2010[1] estimates base (April 1)	2000[1] estimates base (April 1)	1990 census[2] (April 1)	Rank 2015	2010	2000	Persons per square mile of land area[3] 2015	2010	2000
Abilene, TX Metro Area	2,758	2,744	169,578	165,252	160,273	148,004	243	242	230	62	60	58
Akron, OH Metro Area	924	900	704,243	703,207	694,975	657,575	78	74	69	782	781	772
Albany, GA Metro Area	1,958	1,933	153,526	157,500	157,872	146,574	267	254	233	79	82	82
Albany, OR Metro Area	2,307	2,287	120,547	116,672	103,079	91,227	320	323	333	53	51	45
Albany-Schenectady-Troy, NY Metro Area	2,878	2,812	881,830	870,713	825,920	809,443	62	60	57	314	310	294
Albuquerque, NM Metro Area	9,296	9,281	907,301	887,075	729,729	599,416	60	59	66	98	96	79
Alexandria, LA Metro Area	2,026	1,961	154,484	153,922	145,087	149,082	265	259	246	79	79	74
Allentown-Bethlehem-Easton, PA-NJ Metro Area	1,475	1,453	832,327	821,303	740,340	686,688	69	67	65	573	565	510
Altoona, PA Metro Area	527	526	125,593	127,078	129,105	130,542	313	307	278	239	242	246
Amarillo, TX Metro Area	5,184	5,150	262,056	251,933	228,670	198,422	182	181	177	51	49	44
Ames, IA Metro Area	574	573	96,021	89,542	79,988	74,252	362	365	370	168	156	140
Anchorage, AK Metro Area	27,220	26,315	399,790	380,821	319,617	266,021	134	133	144	15	15	12
Ann Arbor, MI Metro Area	722	706	358,880	345,066	322,818	282,937	147	148	141	508	489	457
Anniston-Oxford-Jacksonville, AL Metro Area	612	606	115,620	118,586	111,882	116,034	334	319	313	191	196	185
Appleton, WI Metro Area	1,042	956	233,007	225,666	201,773	174,801	194	195	192	244	236	211
Asheville, NC Metro Area	2,041	2,033	446,840	424,860	369,186	308,001	116	118	124	220	209	182
Athens-Clarke County, GA Metro Area	1,035	1,025	203,189	192,541	166,028	136,025	218	219	224	198	188	162
Atlanta-Sandy Springs-Roswell, GA Metro Area	8,836	8,681	5,710,795	5,286,727	4,263,135	3,082,308	9	9	11	658	609	491
Atlantic City-Hammonton, NJ Metro Area	672	556	274,219	274,549	253,210	224,327	173	167	167	494	494	456
Auburn-Opelika, AL Metro Area	616	608	156,993	140,296	115,014	87,146	260	283	306	258	231	189
Augusta-Richmond County, GA-SC Metro Area	3,582	3,481	590,146	564,873	508,041	443,205	92	94	90	170	162	146
Austin-Round Rock, TX Metro Area	4,280	4,222	2,000,860	1,716,313	1,249,963	846,227	33	35	40	474	407	296
Bakersfield, CA Metro Area	8,163	8,132	882,176	839,631	661,632	543,477	61	63	71	109	103	81
Baltimore-Columbia-Towson, MD Metro Area	3,105	2,602	2,797,407	2,710,575	2,553,137	2,382,172	21	20	19	1,075	1,042	981
Bangor, ME Metro Area	3,557	3,397	152,692	153,920	144,866	146,601	268	260	247	45	45	43
Barnstable Town, MA Metro Area	1,306	394	214,333	215,888	222,239	186,605	204	198	181	544	548	564
Baton Rouge, LA Metro Area	4,203	4,027	830,480	802,500	706,122	623,853	70	69	68	206	199	175
Battle Creek, MI Metro Area	718	706	134,314	136,148	137,991	135,982	298	291	264	190	193	195
Bay City, MI Metro Area	631	442	105,659	107,771	110,271	111,723	343	339	317	239	244	249
Beaumont-Port Arthur, TX Metro Area	3,330	3,034	408,419	403,190	400,130	374,795	131	130	114	135	133	132
Beckley, WV Metro Area	1,278	1,267	122,507	124,901	126,828	124,771	316	312	282	97	99	100
Bellingham, WA Metro Area	2,505	2,108	212,284	201,140	166,822	127,780	209	211	223	101	95	79
Bend-Redmond, OR Metro Area	3,054	3,018	175,268	157,733	115,372	74,958	235	253	305	58	52	38
Billings, MT Metro Area	5,886	5,856	168,283	158,934	139,932	122,411	247	251	260	29	27	24
Binghamton, NY Metro Area	1,238	1,224	246,020	251,723	252,298	264,497	189	182	168	201	206	206
Birmingham-Hoover, AL Metro Area	5,370	5,280	1,145,647	1,128,056	1,051,340	956,844	49	49	49	217	214	199
Bismarck, ND Metro Area	5,473	5,376	129,517	114,778	100,809	89,973	304	328	340	24	21	19
Blacksburg-Christiansburg-Radford, VA Metro Area	1,471	1,453	181,747	178,258	165,161	152,720	228	228	225	125	123	114
Bloomington, IL Metro Area	1,591	1,581	189,413	186,133	167,186	145,696	225	222	222	120	118	106
Bloomington, IN Metro Area	799	780	165,577	159,542	142,342	126,259	252	249	253	212	205	183
Bloomsburg-Berwick, PA Metro Area	623	613	85,229	85,563	82,181	80,937	368	368	366	139	140	134
Boise City, ID Metro Area	11,833	11,765	676,909	616,561	464,872	319,596	81	85	100	58	52	40
Boston-Cambridge-Newton, MA-NH Metro Area	4,511	3,486	4,774,321	4,552,412	4,392,533	4,133,895	10	10	10	1,370	1,306	1,260
Boston, MA Metro Division	1,658	1,113	1,984,537	1,887,745	1,814,170	1,715,269	-	-	-	1,783	1,696	1,630
Cambridge-Newton-Framingham, MA Metro Division	1,676	1,310	2,361,182	2,246,301	2,188,740	2,068,548	-	-	-	1,802	1,715	1,671
Rockingham County-Strafford County, NH Metro Division	1,178	1,063	428,602	418,366	389,623	350,078	-	-	-	403	394	367
Boulder, CO Metro Area	741	726	319,372	294,571	269,784	225,339	156	162	159	440	406	371
Bowling Green, KY Metro Area	1,639	1,615	168,436	158,599	134,951	112,903	246	252	267	104	98	84
Bremerton-Silverdale, WA Metro Area	566	395	260,131	251,133	231,982	189,731	184	184	176	658	636	587
Bridgeport-Stamford-Norwalk, CT Metro Area	837	625	948,053	916,850	882,622	827,645	57	58	52	1,517	1,467	1,412
Brownsville-Harlingen, TX Metro Area	1,276	891	422,156	406,219	334,884	260,120	126	127	138	474	456	376
Brunswick, GA Metro Area	1,606	1,287	116,003	112,368	93,027	82,207	333	332	349	90	87	72
Buffalo-Cheektowaga-Niagara Falls, NY Metro Area	2,367	1,565	1,135,230	1,135,551	1,170,022	1,189,288	50	47	42	725	726	748
Burlington, NC Metro Area	434	423	158,276	151,241	130,750	108,213	259	267	274	374	357	309
Burlington-South Burlington, VT Metro Area	1,506	1,252	217,042	211,262	198,895	177,059	202	200	195	173	169	159
California-Lexington Park, MD Metro Area	764	357	111,413	105,151	86,196	75,974	337	343	360	312	294	241
Canton-Massillon, OH Metro Area	980	970	402,976	404,420	406,966	394,106	133	129	111	416	417	420
Cape Coral-Fort Myers, FL Metro Area	1,212	784	701,982	618,754	440,910	335,113	79	84	104	895	789	562
Cape Girardeau, MO-IL Metro Area	1,460	1,432	97,534	96,275	90,286	82,878	357	357	356	68	67	63
Carbondale-Marion, IL Metro Area	1,047	1,004	126,828	126,580	120,907	118,800	310	309	293	126	126	120
Carson City, NV Metro Area	157	145	54,521	55,274	52,477	40,443	382	382	382	377	382	363
Casper, WY Metro Area	5,376	5,341	82,178	75,450	66,541	61,226	375	378	377	15	14	13
Cedar Rapids, IA Metro Area	2,020	2,009	266,040	257,940	237,267	210,640	179	173	172	132	128	118
Chambersburg-Waynesboro, PA Metro Area	773	772	153,638	149,618	129,495	121,082	266	270	275	199	194	168
Champaign-Urbana, IL Metro Area	1,924	1,921	238,984	231,889	210,299	202,848	191	190	186	124	121	110
Charleston, WV Metro Area	1,758	1,745	220,614	227,071	235,995	243,472	200	194	173	126	130	135

X = Not applicable.

[1] The April 1, 2010 and 2000, population estimates bases reflect modifications to the censuses as documented in the Count Question Resolution program and geographic program revisions.
[2] The April 1, 1990, census counts include corrections processed through August 1997, results of special censuses and test censuses, and do not include adjustments for census coverage errors.
[3] Persons per square mile were calculated on the basis of land area data published for 2016, generally the same as that from the 2010 census.

Table B-1.   Area and Population—*Continued*

Metropolitan statistical area and division	Area, 2016 (square miles)		Population									
	Total	Land	2015 Estimate (July 1)	2010[1] estimates base (April 1)	2000[1] estimates base (April 1)	1990 census[2] (April 1)	Rank			Persons per square mile of land area[3]		
							2015	2010	2000	2015	2010	2000
Charleston-North Charleston, SC Metro Area........	3,163	2,590	744,526	664,643	549,021	506,875	75	78	85	288	257	212
Charlotte-Concord-Gastonia, NC-SC Metro Area...	5,177	5,065	2,426,363	2,217,248	1,717,647	1,341,710	22	24	29	479	438	339
Charlottesville, VA Metro Area..........................	2,241	2,224	229,514	218,707	189,601	156,758	196	197	202	103	98	85
Chattanooga, TN-GA Metro Area.........................	2,138	2,089	547,776	528,145	476,611	433,210	101	98	96	262	253	228
Cheyenne, WY Metro Area	2,688	2,686	97,121	91,881	81,617	73,142	360	364	367	36	34	30
Chicago-Naperville-Elgin, IL-IN-WI Metro Area .	9,579	7,197	9,551,031	9,461,537	9,098,970	8,182,076	3	3	3	1,327	1,315	1,264
Chicago-Naperville-Arlington Heights, IL Metro Division..............................	4,184	3,451	7,340,454	7,263,098	7,135,137	6,499,037	-	-	-	2,127	2,105	2,068
Elgin, IL Metro Division..............................	1,159	1,152	635,199	620,466	493,449	395,403	-	-	-	552	539	429
Gary, IN Metro Division..............................	2,113	1,878	703,031	708,138	676,118	643,037	-	-	-	374	377	360
Lake County-Kenosha County, IL-WI Metro Division..............................	2,122	716	872,347	869,835	794,266	644,599	-	-	-	1,219	1,215	1,110
Chico, CA Metro Area.................................	1,677	1,637	225,411	220,000	203,125	182,120	197	196	191	138	134	124
Cincinnati, OH-KY-IN Metro Area	4,240	4,166	2,157,719	2,114,755	1,994,818	1,832,313	28	28	24	518	508	479
Clarksville, TN-KY Metro Area..........................	1,749	1,698	281,021	260,610	219,727	179,800	166	172	183	166	154	129
Cleveland, TN Metro Area.................................	774	763	120,864	115,788	104,012	87,355	319	326	329	158	152	136
Cleveland-Elyria, OH Metro Area	3,979	1,999	2,060,810	2,077,246	2,148,041	2,102,248	31	29	23	1,031	1,039	1,075
Coeur d'Alene, ID Metro Area	1,309	1,238	150,346	138,494	108,682	69,795	273	285	321	122	112	88
College Station-Bryan, TX Metro Area..................	2,133	2,100	249,156	228,660	184,857	150,998	187	192	205	119	109	88
Colorado Springs, CO Metro Area......................	2,689	2,684	697,856	645,611	537,475	409,482	80	80	86	260	241	200
Columbia, MO Metro Area.................................	691	686	174,974	162,642	135,477	112,379	236	243	266	255	237	198
Columbia, SC Metro Area.................................	3,834	3,703	810,068	767,477	647,216	548,335	71	72	73	219	207	175
Columbus, GA-AL Metro Area.............................	1,960	1,936	313,749	295,531	281,878	266,450	160	161	156	162	153	146
Columbus, IN Metro Area.................................	410	407	81,162	76,786	71,467	63,657	376	377	376	200	189	176
Columbus, OH Metro Area	4,850	4,797	2,021,632	1,902,015	1,675,226	1,462,258	32	32	31	422	397	349
Corpus Christi, TX Metro Area	2,401	1,784	452,422	428,188	403,242	367,786	114	115	112	254	240	226
Corvallis, OR Metro Area.................................	678	675	87,572	85,581	78,143	70,811	366	367	371	130	127	116
Crestview-Fort Walton Beach-Destin, FL Metro Area......................................	2,322	1,968	262,172	235,865	211,081	171,536	181	187	185	133	120	107
Cumberland, MD-WV Metro Area......................	759	752	99,979	103,299	101,995	101,643	351	345	339	133	137	136
Dallas-Fort Worth-Arlington, TX Metro Area......	9,636	9,280	7,102,796	6,426,214	5,204,627	4,018,778	4	4	5	765	693	561
Dallas-Plano-Irving, TX Metro Division............	5,538	5,277	4,707,151	4,230,031	3,443,597	2,617,705	-	-	-	892	802	653
Fort Worth-Arlington, TX Metro Division..........	4,098	4,003	2,395,645	2,196,183	1,761,030	1,401,073	-	-	-	598	549	440
Dalton, GA Metro Area..................................	638	635	143,781	142,227	120,062	98,609	286	280	297	226	224	189
Danville, IL Metro Area..................................	901	898	79,282	81,625	83,929	88,257	378	374	363	88	91	93
Daphne-Fairhope-Foley, AL Metro Area	2,027	1,590	203,709	182,265	140,416	98,280	216	225	258	128	115	88
Davenport-Moline-Rock Island, IA-IL Metro Area .	2,314	2,270	383,606	379,689	376,067	368,151	137	134	122	169	167	166
Dayton, OH Metro Area.................................	1,290	1,282	800,909	799,216	805,971	803,722	72	70	59	625	624	629
Decatur, AL Metro Area.................................	1,316	1,270	152,680	153,825	145,910	131,556	269	261	245	120	121	115
Decatur, IL Metro Area.................................	586	581	107,303	110,768	114,690	117,206	341	337	308	185	191	198
Deltona-Daytona Beach-Ormond Beach, FL Metro Area......................................	2,003	1,587	623,279	590,293	493,203	399,413	89	90	91	393	372	311
Denver-Aurora-Lakewood, CO Metro Area	8,403	8,346	2,814,330	2,543,600	2,179,476	1,650,489	19	21	22	337	305	261
Des Moines-West Des Moines, IA Metro Area	2,912	2,884	622,899	569,633	481,399	416,346	90	91	95	216	198	167
Detroit-Warren-Dearborn, MI Metro Area..........	4,236	3,889	4,302,043	4,296,313	4,452,778	4,248,699	14	12	9	1,106	1,105	1,145
Detroit-Dearborn-Livonia, MI Metro Division....	673	612	1,759,335	1,820,641	2,061,180	2,111,687	-	-	-	2,875	2,975	3,368
Warren-Troy-Farmington Hills, MI Metro Division..............................	3,563	3,277	2,542,708	2,475,672	2,391,598	2,137,012	-	-	-	776	755	730
Dothan, AL Metro Area.................................	1,729	1,716	148,171	145,639	130,828	120,352	280	276	273	86	85	76
Dover, DE Metro Area..................................	798	586	173,533	162,349	126,771	110,993	237	244	283	296	277	216
Dubuque, IA Metro Area.................................	617	608	97,125	93,653	89,133	86,403	359	360	357	160	154	147
Duluth, MN-WI Metro Area.............................	9,215	8,413	279,601	279,771	275,579	269,230	168	166	158	33	33	33
Durham-Chapel Hill, NC Metro Area....................	1,812	1,758	552,493	506,631	423,858	344,625	98	104	107	314	288	241
East Stroudsburg, PA Metro Area	617	608	166,397	169,842	138,615	95,709	250	236	263	274	279	228
Eau Claire, WI Metro Area	1,687	1,646	165,636	161,390	148,345	137,543	251	245	242	101	98	90
El Centro, CA Metro Area.............................	4,482	4,177	180,191	174,528	142,334	109,303	229	233	254	43	42	34
Elizabethtown-Fort Knox, KY Metro Area	1,218	1,190	148,604	148,351	133,981	125,089	278	272	269	125	125	113
Elkhart-Goshen, IN Metro Area........................	468	463	203,474	197,561	182,793	156,198	217	216	207	439	427	395
Elmira, NY Metro Area.................................	411	407	87,071	88,842	91,119	95,195	367	366	352	214	218	224
El Paso, TX Metro Area	5,587	5,584	838,972	804,123	682,917	594,525	68	68	70	150	144	122
Enid, OK Metro Area.....................................	1,060	1,059	63,569	60,580	57,811	56,735	380	381	380	60	57	55
Erie, PA Metro Area......................................	1,558	799	278,045	280,566	280,907	275,572	170	164	157	348	351	352
Eugene, OR Metro Area..................................	4,725	4,556	362,895	351,715	323,011	282,912	144	145	140	80	77	71
Evansville, IN-KY Metro Area	1,513	1,465	315,693	311,552	296,236	278,990	158	154	151	216	213	202
Fairbanks, AK Metro Area...............................	7,450	7,343	99,631	97,581	82,849	77,720	353	353	364	14	13	11
Fargo, ND-MN Metro Area.............................	2,821	2,810	233,836	208,777	174,398	153,296	192	205	215	83	74	62
Farmington, NM Metro Area.............................	5,538	5,513	118,737	130,045	113,812	91,605	325	301	309	22	24	21
Fayetteville, NC Metro Area	1,050	1,043	376,509	366,383	336,686	297,422	141	142	137	361	351	323
Fayetteville-Springdale-Rogers, AR-MO Metro Area................................	3,213	3,163	513,559	463,207	347,040	239,464	105	109	132	162	146	110

X = Not applicable.

[1]The April 1, 2010 and 2000, population estimates bases reflect modifications to the censuses as documented in the Count Question Resolution program and geographic program revisions.

[2]The April 1, 1990, census counts include corrections processed through August 1997, results of special censuses and test censuses, and do not include adjustments for census coverage errors.

[3]Persons per square mile were calculated on the basis of land area data published for 2016, generally the same as that from the 2010 census.

Table B-1.   Area and Population—*Continued*

Metropolitan statistical area and division	Area, 2016 (square miles) Total	Land	2015 Estimate (July 1)	2010[1] estimates base (April 1)	2000[1] estimates base (April 1)	1990 census[2] (April 1)	Rank 2015	Rank 2010	Rank 2000	Persons per square mile of land area[3] 2015	2010	2000
Flagstaff, AZ Metro Area	18,661	18,619	139,097	134,437	116,320	96,591	291	293	304	8	7	6
Flint, MI Metro Area	650	637	410,849	425,790	436,213	430,459	129	116	105	645	668	685
Florence, SC Metro Area	1,371	1,361	206,448	205,571	193,153	176,195	212	208	199	152	151	142
Florence-Muscle Shoals, AL Metro Area	1,343	1,260	146,950	147,137	142,931	131,327	283	274	252	117	117	113
Fond du Lac, WI Metro Area	766	720	101,973	101,633	97,284	90,083	350	347	345	142	141	135
Fort Collins, CO Metro Area	2,634	2,596	333,577	299,630	251,489	186,136	152	159	169	129	115	97
Fort Smith, AR-OK Metro Area	3,473	3,386	280,241	280,515	255,404	219,181	167	165	166	83	83	75
Fort Wayne, IN Metro Area	1,368	1,361	429,820	416,254	390,102	354,435	125	122	118	316	306	287
Fresno, CA Metro Area	6,011	5,959	974,861	930,452	798,766	667,490	56	56	60	164	156	134
Gadsden, AL Metro Area	549	535	103,057	104,427	103,448	99,840	347	344	332	103	195	193
Gainesville, FL Metro Area	1,324	1,225	277,163	264,274	232,393	191,263	172	170	174	226	216	190
Gainesville, GA Metro Area	429	393	193,535	179,684	139,615	95,428	223	226	261	493	457	355
Gettysburg, PA Metro Area	522	519	102,295	101,417	91,207	78,274	349	349	351	197	196	176
Glens Falls, NY Metro Area	1,778	1,698	126,918	128,921	124,295	118,539	308	304	286	75	76	73
Goldsboro, NC Metro Area	558	554	124,132	122,623	113,449	104,666	315	315	310	224	221	205
Grand Forks, ND-MN Metro Area	3,437	3,408	102,449	98,461	97,489	103,181	348	352	344	30	29	29
Grand Island, NE Metro Area	2,169	2,143	85,066	81,850	77,735	71,884	369	373	372	40	38	36
Grand Junction, CO Metro Area	3,341	3,329	148,513	146,723	116,939	93,145	279	275	303	45	44	35
Grand Rapids-Wyoming, MI Metro Area	3,801	2,670	1,038,583	988,940	930,880	791,515	52	52	51	389	370	349
Grants Pass, OR Metro Area	1,641	1,639	84,745	82,713	75,729	62,649	370	372	373	52	51	46
Great Falls, MT Metro Area	2,712	2,698	82,278	81,327	80,356	77,691	374	375	369	31	30	30
Greeley, CO Metro Area	4,017	3,987	285,174	252,831	180,766	131,821	164	177	210	72	63	45
Green Bay, WI Metro Area	2,849	1,869	316,519	306,241	282,489	243,698	157	157	155	169	164	151
Greensboro-High Point, NC Metro Area	2,020	1,994	752,157	723,798	643,369	540,030	74	73	74	377	363	323
Greenville, NC Metro Area	656	652	175,842	168,148	133,759	107,924	234	238	270	270	258	205
Greenville-Anderson-Mauldin, SC Metro Area	2,788	2,711	874,869	824,107	725,544	617,349	63	65	67	323	304	268
Gulfport-Biloxi-Pascagoula, MS Metro Area	2,581	1,771	389,255	370,787	363,961	312,368	136	139	128	220	209	206
Hagerstown-Martinsburg, MD-WV Metro Area	789	779	261,486	251,602	207,810	180,646	183	183	188	336	323	267
Hammond, LA Metro Area	844	791	128,755	121,101	100,481	85,709	305	316	341	163	153	127
Hanford-Corcoran, CA Metro Area	1,392	1,389	150,965	152,982	129,470	101,469	271	262	276	109	110	93
Harrisburg-Carlisle, PA Metro Area	1,664	1,622	565,006	549,473	509,011	474,242	96	96	89	348	339	314
Harrisonburg, VA Metro Area	871	867	131,131	125,217	108,215	88,189	301	311	323	151	145	125
Hartford-West Hartford-East Hartford, CT Metro Area	1,607	1,515	1,211,324	1,212,387	1,148,649	1,123,678	47	44	43	800	800	758
Hattiesburg, MS Metro Area	1,621	1,610	148,839	142,857	123,922	109,603	276	279	287	92	89	77
Hickory-Lenoir-Morganton, NC Metro Area	1,669	1,640	362,510	365,492	341,854	292,409	145	143	136	221	223	209
Hilton Head Island-Bluffton-Beaufort, SC Metro Area	1,623	1,232	207,413	187,010	141,603	101,912	211	221	256	168	152	115
Hinesville, GA Metro Area	1,006	917	80,198	77,917	71,934	58,947	377	376	375	88	85	79
Homosassa Springs, FL Metro Area	773	582	141,058	141,236	118,106	93,515	289	282	301	242	243	203
Hot Springs, AR Metro Area	735	678	97,177	96,000	88,122	73,397	358	358	358	143	142	130
Houma-Thibodaux, LA Metro Area	3,551	2,300	212,297	208,176	194,517	182,842	208	206	196	92	91	85
Houston-The Woodlands-Sugar Land, TX Metro Area	9,444	8,261	6,656,947	5,920,493	4,693,520	3,750,963	5	6	8	806	717	568
Huntington-Ashland, WV-KY-OH Metro Area	2,563	2,527	361,580	364,930	362,350	352,406	146	144	129	143	144	143
Huntsville, AL Metro Area	1,420	1,362	444,752	417,593	342,666	293,047	118	121	135	327	307	252
Idaho Falls, ID Metro Area	5,244	5,196	139,747	133,337	104,559	91,668	290	297	328	27	26	20
Indianapolis-Carmel-Anderson, IN Metro Area	4,341	4,307	1,988,817	1,888,082	1,658,439	1,424,886	34	33	32	462	438	385
Iowa City, IA Metro Area	1,194	1,183	166,498	152,586	131,662	115,731	249	263	272	141	129	111
Ithaca, NY Metro Area	492	475	104,926	101,594	96,487	94,097	344	348	346	221	214	203
Jackson, MI Metro Area	724	702	159,494	160,248	158,426	149,756	257	247	232	227	228	226
Jackson, MS Metro Area	4,729	4,648	578,777	567,645	525,407	472,447	94	92	88	125	122	113
Jackson, TN Metro Area	1,110	1,108	129,682	130,009	121,969	104,179	303	302	290	117	117	110
Jacksonville, FL Metro Area	3,698	3,202	1,449,481	1,345,596	1,122,821	925,213	40	40	44	453	420	351
Jacksonville, NC Metro Area	905	762	186,311	177,772	150,418	149,838	227	229	241	245	233	197
Janesville-Beloit, WI Metro Area	726	718	161,448	160,331	152,315	139,510	255	246	239	225	223	212
Jefferson City, MO Metro Area	2,279	2,248	151,145	149,807	140,033	120,704	270	269	259	67	67	62
Johnson City, TN Metro Area	864	854	200,648	198,716	181,585	160,369	219	215	208	235	233	213
Johnstown, PA Metro Area	694	688	136,411	143,674	152,555	163,029	295	278	238	198	209	222
Jonesboro, AR Metro Area	1,476	1,466	128,394	121,026	107,756	93,620	306	317	324	88	83	74
Joplin, MO Metro Area	1,268	1,263	177,211	175,516	157,300	134,910	233	232	234	140	139	125
Kahului-Wailuku-Lahaina, HI Metro Area	2,451	1,174	164,726	154,925	128,237	100,504	253	257	280	140	132	109
Kalamazoo-Portage, MI Metro Area	1,670	1,170	335,340	326,592	314,841	293,471	151	150	147	287	279	269
Kankakee, IL Metro Area	681	677	110,879	113,449	103,825	96,255	339	331	330	164	168	154
Kansas City, MO-KS Metro Area	7,373	7,256	2,087,471	2,009,338	1,811,788	1,614,530	30	30	26	288	277	250
Kennewick-Richland, WA Metro Area	3,025	2,941	279,116	253,340	191,851	150,033	169	176	201	95	86	65
Killeen-Temple, TX Metro Area	2,859	2,816	431,032	405,303	330,726	268,822	124	128	139	153	144	117
Kingsport-Bristol-Bristol, TN-VA Metro Area	2,047	2,010	307,120	309,542	298,564	275,678	162	155	150	153	154	149
Kingston, NY Metro Area	1,161	1,124	180,143	182,531	177,726	165,304	230	224	212	160	162	158
Knoxville, TN Metro Area	3,650	3,501	861,424	837,579	748,231	651,618	64	64	64	246	239	214

X = Not applicable.
[1] The April 1, 2010 and 2000, population estimates bases reflect modifications to the censuses as documented in the Count Question Resolution program and geographic program revisions.
[2] The April 1, 1990, census counts include corrections processed through August 1997, results of special censuses and test censuses, and do not include adjustments for census coverage errors.
[3] Persons per square mile were calculated on the basis of land area data published for 2016, generally the same as that from the 2010 census.

Table B-1.　Area and Population—*Continued*

Metropolitan statistical area and division	Area, 2016 (square miles) Total	Land	Population 2015 Estimate (July 1)	2010[1] estimates base (April 1)	2000[1] estimates base (April 1)	1990 census[2] (April 1)	Rank 2015	2010	2000	Persons per square mile of land area[3] 2015	2010	2000
Kokomo, IN Metro Area	294	293	82,556	82,752	84,961	80,827	373	371	362	282	282	290
La Crosse-Onalaska, WI-MN Metro Area	1,049	1,004	136,985	133,665	126,881	116,401	294	295	281	137	133	126
Lafayette, LA Metro Area	4,316	3,409	490,488	466,750	424,983	382,974	108	107	106	144	137	125
Lafayette-West Lafayette, IN Metro Area	1,285	1,278	214,363	201,798	178,549	158,848	203	210	211	168	158	140
Lake Charles, LA Metro Area	3,031	2,349	205,605	199,629	193,571	177,394	213	214	198	88	85	82
Lake Havasu City-Kingman, AZ Metro Area	13,461	13,311	204,737	200,186	154,981	93,497	214	212	236	15	15	12
Lakeland-Winter Haven, FL Metro Area	2,011	1,797	650,092	602,095	483,888	405,382	84	88	94	362	335	269
Lancaster, PA Metro Area	984	944	536,624	519,448	470,783	422,822	103	101	98	569	550	499
Lansing-East Lansing, MI Metro Area	1,715	1,698	472,276	464,032	447,845	432,674	110	108	102	278	273	264
Laredo, TX Metro Area	3,376	3,362	269,721	250,304	193,124	133,239	176	185	200	80	75	58
Las Cruces, NM Metro Area	3,815	3,808	214,295	209,241	174,880	135,510	205	204	213	56	55	46
Las Vegas-Henderson-Paradise, NV Metro Area	8,061	7,892	2,114,801	1,951,269	1,375,741	741,459	29	31	38	268	247	174
Lawrence, KS Metro Area	475	456	118,053	110,826	99,953	81,798	326	336	342	259	243	219
Lawton, OK Metro Area	1,726	1,702	130,644	130,291	121,599	118,137	302	300	291	77	77	71
Lebanon, PA Metro Area	363	362	137,067	133,577	120,202	113,744	293	296	295	379	369	332
Lewiston, ID-WA Metro Area	1,497	1,484	62,153	60,888	57,971	51,359	381	380	379	42	41	39
Lewiston-Auburn, ME Metro Area	497	468	107,233	107,702	103,803	105,259	342	340	331	229	230	222
Lexington-Fayette, KY Metro Area	1,484	1,469	500,535	472,099	408,411	348,428	107	106	110	341	322	278
Lima, OH Metro Area	407	403	104,425	106,331	108,464	109,755	345	342	322	259	264	270
Lincoln, NE Metro Area	1,422	1,409	323,578	302,157	266,798	229,091	154	158	161	230	214	189
Little Rock-North Little Rock-Conway, AR Metro Area	4,199	4,084	731,612	699,823	610,470	535,034	76	76	76	179	171	150
Logan, UT-ID Metro Area	1,841	1,828	133,857	125,442	102,722	79,415	299	310	336	73	69	56
Longview, TX Metro Area	1,807	1,780	217,781	214,384	194,046	180,053	201	199	197	122	120	109
Longview, WA Metro Area	1,166	1,140	103,468	102,410	92,945	82,119	346	346	350	91	90	82
Los Angeles-Long Beach-Anaheim, CA Metro Area	5,699	4,849	13,340,068	12,828,966	12,365,597	11,273,720	2	2	2	2,751	2,646	2,550
Anaheim-Santa Ana-Irvine, CA Metro Division	948	791	3,169,776	3,010,266	2,846,282	2,410,556	-	-	-	4,009	3,808	3,600
Los Angeles-Long Beach-Glendale, CA Metro Division	4,751	4,058	10,170,292	9,818,700	9,519,315	8,863,164	-	-	-	2,506	2,420	2,346
Louisville/Jefferson County, KY-IN Metro Area	3,640	3,578	1,278,413	1,235,710	1,121,521	1,023,084	43	43	45	357	345	313
Lubbock, TX Metro Area	2,696	2,688	311,154	290,805	256,263	236,098	161	163	164	116	108	95
Lynchburg, VA Metro Area	2,147	2,120	259,950	252,659	222,120	206,226	185	179	182	123	119	105
Macon, GA Metro Area	1,738	1,723	230,096	232,293	222,479	206,616	195	189	180	134	135	129
Madera, CA Metro Area	2,153	2,137	154,998	150,865	123,179	88,090	263	268	289	73	71	58
Madison, WI Metro Area	3,386	3,309	641,385	605,437	535,453	462,662	87	87	87	194	183	162
Manchester-Nashua, NH Metro Area	893	876	406,678	400,721	380,856	336,073	132	131	120	464	457	435
Manhattan, KS Metro Area	1,484	1,451	98,545	92,735	81,162	83,267	356	362	368	68	64	56
Mankato-North Mankato, MN Metro Area	1,233	1,196	99,134	96,740	85,711	82,120	355	355	361	83	81	72
Mansfield, OH Metro Area	500	495	121,707	124,475	128,932	126,137	318	313	279	246	251	260
McAllen-Edinburg-Mission, TX Metro Area	1,583	1,571	842,304	774,774	569,099	383,545	67	71	82	536	493	362
Medford, OR Metro Area	2,801	2,783	212,567	203,206	181,281	146,389	207	209	209	76	73	65
Memphis, TN-MS-AR Metro Area	5,108	4,986	1,344,127	1,324,829	1,213,285	1,075,309	42	41	41	270	266	243
Merced, CA Metro Area	1,979	1,935	268,455	255,798	211,178	178,403	178	174	184	139	132	109
Miami-Fort Lauderdale-West Palm Beach, FL Metro Area	6,137	5,076	6,012,331	5,566,299	5,007,956	4,056,100	8	8	6	1,185	1,097	987
Fort Lauderdale-Pompano Beach-Deerfield Beach, FL Metro Division	1,323	1,207	1,896,425	1,748,148	1,622,974	1,255,488	-	-	-	1,571	1,448	1,345
Miami-Miami Beach-Kendall, FL Metro Division	2,431	1,899	2,693,117	2,498,017	2,253,793	1,937,094	-	-	-	1,418	1,316	1,187
West Palm Beach-Boca Raton-Delray Beach, FL Metro Division	2,383	1,970	1,422,789	1,320,134	1,131,189	863,518	-	-	-	722	670	574
Michigan City-La Porte, IN Metro Area	613	598	110,884	111,467	110,099	107,066	338	334	318	185	186	184
Midland, MI Metro Area	528	516	83,632	83,629	82,797	75,651	372	369	365	162	162	160
Midland, TX Metro Area	1,818	1,815	166,710	141,674	120,780	111,567	248	281	294	92	78	67
Milwaukee-Waukesha-West Allis, WI Metro Area	3,322	1,455	1,575,747	1,555,954	1,500,788	1,432,149	39	39	36	1,083	1,069	1,032
Minneapolis-St. Paul-Bloomington, MN-WI Metro Area	8,120	7,637	3,524,583	3,348,857	3,032,340	2,595,109	16	16	16	462	439	397
Missoula, MT Metro Area	2,618	2,593	114,181	109,299	95,803	78,687	336	338	347	44	42	37
Mobile, AL Metro Area	1,644	1,229	415,395	413,143	399,887	378,643	127	125	115	338	336	325
Modesto, CA Metro Area	1,514	1,496	538,388	514,451	446,850	370,522	102	102	103	360	344	299
Monroe, LA Metro Area	1,537	1,487	179,238	176,502	170,054	162,881	232	231	218	121	119	114
Monroe, MI Metro Area	680	549	149,568	152,021	145,939	133,600	275	265	244	272	277	266
Montgomery, AL Metro Area	2,786	2,713	373,792	374,529	346,571	305,175	142	137	133	138	138	128
Morgantown, WV Metro Area	1,017	1,009	138,176	129,709	111,201	104,546	292	303	315	137	129	110
Morristown, TN Metro Area	490	436	116,642	114,111	102,444	83,496	330	330	337	268	262	235
Mount Vernon-Anacortes, WA Metro Area	1,917	1,730	121,846	116,901	103,017	79,555	317	322	334	70	68	60
Muncie, IN Metro Area	396	392	116,852	117,671	118,769	119,659	329	321	300	298	300	303
Muskegon, MI Metro Area	1,460	500	172,790	172,188	170,208	158,983	239	235	217	346	344	340
Myrtle Beach-Conway-North Myrtle Beach, SC-NC Metro Area	2,305	1,984	431,964	376,722	269,679	195,038	123	136	160	218	190	136

X = Not applicable.
[1]The April 1, 2010 and 2000, population estimates bases reflect modifications to the censuses as documented in the Count Question Resolution program and geographic program revisions.
[2]The April 1, 1990, census counts include corrections processed through August 1997, results of special censuses and test censuses, and do not include adjustments for census coverage errors.
[3]Persons per square mile were calculated on the basis of land area data published for 2016, generally the same as that from the 2010 census.

Table B-1.   Area and Population—*Continued*

Metropolitan statistical area and division	Area, 2016 (square miles) Total	Land	2015 Estimate (July 1)	2010[1] estimates base (April 1)	2000[1] estimates base (April 1)	1990 census[2] (April 1)	Rank 2015	2010	2000	Persons per square mile of land area[3] 2015	2010	2000
Napa, CA Metro Area	789	748	142,456	136,530	124,344	110,765	288	290	285	190	183	166
Naples-Immokalee-Marco Island, FL Metro Area	2,305	1,999	357,305	321,520	251,412	152,099	148	151	170	179	161	126
Nashville-Davidson—Murfreesboro—Franklin, TN Metro Area	6,378	6,302	1,830,345	1,670,896	1,381,412	1,103,028	36	37	37	290	265	219
New Bern, NC Metro Area	1,809	1,515	126,245	126,802	114,733	102,399	312	308	307	83	84	76
New Haven-Milford, CT Metro Area	862	605	859,470	862,474	823,993	804,219	65	62	58	1,422	1,427	1,363
New Orleans-Metairie, LA Metro Area	7,875	3,202	1,262,888	1,189,863	1,337,740	1,285,270	46	46	39	394	372	418
New York-Newark-Jersey City, NY-NJ-PA Metro Area	10,876	8,295	20,182,305	19,566,387	18,945,888	17,413,155	1	1	1	2,433	2,359	2,284
Dutchess County-Putnam County, NY Metro Division	1,072	1,026	394,796	397,198	375,763	343,403	-	-	-	385	387	366
Nassau County-Suffolk County, NY Metro Division	2,827	1,197	2,862,937	2,833,053	2,754,004	2,609,212	-	-	-	2,393	2,368	2,302
Newark, NJ-PA Metro Division	2,561	2,483	2,511,493	2,469,792	2,395,141	2,200,342	-	-	-	1,012	995	965
New York-Jersey City-White Plains, NY-NJ Metro Division	4,417	3,589	14,413,079	13,866,344	13,420,980	12,260,198	-	-	-	4,016	3,863	3,739
Niles-Benton Harbor, MI Metro Area	1,582	568	154,636	156,817	162,491	161,378	264	256	229	272	276	286
North Port-Sarasota-Bradenton, FL Metro Area	1,618	1,299	768,918	702,268	589,998	489,483	73	75	79	592	541	454
Norwich-New London, CT Metro Area	772	665	271,863	274,046	259,108	254,957	175	168	162	409	412	390
Ocala, FL Metro Area	1,663	1,588	343,254	331,304	258,873	194,833	149	149	163	216	209	163
Ocean City, NJ Metro Area	620	252	94,727	97,265	102,323	95,089	363	354	338	376	386	406
Odessa, TX Metro Area	902	898	159,436	137,133	121,124	118,934	258	289	292	178	153	135
Ogden-Clearfield, UT Metro Area	8,635	7,230	642,850	597,159	485,410	388,284	86	89	93	89	83	67
Oklahoma City, OK Metro Area	5,582	5,512	1,358,452	1,252,992	1,095,553	971,042	41	42	46	247	227	199
Olympia-Tumwater, WA Metro Area	774	723	269,536	252,264	207,392	161,238	177	180	189	373	349	287
Omaha-Council Bluffs, NE-IA Metro Area	4,407	4,350	915,312	865,356	767,175	685,797	59	61	62	210	199	176
Orlando-Kissimmee-Sanford, FL Metro Area	4,012	3,481	2,387,138	2,134,405	1,644,509	1,224,852	24	27	33	686	613	472
Oshkosh-Neenah, WI Metro Area	579	435	169,546	166,994	156,752	140,320	244	240	235	390	384	361
Owensboro, KY Metro Area	932	899	117,463	114,754	109,879	104,681	328	329	319	131	128	122
Oxnard-Thousand Oaks-Ventura, CA Metro Area	2,208	1,843	850,536	823,387	753,230	669,016	66	66	63	462	447	409
Palm Bay-Melbourne-Titusville, FL Metro Area	1,557	1,015	568,088	543,378	476,299	398,978	95	97	97	560	535	469
Panama City, FL Metro Area	1,778	1,312	197,506	184,715	162,818	138,498	220	223	228	151	141	124
Parkersburg-Vienna, WV Metro Area	612	599	92,332	92,673	93,819	92,107	365	363	348	154	155	157
Pensacola-Ferry Pass-Brent, FL Metro Area	2,049	1,669	478,043	448,991	412,167	344,406	109	110	109	287	269	247
Peoria, IL Metro Area	2,518	2,469	378,018	379,186	366,911	358,552	139	135	127	153	154	149
Philadelphia-Camden-Wilmington, PA-NJ-DE-MD Metro Area	4,870	4,603	6,069,875	5,965,379	5,686,329	5,435,468	7	5	4	1,319	1,296	1,236
Camden, NJ Metro Division	1,384	1,342	1,252,628	1,250,694	1,186,350	1,127,972	-	-	-	933	932	884
Montgomery County-Bucks County-Chester County, PA Metro Division	1,868	1,838	1,962,570	1,924,285	1,780,165	1,595,681	-	-	-	1,068	1,047	969
Philadelphia, PA Metro Division	333	318	2,131,336	2,084,732	2,069,284	2,133,228	-	-	-	6,700	6,554	6,505
Wilmington, DE-MD-NJ Metro Division	1,284	1,104	723,341	705,668	650,530	578,587	-	-	-	655	639	589
Phoenix-Mesa-Scottsdale, AZ Metro Area	14,599	14,565	4,574,531	4,193,127	3,251,884	2,238,480	12	14	14	314	288	223
Pine Bluff, AR Metro Area	2,085	2,030	93,696	100,258	107,339	106,958	364	350	325	46	49	53
Pittsburgh, PA Metro Area	5,343	5,282	2,353,045	2,356,283	2,431,233	2,468,289	26	22	20	446	446	460
Pittsfield, MA Metro Area	947	927	127,828	131,272	134,922	139,352	307	299	268	138	142	146
Pocatello, ID Metro Area	1,148	1,113	83,744	82,839	75,562	66,026	371	370	374	75	75	68
Portland-South Portland, ME Metro Area	2,857	2,080	526,295	514,100	487,508	441,257	104	103	92	253	247	234
Portland-Vancouver-Hillsboro, OR-WA Metro Area	6,824	6,687	2,389,228	2,226,011	1,927,904	1,523,741	23	23	25	357	333	288
Port St. Lucie, FL Metro Area	1,441	1,115	454,846	424,107	319,456	251,071	113	119	145	408	380	286
Prescott, AZ Metro Area	8,128	8,124	222,255	211,015	167,377	107,714	199	201	221	27	26	21
Providence-Warwick, RI-MA Metro Area	2,236	1,587	1,613,070	1,601,216	1,582,961	1,509,789	38	38	34	1,016	1,009	998
Provo-Orem, UT Metro Area	5,550	5,395	585,799	526,886	376,775	269,407	93	100	121	109	98	70
Pueblo, CO Metro Area	2,398	2,386	163,591	159,063	141,490	123,051	254	250	257	69	67	59
Punta Gorda, FL Metro Area	858	681	173,115	159,991	141,620	110,975	238	248	255	254	235	208
Racine, WI Metro Area	792	333	195,080	195,428	188,849	175,034	221	218	203	587	588	568
Raleigh, NC Metro Area	2,148	2,118	1,273,568	1,130,491	797,188	541,100	44	48	61	601	534	376
Rapid City, SD Metro Area	7,826	7,805	144,134	134,609	120,117	109,400	285	292	296	19	17	15
Reading, PA Metro Area	866	856	415,271	411,572	373,712	336,523	128	126	123	485	481	436
Redding, CA Metro Area	3,847	3,775	179,533	177,223	163,242	147,036	231	230	227	48	47	43
Reno, NV Metro Area	6,806	6,565	450,890	425,437	342,881	257,193	115	117	134	69	65	52
Richmond, VA Metro Area	4,703	4,576	1,271,334	1,208,080	1,055,796	914,805	45	45	48	278	264	231
Riverside-San Bernardino-Ontario, CA Metro Area	27,408	27,264	4,489,159	4,224,972	3,254,799	2,588,793	13	13	13	165	155	119
Roanoke, VA Metro Area	1,897	1,869	314,560	308,682	288,370	268,398	159	156	153	168	165	154
Rochester, MN Metro Area	2,506	2,477	213,873	206,877	184,745	162,722	206	207	206	86	84	75
Rochester, NY Metro Area	5,246	3,266	1,081,954	1,079,695	1,062,522	1,025,220	51	51	47	331	331	325
Rockford, IL Metro Area	801	794	340,663	349,431	320,229	283,719	150	146	143	429	440	403
Rocky Mount, NC Metro Area	1,050	1,046	148,069	152,390	142,982	133,235	281	264	251	142	146	137
Rome, GA Metro Area	519	510	96,504	96,317	90,622	81,251	361	356	354	189	189	178

X = Not applicable.
[1]The April 1, 2010 and 2000, population estimates bases reflect modifications to the censuses as documented in the Count Question Resolution program and geographic program revisions.
[2]The April 1, 1990, census counts include corrections processed through August 1997, results of special censuses and test censuses, and do not include adjustments for census coverage errors.
[3]Persons per square mile were calculated on the basis of land area data published for 2016, generally the same as that from the 2010 census.

Table B-1.   Area and Population—*Continued*

Metropolitan statistical area and division	Area, 2016 (square miles) Total	Land	Population 2015 Estimate (July 1)	2010[1] estimates base (April 1)	2000[1] estimates base (April 1)	1990 census[2] (April 1)	Rank 2015	2010	2000	Persons per square mile of land area[3] 2015	2010	2000
Sacramento—Roseville—Arden-Arcade, CA Metro Area	5,307	5,095	2,274,194	2,149,143	1,796,822	1,481,102	27	25	27	446	422	353
Saginaw, MI Metro Area	816	801	193,307	200,169	210,051	211,946	224	213	187	242	250	262
St. Cloud, MN Metro Area	1,803	1,751	194,418	189,093	167,441	148,976	222	220	220	111	108	96
St. George, UT Metro Area	2,430	2,427	155,602	138,115	90,325	48,560	262	287	355	64	57	37
St. Joseph, MO-KS Metro Area	1,675	1,656	126,880	127,329	123,841	115,816	309	306	288	77	77	75
St. Louis, MO-IL Metro Area	8,082	7,864	2,811,588	2,787,748	2,675,562	2,560,517	20	18	18	358	355	340
Salem, OR Metro Area	1,935	1,922	410,091	390,738	347,256	278,024	130	132	131	213	203	181
Salinas, CA Metro Area	3,771	3,281	433,898	415,057	401,752	355,660	122	123	113	132	127	123
Salisbury, MD-DE Metro Area	2,902	2,099	395,300	373,764	312,437	246,036	135	138	148	188	178	149
Salt Lake City, UT Metro Area	8,092	7,684	1,170,266	1,087,799	939,169	752,557	48	50	50	152	142	122
San Angelo, TX Metro Area	2,592	2,574	119,659	111,823	105,780	100,087	323	333	326	47	44	41
San Antonio-New Braunfels, TX Metro Area	7,371	7,313	2,384,075	2,142,518	1,711,578	1,407,745	25	26	30	326	293	234
San Diego-Carlsbad, CA Metro Area	4,526	4,207	3,299,521	3,095,308	2,813,839	2,498,016	17	17	17	784	736	669
San Francisco-Oakland-Hayward, CA Metro Area	3,426	2,478	4,656,132	4,335,560	4,123,734	3,686,592	11	11	12	1,879	1,750	1,664
Oakland-Hayward-Berkeley, CA Metro Division	1,625	1,462	2,764,960	2,559,458	2,392,570	2,082,914	-	-	-	1,891	1,751	1,637
San Francisco-Redwood City-South San Francisco, CA Metro Division	973	495	1,629,951	1,523,693	1,483,863	1,373,582	-	-	-	3,290	3,076	2,995
San Rafael, CA Metro Division	828	521	261,221	252,409	247,301	230,096	-	-	-	502	485	475
San Jose-Sunnyvale-Santa Clara, CA Metro Area	2,695	2,680	1,976,836	1,836,941	1,735,995	1,534,274	35	34	28	738	686	648
San Luis Obispo-Paso Robles-Arroyo Grande, CA Metro Area	3,616	3,301	281,401	269,593	246,746	217,162	165	169	171	85	82	75
Santa Cruz-Watsonville, CA Metro Area	607	445	274,146	262,362	255,614	229,734	174	171	165	616	589	574
Santa Fe, NM Metro Area	1,909	1,908	148,686	144,171	129,304	98,928	277	277	277	78	76	68
Santa Maria-Santa Barbara, CA Metro Area	3,789	2,735	444,769	423,939	399,293	369,608	117	120	116	163	155	146
Santa Rosa, CA Metro Area	1,768	1,576	502,146	483,880	458,586	388,222	106	105	101	319	307	291
Savannah, GA Metro Area	1,570	1,343	379,199	347,621	293,324	258,060	138	147	152	282	259	218
Scranton—Wilkes-Barre—Hazleton, PA Metro Area	1,776	1,746	558,166	563,630	560,793	575,264	97	95	84	320	323	321
Seattle-Tacoma-Bellevue, WA Metro Area	6,309	5,871	3,733,580	3,439,815	3,043,934	2,559,164	15	15	15	636	586	519
Seattle-Bellevue-Everett, WA Metro Division	4,503	4,202	2,889,626	2,644,586	2,343,118	1,972,961	-	-	-	688	629	558
Tacoma-Lakewood, WA Metro Division	1,805	1,669	843,954	795,229	700,816	586,203	-	-	-	506	477	420
Sebastian-Vero Beach, FL Metro Area	617	503	147,919	138,028	112,877	90,208	282	288	311	294	275	225
Sebring, FL Metro Area	1,106	1,017	99,491	98,786	87,391	68,432	354	351	359	98	97	86
Sheboygan, WI Metro Area	1,271	511	115,569	115,507	112,663	103,877	335	327	312	226	226	220
Sherman-Denison, TX Metro Area	979	933	125,467	120,873	110,574	95,021	314	318	316	135	130	119
Shreveport-Bossier City, LA Metro Area	3,314	3,188	443,708	439,811	417,787	401,676	119	112	108	139	138	131
Sierra Vista-Douglas, AZ Metro Area	6,218	6,165	126,427	131,357	117,743	97,624	311	298	302	21	21	19
Sioux City, IA-NE-SD Metro Area	2,959	2,937	169,069	168,563	167,860	154,738	245	237	219	58	57	57
Sioux Falls, SD Metro Area	2,586	2,576	251,854	228,264	187,151	153,500	186	193	204	98	89	73
South Bend-Mishawaka, IN-MI Metro Area	970	948	320,098	319,215	316,653	296,529	155	152	146	338	337	334
Spartanburg, SC Metro Area	1,335	1,322	325,079	313,268	283,896	257,137	153	153	154	246	237	215
Spokane-Spokane Valley, WA Metro Area	5,747	5,642	547,824	527,753	469,756	401,227	100	99	99	97	94	83
Springfield, IL Metro Area	1,193	1,183	211,156	210,170	201,457	189,550	210	202	193	179	178	170
Springfield, MA Metro Area	1,179	1,144	631,982	621,705	608,517	602,878	88	83	77	552	543	532
Springfield, MO Metro Area	3,021	3,007	456,456	436,713	368,451	298,818	112	113	125	152	145	123
Springfield, OH Metro Area	403	398	135,959	138,333	144,742	147,548	296	286	248	342	348	364
State College, PA Metro Area	1,113	1,110	160,580	153,981	135,678	123,786	256	258	265	145	139	122
Staunton-Waynesboro, VA Metro Area	1,006	1,002	120,221	118,502	108,953	97,687	322	320	320	120	118	109
Stockton-Lodi, CA Metro Area	1,427	1,392	726,106	685,308	563,660	480,628	77	77	83	522	492	405
Sumter, SC Metro Area	682	665	107,480	107,463	104,687	102,637	340	341	327	162	162	157
Syracuse, NY Metro Area	2,779	2,385	660,458	662,589	650,133	659,864	82	79	72	277	278	273
Tallahassee, FL Metro Area	2,603	2,388	377,924	368,770	320,259	259,096	140	140	142	158	154	134
Tampa-St. Petersburg-Clearwater, FL Metro Area	3,331	2,515	2,975,225	2,783,514	2,396,038	2,067,959	18	19	21	1,183	1,107	953
Terre Haute, IN Metro Area	1,485	1,465	171,019	172,422	170,952	166,578	240	234	216	117	118	117
Texarkana, TX-AR Metro Area	2,125	2,043	149,769	149,195	143,379	134,098	274	271	250	73	73	70
The Villages, FL Metro Area	580	548	118,891	93,420	53,337	31,577	324	361	381	217	171	97
Toledo, OH Metro Area	1,624	1,364	605,956	610,001	618,216	614,128	91	86	75	444	447	453
Topeka, KS Metro Area	3,290	3,233	233,791	233,868	224,568	210,257	193	188	178	72	72	70
Trenton, NJ Metro Area	229	224	371,398	367,508	350,773	325,824	143	141	130	1,655	1,638	1,563
Tucson, AZ Metro Area	9,189	9,187	1,010,025	980,263	843,702	666,880	53	53	56	110	107	92
Tulsa, OK Metro Area	6,460	6,270	981,005	937,528	859,635	761,019	55	55	54	157	150	137
Tuscaloosa, AL Metro Area	2,898	2,847	239,908	230,159	204,116	186,719	190	191	190	84	81	72
Tyler, TX Metro Area	950	922	222,936	209,721	174,861	151,309	198	203	214	242	228	190
Urban Honolulu, HI Metro Area	2,166	601	998,714	953,207	876,159	836,231	54	54	53	1,663	1,587	1,459
Utica-Rome, NY Metro Area	2,716	2,624	295,600	299,376	300,018	316,633	163	160	149	113	114	114
Valdosta, GA Metro Area	1,629	1,589	142,875	139,665	119,570	99,244	287	284	299	90	88	75
Vallejo-Fairfield, CA Metro Area	906	822	436,092	413,344	394,495	340,421	121	124	117	531	503	480
Victoria, TX Metro Area	1,748	1,734	99,913	94,003	91,000	80,341	352	359	353	58	54	53

X = Not applicable.

[1]The April 1, 2010 and 2000, population estimates bases reflect modifications to the censuses as documented in the Count Question Resolution program and geographic program revisions.

[2]The April 1, 1990, census counts include corrections processed through August 1997, results of special censuses and test censuses, and do not include adjustments for census coverage errors.

[3]Persons per square mile were calculated on the basis of land area data published for 2016, generally the same as that from the 2010 census.

Table B-1.   Area and Population—*Continued*

Metropolitan statistical area and division	Area, 2016 (square miles)		Population									
	Total	Land	2015 Estimate (July 1)	2010[1] estimates base (April 1)	2000[1] estimates base (April 1)	1990 census[2] (April 1)	Rank			Persons per square mile of land area[3]		
							2015	2010	2000	2015	2010	2000
Vineland-Bridgeton, NJ Metro Area	678	484	155,854	156,898	146,454	138,053	261	255	243	322	325	303
Virginia Beach-Norfolk-Newport News, VA-NC Metro Area	3,933	2,683	1,724,876	1,676,817	1,580,603	1,452,549	37	36	35	643	625	589
Visalia-Porterville, CA Metro Area	4,839	4,824	459,863	442,182	368,011	311,921	111	111	126	95	92	76
Waco, TX Metro Area	1,834	1,803	262,813	252,772	232,088	206,835	180	178	175	146	140	129
Walla Walla, WA Metro Area	2,172	2,139	64,282	62,859	59,241	52,463	379	379	378	30	29	28
Warner Robins, GA Metro Area	782	775	188,149	179,605	144,046	118,505	226	227	249	243	232	186
Washington-Arlington-Alexandria, DC-VA-MD-WV Metro Area	6,680	6,247	6,097,684	5,636,406	4,837,674	4,157,327	6	7	7	976	902	774
Silver Spring-Frederick-Rockville, MD Metro Division	1,174	1,154	1,285,438	1,205,191	1,069,151	907,235	-	-	-	1,114	1,045	927
Washington-Arlington-Alexandria, DC-VA-MD-WV Metro Division	5,506	5,093	4,812,246	4,431,215	3,768,523	3,250,092	-	-	-	945	870	740
Waterloo-Cedar Falls, IA Metro Area	1,514	1,503	170,612	167,819	163,721	158,640	242	239	226	114	112	109
Watertown-Fort Drum, NY Metro Area	1,857	1,269	117,635	116,232	111,716	110,943	327	324	314	93	92	88
Wausau, WI Metro Area	1,576	1,545	135,868	134,063	125,908	115,400	297	294	284	88	87	82
Weirton-Steubenville, WV-OH Metro Area	592	580	120,512	124,455	131,995	142,523	321	314	271	208	215	228
Wenatchee, WA Metro Area	4,843	4,740	116,178	110,887	99,200	78,455	331	335	343	25	23	21
Wheeling, WV-OH Metro Area	963	943	144,198	147,949	153,200	159,301	284	273	237	153	157	162
Wichita, KS Metro Area	5,048	5,012	644,610	630,919	579,860	519,403	85	82	80	129	126	116
Wichita Falls, TX Metro Area	2,675	2,620	150,780	151,476	151,596	140,375	272	266	240	58	58	58
Williamsport, PA Metro Area	1,244	1,229	116,048	116,108	120,003	118,710	332	325	298	95	95	98
Wilmington, NC Metro Area	1,263	1,063	277,969	254,884	201,386	149,139	171	175	194	261	240	189
Winchester, VA-WV Metro Area	1,069	1,063	133,836	128,473	102,996	84,168	300	305	335	126	121	97
Winston-Salem, NC Metro Area	2,040	2,009	659,330	640,577	569,355	488,125	83	81	81	328	319	284
Worcester, MA-CT Metro Area	2,100	2,024	935,536	916,976	859,106	812,230	58	57	55	462	453	425
Yakima, WA Metro Area	4,310	4,295	248,830	243,231	222,578	188,823	188	186	179	58	57	52
York-Hanover, PA Metro Area	911	904	442,867	434,998	381,791	339,574	120	114	119	490	481	422
Youngstown-Warren-Boardman, OH-PA Metro Area	1,744	1,702	549,885	565,804	603,061	613,622	99	93	78	323	332	354
Yuba City, CA Metro Area	1,253	1,235	170,955	166,892	139,196	122,643	241	241	262	139	135	113
Yuma, AZ Metro Area	5,519	5,514	204,275	195,750	159,995	106,895	215	217	231	37	36	29

X = Not applicable.
[1] The April 1, 2010 and 2000, population estimates bases reflect modifications to the censuses as documented in the Count Question Resolution program and geographic program revisions.
[2] The April 1, 1990, census counts include corrections processed through August 1997, results of special censuses and test censuses, and do not include adjustments for census coverage errors.
[3] Persons per square mile were calculated on the basis of land area data published for 2016, generally the same as that from the 2010 census.

Table B-2. Components of Population Change

Metropolitan statistical area and division	Components of population change, April 1, 2010 (estimates base) to July 1, 2015								Population change, April 1, 2000 to April 1, 2010	
	Number									
	Total population change¹	Natural increase			Total migration	Net International migration	Net domestic migration	Percent change	Number	Percent change
		Total	Births	Deaths						
Abilene, TX Metro Area	4,326	3,744	12,227	8,483	531	2,035	-1,504	2.6	4,979	3.1
Akron, OH Metro Area	1,036	3,857	40,031	36,174	-1,982	7,298	-9,280	0.1	8,232	1.2
Albany, GA Metro Area	-3,974	4,017	11,412	7,395	-7,985	629	-8,614	-2.5	-372	-0.2
Albany, OR Metro Area	3,875	1,452	7,582	6,130	2,237	135	2,102	3.3	13,593	13.2
Albany-Schenectady-Troy, NY Metro Area	11,117	7,670	48,015	40,345	4,462	13,449	-8,987	1.3	44,793	5.4
Albuquerque, NM Metro Area	20,226	20,566	56,632	36,066	-402	6,777	-7,179	2.3	157,346	21.6
Alexandria, LA Metro Area	562	2,347	10,690	8,343	-1,671	734	-2,405	0.4	8,835	6.1
Allentown-Bethlehem-Easton, PA-NJ Metro Area	11,024	4,142	45,117	40,975	6,917	13,532	-6,615	1.3	80,963	10.9
Altoona, PA Metro Area	-1,485	-1,270	7,207	8,477	-485	188	-673	-1.2	-2,027	-1.6
Amarillo, TX Metro Area	10,123	8,412	20,104	11,692	1,632	4,076	-2,444	4.0	23,263	10.2
Ames, IA Metro Area	6,479	2,531	5,020	2,489	4,023	4,072	-49	7.2	9,554	11.9
Anchorage, AK Metro Area	18,969	20,868	31,968	11,100	-1,758	6,719	-8,477	5.0	61,204	19.1
Ann Arbor, MI Metro Area	13,814	8,446	19,637	11,191	5,342	11,051	-5,709	4.0	22,248	6.9
Anniston-Oxford-Jacksonville, AL Metro Area	-2,966	-154	7,055	7,209	-2,686	294	-2,980	-2.5	6,704	6.0
Appleton, WI Metro Area	7,341	6,639	14,941	8,302	670	950	-280	3.3	23,893	11.8
Asheville, NC Metro Area	21,980	-1,203	23,166	24,369	21,899	1,614	20,285	5.2	55,674	15.1
Athens-Clarke County, GA Metro Area	10,648	4,779	11,656	6,877	5,546	2,646	2,900	5.5	26,513	16.0
Atlanta-Sandy Springs-Roswell, GA Metro Area	424,068	205,223	381,487	176,264	215,011	98,784	116,227	8.0	1,023,592	24.0
Atlantic City-Hammonton, NJ Metro Area	-330	3,846	17,369	13,523	-4,110	8,527	-12,637	-0.1	21,339	8.4
Auburn-Opelika, AL Metro Area	16,697	4,316	9,295	4,979	12,044	2,919	9,125	11.9	25,282	22.0
Augusta-Richmond County, GA-SC Metro Area	25,273	11,915	38,755	26,840	12,642	4,932	7,710	4.5	56,832	11.2
Austin-Round Rock, TX Metro Area	284,547	87,389	134,107	46,718	192,904	33,656	159,248	16.6	466,350	37.3
Bakersfield, CA Metro Area	42,545	45,872	75,269	29,397	-2,440	10,173	-12,613	5.1	177,999	26.9
Baltimore-Columbia-Towson, MD Metro Area	86,832	53,248	176,761	123,513	35,502	50,243	-14,741	3.2	157,438	6.2
Bangor, ME Metro Area	-1,228	-138	7,770	7,908	-1,202	695	-1,897	-0.8	9,054	6.2
Barnstable Town, MA Metro Area	-1,555	-6,499	8,293	14,792	4,731	1,625	3,106	-0.7	-6,351	-2.9
Baton Rouge, LA Metro Area	27,980	23,938	57,960	34,022	4,151	6,940	-2,789	3.5	96,378	13.6
Battle Creek, MI Metro Area	-1,834	1,172	8,784	7,612	-2,924	965	-3,889	-1.3	-1,843	-1.3
Bay City, MI Metro Area	-2,112	-425	5,644	6,069	-1,626	349	-1,975	-2.0	-2,500	-2.3
Beaumont-Port Arthur, TX Metro Area	5,229	7,526	28,440	20,914	-2,132	3,167	-5,299	1.3	3,060	0.8
Beckley, WV Metro Area	-2,394	-807	7,927	8,734	-1,500	555	-2,055	-1.9	-1,927	-1.5
Bellingham, WA Metro Area	11,144	4,060	11,960	7,900	7,041	2,022	5,019	5.5	34,318	20.6
Bend-Redmond, OR Metro Area	17,535	2,119	9,073	6,954	15,127	4	15,123	11.1	42,361	36.7
Billings, MT Metro Area	9,349	3,179	10,941	7,762	6,088	342	5,746	5.9	19,002	13.6
Binghamton, NY Metro Area	-5,703	345	13,521	13,176	-5,876	2,844	-8,720	-2.3	-575	-0.2
Birmingham-Hoover, AL Metro Area	17,591	16,301	75,977	59,676	1,718	5,898	-4,180	1.6	76,716	7.3
Bismarck, ND Metro Area	14,739	4,052	9,220	5,168	10,341	197	10,144	12.8	13,969	13.9
Blacksburg-Christiansburg-Radford, VA Metro Area	3,489	1,160	8,798	7,638	2,519	3,813	-1,294	2.0	13,097	7.9
Bloomington, IL Metro Area	3,280	5,195	12,032	6,837	-1,871	3,319	-5,190	1.8	18,947	11.3
Bloomington, IN Metro Area	6,035	2,258	7,979	5,721	3,787	5,204	-1,417	3.8	17,200	12.1
Bloomsburg-Berwick, PA Metro Area	-334	-321	4,307	4,628	-44	780	-824	-0.4	3,382	4.1
Boise City, ID Metro Area	60,348	23,129	45,056	21,927	36,353	4,647	31,706	9.8	151,689	32.6
Boston-Cambridge-Newton, MA-NH Metro Area	221,909	89,720	273,057	183,337	137,505	157,158	-19,653	4.9	159,879	3.6
Boston, MA Metro Division	96,792	38,894	115,223	76,329	59,737	71,670	-11,933	5.1	73,575	4.1
Cambridge-Newton-Framingham, MA Metro Division	114,881	46,714	137,534	90,820	71,440	83,706	-12,266	5.1	57,561	2.6
Rockingham County-Strafford County, NH Metro Division	10,236	4,112	20,300	16,188	6,328	1,782	4,546	2.4	28,743	7.4
Boulder, CO Metro Area	24,801	6,955	15,535	8,580	17,624	5,025	12,599	8.4	24,787	9.2
Bowling Green, KY Metro Area	9,837	3,495	10,724	7,229	6,353	2,679	3,674	6.2	23,648	17.5
Bremerton-Silverdale, WA Metro Area	8,998	4,733	15,499	10,766	3,820	2,396	1,424	3.6	19,151	8.3
Bridgeport-Stamford-Norwalk, CT Metro Area	31,203	19,316	53,486	34,170	13,815	31,563	-17,748	3.4	34,228	3.9
Brownsville-Harlingen, TX Metro Area	15,937	26,317	39,172	12,855	-10,664	3,914	-14,578	3.9	71,335	21.3
Brunswick, GA Metro Area	3,635	1,215	6,940	5,725	2,273	786	1,487	3.2	19,341	20.8
Buffalo-Cheektowaga-Niagara Falls, NY Metro Area	-321	983	63,696	62,713	962	17,244	-16,282	0.0	-34,471	-2.9
Burlington, NC Metro Area	7,035	1,225	9,271	8,046	5,558	1,158	4,400	4.7	20,491	15.7
Burlington-South Burlington, VT Metro Area	5,780	4,040	11,620	7,580	1,818	2,674	-856	2.7	12,367	6.2
California-Lexington Park, MD Metro Area	6,262	3,566	7,454	3,888	2,524	1,119	1,405	6.0	18,955	22.0
Canton-Massillon, OH Metro Area	-1,444	670	23,348	22,678	-1,654	902	-2,556	-0.4	-2,546	-0.6
Cape Coral-Fort Myers, FL Metro Area	83,228	437	33,534	33,097	81,946	15,010	66,936	13.5	177,844	40.3
Cape Girardeau, MO-IL Metro Area	1,259	1,142	6,116	4,974	121	649	-528	1.3	5,989	6.6
Carbondale-Marion, IL Metro Area	248	1,266	7,579	6,313	-1,040	1,557	-2,597	0.2	5,673	4.7
Carson City, NV Metro Area	-753	-458	2,992	3,450	-430	54	-484	-1.4	2,797	5.3
Casper, WY Metro Area	6,728	2,232	5,867	3,635	4,437	301	4,136	8.9	8,909	13.4
Cedar Rapids, IA Metro Area	8,100	6,175	16,991	10,816	2,024	1,837	187	3.1	20,673	8.7
Chambersburg-Waynesboro, PA Metro Area	4,020	2,275	9,793	7,518	1,533	1,143	390	2.7	20,123	15.5
Champaign-Urbana, IL Metro Area	7,095	5,829	14,203	8,374	1,314	9,997	-8,683	3.1	21,590	10.3
Charleston, WV Metro Area	-6,457	-1,389	13,558	14,947	-4,684	548	-5,232	-2.8	-8,924	-3.8
Charleston-North Charleston, SC Metro Area	79,883	21,590	48,410	26,820	55,450	5,541	49,909	12.0	115,622	21.1
Charlotte-Concord-Gastonia, NC-SC Metro Area	209,115	65,198	154,704	89,506	140,115	29,328	110,787	9.4	499,601	29.1

¹Includes residual not shown separately.

Table B-2. Components of Population Change—*Continued*

Metropolitan statistical area and division	Components of population change, April 1, 2010 (estimates base) to July 1, 2015								Population change, April 1, 2000 to April 1, 2010	
	Number									
	Total population change¹	Natural increase			Total migration	Net International migration	Net domestic migration	Percent change	Number	Percent change
		Total	Births	Deaths						
Charlottesville, VA Metro Area	10,807	3,788	12,739	8,951	6,842	4,601	2,241	4.9	29,106	15.4
Chattanooga, TN-GA Metro Area	19,631	5,319	32,754	27,435	14,286	3,029	11,257	3.7	51,534	10.8
Cheyenne, WY Metro Area	5,240	2,680	6,656	3,976	2,566	638	1,928	5.7	10,264	12.6
Chicago-Naperville-Elgin, IL-IN-WI Metro Area	89,494	275,196	633,992	358,796	-175,204	143,616	-318,820	0.9	362,567	4.0
Chicago-Naperville-Arlington Heights, IL Metro Division	77,356	219,326	495,088	275,762	-131,279	126,011	-257,290	1.1	127,961	1.8
Elgin, IL Metro Division	14,733	23,185	42,507	19,322	-9,397	4,495	-13,892	2.4	127,017	25.7
Gary, IN Metro Division	-5,107	9,587	43,857	34,270	-14,034	2,620	-16,654	-0.7	32,020	4.7
Lake County-Kenosha County, IL-WI Metro Division	2,512	23,098	52,540	29,442	-20,494	10,490	-30,984	0.3	75,569	9.5
Chico, CA Metro Area	5,411	911	12,767	11,856	4,237	1,122	3,115	2.5	16,875	8.3
Cincinnati, OH-KY-IN Metro Area	42,964	46,788	143,253	96,465	-2,131	19,024	-21,155	2.0	119,937	6.0
Clarksville, TN-KY Metro Area	20,411	16,196	26,069	9,873	3,700	7,113	-3,413	7.8	40,883	18.6
Cleveland, TN Metro Area	5,076	930	7,050	6,120	3,993	563	3,430	4.4	11,776	11.3
Cleveland-Elyria, OH Metro Area	-16,436	12,546	122,513	109,967	-27,711	20,744	-48,455	-0.8	-70,795	-3.3
Coeur d'Alene, ID Metro Area	11,852	2,574	9,076	6,502	9,123	195	8,928	8.6	29,812	27.4
College Station-Bryan, TX Metro Area	20,496	9,202	15,991	6,789	10,996	7,385	3,611	9.0	43,803	23.7
Colorado Springs, CO Metro Area	52,245	28,037	49,460	21,423	23,500	9,751	13,749	8.1	108,136	20.1
Columbia, MO Metro Area	12,332	5,899	11,190	5,291	6,360	3,771	2,589	7.6	27,165	20.1
Columbia, SC Metro Area	42,591	16,254	49,461	33,207	25,578	8,067	17,511	5.5	120,261	18.6
Columbus, GA-AL Metro Area	18,218	10,274	24,439	14,165	7,484	5,725	1,759	6.2	13,653	4.8
Columbus, IN Metro Area	4,376	1,851	5,551	3,700	2,604	1,459	1,145	5.7	5,319	7.4
Columbus, OH Metro Area	119,617	65,308	142,078	76,770	55,111	30,180	24,931	6.3	226,789	13.5
Corpus Christi, TX Metro Area	24,234	12,493	31,787	19,294	11,880	4,058	7,822	5.7	24,946	6.2
Corvallis, OR Metro Area	1,991	935	3,807	2,872	980	2,153	-1,173	2.3	7,438	9.5
Crestview-Fort Walton Beach-Destin, FL Metro Area	26,307	6,539	17,794	11,255	19,163	3,533	15,630	11.2	24,784	11.7
Cumberland, MD-WV Metro Area	-3,320	-1,327	5,122	6,449	-1,835	443	-2,278	-3.2	1,304	1.3
Dallas-Fort Worth-Arlington, TX Metro Area	676,582	301,315	510,606	209,291	372,601	131,422	241,179	10.5	1,221,587	23.5
Dallas-Plano-Irving, TX Metro Division	477,120	208,792	339,420	130,628	267,888	98,220	169,668	11.3	786,434	22.8
Fort Worth-Arlington, TX Metro Division	199,462	92,523	171,186	78,663	104,713	33,202	71,511	9.1	435,153	24.7
Dalton, GA Metro Area	1,554	4,092	9,998	5,906	-2,607	641	-3,248	1.1	22,165	18.5
Danville, IL Metro Area	-2,343	766	5,629	4,863	-2,968	174	-3,142	-2.9	-2,304	-2.7
Daphne-Fairhope-Foley, AL Metro Area	21,444	1,208	11,382	10,174	19,436	1,031	18,405	11.8	41,849	29.8
Davenport-Moline-Rock Island, IA-IL Metro Area	3,917	6,061	25,016	18,955	-1,727	3,034	-4,761	1.0	3,622	1.0
Dayton, OH Metro Area	1,693	8,218	50,543	42,325	-5,898	8,139	-14,037	0.2	-6,755	-0.8
Decatur, AL Metro Area	-1,145	875	9,333	8,458	-1,925	572	-2,497	-0.7	7,915	5.4
Decatur, IL Metro Area	-3,465	941	7,082	6,141	-4,207	429	-4,636	-3.1	-3,922	-3.4
Deltona-Daytona Beach-Ormond Beach, FL Metro Area	32,986	-10,616	28,888	39,504	42,799	6,656	36,143	5.6	97,090	19.7
Denver-Aurora-Lakewood, CO Metro Area	270,730	97,745	183,019	85,274	169,823	34,858	134,965	10.6	364,124	16.7
Des Moines-West Des Moines, IA Metro Area	53,266	23,591	45,668	22,077	29,159	8,165	20,994	9.4	88,234	18.3
Detroit-Warren-Dearborn, MI Metro Area	5,730	55,465	264,327	208,862	-47,620	63,013	-110,633	0.1	-156,465	-3.5
Detroit-Dearborn-Livonia, MI Metro Division	-61,306	29,875	123,577	93,702	-89,890	22,210	-112,100	-3.4	-240,539	-11.7
Warren-Troy-Farmington Hills, MI Metro Division	67,036	25,590	140,750	115,160	42,270	40,803	1,467	2.7	84,074	3.5
Dothan, AL Metro Area	2,532	860	9,246	8,386	1,665	281	1,384	1.7	14,811	11.3
Dover, DE Metro Area	11,184	3,765	11,447	7,682	7,173	1,929	5,244	6.9	35,578	28.1
Dubuque, IA Metro Area	3,472	1,695	6,293	4,598	1,744	555	1,189	3.7	4,520	5.1
Duluth, MN-WI Metro Area	-170	128	15,020	14,892	115	1,078	-963	-0.1	4,192	1.5
Durham-Chapel Hill, NC Metro Area	45,862	15,631	34,537	18,906	29,255	12,220	17,035	9.1	82,773	19.5
East Stroudsburg, PA Metro Area	-3,445	328	7,487	7,159	-3,585	1,532	-5,117	-2.0	31,227	22.5
Eau Claire, WI Metro Area	4,246	3,149	9,998	6,849	1,205	566	639	2.6	13,045	8.8
El Centro, CA Metro Area	5,663	11,110	16,150	5,040	-5,747	1,777	-7,524	3.2	32,194	22.6
Elizabethtown-Fort Knox, KY Metro Area	253	4,239	10,756	6,517	-4,256	2,163	-6,419	0.2	14,370	10.7
Elkhart-Goshen, IN Metro Area	5,913	7,510	15,789	8,279	-1,498	661	-2,159	3.0	14,768	8.1
Elmira, NY Metro Area	-1,771	367	5,176	4,809	-2,066	500	-2,566	-2.0	-2,277	-2.5
El Paso, TX Metro Area	34,849	46,432	72,178	25,746	-11,748	14,831	-26,579	4.3	121,206	17.7
Enid, OK Metro Area	2,989	1,495	5,067	3,572	1,539	1,199	340	4.9	2,769	4.8
Erie, PA Metro Area	-2,521	2,222	16,756	14,534	-4,356	2,845	-7,201	-0.9	-341	-0.1
Eugene, OR Metro Area	11,180	1,270	18,637	17,367	9,570	3,712	5,858	3.2	28,704	8.9
Evansville, IN-KY Metro Area	4,141	3,418	19,872	16,454	1,017	1,306	-289	1.3	15,316	5.2
Fairbanks, AK Metro Area	2,050	6,558	8,969	2,411	-4,546	2,054	-6,600	2.1	14,732	17.8
Fargo, ND-MN Metro Area	25,059	9,448	16,762	7,314	15,192	4,257	10,935	12.0	34,379	19.7
Farmington, NM Metro Area	-11,308	4,996	9,862	4,866	-16,381	144	-16,525	-8.7	16,233	14.3
Fayetteville, NC Metro Area	10,126	20,984	34,895	13,911	-11,417	10,106	-21,523	2.8	29,697	8.8
Fayetteville-Springdale-Rogers, AR-MO Metro Area	50,352	19,211	37,079	17,868	30,385	7,836	22,549	10.9	116,167	33.5
Flagstaff, AZ Metro Area	4,660	5,064	8,997	3,933	-477	756	-1,233	3.5	18,117	15.6
Flint, MI Metro Area	-14,941	3,901	26,341	22,440	-18,632	1,251	-19,883	-3.5	-10,423	-2.4
Florence, SC Metro Area	877	1,579	13,477	11,898	-531	547	-1,078	0.4	12,418	6.4

¹Includes residual not shown separately.

Table B-2. Components of Population Change—*Continued*

Metropolitan statistical area and division	Components of population change, April 1, 2010 (estimates base) to July 1, 2015								Population change, April 1, 2000 to April 1, 2010	
	Number									
	Total population change[1]	Natural increase			Total migration	Net International migration	Net domestic migration	Percent change	Number	Percent change
		Total	Births	Deaths						
Florence-Muscle Shoals, AL Metro Area	-187	-1,089	8,057	9,146	1,070	397	673	-0.1	4,206	2.9
Fond du Lac, WI Metro Area	340	970	5,818	4,848	-533	696	-1,229	0.3	4,349	4.5
Fort Collins, CO Metro Area	33,947	7,669	17,937	10,268	25,303	2,447	22,856	11.3	48,141	19.1
Fort Smith, AR-OK Metro Area	-274	3,015	18,310	15,295	-3,309	1,253	-4,562	-0.1	25,111	9.8
Fort Wayne, IN Metro Area	13,566	12,747	31,019	18,272	1,125	4,605	-3,480	3.3	26,152	6.7
Fresno, CA Metro Area	44,409	49,889	83,845	33,956	-5,826	9,989	-15,815	4.8	131,686	16.5
Gadsden, AL Metro Area	-1,370	-1,129	6,162	7,291	-210	236	-446	-1.3	979	0.9
Gainesville, FL Metro Area	12,889	5,847	16,101	10,254	6,813	7,322	-509	4.9	31,881	13.7
Gainesville, GA Metro Area	13,851	6,364	13,258	6,894	7,160	1,380	5,780	7.7	40,069	28.7
Gettysburg, PA Metro Area	878	402	5,385	4,983	202	429	-227	0.9	10,210	11.2
Glens Falls, NY Metro Area	-2,003	-175	6,433	6,608	-1,642	246	-1,888	-1.6	4,626	3.7
Goldsboro, NC Metro Area	1,509	3,044	8,988	5,944	-1,505	1,773	-3,278	1.2	9,174	8.1
Grand Forks, ND-MN Metro Area	3,988	2,978	7,222	4,244	925	1,835	-910	4.1	972	1.0
Grand Island, NE Metro Area	3,216	2,492	6,345	3,853	736	1,771	-1,035	3.9	4,115	5.3
Grand Junction, CO Metro Area	1,790	2,505	9,653	7,148	-856	365	-1,221	1.2	29,784	25.5
Grand Rapids-Wyoming, MI Metro Area	49,643	33,738	71,624	37,886	15,943	9,341	6,602	5.0	58,060	6.2
Grants Pass, OR Metro Area	2,032	-1,712	4,335	6,047	3,687	7	3,680	2.5	6,984	9.2
Great Falls, MT Metro Area	951	2,036	6,223	4,187	-1,085	767	-1,852	1.2	971	1.2
Greeley, CO Metro Area	32,343	12,217	20,309	8,092	19,457	1,521	17,936	12.8	72,065	39.9
Green Bay, WI Metro Area	10,278	8,612	20,764	12,152	1,781	2,299	-518	3.4	23,752	8.4
Greensboro-High Point, NC Metro Area	28,359	11,697	45,437	33,740	16,597	9,043	7,554	3.9	80,429	12.5
Greenville, NC Metro Area	7,694	5,005	11,192	6,187	2,731	1,354	1,377	4.6	34,389	25.7
Greenville-Anderson-Mauldin, SC Metro Area	50,762	13,918	54,507	40,589	35,326	7,590	27,736	6.2	98,563	13.6
Gulfport-Biloxi-Pascagoula, MS Metro Area	18,468	7,152	25,538	18,386	11,066	4,533	6,533	5.0	6,826	1.9
Hagerstown-Martinsburg, MD-WV Metro Area	9,884	3,759	16,319	12,560	5,881	1,778	4,103	3.9	43,792	21.1
Hammond, LA Metro Area	7,654	3,931	9,982	6,051	3,574	528	3,046	6.3	20,620	20.5
Hanford-Corcoran, CA Metro Area	-2,017	8,545	12,779	4,234	-10,754	1,884	-12,638	-1.3	23,512	18.2
Harrisburg-Carlisle, PA Metro Area	15,533	7,839	34,328	26,489	8,070	8,336	-266	2.8	40,462	7.9
Harrisonburg, VA Metro Area	5,914	2,333	7,258	4,925	3,174	2,188	986	4.7	17,002	15.7
Hartford-West Hartford-East Hartford, CT Metro Area	-1,063	9,474	63,398	53,924	-8,800	28,349	-37,149	-0.1	63,738	5.5
Hattiesburg, MS Metro Area	5,982	4,110	10,543	6,433	1,648	658	990	4.2	18,935	15.3
Hickory-Lenoir-Morganton, NC Metro Area	-2,982	-238	19,801	20,039	-2,924	1,602	-4,526	-0.8	23,638	6.9
Hilton Head Island-Bluffton-Beaufort, SC Metro Area	20,403	4,064	12,552	8,488	15,819	3,007	12,812	10.9	45,407	32.1
Hinesville, GA Metro Area	2,281	6,695	8,778	2,083	-4,783	2,558	-7,341	2.9	5,983	8.3
Homosassa Springs, FL Metro Area	-178	-7,146	5,440	12,586	6,775	434	6,341	-0.1	23,130	19.6
Hot Springs, AR Metro Area	1,177	-1,272	5,784	7,056	2,640	66	2,574	1.2	7,878	8.9
Houma-Thibodaux, LA Metro Area	4,121	5,492	15,200	9,708	-1,250	1,216	-2,466	2.0	13,659	7.0
Houston-The Woodlands-Sugar Land, TX Metro Area	736,454	306,873	494,164	187,291	428,160	172,955	255,205	12.4	1,226,973	26.1
Huntington-Ashland, WV-KY-OH Metro Area	-3,350	172	21,823	21,651	-3,076	844	-3,920	-0.9	2,580	0.7
Huntsville, AL Metro Area	27,159	8,622	26,782	18,160	17,775	3,238	14,537	6.5	74,927	21.9
Idaho Falls, ID Metro Area	6,410	7,926	12,767	4,841	-1,569	321	-1,890	4.8	28,778	27.5
Indianapolis-Carmel-Anderson, IN Metro Area	100,735	59,449	140,019	80,570	42,037	23,856	18,181	5.3	229,643	13.8
Iowa City, IA Metro Area	13,912	6,331	10,961	4,630	7,436	4,840	2,596	9.1	20,924	15.9
Ithaca, NY Metro Area	3,332	1,254	4,636	3,382	2,081	5,898	-3,817	3.3	5,107	5.3
Jackson, MI Metro Area	-754	1,019	9,339	8,320	-1,677	569	-2,246	-0.5	1,822	1.2
Jackson, MS Metro Area	11,132	13,891	40,066	26,175	-2,593	2,862	-5,455	2.0	42,238	8.0
Jackson, TN Metro Area	-327	1,928	8,525	6,597	-2,252	383	-2,635	-0.3	8,040	6.6
Jacksonville, FL Metro Area	103,885	31,688	92,777	61,089	70,439	21,987	48,452	7.7	222,775	19.8
Jacksonville, NC Metro Area	8,539	17,964	22,825	4,861	-9,895	7,840	-17,735	4.8	27,354	18.2
Janesville-Beloit, WI Metro Area	1,117	2,689	10,178	7,489	-1,580	400	-1,980	0.7	8,016	5.3
Jefferson City, MO Metro Area	1,338	2,939	9,482	6,543	-1,500	765	-2,265	0.9	9,774	7.0
Johnson City, TN Metro Area	1,932	-1,040	10,626	11,666	2,774	551	2,223	1.0	17,131	9.4
Johnstown, PA Metro Area	-7,263	-2,519	6,965	9,484	-4,651	301	-4,952	-5.1	-8,881	-5.8
Jonesboro, AR Metro Area	7,368	2,664	9,012	6,348	4,536	798	3,738	6.1	13,270	12.3
Joplin, MO Metro Area	1,695	3,654	12,841	9,187	-2,111	1,148	-3,259	1.0	18,216	11.6
Kahului-Wailuku-Lahaina, HI Metro Area	9,801	4,712	10,707	5,995	5,060	4,048	1,012	6.3	26,688	20.8
Kalamazoo-Portage, MI Metro Area	8,748	6,885	21,323	14,438	1,883	3,284	-1,401	2.7	11,751	3.7
Kankakee, IL Metro Area	-2,570	1,483	7,110	5,627	-4,105	544	-4,649	-2.3	9,624	9.3
Kansas City, MO-KS Metro Area	78,133	60,024	145,098	85,074	18,666	19,578	-912	3.9	197,550	10.9
Kennewick-Richland, WA Metro Area	25,776	13,640	22,249	8,609	11,638	2,049	9,589	10.2	61,489	32.1
Killeen-Temple, TX Metro Area	25,729	26,578	39,785	13,207	-1,479	10,776	-12,255	6.3	74,577	22.5
Kingsport-Bristol-Bristol, TN-VA Metro Area	-2,422	-4,049	15,779	19,828	1,685	312	1,373	-0.8	10,978	3.7
Kingston, NY Metro Area	-2,388	67	8,562	8,495	-2,337	2,074	-4,411	-1.3	4,805	2.7
Knoxville, TN Metro Area	23,845	2,868	48,897	46,029	20,379	3,976	16,403	2.8	89,348	11.9
Kokomo, IN Metro Area	-196	400	5,182	4,782	-590	283	-873	-0.2	-2,209	-2.6
La Crosse-Onalaska, WI-MN Metro Area	3,320	1,716	7,636	5,920	1,496	538	958	2.5	6,784	5.3
Lafayette, LA Metro Area	23,738	14,627	35,682	21,055	9,013	4,284	4,729	5.1	41,767	9.8
Lafayette-West Lafayette, IN Metro Area	12,565	6,277	13,396	7,119	6,507	8,238	-1,731	6.2	23,249	13.0

[1]Includes residual not shown separately.

Table B-2. Components of Population Change—*Continued*

Metropolitan statistical area and division	Components of population change, April 1, 2010 (estimates base) to July 1, 2015								Population change, April 1, 2000 to April 1, 2010	
	Number									
	Total population change[1]	Natural increase			Total migration	Net International migration	Net domestic migration	Percent change	Number	Percent change
		Total	Births	Deaths						
Lake Charles, LA Metro Area	5,976	4,385	14,560	10,175	1,809	985	824	3.0	6,058	3.1
Lake Havasu City-Kingman, AZ Metro Area	4,551	-3,827	9,767	13,594	7,699	170	7,529	2.3	45,205	29.2
Lakeland-Winter Haven, FL Metro Area	47,997	6,420	38,488	32,068	40,367	14,979	25,388	8.0	118,207	24.4
Lancaster, PA Metro Area	17,176	12,627	37,164	24,537	4,010	6,970	-2,960	3.3	48,665	10.3
Lansing-East Lansing, MI Metro Area	8,244	8,889	27,466	18,577	-659	11,253	-11,912	1.8	16,187	3.6
Laredo, TX Metro Area	19,417	22,476	28,941	6,465	-2,935	3,966	-6,901	7.8	57,180	29.6
Las Cruces, NM Metro Area	5,054	8,436	16,207	7,771	-3,594	1,062	-4,656	2.4	34,361	19.6
Las Vegas-Henderson-Paradise, NV Metro Area	163,532	63,399	139,109	75,710	96,780	36,388	60,392	8.4	575,528	41.8
Lawrence, KS Metro Area	7,227	3,233	6,484	3,251	3,976	3,220	756	6.5	10,873	10.9
Lawton, OK Metro Area	353	5,367	10,923	5,556	-5,105	3,121	-8,226	0.3	8,692	7.1
Lebanon, PA Metro Area	3,490	996	8,500	7,504	2,347	2,284	63	2.6	13,375	11.1
Lewiston, ID-WA Metro Area	1,265	21	3,770	3,749	1,297	109	1,188	2.1	2,917	5.0
Lewiston-Auburn, ME Metro Area	-469	1,447	6,801	5,354	-1,896	648	-2,544	-0.4	3,899	3.8
Lexington-Fayette, KY Metro Area	28,436	13,947	32,906	18,959	14,605	7,575	7,030	6.0	63,688	15.6
Lima, OH Metro Area	-1,906	1,115	6,738	5,623	-2,976	375	-3,351	-1.8	-2,133	-2.0
Lincoln, NE Metro Area	21,421	11,330	22,320	10,990	9,770	5,214	4,556	7.1	35,359	13.3
Little Rock-North Little Rock-Conway, AR Metro Area	31,789	18,484	51,384	32,900	13,198	5,310	7,888	4.5	89,353	14.6
Logan, UT-ID Metro Area	8,415	10,563	13,635	3,072	-2,262	1,670	-3,932	6.7	22,720	22.1
Longview, TX Metro Area	3,397	4,451	15,974	11,523	-999	1,490	-2,489	1.6	20,338	10.5
Longview, WA Metro Area	1,058	700	6,230	5,530	227	236	-9	1.0	9,465	10.2
Los Angeles-Long Beach-Anaheim, CA Metro Area	511,102	467,873	882,218	414,345	54,525	334,867	-280,342	4.0	463,369	3.7
Anaheim-Santa Ana-Irvine, CA Metro Division	159,510	101,053	198,487	97,434	58,490	69,224	-10,734	5.3	163,984	5.8
Los Angeles-Long Beach-Glendale, CA Metro Division	351,592	366,820	683,731	316,911	-3,965	265,643	-269,608	3.6	299,385	3.1
Louisville/Jefferson County, KY-IN Metro Area	42,703	22,004	82,854	60,850	21,756	13,003	8,753	3.5	114,189	10.2
Lubbock, TX Metro Area	20,349	9,557	22,182	12,625	10,396	2,350	8,046	7.0	34,542	13.5
Lynchburg, VA Metro Area	7,291	1,734	14,938	13,204	5,441	1,864	3,577	2.9	30,539	13.7
Macon, GA Metro Area	-2,197	3,581	15,994	12,413	-5,935	1,139	-7,074	-0.9	9,814	4.4
Madera, CA Metro Area	4,133	7,004	12,400	5,396	-2,625	914	-3,539	2.7	27,686	22.5
Madison, WI Metro Area	35,948	17,324	38,885	21,561	17,804	9,580	8,224	5.9	69,984	13.1
Manchester-Nashua, NH Metro Area	5,957	7,183	22,839	15,656	-1,179	5,506	-6,685	1.5	19,865	5.2
Manhattan, KS Metro Area	5,810	4,923	7,485	2,562	696	4,187	-3,491	6.3	11,573	14.3
Mankato-North Mankato, MN Metro Area	2,394	2,430	5,959	3,529	-30	783	-813	2.5	11,029	12.9
Mansfield, OH Metro Area	-2,768	222	7,345	7,123	-2,961	188	-3,149	-2.2	-4,457	-3.5
McAllen-Edinburg-Mission, TX Metro Area	67,530	64,456	84,955	20,499	2,143	10,656	-8,513	8.7	205,675	36.1
Medford, OR Metro Area	9,361	591	12,227	11,636	8,380	367	8,013	4.6	21,925	12.1
Memphis, TN-MS-AR Metro Area	19,298	40,479	99,039	58,560	-20,849	9,618	-30,467	1.5	111,544	9.2
Merced, CA Metro Area	12,657	13,851	22,292	8,441	-893	2,581	-3,474	4.9	44,620	21.1
Miami-Fort Lauderdale-West Palm Beach, FL Metro Area	446,032	102,280	350,163	247,883	338,296	335,637	2,659	8.0	558,343	11.1
Fort Lauderdale-Pompano Beach-Deerfield Beach, FL Metro Division	148,277	35,914	112,725	76,811	112,114	81,778	30,336	8.5	125,174	7.7
Miami-Miami Beach-Kendall, FL Metro Division	195,100	64,003	163,446	99,443	128,596	211,162	-82,566	7.8	244,224	10.8
West Palm Beach-Boca Raton-Delray Beach, FL Metro Division	102,655	2,363	73,992	71,629	97,586	42,697	54,889	7.8	188,945	16.7
Michigan City-La Porte, IN Metro Area	-583	924	6,913	5,989	-1,367	223	-1,590	-0.5	1,368	1.2
Midland, MI Metro Area	3	805	4,467	3,662	-811	818	-1,629	0.0	832	1.0
Midland, TX Metro Area	25,044	8,368	13,926	5,558	16,583	790	15,793	17.7	20,894	17.3
Milwaukee-Waukesha-West Allis, WI Metro Area	19,793	36,606	104,969	68,363	-15,692	15,537	-31,229	1.3	55,166	3.7
Minneapolis-St. Paul-Bloomington, MN-WI Metro Area	175,726	125,864	239,665	113,801	51,228	59,720	-8,492	5.2	316,517	10.4
Missoula, MT Metro Area	4,882	2,267	6,518	4,251	2,558	547	2,011	4.5	13,496	14.1
Mobile, AL Metro Area	2,252	7,084	29,262	22,178	-4,688	3,259	-7,947	0.5	13,256	3.3
Modesto, CA Metro Area	23,937	20,260	40,301	20,041	3,253	6,858	-3,605	4.7	67,601	15.1
Monroe, LA Metro Area	2,736	4,204	13,334	9,130	-1,531	603	-2,134	1.6	6,448	3.8
Monroe, MI Metro Area	-2,453	935	8,146	7,211	-3,420	370	-3,790	-1.6	6,082	4.2
Montgomery, AL Metro Area	-737	7,320	25,272	17,952	-8,232	2,742	-10,974	-0.2	27,958	8.1
Morgantown, WV Metro Area	8,467	2,239	7,428	5,189	6,273	1,802	4,471	6.5	18,508	16.6
Morristown, TN Metro Area	2,531	91	6,815	6,724	2,337	515	1,822	2.2	11,667	11.4
Mount Vernon-Anacortes, WA Metro Area	4,945	1,740	7,601	5,861	3,033	646	2,387	4.2	13,884	13.5
Muncie, IN Metro Area	-819	420	6,640	6,220	-1,119	859	-1,978	-0.7	-1,098	-0.9
Muskegon, MI Metro Area	602	2,457	11,180	8,723	-1,960	360	-2,320	0.3	1,980	1.2
Myrtle Beach-Conway-North Myrtle Beach, SC-NC Metro Area	55,242	219	21,658	21,439	54,080	1,883	52,197	14.7	107,043	39.7
Napa, CA Metro Area	5,926	1,456	7,810	6,354	4,354	2,413	1,941	4.3	12,186	9.8
Naples-Immokalee-Marco Island, FL Metro Area	35,785	1,050	16,903	15,853	34,572	10,816	23,756	11.1	70,108	27.9
Nashville-Davidson—Murfreesboro—Franklin, TN Metro Area	159,449	51,809	121,373	69,564	105,958	22,079	83,879	9.5	289,484	21.0
New Bern, NC Metro Area	-557	2,663	9,302	6,639	-3,580	2,416	-5,996	-0.4	12,069	10.5
New Haven-Milford, CT Metro Area	-3,004	7,614	47,416	39,802	-9,854	19,378	-29,232	-0.3	38,481	4.7

[1]Includes residual not shown separately.

Table B-2. Components of Population Change—*Continued*

Metropolitan statistical area and division	Components of population change, April 1, 2010 (estimates base) to July 1, 2015 — Number								Population change, April 1, 2000 to April 1, 2010	
	Total population change[1]	Natural increase — Total	Natural increase — Births	Natural increase — Deaths	Total migration	Net International migration	Net domestic migration	Percent change	Number	Percent change
New Orleans-Metairie, LA Metro Area	73,025	26,015	82,050	56,035	45,886	17,311	28,575	6.1	-147,877	-11.1
New York-Newark-Jersey City, NY-NJ-PA Metro Area	615,918	571,303	1,317,457	746,154	73,211	773,841	-700,630	3.1	620,499	3.3
Dutchess County-Putnam County, NY Metro Division	-2,402	2,422	18,567	16,145	-4,838	5,733	-10,571	-0.6	21,435	5.7
Nassau County-Suffolk County, NY Metro Division	29,884	38,365	157,818	119,453	-4,763	48,583	-53,346	1.1	79,049	2.9
Newark, NJ-PA Metro Division	41,701	51,681	147,831	96,150	-7,255	73,216	-80,471	1.7	74,651	3.1
New York-Jersey City-White Plains, NY-NJ Metro Division	546,735	478,835	993,241	514,406	90,067	646,309	-556,242	3.9	445,364	3.3
Niles-Benton Harbor, MI Metro Area	-2,181	1,159	9,810	8,651	-3,263	1,703	-4,966	-1.4	-5,674	-3.5
North Port-Sarasota-Bradenton, FL Metro Area	66,650	-12,548	33,088	45,636	77,820	10,659	67,161	9.5	112,270	19.0
Norwich-New London, CT Metro Area	-2,183	2,175	14,404	12,229	-4,063	6,516	-10,579	-0.8	14,938	5.8
Ocala, FL Metro Area	11,950	-6,254	17,540	23,794	17,207	2,679	14,528	3.6	72,431	28.0
Ocean City, NJ Metro Area	-2,538	-2,068	4,690	6,758	-279	1,231	-1,510	-2.6	-5,058	-4.9
Odessa, TX Metro Area	22,303	8,413	14,509	6,096	13,854	625	13,229	16.3	16,009	13.2
Ogden-Clearfield, UT Metro Area	45,691	38,281	56,593	18,312	7,361	3,986	3,375	7.7	111,749	23.0
Oklahoma City, OK Metro Area	105,460	41,907	99,964	58,057	62,378	15,718	46,660	8.4	157,439	14.4
Olympia-Tumwater, WA Metro Area	17,272	5,784	16,252	10,468	11,409	3,952	7,457	6.8	44,872	21.6
Omaha-Council Bluffs, NE-IA Metro Area	49,956	35,608	69,281	33,673	15,351	11,348	4,003	5.8	98,181	12.8
Orlando-Kissimmee-Sanford, FL Metro Area	252,733	60,535	142,721	82,186	189,354	86,472	102,882	11.8	489,896	29.8
Oshkosh-Neenah, WI Metro Area	2,552	2,426	9,868	7,442	34	623	-589	1.5	10,242	6.5
Owensboro, KY Metro Area	2,709	1,827	8,068	6,241	868	326	542	2.4	4,875	4.4
Oxnard-Thousand Oaks-Ventura, CA Metro Area	27,149	27,863	55,951	28,088	-1,072	9,319	-10,391	3.3	70,157	9.3
Palm Bay-Melbourne-Titusville, FL Metro Area	24,710	-6,934	26,746	33,680	30,354	6,149	24,205	4.5	67,079	14.1
Panama City, FL Metro Area	12,791	2,465	12,448	9,983	9,738	1,780	7,958	6.9	21,897	13.4
Parkersburg-Vienna, WV Metro Area	-341	-156	5,538	5,694	-21	57	-78	-0.4	-1,146	-1.2
Pensacola-Ferry Pass-Brent, FL Metro Area	29,052	6,641	29,907	23,266	21,708	6,131	15,577	6.5	36,824	8.9
Peoria, IL Metro Area	-1,168	6,006	25,614	19,608	-6,928	2,392	-9,320	-0.3	12,275	3.3
Philadelphia-Camden-Wilmington, PA-NJ-DE-MD Metro Area	104,496	100,215	379,426	279,211	8,078	107,790	-99,712	1.8	279,050	4.9
Camden, NJ Metro Division	1,934	16,916	73,475	56,559	-14,381	15,797	-30,178	0.2	64,344	5.4
Montgomery County-Bucks County-Chester County, PA Metro Division	38,285	19,554	106,720	87,166	18,084	24,373	-6,289	2.0	144,120	8.1
Philadelphia, PA Metro Division	46,604	50,403	154,714	104,311	-330	57,344	-57,674	2.2	15,448	0.7
Wilmington, DE-MD-NJ Metro Division	17,673	13,342	44,517	31,175	4,705	10,276	-5,571	2.5	55,138	8.5
Phoenix-Mesa-Scottsdale, AZ Metro Area	381,404	154,367	310,615	156,248	220,111	57,686	162,425	9.1	941,243	28.9
Pine Bluff, AR Metro Area	-6,562	569	6,077	5,508	-7,062	130	-7,192	-6.5	-7,081	-6.6
Pittsburgh, PA Metro Area	-3,238	-15,846	125,987	141,833	15,854	18,563	-2,709	-0.1	-74,950	-3.1
Pittsfield, MA Metro Area	-3,444	-1,569	5,865	7,434	-1,754	996	-2,750	-2.6	-3,650	-2.7
Pocatello, ID Metro Area	905	3,465	6,906	3,441	-2,544	558	-3,102	1.1	7,277	9.6
Portland-South Portland, ME Metro Area	12,195	2,072	26,324	24,252	9,426	3,982	5,444	2.4	26,592	5.5
Portland-Vancouver-Hillsboro, OR-WA Metro Area	163,217	61,207	146,121	84,914	99,139	28,913	70,226	7.3	298,107	15.5
Port St. Lucie, FL Metro Area	30,739	-2,544	22,002	24,546	32,613	5,284	27,329	7.2	104,651	32.8
Prescott, AZ Metro Area	11,240	-4,412	9,717	14,129	15,180	880	14,300	5.3	43,638	26.1
Providence-Warwick, RI-MA Metro Area	11,854	10,923	87,599	76,676	1,766	27,410	-25,644	0.7	18,255	1.2
Provo-Orem, UT Metro Area	58,913	52,534	63,888	11,354	6,216	4,764	1,452	11.2	150,111	39.8
Pueblo, CO Metro Area	4,528	1,366	9,975	8,609	3,038	367	2,671	2.8	17,573	12.4
Punta Gorda, FL Metro Area	13,124	-6,987	5,336	12,323	19,957	1,422	18,535	8.2	18,371	13.0
Racine, WI Metro Area	-348	3,794	12,624	8,830	-4,011	710	-4,721	-0.2	6,579	3.5
Raleigh, NC Metro Area	143,077	46,624	80,989	34,365	94,090	21,715	72,375	12.7	333,303	41.8
Rapid City, SD Metro Area	9,525	4,635	10,217	5,582	4,784	876	3,908	7.1	14,492	12.1
Reading, PA Metro Area	3,699	6,156	25,594	19,438	-1,904	7,136	-9,040	0.9	37,860	10.1
Redding, CA Metro Area	2,310	144	11,128	10,984	1,787	1,076	711	1.3	13,981	8.6
Reno, NV Metro Area	25,453	9,752	28,393	18,641	15,010	4,087	10,923	6.0	82,556	24.1
Richmond, VA Metro Area	63,254	25,560	77,847	52,287	36,940	18,944	17,996	5.2	152,284	14.4
Riverside-San Bernardino-Ontario, CA Metro Area	264,187	173,586	320,572	146,986	86,701	42,369	44,332	6.3	970,173	29.8
Roanoke, VA Metro Area	5,878	-73	17,496	17,569	5,624	4,576	1,048	1.9	20,312	7.0
Rochester, MN Metro Area	6,996	7,498	15,272	7,774	-686	3,043	-3,729	3.4	22,132	12.0
Rochester, NY Metro Area	2,259	11,726	61,717	49,991	-9,207	16,005	-25,212	0.2	17,173	1.6
Rockford, IL Metro Area	-8,768	5,758	21,850	16,092	-14,334	2,035	-16,369	-2.5	29,202	9.1
Rocky Mount, NC Metro Area	-4,321	870	9,155	8,285	-5,241	271	-5,512	-2.8	9,408	6.6
Rome, GA Metro Area	187	920	6,228	5,308	-673	607	-1,280	0.2	5,695	6.3
Sacramento—Roseville—Arden-Arcade, CA Metro Area	125,051	59,525	144,413	84,888	63,264	37,057	26,207	5.8	352,321	19.6
Saginaw, MI Metro Area	-6,862	1,336	12,013	10,677	-8,039	981	-9,020	-3.4	-9,882	-4.7
St. Cloud, MN Metro Area	5,325	6,530	13,144	6,614	-1,071	1,362	-2,433	2.8	21,652	12.9
St. George, UT Metro Area	17,487	5,914	11,792	5,878	11,397	247	11,150	12.7	47,790	52.9
St. Joseph, MO-KS Metro Area	-449	1,321	8,151	6,830	-1,725	1,056	-2,781	-0.4	3,488	2.8
St. Louis, MO-IL Metro Area	23,840	47,189	179,251	132,062	-22,381	23,704	-46,085	0.9	112,186	4.2
Salem, OR Metro Area	19,353	10,512	27,656	17,144	8,423	2,072	6,351	5.0	43,482	12.5

[1]Includes residual not shown separately.

Table B-2.   Components of Population Change—*Continued*

Metropolitan statistical area and division	Total population change[1]	Natural increase Total	Births	Deaths	Total migration	Net Inter-national migration	Net domestic migration	Percent change	Number	Percent change
Salinas, CA Metro Area	18,841	22,446	35,039	12,593	-3,146	5,957	-9,103	4.5	13,305	3.3
Salisbury, MD-DE Metro Area	21,536	817	21,846	21,029	20,330	5,400	14,930	5.8	61,327	19.6
Salt Lake City, UT Metro Area	82,467	66,722	99,896	33,174	16,801	17,115	-314	7.6	148,630	15.8
San Angelo, TX Metro Area	7,836	2,951	8,205	5,254	4,961	1,099	3,862	7.0	6,043	5.7
San Antonio-New Braunfels, TX Metro Area	241,557	85,473	167,339	81,866	152,107	30,429	121,678	11.3	430,940	25.2
San Diego-Carlsbad, CA Metro Area	204,213	124,071	231,748	107,677	78,523	84,767	-6,244	6.6	281,469	10.0
San Francisco-Oakland-Hayward, CA Metro Area	320,572	118,724	272,905	154,181	207,569	150,464	57,105	7.4	211,826	5.1
Oakland-Hayward-Berkeley, CA Metro Division	205,502	77,380	166,442	89,062	130,125	82,179	47,946	8.0	166,888	7.0
San Francisco-Redwood City-South San Francisco, CA Metro Division	106,258	38,943	94,242	55,299	70,400	63,884	6,516	7.0	39,830	2.7
San Rafael, CA Metro Division	8,812	2,401	12,221	9,820	7,044	4,401	2,643	3.5	5,108	2.1
San Jose-Sunnyvale-Santa Clara, CA Metro Area	139,895	76,145	128,416	52,271	67,029	92,657	-25,628	7.6	100,946	5.8
San Luis Obispo-Paso Robles-Arroyo Grande, CA Metro Area	11,808	2,249	14,003	11,754	9,089	1,190	7,899	4.4	22,847	9.3
Santa Cruz-Watsonville, CA Metro Area	11,784	6,794	16,009	9,215	4,827	1,995	2,832	4.5	6,748	2.6
Santa Fe, NM Metro Area	4,515	1,602	7,188	5,586	2,689	2,088	601	3.1	14,867	11.5
Santa Maria-Santa Barbara, CA Metro Area	20,830	14,758	30,292	15,534	5,940	7,673	-1,733	4.9	24,646	6.2
Santa Rosa, CA Metro Area	18,266	6,069	27,027	20,958	11,478	3,127	8,351	3.8	25,294	5.5
Savannah, GA Metro Area	31,578	11,805	26,860	15,055	19,131	5,107	14,024	9.1	54,297	18.5
Scranton—Wilkes-Barre—Hazleton, PA Metro Area	-5,464	-6,673	29,680	36,353	1,903	6,517	-4,614		2,837	0.5
Seattle-Tacoma-Bellevue, WA Metro Area	293,765	116,672	239,087	122,415	176,382	100,201	76,181	8.5	395,881	13.0
Seattle-Bellevue-Everett, WA Metro Division	245,040	89,297	180,104	90,807	155,713	88,547	67,166	9.3	301,468	12.9
Tacoma-Lakewood, WA Metro Division	48,725	27,375	58,983	31,608	20,669	11,654	9,015	6.1	94,413	13.5
Sebastian-Vero Beach, FL Metro Area	9,891	-3,049	6,624	9,673	12,758	1,427	11,331	7.2	25,151	22.3
Sebring, FL Metro Area	705	-2,905	4,716	7,621	3,525	1,132	2,393	0.7	11,395	13.0
Sheboygan, WI Metro Area	62	1,098	6,645	5,547	-1,165	540	-1,705	0.1	2,844	2.5
Sherman-Denison, TX Metro Area	4,594	933	7,888	6,955	3,638	788	2,850	3.8	10,299	9.3
Shreveport-Bossier City, LA Metro Area	3,897	10,523	33,826	23,303	-6,454	2,574	-9,028	0.9	22,024	5.3
Sierra Vista-Douglas, AZ Metro Area	-4,930	2,306	8,722	6,416	-7,351	1,780	-9,131	-3.8	13,614	11.6
Sioux City, IA-NE-SD Metro Area	506	5,014	12,757	7,743	-4,255	1,629	-5,884	0.3	703	0.4
Sioux Falls, SD Metro Area	23,590	11,277	19,990	8,713	11,912	3,482	8,430	10.3	41,113	22.0
South Bend-Mishawaka, IN-MI Metro Area	883	5,427	21,107	15,680	-4,220	2,732	-6,952	0.3	2,562	0.8
Spartanburg, SC Metro Area	11,811	3,647	20,406	16,759	8,044	1,215	6,829	3.8	29,372	10.3
Spokane-Spokane Valley, WA Metro Area	20,071	9,320	34,236	24,916	10,411	4,610	5,801	3.8	57,997	12.3
Springfield, IL Metro Area	986	2,221	12,926	10,705	-1,090	1,324	-2,414	0.5	8,713	4.3
Springfield, MA Metro Area	10,277	5,382	34,111	28,729	5,542	19,471	-13,929	1.7	13,188	2.2
Springfield, MO Metro Area	19,743	8,855	29,715	20,860	10,401	1,706	8,695	4.5	68,262	18.5
Springfield, OH Metro Area	-2,374	-302	8,393	8,695	-2,034	304	-2,338	-1.7	-6,409	-4.4
State College, PA Metro Area	6,599	1,800	6,759	4,959	4,868	5,301	-433	4.3	18,303	13.5
Staunton-Waynesboro, VA Metro Area	1,719	-97	6,489	6,586	1,563	398	1,165	1.5	9,549	8.8
Stockton-Lodi, CA Metro Area	40,798	27,059	53,135	26,076	13,029	8,942	4,087	6.0	121,648	21.6
Sumter, SC Metro Area	17	2,586	7,939	5,353	-2,608	919	-3,527	0.0	2,776	2.7
Syracuse, NY Metro Area	-2,131	8,377	38,566	30,189	-9,891	9,936	-19,827	-0.3	12,456	1.9
Tallahassee, FL Metro Area	9,154	7,693	21,231	13,538	1,216	4,273	-3,057	2.5	48,511	15.1
Tampa-St. Petersburg-Clearwater, FL Metro Area	191,711	10,048	164,235	154,187	176,744	59,744	117,000	6.9	387,476	16.2
Terre Haute, IN Metro Area	-1,403	690	10,503	9,813	-2,128	1,043	-3,171	-0.8	1,470	0.9
Texarkana, TX-AR Metro Area	574	2,129	10,293	8,164	-1,416	261	-1,677	0.4	5,816	4.1
The Villages, FL Metro Area	25,471	-4,779	2,414	7,193	30,145	214	29,931	27.3	40,083	75.2
Toledo, OH Metro Area	-4,045	9,388	39,559	30,171	-13,542	3,295	-16,837	-0.7	-8,215	-1.3
Topeka, KS Metro Area	-77	4,064	15,911	11,847	-4,031	895	-4,926	0.0	9,300	4.1
Trenton, NJ Metro Area	3,890	7,472	22,442	14,970	-3,182	13,577	-16,759	1.1	16,735	4.8
Tucson, AZ Metro Area	29,762	16,275	62,878	46,603	12,769	11,894	875	3.0	136,561	16.2
Tulsa, OK Metro Area	43,477	22,373	69,784	47,411	20,540	7,175	13,365	4.6	77,893	9.1
Tuscaloosa, AL Metro Area	9,749	3,967	14,892	10,925	5,647	1,276	4,371	4.2	26,043	12.8
Tyler, TX Metro Area	13,215	5,752	15,984	10,232	7,184	1,715	5,469	6.3	34,860	19.9
Urban Honolulu, HI Metro Area	45,507	32,588	71,809	39,221	13,834	36,923	-23,089	4.8	77,048	8.8
Utica-Rome, NY Metro Area	-3,776	884	17,397	16,513	-4,315	4,187	-8,502	-1.3	-642	-0.2
Valdosta, GA Metro Area	3,210	4,906	10,829	5,923	-2,066	1,580	-3,646	2.3	20,095	16.8
Vallejo-Fairfield, CA Metro Area	22,748	11,468	27,379	15,911	10,833	7,502	3,331	5.5	18,849	4.8
Victoria, TX Metro Area	5,910	2,880	7,239	4,359	3,027	486	2,541	6.3	3,003	3.3
Vineland-Bridgeton, NJ Metro Area	-1,044	3,475	10,987	7,512	-4,179	2,379	-6,558	-0.7	10,444	7.1
Virginia Beach-Norfolk-Newport News, VA-NC Metro Area	48,059	49,582	118,953	69,371	-1,722	30,037	-31,759	2.9	96,214	6.1
Visalia-Porterville, CA Metro Area	17,681	26,300	41,223	14,923	-8,155	1,981	-10,136	4.0	74,171	20.2
Waco, TX Metro Area	10,041	7,818	19,298	11,480	2,380	1,563	817	4.0	20,684	8.9
Walla Walla, WA Metro Area	1,423	626	3,755	3,129	708	365	343	2.3	3,618	6.1
Warner Robins, GA Metro Area	8,544	5,567	12,818	7,251	2,578	2,131	447	4.8	35,559	24.7
Washington-Arlington-Alexandria, DC-VA-MD-WV Metro Area	461,278	251,070	422,676	171,606	211,921	224,507	-12,586	8.2	798,732	16.5

[1]Includes residual not shown separately.

Table B-2.   Components of Population Change—*Continued*

Metropolitan statistical area and division	Components of population change, April 1, 2010 (estimates base) to July 1, 2015								Population change, April 1, 2000 to April 1, 2010	
	Number									
	Total population change[1]	Natural increase			Total migration	Net International migration	Net domestic migration	Percent change	Number	Percent change
		Total	Births	Deaths						
Silver Spring-Frederick-Rockville, MD Metro Division	80,247	44,358	83,461	39,103	36,650	56,163	-19,513	6.7	136,040	12.7
Washington-Arlington-Alexandria, DC-VA-MD-WV Metro Division	381,031	206,712	339,215	132,503	175,271	168,344	6,927	8.6	662,692	17.6
Waterloo-Cedar Falls, IA Metro Area	2,793	3,027	10,945	7,918	-112	1,205	-1,317	1.7	4,098	2.5
Watertown-Fort Drum, NY Metro Area	1,403	6,788	11,491	4,703	-5,617	3,551	-9,168	1.2	4,516	4.0
Wausau, WI Metro Area	1,805	2,535	8,456	5,921	-908	493	-1,401	1.3	8,155	6.5
Weirton-Steubenville, WV-OH Metro Area	-3,943	-2,914	5,874	8,788	-797	78	-875	-3.2	-7,540	-5.7
Wenatchee, WA Metro Area	5,291	2,566	7,635	5,069	2,623	615	2,008	4.8	11,687	11.8
Wheeling, WV-OH Metro Area	-3,751	-1,963	7,839	9,802	-1,455	190	-1,645	-2.5	-5,251	-3.4
Wichita, KS Metro Area	13,691	20,106	48,845	28,739	-6,560	6,633	-13,193	2.2	51,059	8.8
Wichita Falls, TX Metro Area	-696	2,420	10,201	7,781	-3,157	2,565	-5,722	-0.5	-120	-0.1
Williamsport, PA Metro Area	-60	181	6,722	6,541	-162	347	-509	-0.1	-3,895	-3.2
Wilmington, NC Metro Area	23,085	3,353	14,908	11,555	19,017	1,657	17,360	9.1	53,498	26.6
Winchester, VA-WV Metro Area	5,363	2,251	8,097	5,846	3,127	619	2,508	4.2	25,477	24.7
Winston-Salem, NC Metro Area	18,753	7,626	39,237	31,611	10,701	4,618	6,083	2.9	71,222	12.5
Worcester, MA-CT Metro Area	18,560	11,888	51,932	40,044	7,194	20,352	-13,158	2.0	57,870	6.7
Yakima, WA Metro Area	5,599	11,874	21,730	9,856	-6,257	553	-6,810	2.3	20,653	9.3
York-Hanover, PA Metro Area	7,869	6,192	26,031	19,839	2,062	3,710	-1,648	1.8	53,207	13.9
Youngstown-Warren-Boardman, OH-PA Metro Area	-15,919	-6,705	29,566	36,271	-8,422	1,727	-10,149	-2.8	-37,257	-6.2
Yuba City, CA Metro Area	4,063	6,532	13,227	6,695	-2,546	3,204	-5,750	2.4	27,696	19.9
Yuma, AZ Metro Area	8,525	9,185	16,490	7,305	-1,204	3,076	-4,280	4.4	35,755	22.3

[1]Includes residual not shown separately.

Table B-3. Population by Age, Race, and Hispanic Origin

Metropolitan statistical area and division	Under 5 years	5 to 14 years	15 to 24 years	25 to 34 years	35 to 44 years	45 to 54 years	55 to 64 years	65 to 74 years	75 to 84 years	85 years and over	White alone	Black or African American alone	American Indian, Alaska Native alone	Asian alone	Native Hawaiian and Other Pacific Islander alone	Two or more races, not of Hispanic origin (percent)	Hispanic or Latino origin[1] (percent)
Abilene, TX Metro Area	6.8	13.0	17.3	14.5	11.1	11.5	11.2	7.9	4.8	1.9	65.6	7.2	0.4	1.7	0.1	1.8	23.2
Akron, OH Metro Area	5.4	11.6	14.5	12.5	11.5	13.9	14.3	9.2	4.7	2.3	80.8	12.3	0.2	2.8	0.0	2.1	1.8
Albany, GA Metro Area	6.9	13.7	14.4	13.1	12.0	12.6	12.7	8.6	4.1	1.7	42.1	52.7	0.2	1.1	0.1	1.1	2.7
Albany, OR Metro Area	6.1	12.9	12.0	13.0	11.8	12.6	13.9	10.4	5.1	2.1	85.8	0.5	1.1	1.0	0.2	2.7	8.7
Albany-Schenectady-Troy, NY Metro Area	5.2	11.2	15.1	12.7	11.9	14.2	13.8	9.1	4.5	2.4	80.7	7.8	0.2	4.1	0.1	2.1	5.0
Albuquerque, NM Metro Area	6.1	13.0	13.1	14.3	12.4	12.9	13.1	9.0	4.2	1.8	40.2	2.3	5.3	2.1	0.1	1.7	48.3
Alexandrla, LA Metro Area	6.6	13.5	13.2	13.6	12.2	13.0	12.7	8.7	4.6	1.8	63.6	29.4	0.8	1.3	0.0	1.7	3.2
Allentown-Bethlehem-Easton, PA-NJ Metro Area..	5.3	12.2	13.1	12.0	12.0	14.5	13.9	9.4	5.0	2.7	74.9	4.9	0.1	2.9	0.0	1.5	15.7
Altoona, PA Metro Area	5.6	11.5	11.9	11.7	11.5	13.4	14.7	10.6	6.1	3.0	94.8	1.8	0.1	0.7	0.0	1.3	1.3
Amarillo, TX Metro Area	7.4	14.3	13.9	15.0	12.5	12.1	11.9	7.4	4.0	1.6	60.8	6.0	0.5	3.1	0.0	1.5	28.1
Ames, IA Metro Area	4.8	9.4	34.3	13.0	9.3	8.9	9.5	5.9	3.3	1.7	84.7	2.7	0.2	7.8	0.0	1.5	3.1
Anchorage, AK Metro Area	7.4	13.8	15.0	16.9	12.5	12.7	12.1	6.4	2.3	0.8	64.3	4.5	7.2	7.3	1.8	6.8	8.1
Ann Arbor, MI Metro Area	5.2	10.8	21.6	14.2	11.5	12.5	11.7	7.6	3.3	1.6	70.5	12.5	0.3	9.0	0.0	3.1	4.6
Anniston-Oxford-Jacksonville, AL Metro Area	5.8	12.3	13.6	13.0	12.1	13.2	13.8	9.7	4.9	1.8	72.6	20.9	0.4	0.8	0.1	1.6	3.6
Appleton, WI Metro Area	6.3	13.7	12.8	12.7	12.8	15.0	13.1	7.8	4.0	1.8	88.7	1.1	1.3	3.2	0.1	1.4	4.3
Asheville, NC Metro Area	5.0	10.8	11.2	12.1	12.3	13.3	14.4	12.1	6.2	2.7	85.3	4.7	0.4	1.1	0.1	1.6	6.8
Athens-Clarke County, GA Metro Area	5.4	11.3	23.6	14.0	11.7	11.1	10.6	7.4	3.4	1.3	66.3	19.9	0.2	3.7	0.0	1.6	8.3
Atlanta-Sandy Springs-Roswell, GA Metro Area ...	6.5	14.4	13.7	13.9	14.4	14.5	11.5	7.1	3.0	1.1	48.6	33.1	0.2	5.7	0.0	1.8	10.6
Atlantic City-Hammonton, NJ Metro Area	6.0	12.0	13.3	11.9	11.7	14.6	14.1	9.4	4.8	2.1	54.3	14.6	0.2	8.3	0.0	1.8	18.8
Auburn-Opelika, AL Metro Area	5.8	12.0	23.0	14.5	12.1	11.8	10.2	6.6	3.0	1.1	67.5	23.5	0.3	3.4	0.1	1.4	3.8
Augusta-Richmond County, GA-SC Metro Area	6.3	13.3	13.6	14.0	12.0	13.0	13.1	8.9	4.2	1.6	55.2	35.0	0.3	1.9	0.1	2.1	5.4
Austin-Round Rock, TX Metro Area	6.6	13.5	13.8	17.4	15.4	12.9	10.5	6.2	2.6	1.1	53.0	7.1	0.3	5.5	0.1	1.8	32.2
Bakersfield, CA Metro Area	8.2	16.3	15.5	15.2	12.5	11.9	10.3	6.1	2.9	1.1	35.4	5.3	0.6	4.5	0.1	1.9	52.2
Baltimore-Columbia-Towson, MD Metro Area	6.1	12.3	12.9	14.6	12.4	14.2	13.1	8.4	4.0	2.0	57.6	28.8	0.3	5.5	0.1	2.2	5.5
Bangor, ME Metro Area	4.8	10.4	14.2	13.3	11.1	14.2	14.8	9.8	5.1	2.3	94.0	0.9	1.2	1.1	0.0	1.6	1.2
Barnstable Town, MA Metro Area	3.8	8.8	10.2	8.7	8.8	13.7	17.4	15.9	8.5	4.1	91.0	2.5	0.6	1.4	0.0	1.7	2.8
Baton Rouge, LA Metro Area	6.6	13.2	15.7	14.5	12.5	12.7	12.1	7.8	3.5	1.4	57.0	35.5	0.3	2.2	0.0	1.2	3.8
Battle Creek, MI Metro Area	6.2	12.9	13.1	11.9	11.7	13.5	13.9	9.3	5.1	2.4	78.6	10.9	0.6	2.1	0.0	3.0	4.8
Bay City, MI Metro Area	5.1	11.9	11.9	11.9	11.5	13.8	15.2	10.6	5.5	2.7	90.2	1.6	0.5	0.7	0.0	1.9	5.1
Beaumont-Port Arthur, TX Metro Area	6.8	13.2	13.5	13.9	12.4	13.1	12.9	8.1	4.4	1.9	57.2	23.9	0.4	2.7	0.0	1.2	14.6
Beckley, WV Metro Area	6.1	11.6	10.9	11.9	13.1	12.5	15.0	11.0	5.6	2.3	89.2	6.8	0.2	0.8	0.0	1.6	1.4
Bellingham, WA Metro Area	5.5	10.9	18.3	13.0	11.5	12.1	12.8	9.7	4.3	2.0	79.5	1.0	2.5	4.3	0.2	3.3	9.2
Bend-Redmond, OR Metro Area	5.2	12.1	10.7	12.4	12.9	13.0	14.7	11.9	4.9	2.1	87.7	0.4	0.7	1.1	0.1	2.1	7.9
Billings, MT Metro Area	6.2	13.2	12.1	13.6	12.0	12.6	14.0	9.2	4.7	2.4	87.3	0.7	3.7	0.6	0.1	2.4	5.2
Binghamton, NY Metro Area	5.2	11.2	16.8	11.2	10.2	13.4	14.2	9.5	5.6	2.9	86.3	4.3	0.2	3.6	0.0	2.1	3.5
Birmingham-Hoover, AL Metro Area	6.2	13.0	12.5	13.6	13.1	13.4	13.2	8.8	4.3	1.8	63.9	28.8	0.3	1.4	0.0	1.1	4.5
Bismarck, ND Metro Area	6.9	12.8	13.1	14.9	12.1	12.4	13.0	8.0	4.4	2.3	87.7	1.2	6.3	0.6	0.1	1.7	2.4
Blacksburg-Christiansburg-Radford, VA Metro Area	4.6	9.3	24.3	13.1	10.8	11.8	11.6	8.7	4.2	1.7	87.3	4.4	0.2	3.7	0.0	1.8	2.6
Bloomington, IL Metro Area	6.0	12.3	20.5	12.8	12.2	12.3	11.6	7.0	3.6	1.8	81.4	7.0	0.2	4.8	0.0	2.0	4.6
Bloomington, IN Metro Area	4.5	9.2	27.7	14.4	10.3	10.6	10.9	7.3	3.6	1.6	85.5	3.0	0.2	5.9	0.0	2.1	3.3
Bloomsburg-Berwick, PA Metro Area	4.7	10.4	17.6	11.2	10.6	13.1	14.2	9.8	5.7	2.7	92.9	1.8	0.1	1.6	0.0	0.9	2.7
Boise City, ID Metro Area	6.5	15.2	13.3	13.9	13.4	12.7	11.7	8.2	3.6	1.6	80.6	1.0	0.6	2.0	0.2	2.2	13.4
Boston-Cambridge-Newton, MA-NH Metro Area.	5.5	11.3	13.8	14.7	12.6	14.4	13.0	8.3	4.2	2.2	72.2	7.6	0.1	7.8	0.0	1.7	10.6
Boston, MA Metro Division	5.5	11.0	14.3	16.1	12.5	13.9	12.5	8.0	4.1	2.1	66.5	12.8	0.2	7.6	0.1	1.8	11.0
Cambridge-Newton-Framingham, MA Metro Division	5.6	11.5	13.4	14.1	12.8	14.6	13.1	8.3	4.3	2.3	73.3	4.4	0.1	8.9	0.0	1.7	11.6
Rockingham County-Strafford County, NH Metro Division	4.7	11.4	14.3	11.5	11.8	16.1	15.0	9.2	4.2	1.9	92.6	0.8	0.2	2.3	0.0	1.4	2.7
Boulder, CO Metro Area	4.9	11.5	18.8	13.5	12.7	13.3	12.7	7.7	3.3	1.6	78.0	0.9	0.4	4.5	0.1	2.2	13.9
Bowling Green, KY Metro Area	6.3	12.4	18.2	13.0	12.2	12.5	11.8	8.3	3.9	1.5	83.9	7.0	0.2	2.5	0.2	1.9	4.3
Bremerton-Silverdale, WA Metro Area	5.7	11.5	14.2	13.9	11.1	13.0	14.1	10.4	4.2	1.9	77.1	2.8	1.4	5.2	0.9	5.0	7.6
Bridgeport-Stamford-Norwalk, CT Metro Area......	5.6	13.3	13.4	11.5	12.7	15.6	13.2	7.9	4.2	2.4	63.1	10.8	0.1	5.5	0.0	1.4	19.1
Brownsville-Harlingen, TX Metro Area	8.7	17.2	16.0	12.0	12.5	11.1	9.7	7.2	4.1	1.6	9.8	0.4	0.1	0.7	0.0	0.2	88.8
Brunswick, GA Metro Area	5.8	12.8	12.1	11.7	11.7	13.5	14.2	11.2	5.1	1.9	68.0	23.4	0.2	1.2	0.1	1.6	5.5
Buffalo-Cheektowaga-Niagara Falls, NY Metro Area	5.4	11.4	13.4	13.5	11.1	14.0	14.4	9.2	5.0	2.7	77.9	12.0	0.6	3.0	0.0	1.7	4.8
Burlington, NC Metro Area	5.7	13.0	14.0	12.0	12.2	14.1	12.6	9.2	4.9	2.3	65.0	19.0	0.4	1.6	0.0	1.6	12.4
Burlington-South Burlington, VT Metro Area	5.2	10.7	17.5	13.2	11.8	13.9	13.7	8.2	3.8	1.9	90.6	2.0	0.4	2.9	0.0	2.1	2.0
California-Lexington Park, MD Metro Area	6.6	13.9	13.7	14.0	12.3	15.1	12.0	7.3	3.6	1.4	74.9	14.1	0.3	2.8	0.1	2.9	4.9
Canton-Massillon, OH Metro Area	5.5	12.2	12.8	11.6	11.4	13.7	14.6	10.2	5.4	2.7	87.6	7.2	0.2	0.9	0.0	2.2	1.9
Cape Coral-Fort Myers, FL Metro Area	4.7	10.5	10.3	10.8	10.5	12.3	14.0	15.4	8.3	3.2	68.8	8.2	0.2	1.6	0.0	1.2	20.0
Cape Girardeau, MO-IL Metro Area	5.9	12.3	16.8	12.0	11.2	12.4	13.1	9.0	5.1	2.3	85.9	8.5	0.3	1.3	0.0	1.8	2.2
Carbondale-Marion, IL Metro Area	5.5	11.1	18.0	13.9	11.5	11.8	12.4	9.0	4.7	2.1	82.7	9.2	0.3	2.4	0.0	2.1	3.3
Carson City, NV Metro Area	5.2	11.6	11.7	12.2	11.2	13.7	14.6	11.3	5.9	2.6	68.1	1.8	2.0	2.4	0.2	2.1	23.4
Casper, WY Metro Area	7.0	13.5	12.4	15.7	12.6	12.1	13.6	7.5	3.7	1.9	86.6	1.3	1.0	0.8	0.1	1.8	8.4
Cedar Rapids, IA Metro Area	6.2	13.3	13.2	13.0	12.7	13.6	12.9	8.4	4.6	2.2	88.9	4.0	0.2	2.0	0.1	2.0	2.8
Chambersburg-Waynesboro, PA Metro Area	6.1	12.6	11.8	12.0	13.8	13.3	10.3	5.7	2.7	88.7	3.3	0.2	1.0	0.0	1.6	5.2	
Champaign-Urbana, IL Metro Area	5.5	10.6	24.6	14.1	11.0	10.5	11.2	6.8	3.7	1.9	71.8	11.1	0.2	9.2	0.1	2.3	5.3
Charleston, WV Metro Area	5.7	11.4	11.3	11.8	12.5	13.2	15.4	10.7	5.6	2.3	89.3	6.5	0.2	1.0	0.0	2.0	1.0

[1]Persons of Hispanic origin may be any race.

Table B-3. Population by Age, Race, and Hispanic Origin—*Continued*

| | Population characteristics, 2015 | | | | | | | | | | | | | | | |
| Metropolitan statistical area and division | Age (percent) | | | | | | | | | | Race alone, not of Hispanic origin (percent) | | | | | Two or more races, not of Hispanic origin (percent) | Hispanic or Latino origin[1] (percent) |
	Under 5 years	5 to 14 years	15 to 24 years	25 to 34 years	35 to 44 years	45 to 54 years	55 to 64 years	65 to 74 years	75 to 84 years	85 years and over	White alone	Black or African American alone	American Indian, Alaska Native alone	Asian alone	Native Hawaiian and Other Pacific Islander alone		
Charleston-North Charleston, SC Metro Area.......	6.3	12.5	13.0	16.0	12.8	13.2	12.5	8.7	3.6	1.4	64.1	26.3	0.4	1.9	0.1	1.9	5.3
Charlotte-Concord-Gastonia, NC-SC Metro Area...	6.3	13.9	13.1	13.7	14.2	14.4	11.8	7.8	3.5	1.4	62.3	22.2	0.4	3.5	0.0	1.7	9.9
Charlottesville, VA Metro Area..........................	5.4	10.9	15.5	14.2	11.8	12.9	13.1	9.4	4.6	2.1	74.8	13.9	0.2	3.9	0.0	2.2	5.0
Chattanooga, TN-GA Metro Area.......................	5.8	12.1	12.6	13.1	12.6	13.5	13.6	9.8	4.9	2.0	78.5	13.8	0.3	1.7	0.1	1.5	4.1
Cheyenne, WY Metro Area................................	6.5	13.3	13.4	14.6	11.9	12.6	13.0	8.6	4.1	2.0	78.6	2.8	0.7	1.2	0.1	2.1	14.5
Chicago-Naperville-Elgin, IL-IN-WI Metro Area .	6.2	13.2	13.5	14.3	13.4	13.8	12.5	7.6	3.7	1.8	53.4	16.6	0.1	6.5	0.0	1.4	22.0
Chicago-Naperville-Arlington Heights, IL Metro Division	6.3	12.9	13.2	15.0	13.6	13.6	12.4	7.5	3.7	1.8	50.3	18.6	0.1	7.3	0.0	1.4	22.3
Elgin, IL Metro Division..........................	6.4	14.8	15.4	12.3	13.4	13.9	11.7	7.2	3.4	1.5	60.9	5.7	0.1	3.7	0.0	1.3	28.3
Gary, IN Metro Division..........................	6.0	13.4	13.4	12.2	12.7	13.4	13.9	8.7	4.4	2.0	64.0	17.6	0.2	1.4	0.0	1.4	15.4
Lake County-Kenosha County, IL-WI Metro Division....................	5.8	14.3	15.0	11.2	12.8	15.1	13.1	7.4	3.5	1.7	65.4	6.9	0.2	6.2	0.0	1.7	19.6
Chico, CA Metro Area.....................................	5.4	11.3	18.5	12.5	10.4	11.2	13.2	10.0	5.0	2.6	73.0	1.5	1.6	4.5	0.2	3.4	15.8
Cincinnati, OH-KY-IN Metro Area	6.3	13.5	13.5	13.2	12.4	13.9	13.2	8.1	4.1	1.8	80.2	12.3	0.1	2.4	0.1	1.8	3.1
Clarksville, TN-KY Metro Area..........................	8.6	14.4	16.3	18.1	12.4	10.8	9.3	6.0	3.1	1.0	66.1	18.8	0.4	2.1	0.4	3.4	8.8
Cleveland, TN Metro Area...............................	5.6	12.4	13.8	12.2	12.7	14.1	12.7	9.9	5.0	1.6	87.7	4.1	0.3	1.0	0.1	1.6	5.2
Cleveland-Elyria, OH Metro Area	5.6	12.1	12.8	12.3	11.7	14.0	14.5	9.4	5.0	2.6	70.5	19.8	0.2	2.3	0.0	1.8	5.4
Coeur d'Alene, ID Metro Area..........................	6.0	13.2	12.2	12.6	11.8	12.9	13.7	10.6	5.1	1.9	90.9	0.4	1.2	0.9	0.1	2.1	4.4
College Station-Bryan, TX Metro Area.................	6.2	11.5	28.0	15.1	10.5	9.7	9.1	5.7	2.9	1.3	57.5	11.4	0.3	5.0	0.1	1.4	24.3
Colorado Springs, CO Metro Area.....................	6.8	13.6	15.5	15.1	12.3	12.7	11.9	7.4	3.4	1.3	70.5	6.0	0.7	2.7	0.3	3.6	16.2
Columbia, MO Metro Area..............................	6.0	11.2	23.4	15.5	11.5	10.9	10.6	6.4	3.0	1.5	79.5	9.4	0.3	4.7	0.1	2.6	3.4
Columbia, SC Metro Area...............................	5.9	12.7	16.0	13.7	12.5	13.1	12.5	8.4	3.7	1.5	57.1	33.3	0.3	2.1	0.1	1.7	5.4
Columbus, GA-AL Metro Area...........................	7.3	13.0	15.0	15.6	12.4	12.3	11.6	7.5	3.7	1.5	47.9	40.3	0.4	2.0	0.2	2.3	6.9
Columbus, IN Metro Area...............................	6.6	13.5	12.3	13.7	13.0	13.2	12.6	8.7	4.5	1.9	84.2	2.1	0.2	5.8	0.0	1.4	6.3
Columbus, OH Metro Area..............................	6.7	13.3	13.3	15.5	13.5	13.5	12.0	7.3	3.5	1.5	74.6	15.1	0.2	3.8	0.0	2.4	3.9
Corpus Christi, TX Metro Area.........................	6.8	14.0	14.2	14.2	12.2	12.2	12.2	8.3	4.2	1.7	33.9	3.2	0.3	1.8	0.1	0.9	59.8
Corvallis, OR Metro Area................................	4.1	9.5	25.5	12.9	10.0	10.5	12.7	8.7	4.1	2.0	81.6	1.0	0.6	6.1	0.3	3.3	7.1
Crestview-Fort Walton Beach-Destin, FL Metro Area	6.5	11.8	12.2	15.3	11.6	13.1	13.2	9.6	5.0	1.7	76.7	8.6	0.6	2.6	0.2	3.2	8.1
Cumberland, MD-WV Metro Area.......................	4.9	10.1	15.1	12.1	11.6	13.3	13.4	11.0	6.2	2.4	89.1	6.7	0.2	0.9	0.0	1.6	1.5
Dallas-Fort Worth-Arlington, TX Metro Area.......	7.1	15.1	13.7	14.7	14.3	13.7	11.0	6.5	2.9	1.2	47.8	15.3	0.4	6.4	0.1	1.7	28.3
Dallas-Plano-Irving, TX Metro Division	7.1	15.1	13.7	14.9	14.7	13.8	10.8	6.2	2.7	1.1	44.8	16.3	0.4	7.3	0.1	1.6	29.5
Fort Worth-Arlington, TX Metro Division...........	7.0	15.1	13.7	14.3	13.5	13.6	11.5	7.0	3.2	1.3	53.8	13.2	0.4	4.5	0.2	1.7	26.2
Dalton, GA Metro Area....................................	6.8	15.0	14.0	13.0	13.2	13.7	11.2	8.0	3.9	1.3	65.9	3.1	0.2	1.1	0.0	1.1	28.6
Danville, IL Metro Area...................................	6.7	13.3	12.3	11.8	11.7	12.8	13.8	9.8	5.4	2.4	78.8	13.3	0.2	0.8	0.0	2.1	4.8
Daphne-Fairhope-Foley, AL Metro Area...............	5.5	12.5	11.5	11.3	12.4	13.6	13.9	11.6	5.6	2.0	83.0	9.4	0.7	0.9	0.0	1.5	4.5
Davenport-Moline-Rock Island, IA-IL Metro Area .	6.3	12.9	12.4	12.6	12.1	13.1	13.8	9.4	5.0	2.4	79.8	7.2	0.2	2.1	0.0	2.2	8.5
Dayton, OH Metro Area..................................	6.0	12.3	13.6	13.0	11.5	13.2	13.6	9.4	5.1	2.4	77.0	15.6	0.2	2.2	0.0	2.3	2.7
Decatur, AL Metro Area..................................	5.9	12.8	12.1	12.2	12.5	14.5	13.5	9.9	5.0	1.7	76.4	12.0	1.8	0.6	0.0	2.4	6.8
Decatur, IL Metro Area...................................	6.1	12.4	13.0	11.7	11.5	12.6	14.4	10.0	5.5	2.8	76.9	17.0	0.2	1.2	0.0	2.5	2.2
Deltona-Daytona Beach-Ormond Beach, FL Metro Area	4.5	10.1	11.3	10.9	10.4	13.1	15.1	13.8	7.5	3.2	73.5	10.4	0.3	1.9	0.0	1.6	12.3
Denver-Aurora-Lakewood, CO Metro Area...........	6.3	13.4	12.2	16.1	14.4	13.5	12.1	7.3	3.2	1.4	64.7	5.4	0.5	4.1	0.1	2.2	23.0
Des Moines-West Des Moines, IA Metro Area	7.2	14.3	12.6	14.9	13.6	13.3	11.7	7.2	3.5	1.7	81.7	5.2	0.2	3.8	0.1	1.8	7.2
Detroit-Warren-Dearborn, MI Metro Area...........	5.9	12.7	12.9	12.5	12.4	14.6	14.0	8.7	4.2	2.1	67.0	22.3	0.3	4.1	0.0	2.0	4.3
Detroit-Dearborn-Livonia, MI Metro Division....	6.6	13.2	13.7	13.1	12.3	13.7	13.4	8.1	4.0	2.1	50.0	38.6	0.3	3.1	0.0	2.2	5.8
Warren-Troy-Farmington Hills, MI Metro Division	5.4	12.3	12.4	12.1	12.5	15.2	14.4	9.1	4.4	2.2	78.8	11.0	0.3	4.7	0.0	1.9	3.3
Dothan, AL Metro Area...................................	6.0	13.0	11.9	12.4	12.4	13.4	13.4	10.3	5.3	1.9	70.4	23.3	0.5	0.8	0.0	1.6	3.4
Dover, DE Metro Area....................................	6.3	13.0	14.5	13.4	11.6	13.1	12.1	9.5	4.8	1.6	62.8	24.3	0.6	2.2	0.1	3.1	6.9
Dubuque, IA Metro Area.................................	6.2	12.9	14.3	12.7	10.8	13.1	13.4	8.7	5.3	2.5	91.4	3.1	0.2	1.4	0.3	1.3	2.3
Duluth, MN-WI Metro Area	5.2	11.2	15.0	11.9	11.1	13.0	15.2	9.8	5.1	2.5	91.0	1.5	2.6	1.0	0.0	2.3	1.6
Durham-Chapel Hill, NC Metro Area...................	5.9	11.8	15.2	14.9	13.2	12.9	12.4	8.2	3.7	1.8	54.7	26.7	0.3	4.9	0.0	1.9	11.5
East Stroudsburg, PA Metro Area	4.5	11.7	15.5	10.5	10.9	16.1	15.2	9.5	4.4	1.6	67.6	13.0	0.2	2.3	0.1	1.9	14.9
Eau Claire, WI Metro Area...............................	5.8	11.9	16.7	13.4	11.4	12.6	12.9	8.7	4.3	2.2	91.8	1.2	0.5	3.0	0.0	1.4	2.1
El Centro, CA Metro Area...............................	8.5	15.3	15.3	14.3	12.0	11.8	10.3	6.8	3.9	1.7	11.9	2.5	0.8	1.4	0.1	0.6	82.7
Elizabethtown-Fort Knox, KY Metro Area	6.6	13.4	13.6	13.1	12.9	14.2	12.8	8.0	4.0	1.5	80.2	9.6	0.4	1.8	0.3	2.8	4.9
Elkhart-Goshen, IN Metro Area........................	7.4	15.8	13.6	12.6	12.4	12.8	11.7	7.7	4.0	1.9	75.5	5.9	0.2	1.1	0.0	2.0	15.3
Elmira, NY Metro Area	5.9	12.1	12.7	12.2	11.6	13.8	14.3	9.5	5.1	2.6	86.2	6.3	0.3	1.5	0.0	2.7	3.0
El Paso, TX Metro Area..................................	8.2	15.2	16.2	14.4	12.5	11.7	10.2	6.5	3.6	1.5	13.1	3.2	0.3	1.1	0.1	0.8	81.4
Enid, OK Metro Area......................................	7.4	14.6	13.0	14.4	11.2	11.7	12.4	8.1	4.9	2.3	75.3	3.2	2.4	1.4	2.3	3.4	12.0
Erie, PA Metro Area.......................................	5.8	12.1	14.2	13.2	11.2	13.2	14.2	8.9	4.7	2.5	85.0	7.2	0.2	1.6	0.0	2.0	4.0
Eugene, OR Metro Area..................................	4.9	10.6	16.5	12.6	11.6	11.9	14.1	10.7	4.9	2.3	82.7	1.0	1.0	2.9	0.2	3.7	8.5
Evansville, IN-KY Metro Area...........................	6.1	12.8	12.9	13.2	11.9	13.1	14.1	9.0	4.7	2.2	87.3	6.9	0.2	1.3	0.1	2.0	2.2
Fairbanks, AK Metro Area...............................	7.9	12.8	18.3	18.8	11.9	10.9	11.1	5.8	1.9	0.7	70.6	5.2	6.9	3.1	0.5	5.7	8.0
Fargo, ND-MN Metro Area...............................	6.9	12.3	19.2	16.2	12.2	11.0	10.7	6.2	3.4	1.9	88.0	3.4	1.2	2.4	0.0	1.9	3.1
Farmington, NM Metro Area............................	7.4	14.8	13.1	13.9	12.0	12.0	12.7	8.1	4.2	1.7	41.2	0.8	35.4	0.6	0.1	2.0	19.9
Fayetteville, NC Metro Area............................	8.3	13.8	15.7	17.1	12.1	11.6	10.5	6.5	3.3	1.1	44.1	35.7	2.4	2.5	0.3	3.6	11.4
Fayetteville-Springdale-Rogers, AR-MO Metro Area..................................	7.1	14.6	15.2	14.6	13.5	12.3	10.5	7.3	3.6	1.4	73.9	2.4	1.4	3.0	1.3	2.3	15.7

[1]Persons of Hispanic origin may be any race.

Table B-3. Population by Age, Race, and Hispanic Origin—*Continued*

Metropolitan statistical area and division	Age (percent)										Race alone, not of Hispanic origin (percent)					Two or more races, not of Hispanic origin (percent)	Hispanic or Latino origin[1] (percent)
	Under 5 years	5 to 14 years	15 to 24 years	25 to 34 years	35 to 44 years	45 to 54 years	55 to 64 years	65 to 74 years	75 to 84 years	85 years and over	White alone	Black or African American alone	American Indian, Alaska Native alone	Asian alone	Native Hawaiian and Other Pacific Islander alone		
Flagstaff, AZ Metro Area	5.9	12.0	23.6	13.6	10.7	11.0	11.8	7.3	3.0	1.1	54.9	1.5	25.6	1.7	0.1	2.3	13.9
Flint, MI Metro Area	6.0	12.9	13.2	11.7	12.0	13.9	14.1	9.2	4.8	2.1	72.5	20.3	0.5	1.0	0.0	2.3	3.4
Florence, SC Metro Area	6.2	13.4	13.3	12.1	12.3	13.2	13.5	9.8	4.6	1.7	53.4	41.7	0.3	1.1	0.0	1.1	2.4
Florence-Muscle Shoals, AL Metro Area	5.3	11.6	14.1	11.6	11.5	13.4	13.8	10.7	5.8	2.2	82.4	12.4	0.4	0.7	0.0	1.5	2.6
Fond du Lac, WI Metro Area	5.6	12.3	12.7	11.7	11.9	14.3	14.4	9.4	5.0	2.6	90.3	1.5	0.4	1.5	0.0	1.2	5.1
Fort Collins, CO Metro Area	5.3	11.6	18.4	14.0	12.1	11.6	12.8	8.7	3.8	1.7	83.2	0.9	0.5	2.2	0.1	2.0	11.1
Fort Smith, AR-OK Metro Area	6.3	13.7	13.0	12.6	12.3	13.5	12.9	9.4	4.7	1.7	73.0	4.0	6.6	2.6	0.1	4.3	9.4
Fort Wayne, IN Metro Area	7.0	14.4	13.5	13.1	12.4	12.9	12.8	8.0	3.9	2.0	77.5	10.0	0.3	3.2	0.0	2.3	6.7
Fresno, CA Metro Area	8.2	15.9	15.3	15.0	12.2	11.6	10.3	6.6	3.3	1.6	30.4	4.7	0.6	9.9	0.1	1.8	52.5
Gadsden, AL Metro Area	5.7	12.1	12.5	11.8	12.6	13.7	13.8	10.5	5.3	1.9	78.2	15.5	0.4	0.8	0.0	1.5	3.6
Gainesville, FL Metro Area	5.5	9.7	24.0	15.1	10.4	10.5	11.4	7.9	3.6	1.8	63.8	19.0	0.2	5.7	0.1	2.3	8.9
Gainesville, GA Metro Area	6.7	14.9	13.7	12.9	13.1	13.6	11.0	8.5	4.1	1.5	61.5	7.5	0.2	1.9	0.1	1.2	27.6
Gettysburg, PA Metro Area	5.1	11.7	13.4	10.7	11.0	14.8	14.6	10.8	5.5	2.5	89.3	1.7	0.2	0.9	0.0	1.1	6.8
Glens Falls, NY Metro Area	4.8	10.8	11.7	11.7	11.4	15.3	15.3	11.1	5.5	2.5	93.4	2.0	0.2	0.7	0.0	1.2	2.5
Goldsboro, NC Metro Area	6.8	13.3	14.1	13.2	11.8	12.9	13.0	8.6	4.7	1.7	54.1	31.1	0.3	1.3	0.0	1.9	11.3
Grand Forks, ND-MN Metro Area	6.6	11.5	21.5	14.6	10.0	10.7	11.8	7.2	4.0	2.2	86.0	2.9	2.2	2.1	0.1	2.1	4.6
Grand Island, NE Metro Area	7.2	14.7	12.7	12.2	12.1	12.8	12.6	8.4	4.9	2.4	75.8	1.6	0.4	1.0	0.1	1.0	20.1
Grand Junction, CO Metro Area	6.2	12.5	13.5	13.3	11.4	11.9	13.9	9.9	5.2	2.3	81.6	0.8	0.7	0.8	0.1	1.7	14.3
Grand Rapids-Wyoming, MI Metro Area	6.6	13.7	14.8	13.9	12.1	13.1	12.4	7.6	3.8	1.9	79.4	6.5	0.3	2.5	0.0	2.0	9.3
Grants Pass, OR Metro Area	5.0	11.0	10.4	10.0	10.2	12.2	16.0	14.6	7.5	3.1	87.2	0.5	1.2	0.9	0.2	2.8	7.2
Great Falls, MT Metro Area	6.8	12.2	13.7	13.9	10.5	12.0	13.5	9.5	5.5	2.4	85.7	1.5	4.2	0.9	0.1	3.3	4.3
Greeley, CO Metro Area	7.1	15.4	14.1	14.6	13.3	12.5	11.6	7.1	3.1	1.3	66.5	1.1	0.5	1.4	0.1	1.4	29.0
Green Bay, WI Metro Area	6.3	13.3	13.0	12.9	12.3	14.3	13.4	8.3	4.3	1.9	84.3	2.0	2.2	2.7	0.0	1.7	7.1
Greensboro-High Point, NC Metro Area	5.9	12.7	14.0	12.8	12.6	14.1	12.9	8.8	4.4	1.9	59.6	26.4	0.4	3.5	0.0	1.8	8.3
Greenville, NC Metro Area	6.0	12.4	22.1	13.6	11.8	11.4	11.0	7.0	3.3	1.4	55.7	34.3	0.3	2.0	0.1	1.7	5.9
Greenville-Anderson-Mauldin, SC Metro Area	6.1	12.8	14.2	12.8	12.5	13.5	12.7	9.3	4.5	1.8	73.3	16.6	0.2	1.7	0.0	1.5	6.7
Gulfport-Biloxi-Pascagoula, MS Metro Area	6.4	13.6	13.2	13.7	12.4	13.3	12.9	8.7	4.3	1.5	68.2	21.3	0.4	2.5	0.1	2.0	5.5
Hagerstown-Martinsburg, MD-WV Metro Area	6.0	12.9	12.0	13.2	13.0	14.8	12.9	9.0	4.3	1.8	82.3	9.2	0.2	1.5	0.0	2.5	4.3
Hammond, LA Metro Area	7.2	13.5	14.7	14.7	12.0	12.2	12.5	8.2	3.7	1.2	63.8	29.9	0.3	0.7	0.0	1.2	4.1
Hanford-Corcoran, CA Metro Area	7.8	15.3	15.7	16.6	13.6	12.2	9.3	5.4	2.9	1.1	33.2	6.1	0.9	3.9	0.2	2.1	53.6
Harrisburg-Carlisle, PA Metro Area	5.8	11.9	12.8	13.1	12.1	13.9	13.9	9.4	4.8	2.3	78.2	10.0	0.2	3.7	0.0	2.1	5.8
Harrisonburg, VA Metro Area	5.3	11.1	22.1	13.1	10.9	11.7	11.3	7.8	4.5	2.1	80.8	4.0	0.1	2.1	0.1	1.6	11.3
Hartford-West Hartford-East Hartford, CT Metro Area	5.1	11.7	14.3	12.5	11.8	14.7	13.9	8.9	4.6	2.6	68.5	10.7	0.2	4.7	0.0	1.6	14.3
Hattiesburg, MS Metro Area	6.7	13.4	16.2	14.9	12.6	12.1	11.1	7.6	3.9	1.5	65.6	29.0	0.2	1.1	0.1	1.2	2.8
Hickory-Lenoir-Morganton, NC Metro Area	5.2	12.1	12.6	11.0	12.3	14.9	14.0	10.7	5.3	1.9	81.5	6.8	0.2	2.9	0.1	1.5	7.0
Hilton Head Island-Bluffton-Beaufort, SC Metro Area	5.6	11.3	12.5	11.9	10.5	11.1	13.3	14.8	6.7	2.3	64.0	21.5	0.2	1.2	0.1	1.5	11.5
Hinesville, GA Metro Area	10.5	14.2	17.5	18.8	11.4	10.3	9.2	5.4	2.1	0.7	45.3	36.1	0.5	1.9	0.5	3.5	12.2
Homosassa Springs, FL Metro Area	3.8	8.2	8.5	7.8	8.0	11.9	16.2	19.4	12.0	4.2	88.4	2.9	0.3	1.6	0.0	1.4	5.4
Hot Springs, AR Metro Area	5.6	11.4	11.3	11.3	11.1	12.7	14.5	12.5	6.9	2.7	82.5	8.5	0.6	0.9	0.1	2.1	5.3
Houma-Thibodaux, LA Metro Area	6.8	13.9	13.2	14.6	12.0	13.8	12.4	7.9	4.0	1.5	71.4	16.4	4.2	1.0	0.1	2.0	4.9
Houston-The Woodlands-Sugar Land, TX Metro Area	7.4	15.1	13.8	15.1	14.2	13.0	11.2	6.3	2.7	1.1	37.4	16.9	0.2	7.6	0.1	1.4	36.4
Huntington-Ashland, WV-KY-OH Metro Area	5.7	12.0	12.8	11.6	12.6	13.4	13.9	10.4	5.5	2.0	94.1	2.4	0.2	0.7	0.0	1.4	1.2
Huntsville, AL Metro Area	5.8	12.6	13.3	13.7	12.5	15.0	13.0	8.2	4.4	1.5	67.6	22.0	0.7	2.4	0.1	2.2	5.0
Idaho Falls, ID Metro Area	8.5	18.2	13.2	13.5	12.4	10.9	10.9	7.2	3.7	1.5	84.3	0.5	0.6	0.8	0.1	1.4	12.3
Indianapolis-Carmel-Anderson, IN Metro Area	6.8	14.1	13.0	14.2	13.4	13.6	12.2	7.4	3.6	1.6	73.6	14.9	0.2	2.8	0.0	1.9	6.6
Iowa City, IA Metro Area	6.2	11.4	22.3	15.4	11.6	10.7	10.7	6.7	3.1	1.7	81.5	5.2	0.2	5.5	0.0	2.0	5.6
Ithaca, NY Metro Area	4.1	8.1	30.2	12.8	10.1	10.6	11.4	7.6	3.3	1.8	77.5	3.9	0.3	10.6	0.0	2.8	4.9
Jackson, MI Metro Area	5.5	12.4	13.3	12.1	12.0	14.3	14.2	9.4	4.7	2.3	84.8	8.1	0.3	0.9	0.0	2.4	3.5
Jackson, MS Metro Area	6.5	14.0	14.0	14.1	12.9	12.9	12.4	7.8	3.8	1.6	46.8	48.6	0.1	1.2	0.0	0.9	2.4
Jackson, TN Metro Area	6.2	12.7	15.1	12.0	11.7	13.1	13.2	9.2	4.7	2.0	62.6	30.6	0.2	0.9	0.0	1.4	4.3
Jacksonville, FL Metro Area	6.1	12.6	12.7	14.4	12.6	13.8	13.0	8.9	4.0	1.7	64.1	21.2	0.3	3.9	0.1	2.2	8.2
Jacksonville, NC Metro Area	9.8	12.5	23.5	19.1	10.2	8.3	7.7	5.2	2.7	0.9	66.4	14.8	0.6	2.0	0.3	3.5	12.4
Janesville-Beloit, WI Metro Area	6.1	13.4	13.0	12.1	12.4	14.0	13.6	8.6	4.7	2.1	83.2	4.9	0.3	1.3	0.0	1.9	8.4
Jefferson City, MO Metro Area	6.0	12.7	13.5	13.2	12.6	14.0	13.2	8.6	4.3	1.9	86.6	7.8	0.3	0.9	0.1	1.7	2.6
Johnson City, TN Metro Area	5.0	10.9	14.0	11.9	12.1	13.7	13.7	10.9	5.6	2.1	91.2	3.1	0.3	1.0	0.0	1.4	3.0
Johnstown, PA Metro Area	4.9	10.9	12.7	10.4	11.1	13.2	15.8	11.1	6.3	3.5	93.0	3.4	0.1	0.6	0.0	1.3	1.6
Jonesboro, AR Metro Area	6.7	13.8	14.6	14.9	12.6	12.2	11.3	8.1	4.2	1.6	79.2	13.5	0.4	1.0	0.0	1.5	4.4
Joplin, MO Metro Area	6.7	14.1	13.3	13.3	12.2	12.6	12.4	8.8	4.7	1.8	85.1	1.7	1.7	1.3	0.5	2.8	6.9
Kahului-Wailuku-Lahaina, HI Metro Area	6.2	12.4	11.2	13.4	13.1	13.7	14.1	9.8	4.0	2.1	31.1	0.9	0.3	27.5	10.0	19.0	11.2
Kalamazoo-Portage, MI Metro Area	6.0	12.5	18.1	12.6	11.4	12.2	12.7	8.3	4.1	2.0	78.9	9.4	0.4	2.2	0.0	2.8	6.3
Kankakee, IL Metro Area	6.0	13.8	14.6	12.0	12.1	13.3	13.1	8.7	4.5	2.2	72.0	15.1	0.2	1.0	0.0	1.6	10.1
Kansas City, MO-KS Metro Area	6.6	14.0	12.4	14.0	13.1	13.5	12.7	7.9	3.9	1.9	73.1	12.5	0.4	2.7	0.2	2.3	8.8
Kennewick-Richland, WA Metro Area	8.0	16.2	13.7	14.3	12.5	11.8	11.5	7.3	3.3	1.4	62.0	1.6	0.6	2.6	0.2	2.1	30.9
Killeen-Temple, TX Metro Area	8.3	14.7	15.9	17.3	12.9	11.1	9.4	6.2	3.0	1.2	50.7	19.3	0.5	2.7	0.7	3.3	22.8
Kingsport-Bristol-Bristol, TN-VA Metro Area	4.9	11.1	11.4	10.9	12.0	14.3	14.7	12.0	6.4	2.3	94.2	2.1	0.2	0.6	0.0	1.2	1.7
Kingston, NY Metro Area	4.5	10.3	13.2	12.1	11.7	15.1	15.2	10.5	4.9	2.5	79.7	5.8	0.2	2.1	0.0	2.1	10.1

[1]Persons of Hispanic origin may be any race.

Table B-3.   Population by Age, Race, and Hispanic Origin—*Continued*

Metropolitan statistical area and division	Under 5 years	5 to 14 years	15 to 24 years	25 to 34 years	35 to 44 years	45 to 54 years	55 to 64 years	65 to 74 years	75 to 84 years	85 years and over	White alone	Black or African American alone	American Indian, Alaska Native alone	Asian alone	Native Hawaiian and Other Pacific Islander alone	Two or more races, not of Hispanic origin (percent)	Hispanic or Latino origin[1] (percent)
Knoxville, TN Metro Area	5.4	11.8	13.8	12.1	12.2	13.7	13.5	10.2	5.0	2.0	87.1	5.8	0.3	1.5	0.0	1.7	3.6
Kokomo, IN Metro Area	6.0	12.7	12.3	11.5	11.8	13.6	13.8	10.4	5.6	2.4	85.8	7.1	0.3	1.1	0.0	2.4	3.3
La Crosse-Onalaska, WI-MN Metro Area	5.3	11.5	18.7	12.3	10.9	12.3	13.2	8.6	4.7	2.5	91.1	1.3	0.3	4.0	0.0	1.5	1.8
Lafayette, LA Metro Area	6.9	13.9	13.6	15.1	12.3	13.0	12.5	7.4	3.8	1.5	67.8	24.8	0.3	1.8	0.0	1.4	3.9
Lafayette-West Lafayette, IN Metro Area	6.0	11.7	25.3	13.7	10.8	10.6	10.4	6.5	3.3	1.6	79.5	4.3	0.2	6.6	0.0	1.7	7.7
Lake Charles, LA Metro Area	6.7	13.8	13.5	14.3	11.9	12.7	13.0	8.2	4.3	1.5	69.0	24.4	0.5	1.3	0.0	1.6	3.2
Lake Havasu City-Kingman, AZ Metro Area	4.5	10.4	10.1	9.9	9.2	12.1	16.0	16.2	8.8	2.6	77.5	1.2	2.1	1.1	0.2	1.7	16.2
Lakeland-Winter Haven, FL Metro Area	5.8	12.9	12.6	12.5	11.7	12.4	12.4	11.2	6.2	2.3	61.3	14.5	0.3	1.8	0.1	1.6	20.4
Lancaster, PA Metro Area	6.6	13.3	13.2	12.8	11.4	13.0	12.9	8.9	5.1	2.7	82.6	3.5	0.1	2.2	0.0	1.4	10.2
Lansing-East Lansing, MI Metro Area	5.6	11.6	19.2	13.2	11.3	12.4	12.8	8.3	3.8	1.8	76.7	8.8	0.4	4.6	0.0	2.8	6.7
Laredo, TX Metro Area	10.1	18.4	16.9	13.2	13.1	11.1	8.3	5.2	2.6	1.1	3.8	0.3	0.0	0.6	0.0	0.1	95.2
Las Cruces, NM Metro Area	7.2	13.9	19.1	12.5	10.7	11.0	11.0	8.4	4.5	1.7	28.5	1.5	0.8	1.1	0.1	1.0	67.0
Las Vegas-Henderson-Paradise, NV Metro Area	6.2	13.4	12.7	14.8	14.0	13.5	11.6	8.6	3.9	1.3	44.5	10.7	0.5	9.6	0.7	3.4	30.6
Lawrence, KS Metro Area	5.2	10.6	27.5	14.8	11.3	10.0	9.9	6.3	2.9	1.5	79.2	4.3	2.3	4.7	0.1	3.4	6.0
Lawton, OK Metro Area	7.4	13.0	16.8	16.5	12.1	11.6	10.9	6.7	3.7	1.3	57.5	16.1	5.4	2.4	0.6	5.4	12.6
Lebanon, PA Metro Area	6.1	12.9	12.3	11.5	11.7	13.4	13.5	10.1	5.6	2.9	83.5	1.9	0.1	1.3	0.0	1.1	12.1
Lewiston, ID-WA Metro Area	5.9	11.6	12.2	12.3	10.9	12.6	14.5	10.9	6.2	2.9	88.6	0.5	3.9	0.8	0.1	2.2	3.9
Lewiston-Auburn, ME Metro Area	6.0	12.2	12.4	12.3	12.0	14.6	14.0	9.4	4.9	2.1	91.3	3.7	0.4	0.8	0.0	2.0	1.8
Lexington-Fayette, KY Metro Area	6.3	12.3	15.9	14.3	13.3	13.0	12.1	7.6	3.6	1.6	78.0	11.0	0.2	2.8	0.0	2.0	6.0
Lima, OH Metro Area	6.1	13.1	14.5	12.0	11.6	12.7	13.7	9.0	4.8	2.5	81.2	12.3	0.2	0.8	0.0	2.6	2.9
Lincoln, NE Metro Area	6.6	12.9	18.7	13.9	12.1	11.4	11.6	7.4	3.6	1.8	82.9	3.7	0.6	4.0	0.1	2.3	6.4
Little Rock-North Little Rock-Conway, AR Metro Area	6.6	13.3	13.5	14.4	12.9	12.8	12.3	8.5	4.1	1.6	68.0	22.9	0.4	1.7	0.0	1.8	5.2
Logan, UT-ID Metro Area	8.9	17.4	23.1	13.6	11.3	8.5	8.0	5.3	2.9	1.2	84.6	0.6	0.5	2.3	0.3	1.5	10.2
Longview, TX Metro Area	7.1	13.8	13.5	13.1	12.0	12.6	12.8	8.6	4.7	1.9	63.8	17.1	0.5	1.0	0.0	1.6	16.0
Longview, WA Metro Area	5.7	12.9	12.1	11.5	11.6	13.2	14.4	11.1	5.2	2.3	84.4	0.7	1.4	1.6	0.3	3.0	8.6
Los Angeles-Long Beach-Anaheim, CA Metro Area	6.2	12.3	14.0	15.4	13.7	13.9	11.7	7.2	3.8	1.8	30.1	6.6	0.2	15.6	0.2	2.1	45.2
Anaheim-Santa Ana-Irvine, CA Metro Division	6.0	12.6	13.7	14.2	13.3	14.5	12.1	7.7	4.0	1.9	41.4	1.6	0.2	19.6	0.3	2.5	34.4
Los Angeles-Long Beach-Glendale, CA Metro Division	6.3	12.2	14.1	15.7	13.8	13.7	11.6	7.1	3.7	1.8	26.6	8.1	0.2	14.4	0.2	2.0	48.5
Louisville/Jefferson County, KY-IN Metro Area	6.2	12.7	12.4	13.6	13.0	13.9	13.5	8.7	4.2	1.9	77.2	14.3	0.2	1.9	0.0	1.9	4.5
Lubbock, TX Metro Area	6.8	13.6	20.9	14.5	11.1	10.7	10.4	6.7	3.8	1.6	54.2	6.9	0.4	2.2	0.1	1.1	35.1
Lynchburg, VA Metro Area	5.4	11.1	17.0	11.7	10.6	13.0	13.5	10.2	5.3	2.2	76.6	17.1	0.4	1.6	0.0	1.8	2.5
Macon, GA Metro Area	6.4	13.4	13.7	12.7	11.8	13.2	13.4	9.1	4.5	1.8	50.0	44.2	0.2	1.5	0.0	1.2	2.9
Madera, CA Metro Area	7.6	15.4	14.6	13.8	12.5	12.0	11.1	7.9	3.8	1.4	35.1	3.3	1.1	2.1	0.1	1.5	56.8
Madison, WI Metro Area	5.8	11.9	16.1	14.6	12.8	13.0	12.5	7.8	3.6	1.8	82.9	4.4	0.3	4.8	0.0	2.0	5.6
Manchester-Nashua, NH Metro Area	5.4	12.0	12.9	12.8	12.5	15.8	14.2	8.4	4.0	2.0	85.9	2.1	0.2	3.9	0.0	1.6	6.3
Manhattan, KS Metro Area	6.8	10.4	29.6	17.6	9.7	7.9	8.4	5.3	2.7	1.6	79.7	5.3	0.5	3.8	0.2	2.8	7.7
Mankato-North Mankato, MN Metro Area	5.6	11.6	22.2	13.8	10.7	10.8	11.7	7.4	4.0	2.2	89.4	3.1	0.3	2.1	0.0	1.5	3.6
Mansfield, OH Metro Area	5.7	12.2	12.3	12.1	11.9	13.3	14.1	10.1	5.8	2.5	85.9	9.4	0.2	0.7	0.0	1.9	1.9
McAllen-Edinburg-Mission, TX Metro Area	9.7	18.3	16.4	13.1	12.9	10.7	8.2	6.0	3.3	1.3	7.0	0.5	0.1	1.0	0.0	0.2	91.2
Medford, OR Metro Area	5.6	11.6	11.5	12.3	11.2	12.3	14.7	12.2	5.9	2.8	81.7	0.7	0.9	1.3	0.3	2.8	12.3
Memphis, TN-MS-AR Metro Area	6.9	14.0	14.0	13.8	12.9	13.3	12.5	7.6	3.5	1.5	44.5	46.5	0.2	2.1	0.0	1.3	5.4
Merced, CA Metro Area	8.0	16.9	16.5	14.3	12.3	11.6	9.8	6.2	3.1	1.3	28.9	3.1	0.4	7.4	0.2	1.8	58.2
Miami-Fort Lauderdale-West Palm Beach, FL Metro Area	5.7	11.3	12.0	13.4	13.2	14.5	12.4	9.1	5.5	2.8	32.1	20.3	0.1	2.5	0.0	1.1	43.9
Fort Lauderdale-Pompano Beach-Deerfield Beach, FL Metro Division	5.9	11.8	12.0	13.5	13.3	14.8	13.0	8.6	4.6	2.5	38.8	27.6	0.2	3.6	0.1	1.6	28.1
Miami-Miami Beach-Kendall, FL Metro Division	5.9	11.1	12.4	14.3	14.0	14.9	11.8	8.3	5.0	2.3	14.4	16.4	0.1	1.6	0.0	0.7	66.8
West Palm Beach-Boca Raton-Delray Beach, FL Metro Division	5.1	10.9	11.2	11.8	11.6	13.6	12.9	11.2	7.5	4.3	56.7	18.0	0.2	2.7	0.0	1.3	21.1
Michigan City-La Porte, IN Metro Area	6.0	11.9	12.6	12.9	12.5	13.8	14.2	9.6	4.6	2.0	79.8	11.2	0.3	0.6	0.0	1.9	6.2
Midland, MI Metro Area	5.1	12.5	13.0	12.1	11.5	14.7	14.2	9.1	5.2	2.5	91.8	1.4	0.4	2.4	0.1	1.3	2.6
Midland, TX Metro Area	8.5	15.3	14.1	17.4	12.2	11.4	11.1	5.4	3.1	1.5	47.3	5.9	0.4	1.6	0.0	1.0	43.8
Milwaukee-Waukesha-West Allis, WI Metro Area	6.4	13.1	13.2	14.0	12.3	13.6	13.2	7.9	4.1	2.2	67.4	16.4	0.4	3.6	0.0	1.8	10.4
Minneapolis-St. Paul-Bloomington, MN-WI Metro Area	6.6	13.4	12.7	14.7	13.1	14.1	12.8	7.4	3.5	1.8	76.8	7.9	0.6	6.6	0.0	2.4	5.7
Missoula, MT Metro Area	5.4	10.8	17.9	15.4	12.0	11.5	12.8	8.7	3.7	1.7	89.5	0.5	2.6	1.5	0.1	2.6	3.2
Mobile, AL Metro Area	6.6	13.1	13.6	13.7	12.0	12.9	13.1	8.9	4.4	1.7	57.6	35.2	0.9	2.0	0.0	1.5	2.8
Modesto, CA Metro Area	7.2	15.3	14.6	14.2	12.5	12.6	11.1	7.2	3.7	1.6	43.5	2.6	0.5	5.3	0.7	2.6	44.8
Monroe, LA Metro Area	6.9	13.8	14.3	13.7	12.1	12.4	12.4	8.2	4.4	1.7	59.6	35.7	0.3	0.8	0.0	1.1	2.5
Monroe, MI Metro Area	5.4	12.5	12.5	11.3	11.9	15.0	15.2	9.5	4.6	2.1	91.6	2.3	0.3	0.7	0.0	1.6	3.5
Montgomery, AL Metro Area	6.4	13.2	13.9	13.9	12.9	13.2	12.4	8.3	4.2	1.6	49.5	43.7	0.3	2.0	0.1	1.3	3.1
Morgantown, WV Metro Area	5.2	9.1	21.1	16.8	12.0	11.5	11.7	7.5	3.6	1.6	90.5	3.2	0.2	2.5	0.0	1.6	2.0
Morristown, TN Metro Area	5.6	12.5	12.6	11.2	12.4	14.1	13.2	11.1	5.6	1.8	86.7	3.2	0.2	0.7	0.1	1.4	7.7
Mount Vernon-Anacortes, WA Metro Area	6.1	12.4	12.0	12.3	11.3	12.2	14.4	11.4	5.4	2.5	75.2	0.7	1.7	2.1	0.2	2.3	17.8
Muncie, IN Metro Area	5.2	10.2	23.6	11.2	10.2	11.7	11.7	9.0	4.9	2.3	87.1	7.1	0.2	1.3	0.1	2.1	2.1
Muskegon, MI Metro Area	6.1	13.3	13.0	12.6	12.0	13.4	14.1	9.0	4.5	2.0	76.6	14.1	0.8	0.6	0.0	2.4	5.5

[1]Persons of Hispanic origin may be any race.

Table B-3. Population by Age, Race, and Hispanic Origin—*Continued*

| | Population characteristics, 2015 | | | | | | | | | | | | | | | | |
| | Age (percent) | | | | | | | | | | Race alone, not of Hispanic origin (percent) | | | | | Two or more races, not of Hispanic origin (percent) | Hispanic or Latino origin[1] (percent) |
Metropolitan statistical area and division	Under 5 years	5 to 14 years	15 to 24 years	25 to 34 years	35 to 44 years	45 to 54 years	55 to 64 years	65 to 74 years	75 to 84 years	85 years and over	White alone	Black or African American alone	American Indian, Alaska Native alone	Asian alone	Native Hawaiian and Other Pacific Islander alone		
Myrtle Beach-Conway-North Myrtle Beach, SC-NC Metro Area...............	4.9	10.4	10.4	11.4	11.2	12.7	15.8	15.5	6.0	1.8	78.4	12.5	0.5	1.0	0.1	1.7	5.8
Napa, CA Metro Area..............................	5.4	12.3	12.8	12.3	12.6	13.7	13.5	9.9	5.0	2.6	53.3	2.0	0.4	7.9	0.2	2.3	33.9
Naples-Immokalee-Marco Island, FL Metro Area ..	4.7	10.1	9.9	9.8	10.0	12.1	13.3	15.7	10.3	4.1	64.1	6.6	0.2	1.3	0.0	0.9	26.9
Nashville-Davidson—Murfreesboro—Franklin, TN Metro Area......................	6.4	13.2	13.5	14.8	13.7	13.7	12.2	7.6	3.5	1.4	73.0	15.3	0.3	2.6	0.1	1.8	6.9
New Bern, NC Metro Area......................	6.4	11.5	15.3	12.9	10.4	11.4	13.1	10.9	5.8	2.3	66.7	21.7	0.5	2.2	0.1	2.2	6.6
New Haven-Milford, CT Metro Area..............	5.3	11.6	14.1	13.2	11.9	14.5	13.6	8.8	4.5	2.6	64.3	12.4	0.2	4.2	0.0	1.7	17.2
New Orleans-Metairie, LA Metro Area..............	6.2	12.5	12.4	15.2	12.6	13.4	13.6	8.4	3.9	1.7	52.1	34.5	0.4	2.9	0.0	1.4	8.7
New York-Newark-Jersey City, NY-NJ-PA Metro Area....................	6.2	12.0	12.9	14.6	13.2	14.2	12.5	8.0	4.2	2.1	47.2	15.9	0.2	11.1	0.0	1.5	24.1
Dutchess County-Putnam County, NY Metro Division....................	4.6	11.3	14.7	11.0	11.7	16.2	14.6	9.1	4.6	2.1	74.1	8.2	0.2	3.6	0.0	1.7	12.2
Nassau County-Suffolk County, NY Metro Division....................	5.4	12.3	13.4	11.4	12.2	15.5	13.7	8.9	4.7	2.5	65.2	9.2	0.2	6.5	0.0	1.3	17.6
Newark, NJ-PA Metro Division................	5.8	12.9	12.9	11.9	13.3	15.7	13.3	8.0	4.0	2.1	52.4	19.2	0.1	7.5	0.0	1.4	19.4
New York-Jersey City-White Plains, NY-NJ Metro Division....................	6.4	11.7	12.7	15.9	13.5	13.6	12.1	7.8	4.2	2.0	41.9	16.9	0.2	12.9	0.0	1.5	26.6
Niles-Benton Harbor, MI Metro Area..............	6.1	12.3	12.5	11.4	11.3	13.6	13.6	14.6	10.2	5.4	75.1	15.1	0.5	1.9	0.1	2.1	5.2
North Port-Sarasota-Bradenton, FL Metro Area	4.3	9.5	9.4	9.4	9.6	12.4	14.9	16.1	9.8	4.6	78.0	6.5	0.2	1.8	0.0	1.3	12.2
Norwich-New London, CT Metro Area................	5.0	11.2	14.2	12.8	11.3	14.6	14.3	9.5	4.7	2.4	75.9	5.7	0.8	4.4	0.1	2.8	10.3
Ocala, FL Metro Area..............................	4.9	10.5	10.3	10.4	9.8	12.1	13.7	15.8	9.3	3.1	71.8	12.5	0.3	1.6	0.1	1.5	12.2
Ocean City, NJ Metro Area	4.8	9.6	11.5	10.4	9.3	13.5	16.5	14.1	7.3	3.1	85.3	4.3	0.2	1.1	0.0	1.6	7.5
Odessa, TX Metro Area..........................	9.1	16.5	15.4	16.6	12.1	11.1	9.8	5.4	2.9	1.1	34.5	4.2	0.5	1.0	0.1	0.9	58.8
Ogden-Clearfield, UT Metro Area	8.3	18.1	14.5	14.4	13.7	10.8	9.9	6.0	3.1	1.2	81.8	1.2	0.5	1.6	0.5	2.0	12.4
Oklahoma City, OK Metro Area....................	7.1	13.9	14.2	15.1	12.7	12.2	11.9	7.6	3.8	1.6	65.2	10.4	3.8	3.2	0.1	4.6	12.7
Olympia-Tumwater, WA Metro Area................	5.9	12.1	12.4	14.2	12.9	12.9	13.6	9.7	4.2	1.9	75.7	3.1	1.3	5.8	1.0	4.6	8.5
Omaha-Council Bluffs, NE-IA Metro Area..........	7.3	14.5	13.1	14.7	13.0	12.9	12.1	7.3	3.6	1.6	77.0	7.7	0.4	2.7	0.1	2.1	10.0
Orlando-Kissimmee-Sanford, FL Metro Area	5.9	12.5	13.9	15.1	13.5	13.6	11.6	8.2	4.1	1.7	49.2	15.5	0.2	4.4	0.1	1.8	28.8
Oshkosh-Neenah, WI Metro Area..................	5.6	11.6	15.8	13.1	11.9	13.8	13.1	8.2	4.6	2.4	89.2	2.0	0.6	2.8	0.0	1.4	4.0
Owensboro, KY Metro Area......................	6.6	13.7	12.3	12.2	12.0	13.4	13.4	9.3	5.0	2.2	90.2	4.3	0.1	0.9	0.1	1.7	2.7
Oxnard-Thousand Oaks-Ventura, CA Metro Area ..	6.3	13.3	14.0	13.1	12.5	14.0	12.7	8.1	4.0	1.9	46.1	1.7	0.3	7.2	0.2	2.3	42.2
Palm Bay-Melbourne-Titusville, FL Metro Area	4.6	10.4	11.2	10.9	10.2	14.2	15.6	12.4	7.5	3.1	75.4	10.0	0.3	2.4	0.1	2.1	9.7
Panama City, FL Metro Area......................	6.0	11.6	12.1	14.4	12.1	13.9	13.4	9.7	4.9	2.0	76.9	11.6	0.6	2.1	0.1	2.7	6.0
Parkersburg-Vienna, WV Metro Area..............	5.8	11.8	11.4	11.4	12.1	14.2	14.5	11.0	5.7	2.1	95.4	1.2	0.2	0.6	0.0	1.5	1.1
Pensacola-Ferry Pass-Brent, FL Metro Area........	5.9	11.9	14.6	14.1	11.5	13.2	13.2	9.3	4.7	1.8	71.2	16.8	0.8	2.7	0.2	2.8	5.5
Peoria, IL Metro Area............................	6.5	13.0	12.4	12.8	12.3	12.9	13.4	9.2	5.0	2.5	82.8	9.4	0.2	2.3	0.0	1.9	3.4
Philadelphia-Camden-Wilmington, PA-NJ-DE-MD Metro Area....................	6.0	12.3	13.3	14.1	12.3	14.1	13.3	8.3	4.3	2.2	62.8	20.4	0.2	5.9	0.0	1.8	8.9
Camden, NJ Metro Division	5.7	12.6	12.9	12.8	12.6	14.9	13.5	8.6	4.3	2.2	66.5	15.8	0.2	4.9	0.0	1.9	10.7
Montgomery County-Bucks County-Chester County, PA Metro Division	5.4	12.5	12.4	11.7	12.2	15.1	14.3	9.1	4.8	2.6	80.2	6.6	0.1	6.0	0.0	1.6	5.5
Philadelphia, PA Metro Division	6.7	11.9	14.2	17.0	12.2	12.5	12.1	7.4	3.9	2.1	44.1	35.8	0.2	6.8	0.0	1.9	11.2
Wilmington, DE-MD-NJ Metro Division	5.9	12.3	13.5	13.8	12.3	14.4	13.3	8.5	4.1	1.9	64.1	20.6	0.2	4.4	0.0	2.0	8.7
Phoenix-Mesa-Scottsdale, AZ Metro Area..............	6.5	14.0	13.5	14.2	13.2	12.7	11.3	8.6	4.3	1.7	56.6	5.1	2.0	3.7	0.2	2.1	30.3
Pine Bluff, AR Metro Area........................	5.9	12.4	13.8	13.3	12.1	13.3	13.5	9.2	4.7	1.9	47.7	47.5	0.4	0.7	0.1	1.3	2.3
Pittsburgh, PA Metro Area	5.1	10.6	12.1	13.1	11.4	13.8	15.2	10.0	5.6	3.0	85.9	8.4	0.1	2.3	0.0	2.0	1.6
Pittsfield, MA Metro Area........................	4.3	9.7	13.3	10.4	10.4	14.5	15.9	11.9	6.2	3.5	89.3	2.9	0.2	1.5	0.0	1.8	4.1
Pocatello, ID Metro Area........................	7.3	15.1	14.5	15.6	12.0	10.6	11.8	7.9	3.8	1.5	84.7	0.8	2.9	1.3	0.3	1.8	8.2
Portland-South Portland, ME Metro Area..............	4.9	11.0	11.9	12.3	11.9	15.0	15.2	10.3	5.1	2.4	92.6	1.9	0.3	1.8	0.0	1.6	1.8
Portland-Vancouver-Hillsboro, OR-WA Metro Area....................	5.9	12.5	12.1	15.1	14.5	13.5	12.7	8.4	3.5	1.8	74.4	2.8	0.7	6.5	0.5	3.4	11.7
Port St. Lucie, FL Metro Area....................	4.8	10.9	10.8	10.4	10.5	13.2	14.1	13.4	8.4	3.6	65.9	14.4	0.2	1.6	0.1	1.5	16.3
Prescott, AZ Metro Area........................	4.1	9.9	9.9	9.0	8.9	11.7	17.5	17.3	8.5	3.2	80.6	0.8	1.4	1.0	0.1	1.7	14.4
Providence-Warwick, RI-MA Metro Area	5.2	11.4	14.1	13.0	12.0	14.5	13.7	8.9	4.5	2.6	77.6	5.1	0.4	3.0	0.1	1.9	11.9
Provo-Orem, UT Metro Area	9.9	19.4	21.9	14.0	12.4	8.3	6.7	4.4	2.2	0.8	83.2	0.6	0.5	1.6	0.8	2.1	11.2
Pueblo, CO Metro Area..........................	5.9	13.2	13.5	12.5	11.7	12.4	13.4	9.8	5.2	2.4	52.6	1.8	0.7	0.8	0.1	1.3	42.7
Punta Gorda, FL Metro Area......................	3.0	7.3	7.9	7.5	7.6	11.4	16.9	20.8	12.5	5.1	84.5	5.6	0.3	1.4	0.0	1.4	6.8
Racine, WI Metro Area..........................	6.2	13.3	12.7	11.9	12.0	14.7	14.1	8.6	4.4	2.1	72.7	11.1	0.3	1.3	0.0	1.9	12.7
Raleigh, NC Metro Area..........................	6.3	14.3	13.4	14.1	15.1	14.6	11.3	6.8	2.9	1.2	61.9	19.9	0.3	5.4	0.0	1.9	10.6
Rapid City, SD Metro Area	6.6	12.9	12.5	13.6	11.3	12.0	14.5	9.6	4.7	2.2	82.5	1.3	7.5	1.1	0.1	3.0	4.5
Reading, PA Metro Area..........................	5.9	12.7	13.9	12.0	11.7	14.3	13.3	8.9	4.8	2.5	73.4	4.3	0.1	1.5	0.0	1.3	19.4
Redding, CA Metro Area..........................	5.9	11.8	11.9	12.6	10.5	12.7	14.8	11.7	5.8	2.4	80.5	1.0	2.3	2.9	0.1	3.6	9.6
Reno, NV Metro Area	5.9	12.5	13.0	14.6	12.1	13.4	13.4	9.7	4.0	1.5	63.9	2.2	1.3	5.6	0.6	2.6	23.8
Richmond, VA Metro Area........................	5.9	12.4	13.3	14.2	12.7	14.1	13.2	8.5	3.9	1.8	58.1	29.8	0.4	3.9	0.1	2.0	5.7
Riverside-San Bernardino-Ontario, CA Metro Area	6.9	14.8	15.3	14.2	12.8	12.9	11.0	7.1	3.6	1.5	33.5	7.1	0.4	6.5	0.3	2.2	50.0
Roanoke, VA Metro Area........................	5.4	11.6	12.2	12.0	11.7	14.0	14.5	10.9	5.4	2.4	78.8	13.2	0.2	2.2	0.0	1.8	3.8
Rochester, MN Metro Area......................	6.8	13.8	11.5	13.5	12.4	13.2	13.3	8.2	4.7	2.4	85.2	4.1	0.2	4.5	0.0	1.6	4.4
Rochester, NY Metro Area......................	5.4	11.7	14.3	13.0	11.1	14.1	13.9	9.3	4.7	2.4	76.9	11.0	0.2	2.8	0.0	1.9	7.2
Rockford, IL Metro Area........................	6.0	13.6	13.1	12.0	12.3	14.0	13.3	9.1	4.6	2.1	70.8	10.9	0.2	2.5	0.0	2.0	13.6

[1]Persons of Hispanic origin may be any race.

Table B-3. Population by Age, Race, and Hispanic Origin—*Continued*

Metropolitan statistical area and division	Under 5 years	5 to 14 years	15 to 24 years	25 to 34 years	35 to 44 years	45 to 54 years	55 to 64 years	65 to 74 years	75 to 84 years	85 years and over	White alone	Black or African American alone	American Indian, Alaska Native alone	Asian alone	Native Hawaiian and Other Pacific Islander alone	Two or more races, not of Hispanic origin (percent)	Hispanic or Latino origin[1] (percent)
Rocky Mount, NC Metro Area	5.9	12.8	13.0	11.4	11.6	13.8	14.4	10.2	5.0	2.0	45.9	45.8	0.5	0.6	0.1	1.3	5.8
Rome, GA Metro Area	6.1	13.3	14.3	12.5	12.2	13.0	12.5	9.1	4.9	2.0	71.8	14.4	0.2	1.3	0.0	1.5	10.8
Sacramento—Roseville—Arden-Arcade, CA Metro Area	6.1	13.2	13.9	14.0	12.6	13.3	12.5	8.3	4.1	1.9	53.4	7.0	0.6	12.9	0.8	4.1	21.2
Saginaw, MI Metro Area	5.8	12.0	14.0	11.8	11.1	13.3	14.2	10.0	5.3	2.5	69.7	18.5	0.4	1.3	0.0	1.8	8.3
St. Cloud, MN Metro Area	6.4	12.9	18.0	13.1	11.3	12.6	11.9	7.5	4.3	2.0	89.4	3.7	0.3	2.0	0.0	1.5	3.1
St. George, UT Metro Area	7.0	15.9	13.5	12.1	11.1	9.3	10.9	11.2	6.6	2.4	85.0	0.5	1.1	0.8	0.8	1.7	10.1
St. Joseph, MO-KS Metro Area	6.1	12.2	13.2	13.9	12.4	13.4	13.2	8.6	4.7	2.2	85.8	5.6	0.5	1.0	0.2	1.9	5.0
St. Louis, MO-IL Metro Area	6.0	12.6	12.7	13.6	12.3	13.8	13.8	8.6	4.5	2.2	74.2	18.3	0.2	2.5	0.0	1.8	3.0
Salem, OR Metro Area	6.5	14.0	14.4	13.1	12.3	12.1	12.3	8.9	4.4	2.0	68.9	1.0	1.2	2.0	0.8	2.6	23.5
Salinas, CA Metro Area	7.7	14.7	14.5	14.7	13.0	12.1	11.1	7.0	3.5	1.8	30.7	2.6	0.3	5.9	0.5	2.2	57.8
Salisbury, MD-DE Metro Area	5.3	11.0	13.1	11.0	10.2	12.7	14.8	13.2	6.3	2.3	71.2	17.6	0.4	1.7	0.0	1.9	7.2
Salt Lake City, UT Metro Area	8.0	16.0	14.1	16.3	14.4	11.3	10.1	5.9	2.7	1.2	72.8	1.5	0.7	3.8	1.5	2.1	17.6
San Angelo, TX Metro Area	6.7	13.1	16.1	15.7	10.8	11.2	11.6	8.0	4.7	2.0	54.5	3.8	0.4	1.2	0.1	1.4	38.6
San Antonio-New Braunfels, TX Metro Area	6.9	14.4	14.6	14.9	13.1	12.6	11.1	7.4	3.6	1.5	34.5	6.5	0.3	2.4	0.1	1.4	54.8
San Diego-Carlsbad, CA Metro Area	6.5	11.9	14.6	16.3	13.1	12.9	11.6	7.4	3.8	1.9	46.3	4.8	0.4	11.5	0.4	3.2	33.4
San Francisco-Oakland-Hayward, CA Metro Area	5.6	11.3	11.4	15.9	14.5	14.3	12.6	8.2	4.0	2.1	40.5	7.5	0.2	25.4	0.7	3.7	22.0
Oakland-Hayward-Berkeley, CA Metro Division	5.9	12.4	12.4	14.8	14.2	14.3	12.5	7.9	3.7	1.9	37.6	10.1	0.3	23.7	0.7	4.0	23.6
San Francisco-Redwood City-South San Francisco, CA Metro Division	5.3	9.2	10.1	19.0	15.2	14.0	12.4	8.1	4.4	2.3	40.5	3.9	0.2	31.3	0.9	3.4	19.8
San Rafael, CA Metro Division	4.8	12.2	10.0	8.8	12.6	16.0	15.5	11.7	5.3	2.9	71.9	2.6	0.2	6.0	0.2	3.1	16.0
San Jose-Sunnyvale-Santa Clara, CA Metro Area	6.4	12.9	12.3	15.2	14.8	14.4	11.6	7.0	3.7	1.7	32.9	2.3	0.2	34.0	0.3	3.0	27.3
San Luis Obispo-Paso Robles-Arroyo Grande, CA Metro Area	4.9	10.1	18.7	11.6	10.6	11.9	14.1	10.6	5.0	2.6	69.3	1.8	0.5	3.6	0.2	2.5	22.1
Santa Cruz-Watsonville, CA Metro Area	5.4	11.0	18.7	12.1	11.7	13.1	13.9	8.8	3.4	1.9	57.8	1.0	0.4	4.5	0.1	2.9	33.3
Santa Fe, NM Metro Area	4.7	11.0	11.0	11.2	11.6	13.4	16.3	13.5	5.3	2.0	43.0	0.8	2.5	1.3	0.1	1.2	51.1
Santa Maria-Santa Barbara, CA Metro Area	6.5	12.2	19.7	13.2	11.3	11.6	11.2	7.6	4.3	2.3	45.4	1.8	0.4	5.2	0.2	2.2	44.8
Santa Rosa, CA Metro Area	5.2	11.6	12.2	13.1	12.1	13.7	14.7	10.6	4.4	2.4	64.3	1.5	0.7	4.1	0.3	2.8	26.3
Savannah, GA Metro Area	6.8	12.9	14.5	16.0	12.7	12.3	11.6	8.0	3.7	1.5	56.1	33.2	0.2	2.5	0.1	1.9	6.0
Scranton—Wilkes-Barre—Hazleton, PA Metro Area	5.1	11.1	12.7	12.3	11.4	14.1	14.2	10.3	5.7	3.1	85.8	3.1	0.1	1.6	0.0	1.2	8.2
Seattle-Tacoma-Bellevue, WA Metro Area	6.3	12.1	12.3	16.2	14.1	13.9	12.5	7.5	3.4	1.7	65.1	5.8	0.9	13.0	0.9	4.6	9.7
Seattle-Bellevue-Everett, WA Metro Division	6.1	11.8	11.9	16.6	14.5	14.1	12.6	7.4	3.3	1.7	64.3	5.5	0.8	14.9	0.7	4.2	9.6
Tacoma-Lakewood, WA Metro Division	6.8	13.1	13.6	15.1	12.7	13.2	12.4	7.8	3.6	1.6	67.8	6.8	1.1	6.4	1.5	5.9	10.5
Sebastian-Vero Beach, FL Metro Area	4.3	9.6	9.9	9.1	9.1	12.1	14.9	16.0	10.1	4.8	76.0	8.9	0.2	1.5	0.0	1.3	12.1
Sebring, FL Metro Area	4.6	10.0	9.4	9.3	8.5	10.6	13.5	16.9	12.4	4.9	68.5	9.6	0.4	1.4	0.0	1.3	18.8
Sheboygan, WI Metro Area	5.5	12.9	12.6	11.4	11.8	14.6	14.5	9.2	4.9	2.5	85.0	1.7	0.4	5.3	0.0	1.3	6.3
Sherman-Denison, TX Metro Area	6.1	13.5	13.0	11.9	11.4	13.3	13.6	10.0	5.1	2.0	76.2	5.9	1.4	1.2	0.0	2.3	13.0
Shreveport-Bossier City, LA Metro Area	7.1	13.3	12.9	14.3	12.2	12.3	12.8	8.6	4.6	1.9	54.2	38.6	0.4	1.3	0.1	1.6	3.8
Sierra Vista-Douglas, AZ Metro Area	6.4	12.2	12.3	12.7	10.7	11.6	13.5	12.0	6.5	2.2	56.0	4.0	0.8	1.9	0.3	2.3	34.7
Sioux City, IA-NE-SD Metro Area	7.0	14.7	13.8	12.2	11.9	12.7	12.8	8.2	4.5	2.1	76.6	2.3	1.3	2.2	0.1	1.8	15.7
Sioux Falls, SD Metro Area	7.6	14.3	12.6	15.3	12.9	12.6	12.1	7.2	3.5	1.9	86.6	3.6	1.9	1.7	0.0	1.9	4.3
South Bend-Mishawaka, IN-MI Metro Area	6.2	13.1	14.7	12.5	11.7	12.9	13.4	8.8	4.4	2.3	75.7	11.6	0.4	2.0	0.1	2.5	7.7
Spartanburg, SC Metro Area	6.1	13.2	13.5	12.6	12.2	13.8	12.9	9.4	4.6	1.7	68.4	21.6	0.2	2.2	0.0	1.5	6.1
Spokane-Spokane Valley, WA Metro Area	6.0	12.4	13.6	14.0	11.6	12.8	13.6	9.5	4.4	2.0	85.4	1.7	1.8	2.1	0.4	3.4	5.2
Springfield, IL Metro Area	5.9	12.9	12.3	12.7	12.2	13.7	14.1	9.2	4.6	2.3	81.9	11.7	0.2	1.9	0.0	2.1	2.2
Springfield, MA Metro Area	5.2	11.4	17.9	12.2	11.0	13.4	13.4	8.7	4.3	2.4	69.3	6.5	0.2	3.2	0.0	1.6	19.2
Springfield, MO Metro Area	6.2	12.7	15.8	13.3	11.9	12.4	12.1	8.9	4.7	2.1	90.2	2.3	0.6	1.4	0.1	2.2	3.2
Springfield, OH Metro Area	5.8	12.8	12.8	11.5	11.3	13.4	14.0	10.4	5.4	2.5	84.3	8.8	0.2	0.7	0.0	2.6	3.4
State College, PA Metro Area	4.0	8.5	27.3	14.5	10.5	11.5	11.1	7.1	3.9	1.7	86.0	3.7	0.1	5.7	0.1	1.5	2.9
Staunton-Waynesboro, VA Metro Area	5.1	11.3	11.8	12.1	11.7	14.1	14.2	11.3	5.9	2.4	86.7	7.0	0.2	0.8	0.0	1.8	3.5
Stockton-Lodi, CA Metro Area	7.1	15.6	14.8	13.7	12.8	12.8	11.0	7.1	3.4	1.6	33.4	7.0	0.5	14.6	0.5	3.3	40.7
Sumter, SC Metro Area	7.0	13.5	14.7	13.7	11.1	12.6	12.4	8.6	4.6	1.7	46.0	46.6	0.4	1.3	0.1	1.6	4.0
Syracuse, NY Metro Area	5.5	12.0	15.0	12.7	11.1	14.3	13.8	8.7	4.5	2.3	82.0	8.1	0.7	2.9	0.0	2.2	4.1
Tallahassee, FL Metro Area	5.3	10.8	22.4	14.0	11.2	11.6	11.8	7.9	3.4	1.5	56.2	32.6	0.3	2.7	0.0	1.8	6.4
Tampa-St. Petersburg-Clearwater, FL Metro Area	5.4	11.3	11.7	12.9	12.3	13.9	13.4	10.6	5.8	2.7	64.6	11.7	0.2	3.4	0.1	1.8	18.2
Terre Haute, IN Metro Area	5.8	11.5	16.4	12.5	12.1	12.8	13.1	9.0	4.6	2.1	89.2	5.2	0.3	1.4	0.0	1.7	2.2
Texarkana, TX-AR Metro Area	6.5	13.2	12.6	13.2	12.7	13.1	12.6	9.3	4.7	2.0	66.5	24.1	0.7	0.9	0.1	1.8	5.9
The Villages, FL Metro Area	2.0	4.0	4.5	5.8	6.3	7.1	15.6	34.5	16.4	4.0	84.7	7.6	0.3	0.8	0.0	0.8	5.8
Toledo, OH Metro Area	6.1	12.7	15.1	13.2	11.7	12.8	13.5	8.5	4.3	2.1	75.0	14.3	0.2	1.6	0.0	2.2	6.7
Topeka, KS Metro Area	6.4	13.5	12.5	12.2	11.4	13.0	14.1	9.5	5.0	2.4	78.4	6.3	1.3	1.1	0.1	2.9	9.9
Trenton, NJ Metro Area	5.8	12.0	15.1	12.5	13.1	14.5	12.9	7.8	4.0	2.2	51.0	19.5	0.2	10.6	0.1	1.7	16.9
Tucson, AZ Metro Area	5.9	12.1	15.8	12.2	11.3	11.6	12.7	10.4	5.6	2.4	52.9	3.4	2.5	2.9	0.1	1.9	36.3
Tulsa, OK Metro Area	6.8	14.0	13.1	13.7	12.5	12.8	12.6	8.4	4.3	1.8	66.0	8.2	2.5	2.2	0.1	6.0	9.4
Tuscaloosa, AL Metro Area	5.9	11.5	20.0	14.5	11.7	11.7	11.9	7.6	3.7	1.5	60.6	33.5	0.2	1.3	0.0	1.0	3.4
Tyler, TX Metro Area	7.0	13.7	14.2	13.7	11.7	12.0	12.0	8.8	5.0	2.0	60.3	17.4	0.3	1.5	0.0	1.4	19.1
Urban Honolulu, HI Metro Area	6.6	11.7	13.6	16.0	12.4	12.0	11.5	8.7	4.7	2.8	19.5	3.0	0.2	41.0	8.7	17.8	9.8
Utica-Rome, NY Metro Area	5.7	11.8	13.4	12.0	11.1	14.0	14.0	9.8	5.3	3.0	85.1	5.0	0.2	3.3	0.0	1.6	4.8
Valdosta, GA Metro Area	7.1	13.7	19.3	14.5	11.2	11.3	10.4	7.4	3.7	1.3	56.1	33.8	0.3	1.6	0.1	1.8	6.3

[1]Persons of Hispanic origin may be any race.

Table B-3. Population by Age, Race, and Hispanic Origin—*Continued*

| | Population characteristics, 2015 | | | | | | | | | | | | | | | | |
| | Age (percent) | | | | | | | | | | Race alone, not of Hispanic origin (percent) | | | | | Two or more races, not of Hispanic origin (percent) | Hispanic or Latino origin[1] (percent) |
Metropolitan statistical area and division	Under 5 years	5 to 14 years	15 to 24 years	25 to 34 years	35 to 44 years	45 to 54 years	55 to 64 years	65 to 74 years	75 to 84 years	85 years and over	White alone	Black or African American alone	American Indian, Alaska Native alone	Asian alone	Native Hawaiian and Other Pacific Islander alone		
Vallejo-Fairfield, CA Metro Area	6.1	12.8	13.4	14.5	12.3	13.5	13.4	8.5	3.9	1.7	39.1	13.7	0.4	14.8	0.8	5.1	26.1
Victoria, TX Metro Area	7.1	14.2	13.6	13.8	11.6	11.9	12.6	8.7	4.6	1.9	46.8	5.9	0.3	1.2	0.0	0.9	44.9
Vineland-Bridgeton, NJ Metro Area	6.6	13.2	12.3	14.9	13.5	13.6	11.9	8.0	4.0	1.9	47.3	18.9	0.7	1.3	0.0	2.0	29.8
Virginia Beach-Norfolk-Newport News, VA-NC Metro Area	6.4	12.3	15.1	15.7	12.0	13.0	12.2	7.9	3.9	1.6	55.9	30.1	0.3	3.9	0.1	3.1	6.6
Visalia-Porterville, CA Metro Area	8.8	17.7	15.6	14.1	12.3	11.4	9.7	6.2	3.1	1.3	29.6	1.3	0.7	3.3	0.1	1.4	63.6
Waco, TX Metro Area	7.1	13.3	18.9	12.8	11.1	11.6	11.4	7.6	4.3	1.9	56.4	14.9	0.3	1.5	0.1	1.5	25.3
Walla Walla, WA Metro Area	5.7	11.8	16.7	12.5	11.1	11.9	12.8	9.6	5.1	2.9	73.1	1.7	0.8	1.5	0.3	2.0	20.6
Warner Robins, GA Metro Area	6.6	14.0	14.1	14.3	12.6	13.7	11.9	7.6	4.0	1.2	56.3	32.0	0.3	2.5	0.1	2.2	6.6
Washington-Arlington-Alexandria, DC-VA-MD-WV Metro Area	6.7	12.8	12.8	15.3	14.4	14.4	11.9	7.1	3.2	1.5	46.4	25.0	0.2	10.3	0.1	2.7	15.3
Silver Spring-Frederick-Rockville, MD Metro Division	6.4	13.1	12.1	13.1	13.7	14.8	13.0	7.9	3.8	2.1	50.9	16.1	0.2	13.2	0.0	2.6	17.0
Washington-Arlington-Alexandria, DC-VA-MD-WV Metro Division	6.7	12.7	13.0	15.9	14.6	14.4	11.6	6.9	3.0	1.3	45.2	27.4	0.2	9.5	0.1	2.8	14.8
Waterloo-Cedar Falls, IA Metro Area	6.1	12.1	18.0	12.5	11.0	11.5	12.7	8.6	4.8	2.6	85.5	7.1	0.1	1.7	0.2	1.9	3.5
Watertown-Fort Drum, NY Metro Area	8.7	12.3	16.3	17.1	11.5	11.2	10.3	7.4	3.6	1.7	81.9	6.1	0.5	1.5	0.3	2.4	7.3
Wausau, WI Metro Area	6.0	13.0	12.3	11.8	12.0	14.4	14.0	9.1	5.0	2.4	89.1	0.8	0.4	5.7	0.0	1.2	2.8
Weirton-Steubenville, WV-OH Metro Area	4.7	10.9	12.6	10.3	11.4	13.6	16.1	11.2	6.5	2.8	92.5	4.0	0.2	0.4	0.0	1.7	1.2
Wenatchee, WA Metro Area	6.7	13.9	12.6	12.1	11.4	12.3	13.6	10.0	5.1	2.3	67.1	0.5	0.7	1.0	0.2	1.6	28.9
Wheeling, WV-OH Metro Area	5.2	10.7	12.1	11.7	11.6	13.3	15.8	10.9	5.8	2.9	93.5	3.2	0.2	0.6	0.0	1.5	1.0
Wichita, KS Metro Area	7.1	14.6	13.8	13.8	11.9	12.3	12.7	7.7	4.1	2.0	72.4	7.5	0.8	3.7	0.1	2.9	12.6
Wichita Falls, TX Metro Area	6.3	12.3	16.5	14.4	11.1	12.0	12.4	8.1	4.8	2.0	69.1	9.0	0.8	1.9	0.1	1.9	17.2
Williamsport, PA Metro Area	5.7	11.4	13.0	13.1	11.0	13.4	14.5	9.7	5.4	2.8	90.9	4.5	0.2	0.6	0.0	1.8	2.0
Wilmington, NC Metro Area	5.2	11.2	15.4	13.0	12.7	13.0	13.1	9.9	4.6	2.0	76.4	14.4	0.4	1.3	0.1	1.8	5.6
Winchester, VA-WV Metro Area	5.8	12.7	12.5	12.4	12.3	14.7	13.3	9.7	4.9	1.8	82.9	5.0	0.2	1.5	0.0	1.8	8.6
Winston-Salem, NC Metro Area	5.7	13.0	13.3	11.7	12.3	14.4	13.4	9.5	4.8	2.0	68.9	17.5	0.3	1.7	0.1	1.5	10.0
Worcester, MA-CT Metro Area	5.5	12.1	14.0	12.4	12.4	15.3	13.8	8.3	4.1	2.2	44.3	4.1	0.2	4.4	0.0	1.7	10.8
Yakima, WA Metro Area	8.3	16.7	14.8	13.0	11.8	11.4	10.8	7.6	3.8	1.7	44.3	0.8	3.7	1.1	0.1	1.7	48.3
York-Hanover, PA Metro Area	5.7	12.7	12.2	12.2	12.2	14.7	13.9	9.3	4.7	2.2	84.2	5.5	0.2	1.4	0.0	1.7	7.0
Youngstown-Warren-Boardman, OH-PA Metro Area	5.2	11.4	12.6	11.0	11.2	13.5	15.3	10.7	6.0	3.2	83.4	10.7	0.2	0.7	0.0	1.7	3.3
Yuba City, CA Metro Area	7.2	15.2	14.1	14.4	12.0	12.1	11.5	7.8	4.2	1.5	51.0	2.5	1.2	12.1	0.3	3.7	29.2
Yuma, AZ Metro Area	7.4	14.1	15.8	13.2	10.8	10.8	9.8	9.4	6.6	2.0	32.6	2.0	1.0	1.2	0.1	1.1	62.0

[1]Persons of Hispanic origin may be any race.

Table B-4.   Migration and Commuting, 2015

Metropolitan statistical area and division	Migration, 2015			Commuting, 2015					
	Total population age 1 year and older	Percent who lived in the same house in prior year	Percent who lived outside this metro area in prior year	Total residents age 16 and older	Total who worked in this metro area	Lived and worked in this metro area	Employment residence ratio	Mean travel time to work	Percent who drove alone to work
Abilene, TX Metro Area	166,688	78.9	8.9	134,017	76,288	72,820	1.00	15.6	86.2
Akron, OH Metro Area	697,817	87.7	4.6	575,548	336,376	251,934	1.00	24.3	88.0
Albany, GA Metro Area	154,246	86.4	4.2	122,083	59,726	52,954	0.99	20.8	83.7
Albany, OR Metro Area	119,536	81.4	6.7	95,784	42,698	31,026	0.89	21.8	82.6
Albany-Schenectady-Troy, NY Metro Area	873,097	86.6	4.6	725,304	447,749	407,340	1.02	23.5	82.7
Albuquerque, NM Metro Area	896,037	84.3	4.0	722,670	399,634	389,309	0.99	23.3	86.5
Alexandria, LA Metro Area	152,252	89.4	4.3	121,590	63,309	55,980	1.04	21.3	83.4
Allentown-Bethlehem-Easton, PA-NJ Metro Area	825,042	86.7	4.9	675,380	361,013	309,533	0.90	28.3	85.0
Altoona, PA Metro Area	124,591	90.0	2.7	103,116	60,683	47,214	1.11	20.8	86.9
Amarillo, TX Metro Area	259,646	81.2	4.9	201,399	123,489	118,656	0.98	17.8	85.2
Ames, IA Metro Area	95,049	68.3	14.3	81,860	53,373	41,508	1.06	18.2	75.9
Anchorage, AK Metro Area	393,893	79.2	6.4	308,644	195,139	190,410	0.98	22.7	77.9
Ann Arbor, MI Metro Area	355,225	76.0	11.3	297,793	214,903	139,524	1.21	23.5	75.5
Anniston-Oxford-Jacksonville, AL Metro Area	114,243	83.6	6.4	93,323	44,717	34,979	0.98	26.3	87.9
Appleton, WI Metro Area	230,426	90.0	4.5	183,455	122,336	89,808	0.97	19.2	90.2
Asheville, NC Metro Area	442,974	86.9	5.7	371,889	196,980	182,999	1.01	21.0	86.7
Athens-Clarke County, GA Metro Area	200,162	79.0	10.1	166,431	99,510	80,070	1.09	20.2	78.6
Atlanta-Sandy Springs-Roswell, GA Metro Area	5,643,682	84.2	4.3	4,438,171	2,714,535	2,602,409	1.00	31.3	83.2
Atlantic City-Hammonton, NJ Metro Area	271,356	88.6	4.9	220,275	130,992	102,884	1.03	24.6	78.7
Auburn-Opelika, AL Metro Area	155,461	76.9	12.1	127,060	61,146	49,689	0.84	22.3	88.2
Augusta-Richmond County, GA-SC Metro Area	581,925	86.8	4.9	467,608	249,418	234,232	1.01	23.9	86.3
Austin-Round Rock, TX Metro Area	1,975,114	81.9	6.4	1,572,710	1,043,260	1,001,141	1.01	26.5	83.3
Bakersfield, CA Metro Area	870,920	86.2	4.8	651,998	346,743	324,679	1.02	22.8	82.1
Baltimore-Columbia-Towson, MD Metro Area	2,764,004	86.2	4.1	2,250,247	1,360,508	1,196,507	0.99	30.6	80.0
Bangor, ME Metro Area	151,453	83.1	6.1	127,856	70,972	61,126	1.06	22.8	83.4
Barnstable Town, MA Metro Area	212,987	91.2	3.6	185,313	101,803	88,691	0.99	22.1	88.0
Baton Rouge, LA Metro Area	819,483	85.9	4.2	654,581	390,937	357,956	1.03	27.1	87.0
Battle Creek, MI Metro Area	132,742	83.8	4.6	106,973	61,146	43,877	1.11	21.1	84.5
Bay City, MI Metro Area	104,480	90.7	3.6	86,423	35,171	26,092	0.75	22.8	89.9
Beaumont-Port Arthur, TX Metro Area	402,447	85.5	4.5	322,801	170,483	155,212	1.01	22.5	89.8
Beckley, WV Metro Area	120,996	89.9	2.9	99,392	41,856	35,609	0.98	27.0	82.4
Bellingham, WA Metro Area	209,892	78.9	7.2	175,831	97,718	93,127	0.97	20.2	79.7
Bend-Redmond, OR Metro Area	174,047	81.5	6.9	142,062	81,942	76,384	1.03	18.7	86.8
Billings, MT Metro Area	166,895	83.3	5.4	133,825	84,317	80,671	1.00	19.5	84.1
Binghamton, NY Metro Area	243,929	85.7	4.2	203,632	106,959	95,926	0.98	20.8	83.8
Birmingham-Hoover, AL Metro Area	1,132,247	85.0	4.3	910,443	507,672	476,191	1.00	26.2	85.8
Bismarck, ND Metro Area	127,966	84.9	6.1	103,942	68,458	66,243	0.96	17.2	88.4
Blacksburg-Christiansburg-Radford, VA Metro Area	178,466	76.9	10.9	153,285	83,316	72,375	1.03	21.6	84.2
Bloomington, IL Metro Area	186,030	82.1	8.6	152,338	103,107	89,177	1.05	17.6	83.3
Bloomington, IN Metro Area	164,030	65.8	13.2	141,099	83,149	68,909	1.05	21.7	76.2
Bloomsburg-Berwick, PA Metro Area	84,816	86.1	8.2	71,830	41,294	27,507	1.12	23.9	87.4
Boise City, ID Metro Area	668,105	81.6	5.7	520,982	307,601	301,588	1.00	21.1	84.4
Boston-Cambridge-Newton, MA-NH Metro Area	4,723,511	87.1	4.0	3,920,656	2,665,661	2,345,110	1.07	31.4	70.2
Boston, MA Metro Division	1,962,981	86.3	4.3	1,635,248	1,222,042	965,848	1.19	33.2	61.9
Cambridge-Newton-Framingham, MA Metro Division	2,335,933	88.0	3.7	1,929,786	1,239,330	1,183,123	1.00	30.3	73.8
Rockingham County-Strafford County, NH Metro Division	424,597	85.4	4.5	355,622	204,289	196,139	0.87	29.4	88.8
Boulder, CO Metro Area	316,377	78.5	10.5	263,957	194,888	133,146	1.15	23.0	74.8
Bowling Green, KY Metro Area	164,907	80.0	8.8	134,415	76,319	63,159	1.05	22.0	82.8
Bremerton-Silverdale, WA Metro Area	256,694	82.8	8.1	212,479	109,992	98,864	0.92	29.9	73.1
Bridgeport-Stamford-Norwalk, CT Metro Area	936,627	87.8	4.7	754,903	465,556	352,206	1.01	30.6	77.4
Brownsville-Harlingen, TX Metro Area	414,819	91.3	2.4	303,289	145,048	134,219	0.95	19.4	87.7
Brunswick, GA Metro Area	115,753	82.0	8.1	93,346	50,262	44,542	1.00	20.4	87.5
Buffalo-Cheektowaga-Niagara Falls, NY Metro Area	1,122,466	89.0	2.6	930,764	547,225	524,438	1.01	22.0	84.6
Burlington, NC Metro Area	156,163	82.7	7.5	126,500	62,304	46,705	0.87	24.1	85.8
Burlington-South Burlington, VT Metro Area	213,974	82.7	6.4	180,014	123,853	112,191	1.04	22.5	80.3
California-Lexington Park, MD Metro Area	110,323	82.4	9.7	87,166	49,825	41,195	0.88	30.7	87.4
Canton-Massillon, OH Metro Area	399,192	88.1	3.5	326,916	180,402	146,929	0.93	22.6	87.1
Cape Coral-Fort Myers, FL Metro Area	696,450	85.3	6.6	587,162	259,475	239,980	0.95	27.0	83.6
Cape Girardeau, MO-IL Metro Area	95,622	81.6	6.5	77,191	48,249	39,457	1.07	19.9	82.7
Carbondale-Marion, IL Metro Area	125,266	81.8	7.3	104,574	57,434	45,579	1.05	21.4	86.4
Carson City, NV Metro Area	54,049	83.1	7.4	44,744	29,322	-	1.20	18.8	83.2
Casper, WY Metro Area	81,120	84.4	7.4	62,939	41,331	38,777	1.04	17.0	89.4
Cedar Rapids, IA Metro Area	263,171	84.5	5.6	210,205	142,821	127,063	1.03	19.4	87.2
Chambersburg-Waynesboro, PA Metro Area	152,392	91.1	4.3	122,313	63,463	50,108	0.88	23.5	87.6
Champaign-Urbana, IL Metro Area	237,150	81.2	10.5	197,531	120,209	106,685	1.04	18.2	74.0
Charleston, WV Metro Area	217,098	87.8	5.1	179,319	107,659	79,893	1.22	22.0	86.2
Charleston-North Charleston, SC Metro Area	733,513	83.1	6.0	596,344	364,810	350,182	1.01	25.2	84.8
Charlotte-Concord-Gastonia, NC-SC Metro Area	2,398,562	83.7	5.1	1,899,335	1,175,453	1,100,190	1.02	26.9	86.0
Charlottesville, VA Metro Area	228,198	81.8	9.1	189,723	119,532	101,938	1.06	24.0	78.9
Chattanooga, TN-GA Metro Area	539,359	87.3	4.7	444,120	256,258	226,657	1.04	23.4	88.0

Table B-4. Migration and Commuting, 2015—*Continued*

Metropolitan statistical area and division	Migration, 2015			Commuting, 2015					
	Total population age 1 year and older	Percent who lived in the same house in prior year	Percent who lived outside this metro area in prior year	Total residents age 16 and older	Total who worked in this metro area	Lived and worked in this metro area	Employment residence ratio	Mean travel time to work	Percent who drove alone to work
Cheyenne, WY Metro Area....................	96,396	80.1	10.6	77,408	49,358	-	1.07	17.2	84.6
Chicago-Naperville-Elgin, IL-IN-WI Metro Area .	9,434,721	87.2	2.4	7,568,243	4,622,691	4,504,347	1.01	31.8	74.2
Chicago-Naperville-Arlington Heights,									
IL Metro Division................	7,249,665	87.5	2.3	5,837,383	3,637,534	3,488,768	1.03	32.7	71.0
Elgin, IL Metro Division...................	628,219	86.7	2.2	490,816	275,005	303,514	0.89	28.0	85.5
Gary, IN Metro Division....................	694,258	86.6	2.7	556,931	273,806	293,723	0.90	28.4	86.6
Lake County-Kenosha County,									
IL-WI Metro Division................	862,579	86.1	3.4	683,113	436,346	418,342	0.99	29.5	83.1
Chico, CA Metro Area....................	223,466	79.6	5.2	184,984	89,694	81,861	1.00	19.7	81.0
Cincinnati, OH-KY-IN Metro Area..........	2,135,169	84.1	3.7	1,700,094	1,039,750	981,907	1.01	24.9	86.6
Clarksville, TN-KY Metro Area............	275,143	77.4	10.2	210,139	123,918	111,429	0.98	23.0	86.2
Cleveland, TN Metro Area................	120,254	85.2	4.6	97,587	48,902	40,226	0.94	21.8	85.5
Cleveland-Elyria, OH Metro Area...........	2,039,634	85.4	3.3	1,665,876	1,002,809	894,679	1.04	24.7	85.5
Coeur d'Alene, ID Metro Area.............	149,450	81.8	7.1	118,710	63,747	54,658	0.93	20.2	83.4
College Station-Bryan, TX Metro Area.....	247,859	71.5	14.4	202,811	120,828	111,376	1.01	18.6	81.7
Colorado Springs, CO Metro Area..........	689,299	78.0	10.3	546,915	334,351	322,082	0.98	23.4	83.3
Columbia, MO Metro Area................	172,916	77.0	10.7	142,871	95,738	79,769	1.08	19.0	84.8
Columbia, SC Metro Area................	801,560	82.9	7.1	651,177	384,756	356,675	1.01	23.5	84.3
Columbus, GA-AL Metro Area.............	307,577	76.2	10.1	244,657	146,980	121,976	1.10	23.0	85.3
Columbus, IN Metro Area................	79,820	83.3	8.4	63,580	50,101	33,677	1.26	20.5	90.7
Columbus, OH Metro Area................	1,995,879	82.2	4.7	1,591,691	1,020,668	954,440	1.03	23.6	86.3
Corpus Christi, TX Metro Area............	443,929	79.5	7.2	350,205	205,540	189,360	1.03	20.2	84.7
Corvallis, OR Metro Area................	86,869	73.3	12.6	74,777	44,839	32,954	1.09	18.5	73.2
Crestview-Fort Walton Beach-Destin,									
FL Metro Area....................	259,186	78.5	10.1	211,614	127,652	110,325	1.06	25.0	84.7
Cumberland, MD-WV Metro Area..........	99,280	84.8	5.6	84,585	38,707	33,947	1.01	23.0	85.7
Dallas-Fort Worth-Arlington, TX Metro Area......	7,004,222	83.8	4.3	5,419,936	3,480,513	3,388,892	1.01	28.1	85.5
Dallas-Plano-Irving, TX Metro Division...........	4,643,277	83.9	4.2	3,587,803	2,387,174	2,273,789	1.03	28.2	84.7
Fort Worth-Arlington, TX Metro Division..........	2,360,945	83.6	4.4	1,832,133	1,093,339	1,115,103	0.96	27.8	87.1
Dalton, GA Metro Area..................	141,932	88.1	4.8	109,853	68,246	56,080	1.06	23.2	89.7
Danville, IL Metro Area.................	78,251	87.4	3.0	62,729	31,074	26,939	0.98	19.1	88.0
Daphne-Fairhope-Foley, AL Metro Area.....	201,489	89.3	4.5	164,125	73,708	63,943	0.86	26.4	91.8
Davenport-Moline-Rock Island, IA-IL Metro Area .	379,969	87.8	3.9	304,679	185,263	171,162	1.02	20.0	88.1
Dayton, OH Metro Area.................	791,031	81.5	5.4	644,267	378,038	321,288	1.04	21.1	86.2
Decatur, AL Metro Area.................	150,871	86.3	4.2	122,184	51,942	41,564	0.84	25.1	86.9
Decatur, IL Metro Area.................	105,973	85.2	3.1	85,920	52,855	41,592	1.13	17.9	85.9
Deltona-Daytona Beach-Ormond Beach,									
FL Metro Area....................	616,291	87.1	6.4	525,442	213,537	199,660	0.87	25.4	86.5
Denver-Aurora-Lakewood, CO Metro Area...........	2,779,313	82.5	5.5	2,221,193	1,464,080	1,392,338	0.99	27.7	83.3
Des Moines-West Des Moines, IA Metro Area	613,087	80.9	5.6	479,097	337,240	310,962	1.04	20.2	87.8
Detroit-Warren-Dearborn, MI Metro Area......	4,251,552	87.0	2.4	3,443,939	1,939,042	1,820,539	1.01	26.6	87.7
Detroit-Dearborn-Livonia, MI Metro Division....	1,737,388	86.8	2.2	1,383,466	755,506	658,622	1.08	24.9	83.7
Warren-Troy-Farmington Hills,									
MI Metro Division................	2,514,164	87.2	2.6	2,060,473	1,183,536	1,161,917	0.97	27.6	89.9
Dothan, AL Metro Area.................	146,582	87.7	3.8	117,987	61,880	49,613	1.03	23.5	90.1
Dover, DE Metro Area....................	171,221	83.7	7.4	138,948	68,985	54,589	0.89	26.2	87.5
Dubuque, IA Metro Area................	95,625	84.0	6.7	77,964	57,665	46,497	1.17	16.4	87.1
Duluth, MN-WI Metro Area..............	276,529	84.3	4.9	231,145	137,191	129,608	1.02	20.1	82.9
Durham-Chapel Hill, NC Metro Area..............	545,044	79.2	8.7	448,623	321,555	220,623	1.17	23.4	78.4
East Stroudsburg, PA Metro Area	165,174	89.5	5.1	136,679	64,341	46,897	0.85	39.6	83.1
Eau Claire, WI Metro Area...............	163,327	81.1	5.6	133,490	88,194	77,303	1.03	19.9	87.0
El Centro, CA Metro Area...............	177,586	84.8	5.7	134,465	58,623	54,477	0.98	20.5	87.3
Elizabethtown-Fort Knox, KY Metro Area	145,998	80.2	10.3	115,972	63,174	51,981	0.95	24.7	84.1
Elkhart-Goshen, IN Metro Area...........	199,928	90.4	3.1	152,525	119,488	81,019	1.32	18.3	83.0
Elmira, NY Metro Area	85,969	86.5	4.8	70,856	37,926	28,209	0.99	21.3	83.3
El Paso, TX Metro Area	826,121	85.2	5.3	629,911	354,745	337,096	1.00	23.3	82.5
Enid, OK Metro Area..................	62,876	83.5	5.3	48,487	-	-	-	-	86.3
Erie, PA Metro Area	274,091	86.3	4.0	224,110	129,500	120,237	1.04	19.7	81.6
Eugene, OR Metro Area................	358,995	80.0	7.0	302,459	163,633	155,391	1.01	20.5	72.7
Evansville, IN-KY Metro Area............	313,502	84.6	4.1	252,606	153,993	136,999	1.03	20.5	89.3
Fairbanks, AK Metro Area...............	97,865	78.1	9.7	78,057	52,264	-	1.00	18.7	76.6
Fargo, ND-MN Metro Area..............	230,265	77.2	9.7	186,466	135,812	124,204	1.05	16.8	86.1
Farmington, NM Metro Area.............	117,107	87.4	3.5	91,214	49,265	46,306	0.99	22.8	88.1
Fayetteville, NC Metro Area.............	369,648	78.3	9.7	286,941	175,325	143,952	1.08	21.1	83.5
Fayetteville-Springdale-Rogers,									
AR-MO Metro Area.................	507,897	84.5	5.7	396,767	244,028	231,976	1.02	21.4	86.1
Flagstaff, AZ Metro Area................	137,916	77.8	14.3	113,457	65,675	59,547	1.01	19.3	72.1
Flint, MI Metro Area	406,348	85.3	3.9	327,202	148,275	121,300	0.90	26.1	88.0
Florence, SC Metro Area	203,166	88.7	3.2	162,868	89,470	74,342	1.07	24.3	87.6
Florence-Muscle Shoals, AL Metro Area	144,903	86.0	5.4	119,504	55,094	50,481	0.94	23.4	89.6
Fond du Lac, WI Metro Area............	101,053	90.0	4.8	82,435	49,165	36,841	0.94	21.1	86.0
Fort Collins, CO Metro Area............	329,908	80.0	10.0	273,136	163,610	139,299	0.96	22.2	80.5
Fort Smith, AR-OK Metro Area...........	276,091	83.9	5.8	220,662	112,282	104,952	1.00	20.8	86.4

Table B-4. Migration and Commuting, 2015—*Continued*

Metropolitan statistical area and division	Migration, 2015			Commuting, 2015					
	Total population age 1 year and older	Percent who lived in the same house in prior year	Percent who lived outside this metro area in prior year	Total residents age 16 and older	Total who worked in this metro area	Lived and worked in this metro area	Employment residence ratio	Mean travel time to work	Percent who drove alone to work
Fort Wayne, IN Metro Area	423,437	84.7	4.4	330,064	208,110	183,623	1.02	21.1	88.1
Fresno, CA Metro Area	959,794	84.0	3.8	725,355	387,895	351,552	1.01	21.8	80.7
Gadsden, AL Metro Area	102,086	82.8	5.0	82,860	38,438	31,271	0.90	22.5	88.8
Gainesville, FL Metro Area	274,546	75.7	11.1	230,540	139,031	114,564	1.11	22.9	78.4
Gainesville, GA Metro Area	190,560	84.5	6.1	149,148	89,625	59,287	1.06	25.6	85.0
Gettysburg, PA Metro Area	101,378	87.1	5.4	83,698	34,530	24,844	0.69	26.0	84.4
Glens Falls, NY Metro Area	125,886	86.7	4.3	106,056	59,267	46,473	0.97	24.2	81.8
Goldsboro, NC Metro Area	122,109	81.1	7.3	98,376	51,376	40,560	0.97	21.2	85.1
Grand Forks, ND-MN Metro Area	100,626	79.8	10.5	82,829	57,443	52,293	1.02	14.6	85.8
Grand Island, NE Metro Area	83,852	84.6	6.9	65,493	45,914	40,826	1.02	17.8	83.0
Grand Junction, CO Metro Area	146,397	80.0	9.1	119,434	66,873	65,237	0.98	21.0	83.1
Grand Rapids-Wyoming, MI Metro Area	1,025,653	84.8	4.4	811,300	526,353	463,205	1.03	22.3	85.5
Grants Pass, OR Metro Area	84,031	85.7	6.8	70,644	27,449	24,858	0.89	19.7	85.9
Great Falls, MT Metro Area	81,019	84.0	6.6	65,471	39,273	-	1.00	15.3	78.7
Greeley, CO Metro Area	281,553	81.4	10.5	216,693	121,689	89,007	0.89	26.5	86.6
Green Bay, WI Metro Area	312,758	85.3	3.6	250,763	169,594	146,633	1.04	19.9	88.6
Greensboro-High Point, NC Metro Area	745,246	87.5	4.7	602,038	362,373	295,483	1.05	22.3	88.1
Greenville, NC Metro Area	173,962	78.1	12.3	142,012	81,390	66,027	1.00	19.3	88.7
Greenville-Anderson-Mauldin, SC Metro Area	863,872	84.4	5.4	700,221	391,689	346,319	1.01	22.6	87.2
Gulfport-Biloxi-Pascagoula, MS Metro Area	384,429	82.5	6.0	306,505	166,691	149,493	1.03	24.6	87.4
Hagerstown-Martinsburg, MD-WV Metro Area	257,962	85.6	6.1	208,378	105,050	80,506	0.90	29.6	85.0
Hammond, LA Metro Area	128,086	80.9	7.5	100,145	45,159	36,534	0.79	31.3	79.7
Hanford-Corcoran, CA Metro Area	148,159	80.6	8.6	113,391	54,179	43,023	0.98	21.9	82.2
Harrisburg-Carlisle, PA Metro Area	558,014	86.0	6.3	457,024	327,108	244,389	1.18	23.0	83.7
Harrisonburg, VA Metro Area	129,631	80.5	7.6	108,470	67,681	53,707	1.12	19.6	77.7
Hartford-West Hartford-East Hartford, CT Metro Area	1,200,079	87.2	4.2	992,389	633,631	523,295	1.05	23.9	85.3
Hattiesburg, MS Metro Area	147,000	77.9	7.6	115,431	65,183	53,825	1.03	23.2	82.5
Hickory-Lenoir-Morganton, NC Metro Area	358,842	87.3	5.0	293,900	145,007	129,766	0.95	23.4	89.3
Hilton Head Island-Bluffton-Beaufort, SC Metro Area	205,864	80.9	9.7	171,174	88,870	81,003	1.02	24.7	83.8
Hinesville, GA Metro Area	77,117	69.3	15.1	58,506	33,683	24,237	1.03	24.1	80.1
Homosassa Springs, FL Metro Area	139,746	85.2	6.5	122,740	35,608	31,352	0.84	24.7	84.9
Hot Springs, AR Metro Area	96,182	80.0	7.3	80,176	41,462	34,462	1.04	22.9	83.5
Houma-Thibodaux, LA Metro Area	209,357	91.2	3.2	164,504	99,101	79,062	1.10	25.4	86.3
Houston-The Woodlands-Sugar Land, TX Metro Area	6,567,175	84.6	4.4	5,065,851	3,152,152	3,072,099	1.01	30.2	83.9
Huntington-Ashland, WV-KY-OH Metro Area	357,836	87.0	2.9	292,086	135,836	118,178	0.97	22.9	85.8
Huntsville, AL Metro Area	440,495	86.3	5.1	357,481	226,598	191,419	1.13	21.5	91.3
Idaho Falls, ID Metro Area	137,831	82.2	8.7	100,307	62,663	53,821	1.05	21.4	80.9
Indianapolis-Carmel-Anderson, IN Metro Area	1,964,132	84.4	3.6	1,541,162	974,160	916,977	1.01	24.9	88.0
Iowa City, IA Metro Area	163,819	78.3	9.0	135,470	96,114	80,908	1.04	18.2	71.7
Ithaca, NY Metro Area	104,298	80.7	9.2	91,619	61,367	44,869	1.26	18.8	65.3
Jackson, MI Metro Area	157,986	83.7	5.3	128,972	63,246	50,579	0.99	22.0	84.9
Jackson, MS Metro Area	572,113	85.9	4.3	448,743	260,286	239,740	1.03	24.5	89.7
Jackson, TN Metro Area	127,578	91.5	2.9	103,293	70,224	50,551	1.19	20.5	88.4
Jacksonville, FL Metro Area	1,432,594	80.9	6.1	1,155,620	672,803	644,145	1.01	26.2	86.1
Jacksonville, NC Metro Area	182,655	71.8	15.3	142,234	91,564	83,187	1.01	20.5	78.0
Janesville-Beloit, WI Metro Area	159,639	84.2	4.4	127,612	64,984	54,221	0.84	22.7	85.8
Jefferson City, MO Metro Area	149,941	82.5	7.9	120,923	74,979	61,159	1.07	21.4	86.2
Johnson City, TN Metro Area	198,859	83.3	6.0	166,469	81,144	67,616	0.97	20.6	91.0
Johnstown, PA Metro Area	135,348	89.8	3.9	113,741	51,960	42,269	0.92	25.1	85.1
Jonesboro, AR Metro Area	126,349	79.0	6.6	100,723	58,322	49,911	1.05	18.9	83.8
Joplin, MO Metro Area	175,267	85.9	4.1	138,334	87,478	76,270	1.04	19.1	87.2
Kahului-Wailuku-Lahaina, HI Metro Area	163,044	89.8	4.5	131,431	81,256	-	1.00	21.2	78.9
Kalamazoo-Portage, MI Metro Area	331,957	82.3	6.2	267,956	157,651	135,239	0.98	21.9	85.5
Kankakee, IL Metro Area	109,732	89.7	3.9	87,001	44,661	36,519	0.94	25.1	84.5
Kansas City, MO-KS Metro Area	2,063,628	84.5	4.1	1,628,022	1,050,241	1,005,609	1.02	22.8	87.7
Kennewick-Richland, WA Metro Area	275,584	81.6	4.6	207,843	118,503	110,874	0.97	21.4	83.6
Killeen-Temple, TX Metro Area	422,981	74.6	12.8	325,262	186,786	173,161	0.99	21.0	82.8
Kingsport-Bristol-Bristol, TN-VA Metro Area	302,878	87.4	3.2	252,751	126,664	105,343	1.00	22.6	89.2
Kingston, NY Metro Area	178,459	89.7	5.1	151,238	68,773	56,451	0.82	28.0	83.9
Knoxville, TN Metro Area	853,674	84.5	5.3	704,977	400,025	365,932	1.03	23.8	88.2
Kokomo, IN Metro Area	81,680	84.7	4.7	66,010	39,331	27,933	1.12	20.0	86.7
La Crosse-Onalaska, WI-MN Metro Area	135,599	81.0	8.6	112,298	77,375	64,484	1.07	18.7	82.8
Lafayette, LA Metro Area	482,573	84.8	4.4	380,454	225,087	202,811	1.02	24.7	86.1
Lafayette-West Lafayette, IN Metro Area	212,465	74.4	10.5	174,303	112,652	95,809	1.06	18.5	76.9
Lake Charles, LA Metro Area	202,355	84.0	5.3	160,351	100,664	86,561	1.09	21.0	88.0
Lake Havasu City-Kingman, AZ Metro Area	203,748	77.6	9.4	172,689	61,385	58,469	0.89	19.5	85.8
Lakeland-Winter Haven, FL Metro Area	642,842	85.6	6.2	518,961	232,225	205,815	0.91	24.9	86.9
Lancaster, PA Metro Area	529,390	87.2	4.0	423,280	250,225	218,294	0.96	22.8	83.1
Lansing-East Lansing, MI Metro Area	467,926	80.5	7.2	385,406	235,503	199,856	1.06	21.2	83.4
Laredo, TX Metro Area	263,598	89.8	1.2	188,937	104,195	99,688	1.00	21.2	84.8

Table B-4. Migration and Commuting, 2015—*Continued*

Metropolitan statistical area and division	Migration, 2015			Commuting, 2015					
	Total population age 1 year and older	Percent who lived in the same house in prior year	Percent who lived outside this metro area in prior year	Total residents age 16 and older	Total who worked in this metro area	Lived and worked in this metro area	Employment residence ratio	Mean travel time to work	Percent who drove alone to work
Las Cruces, NM Metro Area	212,097	87.1	5.7	165,791	79,119	71,448	0.89	21.5	84.2
Las Vegas-Henderson-Paradise, NV Metro Area	2,091,021	79.8	5.7	1,668,793	966,244	946,112	1.00	25.0	81.6
Lawrence, KS Metro Area	116,663	76.1	13.2	98,265	55,638	46,870	0.88	20.0	81.2
Lawton, OK Metro Area	128,164	71.4	14.5	102,095	63,733	58,800	1.03	16.0	78.5
Lebanon, PA Metro Area	135,491	88.8	4.3	108,946	56,242	40,220	0.87	23.1	84.6
Lewiston, ID-WA Metro Area	61,474	81.2	4.6	51,668	28,409	25,966	1.01	16.7	84.5
Lewiston-Auburn, ME Metro Area	106,410	82.7	6.1	86,334	46,693	35,903	0.88	24.0	83.8
Lexington-Fayette, KY Metro Area	494,685	77.6	8.2	402,690	270,204	223,583	1.10	22.1	83.0
Lima, OII Metro Area	102,900	86.2	6.0	83,188	53,761	39,181	1.10	19.6	88.9
Lincoln, NE Metro Area	318,860	80.2	7.6	255,500	182,036	163,894	1.05	18.5	84.8
Little Rock-North Little Rock-Conway, AR Metro Area	720,652	81.0	5.0	575,157	343,195	315,385	1.03	23.4	86.6
Logan, UT-ID Metro Area	131,271	79.4	8.5	97,411	58,772	56,611	0.94	19.5	78.1
Longview, TX Metro Area	215,201	81.8	7.3	169,086	96,624	77,332	1.07	21.4	89.8
Longview, WA Metro Area	102,703	80.6	5.8	82,099	41,202	32,965	0.95	26.2	85.0
Los Angeles-Long Beach-Anaheim, CA Metro Area	13,184,696	88.3	2.8	10,696,249	6,479,842	6,040,432	1.04	30.0	79.7
Anaheim-Santa Ana-Irvine, CA Metro Division	3,133,599	86.7	3.3	2,539,295	1,625,833	1,476,686	1.06	27.3	83.8
Los Angeles-Long Beach-Glendale, CA Metro Division	10,051,097	88.8	2.7	8,156,954	4,854,009	4,563,746	1.03	30.9	78.3
Louisville/Jefferson County, KY-IN Metro Area	1,263,205	86.6	3.2	1,020,043	625,232	586,188	1.03	24.1	85.5
Lubbock, TX Metro Area	308,538	74.3	8.7	243,242	145,653	137,409	1.00	18.9	81.8
Lynchburg, VA Metro Area	257,923	87.6	4.5	216,625	113,121	102,825	0.96	23.9	83.6
Macon, GA Metro Area	228,502	85.8	5.2	182,186	97,595	73,535	1.08	24.9	87.2
Madera, CA Metro Area	152,913	91.0	4.7	117,782	47,904	33,291	0.92	26.4	80.8
Madison, WI Metro Area	633,876	81.0	6.2	519,875	383,993	334,861	1.08	21.5	79.4
Manchester-Nashua, NH Metro Area	401,820	85.3	6.1	331,285	193,907	142,008	0.90	28.8	86.7
Manhattan, KS Metro Area	97,452	72.9	15.4	80,587	48,330	40,530	0.95	15.8	80.7
Mankato-North Mankato, MN Metro Area	97,696	81.7	8.8	81,664	60,054	48,304	1.09	17.4	84.2
Mansfield, OH Metro Area	121,018	83.7	5.5	98,229	52,913	41,151	1.03	22.9	86.8
McAllen-Edinburg-Mission, TX Metro Area	829,925	90.6	3.1	591,772	289,858	274,695	0.95	23.0	83.2
Medford, OR Metro Area	210,081	80.9	7.0	174,038	91,089	85,124	1.03	19.3	81.3
Memphis, TN-MS-AR Metro Area	1,327,052	85.5	3.3	1,044,114	624,682	593,705	1.03	23.8	87.1
Merced, CA Metro Area	264,589	87.0	5.6	198,216	79,108	66,838	0.85	25.0	78.5
Miami-Fort Lauderdale-West Palm Beach, FL Metro Area	5,947,658	85.6	3.9	4,919,039	2,817,706	2,762,447	1.00	29.1	82.8
Fort Lauderdale-Pompano Beach-Deerfield Beach, FL Metro Division	1,877,165	83.7	4.1	1,535,382	843,487	913,702	0.91	28.0	83.5
Miami-Miami Beach-Kendall, FL Metro Division	2,661,077	88.5	3.0	2,204,515	1,312,125	1,221,903	1.06	31.9	81.5
West Palm Beach-Boca Raton-Delray Beach, FL Metro Division	1,409,416	82.7	5.4	1,179,142	662,094	626,842	1.03	25.4	84.4
Michigan City-La Porte, IN Metro Area	110,272	80.1	8.9	89,265	40,003	31,707	0.87	22.3	83.9
Midland, MI Metro Area	82,525	84.8	5.6	67,364	41,651	28,188	1.11	20.7	88.1
Midland, TX Metro Area	161,298	81.8	8.7	124,168	101,614	73,058	1.22	19.4	88.2
Milwaukee-Waukesha-West Allis, WI Metro Area	1,557,574	85.6	3.2	1,246,149	824,549	749,820	1.06	23.1	83.4
Minneapolis-St. Paul-Bloomington, MN-WI Metro Area	3,478,017	84.7	3.7	2,772,146	1,902,029	1,828,104	1.01	25.4	82.2
Missoula, MT Metro Area	113,440	81.7	9.0	93,433	62,323	-	1.05	19.0	76.0
Mobile, AL Metro Area	409,617	86.6	3.2	326,702	179,636	154,148	1.04	25.0	89.7
Modesto, CA Metro Area	531,049	87.1	3.8	408,949	188,988	159,920	0.90	28.0	85.6
Monroe, LA Metro Area	176,609	88.4	4.6	138,394	74,785	63,716	1.05	21.1	88.9
Monroe, MI Metro Area	148,012	89.3	4.8	121,267	46,169	32,179	0.68	24.3	88.1
Montgomery, AL Metro Area	370,497	82.2	4.7	295,792	165,960	148,007	1.05	22.2	88.4
Morgantown, WV Metro Area	136,417	85.6	7.7	117,974	69,448	52,176	1.16	21.4	81.8
Morristown, TN Metro Area	114,689	88.3	5.4	93,706	45,971	34,051	0.96	25.2	83.7
Mount Vernon-Anacortes, WA Metro Area	120,699	84.7	7.4	97,906	55,537	44,604	1.03	25.6	83.4
Muncie, IN Metro Area	115,669	76.0	9.1	97,275	53,439	42,098	1.04	20.3	80.6
Muskegon, MI Metro Area	171,094	84.3	5.4	136,526	65,673	54,116	0.91	20.9	86.3
Myrtle Beach-Conway-North Myrtle Beach, SC-NC Metro Area	429,529	83.5	7.5	362,000	173,652	156,630	0.96	23.1	86.1
Napa, CA Metro Area	141,442	85.9	5.9	115,251	77,114	52,590	1.13	24.7	81.9
Naples-Immokalee-Marco Island, FL Metro Area	354,015	84.7	7.3	300,290	155,947	133,815	1.05	24.4	82.9
Nashville-Davidson—Murfreesboro—Franklin, TN Metro Area	1,809,800	82.6	5.5	1,446,261	936,353	879,006	1.03	27.4	86.1
New Bern, NC Metro Area	123,504	79.6	10.1	100,744	52,413	44,510	0.95	20.7	86.2
New Haven-Milford, CT Metro Area	851,026	88.0	4.4	704,794	392,701	309,670	0.93	25.7	81.0
New Orleans-Metairie, LA Metro Area	1,246,429	87.4	3.8	1,009,182	610,796	557,797	1.05	25.9	81.6
New York-Newark-Jersey City, NY-NJ-PA Metro Area	19,943,094	90.8	2.1	16,265,767	9,733,145	9,369,168	1.02	36.3	52.0
Dutchess County-Putnam County, NY Metro Division	391,102	89.6	3.0	326,247	141,927	-	0.76	33.1	80.9
Nassau County-Suffolk County, NY Metro Division	2,834,249	93.2	1.3	2,316,694	1,222,342	-	0.87	33.9	76.8
Newark, NJ-PA Metro Division	2,483,236	90.5	1.8	2,005,406	1,209,033	1,176,896	0.99	33.3	75.0

Table B-4.   Migration and Commuting, 2015—*Continued*

	Migration, 2015			Commuting, 2015					
Metropolitan statistical area and division	Total population age 1 year and older	Percent who lived in the same house in prior year	Percent who lived outside this metro area in prior year	Total residents age 16 and older	Total who worked in this metro area	Lived and worked in this metro area	Employment residence ratio	Mean travel time to work	Percent who drove alone to work
New York-Jersey City-White Plains, NY-NJ Metro Division	14,234,507	90.4	2.2	11,617,420	7,159,843	6,625,840	1.06	37.4	41.9
Niles-Benton Harbor, MI Metro Area	152,660	85.3	5.5	124,552	69,514	56,621	1.00	18.5	86.7
North Port-Sarasota-Bradenton, FL Metro Area	763,466	83.2	7.0	654,653	302,012	278,597	1.00	25.2	86.9
Norwich-New London, CT Metro Area	269,580	84.7	6.7	223,781	135,723	108,067	1.00	23.7	83.3
Ocala, FL Metro Area	340,394	84.6	7.3	286,389	99,731	86,152	0.92	27.0	87.6
Ocean City, NJ Metro Area	93,959	90.8	5.4	80,467	42,667	32,037	1.02	22.5	82.5
Odessa, TX Metro Area	156,525	81.0	7.3	116,445	75,912	59,371	1.03	21.4	86.5
Ogden-Clearfield, UT Metro Area	633,974	83.9	5.6	461,810	248,688	228,991	0.84	22.1	84.2
Oklahoma City, OK Metro Area	1,342,128	82.2	5.2	1,053,263	644,140	615,449	1.01	22.5	86.3
Olympia-Tumwater, WA Metro Area	266,822	81.8	9.2	217,609	113,231	88,257	0.93	26.2	84.4
Omaha-Council Bluffs, NE-IA Metro Area	902,374	84.2	4.6	703,448	472,410	450,010	1.01	20.1	87.2
Orlando-Kissimmee-Sanford, FL Metro Area	2,362,844	82.3	6.5	1,917,585	1,190,934	1,087,724	1.05	27.9	85.4
Oshkosh-Neenah, WI Metro Area	168,039	86.0	6.6	138,422	95,737	63,425	1.12	17.8	89.6
Owensboro, KY Metro Area	116,657	86.8	4.5	92,223	51,549	44,730	1.01	21.7	91.2
Oxnard-Thousand Oaks-Ventura, CA Metro Area	839,764	88.3	3.7	672,407	352,011	310,049	0.88	27.2	83.0
Palm Bay-Melbourne-Titusville, FL Metro Area	562,142	83.3	8.2	476,378	228,228	220,283	0.96	23.8	86.6
Panama City, FL Metro Area	195,463	81.8	8.4	158,872	90,517	83,363	1.01	24.1	83.3
Parkersburg-Vienna, WV Metro Area	91,153	88.6	3.8	75,111	42,627	31,442	1.11	20.3	82.6
Pensacola-Ferry Pass-Brent, FL Metro Area	474,690	79.3	9.8	388,577	206,585	198,271	0.94	23.2	85.1
Peoria, IL Metro Area	371,946	86.7	3.7	297,218	177,990	162,963	1.02	20.7	86.3
Philadelphia-Camden-Wilmington, PA-NJ-DE-MD Metro Area	5,999,663	88.3	3.0	4,883,842	2,843,317	2,678,041	0.99	29.6	76.6
Camden, NJ Metro Division	1,239,859	89.1	2.9	1,006,396	514,063	528,953	0.85	28.4	84.5
Montgomery County-Bucks County-Chester County, PA Metro Division	1,940,870	89.7	2.8	1,584,219	1,002,340	920,448	1.00	29.2	85.3
Philadelphia, PA Metro Division	2,102,579	87.1	3.0	1,710,953	977,754	906,705	1.05	32.0	59.4
Wilmington, DE-MD-NJ Metro Division	716,355	86.5	4.0	582,274	349,160	321,935	0.99	26.1	84.6
Phoenix-Mesa-Scottsdale, AZ Metro Area	4,520,222	82.7	4.9	3,576,384	2,031,324	2,006,519	0.99	26.2	81.6
Pine Bluff, AR Metro Area	93,553	89.0	5.7	75,954	32,973	27,407	0.99	20.6	86.4
Pittsburgh, PA Metro Area	2,328,847	87.4	3.2	1,955,221	1,144,356	1,086,149	1.01	26.6	80.6
Pittsfield, MA Metro Area	126,811	89.4	4.5	108,789	63,805	57,973	1.01	19.6	78.6
Pocatello, ID Metro Area	82,728	78.1	9.8	63,487	32,316	29,463	0.94	16.6	78.1
Portland-South Portland, ME Metro Area	522,174	85.6	4.7	437,593	276,057	245,682	1.00	24.2	85.8
Portland-Vancouver-Hillsboro, OR-WA Metro Area	2,363,290	82.7	5.2	1,920,269	1,178,279	1,134,255	1.01	26.6	74.8
Port St. Lucie, FL Metro Area	450,045	84.2	9.2	377,607	157,722	145,878	0.86	27.2	83.9
Prescott, AZ Metro Area	221,064	81.2	7.8	188,960	76,609	73,681	0.93	24.7	81.6
Providence-Warwick, RI-MA Metro Area	1,596,245	87.4	3.8	1,325,178	704,808	644,313	0.90	26.2	82.4
Provo-Orem, UT Metro Area	572,484	79.1	8.0	404,065	245,279	219,883	0.95	21.0	78.4
Pueblo, CO Metro Area	161,931	83.4	7.5	130,047	64,270	57,664	1.00	22.2	84.1
Punta Gorda, FL Metro Area	171,467	83.9	10.0	153,663	50,877	41,972	0.85	23.8	89.0
Racine, WI Metro Area	192,582	88.1	3.8	154,457	80,651	59,415	0.87	23.1	85.4
Raleigh, NC Metro Area	1,258,360	83.4	6.8	992,118	624,089	534,076	0.99	25.9	86.7
Rapid City, SD Metro Area	143,332	82.7	8.3	114,731	72,397	69,094	1.00	19.0	88.0
Reading, PA Metro Area	411,801	88.3	4.1	331,330	180,236	147,586	0.92	23.7	83.0
Redding, CA Metro Area	178,039	84.9	6.1	145,944	72,245	65,385	1.03	18.8	85.8
Reno, NV Metro Area	446,310	80.0	6.2	362,309	218,532	204,050	1.00	20.9	79.4
Richmond, VA Metro Area	1,257,294	82.7	5.6	1,025,345	637,552	598,310	1.01	24.5	85.4
Riverside-San Bernardino-Ontario, CA Metro Area	4,431,662	85.8	4.9	3,445,866	1,578,455	1,456,627	0.87	31.9	82.2
Roanoke, VA Metro Area	308,307	83.2	4.9	253,757	152,466	131,779	1.07	25.4	87.1
Rochester, MN Metro Area	211,570	85.6	5.4	167,202	118,287	102,289	1.06	19.6	78.0
Rochester, NY Metro Area	1,070,622	84.6	4.6	880,839	516,254	491,425	1.02	21.5	84.3
Rockford, IL Metro Area	337,371	86.1	4.8	267,231	152,198	131,596	0.99	22.8	88.5
Rocky Mount, NC Metro Area	146,046	89.3	4.0	117,828	60,082	48,765	0.95	21.5	85.0
Rome, GA Metro Area	95,143	79.5	7.2	76,222	46,283	32,874	1.18	22.1	87.0
Sacramento—Roseville—Arden-Arcade, CA Metro Area	2,246,663	83.8	4.7	1,804,752	980,903	917,074	0.99	26.9	82.2
Saginaw, MI Metro Area	190,128	84.3	4.6	157,282	95,733	64,135	1.20	22.8	84.4
St. Cloud, MN Metro Area	192,188	80.1	8.7	154,284	111,166	90,456	1.05	21.9	85.5
St. George, UT Metro Area	153,143	79.7	8.5	117,406	62,216	59,007	1.01	16.5	82.2
St. Joseph, MO-KS Metro Area	125,324	82.3	8.3	102,589	62,720	53,131	1.04	17.8	86.8
St. Louis, MO-IL Metro Area	2,784,008	85.6	3.1	2,250,742	1,373,561	1,331,226	1.00	25.6	86.9
Salem, OR Metro Area	405,349	82.6	5.6	321,097	168,946	146,986	0.94	23.4	79.1
Salinas, CA Metro Area	427,722	87.0	6.4	331,326	183,717	166,669	0.99	22.3	72.9
Salisbury, MD-DE Metro Area	390,970	83.8	5.9	325,690	165,537	150,461	0.97	24.4	88.0
Salt Lake City, UT Metro Area	1,153,468	84.0	5.2	871,393	646,374	538,400	1.11	22.3	78.7
San Angelo, TX Metro Area	118,730	84.0	9.0	94,722	55,774	52,666	0.99	17.8	85.2
San Antonio-New Braunfels, TX Metro Area	2,348,071	82.6	5.0	1,837,018	1,066,055	1,034,649	0.99	26.4	84.7
San Diego-Carlsbad, CA Metro Area	3,257,856	84.3	5.0	2,652,326	1,609,120	1,538,487	1.01	26.1	81.9
San Francisco-Oakland-Hayward, CA Metro Area	4,603,814	87.1	4.9	3,818,210	2,347,752	2,057,559	1.02	33.2	62.8
Oakland-Hayward-Berkeley, CA Metro Division	2,732,647	87.3	4.2	2,223,173	1,109,087	1,153,291	0.86	34.8	68.9

Table B-4.   Migration and Commuting, 2015—*Continued*

	Migration, 2015			Commuting, 2015					
Metropolitan statistical area and division	Total population age 1 year and older	Percent who lived in the same house in prior year	Percent who lived outside this metro area in prior year	Total residents age 16 and older	Total who worked in this metro area	Lived and worked in this metro area	Employment residence ratio	Mean travel time to work	Percent who drove alone to work
San Francisco-Redwood City-South San Francisco, CA Metro Division	1,612,875	86.7	6.0	1,381,434	1,111,539	782,684	1.25	31.2	53.0
San Rafael, CA Metro Division	258,292	87.1	5.0	213,603	127,126	121,584	0.99	31.6	69.8
San Jose-Sunnyvale-Santa Clara, CA Metro Area..	1,952,483	86.1	6.3	1,574,490	1,092,267	835,970	1.14	28.1	79.6
San Luis Obispo-Paso Robles-Arroyo Grande, CA Metro Area	279,604	80.3	8.5	236,308	127,260	115,094	0.99	21.0	77.6
Santa Cruz-Watsonville, CA Metro Area	270,538	86.1	5.9	226,071	118,980	102,502	0.93	26.2	74.4
Santa Fe, NM Metro Area	147,599	88.4	5.8	123,712	70,829	58,800	1.00	21.9	87.1
Santa Maria-Santa Barbara, CA Metro Area	440,542	81.0	7.8	356,206	223,444	196,483	1.06	20.1	71.6
Santa Rosa, CA Metro Area	496,451	86.7	5.0	411,102	228,261	210,882	0.93	24.5	79.5
Savannah, GA Metro Area	373,964	78.3	9.8	300,506	184,781	165,139	1.05	23.2	80.8
Scranton—Wilkes-Barre—Hazleton, PA Metro Area	552,744	88.4	3.2	460,733	261,106	231,786	1.02	22.1	84.2
Seattle-Tacoma-Bellevue, WA Metro Area	3,689,105	81.4	5.2	3,007,037	1,927,939	1,842,662	1.02	30.2	73.3
Seattle-Bellevue-Everett, WA Metro Division	2,857,330	81.1	5.4	2,343,162	1,599,053	1,475,352	1.07	29.9	70.8
Tacoma-Lakewood, WA Metro Division	831,775	82.6	4.7	663,875	328,886	367,310	0.85	31.6	82.8
Sebastian-Vero Beach, FL Metro Area	146,312	86.7	7.4	124,878	51,702	43,191	1.00	22.1	84.6
Sebring, FL Metro Area	98,958	82.3	7.4	84,228	29,262	26,944	0.93	22.1	85.9
Sheboygan, WI Metro Area	114,370	87.3	3.7	92,339	59,924	49,515	1.03	18.6	85.1
Sherman-Denison, TX Metro Area	124,282	80.7	9.0	99,482	50,793	41,919	0.88	24.7	80.6
Shreveport-Bossier City, LA Metro Area	439,423	88.2	3.2	346,648	192,107	178,105	1.03	22.4	89.0
Sierra Vista-Douglas, AZ Metro Area	124,453	80.5	11.1	102,342	42,533	40,120	0.99	20.6	82.8
Sioux City, IA-NE-SD Metro Area	162,582	88.6	5.0	127,825	81,318	76,124	1.00	18.4	85.9
Sioux Falls, SD Metro Area	248,983	81.8	5.0	192,947	138,814	129,110	1.04	18.7	87.2
South Bend-Mishawaka, IN-MI Metro Area	316,489	85.9	5.4	253,682	134,373	110,586	0.94	20.9	83.4
Spartanburg, SC Metro Area	321,487	84.2	4.7	258,134	152,628	112,486	1.08	22.4	88.3
Spokane-Spokane Valley, WA Metro Area	540,826	82.0	7.3	439,083	232,700	216,789	1.02	21.9	82.7
Springfield, IL Metro Area	209,301	82.1	5.5	168,481	111,136	92,901	1.13	19.6	85.5
Springfield, MA Metro Area	625,730	86.5	4.7	518,816	291,563	260,285	0.98	22.8	83.7
Springfield, MO Metro Area	449,841	81.3	6.8	363,488	215,767	197,874	1.04	22.1	85.2
Springfield, OH Metro Area	133,741	78.4	5.9	108,468	49,612	38,243	0.83	22.1	86.0
State College, PA Metro Area	159,153	75.9	13.9	138,761	83,941	68,793	1.10	20.3	68.7
Staunton-Waynesboro, VA Metro Area	119,262	86.3	6.5	99,298	47,746	41,224	0.88	22.5	89.1
Stockton-Lodi, CA Metro Area	716,791	85.7	5.3	548,879	251,471	202,436	0.89	31.1	79.4
Sumter, SC Metro Area	104,992	82.7	6.2	84,642	45,290	36,139	1.02	22.0	87.2
Syracuse, NY Metro Area	653,726	85.6	4.9	535,993	310,039	283,736	1.02	21.6	84.3
Tallahassee, FL Metro Area	374,514	78.2	8.7	314,083	177,476	167,183	1.03	23.6	83.4
Tampa-St. Petersburg-Clearwater, FL Metro Area	2,946,960	83.9	5.4	2,440,504	1,324,973	1,284,811	0.99	27.0	85.4
Terre Haute, IN Metro Area	170,345	80.6	7.8	140,222	69,616	60,166	0.98	23.6	85.4
Texarkana, TX-AR Metro Area	149,660	82.8	5.1	118,450	58,308	52,836	1.02	20.1	88.7
The Villages, FL Metro Area	118,274	87.3	8.6	111,323	30,849	16,321	1.32	24.0	87.6
Toledo, OH Metro Area	598,585	81.2	5.0	484,139	298,012	254,140	1.06	21.1	86.7
Topeka, KS Metro Area	230,885	83.8	4.4	183,614	107,311	96,704	1.00	19.9	86.9
Trenton, NJ Metro Area	367,294	87.8	6.1	299,994	231,113	117,540	1.32	27.6	77.2
Tucson, AZ Metro Area	997,158	79.0	6.2	817,168	423,278	411,135	1.00	24.5	80.5
Tulsa, OK Metro Area	967,240	83.1	4.4	762,865	462,388	438,536	1.01	21.3	85.9
Tuscaloosa, AL Metro Area	238,000	84.6	6.4	196,841	100,918	87,965	1.03	23.5	89.8
Tyler, TX Metro Area	219,790	86.5	6.5	172,866	105,194	85,443	1.08	23.9	90.2
Urban Honolulu, HI Metro Area	986,125	84.4	6.1	806,782	506,230	500,887	1.00	29.1	66.3
Utica-Rome, NY Metro Area	292,189	88.7	4.5	238,964	123,891	112,855	0.99	21.1	86.5
Valdosta, GA Metro Area	140,397	80.5	6.0	109,622	58,300	51,629	1.04	20.2	86.9
Vallejo-Fairfield, CA Metro Area	433,103	83.4	7.3	348,462	146,047	115,450	0.76	30.9	81.0
Victoria, TX Metro Area	97,783	83.4	5.3	76,674	46,290	38,323	1.05	19.8	84.3
Vineland-Bridgeton, NJ Metro Area	154,014	88.9	4.4	123,260	63,263	47,200	0.99	22.9	88.4
Virginia Beach-Norfolk-Newport News, VA-NC Metro Area	1,701,056	80.7	6.7	1,383,422	854,256	820,483	1.01	24.8	85.6
Visalia-Porterville, CA Metro Area	452,475	87.2	2.7	330,900	152,586	138,548	0.93	25.0	80.8
Waco, TX Metro Area	259,084	82.9	6.6	205,473	118,794	106,129	1.03	20.1	83.6
Walla Walla, WA Metro Area	63,579	81.4	7.1	52,436	33,332	24,997	1.23	15.1	75.8
Warner Robins, GA Metro Area	185,412	81.4	7.1	144,877	82,318	66,730	1.00	20.9	87.5
Washington-Arlington-Alexandria, DC-VA-MD-WV Metro Area	6,018,925	84.3	5.1	4,832,622	3,372,857	3,067,426	1.05	34.4	69.3
Silver Spring-Frederick-Rockville, MD Metro Division	1,269,992	85.7	4.4	1,016,889	625,064	630,853	0.92	34.5	72.6
Washington-Arlington-Alexandria, DC-VA-MD-WV Metro Division	4,748,933	84.0	5.4	3,815,733	2,747,793	2,436,573	1.08	34.4	68.4
Waterloo-Cedar Falls, IA Metro Area	168,233	83.6	7.2	137,204	91,753	80,843	1.05	18.0	83.8
Watertown-Fort Drum, NY Metro Area	115,577	74.5	14.3	90,978	57,399	51,067	1.06	16.5	79.0
Wausau, WI Metro Area	134,373	88.6	5.0	107,859	72,441	59,432	1.02	19.3	87.0
Weirton-Steubenville, WV-OH Metro Area	120,544	87.2	6.0	100,578	45,223	37,256	0.85	24.4	85.8
Wenatchee, WA Metro Area	115,599	86.8	3.9	90,189	50,286	48,275	0.98	16.7	81.8
Wheeling, WV-OH Metro Area	143,206	91.7	3.3	119,803	66,095	53,214	1.09	22.4	89.4
Wichita, KS Metro Area	635,343	86.0	3.2	494,351	307,054	295,530	1.01	19.6	88.3
Wichita Falls, TX Metro Area	148,514	82.7	8.3	121,428	65,674	63,030	0.99	15.9	80.8

Table B-4. Migration and Commuting, 2015—*Continued*

Metropolitan statistical area and division	Migration, 2015			Commuting, 2015					
	Total population age 1 year and older	Percent who lived in the same house in prior year	Percent who lived outside this metro area in prior year	Total residents age 16 and older	Total who worked in this metro area	Lived and worked in this metro area	Employment residence ratio	Mean travel time to work	Percent who drove alone to work
Williamsport, PA Metro Area	114,411	85.5	4.7	94,792	57,191	47,293	1.04	19.9	82.2
Wilmington, NC Metro Area	274,984	82.9	7.2	229,344	136,201	116,987	1.07	21.0	86.3
Winchester, VA-WV Metro Area	131,874	87.6	5.1	107,297	60,789	44,176	0.97	30.8	84.4
Winston-Salem, NC Metro Area	652,125	85.1	4.6	526,838	267,245	227,473	0.92	23.5	88.2
Worcester, MA-CT Metro Area	927,751	87.7	4.4	758,205	394,056	321,978	0.86	28.3	85.2
Yakima, WA Metro Area	245,499	86.0	3.9	181,328	102,156	98,033	1.00	18.0	80.4
York-Hanover, PA Metro Area	437,832	85.6	4.5	355,190	183,277	147,077	0.84	26.5	86.1
Youngstown-Warren-Boardman, OH-PA Metro Area	543,818	89.0	3.0	450,796	234,774	202,735	0.99	21.7	89.5
Yuba City, CA Metro Area	168,573	83.3	7.2	130,171	56,421	45,256	0.87	26.9	84.1
Yuma, AZ Metro Area	201,187	82.5	5.8	158,011	70,010	68,893	0.96	19.1	86.5

Table B-5. Population and Household Characteristics 2015

Metropolitan statistical area and division	Households Total	Family households Total	Family households With own children under 18 Total	Family households With own children under 18 Single parent headed (percent)	Nonfamily households Householder living alone Total	Nonfamily households Householder living alone Percent age 65 or older	Percent of households with one or more persons age 65 years or older	Foreign-born population as a percent of total population	Non-citizens as a percent of total population	Speaking language other than English at home, persons 5 years and over (percent)
Abilene, TX Metro Area	59,372	37,669	15,699	36.9	17,205	39.6	27.1	5.2	2.9	14.9
Akron, OH Metro Area	282,456	177,764	69,567	35.3	85,192	36.6	28.5	5.0	2.9	6.1
Albany, GA Metro Area	57,597	37,713	16,833	52.7	17,094	41.0	28.1	2.2	0.6	3.8
Albany, OR Metro Area	46,315	31,455	13,796	38.0	11,599	39.6	31.5	4.1	2.4	7.9
Albany-Schenectady-Troy, NY Metro Area	342,766	204,094	80,928	31.1	114,424	35.1	27.9	7.4	3.3	9.3
Albuquerque, NM Metro Area	342,590	212,005	90,036	37.3	107,238	34.6	27.7	9.8	6.1	30.4
Alexandria, LA Metro Area	54,406	36,410	15,960	48.6	15,576	41.1	30.8	2.5	1.6	4.1
Allentown-Bethlehem-Easton, PA-NJ Metro Area..	314,985	216,275	89,858	33.4	78,947	44.3	30.4	8.9	3.6	16.2
Altoona, PA Metro Area	52,830	33,350	12,659	31.7	16,850	51.8	33.9	1.4	0.2	NA
Amarillo, TX Metro Area	95,626	62,368	28,948	34.0	28,662	31.2	24.3	8.9	5.9	20.8
Ames, IA Metro Area	37,264	19,644	8,951	22.7	9,250	26.0	18.0	9.8	7.5	10.1
Anchorage, AK Metro Area	135,601	89,458	43,864	36.0	35,047	24.2	19.0	9.0	4.1	14.8
Ann Arbor, MI Metro Area	138,099	78,918	33,776	28.3	41,532	28.0	23.4	12.0	7.0	15.3
Anniston-Oxford-Jacksonville, AL Metro Area	44,323	29,438	10,315	45.3	13,214	39.2	31.0	2.9	1.4	4.8
Appleton, WI Metro Area	90,489	62,809	29,193	30.1	22,871	40.9	24.8	3.6	1.5	6.5
Asheville, NC Metro Area	184,983	112,938	38,868	30.0	60,828	41.7	34.1	6.3	3.8	8.4
Athens-Clarke County, GA Metro Area	76,704	43,444	19,078	36.9	24,294	28.0	22.9	7.7	5.5	11.6
Atlanta-Sandy Springs-Roswell, GA Metro Area ...	2,028,705	1,367,381	642,671	32.1	540,158	26.7	21.9	13.8	7.8	18.1
Atlantic City-Hammonton, NJ Metro Area	101,813	68,091	29,805	38.8	28,018	47.8	33.4	16.4	6.5	27.4
Auburn-Opelika, AL Metro Area	58,191	37,772	18,931	38.5	15,853	22.4	20.8	5.9	3.7	7.1
Augusta-Richmond County, GA-SC Metro Area	210,854	143,773	58,494	37.9	56,082	37.8	28.4	4.3	2.6	6.7
Austin-Round Rock, TX Metro Area	723,914	445,303	217,184	26.2	204,233	22.1	18.5	15.1	9.7	28.3
Bakersfield, CA Metro Area	263,273	198,899	102,034	35.3	51,596	36.8	24.0	20.4	13.5	45.2
Baltimore-Columbia-Towson, MD Metro Area	1,037,443	675,727	288,744	32.8	292,398	37.9	27.5	10.3	5.0	12.5
Bangor, ME Metro Area	59,099	37,433	14,010	43.0	16,357	37.2	28.9	2.4	1.3	3.9
Barnstable Town, MA Metro Area	97,451	59,535	16,844	27.0	30,977	51.3	43.7	7.9	3.5	8.4
Baton Rouge, LA Metro Area	300,535	193,645	84,213	38.8	87,365	34.2	24.9	3.9	2.2	6.7
Battle Creek, MI Metro Area	53,076	33,681	13,322	37.8	16,421	40.0	29.6	3.6	2.3	5.0
Bay City, MI Metro Area	42,799	26,269	9,827	34.3	13,429	46.6	31.8	1.8	0.4	NA
Beaumont-Port Arthur, TX Metro Area	153,283	99,444	44,286	36.5	46,525	36.7	27.5	8.2	5.3	16.2
Beckley, WV Metro Area	49,070	31,298	11,746	35.7	15,204	45.4	33.9	1.4	0.8	3.6
Bellingham, WA Metro Area	80,023	47,905	18,431	27.7	22,982	38.8	28.9	10.6	5.0	12.2
Bend-Redmond, OR Metro Area	69,424	46,165	18,108	22.6	17,131	37.9	32.2	4.6	2.4	6.4
Billings, MT Metro Area	68,021	41,830	18,932	29.2	20,650	33.7	27.7	2.2	0.7	4.1
Binghamton, NY Metro Area	97,883	58,688	23,420	41.3	30,843	45.6	31.5	5.5	2.3	8.1
Birmingham-Hoover, AL Metro Area	441,762	291,948	121,055	34.9	130,400	37.2	27.8	4.1	2.8	6.0
Bismarck, ND Metro Area	55,092	34,461	14,698	26.4	15,442	35.3	23.4	2.2	1.2	4.4
Blacksburg-Christiansburg-Radford, VA Metro Area	69,396	40,755	15,936	38.2	19,179	34.9	26.2	5.6	3.8	7.2
Bloomington, IL Metro Area	72,767	46,428	20,545	19.3	19,946	30.1	22.2	5.9	3.7	6.7
Bloomington, IN Metro Area	62,702	33,184	13,032	27.3	20,757	26.2	23.3	7.1	4.9	9.3
Bloomsburg-Berwick, PA Metro Area	33,140	21,264	7,460	30.6	10,021	38.1	31.7	3.4	1.3	3.4
Boise City, ID Metro Area	245,109	155,558	73,450	29.0	74,500	30.3	24.8	6.4	4.0	11.3
Boston-Cambridge-Newton, MA-NH Metro Area	1,782,655	1,131,612	491,268	27.7	498,988	38.7	27.6	18.3	8.8	24.3
Boston, MA Metro Division	743,723	445,655	191,238	32.0	225,620	37.1	27.0	20.0	9.5	26.2
Cambridge-Newton-Framingham, MA Metro Division	872,640	571,655	254,273	24.3	234,762	40.1	28.1	19.2	9.4	25.8
Rockingham County-Strafford County, NH Metro Division	166,292	114,302	45,757	28.3	38,606	39.8	27.6	5.3	2.2	7.0
Boulder, CO Metro Area	124,615	72,269	32,667	21.3	35,315	33.1	23.0	10.7	6.7	16.9
Bowling Green, KY Metro Area	62,500	42,676	18,819	37.0	16,053	29.5	24.4	7.5	5.5	11.2
Bremerton-Silverdale, WA Metro Area	98,490	66,973	26,201	31.7	24,967	36.4	29.6	6.0	1.5	6.6
Bridgeport-Stamford-Norwalk, CT Metro Area	333,528	232,162	109,068	25.1	82,864	43.1	28.3	21.3	11.4	29.6
Brownsville-Harlingen, TX Metro Area	122,468	96,931	46,345	34.7	21,979	43.9	29.7	23.8	16.0	75.5
Brunswick, GA Metro Area	46,647	32,508	12,589	46.7	12,080	45.3	34.7	2.8	1.6	4.9
Buffalo-Cheektowaga-Niagara Falls, NY Metro Area	467,992	277,851	111,698	38.9	157,660	40.5	29.6	6.6	3.2	9.5
Burlington, NC Metro Area	63,093	39,431	18,538	40.6	20,223	45.9	30.0	7.7	5.0	13.1
Burlington-South Burlington, VT Metro Area	85,553	50,335	21,223	24.7	23,122	40.6	25.0	7.4	3.7	9.8
California-Lexington Park, MD Metro Area	39,029	27,831	13,198	30.2	8,924	33.7	23.2	4.1	1.5	6.3
Canton-Massillon, OH Metro Area	162,868	104,295	40,414	39.8	48,497	43.6	31.9	2.2	0.9	3.8
Cape Coral-Fort Myers, FL Metro Area	263,694	171,923	51,021	39.7	75,796	51.6	45.4	16.0	8.8	21.0
Cape Girardeau, MO-IL Metro Area	35,273	22,479	8,158	31.5	10,220	37.0	29.6	2.0	1.6	NA
Carbondale-Marion, IL Metro Area	48,012	29,294	10,756	34.3	15,804	33.0	27.8	4.1	2.5	6.0
Carson City, NV Metro Area	22,687	13,398	5,278	34.7	7,683	48.3	34.4	10.2	5.5	21.5
Casper, WY Metro Area	32,564	19,018	8,451	35.7	11,040	38.1	24.7	3.6	1.7	NA
Cedar Rapids, IA Metro Area	107,586	67,877	29,607	31.2	31,889	34.2	25.8	2.6	1.6	4.1
Chambersburg-Waynesboro, PA Metro Area	59,486	43,290	17,195	28.6	13,552	50.0	32.7	3.3	2.1	6.8
Champaign-Urbana, IL Metro Area	92,268	49,113	21,006	31.3	33,161	29.6	22.6	10.7	6.9	16.3
Charleston, WV Metro Area	94,533	59,440	22,244	43.2	29,627	37.0	32.3	1.7	0.7	2.1
Charleston-North Charleston, SC Metro Area	273,722	174,328	71,990	35.0	79,645	32.5	25.8	5.1	2.9	6.5

NA = Not available.

Table B-5.   Population and Household Characteristics 2015—*Continued*

Metropolitan statistical area and division	Households Total	Family households Total	With own children under 18 Total	Single parent headed (percent)	Nonfamily Householder living alone Total	Percent age 65 or older	Percent of households with one or more persons age 65 years or older	Foreign-born population as a percent of total population	Non-citizens as a percent of total population	Speaking language other than English at home, persons 5 years and over (percent)
Charlotte-Concord-Gastonia, NC-SC Metro Area...	905,696	602,571	271,056	31.8	245,475	30.4	23.9	9.8	5.9	13.5
Charlottesville, VA Metro Area	87,949	54,552	22,321	26.3	23,640	37.4	29.1	7.7	4.5	9.5
Chattanooga, TN-GA Metro Area	209,340	139,913	55,414	34.3	58,059	43.2	31.3	3.9	2.4	5.3
Cheyenne, WY Metro Area	37,740	24,226	12,100	38.5	11,123	40.4	26.7	4.5	2.9	8.3
Chicago-Naperville-Elgin, IL-IN-WI Metro Area	3,470,993	2,269,030	1,022,662	30.1	988,072	35.0	25.7	18.0	9.1	29.3
Chicago-Naperville-Arlington Heights, IL Metro Division	2,686,830	1,714,648	763,169	30.1	797,998	33.9	25.5	19.5	9.8	31.5
Elgin, IL Metro Division	212,458	152,897	75,970	26.3	47,396	39.8	24.8	16.5	9.8	28.4
Gary, IN Metro Division	266,576	179,617	77,641	38.2	73,765	37.6	28.7	6.2	2.6	12.3
Lake County-Kenosha County, IL-WI Metro Division	305,129	221,868	105,882	27.0	68,913	41.5	25.3	15.9	8.5	24.9
Chico, CA Metro Area	85,289	50,799	18,987	28.9	22,825	42.6	31.4	7.4	2.9	15.0
Cincinnati, OH-KY-IN Metro Area	832,607	540,617	236,903	33.4	240,127	34.1	25.1	4.4	2.3	6.0
Clarksville, TN-KY Metro Area	101,265	68,839	35,532	27.4	26,523	27.9	19.8	4.0	1.7	8.1
Cleveland, TN Metro Area	46,389	31,350	13,231	32.9	13,127	44.2	31.0	3.9	2.5	5.6
Cleveland-Elyria, OH Metro Area	849,475	518,070	210,048	37.9	284,645	37.7	29.7	5.9	2.4	10.3
Coeur d'Alene, ID Metro Area	58,675	39,597	16,309	33.7	15,139	44.7	30.7	2.4	1.0	2.9
College Station-Bryan, TX Metro Area	90,526	51,390	22,068	32.5	25,132	24.8	18.9	13.2	10.2	21.4
Colorado Springs, CO Metro Area	261,435	181,160	82,568	27.8	64,887	33.6	22.8	7.2	3.4	12.4
Columbia, MO Metro Area	69,152	37,099	17,450	23.7	23,057	24.0	18.7	6.5	3.8	7.3
Columbia, SC Metro Area	302,634	193,734	79,579	36.0	91,056	32.0	25.7	4.6	2.7	7.2
Columbus, GA-AL Metro Area	112,983	71,389	34,035	40.9	36,488	35.0	25.8	4.6	2.4	8.4
Columbus, IN Metro Area	31,131	20,243	8,070	29.5	8,545	38.0	26.9	8.4	7.6	9.4
Columbus, OH Metro Area	772,304	493,437	229,077	34.1	219,654	30.9	22.7	7.7	4.2	9.5
Corpus Christi, TX Metro Area	161,634	108,806	44,170	38.0	42,466	38.0	28.5	8.8	5.6	36.4
Corvallis, OR Metro Area	35,062	19,538	8,034	23.4	10,802	35.9	26.0	12.0	9.2	14.2
Crestview-Fort Walton Beach-Destin, FL Metro Area	102,729	65,581	25,567	28.4	30,787	37.8	30.5	6.1	3.0	10.5
Cumberland, MD-WV Metro Area	39,120	23,909	8,177	40.1	12,674	46.6	33.8	1.9	1.2	3.8
Dallas-Fort Worth-Arlington, TX Metro Area	2,479,995	1,724,140	850,026	30.1	617,632	28.4	21.2	18.2	11.7	31.0
Dallas-Plano-Irving, TX Metro Division	1,653,468	1,138,376	570,597	28.9	416,913	26.7	20.3	20.3	13.3	33.7
Fort Worth-Arlington, TX Metro Division	826,527	585,764	279,429	32.6	200,719	32.1	23.1	14.0	8.6	25.6
Dalton, GA Metro Area	48,631	35,392	17,254	34.5	10,337	39.9	26.6	15.2	10.6	25.7
Danville, IL Metro Area	30,927	20,098	8,491	46.1	9,370	45.1	32.4	2.5	1.5	4.6
Daphne-Fairhope-Foley, AL Metro Area	72,269	45,858	15,830	23.5	23,243	43.3	36.3	2.5	1.6	6.1
Davenport-Moline-Rock Island, IA-IL Metro Area	155,753	99,208	40,807	34.1	47,856	39.8	29.2	5.0	3.2	8.9
Dayton, OH Metro Area	330,430	203,858	84,695	38.2	104,366	37.1	29.3	4.3	2.1	5.3
Decatur, AL Metro Area	60,697	42,128	16,590	36.7	16,104	40.6	28.5	4.0	3.1	5.1
Decatur, IL Metro Area	44,429	27,118	10,432	45.9	15,441	37.7	30.5	1.8	0.9	3.3
Deltona-Daytona Beach-Ormond Beach, FL Metro Area	248,938	155,112	47,468	38.2	75,566	49.7	41.4	7.9	3.1	13.4
Denver-Aurora-Lakewood, CO Metro Area	1,075,919	683,260	318,852	27.5	301,542	28.9	22.0	12.3	7.7	20.3
Des Moines-West Des Moines, IA Metro Area	242,022	156,694	73,041	29.4	68,474	32.1	22.5	7.6	4.4	11.5
Detroit-Warren-Dearborn, MI Metro Area	1,674,251	1,076,964	450,869	34.4	507,227	36.0	28.0	9.5	4.1	13.2
Detroit-Dearborn-Livonia, MI Metro Division	667,521	408,977	176,349	47.1	223,645	34.4	27.5	8.6	3.7	14.2
Warren-Troy-Farmington Hills, MI Metro Division	1,006,730	667,987	274,520	26.3	283,582	37.2	28.3	10.2	4.4	12.5
Dothan, AL Metro Area	55,973	37,461	14,805	39.2	16,111	41.3	31.6	1.9	1.0	3.2
Dover, DE Metro Area	62,477	42,633	16,854	35.7	14,971	43.8	30.7	5.1	2.6	9.1
Dubuque, IA Metro Area	37,784	25,213	10,941	29.0	10,526	37.1	27.3	2.5	1.6	4.0
Duluth, MN-WI Metro Area	116,212	68,965	27,284	37.3	38,665	41.9	29.9	2.2	1.2	4.1
Durham-Chapel Hill, NC Metro Area	215,294	126,683	51,568	34.5	68,720	30.5	24.5	12.6	8.7	17.6
East Stroudsburg, PA Metro Area	55,681	39,693	14,846	22.9	12,587	41.6	30.6	11.9	3.0	18.1
Eau Claire, WI Metro Area	63,854	39,247	16,632	31.2	18,749	40.4	27.7	2.6	0.7	5.2
El Centro, CA Metro Area	45,158	34,623	16,310	32.8	9,442	50.1	32.2	31.9	16.2	75.5
Elizabethtown-Fort Knox, KY Metro Area	56,899	39,112	16,062	33.8	15,082	38.0	25.5	2.9	1.3	5.6
Elkhart-Goshen, IN Metro Area	68,498	47,788	20,848	33.2	16,606	39.5	26.9	7.4	5.2	19.4
Elmira, NY Metro Area	34,546	21,753	8,588	38.0	10,303	47.2	29.9	3.1	1.2	3.6
El Paso, TX Metro Area	261,529	194,126	89,688	33.0	59,352	35.2	25.4	24.6	13.8	71.2
Enid, OK Metro Area	23,808	17,092	-	-	5,990	-	-	8.1	5.1	-
Erie, PA Metro Area	110,138	70,215	29,253	45.1	33,006	39.0	28.5	4.0	2.3	6.5
Eugene, OR Metro Area	146,602	87,881	32,534	37.2	44,200	41.3	31.2	6.5	4.2	8.8
Evansville, IN-KY Metro Area	124,936	80,855	32,559	36.4	38,361	36.6	27.8	2.5	1.5	3.1
Fairbanks, AK Metro Area	35,475	22,945	10,758	30.8	9,974	17.0	16.6	5.2	1.5	9.7
Fargo, ND-MN Metro Area	96,142	56,053	26,563	31.0	30,041	28.8	20.3	6.5	3.7	7.9
Farmington, NM Metro Area	43,030	29,729	12,469	41.4	10,809	41.2	29.2	4.5	3.3	33.0
Fayetteville, NC Metro Area	137,158	89,425	42,272	42.9	42,258	27.8	21.4	6.5	3.0	12.4
Fayetteville-Springdale-Rogers, AR-MO Metro Area	190,860	129,383	62,598	24.0	49,376	37.2	23.9	11.2	8.4	14.8

NA = Not available.

Table B-5.   Population and Household Characteristics 2015—*Continued*

Metropolitan statistical area and division	Households						Percent of households with one or more persons age 65 years or older	Foreign-born population		Speaking language other than English at home, persons 5 years and over (percent)
	Family households			Nonfamily households						
			With own children under 18		Householder living alone					
	Total	Total	Total	Single parent headed (percent)	Total	Percent age 65 or older		Foreign-born population as a percent of total population	Non-citizens as a percent of total population	
Flagstaff, AZ Metro Area	45,911	28,210	10,568	30.1	11,711	31.6	24.3	4.6	2.7	24.3
Flint, MI Metro Area	163,488	103,060	43,786	43.5	50,766	36.5	29.1	2.4	0.8	3.6
Florence, SC Metro Area	79,914	51,646	21,431	43.8	24,785	37.2	29.9	2.1	1.1	3.0
Florence-Muscle Shoals, AL Metro Area	60,663	39,207	15,272	37.4	18,121	45.6	31.8	1.6	1.1	3.3
Fond du Lac, WI Metro Area	40,295	27,039	10,480	27.5	11,018	40.5	28.2	2.5	1.4	4.7
Fort Collins, CO Metro Area	129,210	78,049	30,575	24.9	31,139	38.3	25.1	4.8	2.5	8.6
Fort Smith, AR-OK Metro Area	107,375	74,035	31,058	30.7	28,243	42.8	29.5	6.1	4.0	9.7
Fort Wayne, IN Metro Area	165,857	110,297	51,175	35.1	46,862	39.2	25.6	5.4	2.9	8.9
Fresno, CA Metro Area	304,209	218,095	109,655	41.5	67,741	42.0	26.4	21.5	13.5	44.6
Gadsden, AL Metro Area	39,332	27,549	10,014	34.9	10,360	46.7	31.2	2.4	2.0	3.2
Gainesville, FL Metro Area	102,219	60,769	22,943	30.2	30,956	29.0	24.2	10.2	5.6	12.8
Gainesville, GA Metro Area	63,989	49,405	21,338	24.4	12,056	46.6	28.7	16.0	10.9	26.5
Gettysburg, PA Metro Area	38,459	26,965	9,786	25.1	9,763	41.9	33.0	3.6	2.2	5.8
Glens Falls, NY Metro Area	48,814	30,665	10,314	33.3	14,247	40.4	32.8	3.3	1.6	5.2
Goldsboro, NC Metro Area	47,490	30,522	13,756	36.0	14,117	41.9	28.3	7.9	5.1	13.0
Grand Forks, ND-MN Metro Area	42,166	24,416	10,318	32.0	13,069	36.3	22.5	4.6	2.4	8.5
Grand Island, NE Metro Area	31,703	21,561	9,425	32.2	8,185	42.4	27.1	9.5	6.6	15.3
Grand Junction, CO Metro Area	59,066	38,782	15,784	36.2	16,008	40.1	31.0	3.1	1.9	6.8
Grand Rapids-Wyoming, MI Metro Area	383,194	260,720	114,889	30.9	95,325	36.5	24.9	6.8	3.9	11.0
Grants Pass, OR Metro Area	35,918	22,205	6,269	35.3	10,333	51.1	42.4	4.5	2.6	4.2
Great Falls, MT Metro Area	34,375	21,377	8,239	32.4	10,847	46.3	31.3	2.1	0.5	NA
Greeley, CO Metro Area	97,822	71,247	35,750	22.7	20,330	35.6	22.9	8.6	5.6	18.7
Green Bay, WI Metro Area	127,779	81,534	37,659	33.0	37,395	37.1	25.3	5.1	3.1	9.4
Greensboro-High Point, NC Metro Area	291,088	186,434	79,889	36.1	87,793	35.9	27.3	8.2	5.2	11.5
Greenville, NC Metro Area	68,374	40,028	17,983	40.6	20,522	27.4	21.9	4.6	2.3	6.6
Greenville-Anderson-Mauldin, SC Metro Area	332,740	218,237	88,388	31.5	95,163	35.5	28.5	6.3	4.2	8.4
Gulfport-Biloxi-Pascagoula, MS Metro Area	146,228	96,245	38,073	45.0	41,033	38.3	28.4	4.5	2.7	7.0
Hagerstown-Martinsburg, MD-WV Metro Area	97,209	65,176	27,145	33.4	25,758	44.0	29.3	4.5	1.6	6.9
Hammond, LA Metro Area	46,263	30,331	11,218	34.9	13,851	31.9	25.8	1.1	0.6	NA
Hanford-Corcoran, CA Metro Area	42,692	31,355	18,612	35.8	8,308	39.9	22.6	17.7	10.7	38.9
Harrisburg-Carlisle, PA Metro Area	225,810	147,597	59,414	34.6	66,023	39.5	29.1	6.1	3.1	9.4
Harrisonburg, VA Metro Area	47,600	29,587	11,829	30.2	12,525	41.4	27.9	10.9	7.5	14.6
Hartford-West Hartford-East Hartford, CT Metro Area	464,613	304,004	123,290	33.0	129,732	39.8	29.1	13.8	6.4	22.0
Hattiesburg, MS Metro Area	54,780	35,603	17,000	42.9	14,685	38.8	25.3	2.7	1.8	3.4
Hickory-Lenoir-Morganton, NC Metro Area	140,097	90,461	32,306	30.3	43,965	40.1	32.5	5.4	2.9	9.1
Hilton Head Island-Bluffton-Beaufort, SC Metro Area	78,824	55,804	18,014	35.0	18,708	48.4	40.6	8.4	5.1	11.8
Hinesville, GA Metro Area	27,874	19,140	11,400	40.4	7,284	17.6	15.4	6.9	3.8	13.0
Homosassa Springs, FL Metro Area	60,541	38,375	8,426	41.6	19,054	58.2	54.5	5.9	1.9	6.2
Hot Springs, AR Metro Area	40,134	25,513	7,692	43.8	12,487	51.0	36.1	3.4	1.2	6.5
Houma-Thibodaux, LA Metro Area	77,548	51,540	23,536	35.7	20,387	41.5	25.7	3.4	2.5	12.3
Houston-The Woodlands-Sugar Land, TX Metro Area	2,292,992	1,618,476	802,621	31.7	560,764	26.7	20.9	23.7	14.8	38.5
Huntington-Ashland, WV-KY-OH Metro Area	140,735	91,061	33,081	33.5	41,218	42.5	31.2	1.0	0.5	1.8
Huntsville, AL Metro Area	172,549	113,393	49,090	27.2	50,348	33.2	26.2	5.3	2.8	6.6
Idaho Falls, ID Metro Area	45,611	34,319	17,245	24.8	9,670	43.9	26.3	5.2	3.0	11.5
Indianapolis-Carmel-Anderson, IN Metro Area	755,100	473,253	219,623	35.1	235,516	31.5	23.3	6.2	4.0	9.1
Iowa City, IA Metro Area	64,183	37,213	16,161	29.1	17,754	28.2	20.6	9.7	6.9	12.4
Ithaca, NY Metro Area	38,112	19,572	7,193	35.5	13,084	23.8	23.4	14.0	8.9	13.8
Jackson, MI Metro Area	59,292	39,165	16,095	34.7	17,299	32.9	29.2	1.4	0.7	3.3
Jackson, MS Metro Area	210,443	142,992	62,581	43.3	59,514	34.5	25.9	2.4	1.7	3.9
Jackson, TN Metro Area	49,318	34,407	13,361	39.5	12,744	35.9	27.4	2.6	1.3	4.6
Jacksonville, FL Metro Area	536,299	353,312	143,307	36.8	145,797	35.8	27.3	8.6	3.4	11.7
Jacksonville, NC Metro Area	64,771	46,172	25,105	32.5	14,422	22.9	17.2	4.7	2.2	10.4
Janesville-Beloit, WI Metro Area	65,054	42,880	19,634	40.7	17,281	43.3	27.7	3.8	2.5	7.8
Jefferson City, MO Metro Area	55,448	35,264	14,812	27.4	17,709	38.0	28.4	2.1	1.1	4.2
Johnson City, TN Metro Area	83,074	53,662	20,455	31.9	24,555	37.5	30.8	3.0	2.1	3.8
Johnstown, PA Metro Area	57,044	34,744	12,382	30.9	18,929	45.9	34.9	1.5	0.7	2.4
Jonesboro, AR Metro Area	48,943	31,399	12,878	40.7	14,287	30.9	23.9	2.9	2.3	4.7
Joplin, MO Metro Area	67,439	46,450	20,815	23.2	17,393	41.9	27.1	3.5	2.3	6.2
Kahului-Wailuku-Lahaina, HI Metro Area	52,170	36,509	14,406	32.8	12,473	38.1	32.9	18.0	7.9	23.7
Kalamazoo-Portage, MI Metro Area	129,792	80,511	31,585	36.6	38,285	37.7	26.7	4.8	2.2	6.6
Kankakee, IL Metro Area	38,755	25,251	11,012	37.6	11,699	40.2	28.6	5.2	3.9	9.2
Kansas City, MO-KS Metro Area	814,092	522,821	239,887	31.6	242,592	34.3	25.0	6.5	3.9	9.9
Kennewick-Richland, WA Metro Area	94,423	69,309	36,818	33.1	19,496	40.4	23.4	13.6	9.2	29.0
Killeen-Temple, TX Metro Area	151,623	107,754	52,311	33.9	37,096	29.7	21.2	8.5	4.0	19.6
Kingsport-Bristol-Bristol, TN-VA Metro Area	126,840	83,821	29,147	36.7	38,727	46.2	35.3	1.2	0.6	1.9
Kingston, NY Metro Area	69,594	42,046	16,248	27.5	22,425	40.7	32.5	6.9	2.9	10.8
Knoxville, TN Metro Area	343,331	224,411	82,367	33.4	98,851	38.6	30.5	3.9	2.2	4.8
Kokomo, IN Metro Area	34,714	22,244	8,270	36.7	10,660	44.3	32.0	1.3	0.5	NA

NA = Not available.

Table B-5. Population and Household Characteristics 2015—*Continued*

		Households							Foreign-born population		Speaking language other than English at home, persons 5 years and over (percent)
		Family households				Nonfamily households		Percent of households with one or more persons age 65 years or older	Foreign-born population as a percent of total population	Non-citizens as a percent of total population	
			With own children under 18			Householder living alone					
Metropolitan statistical area and division	Total	Total	Total	Single parent headed (percent)		Total	Percent age 65 or older				
La Crosse-Onalaska, WI-MN Metro Area	54,008	32,484	12,859	21.9		16,069	39.7	27.6	2.8	0.5	7.7
Lafayette, LA Metro Area	180,902	120,688	55,806	36.9		48,462	34.6	23.6	2.9	1.9	13.7
Lafayette-West Lafayette, IN Metro Area	81,069	44,446	21,091	28.8		25,612	28.3	20.8	11.0	8.7	15.3
Lake Charles, LA Metro Area	79,853	51,971	22,821	44.9		23,131	35.0	26.0	3.2	2.2	8.4
Lake Havasu City-Kingman, AZ Metro Area	83,801	55,229	16,282	48.9		21,799	52.7	45.5	6.4	3.2	10.1
Lakeland-Winter Haven, FL Metro Area	227,122	157,259	54,606	37.1		56,548	48.4	37.1	9.9	5.8	21.1
Lancaster, PA Metro Area	197,706	138,972	56,178	27.6		46,334	47.1	30.5	4.6	2.4	16.7
Lansing-East Lansing, MI Metro Area	183,888	107,158	43,166	33.4		57,432	32.3	25.3	6.5	4.0	9.4
Laredo, TX Metro Area	72,259	55,992	29,078	38.3		13,464	39.7	22.7	26.8	19.3	90.6
Las Cruces, NM Metro Area	74,631	52,596	23,840	35.7		17,572	41.1	29.2	16.0	10.2	50.3
Las Vegas-Henderson-Paradise, NV Metro Area	740,966	469,005	204,789	38.5		214,406	30.8	26.7	22.2	11.7	34.1
Lawrence, KS Metro Area	42,817	24,012	11,321	24.7		13,158	27.9	21.4	7.6	5.7	10.2
Lawton, OK Metro Area	43,678	28,530	13,191	34.2		12,227	36.5	25.9	5.5	2.9	8.2
Lebanon, PA Metro Area	53,200	35,278	13,014	34.9		14,209	49.0	33.0	4.7	2.1	11.1
Lewiston, ID-WA Metro Area	25,354	17,161	5,985	39.3		6,848	40.7	33.6	1.6	0.6	NA
Lewiston-Auburn, ME Metro Area	45,138	28,562	12,935	42.1		12,574	37.3	27.0	3.6	1.6	11.8
Lexington-Fayette, KY Metro Area	199,299	127,319	54,332	40.3		53,515	27.8	22.5	7.2	5.5	9.5
Lima, OH Metro Area	40,234	26,582	11,944	41.3		11,345	40.1	29.1	1.2	0.5	NA
Lincoln, NE Metro Area	127,316	74,076	33,693	30.0		40,532	29.6	23.3	7.3	4.3	11.1
Little Rock-North Little Rock-Conway, AR Metro Area	282,914	182,963	79,383	36.1		83,271	35.7	25.7	4.2	2.4	6.7
Logan, UT-ID Metro Area	40,927	30,370	15,019	14.2		7,243	41.3	20.2	5.9	3.7	10.1
Longview, TX Metro Area	76,401	52,587	21,092	37.4		19,297	37.7	29.3	7.2	5.2	14.0
Longview, WA Metro Area	40,187	26,804	10,750	29.7		9,996	42.0	31.3	4.6	2.9	7.2
Los Angeles-Long Beach-Anaheim, CA Metro Area	4,315,637	2,938,110	1,283,807	30.1		1,057,690	34.5	27.2	33.8	16.6	54.7
Anaheim-Santa Ana-Irvine, CA Metro Division	1,022,542	732,314	320,030	24.1		217,764	41.5	28.6	31.3	15.5	46.2
Los Angeles-Long Beach-Glendale, CA Metro Division	3,293,095	2,205,796	963,777	32.1		839,926	32.7	26.7	34.6	16.9	57.4
Louisville/Jefferson County, KY-IN Metro Area	496,455	318,075	130,319	33.7		150,482	34.4	26.9	5.0	2.8	6.6
Lubbock, TX Metro Area	112,853	69,397	31,804	40.9		32,496	33.5	23.3	5.3	3.0	24.1
Lynchburg, VA Metro Area	100,497	68,189	24,989	36.9		26,437	40.4	30.8	3.0	2.1	3.6
Macon, GA Metro Area	86,400	54,837	20,085	46.2		27,397	33.9	28.4	3.4	1.7	5.1
Madera, CA Metro Area	45,224	35,580	16,893	38.7		8,662	49.8	30.5	21.5	16.9	44.5
Madison, WI Metro Area	264,340	154,471	69,990	29.4		78,081	31.6	22.6	7.4	4.6	10.9
Manchester-Nashua, NH Metro Area	156,678	103,581	42,882	27.0		39,748	35.4	25.7	9.0	3.9	12.1
Manhattan, KS Metro Area	34,806	19,356	9,469	23.8		9,887	27.8	17.4	8.3	5.9	11.1
Mankato-North Mankato, MN Metro Area	38,444	22,261	9,213	38.0		10,719	32.8	23.4	3.5	2.2	5.4
Mansfield, OH Metro Area	46,989	28,748	10,071	37.1		15,078	46.1	34.3	1.3	0.6	4.4
McAllen-Edinburg-Mission, TX Metro Area	225,692	184,798	97,500	33.5		36,072	42.5	26.7	27.7	20.3	84.0
Medford, OR Metro Area	83,876	52,967	20,592	37.6		23,781	54.8	38.1	5.3	3.2	8.8
Memphis, TN-MS-AR Metro Area	494,270	324,092	139,655	43.9		143,684	31.4	25.1	5.3	3.6	7.6
Merced, CA Metro Area	79,098	60,131	33,152	38.8		14,692	44.3	25.3	26.4	16.4	55.6
Miami-Fort Lauderdale-West Palm Beach, FL Metro Area	2,077,362	1,355,646	557,414	37.5		591,362	43.1	33.7	39.9	17.8	53.6
Fort Lauderdale-Pompano Beach-Deerfield Beach, FL Metro Division	673,870	433,387	184,194	37.6		192,169	41.0	30.7	33.5	14.4	40.7
Miami-Miami Beach-Kendall, FL Metro Division	857,712	577,934	240,377	39.4		231,648	37.8	32.0	52.7	23.4	74.8
West Palm Beach-Boca Raton-Delray Beach, FL Metro Division	545,780	344,325	132,843	33.9		167,545	53.0	40.1	24.2	11.9	30.9
Michigan City-La Porte, IN Metro Area	43,169	26,954	10,162	45.8		13,418	40.4	31.1	2.5	0.5	5.8
Midland, MI Metro Area	32,977	22,721	8,493	24.9		8,751	36.5	28.1	4.2	2.8	4.3
Midland, TX Metro Area	57,867	39,941	16,817	24.9		14,610	28.0	19.4	11.9	7.0	33.6
Milwaukee-Waukesha-West Allis, WI Metro Area	627,842	384,693	169,827	35.5		196,566	34.8	25.4	7.2	4.0	12.4
Minneapolis-St. Paul-Bloomington, MN-WI Metro Area	1,354,766	876,587	406,488	28.0		374,570	34.0	23.2	10.6	5.2	14.1
Missoula, MT Metro Area	47,910	26,407	11,874	36.6		15,954	29.0	23.3	2.9	1.4	NA
Mobile, AL Metro Area	152,938	99,338	40,938	40.9		46,234	33.3	28.3	3.2	1.5	4.8
Modesto, CA Metro Area	171,960	126,194	62,245	34.7		35,013	42.5	27.2	20.6	11.5	42.0
Monroe, LA Metro Area	64,955	41,091	16,944	42.5		21,137	38.0	27.6	1.6	1.1	2.7
Monroe, MI Metro Area	58,886	39,598	15,136	31.2		16,855	41.7	29.8	2.2	0.8	3.6
Montgomery, AL Metro Area	144,379	95,901	41,202	43.2		42,717	35.7	26.6	3.5	2.3	4.6
Morgantown, WV Metro Area	50,274	27,866	11,019	29.9		16,985	29.5	24.2	4.1	3.1	7.1
Morristown, TN Metro Area	44,574	31,002	10,460	33.5		11,023	42.6	33.7	4.2	3.8	6.7
Mount Vernon-Anacortes, WA Metro Area	48,056	33,338	12,607	26.8		11,431	38.8	33.3	11.1	7.2	17.7
Muncie, IN Metro Area	45,278	28,380	11,690	37.9		11,542	37.1	28.3	1.6	0.9	3.1
Muskegon, MI Metro Area	63,215	43,753	17,725	39.2		15,980	42.9	29.9	1.8	0.7	NA
Myrtle Beach-Conway-North Myrtle Beach, SC-NC Metro Area	174,808	115,780	34,084	34.1		48,049	41.6	38.0	5.1	3.0	6.9
Napa, CA Metro Area	49,619	33,093	14,658	26.0		13,149	55.4	34.7	22.9	13.7	35.9
Naples-Immokalee-Marco Island, FL Metro Area	134,906	95,011	27,837	35.9		33,176	57.5	48.9	23.2	13.7	32.2

NA = Not available.

Table B-5. Population and Household Characteristics 2015—*Continued*

Metropolitan statistical area and division	Households							Foreign-born population		Speaking language other than English at home, persons 5 years and over (percent)
	Total	Family households			Nonfamily households		Percent of households with one or more persons age 65 years or older	Foreign-born population as a percent of total population	Non-citizens as a percent of total population	
		Total	With own children under 18		Householder living alone					
			Total	Single parent headed (percent)	Total	Percent age 65 or older				
Nashville-Davidson—Murfreesboro—Franklin, TN Metro Area	686,640	454,873	195,479	29.1	180,767	31.4	23.4	8.2	5.1	10.9
New Bern, NC Metro Area	51,013	33,919	13,435	34.8	15,000	39.1	31.8	4.8	3.0	7.0
New Haven-Milford, CT Metro Area	323,270	197,407	76,186	38.4	104,887	38.1	29.3	12.6	7.0	22.1
New Orleans-Metairie, LA Metro Area	481,754	294,429	123,251	43.1	160,062	30.3	26.3	7.5	4.3	11.1
New York-Newark-Jersey City, NY-NJ-PA Metro Area	7,125,065	4,689,422	2,041,936	30.5	2,008,105	38.5	28.8	29.0	12.9	39.1
Dutchess County-Putnam County, NY Metro Division	140,500	97,570	38,993	26.0	36,337	38.5	29.9	10.5	4.3	16.6
Nassau County-Suffolk County, NY Metro Division	918,363	680,611	282,684	19.4	203,382	51.3	34.0	18.8	7.8	25.7
Newark, NJ-PA Metro Division	886,182	615,177	280,283	29.4	233,009	38.9	27.9	23.2	10.6	30.6
New York-Jersey City-White Plains, NY-NJ Metro Division	5,180,020	3,296,064	1,439,976	33.1	1,535,377	36.7	28.0	32.5	14.6	43.9
Niles-Benton Harbor, MI Metro Area	64,279	39,893	16,678	40.4	20,934	45.9	31.8	7.2	4.2	8.4
North Port-Sarasota-Bradenton, FL Metro Area	312,497	199,518	55,123	38.0	94,712	58.2	48.5	11.9	5.6	14.8
Norwich-New London, CT Metro Area	105,376	66,971	28,739	38.9	32,174	36.6	28.9	7.8	3.5	13.0
Ocala, FL Metro Area	125,227	77,721	19,535	37.6	41,369	57.0	49.5	7.2	2.3	10.5
Ocean City, NJ Metro Area	38,708	25,374	8,123	25.4	11,720	53.3	41.9	6.4	3.3	10.3
Odessa, TX Metro Area	52,023	36,869	18,875	27.7	11,877	29.4	21.3	13.7	9.8	45.9
Ogden-Clearfield, UT Metro Area	201,165	156,642	78,277	21.3	38,423	35.4	22.6	5.8	3.4	11.7
Oklahoma City, OK Metro Area	505,074	328,529	146,420	34.5	144,838	33.9	24.5	8.2	5.3	13.2
Olympia-Tumwater, WA Metro Area	105,159	69,192	29,260	32.9	28,349	38.4	28.2	7.4	2.8	12.8
Omaha-Council Bluffs, NE-IA Metro Area	351,446	229,016	110,369	28.9	98,584	33.3	23.3	7.3	4.4	11.7
Orlando-Kissimmee-Sanford, FL Metro Area	845,295	569,013	242,792	38.0	208,014	33.8	26.6	17.2	8.1	32.5
Oshkosh-Neenah, WI Metro Area	69,636	41,811	17,757	30.0	21,721	33.7	25.6	3.1	1.8	6.5
Owensboro, KY Metro Area	46,415	31,995	13,090	32.6	12,073	36.1	27.7	1.7	1.4	2.2
Oxnard-Thousand Oaks-Ventura, CA Metro Area	269,566	197,572	86,518	24.4	58,239	41.9	30.3	23.3	13.0	39.1
Palm Bay-Melbourne-Titusville, FL Metro Area	225,682	141,500	44,899	40.4	68,220	47.5	38.5	8.6	3.4	10.8
Panama City, FL Metro Area	74,276	45,645	17,055	41.1	23,896	36.4	30.5	5.2	2.0	5.5
Parkersburg-Vienna, WV Metro Area	39,349	25,267	9,981	39.1	12,206	37.5	30.6	1.2	0.5	NA
Pensacola-Ferry Pass-Brent, FL Metro Area	177,675	113,203	39,636	29.8	51,105	32.0	29.6	4.8	2.1	6.2
Peoria, IL Metro Area	150,639	96,647	38,955	34.1	47,092	38.4	29.0	3.4	1.8	5.6
Philadelphia-Camden-Wilmington, PA-NJ-DE-MD Metro Area	2,233,752	1,456,746	606,850	33.9	637,821	38.6	28.5	10.5	4.9	15.6
Camden, NJ Metro Division	452,494	309,924	129,089	31.4	118,898	41.8	29.3	9.3	3.6	15.2
Montgomery County-Bucks County-Chester County, PA Metro Division	732,646	514,209	214,244	21.9	180,343	43.5	30.1	9.7	4.5	12.6
Philadelphia, PA Metro Division	784,807	455,690	190,404	48.4	269,394	33.7	26.7	12.2	5.8	19.4
Wilmington, DE-MD-NJ Metro Division	263,805	176,923	73,113	35.7	69,186	39.4	27.7	9.7	5.3	13.3
Phoenix-Mesa-Scottsdale, AZ Metro Area	1,608,722	1,047,580	462,268	34.5	438,347	35.5	28.1	14.3	8.7	26.4
Pine Bluff, AR Metro Area	34,059	21,628	7,365	45.4	11,400	31.7	31.0	1.3	1.1	3.6
Pittsburgh, PA Metro Area	990,355	608,651	225,231	32.0	321,001	41.5	31.5	3.9	2.0	5.2
Pittsfield, MA Metro Area	55,497	34,193	12,110	44.9	17,491	45.7	35.0	6.3	3.8	8.0
Pocatello, ID Metro Area	30,174	18,815	8,550	29.1	8,175	37.8	25.7	4.0	3.0	6.5
Portland-South Portland, ME Metro Area	212,240	134,410	50,718	30.9	61,149	42.8	30.8	4.8	1.9	6.9
Portland-Vancouver-Hillsboro, OR-WA Metro Area	901,402	568,437	251,879	28.9	248,396	34.8	25.4	12.4	6.6	17.6
Port St. Lucie, FL Metro Area	173,912	112,557	33,881	31.7	50,821	55.8	44.4	14.7	7.1	19.8
Prescott, AZ Metro Area	94,920	60,923	17,343	33.2	26,840	47.4	44.6	5.5	2.4	9.9
Providence-Warwick, RI-MA Metro Area	622,607	387,305	162,221	38.1	192,500	40.3	29.2	12.9	5.5	21.5
Provo-Orem, UT Metro Area	158,270	129,352	71,728	10.8	18,674	41.7	18.7	7.1	4.7	13.6
Pueblo, CO Metro Area	61,876	40,452	15,961	36.3	17,562	40.8	33.1	2.7	1.4	14.9
Punta Gorda, FL Metro Area	72,671	48,022	8,971	34.9	20,558	68.4	58.0	12.0	4.3	10.9
Racine, WI Metro Area	74,960	51,268	22,612	33.5	19,620	43.0	27.6	4.0	1.8	7.3
Raleigh, NC Metro Area	470,527	320,026	162,683	26.3	117,588	27.6	20.4	12.2	7.3	15.2
Rapid City, SD Metro Area	58,598	37,400	15,257	29.5	18,330	36.0	27.5	2.6	1.4	5.1
Reading, PA Metro Area	151,792	103,149	42,870	34.3	40,951	46.3	30.9	7.4	3.7	17.5
Redding, CA Metro Area	69,799	44,399	16,891	41.3	19,740	46.8	35.3	5.2	2.5	7.6
Reno, NV Metro Area	174,571	107,835	47,536	37.7	49,629	41.2	28.6	13.8	7.2	23.1
Richmond, VA Metro Area	483,251	308,248	129,726	35.0	141,914	35.9	27.0	7.6	4.2	9.8
Riverside-San Bernardino-Ontario, CA Metro Area	1,343,526	994,158	467,892	33.2	278,216	39.7	27.9	21.9	11.5	41.7
Roanoke, VA Metro Area	127,273	81,311	31,358	38.7	38,514	39.0	31.3	4.8	3.1	5.8
Rochester, MN Metro Area	83,418	55,636	25,528	24.1	23,569	39.4	26.5	9.1	5.3	10.8
Rochester, NY Metro Area	427,520	267,511	110,173	37.8	128,233	40.8	29.0	7.2	3.4	11.7
Rockford, IL Metro Area	132,190	85,095	35,336	38.3	40,182	39.5	28.7	8.8	5.1	15.0
Rocky Mount, NC Metro Area	57,450	36,750	14,829	55.1	17,808	41.4	32.1	2.4	1.5	4.7
Rome, GA Metro Area	34,931	23,019	8,643	40.1	10,364	47.8	31.8	6.5	4.3	8.4
Sacramento—Roseville—Arden-Arcade, CA Metro Area	809,295	537,141	240,759	31.5	214,501	37.3	28.2	18.2	7.9	28.2
Saginaw, MI Metro Area	77,211	48,763	20,218	44.2	23,787	39.6	30.8	2.8	1.5	5.0

NA = Not available.

Table B-5. Population and Household Characteristics 2015—*Continued*

Metropolitan statistical area and division	Households Total	Family households Total	Family households With own children under 18 Total	Family households With own children under 18 Single parent headed (percent)	Nonfamily households Householder living alone Total	Nonfamily households Householder living alone Percent age 65 or older	Percent of households with one or more persons age 65 years or older	Foreign-born population as a percent of total population	Non-citizens as a percent of total population	Speaking language other than English at home, persons 5 years and over (percent)
St. Cloud, MN Metro Area	74,617	47,983	22,164	37.7	19,370	31.4	22.3	5.5	3.5	8.0
St. George, UT Metro Area	52,453	39,546	16,411	23.9	10,270	59.9	38.2	4.6	2.6	9.4
St. Joseph, MO-KS Metro Area	46,518	30,726	11,919	37.6	12,047	46.2	29.4	3.2	2.8	4.6
St. Louis, MO-IL Metro Area	1,108,303	713,895	304,706	34.1	332,833	38.3	27.3	4.6	2.4	6.2
Salem, OR Metro Area	144,600	99,959	40,851	35.0	34,494	45.7	31.0	11.7	7.7	23.5
Salinas, CA Metro Area	126,904	90,182	43,213	32.5	27,893	44.1	29.0	30.8	22.3	55.5
Salisbury, MD-DE Metro Area	154,242	102,327	34,250	35.6	42,334	44.2	38.0	6.9	3.9	9.6
Salt Lake City, UT Metro Area	377,058	262,957	130,655	23.8	87,977	32.2	21.4	11.7	7.0	19.6
San Angelo, TX Metro Area	45,137	27,773	11,433	34.1	13,532	28.1	25.4	7.6	2.4	29.0
San Antonio-New Braunfels, TX Metro Area	791,273	543,444	246,017	35.5	206,389	33.8	25.4	11.7	7.1	37.0
San Diego-Carlsbad, CA Metro Area	1,113,610	737,052	331,477	29.4	276,876	35.4	26.5	24.2	11.7	38.1
San Francisco-Oakland-Hayward, CA Metro Area	1,689,907	1,079,743	469,133	24.3	449,279	36.3	27.8	30.7	13.6	41.3
Oakland-Hayward-Berkeley, CA Metro Division	963,824	663,722	303,674	25.3	225,071	37.5	27.1	29.5	13.8	40.7
San Francisco-Redwood City-South San Francisco, CA Metro Division	620,196	349,896	137,206	22.4	191,875	32.0	27.4	34.9	14.1	45.4
San Rafael, CA Metro Division	105,887	66,125	28,253	22.0	32,333	53.3	36.7	17.5	9.1	22.3
San Jose-Sunnyvale-Santa Clara, CA Metro Area	651,352	470,389	222,345	19.0	132,996	37.7	25.8	37.8	18.0	52.3
San Luis Obispo-Paso Robles-Arroyo Grande, CA Metro Area	104,760	66,103	24,008	27.3	27,429	44.6	33.7	9.6	5.3	17.2
Santa Cruz-Watsonville, CA Metro Area	93,317	58,166	23,912	25.2	25,857	41.2	30.9	18.6	11.9	31.8
Santa Fe, NM Metro Area	60,642	36,800	12,138	45.5	20,029	40.2	36.1	12.4	8.2	32.8
Santa Maria-Santa Barbara, CA Metro Area	144,261	94,718	43,218	29.0	34,652	51.2	30.8	23.1	15.3	39.6
Santa Rosa, CA Metro Area	190,662	120,760	48,224	31.4	53,210	49.5	33.4	16.7	9.8	25.7
Savannah, GA Metro Area	138,784	91,612	40,194	39.4	36,769	35.9	25.2	6.2	4.0	10.1
Scranton—Wilkes-Barre—Hazleton, PA Metro Area	221,200	137,586	49,867	43.3	70,733	44.2	33.2	4.9	3.0	8.9
Seattle-Tacoma-Bellevue, WA Metro Area	1,437,222	903,536	405,733	26.2	392,806	31.6	23.2	17.8	9.1	22.7
Seattle-Bellevue-Everett, WA Metro Division	1,130,166	699,415	312,146	24.1	311,650	30.8	22.7	20.1	10.4	25.0
Tacoma-Lakewood, WA Metro Division	307,056	204,121	93,587	33.1	81,156	34.6	24.8	9.8	4.4	14.9
Sebastian-Vero Beach, FL Metro Area	55,494	34,361	9,656	24.6	18,696	61.2	52.0	8.6	4.7	12.4
Sebring, FL Metro Area	41,116	27,141	8,064	22.2	12,120	54.6	51.1	9.7	5.9	17.9
Sheboygan, WI Metro Area	47,438	32,177	13,232	25.2	13,048	37.4	28.2	6.1	2.6	10.4
Sherman-Denison, TX Metro Area	47,538	31,698	13,368	38.8	13,898	42.5	30.9	6.4	4.9	11.1
Shreveport-Bossier City, LA Metro Area	171,531	109,589	46,646	40.7	54,217	38.8	28.1	2.8	1.3	3.9
Sierra Vista-Douglas, AZ Metro Area	50,202	34,239	11,267	37.5	13,690	47.2	38.3	12.7	5.5	31.5
Sioux City, IA-NE-SD Metro Area	63,198	41,583	19,768	35.9	17,841	42.6	28.4	8.0	4.8	15.6
Sioux Falls, SD Metro Area	98,273	63,647	30,789	31.1	28,065	35.5	22.7	5.5	3.6	8.5
South Bend-Mishawaka, IN-MI Metro Area	119,494	77,143	32,524	37.0	35,965	40.3	29.0	5.4	3.3	8.8
Spartanburg, SC Metro Area	124,570	82,438	33,186	34.4	36,570	40.2	29.8	6.2	3.5	8.5
Spokane-Spokane Valley, WA Metro Area	215,652	137,450	57,838	35.5	64,497	37.2	28.8	5.3	2.4	7.0
Springfield, IL Metro Area	88,081	53,716	23,344	42.8	28,969	36.3	27.2	2.8	1.6	4.9
Springfield, MA Metro Area	233,619	143,941	59,597	43.3	71,263	41.0	29.6	8.8	4.2	21.9
Springfield, MO Metro Area	179,752	114,682	47,985	29.3	49,411	40.4	27.4	2.9	1.5	5.5
Springfield, OH Metro Area	54,232	35,720	14,173	42.7	15,229	49.0	33.5	1.5	0.8	3.8
State College, PA Metro Area	56,116	31,681	11,896	23.9	15,925	28.1	24.6	8.5	5.3	11.1
Staunton-Waynesboro, VA Metro Area	46,768	30,701	11,436	41.7	13,412	40.8	31.4	2.3	1.1	2.8
Stockton-Lodi, CA Metro Area	223,062	166,266	82,089	30.8	45,508	45.2	27.2	24.1	13.3	42.1
Sumter, SC Metro Area	41,017	27,648	10,000	57.4	11,059	36.5	27.8	3.2	2.3	5.5
Syracuse, NY Metro Area	254,001	156,878	67,788	39.2	74,266	41.8	28.9	6.5	3.0	9.1
Tallahassee, FL Metro Area	142,295	80,261	31,374	42.4	44,851	29.1	24.9	6.7	3.9	10.5
Tampa-St. Petersburg-Clearwater, FL Metro Area	1,166,704	712,385	272,538	38.3	372,319	40.8	33.1	13.4	6.4	20.6
Terre Haute, IN Metro Area	66,685	41,065	17,799	32.2	21,104	41.4	29.1	1.5	1.1	2.2
Texarkana, TX-AR Metro Area	54,440	37,241	15,177	45.0	14,799	45.5	30.1	1.9	1.4	NA
The Villages, FL Metro Area	51,170	33,695	-	-	15,858	67.6	75.6	5.0	2.1	5.6
Toledo, OH Metro Area	242,641	147,276	62,563	41.3	77,400	35.5	26.5	3.2	1.7	6.4
Topeka, KS Metro Area	93,078	59,448	26,575	34.1	29,170	37.7	29.5	3.1	2.1	6.2
Trenton, NJ Metro Area	127,965	88,164	37,814	29.0	33,540	36.1	27.3	22.2	11.6	30.0
Tucson, AZ Metro Area	395,992	241,144	94,965	40.6	122,263	38.4	32.2	13.2	7.0	28.1
Tulsa, OK Metro Area	380,841	254,975	114,467	35.7	102,101	36.6	26.1	6.4	4.3	10.2
Tuscaloosa, AL Metro Area	84,889	54,927	23,481	42.0	25,025	35.1	26.0	3.7	2.8	4.9
Tyler, TX Metro Area	78,380	53,257	22,892	31.1	20,553	43.6	30.1	6.2	4.2	16.8
Urban Honolulu, HI Metro Area	307,703	215,170	81,503	20.1	70,545	39.8	34.1	19.2	8.0	28.5
Utica-Rome, NY Metro Area	114,580	71,930	29,198	44.1	36,477	42.9	32.3	6.2	2.5	10.5
Valdosta, GA Metro Area	48,600	28,889	13,763	35.1	16,137	33.8	25.4	3.1	1.9	4.9
Vallejo-Fairfield, CA Metro Area	145,502	103,104	43,598	35.1	33,174	39.8	29.0	20.0	8.8	29.6
Victoria, TX Metro Area	35,842	26,034	10,473	26.7	8,167	48.5	32.0	5.3	3.9	21.1
Vineland-Bridgeton, NJ Metro Area	50,380	34,807	16,043	42.7	12,257	44.4	28.6	11.3	6.9	26.7
Virginia Beach-Norfolk-Newport News, VA-NC Metro Area	642,911	425,298	184,614	36.6	174,952	35.6	26.0	6.2	2.5	9.0

NA = Not available.

Table B-5.   Population and Household Characteristics 2015—*Continued*

Metropolitan statistical area and division	Households Total	Family households Total	Family households — With own children under 18 Total	Family households — With own children under 18 Single parent headed (percent)	Nonfamily households — Householder living alone Total	Nonfamily households — Householder living alone Percent age 65 or older	Percent of households with one or more persons age 65 years or older	Foreign-born population as a percent of total population	Non-citizens as a percent of total population	Speaking language other than English at home, persons 5 years and over (percent)
Visalia-Porterville, CA Metro Area	134,801	104,781	56,805	34.2	23,886	41.1	25.9	21.9	14.8	50.2
Waco, TX Metro Area	93,239	63,519	26,313	40.6	23,166	37.3	26.8	9.0	6.7	19.3
Walla Walla, WA Metro Area	24,201	15,654	5,714	24.9	7,516	39.1	34.0	10.4	7.0	17.4
Warner Robins, GA Metro Area	69,562	50,769	21,050	36.6	15,332	37.7	24.9	4.3	1.7	9.3
Washington-Arlington-Alexandria, DC-VA-MD-WV Metro Area	2,172,310	1,426,676	667,019	26.5	589,424	29.6	23.3	22.9	11.5	28.7
Silver Spring-Frederick-Rockville, MD Metro Division	461,405	321,317	152,777	25.2	114,449	36.8	27.1	28.7	13.8	35.6
Washington-Arlington-Alexandria, DC-VA-MD-WV Metro Division	1,710,905	1,105,359	514,242	26.9	474,975	27.9	22.2	21.4	10.9	26.9
Waterloo-Cedar Falls, IA Metro Area	66,986	41,837	17,269	32.2	19,417	38.6	28.0	3.8	1.6	7.0
Watertown-Fort Drum, NY Metro Area	43,145	28,987	13,014	33.6	11,844	34.7	23.3	3.9	1.4	5.9
Wausau, WI Metro Area	54,558	36,543	15,089	21.9	14,671	37.7	28.4	4.7	2.3	8.5
Weirton-Steubenville, WV-OH Metro Area	50,699	30,744	11,524	45.3	17,313	45.7	33.0	1.3	0.5	NA
Wenatchee, WA Metro Area	41,304	29,053	11,551	30.6	10,526	41.6	33.6	11.2	7.1	27.3
Wheeling, WV-OH Metro Area	58,313	37,510	14,261	35.2	18,049	45.6	34.0	1.4	0.3	1.8
Wichita, KS Metro Area	244,522	155,457	70,255	35.6	77,358	32.7	25.6	7.3	3.6	12.0
Wichita Falls, TX Metro Area	55,562	34,279	14,670	33.6	17,230	43.6	28.6	7.0	4.0	14.0
Williamsport, PA Metro Area	45,751	29,440	11,218	32.6	13,719	38.4	31.0	1.8	0.9	3.8
Wilmington, NC Metro Area	111,546	68,724	28,149	32.2	33,065	38.7	29.1	5.7	3.5	7.6
Winchester, VA-WV Metro Area	48,995	33,181	13,188	32.0	12,708	47.3	31.1	6.6	5.0	10.6
Winston-Salem, NC Metro Area	260,437	171,954	69,579	33.6	75,428	38.9	29.0	6.7	4.6	11.2
Worcester, MA-CT Metro Area	345,269	225,766	95,254	32.8	94,917	39.8	26.9	10.3	5.1	16.6
Yakima, WA Metro Area	81,709	59,225	29,034	36.0	18,256	40.9	28.6	17.9	13.1	40.5
York-Hanover, PA Metro Area	165,672	114,064	43,783	34.1	39,764	42.5	29.8	4.0	1.8	7.3
Youngstown-Warren-Boardman, OH-PA Metro Area	228,692	142,862	51,186	39.9	74,107	44.4	33.8	1.7	0.5	5.2
Yuba City, CA Metro Area	58,262	41,638	20,626	29.3	12,543	43.9	30.0	17.7	9.3	31.4
Yuma, AZ Metro Area	71,751	52,480	23,318	33.7	15,915	48.8	34.5	26.1	14.2	51.4

NA = Not available.

Table B-6. Enrollment, Teachers, and Educational Attainment

Metropolitan statistical area and division	Public school enrollment[1]				Number of public school teachers,[4]		Pupil/teacher ratio		Educational attainment, 2015		
	2014–2015										
	Total[2]	Pre-Kindergarten to grade 8[3]	Grades 9–12	Total,[2] 2004–2005	2014–2015	2004–2005	2014–2015	2004–2005	Population 25 years and over	High school graduate or less (percent)	Bachelor's degree or higher (percent)
Abilene, TX Metro Area	29,201	21,559	7,642	27,975	2,054	2,192	14.2	12.8	106,507	44.9	20.7
Akron, OH Metro Area	95,820	64,689	31,131	109,390	NA	7,075	NA	15.5	482,473	41.9	30.1
Albany, GA Metro Area	27,076	19,784	7,292	28,593	1,611	1,851	16.8	15.4	101,243	48.9	21.1
Albany, OR Metro Area	21,347	13,636	7,711	17,183	951	797	22.4	21.6	83,387	40.2	17.2
Albany-Schenectady-Troy, NY Metro Area	121,368	81,251	37,474	128,228	8,366	9,298	14.5	13.8	605,021	35.3	35.3
Albuquerque, NM Metro Area	139,943	95,820	41,960	128,378	8,960	8,509	15.6	15.1	612,939	37.9	30.2
Alexandria, LA Metro Area	27,007	19,603	7,404	26,550	1,783	1,811	15.1	14.7	103,271	56.1	17.7
Allentown-Bethlehem-Easton, PA-NJ Metro Area	120,876	82,557	32,420	122,181	8,222	7,849	14.7	15.6	577,040	44.5	28.2
Altoona, PA Metro Area	17,668	12,308	5,360	18,320	1,170	1,219	15.1	15.0	89,411	56.3	21.9
Amarillo, TX Metro Area	49,805	36,104	13,701	43,413	3,466	3,067	14.4	14.2	168,964	40.3	24.5
Ames, IA Metro Area	11,284	8,014	3,270	10,400	771	768	14.6	13.5	49,115	19.9	51.6
Anchorage, AK Metro Area	66,353	46,810	19,543	64,388	3,675	3,507	18.1	18.4	253,453	32.5	31.7
Ann Arbor, MI Metro Area	45,541	31,245	14,282	48,253	2,562	2,723	17.8	17.7	223,966	20.2	55.2
Anniston-Oxford-Jacksonville, AL Metro Area	17,107	12,876	4,231	18,090	1,003	1,175	17.1	15.4	78,387	48.1	17.3
Appleton, WI Metro Area	39,263	27,459	11,804	36,487	NA	2,378	NA	15.3	156,226	40.0	29.0
Asheville, NC Metro Area	54,840	38,064	16,666	53,200	3,696	3,794	14.8	14.0	327,553	37.2	32.8
Athens-Clarke County, GA Metro Area	27,172	19,790	7,382	22,331	1,931	1,624	14.1	13.8	119,110	39.6	38.0
Atlanta-Sandy Springs-Roswell, GA Metro Area	995,805	700,767	278,996	835,017	62,179	56,260	16.0	14.8	3,734,637	35.8	37.0
Atlantic City-Hammonton, NJ Metro Area	45,385	30,394	NA	47,553	4,027	3,838	11.3	12.4	187,759	47.2	27.2
Auburn-Opelika, AL Metro Area	23,404	16,623	6,781	18,759	1,409	1,280	16.6	14.7	92,177	32.0	34.3
Augusta-Richmond County, GA-SC Metro Area	95,386	67,979	17,229	94,484	5,870	6,188	16.2	15.3	393,190	44.6	24.6
Austin-Round Rock, TX Metro Area	334,540	242,818	91,722	243,823	22,375	16,675	15.0	14.6	1,321,572	30.5	42.6
Bakersfield, CA Metro Area	178,341	125,566	52,744	164,805	7,543	7,807	23.6	21.1	528,165	55.8	16.2
Baltimore-Columbia-Towson, MD Metro Area	399,599	284,546	115,053	397,583	26,493	25,002	15.1	15.9	1,921,102	35.2	38.6
Bangor, ME Metro Area	20,385	14,187	6,198	22,606	1,671	1,831	12.2	12.3	107,601	43.7	24.5
Barnstable Town, MA Metro Area	25,430	17,091	8,305	30,728	2,131	2,477	11.9	12.4	165,588	29.3	40.1
Baton Rouge, LA Metro Area	125,697	91,299	34,398	108,761	8,450	7,296	14.9	14.9	534,104	44.9	28.2
Battle Creek, MI Metro Area	20,563	14,297	6,232	24,891	1,185	1,537	17.4	16.2	90,733	48.0	20.0
Bay City, MI Metro Area	14,344	9,553	4,740	16,691	786	891	18.2	18.7	74,816	44.8	18.0
Beaumont-Port Arthur, TX Metro Area	70,734	51,070	19,664	73,364	4,619	5,045	15.3	14.5	271,366	50.7	17.5
Beckley, WV Metro Area	19,116	13,668	5,448	18,628	1,366	1,303	14.0	14.3	87,689	60.0	14.8
Bellingham, WA Metro Area	26,508	17,908	8,600	26,529	1,443	NA	18.4	NA	138,988	31.8	33.0
Bend-Redmond, OR Metro Area	25,161	17,116	8,045	21,798	1,135	977	22.2	22.3	125,575	24.9	36.5
Billings, MT Metro Area	24,632	17,836	6,796	23,619	1,562	1,542	15.8	15.3	116,101	38.2	29.9
Binghamton, NY Metro Area	34,706	23,327	10,726	39,058	2,578	2,992	13.5	13.1	165,142	41.3	27.1
Birmingham-Hoover, AL Metro Area	177,449	124,810	13,423	172,609	10,294	11,473	17.2	15.0	780,402	40.4	28.6
Bismarck, ND Metro Area	17,335	12,393	58	15,872	1,362	1,123	12.7	14.1	88,853	32.8	33.9
Blacksburg-Christiansburg-Radford, VA Metro Area	20,210	9,749	1,116	20,612	1,485	1,575	13.6	13.1	109,450	37.7	35.2
Bloomington, IL Metro Area	28,215	19,975	8,240	26,740	1,803	1,704	15.6	15.7	115,006	32.2	44.0
Bloomington, IN Metro Area	16,774	11,699	5,059	16,636	951	986	17.6	16.9	96,446	33.8	40.4
Bloomsburg-Berwick, PA Metro Area	10,654	6,772	3,882	12,941	830	738	12.8	17.5	57,347	53.3	24.0
Boise City, ID Metro Area	120,408	84,590	35,794	95,273	6,111	5,139	19.7	18.5	439,125	34.6	30.1
Boston-Cambridge-Newton, MA-NH Metro Area	660,496	460,430	199,328	659,290	49,735	49,320	13.3	13.4	3,313,637	32.0	46.0
Boston, MA Metro Division	266,313	186,807	79,093	261,490	19,569	19,491	13.6	13.4	1,373,731	33.7	43.9
Cambridge-Newton-Framingham, MA Metro Division	333,271	232,043	100,906	331,705	25,288	24,972	13.2	13.3	1,640,640	30.6	48.8
Rockingham County-Strafford County, NH Metro Division	60,912	41,580	19,329	66,095	4,878	4,857	12.5	13.6	299,266	31.7	39.9
Boulder, CO Metro Area	47,782	33,680	14,102	41,425	2,599	2,411	18.4	17.2	206,135	18.4	60.6
Bowling Green, KY Metro Area	26,240	15,960	559	22,183	1,597	1,346	16.4	16.5	106,396	45.1	25.7
Bremerton-Silverdale, WA Metro Area	36,114	24,438	11,676	40,689	2,001	2,081	18.0	19.6	178,483	28.3	30.5
Bridgeport-Stamford-Norwalk, CT Metro Area	148,284	103,516	44,768	149,007	10,805	9,781	13.7	15.2	641,084	33.1	46.3
Brownsville-Harlingen, TX Metro Area	106,286	76,577	29,709	92,580	6,930	5,790	15.3	16.0	244,947	59.7	15.2
Brunswick, GA Metro Area	18,305	13,315	1,433	17,319	1,143	1,224	16.0	14.1	81,264	45.3	24.1
Buffalo-Cheektowaga-Niagara Falls, NY Metro Area	157,133	107,344	47,848	175,630	11,267	12,250	13.9	14.3	792,356	39.2	30.3
Burlington, NC Metro Area	24,552	16,997	7,555	22,798	1,571	1,477	15.6	15.4	106,205	43.9	22.9
Burlington-South Burlington, VT Metro Area	30,789	21,720	9,069	32,829	2,536	2,606	12.1	12.6	144,307	31.4	43.4
California-Lexington Park, MD Metro Area	17,887	12,879	NA	16,567	1,026	992	17.4	16.7	74,038	36.3	33.3
Canton-Massillon, OH Metro Area	60,453	41,232	19,221	67,044	NA	4,276	NA	15.7	279,545	48.2	21.2
Cape Coral-Fort Myers, FL Metro Area	89,364	63,044	26,320	70,871	5,560	4,082	16.1	17.4	522,733	44.2	26.2
Cape Girardeau, MO-IL Metro Area	13,042	9,444	3,598	13,121	970	947	13.4	13.9	62,792	44.8	24.9
Carbondale-Marion, IL Metro Area	17,768	12,782	4,986	17,546	1,134	1,030	15.7	17.0	82,220	37.4	27.4
Carson City, NV Metro Area	8,242	5,570	2,672	8,730	443	192	18.6	45.5	38,334	40.6	21.7
Casper, WY Metro Area	13,433	9,771	3,662	11,809	927	782	14.5	15.1	53,528	40.1	22.2
Cedar Rapids, IA Metro Area	43,333	30,514	12,819	40,492	2,889	2,841	15.0	14.3	179,106	36.4	28.1
Chambersburg-Waynesboro, PA Metro Area	21,659	14,887	6,772	20,274	1,328	1,225	16.3	16.6	106,517	56.8	20.2
Champaign-Urbana, IL Metro Area	30,436	22,090	8,346	30,473	2,284	2,067	13.3	14.7	141,822	30.1	42.6
Charleston, WV Metro Area	34,310	24,412	9,898	34,727	2,298	2,307	14.9	15.1	158,868	53.7	22.8
Charleston-North Charleston, SC Metro Area	107,652	78,524	29,128	93,556	7,094	6,065	15.2	15.4	508,644	35.6	34.7
Charlotte-Concord-Gastonia, NC-SC Metro Area	398,464	281,738	116,583	320,145	24,185	19,541	16.5	16.4	1,617,907	36.7	33.5
Charlottesville, VA Metro Area	22,117	15,510	1,206	27,204	1,630	1,958	13.6	13.9	156,796	32.8	40.9
Chattanooga, TN-GA Metro Area	74,253	53,262	20,991	70,549	5,052	4,513	14.7	15.6	378,791	45.9	25.1
Cheyenne, WY Metro Area	14,748	10,537	4,211	13,792	1,159	1,001	12.7	13.8	64,281	33.8	27.5
Chicago-Naperville-Elgin, IL-IN-WI Metro Area	1,551,663	1,077,695	473,769	1,572,335	94,793	92,521	16.4	17.0	6,407,668	36.7	36.0

NA = Not available.
[1]Data obtained from public schools.
[2]Including ungraded students, these are students who are assigned to programs or classes without standard grade designation.
[3]Data for prekindergarten not available in all areas.
[4]Full-time equivalent.

Table B-6. Enrollment, Teachers, and Educational Attainment—*Continued*

Metropolitan statistical area and division	Public school enrollment[1]				Number of public school teachers,[4]		Pupil/teacher ratio		Educational attainment, 2015		
	2014–2015			Total,[2] 2004–2005	2014–2015	2004–2005	2014–2015	2004–2005	Population 25 years and over	High school graduate or less (percent)	Bachelor's degree or higher (percent)
	Total[2]	Pre-Kindergarten to grade 8[3]	Grades 9–12								
Chicago-Naperville-Arlington Heights, IL Metro Division	1,162,622	810,895	351,727	1,191,659	73,097	70,081	15.9	17.0	4,969,082	36.0	37.2
Elgin, IL Metro Division	111,724	78,691	33,033	101,767	6,816	5,854	16.4	17.4	401,765	38.5	31.2
Gary, IN Metro Division	118,207	81,427	36,581	119,370	6,025	6,578	19.6	18.1	471,073	46.4	22.5
Lake County-Kenosha County, IL-WI Metro Division	159,110	106,682	52,428	159,539	8,855	10,008	18.0	15.9	565,748	33.2	40.2
Chico, CA Metro Area	30,982	21,342	9,577	33,385	1,403	1,698	22.1	19.7	146,064	32.7	27.8
Cincinnati, OH-KY-IN Metro Area	315,528	221,553	80,303	317,195	4,671	18,983	67.6	16.7	1,439,532	39.5	32.1
Clarksville, TN-KY Metro Area	43,436	31,444	9,503	36,871	2,163	2,180	20.1	16.9	169,045	41.0	24.0
Cleveland, TN Metro Area	18,501	12,871	5,630	16,565	1,157	1,020	16.0	16.2	81,001	50.3	18.5
Cleveland-Elyria, OH Metro Area	287,164	195,555	91,609	323,015	NA	19,530	NA	16.5	1,432,123	40.1	29.4
Coeur d'Alene, ID Metro Area	21,906	15,116	6,764	20,083	1,051	1,054	20.8	19.1	103,211	35.7	23.2
College Station Bryan, TX Metro Area	35,242	25,786	9,456	29,264	2,464	2,013	14.3	14.5	136,908	35.9	36.3
Colorado Springs, CO Metro Area	121,137	85,765	35,372	104,757	7,159	6,366	16.9	16.5	446,709	27.3	36.5
Columbia, MO Metro Area	23,391	16,721	6,670	21,369	1,629	1,591	14.4	13.4	104,102	27.1	48.5
Columbia, SC Metro Area	136,246	94,884	41,362	118,863	9,086	8,175	15.0	14.5	529,053	37.9	31.4
Columbus, GA-AL Metro Area	49,522	35,079	14,443	48,723	2,809	3,187	17.6	15.3	203,174	41.7	23.3
Columbus, IN Metro Area	12,443	8,574	3,869	11,801	649	656	19.2	18.0	54,548	41.7	29.6
Columbus, OH Metro Area	327,705	227,020	100,685	296,162	NA	17,718	NA	16.7	1,348,258	37.5	35.1
Corpus Christi, TX Metro Area	81,266	58,458	22,808	80,525	5,135	5,155	15.8	15.6	291,482	48.9	20.5
Corvallis, OR Metro Area	10,030	7,008	3,022	10,390	478	435	21.0	23.9	52,894	20.5	55.1
Crestview-Fort Walton Beach-Destin, FL Metro Area	38,850	27,917	10,933	37,567	1,825	2,256	21.3	16.7	183,142	34.8	28.5
Cumberland, MD-WV Metro Area	13,089	9,233	3,856	14,423	913	1,005	14.3	14.4	69,579	55.6	15.3
Dallas-Fort Worth-Arlington, TX Metro Area	1,347,764	972,747	375,017	1,080,483	86,830	70,718	15.5	15.3	4,555,092	38.1	33.4
Dallas-Plano-Irving, TX Metro Division	906,838	651,785	255,053	714,713	58,706	47,438	15.4	15.1	3,016,975	37.2	35.5
Fort Worth-Arlington, TX Metro Division	440,926	320,962	119,964	365,770	28,124	23,280	15.7	15.7	1,538,117	39.8	29.3
Dalton, GA Metro Area	28,986	20,834	8,152	26,248	1,797	1,696	16.1	15.5	92,059	61.3	13.4
Danville, IL Metro Area	13,118	9,446	3,672	14,275	875	926	15.0	15.4	53,843	53.4	13.0
Daphne-Fairhope-Foley, AL Metro Area	30,596	21,568	NA	24,443	1,687	1,749	18.1	14.0	143,738	40.9	29.5
Davenport-Moline-Rock Island, IA-IL Metro Area	61,254	43,076	18,178	61,396	3,964	4,075	15.5	15.1	263,037	41.3	26.0
Dayton, OH Metro Area	113,840	81,098	32,742	122,663	NA	7,091	NA	17.3	544,791	38.8	28.5
Decatur, AL Metro Area	24,418	17,187	NA	25,234	1,475	1,714	16.6	14.7	106,054	49.4	19.9
Decatur, IL Metro Area	16,291	11,829	4,462	17,272	983	894	16.6	19.3	73,158	45.1	23.4
Deltona-Daytona Beach-Ormond Beach, FL Metro Area	74,570	51,515	23,055	74,716	4,899	4,793	15.2	15.6	460,890	42.7	23.1
Denver-Aurora-Lakewood, CO Metro Area	467,399	334,470	132,929	389,370	25,513	21,556	18.3	18.1	1,919,084	29.6	41.8
Des Moines-West Des Moines, IA Metro Area	106,861	76,654	30,207	86,859	7,058	6,066	15.1	14.3	409,801	33.9	35.1
Detroit-Warren-Dearborn, MI Metro Area	657,722	441,402	214,618	777,287	35,353	41,816	18.6	18.6	2,949,395	37.7	29.5
Detroit-Dearborn-Livonia, MI Metro Division	277,944	190,173	87,133	359,259	14,875	19,212	18.7	18.7	1,170,856	44.9	22.6
Warren-Troy-Farmington Hills, MI Metro Division	379,778	251,229	127,485	418,028	20,478	22,604	18.5	18.5	1,778,539	33.0	34.1
Dothan, AL Metro Area	21,939	15,525	1,966	21,544	1,231	1,360	17.8	15.8	102,233	48.8	19.0
Dover, DE Metro Area	28,680	19,810	8,870	24,283	2,062	1,598	13.9	15.2	113,970	47.3	21.3
Dubuque, IA Metro Area	14,004	9,595	4,409	13,018	1,057	961	13.2	13.5	64,517	40.6	30.9
Duluth, MN-WI Metro Area	37,651	26,388	11,263	40,077	1,543	2,093	24.4	19.1	191,463	37.0	26.5
Durham-Chapel Hill, NC Metro Area	75,348	53,079	22,269	65,181	5,239	4,703	14.4	13.9	369,442	31.8	45.1
East Stroudsburg, PA Metro Area	24,147	15,807	8,340	29,912	1,870	1,926	12.9	15.5	113,149	47.1	24.9
Eau Claire, WI Metro Area	23,274	16,636	6,638	22,168	NA	1,586	NA	14.0	108,249	37.0	26.5
El Centro, CA Metro Area	38,258	26,150	12,046	36,196	1,636	1,734	23.4	20.9	109,306	54.7	14.3
Elizabethtown-Fort Knox, KY Metro Area	24,760	16,934	7,807	22,668	729	1,406	34.0	16.1	98,204	44.8	20.1
Elkhart-Goshen, IN Metro Area	36,462	25,884	10,540	34,655	2,053	1,991	17.8	17.4	127,871	55.0	18.3
Elmira, NY Metro Area	12,514	8,860	3,550	13,266	814	922	15.4	14.4	60,894	44.4	24.2
El Paso, TX Metro Area	179,132	124,782	54,350	168,738	11,225	10,998	16.0	15.3	507,644	47.7	22.8
Enid, OK Metro Area	11,564	8,671	2,837	9,729	714	634	16.2	15.3	41,816	47.5	24.5
Erie, PA Metro Area	39,420	27,220	12,200	41,710	2,658	2,695	14.8	15.5	187,773	47.4	26.4
Eugene, OR Metro Area	44,631	30,604	14,027	47,026	1,987	2,181	22.5	21.6	246,605	33.3	29.1
Evansville, IN-KY Metro Area	44,340	31,139	11,109	43,087	2,985	2,626	14.9	16.4	214,725	46.0	23.3
Fairbanks, AK Metro Area	19,052	13,714	5,338	19,409	836	844	22.8	23.0	59,492	24.2	34.5
Fargo, ND-MN Metro Area	32,631	23,490	9,141	27,957	2,386	1,788	13.7	15.6	144,696	28.7	34.5
Farmington, NM Metro Area	24,452	14,743	7,056	23,569	1,544	1,558	15.8	15.1	76,791	51.6	14.1
Fayetteville, NC Metro Area	60,571	42,315	18,244	60,390	4,036	4,386	15.0	13.8	234,567	35.1	25.2
Fayetteville-Springdale-Rogers, AR-MO Metro Area	89,438	63,629	25,784	67,853	5,958	4,426	15.0	15.3	324,727	43.8	30.8
Flagstaff, AZ Metro Area	18,627	12,829	5,789	21,009	NA	NA	NA	NA	80,427	32.8	33.1
Flint, MI Metro Area	67,305	45,409	21,773	85,552	3,463	4,375	19.4	19.6	278,345	42.0	20.8
Florence, SC Metro Area	34,207	24,425	9,782	34,693	2,206	2,281	15.5	15.2	139,053	52.3	19.8
Florence-Muscle Shoals, AL Metro Area	21,227	14,733	3,969	21,521	1,262	1,390	16.8	15.5	101,533	51.3	20.8
Fond du Lac, WI Metro Area	13,964	10,011	3,953	13,440	NA	948	NA	14.2	70,505	46.3	21.7
Fort Collins, CO Metro Area	47,390	33,400	13,990	41,221	2,650	2,420	17.9	17.0	217,339	24.2	46.2
Fort Smith, AR-OK Metro Area	49,379	34,815	14,500	47,826	3,322	3,252	14.9	14.7	187,828	51.8	17.1
Fort Wayne, IN Metro Area	64,686	45,103	19,576	65,301	3,423	3,681	18.9	17.7	279,140	41.2	26.9
Fresno, CA Metro Area	198,551	139,439	58,865	192,373	8,360	9,269	23.8	20.8	590,620	49.0	19.2
Gadsden, AL Metro Area	15,972	10,980	NA	15,971	927	1,105	17.2	14.5	71,551	47.6	17.3
Gainesville, FL Metro Area	32,457	22,880	9,577	33,122	1,895	1,963	17.1	16.9	166,968	30.4	42.0
Gainesville, GA Metro Area	35,099	25,123	9,976	28,858	2,171	1,895	16.2	15.2	125,214	48.4	22.7

NA = Not available.
[1]Data obtained from public schools.
[2]Including ungraded students, these are students who are assigned to programs or classes without standard grade designation.
[3]Data for prekindergarten not available in all areas.
[4]Full-time equivalent.

Table B-6.   Enrollment, Teachers, and Educational Attainment—*Continued*

Metropolitan statistical area and division	Public school enrollment[1] 2014–2015 Total[2]	Public school enrollment[1] Pre-Kindergarten to grade 8[3]	Public school enrollment[1] Grades 9–12	Total,[2] 2004–2005	Number of public school teachers,[4] 2014–2015	Number of public school teachers,[4] 2004–2005	Pupil/teacher ratio 2014–2015	Pupil/teacher ratio 2004–2005	Educational attainment, 2015 Population 25 years and over	Educational attainment, 2015 High school graduate or less (percent)	Educational attainment, 2015 Bachelor's degree or higher (percent)
Gettysburg, PA Metro Area	13,871	9,411	4,460	14,754	919	890	15.1	16.6	71,589	52.2	21.0
Glens Falls, NY Metro Area	18,111	12,289	5,590	21,424	1,483	1,674	12.2	12.8	92,339	45.2	24.6
Goldsboro, NC Metro Area	19,813	14,118	5,667	19,555	1,259	1,374	15.7	14.2	82,719	44.1	21.9
Grand Forks, ND-MN Metro Area	13,820	9,706	1,493	14,927	1,082	1,134	12.8	13.2	62,152	32.5	32.8
Grand Island, NE Metro Area	16,127	11,613	1,147	14,817	1,192	1,042	13.5	14.2	54,583	47.6	19.8
Grand Junction, CO Metro Area	23,047	16,321	6,726	20,806	1,340	1,210	17.2	17.2	99,999	35.1	30.3
Grand Rapids-Wyoming, MI Metro Area	167,330	114,770	52,386	171,782	9,224	9,652	18.1	17.8	673,744	37.2	31.1
Grants Pass, OR Metro Area	10,638	7,150	3,488	11,517	466	501	22.8	23.0	62,429	45.9	14.0
Great Falls, MT Metro Area	11,736	8,389	3,347	12,493	825	860	14.2	14.5	55,591	42.5	25.6
Greeley, CO Metro Area	51,070	37,049	14,021	38,756	2,858	2,404	17.9	16.1	180,362	39.5	25.9
Green Bay, WI Metro Area	51,975	36,641	15,334	48,820	NA	3,406	NA	14.3	214,031	41.9	26.1
Greensboro-High Point, NC Metro Area	114,767	79,584	35,094	107,970	7,260	7,106	15.8	15.2	508,638	40.8	28.0
Greenville, NC Metro Area	24,305	17,200	7,105	21,833	1,601	1,590	15.2	13.7	105,143	35.5	31.6
Greenville-Anderson-Mauldin, SC Metro Area	135,323	96,479	38,844	121,020	8,113	7,307	16.7	16.6	586,353	43.2	26.7
Gulfport-Biloxi-Pascagoula, MS Metro Area	62,761	44,827	17,084	62,869	3,919	3,885	16.0	16.2	258,547	45.1	20.4
Hagerstown-Martinsburg, MD-WV Metro Area	41,071	29,187	11,884	35,835	2,776	2,347	14.8	15.3	180,660	51.5	19.1
Hammond, LA Metro Area	19,937	14,308	5,629	18,483	1,213	1,063	16.4	17.4	80,916	51.2	19.1
Hanford-Corcoran, CA Metro Area	28,182	20,047	8,092	27,372	1,252	1,347	22.5	20.3	92,734	51.2	16.1
Harrisburg-Carlisle, PA Metro Area	82,056	55,755	26,301	94,505	5,598	5,352	14.7	17.7	389,642	45.0	29.6
Harrisonburg, VA Metro Area	17,503	12,404	3,576	15,394	1,224	1,227	14.3	12.5	79,147	48.0	29.0
Hartford-West Hartford-East Hartford, CT Metro Area	184,541	127,262	57,279	195,996	14,193	12,810	13.0	15.3	834,317	36.5	38.3
Hattiesburg, MS Metro Area	23,995	16,974	6,599	21,540	1,659	1,453	14.5	14.8	93,004	41.6	26.8
Hickory-Lenoir-Morganton, NC Metro Area	55,280	37,781	17,436	58,346	3,547	4,206	15.6	13.9	251,942	48.7	18.5
Hilton Head Island-Bluffton-Beaufort, SC Metro Area	25,502	18,882	6,620	22,378	1,709	1,553	14.9	14.4	146,803	33.7	37.3
Hinesville, GA Metro Area	13,338	9,697	837	13,602	814	876	16.4	15.5	45,740	43.9	17.5
Homosassa Springs, FL Metro Area	15,159	10,383	4,776	15,652	1,008	979	15.0	16.0	111,992	53.5	16.2
Hot Springs, AR Metro Area	15,132	10,697	4,434	13,359	1,055	917	14.3	14.6	69,624	44.3	19.4
Houma-Thibodaux, LA Metro Area	33,322	24,553	8,769	33,788	2,078	2,444	16.0	13.8	139,275	61.8	16.0
Houston-The Woodlands-Sugar Land, TX Metro Area	1,286,180	931,111	355,069	1,042,038	77,862	64,281	16.5	16.2	4,241,381	41.1	31.5
Huntington-Ashland, WV-KY-OH Metro Area	57,712	39,907	12,315	56,809	3,249	3,822	17.8	14.9	250,851	49.9	19.1
Huntsville, AL Metro Area	65,314	45,388	19,926	58,003	3,693	3,955	17.7	14.7	303,237	34.2	38.1
Idaho Falls, ID Metro Area	30,695	22,295	8,364	26,242	1,457	1,328	21.1	19.8	83,994	38.3	27.1
Indianapolis-Carmel-Anderson, IN Metro Area	338,770	237,431	100,803	295,328	17,616	17,378	19.2	17.0	1,310,888	39.6	32.9
Iowa City, IA Metro Area	21,101	15,113	5,988	16,935	1,392	1,198	15.2	14.1	99,525	29.2	43.6
Ithaca, NY Metro Area	11,303	7,552	3,658	12,303	973	1,051	11.6	11.7	59,768	24.6	54.9
Jackson, MI Metro Area	23,385	15,984	7,343	27,338	1,351	1,497	17.3	18.3	109,882	44.8	21.9
Jackson, MS Metro Area	92,439	65,483	25,761	90,760	5,862	5,383	15.8	16.9	377,394	37.9	29.0
Jackson, TN Metro Area	19,045	13,644	5,401	19,696	1,203	1,248	15.8	15.8	85,582	47.4	23.5
Jacksonville, FL Metro Area	217,075	153,641	63,434	200,298	12,228	11,858	17.8	16.9	993,223	38.1	30.0
Jacksonville, NC Metro Area	25,948	18,811	7,137	22,230	1,592	1,477	16.3	15.1	101,004	41.2	20.8
Janesville-Beloit, WI Metro Area	28,005	19,401	8,604	27,803	NA	1,926	NA	14.4	109,280	47.0	21.8
Jefferson City, MO Metro Area	20,601	14,272	6,329	20,058	1,556	1,497	13.2	13.4	101,942	44.8	27.1
Johnson City, TN Metro Area	27,291	18,955	3,164	26,746	1,801	1,684	15.2	15.9	141,183	49.0	23.9
Johnstown, PA Metro Area	17,840	12,350	5,490	19,933	1,290	1,378	13.8	14.5	97,536	54.2	21.1
Jonesboro, AR Metro Area	22,399	16,264	6,110	18,975	1,597	1,289	14.0	14.7	82,515	48.1	21.7
Joplin, MO Metro Area	30,250	21,614	8,636	27,752	2,067	1,817	14.6	15.3	115,303	45.4	22.7
Kahului-Wailuku-Lahaina, HI Metro Area	21,908	15,586	6,289	22,082	1,348	1,255	16.3	17.6	116,301	39.9	25.3
Kalamazoo-Portage, MI Metro Area	49,841	33,784	15,902	53,543	2,810	3,157	17.7	17.0	213,504	31.1	34.7
Kankakee, IL Metro Area	18,529	13,242	5,287	19,161	1,216	1,138	15.2	16.8	72,783	47.2	20.8
Kansas City, MO-KS Metro Area	345,639	246,169	99,027	321,365	22,961	21,872	15.1	14.7	1,395,502	35.1	35.8
Kennewick-Richland, WA Metro Area	54,665	38,333	16,332	43,169	2,914	2,141	18.8	20.2	172,291	40.1	26.4
Killeen-Temple, TX Metro Area	83,695	62,268	21,427	68,535	5,574	4,958	15.0	13.8	263,003	37.9	23.2
Kingsport-Bristol-Bristol, TN-VA Metro Area	40,795	22,680	9,159	44,536	2,741	2,803	14.9	15.9	221,665	50.6	20.5
Kingston, NY Metro Area	22,701	14,982	7,510	29,498	1,660	2,060	13.7	14.3	128,981	42.0	31.3
Knoxville, TN Metro Area	121,501	85,460	34,337	114,560	7,783	7,134	15.6	16.1	595,198	44.5	27.9
Kokomo, IN Metro Area	14,005	9,510	4,453	13,973	816	914	17.2	15.3	57,645	49.7	18.8
La Crosse-Onalaska, WI-MN Metro Area	20,600	14,348	6,252	19,517	271	1,391	76.0	14.0	88,227	33.8	30.0
Lafayette, LA Metro Area	73,539	53,608	19,931	70,909	4,697	4,860	15.7	14.6	319,495	52.7	21.2
Lafayette-West Lafayette, IN Metro Area	27,280	19,410	7,834	24,599	1,521	1,504	17.9	16.4	121,172	38.3	32.5
Lake Charles, LA Metro Area	35,143	25,643	9,500	34,246	2,456	2,329	14.3	14.7	135,739	48.5	21.6
Lake Havasu City-Kingman, AZ Metro Area	24,272	17,195	7,074	26,765	NA	NA	NA	NA	153,740	53.3	11.9
Lakeland-Winter Haven, FL Metro Area	99,643	70,803	28,840	87,052	6,085	5,780	16.4	15.1	446,224	52.3	19.1
Lancaster, PA Metro Area	67,018	46,413	20,605	69,310	4,604	4,390	14.6	15.8	358,036	52.0	25.8
Lansing-East Lansing, MI Metro Area	68,206	45,025	23,078	75,263	3,763	4,328	18.1	17.4	299,437	31.7	34.2
Laredo, TX Metro Area	70,163	50,492	19,671	59,525	4,129	3,703	17.0	16.1	147,672	61.0	17.4
Las Cruces, NM Metro Area	38,555	26,391	12,164	39,352	2,534	2,535	15.2	15.5	129,813	43.8	26.4
Las Vegas-Henderson-Paradise, NV Metro Area	340,174	241,064	98,363	282,984	16,123	8,295	21.1	34.1	1,429,567	43.2	23.1
Lawrence, KS Metro Area	14,982	10,714	4,268	13,037	1,079	912	13.9	14.3	67,537	27.5	47.0
Lawton, OK Metro Area	22,938	16,722	6,157	23,138	1,430	1,458	16.0	15.9	81,608	44.5	19.9
Lebanon, PA Metro Area	19,065	13,532	5,533	18,701	1,248	1,161	15.3	16.1	93,143	58.7	18.6

NA = Not available.

[1]Data obtained from public schools.

[2]Including ungraded students, these are students who are assigned to programs or classes without standard grade designation.

[3]Data for prekindergarten not available in all areas.

[4]Full-time equivalent.

Table B-6.   Enrollment, Teachers, and Educational Attainment—*Continued*

Metropolitan statistical area and division	Public school enrollment[1] 2014–2015 Total[2]	Pre-Kindergarten to grade 8[3]	Grades 9–12	Total,[2] 2004–2005	Number of public school teachers,[4] 2014–2015	2004–2005	Pupil/teacher ratio 2014–2015	2004–2005	Educational attainment, 2015 Population 25 years and over	High school graduate or less (percent)	Bachelor's degree or higher (percent)
Lewiston, ID-WA Metro Area	8,663	5,880	2,779	9,079	518	513	16.7	17.7	44,900	39.5	22.9
Lewiston-Auburn, ME Metro Area	15,605	11,360	4,245	16,130	1,255	1,323	12.4	12.2	74,789	47.8	21.1
Lexington-Fayette, KY Metro Area	71,270	50,510	4,021	59,550	4,560	4,025	15.6	14.8	326,802	36.0	35.5
Lima, OH Metro Area	15,510	11,309	4,201	17,486	NA	1,075	NA	16.3	70,033	47.6	19.4
Lincoln, NE Metro Area	46,619	33,353	873	39,229	3,361	2,759	13.9	14.2	200,253	28.3	36.7
Little Rock-North Little Rock-Conway, AR Metro Area	114,837	82,507	32,309	100,957	7,939	6,989	14.5	14.4	485,979	39.0	30.0
Logan, UT-ID Metro Area	28,416	20,422	7,993	22,879	150	1,126	189.4	20.3	68,650	31.1	33.4
Longview, TX Metro Area	39,813	28,964	10,849	37,507	2,837	2,747	14.0	13.7	143,653	46.3	19.1
Longview, WA Metro Area	16,702	11,419	5,283	17,911	931	877	17.9	20.4	71,960	42.9	17.2
Los Angeles-Long Beach-Anaheim, CA Metro Area	2,028,505	1,370,403	656,580	2,248,501	83,005	100,499	24.4	22.4	8,999,070	40.7	32.7
Anaheim-Santa Ana-Irvine, CA Metro Division	499,077	334,911	163,345	515,222	18,780	21,999	26.6	23.4	2,146,420	33.1	38.8
Los Angeles-Long Beach-Glendale, CA Metro Division	1,529,428	1,035,492	493,235	1,733,279	64,225	78,500	23.8	22.1	6,852,650	43.1	30.8
Louisville/Jefferson County, KY-IN Metro Area	184,478	129,706	48,664	168,662	10,050	10,017	18.4	16.8	876,489	40.9	28.7
Lubbock, TX Metro Area	52,914	39,100	13,814	45,290	3,768	3,331	14.0	13.6	182,861	43.8	25.8
Lynchburg, VA Metro Area	24,809	16,149	2,061	35,616	1,630	2,639	15.2	13.5	175,102	44.1	26.0
Macon, GA Metro Area	36,649	26,894	9,755	37,745	2,390	2,388	15.3	15.8	152,373	48.6	23.6
Madera, CA Metro Area	30,859	21,689	9,165	27,805	1,320	1,290	23.4	21.6	97,105	53.6	15.4
Madison, WI Metro Area	96,181	68,234	27,947	83,736	NA	6,492	NA	12.9	424,196	27.0	43.5
Manchester-Nashua, NH Metro Area	60,225	40,479	19,746	67,092	4,400	4,628	13.7	14.5	282,826	34.8	36.9
Manhattan, KS Metro Area	11,472	8,364	3,076	9,167	879	711	13.1	12.9	51,930	26.3	40.0
Mankato-North Mankato, MN Metro Area	12,845	9,145	3,700	12,411	544	763	23.6	16.3	59,064	29.3	33.7
Mansfield, OH Metro Area	17,089	12,183	4,906	19,701	NA	1,351	NA	14.6	84,510	54.3	14.4
McAllen-Edinburg-Mission, TX Metro Area	221,957	160,120	61,837	175,377	14,248	11,182	15.6	15.7	467,992	60.6	17.3
Medford, OR Metro Area	28,705	19,769	8,936	28,884	1,298	1,244	22.1	23.2	152,758	39.8	25.6
Memphis, TN-MS-AR Metro Area	225,149	158,696	65,566	229,700	11,187	13,420	20.1	17.1	873,656	43.4	26.9
Merced, CA Metro Area	56,997	39,838	17,125	54,857	2,469	2,639	23.1	20.8	155,645	56.5	14.4
Miami-Fort Lauderdale-West Palm Beach, FL Metro Area	811,396	563,057	248,339	814,278	48,379	46,485	16.8	17.5	4,271,132	42.3	30.9
Fort Lauderdale-Pompano Beach-Deerfield Beach, FL Metro Division	266,944	185,573	81,371	274,059	14,968	15,671	17.8	17.5	1,332,717	39.1	32.2
Miami-Miami Beach-Kendall, FL Metro Division	356,964	247,562	109,402	365,478	20,417	20,489	17.5	17.8	1,900,999	48.3	27.4
West Palm Beach-Boca Raton-Delray Beach, FL Metro Division	187,488	129,922	57,566	174,741	12,994	10,325	14.4	16.9	1,037,416	35.5	35.7
Michigan City-La Porte, IN Metro Area	17,065	11,568	5,486	17,294	941	1,037	18.1	16.7	77,191	50.9	17.6
Midland, MI Metro Area	12,119	7,914	4,176	15,417	667	809	18.2	19.1	57,912	37.7	34.0
Midland, TX Metro Area	28,785	21,262	7,523	24,347	1,845	1,619	15.6	15.0	103,081	40.7	26.2
Milwaukee-Waukesha-West Allis, WI Metro Area	234,288	162,575	71,713	241,792	NA	15,500	NA	15.6	1,060,667	35.5	33.9
Minneapolis-St. Paul-Bloomington, MN-WI Metro Area	566,123	392,329	173,794	535,856	32,175	19,985	17.6	26.8	2,374,578	28.7	40.3
Missoula, MT Metro Area	13,603	9,697	3,906	13,348	877	814	15.5	16.4	75,225	28.2	42.9
Mobile, AL Metro Area	63,016	44,321	18,695	63,987	3,425	4,107	18.4	15.6	277,665	47.1	23.5
Modesto, CA Metro Area	106,689	74,194	32,446	105,845	4,471	4,959	23.9	21.3	338,947	51.3	16.4
Monroe, LA Metro Area	32,075	23,226	8,849	31,571	2,072	2,102	15.5	15.0	115,167	48.2	25.1
Monroe, MI Metro Area	22,826	14,618	8,138	26,829	1,151	1,507	19.8	17.8	104,204	46.0	18.3
Montgomery, AL Metro Area	46,449	33,135	NA	55,681	3,013	3,044	15.4	18.3	248,483	43.6	28.0
Morgantown, WV Metro Area	15,401	10,905	4,496	14,662	1,017	1,000	15.1	14.7	89,593	44.4	34.3
Morristown, TN Metro Area	17,856	12,747	2,909	16,745	1,124	1,007	15.9	16.6	80,828	60.0	14.9
Mount Vernon-Anacortes, WA Metro Area	19,178	13,200	5,978	19,171	1,099	973	17.5	19.7	84,596	36.8	24.4
Muncie, IN Metro Area	15,955	10,918	5,033	17,156	967	1,139	16.5	15.1	70,810	46.6	23.1
Muskegon, MI Metro Area	27,485	19,017	8,422	33,798	1,544	1,843	17.8	18.3	117,345	45.8	18.7
Myrtle Beach-Conway-North Myrtle Beach, SC-NC Metro Area	55,912	39,809	16,032	45,197	3,467	2,930	16.1	15.4	319,925	42.0	24.9
Napa, CA Metro Area	20,978	14,103	6,826	19,841	959	1,006	21.9	19.7	98,697	33.4	32.8
Naples-Immokalee-Marco Island, FL Metro Area	45,228	32,052	13,176	41,953	2,956	2,511	15.3	16.7	268,250	39.3	35.2
Nashville-Davidson—Murfreesboro—Franklin, TN Metro Area	276,208	198,129	73,686	230,196	17,929	14,371	15.4	16.0	1,224,179	38.9	33.6
New Bern, NC Metro Area	17,504	12,416	5,030	18,189	1,167	1,300	15.0	14.0	82,938	39.0	23.0
New Haven-Milford, CT Metro Area	128,443	88,760	39,683	137,938	9,557	8,891	13.4	15.5	594,403	40.8	34.3
New Orleans-Metairie, LA Metro Area	166,225	121,256	44,969	188,188	10,911	12,381	15.2	15.2	870,010	42.4	28.6
New York-Newark-Jersey City, NY-NJ-PA Metro Area	2,837,254	1,926,666	838,144	2,846,637	209,960	133,962	13.5	21.2	13,918,552	39.7	38.4
Dutchess County-Putnam County, NY Metro Division	56,130	36,546	19,151	64,670	3,938	4,312	14.3	15.0	273,739	36.8	34.2
Nassau County-Suffolk County, NY Metro Division	451,141	300,273	145,094	476,515	31,883	33,882	14.1	14.1	1,973,301	35.9	38.9
Newark, NJ-PA Metro Division	404,255	272,754	111,728	405,101	33,956	31,414	11.9	12.9	1,713,541	37.0	40.9
New York-Jersey City-White Plains, NY-NJ Metro Division	1,925,728	1,317,093	562,171	1,900,351	140,183	64,354	13.7	29.5	9,957,971	41.0	38.0
Niles-Benton Harbor, MI Metro Area	23,903	15,996	7,848	27,950	1,363	1,656	17.5	16.9	106,760	37.7	28.9
North Port-Sarasota-Bradenton, FL Metro Area	89,795	63,597	26,198	82,238	5,930	5,236	15.1	15.7	588,724	40.2	31.3
Norwich-New London, CT Metro Area	39,534	26,882	12,652	44,439	3,089	2,990	12.8	14.9	189,272	39.5	33.4
Ocala, FL Metro Area	42,517	29,658	12,859	41,113	2,492	2,424	17.1	17.0	253,157	49.6	19.7

NA = Not available.
[1]Data obtained from public schools.
[2]Including ungraded students, these are students who are assigned to programs or classes without standard grade designation.
[3]Data for prekindergarten not available in all areas.
[4]Full-time equivalent.

Table B-6. Enrollment, Teachers, and Educational Attainment—*Continued*

Metropolitan statistical area and division	Public school enrollment[1] 2014–2015 Total[2]	Public school enrollment[1] 2014–2015 Pre-Kindergarten to grade 8[3]	Public school enrollment[1] 2014–2015 Grades 9–12	Total,[2] 2004–2005	Number of public school teachers,[4] 2014–2015	Number of public school teachers,[4] 2004–2005	Pupil/teacher ratio 2014–2015	Pupil/teacher ratio 2004–2005	Educational attainment, 2015 Population 25 years and over	Educational attainment, 2015 High school graduate or less (percent)	Educational attainment, 2015 Bachelor's degree or higher (percent)
Ocean City, NJ Metro Area	12,692	8,427	0	13,982	1,182	1,280	10.7	10.9	70,934	41.8	30.7
Odessa, TX Metro Area	33,689	25,604	8,085	26,327	1,834	1,689	18.4	15.6	93,777	52.7	16.2
Ogden-Clearfield, UT Metro Area	143,401	102,812	40,589	113,884	NA	5,231	NA	21.8	380,160	33.4	30.0
Oklahoma City, OK Metro Area	234,146	170,624	62,846	193,570	13,334	11,136	17.6	17.4	880,297	39.8	29.3
Olympia-Tumwater, WA Metro Area	41,141	27,573	13,568	38,422	2,256	1,997	18.2	19.2	186,672	30.7	32.7
Omaha-Council Bluffs, NE-IA Metro Area	153,630	110,122	18,966	134,351	10,296	9,115	14.9	14.7	595,342	32.9	34.7
Orlando-Kissimmee-Sanford, FL Metro Area	365,362	253,801	111,561	325,077	23,662	19,338	15.4	16.8	1,618,272	37.3	29.9
Oshkosh-Neenah, WI Metro Area	22,424	15,758	6,666	23,150	NA	1,555	NA	14.9	113,119	41.7	25.6
Owensboro, KY Metro Area	20,102	14,680	996	17,878	1,209	1,142	16.6	15.7	79,309	49.7	19.5
Oxnard-Thousand Oaks-Ventura, CA Metro Area	156,752	106,089	50,432	145,022	7,806	6,430	20.1	22.6	564,044	35.4	32.7
Palm Bay-Melbourne-Titusville, FL Metro Area	72,285	50,353	21,932	74,492	4,841	4,641	14.9	16.1	418,232	37.8	28.4
Panama City, FL Metro Area	29,513	21,510	8,003	29,181	1,974	1,817	15.0	16.1	138,270	42.2	22.4
Parkersburg-Vienna, WV Metro Area	14,379	10,128	4,251	14,832	985	1,010	14.6	14.7	65,706	48.8	19.7
Pensacola-Ferry Pass-Brent, FL Metro Area	67,065	47,609	19,456	68,782	4,473	4,237	15.0	16.2	324,088	36.9	26.2
Peoria, IL Metro Area	59,449	41,863	17,586	60,163	3,980	3,857	14.9	15.6	256,463	39.5	27.4
Philadelphia-Camden-Wilmington, PA-NJ-DE-MD Metro Area	860,935	593,226	237,996	870,036	60,023	56,236	14.3	15.5	4,154,206	39.7	36.0
Camden, NJ Metro Division	200,319	133,262	37,622	213,975	16,283	16,223	12.3	13.2	861,767	39.4	33.0
Montgomery County-Bucks County-Chester County, PA Metro Division	279,559	190,161	89,398	272,951	19,367	17,506	14.4	15.6	1,367,704	32.0	45.6
Philadelphia, PA Metro Division	276,801	196,575	80,226	283,858	16,724	16,108	16.6	17.6	1,431,025	47.2	29.8
Wilmington, DE-MD-NJ Metro Division	104,256	73,228	30,750	99,252	7,649	6,399	13.6	15.5	493,710	40.1	32.6
Phoenix-Mesa-Scottsdale, AZ Metro Area	778,094	547,627	230,305	688,419	NA	NA	NA	NA	3,021,157	37.1	29.4
Pine Bluff, AR Metro Area	15,076	10,605	4,470	17,540	1,082	1,180	13.9	14.9	64,784	56.3	14.2
Pittsburgh, PA Metro Area	306,094	207,034	99,060	340,162	21,337	22,457	14.3	15.1	1,697,737	41.0	33.0
Pittsfield, MA Metro Area	16,450	11,297	5,137	19,343	1,433	1,595	11.5	12.1	92,514	40.3	32.4
Pocatello, ID Metro Area	14,502	10,339	4,141	13,330	720	699	20.1	19.1	52,113	34.7	24.3
Portland-South Portland, ME Metro Area	69,914	48,586	19,750	77,562	5,627	6,116	12.4	12.7	380,388	33.4	39.6
Portland-Vancouver-Hillsboro, OR-WA Metro Area	341,420	236,296	105,124	322,766	16,854	15,858	20.3	20.4	1,660,565	29.3	37.9
Port St. Lucie, FL Metro Area	60,563	41,769	18,794	52,802	2,460	2,858	24.6	18.5	334,007	44.0	25.0
Prescott, AZ Metro Area	25,757	17,965	7,788	28,373	NA	NA	NA	NA	169,500	34.8	26.5
Providence-Warwick, RI-MA Metro Area	221,284	154,669	66,577	241,909	15,093	18,002	14.7	13.4	1,116,749	42.2	30.6
Provo-Orem, UT Metro Area	140,159	101,575	38,584	94,931	NA	4,167	NA	22.8	285,577	24.6	37.7
Pueblo, CO Metro Area	27,791	19,875	7,916	25,785	1,523	1,529	18.2	16.9	110,570	41.6	21.6
Punta Gorda, FL Metro Area	16,135	10,582	5,553	17,409	988	1,034	16.3	16.8	141,657	48.1	21.0
Racine, WI Metro Area	29,922	20,351	9,571	30,377	NA	1,982	NA	15.3	131,952	40.7	24.0
Raleigh, NC Metro Area	209,537	148,515	60,928	153,698	13,340	10,008	15.7	15.4	839,512	28.4	44.4
Rapid City, SD Metro Area	21,441	15,389	5,273	20,404	1,462	1,368	14.7	14.9	98,648	33.8	30.0
Reading, PA Metro Area	65,242	44,605	20,637	65,998	4,398	4,175	14.8	15.8	280,020	50.7	24.4
Redding, CA Metro Area	26,657	18,010	8,647	29,834	1,222	1,466	21.8	20.4	126,950	35.1	22.0
Reno, NV Metro Area	69,141	48,045	20,981	64,110	3,269	97	21.2	660.9	309,592	35.8	29.6
Richmond, VA Metro Area	178,457	80,023	3,877	189,704	9,503	12,210	18.8	15.5	871,695	36.7	35.2
Riverside-San Bernardino-Ontario, CA Metro Area	833,652	570,061	263,248	804,622	33,602	35,697	24.8	22.5	2,828,883	47.1	20.1
Roanoke, VA Metro Area	36,170	25,623	7,051	44,977	2,486	3,443	14.5	13.1	220,643	41.5	26.5
Rochester, MN Metro Area	33,704	23,700	10,004	32,901	2,161	1,995	15.6	16.5	145,251	30.5	37.3
Rochester, NY Metro Area	157,387	106,705	48,821	175,472	12,159	13,104	12.9	13.4	740,716	37.4	33.0
Rockford, IL Metro Area	55,449	38,969	16,480	56,879	3,483	3,116	15.9	18.3	228,899	45.9	22.1
Rocky Mount, NC Metro Area	25,364	18,058	7,239	27,280	1,486	1,957	17.1	13.9	100,398	50.9	16.4
Rome, GA Metro Area	16,448	11,847	4,601	15,871	1,075	1,139	15.3	13.9	64,448	53.6	18.5
Sacramento—Roseville—Arden-Arcade, CA Metro Area	366,770	252,454	113,552	358,352	15,922	17,171	23.0	20.9	1,519,801	32.7	32.2
Saginaw, MI Metro Area	28,426	18,843	9,547	36,882	1,472	2,026	19.3	18.2	132,337	46.1	19.4
St. Cloud, MN Metro Area	29,916	20,467	9,449	27,360	1,512	NA	19.8	NA	122,610	37.0	25.6
St. George, UT Metro Area	31,418	22,624	8,794	21,795	NA	1,004	NA	21.7	96,848	34.7	26.0
St. Joseph, MO-KS Metro Area	18,540	13,190	5,320	18,433	1,420	1,397	13.1	13.2	86,652	48.6	20.2
St. Louis, MO-IL Metro Area	411,080	287,746	122,410	419,559	26,956	27,923	15.3	15.0	1,929,636	36.1	32.5
Salem, OR Metro Area	66,118	45,717	20,401	61,021	3,065	3,045	21.6	20.0	267,783	40.9	23.0
Salinas, CA Metro Area	78,024	57,043	20,903	73,902	3,310	3,504	23.6	21.1	273,998	50.5	23.3
Salisbury, MD-DE Metro Area	51,855	37,406	13,720	48,281	3,851	3,424	13.5	14.1	278,917	45.9	25.8
Salt Lake City, UT Metro Area	227,458	162,737	64,721	187,782	NA	8,362	NA	22.5	724,009	34.4	32.7
San Angelo, TX Metro Area	20,024	14,512	5,512	18,725	30	30	667.5	624.2	76,641	45.7	23.5
San Antonio-New Braunfels, TX Metro Area	440,204	317,146	123,058	356,942	27,452	22,719	16.0	15.7	1,524,281	42.7	26.6
San Diego-Carlsbad, CA Metro Area	499,452	342,059	157,039	497,959	20,475	23,708	24.4	21.0	2,209,465	32.2	37.2
San Francisco-Oakland-Hayward, CA Metro Area	584,418	406,746	177,134	557,608	25,688	27,486	22.8	20.3	3,336,089	27.9	47.2
Oakland-Hayward-Berkeley, CA Metro Division	398,666	277,342	120,872	382,098	17,034	18,306	23.4	20.9	1,915,653	30.0	43.1
San Francisco-Redwood City-South San Francisco, CA Metro Division	152,749	105,675	47,031	147,109	7,019	7,652	21.8	19.2	1,229,337	26.1	51.6
San Rafael, CA Metro Division	33,003	23,729	9,231	28,401	1,635	1,528	20.2	18.6	191,099	18.5	58.9
San Jose-Sunnyvale-Santa Clara, CA Metro Area	286,532	200,916	85,051	264,787	12,274	12,567	23.3	21.1	1,352,161	27.9	48.7
San Luis Obispo-Paso Robles-Arroyo Grande, CA Metro Area	34,755	23,494	11,209	36,347	1,548	1,864	22.5	19.5	187,193	30.2	34.1
Santa Cruz-Watsonville, CA Metro Area	39,488	27,351	12,096	36,656	1,627	1,669	24.3	22.0	178,043	31.4	37.1
Santa Fe, NM Metro Area	19,524	13,907	5,617	16,375	1,325	1,097	14.7	14.9	108,701	32.8	40.9
Santa Maria-Santa Barbara, CA Metro Area	68,578	48,071	20,507	67,551	2,963	3,213	23.1	21.0	273,982	37.8	33.2
Santa Rosa, CA Metro Area	70,025	49,023	20,834	72,395	3,222	3,529	21.7	20.5	356,680	32.1	32.8

NA = Not available.
[1] Data obtained from public schools.
[2] Including ungraded students, these are students who are assigned to programs or classes without standard grade designation.
[3] Data for prekindergarten not available in all areas.
[4] Full-time equivalent.

Table B-6.   Enrollment, Teachers, and Educational Attainment—*Continued*

Metropolitan statistical area and division	Public school enrollment[1] 2014–2015 Total[2]	Pre-Kindergarten to grade 8[3]	Grades 9–12	Total,[2] 2004–2005	Number of public school teachers,[4] 2014–2015	2004–2005	Pupil/teacher ratio 2014–2015	2004–2005	Population 25 years and over	Educational attainment, 2015 High school graduate or less (percent)	Bachelor's degree or higher (percent)
Savannah, GA Metro Area	58,273	43,585	14,688	50,433	3,785	3,477	15.4	14.5	247,529	37.5	28.9
Scranton—Wilkes-Barre—Hazleton, PA Metro Area	73,961	51,751	22,210	73,984	4,967	4,572	14.9	16.2	396,044	49.3	23.3
Seattle-Tacoma-Bellevue, WA Metro Area	520,944	361,804	159,140	491,027	28,355	23,923	18.4	20.5	2,587,548	28.0	41.2
Seattle-Bellevue-Everett, WA Metro Division	389,403	270,244	119,159	361,811	21,099	17,622	18.5	20.5	2,026,680	25.5	45.4
Tacoma-Lakewood, WA Metro Division	131,541	91,560	39,981	129,216	7,256	6,301	18.1	20.5	560,868	37.2	25.7
Sebastian-Vero Beach, FL Metro Area	18,077	12,656	5,421	16,942	1,044	1,015	17.3	16.7	111,187	45.9	25.6
Sebring, FL Metro Area	12,346	8,850	3,496	12,226	NA	781	NA	15.7	74,414	53.7	17.6
Sheboygan, WI Metro Area	19,178	13,136	6,042	19,329	NA	1,348	NA	14.3	80,718	46.7	23.4
Sherman-Denison, TX Metro Area	21,861	15,655	6,206	21,031	1,619	1,570	13.5	13.4	84,286	46.5	19.2
Shreveport-Bossier City, LA Metro Area	74,917	54,488	20,429	75,021	4,518	4,896	16.6	15.3	295,998	47.6	22.0
Sierra Vista-Douglas, AZ Metro Area	19,974	14,025	5,942	23,314	NA	NA	NA	NA	89,293	36.9	19.8
Sioux City, IA-NE-SD Metro Area	30,102	21,348	8,754	29,546	2,071	2,124	14.5	13.9	107,694	48.2	21.6
Sioux Falls, SD Metro Area	41,036	29,913	11,123	32,857	2,694	2,169	15.2	15.1	165,046	34.7	31.7
South Bend-Mishawaka, IN-MI Metro Area	45,777	31,838	13,851	48,466	1,527	2,782	30.0	17.4	210,158	44.9	25.9
Spartanburg, SC Metro Area	52,528	37,518	15,010	50,201	3,598	3,525	14.6	14.2	217,872	47.0	22.2
Spokane-Spokane Valley, WA Metro Area	82,436	56,533	25,903	80,713	4,694	3,713	17.6	21.7	371,769	33.9	27.2
Springfield, IL Metro Area	32,511	23,245	9,266	32,010	2,095	1,937	15.5	16.5	144,684	35.2	34.1
Springfield, MA Metro Area	92,294	63,877	28,227	98,649	7,202	7,838	12.8	12.6	415,653	41.6	31.1
Springfield, MO Metro Area	67,329	47,939	19,390	60,046	4,666	3,965	14.4	15.1	296,166	40.2	27.1
Springfield, OH Metro Area	20,852	14,803	6,049	24,690	NA	1,504	NA	16.4	93,014	50.1	17.7
State College, PA Metro Area	14,262	9,628	4,634	15,785	1,140	1,141	12.5	13.8	96,414	38.7	43.0
Staunton-Waynesboro, VA Metro Area	16,585	10,643	876	16,668	969	1,082	17.1	15.4	85,521	51.1	22.9
Stockton-Lodi, CA Metro Area	141,795	98,860	42,831	134,989	5,743	6,381	24.7	21.2	452,979	48.4	18.8
Sumter, SC Metro Area	16,943	12,182	4,761	18,503	1,043	1,144	16.2	16.2	68,051	47.3	17.3
Syracuse, NY Metro Area	101,904	68,697	32,118	113,147	7,213	8,170	14.1	13.8	444,565	38.9	31.0
Tallahassee, FL Metro Area	47,866	34,765	13,101	46,878	2,960	2,959	16.2	15.8	232,124	35.2	35.3
Tampa-St. Petersburg-Clearwater, FL Metro Area	402,159	283,102	119,057	382,739	26,846	23,838	15.0	16.1	2,128,909	39.4	28.9
Terre Haute, IN Metro Area	25,109	17,739	7,369	27,423	1,449	1,736	17.3	15.8	113,655	48.9	21.1
Texarkana, TX-AR Metro Area	26,716	19,370	7,346	25,788	2,042	1,895	13.1	13.6	101,312	51.5	14.1
The Villages, FL Metro Area	8,307	6,057	2,250	7,142	NA	428	NA	16.7	105,817	38.1	33.0
Toledo, OH Metro Area	100,098	69,976	30,122	101,851	NA	6,062	NA	16.8	400,219	41.5	25.5
Topeka, KS Metro Area	38,538	26,745	11,407	38,017	2,968	2,851	13.0	13.3	157,312	41.1	27.4
Trenton, NJ Metro Area	54,464	35,811	0	55,820	4,611	4,156	11.8	13.4	248,659	38.6	38.1
Tucson, AZ Metro Area	146,535	101,997	44,515	145,806	NA	NA	NA	NA	668,691	35.6	31.1
Tulsa, OK Metro Area	166,985	121,773	44,825	155,413	9,764	9,197	17.1	16.9	647,291	40.4	26.7
Tuscaloosa, AL Metro Area	33,681	23,919	9,762	32,410	1,894	2,138	17.8	15.2	152,128	46.6	28.1
Tyler, TX Metro Area	34,937	25,499	9,438	33,019	2,388	2,358	14.6	14.0	144,118	42.4	24.6
Urban Honolulu, HI Metro Area	124,021	89,603	34,180	127,234	7,619	7,614	16.3	16.7	681,195	35.2	33.2
Utica-Rome, NY Metro Area	44,456	30,540	13,363	48,462	3,206	3,512	13.9	13.8	205,291	45.8	23.1
Valdosta, GA Metro Area	23,402	17,287	1,167	21,282	1,485	1,417	15.8	15.0	85,916	48.6	21.6
Vallejo-Fairfield, CA Metro Area	64,791	44,547	20,078	72,667	2,657	3,413	24.4	21.3	295,732	37.0	25.7
Victoria, TX Metro Area	17,157	12,704	4,453	16,870	1,195	1,071	14.4	15.8	64,711	46.9	21.8
Vineland-Bridgeton, NJ Metro Area	27,730	19,667	NA	26,448	2,387	2,326	11.6	11.4	106,002	65.2	13.5
Virginia Beach-Norfolk-Newport News, VA-NC Metro Area	265,961	136,197	8,853	280,327	14,376	19,782	18.5	14.2	1,141,907	34.5	30.2
Visalia-Porterville, CA Metro Area	102,206	72,721	29,299	92,124	4,266	4,316	24.0	21.3	267,457	55.2	14.2
Waco, TX Metro Area	46,917	33,540	13,377	44,404	3,222	3,033	14.6	14.6	161,027	45.2	22.5
Walla Walla, WA Metro Area	9,468	6,353	3,115	9,421	544	507	17.4	18.6	42,580	33.5	29.2
Warner Robins, GA Metro Area	29,556	21,225	8,331	29,739	2,198	2,030	13.4	14.6	122,322	39.0	20.7
Washington-Arlington-Alexandria, DC-VA-MD-WV Metro Area	935,173	651,376	137,203	835,181	62,329	54,392	15.0	15.4	4,132,855	28.6	49.3
Silver Spring-Frederick-Rockville, MD Metro Division	195,216	137,068	58,148	178,882	12,776	11,401	15.3	15.7	879,029	25.3	54.3
Washington-Arlington-Alexandria, DC-VA-MD-WV Metro Division	739,957	514,308	79,055	656,299	49,553	42,991	14.9	15.3	3,253,826	29.5	48.0
Waterloo-Cedar Falls, IA Metro Area	24,995	17,223	7,772	23,496	1,818	1,740	13.7	13.5	109,498	39.0	29.0
Watertown-Fort Drum, NY Metro Area	18,604	13,285	5,102	18,340	1,293	1,258	14.4	14.6	73,484	40.8	23.0
Wausau, WI Metro Area	20,010	13,957	6,053	19,805	NA	1,368	NA	14.5	94,391	45.7	23.7
Weirton-Steubenville, WV-OH Metro Area	16,162	11,700	4,462	18,878	535	1,263	30.2	14.9	86,277	53.5	16.5
Wenatchee, WA Metro Area	20,578	14,142	6,436	19,443	1,204	1,006	17.1	19.3	78,300	46.8	21.6
Wheeling, WV-OH Metro Area	19,212	13,854	5,358	19,979	737	1,337	26.1	14.9	104,426	45.6	22.5
Wichita, KS Metro Area	113,569	80,850	31,486	104,577	7,466	6,731	15.2	15.5	416,443	38.4	27.7
Wichita Falls, TX Metro Area	24,350	17,681	6,669	26,139	1,824	1,965	13.3	13.3	97,188	49.4	21.8
Williamsport, PA Metro Area	15,743	10,947	4,796	17,509	1,106	1,212	14.2	14.4	81,534	53.6	22.9
Wilmington, NC Metro Area	36,014	25,241	10,688	30,741	2,257	1,852	16.0	16.6	190,388	31.6	34.3
Winchester, VA-WV Metro Area	21,001	14,567	2,330	19,224	1,533	1,446	13.7	13.3	92,144	46.9	26.3
Winston-Salem, NC Metro Area	100,619	70,029	30,528	95,587	6,584	6,298	15.3	15.2	449,699	43.5	26.9
Worcester, MA-CT Metro Area	144,878	100,765	43,964	152,070	10,474	10,780	13.8	14.1	639,714	39.9	33.3
Yakima, WA Metro Area	53,250	37,995	15,255	48,883	3,017	2,484	17.6	19.7	149,845	57.0	15.7
York-Hanover, PA Metro Area	64,003	44,619	19,384	63,505	4,096	4,018	15.6	15.8	307,046	51.8	22.7
Youngstown-Warren-Boardman, OH-PA Metro Area	76,041	51,987	24,054	90,721	1,088	5,767	69.9	15.7	388,419	52.2	21.2
Yuba City, CA Metro Area	34,528	24,464	10,064	30,582	1,611	1,566	21.4	19.5	109,075	44.8	15.2
Yuma, AZ Metro Area	38,016	26,255	11,752	36,081	NA	1,729	NA	20.9	128,566	53.1	15.4

NA = Not available.
[1]Data obtained from public schools.
[2]Including ungraded students, these are students who are assigned to programs or classes without standard grade designation.
[3]Data for prekindergarten not available in all areas.
[4]Full-time equivalent.

Table B-7. Median Income, Household Income Distribution, and Poverty Status, 2015

Metropolitan statistical area and division	Median family income (in 2015 inflation-adjusted dollars)	Median household income (in 2015 inflation-adjusted dollars)	Total number of households	Percent of households by income level						Percent of group whose income in the past 12 months is below poverty level[1]		
				Under $25,000	$25,000–$49,999	$50,000–$74,999	$75,000–$99,999	$100,000–$199,999	$200,000 and over	Families	Individuals	Children under 18
Abilene, TX Metro Area	60,639	47,420	59,372	25.0	26.7	19.4	11.2	14.5	3.2	9.9	13.9	17.3
Akron, OH Metro Area	69,424	51,580	282,456	23.9	24.4	18.1	11.4	18.4	3.8	10.2	14.2	21.0
Albany, GA Metro Area	50,660	40,143	57,597	34.0	24.6	17.7	8.8	12.9	2.0	19.4	24.6	34.6
Albany, OR Metro Area	56,652	47,527	46,315	25.4	27.1	23.0	10.0	12.8	1.7	12.2	15.9	20.8
Albany-Schenectady-Troy, NY Metro Area	81,972	63,080	342,766	18.1	20.6	19.2	14.1	22.7	5.3	6.5	10.2	13.9
Albuquerque, NM Metro Area	61,696	48,937	342,590	26.9	24.0	18.1	11.6	16.3	3.1	13.1	18.7	25.7
Alexandria, LA Metro Area	52,539	42,778	54,406	30.6	25.8	19.1	9.6	11.7	3.1	18.0	22.0	33.9
Allentown-Bethlehem-Easton, PA-NJ Metro Area	72,206	60,671	314,985	17.7	23.1	19.6	13.8	21.0	4.9	7.1	9.9	15.7
Altoona, PA Metro Area	61,768	45,432	52,830	27.6	25.9	19.2	12.6	12.3	2.4	11.7	15.3	23.4
Amarillo, TX Metro Area	63,337	51,734	95,626	22.4	25.0	19.5	12.6	17.0	3.5	11.6	14.4	20.2
Ames, IA Metro Area	75,697	50,811	37,264	26.4	21.7	18.8	13.1	14.3	5.7	4.3	20.7	8.5
Anchorage, AK Metro Area	92,612	78,238	135,601	11.9	19.1	16.6	14.5	30.1	7.8	6.5	8.7	13.3
Ann Arbor, MI Metro Area	88,162	61,977	138,099	19.8	20.6	17.1	12.0	22.7	7.8	6.8	14.6	13.7
Anniston-Oxford-Jacksonville, AL Metro Area	53,927	42,346	44,323	30.1	25.5	19.6	11.4	13.0	0.4	16.2	20.0	32.1
Appleton, WI Metro Area	73,930	61,245	90,489	16.7	24.0	19.0	15.1	22.3	2.7	8.0	9.4	15.9
Asheville, NC Metro Area	59,335	44,826	184,983	25.8	29.2	18.7	10.1	12.9	3.4	10.6	15.4	23.6
Athens-Clarke County, GA Metro Area	55,915	38,643	76,704	35.7	24.4	14.1	9.2	12.8	3.8	15.9	27.1	31.6
Atlanta-Sandy Springs-Roswell, GA Metro Area	70,603	60,219	2,028,705	19.3	22.4	18.9	12.5	20.6	6.3	10.7	13.9	20.2
Atlantic City-Hammonton, NJ Metro Area	67,976	54,052	101,813	20.9	25.6	16.3	11.3	20.4	5.6	10.8	14.3	22.3
Auburn-Opelika, AL Metro Area	63,485	46,589	58,191	31.8	20.8	17.5	11.6	15.2	3.1	14.6	21.9	21.3
Augusta-Richmond County, GA-SC Metro Area	59,111	49,721	210,854	26.2	24.0	18.1	12.8	15.9	3.0	14.8	19.1	29.0
Austin-Round Rock, TX Metro Area	81,634	67,195	723,914	15.6	21.5	17.8	13.9	23.1	8.1	7.6	11.7	15.2
Bakersfield, CA Metro Area	55,694	51,342	263,273	25.1	23.4	18.0	11.7	18.4	3.5	18.0	21.9	31.9
Baltimore-Columbia-Towson, MD Metro Area	90,008	72,520	1,037,443	16.4	17.7	17.4	13.3	26.8	8.5	7.1	10.6	13.8
Bangor, ME Metro Area	59,355	44,173	59,099	29.0	25.4	18.3	12.3	13.1	1.9	10.7	18.0	20.8
Barnstable Town, MA Metro Area	81,817	66,102	97,451	16.8	20.7	18.7	14.7	22.8	6.3	3.7	6.6	6.6
Baton Rouge, LA Metro Area	70,649	54,774	300,535	24.4	21.7	16.3	11.7	21.5	4.4	11.0	16.2	22.5
Battle Creek, MI Metro Area	52,055	43,084	53,076	29.3	26.2	18.6	11.1	13.1	1.7	12.6	15.8	21.0
Bay City, MI Metro Area	57,331	46,560	42,799	26.6	26.4	23.9	12.2	9.4	1.6	9.1	14.6	20.1
Beaumont-Port Arthur, TX Metro Area	60,803	49,787	153,283	25.8	24.4	19.0	10.7	17.2	3.0	11.5	15.7	20.2
Beckley, WV Metro Area	46,236	37,101	49,070	32.4	32.1	16.0	8.5	10.1	0.9	12.6	18.0	25.7
Bellingham, WA Metro Area	73,501	55,016	80,023	20.9	23.4	20.0	13.6	18.4	3.6	6.4	14.5	12.0
Bend-Redmond, OR Metro Area	66,076	57,373	69,424	19.2	25.2	20.2	12.4	18.2	4.8	9.9	14.8	21.7
Billings, MT Metro Area	67,386	57,249	68,021	19.0	23.6	23.7	13.6	16.3	3.9	6.7	9.6	13.5
Binghamton, NY Metro Area	63,486	49,386	97,883	26.1	24.4	17.9	11.6	16.8	3.2	10.4	16.5	21.0
Birmingham-Hoover, AL Metro Area	65,827	51,459	441,762	25.5	22.7	18.6	12.2	16.7	4.3	11.8	15.7	22.3
Bismarck, ND Metro Area	90,672	65,173	55,092	17.0	22.4	17.1	13.1	24.7	5.7	6.0	10.5	11.4
Blacksburg-Christiansburg-Radford, VA Metro Area	65,283	50,947	69,396	26.5	22.5	20.2	10.9	16.2	3.7	7.1	19.0	11.6
Bloomington, IL Metro Area	84,424	63,842	72,767	18.9	19.6	18.3	13.7	23.2	6.3	4.9	11.5	7.3
Bloomington, IN Metro Area	70,125	44,376	62,702	30.7	24.3	16.5	10.2	15.8	2.5	10.7	24.2	22.1
Bloomsburg-Berwick, PA Metro Area	62,016	46,688	33,140	26.2	26.1	18.2	12.2	14.5	2.7	8.0	13.3	17.1
Boise City, ID Metro Area	66,071	51,925	245,109	23.5	24.3	18.9	12.1	17.9	3.3	8.5	13.4	14.7
Boston-Cambridge-Newton, MA-NH Metro Area	**99,887**	**78,800**	**1,782,655**	**16.9**	**16.2**	**14.8**	**12.0**	**28.0**	**12.1**	**7.0**	**10.2**	**12.6**
Boston, MA Metro Division	*94,252*	*73,628*	*743,723*	*19.4*	*16.8*	*14.3*	*11.7*	*26.6*	*11.2*	*9.0*	*12.6*	*15.9*
Cambridge-Newton-Framingham, MA Metro Division	*104,669*	*82,394*	*872,640*	*15.6*	*15.7*	*14.8*	*11.9*	*28.6*	*13.5*	*6.1*	*8.9*	*10.8*
Rockingham County-Strafford County, NH Metro Division	*96,128*	*80,441*	*166,292*	*12.6*	*16.9*	*17.0*	*14.2*	*30.8*	*8.5*	*3.5*	*6.5*	*8.0*
Boulder, CO Metro Area	103,037	72,009	124,615	15.0	21.4	15.0	11.8	25.1	11.7	5.0	12.9	12.0
Bowling Green, KY Metro Area	53,896	43,437	62,500	28.2	26.9	18.3	10.8	12.8	3.0	15.3	19.7	26.0
Bremerton-Silverdale, WA Metro Area	78,341	66,090	98,490	14.6	21.7	19.5	17.5	22.0	4.7	4.6	9.6	9.3
Bridgeport-Stamford-Norwalk, CT Metro Area	105,514	86,414	333,528	15.5	16.0	12.8	11.9	25.5	18.3	6.1	8.9	10.7
Brownsville-Harlingen, TX Metro Area	36,872	34,074	122,468	38.3	27.3	12.9	9.1	10.4	1.9	28.4	32.4	47.5
Brunswick, GA Metro Area	50,281	44,347	46,647	27.8	28.3	13.7	11.3	15.4	3.5	16.2	19.7	30.5
Buffalo-Cheektowaga-Niagara Falls, NY Metro Area	70,876	51,772	467,992	25.6	22.6	16.8	13.5	18.4	3.1	10.8	15.7	25.4
Burlington, NC Metro Area	52,316	39,541	63,093	31.6	27.9	15.3	10.6	13.0	1.5	15.8	20.1	29.7
Burlington-South Burlington, VT Metro Area	88,201	66,807	85,553	17.6	18.9	19.6	15.3	23.3	5.3	5.6	10.4	12.3
California-Lexington Park, MD Metro Area	98,119	85,163	39,029	9.9	15.8	15.7	15.5	33.7	9.4	6.4	8.0	13.1
Canton-Massillon, OH Metro Area	61,626	49,313	162,868	23.8	26.9	18.9	11.8	15.7	3.0	9.4	13.2	20.2
Cape Coral-Fort Myers, FL Metro Area	60,413	50,651	263,694	22.8	26.3	19.9	12.1	15.0	3.9	11.0	16.4	26.5
Cape Girardeau, MO-IL Metro Area	61,280	47,824	35,273	24.0	28.6	16.3	11.6	15.8	3.8	12.1	19.6	28.2
Carbondale-Marion, IL Metro Area	58,413	42,284	48,012	31.0	26.5	17.0	9.9	12.3	3.2	10.9	18.9	24.7
Carson City, NV Metro Area	58,803	42,251	22,687	26.3	29.8	15.4	8.8	15.8	3.9	13.1	18.7	28.3
Casper, WY Metro Area	70,549	52,886	32,564	20.5	26.3	16.7	13.5	19.9	3.1	7.3	11.6	18.7
Cedar Rapids, IA Metro Area	76,704	58,015	107,586	19.1	24.0	19.3	14.1	19.7	3.9	7.4	11.1	13.4
Chambersburg-Waynesboro, PA Metro Area	67,634	57,960	59,486	15.8	28.1	19.4	16.6	17.3	2.7	7.3	8.9	13.5
Champaign-Urbana, IL Metro Area	75,747	51,600	92,268	26.1	22.5	17.5	12.5	16.9	4.4	6.2	19.0	15.0
Charleston, WV Metro Area	53,608	42,526	94,533	27.8	29.3	18.0	11.5	11.1	2.3	15.0	18.6	29.6
Charleston-North Charleston, SC Metro Area	70,720	56,430	273,722	20.7	22.8	18.9	13.5	18.6	5.5	9.9	14.2	20.1
Charlotte-Concord-Gastonia, NC-SC Metro Area	67,639	54,836	905,696	21.1	24.3	18.2	12.0	18.5	5.9	10.3	14.1	19.4
Charlottesville, VA Metro Area	81,751	63,918	87,949	17.8	21.4	18.8	12.5	22.1	7.5	6.7	13.1	11.3
Chattanooga, TN-GA Metro Area	58,568	47,809	209,340	25.9	25.7	18.7	11.0	15.4	3.4	11.3	15.3	21.3
Cheyenne, WY Metro Area	75,770	60,599	37,740	17.8	23.2	18.4	14.5	22.2	3.9	8.3	12.6	17.9
Chicago-Naperville-Elgin, IL-IN-WI Metro Area	**78,342**	**63,153**	**3,470,993**	**19.7**	**20.4**	**16.8**	**12.6**	**22.7**	**7.8**	**10.0**	**13.3**	**19.3**

[1] The Poverty status was determined for all people except institutionalized people, people in military group quarters, people in college dormitories, and unrelated individuals under 15 years old.

Table B-7. Median Income, Household Income Distribution, and Poverty Status, 2015—*Continued*

Metropolitan statistical area and division	Median family income (in 2015 inflation-adjusted dollars)	Median household income (in 2015 inflation-adjusted dollars)	Total number of households	Percent of households by income level						Percent of group whose income in the past 12 months is below poverty level[1]		
				Under $25,000	$25,000–$49,999	$50,000–$74,999	$75,000–$99,999	$100,000–$199,999	$200,000 and over	Families	Individuals	Children under 18
Chicago-Naperville-Arlington Heights, IL Metro Division	78,191	62,505	2,686,830	20.4	20.1	16.5	12.5	22.6	7.9	10.2	13.7	19.5
Elgin, IL Metro Division	81,693	66,980	212,458	16.3	20.0	19.1	11.8	26.1	6.5	9.1	12.1	17.5
Gary, IN Metro Division	65,880	53,026	266,576	21.9	24.9	18.5	13.2	18.0	3.5	11.8	15.3	25.9
Lake County-Kenosha County, IL-WI Metro Division	91,571	75,548	305,129	13.6	19.7	16.5	12.8	26.0	11.5	7.5	9.7	14.0
Chico, CA Metro Area	57,413	45,644	85,289	28.8	26.5	15.7	10.3	15.7	3.0	13.4	21.8	21.4
Cincinnati, OH-KY-IN Metro Area	73,052	56,826	832,607	21.5	22.6	18.0	12.9	20.0	5.1	9.3	13.2	17.9
Clarksville, TN-KY Metro Area	52,577	46,070	101,265	21.5	33.0	20.5	11.1	12.7	1.2	11.3	15.3	20.4
Cleveland, TN Metro Area	56,047	42,380	46,389	32.2	24.0	18.2	11.7	10.6	3.3	15.6	19.6	27.1
Cleveland-Elyria, OH Metro Area	67,120	51,049	849,475	24.6	24.2	17.8	12.2	16.9	4.4	11.0	14.8	21.7
Coeur d'Alene, ID Metro Area	59,678	47,860	58,675	26.1	27.2	17.2	9.9	16.7	2.9	13.4	15.7	24.0
College Station-Bryan, TX Metro Area	70,071	46,341	90,526	28.8	24.2	15.2	11.0	16.8	4.0	10.9	23.0	16.9
Colorado Springs, CO Metro Area	73,899	60,458	261,435	17.6	23.3	19.5	12.7	22.1	4.8	7.7	10.6	14.7
Columbia, MO Metro Area	72,446	50,520	69,152	26.2	23.1	18.8	11.1	17.8	2.9	6.9	18.5	10.4
Columbia, SC Metro Area	65,276	51,369	302,634	23.4	25.0	19.5	12.8	15.5	3.8	10.8	15.1	21.2
Columbus, GA-AL Metro Area	53,102	41,592	112,983	31.8	26.8	16.9	9.9	12.1	2.6	16.3	21.1	31.4
Columbus, IN Metro Area	67,481	54,447	31,131	18.8	26.1	21.3	13.5	17.2	3.2	9.4	13.9	20.4
Columbus, OH Metro Area	72,068	58,192	772,304	20.4	22.7	18.5	13.2	20.0	5.2	10.2	14.2	19.6
Corpus Christi, TX Metro Area	60,306	50,253	161,634	25.5	24.2	18.6	12.7	15.3	3.7	14.0	19.0	30.2
Corvallis, OR Metro Area	79,763	52,852	35,062	27.0	20.7	11.8	16.4	18.9	5.2	9.1	20.1	16.5
Crestview-Fort Walton Beach-Destin, FL Metro Area	61,077	53,488	102,729	19.9	26.8	20.4	12.7	15.6	4.6	8.1	11.8	19.8
Cumberland, MD-WV Metro Area	52,642	39,408	39,120	34.1	26.9	17.1	11.1	9.0	1.8	13.1	19.2	30.1
Dallas-Fort Worth-Arlington, TX Metro Area	72,350	61,644	2,479,995	17.9	22.5	18.5	12.6	21.4	7.1	10.2	13.4	19.2
Dallas-Plano-Irving, TX Metro Division	73,209	62,142	1,653,468	17.8	22.4	17.9	12.5	21.9	7.5	10.6	13.6	19.5
Fort Worth-Arlington, TX Metro Division	71,188	60,756	826,527	18.0	22.7	19.6	12.8	20.3	6.5	9.5	12.8	18.5
Dalton, GA Metro Area	53,680	45,632	48,631	25.6	28.3	22.2	10.9	9.7	3.1	11.0	15.2	22.6
Danville, IL Metro Area	55,361	45,098	30,927	26.1	28.4	19.8	11.6	12.1	2.1	12.7	18.1	27.8
Daphne-Fairhope-Foley, AL Metro Area	65,855	52,003	72,269	22.2	24.9	19.8	11.4	16.1	5.6	7.5	12.8	18.0
Davenport-Moline-Rock Island, IA-IL Metro Area	68,559	55,496	155,753	21.7	22.9	20.3	14.5	17.8	2.8	8.8	11.9	16.0
Dayton, OH Metro Area	62,301	49,504	330,430	24.2	26.2	19.0	11.4	15.7	3.4	12.0	16.2	24.4
Decatur, AL Metro Area	55,665	46,157	60,697	25.3	29.5	18.8	11.9	12.2	2.3	14.7	17.3	25.2
Decatur, IL Metro Area	63,303	48,040	44,429	28.0	23.7	16.7	13.1	14.5	4.1	13.8	18.3	27.0
Deltona-Daytona Beach-Ormond Beach, FL Metro Area	52,808	43,284	248,938	26.5	30.1	19.5	9.9	11.9	2.2	10.9	15.3	22.8
Denver-Aurora-Lakewood, CO Metro Area	85,344	70,283	1,075,919	14.9	20.0	18.4	13.6	25.2	7.8	7.0	10.3	13.9
Des Moines-West Des Moines, IA Metro Area	75,521	62,024	242,022	17.3	21.7	20.9	13.8	21.1	5.2	6.9	10.7	13.8
Detroit-Warren-Dearborn, MI Metro Area	68,516	53,628	1,674,251	23.4	23.0	17.7	11.9	19.1	4.9	12.2	16.1	24.0
Detroit-Dearborn-Livonia, MI Metro Division	52,657	41,557	667,521	32.2	24.4	16.8	10.1	13.4	3.1	19.7	24.8	37.5
Warren-Troy-Farmington Hills, MI Metro Division	78,972	62,593	1,006,730	17.7	22.1	18.3	13.0	22.9	6.1	7.6	10.1	13.8
Dothan, AL Metro Area	51,008	42,492	55,973	29.6	28.8	18.3	9.1	11.1	3.1	14.0	17.9	27.1
Dover, DE Metro Area	66,755	56,778	62,477	20.6	23.7	20.7	14.6	16.7	3.6	10.5	14.6	22.4
Dubuque, IA Metro Area	71,284	58,487	37,784	19.3	22.6	22.1	15.1	18.3	2.7	8.3	12.9	16.9
Duluth, MN-WI Metro Area	67,723	50,566	116,212	24.2	25.1	19.5	12.4	16.3	2.6	8.6	13.5	14.5
Durham-Chapel Hill, NC Metro Area	74,638	54,160	215,294	22.8	23.4	16.2	11.8	18.6	7.2	9.8	15.9	22.8
East Stroudsburg, PA Metro Area	70,283	57,318	55,681	19.2	24.6	20.2	13.1	20.1	2.7	9.3	12.5	16.2
Eau Claire, WI Metro Area	68,358	52,094	63,854	21.0	25.9	21.5	13.7	15.1	2.7	6.6	12.5	14.9
El Centro, CA Metro Area	45,762	40,852	45,158	34.2	23.5	14.8	8.8	16.8	1.9	23.3	25.1	31.6
Elizabethtown-Fort Knox, KY Metro Area	58,122	48,955	56,899	23.4	27.8	20.7	11.6	15.0	1.4	11.1	15.7	24.7
Elkhart-Goshen, IN Metro Area	58,019	49,556	68,498	22.1	28.5	21.8	11.7	13.4	2.7	11.0	15.1	22.7
Elmira, NY Metro Area	67,329	53,119	34,546	21.8	24.3	23.4	12.1	16.0	2.4	10.5	13.9	20.0
El Paso, TX Metro Area	49,027	43,633	261,529	27.3	29.2	19.2	9.9	12.9	1.5	16.3	20.1	29.3
Enid, OK Metro Area	58,467	48,222	23,808	NA	NA	NA	NA	14.4	3.1	10.9	14.5	19.3
Erie, PA Metro Area	60,487	47,386	110,138	25.9	25.6	18.8	12.0	14.8	3.0	12.8	17.5	27.2
Eugene, OR Metro Area	60,797	47,318	146,602	26.8	25.4	19.1	11.8	14.2	2.7	11.0	19.4	24.6
Evansville, IN-KY Metro Area	61,757	48,662	124,936	25.7	25.4	18.8	12.5	14.3	3.3	11.7	15.2	22.6
Fairbanks, AK Metro Area	88,211	72,975	35,475	12.2	19.4	20.0	17.1	25.3	6.1	3.6	7.4	8.9
Fargo, ND-MN Metro Area	77,776	56,051	96,142	20.8	24.8	16.3	15.1	18.2	4.9	5.1	11.1	8.5
Farmington, NM Metro Area	57,063	49,613	43,030	26.8	23.5	18.2	13.6	15.9	2.0	14.5	19.6	25.2
Fayetteville, NC Metro Area	50,056	41,921	137,158	28.7	29.3	16.6	11.3	12.3	1.7	15.5	19.4	28.2
Fayetteville-Springdale-Rogers, AR-MO Metro Area	61,221	50,788	190,860	21.7	27.2	20.3	10.7	14.9	5.2	9.7	14.3	19.4
Flagstaff, AZ Metro Area	71,254	53,152	45,911	24.8	21.0	17.8	14.2	17.7	4.6	11.5	20.0	17.3
Flint, MI Metro Area	54,952	44,025	163,488	28.7	27.6	18.0	10.8	12.9	2.0	15.6	20.6	30.6
Florence, SC Metro Area	51,081	38,062	79,914	32.9	27.3	17.4	8.4	11.9	2.1	14.3	19.5	26.7
Florence-Muscle Shoals, AL Metro Area	54,575	41,547	60,663	30.7	27.0	18.2	9.8	11.8	2.5	13.4	18.0	26.6
Fond du Lac, WI Metro Area	71,708	57,620	40,295	18.4	24.1	21.2	15.6	18.1	2.6	5.8	9.2	11.0
Fort Collins, CO Metro Area	80,757	64,919	129,210	17.7	21.2	17.9	15.0	22.3	5.9	5.8	12.5	10.8
Fort Smith, AR-OK Metro Area	49,711	41,040	107,375	31.6	27.4	17.5	12.1	9.4	2.1	16.8	20.5	27.5
Fort Wayne, IN Metro Area	62,257	50,856	165,857	20.9	28.0	20.2	12.9	14.4	3.6	9.7	13.7	20.0
Fresno, CA Metro Area	52,651	46,949	304,209	27.7	24.3	18.2	10.6	15.8	3.5	21.1	25.3	36.9
Gadsden, AL Metro Area	51,350	43,346	39,332	29.6	27.4	19.3	13.1	9.7	1.0	15.1	18.1	32.9
Gainesville, FL Metro Area	67,607	46,949	102,219	29.2	23.2	14.4	12.6	16.4	4.3	11.9	21.9	22.4
Gainesville, GA Metro Area	60,909	55,009	63,989	21.3	24.5	19.8	13.0	16.3	5.2	13.3	17.3	26.7

[1]The Poverty status was determined for all people except institutionalized people, people in military group quarters, people in college dormitories, and unrelated individuals under 15 years old.

Table B-7.　Median Income, Household Income Distribution, and Poverty Status, 2015—*Continued*

Metropolitan statistical area and division	Median family income (in 2015 inflation-adjusted dollars)	Median household income (in 2015 inflation-adjusted dollars)	Total number of households	Percent of households by income level						Percent of group whose income in the past 12 months is below poverty level[1]		
				Under $25,000	$25,000–$49,999	$50,000–$74,999	$75,000–$99,999	$100,000–$199,999	$200,000 and over	Families	Individuals	Children under 18
Gettysburg, PA Metro Area	71,055	61,023	38,459	14.9	25.7	21.3	16.2	18.7	3.2	4.6	7.9	13.1
Glens Falls, NY Metro Area	68,801	55,186	48,814	20.7	24.7	21.0	12.9	17.9	2.8	5.7	11.5	14.9
Goldsboro, NC Metro Area	54,132	40,361	47,490	30.2	27.4	17.9	12.0	10.6	1.9	13.7	18.0	29.1
Grand Forks, ND-MN Metro Area	74,094	53,443	42,166	23.8	22.8	17.0	13.0	20.0	3.4	9.6	14.2	17.1
Grand Island, NE Metro Area	64,566	51,371	31,703	22.4	26.0	19.6	13.1	16.6	2.3	10.1	12.7	19.4
Grand Junction, CO Metro Area	60,630	51,465	59,066	23.1	24.8	21.5	11.7	15.4	3.6	11.6	14.4	17.6
Grand Rapids-Wyoming, MI Metro Area	66,743	55,459	383,194	19.6	25.6	19.9	14.0	17.2	3.8	8.3	12.9	17.3
Grants Pass, OR Metro Area	50,844	41,493	35,918	30.3	28.5	22.1	11.0	5.5	2.6	13.3	22.6	38.3
Great Falls, MT Metro Area	59,578	45,606	34,375	28.1	27.4	18.1	8.5	14.4	3.5	10.5	14.3	20.5
Greeley, CO Metro Area	78,222	70,256	97,822	16.1	20.1	18.4	17.6	23.2	4.5	7.5	11.3	13.3
Green Bay, WI Metro Area	71,775	54,847	127,779	19.4	26.0	18.9	15.9	16.5	3.3	7.0	11.0	14.9
Greensboro-High Point, NC Metro Area	56,740	45,749	291,088	25.9	28.0	18.5	11.1	13.1	3.4	11.8	16.1	24.0
Greenville, NC Metro Area	58,292	41,453	68,374	32.9	25.3	14.7	9.8	13.9	3.4	16.8	26.8	32.9
Greenville-Anderson-Mauldin, SC Metro Area	60,912	48,180	332,740	25.8	25.7	18.1	12.7	14.9	2.8	11.3	15.7	20.8
Gulfport-Biloxi-Pascagoula, MS Metro Area	52,315	44,328	146,228	28.8	26.6	17.0	13.5	12.1	2.0	16.4	20.0	29.1
Hagerstown-Martinsburg, MD-WV Metro Area	66,586	55,142	97,209	20.4	25.6	19.8	12.5	19.4	2.4	9.0	12.1	18.7
Hammond, LA Metro Area	60,091	42,962	46,263	32.6	21.5	14.5	12.9	15.9	2.6	19.3	24.6	36.5
Hanford-Corcoran, CA Metro Area	52,557	45,746	42,692	24.5	28.0	14.5	14.6	15.3	3.1	18.1	23.6	32.7
Harrisburg-Carlisle, PA Metro Area	71,380	58,166	225,810	17.0	25.0	20.8	14.2	18.9	4.0	7.2	10.5	17.7
Harrisonburg, VA Metro Area	59,322	47,420	47,600	22.5	29.1	20.1	11.5	13.8	3.0	10.8	20.3	20.2
Hartford-West Hartford-East Hartford, CT Metro Area	91,759	72,275	464,613	17.3	18.8	15.4	13.4	26.0	9.1	7.2	9.9	13.0
Hattiesburg, MS Metro Area	55,228	41,938	54,780	34.1	22.8	17.1	10.6	13.2	2.3	16.9	23.5	25.8
Hickory-Lenoir-Morganton, NC Metro Area	52,162	40,380	140,097	29.2	30.4	17.9	10.9	9.9	1.8	11.2	15.8	19.4
Hilton Head Island-Bluffton-Beaufort, SC Metro Area	66,958	55,923	78,824	20.5	25.5	19.7	11.4	18.1	4.7	9.2	14.3	26.3
Hinesville, GA Metro Area	40,249	37,211	27,874	31.1	32.9	17.7	10.2	7.6	0.6	19.6	22.0	26.2
Homosassa Springs, FL Metro Area	49,705	40,294	60,541	31.9	29.5	17.3	9.8	9.5	2.1	10.1	17.6	32.0
Hot Springs, AR Metro Area	50,006	37,013	40,134	33.1	30.0	16.4	8.8	9.1	2.5	12.7	20.1	26.7
Houma-Thibodaux, LA Metro Area	58,453	48,119	77,548	27.3	24.6	16.9	10.7	17.6	2.8	12.9	17.7	21.3
Houston-The Woodlands-Sugar Land, TX Metro Area	71,729	61,465	2,292,992	19.4	21.6	17.2	11.8	21.5	8.6	12.0	14.6	21.9
Huntington-Ashland, WV-KY-OH Metro Area	54,003	42,237	140,735	32.3	24.6	18.2	10.8	11.7	2.5	16.1	20.1	29.9
Huntsville, AL Metro Area	74,651	57,792	172,549	22.4	21.6	17.2	11.6	22.1	5.1	10.1	13.8	19.6
Idaho Falls, ID Metro Area	58,923	52,689	45,611	20.2	26.7	20.3	13.1	15.6	4.1	9.4	11.9	14.4
Indianapolis-Carmel-Anderson, IN Metro Area	71,303	54,322	755,100	21.3	25.0	17.6	12.4	18.7	4.9	9.7	13.9	20.5
Iowa City, IA Metro Area	80,991	55,332	64,183	23.7	21.1	16.6	14.3	18.9	5.5	9.0	19.4	16.2
Ithaca, NY Metro Area	84,422	58,084	38,112	24.4	18.5	20.2	12.0	18.7	6.3	8.4	22.3	18.1
Jackson, MI Metro Area	59,210	50,783	59,292	24.5	24.8	21.3	11.7	14.3	3.5	11.9	16.6	28.1
Jackson, MS Metro Area	57,602	46,757	210,443	27.1	25.3	16.9	11.4	16.2	3.1	14.0	19.4	27.6
Jackson, TN Metro Area	54,769	46,553	49,318	25.8	27.3	18.3	12.6	13.0	3.0	12.1	18.1	30.9
Jacksonville, FL Metro Area	66,329	53,221	536,299	21.2	25.4	18.8	12.8	16.9	5.0	10.7	14.3	21.0
Jacksonville, NC Metro Area	50,251	45,832	64,771	24.4	29.6	22.2	9.4	13.3	1.1	11.9	15.4	21.7
Janesville-Beloit, WI Metro Area	63,457	53,777	65,054	22.1	23.2	22.1	15.2	14.4	3.0	12.3	14.5	22.3
Jefferson City, MO Metro Area	70,711	55,069	55,448	21.9	22.9	20.6	17.0	15.0	2.5	8.5	13.5	21.9
Johnson City, TN Metro Area	51,303	40,388	83,074	30.3	29.3	19.5	7.9	10.9	2.2	14.6	20.4	27.3
Johnstown, PA Metro Area	60,935	44,179	57,044	28.2	27.1	19.3	12.4	11.5	1.4	9.5	14.9	22.3
Jonesboro, AR Metro Area	50,407	37,378	48,943	31.8	28.7	16.3	11.7	9.7	1.7	12.1	18.2	26.9
Joplin, MO Metro Area	53,763	45,089	67,439	24.3	31.0	19.2	11.0	11.9	2.4	10.7	14.2	19.3
Kahului-Wailuku-Lahaina, HI Metro Area	77,254	70,468	52,170	14.5	18.3	21.0	16.2	24.6	5.3	7.8	9.7	12.5
Kalamazoo-Portage, MI Metro Area	66,746	51,167	129,792	22.6	26.2	18.8	12.0	16.5	3.9	9.1	16.0	19.5
Kankakee, IL Metro Area	64,432	53,850	38,755	23.8	22.0	22.9	10.9	17.1	3.3	12.7	15.1	21.5
Kansas City, MO-KS Metro Area	75,796	60,502	814,092	19.0	22.6	19.0	13.1	21.2	5.1	8.2	11.8	17.2
Kennewick-Richland, WA Metro Area	69,106	61,361	94,423	18.6	22.3	19.1	15.5	20.1	4.4	12.3	15.5	22.1
Killeen-Temple, TX Metro Area	56,831	48,612	151,623	24.2	27.1	20.4	12.1	13.6	2.7	13.0	16.3	23.4
Kingsport-Bristol-Bristol, TN-VA Metro Area	52,002	41,206	126,840	30.5	27.9	19.6	9.3	10.5	2.2	13.1	17.6	27.7
Kingston, NY Metro Area	75,160	59,758	69,594	21.0	22.6	18.1	12.3	22.4	3.5	8.4	13.9	18.3
Knoxville, TN Metro Area	60,823	48,382	343,331	26.3	25.0	18.4	12.0	14.7	3.7	11.7	16.8	24.4
Kokomo, IN Metro Area	60,855	46,793	34,714	25.8	27.4	16.9	13.3	14.6	1.9	15.1	18.9	29.4
La Crosse-Onalaska, WI-MN Metro Area	68,664	50,705	54,008	19.9	29.0	19.2	11.9	15.7	4.3	6.2	14.1	10.9
Lafayette, LA Metro Area	61,438	48,370	180,902	28.7	22.1	15.2	12.1	17.0	4.8	13.8	19.0	25.6
Lafayette-West Lafayette, IN Metro Area	66,271	50,088	81,069	23.5	26.4	20.2	11.3	15.5	3.1	9.2	18.5	17.6
Lake Charles, LA Metro Area	56,961	46,229	79,853	26.8	25.6	16.4	11.5	16.1	3.5	13.5	17.4	27.6
Lake Havasu City-Kingman, AZ Metro Area	47,035	40,908	83,801	28.1	30.5	19.9	8.9	11.1	1.5	9.8	16.2	24.4
Lakeland-Winter Haven, FL Metro Area	50,840	44,061	227,122	25.7	30.1	19.9	10.1	12.4	1.8	11.9	17.2	26.5
Lancaster, PA Metro Area	70,024	59,262	197,706	17.8	23.9	20.4	16.1	18.1	3.7	7.1	10.9	16.5
Lansing-East Lansing, MI Metro Area	70,162	51,839	183,888	23.1	24.8	19.5	12.4	16.8	3.5	10.2	17.5	21.1
Laredo, TX Metro Area	41,970	39,774	72,259	32.3	26.1	16.8	9.4	12.1	3.3	26.5	31.8	44.7
Las Cruces, NM Metro Area	42,416	39,902	74,631	32.2	28.9	14.4	10.6	11.8	2.1	23.1	27.1	44.0
Las Vegas-Henderson-Paradise, NV Metro Area	61,465	51,552	740,966	21.9	26.3	19.1	12.9	16.0	3.7	11.7	15.1	22.0
Lawrence, KS Metro Area	82,967	52,964	42,817	27.1	20.6	15.5	12.9	19.0	4.9	7.7	21.3	11.5
Lawton, OK Metro Area	58,055	47,617	43,678	24.9	27.3	19.9	10.0	15.5	2.3	10.4	14.1	15.8
Lebanon, PA Metro Area	66,524	52,571	53,200	20.0	26.5	22.3	13.9	14.0	3.3	10.1	12.7	20.5
Lewiston, ID-WA Metro Area	65,624	52,735	25,354	23.5	23.4	22.2	12.8	16.6	1.6	8.8	13.5	23.6
Lewiston-Auburn, ME Metro Area	60,671	50,338	45,138	25.2	24.4	21.5	13.6	13.2	2.1	10.6	15.4	22.0

[1]The Poverty status was determined for all people except institutionalized people, people in military group quarters, people in college dormitories, and unrelated individuals under 15 years old.

Table B-7. Median Income, Household Income Distribution, and Poverty Status, 2015—*Continued*

Metropolitan statistical area and division	Median family income (in 2015 inflation-adjusted dollars)	Median household income (in 2015 inflation-adjusted dollars)	Total number of households	Percent of households by income level						Percent of group whose income in the past 12 months is below poverty level[1]		
				Under $25,000	$25,000– $49,999	$50,000– $74,999	$75,000– $99,999	$100,000– $199,999	$200,000 and over	Families	Individuals	Children under 18
Lexington-Fayette, KY Metro Area	66,549	53,117	199,299	24.0	23.3	17.8	12.8	17.6	4.5	13.5	18.7	26.3
Lima, OH Metro Area	59,517	50,332	40,234	27.2	22.4	22.8	13.4	12.1	2.1	11.4	14.6	22.8
Lincoln, NE Metro Area	74,536	54,002	127,316	21.5	23.7	19.3	13.3	18.6	3.6	8.7	13.7	14.0
Little Rock-North Little Rock-Conway, AR Metro Area	62,561	49,066	282,914	25.8	25.0	18.1	11.3	15.8	4.1	11.6	17.0	23.7
Logan, UT-ID Metro Area	61,301	51,555	40,927	20.5	28.2	18.9	13.5	15.6	3.3	12.4	16.6	19.6
Longview, TX Metro Area	56,921	47,532	76,401	24.4	27.0	17.7	12.2	16.4	2.4	13.0	16.6	23.4
Longview, WA Metro Area	60,345	49,949	40,187	21.8	28.2	16.9	12.5	18.7	1.9	11.8	15.1	20.5
Los Angeles-Long Beach-Anaheim, CA Metro Area	71,067	62,544	4,315,637	20.0	20.8	16.2	12.1	22.1	8.8	11.7	15.7	21.7
Anaheim-Santa Ana-Irvine, CA Metro Division	87,942	78,428	1,022,542	15.4	17.1	15.2	13.4	26.6	12.3	8.7	12.7	16.7
Los Angeles-Long Beach-Glendale, CA Metro Division	65,789	59,134	3,293,095	21.4	22.0	16.5	11.7	20.7	7.7	12.6	16.6	23.3
Louisville/Jefferson County, KY-IN Metro Area	66,817	52,898	496,455	22.1	25.1	19.1	12.8	16.9	3.9	9.2	13.4	19.5
Lubbock, TX Metro Area	59,572	47,291	112,853	25.9	25.8	19.4	10.9	14.6	3.4	13.6	20.7	25.3
Lynchburg, VA Metro Area	60,310	48,090	100,497	24.7	27.3	18.2	12.7	14.5	2.6	10.7	14.8	19.2
Macon, GA Metro Area	51,660	40,067	86,400	33.0	25.9	15.8	8.9	13.6	2.9	16.7	23.7	36.6
Madera, CA Metro Area	52,348	47,150	45,224	23.6	28.7	18.7	8.6	17.2	3.2	19.9	23.4	34.4
Madison, WI Metro Area	84,046	64,174	264,340	16.0	22.0	19.6	14.8	21.9	5.8	5.0	10.8	10.4
Manchester-Nashua, NH Metro Area	89,320	74,323	156,678	14.3	18.7	17.3	15.1	26.5	8.2	5.3	8.0	8.8
Manhattan, KS Metro Area	68,483	50,354	34,806	23.7	25.7	18.8	13.7	15.4	2.7	8.4	20.8	10.1
Mankato-North Mankato, MN Metro Area	71,128	52,497	38,444	22.3	25.4	19.3	13.0	17.0	3.0	6.6	16.8	12.2
Mansfield, OH Metro Area	57,093	45,155	46,989	24.3	29.9	20.4	13.2	10.8	1.4	9.1	14.2	22.4
McAllen-Edinburg-Mission, TX Metro Area	38,222	35,730	225,692	35.6	26.8	15.3	8.2	11.2	2.8	27.5	31.5	43.8
Medford, OR Metro Area	55,911	43,948	83,876	29.2	25.2	18.0	11.3	13.6	2.6	15.8	20.3	27.3
Memphis, TN-MS-AR Metro Area	60,191	48,524	494,270	26.2	24.8	17.4	11.2	16.3	4.0	13.8	18.4	28.8
Merced, CA Metro Area	45,768	41,997	79,098	29.5	28.1	17.2	9.9	12.1	3.2	22.5	26.7	38.5
Miami-Fort Lauderdale-West Palm Beach, FL Metro Area	58,530	50,441	2,077,362	25.5	24.0	17.3	10.9	16.6	5.7	12.8	16.5	23.5
Fort Lauderdale-Pompano Beach-Deerfield Beach, FL Metro Division	62,372	53,926	673,870	22.0	24.2	19.0	11.5	18.0	5.4	10.7	13.9	20.2
Miami-Miami Beach-Kendall, FL Metro Division	49,609	43,786	857,712	30.7	24.5	16.0	9.9	13.8	5.0	16.3	20.0	27.3
West Palm Beach-Boca Raton-Delray Beach, FL Metro Division	70,491	56,664	545,780	21.5	23.2	17.0	11.6	19.4	7.3	9.5	13.5	20.9
Michigan City-La Porte, IN Metro Area	57,320	45,838	43,169	26.1	27.6	17.5	11.7	14.0	3.1	12.6	16.4	28.2
Midland, MI Metro Area	69,639	59,292	32,977	18.2	21.2	22.2	12.6	19.6	6.1	6.5	11.5	16.3
Midland, TX Metro Area	95,549	80,761	57,867	12.1	19.3	16.2	13.2	28.8	10.3	4.0	6.6	7.9
Milwaukee-Waukesha-West Allis, WI Metro Area	73,345	56,247	627,842	21.8	22.6	18.8	13.0	19.1	4.8	10.0	14.0	20.3
Minneapolis-St. Paul-Bloomington, MN-WI Metro Area	88,802	71,008	1,354,766	15.2	19.5	17.8	14.2	26.0	7.3	5.9	9.3	12.4
Missoula, MT Metro Area	66,801	42,815	47,910	28.1	26.2	17.8	11.7	12.7	3.4	8.6	16.0	15.4
Mobile, AL Metro Area	56,732	42,699	152,938	30.6	24.1	19.2	9.7	13.8	2.6	14.2	17.7	24.2
Modesto, CA Metro Area	57,631	52,363	171,960	22.3	24.7	19.1	13.6	16.7	3.6	15.0	19.7	27.7
Monroe, LA Metro Area	49,554	36,346	64,955	35.5	25.8	14.7	8.7	12.0	3.3	18.4	23.9	35.0
Monroe, MI Metro Area	71,210	54,396	58,886	19.0	26.4	18.1	14.8	19.2	2.4	7.7	10.5	15.0
Montgomery, AL Metro Area	59,644	45,636	144,379	28.1	25.0	17.4	10.8	14.9	3.8	15.2	19.6	29.4
Morgantown, WV Metro Area	69,106	45,941	50,274	28.3	24.4	15.3	12.1	14.8	5.0	10.8	20.3	17.7
Morristown, TN Metro Area	48,270	40,041	44,574	31.2	28.4	17.3	9.5	11.9	1.6	13.1	17.7	22.7
Mount Vernon-Anacortes, WA Metro Area	65,544	57,122	48,056	19.9	25.2	19.3	14.6	17.6	3.5	11.2	16.0	24.1
Muncie, IN Metro Area	55,251	40,606	45,278	32.3	26.6	19.9	9.3	10.2	1.7	14.9	23.4	33.9
Muskegon, MI Metro Area	56,302	47,453	63,215	25.9	26.5	21.7	11.1	13.0	1.9	12.8	15.5	21.7
Myrtle Beach-Conway-North Myrtle Beach, SC-NC Metro Area	58,500	47,379	174,808	25.7	26.7	20.3	12.1	12.4	2.7	11.7	16.1	28.5
Napa, CA Metro Area	84,009	75,513	49,619	14.9	18.3	16.4	13.2	25.5	11.8	7.3	10.8	13.2
Naples-Immokalee-Marco Island, FL Metro Area	71,195	62,126	134,906	16.4	22.6	19.4	12.9	19.2	9.5	9.3	14.2	24.9
Nashville-Davidson—Murfreesboro—Franklin, TN Metro Area	69,464	57,985	686,640	19.2	23.9	19.7	12.9	18.4	6.0	9.1	12.7	17.4
New Bern, NC Metro Area	55,952	45,971	51,013	22.9	32.1	18.7	10.5	13.6	2.2	8.3	13.7	22.4
New Haven-Milford, CT Metro Area	81,778	61,760	323,270	20.4	20.3	17.4	11.5	23.4	7.0	9.8	13.7	20.6
New Orleans-Metairie, LA Metro Area	62,295	48,343	481,754	27.2	23.9	16.9	11.2	16.7	4.1	13.7	18.0	27.7
New York-Newark-Jersey City, NY-NJ-PA Metro Area	82,374	68,743	7,125,065	20.3	17.9	15.2	11.4	24.2	11.0	11.0	14.1	20.0
Dutchess County-Putnam County, NY Metro Division	92,444	76,877	140,500	15.0	17.1	16.7	14.1	29.2	7.8	5.9	9.0	11.1
Nassau County-Suffolk County, NY Metro Division	110,750	94,079	918,363	11.7	14.0	13.9	12.8	32.7	14.9	4.4	6.7	8.8
Newark, NJ-PA Metro Division	95,591	76,596	886,182	17.3	16.9	14.8	11.9	25.2	13.8	7.8	10.3	15.0
New York-Jersey City-White Plains, NY-NJ Metro Division	73,995	62,452	5,180,020	22.5	18.8	15.4	11.0	22.4	10.0	13.1	16.4	23.3
Niles-Benton Harbor, MI Metro Area	57,732	46,649	64,279	26.3	26.2	17.9	10.6	14.8	4.1	12.9	17.0	26.1
North Port-Sarasota-Bradenton, FL Metro Area	66,723	53,698	312,497	20.0	26.1	19.6	12.3	17.2	4.8	7.2	11.8	20.0
Norwich-New London, CT Metro Area	82,064	65,764	105,376	18.4	19.6	18.1	12.8	25.3	5.7	8.7	11.4	20.3
Ocala, FL Metro Area	50,674	40,050	125,227	30.2	28.6	22.6	7.9	9.2	1.6	13.3	18.8	33.5
Ocean City, NJ Metro Area	74,698	57,116	38,708	20.0	24.2	17.2	14.2	19.2	5.3	5.2	8.7	13.8
Odessa, TX Metro Area	71,424	65,454	52,023	18.3	20.0	19.1	13.8	23.6	5.2	10.8	11.7	15.0
Ogden-Clearfield, UT Metro Area	72,882	65,538	201,165	13.9	21.8	22.4	15.8	22.5	3.7	7.2	8.8	10.7

[1]The Poverty status was determined for all people except institutionalized people, people in military group quarters, people in college dormitories, and unrelated individuals under 15 years old.

Table B-7.   Median Income, Household Income Distribution, and Poverty Status, 2015—*Continued*

Metropolitan statistical area and division	Median family income (in 2015 inflation-adjusted dollars)	Median household income (in 2015 inflation-adjusted dollars)	Total number of households	Percent of households by income level						Percent of group whose income in the past 12 months is below poverty level[1]		
				Under $25,000	$25,000–$49,999	$50,000–$74,999	$75,000–$99,999	$100,000–$199,999	$200,000 and over	Families	Individuals	Children under 18
Oklahoma City, OK Metro Area	65,725	52,221	505,074	22.2	25.1	19.2	12.3	16.9	4.3	10.3	14.5	20.1
Olympia-Tumwater, WA Metro Area	73,715	62,137	105,159	17.9	20.1	21.6	15.3	21.3	3.8	8.9	12.7	16.3
Omaha-Council Bluffs, NE-IA Metro Area	77,180	61,024	351,446	18.3	23.0	18.5	13.6	21.7	4.9	8.8	12.3	18.3
Orlando-Kissimmee-Sanford, FL Metro Area	59,675	51,077	845,295	22.4	26.4	19.8	11.7	15.5	4.2	11.4	15.0	21.8
Oshkosh-Neenah, WI Metro Area	67,477	52,136	69,636	19.6	27.1	22.3	13.4	14.4	3.2	6.2	11.7	13.3
Owensboro, KY Metro Area	59,125	47,751	46,415	24.7	27.3	18.5	11.4	15.3	2.9	10.4	15.3	23.1
Oxnard-Thousand Oaks-Ventura, CA Metro Area	91,112	80,032	269,566	12.7	17.5	16.5	13.6	28.8	10.8	6.7	9.6	13.7
Palm Bay-Melbourne-Titusville, FL Metro Area	61,459	50,416	225,682	22.2	27.4	20.3	11.9	15.1	3.1	9.4	13.2	21.1
Panama City, FL Metro Area	59,080	48,066	74,276	24.8	27.3	17.2	13.2	14.9	2.6	11.7	16.0	25.3
Parkersburg-Vienna, WV Metro Area	50,756	40,547	39,349	30.6	27.9	18.8	10.6	10.1	2.0	13.1	17.3	24.6
Pensacola-Ferry Pass-Brent, FL Metro Area	61,819	50,560	177,675	20.5	28.6	20.2	12.6	15.5	2.5	8.1	13.1	22.3
Peoria, IL Metro Area	72,283	56,350	150,639	19.3	24.1	19.0	14.9	18.3	4.4	8.7	11.9	17.2
Philadelphia-Camden-Wilmington, PA-NJ-DE-MD Metro Area	82,954	65,123	2,233,752	19.5	20.0	16.1	12.8	23.5	8.1	9.3	13.1	18.7
Camden, NJ Metro Division	87,672	71,605	452,494	16.6	19.4	16.0	13.9	26.6	7.5	7.3	9.9	14.5
Montgomery County-Bucks County-Chester County, PA Metro Division	102,372	84,349	732,646	12.1	17.2	15.2	13.6	28.9	13.0	4.1	6.2	7.2
Philadelphia, PA Metro Division	58,532	47,220	784,807	29.0	22.8	16.5	10.5	16.5	4.6	16.9	21.7	31.9
Wilmington, DE-MD-NJ Metro Division	83,434	67,091	263,805	16.6	20.4	17.9	15.3	24.1	5.7	7.9	11.8	18.2
Phoenix-Mesa-Scottsdale, AZ Metro Area	65,556	55,547	1,608,722	20.8	24.2	18.9	12.4	18.7	5.1	11.7	16.2	23.0
Pine Bluff, AR Metro Area	45,473	36,538	34,059	36.1	27.1	16.9	9.1	9.8	1.1	19.5	25.7	41.2
Pittsburgh, PA Metro Area	71,625	54,080	990,355	23.1	23.0	18.0	12.6	18.4	4.8	8.1	12.3	17.6
Pittsfield, MA Metro Area	65,297	50,765	55,497	25.0	24.5	17.9	11.0	17.2	4.4	11.4	14.7	20.1
Pocatello, ID Metro Area	54,347	41,530	30,174	29.2	27.8	18.1	11.0	12.4	1.5	18.9	25.3	26.6
Portland-South Portland, ME Metro Area	77,486	62,074	212,240	18.3	21.1	19.7	15.0	21.2	4.7	6.2	9.6	11.9
Portland-Vancouver-Hillsboro, OR-WA Metro Area	77,208	63,850	901,402	17.4	21.6	18.7	13.7	21.9	6.7	7.4	12.2	14.9
Port St. Lucie, FL Metro Area	57,377	48,002	173,912	25.9	25.5	19.4	11.9	13.4	3.8	10.0	14.4	21.5
Prescott, AZ Metro Area	57,859	48,105	94,920	23.5	27.9	21.7	13.0	11.7	2.2	9.8	15.1	21.9
Providence-Warwick, RI-MA Metro Area	76,482	58,965	622,607	22.8	20.3	16.9	13.3	21.4	5.3	9.8	13.4	18.8
Provo-Orem, UT Metro Area	70,876	65,092	158,270	15.4	21.0	21.3	15.8	21.7	4.7	9.0	12.6	12.2
Pueblo, CO Metro Area	52,495	40,050	61,876	30.2	28.2	15.4	11.0	13.3	1.9	15.8	20.1	28.9
Punta Gorda, FL Metro Area	55,335	45,492	72,671	26.1	29.2	19.0	10.9	11.7	3.0	7.7	11.3	20.6
Racine, WI Metro Area	74,337	57,232	74,960	20.3	21.7	19.3	15.9	18.7	4.1	9.0	11.9	16.7
Raleigh, NC Metro Area	80,001	65,778	470,527	15.6	22.1	18.4	13.4	23.7	6.8	7.9	11.6	16.0
Rapid City, SD Metro Area	68,217	52,809	58,598	21.2	26.5	19.0	15.6	13.8	3.9	6.6	10.5	12.7
Reading, PA Metro Area	68,232	56,122	151,792	21.6	22.3	19.8	14.2	18.3	3.8	9.0	12.8	20.8
Redding, CA Metro Area	58,303	46,693	69,799	27.7	24.3	19.2	10.6	15.2	3.0	12.9	19.6	28.0
Reno, NV Metro Area	69,738	56,611	174,571	19.7	25.4	18.9	13.2	18.0	4.7	9.0	13.6	17.6
Richmond, VA Metro Area	78,974	60,713	483,127	18.6	22.8	18.0	13.2	20.8	6.5	7.7	11.8	16.5
Riverside-San Bernardino-Ontario, CA Metro Area	62,414	56,087	1,343,526	21.3	23.3	18.6	13.3	19.4	4.2	13.8	17.5	25.0
Roanoke, VA Metro Area	61,990	50,571	127,273	21.9	27.5	20.2	12.8	15.2	2.5	10.5	13.2	18.0
Rochester, MN Metro Area	81,798	65,627	83,418	17.0	20.3	19.4	14.7	22.4	6.3	4.8	8.6	11.3
Rochester, NY Metro Area	70,205	53,667	427,520	21.9	24.7	17.4	13.1	18.8	3.9	9.9	13.8	20.2
Rockford, IL Metro Area	62,785	51,036	132,190	22.6	25.8	19.0	14.2	15.9	2.5	9.6	14.3	21.4
Rocky Mount, NC Metro Area	50,272	37,324	57,450	33.0	28.0	16.7	10.4	9.4	2.5	16.5	22.0	32.2
Rome, GA Metro Area	51,573	40,510	34,931	32.9	26.9	15.2	9.7	13.2	2.2	15.8	18.9	28.3
Sacramento—Roseville—Arden-Arcade, CA Metro Area	76,294	62,813	809,295	20.6	19.5	17.7	12.7	23.3	6.2	10.5	15.0	19.4
Saginaw, MI Metro Area	53,636	43,383	77,211	28.6	27.7	17.2	11.6	11.7	3.2	13.3	18.4	26.9
St. Cloud, MN Metro Area	66,961	54,157	74,617	20.1	25.8	21.2	14.4	15.9	2.7	8.8	14.5	19.9
St. George, UT Metro Area	61,338	54,913	52,453	15.3	28.0	24.7	15.1	12.4	4.5	8.9	13.7	19.0
St. Joseph, MO-KS Metro Area	60,991	49,263	46,518	24.1	26.7	21.9	12.8	12.2	2.3	11.4	16.5	23.6
St. Louis, MO-IL Metro Area	72,686	56,483	1,108,303	20.3	23.8	18.4	12.8	19.5	5.3	8.7	12.2	17.4
Salem, OR Metro Area	63,884	52,448	144,600	21.9	25.4	18.4	13.9	17.6	2.8	11.0	16.1	24.4
Salinas, CA Metro Area	65,588	60,494	126,904	15.8	24.6	19.5	13.2	20.9	5.9	11.2	15.3	23.1
Salisbury, MD-DE Metro Area	65,645	54,233	154,242	20.1	25.8	19.7	13.6	17.5	3.3	9.3	12.1	17.5
Salt Lake City, UT Metro Area	75,625	65,792	377,058	14.9	22.0	20.1	14.9	22.6	5.4	7.0	10.2	11.7
San Angelo, TX Metro Area	61,464	48,441	45,137	23.8	27.0	19.9	11.3	13.3	4.7	10.4	16.4	24.1
San Antonio-New Braunfels, TX Metro Area	63,981	55,083	791,273	21.0	24.3	19.4	12.5	18.3	4.5	11.0	14.6	21.1
San Diego-Carlsbad, CA Metro Area	77,653	67,320	1,113,610	17.5	19.5	17.4	13.5	23.9	8.2	9.8	13.8	17.7
San Francisco-Oakland-Hayward, CA Metro Area	103,237	88,518	1,689,907	14.8	14.8	13.6	11.6	28.6	16.6	6.8	10.6	12.2
Oakland-Hayward-Berkeley, CA Metro Division	99,054	82,196	963,824	15.0	15.8	14.8	12.4	28.5	13.6	7.5	10.9	13.4
San Francisco-Redwood City-South San Francisco, CA Metro Division	110,453	96,989	620,196	15.1	13.2	12.1	10.6	28.8	20.2	6.1	10.5	10.6
San Rafael, CA Metro Division	127,900	100,662	105,887	11.9	14.6	11.8	11.2	28.3	22.2	4.2	7.1	7.4
San Jose-Sunnyvale-Santa Clara, CA Metro Area	117,098	101,980	651,352	11.6	13.3	12.2	11.0	31.1	20.7	5.3	8.1	8.3
San Luis Obispo-Paso Robles-Arroyo Grande, CA Metro Area	76,467	62,648	104,760	19.5	19.3	18.3	13.5	22.6	6.8	8.2	14.9	14.6
Santa Cruz-Watsonville, CA Metro Area	77,255	65,139	93,317	19.6	19.0	18.1	11.4	22.3	9.5	9.7	16.1	19.6
Santa Fe, NM Metro Area	68,311	55,676	60,642	20.6	24.4	17.5	11.2	19.9	6.4	8.4	13.0	15.7
Santa Maria-Santa Barbara, CA Metro Area	75,497	63,625	144,261	17.0	22.5	16.1	12.0	23.6	8.7	9.9	15.7	21.0
Santa Rosa, CA Metro Area	79,788	66,674	190,662	15.6	19.8	20.2	13.3	23.2	8.0	7.0	11.1	14.6
Savannah, GA Metro Area	61,909	51,390	138,784	23.3	25.1	18.9	12.4	17.0	3.2	12.5	16.6	22.9
Scranton—Wilkes-Barre—Hazleton, PA Metro Area	63,253	49,670	221,200	25.7	24.6	19.8	11.7	15.5	2.8	10.5	15.2	24.2

[1]The Poverty status was determined for all people except institutionalized people, people in military group quarters, people in college dormitories, and unrelated individuals under 15 years old.

Table B-7.   Median Income, Household Income Distribution, and Poverty Status, 2015—*Continued*

Metropolitan statistical area and division	Median family income (in 2015 inflation-adjusted dollars)	Median household income (in 2015 inflation-adjusted dollars)	Total number of households	Percent of households by income level						Percent of group whose income in the past 12 months is below poverty level[1]		
				Under $25,000	$25,000–$49,999	$50,000–$74,999	$75,000–$99,999	$100,000–$199,999	$200,000 and over	Families	Individuals	Children under 18
Seattle-Tacoma-Bellevue, WA Metro Area.......	91,123	75,331	1,437,222	14.2	18.5	17.1	13.9	26.5	9.8	6.6	10.2	12.3
Seattle-Bellevue-Everett, WA Metro Division.....	98,153	80,688	1,130,166	13.3	17.1	16.2	13.8	28.3	11.3	5.9	9.6	10.8
Tacoma-Lakewood, WA Metro Division.............	70,818	60,167	307,056	17.4	23.5	20.4	14.5	20.0	4.2	8.8	12.3	16.9
Sebastian-Vero Beach, FL Metro Area.................	61,313	49,379	55,494	20.5	30.4	19.2	11.1	13.0	5.7	7.2	12.5	19.6
Sebring, FL Metro Area	41,606	34,242	41,116	33.7	34.3	16.0	7.5	7.3	1.3	16.7	24.6	42.9
Sheboygan, WI Metro Area	70,917	57,047	47,438	20.2	22.3	22.0	14.7	18.7	2.2	6.5	8.9	10.4
Sherman-Denison, TX Metro Area	61,867	48,126	47,538	25.9	25.5	16.0	13.3	16.2	3.0	11.7	15.9	25.4
Shreveport-Bossier City, LA Metro Area...............	56,800	43,292	171,531	31.1	24.0	16.9	11.0	13.7	3.2	15.2	21.0	32.4
Sierra Vista-Douglas, AZ Metro Area.................	55,443	43,291	50,202	29.5	25.0	18.2	10.8	14.0	2.5	12.6	17.0	21.9
Sioux City, IA-NE-SD Metro Area	63,341	52,698	63,198	23.4	23.4	20.6	12.2	16.8	3.5	11.6	13.3	17.3
Sioux Falls, SD Metro Area	74,632	59,844	98,273	19.2	23.3	19.5	14.6	19.3	4.1	7.6	11.5	15.6
South Bend-Mishawaka, IN-MI Metro Area...........	60,196	47,207	119,494	24.6	27.3	19.9	12.0	13.1	3.2	12.2	16.6	25.0
Spartanburg, SC Metro Area	56,608	44,028	124,570	28.7	26.2	19.2	10.7	12.9	2.3	11.5	15.6	22.6
Spokane-Spokane Valley, WA Metro Area	60,735	47,548	215,652	24.9	27.6	18.4	12.4	14.0	2.8	10.8	16.3	21.6
Springfield, IL Metro Area	74,517	57,824	88,081	21.0	21.9	19.4	12.6	20.4	4.7	11.8	16.2	26.4
Springfield, MA Metro Area	70,083	53,393	233,619	24.6	22.3	17.5	11.9	19.4	4.3	12.2	16.9	24.1
Springfield, MO Metro Area	56,472	44,786	179,752	25.5	28.7	19.4	12.4	11.9	2.0	11.1	16.8	21.2
Springfield, OH Metro Area	61,922	47,963	54,232	25.6	26.1	19.0	13.6	13.7	2.1	10.0	14.5	23.8
State College, PA Metro Area	78,211	56,337	56,116	21.1	24.0	17.7	12.2	20.5	4.4	5.3	16.8	12.7
Staunton-Waynesboro, VA Metro Area..............	61,009	49,834	46,768	22.9	27.2	22.5	12.3	12.7	2.5	8.8	12.9	18.0
Stockton-Lodi, CA Metro Area	60,416	53,705	223,062	22.6	23.9	17.9	12.4	19.4	3.7	14.2	17.4	23.9
Sumter, SC Metro Area	47,278	41,169	41,017	26.0	32.4	19.9	12.6	7.9	1.2	13.7	18.5	27.3
Syracuse, NY Metro Area	70,343	56,371	254,001	21.4	23.0	19.0	13.5	19.5	3.6	9.7	15.0	22.3
Tallahassee, FL Metro Area	62,197	44,295	142,295	27.8	28.0	17.5	9.9	13.7	3.1	11.7	22.4	25.3
Tampa-St. Petersburg-Clearwater, FL Metro Area .	60,632	48,911	1,166,704	24.9	25.9	18.0	11.6	15.4	4.2	10.5	14.7	20.4
Terre Haute, IN Metro Area	55,273	40,974	66,685	30.7	27.6	18.3	10.9	10.4	2.2	11.3	17.7	21.5
Texarkana, TX-AR Metro Area	49,775	38,814	54,440	33.4	25.7	16.7	11.9	9.4	2.9	16.4	19.6	26.4
The Villages, FL Metro Area	64,737	51,335	51,170	16.9	31.9	18.5	12.6	17.1	3.0	4.2	8.1	22.0
Toledo, OH Metro Area...................................	63,769	47,093	242,641	26.3	25.6	17.2	11.6	16.3	3.1	12.1	17.2	24.2
Topeka, KS Metro Area	65,043	51,674	93,078	22.8	25.2	21.1	13.8	14.7	2.4	9.0	13.3	18.2
Trenton, NJ Metro Area..................................	93,880	72,417	127,965	17.1	18.3	15.9	12.6	24.1	12.0	7.8	11.2	15.6
Tucson, AZ Metro Area...................................	57,542	47,099	395,992	26.2	26.2	18.5	12.1	13.8	3.2	13.1	18.9	28.3
Tulsa, OK Metro Area	62,412	51,352	380,841	23.7	24.7	18.9	12.0	16.4	4.3	11.8	15.4	23.5
Tuscaloosa, AL Metro Area	57,661	46,470	84,889	29.3	23.4	17.4	11.1	15.6	3.2	13.2	21.0	27.8
Tyler, TX Metro Area.....................................	60,736	49,060	78,380	23.1	27.8	16.3	11.2	17.1	4.4	10.8	16.4	24.2
Urban Honolulu, HI Metro Area........................	91,111	77,273	307,703	13.4	17.0	17.8	14.0	28.9	8.8	5.4	9.2	11.0
Utica-Rome, NY Metro Area............................	61,687	48,935	114,580	24.0	26.5	19.2	12.3	15.0	2.9	11.9	16.5	27.6
Valdosta, GA Metro Area................................	47,004	36,740	48,600	39.3	25.7	15.1	7.8	10.9	1.2	19.1	26.6	34.0
Vallejo-Fairfield, CA Metro Area.......................	79,464	67,443	145,502	16.5	21.0	17.0	14.6	25.4	5.6	9.6	12.1	16.4
Victoria, TX Metro Area..................................	65,993	56,073	35,842	18.7	26.4	16.4	12.6	22.1	3.8	10.2	12.7	16.9
Vineland-Bridgeton, NJ Metro Area..................	59,241	51,315	50,380	23.8	24.7	19.0	11.6	18.7	2.2	12.4	16.9	25.1
Virginia Beach-Norfolk-Newport News, VA-NC Metro Area.................................	71,018	60,093	642,911	18.8	22.5	20.2	14.1	20.4	4.0	9.3	12.3	18.9
Visalia-Porterville, CA Metro Area	46,689	42,413	134,801	30.0	25.6	17.5	9.0	15.1	2.7	24.3	27.6	37.0
Waco, TX Metro Area	56,109	46,307	93,239	27.8	25.3	19.9	10.7	13.1	3.1	13.3	20.3	29.0
Walla Walla, WA Metro Area	63,634	47,283	24,201	24.0	26.8	17.7	13.0	15.0	3.5	10.3	16.6	22.9
Warner Robins, GA Metro Area	61,125	51,954	69,562	21.6	25.0	24.0	10.1	17.3	2.0	14.8	17.8	28.0
Washington-Arlington-Alexandria, DC-VA-MD-WV Metro Area	110,251	93,294	2,172,310	10.9	14.4	14.7	13.1	31.9	15.1	5.7	8.3	10.6
Silver Spring-Frederick-Rockville, MD Metro Division	112,634	95,519	461,405	9.9	15.6	14.6	12.0	31.0	17.1	5.2	7.5	10.6
Washington-Arlington-Alexandria, DC-VA-MD-WV Metro Division	109,048	92,668	1,710,905	11.1	14.0	14.7	13.4	32.2	14.5	5.8	8.5	10.6
Waterloo-Cedar Falls, IA Metro Area	67,858	52,255	66,986	21.0	26.3	19.0	12.8	17.6	3.3	5.8	12.4	13.8
Watertown-Fort Drum, NY Metro Area................	58,924	51,107	43,145	21.9	26.9	20.8	14.1	14.6	1.7	9.8	13.4	18.5
Wausau, WI Metro Area	68,964	55,687	54,558	18.4	26.6	21.2	14.4	16.3	3.1	4.7	8.9	12.4
Weirton-Steubenville, WV-OH Metro Area...........	58,352	43,452	50,699	28.6	28.7	14.9	14.2	12.5	1.0	10.8	16.0	25.7
Wenatchee, WA Metro Area.............................	63,667	56,319	41,304	18.4	26.6	20.7	12.6	18.9	2.8	7.6	11.4	17.0
Wheeling, WV-OH Metro Area..........................	62,311	47,726	58,313	26.8	25.3	18.7	11.6	14.4	3.2	7.2	11.7	13.2
Wichita, KS Metro Area..................................	65,908	51,591	244,522	23.3	24.7	19.8	12.0	16.8	3.4	9.6	14.1	20.3
Wichita Falls, TX Metro Area	59,674	45,641	55,562	26.1	28.6	17.8	10.7	14.2	2.6	13.8	18.7	28.0
Williamsport, PA Metro Area	63,250	51,455	45,751	26.4	22.4	21.0	12.9	15.2	2.1	9.4	15.2	25.8
Wilmington, NC Metro Area.............................	68,893	52,655	111,546	25.4	22.4	18.1	11.6	18.5	4.0	10.2	16.9	21.0
Winchester, VA-WV Metro Area........................	67,470	60,752	48,995	20.0	20.0	20.8	14.3	21.4	3.5	9.3	13.0	20.1
Winston-Salem, NC Metro Area	58,872	45,098	260,437	26.0	28.2	17.4	12.3	12.6	3.5	12.1	16.7	26.9
Worcester, MA-CT Metro Area	82,421	65,427	345,269	19.2	19.1	18.1	12.3	24.4	7.0	7.7	11.9	15.7
Yakima, WA Metro Area	51,921	47,223	81,709	23.9	30.1	20.9	9.9	12.7	2.4	14.7	18.8	28.0
York-Hanover, PA Metro Area..........................	70,532	58,409	165,672	17.8	23.1	21.3	14.8	20.4	2.7	7.9	10.7	16.0
Youngstown-Warren-Boardman, OH-PA Metro Area.................................	57,865	43,127	228,692	27.9	28.1	18.2	11.5	12.1	2.2	12.1	16.4	27.4
Yuba City, CA Metro Area...............................	56,976	51,185	58,262	25.1	23.5	18.2	12.4	18.0	2.8	18.2	20.6	30.1
Yuma, AZ Metro Area....................................	44,552	40,539	71,751	28.2	32.1	19.0	8.7	10.1	1.9	17.3	20.5	30.5

[1]The Poverty status was determined for all people except institutionalized people, people in military group quarters, people in college dormitories, and unrelated individuals under 15 years old.

Table B-8. Health Insurance, Medicare, Social Security and Supplemental Security Income

Metropolitan statistical area and division	Persons with no health insurance, 2015[1]		Persons who enrolled in Affordable Healthcare Act plans, 2016[2]		Persons with a disability, 2015		Medicare program enrollment,[4] 2015		Social security program (OASDI) beneficiaries, December 2015			Supplemental Security Income program recipients, 2015	
	Number	Percent	Number	Percent[3]	Total 5 years and over	18 to 64 years	Total	Rate per 1,000 persons[3]	Number	Rate per 1,000 persons[3]	Retired workers, number	Number	Rate per 1,000 persons[3]
Abilene, TX Metro Area	20,788	13.4	5,182	3.1	22,864	10,420	29,211	172	31,250	184	20,275	4,543	27
Akron, OH Metro Area	38,951	5.6	16,144	2.3	88,333	47,747	128,729	183	137,540	195	90,835	17,014	24
Albany, GA Metro Area	22,150	14.4	6,160	4.0	25,000	14,115	27,050	176	31,130	203	19,590	7,087	46
Albany, OR Metro Area	9,643	8.0	3,224	2.7	22,674	12,906	27,833	231	28,890	240	19,310	3,425	28
Albany-Schenectady-Troy, NY Metro Area	36,011	4.1	NA	NA	108,080	56,945	164,092	186	180,110	204	124,270	19,964	23
Albuquerque, NM Metro Area	91,452	10.2	23,528	2.6	123,692	65,505	155,750	172	169,870	187	111,250	24,019	26
Alexandria, LA Metro Area	17,447	11.8	6,050	3.9	22,737	12,014	30,854	200	32,705	212	17,405	7,755	50
Allentown-Bethlehem-Easton, PA-NJ Metro Area..	48,861	5.9	29,042	3.5	110,038	54,143	167,531	201	181,555	218	124,255	19,285	23
Altoona, PA Metro Area	5,398	4.3	2,926	2.3	22,034	10,715	30,795	245	30,470	243	19,475	4,711	38
Amarillo, TX Metro Area	39,354	15.4	7,529	2.9	30,264	16,263	39,157	149	41,160	157	27,130	4,525	17
Ames, IA Metro Area	2,355	2.5	1,132	1.2	6,654	3,558	12,515	130	12,375	129	9,300	623	6
Anchorage, AK Metro Area	49,744	12.9	12,702	3.2	44,210	25,811	44,847	112	47,810	120	31,835	7,511	19
Ann Arbor, MI Metro Area	14,975	4.2	13,529	3.8	32,430	16,941	51,746	144	56,060	156	38,715	5,585	16
Anniston-Oxford-Jacksonville, AL Metro Area	10,106	8.9	3,966	3.4	28,545	17,450	27,928	242	30,045	260	16,865	4,758	41
Appleton, WI Metro Area	10,039	4.3	9,009	3.9	23,193	12,366	37,379	160	41,835	180	29,310	2,917	13
Asheville, NC Metro Area	48,423	11.0	36,129	8.1	68,550	33,025	106,862	239	115,195	258	81,345	10,131	23
Athens-Clarke County, GA Metro Area	29,390	14.7	7,934	3.9	21,776	11,598	29,797	147	32,950	162	21,870	4,774	23
Atlanta-Sandy Springs-Roswell, GA Metro Area ...	759,403	13.4	386,916	6.8	552,782	301,824	725,922	127	810,330	142	543,025	113,504	20
Atlantic City-Hammonton, NJ Metro Area	23,129	8.5	10,061	3.7	35,982	18,549	52,613	192	57,475	210	39,235	6,917	25
Auburn-Opelika, AL Metro Area	13,087	8.4	5,455	3.5	20,217	12,351	19,003	121	24,080	153	14,395	3,394	22
Augusta-Richmond County, GA-SC Metro Area	66,349	11.6	26,245	4.4	79,571	41,782	101,589	172	116,690	198	75,470	16,810	28
Austin-Round Rock, TX Metro Area	256,428	12.9	113,735	5.7	175,988	98,185	218,444	109	232,125	116	157,645	27,462	14
Bakersfield, CA Metro Area	72,332	8.5	NA	NA	88,731	49,822	106,199	120	116,820	132	72,590	33,746	38
Baltimore-Columbia-Towson, MD Metro Area	146,539	5.3	NA	NA	327,415	172,752	449,060	161	471,465	169	322,330	69,408	25
Bangor, ME Metro Area	14,319	9.5	7,895	5.2	30,030	18,222	34,665	227	36,880	242	21,730	5,468	36
Barnstable Town, MA Metro Area	7,146	3.4	NA	NA	29,047	11,390	70,011	327	69,870	326	53,735	3,271	15
Baton Rouge, LA Metro Area	75,812	9.3	37,159	4.5	119,084	68,232	123,893	149	136,595	164	78,295	25,375	31
Battle Creek, MI Metro Area	8,857	6.7	3,227	2.4	21,644	11,828	29,039	216	32,580	243	20,390	4,943	37
Bay City, MI Metro Area	4,632	4.4	2,977	2.8	17,529	9,592	24,212	229	28,550	270	17,690	3,250	31
Beaumont-Port Arthur, TX Metro Area	76,480	19.5	13,053	3.2	54,934	28,189	71,395	175	78,850	193	45,935	13,458	33
Beckley, WV Metro Area	12,509	10.5	2,415	2.0	29,750	15,930	30,070	245	34,170	279	17,120	6,017	49
Bellingham, WA Metro Area	14,957	7.1	NA	NA	28,715	16,403	39,369	185	41,775	197	29,325	4,423	21
Bend-Redmond, OR Metro Area	15,630	8.9	10,824	6.2	24,433	12,379	37,382	213	41,100	234	30,980	2,346	13
Billings, MT Metro Area	17,168	10.3	6,933	4.1	23,696	12,141	30,674	182	32,710	194	23,115	2,647	16
Binghamton, NY Metro Area	13,518	5.6	NA	NA	37,848	20,345	53,652	218	59,100	240	39,240	7,908	32
Birmingham-Hoover, AL Metro Area	109,319	9.7	45,767	4.0	170,082	96,288	216,320	189	245,865	215	143,575	36,294	32
Bismarck, ND Metro Area	9,323	7.3	3,073	2.4	11,260	5,025	21,222	164	22,520	174	16,105	1,327	10
Blacksburg-Christiansburg-Radford, VA Metro Area	12,152	6.8	7,028	3.9	20,403	11,309	31,470	173	34,810	192	22,665	3,281	18
Bloomington, IL Metro Area	6,304	3.4	4,088	2.2	17,025	8,015	27,194	144	29,035	153	20,465	1,988	10
Bloomington, IN Metro Area	15,640	9.5	5,441	3.3	18,652	10,789	23,650	143	26,325	159	18,210	2,212	13
Bloomsburg-Berwick, PA Metro Area	3,135	3.7	2,157	2.5	11,963	6,757	18,816	221	20,050	235	14,020	1,933	23
Boise City, ID Metro Area	69,961	10.5	NA	NA	80,461	43,130	104,953	155	117,235	173	81,325	12,252	18
Boston-Cambridge-Newton, MA-NH Metro Area	141,958	3.0	NA	NA	500,610	248,388	794,462	166	795,310	167	538,805	107,309	22
Boston, MA Metro Division	56,639	2.9	NA	NA	221,843	115,834	317,216	160	318,640	161	212,130	54,672	28
Cambridge-Newton-Framingham, MA Metro Division	63,705	2.7	NA	NA	229,220	106,611	398,583	169	391,040	166	267,845	48,313	20
Rockingham County-Strafford County, NH Metro Division	21,614	5.1	17,740	4.1	49,547	25,943	78,663	184	85,630	200	58,830	4,324	10
Boulder, CO Metro Area	15,076	4.7	NA	NA	26,896	14,836	49,038	154	42,510	133	31,550	2,426	8
Bowling Green, KY Metro Area	10,553	6.4	NA	NA	27,664	15,766	29,029	172	32,140	191	19,690	5,421	32
Bremerton-Silverdale, WA Metro Area	11,650	4.7	NA	NA	37,538	20,860	48,467	186	49,975	192	35,150	5,048	19
Bridgeport-Stamford-Norwalk, CT Metro Area	87,978	9.4	NA	NA	85,730	39,606	146,357	154	148,805	157	110,215	12,213	13
Brownsville-Harlingen, TX Metro Area	111,306	26.5	20,406	4.8	57,222	25,128	56,400	134	62,795	149	37,900	23,072	55
Brunswick, GA Metro Area	17,729	15.2	7,780	6.7	20,330	10,699	22,598	195	25,540	220	17,015	2,896	25
Buffalo-Cheektowaga-Niagara Falls, NY Metro Area	42,690	3.8	NA	NA	150,827	78,936	233,452	206	256,185	226	167,050	33,301	29
Burlington, NC Metro Area	19,662	12.5	8,028	5.1	24,622	12,182	30,465	192	33,560	212	23,500	3,430	22
Burlington-South Burlington, VT Metro Area	6,615	3.1	NA	NA	26,851	14,418	30,866	142	39,360	181	26,455	4,510	21
California-Lexington Park, MD Metro Area	4,040	3.7	NA	NA	10,599	6,497	14,740	132	15,520	139	10,395	1,599	14
Canton-Massillon, OH Metro Area	25,746	6.5	8,586	2.1	52,277	25,489	89,109	221	92,225	229	60,815	10,331	26
Cape Coral-Fort Myers, FL Metro Area	106,285	15.3	49,821	7.1	96,413	38,081	165,492	236	179,170	255	136,245	12,789	18
Cape Girardeau, MO-IL Metro Area	6,651	7.0	3,267	3.3	15,229	7,842	19,016	195	21,150	217	13,435	2,537	26
Carbondale-Marion, IL Metro Area	5,429	4.4	2,944	2.3	17,800	9,970	23,470	185	24,875	196	16,075	3,225	25
Carson City, NV Metro Area	5,959	11.3	1,746	3.2	20,193	12,543	14,584	267	12,875	236	9,515	1,003	18
Casper, WY Metro Area	12,201	15.0	2,640	3.2	11,940	6,613	12,638	154	13,880	169	9,375	1,161	14
Cedar Rapids, IA Metro Area	11,542	4.4	4,546	1.7	30,275	14,729	45,932	173	50,835	191	36,310	4,286	16
Chambersburg-Waynesboro, PA Metro Area	15,150	9.9	4,416	2.9	17,381	7,799	31,729	207	35,510	231	25,080	2,499	16

[1] Civilian noninstitutionalized population, as estimated in the American Community Survey.
[2] Includes only metropolitan areas located in those 38 states who used the federal marketplace because they did not have state marketplaces. States with their own healthcare marketplaces, not included in this table, are: CA, CO, CT, DC, HI, ID, KY, MD, MA, MN. NV, NM, NY, OR, RI, VT, and WA. ACA numbers refer to enrollments in late 2015 and early 2016 for coverage in 2016; the percentages are based on the July 1, 2015 population estimate.
[3] Based on resident population estimated as of July 1 of the year shown.
[4] Unduplicated count of persons enrolled in either hospital (Part A) and/or supplemental medical insurance (Part B) during the year.

Table B-8. Health Insurance, Medicare, Social Security and Supplemental Security Income—*Continued*

Metropolitan statistical area and division	Persons with no health insurance, 2015[1]		Persons who enrolled in Affordable Healthcare Act plans, 2016[2]		Persons with a disability, 2015		Medicare program enrollment,[4] 2015		Social security program (OASDI) beneficiaries, December 2015			Supplemental Security Income program recipients, 2015	
	Number	Percent	Number	Percent[3]	Total 5 years and over	18 to 64 years	Total	Rate per 1,000 persons[3]	Number	Rate per 1,000 persons	Retired workers, number	Number	Rate per 1,000 persons[3]
Champaign-Urbana, IL Metro Area	11,008	4.6	5,449	2.3	22,149	11,123	33,019	138	33,475	140	22,975	3,434	14
Charleston, WV Metro Area	13,155	6.0	4,316	2.0	41,023	21,595	53,525	243	59,390	269	33,285	9,439	43
Charleston-North Charleston, SC Metro Area	77,831	10.7	38,008	5.1	92,475	48,237	118,583	159	131,390	176	87,090	13,370	18
Charlotte-Concord-Gastonia, NC-SC Metro Area	252,020	10.5	162,698	6.7	268,181	142,904	362,593	149	404,580	167	276,725	42,977	18
Charlottesville, VA Metro Area	18,919	8.4	12,406	5.4	24,015	11,661	40,606	177	42,255	184	30,690	3,302	14
Chattanooga, TN-GA Metro Area	49,408	9.2	23,347	4.3	86,484	45,368	106,699	195	119,005	217	77,635	13,657	25
Cheyenne, WY Metro Area	10,490	11.2	2,820	2.9	11,285	6,043	16,826	173	17,560	181	12,120	1,490	15
Chicago-Naperville-Elgin, IL-IN-WI Metro Area	773,161	8.2	307,950	3.2	916,359	455,749	1,404,239	147	1,463,825	153	1,005,840	206,567	22
Chicago-Naperville-Arlington Heights, IL Metro Division	595,592	8.2	238,301	3.2	693,425	342,994	1,066,558	145	1,103,600	150	761,115	173,083	24
Elgin, IL Metro Division	54,526	8.6	18,309	2.9	53,935	26,098	90,627	143	87,165	137	62,740	5,957	9
Gary, IN Metro Division	59,328	8.5	20,046	2.9	90,256	46,587	123,804	176	141,170	201	89,730	15,662	22
Lake County-Kenosha County, IL-WI Metro Division	63,715	7.5	31,294	3.6	78,743	40,070	123,250	141	131,890	151	92,255	11,865	14
Chico, CA Metro Area	15,136	6.8	NA	NA	37,092	19,755	47,844	212	51,035	226	33,385	11,390	51
Cincinnati, OH-KY-IN Metro Area	123,499	5.8	39,766	1.8	260,501	141,327	358,762	166	386,085	179	247,660	48,734	23
Clarksville, TN-KY Metro Area	17,529	6.9	4,606	1.6	38,715	23,939	35,737	127	42,240	150	24,335	6,140	22
Cleveland, TN Metro Area	12,392	10.3	4,555	3.8	19,689	11,357	25,163	208	28,570	236	18,085	3,164	26
Cleveland-Elyria, OH Metro Area	123,809	6.1	46,805	2.3	293,054	150,797	398,468	193	417,685	203	279,895	63,160	31
Coeur d'Alene, ID Metro Area	14,575	9.8	NA	NA	20,155	10,234	32,230	214	35,530	236	24,715	2,682	18
College Station-Bryan, TX Metro Area	32,598	13.3	7,111	2.9	21,747	10,793	27,555	111	29,140	117	19,060	4,712	19
Colorado Springs, CO Metro Area	49,387	7.4	NA	NA	80,190	46,670	96,600	138	105,505	151	69,665	9,237	13
Columbia, MO Metro Area	10,246	5.9	6,809	3.9	19,643	11,032	23,789	136	25,230	144	16,610	2,692	15
Columbia, SC Metro Area	72,086	9.2	35,138	4.3	98,311	54,361	128,772	159	147,540	182	99,075	16,321	20
Columbus, GA-AL Metro Area	34,224	11.6	10,412	3.3	53,873	31,233	52,675	168	58,710	187	34,710	10,249	33
Columbus, IN Metro Area	6,383	7.9	1,852	2.3	9,199	4,233	15,660	193	16,305	201	10,915	1,255	15
Columbus, OH Metro Area	141,673	7.1	41,098	2.0	234,878	132,332	289,645	143	306,855	152	196,685	45,398	22
Corpus Christi, TX Metro Area	74,536	16.8	16,663	3.7	68,618	35,464	73,394	162	80,175	177	48,625	15,634	35
Corvallis, OR Metro Area	4,661	5.3	2,658	3.0	9,003	4,161	12,465	142	14,940	171	11,195	994	11
Crestview-Fort Walton Beach-Destin, FL Metro Area	29,975	12.1	13,822	5.3	35,989	18,368	47,061	180	53,575	204	36,560	4,123	16
Cumberland, MD-WV Metro Area	5,148	5.5	495	0.5	20,892	9,901	22,769	228	24,215	242	15,430	3,071	31
Dallas-Fort Worth-Arlington, TX Metro Area	1,150,488	16.3	360,191	5.1	685,150	364,347	844,986	119	894,985	126	596,630	130,969	18
Dallas-Plano-Irving, TX Metro Division	773,082	16.5	241,152	5.1	421,714	222,692	540,389	115	563,870	120	376,870	88,589	19
Fort Worth-Arlington, TX Metro Division	377,406	15.9	119,039	5.0	263,436	141,655	304,597	127	331,115	138	219,760	42,380	18
Dalton, GA Metro Area	23,459	16.4	4,816	3.3	17,697	9,474	23,320	162	26,675	186	16,435	3,710	26
Danville, IL Metro Area	3,981	5.2	1,743	2.2	11,792	6,027	17,412	220	18,715	236	11,840	2,789	35
Daphne-Fairhope-Foley, AL Metro Area	16,351	8.1	11,778	5.8	28,094	12,026	44,762	220	50,340	247	34,055	3,510	17
Davenport-Moline-Rock Island, IA-IL Metro Area	15,539	4.1	8,792	2.3	46,743	21,456	73,526	192	79,300	207	56,525	7,540	20
Dayton, OH Metro Area	49,814	6.3	16,747	2.1	117,478	62,369	157,057	196	163,035	204	107,280	20,476	26
Decatur, AL Metro Area	15,597	10.4	6,755	4.4	28,264	13,709	31,896	209	36,995	242	22,270	4,789	31
Decatur, IL Metro Area	5,294	5.1	2,310	2.2	16,219	8,678	23,371	218	24,915	232	16,555	3,276	31
Deltona-Daytona Beach-Ormond Beach, FL Metro Area	73,168	11.8	47,735	7.7	98,943	42,712	164,258	264	180,585	290	130,755	13,926	22
Denver-Aurora-Lakewood, CO Metro Area	224,960	8.1	NA	NA	247,403	126,589	366,858	130	375,295	133	265,995	36,329	13
Des Moines-West Des Moines, IA Metro Area	28,238	4.6	11,899	1.9	63,757	34,082	89,894	144	98,185	158	70,055	9,002	14
Detroit-Warren-Dearborn, MI Metro Area	268,902	6.3	155,651	3.6	607,413	331,356	777,004	181	869,975	202	554,895	133,705	31
Detroit-Dearborn-Livonia, MI Metro Division	130,256	7.5	46,755	2.7	278,541	162,224	318,147	181	356,595	203	207,820	84,892	48
Warren-Troy-Farmington Hills, MI Metro Division	138,646	5.5	108,896	4.3	328,872	169,132	458,857	180	513,380	202	347,075	48,813	19
Dothan, AL Metro Area	16,535	11.3	5,753	3.9	27,551	15,299	32,201	217	37,495	253	22,850	5,937	40
Dover, DE Metro Area	10,404	6.1	3,820	2.2	27,445	15,650	31,562	182	35,740	206	24,160	3,472	20
Dubuque, IA Metro Area	3,773	3.9	1,359	1.4	10,609	4,923	19,210	198	20,540	211	14,540	1,583	16
Duluth, MN-WI Metro Area	10,753	3.9	1,620	0.6	38,978	20,522	59,950	214	64,020	229	43,215	6,912	25
Durham-Chapel Hill, NC Metro Area	63,827	11.7	31,617	5.7	61,399	32,832	79,571	144	89,660	162	63,575	9,808	18
East Stroudsburg, PA Metro Area	12,079	7.3	6,713	4.0	26,208	15,431	30,345	182	34,705	209	22,430	3,045	18
Eau Claire, WI Metro Area	10,080	6.2	7,414	4.5	20,311	11,590	32,370	195	33,775	204	23,360	3,159	19
El Centro, CA Metro Area	16,929	9.9	NA	NA	25,835	12,188	27,626	153	30,815	171	18,930	10,421	58
Elizabethtown-Fort Knox, KY Metro Area	8,556	6.0	NA	NA	24,965	14,106	26,422	178	29,445	198	16,790	4,399	30
Elkhart-Goshen, IN Metro Area	31,238	15.5	5,418	2.7	26,094	14,721	32,267	159	35,415	174	24,410	3,058	15
Elmira, NY Metro Area	4,172	5.0	NA	NA	9,737	5,053	18,998	218	21,295	245	13,640	3,144	36
El Paso, TX Metro Area	164,637	20.3	63,193	7.5	118,612	62,573	115,504	138	124,865	149	71,895	30,043	36
Enid, OK Metro Area			2,124	3.3			11,643	183	12,415	195	8,020	1,303	20
Erie, PA Metro Area	13,318	4.9	6,377	2.3	35,986	19,193	55,505	200	62,080	223	39,935	11,172	40
Eugene, OR Metro Area	25,910	7.2	12,708	3.5	61,578	34,332	75,794	209	82,335	227	57,150	9,236	25
Evansville, IN-KY Metro Area	22,205	7.1	9,180	2.9	48,629	27,165	60,976	193	68,000	215	43,815	7,315	23
Fairbanks, AK Metro Area	8,812	9.5	2,382	2.4	10,154	6,062	9,053	91	10,360	104	7,050	1,055	11
Fargo, ND-MN Metro Area	13,078	5.6	4,339	1.9	24,688	13,162	30,488	130	32,530	139	22,280	2,954	13

[1] Civilian noninstitutionalized population, as estimated in the American Community Survey.
[2] Includes only metropolitan areas located in those 38 states who used the federal marketplace because they did not have state marketplaces. States with their own healthcare marketplaces, not included in this table, are: CA, CO, CT, DC, HI, ID, KY, MD, MA, MN. NV, NM, NY, OR, RI, VT, and WA. ACA numbers refer to enrollments in late 2015 and early 2016 for coverage in 2016; the percentages are based on the July 1, 2015 population estimate.
[3] Based on resident population estimated as of July 1 of the year shown.
[4] Unduplicated count of persons enrolled in either hospital (Part A) and/or supplemental medical insurance (Part B) during the year.

Table B-8.　Health Insurance, Medicare, Social Security and Supplemental Security Income—*Continued*

Metropolitan statistical area and division	Persons with no health insurance, 2015[1]		Persons who enrolled in Affordable Healthcare Act plans, 2016[2]		Persons with a disability, 2015		Medicare program enrollment,[4] 2015		Social security program (OASDI) beneficiaries, December 2015			Supplemental Security Income program recipients, 2015	
	Number	Percent	Number	Percent[3]	Total 5 years and over	18 to 64 years	Total	Rate per 1,000 persons[3]	Number	Rate per 1,000 persons	Retired workers, number	Number	Rate per 1,000 persons[3]
Farmington, NM Metro Area	17,594	15.0	1,676	1.4	17,871	8,261	19,051	160	21,405	180	12,780	3,982	34
Fayetteville, NC Metro Area	37,049	10.6	14,558	3.9	63,548	37,317	53,294	142	61,860	164	35,700	11,414	30
Fayetteville-Springdale-Rogers, AR-MO Metro Area	51,809	10.1	14,370	2.8	49,933	24,445	75,310	147	85,725	167	55,255	9,026	18
Flagstaff, AZ Metro Area	15,607	11.3	4,197	3.0	15,318	8,396	21,868	157	19,330	139	13,375	2,624	19
Flint, MI Metro Area	21,980	5.4	10,931	2.7	71,235	40,934	87,247	212	98,190	239	59,025	17,112	42
Florence, SC Metro Area	22,790	11.2	9,871	4.8	33,038	18,233	42,918	208	47,865	232	29,335	8,847	43
Florence-Muscle Shoals, AL Metro Area	11,643	8.0	6,256	4.3	27,042	14,398	34,122	232	38,745	264	23,115	4,778	33
Fond du Lac, WI Metro Area	3,814	3.8	3,663	3.6	10,425	5,020	21,039	206	21,605	212	15,550	1,513	15
Fort Collins, CO Metro Area	19,150	5.8	NA	NA	31,091	15,528	50,933	153	53,095	159	39,210	2,537	8
Fort Smith, AR-OK Metro Area	33,281	12.0	7,777	2.8	55,400	31,391	57,390	205	65,535	234	37,360	10,302	37
Fort Wayne, IN Metro Area	42,120	9.9	12,173	2.8	52,253	29,525	71,254	166	81,255	189	54,945	8,736	20
Fresno, CA Metro Area	93,044	9.7	NA	NA	126,905	68,040	127,845	131	132,645	136	88,105	43,429	45
Gadsden, AL Metro Area	9,736	9.5	4,639	4.5	20,224	12,515	24,978	242	28,650	278	15,360	4,763	46
Gainesville, FL Metro Area	26,227	9.6	15,573	5.6	28,818	14,143	45,218	163	46,390	167	31,750	7,005	25
Gainesville, GA Metro Area	35,581	18.5	10,352	5.3	20,011	9,687	30,386	157	35,060	181	24,990	3,135	16
Gettysburg, PA Metro Area	5,327	5.3	3,537	3.5	13,621	6,480	20,045	196	23,900	234	17,610	1,112	11
Glens Falls, NY Metro Area	5,916	4.8	NA	NA	18,383	8,916	29,901	236	32,540	256	21,425	3,191	25
Goldsboro, NC Metro Area	13,389	11.1	4,457	3.6	19,373	10,218	23,046	186	25,715	207	15,755	4,541	37
Grand Forks, ND-MN Metro Area	5,854	5.9	1,634	1.6	10,832	5,427	16,157	158	16,815	164	11,585	1,330	13
Grand Island, NE Metro Area	9,757	11.6	3,883	4.6	9,617	4,010	15,604	183	15,965	188	11,425	1,197	14
Grand Junction, CO Metro Area	16,616	11.3	NA	NA	19,601	9,516	29,398	198	30,805	207	21,850	2,505	17
Grand Rapids-Wyoming, MI Metro Area	58,538	5.7	35,091	3.4	125,490	69,615	168,753	162	188,165	181	127,080	19,820	19
Grants Pass, OR Metro Area	6,939	8.3	3,229	3.8	16,943	7,423	24,152	285	26,860	317	19,165	2,793	33
Great Falls, MT Metro Area	8,010	10.2	3,088	3.8	9,069	3,963	16,817	204	18,060	219	12,470	1,862	23
Greeley, CO Metro Area	17,490	6.2	NA	NA	26,122	14,170	34,650	122	39,210	137	26,795	3,410	12
Green Bay, WI Metro Area	17,949	5.7	13,728	4.3	37,288	19,471	53,767	170	60,640	192	42,035	5,556	18
Greensboro-High Point, NC Metro Area	87,388	11.7	48,713	6.5	93,038	48,364	138,382	184	152,040	202	103,825	18,176	24
Greenville, NC Metro Area	21,436	12.3	9,560	5.4	21,175	12,266	26,623	151	29,590	168	18,300	6,015	34
Greenville-Anderson-Mauldin, SC Metro Area	101,825	11.7	43,676	5.0	124,913	65,479	164,328	188	187,260	214	123,795	18,485	21
Gulfport-Biloxi-Pascagoula, MS Metro Area	61,387	16.2	10,820	2.8	66,941	38,422	68,346	176	79,360	204	48,335	10,901	28
Hagerstown-Martinsburg, MD-WV Metro Area	14,904	5.9	2,235	0.9	44,324	25,531	47,423	181	52,905	202	34,260	5,841	22
Hammond, LA Metro Area	15,747	12.3	5,055	3.9	24,319	15,259	22,680	176	22,955	178	12,225	5,260	41
Hanford-Corcoran, CA Metro Area	9,182	7.0	NA	NA	15,301	8,374	15,642	104	17,510	116	10,920	4,591	30
Harrisburg-Carlisle, PA Metro Area	33,944	6.1	16,857	3.0	69,931	37,164	110,381	195	116,030	205	81,885	11,004	19
Harrisonburg, VA Metro Area	15,716	12.1	5,375	4.1	15,722	7,885	18,509	141	22,890	175	16,225	1,858	14
Hartford-West Hartford-East Hartford, CT Metro Area	48,135	4.0	NA	NA	135,287	66,557	218,177	180	229,695	190	166,540	23,661	20
Hattiesburg, MS Metro Area	20,262	13.8	4,859	3.3	26,017	14,606	25,653	172	27,700	186	16,420	4,810	32
Hickory-Lenoir-Morganton, NC Metro Area	40,910	11.5	20,998	5.8	62,495	35,800	76,567	211	88,685	245	60,820	7,639	21
Hilton Head Island-Bluffton-Beaufort, SC Metro Area	25,785	12.9	10,299	5.0	27,455	11,113	48,074	232	51,815	250	40,460	2,699	13
Hinesville, GA Metro Area	11,677	16.2	2,636	3.3	9,343	6,116	6,918	86	9,140	114	5,105	1,460	18
Homosassa Springs, FL Metro Area	12,854	9.2	10,017	7.1	28,830	11,581	47,502	337	57,725	409	42,595	3,326	24
Hot Springs, AR Metro Area	11,890	12.4	3,302	3.4	19,878	11,056	31,497	324	29,755	306	19,735	3,922	40
Houma-Thibodaux, LA Metro Area	28,900	13.8	6,996	3.3	32,375	18,121	35,559	167	40,365	190	19,925	8,014	38
Houston-The Woodlands-Sugar Land, TX Metro Area	1,142,813	17.3	344,776	5.2	623,752	332,702	737,107	111	788,030	118	506,230	141,311	21
Huntington-Ashland, WV-KY-OH Metro Area	24,931	7.0	4,950	1.4	70,374	40,167	82,381	228	89,150	247	48,020	16,941	47
Huntsville, AL Metro Area	45,276	10.4	18,617	4.2	61,237	32,617	74,091	167	81,275	183	52,725	9,096	20
Idaho Falls, ID Metro Area	14,717	10.6	NA	NA	20,553	12,095	20,647	148	23,210	166	15,325	2,584	18
Indianapolis-Carmel-Anderson, IN Metro Area	182,847	9.3	66,098	3.3	246,311	133,864	299,731	151	339,955	171	223,815	37,044	19
Iowa City, IA Metro Area	11,707	7.1	2,599	1.6	12,810	6,822	21,176	127	22,800	137	16,610	1,980	12
Ithaca, NY Metro Area	4,089	3.9	NA	NA	9,942	6,054	15,081	144	15,750	150	11,295	1,473	14
Jackson, MI Metro Area	7,072	4.7	4,260	2.7	22,965	11,662	32,398	203	36,490	229	23,840	4,558	29
Jackson, MS Metro Area	63,160	11.2	31,262	5.4	72,954	37,719	94,589	163	109,455	189	67,945	20,548	36
Jackson, TN Metro Area	11,874	9.3	5,446	4.2	19,583	10,663	25,089	193	29,000	224	18,275	4,274	33
Jacksonville, FL Metro Area	153,310	10.8	85,093	5.9	201,001	103,276	245,499	169	269,975	186	181,325	32,046	22
Jacksonville, NC Metro Area	13,190	8.4	6,385	3.4	30,920	19,473	20,140	108	24,595	132	14,965	3,027	16
Janesville-Beloit, WI Metro Area	12,180	7.6	5,007	3.1	21,237	11,670	30,659	190	34,510	214	23,145	3,926	24
Jefferson City, MO Metro Area	12,022	8.4	4,800	3.2	19,570	10,370	27,166	180	31,345	207	20,320	2,497	17
Johnson City, TN Metro Area	23,347	11.8	8,350	4.2	37,030	19,935	46,163	230	51,475	257	31,830	5,992	30
Johnstown, PA Metro Area	6,678	5.0	3,803	2.8	24,843	12,512	35,019	257	38,305	281	23,920	5,068	37
Jonesboro, AR Metro Area	13,977	11.0	2,998	2.3	24,490	14,111	23,845	186	26,700	208	15,260	5,557	43
Joplin, MO Metro Area	20,940	11.9	6,808	3.8	23,081	11,629	33,691	190	37,570	212	23,325	4,587	26
Kahului-Wailuku-Lahaina, HI Metro Area	8,387	5.1	2,409	1.5	16,923	7,923	25,679	156	28,685	174	21,670	2,056	12
Kalamazoo-Portage, MI Metro Area	18,996	5.7	10,783	3.2	42,660	22,910	60,995	182	67,335	201	44,600	8,581	26
Kankakee, IL Metro Area	7,682	7.1	2,447	2.2	17,254	9,487	20,571	186	22,380	202	14,190	2,658	24
Kansas City, MO-KS Metro Area	183,313	8.9	94,082	4.5	259,746	142,118	331,231	159	359,405	172	244,650	34,205	16

[1]Civilian noninstitutionalized population, as estimated in the American Community Survey.
[2]Includes only metropolitan areas located in those 38 states who used the federal marketplace because they did not have state marketplaces. States with their own healthcare marketplaces, not included in this table, are: CA, CO, CT, DC, HI, ID, KY, MD, MA, MN. NV, NM, NY, OR, RI, VT, and WA. ACA numbers refer to enrollments in late 2015 and early 2016 for coverage in 2016; the percentages are based on the July 1, 2015 population estimate.
[3]Based on resident population estimated as of July 1 of the year shown.
[4]Unduplicated count of persons enrolled in either hospital (Part A) and/or supplemental medical insurance (Part B) during the year.

Table B-8.   Health Insurance, Medicare, Social Security and Supplemental Security Income—*Continued*

Metropolitan statistical area and division	Persons with no health insurance, 2015[1]		Persons who enrolled in Affordable Healthcare Act plans, 2016[2]		Persons with a disability, 2015		Medicare program enrollment,[4] 2015		Social security program (OASDI) beneficiaries, December 2015			Supplemental Security Income program recipients, 2015	
	Number	Percent	Number	Percent[3]	Total 5 years and over	18 to 64 years	Total	Rate per 1,000 persons[3]	Number	Rate per 1,000 persons	Retired workers, number	Number	Rate per 1,000 persons[3]
Kennewick-Richland, WA Metro Area..................	23,326	8.5	NA	NA	35,047	18,040	39,066	140	43,030	154	28,795	5,588	20
Killeen-Temple, TX Metro Area.............................	41,577	10.7	10,589	2.5	59,479	33,375	54,805	127	63,155	147	35,590	9,565	22
Kingsport-Bristol-Bristol, TN-VA Metro Area.......	25,807	8.5	12,082	3.9	61,959	32,320	80,428	262	90,645	295	53,840	10,380	34
Kingston, NY Metro Area..	10,103	5.7	NA	NA	21,900	9,928	36,644	203	40,950	227	27,785	4,111	23
Knoxville, TN Metro Area	80,428	9.4	34,421	4.0	132,041	71,170	177,714	206	197,920	230	127,430	22,859	27
Kokomo, IN Metro Area	6,517	8.0	1,677	2.0	14,417	6,730	19,104	231	21,310	258	14,295	2,199	27
La Crosse-Onalaska, WI-MN Metro Area...........	6,868	5.1	4,154	3.0	16,827	9,553	25,003	183	26,810	196	19,285	2,423	18
Lafayette, LA Metro Area....................................	60,613	12.5	20,809	4.2	67,516	37,868	76,059	155	84,800	173	45,830	15,470	32
Lafayette-West Lafayette, IN Metro Area.............	22,504	10.6	5,178	2.4	22,055	12,062	27,995	131	31,660	148	21,410	2,610	12
Lake Charles, LA Metro Area..............................	23,128	11.4	6,958	3.4	33,937	16,963	36,055	175	39,870	194	21,600	6,411	31
Lake Havasu City-Kingman, AZ Metro Area........	21,669	10.7	6,525	3.2	45,668	20,121	56,863	278	64,295	314	46,900	4,681	23
Lakeland-Winter Haven, FL Metro Area...............	81,699	12.7	34,156	5.3	93,461	43,527	129,259	199	152,835	235	103,675	21,247	33
Lancaster, PA Metro Area...................................	60,437	11.4	17,407	3.2	61,897	30,322	101,147	188	108,810	203	77,235	9,766	18
Lansing-East Lansing, MI Metro Area.................	28,053	6.0	12,667	2.7	63,242	35,015	79,703	169	88,405	187	59,755	10,282	22
Laredo, TX Metro Area..	70,242	26.2	15,805	5.9	32,692	15,119	29,245	108	32,310	120	18,650	12,562	47
Las Cruces, NM Metro Area................................	22,318	10.6	6,466	3.0	26,314	13,115	36,381	170	38,890	181	25,395	8,093	38
Las Vegas-Henderson-Paradise, NV Metro Area...	277,837	13.3	61,644	2.9	257,526	138,039	300,930	142	332,650	157	236,050	41,203	19
Lawrence, KS Metro Area....................................	8,952	7.6	5,332	4.5	13,068	7,586	15,993	135	16,125	137	11,110	1,360	12
Lawton, OK Metro Area..	14,563	12.4	3,466	2.7	19,041	10,705	18,857	144	21,295	163	12,505	3,326	25
Lebanon, PA Metro Area......................................	12,872	9.5	3,838	2.8	19,613	9,100	29,151	213	31,785	232	23,020	2,441	18
Lewiston, ID-WA Metro Area................................	5,113	8.3	NA	NA	11,882	6,594	15,382	247	16,465	265	10,815	1,682	27
Lewiston-Auburn, ME Metro Area........................	8,387	7.9	4,594	4.3	16,109	9,143	23,928	223	25,510	238	15,780	4,113	38
Lexington-Fayette, KY Metro Area.......................	35,235	7.1	NA	NA	60,204	33,516	76,249	152	82,980	166	53,930	11,437	23
Lima, OH Metro Area...	5,767	5.6	1,430	1.4	12,872	6,374	20,425	196	22,500	215	14,370	3,105	30
Lincoln, NE Metro Area.......................................	23,453	7.4	12,412	3.8	34,381	17,615	47,151	146	48,575	150	34,645	4,965	15
Little Rock-North Little Rock-Conway, AR Metro Area...	62,159	8.6	17,620	2.4	107,794	55,540	124,921	171	146,075	200	88,925	24,846	34
Logan, UT-ID Metro Area.....................................	7,813	5.9	7,321	5.5	13,137	7,550	13,676	102	15,365	115	10,605	1,044	8
Longview, TX Metro Area.....................................	42,509	20.2	8,208	3.8	35,009	17,893	41,472	190	43,465	200	26,825	6,938	32
Longview, WA Metro Area....................................	6,288	6.1	NA	NA	19,196	9,170	21,936	212	26,715	258	17,120	3,790	37
Los Angeles-Long Beach-Anaheim, CA Metro Area	1,424,010	10.7	NA	NA	1,258,781	600,765	1,813,385	136	1,733,435	130	1,221,430	493,416	37
Anaheim-Santa Ana-Irvine, CA Metro Division..	285,647	9.1	NA	NA	270,480	117,011	449,813	142	433,330	137	317,720	74,589	24
Los Angeles-Long Beach-Glendale, CA Metro Division	1,138,363	11.3	NA	NA	988,301	483,754	1,363,572	134	1,300,105	128	903,710	418,827	41
Louisville/Jefferson County, KY-IN Metro Area....	74,228	5.9	7,071	0.6	177,764	99,698	229,663	180	253,240	198	159,890	35,264	28
Lubbock, TX Metro Area......................................	44,886	14.6	9,780	3.1	46,863	24,566	43,798	141	47,120	151	29,840	6,909	22
Lynchburg, VA Metro Area...................................	25,506	9.9	12,314	4.7	35,215	19,676	58,039	223	61,535	237	41,215	6,426	25
Macon, GA Metro Area..	30,655	13.6	10,203	4.4	32,975	17,809	43,427	189	49,680	216	30,110	9,716	42
Madera, CA Metro Area.......................................	16,830	11.5	NA	NA	17,435	8,534	23,031	149	24,685	159	17,075	4,806	31
Madison, WI Metro Area......................................	28,327	4.5	20,946	3.3	57,769	30,035	97,871	153	105,775	165	76,820	9,051	14
Manchester-Nashua, NH Metro Area...................	25,566	6.4	15,079	3.7	47,596	24,813	71,344	175	77,720	191	50,695	7,233	18
Manhattan, KS Metro Area..................................	5,830	6.4	2,189	2.2	9,752	6,680	10,885	110	11,220	114	7,895	752	8
Mankato-North Mankato, MN Metro Area	2,854	2.9	NA	NA	10,395	6,146	16,396	165	16,615	168	11,745	1,329	13
Mansfield, OH Metro Area...................................	8,649	7.5	2,308	1.9	17,548	8,297	27,531	226	28,770	236	18,955	3,448	28
McAllen-Edinburg-Mission, TX Metro Area..........	258,068	31.0	38,134	4.5	106,227	52,163	91,786	109	103,115	122	60,960	42,644	51
Medford, OR Metro Area......................................	15,676	7.4	8,352	3.9	36,044	16,694	50,991	240	54,825	258	39,210	4,715	22
Memphis, TN-MS-AR Metro Area........................	158,624	12.0	54,637	4.1	166,104	92,259	205,829	153	233,505	174	144,405	46,875	35
Merced, CA Metro Area.......................................	23,699	8.9	NA	NA	35,440	18,216	32,446	121	36,425	136	22,990	11,291	42
Miami-Fort Lauderdale-West Palm Beach, FL Metro Area	946,358	15.9	783,646	13.0	649,519	268,228	1,015,442	169	1,030,970	171	748,100	231,832	39
Fort Lauderdale-Pompano Beach-Deerfield Beach, FL Metro Division	273,455	14.5	241,784	12.7	201,387	89,347	289,626	153	308,190	163	220,455	44,876	24
Miami-Miami Beach-Kendall, FL Metro Division	488,346	18.3	392,901	14.6	272,856	117,081	428,507	159	414,805	154	292,995	162,767	60
West Palm Beach-Boca Raton-Delray Beach, FL Metro Division	184,557	13.1	148,961	10.5	175,276	61,800	297,309	209	307,975	216	234,650	24,189	17
Michigan City-La Porte, IN Metro Area................	9,657	9.5	3,219	2.9	13,315	6,270	21,126	191	24,230	219	15,965	2,214	20
Midland, MI Metro Area.......................................	3,799	4.6	2,548	3.0	11,290	5,484	15,511	185	18,975	227	12,575	1,605	19
Midland, TX Metro Area.......................................	24,882	15.1	4,800	2.9	16,264	10,016	17,606	106	19,240	115	12,195	2,174	13
Milwaukee-Waukesha-West Allis, WI Metro Area..	93,581	6.0	62,525	4.0	190,256	99,485	265,599	169	288,790	183	198,115	47,852	30
Minneapolis-St. Paul-Bloomington, MN-WI Metro Area......................................	159,196	4.6	5,044	0.1	350,251	181,803	503,907	143	540,260	153	385,575	61,274	17
Missoula, MT Metro Area.....................................	9,650	8.5	7,680	6.7	15,948	9,382	19,308	169	20,575	180	14,160	2,129	19
Mobile, AL Metro Area...	46,888	11.5	19,313	4.6	62,706	33,881	78,070	188	89,650	216	51,395	15,281	37
Modesto, CA Metro Area......................................	34,679	6.5	NA	NA	71,505	38,489	80,094	149	85,825	159	54,935	22,102	41
Monroe, LA Metro Area..	22,343	12.8	8,937	5.0	21,778	12,193	31,763	177	34,350	192	20,295	7,868	44
Monroe, MI Metro Area..	7,339	4.9	4,182	2.8	18,017	9,871	28,563	191	33,860	226	21,525	2,572	17
Montgomery, AL Metro Area................................	36,103	9.9	13,636	3.6	68,584	39,915	68,594	184	77,820	208	45,950	14,560	39
Morgantown, WV Metro Area...............................	5,382	4.0	2,570	1.9	17,129	9,645	19,332	140	21,950	159	14,045	2,783	20

[1]Civilian noninstitutionalized population, as estimated in the American Community Survey.
[2]Includes only metropolitan areas located in those 38 states who used the federal marketplace because they did not have state marketplaces. States with their own healthcare marketplaces, not included in this table, are: CA, CO, CT, DC, HI, ID, KY, MD, MA, MN. NV, NM, NY, OR, RI, VT, and WA. ACA numbers refer to enrollments in late 2015 and early 2016 for coverage in 2016; the percentages are based on the July 1, 2015 population estimate.
[3]Based on resident population estimated as of July 1 of the year shown.
[4]Unduplicated count of persons enrolled in either hospital (Part A) and/or supplemental medical insurance (Part B) during the year.

Table B-8. Health Insurance, Medicare, Social Security and Supplemental Security Income—Continued

Metropolitan statistical area and division	Persons with no health insurance, 2015[1] Number	Persons with no health insurance, 2015[1] Percent	Persons who enrolled in Affordable Healthcare Act plans, 2016[2] Number	Persons who enrolled in Affordable Healthcare Act plans, 2016[2] Percent[3]	Persons with a disability, 2015 Total 5 years and over	Persons with a disability, 2015 18 to 64 years	Medicare program enrollment,[4] 2015 Total	Medicare program enrollment,[4] 2015 Rate per 1,000 persons[3]	Social security program (OASDI) beneficiaries, December 2015 Number	Social security program (OASDI) beneficiaries, December 2015 Rate per 1,000 persons	Social security program (OASDI) beneficiaries, December 2015 Retired workers, number	Supplemental Security Income program recipients, 2015 Number	Supplemental Security Income program recipients, 2015 Rate per 1,000 persons[3]
Morristown, TN Metro Area	12,106	10.5	4,442	3.8	21,537	10,935	28,437	244	30,470	261	18,720	3,570	31
Mount Vernon-Anacortes, WA Metro Area	10,151	8.4	NA	NA	15,818	8,825	27,214	223	28,855	237	20,895	2,486	20
Muncie, IN Metro Area	10,564	9.1	2,705	2.3	18,993	10,291	23,365	200	25,860	221	16,580	3,086	26
Muskegon, MI Metro Area	9,307	5.5	4,958	2.9	26,700	14,601	36,408	211	41,655	241	24,955	6,331	37
Myrtle Beach-Conway-North Myrtle Beach, SC-NC Metro Area	55,380	12.9	30,476	7.1	73,168	36,892	110,877	257	127,640	295	93,685	8,039	19
Napa, CA Metro Area	7,951	5.7	NA	NA	14,191	6,685	27,483	193	26,585	187	19,265	2,362	17
Naples-Immokalee-Marco Island, FL Metro Area	58,990	16.6	28,283	7.9	39,294	12,474	86,812	243	88,625	248	70,360	4,061	11
Nashville-Davidson—Murfreesboro—Franklin, TN Metro Area	176,480	9.7	80,249	4.4	229,639	127,057	269,892	147	300,985	164	200,185	32,494	18
New Bern, NC Metro Area	14,388	12.2	6,352	5.0	21,697	11,648	28,348	225	30,015	238	21,045	3,199	25
New Haven-Milford, CT Metro Area	51,397	6.1	NA	NA	98,279	48,726	155,263	181	161,755	188	113,920	19,858	23
New Orleans-Metairie, LA Metro Area	144,728	11.6	74,438	5.9	170,597	93,864	210,287	167	227,670	180	134,625	44,844	36
New York-Newark-Jersey City, NY-NJ-PA Metro Area	1,695,411	8.5	NA	NA	1,983,112	927,614	3,158,850	157	3,240,325	161	2,268,005	599,843	30
Dutchess County-Putnam County, NY Metro Division	18,436	4.8	NA	NA	51,995	26,165	71,787	182	77,355	196	52,610	6,176	16
Nassau County-Suffolk County, NY Metro Division	161,268	5.7	NA	NA	260,559	114,154	518,141	181	544,890	190	382,260	37,339	13
Newark, NJ-PA Metro Division	230,376	9.3	NA	NA	247,727	116,297	382,183	152	405,630	162	289,695	50,719	20
New York-Jersey City-White Plains, NY-NJ Metro Division	1,285,331	9.0	NA	NA	1,422,831	670,998	2,186,739	152	2,212,450	154	1,543,440	505,609	35
Niles-Benton Harbor, MI Metro Area	12,124	7.9	6,120	4.0	22,224	12,431	37,023	239	37,235	241	25,385	4,851	31
North Port-Sarasota-Bradenton, FL Metro Area	91,659	12.0	49,749	6.5	112,158	40,724	218,755	284	224,775	292	174,040	10,744	14
Norwich-New London, CT Metro Area	10,414	4.0	NA	NA	34,294	18,717	51,404	189	54,575	201	38,170	4,176	15
Ocala, FL Metro Area	38,095	11.4	22,270	6.5	64,155	26,271	103,728	302	112,580	328	82,365	9,610	28
Ocean City, NJ Metro Area	8,407	9.1	4,261	4.5	13,934	6,770	25,859	273	28,205	298	20,780	1,814	19
Odessa, TX Metro Area	31,908	20.2	4,760	3.0	17,975	10,103	18,986	119	19,630	123	11,250	3,453	22
Ogden-Clearfield, UT Metro Area	53,132	8.3	30,797	4.8	69,105	38,070	76,199	119	80,960	126	54,285	6,674	10
Oklahoma City, OK Metro Area	170,443	12.8	57,443	4.2	178,655	100,352	203,115	150	224,225	165	147,625	27,197	20
Olympia-Tumwater, WA Metro Area	15,183	5.8	NA	NA	36,379	19,360	50,659	188	55,735	207	38,000	5,207	19
Omaha-Council Bluffs, NE-IA Metro Area	64,160	7.1	32,772	3.6	95,076	50,776	135,478	148	143,855	157	97,860	14,768	16
Orlando-Kissimmee-Sanford, FL Metro Area	315,091	13.3	216,098	9.1	278,816	141,778	425,134	178	415,815	174	278,270	60,114	25
Oshkosh-Neenah, WI Metro Area	7,604	4.6	6,401	3.8	18,140	9,470	29,048	171	33,535	198	23,485	2,502	15
Owensboro, KY Metro Area	5,411	4.7	NA	NA	18,658	10,829	25,112	214	28,010	238	16,770	4,225	36
Oxnard-Thousand Oaks-Ventura, CA Metro Area	77,501	9.2	NA	NA	88,545	37,646	133,097	156	134,090	158	96,355	16,475	19
Palm Bay-Melbourne-Titusville, FL Metro Area	60,071	10.7	37,779	6.7	82,237	37,421	139,917	246	154,590	272	109,295	11,846	21
Panama City, FL Metro Area	23,724	12.5	12,388	6.3	34,040	17,849	40,370	204	43,205	219	28,060	5,166	26
Parkersburg-Vienna, WV Metro Area	4,933	5.3	1,886	2.0	17,793	10,271	23,014	249	24,970	270	14,410	3,987	43
Pensacola-Ferry Pass-Brent, FL Metro Area	46,242	10.2	21,071	4.4	68,768	34,715	92,868	194	104,170	218	66,375	12,559	26
Peoria, IL Metro Area	14,289	3.9	8,895	2.4	40,154	20,522	70,893	188	77,955	206	54,410	7,301	19
Philadelphia-Camden-Wilmington, PA-NJ-DE-MD Metro Area	377,767	6.3	228,189	3.8	754,058	394,378	1,043,316	172	1,108,445	183	743,265	182,428	30
Camden, NJ Metro Division	72,602	5.9	37,235	3.0	159,639	80,587	220,119	176	242,890	194	161,565	27,178	22
Montgomery County-Bucks County-Chester County, PA Metro Division	90,273	4.7	89,321	4.6	188,047	81,439	355,552	181	370,755	189	270,325	19,618	10
Philadelphia, PA Metro Division	179,401	8.5	83,403	3.9	328,388	192,345	347,074	163	362,535	170	222,510	121,972	57
Wilmington, DE-MD-NJ Metro Division	35,491	5.0	18,230	2.5	77,984	40,007	120,571	167	132,265	183	88,865	13,660	19
Phoenix-Mesa-Scottsdale, AZ Metro Area	491,191	10.9	135,984	3.0	511,800	253,756	666,017	146	733,885	160	521,955	67,685	15
Pine Bluff, AR Metro Area	6,926	8.1	1,693	1.8	17,351	9,427	19,516	208	21,180	226	11,610	5,290	56
Pittsburgh, PA Metro Area	104,430	4.5	73,286	3.1	332,915	165,082	509,170	216	554,050	235	367,515	66,910	28
Pittsfield, MA Metro Area	3,668	2.9	NA	NA	20,579	10,751	32,469	254	34,080	267	22,535	4,070	32
Pocatello, ID Metro Area	9,217	11.1	NA	NA	13,070	7,265	13,874	166	14,295	171	9,035	1,942	23
Portland-South Portland, ME Metro Area	39,694	7.6	32,681	6.2	66,539	34,732	111,156	211	116,775	222	80,270	10,118	19
Portland-Vancouver-Hillsboro, OR-WA Metro Area	152,585	6.4	72,493	3.0	302,021	167,058	370,265	155	392,330	164	278,110	44,471	19
Port St. Lucie, FL Metro Area	59,735	13.3	37,530	8.3	68,983	27,260	108,489	239	120,605	265	88,605	8,574	19
Prescott, AZ Metro Area	20,325	9.2	9,875	4.4	39,023	17,624	65,769	296	74,885	337	57,375	3,713	17
Providence-Warwick, RI-MA Metro Area	76,651	4.8	NA	NA	216,864	115,071	316,684	196	337,740	209	222,045	52,278	32
Provo-Orem, UT Metro Area	55,731	9.6	38,127	6.5	45,188	24,010	48,257	82	54,800	94	34,785	4,275	7
Pueblo, CO Metro Area	10,751	6.7	NA	NA	33,129	17,644	34,641	212	35,720	218	21,850	6,254	38
Punta Gorda, FL Metro Area	17,679	10.4	11,451	6.6	33,165	11,994	54,568	315	64,695	374	50,020	2,681	15
Racine, WI Metro Area	9,934	5.2	7,151	3.7	22,154	10,854	38,290	196	41,265	212	27,425	5,485	28
Raleigh, NC Metro Area	114,574	9.1	79,616	6.3	123,988	68,698	163,202	128	175,945	138	120,750	17,669	14
Rapid City, SD Metro Area	17,797	12.6	3,885	2.7	18,773	9,492	28,663	199	31,430	218	22,720	2,376	16
Reading, PA Metro Area	28,143	6.9	13,972	3.4	54,103	28,293	78,053	188	85,440	206	59,670	10,548	25
Redding, CA Metro Area	14,386	8.1	NA	NA	34,785	18,550	43,801	244	48,495	270	31,065	10,066	56
Reno, NV Metro Area	41,035	9.2	16,808	3.7	55,609	29,644	79,849	177	82,650	183	60,395	7,139	16
Richmond, VA Metro Area	106,607	8.6	70,712	5.6	154,164	79,827	212,202	167	228,870	180	157,630	27,650	22
Riverside-San Bernardino-Ontario, CA Metro Area	416,554	9.4	NA	NA	478,440	250,393	592,424	132	639,490	142	429,330	135,496	30
Roanoke, VA Metro Area	26,828	8.7	14,980	4.8	45,431	23,544	67,779	215	74,615	237	49,605	8,241	26

[1]Civilian noninstitutionalized population, as estimated in the American Community Survey.
[2]Includes only metropolitan areas located in those 38 states who used the federal marketplace because they did not have state marketplaces. States with their own healthcare marketplaces, not included in this table, are: CA, CO, CT, DC, HI, ID, KY, MD, MA, MN, NV, NM, NY, OR, RI, VT, and WA. ACA numbers refer to enrollments in late 2015 and early 2016 for coverage in 2016; the percentages are based on the July 1, 2015 population estimate.
[3]Based on resident population estimated as of July 1 of the year shown.
[4]Unduplicated count of persons enrolled in either hospital (Part A) and/or supplemental medical insurance (Part B) during the year.

Table B-8. Health Insurance, Medicare, Social Security and Supplemental Security Income—*Continued*

Metropolitan statistical area and division	Persons with no health insurance, 2015[1]		Persons who enrolled in Affordable Healthcare Act plans, 2016[2]		Persons with a disability, 2015		Medicare program enrollment,[4] 2015		Social security program (OASDI) beneficiaries, December 2015			Supplemental Security Income program recipients, 2015	
	Number	Percent	Number	Percent[3]	Total 5 years and over	18 to 64 years	Total	Rate per 1,000 persons[3]	Number	Rate per 1,000 persons	Retired workers, number	Number	Rate per 1,000 persons[3]
Rochester, MN Metro Area	7,836	3.7	NA	NA	20,454	10,123	36,507	171	38,910	182	28,965	2,723	13
Rochester, NY Metro Area	52,530	4.9	NA	NA	149,090	78,759	213,433	197	235,405	218	160,465	32,060	30
Rockford, IL Metro Area	18,861	5.6	9,875	2.9	45,717	26,196	63,359	186	70,250	206	46,990	7,817	23
Rocky Mount, NC Metro Area	15,656	10.7	7,802	5.3	25,723	13,884	31,806	215	35,125	237	22,275	6,482	44
Rome, GA Metro Area	13,269	14.1	4,549	4.7	15,003	7,623	19,634	203	21,860	227	13,820	3,340	35
Sacramento—Roseville—Arden-Arcade, CA Metro Area	133,256	5.9	NA	NA	267,825	132,682	372,611	164	378,365	166	255,825	82,240	36
Saginaw, MI Metro Area	11,756	6.2	5,347	2.8	30,095	16,170	43,676	226	49,135	254	30,105	8,577	44
St. Cloud, MN Metro Area	6,641	3.4	NA	NA	21,324	10,545	35,579	183	33,450	172	23,065	2,784	14
St. George, UT Metro Area	25,654	16.6	12,046	7.7	19,599	8,262	30,562	196	33,725	217	25,365	1,338	9
St. Joseph, MO-KS Metro Area	10,648	8.8	4,310	3.4	19,027	10,366	22,967	181	25,655	202	16,650	2,858	23
St. Louis, MO-IL Metro Area	194,259	7.0	126,777	4.5	340,974	173,976	500,753	178	546,675	194	360,250	59,770	21
Salem, OR Metro Area	27,147	6.7	10,509	2.6	60,309	31,853	73,394	179	80,110	195	56,720	8,699	21
Salinas, CA Metro Area	44,537	10.7	NA	NA	39,632	18,502	57,368	132	60,650	140	42,265	8,977	21
Salisbury, MD-DE Metro Area	26,809	6.9	7,736	2.0	49,141	19,881	95,571	242	103,360	261	77,715	7,582	19
Salt Lake City, UT Metro Area	126,747	10.9	67,681	5.8	109,871	59,981	132,508	113	141,820	121	95,500	14,320	12
San Angelo, TX Metro Area	17,125	14.9	4,133	3.5	15,611	8,236	20,337	170	22,000	184	14,765	2,977	25
San Antonio-New Braunfels, TX Metro Area	338,905	14.5	111,787	4.7	321,041	184,914	344,611	145	379,045	159	234,420	63,359	27
San Diego-Carlsbad, CA Metro Area	282,291	8.8	NA	NA	322,891	157,978	472,652	143	475,805	144	336,800	84,965	26
San Francisco-Oakland-Hayward, CA Metro Area	224,584	4.9	NA	NA	468,317	223,037	711,911	153	669,620	144	486,515	137,094	29
Oakland-Hayward-Berkeley, CA Metro Division	139,958	5.1	NA	NA	289,033	146,639	400,803	145	386,665	140	273,005	78,420	28
San Francisco-Redwood City-South San Francisco, CA Metro Division	73,595	4.5	NA	NA	154,870	67,382	257,293	158	232,430	143	174,060	55,161	34
San Rafael, CA Metro Division	11,031	4.3	NA	NA	24,414	9,016	53,815	206	50,525	193	39,450	3,513	13
San Jose-Sunnyvale-Santa Clara, CA Metro Area	99,983	5.1	NA	NA	155,303	70,931	256,317	130	237,490	120	172,695	48,177	24
San Luis Obispo-Paso Robles-Arroyo Grande, CA Metro Area	17,661	6.4	NA	NA	32,318	13,593	55,531	197	57,130	203	42,780	4,777	17
Santa Cruz-Watsonville, CA Metro Area	14,052	5.2	NA	NA	31,332	18,499	43,752	160	44,385	162	31,825	5,928	22
Santa Fe, NM Metro Area	16,754	11.4	7,168	4.8	19,403	8,579	33,936	228	34,820	234	25,375	2,681	18
Santa Maria-Santa Barbara, CA Metro Area	48,725	11.1	NA	NA	39,620	16,834	70,582	159	71,110	160	50,365	9,090	20
Santa Rosa, CA Metro Area	33,736	6.8	NA	NA	62,853	33,380	94,911	189	96,460	192	70,485	9,454	19
Savannah, GA Metro Area	50,586	13.7	24,223	6.4	50,805	28,922	57,422	151	63,680	168	42,175	8,434	22
Scranton—Wilkes-Barre—Hazleton, PA Metro Area	31,536	5.8	18,439	3.3	84,086	41,793	125,917	226	139,250	249	92,435	17,381	31
Seattle-Tacoma-Bellevue, WA Metro Area	220,064	6.0	NA	NA	401,243	219,095	531,402	142	545,085	146	379,735	70,504	19
Seattle-Bellevue-Everett, WA Metro Division	165,321	5.8	NA	NA	289,668	154,700	398,752	138	400,410	139	286,225	50,638	18
Tacoma-Lakewood, WA Metro Division	54,743	6.6	NA	NA	111,575	64,395	132,650	157	144,675	171	93,510	19,866	24
Sebastian-Vero Beach, FL Metro Area	21,047	14.4	10,396	7.0	26,416	9,443	44,709	302	48,065	325	36,345	2,505	17
Sebring, FL Metro Area	8,634	8.8	5,310	5.3	19,016	7,380	30,988	311	33,525	337	25,180	2,838	29
Sheboygan, WI Metro Area	4,206	3.7	4,564	3.9	12,083	6,568	22,372	194	24,955	216	18,080	1,784	15
Sherman-Denison, TX Metro Area	23,047	18.6	4,366	3.5	22,540	11,694	26,388	210	27,255	217	18,185	3,031	24
Shreveport-Bossier City, LA Metro Area	52,182	12.1	18,527	4.2	64,264	34,798	80,394	181	86,865	196	52,415	19,810	45
Sierra Vista-Douglas, AZ Metro Area	7,188	6.4	3,206	2.5	19,272	8,747	28,464	225	31,020	245	21,830	3,086	24
Sioux City, IA-NE-SD Metro Area	11,443	7.0	3,714	2.2	19,067	9,208	29,677	176	31,905	189	21,995	2,621	16
Sioux Falls, SD Metro Area	19,186	7.7	7,264	2.9	25,304	13,501	39,457	157	42,715	170	30,720	3,338	13
South Bend-Mishawaka, IN-MI Metro Area	27,838	8.8	10,325	3.2	47,534	25,607	55,301	173	64,065	200	44,090	6,947	22
Spartanburg, SC Metro Area	33,451	10.4	13,007	4.0	49,467	25,901	70,009	215	74,595	229	46,525	8,334	26
Spokane-Spokane Valley, WA Metro Area	28,450	5.3	NA	NA	83,031	45,914	106,172	194	114,395	209	75,315	16,042	29
Springfield, IL Metro Area	7,828	3.7	4,633	2.2	28,100	14,728	40,451	192	44,005	208	30,235	4,742	22
Springfield, MA Metro Area	18,922	3.0	NA	NA	92,263	47,293	124,125	196	130,320	206	78,800	33,366	53
Springfield, MO Metro Area	53,873	12.0	26,202	5.7	64,215	36,603	88,130	193	95,175	209	60,815	9,930	22
Springfield, OH Metro Area	7,424	5.5	2,282	1.7	25,094	12,890	29,689	218	30,990	228	20,025	4,111	30
State College, PA Metro Area	8,786	5.7	3,438	2.1	15,608	8,551	22,031	137	23,680	147	17,235	1,522	9
Staunton-Waynesboro, VA Metro Area	13,892	12.0	5,974	5.0	17,315	8,583	26,460	220	30,165	251	20,840	2,170	18
Stockton-Lodi, CA Metro Area	52,058	7.3	NA	NA	86,737	46,668	101,027	139	107,155	148	68,965	29,502	41
Sumter, SC Metro Area	12,556	12.0	3,996	3.7	21,246	12,617	20,679	192	23,195	216	14,300	4,373	41
Syracuse, NY Metro Area	28,865	4.4	NA	NA	83,798	44,133	125,761	190	138,660	210	92,040	18,799	28
Tallahassee, FL Metro Area	36,647	10.0	15,610	4.1	46,729	27,492	56,313	149	62,295	165	43,800	9,850	26
Tampa-St. Petersburg-Clearwater, FL Metro Area	347,012	11.8	194,852	6.5	413,113	191,144	603,909	203	660,755	222	453,405	79,069	27
Terre Haute, IN Metro Area	13,797	8.3	4,853	2.8	31,562	17,632	34,137	200	37,960	222	24,045	4,539	27
Texarkana, TX-AR Metro Area	21,158	14.6	3,961	2.6	22,390	12,199	30,103	201	32,490	217	19,270	6,678	45
The Villages, FL Metro Area	4,621	4.2	4,270	3.6	22,078	3,270	20,193	170	64,785	545	56,095	1,623	14
Toledo, OH Metro Area	33,536	5.6	11,160	1.8	88,383	48,290	108,550	179	116,195	192	73,260	19,723	33
Topeka, KS Metro Area	15,171	6.6	6,766	2.9	34,036	17,957	47,272	202	50,755	217	33,690	5,695	24
Trenton, NJ Metro Area	31,197	8.5	9,554	2.6	37,939	19,080	63,143	170	64,860	175	44,425	9,663	26
Tucson, AZ Metro Area	97,064	9.8	31,161	3.1	153,984	75,440	199,539	198	208,665	207	147,520	20,275	20
Tulsa, OK Metro Area	128,189	13.2	37,575	3.8	142,671	76,823	166,037	169	185,705	189	120,415	22,086	23
Tuscaloosa, AL Metro Area	18,533	7.8	7,831	3.3	31,852	17,685	41,437	173	49,220	205	26,620	8,798	37
Tyler, TX Metro Area	34,235	15.5	9,261	4.2	29,271	13,070	41,921	188	43,405	195	29,010	5,554	25
Urban Honolulu, HI Metro Area	33,984	3.6	7,923	0.8	99,841	44,282	167,936	168	171,060	171	131,555	16,308	16

[1]Civilian noninstitutionalized population, as estimated in the American Community Survey.
[2]Includes only metropolitan areas located in those 38 states who used the federal marketplace because they did not have state marketplaces. States with their own healthcare marketplaces, not included in this table, are: CA, CO, CT, DC, HI, ID, KY, MD, MA, MN, NV, NM, NY, OR, RI, VT, and WA. ACA numbers refer to enrollments in late 2015 and early 2016 for coverage in 2016; the percentages are based on the July 1, 2015 population estimate.
[3]Based on resident population estimated as of July 1 of the year shown.
[4]Unduplicated count of persons enrolled in either hospital (Part A) and/or supplemental medical insurance (Part B) during the year.

Table B-8. Health Insurance, Medicare, Social Security and Supplemental Security Income—*Continued*

Metropolitan statistical area and division	Persons with no health insurance, 2015[1]		Persons who enrolled in Affordable Healthcare Act plans, 2016[2]		Persons with a disability, 2015		Medicare program enrollment,[4] 2015		Social security program (OASDI) beneficiaries, December 2015			Supplemental Security Income program recipients, 2015	
	Number	Percent	Number	Percent[3]	Total 5 years and over	18 to 64 years	Total	Rate per 1,000 persons[3]	Number	Rate per 1,000 persons	Retired workers, number	Number	Rate per 1,000 persons[3]
Utica-Rome, NY Metro Area	14,320	5.0	NA	NA	45,962	26,437	63,807	216	70,990	240	46,165	9,835	33
Valdosta, GA Metro Area	22,202	16.2	4,465	3.1	19,218	10,473	21,241	149	24,895	174	15,240	5,044	35
Vallejo-Fairfield, CA Metro Area	19,239	4.5	NA	NA	51,449	27,373	69,287	159	74,015	170	49,440	12,611	29
Victoria, TX Metro Area	13,937	14.2	3,160	3.2	13,846	6,355	18,098	181	19,140	192	11,895	2,757	28
Vineland-Bridgeton, NJ Metro Area	15,144	10.5	3,159	2.0	17,697	8,460	28,115	180	30,570	196	19,180	5,908	38
Virginia Beach-Norfolk-Newport News, VA-NC Metro Area	144,625	8.9	70,320	4.1	200,232	106,489	266,836	155	292,330	169	196,890	34,164	20
Visalia-Porterville, CA Metro Area	44,513	9.8	NA	NA	60,342	32,605	56,580	123	63,130	137	40,900	18,954	41
Waco, TX Metro Area	38,022	14.8	8,454	3.2	32,601	15,851	43,284	165	46,785	178	29,235	8,182	31
Walla Walla, WA Metro Area	4,648	7.7	NA	NA	10,422	5,316	12,924	201	13,675	213	9,765	1,544	24
Warner Robins, GA Metro Area	20,417	11.2	6,765	3.6	26,213	12,938	29,806	158	31,975	170	19,995	5,158	27
Washington-Arlington-Alexandria, DC-VA-MD-WV Metro Area	485,481	8.1	NA	NA	511,372	263,701	753,090	124	722,811	119	521,169	88,081	14
Silver Spring-Frederick-Rockville, MD Metro Division	96,016	7.5	NA	NA	108,720	49,771	180,283	140	168,500	131	125,475	16,173	13
Washington-Arlington-Alexandria, DC-VA-MD-WV Metro Division	389,465	8.2	NA	NA	402,652	213,930	572,807	119	554,311	115	395,694	71,908	15
Waterloo-Cedar Falls, IA Metro Area	10,968	6.5	2,507	1.5	17,073	8,697	32,006	188	34,600	203	24,185	3,424	20
Watertown-Fort Drum, NY Metro Area	6,694	6.3	NA	NA	14,634	7,808	18,945	161	21,570	183	13,685	2,731	23
Wausau, WI Metro Area	7,457	5.5	6,525	4.8	15,645	7,559	23,828	175	27,840	205	19,970	2,026	15
Weirton-Steubenville, WV-OH Metro Area	7,412	6.2	2,641	2.2	20,432	10,941	29,932	248	32,875	273	19,620	4,079	34
Wenatchee, WA Metro Area	8,820	7.6	NA	NA	17,232	8,797	22,860	197	24,270	209	17,860	2,030	17
Wheeling, WV-OH Metro Area	6,403	4.6	2,910	2.0	20,321	10,790	32,335	224	36,215	251	23,195	4,303	30
Wichita, KS Metro Area	78,422	12.4	20,907	3.2	74,916	38,315	104,392	162	115,480	179	77,680	12,647	20
Wichita Falls, TX Metro Area	18,869	13.9	3,893	2.6	21,935	11,320	27,151	180	29,195	194	18,135	4,301	29
Williamsport, PA Metro Area	5,620	5.0	3,429	3.0	16,291	7,869	25,280	218	27,590	238	18,975	3,299	28
Wilmington, NC Metro Area	29,812	10.9	21,498	7.7	35,857	18,044	52,469	189	56,755	204	39,410	5,543	20
Winchester, VA-WV Metro Area	14,630	11.1	5,413	4.0	17,885	9,034	24,927	186	27,000	202	18,855	2,378	18
Winston-Salem, NC Metro Area	73,942	11.3	38,290	5.8	84,273	42,208	123,928	188	140,465	213	96,710	14,066	21
Worcester, MA-CT Metro Area	23,416	2.5	NA	NA	113,031	62,443	164,378	176	173,420	185	111,600	25,173	27
Yakima, WA Metro Area	35,077	14.3	NA	NA	30,108	14,774	39,469	159	43,390	174	28,955	7,487	30
York-Hanover, PA Metro Area	26,614	6.1	14,110	3.2	59,305	29,094	84,001	190	93,000	210	64,950	8,368	19
Youngstown-Warren-Boardman, OH-PA Metro Area	36,057	6.7	12,731	2.3	79,284	40,804	127,133	231	140,535	256	89,310	18,869	34
Yuba City, CA Metro Area	18,349	10.9	NA	NA	25,991	14,135	27,794	163	29,895	175	18,220	8,168	48
Yuma, AZ Metro Area	30,785	15.6	4,558	2.2	21,680	7,996	30,719	150	34,735	170	23,965	4,363	21

[1]Civilian noninstitutionalized population, as estimated in the American Community Survey.
[2]Includes only metropolitan areas located in those 38 states who used the federal marketplace because they did not have state marketplaces. States with their own healthcare marketplaces, not included in this table, are: CA, CO, CT, DC, HI, ID, KY, MD, MA, MN, NV, NM, NY, OR, RI, VT, and WA. ACA numbers refer to enrollments in late 2015 and early 2016 for coverage in 2016; the percentages are based on the July 1, 2015 population estimate.
[3]Based on resident population estimated as of July 1 of the year shown.
[4]Unduplicated count of persons enrolled in either hospital (Part A) and/or supplemental medical insurance (Part B) during the year.

Table B-9. Housing Units and Building Permits

Metropolitan statistical area and division	Housing units 2015 (July 1 estimate)	2010 (July 1 estimate)	2000 (July 1 estimate)	Change, 2010–2015 Number	Percent	Units per square mile of land area,[1] 2015	New private housing units authorized by building permits[2] 2015	Percent single family 2015	2010	Percent single family 2010
Abilene, TX Metro Area	70,931	69,748	65,395	1,183	1.7	25.9	535	56.6	390	69.7
Akron, OH Metro Area	313,488	312,602	291,804	886	0.3	348.2	967	81.9	736	89.3
Albany, GA Metro Area	66,489	66,149	63,901	340	0.5	34.4	203	81.8	248	69.4
Albany, OR Metro Area	49,164	48,843	42,661	321	0.7	21.5	365	94.2	174	92.5
Albany-Schenectady-Troy, NY Metro Area	398,546	393,421	364,471	5,125	1.3	141.7	3,623	32.7	1,429	76.9
Albuquerque, NM Metro Area	381,626	374,974	307,455	6,652	1.8	41.1	2,295	87.7	1,764	88.0
Alexandria, LA Metro Area	66,402	64,663	60,558	1,739	2.7	33.9	289	83.4	434	78.3
Allentown-Bethlehem-Easton, PA-NJ Metro Area	345,227	342,478	308,188	2,749	0.8	237.6	1,356	69.5	1,388	84.8
Altoona, PA Metro Area	56,011	56,262	55,077	-251	-0.4	106.5	117	92.3	159	70.4
Amarillo, TX Metro Area	107,873	103,509	92,624	4,364	4.2	20.9	880	64.1	931	61.9
Ames, IA Metro Area	38,569	36,800	30,708	1,769	4.8	67.3	555	35.3	167	55.7
Anchorage, AK Metro Area	156,278	154,440	128,250	1,838	1.2	5.9	1,767	76.0	533	79.5
Ann Arbor, MI Metro Area	150,075	147,748	131,863	2,327	1.6	212.6	420	92.9	368	86.1
Anniston-Oxford-Jacksonville, AL Metro Area	53,326	53,316	51,309	10	0.0	88.0	61	100.0	107	92.5
Appleton, WI Metro Area	95,885	92,932	78,841	2,953	3.2	100.3	1,119	50.8	587	70.4
Asheville, NC Metro Area	218,117	213,830	176,319	4,287	2.0	107.3	2,161	83.0	2,038	51.3
Athens-Clarke County, GA Metro Area	83,878	81,738	67,872	2,140	2.6	81.8	1,159	48.5	226	100.0
Atlanta-Sandy Springs-Roswell, GA Metro Area	2,239,194	2,173,774	1,666,401	65,420	3.0	257.9	30,342	65.9	7,608	84.3
Atlantic City-Hammonton, NJ Metro Area	127,865	126,785	114,431	1,080	0.9	230.1	710	49.4	512	81.8
Auburn-Opelika, AL Metro Area	66,382	62,686	50,508	3,696	5.9	109.3	838	98.6	971	64.2
Augusta-Richmond County, GA-SC Metro Area	251,168	242,123	209,903	9,045	3.7	72.2	3,035	87.9	2,490	97.2
Austin-Round Rock, TX Metro Area	784,346	708,484	502,748	75,862	10.7	185.8	22,370	53.0	8,786	70.6
Bakersfield, CA Metro Area	293,574	284,771	232,436	8,803	3.1	36.1	2,200	95.4	1,656	73.1
Baltimore-Columbia-Towson, MD Metro Area	1,155,341	1,133,025	1,050,614	22,316	2.0	444.1	8,264	55.5	5,594	63.5
Bangor, ME Metro Area	74,331	73,893	66,999	438	0.6	21.9	555	35.5	272	91.5
Barnstable Town, MA Metro Area	162,118	160,348	147,569	1,770	1.1	411.3	572	96.2	418	91.1
Baton Rouge, LA Metro Area	345,301	330,417	283,453	14,884	4.5	85.7	3,569	97.0	2,962	95.6
Battle Creek, MI Metro Area	60,602	61,011	58,824	-409	-0.7	85.8	59	100.0	33	100.0
Bay City, MI Metro Area	47,973	48,204	46,496	-231	-0.5	108.5	147	33.3	54	100.0
Beaumont-Port Arthur, TX Metro Area	175,558	169,929	164,290	5,629	3.3	57.9	1,132	84.2	1,424	88.2
Beckley, WV Metro Area	57,507	57,582	57,319	-75	-0.1	45.4	100	100.0	149	94.6
Bellingham, WA Metro Area	93,247	90,721	74,335	2,526	2.8	44.2	1,144	52.4	458	87.6
Bend-Redmond, OR Metro Area	83,873	80,189	55,131	3,684	4.6	27.8	2,227	69.6	377	96.8
Billings, MT Metro Area	74,482	71,028	60,720	3,454	4.9	12.7	1,764	72.2	457	70.2
Binghamton, NY Metro Area	111,802	112,740	110,305	-938	-0.8	91.3	249	28.5	108	94.4
Birmingham-Hoover, AL Metro Area	509,664	500,258	455,698	9,406	1.9	96.5	3,733	64.7	1,924	81.2
Bismarck, ND Metro Area	57,904	50,174	41,864	7,730	15.4	10.8	1,082	61.4	651	86.8
Blacksburg-Christiansburg-Radford, VA Metro Area	79,457	78,425	69,695	1,032	1.3	54.7	476	99.6	317	77.9
Bloomington, IL Metro Area	79,033	77,264	67,469	1,769	2.3	50.0	396	61.9	451	75.4
Bloomington, IN Metro Area	70,493	69,231	60,912	1,262	1.8	90.4	395	68.1	263	74.5
Bloomsburg-Berwick, PA Metro Area	37,642	37,488	35,405	154	0.4	61.4	190	71.1	188	100.0
Boise City, ID Metro Area	260,390	246,398	182,764	13,992	5.7	22.1	5,499	78.1	1,693	96.3
Boston-Cambridge-Newton, MA-NH Metro Area	1,917,255	1,884,051	1,754,936	33,204	1.8	550.0	15,036	32.2	6,672	56.2
Boston, MA Metro Division	804,241	786,406	730,598	17,835	2.3	722.5	7,937	20.5	2,842	41.1
Cambridge-Newton-Framingham, MA Metro Division	930,960	919,147	865,154	11,813	1.3	710.6	5,745	38.9	2,981	63.4
Rockingham County-Strafford County, NH Metro Division	182,054	178,498	159,184	3,556	2.0	171.3	1,354	72.8	849	81.4
Boulder, CO Metro Area	132,457	127,118	112,068	5,339	4.2	182.4	1,249	61.5	657	42.0
Bowling Green, KY Metro Area	71,928	68,939	58,620	2,989	4.3	44.5	1,147	47.6	573	63.2
Bremerton-Silverdale, WA Metro Area	109,690	107,444	93,010	2,246	2.1	277.6	918	86.7	623	75.1
Bridgeport-Stamford-Norwalk, CT Metro Area	366,122	361,342	340,078	4,780	1.3	585.8	2,598	30.8	926	59.0
Brownsville-Harlingen, TX Metro Area	147,492	142,142	120,234	5,350	3.8	165.5	1,285	87.9	1,258	84.4
Brunswick, GA Metro Area	59,222	58,066	45,185	1,156	2.0	46.0	535	100.0	404	100.0
Buffalo-Cheektowaga-Niagara Falls, NY Metro Area	520,981	519,147	511,881	1,834	0.4	332.9	1,677	59.2	1,498	69.2
Burlington, NC Metro Area	68,493	66,706	55,721	1,787	2.7	161.8	1,032	71.3	847	52.3
Burlington-South Burlington, VT Metro Area	95,117	92,470	82,989	2,647	2.9	76.0	916	39.0	585	55.6
California-Lexington Park, MD Metro Area	43,625	41,376	34,336	2,249	5.4	122.1	1,282	97.7	413	96.6
Canton-Massillon, OH Metro Area	179,318	178,906	170,237	412	0.2	184.9	558	72.6	452	68.1
Cape Coral-Fort Myers, FL Metro Area	379,018	371,109	247,782	7,909	2.1	483.4	6,879	55.5	1,276	92.1
Cape Girardeau, MO-IL Metro Area	42,912	42,520	39,679	392	0.9	30.0	179	66.5	99	73.7
Carbondale-Marion, IL Metro Area	59,550	58,994	54,661	556	0.9	59.3	137	56.9	193	46.1
Carson City, NV Metro Area	23,445	23,524	21,369	-79	-0.3	162.0	43	90.7	71	15.5
Casper, WY Metro Area	36,067	33,884	29,952	2,183	6.4	6.8	271	83.8	807	32.7
Cedar Rapids, IA Metro Area	115,320	112,487	99,271	2,833	2.5	57.4	1,073	65.5	855	80.8
Chambersburg-Waynesboro, PA Metro Area	64,325	63,304	54,022	1,021	1.6	83.3	231	100.0	570	90.0
Champaign-Urbana, IL Metro Area	104,152	101,200	88,443	2,952	2.9	54.2	1,235	26.6	529	47.4
Charleston, WV Metro Area	108,076	108,250	110,249	-174	-0.2	61.9	283	31.8	226	77.0
Charleston-North Charleston, SC Metro Area	318,456	299,091	234,443	19,365	6.5	123.0	6,590	69.9	3,060	91.1
Charlotte-Concord-Gastonia, NC-SC Metro Area	989,531	937,950	714,058	51,581	5.5	195.4	19,543	63.4	6,102	84.5
Charlottesville, VA Metro Area	100,874	96,504	80,480	4,370	4.5	45.4	989	76.5	1,136	56.2
Chattanooga, TN-GA Metro Area	240,080	234,595	206,170	5,485	2.3	114.9	2,093	73.2	1,086	87.9
Cheyenne, WY Metro Area	41,955	40,530	34,317	1,425	3.5	15.6	440	88.2	238	100.0
Chicago-Naperville-Elgin, IL-IN-WI Metro Area	3,812,136	3,796,957	3,471,602	15,179	0.4	529.7	15,813	48.5	7,267	58.4

[1] Units per square mile was calculated on the basis of land area data as of 2016.
[2] Sample selected from a universe of 20,000 permit-issuing places.

Table B-9.   Housing Units and Building Permits—*Continued*

Metropolitan statistical area and division	Housing units						New private housing units authorized by building permits \2			
	2015 (July 1 estimate)	2010 (July 1 estimate)	2000 (July 1 estimate)	Change, 2010–2015 Number	Change, 2010–2015 Percent	Units per square mile of land area,¹ 2015	2015	Percent single family 2015	2010	Percent single family 2010
Chicago-Naperville-Arlington Heights, IL Metro Division	2,956,521	2,949,916	2,740,284	6,605	0.2	856.7	11,596	38.5	4,538	47.8
Elgin, IL Metro Division	225,916	223,191	173,621	2,725	1.2	196.2	1,589	77.2	616	93.8
Gary, IN Metro Division	297,657	294,238	270,298	3,419	1.2	158.5	1,697	74.7	1,167	78.1
Lake County-Kenosha County, IL-WI Metro Division	332,042	329,612	287,399	2,430	0.7	463.8	931	76.7	946	61.9
Chico, CA Metro Area	98,035	95,923	85,759	2,112	2.2	59.9	621	57.3	512	30.7
Cincinnati, OH-KY-IN Metro Area	922,108	911,493	830,215	10,615	1.2	221.4	4,661	74.6	3,180	88.0
Clarksville, TN-KY Metro Area	115,905	107,680	86,584	8,225	7.6	68.3	1,342	84.4	1,917	56.8
Cleveland, TN Metro Area	51,364	49,449	44,347	1,915	3.9	67.3	732	60.0	550	48.5
Cleveland-Elyria, OH Metro Area	957,499	955,762	912,850	1,737	0.2	479.0	2,938	86.2	1,941	95.5
Coeur d'Alene, ID Metro Area	67,028	63,351	46,939	3,677	5.8	54.2	1,414	77.1	627	75.4
College Station-Bryan, TX Metro Area	102,735	95,199	75,583	7,536	7.9	48.9	1,712	70.6	995	78.1
Colorado Springs, CO Metro Area	281,862	265,717	214,514	16,145	6.1	105.0	3,665	82.5	1,760	95.2
Columbia, MO Metro Area	74,436	69,671	56,980	4,765	6.8	108.6	1,433	53.8	607	90.1
Columbia, SC Metro Area	345,117	332,114	270,721	13,003	3.9	93.2	4,642	79.2	2,942	85.9
Columbus, GA-AL Metro Area	132,443	128,424	116,187	4,019	3.1	68.4	1,244	48.6	1,384	62.8
Columbus, IN Metro Area	33,727	33,104	29,964	623	1.9	82.9	233	100.0	131	100.0
Columbus, OH Metro Area	845,562	821,608	710,597	23,954	2.9	176.3	7,555	46.6	4,479	65.1
Corpus Christi, TX Metro Area	190,999	183,119	161,256	7,880	4.3	107.1	2,153	74.6	1,225	75.5
Corvallis, OR Metro Area	37,695	36,300	32,074	1,395	3.8	55.8	142	97.2	93	80.6
Crestview-Fort Walton Beach-Destin, FL Metro Area	144,245	137,618	108,371	6,627	4.8	73.3	2,027	87.7	935	90.5
Cumberland, MD-WV Metro Area	46,257	46,369	45,158	-112	-0.2	61.5	84	65.5	161	59.0
Dallas-Fort Worth-Arlington, TX Metro Area	2,686,705	2,532,738	2,030,072	153,967	6.1	289.5	57,146	50.8	19,639	73.8
Dallas-Plano-Irving, TX Metro Division	1,777,642	1,660,512	1,337,580	117,130	7.1	336.9	46,785	47.1	13,460	71.4
Fort Worth-Arlington, TX Metro Division	909,063	872,226	692,492	36,837	4.2	227.1	10,361	67.8	6,179	79.2
Dalton, GA Metro Area	55,369	55,865	45,456	-496	-0.9	87.2	159	93.7	101	89.1
Danville, IL Metro Area	35,940	36,305	36,375	-365	-1.0	40.0	10	100.0	13	76.9
Daphne-Fairhope-Foley, AL Metro Area	108,564	104,248	74,907	4,316	4.1	68.3	2,203	73.6	696	98.0
Davenport-Moline-Rock Island, IA-IL Metro Area .	168,600	167,192	158,790	1,408	0.8	74.3	751	57.4	702	60.1
Dayton, OH Metro Area	367,933	367,277	348,098	656	0.2	287.0	980	87.4	731	88.8
Decatur, AL Metro Area	66,743	66,427	62,598	316	0.5	52.6	139	94.2	165	87.9
Decatur, IL Metro Area	50,298	50,469	50,260	-171	-0.3	86.6	47	95.7	101	94.1
Deltona-Daytona Beach-Ormond Beach, FL Metro Area	307,011	302,869	237,753	4,142	1.4	193.5	2,047	93.0	993	81.7
Denver-Aurora-Lakewood, CO Metro Area	1,132,228	1,079,422	897,927	52,806	4.9	135.7	18,326	50.9	5,042	72.6
Des Moines-West Des Moines, IA Metro Area	258,050	240,681	199,774	17,369	7.2	89.5	5,707	59.1	2,815	78.4
Detroit-Warren-Dearborn, MI Metro Area	1,895,743	1,886,329	1,800,731	9,414	0.5	487.5	7,304	71.1	3,210	75.7
Detroit-Dearborn-Livonia, MI Metro Division	814,328	821,165	824,760	-6,837	-0.8	1,330.6	1,774	45.0	735	63.9
Warren-Troy-Farmington Hills, MI Metro Division	1,081,415	1,065,164	975,971	16,251	1.5	330.0	5,530	79.4	2,475	79.2
Dothan, AL Metro Area	68,298	66,952	60,008	1,346	2.0	39.8	327	95.1	321	84.4
Dover, DE Metro Area	68,692	65,503	50,778	3,189	4.9	117.2	1,061	77.9	813	82.9
Dubuque, IA Metro Area	40,588	39,032	35,546	1,556	4.0	66.7	255	92.9	548	59.1
Duluth, MN-WI Metro Area	142,131	141,571	130,247	560	0.4	16.9	841	55.5	486	82.1
Durham-Chapel Hill, NC Metro Area	235,645	223,255	181,268	12,390	5.5	134.1	4,411	59.3	1,913	80.0
East Stroudsburg, PA Metro Area	80,720	80,393	67,936	327	0.4	132.7	152	100.0	263	91.3
Eau Claire, WI Metro Area	71,022	69,402	60,549	1,620	2.3	43.1	677	59.1	357	81.8
El Centro, CA Metro Area	57,216	56,112	44,078	1,104	2.0	13.7	293	38.2	102	100.0
Elizabethtown-Fort Knox, KY Metro Area	64,547	61,311	54,010	3,236	5.3	54.2	308	90.9	1,458	57.8
Elkhart-Goshen, IN Metro Area	78,030	77,763	70,116	267	0.3	168.5	309	99.4	234	74.4
Elmira, NY Metro Area	38,340	38,368	37,805	-28	-0.1	94.1	78	59.0	76	89.5
El Paso, TX Metro Area	290,975	272,522	226,965	18,453	6.8	52.1	4,491	56.1	4,549	65.1
Enid, OK Metro Area	26,856	26,829	26,057	27	0.1	25.4	74	100.0	74	100.0
Erie, PA Metro Area	120,094	119,199	114,508	895	0.8	150.3	267	71.9	586	63.0
Eugene, OR Metro Area	159,288	156,170	139,383	3,118	2.0	35.0	721	80.2	550	84.4
Evansville, IN-KY Metro Area	140,561	138,816	127,819	1,745	1.3	96.0	763	75.9	597	83.8
Fairbanks, AK Metro Area	41,616	41,775	33,472	-159	-0.4	5.7	7	100.0	42	100.0
Fargo, ND-MN Metro Area	103,693	92,272	73,881	11,421	12.4	36.9	2,719	50.0	1,318	57.7
Farmington, NM Metro Area	49,661	49,365	43,448	296	0.6	9.0	118	100.0	273	73.6
Fayetteville, NC Metro Area	164,591	154,281	131,449	10,310	6.7	157.9	1,386	64.1	3,609	44.6
Fayetteville-Springdale-Rogers, AR-MO Metro Area	207,938	198,688	145,424	9,250	4.7	65.7	3,793	74.3	1,221	88.5
Flagstaff, AZ Metro Area	64,446	63,317	53,677	1,129	1.8	3.5	566	58.8	315	59.0
Flint, MI Metro Area	190,887	192,097	184,146	-1,210	-0.6	299.7	413	83.5	78	100.0
Florence, SC Metro Area	89,425	88,979	81,125	446	0.5	65.7	424	98.6	476	74.2
Florence-Muscle Shoals, AL Metro Area	70,684	69,577	65,562	1,107	1.6	56.1	338	60.9	232	66.8
Fond du Lac, WI Metro Area	44,620	43,935	39,365	685	1.6	62.0	195	71.8	229	49.3
Fort Collins, CO Metro Area	140,892	132,784	106,306	8,108	6.1	54.3	2,434	70.7	1,153	41.4
Fort Smith, AR-OK Metro Area	123,514	121,067	108,066	2,447	2.0	36.5	466	70.4	682	75.2
Fort Wayne, IN Metro Area	181,519	178,242	162,905	3,277	1.8	133.4	1,355	73.1	885	91.4
Fresno, CA Metro Area	325,996	316,053	271,364	9,943	3.1	54.7	2,322	88.4	2,248	85.3
Gadsden, AL Metro Area	47,510	47,465	46,035	45	0.1	88.8	83	100.0	105	100.0
Gainesville, FL Metro Area	121,823	120,124	101,576	1,699	1.4	99.5	1,214	51.3	490	74.9
Gainesville, GA Metro Area	70,107	68,844	51,793	1,263	1.8	178.5	946	95.8	184	100.0

¹Units per square mile was calculated on the basis of land area data as of 2016.
²Sample selected from a universe of 20,000 permit-issuing places.

Table B-9.   Housing Units and Building Permits—*Continued*

Metropolitan statistical area and division	Housing units						New private housing units authorized by building permits \2			
	2015 (July 1 estimate)	2010 (July 1 estimate)	2000 (July 1 estimate)	Change, 2010–2015		Units per square mile of land area,[1] 2015	2015	Percent single family 2015	2010	Percent single family 2010
				Number	Percent					
Gettysburg, PA Metro Area	41,462	40,844	35,977	618	1.5	79.9	240	90.8	306	92.8
Glens Falls, NY Metro Area	68,208	67,606	61,760	602	0.9	40.2	381	53.3	279	91.4
Goldsboro, NC Metro Area	53,290	52,963	47,559	327	0.6	96.2	248	98.4	279	79.9
Grand Forks, ND-MN Metro Area	46,961	44,014	41,397	2,947	6.7	13.8	529	46.3	200	77.0
Grand Island, NE Metro Area	35,196	34,197	31,935	999	2.9	16.4	300	74.0	191	88.5
Grand Junction, CO Metro Area	64,247	62,696	49,116	1,551	2.5	19.3	486	91.8	408	85.3
Grand Rapids-Wyoming, MI Metro Area	410,654	404,680	362,218	5,974	1.5	153.8	3,672	67.9	1,271	96.5
Grants Pass, OR Metro Area	38,136	38,004	33,371	132	0.3	23.3	237	73.0	106	88.7
Great Falls, MT Metro Area	37,932	37,310	35,268	622	1.7	14.1	226	67.3	150	89.3
Greeley, CO Metro Area	102,603	96,396	67,151	6,207	6.4	25.7	3,186	82.4	863	91.4
Green Bay, WI Metro Area	141,087	137,346	118,725	3,741	2.7	75.5	1,018	64.4	1,134	53.9
Greensboro-High Point, NC Metro Area	329,921	323,077	276,354	6,844	2.1	165.5	2,212	75.0	1,903	64.8
Greenville, NC Metro Area	77,332	75,078	58,528	2,254	3.0	118.5	538	65.4	669	52.3
Greenville-Anderson-Mauldin, SC Metro Area	372,546	362,390	313,676	10,156	2.8	137.4	5,896	64.1	1,962	89.5
Gulfport-Biloxi-Pascagoula, MS Metro Area	176,197	167,943	153,468	8,254	4.9	99.5	1,712	88.0	2,058	77.5
Hagerstown-Martinsburg, MD-WV Metro Area	108,141	105,679	86,238	2,462	2.3	138.8	978	84.7	656	90.5
Hammond, LA Metro Area	53,138	50,277	40,876	2,861	5.7	67.2	627	99.0	526	89.4
Hanford-Corcoran, CA Metro Area	45,253	43,910	36,687	1,343	3.1	32.6	591	67.9	265	72.8
Harrisburg-Carlisle, PA Metro Area	246,295	241,053	217,567	5,242	2.2	151.8	1,615	74.0	1,612	81.6
Harrisonburg, VA Metro Area	52,898	51,224	41,199	1,674	3.3	61.0	406	98.8	462	84.8
Hartford-West Hartford-East Hartford, CT Metro Area	508,930	507,139	472,786	1,791	0.4	336.0	1,582	49.8	1,279	83.4
Hattiesburg, MS Metro Area	62,545	61,913	50,741	632	1.0	38.8	212	57.5	74	100.0
Hickory-Lenoir-Morganton, NC Metro Area	162,293	162,631	145,651	-338	-0.2	99.0	805	66.8	448	88.8
Hilton Head Island-Bluffton-Beaufort, SC Metro Area	106,364	103,366	69,299	2,998	2.9	86.4	2,102	80.3	412	87.9
Hinesville, GA Metro Area	33,712	32,872	26,370	840	2.6	36.8	545	85.7	111	100.0
Homosassa Springs, FL Metro Area	77,726	78,075	62,527	-349	-0.4	133.6	378	93.7	199	94.0
Hot Springs, AR Metro Area	50,538	50,539	45,085	0	0.0	74.6	59	100.0	38	100.0
Houma-Thibodaux, LA Metro Area	84,850	82,602	75,167	2,248	2.7	36.9	663	92.5	365	98.4
Houston-The Woodlands-Sugar Land, TX Metro Area	2,501,900	2,300,903	1,798,493	200,997	8.7	302.9	56,901	64.6	27,450	81.3
Huntington-Ashland, WV-KY-OH Metro Area	164,657	164,457	161,541	200	0.1	65.1	291	68.7	380	67.9
Huntsville, AL Metro Area	192,458	182,089	147,830	10,369	5.7	141.4	2,607	81.4	2,275	100.0
Idaho Falls, ID Metro Area	51,308	49,860	38,252	1,448	2.9	9.9	862	79.1	391	79.5
Indianapolis-Carmel-Anderson, IN Metro Area	842,432	817,503	705,444	24,929	3.0	195.6	8,735	59.2	6,001	64.5
Iowa City, IA Metro Area	69,357	65,627	54,918	3,730	5.7	58.6	1,327	36.4	553	79.6
Ithaca, NY Metro Area	42,272	41,694	38,758	578	1.4	89.1	279	49.5	153	73.9
Jackson, MI Metro Area	69,016	69,444	63,169	-428	-0.6	98.4	117	94.9	63	100.0
Jackson, MS Metro Area	239,263	232,886	207,201	6,377	2.7	51.5	1,569	100.0	1,393	93.7
Jackson, TN Metro Area	56,214	55,324	50,706	890	1.6	50.7	214	96.3	250	100.0
Jacksonville, FL Metro Area	622,262	599,284	477,477	22,978	3.8	194.3	9,671	75.0	3,606	93.9
Jacksonville, NC Metro Area	76,926	68,687	56,207	8,239	12.0	100.9	894	95.7	2,375	89.9
Janesville-Beloit, WI Metro Area	68,313	68,436	62,377	-123	-0.2	95.1	216	85.2	111	91.0
Jefferson City, MO Metro Area	64,115	63,605	57,024	510	0.8	28.5	270	61.5	222	81.5
Johnson City, TN Metro Area	96,065	93,906	82,219	2,159	2.3	112.5	689	79.4	741	53.7
Johnstown, PA Metro Area	65,126	65,627	65,793	-501	-0.8	94.6	47	100.0	117	100.0
Jonesboro, AR Metro Area	54,908	51,534	46,303	3,374	6.5	37.5	482	83.4	611	66.0
Joplin, MO Metro Area	76,046	74,999	67,733	1,047	1.4	60.2	531	83.8	202	71.3
Kahului-Wailuku-Lahaina, HI Metro Area	71,835	70,567	56,877	1,268	1.8	61.2	502	66.1	277	75.8
Kalamazoo-Portage, MI Metro Area	147,152	146,804	133,741	348	0.2	125.8	623	80.4	367	95.6
Kankakee, IL Metro Area	45,185	45,245	40,716	-60	-0.1	66.8	89	100.0	71	83.1
Kansas City, MO-KS Metro Area	891,296	872,401	760,905	18,895	2.2	122.8	8,954	50.8	2,681	79.3
Kennewick-Richland, WA Metro Area	99,753	93,242	72,410	6,511	7.0	33.9	1,464	83.4	2,022	77.8
Killeen-Temple, TX Metro Area	171,106	159,900	122,885	11,206	7.0	60.8	2,310	79.7	2,241	87.4
Kingsport-Bristol-Bristol, TN-VA Metro Area	147,405	147,039	136,645	366	0.2	73.3	705	59.4	464	93.5
Kingston, NY Metro Area	83,801	83,661	77,790	140	0.2	74.5	307	48.2	334	46.1
Knoxville, TN Metro Area	388,913	381,483	336,727	7,430	1.9	111.1	3,060	84.7	2,427	66.2
Kokomo, IN Metro Area	38,747	38,678	37,685	69	0.2	132.2	441	37.6	13	100.0
La Crosse-Onalaska, WI-MN Metro Area	58,098	57,051	51,795	1,047	1.8	57.9	497	46.9	327	76.1
Lafayette, LA Metro Area	204,102	196,225	172,176	7,877	4.0	59.9	2,483	79.5	1,202	91.6
Lafayette-West Lafayette, IN Metro Area	88,162	84,577	71,349	3,585	4.2	69.0	527	90.1	531	84.9
Lake Charles, LA Metro Area	90,806	85,933	81,511	4,873	5.7	38.7	1,034	76.2	975	88.7
Lake Havasu City-Kingman, AZ Metro Area	112,867	110,965	80,717	1,902	1.7	8.5	636	98.4	262	81.7
Lakeland-Winter Haven, FL Metro Area	284,342	281,212	227,250	3,130	1.1	158.2	3,039	98.8	1,200	92.7
Lancaster, PA Metro Area	207,090	203,154	180,611	3,936	1.9	219.4	1,154	83.9	1,381	83.2
Lansing-East Lansing, MI Metro Area	200,375	198,976	182,411	1,399	0.7	118.0	1,056	47.0	677	66.6
Laredo, TX Metro Area	79,708	73,665	55,740	6,043	8.2	23.7	1,848	55.8	663	95.9
Las Cruces, NM Metro Area	84,646	81,664	65,878	2,982	3.7	22.2	760	94.6	974	82.0
Las Vegas-Henderson-Paradise, NV Metro Area	871,807	841,433	566,405	30,374	3.6	110.5	10,605	73.6	5,474	84.5
Lawrence, KS Metro Area	48,540	46,793	40,436	1,747	3.7	106.5	839	44.3	288	66.0
Lawton, OK Metro Area	54,703	53,895	48,585	808	1.5	32.1	100	96.0	326	91.4
Lebanon, PA Metro Area	56,464	55,647	49,431	817	1.5	156.1	384	90.4	240	100.0
Lewiston, ID-WA Metro Area	27,278	27,311	25,382	-33	-0.1	18.4	139	45.3	75	94.7
Lewiston-Auburn, ME Metro Area	49,105	49,098	46,055	7	0.0	104.9	74	100.0	206	78.6
Lexington-Fayette, KY Metro Area	216,459	209,453	176,228	7,006	3.3	147.4	2,206	62.6	1,361	84.9

[1]Units per square mile was calculated on the basis of land area data as of 2016.
[2]Sample selected from a universe of 20,000 permit-issuing places.

Table B-9.   Housing Units and Building Permits—*Continued*

Metropolitan statistical area and division	Housing units						New private housing units authorized by building permits \2			
	2015 (July 1 estimate)	2010 (July 1 estimate)	2000 (July 1 estimate)	Change, 2010–2015		Units per square mile of land area,[1] 2015	2015	Percent single family 2015	2010	Percent single family 2010
				Number	Percent					
Lima, OH Metro Area	44,799	44,988	44,276	-189	-0.4	111.3	77	83.1	116	37.9
Lincoln, NE Metro Area	133,554	127,868	111,111	5,686	4.4	94.8	2,548	42.8	1,032	62.8
Little Rock-North Little Rock-Conway, AR Metro Area	320,011	307,553	262,950	12,458	4.1	78.3	2,699	55.1	3,559	53.3
Logan, UT-ID Metro Area	44,421	41,662	33,015	2,759	6.6	24.3	614	59.9	655	55.9
Longview, TX Metro Area	89,818	87,361	81,346	2,457	2.8	50.5	248	89.1	491	43.4
Longview, WA Metro Area	43,566	43,454	38,767	112	0.3	38.2	178	94.4	131	88.5
Los Angeles-Long Beach-Anaheim, CA Metro Area	4,585,126	4,495,807	4,247,689	89,319	2.0	945.6	34,034	24.8	10,394	38.6
Anaheim-Santa Ana-Irvine, CA Metro Division	1,080,987	1,049,357	972,611	31,630	3.0	1,367.3	10,771	35.4	3,134	51.8
Los Angeles-Long Beach-Glendale, CA Metro Division	3,504,139	3,446,450	3,275,078	57,689	1.7	863.5	23,263	19.9	7,260	32.8
Louisville/Jefferson County, KY-IN Metro Area	551,210	540,701	478,798	10,509	1.9	154.0	3,979	68.7	2,207	79.9
Lubbock, TX Metro Area	128,688	120,855	106,679	7,833	6.5	47.9	1,856	51.6	1,452	61.8
Lynchburg, VA Metro Area	115,229	112,637	98,404	2,592	2.3	54.3	797	74.2	700	84.9
Macon, GA Metro Area	102,241	101,598	94,363	643	0.6	59.3	317	77.3	368	95.1
Madera, CA Metro Area	50,084	49,160	40,518	924	1.9	23.4	211	100.0	192	58.3
Madison, WI Metro Area	278,423	268,967	227,642	9,456	3.5	84.1	3,498	40.2	1,252	67.4
Manchester-Nashua, NH Metro Area	168,074	166,102	150,436	1,972	1.2	191.8	921	60.5	682	53.8
Manhattan, KS Metro Area	39,371	36,965	30,840	2,406	6.5	27.1	496	68.5	601	55.7
Mankato-North Mankato, MN Metro Area	40,650	39,112	33,338	1,538	3.9	34.0	808	30.3	331	59.2
Mansfield, OH Metro Area	54,199	54,588	53,218	-389	-0.7	109.4	62	100.0	45	100.0
McAllen-Edinburg-Mission, TX Metro Area	264,604	248,966	193,935	15,638	6.3	168.4	4,306	68.0	3,552	87.2
Medford, OR Metro Area	92,844	90,959	76,129	1,885	2.1	33.4	717	84.2	373	78.6
Memphis, TN-MS-AR Metro Area	566,162	555,384	486,838	10,778	1.9	113.6	3,951	65.1	2,429	68.1
Merced, CA Metro Area	84,322	83,717	68,875	605	0.7	43.6	232	98.3	106	98.1
Miami-Fort Lauderdale-West Palm Beach, FL Metro Area	2,508,205	2,464,492	2,158,776	43,713	1.8	494.2	23,450	30.5	5,877	54.0
Fort Lauderdale-Pompano Beach-Deerfield Beach, FL Metro Division	818,623	810,355	743,865	8,268	1.0	678.2	5,452	27.4	1,168	83.8
Miami-Miami Beach-Kendall, FL Metro Division	1,010,556	989,412	855,553	21,144	2.1	532.2	12,617	22.2	3,203	29.4
West Palm Beach-Boca Raton-Delray Beach, FL Metro Division	679,026	664,725	559,358	14,301	2.2	344.7	5,381	52.9	1,506	83.1
Michigan City-La Porte, IN Metro Area	48,782	48,450	45,724	332	0.7	81.5	159	62.3	228	68.4
Midland, MI Metro Area	36,465	35,953	33,906	512	1.4	70.6	130	83.1	123	91.9
Midland, TX Metro Area	61,377	56,267	50,118	5,110	9.1	33.8	1,030	74.4	403	100.0
Milwaukee-Waukesha-West Allis, WI Metro Area	673,016	669,901	619,802	3,115	0.5	462.6	3,048	46.5	1,941	49.8
Minneapolis-St. Paul-Bloomington, MN-WI Metro Area	1,425,849	1,387,263	1,202,766	38,586	2.8	186.7	11,673	58.0	5,788	66.8
Missoula, MT Metro Area	51,869	50,119	41,534	1,750	3.5	20.0	574	50.9	368	51.6
Mobile, AL Metro Area	182,025	178,747	165,520	3,278	1.8	148.1	907	71.4	1,026	87.2
Modesto, CA Metro Area	180,704	179,579	151,433	1,125	0.6	120.8	413	100.0	292	54.5
Monroe, LA Metro Area	78,410	75,891	71,086	2,519	3.3	52.7	605	91.7	441	75.5
Monroe, MI Metro Area	63,654	63,033	56,702	621	1.0	115.9	291	83.5	117	96.6
Montgomery, AL Metro Area	165,497	161,612	145,108	3,885	2.4	61.0	1,099	69.5	993	47.5
Morgantown, WV Metro Area	59,576	58,342	50,360	1,234	2.1	59.1	166	14.5	301	7.0
Morristown, TN Metro Area	50,696	50,490	44,244	206	0.4	116.3	188	98.9	204	96.6
Mount Vernon-Anacortes, WA Metro Area	52,214	51,511	42,904	703	1.4	30.2	438	93.6	207	98.1
Muncie, IN Metro Area	52,489	52,336	51,122	153	0.3	133.9	46	100.0	50	92.0
Muskegon, MI Metro Area	73,331	73,534	68,781	-203	-0.3	146.7	241	100.0	106	79.2
Myrtle Beach-Conway-North Myrtle Beach, SC-NC Metro Area	279,196	263,996	175,248	15,200	5.8	140.8	6,154	93.6	2,587	88.8
Napa, CA Metro Area	55,472	54,787	48,719	685	1.3	74.1	172	98.8	110	100.0
Naples-Immokalee-Marco Island, FL Metro Area	206,375	197,453	146,520	8,922	4.5	103.2	4,060	75.8	1,259	60.8
Nashville-Davidson—Murfreesboro—Franklin, TN Metro Area	744,320	703,938	575,049	40,382	5.7	118.1	18,291	62.4	5,433	78.8
New Bern, NC Metro Area	58,470	57,456	49,745	1,014	1.8	38.6	435	72.4	533	85.7
New Haven-Milford, CT Metro Area	362,679	361,946	341,322	733	0.2	600.0	1,161	36.3	1,019	44.4
New Orleans-Metairie, LA Metro Area	555,843	547,218	557,784	8,625	1.6	173.6	2,495	83.9	2,211	86.4
New York-Newark-Jersey City, NY-NJ-PA Metro Area	7,892,416	7,790,083	7,333,969	102,333	1.3	951.5	86,424	12.9	20,011	39.1
Dutchess County-Putnam County, NY Metro Division	157,569	156,877	141,552	692	0.4	153.6	351	64.1	417	98.3
Nassau County-Suffolk County, NY Metro Division	1,037,488	1,038,223	982,427	-735	-0.1	867.0	2,304	75.3	1,494	87.7
Newark, NJ-PA Metro Division	984,251	975,551	919,578	8,700	0.9	396.4	9,929	24.0	3,362	57.6
New York-Jersey City-White Plains, NY-NJ Metro Division	5,713,108	5,619,432	5,290,412	93,676	1.7	1,591.7	73,840	9.2	14,738	28.2
Niles-Benton Harbor, MI Metro Area	76,793	76,902	73,574	-109	-0.1	135.2	208	80.8	133	100.0
North Port-Sarasota-Bradenton, FL Metro Area	414,742	401,268	322,435	13,474	3.4	319.3	7,141	69.9	1,955	87.2
Norwich-New London, CT Metro Area	121,637	121,036	110,921	601	0.5	182.9	531	44.8	344	82.8
Ocala, FL Metro Area	163,808	163,998	123,249	-190	-0.1	103.2	1,055	100.0	481	100.0
Ocean City, NJ Metro Area	99,010	98,416	91,226	594	0.6	392.7	614	73.8	434	65.4
Odessa, TX Metro Area	57,025	53,071	49,634	3,954	7.5	63.5	612	76.5	708	37.9
Ogden-Clearfield, UT Metro Area	215,183	204,446	161,969	10,737	5.3	29.8	3,120	74.3	1,773	87.8
Oklahoma City, OK Metro Area	564,440	539,738	473,659	24,702	4.6	102.4	6,004	91.9	3,635	83.4

[1]Units per square mile was calculated on the basis of land area data as of 2016.
[2]Sample selected from a universe of 20,000 permit-issuing places.

Table B-9. Housing Units and Building Permits—*Continued*

Metropolitan statistical area and division	Housing units						New private housing units authorized by building permits \2			
	2015 (July 1 estimate)	2010 (July 1 estimate)	2000 (July 1 estimate)	Change, 2010–2015		Units per square mile of land area,[1] 2015	2015	Percent single family 2015	2010	Percent single family 2010
				Number	Percent					
Olympia-Tumwater, WA Metro Area	112,553	108,436	87,059	4,117	3.8	155.8	1,020	86.4	1,156	91.1
Omaha-Council Bluffs, NE-IA Metro Area	377,871	362,986	313,007	14,885	4.1	86.9	4,157	71.5	3,223	71.5
Orlando-Kissimmee-Sanford, FL Metro Area	988,892	942,941	690,045	45,951	4.9	284.1	20,474	58.8	5,254	80.3
Oshkosh-Neenah, WI Metro Area	74,551	73,386	64,945	1,165	1.6	171.6	710	42.7	359	71.6
Owensboro, KY Metro Area	50,749	49,490	46,596	1,259	2.5	56.5	243	95.9	338	81.7
Oxnard-Thousand Oaks-Ventura, CA Metro Area	285,880	281,771	252,796	4,109	1.5	155.1	1,433	47.3	590	35.4
Palm Bay-Melbourne-Titusville, FL Metro Area	273,096	269,967	223,111	3,129	1.2	269.0	1,918	83.9	1,144	80.9
Panama City, FL Metro Area	109,942	108,773	86,425	1,169	1.1	83.8	988	81.8	354	70.1
Parkersburg-Vienna, WV Metro Area	43,497	43,455	43,068	42	0.1	72.6	177	77.4	137	65.7
Pensacola-Ferry Pass-Brent, FL Metro Area	207,629	201,596	174,356	6,033	3.0	124.4	2,634	76.6	1,754	76.2
Peoria, IL Metro Area	166,098	164,333	153,633	1,765	1.1	67.3	502	84.5	793	71.9
Philadelphia-Camden-Wilmington, PA-NJ-DE-MD Metro Area	2,455,432	2,434,040	2,286,358	21,392	0.9	533.5	12,317	53.2	7,053	73.5
Camden, NJ Metro Division	496,585	490,627	457,033	5,958	1.2	370.0	2,670	47.7	1,885	62.5
Montgomery County-Bucks County-Chester County, PA Metro Division	772,551	764,363	689,131	8,188	1.1	420.3	3,767	72.3	2,647	81.7
Philadelphia, PA Metro Division	894,462	892,864	879,239	1,598	0.2	2,811.9	4,015	29.0	1,347	59.5
Wilmington, DE-MD-NJ Metro Division	291,834	286,186	260,955	5,648	2.0	264.2	1,865	74.3	1,174	88.9
Phoenix-Mesa-Scottsdale, AZ Metro Area	1,859,996	1,801,633	1,342,946	58,363	3.2	127.7	22,402	74.2	8,300	86.9
Pine Bluff, AR Metro Area	42,149	41,941	43,145	208	0.5	20.8	31	67.7	126	36.5
Pittsburgh, PA Metro Area	1,107,452	1,102,147	1,079,518	5,305	0.5	209.7	5,264	62.6	3,615	94.0
Pittsfield, MA Metro Area	68,397	68,521	66,317	-124	-0.2	73.8	214	49.5	139	89.9
Pocatello, ID Metro Area	33,457	33,207	29,177	250	0.8	30.1	190	88.4	140	97.9
Portland-South Portland, ME Metro Area	267,081	262,870	234,119	4,211	1.6	128.4	1,980	80.0	1,260	97.2
Portland-Vancouver-Hillsboro, OR-WA Metro Area	959,565	925,679	794,512	33,886	3.7	143.5	13,967	50.8	4,476	75.0
Port St. Lucie, FL Metro Area	217,310	215,151	157,691	2,159	1.0	194.8	1,601	79.2	492	87.8
Prescott, AZ Metro Area	113,083	110,476	82,364	2,607	2.4	13.9	1,377	81.3	339	69.9
Providence-Warwick, RI-MA Metro Area	694,206	693,897	657,795	309	0.0	437.4	1,818	81.5	1,439	83.7
Provo-Orem, UT Metro Area	166,132	152,208	108,093	13,924	9.1	30.8	4,549	68.1	1,985	78.2
Pueblo, CO Metro Area	70,142	69,576	59,251	566	0.8	29.4	282	70.9	234	89.3
Punta Gorda, FL Metro Area	101,775	100,657	80,155	1,118	1.1	149.4	1,129	83.9	425	68.9
Racine, WI Metro Area	82,323	82,206	74,909	117	0.1	247.6	217	87.1	240	65.0
Raleigh, NC Metro Area	509,636	467,062	332,456	42,574	9.1	240.6	11,987	72.5	5,213	89.3
Rapid City, SD Metro Area	63,745	60,677	51,230	3,068	5.1	8.2	798	71.7	676	69.8
Reading, PA Metro Area	164,904	164,825	150,712	79	0.0	192.6	416	82.5	415	84.3
Redding, CA Metro Area	78,101	77,351	69,020	750	1.0	20.7	375	85.6	253	66.0
Reno, NV Metro Area	190,961	186,927	146,669	4,034	2.2	29.1	2,787	71.8	606	77.9
Richmond, VA Metro Area	522,517	507,821	435,440	14,696	2.9	114.2	4,875	74.2	3,248	69.7
Riverside-San Bernardino-Ontario, CA Metro Area	1,538,450	1,501,866	1,191,406	36,584	2.4	56.4	9,926	78.7	6,336	83.4
Roanoke, VA Metro Area	146,071	145,021	130,120	1,050	0.7	78.2	763	53.5	436	92.7
Rochester, MN Metro Area	90,316	88,265	74,524	2,051	2.3	36.5	1,776	37.0	532	72.9
Rochester, NY Metro Area	475,773	469,649	440,207	6,124	1.3	145.7	2,652	52.1	1,493	78.6
Rockford, IL Metro Area	145,395	145,920	130,217	-525	-0.4	183.1	134	67.2	299	98.0
Rocky Mount, NC Metro Area	67,083	67,135	61,297	-52	-0.1	64.1	263	94.7	212	99.1
Rome, GA Metro Area	40,410	40,554	36,742	-144	-0.4	79.3	93	95.7	55	100.0
Sacramento—Roseville—Arden-Arcade, CA Metro Area	889,022	872,422	718,998	16,600	1.9	174.5	6,184	83.7	2,702	80.2
Saginaw, MI Metro Area	86,822	86,821	85,696	1	0.0	108.5	382	40.8	137	82.5
St. Cloud, MN Metro Area	79,798	78,203	64,238	1,595	2.0	45.6	858	43.8	314	100.0
St. George, UT Metro Area	63,947	57,855	36,848	6,092	10.5	26.3	1,658	97.3	893	97.8
St. Joseph, MO-KS Metro Area	53,563	53,647	50,694	-84	-0.2	32.4	211	44.5	131	73.3
St. Louis, MO-IL Metro Area	1,241,161	1,225,851	1,126,418	15,310	1.2	157.8	7,698	65.7	5,654	75.2
Salem, OR Metro Area	154,633	151,369	133,093	3,264	2.2	80.5	1,297	62.2	699	67.0
Salinas, CA Metro Area	140,470	139,091	132,051	1,379	1.0	42.8	587	53.7	279	40.1
Salisbury, MD-DE Metro Area	240,770	231,437	185,724	9,333	4.0	114.7	3,031	82.9	1,841	87.8
Salt Lake City, UT Metro Area	401,449	384,340	326,092	17,109	4.5	52.2	6,755	55.7	2,746	65.4
San Angelo, TX Metro Area	49,133	47,537	44,911	1,596	3.4	19.1	236	100.0	177	100.0
San Antonio-New Braunfels, TX Metro Area	872,477	839,174	652,668	33,303	4.0	119.3	7,824	82.8	6,865	74.9
San Diego-Carlsbad, CA Metro Area	1,194,415	1,165,418	1,044,144	28,997	2.5	283.9	9,883	32.6	3,494	65.0
San Francisco-Oakland-Hayward, CA Metro Area	1,782,303	1,742,786	1,610,766	39,517	2.3	719.3	13,386	35.9	4,621	45.8
Oakland-Hayward-Berkeley, CA Metro Division	1,004,570	983,390	897,252	21,180	2.2	687.2	7,711	51.6	3,403	52.0
San Francisco-Redwood City-South San Francisco, CA Metro Division	665,041	648,133	608,358	16,908	2.6	1,342.4	5,285	11.8	1,032	22.1
San Rafael, CA Metro Division	112,692	111,263	105,156	1,429	1.3	216.5	390	51.5	186	65.1
San Jose-Sunnyvale-Santa Clara, CA Metro Area	678,844	650,022	597,689	28,822	4.4	253.3	5,788	32.8	4,179	20.6
San Luis Obispo-Paso Robles-Arroyo Grande, CA Metro Area	120,137	117,396	102,684	2,741	2.3	36.4	821	84.3	468	65.8
Santa Cruz-Watsonville, CA Metro Area	105,530	104,491	98,986	1,039	1.0	237.0	335	60.3	158	75.3
Santa Fe, NM Metro Area	71,873	71,262	57,920	611	0.9	37.7	110	100.0	96	100.0
Santa Maria-Santa Barbara, CA Metro Area	155,163	152,898	143,164	2,265	1.5	56.7	1,082	38.0	400	57.3
Santa Rosa, CA Metro Area	207,891	204,666	183,846	3,225	1.6	131.9	621	69.4	477	60.2
Savannah, GA Metro Area	157,902	151,350	123,434	6,552	4.3	117.6	2,407	97.9	1,301	78.4
Scranton—Wilkes-Barre—Hazleton, PA Metro Area	259,895	258,832	252,950	1,063	0.4	148.8	831	96.3	687	96.8

[1]Units per square mile was calculated on the basis of land area data as of 2016.
[2]Sample selected from a universe of 20,000 permit-issuing places.

Table B-9.   Housing Units and Building Permits—*Continued*

Metropolitan statistical area and division	Housing units						New private housing units authorized by building permits \2			
	2015 (July 1 estimate)	2010 (July 1 estimate)	2000 (July 1 estimate)	Change, 2010–2015		Units per square mile of land area,[1] 2015	2015	Percent single family 2015	2010	Percent single family 2010
				Number	Percent					
Seattle-Tacoma-Bellevue, WA Metro Area.......	1,529,969	1,464,412	1,261,027	65,557	4.5	260.6	25,008	34.6	10,040	61.1
Seattle-Bellevue-Everett, WA Metro Division.....	1,193,612	1,138,714	982,839	54,898	4.8	284.0	22,111	28.9	8,140	54.4
Tacoma-Lakewood, WA Metro Division............	336,357	325,698	278,188	10,659	3.3	201.6	2,897	77.8	1,900	89.9
Sebastian-Vero Beach, FL Metro Area.................	77,900	76,385	58,305	1,515	2.0	154.9	873	97.3	307	100.0
Sebring, FL Metro Area...................................	54,822	55,363	48,964	-541		53.9	162	96.3	154	47.4
Sheboygan, WI Metro Area.............................	50,589	50,777	46,097	-188	-0.4	98.9	123	82.1	69	94.2
Sherman-Denison, TX Metro Area.....................	54,653	53,740	48,441	913	1.7	58.6	340	94.7	327	22.9
Shreveport-Bossier City, LA Metro Area.............	200,169	193,316	179,029	6,853	3.5	62.8	1,107	92.4	1,357	85.9
Sierra Vista-Douglas, AZ Metro Area..................	60,620	59,130	51,322	1,490	2.5	9.8	215	64.7	347	100.0
Sioux City, IA-NE-SD Metro Area......................	69,537	68,655	66,863	882	1.3	23.7	510	68.4	319	79.3
Sioux Falls, SD Metro Area.............................	103,807	96,192	76,074	7,615	7.9	40.3	1,926	55.5	1,081	69.8
South Bend-Mishawaka, IN-MI Metro Area..........	141,700	140,737	131,341	963	0.7	149.5	524	72.5	383	62.1
Spartanburg, SC Metro Area...........................	139,330	136,852	120,921	2,478	1.8	105.4	1,418	100.0	579	100.0
Spokane-Spokane Valley, WA Metro Area...........	237,474	230,854	199,922	6,620	2.9	42.1	2,738	53.4	1,733	61.0
Springfield, IL Metro Area..............................	96,455	95,605	90,921	850	0.9	81.6	383	75.5	399	71.7
Springfield, MA Metro Area.............................	255,006	254,796	244,775	210	0.1	222.8	458	88.4	575	88.2
Springfield, MO Metro Area.............................	198,901	192,552	157,347	6,349	3.3	66.2	2,223	56.5	1,338	67.6
Springfield, OH Metro Area.............................	61,102	61,397	61,089	-295	-0.5	153.7	63	96.8	57	93.0
State College, PA Metro Area..........................	65,478	63,347	53,367	2,131	3.4	59.0	389	80.7	426	81.5
Staunton-Waynesboro, VA Metro Area.................	54,062	52,683	46,185	1,379	2.6	54.0	287	100.0	376	49.5
Stockton-Lodi, CA Metro Area.........................	238,571	233,929	190,509	4,642	2.0	171.3	2,431	70.3	813	98.5
Sumter, SC Metro Area..................................	47,183	46,074	41,864	1,109	2.4	70.9	217	100.0	353	81.9
Syracuse, NY Metro Area...............................	290,392	287,805	278,406	2,587	0.9	121.8	1,194	51.5	1,139	72.5
Tallahassee, FL Metro Area............................	166,456	163,184	137,424	3,272	2.0	69.7	896	82.3	625	92.3
Tampa-St. Petersburg-Clearwater, FL Metro Area .	1,385,058	1,354,014	1,148,904	31,044	2.3	550.8	15,653	62.2	6,501	67.6
Terre Haute, IN Metro Area.............................	74,638	74,125	72,634	513	0.7	50.9	215	36.7	189	85.2
Texarkana, TX-AR Metro Area..........................	65,106	64,292	60,796	814	1.3	31.9	333	20.7	240	42.1
The Villages, FL Metro Area............................	66,850	53,510	25,696	13,340	24.9	122.1	1,568	100.0	2,420	100.0
Toledo, OH Metro Area..................................	273,761	273,385	260,471	376	0.1	200.8	715	90.8	639	60.6
Topeka, KS Metro Area..................................	104,297	103,872	96,606	425	0.4	32.3	388	91.2	381	92.7
Trenton, NJ Metro Area..................................	144,487	143,220	133,584	1,267	0.9	643.9	896	31.7	655	27.5
Tucson, AZ Metro Area..................................	452,040	441,118	369,335	10,922	2.5	49.2	2,428	91.7	1,938	89.1
Tulsa, OK Metro Area....................................	425,016	410,491	367,312	14,525	3.5	67.8	3,774	76.4	2,616	86.7
Tuscaloosa, AL Metro Area.............................	106,135	102,149	89,000	3,986	3.9	37.3	747	60.6	624	56.6
Tyler, TX Metro Area.....................................	88,852	87,352	72,139	1,500	1.7	96.4	470	89.4	266	75.6
Urban Honolulu, HI Metro Area........................	344,108	337,032	316,367	7,076	2.1	572.9	3,833	25.6	1,891	46.5
Utica-Rome, NY Metro Area............................	137,184	137,569	134,947	-385	-0.3	52.3	246	91.1	314	89.8
Valdosta, GA Metro Area................................	59,395	57,606	48,366	1,789	3.1	37.4	627	96.2	852	58.6
Vallejo-Fairfield, CA Metro Area.......................	155,625	152,840	135,034	2,785	1.8	189.4	1,434	72.2	467	100.0
Victoria, TX Metro Area..................................	40,565	39,131	36,473	1,434	3.7	23.4	139	100.0	47	100.0
Vineland-Bridgeton, NJ Metro Area....................	56,360	55,891	52,909	469	0.8	116.6	237	78.1	246	93.9
Virginia Beach-Norfolk-Newport News, VA-NC Metro Area...................................	711,353	689,080	625,502	22,273	3.2	265.1	6,722	59.9	3,967	79.4
Visalia-Porterville, CA Metro Area.....................	146,520	141,946	120,048	4,574	3.2	30.4	1,275	88.5	1,367	79.4
Waco, TX Metro Area....................................	106,383	102,981	92,693	3,402	3.3	59.0	1,507	39.3	607	73.6
Walla Walla, WA Metro Area............................	26,155	25,597	23,230	558	2.2	12.2	214	90.7	132	53.0
Warner Robins, GA Metro Area........................	77,562	74,685	58,051	2,877	3.9	100.1	1,048	71.4	738	100.0
Washington-Arlington-Alexandria, DC-VA-MD-WV Metro Area	2,324,126	2,237,445	1,916,243	86,681	3.9	372.1	23,007	54.9	13,174	72.8
Silver Spring-Frederick-Rockville, MD Metro Division.............................	483,741	466,296	409,906	17,445	3.7	419.4	3,383	62.3	2,838	61.8
Washington-Arlington-Alexandria, DC-VA-MD-WV Metro Division..............................	1,840,385	1,771,149	1,506,337	69,236	3.9	361.3	19,624	53.7	10,336	75.9
Waterloo-Cedar Falls, IA Metro Area..................	72,824	71,377	66,483	1,447	2.0	48.4	414	79.2	391	94.4
Watertown-Fort Drum, NY Metro Area.................	59,123	57,971	54,136	1,152	2.0	46.6	147	93.2	291	70.4
Wausau, WI Metro Area.................................	58,613	57,773	50,542	840	1.5	37.9	241	95.0	262	95.4
Weirton-Steubenville, WV-OH Metro Area...........	57,779	58,318	59,143	-539	-0.9	99.6	48	100.0	25	100.0
Wenatchee, WA Metro Area............................	52,782	51,519	43,484	1,263	2.5	11.1	593	82.6	320	97.8
Wheeling, WV-OH Metro Area..........................	68,961	69,515	69,420	-554	-0.8	73.1	115	61.7	38	86.8
Wichita, KS Metro Area..................................	271,000	267,179	243,071	3,821	1.4	54.1	2,021	57.1	1,270	83.2
Wichita Falls, TX Metro Area...........................	65,401	64,850	62,223	551	0.8	25.0	80	100.0	187	84.0
Williamsport, PA Metro Area...........................	52,671	52,495	52,482	176	0.3	42.9	159	89.9	207	96.1
Wilmington, NC Metro Area.............................	134,649	128,234	101,048	6,415	5.0	126.6	2,358	69.8	751	78.0
Winchester, VA-WV Metro Area........................	58,497	56,967	45,320	1,530	2.7	55.0	774	82.3	346	100.0
Winston-Salem, NC Metro Area........................	292,303	287,200	246,938	5,103	1.8	145.5	2,044	78.4	1,467	80.2
Worcester, MA-CT Metro Area.........................	379,267	376,058	342,938	3,209	0.9	187.4	1,385	83.2	1,591	76.0
Yakima, WA Metro Area.................................	86,569	85,535	79,292	1,034	1.2	20.2	395	98.7	624	55.0
York-Hanover, PA Metro Area..........................	181,068	178,856	157,223	2,212	1.2	200.3	778	90.9	1,059	81.0
Youngstown-Warren-Boardman, OH-PA Metro Area..	258,212	259,663	257,023	-1,451	-0.6	151.7	311	96.1	325	89.8
Yuba City, CA Metro Area...............................	62,393	61,535	51,023	858	1.4	50.5	371	65.2	150	100.0
Yuma, AZ Metro Area....................................	90,485	87,959	74,476	2,526	2.9	16.4	768	99.6	455	100.0

[1]Units per square mile was calculated on the basis of land area data as of 2016.
[2]Sample selected from a universe of 20,000 permit-issuing places.

Table B-10.   Housing Units, 2015

				Housing Units					
				Owner-occupied				Renter-occupied	
					Housing units with a mortgage				
Metropolitan statistical area and division	Total housing units	1 unit detached, (percent)	With 2 or more vehicles available (percent of occupied units)	Owner-ship rate	Number	Median monthly owner costs (dollars)	Units with costs 30 percent or more of household income (percent)	Number	Median monthly rent (dollars)	Units with rent 30 percent or more of household income (percent)
Abilene, TX Metro Area	70,595	71.5	59.7	60.7	17,649	1,160	22.2	23,326	796	43.2
Akron, OH Metro Area	313,518	68.8	57.7	65.5	119,495	1,231	22.2	97,475	757	48.8
Albany, GA Metro Area	66,857	63.1	51.5	54.7	18,038	1,142	24.3	26,092	711	51.0
Albany, OR Metro Area	49,174	65.8	59.9	59.3	16,911	1,336	35.8	18,851	806	47.2
Albany-Schenectady-Troy, NY Metro Area	398,555	55.7	53.6	63.9	141,283	1,596	25.9	123,804	923	48.1
Albuquerque, NM Metro Area	381,558	66.5	59.7	66.5	150,081	1,274	32.8	114,669	826	53.5
Alexandria, LA Metro Area	66,402	68.3	53.1	57.4	16,637	1,079	20.6	23,178	731	52.2
Allentown-Bethlehem-Easton, PA-NJ Metro Area..	345,251	56.6	60.7	69.0	142,776	1,638	31.3	97,565	995	51.8
Altoona, PA Metro Area	56,007	71.9	54.1	70.6	20,619	1,041	21.4	15,540	655	49.2
Amarillo, TX Metro Area	107,954	71.6	60.2	63.8	34,766	1,216	21.5	34,646	795	49.0
Ames, IA Metro Area	38,558	53.5	63.0	53.3	12,452	1,390	18.9	17,396	832	53.2
Anchorage, AK Metro Area	156,279	56.6	64.5	64.7	62,207	1,880	26.8	47,912	1,210	48.6
Ann Arbor, MI Metro Area	150,083	56.0	56.2	58.7	55,104	1,656	23.8	57,057	978	48.4
Anniston-Oxford-Jacksonville, AL Metro Area	53,323	72.7	61.9	69.4	14,583	1,005	21.1	13,570	711	56.2
Appleton, WI Metro Area	95,890	72.3	65.4	73.7	44,322	1,312	19.2	23,810	775	44.1
Asheville, NC Metro Area	218,917	65.5	58.2	66.6	69,897	1,189	27.1	61,816	777	55.3
Athens-Clarke County, GA Metro Area	84,691	57.9	56.8	53.5	24,928	1,204	28.1	35,701	799	57.9
Atlanta-Sandy Springs-Roswell, GA Metro Area ...	2,240,042	66.5	60.4	61.6	919,180	1,411	27.4	779,979	1,015	48.6
Atlantic City-Hammonton, NJ Metro Area	127,879	58.2	51.8	67.9	47,309	1,940	47.0	32,661	1,070	65.5
Auburn-Opelika, AL Metro Area	66,385	58.2	60.6	58.1	22,522	1,212	20.5	24,402	840	55.8
Augusta-Richmond County, GA-SC Metro Area	250,529	67.8	61.4	66.6	86,735	1,161	26.5	70,334	796	52.7
Austin-Round Rock, TX Metro Area	784,417	59.2	60.6	57.5	287,917	1,698	27.7	307,445	1,131	48.0
Bakersfield, CA Metro Area	293,589	72.0	61.7	56.6	105,985	1,403	32.5	114,282	906	52.4
Baltimore-Columbia-Towson, MD Metro Area	1,155,452	45.0	56.5	65.6	490,634	1,834	28.9	356,772	1,184	49.5
Bangor, ME Metro Area	74,332	64.2	56.0	68.6	23,653	1,167	24.8	18,555	738	54.3
Barnstable Town, MA Metro Area	162,116	82.4	59.5	77.4	46,341	1,811	43.5	22,010	1,187	53.2
Baton Rouge, LA Metro Area	345,319	67.2	58.1	69.5	123,678	1,310	23.2	91,686	850	52.7
Battle Creek, MI Metro Area	60,608	72.8	55.3	69.3	21,098	1,039	24.6	16,313	682	56.3
Bay City, MI Metro Area	47,964	78.4	58.5	76.9	16,541	987	23.2	9,892	626	40.8
Beaumont-Port Arthur, TX Metro Area	175,086	70.6	56.6	67.4	40,485	1,223	25.7	49,978	797	44.8
Beckley, WV Metro Area	57,522	72.1	52.3	72.9	15,539	937	25.1	13,274	599	48.5
Bellingham, WA Metro Area	93,263	64.8	64.9	63.7	33,879	1,616	30.5	29,042	930	55.4
Bend-Redmond, OR Metro Area	83,886	73.0	66.9	64.2	29,755	1,475	34.1	24,860	982	51.9
Billings, MT Metro Area	74,707	65.5	70.0	67.5	30,084	1,325	25.3	22,110	858	45.5
Binghamton, NY Metro Area	111,816	63.5	52.1	67.4	36,429	1,187	27.3	31,915	702	54.0
Birmingham-Hoover, AL Metro Area	510,137	70.2	59.9	68.9	189,968	1,240	24.4	137,264	809	50.7
Bismarck, ND Metro Area	58,103	59.1	65.8	67.8	22,504	1,423	15.2	17,758	796	41.6
Blacksburg-Christiansburg-Radford, VA Metro Area	79,371	62.4	65.1	61.8	25,290	1,193	24.1	26,529	846	53.1
Bloomington, IL Metro Area	78,827	63.4	61.7	65.8	32,023	1,391	14.6	24,920	817	47.1
Bloomington, IN Metro Area	70,027	55.7	58.4	56.9	23,093	1,191	22.9	27,004	833	60.4
Bloomsburg-Berwick, PA Metro Area	37,647	69.6	58.1	71.3	12,012	1,213	28.5	9,516	729	44.0
Boise City, ID Metro Area	260,644	76.2	64.3	68.4	120,316	1,217	26.8	77,505	849	49.7
Boston-Cambridge-Newton, MA-NH Metro Area	1,917,372	47.1	51.3	61.2	776,000	2,249	32.5	691,752	1,316	50.9
Boston, MA Metro Division	804,329	42.4	44.6	56.5	304,965	2,244	34.6	323,419	1,357	53.5
Cambridge-Newton-Framingham, MA Metro Division	930,989	48.2	53.8	62.8	385,593	2,317	31.8	324,558	1,324	48.7
Rockingham County-Strafford County, NH Metro Division	182,054	62.3	68.3	73.7	85,442	1,973	28.4	43,775	1,050	47.5
Boulder, CO Metro Area	132,448	59.1	62.8	60.0	53,109	1,783	24.9	49,815	1,287	57.9
Bowling Green, KY Metro Area	71,676	67.0	62.5	61.5	22,106	1,000	22.0	24,083	710	44.4
Bremerton-Silverdale, WA Metro Area	109,684	71.4	67.5	68.2	47,898	1,603	29.1	31,345	1,057	49.0
Bridgeport-Stamford-Norwalk, CT Metro Area	366,129	56.9	62.6	67.4	161,176	2,641	38.0	108,604	1,428	54.4
Brownsville-Harlingen, TX Metro Area	147,515	63.4	54.4	66.0	32,953	1,113	33.4	41,647	643	54.5
Brunswick, GA Metro Area	57,780	60.8	59.5	62.9	15,443	1,244	26.3	17,327	866	50.4
Buffalo-Cheektowaga-Niagara Falls, NY Metro Area	520,994	59.8	47.9	65.2	187,310	1,228	21.9	162,785	733	50.7
Burlington, NC Metro Area	68,485	65.9	61.3	62.6	23,321	1,133	29.5	23,578	743	57.7
Burlington-South Burlington, VT Metro Area	95,152	57.7	60.8	65.7	38,636	1,689	29.0	29,343	1,118	52.9
California-Lexington Park, MD Metro Area	43,632	73.5	71.9	70.8	19,754	1,900	27.2	11,393	1,361	40.6
Canton-Massillon, OH Metro Area	179,323	75.2	59.4	69.0	69,919	1,111	23.1	50,449	687	43.7
Cape Coral-Fort Myers, FL Metro Area	379,060	54.9	50.9	69.3	92,107	1,321	38.7	80,888	1,003	52.4
Cape Girardeau, MO-IL Metro Area	42,494	71.2	64.5	66.1	14,236	1,021	21.2	11,949	641	40.0
Carbondale-Marion, IL Metro Area	59,565	63.9	56.9	64.8	15,728	956	21.0	16,885	654	54.6
Carson City, NV Metro Area	23,448	52.4	53.2	54.3	7,128	1,363	37.1	10,366	837	45.1
Casper, WY Metro Area	36,077	63.4	66.2	62.0	11,967	1,309	25.4	12,360	812	38.9
Cedar Rapids, IA Metro Area	115,304	68.5	63.7	73.2	50,266	1,252	21.8	28,785	699	43.9
Chambersburg-Waynesboro, PA Metro Area	64,316	68.9	68.2	71.3	26,244	1,317	24.8	17,066	829	32.5
Champaign-Urbana, IL Metro Area	104,370	58.8	55.1	57.6	31,534	1,302	20.9	39,081	854	49.9
Charleston, WV Metro Area	108,087	67.1	51.0	68.9	30,742	940	19.6	29,441	692	40.2
Charleston-North Charleston, SC Metro Area	318,493	60.3	59.6	65.5	120,703	1,425	30.8	94,567	1,034	47.4
Charlotte-Concord-Gastonia, NC-SC Metro Area...	989,593	67.6	61.7	64.6	416,080	1,301	25.8	320,297	915	47.6
Charlottesville, VA Metro Area	101,909	65.6	64.3	65.2	37,465	1,570	29.9	30,631	1,106	47.4
Chattanooga, TN-GA Metro Area	239,343	70.3	61.8	67.1	84,353	1,159	24.1	68,947	744	46.8
Cheyenne, WY Metro Area	41,960	61.1	64.2	65.4	15,375	1,382	24.0	13,072	926	47.1

Table B-10. Housing Units, 2015—*Continued*

Metropolitan statistical area and division	Total housing units	1 unit detached, (percent)	With 2 or more vehicles available (percent of occupied units)	Owner-ship rate	Number	Median monthly owner costs (dollars)	Units with costs 30 percent or more of household income (percent)	Number	Median monthly rent (dollars)	Units with rent 30 percent or more of household income (percent)
					Owner-occupied			Renter-occupied		
					Housing units with a mortgage					
Chicago-Naperville-Elgin, IL-IN-WI Metro Area	3,812,007	52.0	51.8	63.2	1,502,035	1,770	32.2	1,275,844	1,012	50.7
Chicago-Naperville-Arlington Heights, IL Metro Division	2,956,628	47.1	48.3	61.3	1,123,641	1,824	33.8	1,040,875	1,033	51.0
Elgin, IL Metro Division	225,914	66.2	66.4	68.2	101,972	1,733	29.1	67,530	1,008	49.0
Gary, IN Metro Division	297,399	72.9	58.3	70.4	125,057	1,225	25.2	78,779	847	49.6
Lake County-Kenosha County, IL-WI Metro Division	332,066	66.7	66.4	70.9	151,365	1,926	27.9	88,660	1,015	49.8
Chico, CA Metro Area	98,040	60.5	62.9	57.5	30,397	1,523	34.1	36,215	942	61.3
Cincinnati, OH-KY-IN Metro Area	922,355	65.2	59.6	65.4	380,037	1,360	23.3	288,318	775	46.1
Clarksville, TN-KY Metro Area	115,550	68.0	62.2	56.3	38,379	1,102	29.3	44,294	874	45.7
Cleveland, TN Metro Area	51,038	70.1	63.4	62.7	16,444	1,135	25.8	17,317	707	50.0
Cleveland-Elyria, OH Metro Area	957,518	65.3	52.3	64.5	349,827	1,294	25.7	301,225	746	48.2
Coeur d'Alene, ID Metro Area	67,022	71.9	68.5	69.9	27,621	1,199	33.5	17,683	865	52.5
College Station-Bryan, TX Metro Area	102,323	53.4	58.6	49.5	24,802	1,430	25.4	45,686	860	55.8
Colorado Springs, CO Metro Area	281,288	67.3	65.1	61.8	120,943	1,454	28.3	99,818	1,049	51.1
Columbia, MO Metro Area	74,446	60.0	58.0	55.8	27,152	1,248	20.6	30,570	769	52.7
Columbia, SC Metro Area	346,611	64.5	60.0	66.6	128,185	1,181	25.5	101,129	857	51.4
Columbus, GA-AL Metro Area	131,629	63.7	53.1	52.2	38,728	1,234	32.9	54,000	818	52.3
Columbus, IN Metro Area	33,735	72.8	64.4	71.2	-	1,067	22.1	8,966	844	30.1
Columbus, OH Metro Area	845,563	61.9	59.5	60.5	334,813	1,420	24.1	305,013	869	45.8
Corpus Christi, TX Metro Area	190,036	67.4	56.6	57.3	46,219	1,330	26.5	68,941	924	48.2
Corvallis, OR Metro Area	37,695	59.3	60.5	58.2	11,860	1,606	23.5	14,661	885	53.7
Crestview-Fort Walton Beach-Destin, FL Metro Area	144,261	57.8	60.3	62.9	36,387	1,400	30.0	38,082	1,041	52.7
Cumberland, MD-WV Metro Area	46,250	70.1	54.5	65.7	12,417	1,023	22.7	13,418	659	53.8
Dallas-Fort Worth-Arlington, TX Metro Area	2,685,922	63.6	62.5	59.3	978,465	1,585	26.8	1,010,127	992	47.2
Dallas-Plano-Irving, TX Metro Division	1,777,705	61.7	61.5	57.7	643,805	1,652	28.4	699,696	1,009	46.8
Fort Worth-Arlington, TX Metro Division	908,217	67.3	64.4	62.4	334,660	1,464	23.9	310,431	963	48.3
Dalton, GA Metro Area	55,375	62.6	64.9	64.6	17,587	1,043	25.3	17,207	673	40.4
Danville, IL Metro Area	35,941	77.0	51.5	67.0	10,190	937	14.9	10,201	649	38.3
Daphne-Fairhope-Foley, AL Metro Area	108,580	61.5	62.0	73.7	30,606	1,277	25.7	19,037	914	43.8
Davenport-Moline-Rock Island, IA-IL Metro Area	168,737	73.5	60.8	70.4	67,558	1,155	19.1	46,134	712	43.9
Dayton, OH Metro Area	367,957	70.0	56.3	63.0	137,407	1,198	24.4	122,267	748	46.9
Decatur, AL Metro Area	66,748	69.8	64.3	73.1	24,044	1,059	25.4	16,302	597	40.0
Decatur, IL Metro Area	50,307	78.3	52.5	67.5	16,143	1,025	17.9	14,439	630	46.5
Deltona-Daytona Beach-Ormond Beach, FL Metro Area	307,028	66.9	51.0	70.4	91,655	1,179	38.9	73,705	958	58.8
Denver-Aurora-Lakewood, CO Metro Area	1,132,728	59.4	63.1	62.9	515,339	1,647	26.3	398,752	1,184	48.5
Des Moines-West Des Moines, IA Metro Area	258,084	65.8	63.0	68.4	117,254	1,335	19.7	76,548	825	45.2
Detroit-Warren-Dearborn, MI Metro Area	1,895,784	70.3	55.5	68.0	699,075	1,355	25.3	535,144	871	52.0
Detroit-Dearborn-Livonia, MI Metro Division	814,338	69.6	46.5	61.3	217,364	1,219	28.7	258,276	809	56.5
Warren-Troy-Farmington Hills, MI Metro Division	1,081,446	70.7	61.4	72.5	481,711	1,422	23.8	276,868	931	48.0
Dothan, AL Metro Area	68,310	68.1	59.4	66.4	20,734	1,005	23.7	18,786	671	46.1
Dover, DE Metro Area	68,693	66.4	64.4	67.8	27,416	1,414	28.6	20,148	995	52.9
Dubuque, IA Metro Area	40,589	70.2	60.7	71.9	15,778	1,232	19.0	10,630	693	42.4
Duluth, MN-WI Metro Area	142,158	75.4	60.0	72.1	50,656	1,175	25.2	32,411	686	44.5
Durham-Chapel Hill, NC Metro Area	235,649	58.5	57.0	58.3	85,799	1,407	25.6	89,792	915	46.8
East Stroudsburg, PA Metro Area	80,718	83.8	67.1	77.3	30,656	1,672	44.6	12,614	977	54.4
Eau Claire, WI Metro Area	71,011	69.4	63.2	69.0	28,084	1,202	22.9	19,796	763	50.2
El Centro, CA Metro Area	57,229	61.7	62.5	56.3	17,825	1,408	36.0	19,730	783	60.8
Elizabethtown-Fort Knox, KY Metro Area	63,708	66.2	62.8	65.4	24,671	1,042	26.1	19,686	748	43.2
Elkhart-Goshen, IN Metro Area	78,023	70.9	60.7	69.0	29,909	1,019	21.0	21,214	729	45.9
Elmira, NY Metro Area	38,343	69.3	55.9	71.1	14,935	1,027	19.9	9,990	750	50.7
El Paso, TX Metro Area	290,930	67.2	59.5	61.5	93,550	1,125	29.9	100,600	757	43.9
Enid, OK Metro Area	26,862			69.9	8,021			7,160	836	
Erie, PA Metro Area	120,096	64.2	50.5	64.1	42,163	1,104	21.1	39,587	701	48.8
Eugene, OR Metro Area	159,311	60.8	57.1	58.3	55,200	1,436	33.6	61,142	881	57.3
Evansville, IN-KY Metro Area	140,556	72.4	57.7	66.6	53,453	1,054	20.7	41,774	696	50.6
Fairbanks, AK Metro Area	41,627	59.3	64.7	57.2	-	1,811	31.7	15,188	1,194	52.2
Fargo, ND-MN Metro Area	103,691	46.3	60.4	54.5	35,429	1,406	19.0	43,750	756	40.7
Farmington, NM Metro Area	49,659	56.4	64.3	71.3	14,186	1,122	23.3	12,336	770	48.3
Fayetteville, NC Metro Area	164,590	65.0	55.6	52.2	48,084	1,164	33.0	65,624	888	53.4
Fayetteville-Springdale-Rogers, AR-MO Metro Area	209,035	68.8	63.4	60.4	74,655	1,150	21.0	75,550	749	39.5
Flagstaff, AZ Metro Area	64,437	60.6	64.4	61.1	14,765	1,537	26.4	17,861	1,093	53.1
Flint, MI Metro Area	190,896	74.7	52.9	70.5	70,206	1,131	30.0	48,163	727	50.2
Florence, SC Metro Area	89,429	63.2	53.7	65.4	28,884	990	30.3	27,683	699	49.0
Florence-Muscle Shoals, AL Metro Area	70,686	71.6	63.1	69.8	21,716	969	26.6	18,314	640	52.4
Fond du Lac, WI Metro Area	44,625	72.2	63.7	74.2	18,528	1,250	23.2	10,411	667	41.2
Fort Collins, CO Metro Area	140,887	67.5	69.7	64.5	58,657	1,558	27.1	45,872	1,112	55.0
Fort Smith, AR-OK Metro Area	123,523	71.2	60.1	67.5	39,964	945	26.2	34,901	637	44.8
Fort Wayne, IN Metro Area	181,528	74.5	60.1	69.5	77,300	988	17.6	50,626	715	42.5
Fresno, CA Metro Area	326,015	67.7	57.1	52.1	112,019	1,455	33.9	145,790	897	57.8
Gadsden, AL Metro Area	47,509	77.0	61.2	74.5	14,696	977	28.0	10,031	650	39.1
Gainesville, FL Metro Area	121,741	52.3	53.2	55.5	33,589	1,335	26.0	45,485	858	54.8
Gainesville, GA Metro Area	70,098	72.1	67.4	64.5	27,066	1,303	33.3	22,707	901	47.6

Table B-10. Housing Units, 2015—*Continued*

Metropolitan statistical area and division	Total housing units	1 unit detached, (percent)	With 2 or more vehicles available (percent of occupied units)	Owner-occupied Owner-ship rate	Housing units with a mortgage Number	Median monthly owner costs (dollars)	Units with costs 30 percent or more of household income (percent)	Renter-occupied Number	Median monthly rent (dollars)	Units with rent 30 percent or more of household income (percent)
Gettysburg, PA Metro Area	41,454	75.7	70.6	78.7	19,101	1,526	29.5	8,188	840	53.7
Glens Falls, NY Metro Area	68,219	73.3	58.4	71.4	21,170	1,358	34.7	13,978	841	50.9
Goldsboro, NC Metro Area	53,289	56.9	54.9	61.5	14,706	1,135	24.5	18,270	718	46.4
Grand Forks, ND-MN Metro Area	46,960	54.3	62.2	55.1	13,701	1,297	17.8	18,937	812	47.1
Grand Island, NE Metro Area	34,997	72.1	65.3	64.7	11,579	1,212	21.1	11,196	682	41.7
Grand Junction, CO Metro Area	64,245	69.3	62.2	67.0	26,339	1,243	29.3	19,494	897	50.9
Grand Rapids-Wyoming, MI Metro Area	410,633	68.8	62.9	72.1	177,112	1,187	21.2	106,817	794	47.4
Grants Pass, OR Metro Area	38,145	68.3	63.3	65.6	12,394	1,244	39.2	12,352	838	57.8
Great Falls, MT Metro Area	37,932	65.2	60.9	61.2	11,056	1,216	20.1	13,350	713	50.8
Greeley, CO Metro Area	102,606	74.1	73.0	70.3	52,605	1,423	24.2	29,026	983	46.8
Green Bay, WI Metro Area	141,101	67.0	63.4	68.2	55,819	1,291	21.6	40,584	711	45.0
Greensboro-High Point, NC Metro Area	329,927	63.9	59.7	61.3	119,101	1,149	25.9	112,578	768	48.3
Greenville, NC Metro Area	77,329	49.4	58.3	52.3	24,396	1,278	28.2	32,607	759	57.5
Greenville-Anderson-Mauldin, SC Metro Area	372,542	67.4	61.2	66.9	135,498	1,112	24.4	110,249	768	45.8
Gulfport-Biloxi-Pascagoula, MS Metro Area	176,195	67.1	59.0	61.8	47,557	1,170	31.8	55,910	819	47.5
Hagerstown-Martinsburg, MD-WV Metro Area	108,148	63.2	61.2	68.7	45,099	1,377	29.4	30,436	900	41.4
Hammond, LA Metro Area	53,142	62.2	55.8	64.3	16,280	1,067	27.1	16,508	794	58.8
Hanford-Corcoran, CA Metro Area	45,251	65.9	60.4	48.2	14,360	1,347	30.4	22,118	892	50.0
Harrisburg-Carlisle, PA Metro Area	246,280	57.1	58.0	67.3	96,831	1,375	25.0	73,816	884	45.4
Harrisonburg, VA Metro Area	52,901	61.0	62.5	59.9	17,217	1,244	25.2	19,101	801	51.3
Hartford-West Hartford-East Hartford, CT Metro Area	508,982	58.5	57.9	66.5	214,832	1,910	29.4	155,790	1,039	48.8
Hattiesburg, MS Metro Area	61,904	63.6	56.6	59.6	16,037	1,154	22.2	22,117	736	61.4
Hickory-Lenoir-Morganton, NC Metro Area	162,285	65.2	62.7	70.3	56,544	962	26.8	41,617	615	45.5
Hilton Head Island-Bluffton-Beaufort, SC Metro Area	106,442	59.6	58.5	70.1	30,537	1,494	42.5	23,561	1,055	50.4
Hinesville, GA Metro Area	34,902	54.8	55.0	49.7	9,080	1,058	38.2	14,011	911	60.0
Homosassa Springs, FL Metro Area	77,726	68.9	53.3	81.4	22,227	975	35.3	11,249	728	59.1
Hot Springs, AR Metro Area	50,539	64.4	58.7	65.8	13,927	1,035	32.0	13,736	707	61.1
Houma-Thibodaux, LA Metro Area	84,864	69.5	59.8	72.4	26,859	1,204	25.6	21,430	724	45.8
Houston-The Woodlands-Sugar Land, TX Metro Area	2,502,275	61.8	60.4	58.7	832,432	1,580	25.5	947,698	978	48.3
Huntington-Ashland, WV-KY-OH Metro Area	165,093	70.1	56.1	70.8	50,082	1,023	19.7	41,153	653	54.6
Huntsville, AL Metro Area	192,463	72.2	63.8	68.9	78,098	1,180	19.3	53,655	758	48.3
Idaho Falls, ID Metro Area	51,115	73.5	69.8	70.2	20,258	1,150	25.8	13,606	776	42.0
Indianapolis-Carmel-Anderson, IN Metro Area	842,013	68.1	58.6	64.2	352,902	1,205	20.4	270,446	825	49.4
Iowa City, IA Metro Area	69,367	51.2	57.6	59.9	24,907	1,418	19.6	25,715	868	56.9
Ithaca, NY Metro Area	42,265	51.2	46.5	53.9	12,711	1,593	28.0	17,572	1,080	55.3
Jackson, MI Metro Area	69,023	76.8	57.0	70.5	26,369	1,108	21.3	17,483	696	49.6
Jackson, MS Metro Area	239,467	71.3	59.3	67.1	85,647	1,175	27.6	69,222	834	54.3
Jackson, TN Metro Area	56,221	78.7	60.9	66.6	17,954	1,134	24.6	16,455	811	53.6
Jacksonville, FL Metro Area	622,796	63.1	57.6	63.2	227,928	1,344	30.3	197,165	994	51.0
Jacksonville, NC Metro Area	76,912	63.0	64.6	51.9	23,572	1,184	39.0	31,154	937	56.2
Janesville-Beloit, WI Metro Area	68,314	73.1	62.4	69.7	30,795	1,205	22.9	19,718	741	47.4
Jefferson City, MO Metro Area	64,148	71.7	63.6	68.8	21,075	1,113	21.0	17,310	608	36.8
Johnson City, TN Metro Area	95,781	67.5	62.2	69.7	29,949	994	30.9	25,159	662	49.3
Johnstown, PA Metro Area	65,142	75.0	53.6	73.2	19,614	1,013	25.6	15,315	596	44.9
Jonesboro, AR Metro Area	54,902	66.4	53.9	58.8	16,605	953	21.4	20,156	678	50.8
Joplin, MO Metro Area	76,045	78.8	63.9	65.2	24,768	1,024	23.2	23,453	739	41.4
Kahului-Wailuku-Lahaina, HI Metro Area	71,839	55.0	64.0	58.5	20,811	2,225	46.2	21,647	1,416	50.5
Kalamazoo-Portage, MI Metro Area	147,143	67.2	59.1	67.1	55,335	1,224	22.1	42,713	716	45.4
Kankakee, IL Metro Area	45,182	70.0	58.6	67.9	16,878	1,295	26.0	12,424	846	47.7
Kansas City, MO-KS Metro Area	890,891	70.5	60.9	65.3	361,352	1,380	21.9	282,837	859	42.2
Kennewick-Richland, WA Metro Area	99,751	62.3	70.0	67.4	41,247	1,356	19.3	30,791	825	46.1
Killeen-Temple, TX Metro Area	171,503	65.0	59.7	52.9	49,430	1,254	28.1	71,435	858	49.1
Kingsport-Bristol-Bristol, TN-VA Metro Area	147,362	68.3	62.7	70.8	42,767	957	24.0	37,092	621	43.6
Kingston, NY Metro Area	83,808	70.4	59.6	68.5	27,404	1,863	37.8	21,941	996	62.6
Knoxville, TN Metro Area	389,246	69.0	62.6	67.8	132,537	1,159	23.5	110,685	756	47.5
Kokomo, IN Metro Area	38,748	74.6	55.8	68.4	14,791	931	17.0	10,976	640	53.4
La Crosse-Onalaska, WI-MN Metro Area	58,103	64.3	64.1	66.8	22,652	1,298	25.4	17,912	746	49.2
Lafayette, LA Metro Area	204,106	66.2	58.2	68.4	62,405	1,166	21.2	57,089	733	47.6
Lafayette-West Lafayette, IN Metro Area	88,739	63.9	57.3	56.2	31,800	1,093	19.8	35,480	782	49.9
Lake Charles, LA Metro Area	90,582	69.6	55.4	68.7	26,687	1,080	23.3	24,962	764	49.5
Lake Havasu City-Kingman, AZ Metro Area	112,850	60.3	54.4	67.2	29,897	1,007	32.5	27,514	742	45.0
Lakeland-Winter Haven, FL Metro Area	284,364	61.0	52.4	67.1	81,219	1,176	32.2	74,703	890	54.1
Lancaster, PA Metro Area	207,135	54.0	59.2	67.4	82,458	1,451	28.7	64,479	941	48.6
Lansing-East Lansing, MI Metro Area	200,399	66.9	56.8	64.2	79,067	1,237	22.8	65,807	790	48.9
Laredo, TX Metro Area	79,704	65.0	61.1	61.9	24,618	1,270	38.1	27,533	776	57.2
Las Cruces, NM Metro Area	84,640	60.3	64.2	62.9	25,661	1,161	30.6	27,706	741	49.5
Las Vegas-Henderson-Paradise, NV Metro Area	871,866	58.3	52.5	51.6	269,577	1,380	30.7	358,783	1,007	51.7
Lawrence, KS Metro Area	48,537	57.4	62.6	53.8	15,313	1,366	19.9	19,773	827	54.9
Lawton, OK Metro Area	54,704	69.7	58.6	53.5	13,537	1,151	22.6	20,297	766	40.8
Lebanon, PA Metro Area	56,479	59.7	59.3	67.8	21,559	1,295	27.8	17,129	786	43.6
Lewiston, ID-WA Metro Area	27,504	68.4	69.2	70.8	9,956	1,232	19.8	7,405	727	44.4

Table B-10.   Housing Units, 2015—*Continued*

				Housing Units					
				Owner-occupied				Renter-occupied	
					Housing units with a mortgage				
Metropolitan statistical area and division	Total housing units	1 unit detached, (percent)	With 2 or more vehicles available (percent of occupied units)	Owner- ship rate	Number	Median monthly owner costs (dollars)	Units with costs 30 percent or more of household income (percent)	Number	Median monthly rent (dollars)	Units with rent 30 percent or more of household income (percent)
Lewiston-Auburn, ME Metro Area......................	49,096	60.1	55.1	63.0	19,855	1,266	28.1	16,715	721	46.7
Lexington-Fayette, KY Metro Area......................	216,472	64.8	57.7	56.2	77,419	1,207	21.1	87,377	803	47.1
Lima, OH Metro Area	44,802	74.0	58.5	65.9	16,053	1,090	21.8	13,703	642	50.2
Lincoln, NE Metro Area	133,626	61.6	59.8	59.2	51,339	1,316	19.1	51,894	767	48.1
Little Rock-North Little Rock-Conway, AR Metro Area	320,504	67.2	58.0	63.1	111,357	1,168	23.0	104,478	807	49.6
Logan, UT-ID Metro Area	44,286	66.7	70.0	65.5	18,410	1,224	26.0	14,138	705	43.1
Longview, TX Metro Area	89,809	69.7	65.4	66.0	24,237	1,172	21.9	25,955	779	47.4
Longview, WA Metro Area...............................	43,567	73.7	67.0	66.2	18,479	1,364	31.4	13,602	820	48.3
Los Angeles-Long Beach-Anaheim, CA Metro Area	4,585,390	49.3	58.8	47.9	1,495,615	2,331	43.1	2,250,279	1,348	58.6
Anaheim-Santa Ana-Irvine, CA Metro Division..	1,081,042	50.3	67.2	56.6	413,103	2,523	39.5	443,592	1,624	57.7
Los Angeles-Long Beach-Glendale, CA Metro Division	3,504,348	49.0	56.2	45.1	1,082,512	2,261	44.4	1,806,687	1,279	58.8
Louisville/Jefferson County, KY-IN Metro Area......	549,573	69.3	57.8	66.4	217,747	1,180	23.7	166,943	777	46.3
Lubbock, TX Metro Area	128,772	67.2	56.9	54.6	32,751	1,236	21.3	51,208	834	52.1
Lynchburg, VA Metro Area	115,539	67.0	65.2	68.3	41,556	1,159	21.3	31,897	759	56.2
Macon, GA Metro Area...................................	102,735	66.7	54.8	62.0	30,672	1,168	29.5	32,827	751	58.6
Madera, CA Metro Area..................................	50,101	78.9	63.1	61.8	18,299	1,488	31.4	17,277	947	56.5
Madison, WI Metro Area.................................	278,462	57.1	59.5	60.6	113,289	1,639	22.6	104,111	933	46.2
Manchester-Nashua, NH Metro Area..................	168,089	57.0	64.5	66.5	77,092	1,943	29.5	52,528	1,107	44.7
Manhattan, KS Metro Area.............................	39,373	51.6	65.9	50.4	11,327	1,382	23.1	17,251	930	48.8
Mankato-North Mankato, MN Metro Area	40,661	61.2	63.0	66.6	16,209	1,306	24.5	12,833	782	52.9
Mansfield, OH Metro Area..............................	54,204	71.7	57.3	67.9	17,529	962	24.4	15,064	640	41.4
McAllen-Edinburg-Mission, TX Metro Area..........	264,607	65.2	58.0	69.5	67,973	1,078	36.6	68,851	690	51.0
Medford, OR Metro Area.................................	92,845	62.3	61.2	61.0	30,663	1,401	37.4	32,726	882	59.4
Memphis, TN-MS-AR Metro Area	566,812	69.5	55.6	59.7	194,643	1,244	28.2	199,021	852	52.1
Merced, CA Metro Area..................................	84,338	76.2	62.5	51.2	28,307	1,362	35.8	38,622	874	57.7
Miami-Fort Lauderdale-West Palm Beach, FL Metro Area	2,508,362	41.5	50.7	58.5	726,708	1,676	42.5	862,134	1,208	63.9
Fort Lauderdale-Pompano Beach-Deerfield Beach, FL Metro Division	818,697	40.5	52.3	61.5	262,161	1,695	41.5	259,614	1,256	62.4
Miami-Miami Beach-Kendall, FL Metro Division	1,010,631	40.0	49.1	50.6	268,784	1,669	46.5	423,866	1,162	66.5
West Palm Beach-Boca Raton-Delray Beach, FL Metro Division..............................	679,034	45.0	51.3	67.3	195,763	1,664	38.3	178,654	1,241	59.9
Michigan City-La Porte, IN Metro Area................	48,768	75.5	57.5	69.9	19,056	1,043	28.2	12,977	694	49.3
Midland, MI Metro Area	36,465	75.6	62.5	75.5	15,550	1,170	19.4	8,069	739	46.1
Midland, TX Metro Area	61,462	67.6	68.4	70.9	22,933	1,661	22.6	16,824	1,196	44.5
Milwaukee-Waukesha-West Allis, WI Metro Area..	673,012	54.3	54.1	58.9	254,058	1,524	26.4	258,303	848	48.8
Minneapolis-St. Paul-Bloomington, MN-WI Metro Area	1,425,844	61.1	61.9	68.9	671,476	1,601	22.6	421,376	979	47.5
Missoula, MT Metro Area................................	51,865	58.8	57.9	58.7	16,190	1,482	30.9	19,786	770	50.0
Mobile, AL Metro Area	182,024	71.7	55.9	65.4	59,790	1,118	27.0	52,910	797	54.4
Modesto, CA Metro Area.................................	180,748	74.7	63.9	56.5	68,287	1,537	34.3	74,883	1,025	54.4
Monroe, LA Metro Area..................................	79,148	63.7	49.9	61.6	20,024	992	22.8	24,974	697	55.3
Monroe, MI Metro Area..................................	63,643	77.4	65.7	80.1	31,573	1,185	25.9	11,737	731	50.2
Montgomery, AL Metro Area............................	165,532	71.2	57.0	63.1	57,760	1,138	23.9	53,274	819	53.7
Morgantown, WV Metro Area...........................	59,602	55.6	54.8	62.8	14,665	1,154	15.3	18,697	865	56.7
Morristown, TN Metro Area.............................	50,707	70.3	65.1	67.0	15,060	985	27.4	14,688	660	50.9
Mount Vernon-Anacortes, WA Metro Area...........	52,216	74.4	70.1	66.4	19,529	1,623	32.3	16,135	952	54.6
Muncie, IN Metro Area	52,482	74.4	60.1	64.5	17,767	913	18.3	16,077	724	59.0
Muskegon, MI Metro Area	73,317	77.4	60.3	73.3	27,995	984	22.2	16,861	714	50.5
Myrtle Beach-Conway-North Myrtle Beach, SC-NC Metro Area	279,205	52.1	61.3	71.1	69,823	1,234	34.5	50,479	873	55.1
Napa, CA Metro Area	55,480	66.7	65.0	61.8	19,881	2,341	35.4	18,954	1,516	56.1
Naples-Immokalee-Marco Island, FL Metro Area ..	206,384	40.8	55.1	72.2	47,787	1,688	37.5	37,492	1,177	53.6
Nashville-Davidson—Murfreesboro—Franklin, TN Metro Area....................................	744,743	65.7	64.3	65.7	308,832	1,340	25.9	235,531	917	46.3
New Bern, NC Metro Area...............................	57,959	65.3	55.7	61.3	19,938	1,243	30.9	19,719	842	51.8
New Haven-Milford, CT Metro Area....................	362,707	53.7	52.9	61.5	135,895	1,913	34.0	124,604	1,070	55.3
New Orleans-Metairie, LA Metro Area................	555,769	60.7	49.7	60.2	166,158	1,423	31.3	191,901	920	56.7
New York-Newark-Jersey City, NY-NJ-PA Metro Area............................	7,892,766	36.4	37.2	50.8	2,361,371	2,604	42.4	3,503,567	1,308	54.1
Dutchess County-Putnam County, NY Metro Division	157,571	65.6	59.8	70.8	67,337	2,222	37.7	40,983	1,169	55.0
Nassau County-Suffolk County, NY Metro Division	1,037,547	77.5	64.6	79.9	488,277	2,823	44.4	184,790	1,605	60.6
Newark, NJ-PA Metro Division	984,291	52.8	53.9	61.6	379,230	2,570	38.0	340,187	1,172	54.2
New York-Jersey City-White Plains, NY-NJ Metro Division..........................	5,713,357	25.3	28.9	43.3	1,426,527	2,539	43.2	2,937,607	1,314	53.7
Niles-Benton Harbor, MI Metro Area	76,802	75.4	55.0	69.0	26,052	1,109	26.0	19,937	688	46.2
North Port-Sarasota-Bradenton, FL Metro Area	414,730	53.7	49.8	70.6	107,761	1,401	34.2	92,019	1,056	53.6
Norwich-New London, CT Metro Area.................	121,660	63.8	57.9	65.1	44,843	1,782	31.5	36,770	1,061	56.4
Ocala, FL Metro Area....................................	163,801	65.2	44.1	76.0	44,141	1,016	35.1	30,015	776	53.5
Ocean City, NJ Metro Area	99,005	51.9	52.1	76.5	17,132	1,907	49.3	9,100	1,072	60.7
Odessa, TX Metro Area	57,024	61.0	63.1	68.7	18,130	1,341	23.8	16,271	1,045	34.5
Ogden-Clearfield, UT Metro Area	215,344	74.5	73.4	74.1	107,383	1,376	23.0	52,073	886	44.8

Table B-10. Housing Units, 2015—*Continued*

Metropolitan statistical area and division	Total housing units	1 unit detached, (percent)	With 2 or more vehicles available (percent of occupied units)	Owner-ship rate	Housing units with a mortgage — Number	Housing units with a mortgage — Median monthly owner costs (dollars)	Housing units with a mortgage — Units with costs 30 percent or more of household income (percent)	Renter-occupied — Number	Renter-occupied — Median monthly rent (dollars)	Renter-occupied — Units with rent 30 percent or more of household income (percent)
Oklahoma City, OK Metro Area	564,489	72.2	62.0	63.9	200,440	1,262	25.9	182,167	821	46.2
Olympia-Tumwater, WA Metro Area	112,535	68.0	63.8	64.4	45,544	1,601	28.3	37,477	1,044	49.4
Omaha-Council Bluffs, NE-IA Metro Area	377,960	71.5	62.0	65.8	162,613	1,391	22.2	120,272	835	44.2
Orlando-Kissimmee-Sanford, FL Metro Area	988,969	58.7	56.1	59.6	335,214	1,357	32.4	341,491	1,070	56.5
Oshkosh-Neenah, WI Metro Area	74,531	65.4	60.5	64.7	27,553	1,216	26.1	24,606	695	44.1
Owensboro, KY Metro Area	50,821	77.8	60.1	71.4	18,232	999	15.7	13,262	623	45.7
Oxnard-Thousand Oaks-Ventura, CA Metro Area	285,889	63.6	69.6	63.3	127,747	2,351	37.9	98,964	1,564	57.5
Palm Bay-Melbourne-Titusville, FL Metro Area	273,134	63.9	51.9	70.0	89,737	1,213	30.5	67,657	976	50.5
Panama City, FL Metro Area	109,937	51.5	54.8	62.1	25,449	1,379	30.1	28,168	983	50.9
Parkersburg-Vienna, WV Metro Area	43,659	71.5	55.2	68.7	13,608	888	21.5	12,335	642	52.8
Pensacola-Ferry Pass-Brent, FL Metro Area	207,635	69.4	59.5	64.3	71,036	1,234	28.2	63,429	911	45.7
Peoria, IL Metro Area	165,966	77.9	58.2	72.4	66,154	1,194	21.0	41,618	739	41.9
Philadelphia-Camden-Wilmington, PA-NJ-DE-MD Metro Area	2,455,550	44.5	52.2	67.2	1,005,651	1,809	32.0	733,186	1,062	52.8
Camden, NJ Metro Division	496,626	62.3	59.9	71.8	226,804	1,964	36.0	127,767	1,105	54.9
Montgomery County-Bucks County-Chester County, PA Metro Division	772,592	59.1	64.9	74.2	373,115	2,054	28.7	189,132	1,213	48.7
Philadelphia, PA Metro Division	894,525	17.6	33.7	57.2	279,010	1,435	33.8	335,962	962	55.5
Wilmington, DE-MD-NJ Metro Division	291,807	58.4	58.4	69.6	126,722	1,620	30.7	80,325	1,073	48.2
Phoenix-Mesa-Scottsdale, AZ Metro Area	1,860,113	64.5	56.1	60.5	665,975	1,388	28.9	635,678	986	48.7
Pine Bluff, AR Metro Area	42,522	68.8	54.1	64.8	10,603	948	30.5	11,996	688	50.6
Pittsburgh, PA Metro Area	1,107,498	67.0	53.7	69.2	401,776	1,238	21.8	305,188	756	45.5
Pittsfield, MA Metro Area	68,406	62.4	50.1	65.6	24,140	1,437	33.7	19,075	821	54.9
Pocatello, ID Metro Area	33,456	63.9	65.7	62.5	11,010	1,090	26.9	11,326	655	46.3
Portland-South Portland, ME Metro Area	267,097	66.7	60.4	70.6	103,557	1,610	29.6	62,471	958	47.5
Portland-Vancouver-Hillsboro, OR-WA Metro Area	960,500	62.1	58.3	61.1	399,066	1,700	30.8	350,612	1,071	50.0
Port St. Lucie, FL Metro Area	217,326	63.2	51.2	72.9	63,235	1,347	39.1	47,055	997	54.9
Prescott, AZ Metro Area	113,085	65.7	62.9	70.4	39,522	1,222	39.9	28,100	868	47.1
Providence-Warwick, RI-MA Metro Area	694,169	53.8	53.1	59.8	259,043	1,747	31.8	250,379	910	47.4
Provo-Orem, UT Metro Area	165,983	67.0	77.5	67.4	78,739	1,470	23.4	51,545	956	46.1
Pueblo, CO Metro Area	70,142	73.9	60.6	63.4	25,301	1,160	30.6	22,639	752	60.5
Punta Gorda, FL Metro Area	101,781	64.3	49.4	75.9	25,164	1,188	36.2	17,540	932	57.0
Racine, WI Metro Area	82,334	69.9	61.3	69.8	34,756	1,408	21.1	22,668	800	54.3
Raleigh, NC Metro Area	509,680	62.6	65.7	64.6	229,349	1,460	22.2	166,642	971	45.4
Rapid City, SD Metro Area	63,314	64.2	69.3	72.2	25,824	1,321	27.3	16,312	805	44.4
Reading, PA Metro Area	164,907	54.8	61.1	71.6	69,961	1,438	29.2	43,168	865	53.6
Redding, CA Metro Area	78,112	68.6	57.5	61.5	26,276	1,446	39.6	26,853	919	51.5
Reno, NV Metro Area	191,187	59.4	59.3	56.0	67,026	1,535	29.9	76,883	920	45.7
Richmond, VA Metro Area	521,123	68.8	61.6	64.0	221,893	1,486	28.2	173,709	1,019	50.7
Riverside-San Bernardino-Ontario, CA Metro Area	1,538,540	68.8	65.4	60.8	586,210	1,719	40.8	526,394	1,166	58.7
Roanoke, VA Metro Area	145,389	71.8	61.1	67.3	52,784	1,171	27.2	41,588	803	41.4
Rochester, MN Metro Area	90,304	69.5	63.5	75.8	40,273	1,352	18.7	20,176	802	46.1
Rochester, NY Metro Area	475,834	65.7	54.0	67.1	186,781	1,322	24.7	140,565	833	53.0
Rockford, IL Metro Area	145,399	71.6	55.9	67.8	59,369	1,218	25.8	42,614	729	44.9
Rocky Mount, NC Metro Area	67,080	59.3	56.1	60.7	22,396	1,108	33.9	22,599	688	56.0
Rome, GA Metro Area	40,413	70.3	56.3	57.7	11,647	1,094	29.3	14,777	690	52.5
Sacramento—Roseville—Arden-Arcade, CA Metro Area	889,065	68.4	60.4	58.6	343,477	1,833	34.3	335,139	1,109	54.2
Saginaw, MI Metro Area	86,824	73.7	53.5	70.6	28,927	1,074	25.2	22,722	720	54.8
St. Cloud, MN Metro Area	79,770	69.3	65.0	65.4	31,165	1,298	28.2	25,844	751	43.9
St. George, UT Metro Area	63,957	69.6	66.7	66.4	21,696	1,300	32.9	17,635	936	41.7
St. Joseph, MO-KS Metro Area	53,365	73.0	62.7	67.7	16,263	1,065	23.0	15,006	728	38.1
St. Louis, MO-IL Metro Area	1,241,719	69.9	58.8	68.3	500,607	1,337	24.0	351,479	839	47.8
Salem, OR Metro Area	154,626	63.0	63.0	60.1	56,309	1,389	29.1	57,675	817	50.1
Salinas, CA Metro Area	140,491	61.4	64.7	49.1	41,221	2,029	43.1	64,647	1,290	53.7
Salisbury, MD-DE Metro Area	240,002	60.7	60.5	71.4	65,408	1,387	33.2	44,058	981	51.8
Salt Lake City, UT Metro Area	401,482	63.8	66.2	66.2	180,785	1,462	24.1	127,414	964	44.6
San Angelo, TX Metro Area	49,153	67.7	56.8	60.7	13,962	1,243	24.7	17,736	883	52.7
San Antonio-New Braunfels, TX Metro Area	871,757	67.4	59.1	60.8	289,883	1,369	27.1	310,037	926	45.9
San Diego-Carlsbad, CA Metro Area	1,194,494	50.6	62.1	52.0	415,532	2,287	41.3	534,145	1,427	56.7
San Francisco-Oakland-Hayward, CA Metro Area	1,782,375	50.2	54.8	53.5	656,117	2,720	37.8	786,407	1,623	47.6
Oakland-Hayward-Berkeley, CA Metro Division	1,004,654	59.1	61.2	57.2	406,987	2,487	36.5	412,276	1,525	51.2
San Francisco-Redwood City-South San Francisco, CA Metro Division	665,048	35.0	43.7	45.9	201,455	3,131	39.8	335,536	1,765	43.0
San Rafael, CA Metro Division	112,673	61.6	61.7	63.6	47,675	3,264	40.6	38,595	1,782	48.5
San Jose-Sunnyvale-Santa Clara, CA Metro Area	678,834	52.8	68.0	56.2	260,644	2,916	35.1	285,035	1,894	47.4
San Luis Obispo-Paso Robles-Arroyo Grande, CA Metro Area	120,134	67.0	65.4	58.9	40,892	2,166	40.8	43,018	1,254	54.9
Santa Cruz-Watsonville, CA Metro Area	105,525	62.2	61.2	55.4	33,952	2,461	42.9	41,612	1,442	60.7
Santa Fe, NM Metro Area	71,877	62.2	61.4	70.1	25,217	1,573	34.2	18,112	951	54.5
Santa Maria-Santa Barbara, CA Metro Area	155,143	58.2	62.3	51.3	48,468	2,103	38.4	70,308	1,419	53.2
Santa Rosa, CA Metro Area	207,891	66.8	63.0	59.5	76,547	2,099	39.6	77,230	1,376	55.1
Savannah, GA Metro Area	157,523	63.5	56.5	55.1	52,490	1,357	32.7	62,270	989	51.1
Scranton—Wilkes-Barre—Hazleton, PA Metro Area	259,918	64.1	52.1	67.5	83,656	1,212	27.4	71,988	753	46.1

Table B-10. Housing Units, 2015—*Continued*

Metropolitan statistical area and division	Total housing units	1 unit detached, (percent)	With 2 or more vehicles available (percent of occupied units)	Owner-ship rate	Owner-occupied — Housing units with a mortgage — Number	Median monthly owner costs (dollars)	Units with costs 30 percent or more of household income (percent)	Renter-occupied — Number	Median monthly rent (dollars)	Units with rent 30 percent or more of household income (percent)
Seattle-Tacoma-Bellevue, WA Metro Area	1,530,004	58.9	60.3	59.9	632,110	1,977	29.7	575,681	1,263	46.7
Seattle-Bellevue-Everett, WA Metro Division	1,193,642	57.4	59.4	59.9	497,619	2,093	28.9	453,604	1,327	45.2
Tacoma-Lakewood, WA Metro Division	336,362	64.5	63.9	60.2	134,491	1,661	32.6	122,077	1,062	52.4
Sebastian-Vero Beach, FL Metro Area	77,905	62.3	49.1	77.0	20,593	1,192	33.6	12,739	911	46.9
Sebring, FL Metro Area	54,819	60.3	42.9	74.9	11,696	965	29.7	10,302	752	60.6
Sheboygan, WI Metro Area	50,599	65.4	63.1	69.7	22,601	1,206	19.2	14,378	688	37.5
Sherman-Denison, TX Metro Area	54,668	74.2	60.6	68.1	16,669	1,185	21.1	15,151	783	45.7
Shreveport-Bossier City, LA Metro Area	200,198	64.8	55.6	61.4	58,159	1,166	26.8	66,177	754	57.2
Sierra Vista-Douglas, AZ Metro Area	60,600	62.1	63.9	67.6	18,885	1,129	26.2	16,244	746	47.5
Sioux City, IA-NE-SD Metro Area	68,594	75.1	63.6	68.5	25,299	1,102	16.7	19,878	695	42.3
Sioux Falls, SD Metro Area	103,773	64.2	66.2	67.6	44,683	1,249	18.6	31,797	750	40.3
South Bend-Mishawaka, IN-MI Metro Area	141,703	76.2	57.1	71.0	52,953	1,042	22.9	34,629	709	49.2
Spartanburg, SC Metro Area	139,356	69.8	61.8	68.6	50,083	1,046	24.1	39,073	711	49.7
Spokane-Spokane Valley, WA Metro Area	237,012	66.2	61.7	62.0	86,940	1,322	32.1	81,846	781	52.3
Springfield, IL Metro Area	96,342	71.7	55.8	68.3	37,613	1,199	19.3	27,928	748	45.0
Springfield, MA Metro Area	255,002	56.8	51.7	62.5	97,058	1,563	30.4	87,635	906	57.9
Springfield, MO Metro Area	197,902	71.6	60.2	61.4	69,693	1,016	21.2	69,325	711	48.5
Springfield, OH Metro Area	61,113	74.4	61.4	65.5	21,168	1,062	22.6	18,708	696	44.6
State College, PA Metro Area	65,474	57.9	56.1	59.1	19,618	1,475	23.3	22,962	945	51.9
Staunton-Waynesboro, VA Metro Area	53,334	73.7	65.0	65.6	17,835	1,176	26.5	16,074	827	45.7
Stockton-Lodi, CA Metro Area	238,626	73.3	65.2	55.0	88,321	1,696	35.8	100,418	1,036	56.8
Sumter, SC Metro Area	47,181	63.3	61.6	63.9	15,174	1,012	27.3	14,798	775	44.3
Syracuse, NY Metro Area	290,445	64.9	52.9	67.5	109,064	1,276	22.3	82,641	813	47.5
Tallahassee, FL Metro Area	167,160	53.7	53.9	56.8	48,113	1,280	33.1	61,401	904	62.1
Tampa-St. Petersburg-Clearwater, FL Metro Area	1,385,082	55.2	50.2	62.9	428,776	1,360	32.8	432,397	976	53.0
Terre Haute, IN Metro Area	74,229	69.5	56.9	63.2	25,690	916	18.3	24,569	677	52.2
Texarkana, TX-AR Metro Area	65,193	70.2	58.7	65.8	16,121	1,102	32.8	18,628	731	56.0
The Villages, FL Metro Area	66,838	80.9	32.8	90.4	18,305	1,216	37.7	4,894	807	52.8
Toledo, OH Metro Area	273,783	67.6	54.8	62.3	95,010	1,205	22.2	91,462	695	46.5
Topeka, KS Metro Area	104,321	75.0	61.8	66.9	38,674	1,188	23.2	30,828	755	45.4
Trenton, NJ Metro Area	144,485	48.5	58.1	62.9	54,475	2,225	33.8	47,481	1,154	50.1
Tucson, AZ Metro Area	452,104	59.3	53.1	60.8	150,779	1,250	30.6	155,425	824	51.4
Tulsa, OK Metro Area	424,992	71.0	61.1	63.8	148,724	1,214	23.6	137,962	791	44.3
Tuscaloosa, AL Metro Area	105,963	59.9	58.6	64.3	33,909	1,206	25.9	30,280	778	51.0
Tyler, TX Metro Area	88,869	67.0	60.9	66.0	28,192	1,321	24.1	26,636	852	53.1
Urban Honolulu, HI Metro Area	344,075	44.1	56.0	53.5	112,055	2,420	39.4	142,933	1,638	59.2
Utica-Rome, NY Metro Area	137,171	62.5	48.7	66.8	40,519	1,169	22.3	38,025	719	50.2
Valdosta, GA Metro Area	58,987	62.7	54.9	54.6	15,837	1,151	29.8	22,065	723	53.5
Vallejo-Fairfield, CA Metro Area	155,637	70.1	66.3	60.3	65,458	1,906	35.3	57,785	1,320	60.1
Victoria, TX Metro Area	41,107	71.6	63.9	70.0	12,267	1,236	22.3	10,766	792	47.8
Vineland-Bridgeton, NJ Metro Area	56,358	68.5	56.4	65.3	21,163	1,497	37.5	17,503	980	61.5
Virginia Beach-Norfolk-Newport News, VA-NC Metro Area	711,988	59.9	61.1	60.5	283,044	1,596	33.5	254,143	1,106	55.4
Visalia-Porterville, CA Metro Area	146,554	74.3	60.1	54.8	53,378	1,321	36.6	60,907	853	59.5
Waco, TX Metro Area	106,699	67.7	59.5	59.7	28,748	1,293	30.0	37,547	813	52.6
Walla Walla, WA Metro Area	26,252	71.6	61.2	64.6	8,146	1,284	31.3	8,578	825	55.2
Warner Robins, GA Metro Area	76,475	68.8	65.0	62.8	29,612	1,184	22.8	25,850	851	50.0
Washington-Arlington-Alexandria, DC-VA-MD-WV Metro Area	2,324,965	45.8	56.6	62.3	1,069,934	2,243	27.7	819,978	1,553	48.5
Silver Spring-Frederick-Rockville, MD Metro Division	483,789	49.9	60.6	66.0	231,717	2,278	28.5	156,761	1,610	52.3
Washington-Arlington-Alexandria, DC-VA-MD-WV Metro Division	1,841,176	44.7	55.6	61.2	838,217	2,233	27.5	663,217	1,537	47.6
Waterloo-Cedar Falls, IA Metro Area	72,825	71.4	65.0	69.9	27,667	1,138	21.1	20,193	688	47.1
Watertown-Fort Drum, NY Metro Area	59,129	56.2	52.7	55.2	14,573	1,208	22.7	19,317	909	47.1
Wausau, WI Metro Area	58,629	74.2	67.8	72.8	24,182	1,187	23.3	14,854	721	39.7
Weirton-Steubenville, WV-OH Metro Area	58,281	78.4	55.4	71.2	18,257	912	14.9	14,576	616	46.0
Wenatchee, WA Metro Area	52,787	67.4	70.1	69.1	16,595	1,334	28.7	12,762	796	34.4
Wheeling, WV-OH Metro Area	68,950	74.5	59.5	74.7	22,194	894	17.3	14,772	588	45.3
Wichita, KS Metro Area	271,004	72.4	60.9	65.3	97,444	1,239	20.6	84,939	751	43.7
Wichita Falls, TX Metro Area	65,403	73.7	60.6	62.3	17,249	1,127	28.3	20,924	743	45.6
Williamsport, PA Metro Area	52,677	69.0	57.7	69.2	17,905	1,182	26.4	14,113	755	51.4
Wilmington, NC Metro Area	134,640	63.2	61.6	61.8	45,975	1,444	30.1	42,609	935	49.2
Winchester, VA-WV Metro Area	57,858	74.8	70.8	68.9	21,909	1,402	24.5	15,245	928	47.2
Winston-Salem, NC Metro Area	292,333	67.8	62.6	65.0	105,022	1,103	24.4	91,132	725	48
Worcester, MA-CT Metro Area	379,264	58.3	57.8	65.3	157,906	1,765	28.9	119,869	972	49.3
Yakima, WA Metro Area	86,568	69.9	70.5	64.1	30,088	1,190	27.4	29,341	764	49.8
York-Hanover, PA Metro Area	181,066	62.8	65.4	73.8	78,709	1,452	26.7	43,433	890	51.3
Youngstown-Warren-Boardman, OH-PA Metro Area	258,050	75.9	54.6	69.9	89,260	1,009	24.3	68,842	634	49.4
Yuba City, CA Metro Area	62,392	71.8	63.3	58.6	23,311	1,516	32.2	24,094	902	60.5
Yuma, AZ Metro Area	90,485	51.8	52.2	65.3	28,018	1,059	35.5	24,888	756	47.3

Table B-11.   Personal Income and Earnings by Place of Work

Metropolitan statistical area and division	Personal Income								Earnings (million dollars)			
	Total (million dollars)				Percent change, 2005–2015	Per capita[1] (dollars)			Earnings (million dollars)			
	2015	2010	2005	2000		2015	2010	2005	2015	2010	2005	2000
Abilene, TX Metro Area	7,077	5,646	4,540	3,673	55.9	41,732	34,093	28,243	4,765	3,823	3,216	2,568
Akron, OH Metro Area	31,457	26,765	23,745	20,645	32.5	44,668	38,066	33,801	22,335	19,176	17,557	14,463
Albany, GA Metro Area	5,270	4,822	4,130	3,510	27.6	34,326	30,584	26,324	3,421	3,267	3,084	2,670
Albany, OR Metro Area	4,503	3,655	2,952	2,376	52.6	37,355	31,269	27,296	2,611	2,207	2,103	1,706
Albany-Schenectady-Troy, NY Metro Area	46,648	38,836	32,093	26,582	45.3	52,899	44,582	37,553	35,051	30,029	25,835	21,554
Albuquerque, NM Metro Area	34,988	30,334	25,212	19,444	38.8	38,563	34,097	31,143	23,901	21,650	19,303	15,072
Alexandria, LA Metro Area	6,305	5,331	4,505	3,360	39.9	40,812	34,587	30,456	3,973	3,510	2,966	2,220
Allentown-Bethlehem-Easton, PA-NJ Metro Area	39,761	34,374	29,259	22,562	35.9	47,770	41,810	37,143	25,750	21,842	20,022	14,903
Altoona, PA Metro Area	5,139	4,394	3,781	3,205	35.9	40,919	34,581	29,834	3,646	3,137	2,891	2,446
Amarillo, TX Metro Area	11,438	9,352	7,183	5,490	59.2	43,648	37,003	29,881	8,484	7,014	5,352	4,190
Ames, IA Metro Area	3,764	2,889	2,533	2,104	48.6	39,204	32,233	30,556	3,233	2,423	2,103	1,694
Anchorage, AK Metro Area	23,443	19,972	14,817	10,917	58.2	58,638	52,124	42,224	16,789	14,749	11,744	8,449
Ann Arbor, MI Metro Area	18,447	15,448	13,919	11,697	32.5	51,400	44,704	40,672	14,801	12,578	12,318	10,820
Anniston-Oxford-Jacksonville, AL Metro Area	3,864	3,633	3,116	2,451	24.0	33,418	30,677	27,216	2,442	2,556	2,276	1,714
Appleton, WI Metro Area	10,559	8,578	7,427	6,085	42.2	45,314	37,963	34,396	7,751	6,340	5,893	4,719
Asheville, NC Metro Area	17,351	14,035	12,088	9,755	43.5	38,831	32,988	30,494	10,915	8,795	8,007	6,462
Athens-Clarke County, GA Metro Area	7,029	5,595	4,901	3,901	43.4	34,596	28,924	27,386	5,322	4,376	3,918	3,027
Atlanta-Sandy Springs-Roswell, GA Metro Area	257,510	205,462	183,846	145,375	40.1	45,092	38,739	38,535	202,116	162,359	154,385	125,717
Atlantic City-Hammonton, NJ Metro Area	11,982	10,525	8,971	8,055	33.6	43,695	38,305	33,187	8,590	8,054	7,966	7,236
Auburn-Opelika, AL Metro Area	5,278	4,084	3,313	2,402	59.3	33,622	29,011	26,270	2,985	2,340	2,081	1,519
Augusta-Richmond County, GA-SC Metro Area	21,924	18,638	15,398	12,467	42.4	37,151	32,896	28,982	15,057	13,039	11,323	9,181
Austin-Round Rock, TX Metro Area	102,072	69,239	51,986	41,626	96.3	51,014	40,078	35,769	80,171	54,160	43,078	36,321
Bakersfield, CA Metro Area	32,953	25,844	20,142	14,071	63.6	37,355	30,705	26,478	23,895	19,158	15,634	10,669
Baltimore-Columbia-Towson, MD Metro Area	154,626	131,896	110,942	88,091	39.4	55,275	48,570	41,956	114,056	96,198	82,486	63,782
Bangor, ME Metro Area	5,654	5,076	4,355	3,583	29.8	37,032	32,991	29,089	4,020	3,664	3,358	2,779
Barnstable Town, MA Metro Area	13,874	11,308	10,180	8,152	36.3	64,730	52,369	45,857	7,039	5,822	5,628	4,065
Baton Rouge, LA Metro Area	36,104	30,177	23,280	17,567	55.1	43,474	37,519	31,652	27,761	22,746	17,900	14,049
Battle Creek, MI Metro Area	4,964	4,324	3,928	3,477	26.4	36,958	31,786	28,272	3,842	3,397	3,235	2,917
Bay City, MI Metro Area	4,003	3,587	3,104	2,922	29.0	37,884	33,306	28,434	2,168	2,001	1,894	1,820
Beaumont-Port Arthur, TX Metro Area	17,101	13,882	10,916	9,343	56.7	41,872	34,387	27,282	12,541	10,124	8,209	7,106
Beckley, WV Metro Area	4,109	3,748	3,134	2,631	31.1	33,538	30,012	25,155	2,426	2,326	2,040	1,608
Bellingham, WA Metro Area	9,024	7,369	5,738	4,188	57.3	42,511	36,557	30,940	5,880	4,846	4,121	2,844
Bend-Redmond, OR Metro Area	7,788	5,415	4,686	3,255	66.2	44,435	34,304	33,336	5,051	3,193	3,303	2,198
Billings, MT Metro Area	7,750	6,080	4,825	3,668	60.6	46,052	38,151	32,478	5,788	4,438	3,687	2,697
Binghamton, NY Metro Area	9,771	8,894	7,225	6,515	35.2	39,714	35,372	28,659	6,487	6,286	5,484	5,060
Birmingham-Hoover, AL Metro Area	51,059	43,972	38,557	30,515	32.4	44,568	38,952	35,493	36,393	31,275	29,003	23,620
Bismarck, ND Metro Area	7,010	4,822	3,440	2,605	103.8	54,124	41,825	32,472	5,205	3,639	2,707	1,996
Blacksburg-Christiansburg-Radford, VA Metro Area	6,247	5,122	4,416	3,477	41.5	34,370	28,688	25,824	4,249	3,484	3,327	2,647
Bloomington, IL Metro Area	8,409	7,402	5,968	4,977	40.9	44,397	39,700	33,717	7,015	6,430	5,405	4,419
Bloomington, IN Metro Area	5,829	4,832	4,103	3,438	42.1	35,203	30,172	27,333	4,146	3,521	3,131	2,648
Bloomsburg-Berwick, PA Metro Area	3,431	2,960	2,388	1,969	43.7	40,258	34,554	28,528	2,830	2,412	1,973	1,606
Boise City, ID Metro Area	27,047	20,564	17,588	13,835	53.8	39,956	33,274	32,154	19,484	14,978	13,624	11,161
Boston-Cambridge-Newton, MA-NH Metro Area	326,046	265,544	216,762	187,187	50.4	68,292	58,164	49,063	261,620	217,251	179,891	159,959
Boston, MA Metro Division	137,843	115,115	91,016	75,683	51.4	69,458	60,780	49,887	124,752	105,482	86,256	74,503
Cambridge-Newton-Framingham, MA Metro Division	162,946	130,322	108,260	97,006	50.5	69,010	57,846	49,576	121,432	98,936	81,929	75,837
Rockingham County-Strafford County, NH Metro Division	25,257	20,108	17,485	14,498	44.4	58,928	48,041	42,661	15,437	12,833	11,707	9,619
Boulder, CO Metro Area	19,233	14,655	12,447	12,185	54.5	60,220	49,513	44,415	14,920	11,690	10,704	11,137
Bowling Green, KY Metro Area	5,805	4,719	3,904	3,078	48.7	34,461	29,653	26,756	4,106	3,285	3,004	2,328
Bremerton-Silverdale, WA Metro Area	12,474	10,552	9,261	7,088	34.7	47,953	41,920	38,620	7,168	6,372	5,613	3,948
Bridgeport-Stamford-Norwalk, CT Metro Area	100,856	96,824	67,426	55,651	49.6	106,382	105,272	75,114	60,699	65,009	44,922	39,451
Brownsville-Harlingen, TX Metro Area	11,325	9,437	6,992	5,148	62.0	26,826	23,152	18,725	7,068	5,879	4,658	3,505
Brunswick, GA Metro Area	4,141	3,575	3,269	2,484	26.7	35,696	31,771	32,197	2,424	2,242	2,139	1,554
Buffalo-Cheektowaga-Niagara Falls, NY Metro Area	51,958	43,954	36,871	32,688	40.9	45,769	38,706	32,102	36,777	31,470	27,718	24,720
Burlington, NC Metro Area	5,673	4,803	4,012	3,442	41.4	35,839	31,686	28,796	3,291	2,840	2,715	2,466
Burlington-South Burlington, VT Metro Area	11,192	9,163	7,665	6,289	46.0	51,565	43,315	37,096	8,591	7,300	6,385	5,267
California-Lexington Park, MD Metro Area	5,792	4,946	3,654	2,628	58.5	51,990	46,770	37,723	4,274	3,722	2,688	1,953
Canton-Massillon, OH Metro Area	16,408	13,661	12,215	10,936	34.3	40,717	33,790	30,148	10,076	8,320	8,324	7,566
Cape Coral-Fort Myers, FL Metro Area	31,296	24,273	21,188	13,102	47.7	44,583	39,117	38,175	16,050	12,652	12,613	7,136
Cape Girardeau, MO-IL Metro Area	3,713	3,197	2,695	2,175	37.8	38,070	33,148	28,928	2,636	2,353	2,124	1,682
Carbondale-Marion, IL Metro Area	4,703	4,254	3,380	2,737	39.1	37,084	33,542	27,286	3,393	3,079	2,520	1,968
Carson City, NV Metro Area	2,369	2,315	1,349	1,733	75.5	43,443	42,076	24,103	2,130	2,216	1,176	1,495
Casper, WY Metro Area	5,645	3,727	2,758	2,132	104.6	68,692	49,379	39,450	4,135	2,869	1,995	1,538
Cedar Rapids, IA Metro Area	12,628	10,495	8,326	7,290	51.7	47,468	40,613	33,673	9,639	8,131	6,839	6,056
Chambersburg-Waynesboro, PA Metro Area	6,417	5,389	4,391	3,345	46.1	41,768	35,942	31,605	3,691	3,105	2,838	2,039
Champaign-Urbana, IL Metro Area	10,244	8,741	6,793	5,727	50.8	42,863	37,629	30,681	7,919	6,760	5,376	4,374
Charleston, WV Metro Area	9,274	8,528	7,227	6,488	28.3	42,039	37,586	31,552	7,525	7,261	6,398	5,628
Charleston-North Charleston, SC Metro Area	32,307	24,045	19,142	14,432	68.8	43,393	36,022	31,993	23,358	17,140	14,331	10,707
Charlotte-Concord-Gastonia, NC-SC Metro Area	109,028	84,662	70,326	52,812	55.0	44,935	38,073	36,360	88,007	66,816	58,790	44,534
Charlottesville, VA Metro Area	12,117	9,635	7,873	5,947	53.9	52,795	43,975	38,412	8,241	6,797	5,646	4,221
Chattanooga, TN-GA Metro Area	22,582	18,793	15,552	13,326	45.2	41,225	35,511	31,130	16,440	13,674	12,117	10,466
Cheyenne, WY Metro Area	4,836	3,922	3,134	2,348	54.3	49,796	42,509	36,558	3,487	2,864	2,266	1,655
Chicago-Naperville-Elgin, IL-IN-WI Metro Area	514,662	414,871	376,685	328,951	36.6	53,886	43,803	40,607	389,395	311,837	298,101	261,671
Chicago-Naperville-Arlington Heights, IL Metro Division	401,636	321,431	294,856	259,698	36.2	54,715	44,208	41,146	315,851	251,361	243,403	217,120

[1]Based on resident population estimated as of July 1 of the year shown.

Table B-11. Personal Income and Earnings by Place of Work—*Continued*

Metropolitan statistical area and division	Personal Income											
	Total (million dollars)				Percent change, 2005–2015	Per capita[1] (dollars)			Earnings (million dollars)			
	2015	2010	2005	2000		2015	2010	2005	2015	2010	2005	2000
Elgin, IL Metro Division	27,725	23,073	19,640	15,001	41.2	43,647	37,139	34,226	16,828	14,247	13,369	10,138
Gary, IN Metro Division	29,181	24,638	21,308	18,935	37.0	41,507	34,785	30,800	17,253	15,166	13,928	12,354
Lake County-Kenosha County, IL-WI Metro Division	56,121	45,729	40,882	35,317	37.3	64,333	52,507	48,409	39,463	31,062	27,400	22,060
Chico, CA Metro Area	9,010	7,280	6,167	4,681	46.1	39,971	33,093	28,718	5,185	4,362	4,040	2,930
Cincinnati, OH-KY-IN Metro Area	101,960	85,152	74,684	61,977	36.5	47,254	40,207	36,345	75,932	64,747	58,360	48,191
Clarksville, TN-KY Metro Area	10,834	9,395	7,328	5,331	47.9	38,554	35,902	30,836	7,715	7,149	5,822	3,878
Cleveland, TN Metro Area	4,393	3,569	3,001	2,450	46.4	36,344	30,780	27,431	2,746	2,114	1,993	1,732
Cleveland-Elyria, OH Metro Area	98,472	81,783	75,290	68,290	30.8	47,783	39,401	35,654	74,587	62,313	59,998	54,940
Coeur d'Alene, ID Metro Area	5,804	4,396	3,706	2,621	56.6	38,605	31,646	29,421	3,201	2,583	2,386	1,666
College Station-Bryan, TX Metro Area	8,919	6,823	4,960	3,721	79.8	35,797	29,734	24,372	6,498	5,028	3,849	2,878
Colorado Springs, CO Metro Area	30,320	24,527	20,175	16,645	50.3	43,447	37,712	34,325	20,805	17,616	15,473	12,783
Columbia, MO Metro Area	7,402	6,051	4,896	3,776	51.2	42,302	37,075	32,909	5,880	4,729	3,993	3,121
Columbia, SC Metro Area	32,743	26,305	21,905	17,841	49.5	40,420	34,176	31,331	24,653	19,632	17,357	14,195
Columbus, GA-AL Metro Area	11,447	9,775	8,619	7,107	32.8	36,484	32,968	30,099	8,743	7,853	6,649	5,460
Columbus, IN Metro Area	3,699	2,875	2,360	2,238	56.7	45,575	37,411	32,036	3,541	2,557	2,289	2,145
Columbus, OH Metro Area	94,148	73,062	62,370	51,755	51.0	46,570	38,324	34,821	75,364	58,430	51,815	43,826
Corpus Christi, TX Metro Area	19,328	15,231	12,276	9,502	57.4	42,721	35,586	29,489	14,030	11,203	9,514	7,079
Corvallis, OR Metro Area	3,650	3,039	2,701	2,298	35.1	41,676	35,519	33,365	2,584	2,254	2,118	1,780
Crestview-Fort Walton Beach-Destin, FL Metro Area	12,149	9,612	8,647	5,860	40.5	46,340	40,727	37,041	8,028	6,422	6,375	3,899
Cumberland, MD-WV Metro Area	3,683	3,294	2,794	2,140	31.8	36,836	31,904	27,615	2,180	2,050	1,925	1,390
Dallas-Fort Worth-Arlington, TX Metro Area	362,948	262,061	215,828	176,437	68.2	51,099	40,613	37,363	292,806	209,943	182,072	155,428
Dallas-Plano-Irving, TX Metro Division	248,157	176,104	147,423	123,859	68.3	52,719	41,450	38,671	213,808	150,932	131,811	116,873
Fort Worth-Arlington, TX Metro Division	114,790	85,958	68,405	52,578	67.8	47,916	39,001	34,823	78,998	59,010	50,261	38,555
Dalton, GA Metro Area	4,535	3,645	3,508	2,891	29.3	31,539	25,609	26,201	3,872	3,200	3,567	2,888
Danville, IL Metro Area	2,825	2,617	2,193	1,880	28.8	35,630	32,062	26,507	1,776	1,682	1,534	1,309
Daphne-Fairhope-Foley, AL Metro Area	8,173	6,612	5,350	3,771	52.8	40,121	36,090	32,989	3,626	2,789	2,595	1,756
Davenport-Moline-Rock Island, IA-IL Metro Area	17,039	15,153	12,733	10,474	33.8	44,418	39,850	34,149	12,194	11,189	9,929	7,923
Dayton, OH Metro Area	34,205	28,939	26,349	23,618	29.8	42,707	36,160	32,741	25,278	21,578	21,489	19,200
Decatur, AL Metro Area	5,416	4,806	4,037	3,502	34.2	35,472	31,228	27,201	3,152	2,873	2,728	2,360
Decatur, IL Metro Area	4,762	4,308	3,580	3,193	33.0	44,383	38,889	32,227	3,727	3,269	2,969	2,660
Deltona-Daytona Beach-Ormond Beach, FL Metro Area	23,808	19,695	17,317	11,914	37.5	38,197	33,342	30,742	10,409	8,557	8,677	5,729
Denver-Aurora-Lakewood, CO Metro Area	157,532	109,387	98,298	82,628	60.3	55,975	42,822	42,138	124,486	86,369	80,420	69,335
Des Moines-West Des Moines, IA Metro Area	30,781	24,171	20,088	15,578	53.2	49,415	42,259	38,514	24,952	19,904	17,153	13,138
Detroit-Warren-Dearborn, MI Metro Area	201,741	162,372	163,566	154,782	23.3	46,894	37,837	36,914	148,970	119,076	132,517	127,284
Detroit-Dearborn-Livonia, MI Metro Division	67,756	58,536	57,978	57,451	16.9	38,512	32,248	29,577	56,498	47,603	53,108	52,331
Warren-Troy-Farmington Hills, MI Metro Division	133,986	103,836	105,588	97,331	26.9	52,694	41,935	42,735	92,471	71,473	79,409	74,953
Dothan, AL Metro Area	5,464	4,917	4,087	3,054	33.7	36,879	33,705	29,910	3,248	2,882	2,758	2,141
Dover, DE Metro Area	6,625	5,514	4,568	3,498	45.0	38,178	33,831	31,593	4,339	3,758	3,458	2,694
Dubuque, IA Metro Area	4,273	3,453	2,734	2,376	56.3	43,997	36,767	30,117	3,396	2,766	2,278	1,947
Duluth, MN-WI Metro Area	11,610	10,073	8,060	7,100	44.0	41,523	36,007	29,130	7,920	7,004	5,869	5,261
Durham-Chapel Hill, NC Metro Area	26,250	21,211	16,981	13,061	54.6	47,513	41,744	37,053	24,634	21,491	17,156	14,388
East Stroudsburg, PA Metro Area	6,330	5,396	4,767	3,540	32.8	38,043	31,756	29,415	3,547	3,342	2,917	2,003
Eau Claire, WI Metro Area	7,168	5,780	4,638	4,006	54.6	43,276	35,755	29,956	5,218	4,250	3,616	3,142
El Centro, CA Metro Area	6,052	5,052	3,771	2,680	60.5	33,584	28,911	24,157	4,203	3,602	2,900	2,011
Elizabethtown-Fort Knox, KY Metro Area	5,596	5,013	3,967	3,282	41.1	37,656	33,431	28,299	3,833	3,855	2,887	2,230
Elkhart-Goshen, IN Metro Area	8,115	5,976	5,869	5,051	38.3	39,882	30,260	30,529	8,045	5,462	6,429	5,247
Elmira, NY Metro Area	3,496	3,116	2,568	2,291	36.1	40,149	35,020	28,896	2,424	2,239	1,874	1,680
El Paso, TX Metro Area	27,349	22,659	16,585	12,999	64.9	32,598	28,074	22,673	19,012	16,153	12,591	10,059
Enid, OK Metro Area	2,860	2,363	1,791	1,391	59.7	44,985	38,890	31,219	2,016	1,610	1,258	917
Erie, PA Metro Area	11,240	9,662	8,150	7,121	37.9	40,425	34,412	29,400	7,787	6,658	6,220	5,446
Eugene, OR Metro Area	14,469	11,740	10,320	8,422	40.2	39,871	33,355	30,730	9,347	7,616	7,454	5,961
Evansville, IN-KY Metro Area	13,288	11,621	9,821	8,428	35.3	42,091	37,269	32,323	9,718	8,882	7,944	6,701
Fairbanks, AK Metro Area	5,399	4,460	3,308	2,445	63.2	54,185	45,379	36,579	3,877	3,292	2,702	1,959
Fargo, ND-MN Metro Area	11,689	8,356	6,247	4,980	87.1	49,987	39,900	32,999	9,059	6,445	5,168	4,049
Farmington, NM Metro Area	4,485	3,953	3,092	2,169	45.1	37,777	30,373	24,777	3,227	2,904	2,409	1,730
Fayetteville, NC Metro Area	13,727	12,106	10,096	8,175	36.0	36,460	32,932	29,392	12,357	12,139	9,052	6,357
Fayetteville-Springdale-Rogers, AR-MO Metro Area	26,967	17,528	13,731	9,082	96.4	52,509	37,629	33,655	15,534	11,054	9,752	6,643
Flagstaff, AZ Metro Area	5,705	4,563	3,729	2,774	53.0	41,018	33,894	29,356	3,786	3,123	2,613	1,967
Flint, MI Metro Area	15,042	12,835	12,225	11,729	23.0	36,612	30,195	27,626	8,530	7,417	8,229	8,524
Florence, SC Metro Area	7,459	6,426	5,484	4,582	36.0	36,130	31,241	27,537	5,094	4,398	4,074	3,566
Florence-Muscle Shoals, AL Metro Area	5,206	4,621	3,856	3,146	35.0	35,427	31,381	26,832	3,017	2,679	2,421	1,996
Fond du Lac, WI Metro Area	4,463	3,747	3,179	2,802	40.4	43,764	36,838	32,012	3,004	2,492	2,303	2,062
Fort Collins, CO Metro Area	15,117	11,106	9,409	7,794	60.7	45,318	36,955	34,201	10,041	7,567	6,870	5,600
Fort Smith, AR-OK Metro Area	9,546	8,240	6,812	5,570	40.1	34,065	29,357	25,542	6,383	5,651	5,233	4,359
Fort Wayne, IN Metro Area	17,666	14,230	12,561	11,554	40.6	41,102	34,131	31,151	13,164	10,822	10,264	9,686
Fresno, CA Metro Area	37,360	29,472	24,573	18,259	52.0	38,323	31,607	28,165	24,708	20,440	18,747	13,752
Gadsden, AL Metro Area	3,513	3,175	2,686	2,242	30.8	34,086	30,404	26,033	1,897	1,711	1,606	1,393
Gainesville, FL Metro Area	10,990	9,228	7,827	5,760	40.4	39,650	34,871	31,362	8,260	7,075	6,331	4,630
Gainesville, GA Metro Area	7,083	5,472	4,800	3,573	47.5	36,597	30,401	29,820	5,235	3,813	3,656	2,755
Gettysburg, PA Metro Area	4,606	3,817	3,174	2,402	45.1	45,023	37,618	32,190	2,095	1,786	1,726	1,264
Glens Falls, NY Metro Area	5,343	4,668	3,782	3,123	41.3	42,101	36,192	29,623	3,398	3,038	2,634	2,175
Goldsboro, NC Metro Area	4,444	3,892	3,208	2,600	38.5	35,801	31,672	27,415	2,750	2,502	2,170	1,772

[1]Based on resident population estimated as of July 1 of the year shown.

Table B-11. Personal Income and Earnings by Place of Work—*Continued*

Metropolitan statistical area and division	Personal Income											
	Total (million dollars)				Percent change, 2005–2015	Per capita[1] (dollars)			Earnings (million dollars)			
	2015	2010	2005	2000		2015	2010	2005	2015	2010	2005	2000
Grand Forks, ND-MN Metro Area	4,626	3,714	2,897	2,380	59.7	45,158	37,664	29,630	3,393	2,835	2,313	1,833
Grand Island, NE Metro Area	3,460	2,862	2,313	1,936	49.6	40,671	34,872	29,603	2,563	2,101	1,769	1,384
Grand Junction, CO Metro Area	5,772	4,920	3,990	3,022	44.7	38,863	33,584	30,645	3,667	3,257	2,778	2,060
Grand Rapids-Wyoming, MI Metro Area	47,121	35,829	32,730	28,226	44.0	45,371	36,208	33,718	34,699	26,298	26,240	24,057
Grants Pass, OR Metro Area	3,052	2,477	2,187	1,696	39.6	36,013	29,896	27,113	1,447	1,194	1,251	881
Great Falls, MT Metro Area	3,460	3,090	2,470	1,998	40.1	42,053	37,896	30,856	2,324	2,132	1,752	1,345
Greeley, CO Metro Area	12,202	8,252	6,382	4,655	91.2	42,787	32,467	28,635	7,910	4,812	4,225	3,229
Green Bay, WI Metro Area	14,454	11,916	10,109	8,490	43.0	45,665	38,848	34,060	11,517	9,484	8,620	7,275
Greensboro-High Point, NC Metro Area	29,532	24,702	21,644	18,239	36.4	39,263	34,068	31,967	22,664	19,051	17,903	15,567
Greenville, NC Metro Area	6,514	5,403	4,297	3,329	51.6	37,042	32,005	29,050	4,791	3,985	3,233	2,623
Greenville-Anderson-Mauldin, SC Metro Area	34,306	26,793	22,268	19,211	54.1	39,213	32,446	29,183	24,672	18,745	16,887	15,126
Gulfport-Biloxi-Pascagoula, MS Metro Area	13,315	12,599	10,836	8,867	22.9	34,206	33,918	28,262	9,819	9,640	8,093	7,021
Hagerstown-Martinsburg, MD-WV Metro Area	10,454	8,897	7,081	5,121	47.6	39,981	35,250	30,233	6,193	5,212	4,898	3,654
Hammond, LA Metro Area	4,641	3,976	2,792	1,970	66.2	36,043	32,725	26,098	2,340	2,420	1,644	1,121
Hanford-Corcoran, CA Metro Area	5,001	4,059	3,416	2,240	46.4	33,126	26,641	23,536	3,531	2,914	2,638	1,668
Harrisburg-Carlisle, PA Metro Area	27,115	22,340	19,074	15,757	42.2	47,991	40,600	36,277	23,993	19,914	18,135	14,558
Harrisonburg, VA Metro Area	4,681	3,802	3,184	2,512	47.0	35,700	30,312	27,302	3,798	3,182	2,785	2,155
Hartford-West Hartford-East Hartford, CT Metro Area	71,227	60,861	51,413	43,781	38.5	58,801	50,127	43,279	57,307	49,036	44,645	37,764
Hattiesburg, MS Metro Area	5,146	4,317	3,376	2,619	52.4	34,574	30,127	25,808	3,644	3,035	2,512	1,887
Hickory-Lenoir-Morganton, NC Metro Area	12,835	10,977	9,917	8,689	29.4	35,406	30,059	28,001	8,367	7,181	7,272	6,903
Hilton Head Island-Bluffton-Beaufort, SC Metro Area	9,366	7,152	6,239	4,483	50.1	45,158	38,074	38,196	5,025	3,948	3,776	2,706
Hinesville, GA Metro Area	2,491	2,137	1,760	1,288	41.6	31,064	27,626	23,037	2,553	2,569	1,863	1,165
Homosassa Springs, FL Metro Area	4,983	4,352	3,636	2,715	37.0	35,323	30,809	27,178	1,837	1,736	1,594	1,101
Hot Springs, AR Metro Area	3,604	3,080	2,627	2,107	37.2	37,090	32,038	28,524	1,905	1,660	1,526	1,219
Houma-Thibodaux, LA Metro Area	9,636	8,232	5,703	4,290	69.0	45,390	39,532	28,451	7,127	6,298	4,214	3,043
Houston-The Woodlands-Sugar Land, TX Metro Area	361,777	264,687	201,478	156,709	79.6	54,346	44,498	38,496	296,148	215,891	169,799	135,947
Huntington-Ashland, WV-KY-OH Metro Area	13,070	11,732	9,353	7,929	39.7	36,146	32,135	25,847	8,154	7,448	6,288	5,198
Huntsville, AL Metro Area	19,600	16,757	12,770	9,735	53.5	44,068	39,964	34,256	16,276	14,235	11,343	8,766
Idaho Falls, ID Metro Area	5,293	4,408	3,572	2,530	48.2	37,873	32,940	30,742	4,034	3,512	2,841	2,165
Indianapolis-Carmel-Anderson, IN Metro Area	96,004	77,224	63,266	54,617	51.7	48,272	40,803	35,684	75,893	61,405	52,225	44,815
Iowa City, IA Metro Area	7,879	6,040	4,882	3,972	61.4	47,324	39,477	34,466	6,473	5,116	4,161	3,264
Ithaca, NY Metro Area	4,312	3,564	2,912	2,360	48.1	41,095	35,019	29,288	3,688	3,200	2,685	2,097
Jackson, MI Metro Area	5,808	4,896	4,428	4,047	31.2	36,413	30,570	27,157	3,639	3,062	3,077	2,780
Jackson, MS Metro Area	24,251	20,309	17,348	13,445	39.8	41,900	35,705	31,689	17,680	14,780	13,200	10,428
Jackson, TN Metro Area	4,781	4,123	3,510	3,096	36.2	36,870	31,716	27,813	3,875	3,206	3,043	2,719
Jacksonville, FL Metro Area	64,095	52,177	45,532	34,534	40.8	44,219	38,676	36,453	44,248	36,425	34,364	26,525
Jacksonville, NC Metro Area	8,189	7,801	5,120	3,613	59.9	43,952	43,436	32,569	6,077	6,282	3,949	2,617
Janesville-Beloit, WI Metro Area	6,462	5,380	4,664	4,086	38.6	40,026	33,577	29,750	4,074	3,281	3,420	2,978
Jefferson City, MO Metro Area	5,970	5,211	4,338	3,568	37.6	39,497	34,751	30,028	4,620	4,145	3,664	2,923
Johnson City, TN Metro Area	7,326	6,327	5,138	4,096	42.6	36,512	31,800	27,162	4,569	3,949	3,541	2,876
Johnstown, PA Metro Area	5,253	4,668	4,113	3,513	27.7	38,512	32,540	27,983	3,035	2,919	2,647	2,232
Jonesboro, AR Metro Area	4,328	3,580	2,895	2,333	49.5	33,709	29,523	25,719	3,119	2,565	2,195	1,802
Joplin, MO Metro Area	6,386	5,385	4,479	3,659	42.6	36,037	30,619	26,953	4,573	3,910	3,469	2,823
Kahului-Wailuku-Lahaina, HI Metro Area	6,989	5,501	4,690	3,316	49.0	42,430	35,476	32,694	4,923	3,791	3,710	2,554
Kalamazoo-Portage, MI Metro Area	14,004	11,523	10,071	8,614	39.0	41,760	35,248	31,447	9,335	8,007	7,472	6,562
Kankakee, IL Metro Area	4,108	3,695	3,062	2,622	34.2	37,049	32,571	28,375	2,554	2,202	1,969	1,721
Kansas City, MO-KS Metro Area	100,316	82,309	66,355	58,559	51.2	48,056	40,874	34,751	78,723	64,254	54,386	47,730
Kennewick-Richland, WA Metro Area	11,295	9,589	6,591	4,901	71.4	40,468	37,510	30,085	8,602	7,492	5,377	3,853
Killeen-Temple, TX Metro Area	17,343	15,128	10,916	7,817	58.9	40,237	37,048	30,531	12,157	11,312	8,249	5,656
Kingsport-Bristol-Bristol, TN-VA Metro Area	11,462	10,077	8,349	7,071	37.3	37,322	32,551	27,598	7,416	6,654	5,935	4,961
Kingston, NY Metro Area	8,002	6,913	5,742	4,703	39.4	44,422	37,897	31,476	4,122	3,727	3,144	2,578
Knoxville, TN Metro Area	35,206	28,869	24,203	19,927	45.5	40,870	34,419	30,610	25,548	20,948	18,841	15,292
Kokomo, IN Metro Area	3,084	2,570	2,576	2,406	19.7	37,356	31,069	30,523	2,532	2,036	2,638	2,578
La Crosse-Onalaska, WI-MN Metro Area	6,141	5,040	4,131	3,459	48.6	44,831	37,645	31,891	4,643	3,878	3,323	2,766
Lafayette, LA Metro Area	21,250	17,731	13,048	9,848	62.9	43,325	37,918	29,658	15,583	13,085	9,976	7,360
Lafayette-West Lafayette, IN Metro Area	7,528	6,173	5,134	4,557	46.6	35,120	30,546	27,307	5,954	4,857	4,360	3,828
Lake Charles, LA Metro Area	8,788	6,834	5,472	4,439	60.6	42,743	34,171	27,879	7,161	5,123	4,322	3,546
Lake Havasu City-Kingman, AZ Metro Area	6,041	5,135	4,440	2,986	36.0	29,505	25,626	23,521	2,646	2,279	2,296	1,496
Lakeland-Winter Haven, FL Metro Area	21,923	18,510	16,031	11,818	36.8	33,723	30,686	29,287	12,438	10,506	10,353	7,471
Lancaster, PA Metro Area	24,146	19,536	17,212	13,719	40.3	44,995	37,543	34,792	17,033	13,685	13,248	10,316
Lansing-East Lansing, MI Metro Area	17,882	15,448	13,688	12,468	30.6	37,863	33,276	29,581	13,345	12,068	11,424	10,563
Laredo, TX Metro Area	8,032	6,408	4,775	3,048	68.2	29,778	25,497	21,347	5,783	4,599	3,730	2,369
Las Cruces, NM Metro Area	6,907	6,163	4,781	3,226	44.5	32,233	29,321	25,271	4,295	4,090	3,293	2,060
Las Vegas-Henderson-Paradise, NV Metro Area	85,970	69,292	66,358	43,235	29.6	40,652	35,473	38,368	59,901	49,829	50,962	34,261
Lawrence, KS Metro Area	4,567	3,703	3,085	2,481	48.0	38,686	33,286	29,191	2,848	2,386	2,097	1,678
Lawton, OK Metro Area	4,997	4,632	3,464	2,670	44.2	38,246	35,209	28,516	3,566	3,519	2,598	1,888
Lebanon, PA Metro Area	5,906	4,947	4,098	3,239	44.1	43,090	37,010	32,476	3,177	2,717	2,397	1,773
Lewiston, ID-WA Metro Area	2,486	2,122	1,713	1,480	45.1	39,999	34,769	29,045	1,595	1,403	1,211	1,063
Lewiston-Auburn, ME Metro Area	3,979	3,617	3,146	2,632	26.5	37,106	33,580	29,310	2,791	2,480	2,218	1,850
Lexington-Fayette, KY Metro Area	21,555	17,439	14,955	12,611	44.1	43,065	36,832	34,231	17,376	14,072	12,976	11,055
Lima, OH Metro Area	3,913	3,474	3,035	2,675	28.9	37,469	32,650	28,400	3,107	2,851	2,684	2,384
Lincoln, NE Metro Area	14,281	11,585	9,717	8,113	47.0	44,133	38,236	34,039	10,970	9,071	7,943	6,488
Little Rock-North Little Rock-Conway, AR Metro Area	30,042	25,660	21,807	16,747	37.8	41,062	36,531	33,612	22,442	19,367	17,743	13,674

[1]Based on resident population estimated as of July 1 of the year shown.

Table B-11.   Personal Income and Earnings by Place of Work—*Continued*

Metropolitan statistical area and division	Personal Income											
	Total (million dollars)				Percent change, 2005–2015	Per capita[1] (dollars)			Earnings (million dollars)			
	2015	2010	2005	2000		2015	2010	2005	2015	2010	2005	2000
Logan, UT-ID Metro Area	4,300	3,481	2,609	1,971	64.8	32,121	27,589	23,173	3,070	2,512	1,919	1,403
Longview, TX Metro Area	9,173	7,876	5,925	4,827	54.8	42,118	36,678	29,180	6,699	5,957	4,492	3,415
Longview, WA Metro Area	4,177	3,602	2,657	2,222	57.2	40,371	35,169	27,521	2,670	2,314	1,888	1,652
Los Angeles-Long Beach-Anaheim, CA Metro Area	727,377	574,299	506,680	391,911	43.6	54,526	44,714	39,813	541,541	435,757	411,609	322,643
Anaheim-Santa Ana-Irvine, CA Metro Division	183,052	149,486	139,941	107,952	30.8	57,749	49,534	47,598	137,915	114,180	112,948	82,481
Los Angeles-Long Beach-Glendale, CA Metro Division	544,325	424,813	366,739	283,959	48.4	53,521	43,234	37,474	403,625	321,577	298,660	240,162
Louisville/Jefferson County, KY-IN Metro Area	56,960	46,329	39,679	33,753	43.6	44,556	37,428	33,838	42,206	33,691	31,006	26,171
Lubbock, TX Metro Area	11,946	9,679	7,587	6,188	57.5	38,392	33,125	28,050	8,528	6,966	5,749	4,808
Lynchburg, VA Metro Area	9,646	8,308	6,857	5,827	40.7	37,107	32,829	28,747	5,927	5,325	4,738	4,105
Macon, GA Metro Area	8,622	7,585	6,626	5,809	30.1	37,470	32,659	29,046	6,076	5,102	4,860	4,236
Madera, CA Metro Area	5,450	4,270	3,431	2,328	58.9	35,165	28,252	24,449	3,628	2,815	2,436	1,489
Madison, WI Metro Area	33,578	25,998	22,624	18,185	48.4	52,352	42,862	39,481	27,222	20,986	19,152	14,876
Manchester-Nashua, NH Metro Area	23,254	19,344	16,858	14,796	37.9	57,180	48,238	42,529	16,836	14,197	12,935	11,160
Manhattan, KS Metro Area	3,987	3,538	2,426	1,890	64.4	40,455	37,917	28,809	2,349	1,960	1,550	1,169
Mankato-North Mankato, MN Metro Area	4,329	3,328	2,953	2,265	46.6	43,665	34,368	32,409	3,371	2,579	2,501	1,807
Mansfield, OH Metro Area	4,331	3,765	3,536	3,072	22.5	35,588	30,317	27,682	2,825	2,566	2,767	2,439
McAllen-Edinburg-Mission, TX Metro Area	20,703	16,921	12,094	8,064	71.2	24,579	21,718	17,917	13,688	10,828	8,272	5,550
Medford, OR Metro Area	8,651	6,708	5,984	4,652	44.6	40,698	32,978	30,732	5,207	4,070	4,072	3,083
Memphis, TN-MS-AR Metro Area	56,856	48,938	43,478	35,857	30.8	42,300	36,895	34,181	43,567	37,776	36,394	29,906
Merced, CA Metro Area	9,714	7,240	6,116	4,192	58.8	36,185	28,191	25,216	5,729	4,318	4,052	2,582
Miami-Fort Lauderdale-West Palm Beach, FL Metro Area	299,528	240,662	219,732	165,082	36.3	49,819	43,086	40,607	184,869	144,933	142,923	107,155
Fort Lauderdale-Pompano Beach-Deerfield Beach, FL Metro Division	85,167	71,381	66,895	51,373	27.3	44,909	40,713	38,294	55,971	45,985	43,550	31,279
Miami-Miami Beach-Kendall, FL Metro Division	116,553	95,717	81,989	60,858	42.2	43,278	38,162	34,364	84,718	65,834	64,153	49,039
West Palm Beach-Boca Raton-Delray Beach, FL Metro Division	97,807	73,564	70,847	52,851	38.1	68,743	55,555	55,420	44,179	33,114	35,219	26,836
Michigan City-La Porte, IN Metro Area	4,194	3,528	3,038	2,783	38.1	37,827	31,654	27,735	2,407	2,181	2,109	1,918
Midland, MI Metro Area	3,760	3,563	3,098	2,645	21.4	44,954	42,588	36,906	2,449	2,696	2,387	2,096
Midland, TX Metro Area	17,458	10,005	7,621	3,886	129.1	104,714	70,557	60,028	15,196	8,212	6,221	2,742
Milwaukee-Waukesha-West Allis, WI Metro Area	79,861	67,189	58,931	50,816	35.5	50,681	43,161	38,709	61,260	51,893	47,981	40,931
Minneapolis-St. Paul-Bloomington, MN-WI Metro Area	194,372	153,074	135,476	111,992	43.5	55,148	45,618	42,349	152,042	119,772	111,646	93,388
Missoula, MT Metro Area	4,659	3,682	3,071	2,425	51.7	40,803	33,642	30,023	3,390	2,795	2,439	1,898
Mobile, AL Metro Area	14,684	13,138	10,766	8,797	36.4	35,348	31,785	26,986	11,129	9,899	8,431	6,969
Modesto, CA Metro Area	21,237	16,449	14,477	10,807	46.7	39,445	31,918	28,953	12,950	10,339	10,039	7,235
Monroe, LA Metro Area	6,491	5,721	4,681	3,924	38.7	36,214	32,358	27,176	4,377	3,968	3,412	2,937
Monroe, MI Metro Area	6,238	5,164	4,907	4,357	27.1	41,707	33,989	32,201	2,819	2,361	2,539	2,269
Montgomery, AL Metro Area	14,713	13,053	11,309	9,165	30.1	39,362	34,797	31,531	10,324	9,468	8,634	6,911
Morgantown, WV Metro Area	5,442	4,429	3,386	2,523	60.7	39,383	33,979	28,234	4,374	3,586	2,749	1,958
Morristown, TN Metro Area	3,903	3,268	2,718	2,322	43.6	33,463	28,623	25,235	2,518	2,113	2,111	1,837
Mount Vernon-Anacortes, WA Metro Area	5,419	4,405	3,601	2,918	50.5	44,470	37,651	32,535	3,351	2,680	2,439	1,939
Muncie, IN Metro Area	3,844	3,289	3,054	2,987	25.9	32,896	27,950	25,847	2,569	2,179	2,297	2,224
Muskegon, MI Metro Area	5,979	4,918	4,396	4,084	36.0	34,604	28,605	25,319	3,633	3,055	3,059	2,889
Myrtle Beach-Conway-North Myrtle Beach, SC-NC Metro Area	14,608	11,162	9,095	6,534	60.6	33,818	29,474	28,623	7,952	6,177	6,062	4,394
Napa, CA Metro Area	8,759	6,347	5,861	4,769	49.4	61,483	46,396	44,956	6,655	4,709	4,347	3,196
Naples-Immokalee-Marco Island, FL Metro Area	28,039	20,547	18,403	10,926	52.4	78,473	63,677	59,858	9,736	7,409	7,962	4,981
Nashville-Davidson—Murfreesboro—Franklin, TN Metro Area	92,680	69,687	54,830	44,307	69.0	50,635	41,580	36,280	76,850	55,821	46,385	37,645
New Bern, NC Metro Area	5,047	4,562	3,734	2,975	35.2	39,975	35,887	31,700	3,355	3,207	2,755	2,149
New Haven-Milford, CT Metro Area	44,551	38,416	34,037	29,235	30.9	51,835	44,494	40,178	29,461	26,100	24,587	20,828
New Orleans-Metairie, LA Metro Area	60,404	50,308	43,076	36,003	40.2	47,830	42,077	31,069	44,275	38,111	32,419	27,866
New York-Newark-Jersey City, NY-NJ-PA Metro Area	1,303,530	1,045,891	899,710	771,821	44.9	64,588	53,359	46,792	966,007	785,179	692,003	605,510
Dutchess County-Putnam County, NY Metro Division	20,328	17,453	15,567	12,842	30.6	51,490	43,903	39,516	10,427	9,759	8,712	6,941
Nassau County-Suffolk County, NY Metro Division	195,181	162,097	140,607	118,837	38.8	68,175	57,142	50,038	111,833	97,560	81,226	67,906
Newark, NJ-PA Metro Division	173,752	145,466	127,131	109,218	36.7	69,183	58,826	52,042	121,638	102,847	93,034	81,833
New York-Jersey City-White Plains, NY-NJ Metro Division	914,269	720,874	616,405	530,924	48.3	63,433	51,884	45,388	722,109	575,014	509,030	448,829
Niles-Benton Harbor, MI Metro Area	6,485	5,668	4,950	4,407	31.0	41,939	36,148	31,229	4,132	3,722	3,473	3,236
North Port-Sarasota-Bradenton, FL Metro Area	38,553	29,736	29,523	21,840	30.6	50,139	42,277	43,754	17,816	13,513	15,597	10,964
Norwich-New London, CT Metro Area	14,272	12,576	11,078	8,801	28.8	52,498	45,888	41,080	9,881	9,468	8,878	6,956
Ocala, FL Metro Area	11,602	10,036	8,574	6,142	35.3	33,800	30,281	28,244	5,289	4,539	4,603	3,196
Ocean City, NJ Metro Area	5,050	4,318	4,113	3,390	22.8	53,309	44,399	41,433	2,618	2,243	2,360	1,660
Odessa, TX Metro Area	7,303	4,804	3,243	2,561	125.2	45,806	35,047	25,867	6,104	3,788	2,539	1,977
Ogden-Clearfield, UT Metro Area	24,564	19,165	15,559	11,816	57.9	38,212	31,953	29,223	14,885	11,821	10,179	7,689
Oklahoma City, OK Metro Area	62,592	48,744	39,025	29,010	60.4	46,076	38,749	33,604	47,018	36,623	30,841	22,447
Olympia-Tumwater, WA Metro Area	11,901	10,054	8,127	6,345	46.4	44,155	39,730	35,798	7,536	6,271	5,300	4,053
Omaha-Council Bluffs, NE-IA Metro Area	47,178	38,474	30,955	25,194	52.4	51,543	44,317	38,014	36,578	29,725	24,196	19,736
Orlando-Kissimmee-Sanford, FL Metro Area	92,221	71,097	62,324	46,164	48.0	38,632	33,230	31,866	71,727	54,090	52,153	38,226
Oshkosh-Neenah, WI Metro Area	7,189	6,155	5,335	4,563	34.7	42,399	36,845	33,043	6,357	5,458	4,913	4,150
Owensboro, KY Metro Area	4,658	4,039	3,205	2,678	45.3	39,657	35,191	28,755	3,125	2,772	2,347	1,987
Oxnard-Thousand Oaks-Ventura, CA Metro Area	46,060	37,605	33,794	25,625	36.3	54,155	45,566	42,551	27,491	23,953	22,106	15,918
Palm Bay-Melbourne-Titusville, FL Metro Area	23,014	20,021	17,759	13,363	29.6	40,511	36,806	33,513	13,362	12,456	11,937	8,761

[1]Based on resident population estimated as of July 1 of the year shown.

Table B-11.   Personal Income and Earnings by Place of Work—*Continued*

Metropolitan statistical area and division	Personal Income								Earnings (million dollars)			
	Total (million dollars)				Percent change, 2005–2015	Per capita[1] (dollars)						
	2015	2010	2005	2000		2015	2010	2005	2015	2010	2005	2000
Panama City, FL Metro Area	7,692	6,617	5,721	3,941	34.5	38,947	35,755	32,014	4,945	4,273	4,050	2,638
Parkersburg-Vienna, WV Metro Area	3,568	2,987	2,514	2,223	41.9	38,642	32,199	27,134	2,344	2,031	1,905	1,763
Pensacola-Ferry Pass-Brent, FL Metro Area	18,667	15,793	13,481	10,174	38.5	39,048	35,010	30,674	11,029	9,498	8,733	6,611
Peoria, IL Metro Area	17,061	15,060	12,344	10,390	38.2	45,132	39,741	33,382	12,714	11,352	9,851	7,885
Philadelphia-Camden-Wilmington, PA-NJ-DE-MD Metro Area	347,032	288,083	244,915	200,929	41.7	57,173	48,243	42,016	249,636	208,289	185,564	149,570
Camden, NJ Metro Division	63,656	55,042	47,420	37,854	34.2	50,818	43,980	38,417	38,670	34,203	31,543	24,532
Montgomery County-Bucks County-Chester County, PA Metro Division	136,840	112,664	100,034	80,675	36.8	69,725	58,482	53,603	88,666	74,622	71,221	55,763
Philadelphia, PA Metro Division	110,472	89,715	69,385	58,863	59.2	51,832	42,979	33,962	93,473	75,062	59,051	49,382
Wilmington, DE-MD-NJ Metro Division	36,064	30,662	28,076	23,537	28.5	49,858	43,426	40,953	28,827	24,402	23,749	19,892
Phoenix-Mesa-Scottsdale, AZ Metro Area	186,693	146,616	131,424	94,431	42.1	40,811	34,867	34,817	134,303	104,601	101,316	74,871
Pine Bluff, AR Metro Area	2,940	2,766	2,484	2,101	18.3	31,377	27,638	23,905	1,928	1,960	1,870	1,568
Pittsburgh, PA Metro Area	119,432	100,644	85,254	74,537	40.1	50,756	42,700	35,904	88,054	72,954	64,183	55,319
Pittsfield, MA Metro Area	6,482	5,412	4,774	4,112	35.8	50,712	41,228	36,009	4,030	3,510	3,310	2,811
Pocatello, ID Metro Area	2,792	2,381	2,071	1,631	34.8	33,344	28,684	26,748	1,784	1,561	1,485	1,183
Portland-South Portland, ME Metro Area	25,918	21,988	19,113	15,288	35.6	49,246	42,787	37,456	18,267	15,879	14,171	11,226
Portland-Vancouver-Hillsboro, OR-WA Metro Area	115,691	88,151	74,697	63,147	54.9	48,422	39,486	36,132	86,340	65,408	59,431	51,160
Port St. Lucie, FL Metro Area	21,763	16,523	14,950	10,073	45.6	47,847	38,855	38,944	8,301	6,726	6,679	4,169
Prescott, AZ Metro Area	7,900	6,141	5,387	3,676	46.6	35,545	29,088	27,568	3,512	2,789	2,711	1,806
Providence-Warwick, RI-MA Metro Area	79,722	67,310	58,350	47,202	36.6	49,423	42,006	36,167	51,078	43,588	39,820	31,571
Provo-Orem, UT Metro Area	20,050	13,733	10,567	7,590	89.8	34,227	25,898	24,036	13,730	8,921	7,662	5,769
Pueblo, CO Metro Area	5,698	4,678	3,992	3,356	42.8	34,831	29,326	26,642	3,401	2,915	2,560	2,155
Punta Gorda, FL Metro Area	6,534	5,153	4,723	3,778	38.3	37,745	32,216	30,420	2,565	2,059	2,080	1,512
Racine, WI Metro Area	8,483	7,365	6,549	5,556	29.5	43,486	37,682	33,887	4,982	4,348	4,200	3,579
Raleigh, NC Metro Area	61,655	48,483	36,895	27,449	67.1	48,411	42,624	39,053	43,513	32,472	26,334	20,524
Rapid City, SD Metro Area	6,454	5,340	4,337	3,186	48.8	44,775	39,533	34,422	4,274	3,524	3,054	2,196
Reading, PA Metro Area	18,609	15,686	13,015	11,081	43.0	44,813	38,074	32,871	12,157	10,095	9,112	7,773
Redding, CA Metro Area	7,340	6,061	5,262	4,146	39.5	40,882	34,181	29,962	4,183	3,662	3,607	2,713
Reno, NV Metro Area	21,429	17,982	17,706	12,981	21.0	47,526	42,200	44,652	13,665	12,326	12,659	9,672
Richmond, VA Metro Area	64,152	51,533	44,583	34,047	43.9	50,460	42,580	39,278	48,286	39,145	35,672	27,444
Riverside-San Bernardino-Ontario, CA Metro Area	159,429	126,656	111,588	76,375	42.9	35,514	29,844	28,792	94,676	73,753	72,482	46,556
Roanoke, VA Metro Area	13,653	11,646	9,938	8,037	37.4	43,405	37,729	33,527	10,005	8,708	7,838	6,416
Rochester, MN Metro Area	10,454	8,796	7,038	5,560	48.5	48,881	42,459	35,691	8,314	7,205	6,122	4,657
Rochester, NY Metro Area	49,852	42,717	35,708	31,864	39.6	46,076	39,542	33,358	36,131	31,957	27,971	24,986
Rockford, IL Metro Area	13,516	11,741	10,091	8,877	33.9	39,674	33,619	30,042	9,370	7,963	7,785	7,033
Rocky Mount, NC Metro Area	5,398	4,861	4,104	3,503	31.5	36,459	31,888	27,914	3,275	3,110	2,956	2,656
Rome, GA Metro Area	3,383	2,931	2,619	2,165	29.2	35,054	30,395	27,761	2,397	2,095	1,941	1,609
Sacramento—Roseville—Arden-Arcade, CA Metro Area	112,889	87,912	76,666	56,089	47.2	49,639	40,804	37,676	80,780	64,539	61,871	44,234
Saginaw, MI Metro Area	6,849	6,103	5,608	5,435	22.1	35,429	30,527	27,041	5,018	4,509	4,647	4,705
St. Cloud, MN Metro Area	8,054	6,451	5,363	4,237	50.2	41,429	34,090	29,924	6,374	5,022	4,492	3,480
St. George, UT Metro Area	4,881	3,508	2,841	1,746	71.8	31,368	25,343	23,870	2,928	2,002	1,938	1,100
St. Joseph, MO-KS Metro Area	4,516	3,960	3,345	2,915	35.0	35,589	31,120	27,086	3,299	2,877	2,493	2,077
St. Louis, MO-IL Metro Area	137,702	118,065	102,431	85,828	34.4	48,977	42,317	37,516	98,802	85,706	77,241	65,138
Salem, OR Metro Area	15,223	12,085	10,147	8,664	50.0	37,121	30,866	27,571	10,093	8,150	7,265	6,158
Salinas, CA Metro Area	21,624	17,247	14,856	12,717	45.6	49,836	41,418	36,670	15,011	12,203	10,727	8,973
Salisbury, MD-DE Metro Area	17,115	13,594	11,566	8,293	48.0	43,296	36,272	33,455	9,779	7,788	7,623	5,414
Salt Lake City, UT Metro Area	51,558	38,770	31,965	25,880	61.3	44,057	35,513	32,054	48,332	36,017	29,969	24,567
San Angelo, TX Metro Area	5,274	4,100	3,269	2,556	61.3	44,072	36,515	30,672	3,375	2,748	2,287	1,769
San Antonio-New Braunfels, TX Metro Area	103,790	76,786	59,411	46,101	74.7	43,535	35,661	31,329	73,724	53,911	44,079	34,842
San Diego-Carlsbad, CA Metro Area	175,859	136,576	123,685	94,885	42.2	53,298	43,995	42,093	128,209	101,885	97,467	72,196
San Francisco-Oakland-Hayward, CA Metro Area	368,795	264,061	235,798	203,143	56.4	79,206	60,768	56,986	275,320	197,941	180,534	159,873
Oakland-Hayward-Berkeley, CA Metro Division	176,127	128,788	119,209	99,135	47.7	63,700	50,177	48,845	110,681	86,579	84,091	66,796
San Francisco-Redwood City-South San Francisco, CA Metro Division	164,175	114,223	95,788	86,818	71.4	100,724	74,862	65,920	151,223	100,662	86,136	85,365
San Rafael, CA Metro Division	28,493	21,050	20,801	17,190	37.0	109,076	83,232	85,179	13,416	10,700	10,307	7,712
San Jose-Sunnyvale-Santa Clara, CA Metro Area	161,295	111,306	89,936	93,416	79.3	81,592	60,414	51,987	153,129	103,382	86,453	100,444
San Luis Obispo-Paso Robles-Arroyo Grande, CA Metro Area	14,034	10,779	9,266	6,969	51.5	49,873	39,935	35,830	8,636	6,763	6,248	4,517
Santa Cruz-Watsonville, CA Metro Area	15,697	12,565	10,643	10,173	47.5	57,257	47,729	42,339	8,698	7,683	6,358	5,741
Santa Fe, NM Metro Area	7,536	6,145	5,224	4,097	44.3	50,684	42,540	37,963	4,152	3,779	3,343	2,541
Santa Maria-Santa Barbara, CA Metro Area	24,208	19,181	17,212	13,368	40.6	54,428	45,198	42,178	16,579	13,465	12,200	9,154
Santa Rosa, CA Metro Area	26,875	20,627	18,993	16,887	41.5	53,520	42,548	40,763	16,720	13,177	12,729	10,703
Savannah, GA Metro Area	15,894	13,047	10,447	8,058	52.1	41,915	37,411	33,214	11,054	8,828	7,627	5,904
Scranton—Wilkes-Barre—Hazleton, PA Metro Area	23,167	20,492	17,411	15,020	33.1	41,505	36,350	31,278	15,271	13,272	12,268	10,493
Seattle-Tacoma-Bellevue, WA Metro Area	227,827	166,156	142,180	119,112	60.2	61,021	48,180	44,455	178,208	130,401	115,500	100,670
Seattle-Bellevue-Everett, WA Metro Division	190,187	135,899	116,809	98,993	62.8	65,817	51,221	47,675	154,579	110,652	99,144	88,670
Tacoma-Lakewood, WA Metro Division	37,640	30,257	25,371	20,119	48.4	44,600	38,038	33,912	23,629	19,750	16,356	12,000
Sebastian-Vero Beach, FL Metro Area	10,055	7,419	6,875	4,505	46.3	67,978	53,668	53,730	3,274	2,561	2,563	1,808
Sebring, FL Metro Area	3,179	2,850	2,386	1,830	33.2	31,949	28,881	24,958	1,413	1,269	1,185	820
Sheboygan, WI Metro Area	5,304	4,452	3,911	3,364	35.6	45,896	38,555	34,173	3,892	3,342	3,173	2,699
Sherman-Denison, TX Metro Area	4,916	3,875	3,150	2,596	56.1	39,181	32,016	27,231	2,736	2,255	2,010	1,852
Shreveport-Bossier City, LA Metro Area	20,127	16,764	13,145	10,120	53.1	45,360	37,998	30,979	14,026	11,875	9,629	7,294
Sierra Vista-Douglas, AZ Metro Area	4,821	4,607	3,574	2,445	34.9	38,133	34,954	28,411	2,651	2,840	2,243	1,515
Sioux City, IA-NE-SD Metro Area	7,864	6,804	5,671	4,509	38.7	46,514	40,301	34,405	5,806	5,056	4,422	3,486

[1]Based on resident population estimated as of July 1 of the year shown.

Table B-11.   Personal Income and Earnings by Place of Work—*Continued*

| | Personal Income | | | | | | | | | | | |
| | Total (million dollars) | | | | Percent change, 2005–2015 | Per capita[1] (dollars) | | | Earnings (million dollars) | | | |
Metropolitan statistical area and division	2015	2010	2005	2000		2015	2010	2005	2015	2010	2005	2000
Sioux Falls, SD Metro Area	13,542	10,519	7,787	5,802	73.9	53,769	45,895	37,689	10,923	8,209	6,292	4,717
South Bend-Mishawaka, IN-MI Metro Area	13,560	10,788	9,944	8,651	36.4	42,362	33,819	31,348	8,862	7,121	7,125	6,195
Spartanburg, SC Metro Area	12,338	9,814	8,340	6,969	47.9	37,954	31,286	28,394	8,898	7,012	6,449	5,535
Spokane-Spokane Valley, WA Metro Area	21,775	18,155	14,469	12,251	50.5	39,748	34,347	29,266	14,906	12,402	10,886	9,206
Springfield, IL Metro Area	9,204	8,153	6,785	6,202	35.7	43,590	38,731	33,101	6,903	6,323	5,585	5,133
Springfield, MA Metro Area	29,295	24,253	20,631	17,002	42.0	46,354	38,904	33,463	18,712	15,736	14,220	11,569
Springfield, MO Metro Area	16,808	13,940	12,078	8,965	39.2	36,824	31,870	29,978	11,936	9,895	9,471	6,786
Springfield, OH Metro Area	5,055	4,434	3,939	3,785	28.4	37,183	32,074	27,862	2,738	2,453	2,375	2,371
State College, PA Metro Area	6,639	5,415	4,469	3,410	48.5	41,344	35,108	30,707	5,883	4,773	4,052	2,942
Staunton-Waynesboro, VA Metro Area	4,809	4,181	3,423	2,721	40.5	40,000	35,331	30,006	2,868	2,602	2,313	1,894
Stockton-Lodi, CA Metro Area	28,151	22,214	19,484	14,134	44.5	38,769	32,314	29,657	16,517	13,591	13,376	9,214
Sumter, SC Metro Area	3,959	3,250	2,787	2,230	42.1	36,834	30,213	26,269	2,576	2,089	1,986	1,644
Syracuse, NY Metro Area	29,258	25,050	20,968	18,019	39.5	44,299	37,781	32,011	21,444	18,865	16,738	14,336
Tallahassee, FL Metro Area	14,258	12,697	10,843	8,348	31.5	37,728	34,372	31,496	10,331	9,343	8,666	6,845
Tampa-St. Petersburg-Clearwater, FL Metro Area	127,958	107,636	92,138	70,833	38.9	43,008	38,597	34,748	85,385	69,388	66,202	50,828
Terre Haute, IN Metro Area	5,882	5,273	4,501	3,923	30.7	34,396	30,605	26,379	3,841	3,641	3,308	2,803
Texarkana, TX-AR Metro Area	5,246	4,756	3,905	3,191	34.3	35,026	31,845	27,020	3,449	3,291	2,844	2,278
The Villages, FL Metro Area	4,638	2,813	1,666	837	178.3	39,012	29,833	24,061	1,543	1,121	782	358
Toledo, OH Metro Area	25,503	21,560	19,360	17,144	31.7	42,087	35,337	31,388	19,683	16,443	16,102	14,184
Topeka, KS Metro Area	9,905	8,572	7,044	6,149	40.6	42,365	36,591	30,865	6,947	6,060	5,284	4,582
Trenton, NJ Metro Area	23,490	19,548	17,386	14,435	35.1	63,247	53,125	48,025	21,001	17,600	15,626	12,256
Tucson, AZ Metro Area	38,922	33,362	28,572	21,030	36.2	38,536	33,978	31,046	23,659	21,471	18,903	14,286
Tulsa, OK Metro Area	56,631	37,105	31,434	23,637	80.2	57,727	39,474	35,605	43,494	26,910	24,469	18,161
Tuscaloosa, AL Metro Area	8,499	7,278	6,089	4,799	39.6	35,424	31,584	28,647	6,131	5,136	4,517	3,426
Tyler, TX Metro Area	11,197	8,676	6,496	4,767	72.4	50,224	41,224	33,944	8,656	6,647	5,144	3,750
Urban Honolulu, HI Metro Area	52,055	43,244	35,681	27,574	45.9	52,122	45,216	38,860	38,509	31,863	27,937	20,854
Utica-Rome, NY Metro Area	11,572	10,555	8,553	7,438	35.3	39,146	35,268	28,648	7,509	7,191	6,067	5,278
Valdosta, GA Metro Area	4,592	4,028	3,316	2,598	38.5	32,138	28,754	26,232	3,121	2,719	2,464	1,860
Vallejo-Fairfield, CA Metro Area	19,408	15,455	14,055	11,157	38.1	44,504	37,324	34,434	11,283	9,436	8,247	5,916
Victoria, TX Metro Area	4,696	3,418	2,903	2,394	61.8	47,005	36,327	31,716	3,042	2,314	2,017	1,592
Vineland-Bridgeton, NJ Metro Area	5,650	5,184	4,344	3,469	30.1	36,253	32,987	28,576	4,060	3,650	3,370	2,630
Virginia Beach-Norfolk-Newport News, VA-NC Metro Area	80,034	68,253	58,718	44,380	36.3	46,400	40,627	35,608	56,429	50,064	45,517	33,298
Visalia-Porterville, CA Metro Area	16,809	13,264	10,555	7,315	59.3	36,551	29,936	25,871	10,352	8,422	7,467	5,103
Waco, TX Metro Area	9,702	7,888	6,494	5,230	49.4	36,917	31,076	26,971	7,010	5,749	4,970	3,944
Walla Walla, WA Metro Area	2,721	2,220	1,689	1,453	61.1	42,333	35,228	27,896	1,870	1,569	1,275	1,083
Warner Robins, GA Metro Area	7,120	6,101	4,917	3,597	44.8	37,841	33,814	30,383	4,763	4,426	3,714	2,700
Washington-Arlington-Alexandria, DC-VA-MD-WV Metro Area	395,632	329,497	272,340	206,821	45.3	64,882	58,148	51,642	326,298	282,309	235,420	175,172
Silver Spring-Frederick-Rockville, MD Metro Division	93,413	80,648	68,158	51,925	37.1	72,670	66,631	59,644	62,526	55,258	45,798	33,036
Washington-Arlington-Alexandria, DC-VA-MD-WV Metro Division	302,219	248,849	204,183	154,896	48.0	62,802	55,844	49,429	263,772	227,050	189,622	142,136
Waterloo-Cedar Falls, IA Metro Area	7,077	6,025	4,968	4,160	42.4	41,478	35,879	30,431	5,383	4,679	3,998	3,198
Watertown-Fort Drum, NY Metro Area	5,078	4,821	3,542	2,677	43.4	43,170	41,359	31,214	3,923	3,999	2,854	2,023
Wausau, WI Metro Area	5,967	5,057	4,414	3,548	35.2	43,921	37,717	34,226	4,628	3,702	3,577	2,867
Weirton-Steubenville, WV-OH Metro Area	4,402	3,812	3,241	2,982	35.8	36,529	30,669	25,424	2,232	2,101	2,129	1,989
Wenatchee, WA Metro Area	4,860	3,760	2,946	2,440	65.0	41,836	33,786	28,503	3,127	2,398	2,070	1,659
Wheeling, WV-OH Metro Area	5,854	4,870	4,428	3,608	32.2	40,594	32,937	29,628	3,873	3,217	3,125	2,343
Wichita, KS Metro Area	31,148	24,143	19,575	16,861	59.1	48,321	38,207	32,830	21,617	17,915	14,768	13,142
Wichita Falls, TX Metro Area	6,393	5,607	4,572	3,736	39.8	42,398	36,973	30,250	4,206	3,860	3,295	2,650
Williamsport, PA Metro Area	4,778	3,962	3,326	2,823	43.6	41,171	34,091	28,303	3,389	2,753	2,510	2,111
Wilmington, NC Metro Area	10,819	8,586	7,489	5,522	44.5	38,922	33,586	32,433	7,251	5,908	5,351	3,953
Winchester, VA-WV Metro Area	5,680	4,696	3,840	2,751	47.9	42,436	36,490	32,587	3,744	3,032	2,831	2,051
Winston-Salem, NC Metro Area	26,516	22,644	19,686	16,420	34.7	40,217	35,304	32,657	17,180	14,890	13,469	11,601
Worcester, MA-CT Metro Area	47,102	39,330	33,043	27,800	42.5	50,348	42,800	36,841	28,180	23,808	21,439	18,502
Yakima, WA Metro Area	9,587	7,813	5,896	5,003	62.6	38,527	31,981	25,794	6,301	5,113	4,141	3,452
York-Hanover, PA Metro Area	19,774	17,614	14,740	11,153	34.2	44,651	40,442	36,033	11,588	10,761	10,107	7,625
Youngstown-Warren-Boardman, OH-PA Metro Area	21,145	18,519	17,262	14,934	22.5	38,454	32,784	29,547	13,085	11,585	12,038	10,368
Yuba City, CA Metro Area	6,704	5,557	4,332	3,242	54.8	39,216	33,243	27,940	3,689	3,159	2,636	2,018
Yuma, AZ Metro Area	6,450	5,331	4,289	2,881	50.4	31,574	27,049	23,983	4,351	3,548	3,133	2,095

[1]Based on resident population estimated as of July 1 of the year shown.

Table B-12. Employees and Earnings by Selected Major Industries, 2015

Metropolitan statistical area and division	Employees						Earnings					
		Percent by selected major industries						Percent by selected major industries				
	Total[1]	Manu-facturing	Finance and insurance	Professional, scientific and technical services	Health care and social services	Government and government enterprises	Total[1] (million dollars)	Manu-facturing	Finance and insurance	Professional, scientific and technical services	Health care and social services	Government and government enterprises
Abilene, TX Metro Area	102,241	3.3	5.4	3.7	11.2	16.4	4,765	3.9	4.3	4.4	13.3	22.2
Akron, OH Metro Area	427,809	9.7	4.2	6.0	12.8	11.1	22,335	13.5	4.3	6.6	13.7	14.0
Albany, GA Metro Area	82,424	D	D	5.4	12.7	16.4	3,421	D	D	5.3	17.0	23.4
Albany, OR Metro Area	58,968	13.3	2.4	3.3	11.4	11.3	2,611	21.0	2.1	2.6	11.7	15.3
Albany-Schenectady-Troy, NY Metro Area	559,183	4.8	5.7	7.9	12.6	18.5	35,051	7.5	6.1	9.9	11.1	28.8
Albuquerque, NM Metro Area	490,780	3.8	3.9	D	12.2	17.7	23,901	5.5	4.3	D	12.6	25.8
Alexandria, LA Metro Area	82,262	6.2	D	3.9	D	17.2	3,973	8.4	D	4.2	D	22.6
Allentown-Bethlehem-Easton, PA-NJ Metro Area..	459,979	8.3	4.3	4.9	14.7	9.1	25,750	13.3	4.1	5.1	15.9	12.0
Altoona, PA Metro Area	75,748	10.3	2.9	3.9	16.5	11.7	3,646	13.0	2.3	4.2	19.5	16.0
Amarillo, TX Metro Area	163,435	8.2	6.2	D	D	12.8	8,484	10.8	4.7	D	D	15.0
Ames, IA Metro Area	63,312	7.4	2.5	5.6	7.1	32.1	3,233	14.0	2.1	6.5	7.4	38.9
Anchorage, AK Metro Area	246,276	1.5	3.3	6.9	12.6	19.2	16,789	1.1	3.1	8.3	12.9	27.3
Ann Arbor, MI Metro Area	259,217	5.9	3.0	9.6	10.5	28.7	14,801	7.9	3.2	12.9	11.2	35.1
Anniston-Oxford-Jacksonville, AL Metro Area	58,328	10.5	2.8	3.3	9.0	21.8	2,442	14.5	2.7	3.1	10.7	32.8
Appleton, WI Metro Area	152,299	16.2	6.0	D	9.6	8.8	7,751	22.2	7.0	D	11.1	11.7
Asheville, NC Metro Area	260,214	8.3	3.0	D	D	10.2	10,915	12.6	3.1	D	D	14.6
Athens-Clarke County, GA Metro Area	117,382	6.1	3.5	D	11.2	23.8	5,322	9.5	4.9	D	14.7	30.9
Atlanta-Sandy Springs-Roswell, GA Metro Area	3,529,941	4.8	5.2	8.7	8.9	9.5	202,116	6.6	7.2	12.7	8.8	11.4
Atlantic City-Hammonton, NJ Metro Area	165,470	D	3.0	4.4	12.5	14.4	8,590	D	2.7	5.7	15.5	25.1
Auburn-Opelika, AL Metro Area	78,351	9.0	2.8	4.5	5.5	22.7	2,985	12.8	2.9	4.6	6.4	35.0
Augusta-Richmond County, GA-SC Metro Area	304,173	7.0	3.0	D	10.4	20.2	15,057	10.2	3.0	D	11.4	28.5
Austin-Round Rock, TX Metro Area	1,318,500	4.9	5.6	10.9	8.2	12.9	80,171	9.0	6.3	15.2	8.0	15.0
Bakersfield, CA Metro Area	406,153	3.9	2.6	4.2	9.6	16.0	23,895	4.9	2.0	4.3	8.3	24.0
Baltimore-Columbia-Towson, MD Metro Area	1,789,755	3.3	4.8	9.3	13.2	15.3	114,056	4.4	6.2	13.4	12.7	23.3
Bangor, ME Metro Area	91,360	3.6	2.7	3.8	17.4	15.9	4,020	4.7	3.1	3.7	22.3	21.4
Barnstable Town, MA Metro Area	147,639	D	3.8	6.7	13.0	11.0	7,039	D	3.4	7.4	16.1	18.7
Baton Rouge, LA Metro Area	522,387	6.0	D	6.1	10.3	14.2	27,761	11.9	D	8.3	10.6	16.9
Battle Creek, MI Metro Area	71,794	17.0	2.4	D	14.3	15.4	3,842	22.3	1.7	D	13.8	20.7
Bay City, MI Metro Area	47,916	9.1	3.6	6.4	15.4	12.6	2,168	13.6	2.7	12.3	18.3	17.3
Beaumont-Port Arthur, TX Metro Area	216,244	11.2	D	4.7	11.1	11.7	12,541	24.4	D	6.6	9.9	12.4
Beckley, WV Metro Area	55,553	2.5	2.4	3.7	16.8	16.9	2,426	2.8	2.3	4.5	18.7	22.8
Bellingham, WA Metro Area	120,008	8.4	3.0	5.8	11.0	13.4	5,880	13.4	3.1	5.7	12.4	18.8
Bend-Redmond, OR Metro Area	108,348	5.5	3.9	7.1	12.1	8.4	5,051	6.1	4.1	8.1	17.7	12.4
Billings, MT Metro Area	114,272	D	D	D	D	9.1	5,788	D	D	D	D	11.5
Binghamton, NY Metro Area	129,416	9.3	3.3	D	13.8	17.0	6,487	15.8	2.8	D	14.8	26.3
Birmingham-Hoover, AL Metro Area	665,758	6.0	7.1	D	10.9	12.6	36,393	7.5	10.4	D	14.7	14.6
Bismarck, ND Metro Area	97,293	D	D	D	14.6	16.4	5,205	D	D	D	16.6	19.4
Blacksburg-Christiansburg-Radford, VA Metro Area	93,940	13.0	2.2	D	8.3	23.9	4,249	20.9	1.5	D	9.0	33.3
Bloomington, IL Metro Area	120,161	4.2	19.4	D	D	13.9	7,015	5.0	33.9	D	D	15.3
Bloomington, IN Metro Area	94,765	9.4	2.8	4.3	D	24.7	4,146	15.0	2.9	5.1	D	32.9
Bloomsburg-Berwick, PA Metro Area	53,050	10.9	4.6	3.5	D	13.2	2,830	12.2	5.1	3.3	D	15.6
Boise City, ID Metro Area	394,739	6.9	4.7	6.3	D	12.0	19,484	12.7	5.0	7.2	D	14.4
Boston-Cambridge-Newton, MA-NH Metro Area	3,423,787	D	6.5	11.2	13.8	9.3	261,620	D	10.9	17.4	12.5	11.1
Boston, MA Metro Division	1,529,921	D	9.0	10.0	15.7	10.0	124,752	D	18.0	16.1	14.5	12.0
Cambridge-Newton-Framingham, MA Metro Division	1,622,578	7.5	4.2	13.0	12.7	8.5	121,432	12.4	4.0	19.7	10.7	9.9
Rockingham County-Strafford County, NH Metro Division	271,288	D	5.5	7.4	9.6	10.2	15,437	D	7.8	9.7	9.9	12.2
Boulder, CO Metro Area	257,993	7.5	4.2	15.8	9.9	13.4	14,920	12.1	3.7	24.2	9.8	15.0
Bowling Green, KY Metro Area	96,041	D	D	D	10.8	13.2	4,106	D	D	D	13.4	16.7
Bremerton-Silverdale, WA Metro Area	127,849	2.4	2.5	6.3	11.3	33.4	7,168	2.0	1.8	6.1	10.2	52.7
Bridgeport-Stamford-Norwalk, CT Metro Area	654,269	5.5	11.6	8.8	11.6	7.6	60,699	12.1	21.4	10.3	8.0	7.1
Brownsville-Harlingen, TX Metro Area	192,539	3.6	3.5	2.8	20.2	16.5	7,068	5.3	2.8	2.7	19.2	26.8
Brunswick, GA Metro Area	57,403	D	3.2	4.2	6.6	18.4	2,424	D	2.7	4.1	7.6	31.7
Buffalo-Cheektowaga-Niagara Falls, NY Metro Area..	665,283	8.2	6.2	6.0	12.6	13.5	36,777	11.9	6.2	7.0	12.4	22.0
Burlington, NC Metro Area	79,897	11.9	3.3	3.3	13.7	9.3	3,291	16.3	3.6	3.4	20.1	11.5
Burlington-South Burlington, VT Metro Area	162,774	8.6	3.3	D	D	14.6	8,591	12.1	4.2	D	D	20.1
California-Lexington Park, MD Metro Area	60,561	1.1	1.5	17.2	8.2	27.6	4,274	0.7	0.7	23.9	6.3	46.7
Canton-Massillon, OH Metro Area	220,861	13.1	4.2	3.9	14.1	9.4	10,076	20.2	4.1	4.8	15.6	12.7
Cape Coral-Fort Myers, FL Metro Area	352,206	1.9	4.7	6.5	8.4	11.7	16,050	2.6	3.5	8.8	11.4	18.1
Cape Girardeau, MO-IL Metro Area	60,876	7.3	D	3.6	D	12.4	2,636	12.4	D	3.9	D	15.5
Carbondale-Marion, IL Metro Area	73,472	5.3	4.8	D	13.2	24.9	3,393	6.6	3.8	D	17.1	36.2
Carson City, NV Metro Area	38,144	7.4	6.2	4.3	11.0	25.2	2,130	8.6	2.0	5.9	14.0	38.3
Casper, WY Metro Area	57,246	3.3	4.0	4.4	11.9	11.0	4,135	3.5	2.1	4.1	10.9	11.0
Cedar Rapids, IA Metro Area	180,987	11.4	6.5	4.1	10.5	9.7	9,639	21.2	8.0	5.1	10.6	11.3
Chambersburg-Waynesboro, PA Metro Area	79,223	12.6	2.5	3.7	12.0	10.7	3,691	17.9	2.2	3.9	14.7	16.7
Champaign-Urbana, IL Metro Area	139,985	6.1	3.5	5.0	D	28.0	7,919	6.5	2.6	5.2	D	34.9
Charleston, WV Metro Area	139,656	D	D	D	D	18.1	7,525	D	D	D	D	19.0
Charleston-North Charleston, SC Metro Area	446,141	6.1	3.4	7.4	8.3	16.9	23,358	10.1	5.4	10.3	9.5	23.1
Charlotte-Concord-Gastonia, NC-SC Metro Area	1,480,569	7.4	6.6	D	D	10.5	88,000	9.0	11.5	D	D	11.8
Charlottesville, VA Metro Area	150,717	2.9	3.5	8.0	8.5	24.0	8,241	3.6	4.7	10.4	9.7	34.5
Chattanooga, TN-GA Metro Area	312,709	10.7	5.5	D	10.3	12.1	16,440	14.0	6.2	D	12.1	16.5
Cheyenne, WY Metro Area	66,805	2.3	5.5	4.5	7.1	26.2	3,487	3.8	3.7	4.7	7.7	40.1
Chicago-Naperville-Elgin, IL-IN-WI Metro Area	5,956,234	7.2	6.2	D	D	10.0	389,395	10.2	8.5	D	D	12.3

D = Data withheld due to disclosure.
[1]Includes other industry categories not shown separately.

Table B-12. Employees and Earnings by Selected Major Industries, 2015—*Continued*

Metropolitan statistical area and division	Employees Total[1]	Manufacturing	Finance and insurance	Professional, scientific and technical services	Health care and social services	Government and government enterprises	Earnings Total[1] (million dollars)	Manufacturing	Finance and insurance	Professional, scientific and technical services	Health care and social services	Government and government enterprises
Chicago-Naperville-Arlington Heights,												
IL Metro Division	4,749,658	6.2	6.6	8.9	11.4	9.5	315,851	7.8	9.4	14.6	9.7	11.9
Elgin, IL Metro Division	322,612	11.3	4.6	5.4	D	14.2	16,828	16.0	4.1	6.3	D	19.9
Gary, IN Metro Division	343,840	10.8	3.0	4.0	13.2	10.8	17,253	21.2	2.6	3.9	14.6	11.0
Lake County-Kenosha County,												
IL-WI Metro Division	540,124	11.3	6.0	7.2	8.7	12.1	39,463	22.6	5.0	8.4	7.0	13.1
Chico, CA Metro Area	110,348	4.6	3.7	5.0	17.8	14.8	5,185	5.1	3.8	5.0	20.1	22.6
Cincinnati, OH-KY-IN Metro Area	1,318,294	D	5.6	6.6	12.0	10.1	75,932	D	7.0	8.4	12.3	11.6
Clarksville, TN-KY Metro Area	145,978	7.4	2.2	2.9	D	33.8	7,715	8.9	1.9	2.8	D	50.7
Cleveland, TN Metro Area	62,546	15.7	3.2	3.0	D	9.8	2,746	23.5	2.5	2.5	D	12.0
Cleveland-Elyria, OH Metro Area	1,315,898	9.8	5.3	6.5	14.1	10.5	74,587	13.7	6.7	9.1	14.3	14.0
Coeur d'Alene, ID Metro Area	81,990	6.8	4.5	5.4	9.9	13.6	3,201	8.7	5.1	5.7	12.5	21.0
College Station-Bryan, TX Metro Area	146,061	4.1	3.3	D	D	27.0	6,498	4.7	2.7	D	D	33.4
Colorado Springs, CO Metro Area	404,317	D	5.4	8.4	9.0	22.0	20,805	D	4.7	12.5	9.6	32.5
Columbia, MO Metro Area	125,068	3.5	4.6	5.6	9.7	25.3	5,880	4.5	5.8	6.4	11.2	36.3
Columbia, SC Metro Area	487,757	6.7	5.5	5.2	8.9	19.6	24,653	10.8	6.7	7.3	9.3	25.5
Columbus, GA-AL Metro Area	180,203	D	D	4.6	D	25.9	8,743	D	D	5.4	D	37.5
Columbus, IN Metro Area	60,433	32.5	2.6	4.1	7.2	10.9	3,541	48.5	2.8	4.2	7.1	9.2
Columbus, OH Metro Area	1,316,793	5.7	6.3	6.8	11.7	13.2	75,364	8.2	8.3	9.4	10.8	18.2
Corpus Christi, TX Metro Area	260,599	4.0	4.1	4.6	D	14.4	14,030	9.9	2.9	5.9	D	17.8
Corvallis, OR Metro Area	50,570	6.6	2.3	8.1	12.9	22.7	2,584	11.2	2.0	9.0	16.0	31.0
Crestview-Fort Walton Beach-Destin,												
FL Metro Area	161,777	2.5	3.7	6.8	7.6	22.0	8,028	3.6	3.0	10.1	7.9	38.2
Cumberland, MD-WV Metro Area	48,382	9.1	2.9	D	D	16.9	2,180	13.9	3.0	D	D	24.6
Dallas-Fort Worth-Arlington, TX Metro Area	4,647,142	6.1	7.6	7.8	D	9.1	292,806	9.2	8.6	10.7	D	10.2
Dallas-Plano-Irving, TX Metro Division	3,264,219	5.5	8.3	9.0	8.7	8.8	213,808	8.3	9.5	12.5	9.3	9.6
Fort Worth-Arlington, TX Metro Division	1,382,923	7.4	5.9	5.2	9.1	9.9	78,998	11.6	6.2	5.9	9.3	11.8
Dalton, GA Metro Area	79,471	29.2	2.1	D	D	9.3	3,872	35.3	1.5	D	D	10.1
Danville, IL Metro Area	37,723	14.3	4.6	1.9	8.9	15.7	1,776	21.9	4.2	1.6	9.7	22.5
Daphne-Fairhope-Foley, AL Metro Area	103,690	4.4	3.8	4.6	9.2	9.7	3,626	6.9	3.7	5.2	13.0	14.4
Davenport-Moline-Rock Island, IA-IL Metro Area	230,571	10.5	4.3	D	11.6	11.9	12,194	15.4	4.2	D	11.8	16.2
Dayton, OH Metro Area	472,062	8.9	4.1	6.7	14.1	14.4	25,278	12.3	4.5	8.9	15.3	22.6
Decatur, AL Metro Area	73,806	16.8	3.0	3.5	D	12.1	3,152	30.4	3.3	3.9	D	14.9
Decatur, IL Metro Area	63,485	16.3	4.0	3.7	14.1	9.4	3,727	30.8	3.2	3.7	12.5	10.7
Deltona-Daytona Beach-Ormond Beach,												
FL Metro Area	269,100	4.5	4.0	5.5	13.3	8.9	10,409	7.3	3.3	6.2	17.9	15.0
Denver-Aurora-Lakewood, CO Metro Area	1,906,208	4.0	D	9.9	9.2	11.0	124,486	5.0	D	13.2	8.3	12.3
Des Moines-West Des Moines, IA Metro Area	443,133	4.8	13.4	5.8	10.6	10.3	24,952	5.9	20.8	7.7	10.4	12.9
Detroit-Warren-Dearborn, MI Metro Area	2,507,050	9.9	4.6	D	12.7	7.9	148,970	14.6	5.3	D	11.9	9.9
Detroit-Dearborn-Livonia, MI Metro Division	933,073	9.9	3.7	D	15.0	9.7	56,498	15.0	4.3	D	13.6	12.2
Warren-Troy-Farmington Hills,												
MI Metro Division	1,573,977	9.9	5.2	11.7	11.4	6.8	92,471	14.4	5.9	17.1	10.8	8.4
Dothan, AL Metro Area	78,312	5.9	3.1	3.3	D	14.5	3,248	7.3	3.3	4.0	D	18.8
Dover, DE Metro Area	88,423	D	3.6	3.5	11.7	26.4	4,339	D	2.9	4.0	12.3	37.9
Dubuque, IA Metro Area	73,823	12.9	6.8	4.7	12.3	6.9	3,396	20.0	8.9	6.3	14.0	8.4
Duluth, MN-WI Metro Area	163,884	5.0	3.9	4.3	18.3	15.9	7,920	6.9	3.6	4.8	20.7	19.6
Durham-Chapel Hill, NC Metro Area	377,890	8.1	4.4	10.3	14.1	17.5	24,634	15.6	5.6	13.8	15.4	19.9
East Stroudsburg, PA Metro Area	75,839	6.8	3.0	4.1	10.6	15.8	3,547	14.6	1.8	2.3	12.1	26.1
Eau Claire, WI Metro Area	109,186	10.3	4.4	4.0	14.8	11.6	5,218	14.8	4.3	4.0	18.9	15.6
El Centro, CA Metro Area	81,756	1.8	1.9	2.3	12.4	22.5	4,203	1.7	1.4	1.8	6.0	38.8
Elizabethtown-Fort Knox, KY Metro Area	77,182	10.4	D	3.2	D	26.2	3,833	14.5	D	3.3	D	42.8
Elkhart-Goshen, IN Metro Area	152,475	40.7	1.9	2.4	7.7	6.1	8,045	49.1	1.7	2.2	7.8	6.0
Elmira, NY Metro Area	45,197	12.2	3.6	2.9	15.3	13.8	2,424	16.5	4.2	2.4	15.6	25.0
El Paso, TX Metro Area	423,596	D	D	D	10.5	22.8	19,012	D	D	D	9.9	37.1
Enid, OK Metro Area	39,915	6.9	3.5	5.1	10.8	13.2	2,016	7.6	3.2	6.1	10.5	16.7
Erie, PA Metro Area	162,399	14.1	4.8	3.6	15.7	11.0	7,787	21.8	6.4	3.6	17.4	16.0
Eugene, OR Metro Area	201,201	7.4	3.5	5.3	13.6	13.0	9,347	9.8	4.1	5.2	16.4	18.8
Evansville, IN-KY Metro Area	191,655	12.2	2.9	4.2	D	9.3	9,718	20.5	2.8	5.0	D	9.7
Fairbanks, AK Metro Area	58,295	1.6	1.9	4.1	9.8	34.1	3,877	1.1	1.4	3.1	9.4	46.4
Fargo, ND-MN Metro Area	174,274	6.0	6.9	5.2	D	11.3	9,059	8.6	7.5	6.2	D	13.7
Farmington, NM Metro Area	65,503	2.4	2.2	2.7	11.3	17.8	3,227	2.4	1.7	2.3	11.9	21.2
Fayetteville, NC Metro Area	213,544	3.8	1.8	D	D	41.5	12,357	4.6	1.2	D	D	62.6
Fayetteville-Springdale-Rogers,												
AR-MO Metro Area	302,656	9.3	2.6	5.5	8.8	11.0	15,534	9.8	2.2	5.9	8.8	12.0
Flagstaff, AZ Metro Area	83,350	5.7	1.9	3.6	11.8	23.0	3,786	10.4	1.3	2.6	15.0	32.5
Flint, MI Metro Area	188,803	6.8	3.8	4.4	15.0	11.2	8,530	12.3	4.5	4.2	18.2	16.2
Florence, SC Metro Area	110,173	9.0	6.5	3.9	11.9	15.6	5,094	16.6	9.0	4.7	13.0	19.1
Florence-Muscle Shoals, AL Metro Area	75,222	13.1	4.0	3.0	9.5	13.9	3,017	19.3	3.9	2.7	12.8	19.7
Fond du Lac, WI Metro Area	60,083	18.2	4.0	2.7	11.2	9.8	3,004	25.4	3.7	2.6	12.7	12.8
Fort Collins, CO Metro Area	217,529	6.6	4.1	8.5	7.9	16.6	10,041	13.6	3.2	11.3	8.7	22.1
Fort Smith, AR-OK Metro Area	146,452	12.4	2.8	D	11.6	13.1	6,383	15.8	2.5	D	13.8	15.7
Fort Wayne, IN Metro Area	268,118	13.6	4.9	D	14.3	8.6	13,164	19.4	6.3	D	17.8	9.7
Fresno, CA Metro Area	477,798	5.7	3.7	4.0	13.5	14.6	24,708	6.6	3.5	4.2	13.9	22.8
Gadsden, AL Metro Area	50,186	11.3	3.6	2.9	16.0	11.6	1,897	16.0	3.8	2.8	22.4	15.0
Gainesville, FL Metro Area	172,101	2.9	3.8	6.0	D	25.8	8,260	3.8	4.4	6.2	D	38.7
Gainesville, GA Metro Area	106,718	18.0	3.7	3.4	12.5	10.4	5,235	21.1	3.8	3.4	16.9	11.5

D = Data withheld due to disclosure.
[1]Includes other industry categories not shown separately.

Table B-12. Employees and Earnings by Selected Major Industries, 2015—*Continued*

| | Employees | | | | | | Earnings | | | | | |
| | | Percent by selected major industries | | | | | | Percent by selected major industries | | | | |
Metropolitan statistical area and division	Total[1]	Manu-facturing	Finance and insurance	Professional, scientific and technical services	Health care and social services	Government and government enterprises	Total[1] (million dollars)	Manu-facturing	Finance and insurance	Professional, scientific and technical services	Health care and social services	Government and government enterprises
Gettysburg, PA Metro Area	47,893	14.8	2.4	3.9	D	8.9	2,095	19.8	2.3	4.0	D	15.6
Glens Falls, NY Metro Area	72,402	8.9	3.8	D	12.4	13.8	3,398	13.6	3.3	D	12.8	23.7
Goldsboro, NC Metro Area	59,106	10.0	3.0	2.7	12.0	22.9	2,750	12.2	2.5	2.9	12.3	31.4
Grand Forks, ND-MN Metro Area	72,776	5.5	3.0	3.3	D	20.7	3,393	6.8	3.0	4.0	D	27.0
Grand Island, NE Metro Area	57,076	14.2	4.5	2.7	9.5	12.4	2,563	17.8	4.0	2.6	10.0	16.3
Grand Junction, CO Metro Area	86,844	3.8	4.4	5.0	12.3	11.7	3,667	4.4	4.4	5.3	16.0	16.9
Grand Rapids-Wyoming, MI Metro Area	674,933	16.7	4.5	D	D	7.3	34,699	24.4	4.8	D	D	9.4
Grants Pass, OR Metro Area	37,223	9.5	3.7	4.1	15.5	8.7	1,447	11.0	3.7	3.4	19.8	13.9
Great Falls, MT Metro Area	50,559	2.8	4.8	4.0	14.4	18.1	2,324	3.6	5.6	4.9	17.0	26.9
Greeley, CO Metro Area	149,738	9.1	4.7	4.4	7.1	11.6	7,910	11.5	3.2	3.5	6.9	11.1
Green Bay, WI Metro Area	214,163	14.0	6.8	D	D	10.5	11,517	16.9	7.8	D	D	12.5
Greensboro-High Point, NC Metro Area	467,460	12.2	4.8	D	10.5	9.7	22,664	17.1	6.0	D	11.6	11.7
Greenville, NC Metro Area	99,045	6.4	3.4	3.3	9.6	27.1	4,791	9.8	3.2	3.2	10.0	38.0
Greenville-Anderson-Mauldin, SC Metro Area	507,440	11.4	3.8	5.7	D	12.0	24,672	16.5	5.5	7.5	D	15.2
Gulfport-Biloxi-Pascagoula, MS Metro Area	208,003	9.4	2.7	4.2	7.4	20.3	9,819	17.1	2.4	5.5	7.4	29.2
Hagerstown-Martinsburg, MD-WV Metro Area	132,173	6.3	6.0	3.8	12.3	13.8	6,193	9.3	7.3	3.9	13.8	21.1
Hammond, LA Metro Area	61,525	4.4	3.1	3.6	11.7	17.9	2,340	5.6	3.3	3.7	12.2	27.2
Hanford-Corcoran, CA Metro Area	60,802	8.4	1.9	2.2	11.4	32.5	3,531	9.0	1.5	1.7	9.3	45.8
Harrisburg-Carlisle, PA Metro Area	410,644	5.5	6.3	5.8	12.1	15.3	23,993	7.0	7.6	7.6	13.8	21.5
Harrisonburg, VA Metro Area	82,381	12.4	2.6	3.8	9.5	14.0	3,798	17.6	2.4	4.2	11.7	17.7
Hartford-West Hartford-East Hartford, CT Metro Area	816,271	8.2	9.6	7.1	13.2	12.5	57,307	11.5	15.6	9.1	11.7	15.8
Hattiesburg, MS Metro Area	85,409	5.1	D	D	11.3	18.7	3,644	6.8	D	D	17.0	23.3
Hickory-Lenoir-Morganton, NC Metro Area	192,340	21.4	2.4	D	D	12.4	8,367	27.0	1.8	D	D	15.3
Hilton Head Island-Bluffton-Beaufort, SC Metro Area	115,478	1.2	3.5	D	8.0	18.9	5,025	1.2	3.6	D	9.9	30.6
Hinesville, GA Metro Area	41,802	D	1.5	D	4.0	57.5	2,553	D	0.8	D	1.9	76.1
Homosassa Springs, FL Metro Area	47,996	1.4	3.8	4.3	17.9	9.5	1,837	1.4	2.7	5.9	22.7	13.9
Hot Springs, AR Metro Area	52,270	5.2	3.8	4.5	16.0	9.5	1,905	7.5	4.0	4.4	22.4	14.3
Houma-Thibodaux, LA Metro Area	125,199	8.2	2.8	4.2	8.7	10.7	7,127	11.1	1.6	4.7	8.3	10.7
Houston-The Woodlands-Sugar Land, TX Metro Area	4,030,642	6.6	4.8	D	D	9.8	296,148	10.4	5.0	D	D	9.5
Huntington-Ashland, WV-KY-OH Metro Area	170,049	D	2.8	4.1	D	14.3	8,154	D	2.5	4.6	D	17.0
Huntsville, AL Metro Area	281,000	8.7	2.5	13.9	6.9	18.3	16,276	12.1	2.1	22.4	7.2	29.1
Idaho Falls, ID Metro Area	85,621	5.5	D	12.6	D	9.6	4,034	6.6	D	22.4	D	10.5
Indianapolis-Carmel-Anderson, IN Metro Area	1,270,379	7.4	5.3	D	11.1	10.8	75,893	11.7	6.5	D	12.2	11.4
Iowa City, IA Metro Area	126,459	5.2	3.4	3.8	8.2	30.2	6,473	6.8	3.1	3.6	7.2	42.9
Ithaca, NY Metro Area	69,764	5.4	2.5	7.3	D	9.0	3,688	7.7	2.6	7.7	D	13.8
Jackson, MI Metro Area	75,286	13.6	2.9	4.0	12.7	10.5	3,639	19.7	2.5	4.0	14.8	14.6
Jackson, MS Metro Area	372,440	5.3	5.3	5.1	11.8	17.2	17,680	7.4	6.4	6.8	12.8	21.4
Jackson, TN Metro Area	83,672	12.2	3.0	D	11.3	17.1	3,875	17.2	2.5	D	14.3	22.6
Jacksonville, FL Metro Area	838,054	3.8	8.1	6.9	D	10.8	44,248	5.6	11.1	8.7	D	15.4
Jacksonville, NC Metro Area	110,563	1.1	1.6	2.3	4.1	52.2	6,077	0.8	1.2	1.8	3.1	72.2
Janesville-Beloit, WI Metro Area	83,999	11.8	2.7	3.0	12.6	11.1	4,074	17.2	2.5	3.0	16.1	15.4
Jefferson City, MO Metro Area	99,297	5.9	4.0	3.9	8.7	26.3	4,620	9.1	3.9	4.7	8.9	33.1
Johnson City, TN Metro Area	103,922	7.7	4.6	D	D	16.0	4,569	10.9	4.4	D	D	21.8
Johnstown, PA Metro Area	69,769	6.0	5.2	5.0	19.1	11.9	3,035	8.7	5.5	6.3	22.7	18.1
Jonesboro, AR Metro Area	72,421	9.4	3.0	2.9	16.2	13.7	3,119	13.7	3.0	3.2	20.7	15.8
Joplin, MO Metro Area	102,228	13.2	2.8	2.7	13.0	9.9	4,573	20.2	2.9	2.5	15.4	11.2
Kahului-Wailuku-Lahaina, HI Metro Area	105,053	1.9	1.8	4.2	6.6	10.5	4,923	1.5	1.3	3.4	7.2	17.3
Kalamazoo-Portage, MI Metro Area	182,518	11.8	4.9	5.0	12.4	11.0	9,335	20.8	5.7	5.2	14.5	14.7
Kankakee, IL Metro Area	55,985	10.5	4.5	D	15.9	11.6	2,554	19.0	4.1	D	18.0	16.6
Kansas City, MO-KS Metro Area	1,344,634	5.8	6.6	D	10.7	12.0	78,723	9.0	8.3	D	10.8	14.0
Kennewick-Richland, WA Metro Area	145,108	5.9	2.6	8.9	10.5	13.6	8,602	6.2	1.9	13.6	9.5	17.5
Killeen-Temple, TX Metro Area	224,472	3.6	3.9	D	D	34.5	12,157	4.1	2.2	D	D	48.8
Kingsport-Bristol-Bristol, TN-VA Metro Area	158,023	13.9	3.0	D	D	11.0	7,416	24.8	2.5	D	D	12.8
Kingston, NY Metro Area	90,098	4.4	3.4	5.6	12.8	15.2	4,122	6.1	2.7	4.3	12.5	32.1
Knoxville, TN Metro Area	499,194	7.5	D	7.0	10.9	12.2	25,548	10.4	D	10.5	14.9	15.0
Kokomo, IN Metro Area	48,871	24.5	2.7	2.5	12.4	11.1	2,532	47.7	2.7	1.9	12.2	9.9
La Crosse-Onalaska, WI-MN Metro Area	95,918	9.0	4.8	3.3	16.6	12.5	4,643	11.2	5.1	3.2	20.6	15.8
Lafayette, LA Metro Area	297,389	6.6	3.6	5.9	11.5	9.3	15,583	8.8	2.9	7.7	11.7	10.1
Lafayette-West Lafayette, IN Metro Area	120,720	D	3.0	4.3	10.2	21.7	5,954	D	3.3	4.1	12.5	26.1
Lake Charles, LA Metro Area	129,004	8.3	2.8	4.7	10.8	11.5	7,161	17.9	2.2	6.1	10.8	11.8
Lake Havasu City-Kingman, AZ Metro Area	67,304	5.1	3.2	3.7	13.5	12.0	2,646	6.2	2.8	3.3	20.8	17.8
Lakeland-Winter Haven, FL Metro Area	281,099	6.3	5.3	3.9	11.1	10.2	12,438	9.4	6.0	4.7	14.1	13.6
Lancaster, PA Metro Area	325,375	12.3	3.4	5.0	12.4	6.7	17,033	15.9	4.1	5.4	13.3	9.1
Lansing-East Lansing, MI Metro Area	268,870	7.6	6.0	D	11.3	18.7	13,345	11.8	7.6	D	12.5	27.0
Laredo, TX Metro Area	139,136	0.8	3.6	3.4	12.0	16.3	5,783	1.0	2.4	3.2	10.1	26.3
Las Cruces, NM Metro Area	100,215	2.7	2.9	5.9	15.7	20.9	4,295	3.5	2.6	7.0	15.5	32.0
Las Vegas-Henderson-Paradise, NV Metro Area	1,210,053	2.1	5.1	5.4	7.6	9.3	59,901	2.5	3.9	6.5	9.3	15.7
Lawrence, KS Metro Area	70,620	5.8	2.6	8.7	7.6	23.1	2,848	8.5	2.5	8.7	7.3	35.0
Lawton, OK Metro Area	69,359	D	3.1	4.1	6.2	38.0	3,566	D	2.5	3.8	5.2	52.6
Lebanon, PA Metro Area	67,413	13.5	2.4	3.6	11.8	12.3	3,177	17.2	2.9	2.9	12.3	19.9
Lewiston, ID-WA Metro Area	35,346	12.3	5.1	3.4	D	15.5	1,595	18.3	5.9	3.5	D	18.1
Lewiston-Auburn, ME Metro Area	62,027	8.8	4.0	5.0	17.3	9.2	2,791	11.4	4.9	5.6	21.4	11.8
Lexington-Fayette, KY Metro Area	346,135	9.1	3.1	6.1	9.3	15.0	17,376	14.7	3.4	7.5	10.8	21.4

D = Data withheld due to disclosure.
[1]Includes other industry categories not shown separately.

Table B-12. Employees and Earnings by Selected Major Industries, 2015—*Continued*

| | Employees | | | | | | Earnings | | | | |
| | | Percent by selected major industries | | | | | | Percent by selected major industries | | | |
Metropolitan statistical area and division	Total[1]	Manu-facturing	Finance and insurance	Profes-sional, scientific and technical services	Health care and social services	Government and government enterprises	Total[1] (million dollars)	Manu-facturing	Finance and insurance	Profes-sional, scientific and technical services	Health care and social services	Government and government enterprises
Lima, OH Metro Area	64,012	14.2	2.9	2.9	15.9	10.0	3,107	25.7	2.3	2.6	18.5	13.4
Lincoln, NE Metro Area	226,318	6.3	6.8	5.9	D	15.8	10,970	8.7	7.9	7.2	D	21.9
Little Rock-North Little Rock-Conway, AR Metro Area	448,882	4.8	5.2	5.9	11.7	17.3	22,442	6.2	6.9	7.9	12.8	23.2
Logan, UT-ID Metro Area	79,568	14.9	4.4	7.1	D	15.2	3,070	21.7	3.8	6.9	D	21.3
Longview, TX Metro Area	138,601	7.7	4.0	D	11.1	8.8	6,699	10.3	2.8	D	11.6	9.6
Longview, WA Metro Area	48,672	13.8	2.7	3.1	13.8	12.7	2,670	21.1	2.0	2.4	13.9	14.8
Los Angeles-Long Beach-Anaheim, CA Metro Area	8,357,951	6.7	4.9	8.4	11.6	9.0	541,541	8.5	6.4	11.9	9.3	13.9
Anaheim-Santa Ana-Irvine, CA Metro Division	2,150,415	7.8	6.6	9.8	9.4	7.3	137,915	11.1	9.5	13.9	8.8	10.9
Los Angeles-Long Beach-Glendale, CA Metro Division	6,207,536	6.3	4.3	8.0	12.3	9.5	403,625	7.6	5.3	11.3	9.4	14.9
Louisville/Jefferson County, KY-IN Metro Area	802,572	D	D	5.6	10.7	10.0	42,206	D	D	7.2	12.1	12.7
Lubbock, TX Metro Area	188,308	D	D	4.2	11.9	16.2	8,528	D	D	4.5	15.6	23.7
Lynchburg, VA Metro Area	135,633	11.2	4.1	5.4	12.1	10.8	5,927	18.5	4.2	8.1	14.7	13.2
Macon, GA Metro Area	135,883	D	8.6	4.5	14.8	11.1	6,076	D	9.8	6.5	19.7	13.8
Madera, CA Metro Area	61,927	6.4	2.1	2.6	14.0	15.6	3,628	7.6	1.0	1.4	13.9	21.4
Madison, WI Metro Area	489,903	7.2	5.6	D	D	18.1	27,222	9.8	7.0	D	D	22.0
Manchester-Nashua, NH Metro Area	263,887	9.9	5.5	8.3	11.9	8.7	16,836	14.2	8.9	11.4	11.3	10.3
Manhattan, KS Metro Area	55,080	5.9	4.1	4.7	9.4	24.6	2,349	7.8	3.8	4.7	10.4	34.9
Mankato-North Mankato, MN Metro Area	70,106	11.4	3.6	D	D	12.5	3,371	18.1	3.1	D	D	16.1
Mansfield, OH Metro Area	65,652	15.3	3.0	2.6	13.0	12.2	2,825	21.9	2.7	2.6	14.2	18.2
McAllen-Edinburg-Mission, TX Metro Area	361,922	2.4	4.0	2.9	19.2	16.1	13,688	2.8	3.2	2.9	17.8	25.3
Medford, OR Metro Area	117,922	7.2	3.4	5.0	14.5	9.5	5,207	9.0	3.6	4.7	19.3	14.6
Memphis, TN-MS-AR Metro Area	833,237	5.8	3.7	4.7	11.6	10.6	43,567	10.6	5.1	5.0	13.1	14.1
Merced, CA Metro Area	99,946	10.2	2.1	2.6	10.4	18.6	5,729	11.1	1.4	1.7	8.7	26.3
Miami-Fort Lauderdale-West Palm Beach, FL Metro Area	3,695,916	2.7	6.0	7.6	10.5	8.6	184,869	3.3	7.7	10.8	11.6	13.4
Fort Lauderdale-Pompano Beach-Deerfield Beach, FL Metro Division	1,138,684	2.8	6.0	7.6	9.6	9.3	55,971	3.6	6.8	10.2	10.2	14.2
Miami-Miami Beach-Kendall, FL Metro Division	1,681,253	2.7	5.5	7.2	10.5	8.7	84,718	3.0	8.1	10.5	11.5	13.9
West Palm Beach-Boca Raton-Delray Beach, FL Metro Division	875,979	2.3	7.2	8.2	11.8	7.4	44,179	3.6	8.1	12.0	13.3	11.4
Michigan City-La Porte, IN Metro Area	53,548	14.7	2.5	3.0	11.3	13.4	2,407	20.8	2.7	2.9	13.9	15.1
Midland, MI Metro Area	48,206	13.7	2.8	4.3	13.3	7.4	2,449	8.8	2.7	4.2	14.3	9.1
Midland, TX Metro Area	138,830	D	D	5.4	5.2	7.1	15,196	D	D	3.4	2.9	4.4
Milwaukee-Waukesha-West Allis, WI Metro Area	1,038,129	12.0	5.8	5.9	13.8	8.9	61,260	16.2	8.3	8.2	13.1	11.0
Minneapolis-St. Paul-Bloomington, MN-WI Metro Area	2,433,222	8.4	6.6	D	12.0	10.6	152,042	11.7	10.0	D	10.5	12.0
Missoula, MT Metro Area	80,309	3.0	3.8	6.7	13.6	14.0	3,390	3.0	4.8	7.6	18.3	19.4
Mobile, AL Metro Area	234,127	8.7	3.7	5.5	11.2	12.2	11,129	15.9	4.7	7.6	12.2	15.3
Modesto, CA Metro Area	238,233	9.5	2.8	4.1	13.5	12.1	12,950	13.3	2.1	3.4	16.2	18.2
Monroe, LA Metro Area	107,015	D	5.4	D	15.9	11.6	4,377	D	5.5	D	18.2	16.0
Monroe, MI Metro Area	58,428	9.9	2.8	5.7	10.3	9.9	2,819	16.1	1.9	7.3	9.8	12.6
Montgomery, AL Metro Area	223,796	8.6	D	D	9.6	19.7	10,324	12.3	D	D	11.0	29.0
Morgantown, WV Metro Area	84,326	5.8	1.8	D	D	22.6	4,374	9.8	1.6	D	D	26.6
Morristown, TN Metro Area	57,350	19.2	2.5	2.4	D	11.5	2,518	27.6	1.8	2.1	D	13.7
Mount Vernon-Anacortes, WA Metro Area	66,941	9.4	3.7	4.8	9.2	17.1	3,351	15.5	3.4	4.8	8.0	23.2
Muncie, IN Metro Area	59,248	7.6	4.1	4.5	14.9	18.9	2,569	11.0	4.3	5.0	19.1	22.8
Muskegon, MI Metro Area	80,943	17.4	2.4	2.8	14.4	9.7	3,633	27.2	2.1	2.6	17.1	14.0
Myrtle Beach-Conway-North Myrtle Beach, SC-NC Metro Area	216,724	2.3	3.8	D	7.6	10.5	7,952	3.2	5.0	D	11.8	16.5
Napa, CA Metro Area	103,236	13.4	2.9	5.7	9.5	10.3	6,655	22.9	3.1	5.6	9.0	14.9
Naples-Immokalee-Marco Island, FL Metro Area	208,126	2.0	6.1	6.3	10.0	6.5	9,736	3.1	6.6	10.9	11.6	9.9
Nashville-Davidson—Murfreesboro—Franklin, TN Metro Area	1,223,004	6.8	5.3	7.3	10.6	9.3	76,850	7.5	6.1	9.8	20.8	9.7
New Bern, NC Metro Area	67,747	5.8	2.2	3.8	9.3	33.5	3,355	7.6	1.7	4.3	9.1	50.1
New Haven-Milford, CT Metro Area	500,126	6.5	4.7	6.3	15.8	10.4	29,461	8.8	4.1	8.8	15.3	15.3
New Orleans-Metairie, LA Metro Area	792,211	4.2	4.3	6.7	9.9	11.3	44,275	7.5	4.7	9.6	10.4	13.7
New York-Newark-Jersey City, NY-NJ-PA Metro Area	12,535,406	3.2	7.6	9.0	13.2	10.5	966,007	4.0	15.3	13.1	10.3	14.0
Dutchess County-Putnam County, NY Metro Division	193,395	5.8	4.3	6.1	14.2	12.9	10,427	11.6	2.6	5.7	15.8	24.8
Nassau County-Suffolk County, NY Metro Division	1,757,060	4.3	7.3	7.8	13.9	10.7	111,833	5.6	7.0	9.2	14.8	19.5
Newark, NJ-PA Metro Division	1,582,903	5.1	6.6	9.8	11.2	11.3	121,638	8.8	8.3	14.9	9.4	13.8
New York-Jersey City-White Plains, NY-NJ Metro Division	9,002,048	2.6	7.9	9.2	13.3	10.3	722,109	2.9	18.0	13.5	9.7	13.0
Niles-Benton Harbor, MI Metro Area	84,061	16.1	3.3	3.8	10.5	11.4	4,132	31.9	3.0	3.2	11.2	13.6
North Port-Sarasota-Bradenton, FL Metro Area	408,999	4.4	5.4	7.0	12.7	6.9	17,816	6.3	5.2	9.8	15.8	10.8
Norwich-New London, CT Metro Area	165,278	9.4	2.7	5.4	11.7	23.0	9,881	18.1	1.8	7.0	11.3	27.8
Ocala, FL Metro Area	141,617	5.8	4.2	4.6	13.8	10.6	5,289	9.1	3.7	5.1	19.8	16.1
Ocean City, NJ Metro Area	60,569	D	3.3	4.1	8.9	16.3	2,618	D	2.9	4.5	10.9	27.9
Odessa, TX Metro Area	97,279	6.3	2.7	3.5	5.9	10.5	6,104	9.3	1.6	3.3	5.1	10.8
Ogden-Clearfield, UT Metro Area	335,436	9.8	5.4	D	D	16.4	14,885	15.2	3.7	D	D	25.1
Oklahoma City, OK Metro Area	856,818	4.7	4.9	D	9.8	15.7	47,018	5.8	4.5	D	11.6	19.7

D = Data withheld due to disclosure.
[1]Includes other industry categories not shown separately.

Table B-12. Employees and Earnings by Selected Major Industries, 2015—*Continued*

Metropolitan statistical area and division	Employees Total¹	Manu-facturing	Finance and insurance	Profes-sional, scientific and technical services	Health care and social services	Government and government enterprises	Earnings Total¹ (million dollars)	Manu-facturing	Finance and insurance	Profes-sional, scientific and technical services	Health care and social services	Government and government enterprises
Olympia-Tumwater, WA Metro Area	140,775	2.9	3.2	5.4	11.3	26.7	7,536	3.1	3.0	5.2	12.7	39.3
Omaha-Council Bluffs, NE-IA Metro Area	615,529	5.5	7.2	D	11.6	11.7	36,578	6.3	8.2	D	10.8	13.7
Orlando-Kissimmee-Sanford, FL Metro Area	1,492,953	3.1	4.5	6.8	9.6	8.1	71,727	4.7	5.6	9.5	11.5	11.4
Oshkosh-Neenah, WI Metro Area	113,566	20.1	4.6	4.6	10.1	11.2	6,357	29.1	4.6	5.3	9.6	12.5
Owensboro, KY Metro Area	66,499	12.6	D	D	D	10.8	3,125	22.2	D	D	D	12.1
Oxnard-Thousand Oaks-Ventura, CA Metro Area	401,174	7.2	5.8	7.7	9.8	10.7	27,491	15.3	5.8	7.6	9.1	17.0
Palm Bay-Melbourne-Titusville, FL Metro Area	272,003	8.2	3.6	7.4	12.6	11.4	13,362	16.2	2.9	9.8	13.9	16.9
Panama City, FL Metro Area	111,306	3.5	3.1	5.1	D	16.5	4,945	5.5	3.1	6.9	D	26.6
Parkersburg-Vienna, WV Metro Area	50,271	D	D	3.1	14.2	14.6	2,344	D	D	3.1	14.8	20.1
Pensacola-Ferry Pass-Brent, FL Metro Area	234,152	2.9	5.5	5.6	12.2	17.5	11,029	4.4	5.9	7.4	15.1	27.8
Peoria, IL Metro Area	219,182	11.6	D	D	14.5	10.3	12,714	23.8	D	D	14.0	11.5
Philadelphia-Camden-Wilmington, PA-NJ-DE-MD Metro Area	3,643,714	D	6.9	D	14.5	10.0	249,636	D	8.1	D	13.0	12.6
Camden, NJ Metro Division	676,534	5.6	5.3	D	13.5	13.0	38,670	8.0	6.0	D	14.8	19.6
Montgomery County-Bucks County-Chester County, PA Metro Division	1,364,565	7.0	7.4	10.8	12.5	6.5	88,666	9.9	7.3	16.7	11.9	8.4
Philadelphia, PA Metro Division	1,158,898	3.3	5.5	7.2	18.2	11.7	93,473	3.8	7.3	11.1	13.5	13.4
Wilmington, DE-MD-NJ Metro Division	443,717	D	11.4	7.8	12.9	11.8	28,827	D	15.7	13.4	12.6	13.6
Phoenix-Mesa-Scottsdale, AZ Metro Area	2,521,850	5.1	7.4	6.7	10.6	9.8	134,303	8.1	8.8	8.6	12.0	12.9
Pine Bluff, AR Metro Area	44,048	12.5	D	2.0	D	23.6	1,928	17.3	D	1.8	D	29.5
Pittsburgh, PA Metro Area	1,459,831	6.3	5.9	7.9	14.0	8.5	88,054	7.9	6.8	10.5	13.9	11.2
Pittsfield, MA Metro Area	85,078	5.9	3.5	6.1	16.6	10.4	4,030	9.9	4.6	7.5	19.0	15.0
Pocatello, ID Metro Area	46,157	4.3	5.9	4.4	13.9	18.6	1,784	7.8	6.3	4.2	15.4	25.5
Portland-South Portland, ME Metro Area	362,929	D	5.4	6.9	13.5	11.2	18,267	D	7.8	9.1	14.9	16.0
Portland-Vancouver-Hillsboro, OR-WA Metro Area	1,477,395	8.9	4.5	D	D	9.9	86,340	13.6	5.2	D	D	13.2
Port St. Lucie, FL Metro Area	200,778	3.5	4.6	6.3	14.0	9.7	8,301	5.2	3.4	7.6	17.5	15.4
Prescott, AZ Metro Area	96,272	4.4	3.5	5.5	11.6	11.6	3,512	5.5	2.0	4.6	15.1	19.7
Providence-Warwick, RI-MA Metro Area	912,099	D	4.9	5.9	14.8	11.2	51,078	D	6.4	6.8	14.5	16.7
Provo-Orem, UT Metro Area	316,762	6.5	D	8.7	D	10.2	13,730	10.1	D	10.1	D	11.9
Pueblo, CO Metro Area	77,573	6.2	3.0	4.0	16.1	16.6	3,401	9.4	2.2	5.4	20.5	21.5
Punta Gorda, FL Metro Area	67,635	1.6	4.1	5.1	14.9	9.2	2,565	1.8	3.5	6.4	22.2	15.3
Racine, WI Metro Area	95,919	19.8	3.2	3.6	12.3	9.9	4,982	34.1	3.4	3.2	12.3	14.3
Raleigh, NC Metro Area	788,778	4.7	4.5	D	8.7	12.6	43,513	8.8	5.3	D	9.2	14.7
Rapid City, SD Metro Area	94,649	3.5	5.2	D	D	15.9	4,274	4.0	5.3	D	D	23.3
Reading, PA Metro Area	223,732	14.2	3.2	5.5	12.9	10.5	12,157	19.1	3.1	6.2	13.8	13.5
Redding, CA Metro Area	90,465	3.4	3.9	5.4	16.4	14.7	4,183	3.7	3.7	5.2	19.4	24.7
Reno, NV Metro Area	279,105	5.1	D	D	D	10.5	13,665	7.0	D	D	D	17.8
Richmond, VA Metro Area	821,890	D	6.8	6.9	11.2	15.2	48,286	D	9.8	10.2	11.6	18.7
Riverside-San Bernardino-Ontario, CA Metro Area	1,944,918	5.5	3.3	4.5	11.4	13.7	94,676	7.3	2.5	4.0	11.6	24.3
Roanoke, VA Metro Area	197,830	8.6	4.9	5.4	12.6	11.3	10,005	13.8	5.4	6.5	16.0	14.4
Rochester, MN Metro Area	148,189	7.7	2.8	3.3	30.8	8.7	8,314	12.3	1.9	2.4	44.8	9.6
Rochester, NY Metro Area	646,600	9.6	4.4	6.4	13.6	11.9	36,131	13.4	4.3	7.9	12.9	17.9
Rockford, IL Metro Area	188,500	17.4	4.1	3.4	13.5	9.5	9,370	26.8	4.9	3.5	15.3	12.9
Rocky Mount, NC Metro Area	74,473	14.5	2.9	3.9	D	14.5	3,275	22.5	2.6	3.4	D	17.8
Rome, GA Metro Area	51,397	12.0	3.2	D	16.8	11.7	2,397	16.9	3.0	D	24.2	13.5
Sacramento-Roseville—Arden-Arcade, CA Metro Area	1,278,201	3.3	5.1	7.3	11.5	19.9	80,780	4.5	5.5	8.7	11.7	33.6
Saginaw, MI Metro Area	108,893	11.6	3.9	3.7	16.0	10.2	5,018	19.2	4.3	4.4	19.0	14.2
St. Cloud, MN Metro Area	136,118	11.5	4.3	3.3	14.2	10.5	6,374	14.2	4.2	3.6	17.1	14.1
St. George, UT Metro Area	85,410	4.3	5.2	5.5	11.9	10.3	2,928	5.5	3.3	5.8	17.0	15.3
St. Joseph, MO-KS Metro Area	72,689	D	4.4	D	11.6	14.4	3,299	D	4.5	D	14.1	16.2
St. Louis, MO-IL Metro Area	1,734,918	6.9	D	6.5	12.9	10.4	98,802	10.8	D	9.2	12.5	12.7
Salem, OR Metro Area	209,644	6.8	3.3	3.9	12.7	19.4	10,093	6.7	3.2	4.0	15.3	30.0
Salinas, CA Metro Area	244,479	2.7	2.3	4.7	8.1	15.3	15,011	2.6	1.8	4.4	7.5	24.5
Salisbury, MD-DE Metro Area	211,235	7.0	3.4	4.1	11.9	12.0	9,779	8.2	2.7	4.1	15.6	16.5
Salt Lake City, UT Metro Area	865,647	6.7	8.2	D	8.1	12.7	48,332	8.9	8.9	D	7.7	15.6
San Angelo, TX Metro Area	72,479	D	D	D	D	16.6	3,375	D	D	D	D	21.6
San Antonio-New Braunfels, TX Metro Area	1,350,276	3.8	7.4	5.7	10.7	14.8	73,724	4.4	8.9	6.6	10.6	20.3
San Diego-Carlsbad, CA Metro Area	2,025,021	5.7	4.3	10.1	9.4	16.6	128,209	8.8	4.2	15.2	8.6	24.2
San Francisco-Oakland-Hayward, CA Metro Area	3,167,329	4.4	5.4	13.6	10.6	10.1	275,320	6.2	7.6	20.0	8.2	12.9
Oakland-Hayward-Berkeley, CA Metro Division	1,540,266	6.2	4.3	10.7	12.2	10.8	110,681	9.5	4.0	13.9	11.7	15.5
San Francisco-Redwood City-South San Francisco, CA Metro Division	1,431,697	2.8	6.4	16.7	8.7	9.7	151,223	3.9	10.4	24.8	5.4	11.0
San Rafael, CA Metro Division	195,366	2.6	6.0	13.4	11.2	8.2	13,416	4.7	6.5	15.7	10.7	12.8
San Jose-Sunnyvale-Santa Clara, CA Metro Area	1,354,229	12.4	3.6	D	9.6	7.1	153,129	21.4	2.7	D	6.4	6.6
San Luis Obispo-Paso Robles-Arroyo Grande, CA Metro Area	169,905	5.1	3.1	7.4	9.6	12.8	8,636	6.5	2.6	7.2	10.9	21.6
Santa Cruz-Watsonville, CA Metro Area	153,381	5.4	3.1	7.9	12.2	12.5	8,698	7.1	2.6	7.6	12.6	19.0
Santa Fe, NM Metro Area	95,211	1.8	3.5	7.8	11.5	18.2	4,152	1.2	6.5	9.3	14.0	29.6
Santa Maria-Santa Barbara, CA Metro Area	274,020	5.3	2.8	7.9	9.9	14.0	16,579	7.3	2.7	9.4	10.6	20.8
Santa Rosa, CA Metro Area	296,678	8.4	3.5	7.8	12.2	10.1	16,720	13.5	3.3	7.7	12.9	14.6
Savannah, GA Metro Area	222,967	8.1	3.4	D	10.5	13.3	11,054	17.1	3.2	D	13.0	18.5
Scranton—Wilkes-Barre—Hazleton, PA Metro Area	321,846	8.7	4.9	4.3	D	9.8	15,271	11.5	5.6	4.9	D	15.3

D = Data withheld due to disclosure.
¹Includes other industry categories not shown separately.

Table B-12. Employees and Earnings by Selected Major Industries, 2015—*Continued*

| | Employees | | | | | | Earnings | | | | | |
| | Total[1] | Percent by selected major industries | | | | | Total[1] (million dollars) | Percent by selected major industries | | | | |
Metropolitan statistical area and division		Manu-facturing	Finance and insurance	Profes-sional, scientific and technical services	Health care and social services	Government and government enterprises		Manu-facturing	Finance and insurance	Profes-sional, scientific and technical services	Health care and social services	Government and government enterprises
Seattle-Tacoma-Bellevue, WA Metro Area......	2,448,266	8.1	4.1	8.6	10.2	12.9	178,208	11.3	4.3	10.3	9.1	15.0
Seattle-Bellevue-Everett, WA Metro Division.....	2,035,391	8.8	4.2	9.5	9.7	11.1	154,579	12.2	4.4	11.3	8.0	12.4
Tacoma-Lakewood, WA Metro Division...........	412,875	4.6	3.6	4.3	12.4	21.9	23,629	5.9	3.4	3.9	16.0	32.2
Sebastian-Vero Beach, FL Metro Area..................	75,557	3.0	6.1	6.5	13.9	7.0	3,274	4.1	4.9	11.4	16.9	10.6
Sebring, FL Metro Area..................................	38,911	2.0	3.3	3.5	15.6	10.7	1,413	2.4	2.6	3.0	22.5	16.8
Sheboygan, WI Metro Area.............................	73,568	28.6	4.8	2.9	9.6	8.2	3,892	39.8	5.6	2.5	11.8	9.9
Sherman-Denison, TX Metro Area....................	67,554	8.8	6.5	3.7	14.6	10.1	2,736	15.8	6.3	3.6	18.5	13.4
Shreveport-Bossier City, LA Metro Area............	259,547	D	3.9	3.8	13.6	14.9	14,026	D	2.8	3.9	14.4	18.6
Sierra Vista-Douglas, AZ Metro Area.................	52,181	1.6	2.5	5.9	8.2	30.2	2,651	1.1	1.9	7.1	7.7	50.9
Sioux City, IA-NE-SD Metro Area	113,668	D	4.6	2.5	10.9	10.2	5,806	D	4.1	2.9	11.6	11.6
Sioux Falls, SD Metro Area	194,496	D	D	D	D	7.6	10,923	D	D	D	D	8.6
South Bend-Mishawaka, IN-MI Metro Area..........	172,229	10.5	3.5	4.5	D	9.7	8,862	15.8	3.9	7.5	D	10.0
Spartanburg, SC Metro Area...........................	176,184	16.6	3.2	3.8	D	13.4	8,898	24.4	4.0	4.2	D	16.6
Spokane-Spokane Valley, WA Metro Area	307,815	6.1	5.3	5.5	D	14.3	14,906	7.7	6.3	5.8	D	20.6
Springfield, IL Metro Area..............................	130,289	2.5	6.6	5.6	D	16.6	6,903	3.3	7.0	7.0	D	25.6
Springfield, MA Metro Area............................	354,365	6.4	4.4	4.7	18.1	15.4	18,712	8.7	6.6	4.6	18.1	22.8
Springfield, MO Metro Area............................	276,997	5.8	4.9	4.8	13.6	10.8	11,936	8.5	4.9	7.1	17.3	14.2
Springfield, OH Metro Area............................	62,986	11.0	6.5	2.9	13.8	11.7	2,738	16.5	7.0	2.7	14.6	16.2
State College, PA Metro Area	115,484	3.9	2.3	5.4	8.4	42.3	5,883	4.7	1.9	5.8	9.7	49.5
Staunton-Waynesboro, VA Metro Area................	64,394	11.5	2.5	3.6	D	14.0	2,868	17.6	2.2	3.3	D	17.4
Stockton-Lodi, CA Metro Area.........................	310,546	6.4	3.4	3.4	11.7	13.4	16,517	8.1	2.6	3.0	12.2	22.0
Sumter, SC Metro Area..................................	55,163	12.1	2.2	2.9	12.0	22.3	2,576	15.5	1.9	3.2	11.2	36.3
Syracuse, NY Metro Area...............................	384,255	6.8	5.3	D	D	14.5	21,444	10.0	5.3	D	D	21.9
Tallahassee, FL Metro Area............................	221,606	1.7	3.7	7.8	D	27.7	10,331	2.1	4.1	11.6	D	38.1
Tampa-St. Petersburg-Clearwater, FL Metro Area .	1,659,175	4.1	7.2	8.3	11.9	9.6	85,385	5.6	9.0	11.6	13.4	13.4
Terre Haute, IN Metro Area............................	86,687	13.0	D	D	D	14.9	3,841	19.2	D	D	D	18.2
Texarkana, TX-AR Metro Area.........................	78,978	7.1	4.7	D	D	17.5	3,449	11.8	4.8	D	D	24.7
The Villages, FL Metro Area	40,268	3.2	5.6	D	11.5	11.9	1,543	4.3	4.1	D	13.3	22.7
Toledo, OH Metro Area..................................	375,118	12.0	3.4	D	D	12.4	19,683	19.1	3.0	D	D	15.9
Topeka, KS Metro Area..................................	145,666	5.3	6.7	D	13.4	19.6	6,947	7.0	9.4	D	14.5	24.3
Trenton, NJ Metro Area..................................	278,920	3.1	7.8	11.5	10.5	15.0	21,001	4.2	10.0	18.3	8.9	19.5
Tucson, AZ Metro Area..................................	500,592	4.9	4.1	6.5	13.2	17.6	23,659	9.9	3.9	7.7	14.7	25.2
Tulsa, OK Metro Area....................................	595,333	8.9	D	5.8	10.7	9.8	43,494	9.7	D	5.5	8.6	7.4
Tuscaloosa, AL Metro Area............................	133,315	11.9	D	D	6.6	20.5	6,131	19.1	D	D	7.3	27.4
Tyler, TX Metro Area....................................	144,387	4.7	5.7	4.7	16.2	10.0	8,656	6.8	4.0	4.6	16.5	9.6
Urban Honolulu, HI Metro Area.......................	646,514	2.1	3.5	5.5	9.4	23.9	38,509	1.9	3.3	6.2	10.2	33.7
Utica-Rome, NY Metro Area............................	155,414	7.7	6.1	4.1	16.2	19.7	7,509	9.7	6.3	4.5	15.6	32.3
Valdosta, GA Metro Area...............................	76,087	6.0	D	D	D	23.0	3,121	8.3	D	D	D	35.0
Vallejo-Fairfield, CA Metro Area......................	187,017	6.7	3.6	4.7	14.3	16.6	11,283	13.2	2.9	3.5	16.6	25.1
Victoria, TX Metro Area.................................	60,510	4.5	D	3.6	12.5	12.0	3,042	8.8	D	3.9	13.5	13.4
Vineland-Bridgeton, NJ Metro Area...................	75,355	11.6	2.3	D	13.9	18.1	4,060	14.6	1.8	D	15.5	28.5
Virginia Beach-Norfolk-Newport News, VA-NC Metro Area.................................	1,028,584	D	D	6.2	9.9	24.1	56,429	D	D	8.0	9.9	36.1
Visalia-Porterville, CA Metro Area....................	201,423	6.4	2.6	2.6	7.8	15.8	10,352	8.3	2.1	2.2	6.6	24.5
Waco, TX Metro Area....................................	152,403	11.1	D	3.6	9.8	12.6	7,010	18.2	D	4.3	10.5	16.1
Walla Walla, WA Metro Area...........................	37,367	10.7	3.1	D	13.6	16.6	1,870	13.5	2.5	D	14.3	23.2
Warner Robins, GA Metro Area........................	96,789	D	D	5.5	D	31.9	4,763	D	D	6.4	D	52.4
Washington-Arlington-Alexandria, DC-VA-MD-WV Metro Area	4,180,748	1.5	D	D	8.7	18.4	326,298	1.7	D	D	6.8	27.6
Silver Spring-Frederick-Rockville, MD Metro Division................................	835,430	2.3	D	D	11.1	13.8	62,526	3.6	D	16.1	9.1	20.9
Washington-Arlington-Alexandria, DC-VA-MD-WV Metro Division.................................	3,345,318	1.2	3.1	15.1	8.1	19.6	263,772	1.2	3.7	24.0	6.3	29.2
Waterloo-Cedar Falls, IA Metro Area.................	113,937	14.5	D	D	11.9	13.4	5,383	23.7	D	D	12.4	16.1
Watertown-Fort Drum, NY Metro Area................	68,993	3.9	2.0	2.1	10.1	39.6	3,923	4.5	1.3	1.8	9.7	59.3
Wausau, WI Metro Area.................................	90,906	18.2	7.0	3.4	11.9	9.2	4,628	22.2	8.3	4.7	15.8	11.5
Weirton-Steubenville, WV-OH Metro Area...........	51,659	10.9	2.8	D	15.9	11.7	2,232	18.3	2.2	D	17.6	13.7
Wenatchee, WA Metro Area	69,267	4.4	2.6	3.7	10.8	13.3	3,127	5.6	1.8	4.0	14.6	21.0
Wheeling, WV-OH Metro Area.........................	81,621	4.1	3.5	D	D	12.5	3,873	6.0	3.6	D	D	13.7
Wichita, KS Metro Area.................................	398,078	13.6	3.9	4.4	11.3	11.7	21,617	22.5	3.0	4.8	11.2	12.9
Wichita Falls, TX Metro Area..........................	87,983	6.4	4.7	D	D	19.3	4,206	9.0	3.7	D	D	24.2
Williamsport, PA Metro Area...........................	71,299	11.5	3.5	3.8	12.8	13.5	3,389	15.8	3.1	3.8	15.2	18.6
Wilmington, NC Metro Area............................	167,000	3.9	3.7	D	9.2	14.1	7,251	5.8	4.1	D	10.9	20.2
Winchester, VA-WV Metro Area	78,268	9.2	4.2	D	12.5	12.8	3,744	13.4	4.7	D	D	18.1
Winston-Salem, NC Metro Area.......................	348,677	9.6	4.7	D	D	9.6	17,180	13.1	7.2	D	D	10.7
Worcester, MA-CT Metro Area	501,109	8.6	4.7	6.1	16.0	12.4	28,180	13.2	5.5	8.2	15.9	17.3
Yakima, WA Metro Area.................................	128,806	6.9	2.3	2.5	13.0	14.0	6,301	8.0	1.9	2.2	13.2	18.2
York-Hanover, PA Metro Area..........................	232,528	13.9	3.0	4.3	11.5	9.2	11,588	19.5	2.8	4.5	13.7	14.2
Youngstown-Warren-Boardman, OH-PA Metro Area..................................	289,857	11.0	3.4	3.5	15.1	10.7	13,085	17.8	3.0	3.3	16.2	15.2
Yuba City, CA Metro Area..............................	68,853	3.8	2.4	3.3	11.8	22.4	3,689	4.3	1.8	2.7	12.6	35.0
Yuma, AZ Metro Area....................................	84,886	2.8	2.5	3.8	9.5	22.0	4,351	2.7	1.7	4.1	10.2	29.7

D = Data withheld due to disclosure.
[1]Includes other industry categories not shown separately.

Table B-13. Civilian Labor Force

Metropolitan statistical area and division	Civilian labor force											
	Total Labor Force					Number of unemployed			Unemployment rate[1]			
	2015	2010	2005	2000	Change, 2005–2015	2015	2010	2005	2015	2010	2005	2000
Abilene, TX Metro Area	75,160	76,448	80,081	75,325	-6.1	2,918	5,330	3,376	3.9	7.0	4.2	4.1
Akron, OH Metro Area	359,928	372,207	380,527	364,753	-5.4	17,722	39,167	22,421	4.9	10.5	5.9	4.3
Albany, GA Metro Area	65,508	70,765	74,349	71,316	-11.9	4,561	8,318	4,227	7.0	11.8	5.7	4.8
Albany, OR Metro Area	54,608	57,072	51,945	51,531	5.1	3,760	7,321	3,899	6.9	12.8	7.5	6.6
Albany-Schenectady-Troy, NY Metro Area	449,051	459,102	454,313	431,882	-1.2	20,323	33,405	18,042	4.5	7.3	4.0	3.5
Albuquerque, NM Metro Area	413,907	424,972	394,236	368,042	5.0	25,644	34,084	19,015	6.2	8.0	4.8	4.1
Alexandria, LA Metro Area	67,099	67,410	67,767	63,709		4,350	5,197	4,185	6.5	7.7	6.2	5.5
Allentown-Bethlehem-Easton, PA-NJ Metro Area..	429,733	419,501	407,310	386,383	5.5	22,433	38,745	19,882	5.2	9.2	4.9	3.7
Altoona, PA Metro Area	61,018	61,777	64,786	62,587	-5.8	3,053	4,948	3,351	5.0	8.0	5.2	4.6
Amarillo, TX Metro Area	130,021	129,609	127,588	118,977	1.9	4,067	7,355	5,068	3.1	5.7	4.0	3.8
Ames, IA Metro Area	57,365	53,344	46,922	46,236	22.3	1,377	2,240	1,422	2.4	4.2	3.0	1.7
Anchorage, AK Metro Area	203,081	200,237	185,756	169,475	9.3	11,420	14,379	10,988	5.6	7.2	5.9	5.5
Ann Arbor, MI Metro Area	189,852	182,801	189,926	185,811	0.0	6,701	14,832	8,467	3.5	8.1	4.5	2.4
Anniston-Oxford-Jacksonville, AL Metro Area	46,051	51,559	53,955	52,896	-14.6	3,214	5,860	2,431	7.0	11.4	4.5	5.1
Appleton, WI Metro Area	129,446	127,899	119,949	116,829	7.9	5,068	10,026	5,304	3.9	7.8	4.4	3.0
Asheville, NC Metro Area	219,079	209,299	198,283	185,742	10.5	10,085	18,796	8,669	4.6	9.0	4.4	3.2
Athens-Clarke County, GA Metro Area	93,471	93,927	99,200	88,967	-5.8	5,119	8,551	4,280	5.5	9.1	4.3	3.3
Atlanta-Sandy Springs-Roswell, GA Metro Area	2,836,326	2,720,049	2,584,602	2,373,513	9.7	158,458	280,009	138,928	5.6	10.3	5.4	3.1
Atlantic City-Hammonton, NJ Metro Area	127,666	140,600	136,314	128,823	-6.3	11,962	17,268	7,293	9.4	12.3	5.4	4.7
Auburn-Opelika, AL Metro Area	71,548	66,764	63,530	58,023	12.6	3,660	6,006	2,369	5.1	9.0	3.7	4.0
Augusta-Richmond County, GA-SC Metro Area	256,201	255,682	256,395	237,653	-0.1	16,187	24,851	15,708	6.3	9.7	6.1	4.0
Austin-Round Rock, TX Metro Area	1,069,773	930,551	798,312	738,762	34.0	36,048	65,089	36,321	3.4	7.0	4.5	3.0
Bakersfield, CA Metro Area	393,764	371,515	326,748	293,919	20.5	40,212	58,154	27,342	10.2	15.7	8.4	8.3
Baltimore-Columbia-Towson, MD Metro Area	1,472,177	1,425,226	1,366,365	1,326,906	7.7	79,478	116,060	60,205	5.4	8.1	4.4	3.8
Bangor, ME Metro Area	76,643	79,110	77,286	75,494	-0.8	3,649	6,791	3,935	4.8	8.6	5.1	3.7
Barnstable Town, MA Metro Area	111,332	111,013	122,143	112,276	-8.9	7,011	10,981	6,022	6.3	9.9	4.9	3.4
Baton Rouge, LA Metro Area	421,898	390,669	362,526	340,452	16.4	22,770	30,317	25,248	5.4	7.8	7.0	5.1
Battle Creek, MI Metro Area	64,682	64,996	71,724	70,635	-9.8	3,159	7,607	4,799	4.9	11.7	6.7	4.2
Bay City, MI Metro Area	52,570	54,666	55,557	57,036	-5.4	2,902	6,319	3,949	5.5	11.6	7.1	4.2
Beaumont-Port Arthur, TX Metro Area	176,632	183,461	182,725	182,871	-3.3	11,852	20,640	14,089	6.7	11.3	7.7	6.5
Beckley, WV Metro Area	47,037	50,037	49,913	51,228	-5.8	3,652	4,396	2,552	7.8	8.8	5.1	6.5
Bellingham, WA Metro Area	102,918	104,359	102,524	88,217	0.4	6,110	9,892	5,399	5.9	9.5	5.3	5.7
Bend-Redmond, OR Metro Area	84,185	81,238	74,532	62,089	13.0	5,024	11,243	4,282	6.0	13.8	5.7	5.3
Billings, MT Metro Area	87,832	82,163	84,503	76,743	3.9	2,885	4,865	3,009	3.3	5.9	3.6	4.3
Binghamton, NY Metro Area	110,454	124,412	122,597	124,132	-9.9	6,582	10,648	5,943	6.0	8.6	4.8	3.6
Birmingham-Hoover, AL Metro Area	531,231	539,753	530,561	527,296	0.1	29,231	52,966	21,801	5.5	9.8	4.1	3.9
Bismarck, ND Metro Area	67,337	64,565	61,247	56,366	9.9	1,739	2,525	1,915	2.6	3.9	3.1	2.6
Blacksburg-Christiansburg-Radford, VA Metro Area	91,365	88,695	83,789	80,473	9.0	4,211	7,330	3,394	4.6	8.3	4.1	3.3
Bloomington, IL Metro Area	99,036	104,944	95,546	95,544	3.7	4,873	7,552	4,003	4.9	7.2	4.2	3.3
Bloomington, IN Metro Area	76,540	78,053	78,446	74,491	-2.4	3,850	6,551	3,969	5.0	8.4	5.1	2.8
Bloomsburg-Berwick, PA Metro Area	43,034	43,840	42,998	40,690	0.1	2,240	3,850	2,386	5.2	8.8	5.5	4.8
Boise City, ID Metro Area	324,068	297,428	281,557	250,923	15.1	13,105	27,312	10,347	4.0	9.2	3.7	3.8
Boston-Cambridge-Newton, MA-NH Metro Area	2,564,753	2,474,337	2,369,644	2,354,104	8.2	113,599	185,756	107,098	4.4	7.5	4.5	2.5
Boston, MA Metro Division	1,052,776	1,014,231	946,385	949,506	11.2	49,260	80,498	45,077	4.7	7.9	4.8	2.7
Cambridge-Newton-Framingham, MA Metro Division	1,263,377	1,218,157	1,185,870	1,182,231	6.5	55,659	91,019	52,740	4.4	7.5	4.4	2.4
Rockingham County-Strafford County, NH Metro Division	248,600	241,949	237,389	222,367	4.7	8,680	14,239	9,281	3.5	5.9	3.9	2.9
Boulder, CO Metro Area	176,726	170,293	168,036	160,011	5.2	5,599	11,985	7,382	3.2	7.0	4.4	2.4
Bowling Green, KY Metro Area	75,913	77,926	74,979	70,658	1.2	3,704	7,767	4,071	4.9	10.0	5.4	3.9
Bremerton-Silverdale, WA Metro Area	115,211	120,592	120,999	106,205	-4.8	6,315	10,362	6,464	5.5	8.6	5.3	5.6
Bridgeport-Stamford-Norwalk, CT Metro Area	479,044	474,646	451,803	452,280	6.0	25,273	39,824	19,830	5.3	8.4	4.4	2.1
Brownsville-Harlingen, TX Metro Area	164,295	162,316	140,218	127,268	17.2	11,692	18,145	10,675	7.1	11.2	7.6	6.9
Brunswick, GA Metro Area	50,101	52,097	51,706	46,463	-3.1	3,114	5,448	2,439	6.2	10.5	4.7	3.7
Buffalo-Cheektowaga-Niagara Falls, NY Metro Area	550,798	573,522	583,969	575,034	-5.7	30,681	49,093	30,659	5.6	8.6	5.3	4.3
Burlington, NC Metro Area	77,083	76,792	68,710	69,593	12.2	4,123	8,355	4,128	5.3	10.9	6.0	3.1
Burlington-South Burlington, VT Metro Area	126,711	126,352	117,420	112,063	7.9	3,745	6,407	3,886	3.0	5.1	3.3	2.5
California-Lexington Park, MD Metro Area	54,498	53,617	49,151	44,340	10.9	2,701	3,503	1,737	5.0	6.5	3.5	3.3
Canton-Massillon, OH Metro Area	200,293	206,242	204,520	206,940	-2.1	10,635	23,520	13,478	5.3	11.4	6.6	4.4
Cape Coral-Fort Myers, FL Metro Area	319,967	283,236	272,752	207,658	17.3	16,084	35,446	8,780	5.0	12.5	3.2	3.2
Cape Girardeau, MO-IL Metro Area	49,351	49,844	47,208	49,965	4.5	2,306	3,946	2,353	4.7	7.9	5.0	3.6
Carbondale-Marion, IL Metro Area	60,747	62,395	64,840	60,745	-6.3	3,619	5,621	3,213	6.0	9.0	5.0	4.9
Carson City, NV Metro Area	25,103	26,700	27,201	26,590	-7.7	1,821	3,600	1,234	7.3	13.5	4.5	3.5
Casper, WY Metro Area	42,894	39,894	39,124	36,524	9.6	2,053	2,784	1,346	4.8	7.0	3.4	4.0
Cedar Rapids, IA Metro Area	144,526	145,562	138,103	134,964	4.7	5,426	8,775	6,023	3.8	6.0	4.4	2.3
Chambersburg-Waynesboro, PA Metro Area	77,739	75,708	76,938	67,744	1.0	3,723	6,455	2,642	4.8	8.5	3.4	3.7
Champaign-Urbana, IL Metro Area	119,357	125,440	117,505	116,556	1.6	6,229	10,348	4,859	5.2	8.2	4.1	3.3
Charleston, WV Metro Area	99,054	105,062	103,457	110,766	-4.3	6,378	8,131	5,109	6.4	7.7	4.9	5.2
Charleston-North Charleston, SC Metro Area	361,515	327,157	295,680	268,862	22.3	18,526	30,266	15,890	5.1	9.3	5.4	3.3
Charlotte-Concord-Gastonia, NC-SC Metro Area...	1,235,300	1,140,626	1,000,379	939,823	23.5	67,511	133,786	53,908	5.5	11.7	5.4	3.4
Charlottesville, VA Metro Area	116,114	111,065	103,869	94,745	11.8	4,538	7,176	3,328	3.9	6.5	3.2	2.2
Chattanooga, TN-GA Metro Area	253,594	258,365	251,219	245,209	0.9	14,093	22,816	12,077	5.6	8.8	4.8	3.3
Cheyenne, WY Metro Area	48,910	46,182	41,359	40,224	18.3	1,888	3,090	1,701	3.9	6.7	4.1	3.8
Chicago-Naperville-Elgin, IL-IN-WI Metro Area	4,888,023	4,872,834	4,698,563	4,765,447	4.0	285,428	514,411	275,641	5.8	10.6	5.9	4.3

NA = Not available.

[1]Civilian unemployed as percent of total civilian labor force.

Table B-13. Civilian Labor Force—*Continued*

Metropolitan statistical area and division	Total Labor Force					Number of unemployed			Unemployment rate[1]			
	2015	2010	2005	2000	Change, 2005–2015	2015	2010	2005	2015	2010	2005	2000
Chicago-Naperville-Arlington Heights, IL Metro Division	3,772,665	3,759,447	3,628,915	3,742,931	4.0	220,752	398,895	218,931	5.9	10.6	6.0	4.5
Elgin, IL Metro Division	322,262	323,571	302,944	275,528	6.4	18,625	35,388	16,538	5.8	10.9	5.5	3.8
Gary, IN Metro Division	337,557	333,944	328,821	324,855	2.7	21,470	34,953	19,086	6.4	10.5	5.8	3.6
Lake County-Kenosha County, IL-WI Metro Division	455,539	455,872	437,883	422,133	4.0	24,581	45,175	21,086	5.4	9.9	4.8	3.5
Chico, CA Metro Area	101,731	102,568	98,309	93,228	3.5	7,334	14,246	6,632	7.2	13.9	6.7	6.2
Cincinnati, OH-KY-IN Metro Area	1,072,143	1,095,962	1,088,914	1,038,933	-1.5	48,406	108,463	59,327	4.5	9.9	5.4	3.7
Clarksville, TN-KY Metro Area	108,713	109,371	98,089	91,778	10.8	6,586	10,552	5,485	6.1	9.6	5.6	4.1
Cleveland, TN Metro Area	56,372	53,784	53,462	52,689	5.4	3,134	5,184	2,857	5.6	9.6	5.3	3.6
Cleveland-Elyria, OH Metro Area	1,025,539	1,052,045	1,078,484	1,090,462	-4.9	49,618	87,921	55,086	4.8	8.4	5.1	2.7
Coeur d'Alene, ID Metro Area	71,896	68,851	67,178	56,292	7.0	3,582	7,514	3,027	5.0	10.9	4.5	6.3
College Station-Bryan, TX Metro Area	120,844	115,448	102,867	93,405	17.5	4,279	7,609	4,380	3.5	6.6	4.3	3.8
Colorado Springs, CO Metro Area	319,535	318,662	301,904	276,568	5.8	14,713	29,786	15,860	4.6	9.3	5.3	2.9
Columbia, MO Metro Area	100,284	92,559	85,727	78,731	17.0	3,491	5,971	3,055	3.5	6.5	3.6	2.3
Columbia, SC Metro Area	396,021	372,416	355,320	338,250	11.5	21,640	34,814	20,316	5.5	9.3	5.7	3.3
Columbus, GA-AL Metro Area	124,454	127,888	127,552	124,484	-2.4	8,570	12,728	7,622	6.9	10.0	6.0	4.6
Columbus, IN Metro Area	43,649	38,387	37,388	37,297	16.7	1,559	3,660	1,812	3.6	9.5	4.8	2.7
Columbus, OH Metro Area	1,038,547	1,004,299	956,304	909,994	8.6	42,907	90,420	52,557	4.1	9.0	5.5	3.4
Corpus Christi, TX Metro Area	207,775	202,622	197,063	185,311	5.4	10,733	17,271	11,083	5.2	8.5	5.6	5.3
Corvallis, OR Metro Area	45,171	45,075	41,922	41,419	7.8	1,945	3,202	2,052	4.3	7.1	4.9	3.8
Crestview-Fort Walton Beach-Destin, FL Metro Area	119,866	115,030	124,514	99,785	-3.7	5,419	9,936	3,492	4.5	8.6	2.8	3.6
Cumberland, MD-WV Metro Area	44,385	46,779	48,703	45,882	-8.9	3,158	4,367	2,867	7.1	9.3	5.9	5.8
Dallas-Fort Worth-Arlington, TX Metro Area	3,584,196	3,300,763	3,024,615	2,873,061	18.5	145,674	266,593	157,701	4.1	8.1	5.2	3.5
Dallas-Plano-Irving, TX Metro Division	2,400,143	2,192,401	2,004,189	1,916,301	19.8	96,025	175,976	105,630	4.0	8.0	5.3	3.5
Fort Worth-Arlington, TX Metro Division	1,184,053	1,108,362	1,020,426	956,760	16.0	49,649	90,617	52,071	4.2	8.2	5.1	3.5
Dalton, GA Metro Area	60,505	64,820	66,501	63,223	-9.0	4,003	8,030	3,164	6.6	12.4	4.8	3.5
Danville, IL Metro Area	35,642	37,973	37,822	39,183	-5.8	2,542	4,337	2,378	7.1	11.4	6.3	5.5
Daphne-Fairhope-Foley, AL Metro Area	87,316	83,459	76,804	69,533	13.7	4,791	8,339	3,061	5.5	10.0	4.0	3.7
Davenport-Moline-Rock Island, IA-IL Metro Area	192,696	198,838	202,279	200,273	-4.7	10,773	16,383	9,189	5.6	8.2	4.5	3.9
Dayton, OH Metro Area	381,765	401,835	404,463	409,510	-5.6	18,294	44,010	25,277	4.8	11.0	6.2	4.1
Decatur, AL Metro Area	68,970	72,718	71,679	72,821	-3.8	4,280	8,094	3,405	6.2	11.1	4.8	4.4
Decatur, IL Metro Area	50,593	55,189	52,836	56,346	-4.2	3,588	6,160	3,202	7.1	11.2	6.1	4.9
Deltona-Daytona Beach-Ormond Beach, FL Metro Area	282,822	279,521	274,669	230,603	3.0	16,400	34,326	10,374	5.8	12.3	3.8	3.4
Denver-Aurora-Lakewood, CO Metro Area	1,504,945	1,423,355	1,314,305	1,240,724	14.5	55,456	123,630	67,657	3.7	8.7	5.1	2.6
Des Moines-West Des Moines, IA Metro Area	339,509	322,912	296,276	275,098	14.6	11,794	18,708	11,637	3.5	5.8	3.9	2.3
Detroit-Warren-Dearborn, MI Metro Area.......	1,998,430	2,058,555	2,209,029	2,293,212	-9.5	124,239	285,929	153,998	6.2	13.9	7.0	3.4
Detroit-Dearborn-Livonia, MI Metro Division....	750,854	802,754	910,762	955,276	-17.6	54,821	124,328	75,511	7.3	15.5	8.3	3.9
Warren-Troy-Farmington Hills, MI Metro Division,	1,247,576	1,255,801	1,298,267	1,337,936	-3.9	69,418	161,601	78,487	5.6	12.9	6.0	3.0
Dothan, AL Metro Area	62,284	65,232	65,199	64,984	-4.5	3,854	6,231	2,545	6.2	9.6	3.9	4.6
Dover, DE Metro Area	76,887	72,689	72,015	63,479	6.8	4,149	6,461	2,621	5.4	8.9	3.6	4.0
Dubuque, IA Metro Area	55,729	54,224	50,793	48,376	9.7	1,997	3,136	2,196	3.6	5.8	4.3	3.2
Duluth, MN-WI Metro Area	142,600	144,905	141,059	142,105	1.1	7,139	11,852	7,265	5.0	8.2	5.2	4.5
Durham-Chapel Hill, NC Metro Area	281,198	262,690	244,489	232,733	15.0	14,015	21,376	10,507	5.0	8.1	4.3	2.9
East Stroudsburg, PA Metro Area	80,651	82,741	77,999	69,483	3.4	5,046	8,049	4,321	6.3	9.7	5.5	4.1
Eau Claire, WI Metro Area	91,409	90,289	86,404	82,837	5.8	3,827	6,767	3,943	4.2	7.5	4.6	3.7
El Centro, CA Metro Area	78,910	78,665	60,592	56,129	30.2	18,945	22,687	9,672	24.0	28.8	16.0	17.5
Elizabethtown-Fort Knox, KY Metro Area	63,537	65,301	65,279	61,457	-2.7	3,316	6,682	3,982	5.2	10.2	6.1	4.3
Elkhart-Goshen, IN Metro Area	104,616	94,498	101,915	96,750	2.7	4,021	12,599	4,726	3.8	13.3	4.6	2.7
Elmira, NY Metro Area	37,960	41,594	40,595	42,544	-6.5	2,247	3,489	2,157	5.9	8.4	5.3	4.3
El Paso, TX Metro Area	344,725	342,254	291,338	276,681	18.3	18,025	31,324	20,532	5.2	9.2	7.0	6.7
Enid, OK Metro Area	29,973	28,519	28,304	28,105	5.9	1,154	1,572	1,013	3.9	5.5	3.6	2.8
Erie, PA Metro Area	134,873	136,354	140,605	140,747	-4.1	7,185	12,687	7,562	5.3	9.3	5.4	4.5
Eugene, OR Metro Area	171,388	178,303	173,600	170,474	-1.3	10,194	19,648	10,664	5.9	11.0	6.1	5.4
Evansville, IN-KY Metro Area	158,056	159,288	159,088	154,923	-0.6	6,761	14,106	8,159	4.3	8.9	5.1	3.3
Fairbanks, AK Metro Area	46,486	48,285	45,247	41,013	2.7	2,527	3,202	2,641	5.4	6.6	5.8	6.2
Fargo, ND-MN Metro Area	130,873	122,707	113,083	103,433	15.7	3,193	5,018	3,269	2.4	4.1	2.9	2.4
Farmington, NM Metro Area	55,257	54,896	54,461	49,296	1.5	3,893	5,139	2,900	7.0	9.4	5.3	5.7
Fayetteville, NC Metro Area	145,827	149,647	145,555	134,131	0.2	10,879	15,151	7,933	7.5	10.1	5.5	4.5
Fayetteville-Springdale-Rogers, AR-MO Metro Area	253,105	227,616	220,833	176,441	14.6	9,584	15,288	7,441	3.8	6.7	3.4	3.0
Flagstaff, AZ Metro Area	73,041	72,846	67,883	62,612	7.6	4,786	7,196	3,334	6.6	9.9	4.9	4.4
Flint, MI Metro Area	182,886	188,190	212,686	215,846	-14.0	10,653	26,272	16,784	5.8	14.0	7.9	4.5
Florence, SC Metro Area	95,466	94,766	92,386	92,814	3.3	6,524	11,303	8,149	6.8	11.9	8.8	4.5
Florence-Muscle Shoals, AL Metro Area	66,300	67,824	67,023	69,396	-1.1	4,828	7,178	3,508	7.3	10.6	5.2	5.2
Fond du Lac, WI Metro Area	57,286	56,516	55,868	55,532	2.5	2,354	4,801	2,567	4.1	8.5	4.6	3.1
Fort Collins, CO Metro Area	180,306	170,001	165,944	146,317	8.7	5,942	12,976	7,251	3.3	7.6	4.4	2.5
Fort Smith, AR-OK Metro Area	121,212	126,732	126,475	119,078	-4.2	6,684	10,809	5,817	5.5	8.5	4.6	3.7
Fort Wayne, IN Metro Area	210,126	207,683	211,446	207,667	-0.6	9,372	22,233	11,062	4.5	10.7	5.2	2.7
Fresno, CA Metro Area	444,168	439,593	407,163	388,673	9.1	45,262	73,372	36,574	10.2	16.7	9.0	10.4
Gadsden, AL Metro Area	43,203	44,000	46,762	48,177	-7.6	2,644	4,807	2,220	6.1	10.9	4.7	5.8
Gainesville, FL Metro Area	136,632	135,244	131,039	122,570	4.3	6,273	11,040	3,864	4.6	8.2	2.9	3.0
Gainesville, GA Metro Area	92,277	86,546	82,801	73,522	11.4	4,383	8,341	3,702	4.7	9.6	4.5	3.0

NA = Not available.

[1] Civilian unemployed as percent of total civilian labor force.

Table B-13. Civilian Labor Force—*Continued*

Metropolitan statistical area and division	Total Labor Force					Number of unemployed			Unemployment rate[1]			
							Civilian labor force					
	2015	2010	2005	2000	Change, 2005–2015	2015	2010	2005	2015	2010	2005	2000
Gettysburg, PA Metro Area	55,038	54,588	54,495	49,605	1.0	2,241	4,215	1,978	4.1	7.7	3.6	3.1
Glens Falls, NY Metro Area	61,203	64,387	67,615	63,133	-9.5	3,291	5,564	3,055	5.4	8.6	4.5	4.0
Goldsboro, NC Metro Area	53,947	54,798	51,135	51,076	5.5	3,291	5,021	2,675	6.1	9.2	5.2	3.9
Grand Forks, ND-MN Metro Area	54,843	55,022	54,988	51,785	-0.3	1,630	2,454	1,967	3.0	4.5	3.6	3.4
Grand Island, NE Metro Area	43,894	43,870	43,547	41,865	0.8	1,651	1,983	1,589	3.8	4.5	3.6	2.8
Grand Junction, CO Metro Area	72,039	76,113	70,811	58,884	1.7	3,997	8,337	3,461	5.5	11.0	4.9	3.3
Grand Rapids-Wyoming, MI Metro Area	555,088	513,987	518,245	516,726	7.1	20,370	53,501	30,100	3.7	10.4	5.8	3.1
Grants Pass, OR Metro Area	33,162	34,491	34,300	31,473	-3.3	2,605	4,839	2,488	7.9	14.0	7.3	7.0
Great Falls, MT Metro Area	38,888	38,447	38,950	38,200	-0.2	1,553	2,451	1,671	4.0	6.4	4.3	5.1
Greeley, CO Metro Area	147,984	131,910	111,087	93,511	33.2	5,670	12,114	6,068	3.8	9.2	5.5	2.7
Green Bay, WI Metro Area	170,742	169,659	167,690	161,509	1.8	7,226	14,022	7,779	4.2	8.3	4.6	3.0
Greensboro-High Point, NC Metro Area	364,824	365,556	360,977	352,624	1.1	21,596	42,127	18,775	5.9	11.5	5.2	3.5
Greenville, NC Metro Area	87,628	85,902	73,488	70,106	19.2	5,339	8,743	4,253	6.1	10.2	5.8	4.1
Greenville-Anderson-Mauldin, SC Metro Area	415,467	390,078	384,213	382,647	8.1	21,870	40,692	23,672	5.3	10.4	6.2	2.9
Gulfport-Biloxi-Pascagoula, MS Metro Area	163,808	172,825	176,008	174,582	-6.9	10,665	15,694	18,495	6.5	9.1	10.5	5.0
Hagerstown-Martinsburg, MD-WV Metro Area	128,895	126,822	111,364	105,754	15.7	7,048	11,652	4,701	5.5	9.2	4.2	3.6
Hammond, LA Metro Area	54,029	53,664	50,534	45,252	6.9	3,870	5,213	4,825	7.2	9.7	9.5	6.5
Hanford-Corcoran, CA Metro Area	58,354	59,440	53,840	49,264	8.4	6,120	9,583	5,083	10.5	16.1	9.4	10.0
Harrisburg-Carlisle, PA Metro Area	293,252	289,988	277,860	269,318	5.5	12,348	21,806	11,211	4.2	7.5	4.0	3.3
Harrisonburg, VA Metro Area	64,253	63,538	61,197	55,781	5.0	2,931	4,632	2,019	4.6	7.3	3.3	1.9
Hartford-West Hartford-East Hartford, CT Metro Area	649,443	657,562	607,993	598,627	6.8	36,153	59,454	30,391	5.6	9.0	5.0	2.5
Hattiesburg, MS Metro Area	66,575	66,379	63,099	60,583	5.5	3,886	5,946	3,823	5.8	9.0	6.1	4.6
Hickory-Lenoir-Morganton, NC Metro Area	167,395	176,027	176,216	188,941	-5.0	9,538	23,608	11,597	5.7	13.4	6.6	2.9
Hilton Head Island-Bluffton-Beaufort, SC Metro Area	83,077	76,235	71,681	60,933	15.9	4,478	6,725	3,516	5.4	8.8	4.9	3.3
Hinesville, GA Metro Area	32,006	33,158	28,663	23,935	11.7	1,992	2,959	1,584	6.2	8.9	5.5	5.0
Homosassa Springs, FL Metro Area	47,739	52,847	51,324	43,726	-7.0	3,552	7,253	2,198	7.4	13.7	4.3	4.7
Hot Springs, AR Metro Area	40,046	41,563	41,936	38,407	-4.5	2,268	3,517	2,374	5.7	8.5	5.7	4.3
Houma-Thibodaux, LA Metro Area	99,998	95,980	96,374	87,021	3.8	5,632	6,058	6,041	5.6	6.3	6.3	4.6
Houston-The Woodlands-Sugar Land, TX Metro Area	3,252,943	2,970,263	2,592,941	2,383,280	25.5	149,965	245,481	144,992	4.6	8.3	5.6	4.2
Huntington-Ashland, WV-KY-OH Metro Area	147,778	157,968	164,800	160,479	-10.3	9,291	14,199	8,853	6.3	9.0	5.4	5.7
Huntsville, AL Metro Area	209,345	208,154	193,890	181,504	8.0	11,465	17,873	7,254	5.5	8.6	3.7	3.6
Idaho Falls, ID Metro Area	65,172	63,055	61,167	51,855	6.5	2,248	4,404	1,887	3.4	7.0	3.1	3.5
Indianapolis-Carmel-Anderson, IN Metro Area	1,008,205	950,612	941,192	879,224	7.1	45,398	91,213	47,523	4.5	9.6	5.0	2.6
Iowa City, IA Metro Area	96,342	91,689	86,066	78,406	11.9	2,557	3,983	2,777	2.7	4.3	3.2	1.9
Ithaca, NY Metro Area	55,371	54,767	54,600	50,538	1.4	2,255	3,370	1,947	4.1	6.2	3.6	3.3
Jackson, MI Metro Area	73,043	74,673	78,307	79,369	-6.7	3,719	9,109	5,363	5.1	12.2	6.8	3.5
Jackson, MS Metro Area	267,233	266,750	272,411	261,042	-1.9	14,464	23,302	16,035	5.4	8.7	5.9	4.6
Jackson, TN Metro Area	61,636	63,842	60,322	60,978	2.2	3,769	6,516	3,539	6.1	10.2	5.9	3.8
Jacksonville, FL Metro Area	724,881	697,120	635,531	589,093	14.1	38,021	74,912	23,855	5.2	10.7	3.8	3.2
Jacksonville, NC Metro Area	63,959	63,331	55,996	53,363	14.2	3,856	5,240	2,985	6.0	8.3	5.3	4.3
Janesville-Beloit, WI Metro Area	83,596	82,698	83,193	82,306	0.5	4,370	9,315	4,856	5.2	11.3	5.8	4.3
Jefferson City, MO Metro Area	76,650	77,926	77,810	76,186	-1.5	3,259	5,785	3,436	4.3	7.4	4.4	3.0
Johnson City, TN Metro Area	88,392	94,817	94,637	90,636	-6.6	5,452	9,092	5,000	6.2	9.6	5.3	4.4
Johnstown, PA Metro Area	62,363	66,747	67,122	66,867	-7.1	3,981	6,290	4,115	6.4	9.4	6.1	6.1
Jonesboro, AR Metro Area	60,852	58,533	56,567	54,151	7.6	2,906	4,548	2,910	4.8	7.8	5.1	4.2
Joplin, MO Metro Area	87,769	87,785	82,311	81,484	6.6	3,804	7,592	4,035	4.3	8.6	4.9	3.6
Kahului-Wailuku-Lahaina, HI Metro Area	84,233	78,966	74,992	70,949	12.3	3,164	6,743	2,026	3.8	8.5	2.7	3.9
Kalamazoo-Portage, MI Metro Area	165,663	167,416	173,449	173,073	-4.5	7,511	18,072	9,831	4.5	10.8	5.7	3.3
Kankakee, IL Metro Area	55,211	57,454	52,672	52,870	4.8	3,763	7,073	3,348	6.8	12.3	6.4	4.3
Kansas City, MO-KS Metro Area	1,121,621	1,082,274	1,013,562	984,106	10.7	53,595	94,152	57,024	4.8	8.7	5.6	3.4
Kennewick-Richland, WA Metro Area	130,602	132,506	114,306	99,279	14.3	8,941	10,777	7,272	6.8	8.1	6.4	6.1
Killeen-Temple, TX Metro Area	169,589	166,193	149,377	134,039	13.5	7,943	12,704	7,716	4.7	7.6	5.2	4.3
Kingsport-Bristol-Bristol, TN-VA Metro Area	137,222	144,661	140,267	139,486	-2.2	7,860	13,173	7,414	5.7	9.1	5.3	3.7
Kingston, NY Metro Area	88,438	93,606	91,816	88,059	-3.7	4,339	7,296	3,988	4.9	7.8	4.3	3.6
Knoxville, TN Metro Area	405,227	415,146	398,020	373,781	1.8	21,750	35,269	18,719	5.4	8.5	4.7	3.5
Kokomo, IN Metro Area	36,934	35,806	39,174	41,485	-5.7	1,844	4,506	2,567	5.0	12.6	6.6	3.3
La Crosse-Onalaska, WI-MN Metro Area	77,256	76,423	72,515	72,083	6.5	3,005	5,187	2,959	3.9	6.8	4.1	3.4
Lafayette, LA Metro Area	228,600	221,628	208,275	196,692	9.8	14,384	15,537	11,966	6.3	7.0	5.7	4.9
Lafayette-West Lafayette, IN Metro Area	107,381	101,447	94,494	93,248	13.6	4,517	9,112	4,647	4.2	9.0	4.9	2.7
Lake Charles, LA Metro Area	102,160	91,195	95,465	91,140	7.0	5,448	7,252	7,087	5.3	8.0	7.4	5.1
Lake Havasu City-Kingman, AZ Metro Area	79,310	82,726	89,079	68,796	-11.0	6,363	10,727	3,808	8.0	13.0	4.3	4.4
Lakeland-Winter Haven, FL Metro Area	279,903	278,479	258,158	231,202	8.4	17,349	33,811	10,479	6.2	12.1	4.1	4.1
Lancaster, PA Metro Area	275,869	268,001	267,575	251,460	3.1	10,997	20,089	9,773	4.0	7.5	3.7	2.8
Lansing-East Lansing, MI Metro Area	242,918	245,259	248,085	248,419	-2.1	10,391	24,076	14,996	4.3	9.8	6.0	2.9
Laredo, TX Metro Area	112,415	105,016	85,624	70,985	31.3	5,328	8,652	5,140	4.7	8.2	6.0	6.0
Las Cruces, NM Metro Area	93,179	93,661	85,089	75,909	9.5	6,868	7,248	4,792	7.4	7.7	5.6	6.1
Las Vegas-Henderson-Paradise, NV Metro Area	1,047,528	984,004	869,251	730,308	20.5	71,265	135,431	35,332	6.8	13.8	4.1	4.3
Lawrence, KS Metro Area	65,273	64,379	63,186	58,565	3.3	2,411	3,805	2,507	3.7	5.9	4.0	2.7
Lawton, OK Metro Area	53,127	54,506	48,573	46,168	9.4	2,228	3,164	2,164	4.2	5.8	4.5	3.6
Lebanon, PA Metro Area	70,133	70,059	70,117	64,373	0.0	3,071	5,236	2,519	4.4	7.5	3.6	3.1
Lewiston, ID-WA Metro Area	30,473	30,420	29,869	28,554	2.0	1,222	2,317	1,507	4.0	7.6	5.0	5.4
Lewiston-Auburn, ME Metro Area	54,566	55,912	57,033	55,712	-4.3	2,259	4,800	2,821	4.1	8.6	4.9	3.4
Lexington-Fayette, KY Metro Area	254,913	255,705	229,055	230,021	11.3	10,396	20,277	10,576	4.1	7.9	4.6	3.0

NA = Not available.
[1]Civilian unemployed as percent of total civilian labor force.

Table B-13.   Civilian Labor Force—*Continued*

	Civilian labor force										
	Total Labor Force					Number of unemployed			Unemployment rate[1]			
Metropolitan statistical area and division	2015	2010	2005	2000	Change, 2005–2015	2015	2010	2005	2015	2010	2005	2000
Lima, OH Metro Area	48,106	52,009	52,706	51,566	-8.7	2,326	5,567	3,291	4.8	10.7	6.2	4.6
Lincoln, NE Metro Area	177,288	171,332	165,264	157,471	7.3	4,647	7,202	5,800	2.6	4.2	3.5	2.4
Little Rock-North Little Rock-Conway, AR Metro Area	346,926	347,828	334,366	311,459	3.8	16,148	24,877	15,603	4.7	7.2	4.7	3.7
Logan, UT-ID Metro Area	66,786	63,443	63,440	53,435	5.3	1,999	3,808	2,048	3.0	6.0	3.2	2.8
Longview, TX Metro Area	100,907	102,607	101,999	92,866	-1.1	5,019	8,273	5,083	5.0	8.1	5.0	5.2
Longview, WA Metro Area	44,276	46,432	42,978	43,311	3.0	3,359	5,997	3,261	7.6	12.9	7.6	7.0
Los Angeles-Long Beach-Anaheim, CA Metro Area	6,597,679	6,454,562	6,367,520	6,159,692	3.6	403,912	764,850	315,711	6.1	11.8	5.0	4.9
Anaheim-Santa Ana-Irvine, CA Metro Division	1,597,071	1,537,187	1,585,916	1,482,303	0.7	71,507	149,749	59,330	4.5	9.7	3.7	3.5
Los Angeles-Long Beach-Glendale, CA Metro Division	5,000,608	4,917,375	4,781,604	4,677,389	4.6	332,405	615,101	256,381	6.6	12.5	5.4	5.4
Louisville/Jefferson County, KY-IN Metro Area	623,267	626,312	590,223	593,348	5.6	29,471	62,001	33,938	4.7	9.9	5.8	3.6
Lubbock, TX Metro Area	153,745	149,359	143,067	134,145	7.5	5,317	9,404	5,915	3.5	6.3	4.1	3.5
Lynchburg, VA Metro Area	123,006	126,345	116,542	114,195	5.5	6,026	9,890	4,736	4.9	7.8	4.1	2.2
Macon, GA Metro Area	103,239	105,508	110,115	103,931	-6.2	6,542	11,947	6,188	6.3	11.3	5.6	4.2
Madera, CA Metro Area	60,566	61,607	61,881	54,963	-2.1	6,357	10,241	4,866	10.5	16.6	7.9	8.7
Madison, WI Metro Area	376,678	360,360	351,442	327,541	7.2	12,730	22,972	11,816	3.4	6.4	3.4	2.6
Manchester-Nashua, NH Metro Area	228,523	226,154	226,188	212,572	1.0	8,232	13,917	8,202	3.6	6.2	3.6	2.5
Manhattan, KS Metro Area	50,089	47,981	44,806	40,105	11.8	1,675	2,424	1,709	3.3	5.1	3.8	2.9
Mankato-North Mankato, MN Metro Area	59,195	57,896	54,322	52,076	9.0	1,690	3,634	1,784	2.9	6.3	3.3	2.8
Mansfield, OH Metro Area	53,647	59,079	62,761	63,248	-14.5	2,986	7,171	4,227	5.6	12.1	6.7	5.3
McAllen-Edinburg-Mission, TX Metro Area	331,632	318,302	260,575	211,320	27.3	26,299	37,418	20,606	7.9	11.8	7.9	9.1
Medford, OR Metro Area	97,648	100,968	98,727	90,977	-1.1	6,751	12,576	6,113	6.9	12.5	6.2	5.6
Memphis, TN-MS-AR Metro Area	614,498	635,580	600,070	592,573	2.4	39,766	61,598	36,760	6.5	9.7	6.1	3.7
Merced, CA Metro Area	115,086	113,579	98,738	90,390	16.6	13,063	20,388	9,858	11.4	18.0	10.0	9.6
Miami-Fort Lauderdale-West Palm Beach, FL Metro Area	3,003,301	2,807,697	2,710,277	2,489,935	10.8	162,744	302,108	97,777	5.4	10.8	3.6	4.0
Fort Lauderdale-Pompano Beach-Deerfield Beach, FL Metro Division	992,392	936,563	957,619	854,842	3.6	49,980	95,090	35,325	5.0	10.2	3.7	3.6
Miami-Miami Beach-Kendall, FL Metro Division	1,317,274	1,225,397	1,147,797	1,093,542	14.8	77,897	136,171	36,360	5.9	11.1	3.2	4.3
West Palm Beach-Boca Raton-Delray Beach, FL Metro Division	693,635	645,737	604,861	541,551	14.7	34,867	70,847	26,092	5.0	11.0	4.3	4.2
Michigan City-La Porte, IN Metro Area	48,522	51,336	53,070	53,804	-8.6	3,033	6,178	3,221	6.3	12.0	6.1	3.6
Midland, MI Metro Area	41,702	41,219	41,907	42,694	-0.5	1,941	4,023	2,479	4.7	9.8	5.9	3.3
Midland, TX Metro Area	91,038	73,527	68,430	60,409	33.0	3,143	4,308	2,542	3.5	5.9	3.7	4.1
Milwaukee-Waukesha-West Allis, WI Metro Area	822,946	817,477	782,820	801,413	5.1	41,090	73,100	38,774	5.0	8.9	5.0	3.8
Minneapolis-St. Paul-Bloomington, MN-WI Metro Area	1,938,857	1,870,769	1,845,419	1,791,103	5.1	66,767	137,127	70,482	3.4	7.3	3.8	2.7
Missoula, MT Metro Area	61,143	58,536	57,899	54,007	5.6	2,365	4,292	2,282	3.9	7.3	3.9	4.2
Mobile, AL Metro Area	183,097	192,730	180,384	184,951	1.5	12,811	21,787	8,945	7.0	11.3	5.0	4.9
Modesto, CA Metro Area	242,710	243,274	226,627	207,963	7.1	23,073	41,092	19,042	9.5	16.9	8.4	7.8
Monroe, LA Metro Area	81,813	80,403	82,886	80,152	-1.3	5,406	6,848	5,095	6.6	8.5	6.1	4.9
Monroe, MI Metro Area	76,732	75,640	77,855	77,465	-1.4	3,345	8,869	4,826	4.4	11.7	6.2	3.2
Montgomery, AL Metro Area	168,786	175,499	168,497	163,496	0.2	9,994	17,267	7,413	5.9	9.8	4.4	4.2
Morgantown, WV Metro Area	65,696	63,289	58,509	54,644	12.3	3,302	3,949	2,308	5.0	6.2	3.9	4.6
Morristown, TN Metro Area	49,733	52,817	52,907	51,830	-6.0	3,199	6,085	3,106	6.4	11.5	5.9	4.1
Mount Vernon-Anacortes, WA Metro Area	56,856	59,114	56,282	52,076	1.0	3,791	6,456	3,498	6.7	10.9	6.2	6.4
Muncie, IN Metro Area	54,475	54,724	56,113	58,650	-2.9	3,087	6,322	3,851	5.7	11.6	6.9	3.5
Muskegon, MI Metro Area	77,763	77,712	90,054	85,904	-13.6	4,319	11,292	6,309	5.6	14.5	7.0	4.2
Myrtle Beach-Conway-North Myrtle Beach, SC-NC Metro Area	184,985	177,470	164,187	142,282	12.7	13,092	21,915	9,115	7.1	12.3	5.6	3.9
Napa, CA Metro Area	74,752	70,216	71,328	66,678	4.8	3,442	7,227	3,114	4.6	10.3	4.4	3.6
Naples-Immokalee-Marco Island, FL Metro Area	162,124	145,349	145,136	116,066	11.7	8,447	16,922	5,049	5.2	11.6	3.5	3.7
Nashville-Davidson—Murfreesboro—Franklin, TN Metro Area	934,338	878,273	779,926	746,995	19.8	43,150	75,866	35,640	4.6	8.6	4.6	3.1
New Bern, NC Metro Area	51,352	52,370	51,421	48,811	-0.1	3,125	5,612	2,412	6.1	10.7	4.7	4.1
New Haven-Milford, CT Metro Area	454,396	462,233	429,962	420,320	5.7	27,907	46,245	22,898	6.1	10.0	5.3	2.6
New Orleans-Metairie, LA Metro Area	603,674	570,730	NA	636,352	NA	36,072	44,220	-	6.0	7.7	-	5.1
New York-Newark-Jersey City, NY-NJ-PA Metro Area	10,073,374	9,812,850	9,505,717	9,205,334	6.0	532,499	873,734	464,298	5.3	8.9	4.9	4.4
Dutchess County-Putnam County, NY Metro Division	194,132	201,790	203,076	190,469	-4.4	8,769	15,304	7,832	4.5	7.6	3.9	3.1
Nassau County-Suffolk County, NY Metro Division	1,472,173	1,469,298	1,467,327	1,405,225	0.3	67,221	109,582	60,389	4.6	7.5	4.1	3.4
Newark, NJ-PA Metro Division	1,262,102	1,277,890	1,247,158	1,224,595	1.2	68,811	116,216	54,637	5.5	9.1	4.4	3.5
New York-Jersey City-White Plains, NY-NJ Metro Division	7,144,967	6,863,872	6,588,156	6,385,045	8.5	387,698	632,632	341,440	5.4	9.2	5.2	4.8
Niles-Benton Harbor, MI Metro Area	74,150	76,628	79,071	82,832	-6.2	3,684	9,213	5,480	5.0	12.0	6.9	3.9
North Port-Sarasota-Bradenton, FL Metro Area	343,357	314,794	313,922	271,964	9.4	17,042	36,219	10,818	5.0	11.5	3.4	3.2
Norwich-New London, CT Metro Area	136,630	144,517	144,132	133,684	-5.2	7,939	12,834	6,473	5.8	8.9	4.5	2.4
Ocala, FL Metro Area	131,147	132,351	127,862	109,171	2.6	8,358	18,054	4,851	6.4	13.6	3.8	4.1
Ocean City, NJ Metro Area	48,896	50,032	57,700	55,469	-15.3	5,307	7,026	3,805	10.9	14.0	6.6	6.4
Odessa, TX Metro Area	79,869	68,186	62,285	56,621	28.2	3,682	5,661	2,827	4.6	8.3	4.5	5.3
Ogden-Clearfield, UT Metro Area	307,072	288,136	270,310	244,225	13.6	11,071	22,530	11,420	3.6	7.8	4.2	3.6
Oklahoma City, OK Metro Area	668,199	623,505	573,874	552,471	16.4	24,707	36,555	24,948	3.7	5.9	4.3	2.7
Olympia-Tumwater, WA Metro Area	125,603	126,948	121,951	108,427	3.0	7,425	11,398	6,465	5.9	9.0	5.3	5.1
Omaha-Council Bluffs, NE-IA Metro Area	477,954	465,973	440,297	423,946	8.6	15,379	23,631	18,843	3.2	5.1	4.3	2.8

NA = Not available.
[1] Civilian unemployed as percent of total civilian labor force.

Table B-13. Civilian Labor Force—*Continued*

Metropolitan statistical area and division	Civilian labor force											
	Total Labor Force					Number of unemployed			Unemployment rate[1]			
	2015	2010	2005	2000	Change, 2005–2015	2015	2010	2005	2015	2010	2005	2000
Orlando-Kissimmee-Sanford, FL Metro Area........	1,223,514	1,137,389	1,015,778	894,780	20.5	61,540	126,244	36,571	5.0	11.1	3.6	3.1
Oshkosh-Neenah, WI Metro Area.........................	91,499	92,449	91,185	89,268	0.3	3,937	7,224	4,025	4.3	7.8	4.4	2.8
Owensboro, KY Metro Area.................................	52,664	55,465	55,137	56,024	-4.5	2,500	5,237	3,291	4.7	9.4	6.0	4.3
Oxnard-Thousand Oaks-Ventura, CA Metro Area ..	429,784	430,010	415,958	392,984	3.3	24,435	46,586	19,733	5.7	10.8	4.7	4.5
Palm Bay-Melbourne-Titusville, FL Metro Area.....	257,684	265,643	260,435	231,904	-1.1	15,122	29,886	9,466	5.9	11.3	3.6	3.6
Panama City, FL Metro Area...............................	93,702	92,304	88,727	77,213	5.6	5,047	9,659	3,143	5.4	10.5	3.5	4.7
Parkersburg-Vienna, WV Metro Area	39,832	41,640	43,449	44,751	-8.3	2,573	3,785	2,423	6.5	9.1	5.6	4.7
Pensacola-Ferry Pass-Brent, FL Metro Area..........	213,181	211,246	203,128	187,393	4.9	11,259	20,778	7,689	5.3	9.8	3.8	4.0
Peoria, IL Metro Area..	186,547	197,473	191,072	188,931	-2.4	12,100	19,703	8,898	6.5	10.0	4.7	4.0
Philadelphia-Camden-Wilmington,												
PA-NJ-DE-MD Metro Area	3,059,036	3,020,334	2,916,385	2,849,620	4.9	161,303	265,134	138,140	5.3	8.8	4.7	3.9
Camden, NJ Metro Division	637,382	653,792	648,744	609,653	-1.8	36,990	65,915	28,272	5.8	10.1	4.4	3.6
Montgomery County-Bucks County-Chester County, PA Metro Division	1,056,108	1,037,023	1,020,158	977,074	3.5	43,257	72,461	39,862	4.1	7.0	3.9	3.2
Philadelphia, PA Metro Division	988,102	973,948	896,383	915,086	10.2	61,742	95,636	54,190	6.2	9.8	6.0	5.0
Wilmington, DE-MD-NJ Metro Division	377,444	355,571	351,100	347,807	7.5	19,314	31,122	15,816	5.1	8.8	4.5	3.6
Phoenix-Mesa-Scottsdale, AZ Metro Area............	2,165,131	2,073,297	1,943,498	1,667,726	11.4	113,890	199,291	80,003	5.3	9.6	4.1	3.3
Pine Bluff, AR Metro Area	36,709	42,560	46,561	44,828	-21.2	2,572	4,302	3,455	7.0	10.1	7.4	5.8
Pittsburgh, PA Metro Area	1,213,284	1,201,150	1,196,815	1,195,684	1.4	62,419	95,830	62,616	5.1	8.0	5.2	4.3
Pittsfield, MA Metro Area..................................	65,608	68,212	72,664	69,422	-9.7	3,658	5,933	3,170	5.6	8.7	4.4	2.9
Pocatello, ID Metro Area	42,141	41,091	40,549	38,180	3.9	1,673	3,282	1,565	4.0	8.0	3.9	4.7
Portland-South Portland, ME Metro Area.............	283,514	283,853	285,935	272,359	-0.8	10,211	20,132	11,150	3.6	7.1	3.9	2.6
Portland-Vancouver-Hillsboro, OR-WA Metro Area	1,224,063	1,207,837	1,093,793	1,080,370	11.9	64,603	123,713	64,508	5.3	10.2	5.9	4.5
Port St. Lucie, FL Metro Area.............................	201,248	195,326	177,600	143,770	13.3	11,861	24,878	8,004	5.9	12.7	4.5	5.1
Prescott, AZ Metro Area....................................	97,545	96,533	91,442	75,804	6.7	5,434	10,309	4,039	5.6	10.7	4.4	4.0
Providence-Warwick, RI-MA Metro Area	842,619	853,201	853,565	818,661	-1.3	51,268	93,625	45,755	6.1	11.0	5.4	4.0
Provo-Orem, UT Metro Area	271,088	234,432	209,058	184,883	29.7	8,677	17,512	8,217	3.2	7.5	3.9	2.9
Pueblo, CO Metro Area.....................................	71,996	74,396	69,326	63,956	3.9	4,069	7,729	4,720	5.7	10.4	6.8	4.0
Punta Gorda, FL Metro Area..............................	67,559	66,293	66,088	55,138	2.2	3,967	8,447	2,658	5.9	12.7	4.0	3.7
Racine, WI Metro Area......................................	99,446	100,313	98,509	99,119	1.0	5,650	10,193	5,822	5.7	10.2	5.9	4.1
Raleigh, NC Metro Area.....................................	656,759	590,114	500,724	456,161	31.2	31,339	51,012	20,913	4.8	8.6	4.2	2.5
Rapid City, SD Metro Area.................................	71,553	70,045	70,122	65,280	2.0	2,353	3,686	2,563	3.3	5.3	3.7	2.3
Reading, PA Metro Area.....................................	213,249	210,138	198,712	195,287	7.3	10,151	18,230	9,697	4.8	8.7	4.9	3.9
Redding, CA Metro Area	74,858	78,503	81,748	74,906	-8.4	5,842	13,169	5,922	7.8	16.8	7.2	6.1
Reno, NV Metro Area..	230,111	222,838	210,769	197,573	9.2	14,382	28,873	8,320	6.3	13.0	3.9	3.4
Richmond, VA Metro Area..................................	661,671	628,685	592,935	547,951	11.6	30,577	50,190	22,617	4.6	8.0	3.8	2.1
Riverside-San Bernardino-Ontario, CA Metro Area	1,961,819	1,866,722	1,704,048	1,421,291	15.1	129,493	255,547	90,008	6.6	13.7	5.3	5.1
Roanoke, VA Metro Area....................................	158,927	159,127	149,437	149,044	6.4	7,021	12,036	5,268	4.4	7.6	3.5	2.2
Rochester, MN Metro Area.................................	118,535	115,857	113,329	107,078	4.6	3,808	7,320	4,127	3.2	6.3	3.6	2.8
Rochester, NY Metro Area	525,622	546,181	547,998	543,258	-4.1	27,353	44,187	25,332	5.2	8.1	4.6	3.7
Rockford, IL Metro Area....................................	168,616	177,527	165,009	170,016	2.2	11,813	24,870	10,543	7.0	14.0	6.4	4.3
Rocky Mount, NC Metro Area	67,015	72,942	68,411	68,774	-2.0	5,440	9,973	4,699	8.1	13.7	6.9	5.0
Rome, GA Metro Area.......................................	42,787	45,087	50,139	44,685	-14.7	2,812	5,337	2,598	6.6	11.8	5.2	3.9
Sacramento—Roseville—Arden-Arcade, CA Metro Area...	1,060,164	1,049,782	1,011,984	909,969	4.8	62,073	129,718	49,365	5.9	12.4	4.9	4.3
Saginaw, MI Metro Area....................................	89,015	90,722	98,365	100,589	-9.5	4,856	11,097	7,845	5.5	12.2	8.0	4.2
St. Cloud, MN Metro Area	110,552	106,774	102,805	98,982	7.5	4,157	8,017	4,511	3.8	7.5	4.4	3.2
St. George, UT Metro Area.................................	63,906	56,776	56,944	39,358	12.2	2,535	5,955	2,305	4.0	10.5	4.0	3.5
St. Joseph, MO-KS Metro Area	66,285	66,123	64,845	60,230	2.2	3,006	5,942	3,738	4.5	9.0	5.8	3.7
St. Louis, MO-IL Metro Area..............................	1,481,428	1,478,074	1,426,498	1,411,904	3.9	74,872	141,694	78,966	5.1	9.6	5.5	3.7
Salem, OR Metro Area	188,784	191,735	183,380	178,575	2.9	11,377	20,861	11,592	6.0	10.9	6.3	5.3
Salinas, CA Metro Area.....................................	221,383	215,788	206,565	203,392	7.2	17,875	27,449	15,030	8.1	12.7	7.3	7.4
Salisbury, MD-DE Metro Area	184,118	177,111	181,096	162,162	1.7	11,860	17,292	8,031	6.4	9.8	4.4	4.5
Salt Lake City, UT Metro Area............................	616,414	575,832	542,619	506,634	13.6	20,728	44,360	21,872	3.4	7.7	4.0	3.2
San Angelo, TX Metro Area	55,306	53,468	52,796	51,698	4.8	2,279	3,492	2,273	4.1	6.5	4.3	3.9
San Antonio-New Braunfels, TX Metro Area.........	1,099,596	1,017,400	894,737	820,042	22.9	42,059	73,629	44,856	3.8	7.2	5.0	3.9
San Diego-Carlsbad, CA Metro Area....................	1,563,836	1,515,198	1,489,799	1,377,101	5.0	81,308	162,932	64,093	5.2	10.8	4.3	3.9
San Francisco-Oakland-Hayward,												
CA Metro Area	2,505,850	2,320,104	2,146,852	2,284,533	16.7	106,594	229,650	103,004	4.3	9.9	4.8	3.4
Oakland-Hayward-Berkeley, CA Metro Division.	1,374,757	1,308,069	1,244,122	1,271,006	10.5	66,663	143,043	62,132	4.8	10.9	5.0	3.6
San Francisco-Redwood City-South San Francisco, CA Metro Division	989,970	879,023	773,635	871,608	28.0	34,932	76,165	35,871	3.5	8.7	4.6	3.2
San Rafael, CA Metro Division	141,123	133,012	129,095	141,919	9.3	4,999	10,442	5,001	3.5	7.9	3.9	2.9
San Jose-Sunnyvale-Santa Clara, CA Metro Area..	1,048,170	954,431	839,860	968,946	24.8	44,586	100,626	45,288	4.3	10.5	5.4	3.2
San Luis Obispo-Paso Robles-Arroyo Grande, CA Metro Area...	143,293	133,651	131,479	122,563	9.0	6,648	13,442	5,600	4.6	10.1	4.3	4.0
Santa Cruz-Watsonville, CA Metro Area	144,248	141,717	142,992	148,485	0.9	10,816	18,845	8,963	7.5	13.3	6.3	5.1
Santa Fe, NM Metro Area..................................	71,658	73,760	76,704	70,244	-6.6	3,891	5,038	3,144	5.4	6.8	4.1	3.6
Santa Maria-Santa Barbara, CA Metro Area	220,001	212,267	213,206	202,556	3.2	11,608	20,587	9,244	5.3	9.7	4.3	4.4
Santa Rosa, CA Metro Area...............................	260,344	244,634	253,410	253,460	2.7	11,680	26,534	11,205	4.5	10.8	4.4	3.4
Savannah, GA Metro Area.................................	175,755	167,555	165,458	142,165	6.2	9,795	16,398	7,345	5.6	9.8	4.4	3.5
Scranton—Wilkes-Barre—Hazleton, PA Metro Area...	278,915	281,080	277,022	273,882	0.7	16,826	26,742	15,387	6.0	9.5	5.6	4.8
Seattle-Tacoma-Bellevue, WA Metro Area.......	1,971,002	1,888,261	1,727,043	1,652,696	14.1	96,535	182,292	83,495	4.9	9.7	4.8	4.2
Seattle-Bellevue-Everett, WA Metro Division....	1,579,039	1,492,417	1,357,888	1,312,041	16.3	71,708	141,024	60,809	4.5	9.4	4.5	3.8
Tacoma-Lakewood, WA Metro Division..........	391,963	395,844	369,155	340,655	6.2	24,827	41,268	22,686	6.3	10.4	6.1	5.6
Sebastian-Vero Beach, FL Metro Area.................	61,307	61,384	59,484	51,043	3.1	4,140	8,536	2,846	6.8	13.9	4.8	5.1

NA = Not available.
[1]Civilian unemployed as percent of total civilian labor force.

Table B-13.   Civilian Labor Force—*Continued*

	Civilian labor force											
	Total Labor Force					Number of unemployed			Unemployment rate[1]			
Metropolitan statistical area and division	2015	2010	2005	2000	Change, 2005– 2015	2015	2010	2005	2015	2010	2005	2000
Sebring, FL Metro Area	35,272	37,247	39,983	33,162	-11.8	2,602	4,660	1,690	7.4	12.5	4.2	4.8
Sheboygan, WI Metro Area	61,368	62,238	64,550	64,092	-4.9	2,338	5,782	2,557	3.8	9.3	4.0	2.6
Sherman-Denison, TX Metro Area	60,503	59,489	56,416	56,405	7.2	2,422	4,869	3,036	4.0	8.2	5.4	4.0
Shreveport-Bossier City, LA Metro Area	195,684	201,600	199,914	191,537	-2.1	13,356	15,688	12,037	6.8	7.8	6.0	5.2
Sierra Vista-Douglas, AZ Metro Area	50,040	57,023	55,774	48,643	-10.3	3,715	5,329	2,677	7.4	9.3	4.8	4.5
Sioux City, IA-NE-SD Metro Area	92,977	92,723	88,637	90,285	4.9	3,260	5,762	3,999	3.5	6.2	4.5	2.6
Sioux Falls, SD Metro Area	144,580	133,561	120,564	111,252	19.9	3,805	6,348	4,081	2.6	4.8	3.4	1.9
South Bend-Mishawaka, IN-MI Metro Area	155,200	155,046	161,819	161,377	-4.1	7,703	17,869	8,571	5.0	11.5	5.3	3.3
Spartanburg, SC Metro Area	150,795	144,213	144,362	145,423	4.5	8,863	17,803	11,199	5.9	12.3	7.8	3.8
Spokane-Spokane Valley, WA Metro Area	250,194	262,377	247,213	233,881	1.2	16,617	27,306	15,176	6.6	10.4	6.1	6.0
Springfield, IL Metro Area	111,709	115,875	112,103	113,461	-0.4	5,857	8,958	5,053	5.2	7.7	4.5	3.4
Springfield, MA Metro Area	307,893	306,283	311,982	301,997	-1.3	18,802	28,917	16,621	6.1	9.4	5.3	3.0
Springfield, MO Metro Area	233,488	223,668	212,489	197,933	9.9	10,101	19,630	9,213	4.3	8.8	4.3	3.1
Springfield, OH Metro Area	64,200	68,266	70,529	72,332	-9.0	3,207	7,530	4,565	5.0	11.0	6.5	4.5
State College, PA Metro Area	77,888	77,335	72,388	68,658	7.6	2,969	4,599	2,896	3.8	5.9	4.0	3.4
Staunton-Waynesboro, VA Metro Area	58,831	59,146	57,325	55,390	2.6	2,514	4,490	1,863	4.3	7.6	3.2	2.1
Stockton-Lodi, CA Metro Area	316,903	311,437	283,588	259,158	11.7	28,127	51,442	22,299	8.9	16.5	7.9	7.0
Sumter, SC Metro Area	44,413	44,424	46,446	45,279	-4.4	3,047	5,532	3,941	6.9	12.5	8.5	4.4
Syracuse, NY Metro Area	312,827	331,466	330,039	322,788	-5.2	17,010	28,247	16,077	5.4	8.5	4.9	3.8
Tallahassee, FL Metro Area	186,294	190,683	179,409	172,474	3.8	9,624	16,084	5,754	5.2	8.4	3.2	3.2
Tampa-St. Petersburg-Clearwater, FL Metro Area	1,447,077	1,384,699	1,258,615	1,199,515	15.0	74,158	153,386	49,881	5.1	11.1	4.0	3.4
Terre Haute, IN Metro Area	77,277	81,204	80,637	80,985	-4.2	4,697	9,121	5,631	6.1	11.2	7.0	4.4
Texarkana, TX-AR Metro Area	64,636	68,991	68,421	65,061	-5.5	3,248	5,241	3,535	5.0	7.6	5.2	4.7
The Villages, FL Metro Area	28,583	25,310	25,555	16,919	11.8	2,130	3,355	870	7.5	13.3	3.4	4.3
Toledo, OH Metro Area	301,153	309,116	315,736	316,118	-4.6	15,206	34,628	21,024	5.0	11.2	6.7	4.5
Topeka, KS Metro Area	121,135	124,269	123,539	120,506	-1.9	5,188	8,766	6,765	4.3	7.1	5.5	3.9
Trenton, NJ Metro Area	199,062	192,625	193,721	179,928	2.8	9,611	16,103	7,585	4.8	8.4	3.9	3.3
Tucson, AZ Metro Area	464,150	478,743	441,581	409,776	5.1	25,787	44,637	19,766	5.6	9.3	4.5	3.7
Tulsa, OK Metro Area	476,532	462,935	442,814	440,191	7.6	20,166	33,649	19,278	4.2	7.3	4.4	2.9
Tuscaloosa, AL Metro Area	111,973	108,059	99,823	97,228	12.2	6,354	10,626	3,989	5.7	9.8	4.0	4.4
Tyler, TX Metro Area	102,736	101,151	95,360	86,479	7.7	4,648	8,041	4,800	4.5	7.9	5.0	4.4
Urban Honolulu, HI Metro Area	468,885	446,189	439,257	430,891	6.7	15,920	26,558	12,241	3.4	6.0	2.8	4.1
Utica-Rome, NY Metro Area	131,965	143,800	142,904	141,951	-7.7	7,371	11,275	6,957	5.6	7.8	4.9	4.0
Valdosta, GA Metro Area	62,718	64,076	64,829	56,190	-3.3	3,734	6,165	2,613	6.0	9.6	4.0	4.5
Vallejo-Fairfield, CA Metro Area	206,604	202,407	208,486	194,370	-0.9	12,650	25,438	11,145	6.1	12.6	5.3	4.6
Victoria, TX Metro Area	49,508	46,435	47,296	46,491	4.7	2,062	3,549	2,149	4.2	7.6	4.5	3.7
Vineland-Bridgeton, NJ Metro Area	67,387	72,379	69,082	65,461	-2.5	5,846	9,431	4,419	8.7	13.0	6.4	5.8
Virginia Beach-Norfolk-Newport News, VA-NC Metro Area	839,466	833,871	792,283	727,621	6.0	41,373	63,270	31,513	4.9	7.6	4.0	2.5
Visalia-Porterville, CA Metro Area	203,392	203,021	183,305	172,016	11.0	23,721	34,911	17,286	11.7	17.2	9.4	10.4
Waco, TX Metro Area	118,946	120,142	119,278	111,124	-0.3	4,897	8,923	6,079	4.1	7.4	5.1	4.2
Walla Walla, WA Metro Area	29,878	32,489	30,619	29,011	-2.4	1,742	2,630	1,887	5.8	8.1	6.2	6.5
Warner Robins, GA Metro Area	80,533	84,547	78,315	68,761	2.8	4,941	7,654	4,018	6.1	9.1	5.1	3.7
Washington-Arlington-Alexandria, DC-VA-MD-WV Metro Area	3,286,062	3,150,741	2,904,466	2,695,799	13.1	146,010	200,068	100,499	4.4	6.3	3.5	2.7
Silver Spring-Frederick-Rockville, MD Metro Division	678,582	660,456	624,759	597,240	8.6	27,644	38,668	19,512	4.1	5.9	3.1	2.7
Washington-Arlington-Alexandria, DC-VA-MD-WV Metro Division	2,607,480	2,490,285	2,279,707	2,098,559	14.4	118,366	161,400	80,987	4.5	6.5	3.6	2.7
Waterloo-Cedar Falls, IA Metro Area	91,256	91,608	92,114	87,697	-0.9	3,902	5,451	3,867	4.3	6.0	4.2	2.7
Watertown-Fort Drum, NY Metro Area	46,610	50,310	47,105	44,776	-1.1	3,144	4,672	2,886	6.7	9.3	6.1	5.9
Wausau, WI Metro Area	73,833	73,520	74,364	71,794	-0.7	3,000	6,829	3,057	4.1	9.3	4.1	3.4
Weirton-Steubenville, WV-OH Metro Area	52,809	58,426	57,537	59,255	-8.2	3,954	7,781	4,349	7.5	13.3	7.6	5.4
Wenatchee, WA Metro Area	62,791	61,977	59,416	54,731	5.7	3,588	5,678	3,578	5.7	9.2	6	7
Wheeling, WV-OH Metro Area	66,273	69,968	68,509	69,408	-3.3	4,346	6,932	4,045	6.6	9.9	5.9	5.6
Wichita, KS Metro Area	312,386	319,316	311,614	303,633	0.2	14,658	27,385	16,832	4.7	8.6	5.4	4
Wichita Falls, TX Metro Area	64,860	69,420	74,253	71,829	-12.6	2,811	5,320	3,376	4.3	7.7	4.5	4.4
Williamsport, PA Metro Area	60,975	59,483	59,297	59,454	2.8	3,574	5,313	3,215	5.9	8.9	5.4	4.3
Wilmington, NC Metro Area	139,010	132,004	119,805	107,457	16.0	7,629	13,239	5,077	5.5	10	4.2	3.7
Winchester, VA-WV Metro Area	68,991	65,434	61,426	55,186	12.3	2,942	5,174	1,904	4.3	7.9	3.1	2.3
Winston-Salem, NC Metro Area	317,805	314,873	309,332	303,728	2.7	17,332	34,446	15,501	5.5	10.9	5	3.3
Worcester, MA-CT Metro Area	488,301	484,955	459,459	442,260	6.3	26,423	43,901	24,179	5.4	9.1	5.3	2.7
Yakima, WA Metro Area	122,052	122,141	117,560	113,583	3.8	9,716	12,972	9,133	8	10.6	7.8	8.5
York-Hanover, PA Metro Area	232,848	230,390	218,916	209,665	6.4	10,718	19,344	9,232	4.6	8.4	4.2	3.3
Youngstown-Warren-Boardman, OH-PA Metro Area	251,809	268,560	281,253	284,602	-10.5	15,276	31,809	19,330	6.1	11.8	6.9	5.2
Yuba City, CA Metro Area	72,961	75,029	65,683	62,215	11.1	7,424	13,599	6,170	10.2	18.1	9.4	8.8
Yuma, AZ Metro Area	93,702	92,816	76,067	64,337	23.2	20,446	23,316	12,063	21.8	25.1	15.9	16.4

NA = Not available.

[1] Civilian unemployed as percent of total civilian labor force.

Table B-14.   Banking, Government Employment, and Private Business Establishments and Employment

Metropolitan statistical area and division	Banking 2016[1] Number of offices	Banking 2016[1] Deposits (million dollars)	Government Employment Federal Civilian 2015	Federal Civilian 2010	Military 2015	Military 2010	State and Local 2015	State and Local 2010	Private nonfarm business Establishments 2014	Establishments Change, 2010–2014	Employment[2] 2014	Employment Change, 2010–2014	Annual payroll per employee, 2014 (dollars)
Abilene, TX Metro Area	48	2,653	1,188	1,474	4,362	5,128	11,262	11,974	3,858	-1.1	57,611	3.2	34,636
Akron, OH Metro Area	210	14,433	2,122	2,517	1,793	1,821	43,698	46,487	16,419	-0.9	291,083	7.7	43,821
Albany, GA Metro Area	39	2,035	2,767	3,633	743	923	9,984	10,387	3,169	-4.9	46,393	3.8	35,100
Albany, OR Metro Area	26	994	313	346	309	331	6,048	6,612	2,441	-0.1	33,472	5.6	37,011
Albany-Schenectady-Troy, NY Metro Area	304	25,106	6,428	7,241	3,291	3,108	93,481	97,778	21,201	0.7	340,468	5.3	44,749
Albuquerque, NM Metro Area	165	14,606	14,324	15,893	5,640	5,970	66,893	66,950	18,571	-0.6	279,897	0.0	38,285
Alexandria, LA Metro Area	63	2,439	3,028	2,981	659	746	10,491	12,047	3,320	-3.7	49,751	1.8	36,990
Allentown-Bethlehem-Easton, PA-NJ Metro Area..	262	16,454	2,224	2,676	2,082	2,132	37,594	40,410	18,280	-0.1	308,398	8.5	46,208
Altoona, PA Metro Area	56	2,427	999	1,083	321	334	7,569	8,249	3,174	-1.3	50,319	-0.3	34,164
Amarillo, TX Metro Area	73	6,148	2,177	2,330	648	601	18,104	18,075	6,279	4.1	94,941	7.1	37,165
Ames, IA Metro Area	38	2,253	958	1,328	344	382	19,019	18,242	2,003	-1.4	31,660	12.6	38,315
Anchorage, AK Metro Area	44	7,001	8,690	10,078	13,644	14,807	24,835	24,620	10,799	3.6	164,797	2.9	60,378
Ann Arbor, MI Metro Area	98	8,211	4,073	3,738	606	687	69,709	69,424	8,049	1.8	142,761	7.7	51,755
Anniston-Oxford-Jacksonville, AL Metro Area	34	1,713	3,745	5,518	569	636	8,416	8,028	2,309	-4.9	35,096	-5.0	32,401
Appleton, WI Metro Area	69	3,734	663	730	645	637	12,109	12,192	5,795	-0.4	110,641	8.6	42,867
Asheville, NC Metro Area	125	7,342	3,306	3,973	1,107	1,074	22,007	23,955	11,745	2.1	156,217	10.1	36,307
Athens-Clarke County, GA Metro Area	55	3,915	1,128	1,708	612	827	26,183	26,156	4,475	1.9	58,608	9.1	35,041
Atlanta-Sandy Springs-Roswell, GA Metro Area ...	1,284	156,210	45,314	49,811	16,634	19,701	274,746	278,721	134,212	3.5	2,178,578	8.5	52,454
Atlantic City-Hammonton, NJ Metro Area	79	5,798	2,631	2,964	975	892	20,217	21,090	6,365	-1.8	110,726	-2.5	35,949
Auburn-Opelika, AL Metro Area	43	2,482	288	310	726	726	16,744	15,426	2,576	9.5	39,528	13.2	30,971
Augusta-Richmond County, GA-SC Metro Area	127	7,995	9,022	9,038	13,075	12,811	39,491	39,744	10,318	-1.6	179,942	5.1	40,704
Austin-Round Rock, TX Metro Area	467	40,381	12,019	12,627	4,234	4,205	154,415	159,079	46,884	13.8	745,697	16.4	51,744
Bakersfield, CA Metro Area	89	8,109	9,995	10,947	3,854	3,817	51,324	47,583	12,480	4.7	192,765	10.2	44,382
Baltimore-Columbia-Towson, MD Metro Area	728	70,170	79,890	77,142	26,775	24,524	167,892	173,666	66,213	1.6	1,123,100	6.0	51,574
Bangor, ME Metro Area	51	2,541	1,181	1,416	485	489	12,865	13,321	4,138	-1.3	57,535	-0.1	35,192
Barnstable Town, MA Metro Area	111	7,521	1,685	1,918	1,182	1,274	13,356	12,522	8,390	2.1	72,254	5.0	43,378
Baton Rouge, LA Metro Area	233	19,675	2,832	3,383	3,749	4,236	67,688	73,956	17,862	0.6	338,772	9.5	48,572
Battle Creek, MI Metro Area	28	1,065	2,970	3,025	273	288	7,828	7,773	2,617	-2.4	51,908	9.8	47,575
Bay City, MI Metro Area	29	1,050	246	290	231	233	5,568	5,931	2,234	-2.5	30,512	4.0	37,420
Beaumont-Port Arthur, TX Metro Area	85	5,253	2,039	2,385	1,012	1,112	22,318	24,705	7,908	-1.9	129,190	1.2	49,603
Beckley, WV Metro Area	42	1,629	2,010	2,227	573	822	6,793	6,734	2,608	-4.2	38,372	1.6	38,841
Bellingham, WA Metro Area	63	3,527	1,389	1,452	630	683	14,117	14,029	6,279	0.6	71,947	6.7	40,068
Bend-Redmond, OR Metro Area	50	3,235	884	1,021	451	448	7,789	7,346	6,260	7.8	56,454	9.6	37,978
Billings, MT Metro Area	49	4,720	1,817	1,997	800	802	7,725	7,732	5,965	0.9	71,014	2.5	41,576
Binghamton, NY Metro Area	58	3,075	672	874	387	417	20,924	23,575	5,075	-0.8	82,583	-2.0	39,669
Birmingham-Hoover, AL Metro Area	336	37,516	9,042	9,728	5,350	5,607	69,611	71,610	25,260	-1.7	445,333	2.6	46,829
Bismarck, ND Metro Area	59	3,723	1,415	1,525	793	842	13,704	12,794	3,912	12.0	58,623	13.6	46,428
Blacksburg-Christiansburg-Radford, VA Metro Area	63	2,981	455	609	594	610	21,381	20,017	3,475	-2.9	49,430	6.8	36,092
Bloomington, IL Metro Area	62	14,145	510	777	368	370	15,786	16,174	4,035		81,138	0.6	50,571
Bloomington, IN Metro Area	40	2,484	337	442	506	515	22,606	22,965	3,173	-3.6	51,752	1.8	36,746
Bloomsburg-Berwick, PA Metro Area	32	1,263	181	230	212	217	6,621	6,663	1,842	-0.5	37,443	9.6	46,596
Boise City, ID Metro Area	178	9,784	6,118	6,237	2,343	2,395	38,714	36,918	16,914	2.8	234,236	11.7	42,383
Boston-Cambridge-Newton, MA-NH Metro Area	1,527	311,452	35,594	40,092	14,504	14,994	268,310	260,538	125,686	2.9	2,363,791	6.2	64,950
Boston, MA Metro Division	-	-	19,133	20,364	5,968	6,193	127,802	125,591	52,152	3.6	1,068,953	5.9	179,383
Cambridge-Newton-Framingham, MA Metro Division	-	-	15,146	18,056	6,877	7,184	115,769	109,539	61,463	2.6	1,129,471	7.1	66,078
Rockingham County-Strafford County, NH Metro Division	-	-	1,315	1,672	1,659	1,617	24,739	25,408	12,071	0.9	165,367	2.9	46,880
Boulder, CO Metro Area	112	9,269	1,995	2,325	890	900	31,577	28,565	11,932	4.3	145,558	9.2	61,265
Bowling Green, KY Metro Area	69	2,723	647	863	514	512	11,555	11,641	3,502	7.6	55,872	8.3	36,500
Bremerton-Silverdale, WA Metro Area	59	3,006	18,676	16,071	11,130	10,856	12,862	13,264	5,607	-0.9	55,893	-0.6	36,477
Bridgeport-Stamford-Norwalk, CT Metro Area	368	47,808	2,764	3,469	1,899	1,799	45,274	43,931	27,022	0.0	408,854	3.8	77,935
Brownsville-Harlingen, TX Metro Area	77	4,430	3,282	3,050	950	1,051	27,544	27,856	6,312	-0.2	100,798	2.0	26,393
Brunswick, GA Metro Area	38	1,865	1,795	1,976	386	426	8,385	8,305	2,807	-1.9	33,005	2.4	33,113
Buffalo-Cheektowaga-Niagara Falls, NY Metro Area	278	42,106	9,171	10,548	2,053	2,102	78,476	82,898	27,077	0.7	474,220	4.1	41,553
Burlington, NC Metro Area	43	1,983	224	266	369	369	6,866	6,940	3,138	-2.1	51,102	5.9	35,395
Burlington-South Burlington, VT Metro Area	70	4,900	3,840	3,508	1,558	1,461	18,411	16,585	6,739	0.3	99,680	1.8	43,109
California-Lexington Park, MD Metro Area	21	1,310	9,518	8,382	2,521	2,685	4,681	4,702	1,925	0.8	28,959	-0.1	49,587
Canton-Massillon, OH Metro Area	133	6,696	983	1,300	1,041	1,025	18,821	19,443	8,684	-2.5	143,440	4.2	37,039
Cape Coral-Fort Myers, FL Metro Area	214	15,231	2,563	2,844	1,333	1,317	37,394	33,824	16,857	8.3	193,523	15.8	36,496
Cape Girardeau, MO-IL Metro Area	47	1,966	420	534	338	321	6,811	6,952	2,697	-13.7	40,531	-0.6	34,890
Carbondale-Marion, IL Metro Area	66	2,057	1,873	1,958	258	261	16,153	17,257	2,923	-1.7	39,025	-0.7	34,401
Carson City, NV Metro Area	16	1,249	528	593	147	132	8,931	9,071	1,930	-9.9	20,718	-1.8	42,823
Casper, WY Metro Area	19	2,518	638	767	426	436	5,210	5,068	2,982	2.4	36,040	10.4	49,012
Cedar Rapids, IA Metro Area	105	5,517	1,139	1,296	982	1,094	15,433	15,827	6,445	-0.1	125,754	3.5	45,554
Chambersburg-Waynesboro, PA Metro Area	52	2,115	2,205	2,557	401	402	5,892	6,529	3,017	-0.4	48,464	4.7	36,461
Champaign-Urbana, IL Metro Area	102	5,409	1,367	1,486	482	484	37,362	37,483	4,844	-1.4	75,108	0.0	37,883
Charleston, WV Metro Area	70	5,099	2,171	2,202	1,067	1,275	22,026	22,238	5,451	-7.7	93,147	-5.4	41,727
Charleston-North Charleston, SC Metro Area	196	12,356	10,475	9,654	12,997	12,914	51,732	49,083	17,270	5.3	256,192	12.1	41,597
Charlotte-Concord-Gastonia, NC-SC Metro Area...	543	200,932	10,158	10,408	6,416	6,210	138,778	133,353	56,408	4.1	954,262	11.8	50,169
Charlottesville, VA Metro Area	70	4,502	1,409	1,524	1,168	1,030	33,657	31,469	6,005	2.0	80,519	5.4	46,304
Chattanooga, TN-GA Metro Area	150	9,377	5,605	6,284	1,663	1,768	30,440	30,039	11,112	-0.2	213,139	9.7	38,087
Cheyenne, WY Metro Area	30	1,790	2,643	2,683	3,465	3,575	11,395	11,270	3,056	13.1	34,481	12.1	40,859
Chicago-Naperville-Elgin, IL-IN-WI Metro Area	2,863	391,331	54,109	61,516	31,815	36,816	512,060	516,880	241,284	1.9	4,079,228	7.4	55,126

NA = Not available.

[1] As of June 30. Covers all FDIC-insured commercial banks and savings institutions. and does not include U.S. branches of foreign banks.

[2] For pay period as of March 12 of the year shown.

Table B-14. Banking, Government Employment, and Private Business Establishments and Employment—Continued

Metropolitan statistical area and division	Banking 2016[1] Number of offices	Banking 2016[1] Deposits (million dollars)	Federal Civilian 2015	Federal Civilian 2010	Military 2015	Military 2010	State and Local 2015	State and Local 2010	Establishments 2014	Establishments Change, 2010–2014	Employment[2] 2014	Employment[2] Change, 2010–2014	Annual payroll per employee, 2014 (dollars)
Chicago-Naperville-Arlington Heights, IL Metro Division	-	-	44,687	50,723	15,206	15,198	389,747	391,495	190,016	2.3	3,258,595	7.7	55,732
Elgin, IL Metro Division	-	-	1,829	2,114	1,265	1,266	42,650	42,069	14,266	0.7	209,420	7.0	41,293
Gary, IN Metro Division	-	-	1,921	2,267	2,141	2,373	33,178	35,719	14,319	-1.1	231,148	3.0	42,370
Lake County-Kenosha County, IL-WI Metro Division	-	-	5,672	6,412	13,203	17,979	46,485	47,597	22,683	1.2	380,065	7.5	65,307
Chico, CA Metro Area	44	3,717	543	664	335	356	15,445	14,285	4,637	-1.6	57,562	6.8	35,059
Cincinnati, OH-KY-IN Metro Area	754	106,807	15,459	17,831	5,874	5,862	111,366	114,469	45,633	-0.4	896,336	2.9	48,203
Clarksville, TN-KY Metro Area	79	3,461	5,721	6,132	30,013	33,007	13,534	12,819	4,276	3.2	66,687	2.3	32,249
Cleveland, TN Metro Area	34	1,689	279	324	364	384	5,486	5,428	2,104	0.0	40,238	10.4	36,445
Cleveland-Elyria, OH Metro Area	679	64,617	18,098	20,079	5,681	5,887	113,862	119,548	51,260	-1.7	914,102	5.1	47,462
Coeur d'Alene, ID Metro Area	45	2,764	596	635	507	534	10,065	9,297	4,366	-1.4	46,988	8.2	35,334
College Station-Bryan, TX Metro Area	70	5,340	820	1,194	554	593	38,055	34,458	4,698	8.1	67,251	13.9	34,795
Colorado Springs, CO Metro Area	146	7,708	12,680	12,909	38,522	39,199	37,876	36,226	16,965	2.5	229,344	5.2	43,139
Columbia, MO Metro Area	77	3,937	2,515	2,251	596	593	28,535	28,389	4,517	4.2	73,688	10.1	36,482
Columbia, SC Metro Area	192	18,311	10,240	10,863	12,378	13,603	72,788	68,967	16,848	-1.5	279,659	3.3	39,734
Columbus, GA-AL Metro Area	64	6,597	6,893	6,450	22,047	22,149	17,651	17,765	5,621	-1.7	97,888	3.9	35,995
Columbus, IN Metro Area	27	1,167	168	254	247	258	6,143	6,199	1,796	-3.2	44,983	16.3	46,552
Columbus, OH Metro Area	564	63,652	14,018	15,660	5,609	5,483	153,956	151,220	40,850	1.6	826,924	8.9	47,360
Corpus Christi, TX Metro Area	107	6,114	6,115	6,858	4,600	4,636	26,725	27,870	9,463	2.2	159,813	12.6	41,538
Corvallis, OR Metro Area	15	1,143	502	592	250	287	10,731	9,885	2,103	2.1	24,947	1.7	41,071
Crestview-Fort Walton Beach-Destin, FL Metro Area	101	4,854	8,553	7,835	16,003	14,923	10,999	10,937	7,071	5.9	75,717	4.9	34,933
Cumberland, MD-WV Metro Area	27	958	605	659	333	344	7,233	7,971	2,030	-5.1	30,983	2.8	33,876
Dallas-Fort Worth-Arlington, TX Metro Area	**1,711**	**247,237**	**44,374**	**48,516**	**16,579**	**17,128**	**363,823**	**347,798**	**152,400**	**7.5**	**2,869,738**	**13.7**	**53,071**
Dallas-Plano-Irving, TX Metro Division	-	-	29,296	32,669	10,300	11,158	248,771	237,151	104,914	7.6	2,011,934	13.8	55,762
Fort Worth-Arlington, TX Metro Division	-	-	15,078	15,847	6,279	5,970	115,052	110,647	47,486	7.1	857,804	13.4	46,758
Dalton, GA Metro Area	33	2,444	232	356	399	456	6,737	6,877	2,541	-5.7	54,075	-3.6	38,113
Danville, IL Metro Area	30	1,082	1,510	1,516	155	164	4,261	4,433	1,451	-5.7	24,259	-0.1	38,805
Daphne-Fairhope-Foley, AL Metro Area	89	3,956	334	370	898	883	8,876	8,259	4,969	6.5	56,531	10.5	30,943
Davenport-Moline-Rock Island, IA-IL Metro Area	146	7,985	5,707	7,814	1,508	1,440	20,271	20,667	8,960	-2.4	159,530	3.4	43,192
Dayton, OH Metro Area	212	10,992	18,443	18,603	7,158	7,071	42,561	45,286	16,598	-0.9	310,429	3.7	42,421
Decatur, AL Metro Area	42	2,036	393	441	670	740	7,834	8,325	2,963	-4.7	46,068	0.2	40,103
Decatur, IL Metro Area	40	1,917	318	370	219	230	5,457	6,004	2,434	-3.0	46,164	-0.4	41,208
Deltona-Daytona Beach-Ormond Beach, FL Metro Area	160	10,428	1,331	1,710	1,187	1,231	21,548	24,011	14,071	4.1	153,420	7.8	33,286
Denver-Aurora-Lakewood, CO Metro Area	657	75,865	28,418	29,252	10,005	9,769	171,507	156,472	78,126	6.1	1,174,056	13.1	55,128
Des Moines-West Des Moines, IA Metro Area	219	16,699	6,206	6,245	2,445	2,565	37,201	36,482	15,320	3.0	297,427	7.4	47,757
Detroit-Warren-Dearborn, MI Metro Area	**1,049**	**121,738**	**27,749**	**30,134**	**7,985**	**9,115**	**161,902**	**183,803**	**97,940**	**0.7**	**1,658,435**	**10.5**	**51,618**
Detroit-Dearborn-Livonia, MI Metro Division	-	-	14,043	15,948	3,275	3,922	73,079	87,651	31,877	-2.1	605,093	6.6	51,004
Warren-Troy-Farmington Hills, MI Metro Division	-	-	13,706	14,186	4,710	5,193	88,823	96,152	66,063	2.2	1,053,342	12.9	51,971
Dothan, AL Metro Area	56	3,207	399	508	685	703	10,294	10,336	3,394	-2.6	48,817	-1.7	35,668
Dover, DE Metro Area	36	1,867	1,742	1,971	4,164	4,422	17,468	17,010	3,263	2.0	49,311	6.3	38,583
Dubuque, IA Metro Area	38	2,770	259	274	368	407	4,482	4,364	2,779	1.5	53,990	6.7	39,439
Duluth, MN-WI Metro Area	93	4,219	1,665	2,062	1,051	1,123	23,296	23,613	7,001	-4.0	108,003	2.4	39,658
Durham-Chapel Hill, NC Metro Area	119	12,231	6,520	5,937	1,461	1,496	58,201	54,950	12,116	3.7	233,692	7.9	56,330
East Stroudsburg, PA Metro Area	53	2,623	3,243	4,702	455	458	8,254	9,342	3,350	-1.7	45,985	2.7	37,576
Eau Claire, WI Metro Area	59	2,858	527	648	425	442	11,686	11,466	4,248	2.0	71,423	5.6	36,460
El Centro, CA Metro Area	15	1,704	2,228	2,546	374	527	15,783	15,378	2,465	4.1	32,849	12.4	30,535
Elizabethtown-Fort Knox, KY Metro Area	56	2,125	5,996	6,405	5,447	12,012	8,751	8,248	2,904	3.5	40,169	6.7	34,145
Elkhart-Goshen, IN Metro Area	59	2,896	260	307	617	659	8,464	8,269	4,825	-1.3	117,990	25.1	41,671
Elmira, NY Metro Area	21	1,023	214	321	132	139	5,912	6,843	1,810	-2.5	31,795	-2.6	39,287
El Paso, TX Metro Area	96	10,347	12,920	12,910	28,521	23,721	54,930	54,945	13,907	3.9	223,804	8.0	31,170
Enid, OK Metro Area			481	556	1,395	1,536	3,379	3,783	1,700	3.3	22,785	2.4	38,262
Erie, PA Metro Area	79	4,797	1,517	1,694	738	771	15,584	16,396	6,176	-1.8	112,761	1.0	37,759
Eugene, OR Metro Area	88	5,007	1,617	1,917	1,013	1,044	23,484	24,224	9,558	-0.4	120,985	8.3	37,163
Evansville, IN-KY Metro Area	99	5,568	1,285	1,349	953	1,032	15,505	15,094	7,539	-0.8	140,148	-1.9	41,115
Fairbanks, AK Metro Area	20	1,388	2,945	3,502	9,019	8,621	7,921	8,059	2,471	1.1	27,435	1.0	50,978
Fargo, ND-MN Metro Area	94	7,156	2,435	2,455	1,278	1,328	16,041	15,290	6,559	4.2	117,483	8.4	41,941
Farmington, NM Metro Area	27	1,397	1,491	1,704	308	353	9,836	9,491	2,793	-1.1	39,206	3.4	47,002
Fayetteville, NC Metro Area	69	3,166	14,786	13,354	48,640	54,701	25,000	25,501	6,106	-0.1	97,552		32,869
Fayetteville-Springdale-Rogers, AR-MO Metro Area	209	9,610	2,576	2,665	2,148	2,051	28,597	25,577	11,125	4.5	193,752	9.9	48,165
Flagstaff, AZ Metro Area	20	1,679	2,706	3,220	301	292	16,135	14,158	3,522	-1.5	47,538	9.5	37,071
Flint, MI Metro Area	80	4,069	1,059	1,466	657	802	19,420	22,993	7,716	-2.4	115,459	4.6	38,750
Florence, SC Metro Area	56	2,838	693	985	830	898	15,692	15,530	4,142	-3.9	73,195	4.2	37,940
Florence-Muscle Shoals, AL Metro Area	52	2,501	965	1,415	647	710	8,869	9,901	3,197	-2.4	46,611	5.5	32,503
Fond du Lac, WI Metro Area	36	2,061	198	249	266	282	5,405	5,763	2,339	-4.1	42,213	9.0	37,447
Fort Collins, CO Metro Area	101	7,347	2,463	2,543	879	830	32,873	25,308	10,031	7.0	116,753	14.5	44,612
Fort Smith, AR-OK Metro Area	113	4,542	1,326	1,621	1,188	1,247	16,684	17,048	5,829	-2.8	96,280	-3.8	35,992
Fort Wayne, IN Metro Area	129	7,814	2,041	2,202	1,337	1,403	19,757	20,052	10,382	-0.7	187,136	6.3	39,657
Fresno, CA Metro Area	137	13,218	9,673	10,754	1,680	1,802	58,293	56,290	16,119	2.1	244,494	8.6	39,371
Gadsden, AL Metro Area	25	1,139	290	437	449	500	5,080	5,137	1,995	-1.8	28,573	-3.1	32,723
Gainesville, FL Metro Area	70	4,089	4,618	4,729	573	577	39,209	38,852	6,155	2.7	86,989	4.9	38,263
Gainesville, GA Metro Area	50	3,240	467	594	535	573	10,076	9,931	4,040	2.3	66,547	15.1	42,564

NA = Not available.
[1] As of June 30. Covers all FDIC-insured commercial banks and savings institutions. and does not include U.S. branches of foreign banks.
[2] For pay period as of March 12 of the year shown.

Table B-14. Banking, Government Employment, and Private Business Establishments and Employment—*Continued*

Metropolitan statistical area and division	Banking 2016[1] Number of offices	Banking 2016[1] Deposits (million dollars)	Federal Civilian 2015	Federal Civilian 2010	Military 2015	Military 2010	State and Local 2015	State and Local 2010	Establishments 2014	Establishments Change, 2010–2014	Employment[2] 2014	Employment[2] Change, 2010–2014	Annual payroll per employee, 2014 (dollars)
Gettysburg, PA Metro Area	26	1,379	714	760	258	263	3,299	3,719	1,930	0.9	28,076	2.1	35,648
Glens Falls, NY Metro Area	52	2,419	319	431	196	208	9,487	10,057	3,355	-2.8	41,649	2.5	38,352
Goldsboro, NC Metro Area	29	1,454	1,225	1,309	4,290	4,885	8,001	8,486	2,145	-3.4	33,742	-0.2	33,048
Grand Forks, ND-MN Metro Area	44	2,679	1,128	1,363	2,024	2,144	11,916	11,822	2,697	3.3	42,548	4.3	35,834
Grand Island, NE Metro Area	58	2,449	721	854	298	336	6,052	6,140	2,518	0.7	35,599	1.8	35,457
Grand Junction, CO Metro Area	41	2,502	1,470	1,606	396	395	8,337	8,112	4,427	-4.7	50,695	2.4	42,259
Grand Rapids-Wyoming, MI Metro Area	304	20,540	3,282	3,861	1,763	1,932	44,350	44,003	23,512	2.4	457,413	14.8	41,841
Grants Pass, OR Metro Area	24	1,337	273	324	215	232	2,768	3,016	1,906	5.4	20,344	6.0	32,096
Great Falls, MT Metro Area	23	1,392	1,639	1,858	3,466	3,583	4,070	4,212	2,420	-1.4	29,900	-1.3	32,847
Greeley, CO Metro Area	72	3,506	596	858	736	688	16,010	14,992	5,637	9.2	77,367	19.7	47,142
Green Bay, WI Metro Area	115	7,000	1,328	1,320	858	892	20,339	20,394	7,581	-0.5	153,096	6.6	43,137
Greensboro-High Point, NC Metro Area	195	11,757	4,301	4,596	1,817	1,822	39,312	40,654	17,400	-0.9	316,549	6.8	41,010
Greenville, NC Metro Area	45	2,006	685	578	448	419	25,720	23,320	3,533		57,990	2.9	35,563
Greenville-Anderson-Mauldin, SC Metro Area	257	15,359	2,619	2,781	3,466	3,641	54,971	51,050	18,851	0.7	318,675	7.2	38,967
Gulfport-Biloxi-Pascagoula, MS Metro Area	123	5,238	8,722	9,008	9,578	12,640	23,905	24,229	7,039	-2.2	123,516	-3.2	39,845
Hagerstown-Martinsburg, MD-WV Metro Area	80	3,430	4,071	4,565	1,033	1,024	13,152	13,367	5,012	-1.3	83,845	10.5	36,270
Hammond, LA Metro Area	40	1,774	359	455	553	587	10,122	11,273	2,307	2.8	34,530	8.3	35,458
Hanford-Corcoran, CA Metro Area	13	1,157	1,131	1,183	5,146	5,671	13,478	11,618	1,589	-1.5	23,624	4.7	35,626
Harrisburg-Carlisle, PA Metro Area	198	13,574	7,243	7,964	2,296	2,127	53,465	56,719	13,300	-0.8	263,396	1.5	45,504
Harrisonburg, VA Metro Area	51	2,154	349	395	393	398	10,814	9,937	2,968	-0.7	50,872	0.6	35,606
Hartford-West Hartford-East Hartford, CT Metro Area	377	42,874	6,177	6,791	2,449	2,346	93,778	91,850	29,110	-1.5	536,262	1.3	55,932
Hattiesburg, MS Metro Area	63	2,727	803	902	1,281	1,141	13,887	14,105	3,291	-0.8	49,475	1.3	35,236
Hickory-Lenoir-Morganton, NC Metro Area	87	4,294	660	1,011	854	896	22,429	23,685	7,325	-4.1	124,874	3.6	36,015
Hilton Head Island-Bluffton-Beaufort, SC Metro Area	66	4,083	2,265	2,578	10,544	10,103	9,035	8,795	5,516	4.6	58,645	10.9	33,538
Hinesville, GA Metro Area	10	435	3,901	4,316	16,290	18,263	3,860	3,714	886	0.0	12,444	5.5	37,583
Homosassa Springs, FL Metro Area	41	2,154	217	274	256	284	4,096	4,740	2,632	-1.3	26,262	5.0	33,183
Hot Springs, AR Metro Area	52	1,807	496	583	407	424	4,061	4,420	2,648	-2.0	32,870	7.6	30,879
Houma-Thibodaux, LA Metro Area	83	4,538	394	588	988	1,080	11,966	13,533	4,825	-0.2	83,844	9.9	50,966
Houston-The Woodlands-Sugar Land, TX Metro Area	1,482	218,807	27,943	30,568	14,868	15,244	350,371	340,463	132,729	8.5	2,507,620	15.3	61,983
Huntington-Ashland, WV-KY-OH Metro Area	128	5,528	3,241	3,584	1,528	1,587	19,585	20,368	7,097	-2.2	112,452	1.6	39,436
Huntsville, AL Metro Area	121	7,491	19,448	19,489	2,729	3,532	29,366	28,960	9,451	1.0	170,407	3.0	46,959
Idaho Falls, ID Metro Area	36	1,748	892	1,007	491	530	6,797	6,530	3,830	3.0	49,134	5.0	38,556
Indianapolis-Carmel-Anderson, IN Metro Area	553	45,100	16,584	17,493	6,607	6,819	114,252	114,758	45,350	1.5	854,861	10.0	46,172
Iowa City, IA Metro Area	59	3,817	2,052	1,819	638	647	35,443	32,560	3,922	4.7	67,175	4.5	38,955
Ithaca, NY Metro Area	26	1,930	258	314	165	167	5,854	6,460	2,361	1.8	47,972	5.5	36,842
Jackson, MI Metro Area	43	1,674	340	394	244	288	7,316	8,478	2,905	-3.7	48,179	7.8	43,784
Jackson, MS Metro Area	230	13,006	6,589	6,752	3,418	3,473	53,887	54,476	13,095	-1.2	214,422	5.8	40,173
Jackson, TN Metro Area	57	2,162	499	606	384	426	13,437	13,370	3,006	-0.9	56,058	4.4	35,752
Jacksonville, FL Metro Area	317	58,530	17,300	18,071	14,563	18,634	58,824	59,347	35,227	3.4	528,075	9.5	45,129
Jacksonville, NC Metro Area	26	1,076	6,779	6,688	43,028	51,451	7,945	8,025	2,757	2.4	34,547	3.9	27,394
Janesville-Beloit, WI Metro Area	41	2,273	291	339	425	451	8,628	8,995	3,236	-1.7	54,808	7.1	40,706
Jefferson City, MO Metro Area	61	4,496	829	904	501	536	24,750	26,730	3,619	0.6	50,402	0.7	37,138
Johnson City, TN Metro Area	67	2,812	2,832	2,668	637	674	13,152	13,882	3,758	-2.0	63,725	2.2	35,332
Johnstown, PA Metro Area	74	2,922	1,036	1,374	365	473	6,888	8,030	3,286	-4.4	47,647	-5.7	34,546
Jonesboro, AR Metro Area	57	2,644	381	526	537	532	9,019	8,722	2,797	1.1	43,048	8.8	34,336
Joplin, MO Metro Area	81	2,655	434	505	628	627	9,053	9,356	3,980	-6.2	68,025	-6.9	36,352
Kahului-Wailuku-Lahaina, HI Metro Area	38	3,152	813	978	1,155	1,161	9,082	8,854	4,500	3.9	63,431	10.6	36,253
Kalamazoo-Portage, MI Metro Area	86	3,714	840	1,217	536	613	18,692	20,148	6,783	-2.5	119,742	0.8	44,193
Kankakee, IL Metro Area	38	1,886	237	281	214	226	6,062	6,098	2,360	0.1	36,792	4.4	36,103
Kansas City, MO-KS Metro Area	714	52,717	27,188	28,991	11,408	11,674	123,194	126,525	51,485	3.9	908,323	6.7	48,213
Kennewick-Richland, WA Metro Area	51	2,890	1,228	1,446	763	802	17,795	16,680	5,533	5.4	79,211	5.8	46,545
Killeen-Temple, TX Metro Area	89	4,519	10,420	11,448	40,210	48,486	26,870	25,940	6,022	1.8	101,153	6.7	36,130
Kingsport-Bristol-Bristol, TN-VA Metro Area	111	4,264	883	1,205	937	1,033	15,571	15,679	5,988	-1.7	104,930	2.0	40,241
Kingston, NY Metro Area	58	3,044	465	511	286	302	12,926	14,197	4,727	0.4	45,384	0.7	33,688
Knoxville, TN Metro Area	278	16,262	5,374	6,086	2,700	2,872	52,736	53,125	17,489	-1.6	319,576	4.3	41,536
Kokomo, IN Metro Area	28	1,083	197	276	252	278	4,975	6,468	1,742	-3.9	31,758	11.8	42,203
La Crosse-Onalaska, WI-MN Metro Area	48	2,675	527	576	372	391	11,050	10,640	3,440	1.8	65,254	6.8	37,218
Lafayette, LA Metro Area	191	10,883	1,367	1,632	2,176	2,313	24,123	26,452	13,350	5.4	198,883	11.3	46,758
Lafayette-West Lafayette, IN Metro Area	71	2,991	540	740	669	691	24,989	23,834	3,975	0.5	69,505	7.9	39,111
Lake Charles, LA Metro Area	81	3,735	543	739	976	1,082	13,260	15,047	4,532	3.3	73,507	7.1	42,795
Lake Havasu City-Kingman, AZ Metro Area	41	2,671	463	677	448	440	7,167	7,540	3,630	-2.2	40,695	2.5	32,841
Lakeland-Winter Haven, FL Metro Area	122	6,039	1,065	1,595	1,238	1,213	26,233	28,273	11,021	0.7	171,305	7.6	38,285
Lancaster, PA Metro Area	187	10,554	1,216	1,529	1,379	1,374	19,280	20,231	12,414	3.1	220,898	6.6	40,430
Lansing-East Lansing, MI Metro Area	117	6,069	1,921	2,380	928	1,256	47,454	49,076	9,486	-0.7	160,216	5.8	41,704
Laredo, TX Metro Area	56	6,134	3,233	3,418	542	575	18,957	18,682	5,123	8.8	73,755	16.1	29,105
Las Cruces, NM Metro Area	47	1,984	3,507	4,274	559	590	16,910	17,480	3,546	-1.8	50,861	1.5	31,337
Las Vegas-Henderson-Paradise, NV Metro Area	347	53,339	12,686	12,390	15,101	14,203	84,204	83,755	42,031	6.1	797,871	9.0	38,977
Lawrence, KS Metro Area	52	2,162	428	526	469	481	15,406	14,615	2,675	1.8	38,850	3.9	30,424
Lawton, OK Metro Area	42	1,623	4,081	4,752	11,432	14,238	10,812	10,893	2,237	-2.7	33,026	-2.9	33,332
Lebanon, PA Metro Area	42	2,133	3,023	2,621	352	392	4,943	5,514	2,641	0.0	44,254	1.9	35,898
Lewiston, ID-WA Metro Area	21	811	250	280	195	217	5,031	5,018	1,546	-1.8	21,337	2.1	36,269

NA = Not available.
[1]As of June 30. Covers all FDIC-insured commercial banks and savings institutions, and does not include U.S. branches of foreign banks.
[2]For pay period as of March 12 of the year shown.

Table B-14. Banking, Government Employment, and Private Business Establishments and Employment—*Continued*

Metropolitan statistical area and division	Banking 2016[1] Number of offices	Banking 2016[1] Deposits (million dollars)	Federal Civilian 2015	Federal Civilian 2010	Military 2015	Military 2010	State and Local 2015	State and Local 2010	Establishments 2014	Establishments Change, 2010–2014	Employment[2] 2014	Employment Change, 2010–2014	Annual payroll per employee, 2014 (dollars)
Lewiston-Auburn, ME Metro Area	24	1,663	259	326	341	344	5,104	5,162	2,667	-3.6	44,283	1.1	37,968
Lexington-Fayette, KY Metro Area	183	9,396	4,451	4,783	1,569	1,555	46,068	45,323	12,195	3.3	216,411	8.2	40,954
Lima, OH Metro Area	33	1,808	322	406	258	264	5,794	6,289	2,436	-4.4	44,435	-4.5	39,321
Lincoln, NE Metro Area	135	7,987	3,274	3,051	1,132	1,228	31,262	31,092	8,556	4.1	134,985	3.6	38,803
Little Rock-North Little Rock-Conway, AR Metro Area	304	18,885	9,664	9,854	7,441	8,350	60,709	62,214	17,632	0.2	274,359	-0.5	41,414
Logan, UT-ID Metro Area	27	1,543	372	419	543	546	11,218	10,953	3,380	0.8	41,306	5.8	31,484
Longview, TX Metro Area	86	4,683	476	681	424	474	11,237	11,693	5,408	2.2	84,869	8.6	42,496
Longview, WA Metro Area	11	608	226	259	279	317	5,696	5,497	2,119	-3.9	30,038	3.2	45,831
Los Angeles-Long Beach-Anaheim, CA Metro Area	2,456	494,626	59,140	65,195	22,586	23,985	668,221	667,209	349,938	5.7	5,354,029	10.3	52,338
Anaheim-Santa Ana-Irvine, CA Metro Division	-	-	11,271	12,617	5,151	5,628	140,943	137,570	90,956	5.1	1,421,125	11.7	54,141
Los Angeles-Long Beach-Glendale, CA Metro Division	-	-	47,869	52,578	17,435	18,357	527,278	529,639	258,982	5.9	3,932,904	9.9	51,686
Louisville/Jefferson County, KY-IN Metro Area	416	25,223	8,718	11,662	4,145	4,295	67,728	67,338	28,932	-0.3	540,954	7.0	43,131
Lubbock, TX Metro Area	113	8,096	1,335	1,499	648	682	28,584	26,539	7,196	2.0	112,158	7.0	34,290
Lynchburg, VA Metro Area	92	4,747	564	833	817	827	13,240	13,795	5,871	-2.2	95,088	1.2	38,967
Macon, GA Metro Area	56	3,307	1,131	1,499	622	829	13,374	13,881	5,122	-3.1	83,900	4.6	36,227
Madera, CA Metro Area	17	1,076	309	359	223	234	9,137	10,578	1,918	0.4	25,722	5.0	38,910
Madison, WI Metro Area	239	17,668	5,422	5,468	1,777	1,761	81,392	77,257	16,492	2.6	308,317	8.7	47,474
Manchester-Nashua, NH Metro Area	101	11,258	4,018	3,947	1,372	1,410	17,505	18,524	10,889	0.6	180,527	1.7	53,691
Manhattan, KS Metro Area	45	2,517	479	570	393	371	12,705	12,252	2,176	2.9	28,976	0.6	31,129
Mankato-North Mankato, MN Metro Area	42	2,138	284	395	356	355	8,096	7,996	2,573	1.0	47,621	5.1	35,730
Mansfield, OH Metro Area	48	1,815	626	721	295	304	7,108	7,543	2,613	-4.5	43,022	1.2	33,678
McAllen-Edinburg-Mission, TX Metro Area	147	9,261	4,062	3,716	1,739	1,798	52,619	50,420	11,780	6.7	181,601	8.7	27,389
Medford, OR Metro Area	65	3,152	1,834	1,782	542	573	8,837	8,970	5,951	2.9	67,428	5.4	36,285
Memphis, TN-MS-AR Metro Area	376	28,039	14,037	15,338	5,838	6,737	68,274	74,725	25,224	-2.3	523,501	2.6	45,119
Merced, CA Metro Area	31	2,108	763	821	396	415	17,406	16,079	2,903	0.7	42,083	8.3	36,124
Miami-Fort Lauderdale-West Palm Beach, FL Metro Area	1,619	225,882	33,557	36,741	14,088	14,185	268,767	277,301	184,069	7.9	2,052,560	12.7	45,270
Fort Lauderdale-Pompano Beach-Deerfield Beach, FL Metro Division	-	-	6,879	8,964	3,952	3,941	94,919	92,287	58,549	5.4	647,907	9.2	44,523
Miami-Miami Beach-Kendall, FL Metro Division	-	-	19,917	20,892	7,407	7,508	118,473	127,356	80,197	9.2	919,859	14.7	45,318
West Palm Beach-Boca Raton-Delray Beach, FL Metro Division	-	-	6,761	6,885	2,729	2,736	55,375	57,658	45,323	8.7	484,794	14.0	46,177
Michigan City-La Porte, IN Metro Area	28	1,663	171	220	341	376	6,649	7,080	2,290	-7.6	33,509	-1.6	35,998
Midland, MI Metro Area	19	1,568	146	170	133	157	3,270	3,403	1,908	4.6	34,973	3.6	65,880
Midland, TX Metro Area	51	5,980	553	672	336	324	9,024	8,592	5,250	12.6	88,906	46.8	68,087
Milwaukee-Waukesha-West Allis, WI Metro Area	552	64,659	10,680	11,224	4,481	4,841	77,403	79,931	37,739	-1.8	764,662	3.7	48,997
Minneapolis-St. Paul-Bloomington, MN-WI Metro Area	815	178,957	20,635	22,467	12,828	13,310	225,604	221,081	93,843	2.5	1,753,004	10.3	54,146
Missoula, MT Metro Area	33	2,136	1,349	1,604	520	539	9,354	8,732	4,225	1.3	49,006	6.0	34,273
Mobile, AL Metro Area	119	6,565	2,601	2,966	2,687	2,963	23,168	25,265	8,492	-3.8	142,481	-4.1	39,654
Modesto, CA Metro Area	89	7,273	830	992	809	841	27,104	25,584	8,544	2.1	132,417	8.9	41,277
Monroe, LA Metro Area	58	3,243	517	695	765	854	11,088	12,976	4,552	0.3	66,676	1.9	35,146
Monroe, MI Metro Area	32	1,913	228	278	241	288	5,338	5,818	2,260	-5.2	36,169	4.3	42,856
Montgomery, AL Metro Area	116	7,722	6,400	7,131	4,194	4,790	33,478	34,228	7,626	-1.5	130,334	2.6	38,501
Morgantown, WV Metro Area	49	2,539	2,101	2,020	626	634	16,315	17,125	2,819	2.8	49,376	11.2	40,111
Morristown, TN Metro Area	36	1,428	278	335	354	379	5,938	5,855	1,923	-3.0	37,218	0.9	34,497
Mount Vernon-Anacortes, WA Metro Area	42	2,333	388	455	327	360	10,706	10,479	3,361	-2.1	39,626	4.2	41,971
Muncie, IN Metro Area	37	2,010	283	357	338	374	10,601	10,449	2,322	-4.8	38,419	7.0	34,199
Muskegon, MI Metro Area	37	1,482	338	433	295	343	7,254	8,254	3,153	-6.7	52,027	9.1	38,614
Myrtle Beach-Conway-North Myrtle Beach, SC-NC Metro Area	157	7,488	1,041	1,183	1,576	1,519	20,194	18,481	10,592	0.6	123,205	6.9	29,775
Napa, CA Metro Area	45	3,709	207	292	208	217	10,216	9,783	4,075	3.3	60,882	10.8	48,174
Naples-Immokalee-Marco Island, FL Metro Area	156	15,439	643	760	648	648	12,222	12,194	11,003	11.6	114,225	12.6	41,057
Nashville-Davidson—Murfreesboro—Franklin, TN Metro Area	598	52,199	13,078	13,448	6,002	6,249	94,659	95,222	40,484	3.1	774,736	14.6	47,211
New Bern, NC Metro Area	25	1,420	5,696	5,767	8,585	9,853	8,439	8,639	2,521	-6.9	30,794	-0.9	35,821
New Haven-Milford, CT Metro Area	265	27,684	5,414	5,975	1,912	1,855	44,806	44,959	19,467	-0.7	338,587	5.5	49,068
New Orleans-Metairie, LA Metro Area	348	35,695	11,839	13,068	8,493	9,111	68,877	78,857	30,049	2.2	490,361	8.3	47,137
New York-Newark-Jersey City, NY-NJ-PA Metro Area	5,735	1,658,292	112,186	133,817	43,130	43,801	1,161,009	1,200,637	569,055	3.5	8,040,243	7.6	67,740
Dutchess County-Putnam County, NY Metro Division	-	-	1,308	1,599	591	619	22,958	25,900	10,352	0.0	114,736	-2.0	45,094
Nassau County-Suffolk County, NY Metro Division	-	-	16,544	18,725	5,178	5,254	166,898	177,579	96,654	1.9	1,107,585	6.2	51,042
Newark, NJ-PA Metro Division	-	-	18,457	20,455	5,275	5,220	155,230	163,268	67,109	-0.5	1,045,550	1.7	66,466
New York-Jersey City-White Plains, NY-NJ Metro Division	-	-	75,877	93,038	32,086	32,708	815,923	833,890	394,940	4.6	5,772,372	9.2	71,625
Niles-Benton Harbor, MI Metro Area	57	1,944	316	396	265	316	8,967	9,179	3,543	-3.6	53,366	7.8	42,584
North Port-Sarasota-Bradenton, FL Metro Area	290	19,295	1,917	2,183	1,479	1,445	24,683	24,354	21,306	7.2	221,630	11.9	37,440
Norwich-New London, CT Metro Area	89	4,756	2,728	2,664	6,859	8,100	28,499	34,610	5,732		102,281	-4.4	47,734
Ocala, FL Metro Area	84	5,723	670	933	617	662	13,660	16,926	6,842	1.0	76,032	2.8	34,011

NA = Not available.

[1]As of June 30. Covers all FDIC-insured commercial banks and savings institutions. and does not include U.S. branches of foreign banks.

[2]For pay period as of March 12 of the year shown.

Table B-14. Banking, Government Employment, and Private Business Establishments and Employment—*Continued*

Metropolitan statistical area and division	Banking 2016[1] Number of offices	Banking 2016[1] Deposits (million dollars)	Federal Civilian 2015	Federal Civilian 2010	Military 2015	Military 2010	State and Local 2015	State and Local 2010	Establishments 2014	Establishments Change, 2010–2014	Employment[2] 2014	Employment[2] Change, 2010–2014	Annual payroll per employee, 2014 (dollars)
Ocean City, NJ Metro Area	49	2,955	443	527	1,094	1,067	8,307	8,781	3,788	-1.7	25,547	4.4	38,581
Odessa, TX Metro Area	38	2,840	179	217	321	313	9,721	9,618	3,686	13.9	63,283	29.2	55,926
Ogden-Clearfield, UT Metro Area	99	12,019	18,615	20,126	6,128	6,794	30,395	28,696	12,946	4.5	173,052	9.5	37,174
Oklahoma City, OK Metro Area	406	29,692	27,573	28,190	10,700	12,679	96,003	93,780	34,769	5.4	502,066	10.9	44,102
Olympia-Tumwater, WA Metro Area	59	3,306	863	1,010	776	816	36,001	35,799	5,923	1.7	66,373	4.3	38,578
Omaha-Council Bluffs, NE-IA Metro Area	327	31,002	9,419	9,482	9,115	9,554	53,646	54,298	22,855	2.5	402,263	0.9	45,594
Orlando-Kissimmee-Sanford, FL Metro Area	570	44,831	12,968	12,778	4,646	4,573	103,571	100,997	58,984	7.1	959,387	12.1	40,349
Oshkosh-Neenah, WI Metro Area	41	2,258	407	531	437	463	11,858	11,956	3,490	-3.1	81,908	-1.8	47,458
Owensboro, KY Metro Area	52	3,510	306	367	381	390	6,463	9,809	2,533	-1.3	46,605	4.6	37,398
Oxnard-Thousand Oaks-Ventura, CA Metro Area	172	17,639	7,173	7,822	5,059	6,388	37,115	35,247	20,251	3.3	251,566	6.8	50,984
Palm Bay-Melbourne-Titusville, FL Metro Area	120	8,244	6,275	6,755	2,829	2,999	21,865	23,048	13,348	2.8	166,056	1.3	40,976
Panama City, FL Metro Area	53	2,735	3,785	3,819	4,250	4,280	10,290	12,103	4,744	-0.7	62,727	11.3	32,839
Parkersburg-Vienna, WV Metro Area	33	1,553	2,305	2,266	433	477	4,588	4,786	2,111	-3.6	33,284	0.7	34,673
Pensacola-Ferry Pass-Brent, FL Metro Area	90	5,416	6,610	7,247	13,190	13,797	21,112	21,340	9,185	1.1	122,512	5.7	36,869
Peoria, IL Metro Area	155	7,244	2,281	2,423	823	812	19,375	19,783	8,465	-3.4	161,541	0.0	49,831
Philadelphia-Camden-Wilmington, PA-NJ-DE-MD Metro Area	1,732	448,052	51,250	57,922	23,106	22,714	289,150	297,896	145,269	0.4	2,550,162	5.3	54,865
Camden, NJ Metro Division	-	-	7,935	9,193	7,611	7,363	72,641	76,657	27,817	-0.6	439,174	3.2	46,953
Montgomery County-Bucks County-Chester County, PA Metro Division	-	-	6,070	7,918	5,235	5,657	76,808	80,125	58,960	0.9	984,156	6.2	57,244
Philadelphia, PA Metro Division	-	-	31,925	35,577	6,671	6,181	96,455	98,400	40,070	0.9	809,220	4.8	54,763
Wilmington, DE-MD-NJ Metro Division	-	-	5,320	5,234	3,589	3,513	43,246	42,714	18,422	-1.1	317,612	7.0	58,695
Phoenix-Mesa-Scottsdale, AZ Metro Area	867	86,080	21,851	24,086	13,740	14,396	212,037	208,294	90,849	3.6	1,574,007	8.3	45,952
Pine Bluff, AR Metro Area	30	1,527	1,517	2,179	389	439	8,474	9,084	1,590	-6.5	22,935	-10.7	34,471
Pittsburgh, PA Metro Area	825	119,406	17,864	19,484	6,519	6,710	100,362	109,421	59,644	0.7	1,092,675	6.0	47,493
Pittsfield, MA Metro Area	60	4,005	373	501	309	336	8,129	8,104	3,900	-3.2	52,802	-1.7	41,507
Pocatello, ID Metro Area	24	771	549	577	280	315	7,751	7,528	1,943	-3.7	25,273	1.5	30,274
Portland-South Portland, ME Metro Area	193	12,924	8,339	8,324	4,073	4,925	28,089	28,829	17,349	0.1	225,199	3.2	44,096
Portland-Vancouver-Hillsboro, OR-WA Metro Area	546	46,383	17,950	18,622	6,657	6,980	121,607	121,007	65,127	4.3	941,033	8.1	51,527
Port St. Lucie, FL Metro Area	118	8,206	1,000	1,302	897	932	17,661	18,129	10,324	4.7	107,781	8.9	35,951
Prescott, AZ Metro Area	53	3,696	1,497	1,551	500	473	9,188	9,529	5,647	0.1	55,932	10.0	33,444
Providence-Warwick, RI-MA Metro Area	416	38,527	11,627	12,052	8,367	8,736	81,772	81,026	40,615	-1.5	610,632	3.4	45,117
Provo-Orem, UT Metro Area	85	6,990	945	1,218	2,430	2,332	28,809	26,815	11,926	10.4	180,449	16.4	38,960
Pueblo, CO Metro Area	44	1,720	1,098	1,038	436	443	11,341	11,821	3,014	-4.5	47,148	0.6	37,269
Punta Gorda, FL Metro Area	55	3,399	334	485	314	322	5,549	5,827	3,704	5.1	35,818	-3.0	31,235
Racine, WI Metro Area	58	3,010	346	372	510	546	8,680	8,843	3,986	-1.6	68,267	6.4	44,849
Raleigh, NC Metro Area	304	27,589	5,522	5,835	3,580	3,514	89,992	86,869	30,759	6.3	472,872	15.2	49,692
Rapid City, SD Metro Area	39	2,535	3,079	3,207	3,829	4,393	8,110	8,176	4,705	4.6	54,622	9.6	36,734
Reading, PA Metro Area	130	14,989	915	1,227	1,064	1,096	21,503	22,971	8,274	-0.1	149,151	4.6	43,764
Redding, CA Metro Area	38	2,871	1,312	1,512	309	288	11,696	11,689	4,114	-4.8	47,366	1.3	36,912
Reno, NV Metro Area	86	146,687	3,554	3,715	1,291	1,081	24,361	24,525	11,742	-0.5	173,723	4.8	42,708
Richmond, VA Metro Area	347	96,835	16,868	16,288	13,376	12,323	94,514	96,541	30,695	1.5	517,420	10.3	47,493
Riverside-San Bernardino-Ontario, CA Metro Area	562	45,790	20,445	22,916	21,690	25,062	223,926	216,770	68,525	5.4	1,069,244	11.7	38,446
Roanoke, VA Metro Area	120	7,254	3,874	4,089	997	1,044	17,443	17,225	8,065	-1.5	135,834	2.7	39,598
Rochester, MN Metro Area	87	5,146	996	1,183	763	793	11,095	10,543	5,140	2.3	98,888	8.9	46,569
Rochester, NY Metro Area	257	17,374	4,695	5,017	1,749	1,793	70,327	73,340	24,531	1.8	433,909	3.3	42,254
Rockford, IL Metro Area	95	5,847	885	1,207	705	718	16,322	16,680	7,309	-2.6	132,384	4.8	41,191
Rocky Mount, NC Metro Area	39	1,876	377	527	349	373	10,062	10,977	2,787	-7.1	47,893	-3.4	36,256
Rome, GA Metro Area	22	1,386	207	262	261	303	5,521	6,796	1,942	-2.0	33,947	0.0	36,412
Sacramento—Roseville—Arden-Arcade, CA Metro Area	405	49,095	13,817	14,773	4,196	4,340	235,875	237,419	46,077	3.5	669,449	7.8	48,982
Saginaw, MI Metro Area	55	2,078	1,420	1,608	313	387	9,323	10,220	4,368	-2.8	77,998	5.4	37,606
St. Cloud, MN Metro Area	64	4,777	2,304	2,100	674	704	11,260	11,831	5,288	1.0	95,502	6.9	39,792
St. George, UT Metro Area	35	2,049	558	615	647	614	7,552	6,518	4,381	14.8	42,838	19.0	31,273
St. Joseph, MO-KS Metro Area	49	2,154	607	671	432	456	9,421	9,431	2,959	-9.2	47,077	-3.4	39,212
St. Louis, MO-IL Metro Area	917	95,134	28,278	31,214	13,462	14,347	138,660	144,028	73,306	4.7	1,201,903	3.0	47,994
Salem, OR Metro Area	89	5,445	1,352	1,823	1,036	1,091	38,245	39,045	9,096	1.1	111,414	4.0	35,048
Salinas, CA Metro Area	77	8,563	5,186	5,834	5,622	5,953	26,560	25,528	8,420	1.0	102,790	6.6	42,780
Salisbury, MD-DE Metro Area	152	57,403	1,073	1,362	1,863	1,739	22,447	21,510	10,364	-0.3	121,303	7.6	35,308
Salt Lake City, UT Metro Area	230	529,176	12,403	13,050	5,143	5,248	92,038	83,956	31,072	5.2	560,004	11.3	46,890
San Angelo, TX Metro Area	31	2,444	1,176	1,417	3,103	3,446	7,743	7,889	2,850	8.1	40,957	12.6	37,415
San Antonio-New Braunfels, TX Metro Area	437	102,792	34,887	34,875	34,285	36,572	130,702	126,810	43,171	7.1	798,637	11.2	42,566
San Diego-Carlsbad, CA Metro Area	599	79,611	46,442	47,256	98,828	110,957	190,043	180,283	79,958	5.5	1,202,583	9.2	51,349
San Francisco-Oakland-Hayward, CA Metro Area	1,043	335,862	32,596	36,157	9,062	9,165	279,028	266,911	124,273	5.6	1,969,853	11.4	79,655
Oakland-Hayward-Berkeley, CA Metro Division	-	-	13,979	15,819	5,650	5,532	146,730	138,603	60,630	4.6	929,824	8.6	63,417
San Francisco-Redwood City-South San Francisco, CA Metro Division	-	-	17,865	19,422	2,864	3,004	117,609	114,375	53,842	7.1	940,445	14.8	97,959
San Rafael, CA Metro Division	-	-	752	916	548	629	14,689	13,933	9,801	2.9	99,584	7.4	58,405
San Jose-Sunnyvale-Santa Clara, CA Metro Area	361	124,515	10,091	10,821	3,451	3,342	82,289	80,970	47,951	6.5	973,967	13.6	104,438
San Luis Obispo-Paso Robles-Arroyo Grande, CA Metro Area	67	6,114	538	676	533	451	20,699	19,982	8,028	3.2	89,509	11.1	39,213
Santa Cruz-Watsonville, CA Metro Area	49	6,077	531	548	397	415	18,204	17,739	6,830	0.7	72,301	6.2	43,481
Santa Fe, NM Metro Area	37	3,255	950	1,182	388	387	16,027	17,436	4,711	-1.4	45,219	2.5	39,456

NA = Not available.
[1]As of June 30. Covers all FDIC-insured commercial banks and savings institutions. and does not include U.S. branches of foreign banks.
[2]For pay period as of March 12 of the year shown.

Table B-14. Banking, Government Employment, and Private Business Establishments and Employment—*Continued*

Metropolitan statistical area and division	Banking 2016[1] Number of offices	Banking 2016[1] Deposits (million dollars)	Federal Civilian 2015	Federal Civilian 2010	Military 2015	Military 2010	State and Local 2015	State and Local 2010	Establishments 2014	Establishments Change, 2010–2014	Employment[2] 2014	Employment[2] Change, 2010–2014	Annual payroll per employee, 2014 (dollars)
Santa Maria-Santa Barbara, CA Metro Area	102	11,937	3,618	4,138	3,123	3,399	31,536	30,838	11,296	0.8	141,785	5.4	48,152
Santa Rosa, CA Metro Area	122	12,285	1,372	1,796	1,407	1,445	27,275	25,005	13,523	2.6	158,918	11.1	46,494
Savannah, GA Metro Area	98	7,085	2,887	3,235	6,143	7,360	20,535	20,170	8,717	4.0	139,798	11.1	40,534
Scranton—Wilkes-Barre—Hazleton, PA Metro Area	221	11,556	4,213	4,734	1,442	1,508	25,816	27,356	13,208		238,759	5.5	37,518
Seattle-Tacoma-Bellevue, WA Metro Area	903	97,595	34,120	37,691	46,996	51,907	235,474	230,175	99,432	2.7	1,574,478	9.7	63,666
Seattle-Bellevue-Everett, WA Metro Division	-	-	22,243	24,488	13,836	14,286	190,254	184,125	82,823	3.3	1,333,184	10.0	67,592
Tacoma-Lakewood, WA Metro Division	-	-	11,877	13,203	33,160	37,621	45,220	46,050	16,609	0.1	241,294	7.9	41,974
Sebastian-Vero Beach, FL Metro Area	58	4,288	330	388	269	278	4,673	5,249	4,058	4.9	40,165	7.7	36,170
Sebring, FL Metro Area	24	1,480	262	253	180	198	3,736	3,994	1,833	-7.4	19,520	3.7	29,723
Sheboygan, WI Metro Area	42	1,913	200	235	320	341	5,513	5,741	2,635	-1.7	51,649	2.1	40,435
Sherman-Denison, TX Metro Area	43	2,287	331	435	252	276	6,240	6,124	2,517	-0.2	39,698	2.2	33,629
Shreveport-Bossier City, LA Metro Area	139	8,117	4,888	4,974	7,033	7,704	26,683	32,163	9,980	0.0	160,556	2.1	37,132
Sierra Vista-Douglas, AZ Metro Area	19	1,198	5,101	5,554	4,254	5,616	6,385	6,949	2,222	-6.2	26,487	-8.8	33,577
Sioux City, IA-NE-SD Metro Area	89	4,151	928	1,096	652	747	9,984	9,995	4,394	-1.9	76,646	2.0	36,250
Sioux Falls, SD Metro Area	143	437,436	2,646	2,643	1,489	1,516	10,649	10,121	7,302	3.9	133,393	8.7	42,117
South Bend-Mishawaka, IN-MI Metro Area	85	4,381	944	1,265	1,023	1,003	14,692	16,015	6,465	-3.8	123,813	5.5	37,409
Spartanburg, SC Metro Area	76	5,284	561	656	1,262	1,364	21,786	20,667	6,575	-3.6	128,014	11.7	41,466
Spokane-Spokane Valley, WA Metro Area	120	7,238	5,022	5,199	4,222	4,397	34,887	35,108	13,449	-0.4	184,736	1.7	41,796
Springfield, IL Metro Area	91	5,687	1,790	2,102	465	452	19,377	20,196	5,233	-2.5	84,441	1.5	39,832
Springfield, MA Metro Area	194	13,801	5,215	5,598	1,727	1,742	47,644	45,575	13,217	-0.2	225,499	3.0	40,835
Springfield, MO Metro Area	194	9,041	2,424	2,665	1,537	1,559	25,998	24,899	11,601	3.4	175,052	7.1	36,665
Springfield, OH Metro Area	37	1,479	563	714	345	355	6,435	6,439	2,321	-5.2	40,253	-1.1	34,746
State College, PA Metro Area	61	3,146	459	547	450	449	47,937	45,226	3,290	3.2	45,984	6.8	37,296
Staunton-Waynesboro, VA Metro Area	40	1,468	258	314	369	389	8,373	8,477	2,779	-0.6	39,094	3.2	34,947
Stockton-Lodi, CA Metro Area	104	9,150	3,066	4,361	1,146	1,143	37,456	32,387	10,825	0.0	168,367	4.8	41,079
Sumter, SC Metro Area	17	896	1,218	1,256	5,566	5,134	5,493	5,828	1,777	-2.4	31,005	12.3	33,070
Syracuse, NY Metro Area	170	12,243	4,847	4,924	1,155	1,347	49,639	51,847	15,392	0.7	258,096	2.3	41,677
Tallahassee, FL Metro Area	85	6,923	1,963	2,113	702	813	58,655	60,426	8,771	1.0	108,416	4.6	38,235
Tampa-St. Petersburg-Clearwater, FL Metro Area	739	75,962	22,744	23,953	12,064	12,655	124,312	125,891	72,931	5.1	1,038,508	11.4	43,281
Terre Haute, IN Metro Area	57	2,527	1,277	1,411	513	572	11,145	11,612	3,563	-4.8	59,126	1.1	36,265
Texarkana, TX-AR Metro Area	57	2,510	4,310	5,238	437	464	9,086	9,605	3,075	0.3	46,704	4.4	34,722
The Villages, FL Metro Area	28	2,317	1,611	1,510	203	174	2,962	2,995	1,334	17.3	18,994	33.2	36,689
Toledo, OH Metro Area	170	10,034	2,142	2,456	1,624	1,619	42,744	43,286	13,313	-2.5	262,741	5.4	40,560
Topeka, KS Metro Area	112	5,095	3,657	3,911	1,020	1,283	23,845	25,343	5,166	-4.3	85,311	-0.9	39,718
Trenton, NJ Metro Area	144	15,484	2,364	2,502	741	766	38,770	42,599	9,627	-1.3	182,255	3.7	66,109
Tucson, AZ Metro Area	172	14,654	12,506	12,756	8,041	8,656	67,320	68,138	19,931	-1.9	303,841	0.9	38,734
Tulsa, OK Metro Area	289	24,398	4,650	5,121	3,731	4,031	49,897	49,918	24,173	0.4	398,738	8.4	46,699
Tuscaloosa, AL Metro Area	68	3,769	1,900	2,029	1,020	1,081	24,384	23,794	4,454	-0.9	78,365	4.9	39,666
Tyler, TX Metro Area	91	5,922	631	910	468	481	13,278	12,166	5,734	5.4	90,521	6.2	41,087
Urban Honolulu, HI Metro Area	185	33,384	30,403	31,825	55,136	53,162	68,941	67,012	21,195	-1.8	354,302	5.5	42,317
Utica-Rome, NY Metro Area	76	4,088	2,350	3,012	501	542	27,768	30,122	6,035	-0.6	101,751	2.0	35,775
Valdosta, GA Metro Area	44	2,131	1,165	1,170	4,620	5,049	11,726	11,849	3,025	0.2	42,666	6.2	30,315
Vallejo-Fairfield, CA Metro Area	64	4,189	3,765	4,685	6,808	7,379	20,558	20,579	6,745	0.0	105,212	7.3	47,326
Victoria, TX Metro Area	28	2,333	209	435	207	222	6,825	6,852	2,524	6.7	35,847	14.2	44,844
Vineland-Bridgeton, NJ Metro Area	37	2,487	632	713	294	305	12,698	13,910	2,883	-2.9	44,491	-1.2	37,406
Virginia Beach-Norfolk-Newport News, VA-NC Metro Area	334	23,865	56,517	50,236	85,855	95,310	105,379	110,382	36,925	-1.9	597,243	0.7	40,597
Visalia-Porterville, CA Metro Area	58	4,631	1,055	1,498	690	722	30,131	30,013	6,165	0.5	90,454	5.9	36,632
Waco, TX Metro Area	66	4,765	3,053	3,750	604	625	15,479	15,631	5,248	1.9	101,733	4.9	35,218
Walla Walla, WA Metro Area	24	1,176	1,332	1,328	165	187	4,709	4,925	1,494	-0.9	19,755	-3.3	36,392
Warner Robins, GA Metro Area	36	1,671	14,901	16,226	3,891	4,425	12,093	12,237	3,014	0.6	43,911	5.2	32,971
Washington-Arlington-Alexandria, DC-VA-MD-WV Metro Area	1,677	223,332	380,384	395,596	65,072	72,523	324,064	307,174	147,986	4.1	2,545,212	6.8	63,121
Silver Spring-Frederick-Rockville, MD Metro Division	-	-	51,121	52,179	9,926	8,270	54,041	50,673	33,088	2.7	515,716	7.2	61,209
Washington-Arlington-Alexandria, DC-VA-MD-WV Metro Division	-	-	329,263	343,417	55,146	64,253	270,023	256,501	114,898	4.5	2,029,496	6.7	63,607
Waterloo-Cedar Falls, IA Metro Area	68	3,297	629	713	641	698	14,035	14,349	4,126	-0.1	81,935	8.9	37,566
Watertown-Fort Drum, NY Metro Area	36	1,551	3,168	3,762	15,779	18,927	8,370	8,357	2,435	-2.5	29,831	-0.5	34,441
Wausau, WI Metro Area	56	3,104	433	540	361	381	7,598	7,524	3,243	-4.5	62,652	6.4	40,387
Weirton-Steubenville, WV-OH Metro Area	44	1,716	253	392	412	452	5,367	5,775	2,245	-4.9	36,182	-2.6	34,364
Wenatchee, WA Metro Area	37	2,335	857	950	314	348	8,046	7,870	3,136	1.0	32,937	2.6	40,072
Wheeling, WV-OH Metro Area	64	3,645	603	745	509	570	9,124	9,617	3,406	-1.5	56,037	3.5	36,529
Wichita, KS Metro Area	49	2,574	4,880	6,402	5,286	5,424	36,592	36,683	14,605	-2.2	261,043	1.3	43,616
Wichita Falls, TX Metro Area	242	14,922	1,944	2,304	4,619	7,104	10,431	10,533	3,495		48,534	2.5	34,410
Williamsport, PA Metro Area	49	2,282	356	544	293	301	8,957	9,409	2,826	-0.9	46,628	5.1	38,027
Wilmington, NC Metro Area	73	5,896	1,028	1,216	879	795	21,590	20,066	7,902	3.9	95,866	7.8	39,193
Winchester, VA-WV Metro Area	52	2,495	1,991	1,624	466	479	7,307	7,084	3,136	2.1	49,104	10.5	38,652
Winston-Salem, NC Metro Area	158	38,103	2,048	2,208	1,589	1,584	29,857	30,827	12,966	-1.1	224,191	6.2	43,631
Worcester, MA-CT Metro Area	268	17,464	3,275	3,154	2,202	2,306	56,571	56,568	19,713	-0.3	313,932	6.3	45,951
Yakima, WA Metro Area	54	3,049	1,245	1,383	802	844	16,036	16,095	4,653	-0.7	63,154	1.2	37,673
York-Hanover, PA Metro Area	141	6,930	4,136	4,791	1,306	1,609	16,010	16,990	8,611	0.4	159,950	5.1	40,057
Youngstown-Warren-Boardman, OH-PA Metro Area	178	9,204	1,941	2,088	1,431	1,452	27,712	29,346	12,447	-3.1	202,884	2.9	36,650
Yuba City, CA Metro Area	24	2,057	1,573	1,611	4,472	3,704	9,349	9,813	2,498		29,333	1.4	37,584
Yuma, AZ Metro Area	26	1,752	3,465	3,912	4,265	4,264	10,922	10,753	2,907	-1.3	41,082	1.1	31,011

NA = Not available.
[1] As of June 30. Covers all FDIC-insured commercial banks and savings institutions. and does not include U.S. branches of foreign banks.
[2] For pay period as of March 12 of the year shown.

PART C

METROPOLITAN COUNTIES

Page

195   Population and Population Characteristics
216   Population Characteristics and Housing Units
237   Personal Income and Earnings by Industry
260   Labor Force and Private Business Establishments and Employment

193

Table C-1. Population and Population Characteristics

Metropolitan statistical area, division, and component county	Population			Net change		Percent change		Percent in each age group, 2015				Percent female
	2015 estimate (July 1)	2010[1] (estimates base) (April 1)	2000[1] (estimates base) (April 1)	2010–2015[2]	2000–2010[3]	2010–2015[2]	2000–2010[3]	Under 15 years	15 to 44 years	45 to 64 years	65 years and over	
Abilene, TX Metro Area	169,578	165,252	160,273	4,326	4,979	2.6	3.1	19.9	42.9	22.7	14.6	49.4
Callahan County, TX	13,557	13,544	12,873	13	671	0.1	5.2	18.1	33.3	28.4	20.2	50.7
Jones County, TX	19,970	20,198	20,794	-228	-596	-1.1	-2.9	14.6	45.2	26.0	14.2	37.1
Taylor County, TX	136,051	131,510	126,606	4,541	4,904	3.5	3.9	20.8	43.5	21.6	14.1	51.1
Akron, OH Metro Area	704,243	703,207	694,975	1,036	8,232	0.1	1.2	17.1	38.5	28.2	16.2	51.4
Portage County, OH	162,275	161,421	152,126	854	9,295	0.5	6.1	15.4	42.4	27.2	15.0	51.0
Summit County, OH	541,968	541,786	542,849	182	-1,063	0.0	-0.2	17.6	37.4	28.5	16.6	51.5
Albany, GA Metro Area	153,526	157,500	157,872	-3,974	-372	-2.5	-0.2	20.7	39.6	25.4	14.4	52.6
Baker County, GA	3,180	3,451	4,047	-271	-596	-7.9	-14.7	17.3	33.3	31.0	18.4	52.6
Dougherty County, GA	91,332	94,565	96,067	-3,233	-1,502	-3.4	-1.6	20.9	40.8	24.2	14.2	53.6
Lee County, GA	29,202	28,298	24,766	904	3,532	3.2	14.3	21.9	40.8	26.0	11.3	49.9
Terrell County, GA	9,113	9,507	10,963	-394	-1,456	-4.1	-13.3	19.7	34.6	27.4	18.3	52.0
Worth County, GA	20,699	21,679	22,029	-980	-350	-4.5	-1.6	19.0	35.7	27.7	17.6	51.8
Albany, OR Metro Area	120,547	116,672	103,079	3,875	13,593	3.3	13.2	19.0	36.8	26.5	17.7	50.4
Linn County, OR	120,547	116,672	103,079	3,875	13,593	3.3	13.2	19.0	36.8	26.5	17.7	50.4
Albany-Schenectady-Troy, NY Metro Area	881,830	870,713	825,920	11,117	44,793	1.3	5.4	16.4	39.6	28.0	16.0	51.0
Albany County, NY	309,381	304,208	294,601	5,173	9,607	1.7	3.3	15.3	42.7	26.4	15.6	51.6
Rensselaer County, NY	160,266	159,427	152,553	839	6,874	0.5	4.5	16.6	39.5	28.3	15.6	50.6
Saratoga County, NY	226,249	219,613	200,626	6,636	18,987	3.0	9.5	17.0	36.9	29.8	16.3	50.6
Schenectady County, NY	154,604	154,721	146,652	-117	8,069	-0.1	5.5	17.8	38.5	27.8	16.0	51.3
Schoharie County, NY	31,330	32,744	31,488	-1,414	1,256	-4.3	4.0	14.9	35.7	30.3	19.1	50.2
Albuquerque, NM Metro Area	907,301	887,075	729,729	20,226	157,346	2.3	21.6	19.1	39.8	26.0	15.0	50.8
Bernalillo County, NM	676,685	662,555	556,120	14,130	106,435	2.1	19.1	18.9	40.8	25.6	14.7	50.9
Sandoval County, NM	139,394	131,563	90,546	7,831	41,017	6.0	45.3	19.8	37.3	27.0	15.9	50.9
Torrance County, NM	15,485	16,383	16,894	-898	-511	-5.5	-3.0	17.5	34.8	28.8	18.9	47.3
Valencia County, NM	75,737	76,574	66,169	-837	10,405	-1.1	15.7	19.9	36.9	27.2	16.0	49.7
Alexandria, LA Metro Area	154,484	153,922	145,087	562	8,835	0.4	6.1	20.2	39.0	25.7	15.1	50.6
Grant Parish, LA	22,343	22,309	18,697	34	3,612	0.2	19.3	17.5	43.2	25.1	14.2	43.9
Rapides Parish, LA	132,141	131,613	126,390	528	5,223	0.4	4.1	20.6	38.3	25.8	15.3	51.7
Allentown-Bethlehem-Easton, PA-NJ Metro Area..	832,327	821,303	740,340	11,024	80,963	1.3	10.9	17.5	37.0	28.4	17.1	51.1
Warren County, NJ	106,869	108,692	102,383	-1,823	6,309	-1.7	6.2	16.6	35.3	31.7	16.5	51.3
Carbon County, PA	63,960	65,250	58,765	-1,290	6,485	-2.0	11.0	16.0	32.9	31.1	20.0	50.5
Lehigh County, PA	360,685	349,626	311,746	11,059	37,880	3.2	12.2	18.7	38.3	26.9	16.1	51.2
Northampton County, PA	300,813	297,735	267,446	3,078	30,289	1.0	11.3	16.6	37.0	28.5	17.8	50.9
Altoona, PA Metro Area	125,593	127,078	129,105	-1,485	-2,027	-1.2	-1.6	17.1	35.1	28.0	19.8	51.2
Blair County, PA	125,593	127,078	129,105	-1,485	-2,027	-1.2	-1.6	17.1	35.1	28.0	19.8	51.2
Amarillo, TX Metro Area	262,056	251,933	228,670	10,123	23,263	4.0	10.2	21.7	41.4	24.0	13.0	49.6
Armstrong County, TX	1,947	1,901	2,153	46	-252	2.4	-11.7	19.5	32.2	26.7	21.6	50.5
Carson County, TX	5,969	6,182	6,503	-213	-321	-3.4	-4.9	20.3	35.1	27.8	16.8	49.9
Oldham County, TX	2,069	2,052	2,183	17	-131	0.8	-6.0	18.8	39.7	27.6	13.9	48.7
Potter County, TX	121,802	121,073	113,655	729	7,418	0.6	6.5	23.5	41.4	23.4	11.8	48.5
Randall County, TX	130,269	120,725	104,176	9,544	16,549	7.9	15.9	20.1	41.9	24.2	13.8	50.7
Ames, IA Metro Area	96,021	89,542	79,988	6,479	9,554	7.2	11.9	14.2	56.6	18.4	10.8	47.9
Story County, IA	96,021	89,542	79,988	6,479	9,554	7.2	11.9	14.2	56.6	18.4	10.8	47.9
Anchorage, AK Metro Area	399,790	380,821	319,617	18,969	61,204	5.0	19.1	21.2	44.4	24.9	9.5	48.2
Anchorage Municipality, AK	298,695	291,826	260,299	6,869	31,527	2.4	12.1	20.8	45.5	24.4	9.4	48.6
Matanuska-Susitna Borough, AK	101,095	88,995	59,318	12,100	29,677	13.6	50.0	22.5	41.3	26.3	9.9	47.3
Ann Arbor, MI Metro Area	358,880	345,066	322,818	13,814	22,248	4.0	6.9	16.0	47.4	24.1	12.5	50.5
Washtenaw County, MI	358,880	345,066	322,818	13,814	22,248	4.0	6.9	16.0	47.4	24.1	12.5	50.5
Anniston-Oxford-Jacksonville, AL Metro Area	115,620	118,586	111,882	-2,966	6,704	-2.5	6.0	18.0	38.6	27.0	16.3	51.8
Calhoun County, AL	115,620	118,586	111,882	-2,966	6,704	-2.5	6.0	18.0	38.6	27.0	16.3	51.8
Appleton, WI Metro Area	233,007	225,666	201,773	7,341	23,893	3.3	11.8	20.0	38.3	28.1	13.6	50.1
Calumet County, WI	49,762	48,971	40,683	791	8,288	1.6	20.4	20.8	36.1	29.6	13.6	49.8
Outagamie County, WI	183,245	176,695	161,090	6,550	15,605	3.7	9.7	19.8	38.9	27.7	13.6	50.2
Asheville, NC Metro Area	446,840	424,860	369,186	21,980	55,674	5.2	15.1	15.8	35.7	27.6	21.0	51.8
Buncombe County, NC	253,178	238,308	206,365	14,870	31,943	6.2	15.5	15.9	38.3	27.2	18.6	52.0
Haywood County, NC	59,868	59,036	54,025	832	5,011	1.4	9.3	14.9	32.2	28.9	24.0	51.8
Henderson County, NC	112,655	106,742	89,184	5,913	17,558	5.5	19.7	16.1	31.6	27.6	24.8	51.7
Madison County, NC	21,139	20,774	19,612	365	1,162	1.8	5.9	15.0	36.3	28.3	20.4	50.3
Athens-Clarke County, GA Metro Area	203,189	192,541	166,028	10,648	26,513	5.5	16.0	16.8	49.4	21.8	12.1	51.8
Clarke County, GA	123,912	116,707	101,941	7,205	14,766	6.2	14.5	15.0	57.7	17.5	9.9	52.5
Madison County, GA	28,441	28,120	25,705	321	2,415	1.1	9.4	18.9	36.7	28.5	15.9	50.8
Oconee County, GA	35,965	32,815	25,772	3,150	7,043	9.6	27.3	21.1	36.4	28.4	14.1	51.0
Oglethorpe County, GA	14,871	14,899	12,610	-28	2,289	-0.2	18.2	17.6	35.7	28.6	18.1	50.5
Atlanta-Sandy Springs-Roswell, GA Metro Area ...	5,710,795	5,286,727	4,263,135	424,068	1,023,592	8.0	24.0	20.9	42.0	26.0	11.1	51.6
Barrow County, GA	75,370	69,367	46,177	6,003	23,190	8.7	50.2	22.5	41.8	24.2	11.6	50.7
Bartow County, GA	102,747	100,157	76,062	2,590	24,095	2.6	31.7	20.5	39.3	27.0	13.2	50.8
Butts County, GA	23,593	23,655	19,460	-62	4,195	-0.3	21.6	17.4	40.5	27.1	14.9	46.7
Carroll County, GA	114,545	110,591	87,302	3,954	23,289	3.6	26.7	20.0	43.1	24.1	12.8	51.0
Cherokee County, GA	235,900	214,346	142,013	21,554	72,333	10.1	50.9	21.1	39.1	27.3	12.5	50.8
Clayton County, GA	273,955	259,470	236,644	14,485	22,826	5.6	9.6	23.7	43.5	24.3	8.5	52.7
Cobb County, GA	741,334	688,076	607,450	53,258	80,626	7.7	13.3	20.4	42.3	26.4	11.0	51.7
Coweta County, GA	138,427	127,317	89,254	11,110	38,063	8.7	42.6	20.9	39.1	27.2	12.8	51.3
Dawson County, GA	23,312	22,339	15,942	973	6,397	4.4	40.1	17.2	35.2	29.0	18.6	49.9
DeKalb County, GA	734,871	691,891	666,158	42,980	25,733	6.2	3.9	20.2	43.8	25.3	10.7	52.5
Douglas County, GA	140,733	132,339	92,315	8,394	40,024	6.3	43.4	21.8	41.1	26.4	10.7	52.3

0 = represents zero or rounds to zero.
[1]The April 1, 2000 and 2010 population estimates bases reflect modifications to the census populations as documented in the Count Question Resolution program and geographic program revisions.
[2]Based on the April 1, 2010 estimates base and the July 1, 2015 estimates
[3]Based on the April 1, 2000 and April 1, 2010 estimates bases.

Table C-1.   Population and Population Characteristics—*Continued*

Metropolitan statistical area, division, and component county	Population			Net change		Percent change		Percent in each age group, 2015				Percent female
	2015 estimate (July 1)	2010¹ (estimates base) (April 1)	2000¹ (estimates base) (April 1)	2010–2015²	2000–2010³	2010–2015²	2000–2010³	Under 15 years	15 to 44 years	45 to 64 years	65 years and over	
Fayette County, GA	110,714	106,566	91,313	4,148	15,253	3.9	16.7	18.1	34.0	31.0	16.9	51.5
Forsyth County, GA	212,438	175,511	98,360	36,927	77,151	21.0	78.4	23.4	38.3	26.9	11.4	50.2
Fulton County, GA	1,010,562	920,579	815,579	89,983	105,000	9.8	12.9	19.1	45.2	24.9	10.8	51.6
Gwinnett County, GA	895,823	805,324	588,133	90,499	217,191	11.2	36.9	22.8	42.4	25.9	8.9	51.0
Haralson County, GA	28,854	28,780	25,660	74	3,120	0.3	12.2	19.5	37.5	26.8	16.2	51.4
Heard County, GA	11,539	11,834	10,980	-295	854	-2.5	7.8	18.6	36.7	28.8	15.9	50.3
Henry County, GA	217,739	203,879	119,498	13,860	84,381	6.8	70.6	21.2	41.1	26.8	10.9	52.2
Jasper County, GA	13,635	13,900	11,441	-265	2,459	-1.9	21.5	19.9	35.0	29.1	15.9	51.1
Lamar County, GA	18,201	18,317	15,956	-116	2,361	-0.6	14.8	17.1	40.8	25.6	16.5	51.9
Meriwether County, GA	21,190	21,992	22,546	-802	-554	-3.6	-2.5	18.2	34.7	28.0	19.1	52.0
Morgan County, GA	18,046	17,868	15,499	178	2,369	1.0	15.3	18.3	34.2	28.8	18.7	51.7
Newton County, GA	105,473	99,958	61,906	5,515	38,052	5.5	61.5	22.0	40.5	25.3	12.3	52.4
Paulding County, GA	152,238	142,324	81,615	9,914	60,709	7.0	74.4	22.4	41.9	25.8	9.9	51.2
Pickens County, GA	30,309	29,422	23,022	887	6,400	3.0	27.8	16.8	33.2	29.1	20.9	50.7
Pike County, GA	17,941	17,869	13,460	72	4,409	0.4	32.8	19.0	37.9	28.1	15.0	50.6
Rockdale County, GA	88,856	85,215	70,292	3,641	14,923	4.3	21.2	20.6	38.4	27.8	13.2	52.8
Spalding County, GA	64,051	64,073	58,461	-22	5,612	0.0	9.6	20.3	37.5	25.6	16.6	51.7
Walton County, GA	88,399	83,768	60,637	4,631	23,131	5.5	38.1	20.9	37.8	26.7	14.6	51.4
Atlantic City-Hammonton, NJ Metro Area	274,219	274,549	253,210	-330	21,339	-0.1	8.4	18.1	36.9	28.7	16.3	51.8
Atlantic County, NJ	274,219	274,549	253,210	-330	21,339	-0.1	8.4	18.1	36.9	28.7	16.3	51.8
Auburn-Opelika, AL Metro Area	156,993	140,296	115,014	16,697	25,282	11.9	22.0	17.8	49.6	22.0	10.6	50.8
Lee County, AL	156,993	140,296	115,014	16,697	25,282	11.9	22.0	17.8	49.6	22.0	10.6	50.8
Augusta-Richmond County, GA-SC Metro Area	590,146	564,873	508,041	25,273	56,832	4.5	11.2	19.6	39.7	26.1	14.6	51.2
Burke County, GA	22,745	23,316	22,255	-571	1,061	-2.4	4.8	21.7	36.7	26.9	14.7	52.1
Columbia County, GA	144,052	124,059	89,497	19,993	34,562	16.1	38.6	21.2	40.9	25.9	12.0	51.0
Lincoln County, GA	7,673	7,996	8,330	-323	-334	-4.0	-4.0	15.4	31.5	31.5	21.5	51.1
McDuffie County, GA	21,540	21,869	21,263	-329	606	-1.5	2.9	21.0	35.8	26.7	16.5	53.1
Richmond County, GA	201,793	200,549	199,552	1,244	997	0.6	0.5	19.9	42.8	24.3	12.9	51.5
Aiken County, SC	165,829	160,106	142,556	5,723	17,550	3.6	12.3	18.1	36.2	27.6	18.1	51.5
Edgefield County, SC	26,514	26,978	24,588	-464	2,390	-1.7	9.7	15.3	38.2	29.9	16.6	46.0
Austin-Round Rock, TX Metro Area	2,000,860	1,716,313	1,249,963	284,547	466,350	16.6	37.3	20.1	46.6	23.4	9.8	50.0
Bastrop County, TX	80,527	74,169	57,702	6,358	16,467	8.6	28.5	20.9	37.0	28.0	14.1	49.2
Caldwell County, TX	40,522	38,057	32,101	2,465	5,956	6.5	18.6	19.2	42.1	25.1	13.6	49.6
Hays County, TX	194,739	157,127	97,918	37,612	59,209	23.9	60.5	19.3	48.6	21.8	10.3	50.2
Travis County, TX	1,176,558	1,024,347	811,776	152,211	212,571	14.9	26.2	19.4	48.8	23.1	8.7	49.6
Williamson County, TX	508,514	422,613	250,466	85,901	172,147	20.3	68.7	22.2	42.7	23.9	11.3	50.9
Bakersfield, CA Metro Area	882,176	839,631	661,632	42,545	177,999	5.1	26.9	24.5	43.3	22.1	10.1	48.7
Kern County, CA	882,176	839,631	661,632	42,545	177,999	5.1	26.9	24.5	43.3	22.1	10.1	48.7
Baltimore-Columbia-Towson, MD Metro Area	2,797,407	2,710,575	2,553,137	86,832	157,438	3.2	6.2	18.3	40.0	27.3	14.4	51.8
Anne Arundel County, MD	564,195	537,654	489,677	26,541	47,977	4.9	9.8	18.7	40.0	27.6	13.7	50.4
Baltimore County, MD	831,128	804,953	753,947	26,175	51,006	3.3	6.8	17.9	39.0	27.0	16.1	52.6
Carroll County, MD	167,627	167,138	150,881	489	16,257	0.3	10.8	17.5	35.6	31.0	15.8	50.6
Harford County, MD	250,290	244,826	218,914	5,464	25,912	2.2	11.8	18.4	37.4	29.2	15.1	51.1
Howard County, MD	313,414	287,085	247,876	26,329	39,209	9.2	15.8	19.9	39.0	28.4	12.7	51.0
Queen Anne's County, MD	48,904	47,776	40,580	1,128	7,196	2.4	17.7	17.8	32.9	31.5	17.8	50.5
Baltimore city, MD	621,849	621,143	651,262	706	-30,119	0.1	-4.6	18.0	44.5	25.0	12.5	52.9
Bangor, ME Metro Area	152,692	153,920	144,866	-1,228	9,054	-0.8	6.2	15.2	38.7	29.0	17.2	50.6
Penobscot County, ME	152,692	153,920	144,866	-1,228	9,054	-0.8	6.2	15.2	38.7	29.0	17.2	50.6
Barnstable Town, MA Metro Area	214,333	215,888	222,239	-1,555	-6,351	-0.7	-2.9	12.6	27.7	31.1	28.5	52.4
Barnstable County, MA	214,333	215,888	222,239	-1,555	-6,351	-0.7	-2.9	12.6	27.7	31.1	28.5	52.4
Baton Rouge, LA Metro Area	830,480	802,500	706,122	27,980	96,378	3.5	13.6	19.8	42.7	24.8	12.7	51.0
Ascension Parish, LA	119,455	107,194	76,639	12,261	30,555	11.4	39.9	22.9	41.3	25.3	10.5	50.6
East Baton Rouge Parish, LA	446,753	440,178	412,899	6,575	27,279	1.5	6.6	19.0	44.6	23.5	12.8	52.1
East Feliciana Parish, LA	19,696	20,263	21,348	-567	-1,085	-2.8	-5.1	15.8	37.4	30.4	16.5	46.1
Iberville Parish, LA	33,095	33,407	33,319	-312	88	-0.9	0.3	17.4	40.8	27.8	14.0	49.1
Livingston Parish, LA	137,788	128,040	91,889	9,748	36,151	7.6	39.3	21.7	41.2	25.1	12.0	50.7
Pointe Coupee Parish, LA	22,251	22,802	22,761	-551	41	-2.4	0.2	18.4	34.2	28.7	18.7	51.8
St. Helena Parish, LA	10,567	11,203	10,553	-636	650	-5.7	6.2	18.3	36.0	27.6	18.2	51.3
West Baton Rouge Parish, LA	25,490	23,788	21,604	1,702	2,184	7.2	10.1	20.7	40.5	26.6	12.2	50.9
West Feliciana Parish, LA	15,385	15,625	15,110	-240	515	-1.5	3.4	13.1	41.1	32.3	13.4	34.2
Battle Creek, MI Metro Area	134,314	136,148	137,991	-1,834	-1,843	-1.3	-1.3	19.1	36.7	27.4	16.8	51.1
Calhoun County, MI	134,314	136,148	137,991	-1,834	-1,843	-1.3	-1.3	19.1	36.7	27.4	16.8	51.1
Bay City, MI Metro Area	105,659	107,771	110,271	-2,112	-2,500	-2.0	-2.3	16.9	35.3	28.9	18.8	50.7
Bay County, MI	105,659	107,771	110,271	-2,112	-2,500	-2.0	-2.3	16.9	35.3	28.9	18.8	50.7
Beaumont-Port Arthur, TX Metro Area	408,419	403,190	400,130	5,229	3,060	1.3	0.8	20.0	39.7	25.9	14.4	49.4
Hardin County, TX	55,865	54,635	48,075	1,230	6,560	2.3	13.6	20.3	37.1	26.8	15.7	50.6
Jefferson County, TX	254,308	252,273	251,968	2,035	305	0.8	0.1	19.9	41.2	25.4	13.5	48.8
Newton County, TX	13,986	14,445	15,054	-459	-609	-3.2	-4.0	17.2	36.3	28.2	18.2	48.3
Orange County, TX	84,260	81,837	85,033	2,423	-3,196	3.0	-3.8	20.6	37.6	26.5	15.3	50.4
Beckley, WV Metro Area	122,507	124,901	126,828	-2,394	-1,927	-1.9	-1.5	17.7	35.9	27.5	18.9	49.8
Fayette County, WV	44,997	46,039	47,591	-1,042	-1,552	-2.3	-3.3	17.5	34.7	28.5	19.2	49.5
Raleigh County, WV	77,510	78,862	79,237	-1,352	-375	-1.7	-0.5	17.9	36.6	26.8	18.7	49.9
Bellingham, WA Metro Area	212,284	201,140	166,822	11,144	34,318	5.5	20.6	16.4	42.8	24.9	16.0	50.4
Whatcom County, WA	212,284	201,140	166,822	11,144	34,318	5.5	20.6	16.4	42.8	24.9	16.0	50.4
Bend-Redmond, OR Metro Area	175,268	157,733	115,372	17,535	42,361	11.1	36.7	17.4	36.0	27.8	18.9	50.7
Deschutes County, OR	175,268	157,733	115,372	17,535	42,361	11.1	36.7	17.4	36.0	27.8	18.9	50.7
Billings, MT Metro Area	168,283	158,934	139,932	9,349	19,002	5.9	13.6	19.4	37.7	26.6	16.3	50.8

0 = represents zero or rounds to zero.
¹The April 1, 2000 and 2010 population estimates bases reflect modifications to the census populations as documented in the Count Question Resolution program and geographic program revisions.
²Based on the April 1, 2010 estimates base and the July 1, 2015 estimates
³Based on the April 1, 2000 and April 1, 2010 estimates bases.

Table C-1.   Population and Population Characteristics—*Continued*

Metropolitan statistical area, division, and component county	2015 estimate (July 1)	2010[1] (estimates base) (April 1)	2000[1] (estimates base) (April 1)	Net change 2010–2015[2]	Net change 2000–2010[3]	Percent change 2010–2015[2]	Percent change 2000–2010[3]	Under 15 years	15 to 44 years	45 to 64 years	65 years and over	Percent female
Carbon County, MT	10,408	10,078	9,545	330	533	3.3	5.6	14.4	30.0	32.6	23.0	49.2
Golden Valley County, MT	827	884	1,040	-57	-156	-6.4	-15.0	15.5	27.0	31.2	26.4	48.1
Yellowstone County, MT	157,048	147,972	129,347	9,076	18,625	6.1	14.4	19.8	38.3	26.2	15.8	50.9
Binghamton, NY Metro Area	246,020	251,723	252,298	-5,703	-575	-2.3	-0.2	16.3	38.1	27.6	18.0	50.7
Broome County, NY	196,567	200,600	200,415	-4,033	185	-2.0	0.1	16.0	39.3	26.9	17.9	50.8
Tioga County, NY	49,453	51,123	51,883	-1,670	-760	-3.3	-1.5	17.7	33.6	30.4	18.3	50.2
Birmingham-Hoover, AL Metro Area	1,145,647	1,128,056	1,051,340	17,591	76,716	1.6	7.3	19.2	39.3	26.6	14.9	51.9
Bibb County, AL	22,583	22,919	19,856	-336	3,063	-1.5	15.4	16.8	40.9	27.3	15.0	46.1
Blount County, AL	57,673	57,322	50,982	351	6,340	0.6	12.4	19.0	36.6	26.9	17.5	50.6
Chilton County, AL	43,943	43,631	39,604	312	4,027	0.7	10.2	20.2	37.7	26.5	15.5	50.9
Jefferson County, AL	660,367	658,350	662,041	2,017	-3,691	0.3	-0.6	19.2	39.9	26.2	14.6	52.8
St. Clair County, AL	87,074	83,593	64,740	3,481	18,853	4.2	29.1	18.9	38.0	27.2	15.9	50.1
Shelby County, AL	208,713	195,218	143,429	13,495	51,789	6.9	36.1	19.7	39.6	27.2	13.5	51.4
Walker County, AL	65,294	67,023	70,688	-1,729	-3,665	-2.6	-5.2	18.0	35.6	27.9	18.5	51.4
Bismarck, ND Metro Area	129,517	114,778	100,809	14,739	13,969	12.8	13.9	19.8	40.2	25.4	14.6	49.8
Burleigh County, ND	92,991	81,308	69,408	11,683	11,900	14.4	17.1	19.4	40.7	25.3	14.6	50.0
Morton County, ND	30,310	27,471	25,301	2,839	2,170	10.3	8.6	19.3	39.3	26.1	15.3	49.4
Oliver County, ND	1,846	1,846	2,057	0	-211	0.0	-10.3	19.3	29.1	32.3	19.3	49.2
Sioux County, ND	4,370	4,153	4,043	217	110	5.2	2.7	32.0	39.1	21.3	7.6	50.0
Blacksburg-Christiansburg-Radford, VA Metro Area	181,747	178,258	165,161	3,489	13,097	2.0	7.9	13.9	48.2	23.4	14.5	49.1
Floyd County, VA	15,651	15,293	13,840	358	1,453	2.3	10.5	16.7	31.6	30.5	21.2	49.7
Giles County, VA	16,708	17,286	16,682	-578	604	-3.3	3.6	16.4	34.3	28.9	20.5	50.9
Montgomery County, VA	97,653	94,412	83,632	3,241	10,780	3.4	12.9	13.3	55.3	20.1	11.3	47.9
Pulaski County, VA	34,332	34,859	35,129	-527	-270	-1.5	-0.8	14.9	34.0	30.0	21.1	49.8
Radford city, VA	17,403	16,408	15,878	995	530	6.1	3.3	11.0	64.0	17.1	8.0	52.4
Bloomington, IL Metro Area	189,413	186,133	167,186	3,280	18,947	1.8	11.3	18.3	45.5	23.8	12.4	51.2
De Witt County, IL	16,247	16,561	16,802	-314	-241	-1.9	-1.4	17.4	35.0	29.1	18.5	50.0
McLean County, IL	173,166	169,572	150,384	3,594	19,188	2.1	12.8	18.4	46.5	23.3	11.8	51.4
Bloomington, IN Metro Area	165,577	159,542	142,342	6,035	17,200	3.8	12.1	13.7	52.3	21.5	12.4	50.1
Monroe County, IN	144,705	137,959	120,561	6,746	17,398	4.9	14.4	13.1	55.1	20.1	11.6	50.1
Owen County, IN	20,872	21,583	21,781	-711	-198	-3.3	-0.9	17.6	33.3	31.3	17.8	49.6
Bloomsburg-Berwick, PA Metro Area	85,229	85,563	82,181	-334	3,382	-0.4	4.1	15.1	39.4	27.3	18.2	51.8
Columbia County, PA	66,672	67,296	63,947	-624	3,349	-0.9	5.2	14.6	40.7	26.9	17.7	51.6
Montour County, PA	18,557	18,267	18,234	290	33	1.6	0.2	16.8	34.5	28.6	20.1	52.3
Boise City, ID Metro Area	676,909	616,561	464,872	60,348	151,689	9.8	32.6	21.7	40.5	24.4	13.4	50.1
Ada County, ID	434,211	392,365	300,953	41,846	91,412	10.7	30.4	20.5	41.3	25.1	13.0	49.9
Boise County, ID	7,058	7,028	6,644	30	384	0.4	5.8	13.5	26.4	37.3	22.8	48.8
Canyon County, ID	207,478	188,923	131,452	18,555	57,471	9.8	43.7	24.8	40.3	22.1	12.8	50.6
Gem County, ID	16,852	16,719	15,179	133	1,540	0.8	10.1	18.8	31.1	28.1	22.1	50.3
Owyhee County, ID	11,310	11,526	10,644	-216	882	-1.9	8.3	21.5	35.9	25.9	16.7	49.5
Boston-Cambridge-Newton, MA-NH Metro Area	4,774,321	4,552,412	4,392,533	221,909	159,879	4.9	3.6	16.8	41.1	27.5	14.6	51.4
Boston, MA Division	*1,984,537*	*1,887,745*	*1,814,170*	*96,792*	*73,575*	*5.1*	*4.1*	*16.5*	*42.9*	*26.4*	*14.3*	*51.7*
Norfolk County, MA	696,023	670,743	650,265	25,280	20,478	3.8	3.1	17.5	37.7	28.8	16.0	52.1
Plymouth County, MA	510,393	494,915	472,858	15,478	22,057	3.1	4.7	17.9	35.3	30.1	16.7	51.3
Suffolk County, MA	778,121	722,087	691,047	56,034	31,040	7.8	4.5	14.5	52.5	21.8	11.1	51.6
Cambridge-Newton-Framingham, MA Division	*2,361,182*	*2,246,301*	*2,188,740*	*114,881*	*57,561*	*5.1*	*2.6*	*17.1*	*40.3*	*27.8*	*14.8*	*51.4*
Essex County, MA	776,043	743,175	723,496	32,868	19,679	4.4	2.7	17.8	37.4	28.8	16.0	51.8
Middlesex County, MA	1,585,139	1,503,126	1,465,244	82,013	37,882	5.5	2.6	16.8	41.7	27.2	14.3	51.2
Rockingham County-Strafford County, NH Division	*428,602*	*418,366*	*389,623*	*10,236*	*28,743*	*2.4*	*7.4*	*16.1*	*37.5*	*31.1*	*15.3*	*50.7*
Rockingham County, NH	301,777	295,220	277,388	6,557	17,832	2.2	6.4	16.2	35.1	32.9	15.8	50.5
Strafford County, NH	126,825	123,146	112,235	3,679	10,911	3.0	9.7	15.8	43.3	26.9	14.0	51.3
Boulder, CO Metro Area	319,372	294,571	269,784	24,801	24,787	8.4	9.2	16.4	45.0	26.0	12.6	49.7
Boulder County, CO	319,372	294,571	269,784	24,801	24,787	8.4	9.2	16.4	45.0	26.0	12.6	49.7
Bowling Green, KY Metro Area	168,436	158,599	134,951	9,837	23,648	6.2	17.5	18.7	43.4	24.3	13.7	50.9
Allen County, KY	20,640	19,967	17,792	673	2,175	3.4	12.2	19.8	36.6	27.3	16.3	50.8
Butler County, KY	12,938	12,690	12,981	248	-291	2.0	-2.2	19.2	35.7	27.5	17.6	50.3
Edmonson County, KY	12,007	12,161	11,632	-154	529	-1.3	4.5	15.3	36.3	28.4	20.0	49.9
Warren County, KY	122,851	113,781	92,546	9,070	21,235	8.0	22.9	18.8	46.0	23.0	12.2	51.1
Bremerton-Silverdale, WA Metro Area	260,131	251,133	231,982	8,998	19,151	3.6	8.3	17.1	39.2	27.1	16.5	49.0
Kitsap County, WA	260,131	251,133	231,982	8,998	19,151	3.6	8.3	17.1	39.2	27.1	16.5	49.0
Bridgeport-Stamford-Norwalk, CT Metro Area	948,053	916,850	882,622	31,203	34,228	3.4	3.9	19.0	37.7	28.8	14.5	51.3
Fairfield County, CT	948,053	916,850	882,622	31,203	34,228	3.4	3.9	19.0	37.7	28.8	14.5	51.3
Brownsville-Harlingen, TX Metro Area	422,156	406,219	334,884	15,937	71,335	3.9	21.3	26.0	40.4	20.8	12.8	51.7
Cameron County, TX	422,156	406,219	334,884	15,937	71,335	3.9	21.3	26.0	40.4	20.8	12.8	51.7
Brunswick, GA Metro Area	116,003	112,368	93,027	3,635	19,341	3.2	20.8	18.6	35.5	27.7	18.2	52.0
Brantley County, GA	18,455	18,410	14,608	45	3,802	0.2	26.0	19.9	37.1	28.0	15.0	50.7
Glynn County, GA	83,579	79,626	67,580	3,953	12,046	5.0	17.8	19.0	35.9	26.9	18.2	52.6
McIntosh County, GA	13,969	14,332	10,839	-363	3,493	-2.5	32.2	15.0	30.8	31.6	22.6	50.5
Buffalo-Cheektowaga-Niagara Falls, NY Metro Area	1,135,230	1,135,551	1,170,022	-321	-34,471	0.0	-2.9	16.7	38.0	28.3	16.9	51.5
Erie County, NY	922,578	919,064	950,227	3,514	-31,163	0.4	-3.3	16.8	38.5	28.0	16.8	51.6
Niagara County, NY	212,652	216,487	219,795	-3,835	-3,308	-1.8	-1.5	16.5	35.9	29.9	17.7	51.3
Burlington, NC Metro Area	158,276	151,241	130,750	7,035	20,491	4.7	15.7	18.7	38.2	26.7	16.4	52.4
Alamance County, NC	158,276	151,241	130,750	7,035	20,491	4.7	15.7	18.7	38.2	26.7	16.4	52.4
Burlington-South Burlington, VT Metro Area	217,042	211,262	198,895	5,780	12,367	2.7	6.2	15.9	42.5	27.6	14.0	50.9
Chittenden County, VT	161,382	156,540	146,615	4,842	9,925	3.1	6.8	15.1	44.6	26.6	13.7	51.1
Franklin County, VT	48,799	47,752	45,395	1,047	2,357	2.2	5.2	18.6	37.1	29.9	14.3	50.3

0 = represents zero or rounds to zero.
[1]The April 1, 2000 and 2010 population estimates bases reflect modifications to the census populations as documented in the Count Question Resolution program and geographic program revisions.
[2]Based on the April 1, 2010 estimates base and the July 1, 2015 estimates
[3]Based on the April 1, 2000 and April 1, 2010 estimates bases.

Table C-1. Population and Population Characteristics—*Continued*

Metropolitan statistical area, division, and component county	Population 2015 estimate (July 1)	Population 2010[1] (estimates base) (April 1)	Population 2000[1] (estimates base) (April 1)	Net change 2010–2015[2]	Net change 2000–2010[3]	Percent change 2010–2015[2]	Percent change 2000–2010[3]	Under 15 years	15 to 44 years	45 to 64 years	65 years and over	Percent female
Grand Isle County, VT	6,861	6,970	6,885	-109	85	-1.6	1.2	14.7	31.8	34.8	18.7	50.5
California-Lexington Park, MD Metro Area	111,413	105,151	86,196	6,262	18,955	6.0	22.0	20.5	40.0	27.2	12.3	50.1
St. Mary's County, MD	111,413	105,151	86,196	6,262	18,955	6.0	22.0	20.5	40.0	27.2	12.3	50.1
Canton-Massillon, OH Metro Area	402,976	404,420	406,966	-1,444	-2,546	-0.4	-0.6	17.7	35.8	28.3	18.2	51.4
Carroll County, OH	27,811	28,836	28,822	-1,025	14	-3.6	0.0	17.1	33.1	30.0	19.8	49.8
Stark County, OH	375,165	375,584	378,144	-419	-2,560	-0.1	-0.7	17.8	36.0	28.1	18.1	51.5
Cape Coral-Fort Myers, FL Metro Area	701,982	618,754	440,910	83,228	177,844	13.5	40.3	15.2	31.6	26.2	26.9	51.0
Lee County, FL	701,982	618,754	440,910	83,228	177,844	13.5	40.3	15.2	31.6	26.2	26.9	51.0
Cape Girardeau, MO-IL Metro Area	97,534	96,275	90,286	1,259	5,989	1.3	6.6	18.2	39.9	25.5	16.4	51.5
Alexander County, IL	6,780	8,238	9,583	-1,458	-1,345	-17.7	-14.0	20.5	30.9	29.2	19.5	52.8
Bollinger County, MO	12,182	12,363	12,012	-181	351	-1.5	2.9	18.4	33.9	29.8	17.9	50.1
Cape Girardeau County, MO	78,572	75,674	68,691	2,898	6,983	3.8	10.2	18.0	41.6	24.5	15.8	51.5
Carbondale-Marion, IL Metro Area	126,828	126,580	120,907	248	5,673	0.2	4.7	16.6	43.4	24.2	15.8	50.0
Jackson County, IL	59,362	60,218	59,607	-856	611	-1.4	1.0	14.8	50.3	21.5	13.5	49.8
Williamson County, IL	67,466	66,362	61,300	1,104	5,062	1.7	8.3	18.1	37.4	26.6	17.9	50.1
Carson City, NV Metro Area	54,521	55,274	52,477	-753	2,797	-1.4	5.3	16.8	35.1	28.3	19.8	48.9
Carson City, NV	54,521	55,274	52,477	-753	2,797	-1.4	5.3	16.8	35.1	28.3	19.8	48.9
Casper, WY Metro Area	82,178	75,450	66,541	6,728	8,909	8.9	13.4	20.5	40.7	25.7	13.1	49.5
Natrona County, WY	82,178	75,450	66,541	6,728	8,909	8.9	13.4	20.5	40.7	25.7	13.1	49.5
Cedar Rapids, IA Metro Area	266,040	257,940	237,267	8,100	20,673	3.1	8.7	19.4	38.8	26.5	15.2	50.4
Benton County, IA	25,658	26,076	25,312	-418	764	-1.6	3.0	19.6	34.0	29.3	17.2	50.2
Jones County, IA	20,466	20,638	20,227	-172	411	-0.8	2.0	18.0	34.3	28.8	19.0	47.8
Linn County, IA	219,916	211,226	191,728	8,690	19,498	4.1	10.2	19.6	39.8	25.9	14.7	50.7
Chambersburg-Waynesboro, PA Metro Area	153,638	149,618	129,495	4,020	20,123	2.7	15.5	18.6	35.7	27.1	18.6	50.9
Franklin County, PA	153,638	149,618	129,495	4,020	20,123	2.7	15.5	18.6	35.7	27.1	18.6	50.9
Champaign-Urbana, IL Metro Area	238,984	231,889	210,299	7,095	21,590	3.1	10.3	16.1	49.8	21.7	12.3	50.2
Champaign County, IL	208,861	201,081	179,687	7,780	21,394	3.9	11.9	15.8	52.1	20.8	11.3	50.2
Ford County, IL	13,736	14,081	14,227	-345	-146	-2.5		18.7	34.2	27.5	19.6	50.9
Piatt County, IL	16,387	16,727	16,385	-340	342	-2.0	2.1	18.1	34.1	29.3	18.5	50.3
Charleston, WV Metro Area	220,614	227,071	235,995	-6,457	-8,924	-2.8	-3.8	17.1	35.6	28.7	18.6	51.6
Boone County, WV	23,372	24,627	25,548	-1,255	-921	-5.1	-3.6	18.3	35.3	29.1	17.4	50.4
Clay County, WV	8,910	9,386	10,336	-476	-950	-5.1	-9.2	18.9	32.8	28.9	19.3	49.7
Kanawha County, WV	188,332	193,058	200,111	-4,726	-7,053	-2.4	-3.5	16.9	35.8	28.6	18.7	51.8
Charleston-North Charleston, SC Metro Area	744,526	664,643	549,021	79,883	115,622	12.0	21.1	18.7	41.8	25.7	13.7	51.1
Berkeley County, SC	202,786	177,850	142,747	24,936	35,103	14.0	24.6	20.3	41.6	25.3	12.7	50.1
Charleston County, SC	389,262	350,204	309,921	39,058	40,283	11.2	13.0	17.1	42.4	25.6	14.9	51.6
Dorchester County, SC	152,478	136,589	96,353	15,889	40,236	11.6	41.8	20.9	40.6	26.4	12.1	51.3
Charlotte-Concord-Gastonia, NC-SC Metro Area	2,426,363	2,217,248	1,717,647	209,115	499,601	9.4	29.1	20.2	40.9	26.1	12.7	51.4
Cabarrus County, NC	196,762	178,182	131,043	18,580	47,139	10.4	36.0	21.5	39.6	26.1	12.7	51.2
Gaston County, NC	213,442	206,083	190,445	7,359	15,638	3.6	8.2	18.8	38.1	27.7	15.4	51.5
Iredell County, NC	169,866	159,440	122,631	10,426	36,809	6.5	30.0	19.1	37.6	28.4	14.9	50.7
Lincoln County, NC	81,035	78,265	63,810	2,770	14,455	3.5	22.7	17.7	35.8	30.2	16.3	50.1
Mecklenburg County, NC	1,034,070	919,666	695,348	114,404	224,318	12.4	32.3	20.5	44.8	24.4	10.3	51.9
Rowan County, NC	139,142	138,442	130,364	700	8,078	0.5	6.2	18.5	37.2	27.5	16.7	50.7
Union County, NC	222,742	201,307	123,834	21,435	77,473	10.6	62.6	22.7	38.4	27.3	11.6	50.6
Chester County, SC	32,267	33,140	34,112	-873	-972	-2.6	-2.8	19.1	34.9	28.9	17.1	51.5
Lancaster County, SC	85,842	76,652	61,404	9,190	15,248	12.0	24.8	18.2	36.2	26.1	19.5	51.1
York County, SC	251,195	226,071	164,656	25,124	61,415	11.1	37.3	20.3	39.2	27.1	13.4	51.7
Charlottesville, VA Metro Area	229,514	218,707	189,601	10,807	29,106	4.9	15.4	16.3	41.5	26.0	16.2	51.6
Albemarle County, VA	105,703	98,998	83,024	6,705	15,974	6.8	19.2	17.0	39.9	26.0	17.1	52.2
Buckingham County, VA	17,032	17,140	15,614	-108	1,526	-0.6	9.8	15.6	37.5	29.5	17.3	45.4
Fluvanna County, VA	26,235	25,704	20,012	531	5,692	2.1	28.4	17.1	35.7	28.3	18.8	54.4
Greene County, VA	19,162	18,410	15,231	752	3,179	4.1	20.9	19.9	35.6	28.2	16.3	50.6
Nelson County, VA	14,785	15,020	14,440	-235	580	-1.6	4.0	15.3	29.3	30.9	24.6	51.2
Charlottesville city, VA	46,597	43,435	41,280	3,162	2,155	7.3	5.2	13.6	56.1	20.7	9.6	51.6
Chattanooga, TN-GA Metro Area	547,776	528,145	476,611	19,631	51,534	3.7	10.8	17.8	38.4	27.1	16.7	51.5
Catoosa County, GA	66,050	63,940	53,188	2,110	10,752	3.3	20.2	19.1	37.8	26.6	16.5	51.6
Dade County, GA	16,264	16,633	15,141	-369	1,492	-2.2	9.9	15.9	38.8	27.7	17.6	51.0
Walker County, GA	68,066	68,756	61,140	-690	7,616		12.5	18.0	37.4	27.6	17.0	50.5
Hamilton County, TN	354,098	336,465	308,115	17,633	28,350	5.2	9.2	17.7	39.1	26.9	16.4	51.7
Marion County, TN	28,487	28,232	27,765	255	467	0.9	1.7	17.3	35.1	28.8	18.7	51.0
Sequatchie County, TN	14,811	14,119	11,262	692	2,857	4.9	25.4	18.1	34.0	28.1	19.8	50.8
Cheyenne, WY Metro Area	97,121	91,881	81,617	5,240	10,264	5.7	12.6	19.8	39.9	25.6	14.7	49.5
Laramie County, WY	97,121	91,881	81,617	5,240	10,264	5.7	12.6	19.8	39.9	25.6	14.7	49.5
Chicago-Naperville-Elgin, IL-IN-WI Metro Area	**9,551,031**	**9,461,537**	**9,098,970**	**89,494**	**362,567**	**0.9**	**4.0**	**19.4**	**41.2**	**26.3**	**13.1**	**51.1**
Chicago-Naperville-Arlington Heights, IL Division	*7,340,454*	*7,263,098*	*7,135,137*	*77,356*	*127,961*	*1.1*	*1.8*	*19.1*	*41.8*	*26.0*	*13.1*	*51.2*
Cook County, IL	5,238,216	5,195,022	5,376,741	43,194	-181,719	0.8	-3.4	18.7	42.9	25.2	13.2	51.5
DuPage County, IL	933,736	916,892	904,594	16,844	12,298	1.8	1.4	19.0	38.7	28.4	13.9	50.9
Grundy County, IL	50,541	50,063	37,528	478	12,535	1.0	33.4	21.1	39.1	26.6	13.2	50.1
Kendall County, IL	123,355	114,721	54,539	8,634	60,182	7.5	110.3	24.6	42.8	23.4	9.3	50.5
McHenry County, IL	307,343	308,826	259,524	-1,483	49,302	-0.5	19.0	19.7	37.5	30.2	12.7	50.2
Will County, IL	687,263	677,574	502,211	9,689	175,363	1.4	34.9	21.1	39.9	27.3	11.6	50.4
Elgin, IL Division	*635,199*	*620,466*	*493,449*	*14,733*	*127,017*	*2.4*	*25.7*	*21.2*	*41.0*	*25.7*	*12.1*	*50.3*
DeKalb County, IL	104,352	105,160	88,941	-808	16,219	-0.8	18.2	18.0	48.3	22.1	11.6	50.5
Kane County, IL	530,847	515,306	404,508	15,541	110,798	3.0	27.4	21.8	39.6	26.4	12.2	50.2
Gary, IN Division	*703,031*	*708,138*	*676,118*	*-5,107*	*32,020*	*-0.7*	*4.7*	*19.4*	*38.2*	*27.3*	*15.1*	*51.3*
Jasper County, IN	33,470	33,478	30,192	-8	3,286	0.0	10.9	19.4	37.7	26.9	16.0	50.2

0 = represents zero or rounds to zero.
[1]The April 1, 2000 and 2010 population estimates bases reflect modifications to the census populations as documented in the Count Question Resolution program and geographic program revisions.
[2]Based on the April 1, 2010 estimates base and the July 1, 2015 estimates
[3]Based on the April 1, 2000 and April 1, 2010 estimates bases.

Table C-1. Population and Population Characteristics—*Continued*

Metropolitan statistical area, division, and component county	Population 2015 estimate (July 1)	Population 2010[1] (estimates base) (April 1)	Population 2000[1] (estimates base) (April 1)	Net change 2010–2015[2]	Net change 2000–2010[3]	Percent change 2010–2015[2]	Percent change 2000–2010[3]	Under 15 years	15 to 44 years	45 to 64 years	65 years and over	Percent female
Lake County, IN	487,865	496,069	484,582	-8,204	11,487	-1.7	2.4	19.9	38.1	27.0	15.0	51.6
Newton County, IN	14,008	14,244	14,538	-236	-294	-1.7	-2.0	17.2	34.7	29.7	18.3	49.1
Porter County, IN	167,688	164,347	146,806	3,341	17,541	2.0	11.9	18.3	38.9	27.9	14.9	50.8
Lake County-Kenosha County, IL-WI Division	*872,347*	*869,835*	*794,266*	*2,512*	*75,569*	*0.3*	*9.5*	*20.1*	*38.9*	*28.3*	*12.7*	*50.2*
Lake County, IL	703,910	703,409	644,682	501	58,727	0.1	9.1	20.3	38.7	28.3	12.6	50.1
Kenosha County, WI	168,437	166,426	149,584	2,011	16,842	1.2	11.3	19.5	39.7	28.0	12.8	50.8
Chico, CA Metro Area	225,411	220,000	203,125	5,411	16,875	2.5	8.3	16.6	41.4	24.4	17.5	50.5
Butte County, CA	225,411	220,000	203,125	5,411	16,875	2.5	8.3	16.6	41.4	24.4	17.5	50.5
Cincinnati, OH-KY-IN Metro Area	2,157,719	2,114,755	1,994,818	42,964	119,937	2.0	6.0	19.8	39.1	27.1	14.0	51.0
Dearborn County, IN	49,455	50,047	46,163	-592	3,884	-1.2	8.4	18.6	35.6	29.9	15.9	50.1
Ohio County, IN	5,938	6,128	5,568	-190	560	-3.1	10.1	15.5	32.4	31.7	20.5	49.8
Union County, IN	7,182	7,516	7,341	-334	175	-4.4	2.4	16.9	35.6	29.8	17.7	50.8
Boone County, KY	127,712	118,811	86,051	8,901	32,760	7.5	38.1	22.6	39.1	26.7	11.6	50.5
Bracken County, KY	8,321	8,488	8,276	-167	212	-2.0	2.6	19.9	35.0	29.3	15.8	50.1
Campbell County, KY	92,066	90,336	88,627	1,730	1,709	1.9	1.9	17.9	40.5	27.3	14.2	50.8
Gallatin County, KY	8,636	8,589	7,845	47	744	0.5	9.5	20.1	37.4	29.8	12.7	49.3
Grant County, KY	24,757	24,662	22,350	95	2,312	0.4	10.3	22.1	38.5	26.5	12.9	50.0
Kenton County, KY	165,012	159,721	151,449	5,291	8,272	3.3	5.5	20.4	39.9	26.6	13.1	50.6
Pendleton County, KY	14,408	14,876	14,384	-468	492	-3.1	3.4	18.1	36.4	30.5	15.0	49.5
Brown County, OH	43,839	44,846	42,261	-1,007	2,585	-2.2	6.1	18.9	35.4	28.4	17.3	50.2
Butler County, OH	376,353	368,130	332,341	8,223	35,789	2.2	10.8	19.8	40.3	26.3	13.6	51.0
Clermont County, OH	201,973	197,363	177,322	4,610	20,041	2.3	11.3	19.6	37.0	28.9	14.6	50.7
Hamilton County, OH	807,598	802,374	845,289	5,224	-42,915	0.7	-5.1	19.4	39.7	26.5	14.4	51.9
Warren County, OH	224,469	212,868	159,551	11,601	53,317	5.4	33.4	20.7	37.6	28.2	13.5	49.8
Clarksville, TN-KY Metro Area	281,021	260,610	219,727	20,411	40,883	7.8	18.6	23.0	46.8	20.1	10.1	49.3
Christian County, KY	73,309	73,939	72,402	-630	1,537	-0.9	2.1	24.0	46.5	18.0	11.5	47.1
Trigg County, KY	14,233	14,334	12,600	-101	1,734	-0.7	13.8	17.5	31.4	29.5	21.6	51.0
Montgomery County, TN	193,479	172,337	134,725	21,142	37,612	12.3	27.9	23.1	48.0	20.1	8.8	50.0
Cleveland, TN Metro Area	120,864	115,788	104,012	5,076	11,776	4.4	11.3	18.0	38.7	26.7	16.6	51.2
Bradley County, TN	104,091	98,963	87,973	5,128	10,990	5.2	12.5	18.3	39.4	26.3	16.1	51.4
Polk County, TN	16,773	16,825	16,039	-52	786	-0.3	4.9	16.3	34.4	29.6	19.7	50.2
Cleveland-Elyria, OH Metro Area	2,060,810	2,077,246	2,148,041	-16,436	-70,795	-0.8	-3.3	17.7	36.8	28.5	17.0	51.8
Cuyahoga County, OH	1,255,921	1,280,109	1,393,871	-24,188	-113,762	-1.9	-8.2	17.5	37.8	27.9	16.8	52.4
Geauga County, OH	94,102	93,410	90,935	692	2,475	0.7	2.7	18.9	31.9	30.7	18.6	50.6
Lake County, OH	229,245	230,038	227,482	-793	2,556	-0.3	1.1	16.9	34.8	29.9	18.5	51.1
Lorain County, OH	305,147	301,356	284,657	3,791	16,699	1.3	5.9	18.4	36.3	28.5	16.8	50.6
Medina County, OH	176,395	172,333	151,096	4,062	21,237	2.4	14.1	18.6	35.6	29.6	16.1	50.6
Coeur d'Alene, ID Metro Area	150,346	138,494	108,682	11,852	29,812	8.6	27.4	19.2	36.5	26.7	17.6	50.6
Kootenai County, ID	150,346	138,494	108,682	11,852	29,812	8.6	27.4	19.2	36.5	26.7	17.6	50.6
College Station-Bryan, TX Metro Area	249,156	228,660	184,857	20,496	43,803	9.0	23.7	17.6	53.7	18.8	9.9	49.4
Brazos County, TX	215,037	194,851	152,436	20,186	42,415	10.4	27.8	17.4	56.8	17.3	8.4	49.3
Burleson County, TX	17,460	17,187	16,449	273	738	1.6	4.5	18.6	32.7	29.1	19.7	50.1
Robertson County, TX	16,659	16,622	15,972	37	650	0.2	4.1	20.0	34.7	26.8	18.5	50.6
Colorado Springs, CO Metro Area	697,856	645,611	537,475	52,245	108,136	8.1	20.1	20.4	42.9	24.6	12.1	49.4
El Paso County, CO	674,471	622,261	516,934	52,210	105,327	8.4	20.4	20.6	43.4	24.1	11.8	49.5
Teller County, CO	23,385	23,350	20,541	35	2,809	0.1	13.7	14.3	29.4	37.4	19.0	49.2
Columbia, MO Metro Area	174,974	162,642	135,477	12,332	27,165	7.6	20.1	17.3	50.4	21.5	10.9	51.6
Boone County, MO	174,974	162,642	135,477	12,332	27,165	7.6	20.1	17.3	50.4	21.5	10.9	51.6
Columbia, SC Metro Area	810,068	767,477	647,216	42,591	120,261	5.5	18.6	18.5	42.2	25.6	13.6	51.3
Calhoun County, SC	14,781	15,176	15,132	-395	44	-2.6	0.3	16.6	32.3	30.5	20.6	51.5
Fairfield County, SC	22,747	23,956	23,388	-1,209	568	-5.0	2.4	16.5	33.3	31.6	18.5	52.3
Kershaw County, SC	63,603	61,570	52,649	2,033	8,921	3.3	16.9	19.3	35.6	28.3	16.9	51.6
Lexington County, SC	281,833	262,397	216,031	19,436	46,366	7.4	21.5	19.4	38.6	27.4	14.6	51.2
Richland County, SC	407,051	384,506	320,836	22,545	63,670	5.9	19.8	18.0	47.0	23.4	11.7	51.5
Saluda County, SC	20,053	19,872	19,180	181	692	0.9	3.6	18.6	34.9	27.5	18.9	49.7
Columbus, GA-AL Metro Area	313,749	295,531	281,878	18,218	13,653	6.2	4.8	20.3	43.0	23.9	12.8	50.0
Russell County, AL	59,660	52,951	49,854	6,709	3,097	12.7	6.2	21.6	40.9	24.8	12.7	51.3
Chattahoochee County, GA	11,368	11,267	14,895	101	-3,628	0.9	-24.4	19.2	69.0	7.5	4.3	31.6
Harris County, GA	33,381	32,026	23,783	1,355	8,243	4.2	34.7	17.3	34.8	30.7	17.3	50.0
Marion County, GA	8,761	8,742	7,133	19	1,609	0.2	22.6	17.6	34.6	29.8	18.1	49.8
Muscogee County, GA	200,579	190,545	186,213	10,034	4,332	5.3	2.3	20.6	43.9	23.2	12.3	50.7
Columbus, IN Metro Area	81,162	76,786	71,467	4,376	5,319	5.7	7.4	20.1	39.0	25.8	15.1	50.1
Bartholomew County, IN	81,162	76,786	71,467	4,376	5,319	5.7	7.4	20.1	39.0	25.8	15.1	50.1
Columbus, OH Metro Area	2,021,632	1,902,015	1,675,226	119,617	226,789	6.3	13.5	20.0	42.2	25.5	12.3	50.8
Delaware County, OH	193,013	174,189	109,974	18,824	64,215	10.8	58.4	22.5	38.0	27.4	12.0	50.4
Fairfield County, OH	151,408	146,152	122,943	5,256	23,209	3.6	18.9	19.5	37.9	27.7	14.9	50.3
Franklin County, OH	1,251,722	1,163,545	1,068,736	88,177	94,809	7.6	8.9	20.0	44.9	24.1	11.1	51.3
Hocking County, OH	28,491	29,375	28,263	-884	1,112	-3.0	3.9	18.4	35.0	28.9	17.7	50.3
Licking County, OH	170,570	166,480	145,699	4,090	20,781	2.5	14.3	19.3	37.0	28.1	15.6	50.9
Madison County, OH	44,094	43,430	40,210	664	3,220	1.5	8.0	17.1	40.2	28.5	14.2	45.4
Morrow County, OH	35,074	34,827	31,646	247	3,181	0.7	10.1	19.4	35.2	29.3	16.1	49.8
Perry County, OH	35,985	36,052	34,052	-67	2,000	-0.2	5.9	19.7	36.5	28.7	15.2	49.9
Pickaway County, OH	56,998	55,698	52,728	1,300	2,970	2.3	5.6	17.9	39.9	27.4	14.9	47.4
Union County, OH	54,277	52,267	40,975	2,010	11,292	3.8	27.6	20.5	40.5	27.4	11.5	52.2
Corpus Christi, TX Metro Area	452,422	428,188	403,242	24,234	24,946	5.7	6.2	20.8	40.6	24.4	14.2	50.5
Aransas County, TX	25,350	23,158	22,457	2,192	701	9.5	3.1	15.3	30.6	27.0	27.1	50.3
Nueces County, TX	359,715	340,223	313,512	19,492	26,711	5.7	8.5	20.8	41.6	24.3	13.2	50.7

0 = represents zero or rounds to zero.
[1] The April 1, 2000 and 2010 population estimates bases reflect modifications to the census populations as documented in the Count Question Resolution program and geographic program revisions.
[2] Based on the April 1, 2010 estimates base and the July 1, 2015 estimates
[3] Based on the April 1, 2000 and April 1, 2010 estimates bases.

Table C-1. Population and Population Characteristics—*Continued*

Metropolitan statistical area, division, and component county	Population 2015 estimate (July 1)	Population 2010[1] (estimates base) (April 1)	Population 2000[1] (estimates base) (April 1)	Net change 2010–2015[2]	Net change 2000–2010[3]	Percent change 2010–2015[2]	Percent change 2000–2010[3]	Under 15 years	15 to 44 years	45 to 64 years	65 years and over	Percent female
San Patricio County, TX	67,357	64,807	67,273	2,550	-2,466	3.9	-3.7	22.4	39.4	23.8	14.4	50.0
Corvallis, OR Metro Area	87,572	85,581	78,143	1,991	7,438	2.3	9.5	13.5	48.5	23.2	14.8	50.0
Benton County, OR	87,572	85,581	78,143	1,991	7,438	2.3	9.5	13.5	48.5	23.2	14.8	50.0
Crestview-Fort Walton Beach-Destin, FL Metro Area	262,172	235,865	211,081	26,307	24,784	11.2	11.7	18.3	39.1	26.3	16.3	49.2
Okaloosa County, FL	198,664	180,822	170,520	17,842	10,302	9.9	6.0	18.7	40.6	25.3	15.4	49.2
Walton County, FL	63,508	55,043	40,561	8,465	14,482	15.4	35.7	17.0	34.7	29.2	19.1	49.3
Cumberland, MD-WV Metro Area	99,979	103,299	101,995	-3,320	1,304	-3.2	1.3	15.0	38.8	26.6	19.6	48.6
Allegany County, MD	72,528	75,087	74,909	-2,559	178	-3.4	0.2	14.4	40.2	26.0	19.4	47.9
Mineral County, WV	27,451	28,212	27,086	-761	1,126	-2.7	4.2	16.5	34.9	28.2	20.3	50.3
Dallas-Fort Worth-Arlington, TX Metro Area	**7,102,796**	**6,426,214**	**5,204,627**	**676,582**	**1,221,587**	**10.5**	**23.5**	**22.2**	**42.6**	**24.7**	**10.5**	**50.8**
Dallas-Plano-Irving, TX Division	*4,707,151*	*4,230,031*	*3,443,597*	*477,120*	*786,434*	*11.3*	*22.8*	*22.2*	*43.2*	*24.5*	*10.1*	*50.8*
Collin County, TX	914,127	782,351	491,272	131,776	291,079	16.8	59.3	22.2	41.8	26.0	10.1	50.9
Dallas County, TX	2,553,385	2,367,643	2,216,808	185,742	150,835	7.8	6.8	22.6	44.0	23.6	9.9	50.8
Denton County, TX	780,612	662,615	433,065	117,997	229,550	17.8	53.0	21.4	44.4	25.0	9.1	50.8
Ellis County, TX	163,632	149,610	111,415	14,022	38,195	9.4	34.3	22.0	39.9	26.0	12.2	50.7
Hunt County, TX	89,844	86,129	76,562	3,715	9,567	4.3	12.5	19.6	38.0	26.8	15.5	50.5
Kaufman County, TX	114,690	103,346	71,452	11,344	31,894	11.0	44.6	22.8	39.8	25.3	12.0	50.8
Rockwall County, TX	90,861	78,337	43,023	12,524	35,314	16.0	82.1	22.2	39.2	26.4	12.1	50.9
Fort Worth-Arlington, TX Division	*2,395,645*	*2,196,183*	*1,761,030*	*199,462*	*435,153*	*9.1*	*24.7*	*22.1*	*41.4*	*25.1*	*11.4*	*50.9*
Hood County, TX	55,423	51,173	40,987	4,250	10,186	8.3	24.9	17.1	31.1	27.6	24.2	51.0
Johnson County, TX	159,990	150,943	126,622	9,047	24,321	6.0	19.2	21.5	39.0	26.0	13.5	50.1
Parker County, TX	126,042	116,927	88,429	9,115	28,498	7.8	32.2	19.9	36.4	28.5	15.1	50.2
Somervell County, TX	8,739	8,490	6,913	249	1,577	2.9	22.8	18.2	35.6	27.5	18.8	51.0
Tarrant County, TX	1,982,498	1,809,531	1,449,290	172,967	360,241	9.6	24.9	22.5	42.4	24.6	10.5	51.1
Wise County, TX	62,953	59,119	48,789	3,834	10,330	6.5	21.2	20.6	36.8	28.0	14.7	49.7
Dalton, GA Metro Area	143,781	142,227	120,062	1,554	22,165	1.1	18.5	21.7	40.1	24.9	13.2	50.3
Murray County, GA	39,565	39,628	36,501	-63	3,127	-0.2	8.6	20.9	39.0	26.3	13.8	50.3
Whitfield County, GA	104,216	102,599	83,561	1,617	19,038	1.6	22.8	22.1	40.6	24.3	13.0	50.3
Danville, IL Metro Area	79,282	81,625	83,929	-2,343	-2,304	-2.9	-2.7	19.9	35.9	26.6	17.6	50.2
Vermilion County, IL	79,282	81,625	83,929	-2,343	-2,304	-2.9	-2.7	19.9	35.9	26.6	17.6	50.2
Daphne-Fairhope-Foley, AL Metro Area	203,709	182,265	140,416	21,444	41,849	11.8	29.8	18.0	35.2	27.6	19.2	51.3
Baldwin County, AL	203,709	182,265	140,416	21,444	41,849	11.8	29.8	18.0	35.2	27.6	19.2	51.3
Davenport-Moline-Rock Island, IA-IL Metro Area	383,606	379,689	376,067	3,917	3,622	1.0	1.0	19.1	37.2	26.9	16.8	50.8
Henry County, IL	49,489	50,485	51,032	-996	-547	-2.0	-1.1	18.3	34.7	28.1	18.9	50.2
Mercer County, IL	15,858	16,434	16,940	-576	-506	-3.5	-3.0	17.5	32.6	29.1	20.8	50.3
Rock Island County, IL	146,133	147,546	149,390	-1,413	-1,844	-1.0	-1.2	18.6	36.9	26.6	17.9	50.8
Scott County, IA	172,126	165,224	158,705	6,902	6,519	4.2	4.1	20.0	38.6	26.5	14.8	51.0
Dayton, OH Metro Area	800,909	799,216	805,791	1,693	-6,755	0.2	-0.8	18.3	38.0	26.8	16.9	51.5
Greene County, OH	164,427	161,569	147,931	2,858	13,638	1.8	9.2	17.0	40.4	26.6	16.0	50.8
Miami County, OH	104,224	102,506	98,899	1,718	3,607	1.7	3.6	18.9	35.5	27.9	17.7	50.7
Montgomery County, OH	532,258	535,141	559,141	-2,883	-24,000	-0.5	-4.3	18.5	37.8	26.7	17.0	51.9
Decatur, AL Metro Area	152,680	153,825	145,910	-1,145	7,915	-0.7	5.4	18.7	36.8	27.9	16.6	50.9
Lawrence County, AL	33,115	34,339	34,834	-1,224	-495	-3.6	-1.4	17.8	35.6	29.2	17.4	51.3
Morgan County, AL	119,565	119,486	111,076	79	8,410	0.1	7.6	18.9	37.2	27.6	16.3	50.7
Decatur, IL Metro Area	107,303	110,768	114,690	-3,465	-3,922	-3.1	-3.4	18.5	36.2	26.9	18.3	52.1
Macon County, IL	107,303	110,768	114,690	-3,465	-3,922	-3.1	-3.4	18.5	36.2	26.9	18.3	52.1
Deltona-Daytona Beach-Ormond Beach, FL Metro Area	623,279	590,293	493,203	32,986	97,090	5.6	19.7	14.6	32.6	28.2	24.6	51.3
Flagler County, FL	105,392	95,696	49,818	9,696	45,878	10.1	92.1	14.4	28.9	27.5	29.1	52.0
Volusia County, FL	517,887	494,597	443,385	23,290	51,212	4.7	11.6	14.6	33.3	28.4	23.7	51.2
Denver-Aurora-Lakewood, CO Metro Area	2,814,330	2,543,600	2,179,476	270,730	364,124	10.6	16.7	19.7	42.8	25.6	11.9	50.1
Adams County, CO	491,337	441,687	348,076	49,650	93,611	11.2	26.9	23.2	43.8	23.2	9.8	49.6
Arapahoe County, CO	631,096	572,155	488,829	58,941	83,326	10.3	17.0	20.2	41.9	25.7	12.2	50.7
Broomfield County, CO	65,065	55,866	39,202	9,199	16,664	16.5	42.5	20.0	41.6	25.9	12.5	50.3
Clear Creek County, CO	9,303	9,075	9,263	228	-188	2.5	-2.0	13.2	31.1	37.0	18.7	48.1
Denver County, CO	682,545	599,860	553,805	82,685	46,055	13.8	8.3	17.9	49.1	22.0	11.0	49.9
Douglas County, CO	322,387	285,465	175,732	36,922	109,733	12.9	62.4	22.8	38.4	28.3	10.5	50.3
Elbert County, CO	24,735	23,086	19,855	1,649	3,231	7.1	16.3	17.0	32.0	36.2	14.7	49.6
Gilpin County, CO	5,828	5,441	4,746	387	695	7.1	14.6	14.0	32.2	39.6	14.2	47.1
Jefferson County, CO	565,524	534,764	525,449	30,760	9,315	5.8	1.8	16.9	38.9	29.1	15.1	50.3
Park County, CO	16,510	16,201	14,519	309	1,682	1.9	11.6	13.5	28.2	41.1	17.2	47.3
Des Moines-West Des Moines, IA Metro Area	622,899	569,633	481,399	53,266	88,234	9.4	18.3	21.5	41.1	25.0	12.4	50.8
Dallas County, IA	80,133	66,137	41,109	13,996	25,028	21.2	60.9	24.1	41.5	22.9	11.5	51.0
Guthrie County, IA	10,676	10,954	11,348	-278	-394	-2.5	-3.5	18.2	31.1	29.2	21.6	50.4
Madison County, IA	15,753	15,679	14,012	74	1,667	0.5	11.9	20.8	34.3	28.4	16.5	50.2
Polk County, IA	467,711	430,635	374,258	37,076	56,377	8.6	15.1	21.2	41.9	24.9	12.0	50.8
Warren County, IA	48,626	46,228	40,672	2,398	5,556	5.2	13.7	20.4	37.5	26.9	15.2	50.6
Detroit-Warren-Dearborn, MI Metro Area	**4,302,043**	**4,296,313**	**4,452,778**	**5,730**	**-156,465**	**0.1**	**-3.5**	**18.5**	**37.9**	**28.5**	**15.1**	**51.4**
Detroit-Dearborn-Livonia, MI Division	*1,759,335*	*1,820,641*	*2,061,180*	*-61,306*	*-240,539*	*-3.4*	*-11.7*	*19.8*	*39.0*	*27.0*	*14.1*	*51.9*
Wayne County, MI	1,759,335	1,820,641	2,061,180	-61,306	-240,539	-3.4	-11.7	19.8	39.0	27.0	14.1	51.9
Warren-Troy-Farmington Hills, MI Division	*2,542,708*	*2,475,672*	*2,391,598*	*67,036*	*84,074*	*2.7*	*3.5*	*17.6*	*37.1*	*29.6*	*15.7*	*51.1*
Lapeer County, MI	88,373	88,316	87,947	57	369	0.1	0.4	17.2	34.5	31.9	16.4	49.3
Livingston County, MI	187,316	180,967	156,943	6,349	24,024	3.5	15.3	17.8	34.9	31.9	15.3	49.9
Macomb County, MI	864,840	840,987	788,120	23,853	52,867	2.8	6.7	17.6	37.6	28.9	15.9	51.3
Oakland County, MI	1,242,304	1,202,362	1,194,346	39,942	8,016	3.3	0.7	17.7	37.4	29.3	15.5	51.3
St. Clair County, MI	159,875	163,040	164,242	-3,165	-1,202	-1.9	-0.7	17.4	34.7	30.7	17.2	50.4
Dothan, AL Metro Area	148,171	145,639	130,828	2,532	14,811	1.7	11.3	19.0	36.7	26.7	17.6	51.8

0 = represents zero or rounds to zero.
[1] The April 1, 2000 and 2010 population estimates bases reflect modifications to the census populations as documented in the Count Question Resolution program and geographic program revisions.
[2] Based on the April 1, 2010 estimates base and the July 1, 2015 estimates
[3] Based on the April 1, 2000 and April 1, 2010 estimates bases.

Table C-1. Population and Population Characteristics—*Continued*

Metropolitan statistical area, division, and component county	Population 2015 estimate (July 1)	Population 2010[1] (estimates base) (April 1)	Population 2000[1] (estimates base) (April 1)	Net change 2010– 2015[2]	Net change 2000– 2010[3]	Percent change 2010– 2015[2]	Percent change 2000– 2010[3]	Percent in each age group, 2015 Under 15 years	Percent in each age group, 2015 15 to 44 years	Percent in each age group, 2015 45 to 64 years	Percent in each age group, 2015 65 years and over	Percent female
Geneva County, AL	26,777	26,790	25,700	-13	1,090	0.0	4.2	18.2	34.2	27.9	19.7	50.7
Henry County, AL	17,221	17,302	16,297	-81	1,005	-0.5	6.2	17.2	34.0	27.5	21.3	51.6
Houston County, AL	104,173	101,547	88,831	2,626	12,716	2.6	14.3	19.5	37.8	26.3	16.5	52.1
Dover, DE Metro Area	173,533	162,349	126,771	11,184	35,578	6.9	28.1	19.3	39.5	25.2	16.0	51.8
Kent County, DE	173,533	162,349	126,771	11,184	35,578	6.9	28.1	19.3	39.5	25.2	16.0	51.8
Dubuque, IA Metro Area	97,125	93,653	89,133	3,472	4,520	3.7	5.1	19.1	37.8	26.5	16.5	50.6
Dubuque County, IA	97,125	93,653	89,133	3,472	4,520	3.7	5.1	19.1	37.8	26.5	16.5	50.6
Duluth, MN-WI Metro Area	279,601	279,771	275,579	-170	4,192	-0.1	1.5	16.4	38.0	28.2	17.4	49.5
Carlton County, MN	35,569	35,386	31,705	183	3,681	0.5	11.6	18.7	36.0	28.5	16.7	47.8
St. Louis County, MN	200,431	200,226	200,586	205	-360	0.1	-0.2	15.9	38.6	27.9	17.7	49.7
Douglas County, WI	43,601	44,159	43,288	-558	871	-1.3	2.0	16.7	37.1	29.2	16.9	50.0
Durham-Chapel Hill, NC Metro Area	552,493	506,631	423,858	45,862	82,773	9.1	19.5	17.7	43.3	25.3	13.7	52.0
Chatham County, NC	70,928	63,491	49,396	7,437	14,095	11.7	28.5	16.5	30.2	28.3	25.0	52.1
Durham County, NC	300,952	269,974	223,270	30,978	46,704	11.5	20.9	18.6	46.0	24.0	11.5	52.1
Orange County, NC	141,354	133,702	115,509	7,652	10,113	5.7	15.7	16.0	46.4	25.5	11.5	52.0
Person County, NC	39,259	39,464	35,603	-205	3,861	-0.5	10.8	17.7	34.8	29.6	17.9	51.3
East Stroudsburg, PA Metro Area	166,397	169,842	138,615	-3,445	31,227	-2.0	22.5	16.2	37.0	31.3	15.5	50.6
Monroe County, PA	166,397	169,842	138,615	-3,445	31,227	-2.0	22.5	16.2	37.0	31.3	15.5	50.6
Eau Claire, WI Metro Area	165,636	161,390	148,345	4,246	13,045	2.6	8.8	17.7	41.5	25.5	15.3	49.6
Chippewa County, WI	63,531	62,505	55,217	1,026	7,288	1.6	13.2	18.6	36.1	28.5	16.7	48.2
Eau Claire County, WI	102,105	98,885	93,128	3,220	5,757	3.3	6.2	17.2	44.8	23.6	14.4	50.5
El Centro, CA Metro Area	180,191	174,528	142,334	5,663	32,194	3.2	22.6	23.8	41.6	22.2	12.5	49.0
Imperial County, CA	180,191	174,528	142,334	5,663	32,194	3.2	22.6	23.8	41.6	22.2	12.5	49.0
Elizabethtown-Fort Knox, KY Metro Area	148,604	148,351	133,981	253	14,370	0.2	10.7	20.0	39.6	26.9	13.5	50.1
Hardin County, KY	106,439	105,537	92,629	902	12,908	0.9	13.9	20.4	40.1	26.4	13.1	50.0
Larue County, KY	14,241	14,193	13,363	48	830	0.3	6.2	18.2	36.0	28.4	17.4	50.6
Meade County, KY	27,924	28,621	27,989	-697	632	-2.4	2.3	19.3	39.2	28.2	13.2	50.2
Elkhart-Goshen, IN Metro Area	203,474	197,561	182,793	5,913	14,768	3.0	8.1	23.3	38.6	24.5	13.6	50.5
Elkhart County, IN	203,474	197,561	182,793	5,913	14,768	3.0	8.1	23.3	38.6	24.5	13.6	50.5
Elmira, NY Metro Area	87,071	88,842	91,119	-1,771	-2,277	-2.0	-2.5	18.0	36.6	28.1	17.3	50.4
Chemung County, NY	87,071	88,842	91,119	-1,771	-2,277	-2.0	-2.5	18.0	36.6	28.1	17.3	50.4
El Paso, TX Metro Area	838,972	804,123	682,917	34,849	121,206	4.3	17.7	23.3	43.0	22.0	11.7	51.0
El Paso County, TX	835,593	800,647	679,568	34,946	121,079	4.4	17.8	23.3	43.1	22.0	11.6	51.0
Hudspeth County, TX	3,379	3,476	3,349	-97	127	-2.8	3.8	18.9	36.8	26.5	17.9	50.2
Enid, OK Metro Area	63,569	60,580	57,811	2,989	2,769	4.9	4.8	22.0	38.7	24.0	15.3	50.1
Garfield County, OK	63,569	60,580	57,811	2,989	2,769	4.9	4.8	22.0	38.7	24.0	15.3	50.1
Erie, PA Metro Area	278,045	280,566	280,907	-2,521	341	0.9	0.1	17.9	38.6	27.4	16.1	50.6
Erie County, PA	278,045	280,566	280,907	-2,521	-341	-0.9	-0.1	17.9	38.6	27.4	16.1	50.6
Eugene, OR Metro Area	362,895	351,715	323,011	11,180	28,704	3.2	8.9	15.5	40.7	25.9	17.9	50.9
Lane County, OR	362,895	351,715	323,011	11,180	28,704	3.2	8.9	15.5	40.7	25.9	17.9	50.9
Evansville, IN-KY Metro Area	315,693	311,552	296,236	4,141	15,316	1.3	5.2	18.9	38.0	27.2	15.9	51.3
Posey County, IN	25,512	25,910	27,078	-398	-1,168	-1.5	-4.3	18.5	34.6	30.4	16.5	50.4
Vanderburgh County, IN	181,877	179,703	171,941	2,174	7,762	1.2	4.5	18.4	39.6	26.5	15.5	51.7
Warrick County, IN	61,897	59,689	52,380	2,208	7,309	3.7	14.0	19.9	35.9	27.6	16.6	50.6
Henderson County, KY	46,407	46,250	44,837	157	1,413	0.3	3.2	19.5	36.4	28.1	16.0	51.5
Fairbanks, AK Metro Area	99,631	97,581	82,849	2,050	14,732	2.1	17.8	20.7	49.0	21.9	8.4	45.6
Fairbanks North Star Borough, AK	99,631	97,581	82,849	2,050	14,732	2.1	17.8	20.7	49.0	21.9	8.4	45.6
Fargo, ND-MN Metro Area	233,836	208,777	174,398	25,059	34,379	12.0	19.7	19.2	47.6	21.7	11.5	49.8
Clay County, MN	62,324	58,999	51,227	3,325	7,772	5.6	15.2	19.8	45.5	22.0	12.8	50.8
Cass County, ND	171,512	149,778	123,171	21,734	26,607	14.5	21.6	19.0	48.3	21.6	11.0	49.4
Farmington, NM Metro Area	118,737	130,045	113,812	-11,308	16,233	-8.7	14.3	22.2	39.0	24.7	14.0	50.4
San Juan County, NM	118,737	130,045	113,812	-11,308	16,233	-8.7	14.3	22.2	39.0	24.7	14.0	50.4
Fayetteville, NC Metro Area	376,509	366,383	336,686	10,126	29,697	2.8	8.8	22.1	44.9	22.1	10.9	51.0
Cumberland County, NC	323,838	319,431	302,978	4,407	16,453	1.4	5.4	21.7	44.9	22.1	11.3	51.1
Hoke County, NC	52,671	46,952	33,708	5,719	13,244	12.2	39.3	24.5	44.9	22.0	8.6	50.5
Fayetteville-Springdale-Rogers, AR-MO Metro Area	513,559	463,207	347,040	50,352	116,167	10.9	33.5	21.7	43.3	22.7	12.3	50.2
Benton County, AR	249,672	221,344	153,323	28,328	68,021	12.8	44.4	22.4	41.2	23.4	13.0	50.5
Madison County, AR	15,767	15,720	14,228	47	1,492	0.3	10.5	19.3	34.2	28.4	18.1	50.0
Washington County, AR	225,477	203,060	157,805	22,417	45,255	11.0	28.7	21.0	46.8	21.2	11.0	50.0
McDonald County, MO	22,643	23,083	21,684	-440	1,399	-1.9	6.5	21.3	37.0	27.5	14.2	49.3
Flagstaff, AZ Metro Area	139,097	134,437	116,320	4,660	18,117	3.5	15.6	17.9	47.9	22.8	11.5	50.6
Coconino County, AZ	139,097	134,437	116,320	4,660	18,117	3.5	15.6	17.9	47.9	22.8	11.5	50.6
Flint, MI Metro Area	410,849	425,790	436,213	-14,941	-10,423	-3.5	-2.4	19.0	37.0	28.0	16.1	51.8
Genesee County, MI	410,849	425,790	436,213	-14,941	-10,423	-3.5	-2.4	19.0	37.0	28.0	16.1	51.8
Florence, SC Metro Area	206,448	205,571	193,153	877	12,418	0.4	6.4	19.6	37.7	26.7	16.0	53.0
Darlington County, SC	67,548	68,683	67,444	-1,135	1,239	-1.7	1.8	18.7	36.4	27.9	17.1	52.8
Florence County, SC	138,900	136,888	125,709	2,012	11,179	1.5	8.9	20.0	38.3	26.2	15.5	53.1
Florence-Muscle Shoals, AL Metro Area	146,950	147,137	142,931	-187	4,206	-0.1	2.9	16.9	37.2	27.2	18.7	52.0
Colbert County, AL	54,354	54,428	54,979	-74	-551	-0.1		17.5	35.9	27.8	18.8	51.8
Lauderdale County, AL	92,596	92,709	87,952	-113	4,757	-0.1	5.4	16.6	37.9	26.8	18.7	52.1
Fond du Lac, WI Metro Area	101,973	101,633	97,284	340	4,349	0.3	4.5	18.0	36.3	28.8	17.0	50.9
Fond du Lac County, WI	101,973	101,633	97,284	340	4,349	0.3	4.5	18.0	36.3	28.8	17.0	50.9
Fort Collins, CO Metro Area	333,577	299,630	251,489	33,947	48,141	11.3	19.1	16.9	44.5	24.4	14.3	50.1
Larimer County, CO	333,577	299,630	251,489	33,947	48,141	11.3	19.1	16.9	44.5	24.4	14.3	50.1
Fort Smith, AR-OK Metro Area	280,241	280,515	255,404	-274	25,111	-0.1	9.8	20.0	37.9	26.3	15.8	50.7
Crawford County, AR	61,703	61,948	53,252	-245	8,696	-0.4	16.3	20.1	37.3	26.8	15.7	50.8

0 = represents zero or rounds to zero.
[1]The April 1, 2000 and 2010 population estimates bases reflect modifications to the census populations as documented in the Count Question Resolution program and geographic program revisions.
[2]Based on the April 1, 2010 estimates base and the July 1, 2015 estimates
[3]Based on the April 1, 2000 and April 1, 2010 estimates bases.

Table C-1. Population and Population Characteristics—*Continued*

Metropolitan statistical area, division, and component county	Population 2015 estimate (July 1)	Population 2010[1] (estimates base) (April 1)	Population 2000[1] (estimates base) (April 1)	Net change 2010–2015[2]	Net change 2000–2010[3]	Percent change 2010–2015[2]	Percent change 2000–2010[3]	Under 15 years	15 to 44 years	45 to 64 years	65 years and over	Percent female
Sebastian County, AR	127,780	125,744	115,101	2,036	10,643	1.6	9.2	20.2	39.1	25.9	14.7	51.1
Le Flore County, OK	49,605	50,384	48,099	-779	2,285	-1.5	4.8	20.0	36.5	26.2	17.3	49.9
Sequoyah County, OK	41,153	42,439	38,952	-1,286	3,487	-3.0	9.0	19.3	36.3	27.0	17.4	50.6
Fort Wayne, IN Metro Area	429,820	416,254	390,102	13,566	26,152	3.3	6.7	21.4	39.0	25.7	13.9	51.0
Allen County, IN	368,450	355,327	331,859	13,123	23,468	3.7	7.1	21.7	39.7	25.2	13.4	51.2
Wells County, IN	27,964	27,636	27,626	328	10	1.2	0.0	20.1	34.7	27.7	17.4	50.5
Whitley County, IN	33,406	33,291	30,617	115	2,674	0.3	8.7	19.1	35.7	28.9	16.3	50.1
Fresno, CA Metro Area	974,861	930,452	798,766	44,409	131,686	4.8	16.5	24.1	42.5	21.9	11.5	50.1
Fresno County, CA	974,861	930,452	798,766	44,409	131,686	4.8	16.5	24.1	42.5	21.9	11.5	50.1
Gadsden, AL Metro Area	103,057	104,427	103,448	-1,370	979	-1.3	0.9	17.8	36.9	27.5	17.7	51.7
Etowah County, AL	103,057	104,427	103,448	-1,370	979	-1.3	0.9	17.8	36.9	27.5	17.7	51.7
Gainesville, FL Metro Area	277,163	264,274	232,393	12,889	31,881	4.9	13.7	15.3	49.5	21.9	13.3	51.4
Alachua County, FL	259,964	247,335	217,964	12,629	29,371	5.1	13.5	15.2	50.4	21.5	12.9	51.6
Gilchrist County, FL	17,199	16,939	14,429	260	2,510	1.5	17.4	16.8	36.0	27.5	19.7	48.6
Gainesville, GA Metro Area	193,535	179,684	139,615	13,851	40,069	7.7	28.7	21.6	39.7	24.6	14.1	50.0
Hall County, GA	193,535	179,684	139,615	13,851	40,069	7.7	28.7	21.6	39.7	24.6	14.1	50.0
Gettysburg, PA Metro Area	102,295	101,417	91,207	878	10,210	0.9	11.2	16.8	35.1	29.3	18.8	50.6
Adams County, PA	102,295	101,417	91,207	878	10,210	0.9	11.2	16.8	35.1	29.3	18.8	50.6
Glens Falls, NY Metro Area	126,918	128,921	124,295	-2,003	4,626	-1.6	3.7	15.6	34.7	30.6	19.0	49.6
Warren County, NY	64,688	65,705	63,263	-1,017	2,442	-1.5	3.9	15.3	33.4	31.0	20.3	51.1
Washington County, NY	62,230	63,216	61,032	-986	2,184	-1.6	3.6	16.0	36.1	30.2	17.7	48.1
Goldsboro, NC Metro Area	124,132	122,623	113,449	1,509	9,174	1.2	8.1	20.1	39.1	25.8	15.0	50.8
Wayne County, NC	124,132	122,623	113,449	1,509	9,174	1.2	8.1	20.1	39.1	25.8	15.0	50.8
Grand Forks, ND-MN Metro Area	102,449	98,461	97,489	3,988	972	4.1	1.0	18.1	46.0	22.6	13.3	48.9
Polk County, MN	31,533	31,600	31,370	-67	230	-0.2	0.7	19.5	36.5	26.6	17.3	49.8
Grand Forks County, ND	70,916	66,861	66,119	4,055	742	6.1	1.1	17.4	50.3	20.7	11.6	48.5
Grand Island, NE Metro Area	85,066	81,850	77,735	3,216	4,115	3.9	5.3	21.9	37.0	25.4	15.7	49.6
Hall County, NE	61,680	58,607	53,577	3,073	5,030	5.2	9.4	22.8	38.4	24.4	14.4	49.6
Hamilton County, NE	9,190	9,114	9,408	76	-294	0.8	-3.1	19.4	34.1	28.2	18.3	49.7
Howard County, NE	6,409	6,274	6,561	135	-287	2.2	-4.4	19.9	32.1	27.2	20.8	49.4
Merrick County, NE	7,787	7,855	8,189	-68	-334	-0.9	-4.1	18.8	34.0	28.4	18.7	50.0
Grand Junction, CO Metro Area	148,513	146,723	116,939	1,790	29,784	1.2	25.5	18.6	38.2	25.8	17.4	50.4
Mesa County, CO	148,513	146,723	116,939	1,790	29,784	1.2	25.5	18.6	38.2	25.8	17.4	50.4
Grand Rapids-Wyoming, MI Metro Area	1,038,583	988,940	930,880	49,643	58,060	5.0	6.2	20.4	40.8	25.6	13.3	50.5
Barry County, MI	59,314	59,175	56,776	139	2,399	0.2	4.2	18.1	34.5	30.0	17.5	49.7
Kent County, MI	636,369	602,622	574,421	33,747	28,201	5.6	4.9	20.8	41.4	25.3	12.5	50.8
Montcalm County, MI	62,945	63,342	61,270	-397	2,072	-0.6	3.4	18.6	36.8	28.3	16.4	48.4
Ottawa County, MI	279,955	263,801	238,413	16,154	25,388	6.1	10.6	20.4	41.5	24.6	13.6	50.6
Grants Pass, OR Metro Area	84,745	82,713	75,729	2,032	6,984	2.5	9.2	16.0	30.6	28.2	25.2	51.2
Josephine County, OR	84,745	82,713	75,729	2,032	6,984	2.5	9.2	16.0	30.6	28.2	25.2	51.2
Great Falls, MT Metro Area	82,278	81,327	80,356	951	971	1.2	1.2	19.0	38.1	25.5	17.4	49.6
Cascade County, MT	82,278	81,327	80,356	951	971	1.2	1.2	19.0	38.1	25.5	17.4	49.6
Greeley, CO Metro Area	285,174	252,831	180,766	32,343	72,065	12.8	39.9	22.5	41.9	24.2	11.4	49.6
Weld County, CO	285,174	252,831	180,766	32,343	72,065	12.8	39.9	22.5	41.9	24.2	11.4	49.6
Green Bay, WI Metro Area	316,519	306,241	282,489	10,278	23,752	3.4	8.4	19.6	38.2	27.7	14.5	50.1
Brown County, WI	258,718	248,007	226,633	10,711	21,374	4.3	9.4	20.2	39.5	26.8	13.5	50.4
Kewaunee County, WI	20,366	20,574	20,199	-208	375		1.9	17.7	33.2	29.9	19.3	49.4
Oconto County, WI	37,435	37,660	35,657	-225	2,003	-0.6	5.6	16.7	31.6	32.7	18.9	49.0
Greensboro-High Point, NC Metro Area	752,157	723,798	643,369	28,359	80,429	3.9	12.5	18.6	39.4	26.9	15.1	52.0
Guilford County, NC	517,600	488,406	420,848	29,194	67,558	6.0	16.1	18.8	41.1	26.0	14.1	52.5
Randolph County, NC	142,799	141,752	130,503	1,047	11,249	0.7	8.6	19.0	36.3	28.3	16.4	50.5
Rockingham County, NC	91,758	93,640	92,018	-1,882	1,622	-2.0	1.8	17.0	34.2	30.1	18.7	51.7
Greenville, NC Metro Area	175,842	168,148	133,759	7,694	34,389	4.6	25.7	18.4	47.4	22.5	11.7	52.8
Pitt County, NC	175,842	168,148	133,759	7,694	34,389	4.6	25.7	18.4	47.4	22.5	11.7	52.8
Greenville-Anderson-Mauldin, SC Metro Area	874,869	824,107	725,544	50,762	98,563	6.2	13.6	18.8	39.4	26.2	15.5	51.3
Anderson County, SC	194,692	187,123	165,734	7,569	21,389	4.0	12.9	19.0	36.6	27.1	17.4	51.8
Greenville County, SC	491,863	451,219	379,648	40,644	71,571	9.0	18.9	19.5	39.8	26.1	14.6	51.4
Laurens County, SC	66,623	66,539	69,407	84	-2,868	0.1	-4.1	18.2	36.6	28.0	17.2	51.4
Pickens County, SC	121,691	119,226	110,755	2,465	8,471	2.1	7.6	16.0	43.9	24.5	15.5	50.2
Gulfport-Biloxi-Pascagoula, MS Metro Area	389,255	370,787	363,961	18,468	6,826	5.0	1.9	20.0	39.3	26.2	14.5	50.7
Hancock County, MS	46,420	44,014	42,945	2,406	1,069	5.5	2.5	17.8	35.4	29.2	17.6	50.7
Harrison County, MS	201,410	187,105	189,577	14,305	-2,472	7.6	-1.3	20.5	40.7	25.1	13.7	50.6
Jackson County, MS	141,425	139,668	131,439	1,757	8,229	1.3	6.3	19.9	38.6	26.9	14.6	50.9
Hagerstown-Martinsburg, MD-WV Metro Area	261,486	251,602	207,810	9,884	43,792	3.9	21.1	18.9	38.3	27.7	15.1	49.7
Washington County, MD	149,585	147,430	131,911	2,155	15,519	1.5	11.8	18.2	37.8	27.8	16.2	49.1
Berkeley County, WV	111,901	104,172	75,899	7,729	28,273	7.4	37.3	19.9	38.9	27.6	13.6	50.6
Hammond, LA Metro Area	128,755	121,101	100,481	7,654	20,620	6.3	20.5	20.7	41.4	24.8	13.2	51.5
Tangipahoa Parish, LA	128,755	121,101	100,481	7,654	20,620	6.3	20.5	20.7	41.4	24.8	13.2	51.5
Hanford-Corcoran, CA Metro Area	150,965	152,982	129,470	-2,017	23,512	-1.3	18.2	23.1	46.0	21.5	9.4	44.8
Kings County, CA	150,965	152,982	129,470	-2,017	23,512	-1.3	18.2	23.1	46.0	21.5	9.4	44.8
Harrisburg-Carlisle, PA Metro Area	565,006	549,473	509,011	15,533	40,462	2.8	7.9	17.7	38.0	27.8	16.5	50.9
Cumberland County, PA	246,338	235,408	213,605	10,930	21,803	4.6	10.2	16.8	38.6	27.2	17.4	50.5
Dauphin County, PA	272,983	268,100	251,770	4,883	16,330	1.8	6.5	18.5	37.9	28.0	15.6	51.5
Perry County, PA	45,685	45,965	43,636	-280	2,329	-0.6	5.3	17.6	35.5	30.5	16.4	49.6
Harrisonburg, VA Metro Area	131,131	125,217	108,215	5,914	17,002	4.7	15.7	16.4	46.2	23.0	14.4	51.3

0 = represents zero or rounds to zero.
[1]The April 1, 2000 and 2010 population estimates bases reflect modifications to the census populations as documented in the Count Question Resolution program and geographic program revisions.
[2]Based on the April 1, 2010 estimates base and the July 1, 2015 estimates
[3]Based on the April 1, 2000 and April 1, 2010 estimates bases.

Table C-1. Population and Population Characteristics—*Continued*

Metropolitan statistical area, division, and component county	Population 2015 estimate (July 1)	Population 2010[1] (estimates base) (April 1)	Population 2000[1] (estimates base) (April 1)	Net change 2010–2015[2]	Net change 2000–2010[3]	Percent change 2010–2015[2]	Percent change 2000–2010[3]	Percent in each age group, 2015 — Under 15 years	15 to 44 years	45 to 64 years	65 years and over	Percent female
Rockingham County, VA	78,593	76,310	67,825	2,283	8,485	3.0	12.5	18.2	36.2	27.4	18.3	50.9
Harrisonburg city, VA	52,538	48,907	40,390	3,631	8,517	7.4	21.1	13.8	61.1	16.6	8.5	52.0
Hartford-West Hartford-East Hartford, CT Metro Area	1,211,324	1,212,387	1,148,649	-1,063	63,738	-0.1	5.5	16.8	38.6	28.6	16.0	51.2
Hartford County, CT	895,841	894,029	857,184	1,812	36,845	0.2	4.3	17.5	38.5	28.1	15.9	51.4
Middlesex County, CT	164,063	165,676	155,088	-1,613	10,588		6.8	15.1	34.9	31.8	18.3	51.2
Tolland County, CT	151,420	152,682	136,377	-1,262	16,305	-0.8	12.0	14.3	43.6	27.9	14.3	49.9
Hattiesburg, MS Metro Area	148,839	142,857	123,922	5,982	18,935	4.2	15.3	20.2	43.7	23.2	13.0	52.1
Forrest County, MS	75,944	74,932	71,934	1,012	2,998	1.4	4.2	19.5	45.4	22.0	13.1	52.4
Lamar County, MS	60,618	55,675	39,877	4,943	15,798	8.9	39.6	21.2	43.1	23.9	11.9	51.9
Perry County, MS	12,277	12,250	12,111	27	139	0.2	1.1	19.3	36.0	27.1	17.5	51.2
Hickory-Lenoir-Morganton, NC Metro Area	362,510	365,492	341,854	-2,982	23,638	-0.8	6.9	17.3	35.9	28.9	17.8	50.5
Alexander County, NC	37,325	37,193	33,566	132	3,627	0.4	10.8	16.9	35.2	28.5	19.5	49.1
Burke County, NC	88,842	90,914	89,163	-2,072	1,751	-2.3	2.0	15.7	35.8	29.6	19.0	50.4
Caldwell County, NC	81,287	83,029	77,425	-1,742	5,604	-2.1	7.2	16.8	35.2	29.8	18.2	50.6
Catawba County, NC	155,056	154,356	141,700	700	12,656	0.5	8.9	18.6	36.6	28.2	16.6	50.9
Hilton Head Island-Bluffton-Beaufort, SC Metro Area	207,413	187,010	141,603	20,403	45,407	10.9	32.1	16.9	34.9	24.4	23.8	50.6
Beaufort County, SC	179,589	162,233	120,931	17,356	41,302	10.7	34.2	16.7	34.4	24.0	24.8	50.8
Jasper County, SC	27,824	24,777	20,672	3,047	4,105	12.3	19.9	18.0	38.2	26.8	17.1	49.0
Hinesville, GA Metro Area	80,198	77,917	71,934	2,281	5,983	2.9	8.3	24.7	47.8	19.5	8.1	48.7
Liberty County, GA	62,467	63,472	61,661	-1,005	1,811	-1.6	2.9	24.9	48.3	18.6	8.2	48.4
Long County, GA	17,731	14,445	10,273	3,286	4,172	22.7	40.6	23.8	45.7	22.7	7.9	49.7
Homosassa Springs, FL Metro Area	141,058	141,236	118,106	-178	23,130	-0.1	19.6	12.0	24.3	28.1	35.6	51.6
Citrus County, FL	141,058	141,236	118,106	-178	23,130	-0.1	19.6	12.0	24.3	28.1	35.6	51.6
Hot Springs, AR Metro Area	97,177	96,000	88,122	1,177	7,878	1.2	8.9	17.0	33.7	27.3	22.0	51.8
Garland County, AR	97,177	96,000	88,122	1,177	7,878	1.2	8.9	17.0	33.7	27.3	22.0	51.8
Houma-Thibodaux, LA Metro Area	212,297	208,176	194,517	4,121	13,659	2.0	7.0	20.7	39.7	26.2	13.4	50.6
Lafourche Parish, LA	98,325	96,592	89,745	1,733	6,847	1.8	7.6	19.6	39.7	26.6	14.0	50.8
Terrebonne Parish, LA	113,972	111,584	104,772	2,388	6,812	2.1	6.5	21.6	39.8	25.8	12.9	50.5
Houston-The Woodlands-Sugar Land, TX Metro Area	6,656,947	5,920,493	4,693,520	736,454	1,226,973	12.4	26.1	22.5	43.2	24.2	10.1	50.3
Austin County, TX	29,563	28,411	23,586	1,152	4,825	4.1	20.5	19.7	34.5	27.8	18.0	50.4
Brazoria County, TX	346,312	313,127	241,805	33,185	71,322	10.6	29.5	22.3	41.4	25.2	11.1	49.3
Chambers County, TX	38,863	35,096	26,006	3,767	9,090	10.7	35.0	22.6	41.0	25.5	10.9	49.7
Fort Bend County, TX	716,087	584,832	354,286	131,255	230,546	22.4	65.1	22.8	41.1	26.1	9.9	50.8
Galveston County, TX	322,225	291,304	250,178	30,921	41,126	10.6	16.4	20.3	39.4	27.2	13.1	50.6
Harris County, TX	4,538,028	4,093,076	3,401,139	444,952	691,937	10.9	20.3	22.7	44.5	23.3	9.4	50.3
Liberty County, TX	79,654	75,646	70,196	4,008	5,450	5.3	7.8	20.9	40.2	26.0	12.9	50.8
Montgomery County, TX	537,559	455,764	293,779	81,795	161,985	17.9	55.1	22.0	39.4	26.3	12.3	50.4
Waller County, TX	48,656	43,237	32,545	5,419	10,692	12.5	32.9	20.0	46.2	22.1	11.7	50.0
Huntington-Ashland, WV-KY-OH Metro Area	361,580	364,930	362,350	-3,350	2,580	-0.9	0.7	17.7	37.1	27.4	17.9	51.0
Boyd County, KY	48,325	49,538	49,721	-1,213	-183	-2.4	-0.4	17.4	36.1	28.3	18.3	50.2
Greenup County, KY	36,068	36,914	36,927	-846	-13	-2.3	0.0	18.0	34.3	28.2	19.5	51.5
Lawrence County, OH	61,109	62,450	62,330	-1,341	120	-2.1	0.2	18.1	36.2	28.1	17.6	51.1
Cabell County, WV	96,844	96,316	96,783	528	-467	0.5	-0.5	16.9	41.1	24.6	17.3	51.2
Lincoln County, WV	21,415	21,720	22,107	-305	-387	-1.4	-1.8	18.6	34.4	29.1	18.0	50.2
Putnam County, WV	56,848	55,508	51,563	1,340	3,945	2.4	7.7	18.6	35.8	28.5	17.1	50.8
Wayne County, WV	40,971	42,484	42,919	-1,513	-435	-3.6		17.3	35.4	28.5	18.8	51.3
Huntsville, AL Metro Area	444,752	417,593	342,666	27,159	74,927	6.5	21.9	18.4	39.5	28.0	14.1	50.9
Limestone County, AL	91,663	82,782	65,668	8,881	17,114	10.7	26.1	19.0	39.0	27.8	14.2	49.7
Madison County, AL	353,089	334,811	276,998	18,278	57,813	5.5	20.9	18.3	39.7	28.0	14.1	51.2
Idaho Falls, ID Metro Area	139,747	133,337	104,559	6,410	28,778	4.8	27.5	26.7	39.1	21.8	12.4	50.3
Bonneville County, ID	110,089	104,304	82,545	5,785	21,759	5.5	26.4	26.3	39.4	21.8	12.5	50.5
Butte County, ID	2,501	2,893	2,897	-392	-4	-13.5	-0.1	20.2	31.5	27.9	20.5	50.0
Jefferson County, ID	27,157	26,140	19,117	1,017	7,023	3.9	36.7	28.8	38.6	21.3	11.3	49.5
Indianapolis-Carmel-Anderson, IN Metro Area	1,988,817	1,888,082	1,658,439	100,735	229,643	5.3	13.8	20.9	40.6	25.8	12.7	51.1
Boone County, IN	63,344	56,638	46,145	6,706	10,493	11.8	22.7	22.0	37.8	27.4	12.8	50.5
Brown County, IN	14,977	15,242	14,953	-265	289	-1.7	1.9	15.4	30.4	32.4	21.8	50.3
Hamilton County, IN	309,697	274,569	182,763	35,128	91,806	12.8	50.2	23.3	39.6	26.2	10.9	51.1
Hancock County, IN	72,520	70,045	55,439	2,475	14,606	3.5	26.3	19.1	37.0	28.4	15.4	51.0
Hendricks County, IN	158,192	145,412	104,051	12,780	41,361	8.8	39.8	21.1	39.7	26.5	12.7	50.2
Johnson County, IN	149,633	139,867	115,181	9,766	24,686	7.0	21.4	20.6	39.6	25.7	14.1	50.7
Madison County, IN	129,723	131,636	133,322	-1,913	-1,686	-1.5	-1.3	18.0	37.7	27.0	17.2	50.2
Marion County, IN	939,020	903,389	860,440	35,631	42,949	3.9	5.0	21.1	42.8	24.6	11.5	51.8
Morgan County, IN	69,648	68,939	66,705	709	2,234	1.0	3.3	18.8	35.8	29.7	15.6	50.5
Putnam County, IN	37,585	37,952	36,060	-367	1,892		5.2	15.8	41.6	27.0	15.6	47.0
Shelby County, IN	44,478	44,393	43,380	85	1,013	0.2	2.3	18.9	36.0	29.2	15.9	50.5
Iowa City, IA Metro Area	166,498	152,586	131,662	13,912	20,924	9.1	15.9	17.7	49.3	21.5	11.5	50.3
Johnson County, IA	144,251	130,882	110,983	13,369	19,899	10.2	17.9	17.2	51.7	20.7	10.4	50.3
Washington County, IA	22,247	21,704	20,679	543	1,025	2.5	5.0	20.6	33.9	26.8	18.7	50.6
Ithaca, NY Metro Area	104,926	101,594	96,487	3,332	5,107	3.3	5.3	12.1	53.1	22.0	12.7	50.8
Tompkins County, NY	104,926	101,594	96,487	3,332	5,107	3.3	5.3	12.1	53.1	22.0	12.7	50.8
Jackson, MI Metro Area	159,494	160,248	158,426	-754	1,822	-0.5	1.2	17.8	37.3	28.5	16.4	48.9
Jackson County, MI	159,494	160,248	158,426	-754	1,822	-0.5	1.2	17.8	37.3	28.5	16.4	48.9
Jackson, MS Metro Area	578,777	567,645	525,407	11,132	42,238	2.0	8.0	20.5	41.0	25.3	13.2	52.1
Copiah County, MS	28,773	29,449	28,763	-676	686	-2.3	2.4	19.8	37.7	26.7	15.9	51.6
Hinds County, MS	242,891	245,365	250,752	-2,474	-5,387		-2.1	20.7	42.3	24.5	12.5	53.3

0 = represents zero or rounds to zero.
[1]The April 1, 2000 and 2010 population estimates bases reflect modifications to the census populations as documented in the Count Question Resolution program and geographic program revisions.
[2]Based on the April 1, 2010 estimates base and the July 1, 2015 estimates
[3]Based on the April 1, 2000 and April 1, 2010 estimates bases.

Table C-1. Population and Population Characteristics—*Continued*

Metropolitan statistical area, division, and component county	Population 2015 estimate (July 1)	Population 2010[1] (estimates base) (April 1)	Population 2000[1] (estimates base) (April 1)	Net change 2010–2015[2]	Net change 2000–2010[3]	Percent change 2010–2015[2]	Percent change 2000–2010[3]	Percent in each age group, 2015 Under 15 years	15 to 44 years	45 to 64 years	65 years and over	Percent female
Madison County, MS	103,465	95,203	74,711	8,262	20,492	8.7	27.4	20.9	39.9	26.5	12.7	52.2
Rankin County, MS	149,039	142,061	115,403	6,978	26,658	4.9	23.1	19.9	40.9	25.5	13.7	51.7
Simpson County, MS	27,222	27,502	27,634	-280	-132		-0.5	20.8	36.8	26.4	16.1	51.3
Yazoo County, MS	27,387	28,065	28,144	-678	-79	-2.4	-0.3	20.2	43.2	23.8	12.8	44.9
Jackson, TN Metro Area	129,682	130,009	121,969	-327	8,040	-0.3	6.6	19.0	38.8	26.3	15.9	52.7
Chester County, TN	17,471	17,131	15,540	340	1,591	2.0	10.2	17.5	41.1	24.4	17.0	52.2
Crockett County, TN	14,601	14,584	14,529	17	55	0.1	0.4	19.7	36.0	26.6	17.7	52.3
Madison County, TN	97,610	98,294	91,900	-684	6,394	-0.7	7.0	19.1	38.8	26.6	15.5	52.8
Jacksonville, FL Metro Area	1,449,481	1,345,596	1,122,821	103,885	222,775	7.7	19.8	18.8	39.8	26.9	14.6	51.3
Baker County, FL	27,420	27,115	22,255	305	4,860	1.1	21.8	20.2	39.9	26.6	13.3	47.7
Clay County, FL	203,967	190,865	140,788	13,102	50,077	6.9	35.6	19.1	38.4	27.9	14.6	50.8
Duval County, FL	913,010	864,263	778,896	48,747	85,367	5.6	11.0	19.1	41.9	25.9	13.1	51.5
Nassau County, FL	78,444	73,314	57,645	5,130	15,669	7.0	27.2	16.3	33.5	29.5	20.7	50.9
St. Johns County, FL	226,640	190,039	123,237	36,601	66,802	19.3	54.2	17.7	34.7	29.0	18.6	51.2
Jacksonville, NC Metro Area	186,311	177,772	150,418	8,539	27,354	4.8	18.2	22.3	52.8	16.0	8.9	45.7
Onslow County, NC	186,311	177,772	150,418	8,539	27,354	4.8	18.2	22.3	52.8	16.0	8.9	45.7
Janesville-Beloit, WI Metro Area	161,448	160,331	152,315	1,117	8,016	0.7	5.3	19.5	37.5	27.6	15.5	50.9
Rock County, WI	161,448	160,331	152,315	1,117	8,016	0.7	5.3	19.5	37.5	27.6	15.5	50.9
Jefferson City, MO Metro Area	151,145	149,807	140,033	1,338	9,774	0.9	7.0	18.7	39.3	27.2	14.9	49.0
Callaway County, MO	44,834	44,332	40,762	502	3,570	1.1	8.8	17.4	40.5	27.5	14.6	49.1
Cole County, MO	76,720	75,983	71,423	737	4,560	1.0	6.4	19.0	39.3	27.1	14.6	49.4
Moniteau County, MO	15,963	15,607	14,829	356	778	2.3	5.2	20.7	38.9	25.4	15.0	46.8
Osage County, MO	13,628	13,885	13,019	-257	866	-1.9	6.7	18.9	35.7	28.1	17.3	48.2
Johnson City, TN Metro Area	200,648	198,716	181,585	1,932	17,131	1.0	9.4	15.9	38.0	27.4	18.6	51.0
Carter County, TN	56,486	57,424	56,731	-938	693	-1.6	1.2	15.6	35.0	29.1	20.3	50.9
Unicoi County, TN	17,860	18,313	17,666	-453	647	-2.5	3.7	15.2	32.8	29.8	22.1	50.9
Washington County, TN	126,302	122,979	107,188	3,323	15,791	2.7	14.7	16.1	40.1	26.4	17.4	51.1
Johnstown, PA Metro Area	136,411	143,674	152,555	-7,263	-8,881	-5.1	-5.8	15.8	34.2	29.0	20.9	50.8
Cambria County, PA	136,411	143,674	152,555	-7,263	-8,881	-5.1	-5.8	15.8	34.2	29.0	20.9	50.8
Jonesboro, AR Metro Area	128,394	121,026	107,756	7,368	13,270	6.1	12.3	20.5	42.1	23.5	13.9	51.4
Craighead County, AR	104,354	96,443	82,139	7,911	14,304	8.2	17.4	20.8	43.3	22.8	13.1	51.4
Poinsett County, AR	24,040	24,583	25,617	-543	-1,034	-2.2	-4.0	19.3	36.6	26.6	17.5	51.4
Joplin, MO Metro Area	177,211	175,516	157,300	1,695	18,216	1.0	11.6	20.8	38.9	25.0	15.3	50.9
Jasper County, MO	118,596	117,404	104,704	1,192	12,700	1.0	12.1	21.3	40.3	24.3	14.2	51.2
Newton County, MO	58,615	58,112	52,596	503	5,516	0.9	10.5	19.9	36.0	26.5	17.7	50.4
Kahului-Wailuku-Lahaina, HI Metro Area	164,726	154,925	128,237	9,801	26,688	6.3	20.8	18.6	37.7	27.8	15.9	49.6
Kalawao County, HI	89	90	147		-57	-1.1	-38.8	0.0	20.2	47.2	32.6	52.8
Maui County, HI	164,637	154,835	128,090	9,802	26,745	6.3	20.9	18.6	37.7	27.7	15.9	49.6
Kalamazoo-Portage, MI Metro Area	335,340	326,592	314,841	8,748	11,751	2.7	3.7	18.5	42.1	24.9	14.4	50.8
Kalamazoo County, MI	260,263	250,327	238,602	9,936	11,725	4.0	4.9	18.2	44.3	23.7	13.8	50.9
Van Buren County, MI	75,077	76,265	76,239	-1,188	26	-1.6	0.0	19.6	34.7	29.2	16.5	50.4
Kankakee, IL Metro Area	110,879	113,449	103,825	-2,570	9,624	-2.3	9.3	19.6	38.7	26.3	15.4	50.9
Kankakee County, IL	110,879	113,449	103,825	-2,570	9,624	-2.3	9.3	19.6	38.7	26.3	15.4	50.9
Kansas City, MO-KS Metro Area	2,087,471	2,009,338	1,811,788	78,133	197,550	3.9	10.9	20.6	39.6	26.2	13.7	50.9
Johnson County, KS	580,159	544,179	451,541	35,980	92,638	6.6	20.5	20.8	39.9	26.2	13.1	51.0
Leavenworth County, KS	79,315	76,227	68,684	3,088	7,543	4.1	11.0	20.0	40.8	26.2	13.1	46.5
Linn County, KS	9,536	9,656	9,541	-120	115	-1.2	1.2	18.7	32.2	28.1	21.0	50.5
Miami County, KS	32,553	32,783	28,340	-230	4,443	-0.7	15.7	20.4	34.6	29.3	15.7	50.3
Wyandotte County, KS	163,369	157,505	157,924	5,864	-419	3.7	-0.3	23.9	41.0	23.7	11.4	50.4
Bates County, MO	16,446	17,049	16,648	-603	401	-3.5	2.4	19.7	33.8	27.6	18.9	50.6
Caldwell County, MO	9,014	9,424	8,964	-410	460	-4.4	5.1	19.4	33.6	27.9	19.1	49.6
Cass County, MO	101,603	99,475	82,123	2,128	17,352	2.1	21.1	20.1	36.8	27.2	15.9	51.1
Clay County, MO	235,637	221,874	183,941	13,763	37,933	6.2	20.6	20.6	40.4	25.9	13.1	51.0
Clinton County, MO	20,609	20,743	19,002	-134	1,741	-0.6	9.2	19.2	35.0	28.2	17.6	49.4
Jackson County, MO	687,623	674,231	654,941	13,392	19,290	2.0	2.9	20.2	40.1	25.9	13.8	51.6
Lafayette County, MO	32,701	33,381	32,939	-680	442	-2.0	1.3	18.7	35.1	28.0	18.3	50.4
Platte County, MO	96,096	89,317	73,826	6,779	15,491	7.6	21.0	19.5	39.6	27.6	13.3	50.6
Ray County, MO	22,810	23,494	23,374	-684	120	-2.9	0.5	18.5	34.8	29.0	17.6	49.8
Kennewick-Richland, WA Metro Area	279,116	253,340	191,851	25,776	61,489	10.2	32.1	24.2	40.5	23.3	12.0	49.3
Benton County, WA	190,309	175,177	142,473	15,132	32,704	8.6	23.0	22.2	39.0	25.1	13.8	49.8
Franklin County, WA	88,807	78,163	49,378	10,644	28,785	13.6	58.3	28.4	43.7	19.6	8.3	48.1
Killeen-Temple, TX Metro Area	431,032	405,303	330,726	25,729	74,577	6.3	22.5	23.0	46.1	20.5	10.4	50.0
Bell County, TX	334,941	310,238	238,000	24,703	72,238	8.0	30.4	23.7	45.9	20.3	10.1	50.0
Coryell County, TX	75,503	75,388	74,899	115	489	0.2	0.7	20.9	50.2	19.6	9.3	50.3
Lampasas County, TX	20,588	19,677	17,827	911	1,850	4.6	10.4	19.0	34.8	27.8	18.5	50.8
Kingsport-Bristol-Bristol, TN-VA Metro Area	307,120	309,542	298,564	-2,422	10,978	-0.8	3.7	16.0	34.3	29.0	20.6	51.2
Hawkins County, TN	56,471	56,836	53,582	-365	3,254	-0.6	6.1	16.7	34.3	29.2	19.8	50.8
Sullivan County, TN	156,791	156,823	153,089	-32	3,734	0.0	2.4	16.0	34.3	29.0	20.7	51.5
Scott County, VA	22,126	23,172	23,395	-1,046	-223	-4.5		15.3	33.2	29.3	22.2	49.8
Washington County, VA	54,591	54,870	51,152	-279	3,718	-0.5	7.3	15.6	34.2	29.5	20.8	50.8
Bristol city, VA	17,141	17,841	17,346	-700	495	-3.9	2.9	16.1	37.1	26.9	19.9	52.5
Kingston, NY Metro Area	180,143	182,531	177,726	-2,388	4,805	-1.3	2.7	14.8	37.0	30.3	17.9	50.3
Ulster County, NY	180,143	182,531	177,726	-2,388	4,805	-1.3	2.7	14.8	37.0	30.3	17.9	50.3
Knoxville, TN Metro Area	861,424	837,579	748,223	23,845	89,348	2.8	11.9	17.2	38.2	27.3	17.3	51.1
Anderson County, TN	75,749	75,126	71,470	623	3,656	0.8	5.1	17.2	35.0	28.6	19.2	51.5
Blount County, TN	127,253	123,016	105,824	4,237	17,192	3.4	16.2	17.0	35.4	28.8	18.9	51.5
Campbell County, TN	39,752	40,716	39,839	-964	877	-2.4	2.2	17.0	35.0	28.2	19.8	51.4

0 = represents zero or rounds to zero.
[1]The April 1, 2000 and 2010 population estimates bases reflect modifications to the census populations as documented in the Count Question Resolution program and geographic program revisions.
[2]Based on the April 1, 2010 estimates base and the July 1, 2015 estimates
[3]Based on the April 1, 2000 and April 1, 2010 estimates bases.

Table C-1. Population and Population Characteristics—*Continued*

Metropolitan statistical area, division, and component county	2015 estimate (July 1)	2010[1] (estimates base) (April 1)	2000[1] (estimates base) (April 1)	Net change 2010–2015[2]	Net change 2000–2010[3]	Percent change 2010–2015[2]	Percent change 2000–2010[3]	Under 15 years	15 to 44 years	45 to 64 years	65 years and over	Percent female
Grainger County, TN	22,846	22,652	20,610	194	2,042	0.9	9.9	16.9	34.1	29.9	19.1	49.7
Knox County, TN	451,324	432,234	381,884	19,090	50,350	4.4	13.2	17.7	41.7	25.8	14.8	51.4
Loudon County, TN	51,130	48,559	39,086	2,571	9,473	5.3	24.2	16.3	30.7	27.8	25.1	50.9
Morgan County, TN	21,498	21,987	19,754	-489	2,233	-2.2	11.3	15.9	39.0	28.7	16.4	45.4
Roane County, TN	52,753	54,180	51,921	-1,427	2,259	-2.6	4.4	15.6	32.1	30.6	21.8	50.9
Union County, TN	19,119	19,109	17,843	10	1,266	0.1	7.1	18.7	35.2	29.2	16.9	50.4
Kokomo, IN Metro Area	82,556	82,752	84,961	-196	-2,209	-0.2	-2.6	18.7	35.5	27.4	18.4	51.6
Howard County, IN	82,556	82,752	84,961	-196	-2,209	-0.2	-2.6	18.7	35.5	27.4	18.4	51.6
La Crosse-Onalaska, WI-MN Metro Area	136,985	133,665	126,881	3,320	6,784	2.5	5.3	16.9	41.9	25.4	15.8	50.9
Houston County, MN	18,773	19,027	19,725	-254	-698	-1.3	-3.5	17.9	32.1	30.3	19.8	50.4
La Crosse County, WI	118,212	114,638	107,156	3,574	7,482	3.1	7.0	16.7	43.4	24.7	15.2	51.0
Lafayette, LA Metro Area	490,488	466,750	424,983	23,738	41,767	5.1	9.8	20.9	40.9	25.5	12.7	51.2
Acadia Parish, LA	62,577	61,773	58,833	804	2,940	1.3	5.0	22.1	38.2	25.9	13.8	51.5
Iberia Parish, LA	74,103	73,240	73,277	863	-37	1.2	-0.1	21.9	38.3	26.2	13.6	51.1
Lafayette Parish, LA	240,098	221,571	190,234	18,527	31,337	8.4	16.5	20.1	43.8	24.6	11.5	51.1
St. Martin Parish, LA	53,835	52,167	48,535	1,668	3,632	3.2	7.5	20.5	38.7	27.2	13.6	50.7
Vermilion Parish, LA	59,875	57,999	54,104	1,876	3,895	3.2	7.2	21.6	37.9	26.3	14.2	51.4
Lafayette-West Lafayette, IN Metro Area	214,363	201,798	178,549	12,565	23,249	6.2	13.0	17.7	49.8	21.1	11.4	49.1
Benton County, IN	8,681	8,836	9,427	-155	-591	-1.8	-6.3	20.9	34.9	27.9	16.3	50.1
Carroll County, IN	19,856	20,159	20,168	-303	-9	-1.5	0.0	18.2	35.0	28.7	18.2	50.2
Tippecanoe County, IN	185,826	172,803	148,954	13,023	23,849	7.5	16.0	17.5	52.1	19.9	10.5	48.9
Lake Charles, LA Metro Area	205,605	199,629	193,571	5,976	6,058	3.0	3.1	20.6	39.8	25.6	14.0	51.2
Calcasieu Parish, LA	198,788	192,770	183,606	6,018	9,164	3.1	5.0	20.6	39.9	25.5	14.0	51.2
Cameron Parish, LA	6,817	6,859	9,965	-42	-3,106	-0.6	-31.2	18.2	37.2	29.6	15.1	50.0
Lake Havasu City-Kingman, AZ Metro Area	204,737	200,186	154,981	4,551	45,205	2.3	29.2	14.9	29.3	28.1	27.7	49.7
Mohave County, AZ	204,737	200,186	154,981	4,551	45,205	2.3	29.2	14.9	29.3	28.1	27.7	49.7
Lakeland-Winter Haven, FL Metro Area	650,092	602,095	483,888	47,997	118,207	8.0	24.4	18.7	36.8	24.8	19.7	51.0
Polk County, FL	650,092	602,095	483,888	47,997	118,207	8.0	24.4	18.7	36.8	24.8	19.7	51.0
Lancaster, PA Metro Area	536,624	519,448	470,783	17,176	48,665	3.3	10.3	19.9	37.5	25.9	16.7	51.1
Lancaster County, PA	536,624	519,448	470,783	17,176	48,665	3.3	10.3	19.9	37.5	25.9	16.7	51.1
Lansing-East Lansing, MI Metro Area	472,276	464,032	447,845	8,244	16,187	1.8	3.6	17.1	43.7	25.3	13.9	51.2
Clinton County, MI	77,390	75,382	64,715	2,008	10,667	2.7	16.5	18.5	36.8	28.9	15.8	50.5
Eaton County, MI	108,801	107,759	103,721	1,042	4,038	1.0	3.9	17.4	37.1	28.7	16.9	51.1
Ingham County, MI	286,085	280,891	279,409	5,194	1,482	1.8	0.5	16.7	48.1	23.0	12.3	51.5
Laredo, TX Metro Area	269,721	250,304	193,124	19,417	57,180	7.8	29.6	28.5	43.2	19.4	8.9	51.1
Webb County, TX	269,721	250,304	193,124	19,417	57,180	7.8	29.6	28.5	43.2	19.4	8.9	51.1
Las Cruces, NM Metro Area	214,295	209,241	174,880	5,054	34,361	2.4	19.6	21.1	42.3	22.0	14.7	50.7
Doña Ana County, NM	214,295	209,241	174,880	5,054	34,361	2.4	19.6	21.1	42.3	22.0	14.7	50.7
Las Vegas-Henderson-Paradise, NV Metro Area	2,114,801	1,951,269	1,375,741	163,532	575,528	8.4	41.8	19.7	41.5	25.1	13.7	50.0
Clark County, NV	2,114,801	1,951,269	1,375,741	163,532	575,528	8.4	41.8	19.7	41.5	25.1	13.7	50.0
Lawrence, KS Metro Area	118,053	110,826	99,953	7,227	10,873	6.5	10.9	15.8	53.6	19.9	10.8	50.0
Douglas County, KS	118,053	110,826	99,953	7,227	10,873	6.5	10.9	15.8	53.6	19.9	10.8	50.0
Lawton, OK Metro Area	130,644	130,291	121,599	353	8,692	0.3	7.1	20.4	45.4	22.5	11.7	48.2
Comanche County, OK	124,648	124,098	114,996	550	9,102	0.4	7.9	20.4	45.9	22.3	11.4	48.1
Cotton County, OK	5,996	6,193	6,603	-197	-410	-3.2	-6.2	19.2	34.3	27.8	18.6	49.7
Lebanon, PA Metro Area	137,067	133,577	120,202	3,490	13,375	2.6	11.1	19.0	35.5	26.8	18.7	50.8
Lebanon County, PA	137,067	133,577	120,202	3,490	13,375	2.6	11.1	19.0	35.5	26.8	18.7	50.8
Lewiston, ID-WA Metro Area	62,153	60,888	57,971	1,265	2,917	2.1	5.0	17.5	35.4	27.1	20.0	50.8
Nez Perce County, ID	40,048	39,265	37,418	783	1,847	2.0	4.9	17.7	36.5	26.4	19.4	50.4
Asotin County, WA	22,105	21,623	20,553	482	1,070	2.2	5.2	17.1	33.2	28.5	21.2	51.5
Lewiston-Auburn, ME Metro Area	107,233	107,702	103,803	-469	3,899	-0.4	3.8	18.2	36.7	28.7	16.4	50.9
Androscoggin County, ME	107,233	107,702	103,803	-469	3,899	-0.4	3.8	18.2	36.7	28.7	16.4	50.9
Lexington-Fayette, KY Metro Area	500,535	472,099	408,411	28,436	63,688	6.0	15.6	18.6	43.5	25.1	12.8	51.0
Bourbon County, KY	20,116	19,985	19,360	131	625	0.7	3.2	18.7	35.6	28.0	17.8	51.3
Clark County, KY	35,757	35,613	33,180	144	2,433	0.4	7.3	18.6	36.6	28.1	16.6	51.4
Fayette County, KY	314,488	295,803	260,527	18,685	35,276	6.3	13.5	17.8	46.3	23.8	12.0	50.8
Jessamine County, KY	51,961	48,586	39,043	3,375	9,543	6.9	24.4	20.5	39.6	26.2	13.7	51.5
Scott County, KY	52,420	47,173	33,076	5,247	14,097	11.1	42.6	21.4	41.6	26.0	10.9	50.8
Woodford County, KY	25,793	24,939	23,225	854	1,714	3.4	7.4	18.1	35.3	30.1	16.4	52.1
Lima, OH Metro Area	104,425	106,331	108,464	-1,906	-2,133	-1.8	-2.0	19.2	38.1	26.4	16.3	49.7
Allen County, OH	104,425	106,331	108,464	-1,906	-2,133	-1.8	-2.0	19.2	38.1	26.4	16.3	49.7
Lincoln, NE Metro Area	323,578	302,157	266,798	21,421	35,359	7.1	13.3	19.5	44.8	23.0	12.8	49.8
Lancaster County, NE	306,468	285,407	250,307	21,061	35,100	7.4	14.0	19.5	45.1	22.8	12.5	49.8
Seward County, NE	17,110	16,750	16,491	360	259	2.1	1.6	19.2	38.4	25.4	17.0	48.5
Little Rock-North Little Rock-Conway, AR Metro Area	731,612	699,823	610,470	31,789	89,353	4.5	14.6	19.9	40.8	25.1	14.2	51.5
Faulkner County, AR	121,552	113,237	86,036	8,315	27,201	7.3	31.6	19.7	46.4	22.3	11.6	51.0
Grant County, AR	18,102	17,853	16,457	249	1,396	1.4	8.5	19.0	36.7	27.7	16.6	50.4
Lonoke County, AR	71,645	68,354	52,849	3,291	15,505	4.8	29.3	21.4	40.9	24.7	13.0	50.6
Perry County, AR	10,189	10,441	10,199	-252	242	-2.4	2.4	18.0	34.5	29.4	18.1	50.2
Pulaski County, AR	392,664	382,789	361,370	9,875	21,419	2.6	5.9	19.8	40.4	25.7	14.0	52.1
Saline County, AR	117,460	107,149	83,559	10,311	23,590	9.6	28.2	19.6	37.6	25.4	17.5	51.0
Logan, UT-ID Metro Area	133,857	125,442	102,722	8,415	22,720	6.7	22.1	26.2	48.0	16.4	9.3	50.1
Franklin County, ID	13,074	12,786	11,333	288	1,453	2.3	12.8	27.5	37.2	21.5	13.8	49.3
Cache County, UT	120,783	112,656	91,389	8,127	21,267	7.2	23.3	26.1	49.2	15.9	8.8	50.2
Longview, TX Metro Area	217,781	214,384	194,046	3,397	20,338	1.6	10.5	20.8	38.6	25.4	15.2	50.0
Gregg County, TX	124,108	121,764	111,328	2,344	10,436	1.9	9.4	21.8	39.7	24.2	14.3	51.0
Rusk County, TX	53,070	53,304	47,410	-234	5,894	-0.4	12.4	19.4	38.6	26.3	15.6	47.5

0 = represents zero or rounds to zero.
[1]The April 1, 2000 and 2010 population estimates bases reflect modifications to the census populations as documented in the Count Question Resolution program and geographic program revisions.
[2]Based on the April 1, 2010 estimates base and the July 1, 2015 estimates
[3]Based on the April 1, 2000 and April 1, 2010 estimates bases.

Table C-1. Population and Population Characteristics—*Continued*

Metropolitan statistical area, division, and component county	Population 2015 estimate (July 1)	Population 2010¹ (estimates base) (April 1)	Population 2000¹ (estimates base) (April 1)	Net change 2010–2015²	Net change 2000–2010³	Percent change 2010–2015²	Percent change 2000–2010³	Under 15 years	15 to 44 years	45 to 64 years	65 years and over	Percent female
Upshur County, TX	40,603	39,316	35,308	1,287	4,008	3.3	11.4	19.8	35.0	27.8	17.3	50.3
Longview, WA Metro Area	103,468	102,410	92,945	1,058	9,465	1.0	10.2	18.7	35.3	27.6	18.5	50.4
Cowlitz County, WA	103,468	102,410	92,945	1,058	9,465	1.0	10.2	18.7	35.3	27.6	18.5	50.4
Los Angeles-Long Beach-Anaheim, CA Metro Area	**13,340,068**	**12,828,966**	**12,365,597**	**511,102**	**463,369**	**4.0**	**3.7**	**18.5**	**43.1**	**25.6**	**12.8**	**50.7**
Anaheim-Santa Ana-Irvine, CA Division	*3,169,776*	*3,010,266*	*2,846,282*	*159,510*	*163,984*	*5.3*	*5.8*	*18.6*	*41.2*	*26.6*	*13.6*	*50.6*
Orange County, CA	3,169,776	3,010,266	2,846,282	159,510	163,984	5.3	5.8	18.6	41.2	26.6	13.6	50.6
Los Angeles-Long Beach-Glendale, CA Division	*10,170,292*	*9,818,700*	*9,519,315*	*351,592*	*299,385*	*3.6*	*3.1*	*18.5*	*43.6*	*25.3*	*12.6*	*50.7*
Los Angeles County, CA	10,170,292	9,818,700	9,519,315	351,592	299,385	3.6	3.1	18.5	43.6	25.3	12.6	50.7
Louisville/Jefferson County, KY-IN Metro Area	1,278,413	1,235,710	1,121,521	42,703	114,189	3.5	10.2	18.9	39.0	27.4	14.7	51.1
Clark County, IN	115,371	110,234	96,446	5,137	13,788	4.7	14.3	19.2	39.3	26.9	14.6	51.0
Floyd County, IN	76,778	74,578	70,815	2,200	3,763	2.9	5.3	18.9	37.7	28.5	14.9	51.4
Harrison County, IN	39,578	39,364	34,354	214	5,010	0.5	14.6	18.5	35.8	29.3	16.4	49.8
Scott County, IN	23,744	24,181	22,976	-437	1,205	-1.8	5.2	18.3	36.9	28.7	16.1	50.8
Washington County, IN	27,827	28,262	27,204	-435	1,058	-1.5	3.9	18.9	36.2	28.9	16.0	50.3
Bullitt County, KY	78,702	74,321	61,178	4,381	13,143	5.9	21.5	18.5	38.8	28.6	14.1	50.6
Henry County, KY	15,620	15,414	15,010	206	404	1.3	2.7	19.5	34.9	29.1	16.5	50.4
Jefferson County, KY	763,623	741,085	693,775	22,538	47,310	3.0	6.8	18.8	39.6	26.7	14.9	51.7
Oldham County, KY	64,875	60,335	46,495	4,540	13,840	7.5	29.8	20.3	38.5	29.2	12.0	46.9
Shelby County, KY	45,632	42,066	33,386	3,566	8,680	8.5	26.0	19.9	38.3	27.7	14.2	51.4
Spencer County, KY	17,894	17,061	11,699	833	5,362	4.9	45.8	19.0	36.9	31.4	12.8	49.5
Trimble County, KY	8,769	8,809	8,183	-40	626	-0.5	7.7	18.5	36.2	29.2	16.1	49.8
Lubbock, TX Metro Area	311,154	290,805	256,263	20,349	34,542	7.0	13.5	20.4	46.5	21.1	12.1	50.6
Crosby County, TX	5,977	6,059	7,072	-82	-1,013	-1.4	-14.3	22.1	35.4	24.0	18.6	50.5
Lubbock County, TX	299,453	278,831	242,644	20,622	36,187	7.4	14.9	20.3	46.9	20.9	11.9	50.6
Lynn County, TX	5,724	5,915	6,547	-191	-632	-3.2	-9.7	22.6	34.8	26.4	16.2	49.2
Lynchburg, VA Metro Area	259,950	252,659	222,120	7,291	30,539	2.9	13.7	16.4	39.3	26.6	17.8	51.8
Amherst County, VA	31,914	32,354	31,888	-440	466	-1.4	1.5	16.1	35.1	29.5	19.4	52.1
Appomattox County, VA	15,414	14,975	13,703	439	1,272	2.9	9.3	17.7	34.9	27.9	19.5	51.6
Bedford County, VA	77,724	74,871	60,226	2,853	14,645	3.8	24.3	16.4	32.4	31.3	19.9	50.6
Campbell County, VA	55,086	54,851	50,997	235	3,854	0.4	7.6	16.1	36.8	28.5	18.6	51.5
Lynchburg city, VA	79,812	75,608	65,306	4,204	10,302	5.6	15.8	16.5	50.2	19.3	14.1	53.2
Macon, GA Metro Area	230,096	232,293	222,479	-2,197	9,814	-0.9	4.4	19.8	38.2	26.6	15.4	52.2
Bibb County, GA	153,721	155,512	153,955	-1,791	1,557	-1.2	1.0	21.0	39.5	25.1	14.4	53.0
Crawford County, GA	12,388	12,630	12,481	-242	149	-1.9	1.2	17.2	34.1	31.1	17.5	49.3
Jones County, GA	28,494	28,669	23,691	-175	4,978	-0.6	21.0	19.1	37.0	27.8	16.0	51.7
Monroe County, GA	27,103	26,459	21,751	644	4,708	2.4	21.6	16.4	36.3	29.9	17.4	49.7
Twiggs County, GA	8,390	9,023	10,601	-633	-1,578	-7.0	-14.9	16.2	31.3	32.0	20.5	50.8
Madera, CA Metro Area	154,998	150,865	123,179	4,133	27,686	2.7	22.5	22.9	40.8	23.1	13.1	51.8
Madera County, CA	154,998	150,865	123,179	4,133	27,686	2.7	22.5	22.9	40.8	23.1	13.1	51.8
Madison, WI Metro Area	641,385	605,437	535,453	35,948	69,984	5.9	13.1	17.8	43.5	25.5	13.2	50.2
Columbia County, WI	56,743	56,833	52,510	-90	4,323	-0.2	8.2	17.9	35.7	29.7	16.8	49.4
Dane County, WI	523,643	488,075	426,475	35,568	61,600	7.3	14.4	17.6	45.5	24.6	12.3	50.4
Green County, WI	37,186	36,842	33,678	344	3,164	0.9	9.4	18.8	34.0	29.8	17.4	50.3
Iowa County, WI	23,813	23,687	22,790	126	897	0.5	3.9	19.2	33.2	30.2	17.4	49.9
Manchester-Nashua, NH Metro Area	406,678	400,721	380,856	5,957	19,865	1.5	5.2	17.4	38.2	30.0	14.4	50.3
Hillsborough County, NH	406,678	400,721	380,856	5,957	19,865	1.5	5.2	17.4	38.2	30.0	14.4	50.3
Manhattan, KS Metro Area	98,545	92,735	81,162	5,810	11,573	6.3	14.3	17.3	56.9	16.3	9.5	47.3
Pottawatomie County, KS	23,298	21,604	18,208	1,694	3,396	7.8	18.7	24.4	38.5	23.7	13.4	50.2
Riley County, KS	75,247	71,131	62,954	4,116	8,177	5.8	13.0	15.1	62.5	14.1	8.3	46.4
Mankato-North Mankato, MN Metro Area	99,134	96,740	85,711	2,394	11,029	2.5	12.9	17.2	46.7	22.5	13.6	49.7
Blue Earth County, MN	65,787	64,013	55,931	1,774	8,082	2.8	14.4	16.7	48.9	21.3	13.2	49.7
Nicollet County, MN	33,347	32,727	29,780	620	2,947	1.9	9.9	18.2	42.4	24.8	14.5	49.6
Mansfield, OH Metro Area	121,707	124,475	128,932	-2,768	-4,457	-2.2	-3.5	17.9	36.3	27.4	18.4	49.1
Richland County, OH	121,707	124,475	128,932	-2,768	-4,457	-2.2	-3.5	17.9	36.3	27.4	18.4	49.1
McAllen-Edinburg-Mission, TX Metro Area	842,304	774,774	569,099	67,530	205,675	8.7	36.1	28.0	42.4	18.9	10.7	51.2
Hidalgo County, TX	842,304	774,774	569,099	67,530	205,675	8.7	36.1	28.0	42.4	18.9	10.7	51.2
Medford, OR Metro Area	212,567	203,206	181,281	9,361	21,925	4.6	12.1	17.2	35.0	27.0	20.8	51.3
Jackson County, OR	212,567	203,206	181,281	9,361	21,925	4.6	12.1	17.2	35.0	27.0	20.8	51.3
Memphis, TN-MS-AR Metro Area	1,344,127	1,324,829	1,213,285	19,298	111,544	1.5	9.2	21.0	40.7	25.8	12.6	52.1
Crittenden County, AR	48,963	50,902	50,855	-1,939	47	-3.8	0.1	23.1	39.0	25.4	12.5	52.6
Benton County, MS	8,182	8,730	8,031	-548	699	-6.3	8.7	18.1	35.4	27.9	18.6	50.1
DeSoto County, MS	173,323	161,264	107,252	12,059	54,012	7.5	50.4	21.5	41.2	25.2	12.2	51.6
Marshall County, MS	35,916	37,139	34,947	-1,223	2,192	-3.3	6.3	18.2	37.5	28.6	15.6	50.6
Tate County, MS	28,296	28,882	25,386	-586	3,496	-2.0	13.8	19.4	39.6	25.8	15.3	51.9
Tunica County, MS	10,343	10,778	9,240	-435	1,538	-4.0	16.6	25.0	40.8	23.2	11.0	53.1
Fayette County, TN	39,165	38,413	28,799	752	9,614	2.0	33.4	16.6	33.3	30.6	19.5	50.7
Shelby County, TN	938,069	927,640	897,466	10,429	30,174	1.1	3.4	21.1	41.3	25.5	12.1	52.4
Tipton County, TN	61,870	61,081	51,309	789	9,772	1.3	19.0	20.5	38.9	27.1	13.5	50.8
Merced, CA Metro Area	268,455	255,798	211,178	12,657	44,620	4.9	21.1	24.9	43.1	21.4	10.6	49.5
Merced County, CA	268,455	255,798	211,178	12,657	44,620	4.9	21.1	24.9	43.1	21.4	10.6	49.5
Miami-Fort Lauderdale-West Palm Beach, FL Metro Area	**6,012,331**	**5,566,299**	**5,007,956**	**446,032**	**558,343**	**8.0**	**11.1**	**17.0**	**38.7**	**27.0**	**17.4**	**51.5**
Fort Lauderdale-Pompano Beach-Deerfield Beach, FL Division	*1,896,425*	*1,748,148*	*1,622,974*	*148,277*	*125,174*	*8.5*	*7.7*	*17.7*	*38.8*	*27.8*	*15.7*	*51.4*
Broward County, FL	1,896,425	1,748,148	1,622,974	148,277	125,174	8.5	7.7	17.7	38.8	27.8	15.7	51.4
Miami-Miami Beach-Kendall, FL Division	*2,693,117*	*2,498,017*	*2,253,793*	*195,100*	*244,224*	*7.8*	*10.8*	*17.0*	*40.7*	*26.7*	*15.6*	*51.5*
Miami-Dade County, FL	2,693,117	2,498,017	2,253,793	195,100	244,224	7.8	10.8	17.0	40.7	26.7	15.6	51.5

0 = represents zero or rounds to zero.
¹The April 1, 2000 and 2010 population estimates bases reflect modifications to the census populations as documented in the Count Question Resolution program and geographic program revisions.
²Based on the April 1, 2010 estimates base and the July 1, 2015 estimates
³Based on the April 1, 2000 and April 1, 2010 estimates bases.

Table C-1. Population and Population Characteristics—*Continued*

Metropolitan statistical area, division, and component county	2015 estimate (July 1)	2010[1] (estimates base) (April 1)	2000[1] (estimates base) (April 1)	Net change 2010–2015[2]	Net change 2000–2010[3]	Percent change 2010–2015[2]	Percent change 2000–2010[3]	Under 15 years	15 to 44 years	45 to 64 years	65 years and over	Percent female
West Palm Beach-Boca Raton-Delray Beach, FL Division...............	*1,422,789*	*1,320,134*	*1,131,189*	*102,655*	*188,945*	*7.8*	*16.7*	*16.0*	*34.6*	*26.5*	*23.0*	*51.7*
Palm Beach County, FL	1,422,789	1,320,134	1,131,189	102,655	188,945	7.8	16.7	16.0	34.6	26.5	23.0	51.7
Michigan City-La Porte, IN Metro Area.................	110,884	111,467	110,099	-583	1,368	-0.5	1.2	17.9	38.0	28.0	16.2	48.5
LaPorte County, IN	110,884	111,467	110,099	-583	1,368	-0.5	1.2	17.9	38.0	28.0	16.2	48.5
Midland, MI Metro Area	83,632	83,629	82,797	3	832	0.0	1.0	17.6	36.6	28.9	16.8	50.8
Midland County, MI	83,632	83,629	82,797	3	832	0.0	1.0	17.6	36.6	28.9	16.8	50.8
Midland, TX Metro Area	166,718	141,674	120,780	25,044	20,894	17.7	17.3	23.8	43.6	22.6	10.0	49.7
Martin County, TX	5,641	4,799	4,746	842	53	17.5	1.1	25.8	39.4	22.8	11.9	50.0
Midland County, TX	161,077	136,875	116,034	24,202	20,841	17.7	18.0	23.8	43.8	22.6	9.9	49.7
Milwaukee-Waukesha-West Allis, WI Metro Area..	1,575,747	1,555,954	1,500,788	19,793	55,166	1.3	3.7	19.5	39.5	26.8	14.2	51.3
Milwaukee County, WI	957,735	947,736	940,127	9,999	7,609	1.1	0.8	20.5	42.8	24.3	12.4	51.7
Ozaukee County, WI	87,850	86,395	82,322	1,455	4,073	1.7	4.9	17.5	34.0	30.5	18.0	50.8
Washington County, WI	133,674	131,885	117,529	1,789	14,356	1.4	12.2	18.4	34.6	30.8	16.3	50.3
Waukesha County, WI	396,488	389,938	360,810	6,550	29,128	1.7	8.1	17.8	34.5	30.6	17.0	50.9
Minneapolis-St. Paul-Bloomington, MN-WI Metro	3,524,583	3,348,857	3,032,340	175,726	316,517	5.2	10.4	20.0	40.4	26.9	12.7	50.5
Anoka County, MN	344,151	330,844	298,164	13,307	32,680	4.0	11.0	20.0	38.7	28.8	12.4	49.9
Carver County, MN	98,741	91,079	70,243	7,662	20,836	8.4	29.7	22.5	38.1	28.8	10.5	50.4
Chisago County, MN	54,293	53,887	41,116	406	12,771	0.8	31.1	18.6	37.0	30.0	14.4	48.3
Dakota County, MN	414,686	398,552	355,923	16,134	42,629	4.0	12.0	20.5	38.7	28.2	12.7	50.9
Hennepin County, MN	1,223,149	1,152,388	1,116,162	70,761	36,226	6.1	3.2	18.7	42.4	26.0	12.8	50.7
Isanti County, MN	38,429	37,816	31,280	613	6,536	1.6	20.9	19.7	36.5	28.7	15.1	49.5
Le Sueur County, MN	27,663	27,703	25,416	-40	2,287	-0.1	9.0	19.9	35.0	28.8	16.4	49.6
Mille Lacs County, MN	25,788	26,097	22,304	-309	3,793	-1.2	17.0	19.6	34.6	27.4	18.4	49.7
Ramsey County, MN	538,133	508,640	511,272	29,493	-2,632	5.8	-0.5	19.8	42.4	24.6	13.3	51.3
Scott County, MN	141,660	129,928	89,510	11,732	40,418	9.0	45.2	23.6	40.0	26.8	9.6	50.1
Sherburne County, MN	91,705	88,499	64,472	3,206	24,027	3.6	37.3	22.2	40.6	26.7	10.5	48.9
Sibley County, MN	14,875	15,226	15,361	-351	-135	-2.3	-0.9	19.6	34.2	28.4	17.9	49.6
Washington County, MN	251,597	238,134	201,214	13,463	36,920	5.7	18.3	20.4	37.2	29.0	13.4	50.5
Wright County, MN	131,311	124,700	90,022	6,611	34,678	5.3	38.5	23.8	38.4	26.1	11.6	49.6
Pierce County, WI	40,889	41,019	36,726	-130	4,293	-0.3	11.7	17.3	42.2	27.4	13.1	50.3
St. Croix County, WI	87,513	84,345	63,155	3,168	21,190	3.8	33.6	21.3	37.7	28.3	12.7	50.1
Missoula, MT Metro Area	114,181	109,299	95,803	4,882	13,496	4.5	14.1	16.3	45.3	24.3	14.2	49.8
Missoula County, MT	114,181	109,299	95,803	4,882	13,496	4.5	14.1	16.3	45.3	24.3	14.2	49.8
Mobile, AL Metro Area	415,395	413,143	399,887	2,252	13,256	0.5	3.3	19.7	39.3	26.0	14.9	52.2
Mobile County, AL	415,395	413,143	399,887	2,252	13,256	0.5	3.3	19.7	39.3	26.0	14.9	52.2
Modesto, CA Metro Area	538,388	514,451	446,850	23,937	67,601	4.7	15.1	22.5	41.3	23.7	12.5	50.5
Stanislaus County, CA	538,388	514,451	446,850	23,937	67,601	4.7	15.1	22.5	41.3	23.7	12.5	50.5
Monroe, LA Metro Area	179,238	176,502	170,054	2,736	6,448	1.6	3.8	20.8	40.1	24.8	14.3	51.9
Ouachita Parish, LA	156,761	153,720	147,256	3,041	6,464	2.0	4.4	21.1	40.9	24.4	13.7	52.1
Union Parish, LA	22,477	22,782	22,798	-305	-16	-1.3	-0.1	18.7	34.5	28.1	18.8	50.4
Monroe, MI Metro Area	149,568	152,021	145,939	-2,453	6,082	-1.6	4.2	17.9	35.7	30.2	16.3	50.6
Monroe County, MI	149,568	152,021	145,939	-2,453	6,082	-1.6	4.2	17.9	35.7	30.2	16.3	50.6
Montgomery, AL Metro Area	373,792	374,529	346,571	-737	27,958	-0.2	8.1	19.7	40.7	25.5	14.0	52.2
Autauga County, AL	55,347	54,571	43,751	776	10,820	1.4	24.7	20.1	39.2	26.4	14.3	51.5
Elmore County, AL	81,468	79,296	65,819	2,172	13,477	2.7	20.5	18.7	40.3	26.6	14.4	51.4
Lowndes County, AL	10,458	11,299	13,483	-841	-2,184	-7.4	-16.2	19.3	35.0	27.8	17.9	52.6
Montgomery County, AL	226,519	229,363	223,518	-2,844	5,845	-1.2	2.6	20.0	41.5	24.8	13.7	52.6
Morgantown, WV Metro Area	138,176	129,709	111,201	8,467	18,508	6.5	16.6	14.2	49.9	23.2	12.7	48.5
Monongalia County, WV	104,236	96,189	81,886	8,047	14,303	8.4	17.5	13.7	53.9	21.3	11.0	48.5
Preston County, WV	33,940	33,520	29,315	420	4,205	1.3	14.3	16.0	37.4	28.8	17.8	48.3
Morristown, TN Metro Area	116,642	114,111	102,444	2,531	11,667	2.2	11.4	18.1	36.1	27.3	18.6	51.0
Hamblen County, TN	63,402	62,541	58,136	861	4,405	1.4	7.6	19.3	36.3	26.4	17.9	51.0
Jefferson County, TN	53,240	51,570	44,308	1,670	7,262	3.2	16.4	16.6	35.8	28.3	19.3	51.0
Mount Vernon-Anacortes, WA Metro Area	121,846	116,901	103,017	4,945	13,884	4.2	13.5	18.5	35.6	26.6	19.3	50.4
Skagit County, WA	121,846	116,901	103,017	4,945	13,884	4.2	13.5	18.5	35.6	26.6	19.3	50.4
Muncie, IN Metro Area	116,852	117,671	118,769	-819	-1,098	-0.7	-0.9	15.4	44.9	23.5	16.2	51.7
Delaware County, IN	116,852	117,671	118,769	-819	-1,098	-0.7	-0.9	15.4	44.9	23.5	16.2	51.7
Muskegon, MI Metro Area	172,790	172,188	170,208	602	1,980	0.3	1.2	19.4	37.5	27.6	15.5	50.3
Muskegon County, MI	172,790	172,188	170,208	602	1,980	0.3	1.2	19.4	37.5	27.6	15.5	50.3
Myrtle Beach-Conway-North Myrtle Beach, SC-NC Metro Area................................	431,964	376,722	269,679	55,242	107,043	14.7	39.7	15.2	33.0	28.5	23.3	51.6
Brunswick County, NC	122,765	107,431	73,121	15,334	34,310	14.3	46.9	13.9	28.6	29.5	28.0	51.5
Horry County, SC	309,199	269,291	196,558	39,908	72,733	14.8	37.0	15.8	34.8	28.0	21.4	51.6
Napa, CA Metro Area	142,456	136,530	124,344	5,926	12,186	4.3	9.8	17.6	37.8	27.2	17.4	50.4
Napa County, CA	142,456	136,530	124,344	5,926	12,186	4.3	9.8	17.6	37.8	27.2	17.4	50.4
Naples-Immokalee-Marco Island, FL Metro Area ..	357,305	321,520	251,412	35,785	70,108	11.1	27.9	14.8	29.7	25.4	30.1	50.7
Collier County, FL	357,305	321,520	251,412	35,785	70,108	11.1	27.9	14.8	29.7	25.4	30.1	50.7
Nashville-Davidson--Murfreesboro--Franklin, TN Metro Area................................	1,830,345	1,670,896	1,381,412	159,449	289,484	9.5	21.0	19.7	42.1	25.8	12.4	51.2
Cannon County, TN	13,840	13,801	12,836	39	965	0.3	7.5	17.2	35.4	29.1	18.3	50.3
Cheatham County, TN	39,741	39,108	35,843	633	3,265	1.6	9.1	18.7	37.2	30.1	14.0	50.1
Davidson County, TN	678,889	626,662	569,927	52,227	56,735	8.3	10.0	18.4	46.4	24.0	11.2	51.9
Dickson County, TN	51,487	49,654	43,152	1,833	6,502	3.7	15.1	19.3	37.3	28.0	15.4	50.9
Hickman County, TN	24,363	24,699	22,311	-336	2,388	-1.4	10.7	17.5	37.9	28.7	15.9	47.6
Macon County, TN..................................	23,177	22,242	20,407	935	1,835	4.2	9.0	20.2	37.4	26.8	15.7	51.7
Maury County, TN	87,757	80,959	69,542	6,798	11,417	8.4	16.4	19.7	37.9	27.2	15.2	51.6
Robertson County, TN..............................	68,570	66,288	54,430	2,282	11,858	3.4	21.8	20.5	37.9	27.8	13.9	50.8

0 = represents zero or rounds to zero.
[1] The April 1, 2000 and 2010 population estimates bases reflect modifications to the census populations as documented in the Count Question Resolution program and geographic program revisions.
[2] Based on the April 1, 2010 estimates base and the July 1, 2015 estimates
[3] Based on the April 1, 2000 and April 1, 2010 estimates bases.

Table C-1.   Population and Population Characteristics—*Continued*

Metropolitan statistical area, division, and component county	Population 2015 estimate (July 1)	Population 2010[1] (estimates base) (April 1)	Population 2000[1] (estimates base) (April 1)	Net change 2010–2015[2]	Net change 2000–2010[3]	Percent change 2010–2015[2]	Percent change 2000–2010[3]	Percent in each age group, 2015 Under 15 years	Percent in each age group, 2015 15 to 44 years	Percent in each age group, 2015 45 to 64 years	Percent in each age group, 2015 65 years and over	Percent female
Rutherford County, TN	298,612	262,604	182,029	36,008	80,575	13.7	44.3	20.7	45.9	23.5	9.8	50.7
Smith County, TN	19,295	19,162	17,708	133	1,454	0.7	8.2	19.1	36.1	29.0	15.7	50.2
Sumner County, TN	175,989	160,657	130,528	15,332	30,129	9.5	23.1	19.7	37.8	27.4	15.1	51.1
Trousdale County, TN	8,042	7,869	7,256	173	613	2.2	8.4	18.4	37.1	28.9	15.6	50.3
Williamson County, TN	211,672	183,180	126,649	28,492	56,531	15.6	44.6	22.5	36.7	28.7	12.1	51.2
Wilson County, TN	128,911	114,011	88,794	14,900	25,217	13.1	28.4	19.7	37.2	28.2	14.9	50.9
New Bern, NC Metro Area	126,245	126,802	114,733	-557	12,069	-0.4	10.5	17.9	38.6	24.5	19.1	49.4
Craven County, NC	103,451	103,505	91,526	-54	11,979	-0.1	13.1	18.7	40.3	23.2	17.8	49.3
Jones County, NC	10,013	10,153	10,311	-140	-158	-1.4	-1.5	15.3	32.2	30.5	22.1	51.8
Pamlico County, NC	12,781	13,144	12,896	-363	248	-2.8	1.9	12.9	29.7	30.2	27.1	48.7
New Haven-Milford, CT Metro Area	859,470	862,474	823,993	-3,004	38,481	-0.3	4.7	16.9	39.1	28.0	15.9	51.8
New Haven County, CT	859,470	862,474	823,993	-3,004	38,481	-0.3	4.7	16.9	39.1	28.0	15.9	51.8
New Orleans-Metairie, LA Metro Area	1,262,888	1,189,863	1,337,740	73,025	-147,877	6.1	-11.1	18.7	40.2	27.0	14.1	51.7
Jefferson Parish, LA	436,275	432,552	455,406	3,723	-22,854	0.9	-5.0	18.2	39.0	27.3	15.5	51.5
Orleans Parish, LA	389,617	343,829	484,692	45,788	-140,863	13.3	-29.1	17.3	44.4	25.8	12.5	52.3
Plaquemines Parish, LA	23,495	23,042	26,749	453	-3,707	2.0	-13.9	22.0	39.4	26.1	12.5	49.7
St. Bernard Parish, LA	45,408	35,897	67,230	9,511	-31,333	26.5	-46.6	23.3	42.2	24.5	10.0	50.7
St. Charles Parish, LA	52,812	52,887	48,019	-75	4,868	-0.1	10.1	20.6	38.9	28.6	12.0	50.8
St. James Parish, LA	21,567	22,102	21,193	-535	909	-2.4	4.3	19.2	36.6	28.7	15.5	51.8
St. John the Baptist Parish, LA	43,626	45,817	43,181	-2,191	2,636	-4.8	6.1	20.7	38.8	27.5	13.0	51.4
St. Tammany Parish, LA	250,088	233,737	191,270	16,351	42,467	7.0	22.2	19.8	36.5	28.3	15.4	51.4
New York-Newark-Jersey City, NY-NJ-PA Metro Area	**20,182,305**	**19,566,387**	**18,945,888**	**615,918**	**620,499**	**3.1**	**3.3**	**18.1**	**40.8**	**26.7**	**14.4**	**51.6**
Dutchess County-Putnam County, NY Division	*394,796*	*397,198*	*375,763*	*-2,402*	*21,435*	*-0.6*	*5.7*	*15.9*	*37.5*	*30.8*	*15.8*	*50.3*
Dutchess County, NY	295,754	297,448	280,032	-1,694	17,416	-0.6	6.2	15.7	38.2	30.0	16.0	50.3
Putnam County, NY	99,042	99,750	95,731	-708	4,019	-0.7	4.2	16.5	35.3	32.9	15.2	50.2
Nassau County-Suffolk County, NY Division	*2,862,937*	*2,833,053*	*2,754,004*	*29,884*	*79,049*	*1.1*	*2.9*	*17.7*	*36.9*	*29.2*	*16.1*	*51.1*
Nassau County, NY	1,361,350	1,339,762	1,334,625	21,588	5,137	1.6	0.4	17.7	36.6	29.0	16.7	51.5
Suffolk County, NY	1,501,587	1,493,291	1,419,379	8,296	73,912	0.6	5.2	17.7	37.2	29.4	15.6	50.8
Newark, NJ-PA Division	*2,511,493*	*2,469,792*	*2,395,141*	*41,701*	*74,651*	*1.7*	*3.1*	*18.7*	*38.1*	*29.0*	*14.1*	*51.3*
Essex County, NJ	797,434	783,987	792,235	13,447	-8,248	1.7		20.0	41.0	26.4	12.6	51.9
Hunterdon County, NJ	125,488	127,351	122,110	-1,863	5,241	-1.5	4.3	16.0	32.8	35.0	16.3	50.5
Morris County, NJ	499,509	492,279	470,277	7,230	22,002	1.5	4.7	17.7	36.0	30.6	15.7	51.0
Somerset County, NJ	333,654	323,441	297,544	10,213	25,897	3.2	8.7	18.4	36.6	30.6	14.4	51.3
Sussex County, NJ	143,673	148,869	144,343	-5,196	4,526	-3.5	3.1	16.7	34.4	33.6	15.3	50.4
Union County, NJ	555,786	536,499	522,507	19,287	13,992	3.6	2.7	19.7	39.6	27.5	13.3	51.2
Pike County, PA	55,949	57,366	46,125	-1,417	11,241	-2.5	24.4	15.0	31.8	32.1	21.2	49.8
New York-Jersey City-White Plains, NY-NJ Division	*14,413,079*	*13,866,344*	*13,420,980*	*546,735*	*445,364*	*3.9*	*3.3*	*18.2*	*42.1*	*25.7*	*14.0*	*51.8*
Bergen County, NJ	938,506	905,117	884,179	33,389	20,938	3.7	2.4	17.4	37.2	29.1	16.2	51.6
Hudson County, NJ	674,836	634,277	609,041	40,559	25,236	6.4	4.1	17.3	48.5	23.4	10.9	50.3
Middlesex County, NJ	840,900	809,860	750,275	31,040	59,585	3.8	7.9	18.1	41.3	26.9	13.7	50.8
Monmouth County, NJ	628,715	630,378	615,253	-1,663	15,125	-0.3	2.5	17.7	35.2	31.1	16.1	51.4
Ocean County, NJ	588,721	576,565	510,950	12,156	65,615	2.1	12.8	19.8	32.4	25.7	22.1	51.8
Passaic County, NJ	510,916	501,624	490,285	9,292	11,339	1.9	2.3	20.2	40.4	26.1	13.4	51.3
Bronx County, NY	1,455,444	1,385,107	1,332,244	70,337	52,863	5.1	4.0	21.2	43.6	23.8	11.4	52.8
Kings County, NY	2,636,735	2,504,710	2,465,689	132,025	39,021	5.3	1.6	19.7	44.7	23.2	12.3	52.6
New York County, NY	1,644,518	1,585,874	1,538,096	58,644	47,778	3.7	3.1	12.5	48.8	24.0	14.6	52.7
Orange County, NY	377,647	372,782	341,397	4,865	31,385	1.3	9.2	21.1	38.8	27.2	12.9	49.9
Queens County, NY	2,339,150	2,230,541	2,229,394	108,609	1,147	4.9	0.1	17.2	42.4	26.6	13.8	51.5
Richmond County, NY	474,558	468,730	443,762	5,828	24,968	1.2	5.6	18.2	38.8	28.0	15.0	51.6
Rockland County, NY	326,037	311,687	286,794	14,350	24,893	4.6	8.7	23.0	36.7	25.2	15.1	51.0
Westchester County, NY	976,396	949,092	923,621	27,304	25,471	2.9	2.8	18.5	37.5	28.3	15.8	51.6
Niles-Benton Harbor, MI Metro Area	154,636	156,817	162,491	-2,181	-5,674	-1.4	-3.5	18.4	35.2	28.2	18.2	51.0
Berrien County, MI	154,636	156,817	162,491	-2,181	-5,674	-1.4	-3.5	18.4	35.2	28.2	18.2	51.0
North Port-Sarasota-Bradenton, FL Metro Area	768,918	702,268	589,998	66,650	112,270	9.5	19.0	13.8	28.4	27.4	30.5	52.0
Manatee County, FL	363,369	322,833	263,996	40,536	58,837	12.6	22.3	15.8	31.2	27.1	25.9	51.7
Sarasota County, FL	405,549	379,435	326,002	26,114	53,433	6.9	16.4	12.0	25.9	27.6	34.6	52.2
Norwich-New London, CT Metro Area	271,863	274,046	259,108	-2,183	14,938	-0.8	5.8	16.3	38.3	28.9	16.6	50.0
New London County, CT	271,863	274,046	259,108	-2,183	14,938	-0.8	5.8	16.3	38.3	28.9	16.6	50.0
Ocala, FL Metro Area	343,254	331,304	258,873	11,950	72,431	3.6	28.0	15.4	30.6	25.8	28.3	52.0
Marion County, FL	343,254	331,304	258,873	11,950	72,431	3.6	28.0	15.4	30.6	25.8	28.3	52.0
Ocean City, NJ Metro Area	94,727	97,265	102,323	-2,538	-5,058	-2.6	-4.9	14.4	31.2	29.9	24.5	51.1
Cape May County, NJ	94,727	97,265	102,323	-2,538	-5,058	-2.6	-4.9	14.4	31.2	29.9	24.5	51.1
Odessa, TX Metro Area	159,436	137,133	121,124	22,303	16,009	16.3	13.2	25.6	44.1	20.9	9.4	49.3
Ector County, TX	159,436	137,133	121,124	22,303	16,009	16.3	13.2	25.6	44.1	20.9	9.4	49.3
Ogden-Clearfield, UT Metro Area	642,850	597,159	485,410	45,691	111,749	7.7	23.0	26.4	42.5	20.7	10.4	49.7
Box Elder County, UT	52,097	49,975	42,755	2,122	7,220	4.2	16.9	27.0	39.0	21.6	12.4	49.3
Davis County, UT	336,043	306,486	238,997	29,557	67,489	9.6	28.2	27.8	43.0	19.8	9.3	49.6
Morgan County, UT	11,065	9,469	7,132	1,596	2,337	16.9	32.8	29.3	37.7	21.6	11.4	48.9
Weber County, UT	243,645	231,229	196,526	12,416	34,703	5.4	17.7	24.2	42.8	21.7	11.3	49.8
Oklahoma City, OK Metro Area	1,358,452	1,252,992	1,095,553	105,460	157,439	8.4	14.4	21.0	41.9	24.1	12.9	50.7
Canadian County, OK	133,378	115,541	87,729	17,837	27,812	15.4	31.7	22.0	41.2	24.6	12.2	50.5
Cleveland County, OK	274,458	255,761	208,036	18,697	47,725	7.3	22.9	18.4	46.2	23.1	12.3	50.2
Grady County, OK	54,648	52,431	45,476	2,217	6,955	4.2	15.3	20.2	37.7	27.1	15.0	50.2
Lincoln County, OK	35,042	34,273	32,070	769	2,203	2.2	6.9	20.2	34.8	27.8	17.2	50.1
Logan County, OK	45,996	41,853	33,911	4,143	7,942	9.9	23.4	19.1	38.8	26.5	15.6	50.4

0 = represents zero or rounds to zero.

[1]The April 1, 2000 and 2010 population estimates bases reflect modifications to the census populations as documented in the Count Question Resolution program and geographic program revisions.

[2]Based on the April 1, 2010 estimates base and the July 1, 2015 estimates

[3]Based on the April 1, 2000 and April 1, 2010 estimates bases.

Table C-1. Population and Population Characteristics—*Continued*

Metropolitan statistical area, division, and component county	2015 estimate (July 1)	2010[1] (estimates base) (April 1)	2000[1] (estimates base) (April 1)	Net change 2010–2015[2]	Net change 2000–2010[3]	Percent change 2010–2015[2]	Percent change 2000–2010[3]	Under 15 years	15 to 44 years	45 to 64 years	65 years and over	Percent female
McClain County, OK	38,066	34,506	27,750	3,560	6,756	10.3	24.3	21.4	37.3	26.4	14.9	50.6
Oklahoma County, OK	776,864	718,627	660,581	58,237	58,046	8.1	8.8	21.9	41.6	23.8	12.7	51.1
Olympia-Tumwater, WA Metro Area	269,536	252,264	207,392	17,272	44,872	6.8	21.6	18.1	39.6	26.5	15.9	50.9
Thurston County, WA	269,536	252,264	207,392	17,272	44,872	6.8	21.6	18.1	39.6	26.5	15.9	50.9
Omaha-Council Bluffs, NE-IA Metro Area	915,312	865,356	767,175	49,956	98,181	5.8	12.8	21.7	40.7	25.0	12.6	50.5
Harrison County, IA	14,265	14,937	15,674	-672	-737	-4.5	-4.7	18.5	32.7	29.2	19.6	50.3
Mills County, IA	14,844	15,059	14,543	-215	516	-1.4	3.5	19.3	33.5	30.7	16.5	49.9
Pottawattamie County, IA	93,671	93,149	87,825	522	5,324	0.6	6.1	19.7	37.0	27.3	15.9	50.7
Cass County, NE	25,512	25,241	24,319	271	922	1.1	3.8	19.8	34.1	29.5	16.5	49.6
Douglas County, NE	550,064	517,116	463,567	32,948	53,549	6.4	11.6	21.8	42.2	24.2	11.8	50.7
Sarpy County, NE	175,692	158,840	122,633	16,852	36,207	10.6	29.5	23.6	41.9	23.8	10.6	50.0
Saunders County, NE	21,016	20,780	19,827	236	953	1.1	4.8	20.1	33.3	28.8	17.8	49.3
Washington County, NE	20,248	20,234	18,787	14	1,447	0.1	7.7	19.4	34.9	29.1	16.6	50.0
Orlando-Kissimmee-Sanford, FL Metro Area	2,387,138	2,134,405	1,644,509	252,733	489,896	11.8	29.8	18.3	42.4	25.3	14.0	51.1
Lake County, FL	325,875	297,046	210,418	28,829	86,628	9.7	41.2	16.2	31.7	25.9	26.1	51.6
Orange County, FL	1,288,126	1,145,954	896,123	142,172	249,831	12.4	27.9	18.7	45.7	24.5	11.0	50.9
Osceola County, FL	323,993	268,687	172,520	55,306	96,167	20.6	55.7	20.3	42.6	24.1	12.9	50.9
Seminole County, FL	449,144	422,718	365,448	26,426	57,270	6.3	15.7	17.2	40.5	27.7	14.7	51.7
Oshkosh-Neenah, WI Metro Area	169,546	166,994	156,752	2,552	10,242	1.5	6.5	17.2	40.8	26.9	15.2	49.6
Winnebago County, WI	169,546	166,994	156,752	2,552	10,242	1.5	6.5	17.2	40.8	26.9	15.2	49.6
Owensboro, KY Metro Area	117,463	114,754	109,879	2,709	4,875	2.4	4.4	20.2	36.5	26.7	16.5	51.2
Daviess County, KY	99,259	96,658	91,542	2,601	5,116	2.7	5.6	20.2	37.0	26.6	16.2	51.5
Hancock County, KY	8,692	8,565	8,395	127	170	1.5	2.0	20.8	34.9	27.3	17.0	48.6
McLean County, KY	9,512	9,531	9,942	-19	-411	-0.2	-4.1	19.8	33.5	27.8	19.0	50.4
Oxnard-Thousand Oaks-Ventura, CA Metro Area	850,536	823,387	753,230	27,149	70,157	3.3	9.3	19.6	39.6	26.7	14.1	50.5
Ventura County, CA	850,536	823,387	753,230	27,149	70,157	3.3	9.3	19.6	39.6	26.7	14.1	50.5
Palm Bay-Melbourne-Titusville, FL Metro Area	568,088	543,378	476,299	24,710	67,079	4.5	14.1	15.1	32.2	29.8	22.9	51.2
Brevard County, FL	568,088	543,378	476,299	24,710	67,079	4.5	14.1	15.1	32.2	29.8	22.9	51.2
Panama City, FL Metro Area	197,506	184,715	162,818	12,791	21,897	6.9	13.4	17.6	38.5	27.3	16.6	49.4
Bay County, FL	181,635	168,852	148,270	12,783	20,582	7.6	13.9	18.0	38.5	27.1	16.4	50.1
Gulf County, FL	15,871	15,863	14,548	8	1,315	0.1	9.0	12.7	39.1	29.4	18.8	40.2
Parkersburg-Vienna, WV Metro Area	92,332	92,673	93,819	-341	-1,146	-0.4	-1.2	17.6	34.9	28.7	18.8	51.4
Wirt County, WV	5,880	5,717	5,865	163	-148	2.9	-2.5	17.4	32.7	31.4	18.5	49.6
Wood County, WV	86,452	86,956	87,954	-504	-998	-0.6	-1.1	17.6	35.1	28.5	18.8	51.6
Pensacola-Ferry Pass-Brent, FL Metro Area	478,043	448,991	412,167	29,052	36,824	6.5	8.9	17.8	40.1	26.4	15.7	49.7
Escambia County, FL	311,003	297,619	294,415	13,384	3,204	4.5	1.1	17.5	40.7	25.6	16.2	50.2
Santa Rosa County, FL	167,040	151,372	117,752	15,668	33,620	10.4	28.6	18.2	39.0	27.9	14.9	48.8
Peoria, IL Metro Area	378,018	379,186	366,911	-1,168	12,275	-0.3	3.3	19.5	37.5	26.3	16.6	51.1
Marshall County, IL	11,982	12,640	13,159	-658	-519	-5.2	-3.9	16.5	32.1	29.1	22.3	50.5
Peoria County, IL	186,221	186,494	183,466	-273	3,028	-0.1	1.7	20.0	39.2	25.4	15.4	51.6
Stark County, IL	5,788	5,994	6,330	-206	-336	-3.4	-5.3	16.6	31.1	27.5	24.8	50.8
Tazewell County, IL	134,800	135,394	128,465	-594	6,929	-0.4	5.4	19.0	36.5	26.9	17.5	50.7
Woodford County, IL	39,227	38,664	35,491	563	3,173	1.5	8.9	20.2	35.5	27.7	16.6	50.5
Philadelphia-Camden-Wilmington, PA-NJ-DE-MD Metro Area	**6,069,875**	**5,965,379**	**5,686,329**	**104,496**	**279,050**	**1.8**	**4.9**	**18.3**	**39.6**	**27.3**	**14.8**	**51.7**
Camden, NJ Division	*1,252,628*	*1,250,694*	*1,186,350*	*1,934*	*64,344*	*0.2*	*5.4*	*18.3*	*38.3*	*28.4*	*15.1*	*51.3*
Burlington County, NJ	450,226	448,728	423,329	1,498	25,399	0.3	6.0	17.4	37.4	29.3	15.9	50.8
Camden County, NJ	510,923	513,678	507,075	-2,755	6,603	-0.5	1.3	19.1	39.0	27.3	14.6	51.7
Gloucester County, NJ	291,479	288,288	255,946	3,191	32,342	1.1	12.6	18.3	38.2	28.9	14.6	51.4
Montgomery County-Bucks County-Chester County, PA Division	*1,962,570*	*1,924,285*	*1,780,165*	*38,285*	*144,120*	*2.0*	*8.1*	*17.9*	*36.3*	*29.4*	*16.4*	*51.1*
Bucks County, PA	627,367	625,255	597,548	2,112	27,707	0.3	4.6	17.0	34.8	31.1	17.2	51.0
Chester County, PA	515,939	499,146	433,208	16,793	65,938	3.4	15.2	19.1	37.0	28.9	15.0	50.8
Montgomery County, PA	819,264	799,884	749,409	19,380	50,475	2.4	6.7	17.9	36.9	28.5	16.8	51.4
Philadelphia, PA Division	*2,131,336*	*2,084,732*	*2,069,284*	*46,604*	*15,448*	*2.2*	*0.7*	*18.6*	*43.4*	*24.6*	*13.4*	*52.5*
Delaware County, PA	563,894	558,726	551,722	5,168	7,004	0.9	1.3	18.3	38.9	27.6	15.3	52.0
Philadelphia County, PA	1,567,442	1,526,006	1,517,562	41,436	8,444	2.7	0.6	18.7	45.0	23.6	12.7	52.7
Wilmington, DE-MD-NJ Division	*723,341*	*705,668*	*650,530*	*17,673*	*55,138*	*2.5*	*8.5*	*18.2*	*39.6*	*27.7*	*14.5*	*51.4*
New Castle County, DE	556,779	538,477	500,294	18,302	38,183	3.4	7.6	18.1	40.5	27.2	14.2	51.6
Cecil County, MD	102,382	101,108	85,964	1,274	15,144	1.3	17.6	18.8	37.2	29.7	14.3	50.3
Salem County, NJ	64,180	66,083	64,272	-1,903	1,811	-2.9	2.8	17.9	35.5	28.8	17.8	51.3
Phoenix-Mesa-Scottsdale, AZ Metro Area	4,574,531	4,193,127	3,251,884	381,404	941,243	9.1	28.9	20.5	40.8	24.0	14.7	50.3
Maricopa County, AZ	4,167,947	3,817,357	3,072,415	350,590	744,942	9.2	24.2	20.5	41.1	24.1	14.2	50.6
Pinal County, AZ	406,584	375,770	179,469	30,814	196,301	8.2	109.4	19.9	38.1	22.9	19.1	47.9
Pine Bluff, AR Metro Area	93,696	100,258	107,339	-6,562	-7,081	-6.5	-6.6	18.2	39.2	26.9	15.7	48.9
Cleveland County, AR	8,311	8,689	8,562	-378	127	-4.4	1.5	18.2	34.5	27.4	19.9	50.9
Jefferson County, AR	71,565	77,435	84,295	-5,870	-6,860	-7.6	-8.1	19.0	38.5	26.9	15.6	50.7
Lincoln County, AR	13,820	14,134	14,482	-314	-348	-2.2	-2.4	14.3	45.4	26.3	14.0	38.7
Pittsburgh, PA Metro Area	2,353,045	2,356,283	2,431,233	-3,238	-74,950	-0.1	-3.1	15.8	36.6	29.0	18.7	51.4
Allegheny County, PA	1,230,459	1,223,348	1,281,795	7,111	-58,447	0.6	-4.6	15.7	38.9	27.7	17.7	51.7
Armstrong County, PA	67,052	68,938	72,345	-1,886	-3,407	-2.7	-4.7	15.8	32.7	30.8	20.7	50.3
Beaver County, PA	168,871	170,539	181,448	-1,668	-10,909		-6.0	16.1	33.9	29.9	20.1	51.6
Butler County, PA	186,818	183,862	174,105	2,956	9,757	1.6	5.6	16.6	35.8	30.2	17.4	50.7
Fayette County, PA	133,628	136,607	148,536	-2,979	-11,929	-2.2	-8.0	15.9	34.5	29.8	19.9	50.6
Washington County, PA	208,261	207,820	203,014	441	4,806	0.2	2.4	16.1	34.7	29.8	19.3	51.0
Westmoreland County, PA	357,956	365,169	369,990	-7,213	-4,821	-2.0	-1.3	15.2	32.7	31.0	21.2	51.1

0 = represents zero or rounds to zero.
[1] The April 1, 2000 and 2010 population estimates bases reflect modifications to the census populations as documented in the Count Question Resolution program and geographic program revisions.
[2] Based on the April 1, 2010 estimates base and the July 1, 2015 estimates
[3] Based on the April 1, 2000 and April 1, 2010 estimates bases.

Table C-1.   Population and Population Characteristics—*Continued*

Metropolitan statistical area, division, and component county	2015 estimate (July 1)	2010[1] (estimates base) (April 1)	2000[1] (estimates base) (April 1)	Net change 2010–2015[2]	Net change 2000–2010[3]	Percent change 2010–2015[2]	Percent change 2000–2010[3]	Under 15 years	15 to 44 years	45 to 64 years	65 years and over	Percent female
Pittsfield, MA Metro Area	127,828	131,272	134,922	-3,444	-3,650	-2.6	-2.7	14.0	34.0	30.4	21.6	51.6
Berkshire County, MA	127,828	131,272	134,922	-3,444	-3,650	-2.6	-2.7	14.0	34.0	30.4	21.6	51.6
Pocatello, ID Metro Area	83,744	82,839	75,562	905	7,277	1.1	9.6	22.3	42.1	22.4	13.2	50.3
Bannock County, ID	83,744	82,839	75,562	905	7,277	1.1	9.6	22.3	42.1	22.4	13.2	50.3
Portland-South Portland, ME Metro Area	526,295	514,100	487,508	12,195	26,592	2.4	5.5	15.8	36.1	30.2	17.8	51.3
Cumberland County, ME	289,977	281,673	265,612	8,304	16,061	2.9	6.0	15.8	37.7	29.5	17.0	51.4
Sagadahoc County, ME	35,149	35,293	35,187	-144	106	-0.4	0.3	15.8	32.7	31.2	20.3	51.5
York County, ME	201,169	197,134	186,709	4,035	10,425	2.0	5.6	15.9	34.4	31.2	18.6	51.3
Portland-Vancouver-Hillsboro, OR-WA Metro Area	2,389,228	2,226,011	1,927,904	163,217	298,107	7.3	15.5	18.4	41.7	26.2	13.7	50.6
Clackamas County, OR	401,515	375,998	338,407	25,517	37,591	6.8	11.1	17.8	36.8	28.7	16.7	50.9
Columbia County, OR	49,600	49,353	43,553	247	5,800	0.5	13.3	17.6	34.5	30.1	17.8	50.3
Multnomah County, OR	790,294	735,189	660,602	55,105	74,587	7.5	11.3	16.6	46.0	25.2	12.2	50.5
Washington County, OR	574,326	529,849	445,256	44,477	84,593	8.4	19.0	20.0	42.4	25.4	12.2	50.7
Yamhill County, OR	102,659	99,193	84,975	3,466	14,218	3.5	16.7	18.6	39.5	25.8	16.2	49.9
Clark County, WA	459,495	425,363	345,235	34,132	80,128	8.0	23.2	20.4	39.0	26.3	14.2	50.5
Skamania County, WA	11,339	11,066	9,876	273	1,190	2.5	12.0	16.2	32.3	33.6	18.0	49.4
Port St. Lucie, FL Metro Area	454,846	424,107	319,456	30,739	104,651	7.2	32.8	15.6	31.7	27.3	25.3	50.9
Martin County, FL	156,283	146,850	126,777	9,433	20,073	6.4	15.8	13.5	28.2	28.6	29.7	50.4
St. Lucie County, FL	298,563	277,257	192,679	21,306	84,578	7.7	43.9	16.8	33.5	26.7	23.0	51.2
Prescott, AZ Metro Area	222,255	211,015	167,377	11,240	43,638	5.3	26.1	13.9	27.8	29.2	29.1	51.2
Yavapai County, AZ	222,255	211,015	167,377	11,240	43,638	5.3	26.1	13.9	27.8	29.2	29.1	51.2
Providence-Warwick, RI-MA Metro Area	1,613,070	1,601,216	1,582,961	11,854	18,255	0.7	1.2	16.6	39.2	28.2	16.1	51.5
Bristol County, MA	556,772	548,285	534,702	8,487	13,583	1.5	2.5	17.1	38.2	28.7	16.0	51.5
Bristol County, RI	49,084	49,875	50,653	-791	-778	-1.6	-1.5	15.3	35.4	30.2	19.1	51.8
Kent County, RI	164,801	166,158	167,220	-1,357	-1,062	-0.8	-0.6	15.6	35.8	30.8	17.8	51.8
Newport County, RI	82,423	83,141	85,442	-718	-2,301	-0.9	-2.7	14.8	36.2	29.2	19.8	50.8
Providence County, RI	633,473	626,663	621,404	6,810	5,259	1.1	0.8	17.3	42.0	26.3	14.4	51.5
Washington County, RI	126,517	127,094	123,540	-577	3,554	-0.5	2.9	13.9	37.2	30.3	18.6	51.7
Provo-Orem, UT Metro Area	585,799	526,886	376,775	58,913	150,111	11.2	39.8	29.3	48.4	14.9	7.4	49.5
Juab County, UT	10,594	10,246	8,236	348	2,010	3.4	24.4	28.3	39.9	19.7	12.0	48.8
UT County, UT	575,205	516,640	368,539	58,565	148,101	11.3	40.2	29.3	48.5	14.9	7.3	49.5
Pueblo, CO Metro Area	163,591	159,063	141,490	4,528	17,573	2.8	12.4	19.0	37.7	25.9	17.4	50.6
Pueblo County, CO	163,591	159,063	141,490	4,528	17,573	2.8	12.4	19.0	37.7	25.9	17.4	50.6
Punta Gorda, FL Metro Area	173,115	159,991	141,620	13,124	18,371	8.2	13.0	10.3	23.1	28.3	38.4	51.3
Charlotte County, FL	173,115	159,991	141,620	13,124	18,371	8.2	13.0	10.3	23.1	28.3	38.4	51.3
Racine, WI Metro Area	195,080	195,428	188,849	-348	6,579	-0.2	3.5	19.4	36.6	28.8	15.2	50.5
Racine County, WI	195,080	195,428	188,849	-348	6,579	-0.2	3.5	19.4	36.6	28.8	15.2	50.5
Raleigh, NC Metro Area	1,273,568	1,130,491	797,188	143,077	333,303	12.7	41.8	20.7	42.6	25.9	10.9	51.2
Franklin County, NC	63,710	60,592	47,284	3,118	13,308	5.1	28.1	18.7	36.7	29.0	15.6	50.3
Johnston County, NC	185,660	168,878	121,998	16,782	46,880	9.9	38.4	21.7	38.8	26.8	12.7	51.0
Wake County, NC	1,024,198	901,021	627,906	123,177	273,115	13.7	43.5	20.6	43.6	25.5	10.3	51.3
Rapid City, SD Metro Area	144,134	134,609	120,117	9,525	14,492	7.1	12.1	19.5	37.5	26.6	16.4	49.5
Custer County, SD	8,446	8,216	7,268	230	948	2.8	13.0	12.4	25.8	35.4	26.5	50.4
Meade County, SD	26,986	25,456	24,230	1,530	1,226	6.0	5.1	20.0	40.7	25.2	14.2	47.8
Pennington County, SD	108,702	100,937	88,619	7,765	12,318	7.7	13.9	20.0	37.6	26.2	16.2	49.8
Reading, PA Metro Area	415,271	411,572	373,712	3,699	37,860	0.9	10.1	18.6	37.6	27.6	16.2	50.9
Berks County, PA	415,271	411,572	373,712	3,699	37,860	0.9	10.1	18.6	37.6	27.6	16.2	50.9
Redding, CA Metro Area	179,533	177,223	163,242	2,310	13,981	1.3	8.6	17.7	35.0	27.5	19.8	51.0
Shasta County, CA	179,533	177,223	163,242	2,310	13,981	1.3	8.6	17.7	35.0	27.5	19.8	51.0
Reno, NV Metro Area	450,890	425,437	342,881	25,453	82,556	6.0	24.1	18.4	39.7	26.7	15.2	49.7
Storey County, NV	3,987	4,010	3,408	-23	602	-0.6	17.7	10.1	25.1	35.7	29.1	48.1
Washoe County, NV	446,903	421,427	339,473	25,476	81,954	6.0	24.1	18.5	39.8	26.6	15.1	49.7
Richmond, VA Metro Area	1,271,334	1,208,080	1,055,796	63,254	152,284	5.2	14.4	18.2	40.2	27.3	14.2	51.7
Amelia County, VA	12,903	12,695	11,378	208	1,317	1.6	11.6	17.2	32.7	31.1	19.0	50.9
Caroline County, VA	29,984	28,558	22,122	1,426	6,436	5.0	29.1	20.0	37.3	27.1	15.6	50.9
Charles City County, VA	7,040	7,256	6,932	-216	324	-3.0	4.7	12.3	30.3	35.3	22.1	51.1
Chesterfield County, VA	335,687	316,231	259,879	19,456	56,352	6.2	21.7	19.7	39.1	27.8	13.4	51.8
Dinwiddie County, VA	27,852	28,001	24,540	-149	3,461	-0.5	14.1	16.4	36.7	30.1	16.8	51.1
Goochland County, VA	22,253	21,699	16,866	554	4,833	2.6	28.7	14.7	31.6	33.6	20.0	50.7
Hanover County, VA	103,227	99,850	86,331	3,377	13,519	3.4	15.7	17.8	35.7	30.4	16.2	51.0
Henrico County, VA	325,155	306,979	263,195	18,176	43,784	5.9	16.6	19.3	39.8	26.7	14.2	52.8
King William County, VA	16,269	15,927	13,155	342	2,772	2.1	21.1	19.4	37.0	28.7	14.9	51.1
New Kent County, VA	20,392	18,432	13,472	1,960	4,960	10.6	36.8	16.6	35.5	32.2	15.7	48.9
Powhatan County, VA	28,031	28,046	22,377	-15	5,669	-0.1	25.3	14.9	35.5	32.8	16.8	47.6
Prince George County, VA	37,862	35,724	33,112	2,138	2,612	6.0	7.9	17.5	43.9	25.8	12.7	45.3
Sussex County, VA	11,715	12,083	12,507	-368	-424	-3.0	-3.4	13.3	42.4	27.8	16.5	40.6
Colonial Heights city, VA	17,820	17,413	16,909	407	504	2.3	3.0	19.4	35.4	24.9	20.3	53.5
Hopewell city, VA	22,378	22,591	22,278	-213	313	-0.9	1.4	21.7	38.1	24.4	15.8	53.1
Petersburg city, VA	32,477	32,420	33,752	57	-1,332	0.2	-3.9	18.9	38.3	27.3	15.6	53.9
Richmond city, VA	220,289	204,175	196,991	16,114	7,184	7.9	3.6	15.7	48.7	24.0	11.6	52.4
Riverside-San Bernardino-Ontario, CA Metro Area	4,489,159	4,224,972	3,254,799	264,187	970,173	6.3	29.8	21.8	42.2	23.8	12.2	50.2
Riverside County, CA	2,361,026	2,189,760	1,545,320	171,266	644,440	7.8	41.7	21.3	41.2	23.9	13.6	50.3
San Bernardino County, CA	2,128,133	2,035,212	1,709,479	92,921	325,733	4.6	19.1	22.2	43.3	23.8	10.7	50.2
Roanoke, VA Metro Area	314,560	308,682	288,370	5,878	20,312	1.9	7.0	17.1	35.8	28.5	18.7	51.6
Botetourt County, VA	33,347	33,148	30,554	199	2,594	0.6	8.5	15.6	31.6	32.3	20.5	50.7
Craig County, VA	5,211	5,173	5,076	38	97	0.7	1.9	15.3	31.6	31.7	21.4	49.6

0 = represents zero or rounds to zero.
[1]The April 1, 2000 and 2010 population estimates bases reflect modifications to the census populations as documented in the Count Question Resolution program and geographic program revisions.
[2]Based on the April 1, 2010 estimates base and the July 1, 2015 estimates
[3]Based on the April 1, 2000 and April 1, 2010 estimates bases.

Table C-1. Population and Population Characteristics—*Continued*

Metropolitan statistical area, division, and component county	2015 estimate (July 1)	2010[1] (estimates base) (April 1)	2000[1] (estimates base) (April 1)	Net change 2010–2015[2]	Net change 2000–2010[3]	Percent change 2010–2015[2]	Percent change 2000–2010[3]	Under 15 years	15 to 44 years	45 to 64 years	65 years and over	Percent female
Franklin County, VA	56,264	56,155	47,311	109	8,844	0.2	18.7	15.8	32.6	30.1	21.5	50.8
Roanoke County, VA	94,409	92,439	85,700	1,970	6,739	2.1	7.9	16.7	34.8	28.4	20.1	52.0
Roanoke city, VA	99,897	96,919	95,006	2,978	1,913	3.1	2.0	19.1	39.2	26.6	15.2	52.1
Salem city, VA	25,432	24,848	24,723	584	125	2.4	0.5	15.7	39.7	27.0	17.6	52.3
Rochester, MN Metro Area	213,873	206,877	184,745	6,996	22,132	3.4	12.0	20.6	37.4	26.6	15.4	50.7
Dodge County, MN	20,364	20,087	17,735	277	2,352	1.4	13.3	22.0	37.6	26.9	13.4	49.8
Fillmore County, MN	20,834	20,866	21,113	-32	-247	-0.2	-1.2	20.0	32.1	27.3	20.6	49.7
Olmsted County, MN	151,436	144,260	124,287	7,176	19,973	5.0	16.1	20.9	38.8	25.9	14.4	51.1
Wabasha County, MN	21,239	21,664	21,610	-425	54	-2.0	0.2	18.3	32.6	29.9	19.2	50.2
Rochester, NY Metro Area	1,081,954	1,079,695	1,062,522	2,259	17,173	0.2	1.6	17.2	38.4	28.0	16.4	51.3
Livingston County, NY	64,717	65,219	64,631	-502	588	-0.8	0.9	14.7	40.2	28.8	16.3	49.8
Monroe County, NY	749,600	744,402	735,328	5,198	9,074	0.7	1.2	17.4	39.5	27.2	15.9	51.7
Ontario County, NY	109,561	108,097	100,009	1,464	8,088	1.4	8.1	16.7	35.1	29.9	18.3	50.9
Orleans County, NY	41,582	42,876	44,184	-1,294	-1,308	-3.0	-3.0	16.1	37.0	30.3	16.7	50.3
Wayne County, NY	91,446	93,750	93,779	-2,304	-29	-2.5	0.0	17.8	34.5	30.7	17.0	50.5
Yates County, NY	25,048	25,351	24,591	-303	760	-1.2	3.1	18.3	35.1	27.7	18.9	51.3
Rockford, IL Metro Area	340,663	349,431	320,229	-8,768	29,202	-2.5	9.1	19.6	37.3	27.3	15.8	51.1
Boone County, IL	53,585	54,167	41,788	-582	12,379	-1.1	29.6	20.7	37.8	27.1	14.4	50.3
Winnebago County, IL	287,078	295,264	278,441	-8,186	16,823	-2.8	6.0	19.4	37.2	27.3	16.0	51.2
Rocky Mount, NC Metro Area	148,069	152,390	142,982	-4,321	9,408	-2.8	6.6	18.7	35.9	28.2	17.2	52.6
Edgecombe County, NC	54,150	56,551	55,604	-2,401	947	-4.2	1.7	19.2	35.3	27.9	17.6	53.7
Nash County, NC	93,919	95,839	87,378	-1,920	8,461	-2.0	9.7	18.4	36.3	28.3	17.0	51.9
Rome, GA Metro Area	96,504	96,317	90,622	187	5,695	0.2	6.3	19.4	39.0	25.5	16.1	51.7
Floyd County, GA	96,504	96,317	90,622	187	5,695	0.2	6.3	19.4	39.0	25.5	16.1	51.7
Sacramento--Roseville--Arden-Arcade, CA Metro Area	2,274,194	2,149,143	1,796,822	125,051	352,321	5.8	19.6	19.3	40.5	25.8	14.4	51.1
El Dorado County, CA	184,452	181,057	156,314	3,395	24,743	1.9	15.8	16.4	33.0	32.0	18.6	49.9
Placer County, CA	375,391	348,494	248,270	26,897	100,224	7.7	40.4	18.4	35.6	27.5	18.5	51.3
Sacramento County, CA	1,501,335	1,418,742	1,223,578	82,593	195,164	5.8	16.0	20.1	41.5	25.2	13.2	51.1
Yolo County, CA	213,016	200,850	168,660	12,166	32,190	6.1	19.1	17.8	48.6	21.8	11.7	51.4
Saginaw, MI Metro Area	193,307	200,169	210,051	-6,862	-9,882	-3.4	-4.7	17.8	36.9	27.5	17.8	51.5
Saginaw County, MI	193,307	200,169	210,051	-6,862	-9,882	-3.4	-4.7	17.8	36.9	27.5	17.8	51.5
St. Cloud, MN Metro Area	194,418	189,093	167,441	5,325	21,652	2.8	12.9	19.2	42.3	24.6	13.8	49.7
Benton County, MN	39,710	38,451	34,242	1,259	4,209	3.3	12.3	20.6	40.4	24.9	14.2	49.9
Stearns County, MN	154,708	150,642	133,199	4,066	17,443	2.7	13.1	18.9	42.9	24.5	13.8	49.6
St. George, UT Metro Area	155,602	138,115	90,325	17,487	47,790	12.7	52.9	22.9	36.7	20.2	20.2	50.5
Washington County, UT	155,602	138,115	90,325	17,487	47,790	12.7	52.9	22.9	36.7	20.2	20.2	50.5
St. Joseph, MO-KS Metro Area	126,880	127,329	123,841	-449	3,488	-0.4	2.8	18.3	39.5	26.6	15.6	48.5
Doniphan County, KS	7,797	7,945	8,249	-148	-304	-1.9	-3.7	17.6	38.3	26.3	17.9	49.6
Andrew County, MO	17,296	17,291	16,489	5	802	0.0	4.9	18.4	35.6	28.5	17.5	50.4
Buchanan County, MO	89,100	89,201	86,013	-101	3,188	-0.1	3.7	19.0	39.9	26.1	15.0	49.7
DeKalb County, MO	12,687	12,892	13,090	-205	-198	-1.6	-1.5	13.8	42.9	27.6	15.8	37.0
St. Louis, MO-IL Metro Area	2,811,588	2,787,748	2,675,562	23,840	112,186	0.9	4.2	18.7	38.6	27.5	15.2	51.5
Bond County, IL	16,950	17,768	17,636	-818	132	-4.6	0.7	15.7	39.2	28.2	17.0	47.2
Calhoun County, IL	4,899	5,089	5,079	-190	10	-3.7	0.2	16.7	30.6	29.6	23.2	49.8
Clinton County, IL	37,786	37,762	35,536	24	2,226	0.1	6.3	17.4	37.9	28.4	16.3	48.2
Jersey County, IL	22,372	22,985	21,649	-613	1,336	-2.7	6.2	17.2	35.8	29.1	18.0	51.3
Macoupin County, IL	46,045	47,765	49,008	-1,720	-1,243	-3.6	-2.5	17.3	34.7	28.7	19.3	50.5
Madison County, IL	266,209	269,328	259,019	-3,119	10,309	-1.2	4.0	18.4	38.0	27.7	15.9	51.2
Monroe County, IL	33,879	32,957	27,625	922	5,332	2.8	19.3	18.3	35.0	30.4	16.4	50.4
St. Clair County, IL	264,052	270,063	256,043	-6,011	14,020	-2.2	5.5	19.8	38.7	27.3	14.3	51.8
Franklin County, MO	102,426	101,491	93,820	935	7,671	0.9	8.2	19.3	35.7	28.9	16.1	50.3
Jefferson County, MO	224,124	218,729	198,362	5,395	20,367	2.5	10.3	19.6	38.0	28.6	13.8	50.3
Lincoln County, MO	54,696	52,565	38,916	2,131	13,649	4.1	35.1	21.4	38.3	27.5	12.7	49.8
St. Charles County, MO	385,590	360,485	283,939	25,105	76,546	7.0	27.0	19.8	39.3	27.2	13.7	50.8
St. Louis County, MO	1,003,362	998,883	1,016,202	4,479	-17,319	0.4	-1.7	18.2	37.3	27.7	16.8	52.6
Warren County, MO	33,513	32,513	24,536	1,000	7,977	3.1	32.5	20.2	34.9	28.2	16.7	50.1
St. Louis city, MO	315,685	319,365	348,192	-3,680	-28,827	-1.2	-8.3	17.2	45.7	25.5	11.6	51.6
Salem, OR Metro Area	410,091	390,738	347,256	19,353	43,482	5.0	12.5	20.5	39.8	24.4	15.3	50.5
Marion County, OR	330,700	315,335	284,844	15,365	30,491	4.9	10.7	20.9	39.9	24.4	14.8	50.2
Polk County, OR	79,391	75,403	62,412	3,988	12,991	5.3	20.8	18.7	39.7	24.2	17.4	51.7
Salinas, CA Metro Area	433,898	415,057	401,752	18,841	13,305	4.5	3.3	22.3	42.2	23.2	12.3	49.1
Monterey County, CA	433,898	415,057	401,752	18,841	13,305	4.5	3.3	22.3	42.2	23.2	12.3	49.1
Salisbury, MD-DE Metro Area	395,300	373,764	312,437	21,536	61,327	5.8	19.6	16.3	34.3	27.5	21.8	51.4
Sussex County, DE	215,622	197,110	156,494	18,512	40,616	9.4	26.0	16.2	30.3	28.5	24.9	51.5
Somerset County, MD	25,768	26,470	24,746	-702	1,724	-2.7	7.0	14.2	44.8	25.3	15.6	46.3
Wicomico County, MD	102,370	98,733	84,638	3,637	14,095	3.7	16.7	18.1	42.3	25.0	14.6	52.4
Worcester County, MD	51,540	51,451	46,559	89	4,892	0.2	10.5	14.3	30.1	29.6	26.0	51.5
Salt Lake City, UT Metro Area	1,170,266	1,087,799	939,169	82,467	148,630	7.6	15.8	24.0	44.8	21.4	9.8	49.8
Salt Lake County, UT	1,107,314	1,029,581	898,429	77,733	131,152	7.5	14.6	23.7	44.9	21.5	9.9	49.8
Tooele County, UT	62,952	58,218	40,740	4,734	17,478	8.1	42.9	28.3	42.6	20.3	8.8	49.5
San Angelo, TX Metro Area	119,659	111,823	105,780	7,836	6,043	7.0	5.7	19.9	42.6	22.9	14.6	50.2
Irion County, TX	1,554	1,599	1,765	-45	-166	-2.8	-9.4	18.9	32.9	28.7	19.5	48.1
Tom Green County, TX	118,105	110,224	104,015	7,881	6,209	7.1	6.0	19.9	42.7	22.8	14.6	50.2
San Antonio-New Braunfels, TX Metro Area	2,384,075	2,142,518	1,711,578	241,557	430,940	11.3	25.2	21.3	42.6	23.7	12.4	50.7
Atascosa County, TX	48,435	44,911	38,564	3,524	6,347	7.8	16.5	22.8	39.1	23.9	14.2	50.2
Bandera County, TX	21,269	20,485	17,589	784	2,896	3.8	16.5	13.7	27.4	33.5	25.4	50.6

0 = represents zero or rounds to zero.
[1]The April 1, 2000 and 2010 population estimates bases reflect modifications to the census populations as documented in the Count Question Resolution program and geographic program revisions.
[2]Based on the April 1, 2010 estimates base and the July 1, 2015 estimates
[3]Based on the April 1, 2000 and April 1, 2010 estimates bases.

Table C-1. Population and Population Characteristics—*Continued*

Metropolitan statistical area, division, and component county	2015 estimate (July 1)	2010[1] (estimates base) (April 1)	2000[1] (estimates base) (April 1)	Net change 2010–2015[2]	Net change 2000–2010[3]	Percent change 2010–2015[2]	Percent change 2000–2010[3]	Under 15 years	15 to 44 years	45 to 64 years	65 years and over	Percent female
Bexar County, TX	1,897,753	1,714,774	1,393,035	182,979	321,739	10.7	23.1	21.7	44.0	22.8	11.5	50.7
Comal County, TX	129,048	108,477	78,022	20,571	30,455	19.0	39.0	18.7	34.9	28.6	17.7	50.6
Guadalupe County, TX	151,249	131,537	88,856	19,712	42,681	15.0	48.0	21.1	40.3	25.3	13.3	50.6
Kendall County, TX	40,384	33,415	23,793	6,969	9,622	20.9	40.4	18.3	33.9	28.4	19.4	51.2
Medina County, TX	48,417	46,006	39,318	2,411	6,688	5.2	17.0	19.1	38.3	26.8	15.8	48.3
Wilson County, TX	47,520	42,913	32,401	4,607	10,512	10.7	32.4	19.7	36.8	28.3	15.2	49.7
San Diego-Carlsbad, CA Metro Area	3,299,521	3,095,308	2,813,839	204,213	281,469	6.6	10.0	18.4	43.9	24.5	13.1	49.7
San Diego County, CA	3,299,521	3,095,308	2,813,839	204,213	281,469	6.6	10.0	18.4	43.9	24.5	13.1	49.7
San Francisco-Oakland-Hayward, CA Metro Area	**4,656,132**	**4,335,560**	**4,123,734**	**320,572**	**211,826**	**7.4**	**5.1**	**16.9**	**41.9**	**26.9**	**14.3**	**50.6**
Oakland-Hayward-Berkeley, CA Division	*2,764,960*	*2,559,458*	*2,392,570*	*205,502*	*166,888*	*8.0*	*7.0*	*18.3*	*41.4*	*26.8*	*13.5*	*51.1*
Alameda County, CA	1,638,215	1,510,261	1,443,705	127,954	66,556	8.5	4.6	17.8	43.3	26.1	12.7	50.9
Contra Costa County, CA	1,126,745	1,049,197	948,865	77,548	100,332	7.4	10.6	19.1	38.6	27.7	14.6	51.2
San Francisco-Redwood City-South San Franciso, CA Division	*1,629,951*	*1,523,693*	*1,483,863*	*106,258*	*39,830*	*7.0*	*2.7*	*14.5*	*44.3*	*26.5*	*14.8*	*49.8*
San Francisco County, CA	864,816	805,195	776,764	59,621	28,431	7.4	3.7	11.5	48.4	25.5	14.6	49.0
San Mateo County, CA	765,135	718,498	707,099	46,637	11,399	6.5	1.6	17.8	39.6	27.6	15.0	50.8
San Rafael, CA Division	*261,221*	*252,409*	*247,301*	*8,812*	*5,108*	*3.5*	*2.1*	*17.0*	*31.4*	*31.5*	*20.0*	*51.2*
Marin County, CA	261,221	252,409	247,301	8,812	5,108	3.5	2.1	17.0	31.4	31.5	20.0	51.2
San Jose-Sunnyvale-Santa Clara, CA Metro Area	1,976,836	1,836,941	1,735,995	139,895	100,946	7.6	5.8	19.2	42.3	26.0	12.5	49.7
San Benito County, CA	58,792	55,269	53,214	3,523	2,055	6.4	3.9	21.8	40.4	26.0	11.8	49.8
Santa Clara County, CA	1,918,044	1,781,672	1,682,781	136,372	98,891	7.7	5.9	19.1	42.4	26.0	12.5	49.7
San Luis Obispo-Paso Robles-Arroyo Grande, CA Metro Area	281,401	269,593	246,746	11,808	22,847	4.4	9.3	14.9	40.9	26.0	18.2	49.2
San Luis Obispo County, CA	281,401	269,593	246,746	11,808	22,847	4.4	9.3	14.9	40.9	26.0	18.2	49.2
Santa Cruz-Watsonville, CA Metro Area	274,146	262,362	255,614	11,784	6,748	4.5	2.6	16.4	42.5	27.0	14.2	50.4
Santa Cruz County, CA	274,146	262,362	255,614	11,784	6,748	4.5	2.6	16.4	42.5	27.0	14.2	50.4
Santa Fe, NM Metro Area	148,686	144,171	129,304	4,515	14,867	3.1	11.5	15.7	33.7	29.7	20.9	51.4
Santa Fe County, NM	148,686	144,171	129,304	4,515	14,867	3.1	11.5	15.7	33.7	29.7	20.9	51.4
Santa Maria-Santa Barbara, CA Metro Area	444,769	423,939	399,293	20,830	24,646	4.9	6.2	18.7	44.2	22.8	14.3	49.9
Santa Barbara County, CA	444,769	423,939	399,293	20,830	24,646	4.9	6.2	18.7	44.2	22.8	14.3	49.9
Santa Rosa, CA Metro Area	502,146	483,880	458,586	18,266	25,294	3.8	5.5	16.8	37.4	28.3	17.5	51.1
Sonoma County, CA	502,146	483,880	458,586	18,266	25,294	3.8	5.5	16.8	37.4	28.3	17.5	51.1
Savannah, GA Metro Area	379,199	347,621	293,324	31,578	54,297	9.1	18.5	19.7	43.2	23.9	13.2	51.4
Bryan County, GA	35,137	30,238	23,430	4,899	6,808	16.2	29.1	24.1	42.1	23.4	10.4	50.6
Chatham County, GA	286,956	265,133	232,372	21,823	32,761	8.2	14.1	18.8	43.8	23.5	14.0	51.8
Effingham County, GA	57,106	52,250	37,522	4,856	14,728	9.3	39.3	21.7	41.0	26.2	11.0	50.2
Scranton--Wilkes-Barre--Hazleton, PA Metro Are	558,166	563,630	560,793	-5,464	2,837	-1.0	0.5	16.2	36.4	28.3	19.1	51.0
Lackawanna County, PA	211,917	214,436	213,292	-2,519	1,144	-1.2	0.5	16.5	36.5	27.9	19.1	51.7
Luzerne County, PA	318,449	320,918	319,429	-2,469	1,489	-0.8	0.5	16.0	36.5	28.4	19.2	50.6
Wyoming County, PA	27,800	28,276	28,072	-476	204	-1.7	0.7	16.3	35.0	29.6	19.1	49.5
Seattle-Tacoma-Bellevue, WA Metro Area	**3,733,580**	**3,439,815**	**3,043,934**	**293,765**	**395,881**	**8.5**	**13.0**	**18.3**	**42.6**	**26.4**	**12.6**	**50.0**
Seattle-Bellevue-Everett, WA Division	*2,889,626*	*2,644,586*	*2,343,118*	*245,040*	*301,468*	*9.3*	*12.9*	*17.9*	*43.0*	*26.7*	*12.4*	*49.9*
King County, WA	2,117,125	1,931,256	1,737,075	185,869	194,181	9.6	11.2	17.4	43.9	26.2	12.4	50.0
Snohomish County, WA	772,501	713,330	606,043	59,171	107,287	8.3	17.7	19.0	40.6	27.9	12.5	49.7
Tacoma-Lakewood, WA Division	*843,954*	*795,229*	*700,816*	*48,725*	*94,413*	*6.1*	*13.5*	*19.9*	*41.4*	*25.6*	*13.1*	*50.2*
Pierce County, WA	843,954	795,229	700,816	48,725	94,413	6.1	13.5	19.9	41.4	25.6	13.1	50.2
Sebastian-Vero Beach, FL Metro Area	147,919	138,028	112,877	9,891	25,151	7.2	22.3	13.9	28.1	27.1	30.9	52.0
Indian River County, FL	147,919	138,028	112,877	9,891	25,151	7.2	22.3	13.9	28.1	27.1	30.9	52.0
Sebring, FL Metro Area	99,491	98,786	87,391	705	11,395	0.7	13.0	14.6	27.2	24.1	34.1	51.4
Highlands County, FL	99,491	98,786	87,391	705	11,395	0.7	13.0	14.6	27.2	24.1	34.1	51.4
Sheboygan, WI Metro Area	115,569	115,507	112,663	62	2,844	0.1	2.5	18.4	35.8	29.1	16.7	49.8
Sheboygan County, WI	115,569	115,507	112,663	62	2,844	0.1	2.5	18.4	35.8	29.1	16.7	49.8
Sherman-Denison, TX Metro Area	125,467	120,873	110,574	4,594	10,299	3.8	9.3	19.6	36.4	26.9	17.1	51.1
Grayson County, TX	125,467	120,873	110,574	4,594	10,299	3.8	9.3	19.6	36.4	26.9	17.1	51.1
Shreveport-Bossier City, LA Metro Area	443,708	439,811	417,787	3,897	22,024	0.9	5.3	20.5	39.3	25.1	15.1	51.8
Bossier Parish, LA	125,175	116,979	99,355	8,196	17,624	7.0	17.7	21.1	42.0	23.7	13.2	50.6
Caddo Parish, LA	251,460	254,969	251,129	-3,509	3,840	-1.4	1.5	20.5	38.9	25.4	15.3	52.5
De Soto Parish, LA	27,052	26,656	25,489	396	1,167	1.5	4.6	20.2	36.1	27.1	16.6	51.8
Webster Parish, LA	40,021	41,207	41,814	-1,186	-607	-2.9	-1.5	18.8	35.9	26.7	18.6	51.3
Sierra Vista-Douglas, AZ Metro Area	126,427	131,357	117,743	-4,930	13,614	-3.8	11.6	18.6	35.7	25.0	20.7	49.1
Cochise County, AZ	126,427	131,357	117,743	-4,930	13,614	-3.8	11.6	18.6	35.7	25.0	20.7	49.1
Sioux City, IA-NE-SD Metro Area	169,069	168,563	167,860	506	703	0.3	0.4	21.7	37.9	25.6	14.8	50.3
Plymouth County, IA	24,800	24,981	24,859	-181	122	-0.7	0.5	20.1	34.0	28.0	17.9	50.4
Woodbury County, IA	102,782	102,177	103,876	605	-1,699	0.6	-1.6	22.0	39.2	24.8	13.9	50.4
Dakota County, NE	20,781	21,006	20,265	-225	741	-1.1	3.7	24.1	39.0	23.7	13.3	50.2
Dixon County, NE	5,797	6,000	6,277	-203	-277	-3.4	-4.4	20.2	32.7	27.3	19.8	49.6
Union County, SD	14,909	14,399	12,583	510	1,816	3.5	14.4	20.1	35.3	28.6	16.1	49.4
Sioux Falls, SD Metro Area	251,854	228,264	187,151	23,590	41,113	10.3	22.0	22.0	40.7	24.7	12.6	49.8
Lincoln County, SD	52,849	44,823	24,158	8,026	20,665	17.9	85.5	24.9	41.2	23.0	10.9	50.4
McCook County, SD	5,599	5,618	5,825	-19	-207	-0.3	-3.6	22.3	31.8	26.2	19.7	49.8
Minnehaha County, SD	185,197	169,476	148,321	15,721	21,155	9.3	14.3	21.2	41.3	24.9	12.6	49.7
Turner County, SD	8,209	8,347	8,847	-138	-500	-1.7	-5.7	19.1	31.7	28.2	20.9	49.6
South Bend-Mishawaka, IN-MI Metro Area	320,098	319,215	316,653	883	2,562	0.3	0.8	19.3	38.9	26.3	15.5	51.2
St. Joseph County, IN	268,441	266,929	265,567	1,512	1,362	0.6	0.5	19.8	40.0	25.5	14.6	51.4
Cass County, MI	51,657	52,286	51,086	-629	1,200	-1.2	2.3	17.0	33.1	30.1	19.9	50.0
Spartanburg, SC Metro Area	325,079	313,268	283,896	11,811	29,372	3.8	10.3	19.3	38.4	26.7	15.7	51.6
Spartanburg County, SC	297,302	284,305	253,957	12,997	30,348	4.6	12.0	19.4	38.8	26.5	15.3	51.5

0 = represents zero or rounds to zero.
[1]The April 1, 2000 and 2010 population estimates bases reflect modifications to the census populations as documented in the Count Question Resolution program and geographic program revisions.
[2]Based on the April 1, 2010 estimates base and the July 1, 2015 estimates
[3]Based on the April 1, 2000 and April 1, 2010 estimates bases.

Table C-1.   Population and Population Characteristics—*Continued*

Metropolitan statistical area, division, and component county	2015 estimate (July 1)	2010[1] (estimates base) (April 1)	2000[1] (estimates base) (April 1)	Net change 2010–2015[2]	Net change 2000–2010[3]	Percent change 2010–2015[2]	Percent change 2000–2010[3]	Under 15 years	15 to 44 years	45 to 64 years	65 years and over	Percent female
Union County, SC	27,777	28,963	29,939	-1,186	-976	-4.1	-3.3	17.4	34.3	29.2	19.1	52.6
Spokane-Spokane Valley, WA Metro Area	547,824	527,753	469,756	20,071	57,997	3.8	12.3	18.4	39.3	26.4	15.9	50.3
Pend Oreille County, WA	13,088	13,001	11,706	87	1,295	0.7	11.1	15.6	28.5	32.1	23.8	48.8
Spokane County, WA	490,945	471,221	417,968	19,724	53,253	4.2	12.7	18.6	40.4	25.9	15.2	50.4
Stevens County, WA	43,791	43,531	40,082	260	3,449	0.6	8.6	17.6	30.4	30.5	21.5	50.0
Springfield, IL Metro Area	211,156	210,170	201,457	986	8,713	0.5	4.3	18.8	37.2	27.8	16.2	51.9
Menard County, IL	12,444	12,705	12,483	-261	222	-2.1	1.8	18.0	33.7	29.6	18.6	51.4
Sangamon County, IL	198,712	197,465	188,974	1,247	8,491	0.6	4.5	18.9	37.4	27.7	16.0	51.9
Springfield, MA Metro Area	631,982	621,705	608,517	10,277	13,188	1.7	2.2	16.7	41.1	26.8	15.4	52.1
Hampden County, MA	470,690	463,625	456,280	7,065	7,345	1.5	1.6	18.2	39.2	27.1	15.5	51.7
Hampshire County, MA	161,292	158,080	152,237	3,212	5,843	2.0	3.8	12.2	46.7	25.8	15.3	53.4
Springfield, MO Metro Area	456,456	436,713	368,451	19,743	68,262	4.5	18.5	18.8	41.0	24.5	15.6	51.0
Christian County, MO	83,279	77,419	54,303	5,860	23,116	7.6	42.6	21.4	38.6	25.4	14.6	51.0
Dallas County, MO	16,393	16,777	15,725	-384	1,052	-2.3	6.7	19.3	32.4	28.5	19.9	50.3
Greene County, MO	288,072	275,178	240,460	12,894	34,718	4.7	14.4	17.6	43.0	23.8	15.6	51.2
Polk County, MO	31,229	31,137	26,922	92	4,215	0.3	15.7	19.0	39.0	24.7	17.3	51.2
Webster County, MO	37,483	36,202	31,041	1,281	5,161	3.5	16.6	22.3	36.7	26.2	14.8	49.1
Springfield, OH Metro Area	135,959	138,333	144,742	-2,374	-6,409	-1.7	-4.4	18.7	35.6	27.5	18.3	51.5
Clark County, OH	135,959	138,333	144,742	-2,374	-6,409	-1.7	-4.4	18.7	35.6	27.5	18.3	51.5
State College, PA Metro Area	160,580	153,981	135,678	6,599	18,303	4.3	13.5	12.5	52.3	22.6	12.7	47.4
Centre County, PA	160,580	153,981	135,678	6,599	18,303	4.3	13.5	12.5	52.3	22.6	12.7	47.4
Staunton-Waynesboro, VA Metro Area	120,221	118,502	108,953	1,719	9,549	1.5	8.8	16.5	35.6	28.3	19.6	51.0
Augusta County, VA	74,314	73,736	65,385	578	8,351	0.8	12.8	15.8	34.5	30.0	19.7	49.4
Staunton city, VA	24,416	23,746	23,951	670	-205	2.8	-0.9	15.5	37.4	26.2	21.0	54.6
Waynesboro city, VA	21,491	21,020	19,617	471	1,403	2.2	7.2	20.0	37.5	24.8	17.7	52.4
Stockton-Lodi, CA Metro Area	726,106	685,308	563,660	40,798	121,648	6.0	21.6	22.8	41.4	23.8	12.1	50.2
San Joaquin County, CA	726,106	685,308	563,660	40,798	121,648	6.0	21.6	22.8	41.4	23.8	12.1	50.2
Sumter, SC Metro Area	107,480	107,463	104,687	17	2,776	0.0	2.7	20.5	39.5	25.0	15.0	51.8
Sumter County, SC	107,480	107,463	104,687	17	2,776	0.0	2.7	20.5	39.5	25.0	15.0	51.8
Syracuse, NY Metro Area	660,458	662,589	650,133	-2,131	12,456	-0.3	1.9	17.5	38.7	28.1	15.6	51.3
Madison County, NY	71,849	73,453	69,420	-1,604	4,033	-2.2	5.8	16.0	38.2	29.5	16.3	50.9
Onondaga County, NY	468,463	467,027	458,326	1,436	8,701	0.3	1.9	17.8	38.9	27.6	15.7	51.7
Oswego County, NY	120,146	122,109	122,387	-1,963	-278	-1.6	-0.2	17.6	38.3	29.3	14.9	50.0
Tallahassee, FL Metro Area	377,924	368,770	320,259	9,154	48,511	2.5	15.1	16.2	47.6	23.4	12.9	51.7
Gadsden County, FL	46,036	47,746	45,017	-1,710	2,729	-3.6	6.1	18.5	37.2	28.3	15.9	52.5
Jefferson County, FL	14,081	14,761	12,876	-680	1,885	-4.6	14.6	14.7	33.4	31.2	20.8	47.6
Leon County, FL	286,272	275,480	239,509	10,792	35,971	3.9	15.0	15.8	50.8	21.6	11.9	52.6
Wakulla County, FL	31,535	30,783	22,857	752	7,926	2.4	34.7	17.0	40.3	28.9	13.8	45.1
Tampa-St. Petersburg-Clearwater, FL Metro Area	2,975,225	2,783,514	2,396,038	191,711	387,476	6.9	16.2	16.8	36.9	27.3	19.0	51.6
Hernando County, FL	178,439	172,775	130,795	5,664	41,980	3.3	32.1	15.0	30.2	27.1	27.7	52.0
Hillsborough County, FL	1,349,050	1,229,224	998,994	119,826	230,230	9.7	23.0	19.1	41.9	25.6	13.4	51.3
Pasco County, FL	497,909	464,703	344,749	33,206	119,954	7.1	34.8	16.7	33.8	26.9	22.7	51.5
Pinellas County, FL	949,827	916,812	921,500	33,015	-4,688	3.6	-0.5	13.8	32.8	30.0	23.4	52.1
Terre Haute, IN Metro Area	171,019	172,422	170,762	-1,403	1,470	-0.8	0.9	17.3	41.0	25.8	15.8	49.1
Clay County, IN	26,503	26,887	26,567	-384	320	-1.4	1.2	18.8	36.3	27.9	16.9	50.8
Sullivan County, IN	20,928	21,475	21,736	-547	-261	-2.5	-1.2	16.3	39.9	27.2	16.6	45.7
Vermillion County, IN	15,692	16,212	16,790	-520	-578	-3.2	-3.4	17.9	34.6	28.4	19.1	50.5
Vigo County, IN	107,896	107,848	105,859	48	1,989	0.0	1.9	17.1	43.3	24.6	14.9	49.2
Texarkana, TX-AR Metro Area	149,769	149,195	143,379	574	5,816	0.4	4.1	19.7	38.6	25.6	16.0	50.1
Little River County, AR	12,472	13,168	13,628	-696	-460	-5.3	-3.4	17.8	34.8	27.3	20.1	51.1
Miller County, AR	43,908	43,462	40,455	446	3,007	1.0	7.4	20.3	38.2	26.1	15.5	50.7
Bowie County, TX	93,389	92,565	89,296	824	3,269	0.9	3.7	19.7	39.3	25.2	15.8	49.6
The Villages, FL Metro Area	118,891	93,420	53,337	25,471	40,083	27.3	75.2	5.9	16.5	22.7	54.8	49.6
Sumter County, FL	118,891	93,420	53,337	25,471	40,083	27.3	75.2	5.9	16.5	22.7	54.8	49.6
Toledo, OH Metro Area	605,956	610,001	618,216	-4,045	-8,215	-0.7	-1.3	18.8	39.9	26.3	15.0	51.3
Fulton County, OH	42,537	42,698	42,051	-161	647	-0.4	1.5	19.7	35.1	28.6	16.6	50.5
Lucas County, OH	433,689	441,815	455,093	-8,126	-13,278	-1.8	-2.9	19.3	39.0	26.7	15.0	51.5
Wood County, OH	129,730	125,488	121,072	4,242	4,416	3.4	3.6	16.9	44.5	24.2	14.4	50.6
Topeka, KS Metro Area	233,791	233,868	224,568	-77	9,300	0.0	4.1	19.9	36.1	27.1	16.9	51.0
Jackson County, KS	13,338	13,462	12,650	-124	812	-0.9	6.4	20.6	33.7	27.7	18.1	49.7
Jefferson County, KS	18,930	19,124	18,450	-194	674		3.7	18.7	33.0	30.6	17.7	49.1
Osage County, KS	15,847	16,295	16,713	-448	-418	-2.7	-2.5	18.8	33.2	29.1	18.9	50.1
Shawnee County, KS	178,725	177,934	169,879	791	8,055	0.4	4.7	20.1	37.0	26.4	16.5	51.4
Wabaunsee County, KS	6,951	7,053	6,876	-102	177	-1.4	2.6	20.6	31.8	29.3	18.2	49.2
Trenton, NJ Metro Area	371,398	367,508	350,773	3,890	16,735	1.1	4.8	17.9	40.7	27.4	14.0	51.1
Mercer County, NJ	371,398	367,508	350,773	3,890	16,735	1.1	4.8	17.9	40.7	27.4	14.0	51.1
Tucson, AZ Metro Area	1,010,025	980,263	843,702	29,762	136,561	3.0	16.2	17.9	39.4	24.3	18.4	50.8
Pima County, AZ	1,010,025	980,263	843,702	29,762	136,561	3.0	16.2	17.9	39.4	24.3	18.4	50.8
Tulsa, OK Metro Area	981,005	937,528	859,635	43,477	77,893	4.6	9.1	20.8	39.3	25.4	14.4	50.9
Creek County, OK	70,892	69,967	67,340	925	2,627	1.3	3.9	19.7	35.9	27.1	17.3	50.3
Okmulgee County, OK	39,187	40,069	39,672	-882	397	-2.2	1.0	19.9	36.7	25.9	17.5	50.7
Osage County, OK	47,887	47,480	44,413	407	3,067	0.9	6.9	18.5	34.5	28.0	19.0	49.8
Pawnee County, OK	16,436	16,579	16,610	-143	-31	-0.9	-0.2	19.3	34.3	27.9	18.5	50.1
Rogers County, OK	90,802	86,906	70,649	3,896	16,257	4.5	23.0	19.6	37.6	27.0	15.7	50.1
Tulsa County, OK	639,242	603,440	563,475	35,802	39,965	5.9	7.1	21.4	40.8	24.6	13.2	51.3
Wagoner County, OK	76,559	73,087	57,476	3,472	15,611	4.8	27.2	20.5	37.9	26.3	15.2	50.5
Tuscaloosa, AL Metro Area	239,908	230,159	204,116	9,749	26,043	4.2	12.8	17.4	46.1	23.6	12.9	51.8

0 = represents zero or rounds to zero.
[1]The April 1, 2000 and 2010 population estimates bases reflect modifications to the census populations as documented in the Count Question Resolution program and geographic program revisions.
[2]Based on the April 1, 2010 estimates base and the July 1, 2015 estimates
[3]Based on the April 1, 2000 and April 1, 2010 estimates bases.

Table C-1. Population and Population Characteristics—*Continued*

Metropolitan statistical area, division, and component county	Population			Net change		Percent change		Percent in each age group, 2015				Percent female
	2015 estimate (July 1)	2010¹ (estimates base) (April 1)	2000¹ (estimates base) (April 1)	2010–2015²	2000–2010³	2010–2015²	2000–2010³	Under 15 years	15 to 44 years	45 to 64 years	65 years and over	
Hale County, AL	15,068	15,760	18,270	-692	-2,510	-4.4	-13.7	18.8	35.7	27.7	17.8	52.9
Pickens County, AL	20,864	19,746	20,914	1,118	-1,168	5.7	-5.6	16.1	38.0	28.2	17.7	50.1
Tuscaloosa County, AL	203,976	194,653	164,932	9,323	29,721	4.8	18.0	17.4	47.7	22.8	12.0	51.9
Tyler, TX Metro Area	222,936	209,721	174,861	13,215	34,860	6.3	19.9	20.7	39.5	24.1	15.7	51.7
Smith County, TX	222,936	209,721	174,861	13,215	34,860	6.3	19.9	20.7	39.5	24.1	15.7	51.7
Urban Honolulu, HI Metro Area	998,714	953,207	876,159	45,507	77,048	4.8	8.8	18.2	42.0	23.5	16.2	49.1
Honolulu County, HI	998,714	953,207	876,159	45,507	77,048	4.8	8.8	18.2	42.0	23.5	16.2	49.1
Utica-Rome, NY Metro Area	295,600	299,376	300,018	-3,776	-642	-1.3	-0.2	17.5	36.4	28.0	18.1	50.3
Herkimer County, NY	63,100	64,486	64,502	-1,386	-16	-2.1	0.0	17.2	34.5	29.0	19.2	50.7
Oneida County, NY	232,500	234,890	235,516	-2,390	-626		-0.3	17.6	36.9	27.7	17.8	50.2
Valdosta, GA Metro Area	142,875	139,665	119,570	3,210	20,095	2.3	16.8	20.8	45.1	21.7	12.4	50.8
Brooks County, GA	15,658	16,324	16,456	-666	-132	-4.1	-0.8	18.6	34.6	27.9	18.9	50.6
Echols County, GA	4,040	4,034	3,747	6	287	0.1	7.7	24.0	41.3	23.3	11.3	50.2
Lanier County, GA	10,312	10,074	7,246	238	2,828	2.4	39.0	21.2	41.7	24.3	12.8	49.6
Lowndes County, GA	112,865	109,233	92,121	3,632	17,112	3.3	18.6	20.9	47.0	20.6	11.5	51.0
Vallejo-Fairfield, CA Metro Area	436,092	413,344	394,495	22,748	18,849	5.5	4.8	18.8	40.1	26.9	14.1	50.3
Solano County, CA	436,092	413,344	394,495	22,748	18,849	5.5	4.8	18.8	40.1	26.9	14.1	50.3
Victoria, TX Metro Area	99,913	94,003	91,000	5,910	3,003	6.3	3.3	21.3	39.0	24.4	15.2	50.8
Goliad County, TX	7,531	7,210	6,923	321	287	4.5	4.1	17.2	32.4	29.7	20.7	50.1
Victoria County, TX	92,382	86,793	84,077	5,589	2,716	6.4	3.2	21.6	39.6	24.0	14.8	50.8
Vineland-Bridgeton, NJ Metro Area	155,854	156,898	146,454	-1,044	10,444	-0.7	7.1	19.8	40.7	25.5	14.0	48.5
Cumberland County, NJ	155,854	156,898	146,454	-1,044	10,444	-0.7	7.1	19.8	40.7	25.5	14.0	48.5
Virginia Beach-Norfolk-Newport News, VA-NC Metro Area	1,724,876	1,676,817	1,580,603	48,059	96,214	2.9	6.1	18.7	42.7	25.2	13.4	50.7
Currituck County, NC	25,263	23,547	18,179	1,716	5,368	7.3	29.5	18.0	35.1	31.6	15.3	50.3
Gates County, NC	11,431	12,186	10,521	-755	1,665	-6.2	15.8	16.9	32.8	32.3	18.0	51.1
Gloucester County, VA	37,143	36,858	34,772	285	2,086	0.8	6.0	16.6	34.7	30.8	17.9	50.8
Isle of Wight County, VA	36,314	35,270	29,724	1,044	5,546	3.0	18.7	16.9	33.8	31.5	17.8	51.4
James City County, VA	73,147	67,401	48,096	5,746	19,305	8.5	40.1	16.4	32.5	27.4	23.6	51.7
Mathews County, VA	8,862	8,976	9,160	-114	-184	-1.3	-2.0	12.7	27.2	30.7	29.4	51.7
York County, VA	67,837	65,191	56,748	2,646	8,443	4.1	14.9	19.6	38.2	27.2	14.9	50.7
Chesapeake city, VA	235,429	222,209	199,153	13,220	23,056	5.9	11.6	19.8	41.0	27.0	12.2	51.1
Hampton city, VA	136,454	137,510	146,436	-1,056	-8,926	-0.8	-6.1	18.1	42.3	25.6	14.1	51.8
Newport News city, VA	182,385	180,911	180,272	1,474	639	0.8	0.4	19.8	44.9	23.3	12.0	51.5
Norfolk city, VA	246,393	242,831	234,463	3,562	8,368	1.5	3.6	17.4	51.5	20.9	10.2	47.7
Poquoson city, VA	12,059	12,157	11,566	-98	591	-0.8	5.1	16.5	35.2	29.7	18.6	50.5
Portsmouth city, VA	96,201	95,535	100,580	666	-5,045	0.7	-5.0	20.3	41.4	24.3	14.1	52.2
Suffolk city, VA	88,161	84,596	63,699	3,565	20,897	4.2	32.8	20.5	39.0	27.1	13.3	51.5
Virginia Beach city, VA	452,745	437,966	425,236	14,779	12,730	3.4	3.0	18.8	43.5	24.9	12.7	50.8
Williamsburg city, VA	15,052	13,673	11,998	1,379	1,675	10.1	14.0	9.0	58.2	17.0	15.8	54.1
Visalia-Porterville, CA Metro Area	459,863	442,182	368,011	17,681	74,171	4.0	20.2	26.3	42.0	21.1	10.7	49.9
Tulare County, CA	459,863	442,182	368,011	17,681	74,171	4.0	20.2	26.3	42.0	21.1	10.7	49.9
Waco, TX Metro Area	262,813	252,772	232,088	10,041	20,684	4.0	8.9	20.4	42.8	22.9	13.8	51.3
Falls County, TX	17,142	17,866	18,563	-724	-697	-4.1	-3.8	17.6	38.8	26.6	17.0	52.5
McLennan County, TX	245,671	234,906	213,525	10,765	21,381	4.6	10.0	20.6	43.1	22.7	13.6	51.2
Walla Walla, WA Metro Area	64,282	62,859	59,241	1,423	3,618	2.3	6.1	17.5	40.3	24.7	17.5	48.9
Columbia County, WA	3,944	4,078	4,064	-134	14	-3.3	0.3	14.3	28.9	29.4	27.4	50.3
Walla Walla County, WA	60,338	58,781	55,177	1,557	3,604	2.6	6.5	17.7	41.1	24.4	16.9	48.8
Warner Robins, GA Metro Area	188,149	179,605	144,046	8,544	35,559	4.8	24.7	20.6	40.9	25.6	12.8	51.7
Houston County, GA	150,033	139,912	110,740	10,121	29,172	7.2	26.3	21.3	41.3	25.3	12.1	51.3
Peach County, GA	26,720	27,694	23,702	-974	3,992	-3.5	16.8	18.6	41.0	26.4	14.0	52.0
Pulaski County, GA	11,396	11,999	9,604	-603	2,395	-5.0	24.9	15.9	36.2	28.4	19.5	56.7
Washington-Arlington-Alexandria, DC-VA-MD-WV Metro Area	**6,097,684**	**5,636,406**	**4,837,674**	**461,278**	**798,732**	**8.2**	**16.5**	**19.4**	**42.5**	**26.4**	**11.8**	**51.1**
Silver Spring-Frederick-Rockville, MD Division	*1,285,438*	*1,205,191*	*1,069,151*	*80,247*	*136,040*	*6.7*	*12.7*	*19.5*	*38.9*	*27.8*	*13.9*	*51.6*
Frederick County, MD	245,322	233,385	195,277	11,937	38,108	5.1	19.5	19.3	38.6	28.8	13.3	50.6
Montgomery County, MD	1,040,116	971,806	873,874	68,310	97,932	7.0	11.2	19.5	38.9	27.5	14.1	51.8
Washington-Arlington-Alexandria, DC-VA-MD-WV Division	*4,812,246*	*4,431,215*	*3,768,523*	*381,031*	*662,692*	*8.6*	*17.6*	*19.4*	*43.4*	*26.0*	*11.2*	*51.0*
District of Columbia, DC	672,228	601,767	572,086	70,461	29,681	11.7	5.2	15.3	51.4	21.9	11.5	52.6
Calvert County, MD	90,595	88,737	74,556	1,858	14,181	2.1	19.0	19.0	36.3	31.2	13.5	50.6
Charles County, MD	156,118	146,551	120,524	9,567	26,027	6.5	21.6	19.8	39.9	28.8	11.5	51.8
Prince George's County, MD	909,535	863,519	801,091	46,016	62,428	5.3	7.8	18.9	42.6	26.8	11.7	51.8
Arlington County, VA	229,164	207,676	189,211	21,488	18,465	10.3	9.8	15.3	52.9	22.4	9.5	49.9
Clarke County, VA	14,363	14,029	12,638	334	1,391	2.4	11.0	17.0	31.3	32.7	19.0	50.2
Culpeper County, VA	49,432	46,691	34,260	2,741	12,431	5.9	36.3	20.9	37.1	27.6	14.4	49.9
Fairfax County, VA	1,142,234	1,081,685	969,987	60,549	111,698	5.6	11.5	19.8	40.7	27.5	11.9	50.5
Fauquier County, VA	68,782	65,275	55,145	3,507	10,130	5.4	18.4	19.2	35.0	30.4	15.4	50.6
Loudoun County, VA	375,629	312,336	169,599	63,293	142,737	20.3	84.2	24.5	41.7	25.5	8.3	50.4
Prince William County, VA	451,721	401,972	281,317	49,749	120,655	12.4	42.9	23.4	42.8	25.1	8.7	50.1
Rappahannock County, VA	7,378	7,506	6,994	-128	512	-1.7	7.3	13.6	30.1	31.8	24.6	50.7
Spotsylvania County, VA	130,475	122,660	90,289	7,815	32,371	6.4	35.9	20.6	39.1	27.5	12.8	50.7
Stafford County, VA	142,003	128,952	92,456	13,051	36,496	10.1	39.5	21.5	42.2	26.9	9.5	49.7
Warren County, VA	39,083	37,431	31,553	1,652	5,878	4.4	18.6	18.6	36.9	29.5	15.0	50.0
Alexandria city, VA	153,511	140,006	128,278	13,505	11,728	9.6	9.1	15.9	49.0	24.7	10.3	51.8

0 = represents zero or rounds to zero.
¹The April 1, 2000 and 2010 population estimates bases reflect modifications to the census populations as documented in the Count Question Resolution program and geographic program revisions.
²Based on the April 1, 2010 estimates base and the July 1, 2015 estimates
³Based on the April 1, 2000 and April 1, 2010 estimates bases.

Table C-1. Population and Population Characteristics—*Continued*

Metropolitan statistical area, division, and component county	Population 2015 estimate (July 1)	Population 2010[1] (estimates base) (April 1)	Population 2000[1] (estimates base) (April 1)	Net change 2010–2015[2]	Net change 2000–2010[3]	Percent change 2010–2015[2]	Percent change 2000–2010[3]	Under 15 years	15 to 44 years	45 to 64 years	65 years and over	Percent female
Fairfax city, VA	24,013	22,542	21,576	1,471	966	6.5	4.5	18.7	38.8	26.2	16.2	50.4
Falls Church city, VA	13,892	12,289	10,432	1,603	1,857	13.0	17.8	21.8	38.3	28.5	11.4	50.8
Fredericksburg city, VA	28,118	24,023	19,367	4,095	4,656	17.0	24.0	18.0	51.1	20.4	10.5	54.5
Manassas city, VA	41,764	37,839	34,692	3,925	3,147	10.4	9.1	22.9	43.8	24.6	8.7	49.8
Manassas Park city, VA	15,726	14,241	10,226	1,485	4,015	10.4	39.3	21.7	46.8	24.0	7.5	48.9
Jefferson County, WV	56,482	53,488	42,246	2,994	11,242	5.6	26.6	19.0	37.2	29.3	14.5	50.7
Waterloo-Cedar Falls, IA Metro Area	170,612	167,819	163,721	2,793	4,098	1.7	2.5	18.2	41.6	24.2	16.0	51.0
Black Hawk County, IA	133,455	131,090	127,990	2,365	3,100	1.8	2.4	18.1	42.9	23.8	15.2	51.0
Bremer County, IA	24,722	24,276	23,361	446	915	1.8	3.9	17.9	38.1	25.1	18.9	50.7
Grundy County, IA	12,435	12,453	12,370	-18	83	-0.1	0.7	19.3	33.5	27.3	19.9	50.9
Watertown-Fort Drum, NY Metro Area	117,635	116,232	111,716	1,403	4,516	1.2	4.0	21.1	44.8	21.5	12.6	47.5
Jefferson County, NY	117,635	116,232	111,716	1,403	4,516	1.2	4.0	21.1	44.8	21.5	12.6	47.5
Wausau, WI Metro Area	135,868	134,063	125,908	1,805	8,155	1.3	6.5	19.0	36.1	28.4	16.4	49.8
Marathon County, WI	135,868	134,063	125,908	1,805	8,155	1.3	6.5	19.0	36.1	28.4	16.4	49.8
Weirton-Steubenville, WV-OH Metro Area	120,512	124,455	131,995	-3,943	-7,540	-3.2	-5.7	15.5	34.3	29.7	20.5	51.3
Jefferson County, OH	67,347	69,709	73,886	-2,362	-4,177	-3.4	-5.7	15.9	34.9	29.4	19.8	51.3
Brooke County, WV	23,350	24,071	25,427	-721	-1,356	-3.0	-5.3	14.1	34.4	29.4	22.1	50.9
Hancock County, WV	29,815	30,675	32,682	-860	-2,007	-2.8	-6.1	15.9	32.8	30.6	20.7	51.6
Wenatchee, WA Metro Area	116,178	110,887	99,200	5,291	11,687	4.8	11.8	20.6	36.2	25.9	17.4	49.9
Chelan County, WA	75,644	72,456	66,611	3,188	5,845	4.4	8.8	20.0	35.8	26.3	17.9	50.1
Douglas County, WA	40,534	38,431	32,589	2,103	5,842	5.5	17.9	21.6	36.9	25.1	16.4	49.6
Wheeling, WV-OH Metro Area	144,198	147,949	153,200	-3,751	-5,251	-2.5	-3.4	15.9	35.4	29.1	19.6	50.2
Belmont County, OH	69,154	70,400	70,239	-1,246	161	-1.8	0.2	15.6	35.7	29.4	19.3	48.9
Marshall County, WV	31,978	33,107	35,529	-1,129	-2,422	-3.4	-6.8	16.3	33.6	29.8	20.2	50.8
Ohio County, WV	43,066	44,442	47,432	-1,376	-2,990	-3.1	-6.3	16.0	36.2	28.0	19.8	52.0
Wichita, KS Metro Area	644,610	630,919	579,860	13,691	51,059	2.2	8.8	21.7	39.5	25.0	13.8	50.3
Butler County, KS	66,741	65,880	59,455	861	6,425	1.3	10.8	20.7	38.2	26.8	14.3	49.7
Harvey County, KS	35,073	34,684	32,885	389	1,799	1.1	5.5	20.7	36.3	24.8	18.2	50.8
Kingman County, KS	7,687	7,858	8,675	-171	-817	-2.2	-9.4	17.8	31.9	28.5	21.8	50.0
Sedgwick County, KS	511,574	498,365	452,901	13,209	45,464	2.7	10.0	22.0	40.2	24.6	13.1	50.3
Sumner County, KS	23,535	24,132	25,944	-597	-1,812	-2.5	-7.0	20.5	34.4	27.6	17.6	50.3
Wichita Falls, TX Metro Area	150,780	151,476	151,596	-696	-120	-0.5	-0.1	18.7	42.0	24.4	14.9	48.5
Archer County, TX	8,715	9,055	8,904	-340	151	-3.8	1.7	16.6	34.4	30.1	18.9	50.1
Clay County, TX	10,360	10,752	10,997	-392	-245	-3.6	-2.2	17.4	31.3	31.0	20.4	49.8
Wichita County, TX	131,705	131,669	131,695	36	-26	0.0	0.0	18.9	43.4	23.6	14.2	48.3
Williamsport, PA Metro Area	116,048	116,108	120,003	-60	-3,895	-0.1	-3.2	17.1	37.1	27.9	17.9	50.8
Lycoming County, PA	116,048	116,108	120,003	-60	-3,895	-0.1	-3.2	17.1	37.1	27.9	17.9	50.8
Wilmington, NC Metro Area	277,969	254,884	201,386	23,085	53,498	9.1	26.6	16.5	41.0	26.1	16.4	51.6
New Hanover County, NC	220,358	202,683	160,315	17,675	42,368	8.7	26.4	16.0	42.4	25.4	16.2	52.0
Pender County, NC	57,611	52,201	41,071	5,410	11,130	10.4	27.1	18.2	35.6	28.8	17.4	50.1
Winchester, VA-WV Metro Area	133,836	128,473	102,996	5,363	25,477	4.2	24.7	18.5	37.1	28.0	16.4	50.1
Frederick County, VA	83,199	78,308	59,226	4,891	19,082	6.2	32.2	19.2	36.9	28.1	15.7	50.2
Winchester city, VA	27,284	26,201	23,599	1,083	2,602	4.1	11.0	18.6	41.0	25.2	15.1	50.6
Hampshire County, WV	23,353	23,964	20,171	-611	3,793	-2.5	18.8	15.8	33.2	30.6	20.3	49.3
Winston-Salem, NC Metro Area	659,330	640,577	569,355	18,753	71,222	2.9	12.5	18.7	37.3	27.7	16.3	51.8
Davidson County, North Carolina	164,622	162,878	147,248	1,744	15,630	1.1	10.6	18.2	35.6	28.9	17.3	51.0
Davie County, North Carolina	41,753	41,222	34,841	531	6,381	1.3	18.3	17.3	33.2	30.0	19.6	51.0
Forsyth County, North Carolina	369,019	350,670	306,274	18,349	44,396	5.2	14.5	19.6	39.2	26.4	14.7	52.5
Stokes County, North Carolina	46,351	47,401	44,640	-1,050	2,761	-2.2	6.2	15.6	33.7	30.9	19.7	50.8
Yadkin County, North Carolina	37,585	38,406	36,352	-821	2,054	-2.1	5.7	17.4	34.3	29.4	18.8	50.4
Worcester, MA-CT Metro Area	935,536	916,976	859,106	18,560	57,870	2.0	6.7	17.6	38.7	29.1	14.5	50.7
Windham County, CT	116,573	118,434	109,095	-1,861	9,339	-1.6	8.6	16.5	38.6	29.6	15.3	50.4
Worcester County, MA	818,963	798,542	750,011	20,421	48,531	2.6	6.5	17.7	38.8	29.1	14.4	50.7
Yakima, WA Metro Area	248,830	243,231	222,578	5,599	20,653	2.3	9.3	25.0	39.6	22.2	13.1	50.0
Yakima County, WA	248,830	243,231	222,578	5,599	20,653	2.3	9.3	25.0	39.6	22.2	13.1	50.0
York-Hanover, PA Metro Area	442,867	434,998	381,751	7,869	53,207	1.8	13.9	18.4	36.7	28.7	16.2	50.6
York County, PA	442,867	434,998	381,751	7,869	53,207	1.8	13.9	18.4	36.7	28.7	16.2	50.6
Youngstown-Warren-Boardman, OH-PA Metro Area	549,885	565,804	603,061	-15,919	-37,257	-2.8	-6.2	16.6	34.8	28.8	19.8	51.1
Mahoning County, OH	231,900	238,823	257,588	-6,923	-18,765	-2.9	-7.3	16.6	35.2	28.7	19.4	51.3
Trumbull County, OH	203,751	210,307	225,105	-6,556	-14,798	-3.1	-6.6	16.9	34.2	29.0	19.9	51.2
Mercer County, PA	114,234	116,674	120,368	-2,440	-3,694	-2.1	-3.1	16.0	35.1	28.7	20.3	50.8
Yuba City, CA Metro Area	170,955	166,892	139,196	4,063	27,696	2.4	19.9	22.4	40.4	23.7	13.5	49.8
Sutter County, CA	96,463	94,737	78,947	1,726	15,790	1.8	20.0	21.6	39.3	24.3	14.9	50.4
Yuba County, CA	74,492	72,155	60,249	2,337	11,906	3.2	19.8	23.5	41.9	22.9	11.8	49.2
Yuma, AZ Metro Area	204,275	195,750	159,995	8,525	35,755	4.4	22.3	21.5	39.8	20.6	18.0	48.6
Yuma County, AZ	204,275	195,750	159,995	8,525	35,755	4.4	22.3	21.5	39.8	20.6	18.0	48.6

0 = represents zero or rounds to zero.
[1] The April 1, 2000 and 2010 population estimates bases reflect modifications to the census populations as documented in the Count Question Resolution program and geographic program revisions.
[2] Based on the April 1, 2010 estimates base and the July 1, 2015 estimates
[3] Based on the April 1, 2000 and April 1, 2010 estimates bases.

Table C-2.   Population Characteristics and Housing Units

| Metropolitan statistical area, division, and component county | Population characteristics, 2015 | | | | | | Housing units | | | | | |
| | Race alone or in combination (percent) | | | | | Hispanic or Latino origin[1] (percent) | 2015 (July 1 estimate) | 2010 (July 1 estimate) | 2005 (July 1 estimate) | 2000 (July 1 estimate) | Percent change | |
	White	Black or African American	Asian	American Indian, Alaska Native	Native Hawaiian and Other Pacific Islander						2010–2015	2005–2010
Abilene, TX Metro Area	88.8	9.3	1.8	2.5	0.3	23.2	70,931	69,748	67,934	65,395	1.7	2.7
Callahan County, TX	96.8	2.4	1.6	0.9	0.1	9.9	6,595	6,551	6,279	5,932	0.7	4.3
Jones County, TX	84.2	14.2	1.9	1.2	0.2	27.4	7,403	7,417	7,377	7,253	-0.2	0.5
Taylor County, TX	88.7	9.2	1.7	2.9	0.3	23.9	56,933	55,780	54,278	52,210	2.1	2.8
Akron, OH Metro Area	84.3	13.9	0.8	3.3	0.1	1.9	313,488	312,602	306,332	291,804	0.3	2.0
Portage County, OH	93.1	5.6	0.7	2.4	0.1	1.7	68,194	67,477	65,105	60,339	1.1	3.6
Summit County, OH	81.7	16.4	0.8	3.5	0.1	2.0	245,294	245,125	241,227	231,465	0.1	1.6
Albany, GA Metro Area	45.0	54.0	0.7	1.4	0.2	2.7	66,489	66,149	66,098	63,901	0.5	0.1
Baker County, GA	51.9	47.4	0.7	1.3	0.1	4.9	1,623	1,651	1,715	1,731	-1.7	-3.7
Dougherty County, GA	29.6	69.5	0.7	1.2	0.3	2.7	40,701	40,794	40,825	39,737	-0.2	-0.1
Lee County, GA	76.3	21.5	0.8	2.8	0.2	2.8	10,848	10,296	10,006	8,855	5.4	2.9
Terrell County, GA	39.1	60.4	0.9	0.8	0.3	2.7	4,147	4,161	4,298	4,455	-0.3	-3.2
Worth County, GA	70.0	29.6	0.7	0.7	0.1	2.2	9,170	9,247	9,254	9,123	-0.8	-0.1
Albany, OR Metro Area	96.3	1.3	3.4	1.9	0.4	8.7	49,164	48,843	45,748	42,661	0.7	6.8
Linn County, OR	96.3	1.3	3.4	1.9	0.4	8.7	49,164	48,843	45,748	42,661	0.7	6.8
Albany-Schenectady-Troy, NY Metro Area	86.5	10.2	0.9	5.0	0.2	5.0	398,546	393,421	380,940	364,471	1.3	3.3
Albany County, NY	79.3	15.5	0.8	7.1	0.2	5.9	138,713	137,731	134,778	130,211	0.7	2.2
Rensselaer County, NY	89.4	8.9	0.8	3.3	0.1	4.7	71,872	71,492	69,173	66,242	0.5	3.4
Saratoga County, NY	95.3	2.5	0.7	3.3	0.1	3.1	102,564	98,777	93,716	87,017	3.8	5.4
Schenectady County, NY	82.7	13.7	1.4	5.7	0.3	6.7	68,180	68,188	66,682	65,132	0.0	2.3
Schoharie County, NY	97.1	2.2	0.9	1.1	0.1	3.2	17,217	17,233	16,591	15,869	-0.1	3.9
Albuquerque, NM Metro Area	86.8	4.1	8.5	3.4	0.4	48.2	381,626	374,974	345,258	307,455	1.8	8.6
Bernalillo County, NM	87.3	4.5	7.3	3.8	0.4	49.2	288,992	284,696	267,601	239,649	1.5	6.4
Sandoval County, NM	81.5	3.4	15.2	2.5	0.4	37.8	54,690	52,375	42,919	35,726	4.4	22.0
Torrance County, NM	92.5	3.0	5.8	1.1	0.5	41.6	7,735	7,793	7,624	7,276	-0.7	2.2
Valencia County, NM	91.3	2.2	7.1	1.4	0.3	59.9	30,209	30,110	27,114	24,804	0.3	11.0
Alexandria, LA Metro Area	67.8	30.6	1.7	1.7	0.1	3.2	66,402	64,663	62,425	60,558	2.7	3.6
Grant Parish, LA	82.4	16.7	2.0	0.7	0.1	4.7	9,074	8,900	8,664	8,544	2.0	2.7
Rapides Parish, LA	65.3	32.9	1.6	1.9	0.1	3.0	57,328	55,763	53,761	52,014	2.8	3.7
Allentown-Bethlehem-Easton, PA-NJ Metro Area	89.2	8.2	1.1	3.6	0.2	15.6	345,227	342,478	328,836	308,188	0.8	4.1
Warren County, NJ	91.8	5.5	0.6	3.5	0.2	8.7	45,412	45,005	44,217	41,321	0.9	1.8
Carbon County, PA	97.0	2.4	0.7	0.8	0.2	4.2	34,387	34,321	32,386	30,546	0.2	6.0
Lehigh County, PA	86.5	10.5	1.4	4.2	0.2	22.4	143,847	142,737	136,961	129,237	0.8	4.2
Northampton County, PA	90.0	7.8	0.9	3.5	0.2	12.4	121,581	120,415	115,272	107,084	1.0	4.5
Altoona, PA Metro Area	97.1	2.8	0.4	1.0	0.1	1.2	56,011	56,262	56,145	55,077	-0.4	0.2
Blair County, PA	97.1	2.8	0.4	1.0	0.1	1.2	56,011	56,262	56,145	55,077	-0.4	0.2
Amarillo, TX Metro Area	88.7	7.6	1.8	3.7	0.2	28.1	107,873	103,509	98,095	92,624	4.2	5.5
Armstrong County, TX	96.7	2.2	1.8	0.4	0.0	9.5	900	904	921	920	-0.4	-1.8
Carson County, TX	96.9	1.6	2.4	0.7	0.1	10.1	2,773	2,784	2,823	2,813	-0.4	-1.4
Oldham County, TX	93.9	4.2	2.0	1.9	0.1	15.7	846	842	834	815	0.5	1.0
Potter County, TX	82.5	11.7	2.0	5.7	0.2	37.7	49,435	47,328	46,087	44,680	4.5	2.7
Randall County, TX	93.9	4.1	1.6	2.1	0.1	20.4	53,919	51,651	47,430	43,396	4.4	8.9
Ames, IA Metro Area	89.0	3.6	0.7	8.5	0.1	3.1	38,569	36,800	34,306	30,708	4.8	7.3
Story County, IA	89.0	3.6	0.7	8.5	0.1	3.1	38,569	36,800	34,306	30,708	4.8	7.3
Anchorage, AK Metro Area	76.8	7.0	12.4	9.8	2.6	8.0	156,278	154,440	143,236	128,250	1.2	7.8
Anchorage Municipality, AK	72.4	8.5	12.7	12.0	3.2	9.1	114,908	113,109	109,159	100,661	1.6	3.6
Matanuska-Susitna Borough, AK	89.7	2.4	11.5	3.0	0.8	4.8	41,370	41,331	34,077	27,589	0.1	21.3
Ann Arbor, MI Metro Area	77.4	14.5	1.3	10.4	0.2	4.6	150,075	147,748	144,845	131,863	1.6	2.0
Washtenaw County, MI	77.4	14.5	1.3	10.4	0.2	4.6	150,075	147,748	144,845	131,863	1.6	2.0
Anniston-Oxford-Jacksonville, AL Metro Area	77.2	22.1	1.2	1.3	0.2	3.6	53,326	53,316	52,620	51,309	0.0	1.3
Calhoun County, AL	77.2	22.1	1.2	1.3	0.2	3.6	53,326	53,316	52,620	51,309	0.0	1.3
Appleton, WI Metro Area	93.8	1.9	2.1	3.7	0.1	4.1	95,885	92,932	88,627	78,841	3.2	4.9
Calumet County, WI	96.3	1.3	1.0	2.7	0.1	4.3	20,192	19,717	18,713	15,900	2.4	5.4
Outagamie County, WI	93.2	2.1	2.4	3.9	0.1	4.1	75,693	73,215	69,914	62,941	3.4	4.7
Asheville, NC Metro Area	93.2	5.7	1.3	1.4	0.2	6.8	218,117	213,830	196,856	176,319	2.0	8.6
Buncombe County, NC	91.3	7.6	1.3	1.7	0.2	6.6	116,638	113,493	104,819	94,451	2.8	8.3
Haywood County, NC	97.4	1.7	1.3	0.7	0.1	3.7	35,111	34,971	32,119	28,812	0.4	8.9
Henderson County, NC	94.4	4.4	1.4	1.5	0.2	10.0	55,664	54,747	49,612	43,299	1.7	10.4
Madison County, NC	97.0	2.3	1.2	0.7	0.1	2.4	10,704	10,619	10,306	9,757	0.8	3.0
Athens-Clarke County, GA Metro Area	75.2	21.3	0.8	4.4	0.2	8.3	83,878	81,738	77,157	67,872	2.6	5.9
Clarke County, GA	67.2	28.6	0.8	5.3	0.2	10.6	52,221	51,067	48,812	42,481	2.3	4.6
Madison County, GA	88.4	10.3	0.9	1.8	0.1	4.9	11,749	11,784	11,261	10,565	-0.3	4.6
Oconee County, GA	89.8	6.2	0.6	4.7	0.1	4.9	13,418	12,397	11,147	9,450	8.2	11.2
Oglethorpe County, GA	81.2	18.7	0.8	1.0	0.1	3.9	6,490	6,490	5,937	5,376	0.0	9.3
Atlanta-Sandy Springs-Roswell, GA Metro Area	59.1	35.5	1.1	6.5	0.2	10.5	2,239,194	2,173,774	1,990,471	1,666,401	3.0	9.2
Barrow County, GA	83.7	13.0	1.1	4.2	0.2	10.0	27,241	26,404	23,094	17,532	3.2	14.3
Bartow County, GA	87.2	12.1	1.3	1.3	0.1	8.3	39,945	39,826	36,116	29,150	0.3	10.3
Butts County, GA	70.8	28.9	0.8	0.7	0.0	3.1	9,269	9,353	8,813	7,441	-0.9	6.1
Carroll County, GA	79.2	20.5	1.0	1.3	0.1	6.7	44,735	44,613	42,365	34,476	0.3	5.3
Cherokee County, GA	90.6	7.7	1.0	2.6	0.2	10.1	87,486	82,428	71,690	52,924	6.1	15.0
Clayton County, GA	24.6	70.4	1.3	5.8	0.2	13.0	104,719	104,704	100,665	87,260	0.0	4.0
Cobb County, GA	66.0	29.3	1.1	6.1	0.2	12.8	295,622	286,543	270,749	239,141	3.2	5.8
Coweta County, GA	79.3	19.0	1.0	2.5	0.2	6.8	52,660	50,228	43,384	33,555	4.8	15.8
Dawson County, GA	97.6	1.7	1.2	0.9	0.1	4.0	10,747	10,434	9,178	7,228	3.0	13.7
DeKalb County, GA	38.1	55.9	1.2	6.9	0.2	8.8	308,118	304,965	290,881	262,573	1.0	4.8
Douglas County, GA	52.7	46.3	1.2	2.2	0.3	9.1	52,012	51,667	45,596	35,166	0.7	13.3

0 = represents zero or rounds to zero.
[1]Persons of Hispanic origin may be of any race.

Table C-2.   Population Characteristics and Housing Units—*Continued*

Metropolitan statistical area, division, and component county	Population characteristics, 2015						Housing units					
	Race alone or in combination (percent)					Hispanic or Latino origin[1] (percent)	2015 (July 1 estimate)	2010 (July 1 estimate)	2005 (July 1 estimate)	2000 (July 1 estimate)	Percent change	
	White	Black or African American	Asian	American Indian, Alaska Native	Native Hawaiian and Other Pacific Islander						2010– 2015	2005– 2010
Fayette County, GA	71.9	23.7	1.1	5.4	0.3	7.3	41,613	40,799	38,171	33,003	2.0	6.9
Forsyth County, GA	85.2	4.4	0.9	11.1	0.2	9.6	74,095	64,225	51,367	37,341	15.4	25.0
Fulton County, GA	48.0	45.6	0.9	7.7	0.1	7.5	455,996	437,310	399,595	350,513	4.3	9.4
Gwinnett County, GA	59.2	29.2	1.5	12.7	0.2	20.5	301,824	291,662	266,330	212,550	3.5	9.5
Haralson County, GA	93.4	6.2	1.0	0.9	0.1	1.4	12,232	12,281	11,737	10,763	-0.4	4.6
Heard County, GA	88.0	11.8	1.2	0.8	0.1	2.6	5,097	5,145	4,964	4,528	-0.9	3.6
Henry County, GA	54.0	43.3	1.0	4.1	0.2	6.5	78,469	76,552	65,629	44,273	2.5	16.6
Jasper County, GA	77.6	22.5	1.1	0.6	0.1	4.0	6,264	6,159	5,714	4,852	1.7	7.8
Lamar County, GA	67.8	32.2	0.9	0.8	0.1	2.5	7,500	7,474	7,051	6,185	0.3	6.0
Meriwether County, GA	59.6	40.0	0.8	0.8	0.1	2.2	9,902	9,957	9,895	9,245	-0.6	0.6
Morgan County, GA	74.8	24.4	1.2	0.9	0.1	3.0	7,526	7,474	6,978	6,191	0.7	7.1
Newton County, GA	54.5	45.0	0.9	1.5	0.2	5.3	38,467	38,338	33,560	23,475	0.3	14.2
Paulding County, GA	79.7	19.9	1.0	1.6	0.2	5.8	53,948	52,185	43,517	29,939	3.4	19.9
Pickens County, GA	96.9	2.2	1.2	1.1	0.1	3.2	13,705	13,684	12,852	10,800	0.2	6.5
Pike County, GA	88.7	11.1	0.9	0.7	0.1	1.6	6,828	6,831	6,108	5,031	0.0	11.8
Rockdale County, GA	44.9	53.7	1.1	2.4	0.3	10.0	33,375	33,277	29,960	25,357	0.3	11.1
Spalding County, GA	64.8	34.7	1.0	1.2	0.2	4.5	27,063	26,807	25,447	23,114	1.0	5.3
Walton County, GA	80.7	18.0	0.8	1.8	0.2	4.1	32,736	32,449	29,065	22,795	0.9	11.6
Atlantic City-Hammonton, NJ Metro Area	73.2	18.6	1.3	9.3	0.2	18.7	127,865	126,785	122,432	114,431	0.9	3.6
Atlantic County, NJ	73.2	18.6	1.3	9.3	0.2	18.7	127,865	126,785	122,432	114,431	0.9	3.6
Auburn-Opelika, AL Metro Area	72.1	24.6	0.9	3.9	0.2	3.9	66,382	62,686	56,323	50,508	5.9	11.3
Lee County, AL	72.1	24.6	0.9	3.9	0.2	3.9	66,382	62,686	56,323	50,508	5.9	11.3
Augusta-Richmond County, GA-SC Metro Area	61.3	37.1	1.1	2.7	0.3	5.3	251,168	242,123	227,502	209,903	3.7	6.4
Burke County, GA	50.9	48.9	0.8	0.8	0.1	3.1	9,835	9,865	9,428	8,879	-0.3	4.6
Columbia County, GA	77.5	18.8	1.1	5.5	0.3	6.5	54,554	48,872	41,448	33,713	11.6	17.9
Lincoln County, GA	68.0	31.5	0.9	0.6	0.0	1.4	4,775	4,784	4,711	4,525	-0.2	1.5
McDuffie County, GA	57.4	42.4	0.8	0.8	0.1	2.8	9,233	9,313	9,237	8,946	-0.9	0.8
Richmond County, GA	41.4	57.4	1.1	2.6	0.4	4.8	87,612	86,400	85,223	82,336	1.4	1.4
Aiken County, SC	73.0	26.3	1.3	1.3	0.1	5.5	74,504	72,330	67,477	62,250	3.0	7.2
Edgefield County, SC	62.5	37.3	1.0	0.6	0.2	5.9	10,655	10,559	9,978	9,254	0.9	5.8
Austin-Round Rock, TX Metro Area	84.9	8.8	2.0	6.8	0.3	32.2	784,346	708,484	605,684	502,748	10.7	17.0
Bastrop County, TX	89.0	8.8	2.7	1.3	0.3	35.8	29,796	29,321	26,304	22,429	1.6	11.5
Caldwell County, TX	90.2	7.7	2.3	1.2	0.1	50.3	14,087	13,783	13,131	11,926	2.2	5.0
Hays County, TX	92.6	5.0	2.0	2.3	0.3	37.6	72,978	59,739	46,802	36,310	22.2	27.6
Travis County, TX	82.8	9.8	2.1	7.7	0.2	33.9	486,517	442,369	392,344	339,194	10.0	12.8
Williamson County, TX	85.6	7.9	1.6	7.5	0.3	24.1	180,968	163,272	127,103	92,889	10.8	28.5
Bakersfield, CA Metro Area	85.4	7.3	4.0	6.2	0.5	52.2	293,574	284,771	258,904	232,436	3.1	10.0
Kern County, CA	85.4	7.3	4.0	6.2	0.5	52.2	293,574	284,771	258,904	232,436	3.1	10.0
Baltimore-Columbia-Towson, MD Metro Area	64.0	31.0	1.1	6.5	0.2	5.5	1,155,341	1,133,025	1,099,693	1,050,614	2.0	3.0
Anne Arundel County, MD	78.2	18.6	1.1	5.1	0.3	7.3	220,989	212,763	203,071	187,804	3.9	4.8
Baltimore County, MD	64.8	29.7	1.0	6.9	0.2	5.2	337,439	335,688	327,876	314,305	0.5	2.4
Carroll County, MD	94.2	4.4	0.6	2.4	0.1	3.2	63,403	62,427	60,711	54,589	1.6	2.8
Harford County, MD	82.6	15.1	0.9	4.0	0.2	4.3	98,938	95,703	91,207	83,607	3.4	4.9
Howard County, MD	62.4	20.9	1.2	19.3	0.2	6.5	116,614	109,607	102,180	93,391	6.4	7.3
Queen Anne's County, MD	91.2	8.0	0.9	1.8	0.1	3.6	20,895	20,164	18,883	16,785	3.6	6.8
Baltimore city, MD	33.3	64.3	1.2	3.4	0.2	4.8	297,063	296,673	295,765	300,133	0.1	0.3
Bangor, ME Metro Area	96.7	1.4	2.1	1.5	0.1	1.3	74,331	73,893	70,673	66,999	0.6	4.6
Penobscot County, ME	96.7	1.4	2.1	1.5	0.1	1.3	74,331	73,893	70,673	66,999	0.6	4.6
Barnstable Town, MA Metro Area	94.9	3.6	1.3	1.9	0.1	2.8	162,118	160,348	155,798	147,569	1.1	2.9
Barnstable County, MA	94.9	3.6	1.3	1.9	0.1	2.8	162,118	160,348	155,798	147,569	1.1	2.9
Baton Rouge, LA Metro Area	61.4	36.6	0.8	2.6	0.1	3.8	345,301	330,417	303,788	283,453	4.5	8.8
Ascension Parish, LA	74.7	23.8	0.8	1.8	0.2	5.2	45,024	40,972	34,966	29,398	9.9	17.2
East Baton Rouge Parish, LA	50.0	46.9	0.7	3.8	0.1	4.0	192,436	187,522	177,044	169,395	2.6	5.9
East Feliciana Parish, LA	54.9	.44.8	1.0	0.6	0.1	1.4	8,216	8,027	7,919	7,920	2.4	1.4
Iberville Parish, LA	50.3	49.4	0.6	0.6	0.1	2.5	13,097	12,716	12,333	11,935	3.0	3.1
Livingston Parish, LA	92.2	7.0	1.0	0.9	0.1	3.6	54,438	50,415	42,483	36,552	8.0	18.7
Pointe Coupee Parish, LA	63.6	36.5	0.7	0.6	0.0	2.5	11,337	11,143	10,745	10,318	1.7	3.7
St. Helena Parish, LA	46.6	53.5	1.2	0.4	0.1	1.5	5,163	5,157	4,958	5,049	0.1	4.0
West Baton Rouge Parish, LA	60.2	39.6	0.6	0.8	0.1	3.0	10,297	9,358	8,584	8,386	10.0	9.0
West Feliciana Parish, LA	53.9	46.1	0.5	0.4	0.1	1.6	5,293	5,107	4,756	4,500	3.6	7.4
Battle Creek, MI Metro Area	85.6	13.3	1.8	2.6	0.2	4.8	60,602	61,011	60,740	58,824	-0.7	0.4
Calhoun County, MI	85.6	13.3	1.8	2.6	0.2	4.8	60,602	61,011	60,740	58,824	-0.7	0.4
Bay City, MI Metro Area	96.8	3.0	1.4	1.0	0.1	5.1	47,973	48,204	47,988	46,496	-0.5	0.5
Bay County, MI	96.8	3.0	1.4	1.0	0.1	5.1	47,973	48,204	47,988	46,496	-0.5	0.5
Beaumont-Port Arthur, TX Metro Area	71.6	25.2	1.4	3.2	0.2	14.5	175,558	169,929	167,496	164,290	3.3	1.5
Hardin County, TX	93.0	6.0	1.1	1.0	0.1	5.6	23,782	22,645	21,384	19,936	5.0	5.9
Jefferson County, TX	60.7	34.9	1.5	4.4	0.2	19.5	108,123	104,764	103,440	102,156	3.2	1.3
Newton County, TX	78.3	21.1	1.4	0.9	0.1	3.7	7,171	7,143	7,401	7,339	0.4	-3.5
Orange County, TX	89.1	9.5	1.4	1.4	0.1	7.1	36,482	35,377	35,271	34,859	3.1	0.3
Beckley, WV Metro Area	91.9	7.9	0.9	1.0	0.1	1.4	57,507	57,582	57,652	57,319	-0.1	-0.1
Fayette County, WV	94.7	5.5	0.8	0.3	0.0	1.1	21,494	21,620	21,853	21,628	-0.6	-1.1
Raleigh County, WV	90.2	9.3	0.9	1.4	0.1	1.5	36,013	35,962	35,799	35,691	0.1	0.5
Bellingham, WA Metro Area	90.5	2.2	4.8	6.1	0.7	9.2	93,247	90,721	84,216	74,335	2.8	7.7
Whatcom County, WA	90.5	2.2	4.8	6.1	0.7	9.2	93,247	90,721	84,216	74,335	2.8	7.7
Bend-Redmond, OR Metro Area	97.0	1.0	2.3	2.0	0.4	7.9	83,873	80,189	69,372	55,131	4.6	15.6
Deschutes County, OR	97.0	1.0	2.3	2.0	0.4	7.9	83,873	80,189	69,372	55,131	4.6	15.6

0 = represents zero or rounds to zero.
[1]Persons of Hispanic origin may be of any race.

Table C-2. Population Characteristics and Housing Units—*Continued*

| | Population characteristics, 2015 | | | | | | Housing units | | | | | |
| | Race alone or in combination (percent) | | | | | | | | | | Percent change | |
Metropolitan statistical area, division, and component county	White	Black or African American	Asian	American Indian, Alaska Native	Native Hawaiian and Other Pacific Islander	Hispanic or Latino origin[1] (percent)	2015 (July 1 estimate)	2010 (July 1 estimate)	2005 (July 1 estimate)	2000 (July 1 estimate)	2010– 2015	2005– 2010
Billings, MT Metro Area	93.9	1.5	5.9	1.3	0.2	5.3	74,482	71,028	66,272	60,720	4.9	7.2
Carbon County, MT	97.8	0.7	2.2	0.5	0.1	2.4	6,452	6,456	5,993	5,511	-0.1	7.7
Golden Valley County, MT	97.1	2.2	3.3	1.0	0.0	4.6	478	477	466	449	0.2	2.4
Yellowstone County, MT	93.7	1.6	6.2	1.3	0.2	5.4	67,552	64,095	59,813	54,760	5.4	7.2
Binghamton, NY Metro Area	91.0	6.2	0.8	4.3	0.2	3.6	111,802	112,740	111,866	110,305	-0.8	0.8
Broome County, NY	89.3	7.4	0.8	5.1	0.2	4.0	89,640	90,536	89,931	88,830		0.7
Tioga County, NY	97.9	1.6	0.7	1.1	0.1	1.7	22,162	22,204	21,935	21,475	-0.2	1.2
Birmingham-Hoover, AL Metro Area	68.8	29.8	0.9	1.8	0.1	4.4	509,664	500,258	481,883	455,698	1.9	3.8
Bibb County, AL	76.9	22.7	0.9	0.4	0.2	2.4	8,986	8,982	8,735	8,362	0.0	2.8
Blount County, AL	97.0	2.3	1.4	0.5	0.2	9.0	23,817	23,887	22,757	21,235	-0.3	5.0
Chilton County, AL	88.3	11.3	1.0	0.6	0.3	7.7	19,279	19,268	18,683	17,725	0.1	3.1
Jefferson County, AL	54.8	43.7	0.8	1.9	0.1	3.8	306,664	300,611	296,036	288,547	2.0	1.5
St. Clair County, AL	89.0	10.2	1.0	1.0	0.1	2.3	35,904	35,565	31,655	27,498	1.0	12.4
Shelby County, AL	84.8	13.1	0.8	2.6	0.1	5.8	84,365	81,135	72,041	59,907	4.0	12.6
Walker County, AL	92.5	7.1	1.1	0.6	0.1	2.4	30,649	30,810	31,976	32,424	-0.5	-3.6
Bismarck, ND Metro Area	91.1	1.8	7.8	1.0	0.1	2.4	57,904	50,174	46,034	41,864	15.4	9.0
Burleigh County, ND	93.4	2.0	5.1	1.1	0.1	2.1	41,248	35,858	32,560	29,137	15.0	10.1
Morton County, ND	94.3	1.5	5.3	0.7	0.2	2.7	14,393	12,100	11,284	10,608	19.0	7.2
Oliver County, ND	96.0	0.8	3.7	0.6	0.0	2.5	930	905	902	900	2.8	0.3
Sioux County, ND	18.6	0.8	83.2	0.5	0.1	4.3	1,333	1,311	1,288	1,219	1.7	1.8
Blacksburg-Christiansburg-Radford, VA Metro Area	91.3	5.4	0.7	4.5	0.1	2.6	79,457	78,425	74,312	69,695	1.3	5.5
Floyd County, VA	97.2	2.5	0.7	0.8	0.1	2.5	7,943	7,812	7,365	6,783	1.7	6.1
Giles County, VA	97.5	2.2	0.6	0.7	0.1	1.6	8,327	8,320	8,136	7,763	0.1	2.3
Montgomery County, VA	89.1	5.1	0.8	7.2	0.2	3.1	39,365	38,630	35,632	32,641	1.9	8.4
Pulaski County, VA	93.7	6.3	0.7	0.8	0.1	1.7	17,264	17,237	16,855	16,362	0.2	2.3
Radford city, VA	87.6	11.0	0.8	3.0	0.1	3.2	6,558	6,426	6,324	6,146	2.1	1.6
Bloomington, IL Metro Area	87.5	8.5	0.7	5.5	0.1	4.6	79,033	77,264	74,349	67,469	2.3	3.9
De Witt County, IL	98.3	1.5	0.7	0.8	0.1	2.4	7,506	7,519	7,470	7,293	-0.2	0.7
McLean County, IL	86.4	9.2	0.7	6.0	0.1	4.8	71,527	69,745	66,879	60,176	2.6	4.3
Bloomington, IN Metro Area	90.4	4.1	0.9	6.9	0.1	3.2	70,493	69,231	66,245	60,912	1.8	4.5
Monroe County, IN	89.2	4.6	0.9	7.8	0.2	3.5	60,523	59,135	56,209	51,034	2.3	5.2
Owen County, IN	98.5	1.0	0.9	0.8	0.1	1.3	9,970	10,096	10,036	9,878	-1.2	0.6
Bloomsburg-Berwick, PA Metro Area	96.1	2.5	0.5	1.8	0.1	2.7	37,642	37,488	36,815	35,405	0.4	1.8
Columbia County, PA	96.4	2.5	0.6	1.4	0.1	2.7	29,594	29,517	28,956	27,769	0.3	1.9
Montour County, PA	95.0	2.3	0.5	3.3	0.1	2.8	8,048	7,971	7,859	7,636	1.0	1.4
Boise City, ID Metro Area	95.2	1.7	2.2	3.2	0.5	13.4	260,390	246,398	218,857	182,764	5.7	12.6
Ada County, ID	94.8	2.0	1.7	4.0	0.5	8.0	170,868	159,754	141,931	119,537	7.0	12.6
Boise County, ID	96.9	0.8	2.6	0.9	0.9	3.7	5,358	5,298	4,835	4,361	1.1	9.6
Canyon County, ID	96.0	1.3	3.0	1.9	0.5	24.8	72,278	69,464	60,884	48,483	4.1	14.1
Gem County, ID	97.4	0.6	2.4	1.7	0.3	8.0	7,118	7,099	6,557	5,919	0.3	8.3
Owyhee County, ID	93.6	1.3	5.7	1.3	0.2	26.5	4,768	4,783	4,650	4,464	-0.3	2.9
Boston-Cambridge-Newton, MA-NH Metro Area...	82.2	10.4	1.0	8.7	0.2	10.6	1,917,255	1,884,051	1,825,947	1,754,936	1.8	3.2
Boston, MA Division	*76.6*	*16.2*	*1.0*	*8.5*	*0.3*	*11.1*	*804,241*	*786,406*	*760,506*	*730,598*	*2.3*	*3.4*
Norfolk County, MA	81.8	7.9	0.5	11.6	0.1	4.2	273,949	270,482	263,708	255,470	1.3	2.6
Plymouth County, MA	87.5	11.3	0.8	2.0	0.3	3.8	203,357	200,281	192,961	181,991	1.5	3.8
Suffolk County, MA	64.7	26.9	1.6	10.0	0.4	22.1	326,935	315,643	303,837	293,137	3.6	3.9
Cambridge-Newton-Framingham, MA Division...	*84.4*	*7.1*	*0.9*	*10.0*	*0.2*	*11.5*	*930,960*	*919,147*	*893,723*	*865,154*	*1.3*	*2.8*
Essex County, MA	88.4	8.1	1.4	4.4	0.3	19.2	309,219	306,763	299,114	287,647	0.8	2.6
Middlesex County, MA	82.4	6.5	0.7	12.7	0.2	7.8	621,741	612,384	594,609	577,507	1.5	3.0
Rockingham County-Strafford County, NH Division	*96.3*	*1.6*	*0.8*	*3.0*	*0.1*	*2.6*	*182,054*	*178,498*	*171,718*	*159,184*	*2.0*	*3.9*
Rockingham County, NH	96.8	1.4	0.7	2.5	0.1	2.7	129,359	126,762	122,173	113,497	2.0	3.8
Strafford County, NH	95.1	2.0	0.9	3.9	0.1	2.3	52,695	51,736	49,545	45,687	1.9	4.4
Boulder, CO Metro Area	93.1	1.8	1.7	6.0	0.2	13.9	132,457	127,118	122,756	112,068	4.2	3.6
Boulder County, CO	93.1	1.8	1.7	6.0	0.2	13.9	132,457	127,118	122,756	112,068	4.2	3.6
Bowling Green, KY Metro Area	89.6	8.5	0.9	2.9	0.3	4.3	71,928	68,939	64,448	58,620	4.3	7.0
Allen County, KY	98.2	1.7	0.8	0.5	0.1	2.1	9,325	9,311	8,813	8,098	0.2	5.7
Butler County, KY	98.4	1.1	1.1	0.4	0.0	3.8	5,858	5,876	5,896	5,817	-0.3	-0.3
Edmonson County, KY	97.5	2.2	0.9	0.4	0.0	1.0	6,450	6,467	6,382	6,120	-0.3	1.3
Warren County, KY	86.5	11.0	0.9	3.9	0.4	5.1	50,295	47,285	43,357	38,585	6.4	9.1
Bremerton-Silverdale, WA Metro Area	88.3	4.5	3.6	8.3	1.8	7.5	109,690	107,444	100,774	93,010	2.1	6.6
Kitsap County, WA	88.3	4.5	3.6	8.3	1.8	7.5	109,690	107,444	100,774	93,010	2.1	6.6
Bridgeport-Stamford-Norwalk, CT Metro Area...	81.1	13.5	1.0	6.3	0.2	19.1	366,122	361,342	351,146	340,078	1.3	2.9
Fairfield County, CT	81.1	13.5	1.0	6.3	0.2	19.1	366,122	361,342	351,146	340,078	1.3	2.9
Brownsville-Harlingen, TX Metro Area	97.6	1.1	0.8	0.9	0.1	88.8	147,492	142,142	134,625	120,234	3.8	5.6
Cameron County, TX	97.6	1.1	0.8	0.9	0.1	88.8	147,492	142,142	134,625	120,234	3.8	5.6
Brunswick, GA Metro Area	74.0	24.9	1.1	1.6	0.2	5.5	59,222	58,066	51,904	45,185	2.0	11.9
Brantley County, GA	95.6	4.3	1.2	0.4	0.0	2.1	7,888	8,073	7,430	6,540	-2.3	8.7
Glynn County, GA	70.9	27.7	1.1	2.0	0.3	6.9	42,053	40,765	37,113	32,836	3.2	9.8
McIntosh County, GA	64.3	35.2	1.0	0.7	0.2	2.1	9,281	9,228	7,361	5,809	0.6	25.4
Buffalo-Cheektowaga-Niagara Falls, NY Metro Area	83.3	13.9	1.3	3.6	0.1	4.8	520,981	519,147	518,229	511,881	0.4	0.2
Erie County, NY	81.7	15.1	1.2	4.0	0.1	5.2	421,840	419,982	420,401	416,085	0.4	-0.1
Niagara County, NY	90.3	8.7	1.8	1.5	0.1	2.8	99,141	99,165	97,828	95,796	0.0	1.4
Burlington, NC Metro Area	76.8	21.0	2.1	2.1	0.2	12.4	68,493	66,706	61,417	55,721	2.7	8.6
Alamance County, NC	76.8	21.0	2.1	2.1	0.2	12.4	68,493	66,706	61,417	55,721	2.7	8.6
Burlington-South Burlington, VT Metro Area	94.4	2.8	1.4	3.6	0.1	2.1	95,117	92,470	88,800	82,989	2.9	4.1

0 = represents zero or rounds to zero.
[1]Persons of Hispanic origin may be of any race.

Table C-2. Population Characteristics and Housing Units—*Continued*

Metropolitan statistical area, division, and component county	White	Black or African American	Asian	American Indian, Alaska Native	Native Hawaiian and Other Pacific Islander	Hispanic or Latino origin[1] (percent)	2015 (July 1 estimate)	2010 (July 1 estimate)	2005 (July 1 estimate)	2000 (July 1 estimate)	2010–2015	2005–2010
Chittenden County, VT	93.3	3.4	1.0	4.6	0.1	2.3	67,897	65,797	63,177	59,077	3.2	4.1
Franklin County, VT	97.7	1.2	2.5	0.9	0.1	1.4	22,090	21,618	20,699	19,242	2.2	4.4
Grand Isle County, VT	97.3	1.6	3.2	0.8	0.2	1.9	5,130	5,055	4,924	4,670	1.5	2.7
California-Lexington Park, MD Metro Area	81.8	16.4	1.1	4.0	0.2	4.9	43,625	41,376	38,657	34,336	5.4	7.0
St. Mary's County, MD	81.8	16.4	1.1	4.0	0.2	4.9	43,625	41,376	38,657	34,336	5.4	7.0
Canton-Massillon, OH Metro Area	91.3	9.0	0.9	1.2	0.1	1.9	179,318	178,906	176,333	170,237	0.2	1.5
Carroll County, OH	98.5	1.3	0.9	0.5	0.0	1.3	13,572	13,697	13,499	13,036	-0.9	1.5
Stark County, OH	90.8	9.0	0.9	1.2	0.1	1.9	165,746	165,209	162,834	157,201	0.3	1.5
Cape Coral-Fort Myers, FL Metro Area	88.4	10.0	0.9	2.2	0.2	19.9	379,018	371,109	316,255	247,782	2.1	17.3
Lee County, FL	88.4	10.0	0.9	2.2	0.2	19.9	379,018	371,109	316,255	247,782	2.1	17.3
Cape Girardeau, MO-IL Metro Area	89.5	9.7	1.0	1.6	0.1	2.1	42,912	42,520	41,589	39,679	0.9	2.2
Alexander County, IL	65.1	35.7	1.0	0.6	0.2	1.3	3,945	4,004	4,318	4,578	-1.5	-7.3
Bollinger County, MO	98.6	0.7	1.4	0.4	0.0	1.0	5,814	5,876	5,806	5,537	-1.1	1.2
Cape Girardeau County, MO	90.2	8.9	0.9	1.9	0.1	2.4	33,153	32,640	31,465	29,564	1.6	3.7
Carbondale-Marion, IL Metro Area	87.4	10.7	1.1	2.9	0.2	3.3	59,550	58,994	56,998	54,661	0.9	3.5
Jackson County, IL	80.1	16.6	1.4	4.8	0.2	4.2	28,692	28,612	27,652	26,888	0.3	3.5
Williamson County, IL	93.9	5.5	0.8	1.3	0.1	2.6	30,858	30,382	29,346	27,773	1.6	3.5
Carson City, NV Metro Area	92.0	2.8	4.2	3.5	0.6	23.4	23,445	23,524	22,985	21,369	-0.3	2.3
Carson City, NV	92.0	2.8	4.2	3.5	0.6	23.4	23,445	23,524	22,985	21,369	-0.3	2.3
Casper, WY Metro Area	96.0	2.3	2.4	1.4	0.3	8.4	36,067	33,884	31,421	29,952	6.4	7.8
Natrona County, WY	96.0	2.3	2.4	1.4	0.3	8.4	36,067	33,884	31,421	29,952	6.4	7.8
Cedar Rapids, IA Metro Area	93.4	5.4	0.8	2.5	0.2	2.8	115,320	112,487	108,190	99,271	2.5	4.0
Benton County, IA	98.8	1.1	0.6	0.5	0.1	1.5	11,085	11,094	10,961	10,393	-0.1	1.2
Jones County, IA	96.6	2.8	0.5	0.6	0.1	1.9	8,902	8,914	8,621	8,137	-0.1	3.4
Linn County, IA	92.4	6.2	0.8	2.9	0.2	3.0	95,333	92,479	88,608	80,741	3.1	4.4
Chambersburg-Waynesboro, PA Metro Area	94.5	5.1	0.7	1.5	0.1	5.2	64,325	63,304	58,950	54,022	1.6	7.4
Franklin County, PA	94.5	5.1	0.7	1.5	0.1	5.2	64,325	63,304	58,950	54,022	1.6	7.4
Champaign-Urbana, IL Metro Area	78.5	12.8	0.8	10.3	0.2	5.3	104,152	101,200	94,633	88,443	2.9	6.9
Champaign County, IL	75.7	14.5	0.8	11.7	0.2	5.7	90,478	87,647	81,312	75,562	3.2	7.8
Ford County, IL	98.1	1.6	0.8	0.6	0.1	3.0	6,330	6,284	6,206	6,063	0.7	1.3
Piatt County, IL	98.6	1.1	0.6	0.8	0.1	1.2	7,344	7,269	7,115	6,818	1.0	2.2
Charleston, WV Metro Area	92.1	7.8	0.8	1.4	0.1	1.0	108,076	108,250	109,716	110,249	-0.2	-1.3
Boone County, WV	99.0	1.0	0.4	0.2	0.0	0.5	11,012	11,069	11,458	11,575	-0.5	-3.4
Clay County, WV	99.3	0.8	0.9	0.2	0.1	0.6	4,570	4,577	4,737	4,838	-0.2	-3.4
Kanawha County, WV	90.9	9.0	0.9	1.6	0.1	1.1	92,494	92,604	93,521	93,836	-0.1	
Charleston-North Charleston, SC Metro Area	70.3	27.9	1.2	2.7	0.2	5.3	318,456	299,091	266,273	234,443	6.5	12.3
Berkeley County, SC	71.2	26.5	1.5	3.5	0.3	6.2	79,154	73,610	63,298	55,081	7.5	16.3
Charleston County, SC	69.5	28.9	0.9	2.2	0.2	5.0	180,681	170,167	157,166	141,817	6.2	8.3
Dorchester County, SC	71.0	27.4	1.5	2.8	0.3	5.0	58,621	55,314	45,809	37,545	6.0	20.7
Charlotte-Concord-Gastonia, NC-SC Metro Area	72.4	24.3	1.3	4.0	0.2	9.8	989,531	937,950	836,192	714,058	5.5	12.2
Cabarrus County, NC	78.4	18.9	1.2	3.5	0.2	10.1	76,892	72,174	63,168	53,302	6.5	14.3
Gaston County, NC	81.4	17.5	1.1	1.8	0.1	6.6	90,398	88,793	84,559	79,193	1.8	5.0
Iredell County, NC	84.4	13.4	1.1	2.9	0.1	7.4	70,906	69,101	61,222	52,362	2.6	12.9
Lincoln County, NC	92.9	6.6	0.9	0.9	0.1	7.2	34,241	33,654	30,457	26,006	1.7	10.5
Mecklenburg County, NC	60.8	33.8	1.5	6.3	0.2	12.8	427,826	399,096	352,974	296,038	7.2	13.1
Rowan County, NC	81.4	17.6	1.2	1.4	0.1	8.3	60,241	60,216	57,915	54,235	0.0	4.0
Union County, NC	84.4	13.3	1.2	3.0	0.1	11.0	77,794	72,984	60,880	46,441	6.6	19.9
Chester County, SC	61.9	38.0	1.0	0.7	0.1	1.9	14,582	14,697	14,691	14,416	-0.8	0.0
Lancaster County, SC	75.9	23.4	0.8	1.3	0.1	5.1	35,063	32,692	29,173	25,198	7.3	12.1
York County, SC	77.4	20.7	1.5	2.3	0.1	5.1	101,588	94,543	81,153	66,867	7.5	16.5
Charlottesville, VA Metro Area	81.2	15.5	1.0	4.8	0.2	4.9	100,874	96,504	90,245	80,480	4.5	6.9
Albemarle County, VA	84.5	11.1	1.0	5.9	0.2	5.8	44,258	42,175	39,232	33,867	4.9	7.5
Buckingham County, VA	64.4	36.1	0.7	0.6	0.1	2.4	7,290	7,243	6,774	6,312	0.6	6.9
Fluvanna County, VA	83.4	16.6	0.8	1.2	0.2	3.2	10,739	10,410	9,765	8,081	3.2	6.6
Greene County, VA	90.9	8.4	1.0	2.1	0.2	5.2	8,091	7,533	6,906	6,032	7.4	9.1
Nelson County, VA	86.3	13.7	1.1	0.8	0.1	3.7	10,073	9,938	9,344	8,586	1.4	6.4
Charlottesville city, VA	73.0	20.6	1.0	8.4	0.2	5.0	20,423	19,205	18,224	17,602	6.3	5.4
Chattanooga, TN-GA Metro Area	83.5	14.8	1.1	2.1	0.2	4.2	240,080	234,595	222,445	206,170	2.3	5.5
Catoosa County, GA	95.0	3.7	1.0	1.8	0.1	2.9	26,882	26,620	24,782	21,879	1.0	7.4
Dade County, GA	96.7	1.9	1.2	1.4	0.1	2.4	7,252	7,303	6,822	6,253	-0.7	7.1
Walker County, GA	94.3	5.6	0.9	0.7	0.1	2.0	30,097	30,102	28,324	25,750	0.0	6.3
Hamilton County, TN	77.2	20.6	1.2	2.6	0.2	5.2	156,385	151,234	143,973	135,179	3.4	5.0
Marion County, TN	94.8	4.8	1.1	0.7	0.1	1.6	13,078	12,963	12,874	12,202	0.9	0.7
Sequatchie County, TN	98.1	1.3	1.2	0.5	0.1	3.4	6,386	6,373	5,670	4,907	0.2	12.4
Cheyenne, WY Metro Area	94.0	4.1	2.3	2.1	0.3	14.5	41,955	40,530	37,744	34,317	3.5	7.4
Laramie County, WY	94.0	4.1	2.3	2.1	0.3	14.5	41,955	40,530	37,744	34,317	3.5	7.4
Chicago-Naperville-Elgin, IL-IN-WI Metro Area	**75.1**	**18.1**	**1.2**	**7.4**	**0.2**	**21.9**	**3,812,136**	**3,796,957**	**3,675,474**	**3,471,602**	**0.4**	**3.3**
Chicago-Naperville-Arlington Heights, IL Division	*72.3*	*20.1*	*1.2*	*8.2*	*0.1*	*22.3*	*2,956,521*	*2,949,916*	*2,869,278*	*2,740,284*	*0.2*	*2.8*
Cook County, IL	67.3	25.1	1.3	8.2	0.2	25.2	2,178,274	2,179,702	2,141,972	2,097,845	-0.1	1.8
DuPage County, IL	82.5	6.0	0.8	12.6	0.1	14.3	358,144	356,163	351,270	336,656	0.6	1.4
Grundy County, IL	97.1	2.1	0.7	1.2	0.1	9.6	20,487	20,008	18,011	15,114	2.4	11.1
Kendall County, IL	88.9	8.1	0.9	4.1	0.1	17.6	41,442	40,364	30,246	19,872	2.7	33.5
McHenry County, IL	94.9	2.1	0.9	3.6	0.1	12.6	117,351	116,113	109,294	93,422	1.1	6.2
Will County, IL	81.8	12.8	0.9	6.3	0.1	16.8	240,823	237,566	218,483	177,375	1.4	8.7
Elgin, IL Division	*88.6*	*7.3*	*1.4*	*4.5*	*0.1*	*28.1*	*225,916*	*223,191*	*204,527*	*173,621*	*1.2*	*9.1*
DeKalb County, IL	89.0	8.5	0.9	3.4	0.1	10.9	40,976	41,092	37,310	33,141	-0.3	10.1
Kane County, IL	88.5	7.0	1.5	4.8	0.1	31.5	184,940	182,099	167,217	140,480	1.6	8.9

0 = represents zero or rounds to zero.
[1]Persons of Hispanic origin may be of any race.

Table C-2. Population Characteristics and Housing Units—*Continued*

| | Population characteristics, 2015 | | | | | | Housing units | | | | | |
| | Race alone or in combination (percent) | | | | | | | | | | Percent change | |
Metropolitan statistical area, division, and component county	White	Black or African American	Asian	American Indian, Alaska Native	Native Hawaiian and Other Pacific Islander	Hispanic or Latino origin[1] (percent)	2015 (July 1 estimate)	2010 (July 1 estimate)	2005 (July 1 estimate)	2000 (July 1 estimate)	2010– 2015	2005– 2010
Gary, IN Division	*79.5*	*19.3*	*1.1*	*1.9*	*0.1*	*15.4*	*297,657*	*294,238*	*285,660*	*270,298*	*1.2*	*3.0*
Jasper County, IN	98.2	1.4	0.8	0.7	0.1	6.0	13,371	13,181	12,467	11,287	1.4	5.7
Lake County, IN	72.6	26.1	1.2	2.0	0.1	18.3	210,868	208,809	204,050	195,352	1.0	2.3
Newton County, IN	98.2	1.2	1.0	0.6	0.1	5.9	6,035	6,030	5,980	5,765	0.1	0.8
Porter County, IN	94.0	4.6	0.9	2.0	0.1	9.7	67,383	66,218	63,163	57,894	1.8	4.8
Lake County-Kenosha County, IL-WI Division	*85.1*	*8.5*	*1.4*	*7.2*	*0.2*	*19.6*	*332,042*	*329,612*	*316,009*	*287,399*	*0.7*	*4.3*
Lake County, IL	83.9	8.3	1.4	8.4	0.2	21.3	262,331	260,318	249,613	227,135	0.8	4.3
Kenosha County, WI	89.9	8.9	1.5	2.3	0.2	12.8	69,711	69,294	66,396	60,264	0.6	4.4
Chico, CA Metro Area	90.5	3.0	4.5	6.1	0.6	15.7	98,035	95,923	92,258	85,759	2.2	4.0
Butte County, CA	90.5	3.0	4.5	6.1	0.6	15.7	98,035	95,923	92,258	85,759	2.2	4.0
Cincinnati, OH-KY-IN Metro Area	84.6	13.8	0.8	2.9	0.2	3.0	922,108	911,493	886,063	830,215	1.2	2.9
Dearborn County, IN	98.4	1.3	0.6	0.7	0.1	1.2	20,262	20,180	19,528	17,901	0.4	3.3
Ohio County, IN	98.8	1.0	0.7	0.6	0.1	1.1	2,805	2,783	2,658	2,410	0.8	4.7
Union County, IN	98.5	1.3	1.0	0.6	0.1	1.5	3,218	3,239	3,276	3,086	-0.6	-1.1
Boone County, KY	93.6	4.1	0.7	3.3	0.2	4.1	48,239	46,257	41,959	33,744	4.3	10.2
Bracken County, KY	98.8	1.5	0.8	0.3	0.0	1.6	3,825	3,840	3,825	3,721	-0.4	0.4
Campbell County, KY	95.4	4.3	0.7	1.4	0.1	1.9	39,942	39,559	38,447	36,963	1.0	2.9
Gallatin County, KY	97.2	2.8	0.9	0.7	0.1	5.5	3,836	3,791	3,592	3,368	1.2	5.5
Grant County, KY	98.1	1.7	0.7	0.6	0.2	2.6	9,983	9,944	9,914	9,347	0.4	0.3
Kenton County, KY	93.2	6.3	0.7	1.7	0.2	3.1	69,689	69,011	67,181	63,683	1.0	2.7
Pendleton County, KY	98.8	0.9	0.7	0.5	0.1	1.2	6,308	6,337	6,125	5,781	-0.5	3.5
Brown County, OH	98.4	1.5	0.8	0.4	0.0	0.9	19,409	19,305	17,657	17,146	0.5	9.3
Butler County, OH	88.1	9.7	0.8	3.5	0.2	4.5	149,891	148,346	141,665	130,273	1.0	4.7
Clermont County, OH	97.0	2.2	0.7	1.5	0.1	1.8	82,250	80,727	77,569	69,284	1.9	4.1
Hamilton County, OH	70.8	27.8	0.8	3.0	0.2	3.0	377,685	377,262	379,153	373,586	0.1	-0.5
Warren County, OH	91.1	4.2	0.6	5.7	0.1	2.6	84,766	80,912	73,514	59,922	4.8	10.1
Clarksville, TN-KY Metro Area	76.6	21.9	1.7	3.4	0.7	8.8	115,905	107,680	97,164	86,584	7.6	10.8
Christian County, KY	75.6	23.2	1.5	2.5	0.7	7.5	29,763	29,458	28,710	27,325	1.0	2.6
Trigg County, KY	91.6	8.6	1.0	0.7	0.1	2.0	7,837	7,812	7,337	6,734	0.3	6.5
Montgomery County, TN	75.9	22.4	1.8	3.9	0.7	9.9	78,305	70,410	61,117	52,525	11.2	15.2
Cleveland, TN Metro Area	93.8	5.2	1.3	1.3	0.2	5.3	51,364	49,449	47,200	44,347	3.9	4.8
Bradley County, TN	93.1	5.9	1.3	1.5	0.2	5.8	42,878	41,438	39,570	36,962	3.5	4.7
Polk County, TN	98.2	1.2	1.5	0.5	0.1	1.8	8,486	8,011	7,630	7,385	5.9	5.0
Cleveland-Elyria, OH Metro Area	76.7	21.8	0.8	2.8	0.1	5.5	957,499	955,762	941,938	912,850	0.2	1.5
Cuyahoga County, OH	66.0	31.7	0.8	3.6	0.1	5.6	618,165	621,535	622,194	617,165	-0.5	-0.1
Geauga County, OH	97.8	1.8	0.4	1.0	0.0	1.4	36,838	36,580	35,440	33,004	0.7	3.2
Lake County, OH	94.3	5.0	0.6	1.7	0.1	4.1	102,068	101,216	98,142	93,679	0.8	3.1
Lorain County, OH	89.2	10.9	1.2	1.7	0.1	9.5	129,295	127,114	121,471	111,814	1.7	4.6
Medina County, OH	97.1	2.1	0.6	1.5	0.0	2.0	71,133	69,317	64,691	57,188	2.6	7.2
Coeur d'Alene, ID Metro Area	96.9	0.8	2.7	1.7	0.3	4.4	67,028	63,351	55,596	46,939	5.8	13.9
Kootenai County, ID	96.9	0.8	2.7	1.7	0.3	4.4	67,028	63,351	55,596	46,939	5.8	13.9
College Station-Bryan, TX Metro Area	81.8	12.8	1.3	5.8	0.2	24.3	102,735	95,199	85,495	75,583	7.9	11.4
Brazos County, TX	81.9	12.0	1.2	6.6	0.2	24.9	85,223	77,878	68,619	59,480	9.4	13.5
Burleson County, TX	85.4	13.8	1.7	0.6	0.1	20.5	8,925	8,835	8,628	8,218	1.0	2.4
Robertson County, TX	77.7	21.3	1.5	1.0	0.1	20.1	8,587	8,486	8,248	7,885	1.2	2.9
Colorado Springs, CO Metro Area	88.1	8.8	2.7	4.7	0.8	16.2	281,862	265,717	248,013	214,514	6.1	7.1
El Paso County, CO	87.8	9.1	2.8	4.8	0.8	16.6	268,981	253,071	236,071	204,051	6.3	7.2
Teller County, CO	96.8	1.4	2.4	1.5	0.2	6.4	12,881	12,646	11,942	10,463	1.9	5.9
Columbia, MO Metro Area	85.0	11.2	1.2	5.5	0.2	3.3	74,436	69,671	64,653	56,980	6.8	7.8
Boone County, MO	85.0	11.2	1.2	5.5	0.2	3.3	74,436	69,671	64,653	56,980	6.8	7.8
Columbia, SC Metro Area	63.0	35.2	1.1	2.7	0.2	5.4	345,117	332,114	301,929	270,721	3.9	10.0
Calhoun County, SC	57.0	42.4	1.1	0.5	0.2	3.2	7,298	7,336	7,249	6,871	-0.5	1.2
Fairfield County, SC	41.1	59.1	0.8	0.6	0.1	1.9	11,677	11,677	11,157	10,406	0.0	4.7
Kershaw County, SC	73.2	26.3	0.9	1.1	0.1	4.2	28,191	27,534	25,183	22,808	2.4	9.3
Lexington County, SC	82.0	16.3	1.1	2.3	0.2	5.8	119,716	114,306	102,332	91,483	4.7	11.7
Richland County, SC	49.2	48.5	1.0	3.5	0.3	5.1	168,973	161,972	146,994	130,581	4.3	10.2
Saluda County, SC	71.4	26.6	1.9	0.5	1.1	15.0	9,262	9,289	9,014	8,572	-0.3	3.1
Columbus, GA-AL Metro Area	55.3	43.1	1.3	2.9	0.5	7.0	132,443	128,424	123,192	116,187	3.1	4.2
Russell County, AL	54.2	45.2	1.4	1.5	0.4	5.3	26,962	24,745	23,496	22,925	9.0	5.3
Chattahoochee County, GA	74.6	21.3	2.3	4.3	1.0	15.7	3,336	3,374	3,354	3,324	-1.1	0.6
Harris County, GA	80.9	18.2	1.0	1.5	0.1	3.3	13,772	13,416	12,343	10,417	2.7	8.7
Marion County, GA	64.9	31.8	1.5	1.5	2.1	7.9	4,099	4,155	3,691	3,158	-1.3	12.6
Muscogee County, GA	49.8	48.3	1.2	3.6	0.4	7.6	84,274	82,734	80,308	76,363	1.9	3.0
Columbus, IN Metro Area	91.2	3.2	1.0	6.1	0.1	6.3	33,727	33,104	31,697	29,964	1.9	4.4
Bartholomew County, IN	91.2	3.2	1.0	6.1	0.1	6.3	33,727	33,104	31,697	29,964	1.9	4.4
Columbus, OH Metro Area	80.1	17.1	1.0	4.5	0.1	3.9	845,562	821,608	787,881	710,597	2.9	4.3
Delaware County, OH	90.4	4.4	0.6	6.5	0.1	2.4	70,560	66,489	59,187	43,212	6.1	12.3
Fairfield County, OH	91.0	8.4	0.9	1.8	0.1	2.1	59,977	58,709	55,625	48,781	2.2	5.5
Franklin County, OH	72.0	24.5	1.1	5.5	0.2	5.2	545,058	527,680	512,279	472,954	3.3	3.0
Hocking County, OH	98.5	1.3	1.0	0.4	0.1	0.9	13,301	13,418	12,908	12,177	-0.9	4.0
Licking County, OH	94.7	5.1	0.9	1.3	0.1	1.8	70,092	69,301	65,871	59,171	1.1	5.2
Madison County, OH	91.7	7.7	0.9	1.5	0.1	1.7	15,943	15,934	15,493	14,407	0.1	2.8
Morrow County, OH	98.6	1.3	0.9	0.6	0.1	1.4	14,093	14,154	13,345	12,182	-0.4	6.1
Perry County, OH	98.9	1.0	1.2	0.3	0.1	0.8	15,124	15,211	14,597	13,683	-0.6	4.2
Pickaway County, OH	95.6	4.3	0.8	0.7	0.1	1.4	21,137	21,268	20,357	18,689	-0.6	4.5
Union County, OH	93.5	3.3	0.7	3.8	0.1	1.6	20,277	19,444	18,219	15,341	4.3	6.7

0 = represents zero or rounds to zero.
[1]Persons of Hispanic origin may be of any race.

Table C-2. Population Characteristics and Housing Units—*Continued*

Metropolitan statistical area, division, and component county	White	Black or African American	Asian	American Indian, Alaska Native	Native Hawaiian and Other Pacific Islander	Hispanic or Latino origin[1] (percent)	2015 (July 1 estimate)	2010 (July 1 estimate)	2005 (July 1 estimate)	2000 (July 1 estimate)	2010–2015	2005–2010
Corpus Christi, TX Metro Area	92.9	4.5	1.5	2.4	0.2	59.8	190,999	183,119	172,381	161,256	4.3	6.2
Aransas County, TX	94.5	2.7	2.3	2.4	0.2	26.9	15,844	15,374	14,167	12,912	3.1	8.5
Nueces County, TX	92.3	5.0	1.4	2.6	0.2	62.8	147,925	141,195	132,001	123,317	4.8	7.0
San Patricio County, TX	95.4	2.7	1.6	1.5	0.2	56.6	27,230	26,550	26,213	25,027	2.6	1.3
Corvallis, OR Metro Area	91.2	1.9	2.2	7.9	0.7	7.3	37,695	36,300	34,767	32,074	3.8	4.4
Benton County, OR	91.2	1.9	2.2	7.9	0.7	7.3	37,695	36,300	34,767	32,074	3.8	4.4
Crestview-Fort Walton Beach-Destin, FL Metro Area	86.8	10.7	1.7	4.3	0.5	8.0	144,245	137,618	125,510	108,371	4.8	9.6
Okaloosa County, FL	85.1	12.0	1.6	5.1	0.5	8.6	95,494	92,465	86,889	79,225	3.3	6.4
Walton County, FL	91.8	6.6	2.1	1.8	0.3	6.0	48,751	45,153	38,621	29,146	8.0	16.9
Cumberland, MD-WV Metro Area	92.0	8.0	0.6	1.1	0.1	1.5	46,257	46,369	45,887	45,158	-0.2	1.1
Allegany County, MD	90.4	9.5	0.6	1.3	0.1	1.7	33,155	33,322	33,113	32,984	-0.5	0.6
Mineral County, WV	96.1	4.2	0.6	0.6	0.0	0.9	13,102	13,047	12,774	12,174	0.4	2.1
Dallas-Fort Worth-Arlington, TX Metro Area	**76.2**	**16.9**	**1.6**	**7.3**	**0.3**	**28.4**	**2,686,705**	**2,532,738**	**2,301,804**	**2,030,072**	**6.1**	**10.0**
Dallas-Plano-Irving, TX Division	*74.2*	*17.9*	*1.6*	*8.3*	*0.2*	*29.6*	*1,777,642*	*1,660,512*	*1,513,998*	*1,337,580*	*7.1*	*9.7*
Collin County, TX	75.7	10.7	1.3	14.8	0.2	15.2	337,778	302,034	252,918	197,215	11.8	19.4
Dallas County, TX	69.2	24.0	1.8	6.8	0.2	39.5	985,403	943,664	905,350	855,824	4.4	4.2
Denton County, TX	80.8	10.9	1.6	9.2	0.2	19.2	288,294	257,059	218,461	170,445	12.2	17.7
Ellis County, TX	88.2	10.6	1.7	1.1	0.2	25.5	58,088	54,469	47,420	39,443	6.6	14.9
Hunt County, TX	88.5	9.2	2.2	1.9	0.3	15.4	37,012	36,743	34,801	32,600	0.7	5.6
Kaufman County, TX	86.8	11.7	1.7	1.4	0.2	20.0	39,457	38,352	32,650	26,441	2.9	17.5
Rockwall County, TX	89.9	7.0	1.3	3.5	0.2	17.1	31,610	28,191	22,398	15,612	12.1	25.9
Fort Worth-Arlington, TX Division	*80.1*	*14.9*	*1.7*	*5.3*	*0.4*	*26.1*	*909,063*	*872,226*	*787,806*	*692,492*	*4.2*	*10.7*
Hood County, TX	97.3	1.3	1.7	0.9	0.1	12.0	25,673	24,985	22,098	19,263	2.8	13.1
Johnson County, TX	94.3	4.0	1.8	1.2	0.6	20.5	59,690	56,815	51,461	46,486	5.1	10.4
Parker County, TX	96.6	2.1	1.8	1.0	0.1	11.7	48,246	46,730	40,193	34,361	3.2	16.3
Somervell County, TX	96.2	2.1	2.4	1.4	0.2	19.6	3,738	3,682	3,203	2,771	1.5	15.0
Tarrant County, TX	76.8	17.4	1.6	6.2	0.4	28.2	747,684	716,227	649,082	570,237	4.4	10.3
Wise County, TX	96.6	2.1	1.9	0.8	0.1	18.8	24,032	23,787	21,769	19,374	1.0	9.3
Dalton, GA Metro Area	93.4	4.5	1.9	1.6	0.3	28.6	55,369	55,865	51,584	45,456	-0.9	8.3
Murray County, GA	96.8	2.2	1.5	0.7	0.3	14.5	15,732	15,970	15,437	14,391	-1.5	3.5
Whitfield County, GA	92.1	5.4	2.0	1.9	0.3	33.9	39,637	39,895	36,147	31,065	-0.6	10.4
Danville, IL Metro Area	84.9	15.3	0.9	1.2	0.1	4.8	35,940	36,305	36,701	36,375		-1.1
Vermilion County, IL	84.9	15.3	0.9	1.2	0.1	4.8	35,940	36,305	36,701	36,375		-1.1
Daphne-Fairhope-Foley, AL Metro Area	88.6	10.2	1.5	1.3	0.1	4.5	108,564	104,248	89,106	74,907	4.1	17.0
Baldwin County, AL	88.6	10.2	1.5	1.3	0.1	4.5	108,564	104,248	89,106	74,907	4.1	17.0
Davenport-Moline-Rock Island, IA-IL Metro Area	89.6	9.2	1.1	2.6	0.1	8.5	168,600	167,192	163,437	158,790	0.8	2.3
Henry County, IL	97.2	2.7	0.7	0.7	0.1	5.5	22,101	22,156	21,845	21,304	-0.2	1.4
Mercer County, IL	98.8	1.1	0.4	0.5	0.0	2.3	7,356	7,359	7,267	7,111	0.0	1.3
Rock Island County, IL	86.6	12.0	1.2	2.9	0.1	12.7	65,864	65,756	65,154	64,525	0.2	0.9
Scott County, IA	89.2	9.5	1.1	3.2	0.2	6.4	73,279	71,921	69,171	65,850	1.9	4.0
Dayton, OH Metro Area	81.4	17.4	0.9	2.9	0.1	2.6	367,933	367,277	360,742	348,098	0.2	1.8
Greene County, OH	89.0	8.7	1.1	4.1	0.2	2.8	69,320	68,287	64,390	58,707	1.5	6.1
Miami County, OH	95.9	3.5	0.7	1.7	0.1	1.6	44,290	44,260	42,795	40,621	0.1	3.4
Montgomery County, OH	76.2	22.8	1.0	2.8	0.1	2.7	254,323	254,730	253,557	248,770	-0.2	0.5
Decatur, AL Metro Area	84.6	13.2	3.7	0.9	0.2	6.7	66,743	66,427	65,227	62,598	0.5	1.8
Lawrence County, AL	82.6	11.9	9.5	0.5	0.1	2.2	15,163	15,228	15,368	15,061	-0.4	-0.9
Morgan County, AL	85.2	13.6	2.1	1.1	0.2	8.0	51,580	51,199	49,859	47,537	0.7	2.7
Decatur, IL Metro Area	81.2	19.2	0.7	1.6	0.1	2.2	50,298	50,469	50,641	50,260	-0.3	-0.3
Macon County, IL	81.2	19.2	0.7	1.6	0.1	2.2	50,298	50,469	50,641	50,260	-0.3	-0.3
Deltona-Daytona Beach-Ormond Beach, FL Metro Area	86.0	12.3	1.1	2.5	0.2	12.3	307,011	302,869	280,131	237,753	1.4	8.1
Flagler County, FL	85.5	12.5	0.9	2.9	0.3	10.1	50,044	48,618	40,479	24,830	2.9	20.1
Volusia County, FL	86.2	12.3	1.1	2.5	0.2	12.7	256,967	254,251	239,652	212,923	1.1	6.1
Denver-Aurora-Lakewood, CO Metro Area	87.8	7.2	2.5	5.4	0.4	22.9	1,132,228	1,079,422	1,016,179	897,927	4.9	6.2
Adams County, CO	89.5	4.8	3.5	5.1	0.4	39.2	167,043	163,201	154,554	128,660	2.4	5.6
Arapahoe County, CO	81.3	13.0	2.2	7.2	0.5	18.9	244,501	238,516	224,874	198,807	2.5	6.1
Broomfield County, CO	91.2	2.1	1.6	7.5	0.2	12.4	26,680	22,668	18,748	14,786	17.7	20.9
Clear Creek County, CO	96.3	1.5	2.5	1.5	0.2	6.0	5,683	5,677	5,510	5,119	0.1	3.0
Denver County, CO	83.5	11.5	3.2	4.9	0.3	30.5	304,037	285,720	271,670	252,034	6.4	5.2
Douglas County, CO	93.4	2.1	1.1	5.8	0.3	8.5	121,665	107,049	91,672	64,930	13.7	16.8
Elbert County, CO	97.0	1.4	1.8	1.7	0.3	6.6	9,184	8,946	8,326	7,190	2.7	7.4
Gilpin County, CO	95.6	1.7	2.5	2.1	0.5	6.5	3,589	3,563	3,303	2,952	0.7	7.9
Jefferson County, CO	94.3	2.0	2.2	3.9	0.3	15.3	235,607	230,117	224,762	212,645	2.4	2.4
Park County, CO	96.9	1.1	2.5	1.6	0.2	6.2	14,239	13,965	12,760	10,804	2.0	9.4
Des Moines-West Des Moines, IA Metro Area	90.2	6.5	0.9	4.4	0.2	7.2	258,050	240,681	223,789	199,774	7.2	7.5
Dallas County, IA	93.6	2.5	0.8	4.5	0.2	6.2	31,144	27,346	21,788	16,883	13.9	25.5
Guthrie County, IA	98.7	1.0	0.8	0.6	0.1	2.3	5,749	5,756	5,683	5,482	-0.1	1.3
Madison County, IA	98.5	0.9	0.8	0.8	0.0	1.6	6,728	6,559	6,229	5,685	2.6	5.3
Polk County, IA	88.3	8.1	1.0	5.0	0.1	8.2	195,114	182,599	173,190	156,480	6.9	5.4
Warren County, IA	98.1	1.3	0.7	1.0	0.3	2.6	19,315	18,421	16,899	15,244	4.9	9.0
Detroit-Warren-Dearborn, MI Metro Area	**72.6**	**23.7**	**1.1**	**4.8**	**0.1**	**4.3**	**1,895,743**	**1,886,329**	**1,875,314**	**1,800,731**	**0.5**	**0.6**
Detroit-Dearborn-Livonia, MI Division	*56.9*	*40.5*	*1.3*	*3.9*	*0.1*	*5.7*	*814,328*	*821,165*	*829,100*	*824,760*	*-0.8*	
Wayne County, MI	56.9	40.5	1.3	3.9	0.1	5.7	814,328	821,165	829,100	824,760	-0.8	
Warren-Troy-Farmington Hills, MI Division	*83.6*	*12.1*	*1.0*	*5.4*	*0.1*	*3.3*	*1,081,415*	*1,065,164*	*1,046,214*	*975,971*	*1.5*	*1.8*
Lapeer County, MI	97.6	1.7	1.2	0.9	0.0	4.7	36,263	36,321	35,598	32,909	-0.2	2.0

0 = represents zero or rounds to zero.
[1]Persons of Hispanic origin may be of any race.

Table C-2.   Population Characteristics and Housing Units—*Continued*

| Metropolitan statistical area, division, and component county | Population characteristics, 2015 | | | | | | Housing units | | | | | |
| | Race alone or in combination (percent) | | | | | Hispanic or Latino origin[1] (percent) | 2015 (July 1 estimate) | 2010 (July 1 estimate) | 2005 (July 1 estimate) | 2000 (July 1 estimate) | Percent change | |
	White	Black or African American	Asian	American Indian, Alaska Native	Native Hawaiian and Other Pacific Islander						2010–2015	2005–2010
Livingston County, MI	97.9	1.0	1.1	1.4	0.1	2.3	75,466	72,946	70,496	59,671	3.5	3.5
Macomb County, MI	84.4	12.4	1.0	4.5	0.1	2.5	362,513	356,699	348,371	321,951	1.6	2.4
Oakland County, MI	78.2	15.5	0.9	7.6	0.1	3.9	535,285	527,373	520,284	493,966	1.5	1.4
St. Clair County, MI	96.2	3.7	1.3	0.9	0.1	3.2	71,888	71,825	71,465	67,474	0.1	0.5
Dothan, AL Metro Area	74.7	24.6	1.3	1.1	0.2	3.4	68,298	66,952	64,038	60,008	2.0	4.6
Geneva County, AL	88.7	10.6	1.8	0.6	0.1	3.9	12,640	12,686	12,523	12,127	-0.4	1.3
Henry County, AL	71.7	27.8	0.8	0.9	0.1	2.6	8,967	8,898	8,580	8,064	0.8	3.7
Houston County, AL	71.6	27.6	1.2	1.3	0.2	3.4	46,691	45,368	42,935	39,817	2.9	5.7
Dover, DE Metro Area	70.7	27.9	1.7	3.2	0.3	7.0	68,692	65,503	58,841	50,778	4.9	11.3
Kent County, DE	70.7	27.9	1.7	3.2	0.3	7.0	68,692	65,503	58,841	50,778	4.9	11.3
Dubuque, IA Metro Area	94.8	4.0	0.6	1.8	0.4	2.3	40,588	39,032	37,838	35,546	4.0	3.2
Dubuque County, IA	94.8	4.0	0.6	1.8	0.4	2.3	40,588	39,032	37,838	35,546	4.0	3.2
Duluth, MN-WI Metro Area	94.5	2.4	4.1	1.5	0.1	1.6	142,131	141,571	136,906	130,247	0.4	3.4
Carlton County, MN	91.7	2.2	7.6	0.8	0.1	1.7	15,819	15,669	14,951	13,809	1.0	4.8
St. Louis County, MN	94.8	2.5	3.6	1.6	0.1	1.5	103,411	103,066	100,146	96,019	0.3	2.9
Douglas County, WI	95.6	2.1	3.6	1.4	0.1	1.5	22,901	22,836	21,809	20,419	0.3	4.7
Durham-Chapel Hill, NC Metro Area	66.0	28.9	1.7	5.8	0.2	11.4	235,645	223,255	206,887	181,268	5.5	7.9
Chatham County, NC	83.5	13.9	1.8	2.3	0.2	12.4	30,498	28,788	25,453	21,569	5.9	13.1
Durham County, NC	55.0	39.8	1.8	5.8	0.2	13.4	130,230	120,572	110,995	96,123	8.0	8.6
Orange County, NC	79.0	13.3	1.5	8.9	0.2	8.5	56,697	55,694	53,290	47,999	1.8	4.5
Person County, NC	71.4	28.1	1.3	0.7	0.1	4.3	18,220	18,201	17,149	15,577	0.1	6.1
East Stroudsburg, PA Metro Area	81.3	17.0	1.4	3.0	0.2	14.9	80,720	80,393	75,954	67,936	0.4	5.8
Monroe County, PA	81.3	17.0	1.4	3.0	0.2	14.9	80,720	80,393	75,954	67,936	0.4	5.8
Eau Claire, WI Metro Area	95.0	2.0	1.1	3.4	0.1	2.1	71,022	69,402	66,336	60,549	2.3	4.6
Chippewa County, WI	96.3	2.1	1.1	1.7	0.1	1.6	27,829	27,216	25,594	22,940	2.3	6.3
Eau Claire County, WI	94.2	1.9	1.2	4.5	0.1	2.3	43,193	42,186	40,742	37,609	2.4	3.5
El Centro, CA Metro Area	91.2	3.9	3.4	3.0	0.4	82.7	57,216	56,112	50,138	44,078	2.0	11.9
Imperial County, CA	91.2	3.9	3.4	3.0	0.4	82.7	57,216	56,112	50,138	44,078	2.0	11.9
Elizabethtown-Fort Knox, KY Metro Area	87.1	11.8	1.3	2.7	0.5	5.0	64,547	61,311	57,809	54,010	5.3	6.1
Hardin County, KY	84.0	14.6	1.3	3.3	0.6	5.5	46,006	43,339	40,221	36,996	6.2	7.8
Larue County, KY	96.1	4.1	0.9	0.4	0.1	3.1	6,307	6,181	6,138	5,881	2.0	0.7
Meade County, KY	94.4	4.7	1.6	1.6	0.3	4.0	12,234	11,791	11,450	11,133	3.8	3.0
Elkhart-Goshen, IN Metro Area	91.8	7.7	1.2	1.6	0.1	15.3	78,030	77,763	75,700	70,116	0.3	2.7
Elkhart County, IN	91.8	7.7	1.2	1.6	0.1	15.3	78,030	77,763	75,700	70,116	0.3	2.7
Elmira, NY Metro Area	91.1	8.9	0.9	2.0	0.1	3.0	38,340	38,368	38,287	37,805	-0.1	0.2
Chemung County, NY	91.1	8.9	0.9	2.0	0.1	3.0	38,340	38,368	38,287	37,805	-0.1	0.2
El Paso, TX Metro Area	93.2	4.7	1.4	1.9	0.3	81.3	290,975	272,522	249,635	226,965	6.8	9.2
El Paso County, TX	93.2	4.7	1.4	1.9	0.3	81.3	289,443	270,995	248,113	225,486	6.8	9.2
Hudspeth County, TX	95.4	2.4	2.2	1.1	0.1	78.0	1,532	1,527	1,522	1,479	0.3	0.3
Enid, OK Metro Area	89.4	5.0	5.5	2.1	2.5	12.0	26,856	26,829	26,626	26,057	0.1	0.8
Garfield County, OK	89.4	5.0	5.5	2.1	2.5	12.0	26,856	26,829	26,626	26,057	0.1	0.8
Erie, PA Metro Area	90.2	9.3	0.7	2.0	0.1	4.0	120,094	119,199	117,392	114,508	0.8	1.5
Erie County, PA	90.2	9.3	0.7	2.0	0.1	4.0	120,094	119,199	117,392	114,508	0.8	1.5
Eugene, OR Metro Area	94.0	2.1	3.6	4.4	0.6	8.5	159,288	156,170	148,578	139,383	2.0	5.1
Lane County, OR	94.0	2.1	3.6	4.4	0.6	8.5	159,288	156,170	148,578	139,383	2.0	5.1
Evansville, IN-KY Metro Area	91.2	8.5	0.7	1.7	0.2	2.3	140,561	138,816	134,962	127,819	1.3	2.9
Posey County, IN	98.2	1.8	0.5	0.7	0.0	1.1	11,358	11,209	11,302	11,098	1.3	-0.8
Vanderburgh County, IN	88.7	11.2	0.7	1.8	0.2	2.6	83,545	83,022	80,985	76,568	0.6	2.5
Warrick County, IN	95.7	2.4	0.7	2.6	0.1	1.8	25,191	24,234	22,695	20,648	3.9	6.8
Henderson County, KY	91.1	9.4	0.6	0.7	0.1	2.3	20,467	20,351	19,980	19,505	0.6	1.9
Fairbanks, AK Metro Area	82.7	7.2	10.9	5.0	1.0	8.0	41,616	41,775	37,677	33,472	-0.4	10.9
Fairbanks North Star Borough, AK	82.7	7.2	10.9	5.0	1.0	8.0	41,616	41,775	37,677	33,472	-0.4	10.9
Fargo, ND-MN Metro Area	92.4	4.3	2.3	3.1	0.2	3.0	103,693	92,272	83,587	73,881	12.4	10.4
Clay County, MN	94.9	2.8	2.5	1.9	0.1	4.2	25,452	24,024	21,858	19,798	5.9	9.9
Cass County, ND	91.5	4.8	2.2	3.5	0.2	2.6	78,241	68,248	61,729	54,083	14.6	10.6
Farmington, NM Metro Area	60.4	1.6	39.6	1.1	0.2	20.0	49,661	49,365	46,668	43,448	0.6	5.8
San Juan County, NM	60.4	1.6	39.6	1.1	0.2	20.0	49,661	49,365	46,668	43,448	0.6	5.8
Fayetteville, NC Metro Area	56.0	40.1	4.3	3.8	0.7	11.4	164,591	154,281	142,082	131,449	6.7	8.6
Cumberland County, NC	56.4	40.7	3.2	4.0	0.7	11.3	144,426	135,974	126,847	118,799	6.2	7.2
Hoke County, NC	53.9	36.5	10.9	2.6	0.6	12.4	20,165	18,307	15,235	12,650	10.1	20.2
Fayetteville-Springdale-Rogers, AR-MO Metro Area	91.0	3.3	3.2	3.7	1.5	15.8	207,938	198,688	173,404	145,424	4.7	14.6
Benton County, AR	91.9	2.6	3.3	4.3	0.5	16.4	99,875	93,342	78,431	64,682	7.0	19.0
Madison County, AR	96.5	0.8	3.0	1.0	0.4	5.3	7,483	7,483	7,093	6,555	0.0	5.5
Washington County, AR	89.6	4.4	2.9	3.4	2.6	16.4	90,776	87,940	78,068	64,865	3.2	12.6
McDonald County, MO	92.0	2.4	5.7	1.8	1.7	11.7	9,804	9,923	9,812	9,322	-1.2	1.1
Flagstaff, AZ Metro Area	68.9	2.4	28.5	2.8	0.5	13.9	64,446	63,317	59,358	53,677	1.8	6.7
Coconino County, AZ	68.9	2.4	28.5	2.8	0.5	13.9	64,446	63,317	59,358	53,677	1.8	6.7
Flint, MI Metro Area	77.5	22.2	1.5	1.5	0.1	3.3	190,887	192,097	193,310	184,146	-0.6	-0.6
Genesee County, MI	77.5	22.2	1.5	1.5	0.1	3.3	190,887	192,097	193,310	184,146	-0.6	-0.6
Florence, SC Metro Area	56.1	42.9	0.8	1.4	0.1	2.3	89,425	88,979	84,925	81,125	0.5	4.8
Darlington County, SC	57.6	42.0	0.8	0.8	0.1	2.1	30,215	30,283	30,089	29,050	-0.2	0.6
Florence County, SC	55.4	43.3	0.8	1.7	0.1	2.5	59,210	58,696	54,836	52,075	0.9	7.0
Florence-Muscle Shoals, AL Metro Area	86.0	13.5	1.2	0.9	0.1	2.5	70,684	69,577	68,019	65,562	1.6	2.3
Colbert County, AL	82.3	17.4	1.4	0.7	0.1	2.6	26,307	25,776	25,459	25,016	2.1	1.2
Lauderdale County, AL	88.2	11.1	1.1	1.1	0.1	2.5	44,377	43,801	42,560	40,546	1.3	2.9

0 = represents zero or rounds to zero.
[1] Persons of Hispanic origin may be of any race.

Table C-2. Population Characteristics and Housing Units—*Continued*

Metropolitan statistical area, division, and component county	Population characteristics, 2015 Race alone or in combination (percent) White	Black or African American	Asian	American Indian, Alaska Native	Native Hawaiian and Other Pacific Islander	Hispanic or Latino origin[1] (percent)	Housing units 2015 (July 1 estimate)	2010 (July 1 estimate)	2005 (July 1 estimate)	2000 (July 1 estimate)	Percent change 2010–2015	2005–2010
Fond du Lac, WI Metro Area	96.2	2.3	1.0	1.8	0.1	5.0	44,620	43,935	42,193	39,365	1.6	4.1
Fond du Lac County, WI	96.2	2.3	1.0	1.8	0.1	5.0	44,620	43,935	42,193	39,365	1.6	4.1
Fort Collins, CO Metro Area	95.4	1.8	2.0	3.3	0.2	11.2	140,892	132,784	124,032	106,306	6.1	7.1
Larimer County, CO	95.4	1.8	2.0	3.3	0.2	11.2	140,892	132,784	124,032	106,306	6.1	7.1
Fort Smith, AR-OK Metro Area	85.6	5.2	10.5	3.2	0.3	9.5	123,514	121,067	114,744	108,066	2.0	5.5
Crawford County, AR	94.1	2.4	4.3	2.1	0.1	6.9	26,484	26,138	23,783	21,434	1.3	9.9
Sebastian County, AR	85.8	8.1	4.1	5.3	0.4	13.7	56,372	54,781	52,082	49,453	2.9	5.2
Le Flore County, OK	83.2	3.1	18.6	0.9	0.3	6.8	21,754	21,475	20,910	20,186	1.3	2.7
Sequoyah County, OK	75.5	2.9	30.1	1.0	0.2	3.9	18,904	18,673	17,969	16,993	1.2	3.9
Fort Wayne, IN Metro Area	85.5	12.2	1.1	3.8	0.2	6.6	181,519	178,242	173,944	162,905	1.8	2.5
Allen County, IN	83.4	14.0	1.1	4.3	0.2	7.3	155,295	152,280	148,702	139,325	2.0	2.4
Wells County, IN	98.3	1.2	0.7	0.8	0.1	2.7	11,712	11,659	11,533	11,011	0.5	1.1
Whitley County, IN	98.6	1.0	0.9	0.7	0.1	2.2	14,512	14,303	13,709	12,569	1.5	4.3
Fresno, CA Metro Area	79.8	6.8	4.2	12.0	0.5	52.4	325,996	316,053	294,828	271,364	3.1	7.2
Fresno County, CA	79.8	6.8	4.2	12.0	0.5	52.4	325,996	316,053	294,828	271,364	3.1	7.2
Gadsden, AL Metro Area	82.5	16.4	1.3	1.0	0.3	3.7	47,510	47,465	47,079	46,035	0.1	0.8
Etowah County, AL	82.5	16.4	1.3	1.0	0.3	3.7	47,510	47,465	47,079	46,035	0.1	0.8
Gainesville, FL Metro Area	74.0	20.9	0.9	6.8	0.2	8.9	121,823	120,124	112,571	101,576	1.4	6.7
Alachua County, FL	72.7	21.9	0.8	7.2	0.2	9.2	114,596	112,826	105,843	95,637	1.6	6.6
Gilchrist County, FL	93.2	5.9	1.3	0.7	0.1	5.1	7,227	7,298	6,728	5,939		8.5
Gainesville, GA Metro Area	88.6	9.0	1.4	2.4	0.3	27.7	70,107	68,844	61,166	51,793	1.8	12.6
Hall County, GA	88.6	9.0	1.4	2.4	0.3	27.7	70,107	68,844	61,166	51,793	1.8	12.6
Gettysburg, PA Metro Area	96.6	2.8	0.8	1.2	0.1	6.8	41,462	40,844	39,035	35,977	1.5	4.6
Adams County, PA	96.6	2.8	0.8	1.2	0.1	6.8	41,462	40,844	39,035	35,977	1.5	4.6
Glens Falls, NY Metro Area	96.6	2.9	0.8	1.0	0.1	2.5	68,208	67,606	64,965	61,760	0.9	4.1
Warren County, NY	97.5	1.9	0.8	1.2	0.1	2.3	39,180	38,748	37,159	34,940	1.1	4.3
Washington County, NY	95.6	3.9	0.8	0.8	0.1	2.6	29,028	28,858	27,806	26,820	0.6	3.8
Goldsboro, NC Metro Area	65.2	33.3	1.4	2.2	0.3	11.2	53,290	52,963	50,856	47,559	0.6	4.1
Wayne County, NC	65.2	33.3	1.4	2.2	0.3	11.2	53,290	52,963	50,856	47,559	0.6	4.1
Grand Forks, ND-MN Metro Area	92.1	3.9	3.7	2.7	0.2	4.7	46,961	44,014	42,686	41,397	6.7	3.1
Polk County, MN	95.4	2.3	2.9	1.5	0.1	6.1	14,723	14,611	14,453	14,027	0.8	1.1
Grand Forks County, ND	90.7	4.6	4.0	3.3	0.3	4.0	32,238	29,403	28,233	27,370	9.6	4.1
Grand Island, NE Metro Area	95.0	2.6	2.0	1.5	0.4	20.1	35,196	34,197	33,101	31,935	2.9	3.3
Hall County, NE	93.7	3.2	2.4	1.8	0.6	26.4	24,333	23,570	22,611	21,637	3.2	4.2
Hamilton County, NE	99.0	0.8	0.6	0.5	0.1	3.5	4,066	3,970	3,915	3,863	2.4	1.4
Howard County, NE	98.7	0.8	1.0	0.5	0.1	2.4	3,026	2,953	2,909	2,793	2.5	1.5
Merrick County, NE	97.6	1.0	1.2	1.4	0.1	4.3	3,771	3,704	3,666	3,642	1.8	1.0
Grand Junction, CO Metro Area	96.2	1.7	2.7	1.6	0.3	14.4	64,247	62,696	56,947	49,116	2.5	10.1
Mesa County, CO	96.2	1.7	2.7	1.6	0.3	14.4	64,247	62,696	56,947	49,116	2.5	10.1
Grand Rapids-Wyoming, MI Metro Area	89.4	8.5	1.4	3.2	0.1	9.2	410,654	404,680	392,719	362,218	1.5	3.0
Barry County, MI	98.4	1.1	1.2	0.7	0.1	2.7	27,094	27,011	26,028	23,994	0.3	3.8
Kent County, MI	85.7	12.3	1.6	3.4	0.2	10.3	249,972	246,919	240,898	224,821	1.2	2.5
Montcalm County, MI	96.5	2.8	1.4	0.7	0.1	3.5	28,095	28,214	27,694	26,002	-0.4	1.9
Ottawa County, MI	94.4	2.7	1.1	3.6	0.1	9.5	105,493	102,536	98,099	87,401	2.9	4.5
Grants Pass, OR Metro Area	96.4	1.1	3.7	1.8	0.5	7.3	38,136	38,004	36,067	33,371	0.3	5.4
Josephine County, OR	96.4	1.1	3.7	1.8	0.5	7.3	38,136	38,004	36,067	33,371	0.3	5.4
Great Falls, MT Metro Area	92.3	2.6	7.0	1.8	0.3	4.2	37,932	37,310	36,117	35,268	1.7	3.3
Cascade County, MT	92.3	2.6	7.0	1.8	0.3	4.2	37,932	37,310	36,117	35,268	1.7	3.3
Greeley, CO Metro Area	95.1	2.0	2.7	2.2	0.3	29.0	102,603	96,396	87,428	67,151	6.4	10.3
Weld County, CO	95.1	2.0	2.7	2.2	0.3	29.0	102,603	96,396	87,428	67,151	6.4	10.3
Green Bay, WI Metro Area	92.0	3.2	3.7	3.1	0.1	7.1	141,087	137,346	131,248	118,725	2.7	4.6
Brown County, WI	90.7	3.7	4.1	3.7	0.2	8.3	107,992	104,499	100,127	90,546	3.3	4.4
Kewaunee County, WI	98.4	0.8	1.1	0.6	0.1	2.6	9,344	9,306	9,009	8,252	0.4	3.3
Oconto County, WI	97.8	0.7	2.0	0.6	0.0	1.7	23,751	23,541	22,112	19,927	0.9	6.5
Greensboro-High Point, NC Metro Area	68.1	28.4	1.5	4.1	0.2	8.3	329,921	323,077	302,820	276,354	2.1	6.7
Guilford County, NC	59.8	35.7	1.5	5.3	0.2	7.8	225,123	218,316	201,365	181,211	3.1	8.4
Randolph County, NC	91.0	7.3	1.7	1.5	0.1	11.3	61,232	61,072	58,903	54,754	0.3	3.7
Rockingham County, NC	79.6	20.2	1.2	0.8	0.2	6.1	43,566	43,689	42,552	40,389	-0.3	2.7
Greenville, NC Metro Area	62.0	36.3	1.0	2.6	0.2	6.0	77,332	75,078	67,297	58,528	3.0	11.6
Pitt County, NC	62.0	36.3	1.0	2.6	0.2	6.0	77,332	75,078	67,297	58,528	3.0	11.6
Greenville-Anderson-Mauldin, SC Metro Area	80.5	18.1	0.9	2.2	0.1	6.6	372,546	362,390	340,898	313,676	2.8	6.3
Anderson County, SC	82.0	17.6	0.7	1.2	0.1	3.6	86,084	84,779	79,997	73,550	1.5	6.0
Greenville County, SC	78.5	19.6	1.0	2.7	0.1	8.8	203,433	195,625	180,361	163,693	4.0	8.5
Laurens County, SC	73.0	26.8	0.8	0.6	0.2	4.5	30,613	30,708	30,874	30,276	-0.3	-0.5
Pickens County, SC	90.7	7.9	0.8	2.3	0.1	3.5	52,416	51,278	49,666	46,157	2.2	3.2
Gulfport-Biloxi-Pascagoula, MS Metro Area	74.9	22.8	1.2	3.3	0.2	5.5	176,197	167,943	169,949	153,468	4.9	-1.2
Hancock County, MS	89.3	9.6	1.5	1.5	0.2	3.8	24,083	21,999	24,179	21,259	9.5	-9.0
Harrison County, MS	71.6	25.7	1.3	3.9	0.3	5.5	90,749	85,699	88,281	80,218	5.9	-2.9
Jackson County, MS	74.7	23.0	1.0	3.0	0.2	6.0	61,365	60,245	57,489	51,991	1.9	4.8
Hagerstown-Martinsburg, MD-WV Metro Area	88.4	11.4	0.9	2.0	0.1	4.3	108,141	105,679	97,396	86,238	2.3	8.5
Washington County, MD	86.4	13.0	0.8	2.3	0.2	4.5	61,344	60,820	57,880	53,123	0.9	5.1
Berkeley County, WV	91.0	9.3	0.9	1.6	0.1	4.0	46,797	44,859	39,516	33,115	4.3	13.5
Hammond, LA Metro Area	68.4	31.0	1.0	1.1	0.1	4.0	53,138	50,277	43,524	40,876	5.7	15.5
Tangipahoa Parish, LA	68.4	31.0	1.0	1.1	0.1	4.0	53,138	50,277	43,524	40,876	5.7	15.5
Hanford-Corcoran, CA Metro Area	84.5	8.4	4.3	6.0	0.7	53.6	45,253	43,910	40,678	36,687	3.1	7.9
Kings County, CA	84.5	8.4	4.3	6.0	0.7	53.6	45,253	43,910	40,678	36,687	3.1	7.9

0 = represents zero or rounds to zero.
[1]Persons of Hispanic origin may be of any race.

Table C-2. Population Characteristics and Housing Units—*Continued*

Metropolitan statistical area, division, and component county	White	Black or African American	Asian	American Indian, Alaska Native	Native Hawaiian and Other Pacific Islander	Hispanic or Latino origin[1] (percent)	2015 (July 1 estimate)	2010 (July 1 estimate)	2005 (July 1 estimate)	2000 (July 1 estimate)	2010–2015	2005–2010
Harrisburg-Carlisle, PA Metro Area	84.9	12.5	0.8	4.3	0.1	5.9	246,295	241,053	230,395	217,567	2.2	4.6
Cumberland County, PA	91.7	5.0	0.6	4.6	0.1	3.6	103,561	100,138	93,911	87,223	3.4	6.6
Dauphin County, PA	76.5	21.1	1.0	4.6	0.2	8.6	122,194	120,489	116,565	111,348	1.4	3.4
Perry County, PA	98.2	1.5	0.6	0.8	0.1	1.8	20,540	20,426	19,919	18,996	0.6	2.5
Harrisonburg, VA Metro Area	92.2	5.7	1.2	2.8	0.2	11.3	52,898	51,224	45,778	41,199	3.3	11.9
Rockingham County, VA	96.2	3.0	1.1	1.1	0.1	6.4	34,709	33,710	30,657	27,448	3.0	10.0
Harrisonburg city, VA	86.1	9.7	1.2	5.4	0.3	18.6	18,189	17,514	15,121	13,751	3.9	15.8
Hartford-West Hartford-East Hartford, CT Metro Area	81.8	13.9	1.0	5.5	0.2	14.3	508,930	507,139	492,867	472,786	0.4	2.9
Hartford County, CT	78.5	16.9	1.1	5.8	0.2	17.4	374,933	374,272	365,392	353,505	0.2	2.4
Middlesex County, CT	90.9	6.5	0.7	3.7	0.2	6.1	75,365	74,874	72,046	67,517	0.7	3.9
Tolland County, CT	91.5	4.5	0.7	5.1	0.2	5.2	58,632	57,993	55,429	51,764	1.1	4.6
Hattiesburg, MS Metro Area	69.0	30.1	0.8	1.4	0.1	2.7	62,545	61,913	55,129	50,741	1.0	12.3
Forrest County, MS	60.9	38.2	0.8	1.4	0.2	3.2	32,722	32,304	30,388	29,610	1.3	6.3
Lamar County, MS	77.1	21.7	0.7	1.7	0.1	2.4	24,298	24,087	19,382	16,013	0.9	24.3
Perry County, MS	79.0	21.1	0.7	0.4	0.1	1.3	5,525	5,522	5,359	5,118	0.1	3.0
Hickory-Lenoir-Morganton, NC Metro Area	88.9	8.1	1.1	3.3	0.3	7.0	162,293	162,631	157,152	145,651	-0.2	3.5
Alexander County, NC	92.4	6.8	0.9	1.2	0.1	4.5	16,163	16,204	15,302	14,163	-0.3	5.9
Burke County, NC	88.1	7.3	1.4	4.1	0.8	6.1	40,615	40,877	39,710	37,600	-0.6	2.9
Caldwell County, NC	93.4	6.0	1.1	0.9	0.1	5.0	37,643	37,661	36,238	33,612	0.0	3.9
Catawba County, NC	86.2	10.0	1.0	4.5	0.1	9.2	67,872	67,889	65,902	60,276	0.0	3.0
Hilton Head Island-Bluffton-Beaufort, SC Metro Area	75.6	23.3	1.0	1.8	0.2	11.6	106,364	103,366	86,268	69,299	2.9	19.8
Beaufort County, SC	78.8	20.1	1.0	1.9	0.2	11.2	95,287	93,050	77,706	61,334	2.4	19.7
Jasper County, SC	55.0	43.9	1.2	1.1	0.1	13.8	11,077	10,316	8,562	7,965	7.4	20.5
Hinesville, GA Metro Area	58.0	40.8	1.8	3.3	0.9	12.2	33,712	32,872	29,389	26,370	2.6	11.9
Liberty County, GA	54.4	44.3	1.8	3.6	1.0	12.5	27,365	26,815	24,417	22,105	2.1	9.8
Long County, GA	70.7	28.4	1.8	2.4	0.8	11.3	6,347	6,057	4,972	4,265	4.8	21.8
Homosassa Springs, FL Metro Area	94.6	3.9	1.1	1.9	0.1	5.3	77,726	78,075	70,882	62,527	-0.4	10.1
Citrus County, FL	94.6	3.9	1.1	1.9	0.1	5.3	77,726	78,075	70,882	62,527	-0.4	10.1
Hot Springs, AR Metro Area	89.5	9.8	1.8	1.3	0.2	5.4	50,538	50,539	48,028	45,085	0.0	5.2
Garland County, AR	89.5	9.8	1.8	1.3	0.2	5.4	50,538	50,539	48,028	45,085	0.0	5.2
Houma-Thibodaux, LA Metro Area	77.5	17.8	5.5	1.3	0.2	4.9	84,850	82,602	78,659	75,167	2.7	5.0
Lafourche Parish, LA	82.0	14.8	3.8	1.2	0.1	4.6	40,009	38,749	36,478	35,045	3.3	6.2
Terrebonne Parish, LA	73.5	20.3	7.0	1.5	0.3	5.2	44,841	43,853	42,181	40,122	2.3	4.0
Houston-The Woodlands-Sugar Land, TX Metro Area	73.1	18.6	1.6	8.5	0.2	36.5	2,501,900	2,300,903	2,040,715	1,798,493	8.7	12.7
Austin County, TX	88.8	10.3	1.4	0.8	0.1	26.2	13,036	12,933	11,681	10,293	0.8	10.7
Brazoria County, TX	78.7	14.6	1.4	7.1	0.2	29.7	129,521	118,817	105,146	91,210	9.0	13.0
Chambers County, TX	88.4	9.5	1.7	1.7	0.1	21.9	14,799	13,387	11,992	10,418	10.5	11.6
Fort Bend County, TX	58.6	21.8	1.1	20.6	0.2	24.1	233,243	198,056	148,758	117,523	17.8	33.1
Galveston County, TX	81.9	14.4	1.5	4.2	0.2	24.0	142,337	132,782	123,955	112,369	7.2	7.1
Harris County, TX	71.8	20.4	1.7	7.9	0.2	42.0	1,720,441	1,601,873	1,452,850	1,304,076	7.4	10.3
Liberty County, TX	87.2	11.5	1.8	1.0	0.2	21.5	29,811	28,802	27,829	26,479	3.5	3.5
Montgomery County, TX	91.0	5.7	1.6	3.4	0.2	23.1	202,474	178,397	144,297	114,095	13.5	23.6
Waller County, TX	71.1	27.2	1.9	1.2	0.2	29.6	16,238	15,856	14,207	12,030	2.4	11.6
Huntington-Ashland, WV-KY-OH Metro Area	96.4	3.3	0.8	1.0	0.1	1.1	164,657	164,457	163,649	161,541	0.1	0.5
Boyd County, KY	96.1	3.8	0.8	0.8	0.1	1.5	21,666	21,795	21,811	21,971	-0.6	-0.1
Greenup County, KY	98.2	1.4	0.9	0.7	0.0	1.1	16,279	16,326	16,267	16,016	-0.3	0.4
Lawrence County, OH	97.0	3.1	0.7	0.6	0.1	0.9	27,349	27,592	27,718	27,250	-0.9	-0.5
Cabell County, WV	93.2	6.5	0.8	1.7	0.1	1.4	46,485	46,174	45,901	45,645	0.7	0.6
Lincoln County, WV	99.4	0.6	0.6	0.2	0.0	0.7	9,799	9,887	9,979	9,856	-0.9	-0.9
Putnam County, WV	97.6	1.7	0.7	1.1	0.1	1.1	23,883	23,456	22,740	21,674	1.8	3.1
Wayne County, WV	98.8	0.9	0.7	0.5	0.1	0.7	19,196	19,227	19,233	19,129	-0.2	0.0
Huntsville, AL Metro Area	73.9	23.6	1.8	3.1	0.2	5.1	192,458	182,089	162,844	147,830	5.7	11.8
Limestone County, AL	83.8	14.5	1.8	1.9	0.3	6.1	35,602	35,013	30,919	27,082	1.7	13.2
Madison County, AL	71.4	25.9	1.8	3.4	0.2	4.8	156,856	147,076	131,925	120,748	6.6	11.5
Idaho Falls, ID Metro Area	97.0	1.1	2.2	1.4	0.3	12.2	51,308	49,860	43,937	38,252	2.9	13.5
Bonneville County, ID	96.8	1.2	2.2	1.6	0.3	12.8	41,026	39,767	35,223	30,656	3.2	12.9
Butte County, ID	98.2	1.0	2.3	0.7	0.4	5.2	1,351	1,356	1,325	1,290	-0.4	2.3
Jefferson County, ID	97.4	0.7	2.3	1.0	0.3	10.4	8,931	8,737	7,389	6,306	2.2	18.2
Indianapolis-Carmel-Anderson, IN Metro Area	81.2	16.7	0.9	3.4	0.1	6.5	842,432	817,503	779,736	705,444	3.0	4.8
Boone County, IN	95.6	2.2	0.7	3.0	0.1	2.7	25,684	22,806	20,707	18,115	12.6	10.1
Brown County, IN	98.5	1.1	1.2	0.6	0.0	1.6	8,538	8,321	7,782	7,206	2.6	6.9
Hamilton County, IN	89.6	4.9	0.5	6.8	0.1	3.9	119,799	107,267	92,165	70,555	11.7	16.4
Hancock County, IN	96.3	3.1	0.7	1.2	0.1	2.2	29,207	28,197	26,171	21,927	3.6	7.7
Hendricks County, IN	90.7	7.1	0.7	3.2	0.1	3.7	59,371	55,593	50,502	39,658	6.8	10.1
Johnson County, IN	95.0	2.8	0.7	3.0	0.1	3.5	59,309	56,787	52,135	45,438	4.4	8.9
Madison County, IN	90.3	9.7	0.9	0.9	0.1	3.9	58,735	59,050	58,719	57,003	-0.5	0.6
Marion County, IN	68.4	29.9	1.2	3.4	0.2	10.0	419,801	417,931	411,073	388,302	0.4	1.7
Morgan County, IN	98.5	1.0	0.8	0.7	0.1	1.5	28,025	27,778	27,672	26,038	0.9	0.4
Putnam County, IN	94.4	4.6	0.7	1.4	0.1	1.9	14,857	14,704	14,269	13,544	1.0	3.0
Shelby County, IN	97.4	1.8	0.7	1.1	0.2	4.0	19,106	19,069	18,541	17,658	0.2	2.8
Iowa City, IA Metro Area	88.5	6.4	0.8	6.4	0.1	5.5	69,357	65,627	61,454	54,918	5.7	6.8
Johnson County, IA	87.1	7.2	0.8	7.3	0.1	5.5	59,787	56,108	52,329	46,355	6.6	7.2
Washington County, IA	98.2	1.6	0.7	0.8	0.1	5.8	9,570	9,519	9,125	8,563	0.5	4.3
Ithaca, NY Metro Area	84.2	5.7	1.1	12.2	0.2	4.9	42,272	41,694	40,587	38,758	1.4	2.7
Tompkins County, NY	84.2	5.7	1.1	12.2	0.2	4.9	42,272	41,694	40,587	38,758	1.4	2.7
Jackson, MI Metro Area	90.2	10.1	1.1	1.2	0.1	3.4	69,016	69,444	67,659	63,169	-0.6	2.6
Jackson County, MI	90.2	10.1	1.1	1.2	0.1	3.4	69,016	69,444	67,659	63,169	-0.6	2.6

0 = represents zero or rounds to zero.
[1]Persons of Hispanic origin may be of any race.

Table C-2. Population Characteristics and Housing Units—*Continued*

Metropolitan statistical area, division, and component county	Population characteristics, 2015						Housing units				Percent change	
	Race alone or in combination (percent)					Hispanic or Latino origin[1] (percent)	2015 (July 1 estimate)	2010 (July 1 estimate)	2005 (July 1 estimate)	2000 (July 1 estimate)	2010– 2015	2005– 2010
	White	Black or African American	Asian	American Indian, Alaska Native	Native Hawaiian and Other Pacific Islander							
Jackson, MS Metro Area	49.4	49.6	0.6	1.4	0.1	2.4	239,263	232,886	221,701	207,201	2.7	5.0
Copiah County, MS	47.8	52.1	0.6	0.5	0.1	2.9	12,139	12,182	11,749	11,148	-0.4	3.7
Hinds County, MS	27.6	71.8	0.5	1.1	0.1	1.6	104,544	103,446	102,652	100,417	1.1	0.8
Madison County, MS	58.7	38.8	0.6	2.7	0.1	2.8	41,842	38,656	34,325	28,957	8.2	12.6
Rankin County, MS	77.8	21.1	0.6	1.5	0.1	2.7	58,726	56,593	51,330	45,320	3.8	10.3
Simpson County, MS	63.3	36.3	0.6	0.6	0.2	1.8	11,944	11,934	11,621	11,332	0.1	2.7
Yazoo County, MS	41.5	58.0	0.8	0.8	0.1	5.5	10,068	10,075	10,024	10,027	-0.1	0.5
Jackson, TN Metro Area	67.6	31.9	0.8	1.2	0.1	4.2	56,214	55,324	53,747	50,706	1.6	2.9
Chester County, TN	89.5	10.6	1.1	0.7	0.1	2.4	7,023	6,986	6,649	6,210	0.5	5.1
Crockett County, TN	85.1	15.1	1.3	0.6	0.1	9.9	6,386	6,424	6,322	6,148	-0.6	1.6
Madison County, TN	61.1	38.2	0.7	1.4	0.1	3.6	42,805	41,914	40,776	38,348	2.1	2.8
Jacksonville, FL Metro Area	73.2	23.3	1.0	5.0	0.3	8.2	622,262	599,284	544,478	477,477	3.8	10.1
Baker County, FL	85.1	14.4	1.1	0.9	0.1	2.5	9,623	9,685	8,683	7,629	-0.6	11.5
Clay County, FL	84.7	12.5	1.3	4.4	0.4	9.6	78,179	75,558	66,648	54,138	3.5	13.4
Duval County, FL	64.2	31.6	1.1	5.9	0.3	8.9	398,541	388,947	362,194	330,917	2.5	7.4
Nassau County, FL	91.8	7.1	1.0	1.4	0.2	4.0	36,450	35,039	30,790	26,108	4.0	13.8
St. Johns County, FL	91.1	6.4	0.8	3.6	0.1	6.4	99,469	90,055	76,163	58,685	10.5	18.2
Jacksonville, NC Metro Area	80.1	18.4	2.0	3.7	0.6	12.3	76,926	68,687	61,663	56,207	12.0	11.4
Onslow County, NC	80.1	18.4	2.0	3.7	0.6	12.3	76,926	68,687	61,663	56,207	12.0	11.4
Janesville-Beloit, WI Metro Area	92.8	6.5	1.1	1.7	0.1	8.4	68,313	68,436	66,336	62,377	-0.2	3.2
Rock County, WI	92.8	6.5	1.1	1.7	0.1	8.4	68,313	68,436	66,336	62,377	-0.2	3.2
Jefferson City, MO Metro Area	90.4	8.9	1.1	1.3	0.2	2.7	64,115	63,605	61,533	57,024	0.8	3.4
Callaway County, MO	93.7	5.5	1.5	1.2	0.1	2.2	18,535	18,537	17,698	16,260	0.0	4.7
Cole County, MO	86.1	13.3	0.9	1.6	0.2	2.8	32,925	32,302	31,414	29,099	1.9	2.8
Moniteau County, MO	94.9	4.5	1.2	0.6	0.1	5.0	6,121	6,175	6,087	5,766	-0.9	1.4
Osage County, MO	99.1	0.8	0.5	0.2	0.1	0.8	6,534	6,591	6,334	5,899	-0.9	4.1
Johnson City, TN Metro Area	95.2	4.1	0.9	1.3	0.1	3.0	96,065	93,906	88,035	82,219	2.3	6.7
Carter County, TN	97.7	2.1	0.8	0.5	0.1	1.7	27,822	27,756	27,017	25,989	0.2	2.7
Unicoi County, TN	98.9	0.9	0.8	0.3	0.0	4.4	8,839	8,829	8,667	8,242	0.1	1.9
Washington County, TN	93.6	5.4	1.0	1.8	0.1	3.4	59,404	57,321	52,351	47,988	3.6	9.5
Johnstown, PA Metro Area	95.6	4.7	0.4	0.8	0.1	1.6	65,126	65,627	65,920	65,793	-0.8	-0.4
Cambria County, PA	95.6	4.7	0.4	0.8	0.1	1.6	65,126	65,627	65,920	65,793	-0.8	-0.4
Jonesboro, AR Metro Area	84.7	14.5	1.1	1.3	0.1	4.5	54,908	51,534	48,891	46,303	6.5	5.4
Craighead County, AR	83.2	15.8	1.1	1.5	0.1	4.9	43,976	40,605	37,857	35,241	8.3	7.3
Poinsett County, AR	91.0	9.2	0.9	0.4	0.1	2.8	10,932	10,929	11,034	11,062	0.0	
Joplin, MO Metro Area	93.9	3.0	3.8	1.7	0.8	7.0	76,046	74,999	72,580	67,733	1.4	3.3
Jasper County, MO	93.9	3.5	3.4	1.6	0.7	7.9	51,694	50,682	48,970	45,729	2.0	3.5
Newton County, MO	93.9	1.8	4.5	1.9	1.1	5.1	24,352	24,317	23,610	22,004	0.1	3.0
Kahului-Wailuku-Lahaina, HI Metro Area	52.2	2.0	2.7	47.1	27.8	11.2	71,835	70,567	63,966	56,877	1.8	10.3
Kalawao County, HI	42.7	3.4	3.4	13.5	52.8	1.1	113	113	141	170	0.0	-19.9
Maui County, HI	52.2	2.0	2.7	47.1	27.8	11.2	71,722	70,454	63,825	56,707	1.8	10.4
Kalamazoo-Portage, MI Metro Area	87.0	11.8	1.7	2.8	0.2	6.3	147,152	146,804	143,083	133,741	0.2	2.6
Kalamazoo County, MI	85.0	13.6	1.5	3.4	0.2	4.8	110,509	110,025	106,824	99,633	0.4	3.0
Van Buren County, MI	93.9	5.3	2.3	0.9	0.1	11.3	36,643	36,779	36,259	34,108	-0.4	1.4
Kankakee, IL Metro Area	82.9	16.6	0.9	1.4	0.1	10.1	45,185	45,245	43,337	40,716	-0.1	4.4
Kankakee County, IL	82.9	16.6	0.9	1.4	0.1	10.1	45,185	45,245	43,337	40,716	-0.1	4.4
Kansas City, MO-KS Metro Area	83.3	14.2	1.6	3.4	0.3	8.9	891,296	872,401	831,292	760,905	2.2	4.9
Johnson County, KS	89.6	6.1	1.2	5.6	0.1	7.4	235,548	226,864	210,985	183,263	3.8	7.5
Leavenworth County, KS	87.6	11.1	2.0	2.3	0.4	7.0	29,252	28,726	27,010	24,502	1.8	6.4
Linn County, KS	97.9	1.2	2.1	0.7	0.1	2.3	5,471	5,447	5,149	4,724	0.4	5.8
Miami County, KS	97.3	2.0	1.6	0.8	0.1	3.1	13,361	13,190	12,311	11,043	1.3	7.1
Wyandotte County, KS	69.7	26.2	2.7	4.6	0.4	27.7	67,675	66,739	66,043	65,921	1.4	1.1
Bates County, MO	97.9	1.6	1.7	0.4	0.1	2.4	7,800	7,841	7,708	7,268	-0.5	1.7
Caldwell County, MO	98.2	1.4	1.5	0.6	0.1	2.2	4,600	4,605	4,604	4,501	-0.1	0.0
Cass County, MO	94.3	4.9	1.6	1.3	0.2	4.4	40,731	40,050	36,960	31,905	1.7	8.4
Clay County, MO	90.3	7.5	1.5	3.1	0.4	6.7	95,600	93,928	86,652	76,638	1.8	8.4
Clinton County, MO	97.2	2.3	1.5	0.8	0.1	2.0	8,894	8,878	8,653	7,920	0.2	2.6
Jackson County, MO	72.9	25.8	1.7	2.5	0.5	8.9	317,140	312,181	305,092	288,963	1.6	2.3
Lafayette County, MO	96.4	3.3	1.4	0.7	0.3	2.7	14,686	14,718	14,410	13,727	-0.2	2.1
Platte County, MO	89.5	7.8	1.5	3.5	0.6	5.8	40,572	39,245	35,850	31,133	3.4	9.5
Ray County, MO	97.4	2.2	1.3	0.6	0.1	2.5	9,966	9,989	9,865	9,397	-0.2	1.3
Kennewick-Richland, WA Metro Area	93.3	2.9	2.4	3.8	0.5	31.0	99,753	93,242	84,183	72,410	7.0	10.8
Benton County, WA	93.5	2.6	2.4	4.1	0.4	21.0	73,065	68,706	63,309	56,218	6.3	8.5
Franklin County, WA	92.9	3.6	2.4	2.9	0.7	52.4	26,688	24,536	20,874	16,192	8.8	17.5
Killeen-Temple, TX Metro Area	73.4	23.6	2.2	4.4	1.2	22.8	171,106	159,900	140,187	122,885	7.0	14.1
Bell County, TX	71.2	25.6	2.2	4.8	1.2	24.1	135,698	125,961	108,794	93,430	7.7	15.8
Coryell County, TX	77.8	19.6	2.2	3.5	1.2	18.1	26,168	25,217	23,209	21,809	3.8	8.7
Lampasas County, TX	92.5	5.3	2.6	2.2	0.5	19.6	9,240	8,722	8,184	7,646	5.9	6.6
Kingsport-Bristol-Bristol, TN-VA Metro Area	96.7	2.8	0.8	0.8	0.1	1.6	147,405	147,039	143,100	136,645	0.2	2.8
Hawkins County, TN	97.6	2.0	0.9	0.6	0.1	1.4	26,843	26,876	26,032	24,530	-0.1	3.2
Sullivan County, TN	96.4	3.1	0.9	1.0	0.1	1.8	74,191	73,804	71,954	69,225	0.5	2.6
Scott County, VA	98.5	1.1	0.7	0.3	0.1	1.2	11,845	11,915	11,806	11,377	-0.6	0.9
Washington County, VA	97.6	1.9	0.6	0.8	0.1	1.4	25,714	25,612	24,643	23,050	0.4	3.9
Bristol city, VA	92.4	7.2	0.9	1.6	0.1	1.8	8,812	8,832	8,665	8,463	-0.2	1.9
Kingston, NY Metro Area	90.2	8.4	1.2	2.8	0.2	10.1	83,801	83,661	81,321	77,790	0.2	2.9
Ulster County, NY	90.2	8.4	1.2	2.8	0.2	10.1	83,801	83,661	81,321	77,790	0.2	2.9

0 = represents zero or rounds to zero.
[1]Persons of Hispanic origin may be of any race.

Table C-2.　Population Characteristics and Housing Units—*Continued*

Metropolitan statistical area, division, and component county	Population characteristics, 2015						Housing units					
	Race alone or in combination (percent)										Percent change	
	White	Black or African American	Asian	American Indian, Alaska Native	Native Hawaiian and Other Pacific Islander	Hispanic or Latino origin[1] (percent)	2015 (July 1 estimate)	2010 (July 1 estimate)	2005 (July 1 estimate)	2000 (July 1 estimate)	2010– 2015	2005– 2010
Knoxville, TN Metro Area	91.9	6.9	1.1	1.9	0.2	3.6	388,913	381,483	361,122	336,727	1.9	5.6
Anderson County, TN	93.8	5.3	1.1	1.8	0.1	2.7	34,835	34,724	33,908	32,592	0.3	2.4
Blount County, TN	95.5	3.8	1.1	1.3	0.1	3.1	56,378	55,294	51,615	47,243	2.0	7.1
Campbell County, TN	98.7	0.9	1.1	0.4	0.1	1.3	20,438	20,001	19,222	18,571	2.2	4.1
Grainger County, TN	98.5	1.2	0.9	0.3	0.1	2.9	10,868	10,892	10,489	9,766	-0.2	3.8
Knox County, TN	88.1	10.2	1.0	2.7	0.2	4.0	200,478	195,210	184,933	172,009	2.7	5.6
Loudon County, TN	96.8	2.2	1.1	1.1	0.2	8.0	22,403	21,751	19,260	17,376	3.0	12.9
Morgan County, TN	95.6	4.0	1.3	0.4	0.1	1.2	8,882	8,920	8,455	7,759	-0.4	5.5
Roane County, TN	96.1	3.5	1.2	0.8	0.1	1.7	25,523	25,724	24,694	23,447	-0.8	4.2
Union County, TN	98.9	0.7	1.3	0.3	0.1	1.5	9,108	8,967	8,546	7,964	1.6	4.9
Kokomo, IN Metro Area	91.0	9.0	1.1	1.5	0.2	3.2	38,747	38,678	38,903	37,685	0.2	-0.6
Howard County, IN	91.0	9.0	1.1	1.5	0.2	3.2	38,747	38,678	38,903	37,685	0.2	-0.6
La Crosse-Onalaska, WI-MN Metro Area	94.0	2.2	0.8	4.5	0.1	1.7	58,098	57,051	54,725	51,795	1.8	4.3
Houston County, MN	98.4	1.4	0.7	0.9	0.1	1.0	8,655	8,601	8,500	8,186	0.6	1.2
La Crosse County, WI	93.3	2.3	0.9	5.1	0.1	1.8	49,443	48,450	46,225	43,609	2.0	4.8
Lafayette, LA Metro Area	72.4	26.1	0.9	2.1	0.1	3.9	204,102	196,225	183,225	172,176	4.0	7.1
Acadia Parish, LA	80.7	19.5	0.7	0.5	0.1	2.3	25,956	25,415	24,192	23,244	2.1	5.1
Iberia Parish, LA	63.7	33.4	1.0	3.5	0.1	4.1	30,169	29,732	28,514	27,866	1.5	4.3
Lafayette Parish, LA	71.5	27.0	0.9	2.2	0.1	4.6	99,227	93,811	85,774	78,232	5.8	9.4
St. Martin Parish, LA	67.7	31.5	1.0	1.2	0.1	2.7	22,707	21,984	21,016	20,271	3.3	4.6
Vermilion Parish, LA	82.4	15.6	0.9	2.6	0.1	3.3	26,043	25,283	23,729	22,563	3.0	6.5
Lafayette-West Lafayette, IN Metro Area	88.2	5.5	0.8	7.4	0.1	7.6	88,162	84,577	80,068	71,349	4.2	5.6
Benton County, IN	98.3	1.7	0.6	0.5	0.0	5.2	3,907	3,929	3,915	3,828	-0.6	0.4
Carroll County, IN	98.9	1.1	0.8	0.3	0.0	4.1	9,433	9,472	9,222	8,700	-0.4	2.7
Tippecanoe County, IN	86.6	6.1	0.8	8.4	0.2	8.1	74,822	71,176	66,931	58,821	5.1	6.3
Lake Charles, LA Metro Area	73.2	25.9	1.2	1.6	0.1	3.2	90,806	85,933	85,344	81,511	5.7	0.7
Calcasieu Parish, LA	72.5	26.6	1.2	1.7	0.1	3.2	86,931	82,314	80,569	76,214	5.6	2.2
Cameron Parish, LA	94.4	5.2	1.2	0.3	0.1	3.7	3,875	3,619	4,775	5,297	7.1	-24.2
Lake Havasu City-Kingman, AZ Metro Area	94.0	1.9	4.2	1.9	0.4	16.2	112,867	110,965	99,091	80,717	1.7	12.0
Mohave County, AZ	94.0	1.9	4.2	1.9	0.4	16.2	112,867	110,965	99,091	80,717	1.7	12.0
Lakeland-Winter Haven, FL Metro Area	81.4	17.0	1.2	2.4	0.2	20.5	284,342	281,212	256,428	227,250	1.1	9.7
Polk County, FL	81.4	17.0	1.2	2.4	0.2	20.5	284,342	281,212	256,428	227,250	1.1	9.7
Lancaster, PA Metro Area	92.2	6.2	0.8	2.7	0.2	10.1	207,090	203,154	194,015	180,611	1.9	4.7
Lancaster County, PA	92.2	6.2	0.8	2.7	0.2	10.1	207,090	203,154	194,015	180,611	1.9	4.7
Lansing-East Lansing, MI Metro Area	85.1	11.3	1.5	5.4	0.2	6.6	200,375	198,976	195,433	182,411	0.7	1.8
Clinton County, MI	95.8	2.9	1.1	2.0	0.1	4.5	31,150	30,693	29,353	24,796	1.5	4.6
Eaton County, MI	90.2	8.3	1.4	2.5	0.1	5.3	47,075	47,041	45,798	42,294	0.1	2.7
Ingham County, MI	80.3	14.7	1.7	7.3	0.2	7.7	122,150	121,242	120,282	115,321	0.7	0.8
Laredo, TX Metro Area	97.9	0.9	0.8	0.8	0.1	95.2	79,708	73,665	65,604	55,740	8.2	12.3
Webb County, TX	97.9	0.9	0.8	0.8	0.1	95.2	79,708	73,665	65,604	55,740	8.2	12.3
Las Cruces, NM Metro Area	93.7	2.8	3.3	1.9	0.3	67.1	84,646	81,664	74,143	65,878	3.7	10.1
Doña Ana County, NM	93.7	2.8	3.3	1.9	0.3	67.1	84,646	81,664	74,143	65,878	3.7	10.1
Las Vegas-Henderson-Paradise, NV Metro Area	75.3	13.6	2.2	12.4	1.6	30.6	871,807	841,433	726,134	566,405	3.6	15.9
Clark County, NV	75.3	13.6	2.2	12.4	1.6	30.6	871,807	841,433	726,134	566,405	3.6	15.9
Lawrence, KS Metro Area	87.5	6.3	4.3	5.8	0.3	6.0	48,540	46,793	44,678	40,436	3.7	4.7
Douglas County, KS	87.5	6.3	4.3	5.8	0.3	6.0	48,540	46,793	44,678	40,436	3.7	4.7
Lawton, OK Metro Area	72.1	20.3	9.5	4.3	1.1	12.6	54,703	53,895	50,233	48,585	1.5	7.3
Comanche County, OK	71.5	21.0	9.3	4.5	1.1	12.9	51,696	50,879	47,174	45,508	1.6	7.9
Cotton County, OK	85.5	3.9	15.2	0.7	0.3	7.5	3,007	3,016	3,059	3,077	-0.3	-1.4
Lebanon, PA Metro Area	94.8	4.2	0.7	1.7	0.1	12.0	56,464	55,647	53,053	49,431	1.5	4.9
Lebanon County, PA	94.8	4.2	0.7	1.7	0.1	12.0	56,464	55,647	53,053	49,431	1.5	4.9
Lewiston, ID-WA Metro Area	93.9	1.1	5.9	1.5	0.3	3.8	27,278	27,311	26,401	25,382	-0.1	3.4
Nez Perce County, ID	92.5	1.0	7.6	1.5	0.3	3.8	17,427	17,438	16,890	16,253	-0.1	3.2
Asotin County, WA	96.5	1.3	2.9	1.5	0.4	3.8	9,851	9,873	9,511	9,129	-0.2	3.8
Lewiston-Auburn, ME Metro Area	94.8	4.8	1.2	1.4	0.1	1.8	49,105	49,098	47,996	46,055	0.0	2.3
Androscoggin County, ME	94.8	4.8	1.2	1.4	0.1	1.8	49,105	49,098	47,996	46,055	0.0	2.3
Lexington-Fayette, KY Metro Area	85.3	12.7	0.9	3.3	0.1	6.0	216,459	209,453	195,267	176,228	3.3	7.3
Bourbon County, KY	92.8	7.6	0.8	0.6	0.1	7.0	9,025	8,929	8,768	8,385	1.1	1.8
Clark County, KY	94.1	5.8	0.7	0.7	0.1	3.0	15,749	15,710	15,258	13,835	0.2	3.0
Fayette County, KY	80.5	16.6	0.9	4.6	0.2	6.9	139,842	135,378	127,426	116,750	3.3	6.2
Jessamine County, KY	94.1	5.2	0.9	1.7	0.1	3.1	20,066	19,351	17,703	14,769	3.7	9.3
Scott County, KY	92.7	6.8	0.8	1.6	0.1	4.4	20,767	19,361	15,946	13,065	7.3	21.4
Woodford County, KY	93.6	6.2	0.6	0.9	0.2	6.5	11,010	10,724	10,166	9,424	2.7	5.5
Lima, OH Metro Area	86.1	14.7	0.8	1.2	0.1	2.9	44,799	44,988	44,973	44,276	-0.4	0.0
Allen County, OH	86.1	14.7	0.8	1.2	0.1	2.9	44,799	44,988	44,973	44,276	-0.4	0.0
Lincoln, NE Metro Area	90.8	5.3	1.7	4.8	0.2	6.5	133,554	127,868	121,957	111,111	4.4	4.8
Lancaster County, NE	90.4	5.5	1.7	5.0	0.2	6.7	126,503	120,989	115,226	104,669	4.6	5.0
Seward County, NE	98.4	1.1	0.9	0.8	0.1	2.5	7,051	6,879	6,731	6,442	2.5	2.2
Little Rock-North Little Rock-Conway, AR Metro Area	74.2	24.2	1.3	2.2	0.2	5.1	320,011	307,553	286,130	262,950	4.1	7.5
Faulkner County, AR	86.2	12.5	1.5	1.8	0.3	4.1	49,143	46,891	40,221	34,785	4.8	16.6
Grant County, AR	95.9	3.5	1.4	0.6	0.1	2.7	7,840	7,764	7,394	6,978	1.0	5.0
Lonoke County, AR	91.9	6.8	1.5	1.5	0.2	4.2	28,850	27,311	24,239	20,908	5.6	12.7
Perry County, AR	96.6	2.7	2.1	0.5	0.1	2.8	4,899	4,907	4,831	4,709	-0.2	1.6
Pulaski County, AR	60.6	37.5	1.3	2.8	0.1	6.0	182,285	175,756	169,648	161,426	3.7	3.6
Saline County, AR	91.2	7.5	1.2	1.5	0.1	4.3	46,994	44,924	39,797	34,144	4.6	12.9

0 = represents zero or rounds to zero.
[1]Persons of Hispanic origin may be of any race.

Table C-2. Population Characteristics and Housing Units—*Continued*

Metropolitan statistical area, division, and component county	White	Black or African American	Asian	American Indian, Alaska Native	Native Hawaiian and Other Pacific Islander	Hispanic or Latino origin[1] (percent)	2015 (July 1 estimate)	2010 (July 1 estimate)	2005 (July 1 estimate)	2000 (July 1 estimate)	2010–2015	2005–2010
Logan, UT-ID Metro Area	95.2	1.2	1.7	3.1	0.7	10.2	44,421	41,662	37,817	33,015	6.6	10.2
Franklin County, ID	98.6	0.6	1.8	0.5	0.2	7.1	4,676	4,540	4,241	3,894	3.0	7.1
Cache County, UT	94.9	1.2	1.7	3.4	0.8	10.6	39,745	37,122	33,576	29,121	7.1	10.6
Longview, TX Metro Area	80.1	18.6	1.7	1.4	0.2	16.1	89,818	87,361	84,660	81,346	2.8	3.2
Gregg County, TX	76.7	21.7	1.6	1.8	0.2	18.5	51,648	49,558	47,985	46,426	4.2	3.3
Rusk County, TX	80.8	18.3	1.6	0.8	0.1	16.5	21,378	21,184	20,752	19,930	0.9	2.1
Upshur County, TX	89.7	9.5	1.9	0.8	0.1	8.3	16,792	16,619	15,923	14,990	1.0	4.4
Longview, WA Metro Area	94.9	1.6	3.9	2.5	0.6	8.6	43,566	43,454	41,178	38,767	0.3	5.5
Cowlitz County, WA	94.9	1.6	3.9	2.5	0.6	8.6	43,566	43,454	41,178	38,767	0.3	5.5
Los Angeles-Long Beach-Anaheim, CA Metro Area	**74.2**	**8.3**	**2.2**	**17.9**	**0.7**	**45.1**	**4,585,126**	**4,495,807**	**4,394,076**	**4,247,689**	**2.0**	**2.3**
Anaheim-Santa Ana-Irvine, CA Division	*76.1*	*2.7*	*1.8*	*22.2*	*0.8*	*34.4*	*1,080,987*	*1,049,357*	*1,023,742*	*972,611*	*3.0*	*2.5*
Orange County, CA	76.1	2.7	1.8	22.2	0.8	34.4	1,080,987	1,049,357	1,023,742	972,611	3.0	2.5
Los Angeles-Long Beach-Glendale, CA Division	*73.7*	*10.0*	*2.3*	*16.6*	*0.7*	*48.4*	*3,504,139*	*3,446,450*	*3,370,334*	*3,275,078*	*1.7*	*2.3*
Los Angeles County, CA	73.7	10.0	2.3	16.6	0.7	48.4	3,504,139	3,446,450	3,370,334	3,275,078	1.7	2.3
Louisville/Jefferson County, KY-IN Metro Area	82.9	15.9	0.9	2.4	0.1	4.4	551,210	540,701	517,131	478,798	1.9	4.6
Clark County, IN	90.7	9.2	1.0	1.5	0.2	5.3	49,410	47,840	45,547	41,354	3.3	5.0
Floyd County, IN	93.0	6.8	0.8	1.5	0.1	2.9	32,407	31,986	31,038	29,199	1.3	3.1
Harrison County, IN	98.5	1.1	0.8	0.7	0.1	1.9	16,708	16,539	15,464	13,798	1.0	7.0
Scott County, IN	98.5	0.9	0.6	0.8	0.1	1.9	10,441	10,437	10,385	9,795	0.0	0.5
Washington County, IN	98.9	0.8	0.7	0.5	0.0	1.5	12,187	12,219	12,014	11,240	-0.3	1.7
Bullitt County, KY	97.8	1.7	1.0	0.9	0.1	1.8	30,650	29,384	27,214	23,322	4.3	8.0
Henry County, KY	96.2	4.0	1.0	0.6	0.1	3.0	6,679	6,640	6,651	6,394	0.6	-0.2
Jefferson County, KY	75.2	23.1	0.8	3.2	0.1	4.9	343,241	337,667	324,856	306,844	1.7	3.9
Oldham County, KY	92.8	5.4	1.2	2.1	0.2	4.1	21,399	20,717	19,169	15,793	3.3	8.1
Shelby County, KY	90.4	9.0	1.0	1.5	0.3	8.8	17,171	16,625	15,223	12,975	3.3	9.2
Spencer County, KY	97.4	2.5	0.8	0.6	0.1	2.0	6,994	6,717	5,822	4,609	4.1	15.4
Trimble County, KY	97.6	1.7	1.0	0.8	0.2	3.1	3,923	3,930	3,748	3,475	-0.2	4.9
Lubbock, TX Metro Area	88.6	8.4	1.8	2.8	0.3	35.1	128,688	120,855	116,177	106,679	6.5	4.0
Crosby County, TX	93.9	4.8	2.2	0.3	0.2	54.5	2,913	2,902	3,039	3,196	0.4	-4.5
Lubbock County, TX	88.4	8.5	1.7	2.9	0.3	34.5	123,099	115,277	110,457	100,814	6.8	4.4
Lynn County, TX	95.1	3.5	2.7	0.6	0.1	48.5	2,676	2,676	2,681	2,669	0.0	-0.2
Lynchburg, VA Metro Area	80.3	18.6	0.9	2.1	0.1	2.5	115,229	112,637	105,869	98,404	2.3	6.4
Amherst County, VA	79.2	20.5	1.5	1.0	0.1	2.3	14,102	13,989	13,555	12,989	0.8	3.2
Appomattox County, VA	79.5	21.0	0.7	0.7	0.1	1.4	7,122	6,938	6,348	5,850	2.7	9.3
Bedford County, VA	91.2	7.9	0.8	1.6	0.1	2.1	36,114	34,892	32,570	29,655	3.5	7.1
Campbell County, VA	83.9	15.8	0.9	1.3	0.1	2.2	25,517	24,789	23,568	22,092	2.9	5.2
Lynchburg city, VA	67.7	29.7	1.0	3.8	0.2	3.4	32,374	32,029	29,828	27,818	1.1	7.4
Macon, GA Metro Area	53.1	45.5	0.7	1.9	0.2	2.8	102,241	101,598	98,972	94,363	0.6	2.7
Bibb County, GA	43.2	55.0	0.7	2.4	0.2	3.2	70,267	69,647	69,188	67,328	0.9	0.7
Crawford County, GA	77.1	22.1	1.2	0.9	0.1	3.0	5,246	5,289	5,279	4,890	-0.8	0.2
Jones County, GA	74.1	25.4	0.7	0.9	0.1	1.5	11,562	11,691	10,872	9,373	-1.1	7.5
Monroe County, GA	74.8	24.4	0.7	1.2	0.1	2.3	10,993	10,738	9,310	8,470	2.4	15.3
Twiggs County, GA	58.7	41.4	0.8	0.5	0.0	2.0	4,173	4,233	4,323	4,302	-1.4	-2.1
Madera, CA Metro Area	88.2	4.8	5.8	3.2	0.5	56.7	50,084	49,160	45,362	40,518	1.9	8.4
Madera County, CA	88.2	4.8	5.8	3.2	0.5	56.7	50,084	49,160	45,362	40,518	1.9	8.4
Madison, WI Metro Area	89.9	5.8	1.0	5.6	0.1	5.7	278,423	268,967	254,973	227,642	3.5	5.5
Columbia County, WI	96.9	2.0	1.2	1.0	0.1	3.0	26,287	26,142	24,965	22,790	0.6	4.7
Dane County, WI	88.1	6.8	1.1	6.6	0.1	6.3	225,514	216,246	204,406	181,311	4.3	5.8
Green County, WI	98.2	1.1	0.7	0.9	0.1	3.0	15,851	15,861	15,215	13,931	-0.1	4.2
Iowa County, WI	98.6	1.0	0.6	0.9	0.1	1.8	10,771	10,718	10,387	9,610	0.5	3.2
Manchester-Nashua, NH Metro Area	93.0	3.5	0.9	4.5	0.1	6.2	168,074	166,102	160,727	150,436	1.2	3.3
Hillsborough County, NH	93.0	3.5	0.9	4.5	0.1	6.2	168,074	166,102	160,727	150,436	1.2	3.3
Manhattan, KS Metro Area	89.1	7.2	1.7	4.9	0.4	7.6	39,371	36,965	33,387	30,840	6.5	10.7
Pottawatomie County, KS	96.3	2.5	2.0	1.6	0.2	5.4	9,236	8,653	7,875	7,334	6.7	9.9
Riley County, KS	86.9	8.7	1.7	6.0	0.4	8.3	30,135	28,312	25,512	23,506	6.4	11.0
Mankato-North Mankato, MN Metro Area	94.1	4.0	0.8	2.7	0.1	3.6	40,650	39,112	37,241	33,338	3.9	5.0
Blue Earth County, MN	93.5	4.5	0.8	3.0	0.1	3.3	27,388	26,232	24,788	22,063	4.4	5.8
Nicollet County, MN	95.5	3.1	0.8	2.0	0.1	4.2	13,262	12,880	12,453	11,275	3.0	3.4
Mansfield, OH Metro Area	89.3	10.9	0.8	1.0	0.1	1.8	54,199	54,588	54,701	53,218	-0.7	-0.2
Richland County, OH	89.3	10.9	0.8	1.0	0.1	1.8	54,199	54,588	54,701	53,218	-0.7	-0.2
McAllen-Edinburg-Mission, TX Metro Area	97.3	1.1	0.7	1.3	0.1	91.3	264,604	248,966	226,956	193,935	6.3	9.7
Hidalgo County, TX	97.3	1.1	0.7	1.3	0.1	91.3	264,604	248,966	226,956	193,935	6.3	9.7
Medford, OR Metro Area	95.6	1.6	3.4	2.3	0.7	12.4	92,844	90,959	85,608	76,129	2.1	6.3
Jackson County, OR	95.6	1.6	3.4	2.3	0.7	12.4	92,844	90,959	85,608	76,129	2.1	6.3
Memphis, TN-MS-AR Metro Area	50.3	47.8	0.8	2.5	0.2	5.4	566,162	555,384	528,489	486,838	1.9	5.1
Crittenden County, AR	46.7	52.8	0.8	1.0	0.1	2.4	21,686	21,495	21,051	20,571	0.9	2.1
Benton County, MS	63.0	36.8	0.9	0.2	0.1	2.4	4,200	4,188	3,836	3,479	0.3	9.2
DeSoto County, MS	72.1	26.6	0.7	1.9	0.1	5.0	64,856	61,746	53,238	41,441	5.0	16.0
Marshall County, MS	51.2	48.6	0.7	0.4	0.1	3.5	15,139	14,898	13,925	13,275	1.6	7.0
Tate County, MS	67.7	32.3	0.7	0.6	0.1	2.6	11,198	10,956	10,250	9,409	2.2	6.9
Tunica County, MS	22.9	76.3	0.5	1.1	0.2	2.5	4,834	4,804	4,515	3,776	0.6	6.4
Fayette County, TN	71.2	28.1	0.7	0.8	0.1	2.5	16,433	15,690	13,085	11,280	4.7	19.9
Shelby County, TN	43.2	54.4	0.8	3.1	0.1	6.1	404,386	398,346	386,849	364,403	1.5	3.0
Tipton County, TN	79.8	19.5	1.2	1.1	0.5	2.6	23,530	23,261	21,740	19,204	1.2	7.0
Merced, CA Metro Area	84.6	5.0	3.7	9.3	0.7	58.2	84,322	83,717	77,686	68,875	0.7	7.8
Merced County, CA	84.6	5.0	3.7	9.3	0.7	58.2	84,322	83,717	77,686	68,875	0.7	7.8

0 = represents zero or rounds to zero.
[1]Persons of Hispanic origin may be of any race.

Table C-2. Population Characteristics and Housing Units—*Continued*

Metropolitan statistical area, division, and component county	Population characteristics, 2015						Housing units				Percent change	
	Race alone or in combination (percent)					Hispanic or Latino origin[1] (percent)	2015 (July 1 estimate)	2010 (July 1 estimate)	2005 (July 1 estimate)	2000 (July 1 estimate)		
	White	Black or African American	Asian	American Indian, Alaska Native	Native Hawaiian and Other Pacific Islander						2010–2015	2005–2010
Miami-Fort Lauderdale-West Palm Beach, FL Metro Area	74.5	23.2	0.7	3.2	0.3	43.8	2,508,205	2,464,492	2,358,423	2,158,776	1.8	4.5
Fort Lauderdale-Pompano Beach-Deerfield Beach, FL Division	66.0	30.7	0.8	4.6	0.3	28.0	818,623	810,355	793,132	743,865	1.0	2.2
Broward County, FL	66.0	30.7	0.8	4.6	0.3	28.0	818,623	810,355	793,132	743,865	1.0	2.2
Miami-Miami Beach-Kendall, FL Division	*79.0*	*19.5*	*0.5*	*2.1*	*0.2*	*66.8*	*1,010,556*	*989,412*	*934,527*	*855,553*	*2.1*	*5.9*
Miami-Dade County, FL	79.0	19.5	0.5	2.1	0.2	66.8	1,010,556	989,412	934,527	855,553	2.1	5.9
West Palm Beach-Boca Raton-Delray Beach, FL Division	*77.2*	*20.1*	*1.0*	*3.4*	*0.3*	*21.1*	*679,026*	*664,725*	*630,764*	*559,358*	*2.2*	*5.4*
Palm Beach County, FL	77.2	20.1	1.0	3.4	0.3	21.1	679,026	664,725	630,764	559,358	2.2	5.4
Michigan City-La Porte, IN Metro Area	87.4	12.8	1.0	1.0	0.1	6.3	48,782	48,450	47,552	45,724	0.7	1.9
LaPorte County, IN	87.4	12.8	1.0	1.0	0.1	6.3	48,782	48,450	47,552	45,724	0.7	1.9
Midland, MI Metro Area	95.4	2.1	1.1	2.8	0.1	2.6	36,465	35,953	35,499	33,906	1.4	1.3
Midland County, MI	95.4	2.1	1.1	2.8	0.1	2.6	36,465	35,953	35,499	33,906	1.4	1.3
Midland, TX Metro Area	90.3	7.4	1.8	2.0	0.2	43.7	61,377	56,267	52,788	50,118	9.1	6.6
Martin County, TX	95.7	3.3	1.7	0.5	0.2	46.2	1,866	1,852	1,862	1,898	0.8	-0.5
Midland County, TX	90.1	7.5	1.8	2.0	0.2	43.7	59,511	54,415	50,926	48,220	9.4	6.9
Milwaukee-Waukesha-West Allis, WI Metro Area	78.4	18.3	1.3	4.2	0.1	10.4	673,016	669,901	651,555	619,802	0.5	2.8
Milwaukee County, WI	67.5	28.8	1.8	4.7	0.1	14.5	416,951	417,963	410,724	400,572	-0.2	1.8
Ozaukee County, WI	95.7	1.9	0.7	2.9	0.1	2.8	36,930	36,294	35,082	32,155	1.8	3.5
Washington County, WI	97.1	1.7	0.7	1.6	0.1	3.1	55,759	54,736	51,330	46,072	1.9	6.6
Waukesha County, WI	94.7	2.1	0.7	3.9	0.1	4.7	163,376	160,908	154,419	141,003	1.5	4.2
Minneapolis-St. Paul-Bloomington, MN-WI Metro	84.0	9.6	1.7	7.5	0.2	5.7	1,425,849	1,387,263	1,331,934	1,202,766	2.8	4.2
Anoka County, MN	88.9	6.9	1.7	5.3	0.1	4.2	130,080	126,762	121,366	108,640	2.6	4.4
Carver County, MN	94.9	2.4	0.7	3.7	0.1	4.1	36,901	34,606	31,848	25,228	6.6	8.7
Chisago County, MN	96.7	1.8	1.3	1.5	0.1	2.0	21,518	21,174	19,584	15,732	1.6	8.1
Dakota County, MN	88.3	7.4	1.3	5.9	0.2	6.7	164,056	159,681	152,797	134,574	2.7	4.5
Hennepin County, MN	78.4	14.5	2.1	8.3	0.2	6.9	526,537	509,530	496,739	469,998	3.3	2.6
Isanti County, MN	97.6	1.3	1.3	1.4	0.1	1.9	15,553	15,326	14,598	12,129	1.5	5.0
Le Sueur County, MN	98.1	1.0	1.0	1.1	0.1	5.8	12,516	12,418	12,009	10,896	0.8	3.4
Mille Lacs County, MN	92.7	1.1	7.2	0.8	0.1	2.1	12,719	12,748	12,068	10,518	-0.2	5.6
Ramsey County, MN	72.4	13.8	2.0	15.3	0.2	7.4	218,430	217,149	214,394	206,701	0.6	1.3
Scott County, MN	88.7	4.6	1.7	7.1	0.2	4.9	49,999	47,239	43,072	32,140	5.8	9.7
Sherburne County, MN	95.8	3.0	1.1	1.8	0.1	2.5	33,098	32,392	30,009	23,146	2.2	7.9
Sibley County, MN	98.2	1.3	0.8	1.0	0.1	8.6	6,548	6,581	6,424	6,042	-0.5	2.4
Washington County, MN	89.0	5.5	1.1	6.6	0.2	4.0	96,289	92,487	85,547	74,218	4.1	8.1
Wright County, MN	96.9	2.0	0.8	1.9	0.1	2.7	50,345	49,032	44,694	34,773	2.7	9.7
Pierce County, WI	97.9	1.2	1.0	1.3	0.1	2.0	16,328	16,140	15,260	13,521	1.2	5.8
St. Croix County, WI	97.6	1.3	0.9	1.6	0.1	2.3	34,932	33,998	31,525	24,510	2.7	7.8
Missoula, MT Metro Area	94.7	1.1	4.5	2.4	0.3	3.2	51,869	50,119	46,557	41,534	3.5	7.7
Missoula County, MT	94.7	1.1	4.5	2.4	0.3	3.2	51,869	50,119	46,557	41,534	3.5	7.7
Mobile, AL Metro Area	61.2	36.3	1.6	2.5	0.1	2.8	182,025	178,747	171,626	165,520	1.8	4.1
Mobile County, AL	61.2	36.3	1.6	2.5	0.1	2.8	182,025	178,747	171,626	165,520	1.8	4.1
Modesto, CA Metro Area	87.3	4.3	3.4	7.7	1.5	44.8	180,704	179,579	169,253	151,433	0.6	6.1
Stanislaus County, CA	87.3	4.3	3.4	7.7	1.5	44.8	180,704	179,579	169,253	151,433	0.6	6.1
Monroe, LA Metro Area	62.5	36.7	0.8	1.2	0.1	2.4	78,410	75,891	73,282	71,086	3.3	3.6
Ouachita Parish, LA	61.0	38.2	0.8	1.3	0.1	2.1	66,953	64,537	62,175	60,217	3.7	3.8
Union Parish, LA	73.0	26.5	0.8	0.4	0.1	4.4	11,457	11,354	11,107	10,869	0.9	2.2
Monroe, MI Metro Area	96.4	3.3	1.1	1.0	0.1	3.5	63,654	63,033	61,751	56,702	1.0	2.1
Monroe County, MI	96.4	3.3	1.1	1.0	0.1	3.5	63,654	63,033	61,751	56,702	1.0	2.1
Montgomery, AL Metro Area	53.2	44.9	0.9	2.4	0.2	3.1	165,497	161,612	154,559	145,108	2.4	4.6
Autauga County, AL	78.9	20.1	1.1	1.7	0.2	2.8	22,847	22,152	20,275	17,845	3.1	9.3
Elmore County, AL	77.2	22.1	1.1	1.1	0.2	2.8	33,570	32,668	29,768	25,862	2.8	9.7
Lowndes County, AL	26.9	72.8	0.7	0.4	0.1	1.3	5,085	5,137	5,478	5,795		-6.2
Montgomery County, AL	39.5	57.8	0.8	3.2	0.2	3.4	103,995	101,655	99,038	95,606	2.3	2.6
Morgantown, WV Metro Area	93.8	4.2	0.7	3.0	0.1	1.9	59,576	58,342	54,511	50,360	2.1	7.0
Monongalia County, WV	92.4	5.0	0.7	3.9	0.1	2.2	44,545	43,245	40,124	36,869	3.0	7.8
Preston County, WV	98.1	1.7	0.7	0.3	0.1	1.0	15,031	15,097	14,387	13,491	-0.4	4.9
Morristown, TN Metro Area	94.7	4.5	1.2	0.9	0.2	7.7	50,696	50,490	47,881	44,244	0.4	5.4
Hamblen County, TN	93.3	5.7	1.5	1.2	0.3	11.2	27,024	26,969	26,083	24,790	0.2	3.4
Jefferson County, TN	96.5	3.1	1.0	0.6	0.1	3.5	23,672	23,521	21,798	19,454	0.6	7.9
Mount Vernon-Anacortes, WA Metro Area	93.4	1.7	4.3	3.2	0.6	17.9	52,214	51,511	47,554	42,904	1.4	8.3
Skagit County, WA	93.4	1.7	4.3	3.2	0.6	17.9	52,214	51,511	47,554	42,904	1.4	8.3
Muncie, IN Metro Area	91.0	8.5	0.8	1.8	0.2	2.2	52,489	52,336	52,502	51,122	0.3	-0.3
Delaware County, IN	91.0	8.5	0.8	1.8	0.2	2.2	52,489	52,336	52,502	51,122	0.3	-0.3
Muskegon, MI Metro Area	83.7	16.1	2.0	1.1	0.1	5.4	73,331	73,534	72,793	68,781	-0.3	1.0
Muskegon County, MI	83.7	16.1	2.0	1.1	0.1	5.4	73,331	73,534	72,793	68,781	-0.3	1.0
Myrtle Beach-Conway-North Myrtle Beach, SC-NC Metro Area	85.0	14.0	1.3	1.5	0.2	5.7	279,196	263,996	216,238	175,248	5.8	22.1
Brunswick County, NC	87.0	12.0	1.6	1.0	0.2	4.8	83,080	77,701	64,429	51,833	6.9	20.6
Horry County, SC	84.2	14.7	1.2	1.7	0.2	6.1	196,116	186,295	151,809	123,415	5.3	22.7
Napa, CA Metro Area	87.3	3.1	2.4	9.8	0.7	33.9	55,472	54,787	52,882	48,719	1.3	3.6
Napa County, CA	87.3	3.1	2.4	9.8	0.7	33.9	55,472	54,787	52,882	48,719	1.3	3.6
Naples-Immokalee-Marco Island, FL Metro Area	90.6	7.8	0.8	1.8	0.3	26.8	206,375	197,453	182,515	146,520	4.5	8.2
Collier County, FL	90.6	7.8	0.8	1.8	0.3	26.8	206,375	197,453	182,515	146,520	4.5	8.2
Nashville-Davidson--Murfreesboro--Franklin, TN Metro Area	81.0	16.7	1.1	3.2	0.2	7.0	744,320	703,938	644,661	575,049	5.7	9.2

0 = represents zero or rounds to zero.
[1] Persons of Hispanic origin may be of any race.

Table C-2. Population Characteristics and Housing Units—*Continued*

Metropolitan statistical area, division, and component county	Population characteristics, 2015						Housing units					
	Race alone or in combination (percent)										Percent change	
	White	Black or African American	Asian	American Indian, Alaska Native	Native Hawaiian and Other Pacific Islander	Hispanic or Latino origin[1] (percent)	2015 (July 1 estimate)	2010 (July 1 estimate)	2005 (July 1 estimate)	2000 (July 1 estimate)	2010– 2015	2005– 2010
Cannon County, TN	97.1	2.5	1.1	0.6	0.2	2.0	6,058	6,037	5,819	5,452	0.3	3.7
Cheatham County, TN	96.9	2.6	1.1	0.7	0.1	2.8	15,869	15,726	14,893	13,548	0.9	5.6
Davidson County, TN	67.6	29.3	1.2	4.3	0.2	10.0	298,788	284,265	269,181	253,627	5.1	5.6
Dickson County, TN	94.3	5.5	1.1	0.8	0.1	3.3	21,229	20,829	19,627	17,720	1.9	6.1
Hickman County, TN	93.9	5.7	1.3	0.6	0.1	2.1	10,294	10,315	9,773	8,965	-0.2	5.5
Macon County, TN	97.5	1.4	1.3	0.9	0.1	5.1	9,992	9,863	9,495	8,940	1.3	3.9
Maury County, TN	86.6	13.2	1.0	1.2	0.1	5.5	36,251	35,296	32,325	28,818	2.7	9.2
Robertson County, TN	91.0	8.5	1.0	0.9	0.2	6.4	26,612	26,113	24,163	21,155	1.9	8.1
Rutherford County, TN	81.4	15.9	1.1	4.0	0.2	7.5	112,105	103,200	89,459	71,472	8.6	15.4
Smith County, TN	96.9	2.9	1.1	0.5	0.0	2.5	8,617	8,533	8,105	7,690	1.0	5.3
Sumner County, TN	90.8	8.1	0.9	1.8	0.2	4.5	68,854	66,093	59,263	51,969	4.2	11.5
Trousdale County, TN	90.0	10.1	1.3	0.6	0.0	3.2	3,442	3,370	3,239	3,100	2.1	4.0
Williamson County, TN	91.1	5.1	0.7	4.5	0.1	4.8	75,994	68,621	58,890	47,442	10.7	16.5
Wilson County, TN	90.9	7.9	1.0	1.9	0.2	3.9	50,215	45,677	40,429	35,151	9.9	13.0
New Bern, NC Metro Area	74.3	23.6	1.4	3.0	0.3	6.6	58,470	57,456	53,956	49,745	1.8	6.5
Craven County, NC	74.5	23.1	1.4	3.5	0.3	7.2	46,055	45,078	42,050	38,301	2.2	7.2
Jones County, NC	67.7	32.0	1.4	0.7	0.1	4.4	4,851	4,840	4,709	4,652	0.2	2.8
Pamlico County, NC	78.4	21.0	1.1	0.7	0.2	3.8	7,564	7,538	7,197	6,792	0.3	4.7
New Haven-Milford, CT Metro Area	80.5	15.9	1.1	4.8	0.2	17.2	362,679	361,946	353,296	341,322	0.2	2.4
New Haven County, CT	80.5	15.9	1.1	4.8	0.2	17.2	362,679	361,946	353,296	341,322	0.2	2.4
New Orleans-Metairie, LA Metro Area	60.9	36.1	1.2	3.5	0.2	8.7	555,843	547,218	592,800	557,784	1.6	-7.7
Jefferson Parish, LA	67.6	28.1	1.2	4.8	0.1	14.2	189,161	189,166	196,381	188,204	0.0	-3.7
Orleans Parish, LA	36.6	60.4	1.0	3.6	0.1	5.6	193,035	190,166	227,110	215,500	1.5	-16.3
Plaquemines Parish, LA	73.0	22.1	3.0	4.7	0.3	6.7	9,954	9,614	11,650	10,532	3.5	-17.5
St. Bernard Parish, LA	73.7	23.9	1.8	2.9	0.2	9.9	16,857	16,799	26,931	26,801	0.3	-37.6
St. Charles Parish, LA	71.7	27.4	1.0	1.5	0.1	6.1	20,372	19,971	18,503	17,447	2.0	7.9
St. James Parish, LA	50.2	49.6	0.5	0.5	0.1	1.8	8,756	8,467	7,916	7,612	3.4	7.0
St. John the Baptist Parish, LA	42.5	56.6	0.8	1.0	0.4	5.7	17,647	17,483	16,826	15,646	0.9	3.9
St. Tammany Parish, LA	85.5	13.0	1.2	2.1	0.1	5.5	100,061	95,552	87,483	76,042	4.7	9.2
New York-Newark-Jersey City, NY-NJ-PA Metro Area	**67.7**	**20.8**	**1.6**	**12.3**	**0.3**	**24.1**	**7,892,416**	**7,790,083**	**7,571,893**	**7,333,969**	**1.3**	**2.9**
Dutchess County-Putnam County, NY Division	*86.3*	*10.6*	*1.0*	*4.3*	*0.2*	*12.2*	*157,569*	*156,877*	*150,718*	*141,552*	*0.4*	*4.1*
Dutchess County, NY	83.8	12.7	1.0	4.7	0.2	11.8	119,233	118,644	113,493	106,418	0.5	4.5
Putnam County, NY	93.6	4.1	0.9	3.1	0.1	13.5	38,336	38,233	37,225	35,134	0.3	2.7
Nassau County-Suffolk County, NY Division	*81.9*	*11.4*	*1.0*	*7.4*	*0.2*	*17.6*	*1,037,488*	*1,038,223*	*1,014,822*	*982,427*	*-0.1*	*2.3*
Nassau County, NY	77.0	13.5	0.9	10.3	0.2	16.5	466,818	468,246	463,425	458,537	-0.3	1.0
Suffolk County, NY	86.4	9.5	1.1	4.8	0.2	18.6	570,670	569,977	551,397	523,890	0.1	3.4
Newark, NJ-PA Division	*70.5*	*22.1*	*1.0*	*8.4*	*0.2*	*19.4*	*984,251*	*975,551*	*952,333*	*919,578*	*0.9*	*2.4*
Essex County, NJ	51.4	43.4	1.3	6.2	0.3	22.4	314,763	313,044	306,703	301,201	0.5	2.1
Hunterdon County, NJ	92.8	3.2	0.5	4.6	0.3	6.3	49,964	49,504	48,276	45,223	0.9	2.5
Morris County, NJ	85.5	4.4	0.6	11.4	0.1	13.0	191,287	189,911	184,423	175,022	0.7	3.0
Somerset County, NJ	72.2	10.9	0.7	18.2	0.2	14.5	125,877	123,230	119,800	113,684	2.1	2.9
Sussex County, NJ	95.2	2.9	0.6	2.6	0.1	7.5	62,327	61,931	60,162	56,760	0.6	2.9
Union County, NJ	69.7	24.9	1.2	6.2	0.2	30.6	201,486	199,548	196,116	193,056	1.0	1.7
Pike County, PA	91.5	7.4	1.2	1.8	0.1	10.5	38,547	38,383	36,853	34,632	0.4	4.2
New York-Jersey City-White Plains, NY-NJ Division	*63.9*	*22.7*	*1.8*	*14.1*	*0.3*	*26.5*	*5,713,108*	*5,619,432*	*5,454,020*	*5,290,412*	*1.7*	*3.0*
Bergen County, NJ	75.6	7.9	0.8	17.6	0.2	18.9	355,116	352,450	346,713	340,394	0.8	1.7
Hudson County, NJ	67.6	16.7	1.8	16.4	0.3	43.0	277,811	270,979	252,622	241,063	2.5	7.3
Middlesex County, NJ	63.2	12.4	1.1	25.4	0.2	20.3	299,592	295,148	285,760	274,311	1.5	3.3
Monmouth County, NJ	86.1	8.6	0.7	6.3	0.1	10.7	260,686	258,691	251,726	240,869	0.8	3.1
Ocean County, NJ	94.0	4.2	0.6	2.5	0.1	9.1	280,494	278,427	269,962	250,088	0.7	3.1
Passaic County, NJ	77.3	16.7	2.1	6.4	0.3	40.2	176,850	176,164	173,322	170,116	0.4	1.6
Bronx County, NY	48.1	46.2	4.1	4.9	0.6	55.1	523,690	512,712	501,921	490,845	2.1	2.1
Kings County, NY	51.1	36.3	1.6	13.4	0.3	19.5	1,025,752	1,002,497	959,666	932,114	2.3	4.5
New York County, NY	67.2	20.1	2.0	14.0	0.3	26.0	869,866	847,856	820,501	799,670	2.6	3.3
Orange County, NY	83.9	13.9	1.6	3.5	0.2	19.8	140,297	137,090	131,862	123,220	2.3	4.0
Queens County, NY	50.5	22.3	2.1	27.8	0.4	28.0	849,505	835,853	823,437	817,540	1.6	1.5
Richmond County, NY	78.4	13.1	1.1	9.4	0.2	18.3	179,001	176,793	173,464	164,640	1.2	1.9
Rockland County, NY	79.1	14.4	1.0	7.4	0.2	17.4	104,825	104,051	99,753	95,391	0.7	4.3
Westchester County, NY	76.2	17.6	1.5	7.2	0.2	24.2	369,623	370,721	363,311	350,151	-0.3	2.0
Niles-Benton Harbor, MI Metro Area	81.7	16.7	1.4	2.5	0.2	5.3	76,793	76,902	75,885	73,574	-0.1	1.3
Berrien County, MI	81.7	16.7	1.4	2.5	0.2	5.3	76,793	76,902	75,885	73,574	-0.1	1.3
North Port-Sarasota-Bradenton, FL Metro Area	90.5	7.8	0.9	2.3	0.2	12.2	414,742	401,268	374,109	322,435	3.4	7.3
Manatee County, FL	87.9	10.2	1.0	2.5	0.2	16.0	182,119	172,855	161,602	138,951	5.4	7.0
Sarasota County, FL	92.9	5.7	0.8	2.1	0.1	8.8	232,623	228,413	212,507	183,484	1.8	7.5
Norwich-New London, CT Metro Area	86.7	8.9	2.4	5.6	0.3	10.3	121,637	121,036	116,755	110,921	0.5	3.7
New London County, CT	86.7	8.9	2.4	5.6	0.3	10.3	121,637	121,036	116,755	110,921	0.5	3.7
Ocala, FL Metro Area	84.2	14.3	1.1	2.1	0.2	12.2	163,808	163,998	146,909	123,249	-0.1	11.6
Marion County, FL	84.2	14.3	1.1	2.1	0.2	12.2	163,808	163,998	146,909	123,249	-0.1	11.6
Ocean City, NJ Metro Area	93.2	6.2	0.8	1.6	0.2	7.6	99,010	98,416	96,139	91,226	0.6	2.4
Cape May County, NJ	93.2	6.2	0.8	1.6	0.2	7.6	99,010	98,416	96,139	91,226	0.6	2.4
Odessa, TX Metro Area	92.1	5.7	2.1	1.4	0.3	58.7	57,025	53,071	51,155	49,634	7.5	3.7
Ector County, TX	92.1	5.7	2.1	1.4	0.3	58.7	57,025	53,071	51,155	49,634	7.5	3.7
Ogden-Clearfield, UT Metro Area	95.2	2.1	1.7	2.8	0.9	12.5	215,183	204,446	185,281	161,969	5.3	10.3
Box Elder County, UT	97.0	0.9	2.0	1.6	0.4	9.3	18,223	17,362	15,721	14,279	5.0	10.4
Davis County, UT	95.0	2.1	1.3	3.3	1.2	9.4	104,982	97,774	87,595	74,596	7.4	11.6
Morgan County, UT	98.4	0.6	0.8	0.9	0.2	2.6	3,382	3,013	2,522	2,173	12.2	19.5
Weber County, UT	95.1	2.4	2.1	2.5	0.7	17.9	88,596	86,297	79,443	70,921	2.7	8.6

0 = represents zero or rounds to zero.
[1]Persons of Hispanic origin may be of any race.

Table C-2. Population Characteristics and Housing Units—*Continued*

| | Population characteristics, 2015 | | | | | | Housing units | | | | | |
| | Race alone or in combination (percent) | | | | | | | | | | Percent change | |
Metropolitan statistical area, division, and component county	White	Black or African American	Asian	American Indian, Alaska Native	Native Hawaiian and Other Pacific Islander	Hispanic or Latino origin[1] (percent)	2015 (July 1 estimate)	2010 (July 1 estimate)	2005 (July 1 estimate)	2000 (July 1 estimate)	2010–2015	2005–2010
Oklahoma City, OK Metro Area	80.6	12.6	8.0	4.1	0.2	12.7	564,440	539,738	509,817	473,659	4.6	5.9
Canadian County, OK	88.3	4.2	8.1	3.9	0.2	8.3	47,635	45,864	40,060	34,213	3.9	14.5
Cleveland County, OK	84.8	6.5	8.7	5.6	0.3	8.2	112,393	105,046	95,962	85,247	7.0	9.5
Grady County, OK	90.6	3.4	10.0	0.8	0.2	5.7	22,584	22,229	20,953	19,497	1.6	6.1
Lincoln County, OK	90.4	2.7	11.6	0.6	0.1	3.3	15,225	15,210	14,571	13,756	0.1	4.4
Logan County, OK	86.6	10.2	6.6	1.1	0.2	5.8	17,265	17,207	15,612	13,989	0.3	10.2
McClain County, OK	91.4	1.5	11.5	0.8	0.2	7.8	15,011	14,019	12,619	11,251	7.1	11.1
Oklahoma County, OK	75.7	18.0	7.4	4.4	0.3	16.6	334,327	320,163	310,040	295,706	4.4	3.3
Olympia-Tumwater, WA Metro Area	87.3	5.1	3.5	8.3	1.7	8.6	112,553	108,436	96,943	87,059	3.8	11.9
Thurston County, WA	87.3	5.1	3.5	8.3	1.7	8.6	112,553	108,436	96,943	87,059	3.8	11.9
Omaha-Council Bluffs, NE-IA Metro Area	88.0	9.4	1.7	3.4	0.2	10.0	377,871	362,986	341,191	313,007	4.1	6.4
Harrison County, IA	98.9	0.7	0.9	0.6	0.0	1.3	6,755	6,734	6,773	6,614	0.3	-0.6
Mills County, IA	98.3	1.2	1.0	0.8	0.2	2.7	6,080	6,109	5,986	5,684	-0.5	2.1
Pottawattamie County, IA	96.6	2.6	1.3	1.2	0.2	7.5	39,616	39,350	38,386	35,959	0.7	2.5
Cass County, NE	98.3	1.1	1.2	0.7	0.1	3.1	11,283	11,122	10,888	10,212	1.4	2.1
Douglas County, NE	83.4	13.1	2.0	4.2	0.2	12.2	229,086	219,944	207,427	193,366	4.2	6.0
Sarpy County, NE	92.1	5.9	1.4	3.6	0.3	8.7	67,144	62,196	54,910	45,449	8.0	13.3
Saunders County, NE	98.4	1.1	0.8	0.7	0.1	2.3	9,447	9,227	8,830	8,282	2.4	4.5
Washington County, NE	98.4	1.3	0.8	0.6	0.2	2.6	8,460	8,304	7,991	7,441	1.9	3.9
Orlando-Kissimmee-Sanford, FL Metro Area	76.7	19.1	1.2	5.4	0.4	28.7	988,892	942,941	835,957	690,045	4.9	12.8
Lake County, FL	85.9	11.8	1.3	2.7	0.3	14.4	148,706	145,058	127,874	103,959	2.5	13.4
Orange County, FL	70.9	23.9	1.1	6.6	0.4	29.8	516,477	488,117	434,446	364,211	5.8	12.4
Osceola County, FL	82.2	15.2	1.5	3.7	0.4	51.0	137,090	128,356	104,562	73,608	6.8	22.8
Seminole County, FL	82.6	13.8	1.1	5.3	0.3	19.8	186,619	181,410	169,075	148,267	2.9	7.3
Oshkosh-Neenah, WI Metro Area	94.2	2.9	1.2	3.3	0.1	4.1	74,551	73,386	70,659	64,945	1.6	3.9
Winnebago County, WI	94.2	2.9	1.2	3.3	0.1	4.1	74,551	73,386	70,659	64,945	1.6	3.9
Owensboro, KY Metro Area	94.3	5.8	0.5	1.1	0.2	2.7	50,749	49,490	49,191	46,596	2.5	0.6
Daviess County, KY	93.6	6.5	0.4	1.3	0.2	2.9	42,785	41,493	41,110	38,591	3.1	0.9
Hancock County, KY	98.1	1.7	0.6	0.5	0.0	1.5	3,714	3,733	3,704	3,610	-0.5	0.8
McLean County, KY	98.6	1.4	0.7	0.3	0.0	1.4	4,250	4,264	4,377	4,395	-0.3	-2.6
Oxnard-Thousand Oaks-Ventura, CA Metro Area	87.7	3.0	2.9	9.4	0.6	42.3	285,880	281,771	270,687	252,796	1.5	4.1
Ventura County, CA	87.7	3.0	2.9	9.4	0.6	42.3	285,880	281,771	270,687	252,796	1.5	4.1
Palm Bay-Melbourne-Titusville, FL Metro Area	86.0	12.0	1.1	3.4	0.3	9.7	273,096	269,967	253,057	223,111	1.2	6.7
Brevard County, FL	86.0	12.0	1.1	3.4	0.3	9.7	273,096	269,967	253,057	223,111	1.2	6.7
Panama City, FL Metro Area	84.6	13.4	1.8	3.2	0.3	6.0	109,942	108,773	98,676	86,425	1.1	10.2
Bay County, FL	85.0	12.8	1.8	3.4	0.3	6.0	100,697	99,670	90,008	78,783	1.0	10.7
Gulf County, FL	80.0	19.7	1.4	0.7	0.1	5.2	9,245	9,103	8,668	7,642	1.6	5.0
Parkersburg-Vienna, WV Metro Area	97.8	2.1	0.8	0.9	0.1	1.0	43,497	43,455	43,440	43,068	0.1	0.0
Wirt County, WV	99.1	1.0	0.8	0.4	0.0	0.8	3,237	3,236	3,257	3,263	0.0	-0.6
Wood County, WV	97.7	2.1	0.8	0.9	0.1	1.1	40,260	40,219	40,183	39,805	0.1	0.1
Pensacola-Ferry Pass-Brent, FL Metro Area	78.6	18.5	1.9	4.1	0.4	5.5	207,629	201,596	191,771	174,356	3.0	5.1
Escambia County, FL	72.5	24.3	1.9	4.4	0.4	5.6	139,055	136,771	132,685	124,889	1.7	3.1
Santa Rosa County, FL	89.9	7.8	1.9	3.5	0.3	5.4	68,574	64,825	59,086	49,467	5.8	9.7
Peoria, IL Metro Area	87.6	10.9	0.8	2.8	0.1	3.4	166,098	164,333	159,910	153,633	1.1	2.8
Marshall County, IL	98.6	0.9	0.7	0.7	0.1	3.4	5,886	5,912	5,986	5,893	-0.4	-1.2
Peoria County, IL	77.2	20.4	0.8	4.4	0.1	4.6	83,560	83,045	81,088	78,421	0.6	2.4
Stark County, IL	98.6	1.3	0.6	0.7	0.1	1.2	2,660	2,674	2,747	2,724	-0.5	-2.7
Tazewell County, IL	97.4	2.0	0.7	1.3	0.1	2.3	58,581	57,546	55,544	53,057	1.8	3.6
Woodford County, IL	98.2	1.2	0.6	1.0	0.1	1.8	15,411	15,156	14,545	13,538	1.7	4.2
Philadelphia-Camden-Wilmington, PA-NJ-DE-MD Metro Area	**71.3**	**23.3**	**1.1**	**6.6**	**0.2**	**9.0**	**2,455,432**	**2,434,040**	**2,376,909**	**2,286,358**	**0.9**	**2.4**
Camden, NJ Division	*76.5*	*19.1*	*1.0*	*5.8*	*0.2*	*10.7*	*496,585*	*490,627*	*477,757*	*457,033*	*1.2*	*2.7*
Burlington County, NJ	76.2	19.4	1.0	6.1	0.2	7.8	177,994	175,683	170,796	161,925	1.3	2.9
Camden County, NJ	71.7	22.8	1.2	6.6	0.2	16.0	206,210	204,998	202,463	199,227	0.6	1.3
Gloucester County, NJ	85.4	12.2	0.7	3.7	0.1	5.9	112,381	109,946	104,498	95,881	2.2	5.2
Montgomery County-Bucks County-Chester County, PA Division	*86.5*	*8.0*	*0.7*	*6.7*	*0.1*	*5.5*	*772,551*	*764,363*	*735,122*	*689,131*	*1.1*	*4.0*
Bucks County, PA	90.6	5.0	0.7	5.4	0.1	5.0	247,207	245,971	239,738	226,193	0.5	2.6
Chester County, PA	88.0	7.4	0.7	5.7	0.1	7.3	196,755	192,613	181,559	164,578	2.2	6.1
Montgomery County, PA	82.4	10.7	0.6	8.4	0.1	4.9	328,589	325,779	313,825	298,360	0.9	3.8
Philadelphia, PA Division	53.8	39.7	1.4	7.6	0.2	11.3	894,462	892,864	886,649	879,239	0.2	0.7
Delaware County, PA	72.4	22.8	0.7	6.3	0.1	3.7	221,874	222,903	221,255	217,129	-0.5	0.7
Philadelphia County, PA	47.1	45.8	1.7	8.1	0.3	14.0	672,588	669,961	665,394	662,110	0.4	0.7
Wilmington, DE-MD-NJ Division	*73.1*	*23.2*	*1.0*	*5.1*	*0.1*	*8.6*	*291,834*	*286,186*	*277,381*	*260,955*	*2.0*	*3.2*
New Castle County, DE	68.6	26.8	1.0	6.1	0.1	9.5	221,637	217,608	211,385	200,131	1.9	2.9
Cecil County, MD	91.0	8.3	1.0	1.8	0.2	4.2	42,565	41,138	39,109	34,658	3.5	5.2
Salem County, NJ	83.4	16.2	1.0	1.5	0.2	8.2	27,632	27,440	26,887	26,166	0.7	2.1
Phoenix-Mesa-Scottsdale, AZ Metro Area	86.4	7.0	4.0	5.1	0.5	30.4	1,859,996	1,801,633	1,591,299	1,342,946	3.2	13.2
Maricopa County, AZ	86.5	7.1	3.6	5.3	0.5	30.5	1,693,581	1,641,906	1,478,079	1,261,150	3.1	11.1
Pinal County, AZ	85.6	6.1	8.0	2.7	0.7	29.3	166,415	159,727	113,220	81,796	4.2	41.1
Pine Bluff, AR Metro Area	50.7	48.6	1.0	1.0	0.2	2.3	42,149	41,941	42,688	43,145	0.5	-1.7
Cleveland County, AR	87.9	12.2	1.0	0.2	0.1	2.2	4,045	4,064	3,978	3,842	-0.5	2.2
Jefferson County, AR	42.9	56.2	1.0	1.2	0.2	2.0	33,252	33,016	33,790	34,344	0.7	-2.3
Lincoln County, AR	68.8	30.9	1.1	0.5	0.1	3.6	4,852	4,861	4,920	4,959	-0.2	-1.2
Pittsburgh, PA Metro Area	88.8	9.7	0.6	2.7	0.1	1.7	1,107,452	1,102,147	1,097,589	1,079,518	0.5	0.4
Allegheny County, PA	82.6	14.8	0.6	4.2	0.1	2.0	590,680	589,168	589,267	583,990	0.3	0.0
Armstrong County, PA	98.6	1.4	0.4	0.4	0.0	0.7	32,338	32,523	32,717	32,382	-0.6	-0.6
Beaver County, PA	92.8	7.8	0.5	0.8	0.1	1.5	78,327	78,203	78,600	77,827	0.2	-0.5

0 = represents zero or rounds to zero.
[1] Persons of Hispanic origin may be of any race.

Table C-2. Population Characteristics and Housing Units—*Continued*

Metropolitan statistical area, division, and component county	White	Black or African American	Asian	American Indian, Alaska Native	Native Hawaiian and Other Pacific Islander	Hispanic or Latino origin[1] (percent)	2015 (July 1 estimate)	2010 (July 1 estimate)	2005 (July 1 estimate)	2000 (July 1 estimate)	2010–2015	2005–2010
Butler County, PA	97.3	1.8	0.4	1.5	0.1	1.4	80,787	78,225	74,913	70,123	3.3	4.4
Fayette County, PA	94.5	5.9	0.6	0.6	0.1	1.1	62,971	62,778	64,997	66,409	0.3	-3.4
Washington County, PA	95.5	4.4	0.5	1.2	0.1	1.6	94,124	93,039	91,162	87,501	1.2	2.1
Westmoreland County, PA	96.3	3.5	0.4	1.2	0.1	1.1	168,225	168,211	165,933	161,286	0.0	1.4
Pittsfield, MA Metro Area	94.8	4.6	0.8	2.0	0.1	4.3	68,397	68,521	67,755	66,317	-0.2	1.1
Berkshire County, MA	94.8	4.6	0.8	2.0	0.1	4.3	68,397	68,521	67,755	66,317	-0.2	1.1
Pocatello, ID Metro Area	93.6	1.4	4.7	2.1	0.5	8.3	33,457	33,207	31,184	29,177	0.8	6.5
Bannock County, ID	93.6	1.4	4.7	2.1	0.5	8.3	33,457	33,207	31,184	29,177	0.8	6.5
Portland-South Portland, ME Metro Area	95.8	2.5	1.0	2.4	0.1	1.9	267,081	262,870	251,402	234,119	1.6	4.6
Cumberland County, ME	94.4	3.6	1.0	3.0	0.1	2.0	140,875	138,721	132,437	123,077	1.6	4.7
Sagadahoc County, ME	97.8	1.5	1.1	1.3	0.1	1.6	18,463	18,302	17,558	16,524	0.9	4.2
York County, ME	97.4	1.3	1.1	1.8	0.1	1.7	107,743	105,847	101,407	94,518	1.8	4.4
Portland-Vancouver-Hillsboro, OR-WA Metro Area	88.1	4.3	2.6	8.4	1.0	11.7	959,565	925,679	867,939	794,512	3.7	6.7
Clackamas County, OR	93.1	1.8	2.3	5.8	0.6	8.5	162,217	157,097	148,262	137,556	3.3	6.0
Columbia County, OR	96.4	1.2	3.5	2.2	0.5	4.8	20,764	20,704	19,532	17,650	0.3	6.0
Multnomah County, OR	84.2	7.3	3.0	9.4	1.1	11.3	336,248	324,838	307,389	289,311	3.5	5.7
Washington County, OR	85.7	3.3	2.3	12.3	1.1	16.4	222,015	212,751	198,104	179,873	4.4	7.4
Yamhill County, OR	94.6	1.7	3.5	2.9	0.5	15.9	37,966	37,147	34,064	30,457	2.2	9.1
Clark County, WA	90.8	3.5	2.5	6.4	1.4	9.0	174,688	167,512	155,544	135,069	4.3	7.7
Skamania County, WA	95.7	1.3	3.8	1.7	0.4	6.1	5,667	5,630	5,044	4,596	0.7	11.6
Port St. Lucie, FL Metro Area	81.9	16.4	1.2	2.2	0.3	16.3	217,310	215,151	193,096	157,691	1.0	11.4
Martin County, FL	91.7	6.3	1.4	1.7	0.3	13.2	79,239	78,350	74,124	65,864	1.1	5.7
St. Lucie County, FL	76.8	21.7	1.1	2.5	0.3	17.9	138,071	136,801	118,972	91,827	0.9	15.0
Prescott, AZ Metro Area	95.4	1.5	3.5	1.7	0.3	14.4	113,083	110,476	99,236	82,364	2.4	11.3
Yavapai County, AZ	95.4	1.5	3.5	1.7	0.3	14.4	113,083	110,476	99,236	82,364	2.4	11.3
Providence-Warwick, RI-MA Metro Area	88.7	8.4	1.6	3.7	0.3	11.9	694,206	693,897	680,123	657,795	0.0	2.0
Bristol County, MA	91.9	6.1	1.2	2.8	0.2	7.2	231,628	230,523	226,090	217,298	0.5	2.0
Bristol County, RI	96.5	1.8	0.7	2.5	0.2	2.7	20,787	20,847	20,449	19,907	-0.3	1.9
Kent County, RI	94.8	2.9	1.0	3.2	0.1	4.4	73,593	73,687	72,389	70,507	-0.1	1.8
Newport County, RI	92.9	5.7	1.3	2.8	0.3	5.7	41,951	41,813	40,957	39,639	0.3	2.1
Providence County, RI	81.9	13.8	2.1	5.2	0.4	21.3	263,219	264,786	260,032	253,451	-0.6	1.8
Washington County, RI	95.3	2.3	1.6	2.6	0.1	3.1	63,028	62,241	60,206	56,993	1.3	3.4
Provo-Orem, UT Metro Area	96.7	1.2	1.4	2.8	1.6	11.3	166,132	152,208	130,457	108,093	9.1	16.7
Juab County, UT	97.7	1.0	1.9	0.7	0.4	4.5	3,587	3,504	3,173	2,829	2.4	10.4
UT County, UT	95.7	1.2	1.4	2.8	1.7	11.4	162,545	148,704	127,284	105,264	9.3	16.8
Pueblo, CO Metro Area	93.0	3.2	4.7	1.6	0.3	42.7	70,142	69,576	65,843	59,251	0.8	5.7
Pueblo County, CO	93.0	3.2	4.7	1.6	0.3	42.7	70,142	69,576	65,843	59,251	0.8	5.7
Punta Gorda, FL Metro Area	91.9	6.9	0.9	1.9	0.2	6.8	101,775	100,657	91,271	80,155	1.1	10.3
Charlotte County, FL	91.9	6.9	0.9	1.9	0.2	6.8	101,775	100,657	91,271	80,155	1.1	10.3
Racine, WI Metro Area	86.1	13.3	1.2	1.7	0.1	12.7	82,323	82,206	79,497	74,909	0.1	3.4
Racine County, WI	86.1	13.3	1.2	1.7	0.1	12.7	82,323	82,206	79,497	74,909	0.1	3.4
Raleigh, NC Metro Area	72.5	22.1	1.5	6.3	0.2	10.5	509,636	467,062	401,896	332,456	9.1	16.2
Franklin County, NC	71.5	27.7	1.7	0.9	0.2	8.1	27,057	26,575	23,837	20,550	1.8	11.5
Johnston County, NC	81.9	17.2	1.6	1.2	0.2	13.4	71,144	67,781	60,047	50,692	5.0	12.9
Wake County, NC	70.8	22.6	1.5	7.6	0.2	10.1	411,435	372,706	318,012	261,214	10.4	17.2
Rapid City, SD Metro Area	88.6	2.3	10.7	1.8	0.2	4.6	63,745	60,677	56,464	51,230	5.1	7.5
Custer County, SD	95.2	0.9	5.3	0.7	0.1	3.3	4,949	4,637	4,196	3,646	6.7	10.5
Meade County, SD	93.9	2.6	4.7	1.6	0.1	4.3	11,616	11,035	10,788	10,156	5.3	2.3
Pennington County, SD	86.8	2.3	12.6	1.9	0.3	4.7	47,180	45,005	41,480	37,428	4.8	8.5
Reading, PA Metro Area	90.5	8.4	1.3	2.0	0.2	19.4	164,904	164,825	160,323	150,712	0.0	2.8
Berks County, PA	90.5	8.4	1.3	2.0	0.2	19.4	164,904	164,825	160,323	150,712	0.0	2.8
Redding, CA Metro Area	92.3	2.1	5.4	4.2	0.5	9.6	78,101	77,351	74,271	69,020	1.0	4.1
Shasta County, CA	92.3	2.1	5.4	4.2	0.5	9.6	78,101	77,351	74,271	69,020	1.0	4.1
Reno, NV Metro Area	88.3	3.6	3.2	7.5	1.2	23.8	190,961	186,927	172,148	146,669	2.2	8.6
Storey County, NV	93.7	2.3	2.8	2.8	0.6	8.3	1,984	1,989	1,833	1,610	-0.3	8.5
Washoe County, NV	88.2	3.6	3.2	7.6	1.2	23.9	188,977	184,938	170,315	145,059	2.2	8.6
Richmond, VA Metro Area	64.6	31.9	1.3	4.7	0.2	5.9	522,517	507,821	477,618	435,440	2.9	6.3
Amelia County, VA	76.7	22.8	1.1	1.1	0.1	2.9	5,451	5,366	5,012	4,619	1.6	7.1
Caroline County, VA	69.8	30.0	1.8	1.6	0.3	4.5	12,046	11,750	10,347	8,916	2.5	13.6
Charles City County, VA	44.8	48.2	8.4	1.2	0.2	1.8	3,313	3,233	3,104	2,912	2.5	4.2
Chesterfield County, VA	71.8	25.1	1.3	4.6	0.2	8.2	127,895	122,714	112,972	98,229	4.2	8.6
Dinwiddie County, VA	66.1	33.6	0.9	1.0	0.2	3.1	11,593	11,446	10,725	9,751	1.3	6.7
Goochland County, VA	80.6	18.2	0.8	1.7	0.1	2.5	9,012	8,625	7,804	6,608	4.5	10.5
Hanover County, VA	88.1	10.3	1.0	2.2	0.1	2.8	40,329	38,404	36,458	32,430	5.0	5.3
Henrico County, VA	60.8	31.6	1.0	9.0	0.1	5.5	135,555	132,870	125,353	113,115	2.0	6.0
King William County, VA	80.1	18.4	2.4	1.4	0.2	2.6	6,737	6,534	5,849	5,219	3.1	11.7
New Kent County, VA	83.9	14.5	2.1	1.9	0.2	2.6	8,045	7,325	6,248	5,239	9.8	17.2
Powhatan County, VA	87.7	11.8	0.8	0.9	0.1	2.1	10,551	10,057	9,061	7,572	4.9	11.0
Prince George County, VA	63.8	34.4	1.6	2.9	0.7	7.8	12,325	12,068	11,590	10,750	2.1	4.1
Sussex County, VA	41.3	58.2	0.8	0.8	0.1	2.8	4,722	4,698	4,608	4,655	0.5	2.0
Colonial Heights city, VA	80.8	15.7	1.2	4.3	0.3	5.5	7,803	7,830	7,697	7,352	-0.3	1.7
Hopewell city, VA	57.5	42.2	1.3	2.0	0.4	7.1	10,324	10,157	9,743	9,755	1.6	4.2
Petersburg city, VA	20.5	78.9	1.1	1.9	0.4	4.6	16,423	16,383	16,005	15,973	0.2	2.4
Richmond city, VA	46.9	50.8	1.3	3.2	0.3	6.5	100,393	98,361	95,042	92,345	2.1	3.5
Riverside-San Bernardino-Ontario, CA Metro Area	81.8	9.5	3.1	8.6	0.8	49.9	1,538,450	1,501,866	1,373,390	1,191,406	2.4	9.4
Riverside County, CA	83.3	8.3	2.9	8.4	0.8	47.9	826,790	801,721	714,686	588,488	3.1	12.2

0 = represents zero or rounds to zero.
[1]Persons of Hispanic origin may be of any race.

Table C-2. Population Characteristics and Housing Units—*Continued*

Metropolitan statistical area, division, and component county	Population characteristics, 2015						Housing units				Percent change	
	Race alone or in combination (percent)					Hispanic or Latino origin[1] (percent)	2015 (July 1 estimate)	2010 (July 1 estimate)	2005 (July 1 estimate)	2000 (July 1 estimate)	2010–2015	2005–2010
	White	Black or African American	Asian	American Indian, Alaska Native	Native Hawaiian and Other Pacific Islander							
San Bernardino County, CA	80.2	10.8	3.3	8.7	0.8	52.2	711,660	700,145	658,704	602,918	1.6	6.3
Roanoke, VA Metro Area	83.6	14.8	0.8	2.7	0.1	3.8	146,071	145,021	139,354	130,120	0.7	4.1
Botetourt County, VA	95.3	4.1	0.8	1.0	0.1	1.6	14,749	14,570	13,864	12,645	1.2	5.1
Craig County, VA	99.2	0.6	0.6	0.4	0.0	1.0	2,876	2,807	2,726	2,561	2.5	3.0
Franklin County, VA	90.6	9.1	0.7	0.7	0.1	2.7	29,500	29,329	26,458	22,900	0.6	10.9
Roanoke County, VA	90.1	7.0	0.7	4.0	0.1	3.0	40,746	40,086	38,754	36,224	1.6	3.4
Roanoke city, VA	67.3	31.3	1.0	3.2	0.2	6.1	47,329	47,382	46,862	45,379	-0.1	1.1
Salem city, VA	89.8	8.8	0.9	2.5	0.1	3.5	10,871	10,847	10,690	10,411	0.2	1.5
Rochester, MN Metro Area	90.7	5.1	0.7	5.3	0.1	4.3	90,316	88,265	84,378	74,524	2.3	4.6
Dodge County, MN	98.3	1.2	0.8	0.8	0.1	5.1	8,068	7,952	7,625	6,691	1.5	4.3
Fillmore County, MN	98.8	0.8	0.5	0.7	0.0	1.2	9,859	9,731	9,523	8,929	1.3	2.2
Olmsted County, MN	87.4	6.7	0.8	7.1	0.2	4.8	62,299	60,587	57,412	49,818	2.8	5.5
Wabasha County, MN	98.3	1.1	0.7	0.9	0.0	3.1	10,090	9,995	9,818	9,086	1.0	1.8
Rochester, NY Metro Area	84.2	13.6	0.9	3.5	0.1	7.0	475,773	469,649	457,802	440,207	1.3	2.6
Livingston County, NY	94.9	3.7	0.9	1.9	0.1	3.7	27,353	27,066	25,965	24,257	1.1	4.2
Monroe County, NY	79.3	17.8	0.9	4.5	0.1	8.3	324,824	320,922	315,019	304,908	1.2	1.9
Ontario County, NY	95.6	3.7	0.8	1.7	0.1	4.4	49,903	48,571	45,737	42,697	2.7	6.2
Orleans County, NY	91.8	7.9	1.3	0.8	0.1	4.8	18,503	18,440	18,023	17,385	0.3	2.3
Wayne County, NY	95.5	4.5	0.9	1.1	0.1	4.2	41,447	41,124	40,184	38,861	0.8	2.3
Yates County, NY	98.1	1.6	0.6	0.7	0.1	2.2	13,743	13,526	12,874	12,099	1.6	5.1
Rockford, IL Metro Area	85.3	12.9	1.2	3.1	0.1	13.6	145,395	145,920	140,190	130,217	-0.4	4.1
Boone County, IL	95.1	3.5	1.7	1.8	0.2	20.9	19,949	19,976	18,293	15,524	-0.1	9.2
Winnebago County, IL	83.5	14.7	1.2	3.3	0.1	12.3	125,446	125,944	121,897	114,693	-0.4	3.3
Rocky Mount, NC Metro Area	51.6	47.4	1.5	1.0	0.2	5.8	67,083	67,135	65,224	61,297	-0.1	2.9
Edgecombe County, NC	40.9	58.2	1.2	0.5	0.3	4.3	24,627	24,829	24,845	24,059	-0.8	-0.1
Nash County, NC	57.7	41.1	1.6	1.3	0.1	6.6	42,456	42,306	40,379	37,238	0.4	4.8
Rome, GA Metro Area	82.4	16.0	1.4	1.8	0.3	10.7	40,410	40,554	39,200	36,742	-0.4	3.5
Floyd County, GA	82.4	16.0	1.4	1.8	0.3	10.7	40,410	40,554	39,200	36,742	-0.4	3.5
Sacramento--Roseville--Arden-Arcade, CA Metro Area	75.5	9.7	3.0	16.2	1.5	21.3	889,022	872,422	825,979	718,998	1.9	5.6
El Dorado County, CA	93.0	1.6	2.8	5.9	0.5	12.8	89,010	88,190	82,697	71,727	0.9	6.6
Placer County, CA	89.3	2.6	2.2	9.5	0.6	13.8	159,406	152,966	138,611	108,665	4.2	10.4
Sacramento County, CA	69.3	13.3	3.3	19.0	1.9	22.7	563,656	556,133	534,429	476,695	1.4	4.1
Yolo County, CA	79.9	4.1	3.2	17.2	1.1	31.5	76,950	75,133	70,242	61,911	2.4	7.0
Saginaw, MI Metro Area	78.5	20.8	1.2	1.7	0.1	8.2	86,822	86,821	87,482	85,696	0.0	-0.8
Saginaw, MI	78.5	20.8	1.2	1.7	0.1	8.2	86,822	86,821	87,482	85,696	0.0	-0.8
St. Cloud, MN Metro Area	93.5	4.7	0.9	2.6	0.1	3.0	79,798	78,203	73,901	64,238	2.0	5.8
Benton County, MN	95.6	3.6	1.0	1.6	0.1	2.1	16,580	16,149	15,587	13,719	2.7	3.6
Stearns County, MN	93.0	5.0	0.9	2.8	0.1	3.2	63,218	62,054	58,314	50,519	1.9	6.4
St. George, UT Metro Area	95.5	1.3	2.4	1.6	1.4	10.1	63,947	57,855	48,914	36,848	10.5	18.3
Washington County, UT	95.5	1.3	2.4	1.6	1.4	10.1	63,947	57,855	48,914	36,848	10.5	18.3
St. Joseph, MO-KS Metro Area	92.2	7.0	1.3	1.3	0.3	5.1	53,563	53,647	52,698	50,694	-0.2	1.8
Doniphan County, KS	94.4	4.5	2.5	0.8	0.1	2.7	3,548	3,577	3,573	3,493	-0.8	0.1
Andrew County, MO	98.3	1.4	0.9	0.7	0.1	2.4	7,274	7,308	7,095	6,690	-0.5	3.0
Buchanan County, MO	91.6	7.6	1.3	1.6	0.4	6.2	38,449	38,432	37,873	36,652	0.0	1.5
DeKalb County, MO	87.3	12.1	0.9	0.5	0.2	2.2	4,292	4,330	4,157	3,859	-0.9	4.2
St. Louis, MO-IL Metro Area	78.5	19.5	0.8	3.2	0.1	3.0	1,241,161	1,225,851	1,188,971	1,126,418	1.2	3.1
Bond County, IL	91.9	7.3	0.9	1.1	0.1	3.6	7,087	7,090	6,978	6,713	0.0	1.6
Calhoun County, IL	99.1	0.6	0.3	0.4	0.0	1.0	2,839	2,839	2,791	2,681	0.0	1.7
Clinton County, IL	95.2	4.3	0.7	0.8	0.1	3.1	15,588	15,333	14,681	13,849	1.7	4.4
Jersey County, IL	98.2	1.1	0.8	1.0	0.1	1.3	10,037	9,854	9,456	8,932	1.9	4.2
Macoupin County, IL	98.1	1.5	0.8	0.6	0.0	1.1	21,529	21,585	21,713	21,132	-0.3	-0.6
Madison County, IL	90.0	9.7	0.8	1.5	0.1	3.1	118,471	117,171	114,604	109,185	1.1	2.2
Monroe County, IL	98.7	0.7	0.5	0.8	0.1	1.6	13,857	13,415	12,390	10,821	3.3	8.3
St. Clair County, IL	67.6	31.6	0.8	2.2	0.2	3.9	118,841	116,408	111,506	104,692	2.1	4.4
Franklin County, MO	97.9	1.7	0.9	0.7	0.1	1.8	44,058	43,453	41,536	38,456	1.4	4.6
Jefferson County, MO	97.7	1.8	0.9	1.1	0.1	1.9	89,111	87,717	83,387	76,057	1.6	5.2
Lincoln County, MO	96.8	2.9	1.1	0.9	0.1	2.3	21,087	21,022	18,549	15,642	0.3	13.3
St. Charles County, MO	92.2	5.7	0.8	3.1	0.1	3.2	149,648	141,318	128,187	106,554	5.9	10.2
St. Louis County, MO	71.3	25.2	0.8	4.9	0.1	2.8	438,425	437,967	433,709	424,238	0.1	1.0
Warren County, MO	96.3	3.5	1.2	0.9	0.1	3.3	14,957	14,705	13,254	11,147	1.7	10.9
St. Louis city, MO	49.1	48.3	1.1	4.0	0.2	3.9	175,626	175,974	176,230	176,319	-0.2	-0.1
Salem, OR Metro Area	92.8	2.2	4.2	3.3	1.2	23.5	154,633	151,369	143,341	133,093	2.2	5.6
Marion County, OR	92.6	2.3	4.2	3.3	1.3	26.0	123,467	121,040	115,585	108,488	2.0	4.7
Polk County, OR	94.0	1.6	4.2	3.2	0.8	13.3	31,166	30,329	27,756	24,605	2.8	9.3
Salinas, CA Metro Area	85.8	4.4	4.0	8.9	1.1	57.8	140,470	139,091	136,963	132,051	1.0	1.6
Monterey County, CA	85.8	4.4	4.0	8.9	1.1	57.8	140,470	139,091	136,963	132,051	1.0	1.6
Salisbury, MD-DE Metro Area	78.9	19.6	1.4	2.2	0.2	7.2	240,770	231,437	211,254	185,724	4.0	9.6
Sussex County, DE	84.3	14.2	1.9	1.6	0.2	9.5	131,418	123,319	109,353	93,535	6.6	12.8
Somerset County, MD	55.9	43.9	1.0	1.4	0.2	3.5	11,271	11,152	10,606	10,099	1.1	5.1
Wicomico County, MD	70.4	27.4	0.9	3.8	0.2	5.2	42,225	41,219	38,503	34,512	2.4	7.1
Worcester County, MD	84.3	14.8	0.8	1.8	0.1	3.4	55,856	55,747	52,792	47,578	0.2	5.6
Salt Lake City, UT Metro Area	91.0	2.6	2.1	5.0	2.1	17.6	401,449	384,340	357,417	326,092	4.5	7.5
Salt Lake County, UT	90.7	2.7	2.1	5.2	2.2	18.0	380,749	364,851	340,244	312,065	4.4	7.2
Tooele County, UT	96.4	1.4	2.2	1.4	0.8	11.8	20,700	19,489	17,173	14,027	6.2	13.5
San Angelo, TX Metro Area	92.7	5.5	1.7	2.0	0.3	38.7	49,133	47,537	46,041	44,911	3.4	3.2

0 = represents zero or rounds to zero.
[1]Persons of Hispanic origin may be of any race.

Table C-2. Population Characteristics and Housing Units—*Continued*

Metropolitan statistical area, division, and component county	White	Black or African American	Asian	American Indian, Alaska Native	Native Hawaiian and Other Pacific Islander	Hispanic or Latino origin[1] (percent)	2015 (July 1 estimate)	2010 (July 1 estimate)	2005 (July 1 estimate)	2000 (July 1 estimate)	2010–2015	2005–2010
				Race alone or in combination (percent)				Housing units			Percent change	
Irion County, TX	97.0	2.5	1.9	0.5	0.0	26.4	857	856	889	909	0.1	-3.7
Tom Green County, TX	92.6	5.5	1.7	2.0	0.3	38.8	48,276	46,681	45,152	44,002	3.4	3.4
San Antonio-New Braunfels, TX Metro Area	88.3	8.4	1.9	3.5	0.3	54.9	872,477	839,174	744,861	652,668	4.0	12.7
Atascosa County, TX	96.5	1.8	1.9	0.8	0.2	63.5	17,929	17,637	16,446	14,951	1.7	7.2
Bandera County, TX	97.2	1.4	2.1	0.8	0.1	18.0	11,626	11,562	10,632	9,550	0.6	8.7
Bexar County, TX	86.9	9.3	1.9	3.9	0.4	59.5	684,164	663,602	593,569	524,467	3.1	11.8
Comal County, TX	95.5	2.8	1.7	1.6	0.2	27.1	53,248	47,282	39,939	33,022	12.6	18.4
Guadalupe County, TX	88.7	9.2	1.8	2.7	0.4	37.4	55,007	50,223	41,087	33,817	9.5	22.2
Kendall County, TX	96.9	1.6	1.5	1.5	0.2	22.8	15,291	14,088	11,986	9,709	8.5	17.5
Medina County, TX	95.0	3.3	1.7	1.2	0.2	51.5	18,157	17,999	16,657	14,926	0.9	8.1
Wilson County, TX	96.5	2.3	1.8	0.8	0.1	39.0	17,055	16,781	14,545	12,226	1.6	15.4
San Diego-Carlsbad, CA Metro Area	79.9	6.8	2.3	14.6	1.1	33.4	1,194,415	1,165,418	1,125,143	1,044,144	2.5	3.6
San Diego County, CA	79.9	6.8	2.3	14.6	1.1	33.4	1,194,415	1,165,418	1,125,143	1,044,144	2.5	3.6
San Francisco-Oakland-Hayward, CA Metro Area	**63.3**	**9.6**	**2.1**	**29.0**	**1.4**	**21.9**	**1,782,303**	**1,742,786**	**1,690,008**	**1,610,766**	**2.3**	**3.1**
Oakland-Hayward-Berkeley, CA Division	*62.1*	*12.6*	*2.3*	*27.4*	*1.4*	*23.7*	*1,004,570*	*983,390*	*949,417*	*897,252*	*2.2*	*3.6*
Alameda County, CA	55.7	13.6	2.4	32.6	1.7	22.6	595,822	582,869	564,447	541,385	2.2	3.3
Contra Costa County, CA	71.3	11.2	2.2	19.9	1.1	25.3	408,748	400,521	384,970	355,867	2.1	4.0
San Francisco-Redwood City-South San Francisco, CA Division	*61.2*	*5.4*	*1.7*	*34.9*	*1.5*	*19.9*	*665,041*	*648,133*	*631,818*	*608,358*	*2.6*	*2.6*
San Francisco County, CA	57.2	6.9	1.7	38.0	0.9	15.3	390,204	377,013	363,667	347,258	3.5	3.7
San Mateo County, CA	65.8	3.9	1.6	31.5	2.2	25.1	274,837	271,120	268,151	261,100	1.4	1.1
San Rafael, CA Division	*89.3*	*3.8*	*2.0*	*8.4*	*0.5*	*16.0*	*112,692*	*111,263*	*108,773*	*105,156*	*1.3*	*2.3*
Marin County, CA	89.3	3.8	2.0	8.4	0.5	16.0	112,692	111,263	108,773	105,156	1.3	2.3
San Jose-Sunnyvale-Santa Clara, CA Metro Area	60.3	3.7	2.2	37.4	0.9	27.3	678,844	650,022	629,350	597,689	4.4	3.3
San Benito County, CA	91.1	2.1	4.6	4.7	0.7	58.7	18,217	17,881	17,747	16,617	1.9	0.8
Santa Clara County, CA	59.3	3.7	2.2	38.4	0.9	26.3	660,627	632,141	611,603	581,072	4.5	3.4
San Luis Obispo-Paso Robles-Arroyo Grande, CA Metro Area	92.2	2.8	2.7	5.5	0.5	22.2	120,137	117,396	112,226	102,684	2.3	4.6
San Luis Obispo County, CA	92.2	2.8	2.7	5.5	0.5	22.2	120,137	117,396	112,226	102,684	2.3	4.6
Santa Cruz-Watsonville, CA Metro Area	91.2	2.4	3.3	7.1	0.6	33.3	105,530	104,491	102,268	98,986	1.0	2.2
Santa Cruz County, CA	91.2	2.4	3.3	7.1	0.6	33.3	105,530	104,491	102,268	98,986	1.0	2.2
Santa Fe, NM Metro Area	92.8	1.6	5.4	2.1	0.3	51.2	71,873	71,262	65,282	57,920	0.9	9.2
Santa Fe County, NM	92.8	1.6	5.4	2.1	0.3	51.2	71,873	71,262	65,282	57,920	0.9	9.2
Santa Maria-Santa Barbara, CA Metro Area	89.0	3.3	3.5	7.6	0.6	44.8	155,163	152,898	150,576	143,164	1.5	1.5
Santa Barbara County, CA	89.0	3.3	3.5	7.6	0.6	44.8	155,163	152,898	150,576	143,164	1.5	1.5
Santa Rosa, CA Metro Area	90.8	2.9	3.7	6.0	0.8	26.3	207,891	204,666	196,459	183,846	1.6	4.2
Sonoma County, CA	90.8	2.9	3.7	6.0	0.8	26.3	207,891	204,666	196,459	183,846	1.6	4.2
Savannah, GA Metro Area	62.7	35.2	1.0	3.2	0.3	5.9	157,902	151,350	136,781	123,434	4.3	10.7
Bryan County, GA	81.5	17.1	1.3	2.9	0.3	6.8	13,278	11,888	10,427	8,759	11.7	14.0
Chatham County, GA	56.1	41.5	0.9	3.6	0.3	6.2	123,669	119,536	109,063	100,374	3.5	9.6
Effingham County, GA	84.1	15.0	1.1	1.5	0.2	4.0	20,955	19,926	17,291	14,301	5.2	15.2
Scranton--Wilkes-Barre--Hazleton, PA Metro Area	93.5	5.3	0.8	2.0	0.1	8.2	259,895	258,832	256,976	252,950	0.4	0.7
Lackawanna County, PA	93.8	4.4	0.7	2.7	0.1	6.6	98,370	96,841	96,429	95,415	1.6	0.4
Luzerne County, PA	92.9	6.2	0.9	1.6	0.1	9.8	148,211	148,732	147,386	144,811	-0.4	0.9
Wyoming County, PA	98.1	1.5	0.7	0.8	0.1	1.9	13,314	13,259	13,161	12,724	0.4	0.7
Seattle-Tacoma-Bellevue, WA Metro Area	**77.7**	**8.0**	**2.8**	**15.9**	**1.5**	**9.8**	**1,529,969**	**1,464,412**	**1,372,178**	**1,261,027**	**4.5**	**6.7**
Seattle-Bellevue-Everett, WA Division	*76.5*	*7.3*	*2.5*	*17.7*	*1.3*	*9.6*	*1,193,612*	*1,138,714*	*1,067,086*	*982,839*	*4.8*	*6.7*
King County, WA	73.9	8.4	2.4	19.6	1.4	9.5	893,157	851,658	800,953	745,080	4.9	6.3
Snohomish County, WA	83.9	4.4	3.0	12.7	1.1	9.9	300,455	287,056	266,133	237,759	4.7	7.9
Tacoma-Lakewood, WA Division	*81.9*	*10.3*	*3.6*	*9.6*	*2.4*	*10.5*	*336,357*	*325,698*	*305,092*	*278,188*	*3.3*	*6.8*
Pierce County, WA	81.9	10.3	3.6	9.6	2.4	10.5	336,357	325,698	305,092	278,188	3.3	6.8
Sebastian-Vero Beach, FL Metro Area	88.5	10.1	0.9	1.9	0.1	12.1	77,900	76,385	69,401	58,305	2.0	10.1
Indian River County, FL	88.5	10.1	0.9	1.9	0.1	12.1	77,900	76,385	69,401	58,305	2.0	10.1
Sebring, FL Metro Area	87.1	11.4	1.2	1.8	0.2	18.8	54,822	55,363	52,047	48,964		6.4
Highlands County, FL	87.1	11.4	1.2	1.8	0.2	18.8	54,822	55,363	52,047	48,964		6.4
Sheboygan, WI Metro Area	92.0	2.6	1.0	5.8	0.1	6.2	50,589	50,777	49,291	46,097	-0.4	3.0
Sheboygan County, WI	92.0	2.6	1.0	5.8	0.1	6.2	50,589	50,777	49,291	46,097	-0.4	3.0
Sherman-Denison, TX Metro Area	90.5	7.3	3.0	1.7	0.2	13.0	54,653	53,740	51,213	48,441	1.7	4.9
Grayson County, TX	90.5	7.3	3.0	1.7	0.2	13.0	54,653	53,740	51,213	48,441	1.7	4.9
Shreveport-Bossier City, LA Metro Area	58.8	39.9	1.2	1.8	0.2	3.8	200,169	193,316	185,811	179,029	3.5	4.0
Bossier Parish, LA	75.2	23.1	1.4	2.6	0.3	6.6	55,362	49,592	44,946	40,990	11.6	10.3
Caddo Parish, LA	49.4	49.3	1.1	1.6	0.1	2.8	112,860	112,069	109,950	107,820	0.7	1.9
De Soto Parish, LA	60.9	38.1	1.5	0.5	0.1	2.8	12,498	12,298	11,767	11,250	1.6	4.5
Webster Parish, LA	64.8	34.8	1.1	0.7	0.1	1.8	19,449	19,357	19,148	18,969	0.5	1.1
Sierra Vista-Douglas, AZ Metro Area	90.6	5.8	3.0	3.4	0.7	34.7	60,620	59,130	55,515	51,322	2.5	6.5
Cochise County, AZ	90.6	5.8	3.0	3.4	0.7	34.7	60,620	59,130	55,515	51,322	2.5	6.5
Sioux City, IA-NE-SD Metro Area	92.5	3.7	3.2	2.8	0.3	15.6	69,537	68,655	68,297	66,863	1.3	0.5
Plymouth County, IA	98.0	1.1	0.9	0.9	0.2	4.3	10,688	10,549	10,330	9,897	1.3	2.1
Woodbury County, IA	91.1	4.5	3.8	3.4	0.3	15.7	41,560	41,483	41,639	41,396	0.2	-0.4
Dakota County, NE	88.0	4.6	4.9	3.9	0.4	38.3	7,755	7,632	7,681	7,549	1.6	-0.6
Dixon County, NE	98.2	1.0	1.2	0.5	0.2	12.3	2,700	2,688	2,716	2,657	0.4	
Union County, SD	96.9	1.5	1.5	1.4	0.1	3.3	6,834	6,303	5,931	5,364	8.4	6.3
Sioux Falls, SD Metro Area	92.1	4.6	3.1	2.2	0.2	4.1	103,807	96,192	86,956	76,074	7.9	10.6
Lincoln County, SD	96.6	2.0	1.2	1.7	0.1	1.9	19,539	17,946	14,165	9,343	8.9	26.7
McCook County, SD	98.2	0.8	1.5	0.4	0.1	3.1	2,525	2,491	2,469	2,388	1.4	0.9

0 = represents zero or rounds to zero.
[1] Persons of Hispanic origin may be of any race.

Table C-2. Population Characteristics and Housing Units—*Continued*

Metropolitan statistical area, division, and component county	Population characteristics, 2015						Housing units					
	Race alone or in combination (percent)										Percent change	
	White	Black or African American	Asian	American Indian, Alaska Native	Native Hawaiian and Other Pacific Islander	Hispanic or Latino origin[1] (percent)	2015 (July 1 estimate)	2010 (July 1 estimate)	2005 (July 1 estimate)	2000 (July 1 estimate)	2010–2015	2005–2010
Minnehaha County, SD	90.3	5.7	3.8	2.5	0.2	4.9	77,750	71,813	66,416	60,489	8.3	8.1
Turner County, SD	98.1	0.8	1.8	0.4	0.1	2.2	3,993	3,942	3,906	3,854	1.3	0.9
South Bend-Mishawaka, IN-MI Metro Area	85.0	13.8	1.4	2.6	0.2	7.7	141,700	140,737	137,497	131,341	0.7	2.4
St. Joseph County, IN	83.5	15.1	1.3	2.9	0.2	8.4	115,778	114,852	112,250	107,388	0.8	2.3
Cass County, MI	92.3	7.1	2.4	1.2	0.1	3.6	25,922	25,885	25,247	23,953	0.1	2.5
Spartanburg, SC Metro Area	75.2	23.1	0.9	2.6	0.1	6.1	139,330	136,852	130,560	120,921	1.8	4.8
Spartanburg County, SC	75.9	22.1	0.9	2.8	0.1	6.5	125,343	122,705	116,644	107,505	2.1	5.2
Union County, SC	67.5	33.0	0.6	0.4	0.1	1.3	13,987	14,147	13,916	13,416	-1.1	1.7
Spokane-Spokane Valley, WA Metro Area	93.1	3.1	3.7	3.5	0.8	5.2	237,474	230,854	215,301	199,922	2.9	7.2
Pend Oreille County, WA	94.1	1.4	5.9	1.3	0.4	3.7	8,029	7,947	7,193	6,631	1.0	10.5
Spokane County, WA	93.1	3.3	3.2	3.7	0.8	5.4	208,296	201,747	188,703	175,610	3.2	6.9
Stevens County, WA	92.5	1.1	8.0	1.4	0.4	3.5	21,149	21,160	19,405	17,681	-0.1	9.0
Springfield, IL Metro Area	85.8	13.4	0.7	2.4	0.1	2.2	96,455	95,605	94,139	90,921	0.9	1.6
Menard County, IL	98.1	1.8	0.8	0.5	0.1	1.4	5,670	5,657	5,574	5,299	0.2	1.5
Sangamon County, IL	85.1	14.2	0.7	2.5	0.1	2.3	90,785	89,948	88,565	85,622	0.9	1.6
Springfield, MA Metro Area	86.8	10.4	1.4	3.9	0.3	19.2	255,006	254,796	251,192	244,775	0.1	1.4
Hampden County, MA	85.5	12.5	1.6	2.9	0.3	24.0	192,002	192,178	189,959	186,025	-0.1	1.2
Hampshire County, MA	90.8	4.1	0.8	6.6	0.2	5.4	63,004	62,618	61,233	58,750	0.6	2.3
Springfield, MO Metro Area	95.2	3.4	1.7	2.0	0.2	3.2	198,901	192,552	176,295	157,347	3.3	9.2
Christian County, MO	97.7	1.5	1.5	1.0	0.1	2.9	32,952	31,622	26,914	22,017	4.2	17.5
Dallas County, MO	98.3	0.9	2.2	0.4	0.1	2.0	7,563	7,660	7,460	6,943	-1.3	2.7
Greene County, MO	93.8	4.6	1.8	2.6	0.2	3.6	130,516	125,550	115,828	105,011	4.0	8.4
Polk County, MO	97.1	1.6	1.6	1.3	0.1	2.2	13,372	13,303	12,552	11,253	0.5	6.0
Webster County, MO	97.8	1.6	1.7	0.5	0.1	2.0	14,498	14,417	13,541	12,123	0.6	6.5
Springfield, OH Metro Area	89.6	11.1	1.1	1.1	0.1	3.2	61,102	61,397	61,536	61,089	-0.5	-0.2
Clark County, OH	89.6	11.1	1.1	1.1	0.1	3.2	61,102	61,397	61,536	61,089	-0.5	-0.2
State College, PA Metro Area	90.0	4.6	0.6	6.6	0.1	3.0	65,478	63,347	59,101	53,367	3.4	7.2
Centre County, PA	90.0	4.6	0.6	6.6	0.1	3.0	65,478	63,347	59,101	53,367	3.4	7.2
Staunton-Waynesboro, VA Metro Area	91.4	8.5	0.8	1.2	0.1	3.4	54,062	52,683	50,027	46,185	2.6	5.3
Augusta County, VA	94.7	5.0	0.7	0.9	0.1	2.6	32,139	31,214	29,619	26,773	3.0	5.4
Staunton city, VA	86.1	13.9	0.8	1.8	0.1	2.8	11,864	11,741	11,034	10,472	1.0	6.4
Waynesboro city, VA	86.0	14.6	1.2	1.5	0.2	7.1	10,059	9,728	9,374	8,940	3.4	3.8
Stockton-Lodi, CA Metro Area	72.2	9.7	3.7	18.9	1.3	40.8	238,571	233,929	220,356	190,509	2.0	6.2
San Joaquin County, CA	72.2	9.7	3.7	18.9	1.3	40.8	238,571	233,929	220,356	190,509	2.0	6.2
Sumter, SC Metro Area	50.5	48.2	1.0	2.0	0.2	4.0	47,183	46,074	43,996	41,864	2.4	4.7
Sumter County, SC	50.5	48.2	1.0	2.0	0.2	4.0	47,183	46,074	43,996	41,864	2.4	4.7
Syracuse, NY Metro Area	87.1	10.3	1.5	3.6	0.1	4.1	290,392	287,805	284,290	278,406	0.9	1.2
Madison County, NY	96.2	2.7	1.1	1.4	0.1	2.1	31,761	31,764	30,303	28,706	0.0	4.8
Onondaga County, NY	83.1	13.7	1.6	4.6	0.1	4.8	204,970	202,425	200,372	196,811	1.3	1.0
Oswego County, NY	97.5	1.7	1.0	1.1	0.1	2.5	53,661	53,616	53,615	52,889	0.1	0.0
Tallahassee, FL Metro Area	63.3	34.3	1.0	3.4	0.2	6.4	166,456	163,184	152,781	137,424	2.0	6.8
Gadsden County, FL	43.1	56.0	0.9	0.9	0.3	10.1	19,383	19,510	18,444	17,725	-0.7	5.8
Jefferson County, FL	63.8	35.8	1.0	0.8	0.2	4.3	6,580	6,630	5,966	5,277	-0.8	11.1
Leon County, FL	64.3	32.8	0.9	4.2	0.2	6.2	127,601	124,232	116,751	104,525	2.7	6.4
Wakulla County, FL	83.7	15.8	1.5	0.9	0.2	3.8	12,892	12,812	11,620	9,897	0.6	10.3
Tampa-St. Petersburg-Clearwater, FL Metro Area .	82.9	14.1	1.0	4.2	0.2	18.2	1,385,058	1,354,014	1,274,106	1,148,904	2.3	6.3
Hernando County, FL	92.2	6.7	1.0	1.8	0.2	12.0	84,801	84,490	74,662	63,113	0.4	13.2
Hillsborough County, FL	77.3	19.2	1.1	4.9	0.3	27.0	560,454	536,716	494,675	428,883	4.4	8.5
Pasco County, FL	91.0	6.8	1.0	3.1	0.2	14.0	234,450	229,170	206,879	174,667	2.3	10.8
Pinellas County, FL	84.8	12.1	0.9	4.2	0.2	9.1	505,353	503,638	497,890	482,241	0.3	1.2
Terre Haute, IN Metro Area	92.9	6.4	0.8	1.7	0.1	2.2	74,638	74,125	74,265	72,634	0.7	-0.2
Clay County, IN	98.6	1.1	0.7	0.5	0.1	1.3	11,684	11,700	11,664	11,145	-0.1	0.3
Sullivan County, IN	94.7	5.2	0.8	0.5	0.1	1.7	8,846	8,938	9,087	8,826	-1.0	-1.6
Vermillion County, IN	98.9	0.9	0.7	0.5	0.1	1.2	7,459	7,487	7,558	7,419	-0.4	-0.9
Vigo County, IN	90.2	8.8	0.9	2.4	0.1	2.6	46,649	46,000	45,956	45,244	1.4	0.1
Texarkana, TX-AR Metro Area	73.2	25.6	1.9	1.3	0.2	5.9	65,106	64,292	63,178	60,796	1.3	1.8
Little River County, AR	77.6	20.9	3.1	0.6	0.1	3.3	6,442	6,458	6,472	6,443	-0.2	-0.2
Miller County, AR	73.2	26.2	1.6	0.9	0.1	3.2	19,426	19,301	18,794	17,784	0.6	2.7
Bowie County, TX	72.7	26.0	1.9	1.6	0.2	7.5	39,238	38,533	37,912	36,569	1.8	1.6
The Villages, FL Metro Area	90.5	8.5	0.9	1.1	0.1	5.7	66,850	53,510	37,045	25,696	24.9	44.4
Sumter County, FL	90.5	8.5	0.9	1.1	0.1	5.7	66,850	53,510	37,045	25,696	24.9	44.4
Toledo, OH Metro Area	82.9	16.6	1.0	2.1	0.1	6.6	273,761	273,385	269,798	260,471	0.1	1.3
Fulton County, OH	98.4	1.3	0.9	0.6	0.1	8.4	17,363	17,422	17,113	16,269	-0.3	1.8
Lucas County, OH	77.8	21.9	1.1	2.3	0.1	6.8	202,471	202,589	201,352	196,487	-0.1	0.6
Wood County, OH	94.9	3.7	0.8	2.2	0.1	5.4	53,927	53,374	51,333	47,715	1.0	4.0
Topeka, KS Metro Area	89.8	8.9	3.3	1.7	0.2	9.9	104,297	103,872	101,281	96,606	0.4	2.6
Jackson County, KS	89.9	1.8	11.0	0.8	0.1	4.8	5,777	5,781	5,513	5,113	-0.1	4.9
Jefferson County, KS	97.8	1.2	2.4	0.5	0.1	2.6	8,230	8,163	7,957	7,530	0.8	2.6
Osage County, KS	98.0	1.5	1.8	0.6	0.1	2.9	7,484	7,504	7,380	7,038	-0.3	1.7
Shawnee County, KS	87.9	11.2	3.0	2.0	0.2	11.9	79,547	79,197	77,248	73,887	0.4	2.5
Wabaunsee County, KS	98.2	1.7	1.9	0.5	0.1	3.4	3,259	3,227	3,183	3,038	1.0	1.4
Trenton, NJ Metro Area	66.8	22.5	1.1	11.7	0.4	17.0	144,487	143,220	140,004	133,584	0.9	2.3
Mercer County, NJ	66.8	22.5	1.1	11.7	0.4	17.0	144,487	143,220	140,004	133,584	0.9	2.3
Tucson, AZ Metro Area	87.9	5.2	5.4	4.2	0.4	36.4	452,040	441,118	413,357	369,335	2.5	6.7
Pima County, AZ	87.9	5.2	5.4	4.2	0.4	36.4	452,040	441,118	413,357	369,335	2.5	6.7
Tulsa, OK Metro Area	79.7	10.1	14.0	2.9	0.2	9.4	425,016	410,491	388,954	367,312	3.5	5.5
Creek County, OK	86.2	3.5	16.3	0.8	0.2	3.9	30,092	29,795	28,957	28,038	1.0	2.9

0 = represents zero or rounds to zero.
[1] Persons of Hispanic origin may be of any race.

Table C-2. Population Characteristics and Housing Units—Continued

	Population characteristics, 2015						Housing units				Percent change	
	Race alone or in combination (percent)					Hispanic or Latino origin[1] (percent)	2015 (July 1 estimate)	2010 (July 1 estimate)	2005 (July 1 estimate)	2000 (July 1 estimate)		
Metropolitan statistical area, division, and component county	White	Black or African American	Asian	American Indian, Alaska Native	Native Hawaiian and Other Pacific Islander						2010– 2015	2005– 2010
Okmulgee County, OK	72.8	10.7	24.3	0.9	0.2	4.0	17,799	17,888	17,751	17,342	-0.5	0.8
Osage County, OK	72.8	12.5	21.5	0.7	0.1	3.4	21,528	21,168	20,032	18,867	1.7	5.7
Pawnee County, OK	84.9	1.9	18.6	0.8	0.1	3.1	7,722	7,745	7,635	7,478	-0.3	1.4
Rogers County, OK	83.8	2.0	20.9	1.7	0.2	4.4	36,835	35,226	31,264	27,664	4.6	12.7
Tulsa County, OK	78.7	12.6	11.1	3.7	0.2	12.1	279,871	268,897	256,526	244,615	4.1	4.8
Wagoner County, OK	83.8	5.0	16.6	2.1	0.2	5.9	31,169	29,772	26,789	23,308	4.7	11.1
Tuscaloosa, AL Metro Area	64.4	34.4	0.7	1.6	0.1	3.3	106,135	102,149	95,157	89,000	3.9	7.3
Hale County, AL	41.8	58.1	0.5	0.4	0.0	1.2	7,036	7,657	7,774	7,763	-0.3	-1.5
Pickens County, AL	59.0	40.6	0.5	0.5	0.3	4.9	9,434	9,482	9,596	9,525	-0.5	-1.2
Tuscaloosa County, AL	66.6	32.0	0.7	1.8	0.1	3.3	89,065	85,010	77,787	71,712	4.8	9.3
Tyler, TX Metro Area	79.4	18.8	1.3	2.0	0.2	19.1	88,852	87,352	80,345	72,139	1.7	8.7
Smith County, TX	79.4	18.8	1.3	2.0	0.2	19.1	88,852	87,352	80,345	72,139	1.7	8.7
Urban Honolulu, HI Metro Area	39.2	4.7	2.2	60.0	24.1	9.8	344,108	337,032	327,967	316,367	2.1	2.8
Honolulu County, HI	39.2	4.7	2.2	60.0	24.1	9.8	344,108	337,032	327,967	316,367	2.1	2.8
Utica-Rome, NY Metro Area	90.5	6.9	0.8	3.8	0.1	4.8	137,184	137,569	136,438	134,947	-0.3	0.8
Herkimer County, NY	97.7	2.1	0.7	0.8	0.1	2.1	33,323	33,368	32,826	32,058	-0.1	1.7
Oneida County, NY	88.5	8.2	0.8	4.6	0.1	5.5	103,861	104,201	103,612	102,889	-0.3	0.6
Valdosta, GA Metro Area	62.8	35.6	1.2	2.4	0.3	6.3	59,395	57,606	51,657	48,366	3.1	11.5
Brooks County, GA	63.4	35.7	0.9	0.9	0.2	5.8	7,642	7,714	7,311	7,139	-0.9	5.5
Echols County, GA	90.4	6.2	4.0	0.9	0.2	29.6	1,529	1,557	1,544	1,486	-1.8	0.8
Lanier County, GA	74.5	23.9	2.0	2.2	0.3	5.6	4,291	4,259	3,445	3,035	0.8	23.6
Lowndes County, GA	60.7	37.7	1.1	2.6	0.3	5.6	45,933	44,076	39,357	36,706	4.2	12.0
Vallejo-Fairfield, CA Metro Area	66.1	17.5	2.9	19.3	2.1	26.0	155,625	152,840	147,570	135,034	1.8	3.6
Solano County, CA	66.1	17.5	2.9	19.3	2.1	26.0	155,625	152,840	147,570	135,034	1.8	3.6
Victoria, TX Metro Area	90.9	7.5	1.4	1.6	0.1	44.9	40,565	39,131	38,251	36,473	3.7	2.3
Goliad County, TX	93.3	5.8	1.4	0.6	0.1	35.5	3,720	3,710	3,611	3,439	0.3	2.7
Victoria County, TX	90.7	7.6	1.4	1.7	0.2	45.7	36,845	35,421	34,640	33,034	4.0	2.3
Vineland-Bridgeton, NJ Metro Area	74.1	24.0	2.7	1.9	0.3	29.7	56,360	55,891	54,114	52,909	0.8	3.3
Cumberland County, NJ	74.1	24.0	2.7	1.9	0.3	29.7	56,360	55,891	54,114	52,909	0.8	3.3
Virginia Beach-Norfolk-Newport News, VA-NC Metro Area	63.6	33.2	1.4	5.3	0.4	6.5	711,353	689,080	663,738	625,502	3.2	3.8
Currituck County, NC	92.4	7.2	1.3	1.2	0.2	3.7	15,218	14,470	13,287	10,783	5.2	8.9
Gates County, NC	66.2	33.6	1.5	0.7	0.3	2.1	5,222	5,208	4,766	4,417	0.3	9.3
Gloucester County, VA	89.9	9.6	1.3	1.5	0.2	3.4	16,253	15,871	15,258	14,525	2.4	4.0
Isle of Wight County, VA	74.8	24.4	1.1	1.7	0.2	3.0	15,159	14,657	13,534	12,136	3.4	8.3
James City County, VA	83.0	14.9	1.1	3.8	0.3	5.5	32,401	30,137	26,108	21,046	7.5	15.4
Mathews County, VA	89.3	10.5	1.3	1.2	0.1	2.3	5,731	5,673	5,540	5,318	1.0	2.4
York County, VA	79.7	15.1	1.2	7.2	0.4	6.1	27,654	26,746	24,703	21,003	3.4	8.3
Chesapeake city, VA	65.4	31.9	1.3	4.8	0.3	5.5	88,880	83,367	78,992	72,906	6.6	5.5
Hampton city, VA	46.2	52.5	1.8	3.6	0.3	5.5	60,392	59,738	58,254	57,348	1.1	2.5
Newport News city, VA	53.9	44.0	1.7	4.6	0.4	8.7	77,589	76,393	75,849	74,312	1.6	0.7
Norfolk city, VA	52.3	44.6	1.7	5.0	0.5	7.6	97,123	95,121	94,495	94,375	2.1	0.7
Poquoson city, VA	95.7	2.0	0.9	3.1	0.1	2.5	4,765	4,730	4,538	4,304	0.7	4.2
Portsmouth city, VA	43.9	55.3	1.4	2.2	0.3	4.0	41,142	40,807	41,250	41,581	0.8	-1.1
Suffolk city, VA	54.4	44.3	1.0	2.7	0.2	4.0	35,481	33,119	30,412	24,891	7.1	8.9
Virginia Beach city, VA	71.8	22.2	1.4	8.8	0.4	8.0	183,119	178,119	172,019	162,628	2.8	3.5
Williamsburg city, VA	77.0	16.9	1.0	8.2	0.2	7.3	5,224	4,924	4,733	3,929	6.1	4.0
Visalia-Porterville, CA Metro Area	90.6	2.8	4.0	4.9	0.5	63.6	146,520	141,946	130,319	120,048	3.2	8.9
Tulare County, CA	90.6	2.8	4.0	4.9	0.5	63.6	146,520	141,946	130,319	120,048	3.2	8.9
Waco, TX Metro Area	81.3	16.7	1.7	2.1	0.2	25.4	106,383	102,981	98,149	92,693	3.3	4.9
Falls County, TX	73.1	25.8	1.7	0.9	0.2	22.7	7,727	7,723	7,722	7,656	0.1	0.0
McLennan County, TX	81.8	16.1	1.7	2.2	0.2	25.6	98,656	95,258	90,427	85,037	3.6	5.3
Walla Walla, WA Metro Area	94.4	2.7	2.4	2.4	0.6	20.7	26,155	25,597	24,556	23,230	2.2	4.2
Columbia County, WA	96.2	1.6	2.8	1.5	0.5	6.9	2,119	2,135	2,102	2,028	-0.7	1.6
Walla Walla County, WA	94.3	2.7	2.4	2.5	0.6	21.6	24,036	23,462	22,454	21,202	2.4	4.5
Warner Robins, GA Metro Area	63.9	34.1	1.2	3.5	0.3	6.6	77,562	74,685	67,501	58,051	3.9	10.6
Houston County, GA	65.4	32.3	1.2	4.0	0.3	6.7	61,023	58,468	52,894	44,914	4.4	10.5
Peach County, GA	54.3	44.9	1.1	1.5	0.3	7.4	11,401	11,071	9,976	9,150	3.0	11.0
Pulaski County, GA	66.5	32.5	0.7	1.3	0.1	3.6	5,138	5,146	4,631	3,987	-0.2	11.1
Washington-Arlington-Alexandria, DC-VA-MD-WV Metro Area	**62.0**	**27.9**	**1.5**	**11.9**	**0.3**	**15.3**	**2,324,126**	**2,237,445**	**2,114,404**	**1,916,243**	**3.9**	**5.8**
Silver Spring-Frederick-Rockville, MD Division	*68.2*	*18.9*	*1.4*	*14.9*	*0.2*	*17.0*	*483,741*	*466,296*	*445,791*	*409,906*	*3.7*	*4.6*
Frederick County, MD	84.9	11.2	1.0	5.7	0.2	8.7	94,741	90,308	84,121	73,727	4.9	7.4
Montgomery County, MD	64.2	20.7	1.5	17.1	0.2	19.0	389,000	375,988	361,670	336,179	3.5	4.0
Washington-Arlington-Alexandria, DC-VA-MD-WV Division	*60.4*	*30.3*	*1.5*	*11.2*	*0.3*	*14.8*	*1,840,385*	*1,771,149*	*1,668,613*	*1,506,337*	*3.9*	*6.1*
District of Columbia, DC	46.2	50.0	1.4	5.3	0.3	10.6	309,574	296,829	284,844	275,210	4.3	4.2
Calvert County, MD	84.3	14.7	1.2	2.6	0.2	3.7	34,766	33,832	32,035	27,809	2.8	5.6
Charles County, MD	50.0	47.6	1.9	4.5	0.3	5.5	58,865	55,118	50,380	44,193	6.8	9.4
Prince George's County, MD	28.8	66.6	2.0	5.4	0.3	17.2	331,325	328,366	317,264	303,078	0.9	3.5
Arlington County, VA	79.2	10.2	1.5	12.5	0.3	15.7	112,529	105,522	95,478	90,547	6.6	10.5
Clarke County, VA	93.0	6.3	1.2	1.8	0.2	4.8	6,299	6,236	5,928	5,403	1.0	5.2
Culpeper County, VA	81.9	17.5	1.4	2.1	0.2	9.5	18,298	17,665	15,341	12,919	3.6	15.1
Fairfax County, VA	69.4	11.2	1.3	21.7	0.3	16.4	412,045	408,041	393,974	361,254	1.0	3.6
Fauquier County, VA	89.5	9.6	1.1	2.2	0.2	7.5	26,451	25,643	24,254	21,167	3.2	5.7
Loudoun County, VA	73.2	9.3	1.1	20.2	0.3	13.6	126,479	109,943	94,045	63,714	15.0	16.9
Prince William County, VA	67.6	24.1	2.1	10.6	0.4	22.3	145,848	137,569	124,598	99,170	6.0	10.4
Rappahannock County, VA	94.1	5.7	0.9	1.2	0.2	3.8	3,964	3,901	3,620	3,319	1.6	7.8

0 = represents zero or rounds to zero.
[1] Persons of Hispanic origin may be of any race.

Table C-2.   Population Characteristics and Housing Units—*Continued*

| | Population characteristics, 2015 | | | | | | Housing units | | | | Percent change | |
| | Race alone or in combination (percent) | | | | | | | | | | | |
Metropolitan statistical area, division, and component county	White	Black or African American	Asian	American Indian, Alaska Native	Native Hawaiian and Other Pacific Islander	Hispanic or Latino origin[1] (percent)	2015 (July 1 estimate)	2010 (July 1 estimate)	2005 (July 1 estimate)	2000 (July 1 estimate)	2010–2015	2005–2010
Spotsylvania County, VA	80.0	18.4	1.2	3.7	0.3	8.9	46,554	45,332	41,815	33,647	2.7	8.4
Stafford County, VA	77.0	20.5	1.6	4.9	0.4	11.8	47,235	44,076	40,243	31,823	7.2	9.5
Warren County, VA	92.9	6.4	1.1	1.8	0.1	4.2	16,181	15,979	14,899	13,340	1.3	7.2
Alexandria city, VA	69.1	24.0	1.5	8.6	0.3	16.7	76,512	72,426	69,226	64,533	5.6	4.6
Fairfax city, VA	76.2	6.7	1.6	18.9	0.3	16.8	8,850	8,675	8,631	8,244	2.0	0.5
Falls Church city, VA	84.6	6.4	1.3	12.2	0.2	10.2	6,025	5,474	5,093	4,764	10.1	7.5
Fredericksburg city, VA	71.7	26.5	1.5	4.1	0.3	11.5	11,471	10,423	9,398	8,935	10.1	10.9
Manassas city, VA	76.5	17.4	2.2	7.3	0.4	34.7	13,491	13,136	12,719	12,139	2.7	3.3
Manassas Park city, VA	72.3	17.2	2.2	11.9	0.4	37.1	4,906	4,894	4,444	3,404	0.2	10.1
Jefferson County, WV	90.8	8.2	1.1	2.5	0.2	5.6	22,717	22,069	20,384	17,725	2.9	8.3
Waterloo-Cedar Falls, IA Metro Area	90.5	8.5	0.7	2.2	0.3	3.6	72,824	71,377	69,615	66,483	2.0	2.5
Black Hawk County, IA	88.3	10.6	0.8	2.5	0.3	4.2	57,069	55,917	54,338	51,814	2.1	2.9
Bremer County, IA	98.0	1.5	0.5	1.2	0.1	1.5	10,200	9,930	9,771	9,361	2.7	1.6
Grundy County, IA	99.0	0.9	0.4	0.5	0.1	1.3	5,555	5,530	5,506	5,308	0.5	0.4
Watertown-Fort Drum, NY Metro Area	90.3	8.3	1.3	2.5	0.5	7.3	59,123	57,971	55,670	54,136	2.0	4.1
Jefferson County, NY	90.3	8.3	1.3	2.5	0.5	7.3	59,123	57,971	55,670	54,136	2.0	4.1
Wausau, WI Metro Area	92.6	1.4	1.0	6.3	0.1	2.7	58,613	57,773	54,997	50,542	1.5	5.0
Marathon County, WI	92.6	1.4	1.0	6.3	0.1	2.7	58,613	57,773	54,997	50,542	1.5	5.0
Weirton-Steubenville, WV-OH Metro Area	95.2	5.2	0.7	0.7	0.1	1.2	57,779	58,318	59,064	59,143	-0.9	-1.3
Jefferson County, OH	93.7	6.9	0.7	0.7	0.1	1.3	32,483	32,817	33,324	33,275		-1.5
Brooke County, WV	97.7	2.4	0.5	0.6	0.1	0.9	10,884	10,966	11,068	11,124	-0.7	-0.9
Hancock County, WV	96.9	3.4	0.7	0.6	0.1	1.3	14,412	14,535	14,672	14,744	-0.8	-0.9
Wenatchee, WA Metro Area	95.6	1.3	3.2	1.8	0.4	28.8	52,782	51,519	47,065	43,484	2.5	9.5
Chelan County, WA	95.7	1.3	3.2	1.7	0.4	27.7	36,452	35,503	32,738	30,497	2.7	8.4
Douglas County, WA	95.3	1.4	3.3	1.9	0.5	30.9	16,330	16,016	14,327	12,987	2.0	11.8
Wheeling, WV-OH Metro Area	95.9	4.2	0.7	0.8	0.1	1.0	68,961	69,515	69,747	69,420	-0.8	-0.3
Belmont County, OH	95.1	5.1	0.6	0.6	0.1	0.9	32,072	32,439	32,158	31,446	-1.1	0.9
Marshall County, WV	98.6	1.3	0.7	0.6	0.0	1.1	15,801	15,914	15,933	15,830	-0.7	-0.1
Ohio County, WV	95.1	5.1	0.7	1.2	0.1	1.1	21,088	21,162	21,656	22,144	-0.3	-2.3
Wichita, KS Metro Area	86.6	9.6	2.7	4.5	0.2	12.6	271,000	267,179	256,503	243,071	1.4	4.2
Butler County, KS	95.6	2.8	2.3	1.6	0.2	4.7	26,476	26,078	25,148	23,296	1.5	3.7
Harvey County, KS	96.0	3.0	2.0	1.3	0.1	11.9	14,650	14,533	14,109	13,419	0.8	3.0
Kingman County, KS	98.3	0.9	1.8	0.7	0.1	3.6	3,811	3,818	3,867	3,855	-0.2	-1.3
Sedgwick County, KS	84.1	11.5	2.8	5.4	0.2	14.1	215,200	211,885	202,407	191,611	1.6	4.7
Sumner County, KS	97.0	2.1	2.9	0.7	0.1	5.6	10,863	10,865	10,972	10,890	0.0	
Wichita Falls, TX Metro Area	86.7	10.7	2.1	2.7	0.3	17.2	65,401	64,850	63,688	62,223	0.8	1.8
Archer County, TX	96.8	1.9	2.0	0.8	0.2	8.3	4,139	4,109	3,983	3,847	0.7	3.2
Clay County, TX	97.3	1.5	2.6	0.6	0.1	6.1	5,156	5,150	5,113	5,002	0.1	0.7
Wichita County, TX	85.2	12.0	2.1	3.0	0.3	18.6	56,106	55,591	54,592	53,374	0.9	1.8
Williamsport, PA Metro Area	94.2	6.2	0.7	0.9	0.1	1.9	52,671	52,495	52,862	52,482	0.3	-0.7
Lycoming County, PA	94.2	6.2	0.7	0.9	0.1	1.9	52,671	52,495	52,862	52,482	0.3	-0.7
Wilmington, NC Metro Area	82.8	15.9	1.4	1.9	0.2	5.7	134,649	128,234	117,074	101,048	5.0	9.5
New Hanover County, NC	83.2	15.4	1.3	2.2	0.2	5.5	107,090	101,504	93,062	80,109	5.5	9.1
Pender County, NC	81.6	17.5	1.7	1.1	0.2	6.5	27,559	26,730	24,012	20,939	3.1	11.3
Winchester, VA-WV Metro Area	92.3	6.7	1.0	2.1	0.1	8.4	58,497	56,967	51,616	45,320	2.7	10.4
Frederick County, VA	93.3	5.8	0.9	2.1	0.1	7.7	32,775	31,401	27,774	23,481	4.4	13.1
Winchester city, VA	84.3	13.6	1.5	3.5	0.2	16.6	11,916	11,872	11,430	10,616	0.4	3.9
Hampshire County, WV	98.1	1.8	0.7	0.5	0.1	1.4	13,806	13,694	12,412	11,223	0.8	10.3
Winston-Salem, NC Metro Area	78.6	19.7	1.4	2.2	0.2	10.1	292,303	287,200	270,024	246,938	1.8	6.4
Davidson County, North Carolina	88.0	10.3	1.3	1.8	0.1	6.9	73,136	72,674	68,412	62,800	0.6	6.2
Davie County, North Carolina	91.8	7.7	1.1	1.0	0.1	6.5	18,222	18,230	16,965	15,065	0.0	7.5
Forsyth County, North Carolina	69.2	28.6	1.6	2.9	0.2	12.7	161,895	157,036	146,998	133,852	3.1	6.8
Stokes County, North Carolina	94.8	4.8	1.0	0.5	0.0	3.0	21,842	21,922	20,851	19,332	-0.4	5.1
Yadkin County, North Carolina	95.2	4.2	1.0	0.5	0.2	10.9	17,208	17,338	16,798	15,889	-0.7	3.2
Worcester, MA-CT Metro Area	89.7	6.3	1.0	5.1	0.2	10.8	379,267	376,058	363,458	342,938	0.9	3.5
Windham County, CT	94.7	4.1	1.5	1.9	0.2	11.1	49,178	49,086	47,032	44,066	0.2	4.4
Worcester County, MA	89.0	6.6	0.9	5.6	0.1	10.8	330,089	326,972	316,426	298,872	1.0	3.3
Yakima, WA Metro Area	90.4	2.2	7.9	2.3	0.5	48.3	86,569	85,535	82,261	79,292	1.2	4.0
Yakima County, WA	90.4	2.2	7.9	2.3	0.5	48.3	86,569	85,535	82,261	79,292	1.2	4.0
York-Hanover, PA Metro Area	91.4	8.0	0.8	1.9	0.1	7.0	181,068	178,856	169,786	157,223	1.2	5.3
York County, PA	91.4	8.0	0.8	1.9	0.1	7.0	181,068	178,856	169,786	157,223	1.2	5.3
Youngstown-Warren-Boardman, OH-PA Metro Area	87.7	12.4	0.8	1.1	0.1	3.2	258,212	259,663	260,443	257,023	-0.6	-0.3
Mahoning County, OH	82.7	17.3	0.9	1.3	0.1	5.5	111,305	111,800	112,640	111,853	-0.4	-0.7
Trumbull County, OH	90.5	9.9	0.7	0.8	0.1	1.7	95,345	96,120	96,354	95,182	-0.8	-0.2
Mercer County, PA	93.1	6.9	0.6	1.0	0.1	1.4	51,562	51,743	51,449	49,988	-0.3	0.6
Yuba City, CA Metro Area	80.6	4.6	4.8	14.6	0.9	29.1	62,393	61,535	56,927	51,023	1.4	8.1
Sutter County, CA	77.6	3.6	4.0	18.6	0.9	30.3	34,176	33,873	31,950	28,383	0.9	6.0
Yuba County, CA	84.5	5.9	5.8	9.5	1.0	27.5	28,217	27,662	24,977	22,640	2.0	10.7
Yuma, AZ Metro Area	93.0	3.4	3.1	2.3	0.5	62.0	90,485	87,959	83,150	74,476	2.9	5.8
Yuma County, AZ	93.0	3.4	3.1	2.3	0.5	62.0	90,485	87,959	83,150	74,476	2.9	5.8

0 = represents zero or rounds to zero.
[1]Persons of Hispanic origin may be of any race.

Table C-3. Personal Income and Earnings by Industry

Metropolitan statistical area, division, and component county	Total (million dollars) 2015	2010	2005	Per capita[1] (dollars) 2015	2010	Percent change, 2010–2015	Earnings 2015 Total[2] (million dollars)	Manu-facturing	Retail trade	Finance and insurance	Professional and technical services	Health care and social services	Government and government enterprises
Abilene, TX Metro Area	7,077	5,646	4,540	41,732	34,093	22.4	4,765	3.9	6.9	4.3	4.4	13.3	22.2
Callahan County, TX	514	399	313	37,919	29,507	28.5	162	5.2	10.7	2.3	2.9	5.2	20.5
Jones County, TX	595	513	423	29,819	25,357	17.6	302	3.4	4.5	3.5	1.7	3.7	38.8
Taylor County, TX	5,967	4,734	3,804	43,861	35,903	22.2	4,302	3.9	6.9	4.4	4.7	14.3	21.1
Akron, OH Metro Area	31,457	26,765	23,745	44,668	38,066	17.3	22,335	13.5	7.5	4.3	6.6	13.7	14.0
Portage County, OH	6,488	5,457	4,841	39,982	33,800	18.3	3,688	21.4	5.9	1.3	4.2	7.7	25.1
Summit County, OH	24,969	21,308	18,904	46,071	39,337	17.1	18,647	11.9	7.8	4.8	7.1	14.8	11.8
Albany, GA Metro Area	5,270	4,822	4,130	34,326	30,584	12.2	3,421	D	6.3	D	5.3	17.0	23.4
Baker County, GA	105	106	99	33,167	30,762	7.8	47	D	3.3	D	D	4.0	11.0
Dougherty County, GA	2,985	2,807	2,387	32,682	29,683	10.1	2,730	9.6	6.2	3.4	5.6	19.6	23.5
Lee County, GA	1,216	1,016	860	41,628	35,743	16.5	329	3.8	6.9	2.2	D	D	23.1
Terrell County, GA	348	294	256	38,174	30,877	23.6	134	14.4	8.0	5.1	1.9	D	22.3
Worth County, GA	616	600	529	29,763	27,598	7.8	182	10.8	7.0	D	D	D	26.1
Albany, OR Metro Area	4,503	3,655	2,952	37,355	31,269	19.5	2,611	21.0	8.6	2.1	2.6	11.7	15.3
Linn County, OR	4,503	3,655	2,952	37,355	31,269	19.5	2,611	21.0	8.6	2.1	2.6	11.7	15.3
Albany-Schenectady-Troy, NY Metro Area	46,648	38,836	32,093	52,899	44,582	18.7	35,051	7.5	6.1	6.1	9.9	11.1	28.8
Albany County, NY	17,539	14,168	11,574	56,692	46,596	21.7	19,350	3.3	6.1	6.8	9.5	10.8	35.1
Rensselaer County, NY	7,184	6,214	5,044	44,823	38,993	15.0	3,895	11.2	5.5	3.5	5.8	11.7	27.1
Saratoga County, NY	13,344	10,815	8,709	58,979	49,140	20.0	6,147	14.1	6.9	8.2	8.6	10.0	18.2
Schenectady County, NY	7,453	6,633	5,878	48,206	42,825	12.6	5,125	13.0	5.5	3.0	16.8	13.3	17.8
Schoharie County, NY	1,128	1,005	888	35,998	30,732	17.1	534	3.4	7.6	4.8	2.4	10.1	37.1
Albuquerque, NM Metro Area	34,988	30,334	25,212	38,563	34,097	13.1	23,901	5.5	6.8	4.3	D	12.6	25.8
Bernalillo County, NM	26,934	23,370	19,845	39,804	35,190	13.1	21,030	4.0	6.7	4.6	14.2	13.3	25.9
Sandoval County, NM	5,281	4,456	3,280	37,885	33,669	12.5	1,931	21.5	7.0	2.0	5.4	7.8	22.2
Torrance County, NM	445	400	374	28,753	24,424	17.7	201	12.2	8.3	1.0	D	5.8	27.0
Valencia County, NM	2,328	2,108	1,712	30,733	27,449	12.0	739	4.5	9.6	2.1	3.0	9.1	31.9
Alexandria, LA Metro Area	6,305	5,331	4,505	40,812	34,587	18.0	3,973	8.4	10.0	D	4.2	D	22.6
Grant Parish, LA	660	584	467	29,548	26,128	13.1	231	7.4	3.4	D	1.0	D	50.1
Rapides Parish, LA	5,645	4,747	4,039	42,716	36,021	18.6	3,742	8.4	10.4	3.0	4.4	20.5	20.9
Allentown-Bethlehem-Easton, PA-NJ Metro Area	39,761	34,374	29,259	47,770	41,810	14.3	25,750	13.3	5.8	4.1	D	15.9	12.0
Warren County, NJ	5,440	4,783	4,245	50,902	44,009	15.7	2,577	11.3	8.9	1.7	5.6	13.1	18.7
Carbon County, PA	2,803	2,332	1,957	43,829	35,750	22.6	1,341	8.9	5.4	1.7	D	13.0	13.7
Lehigh County, PA	17,146	15,172	12,595	47,537	43,325	9.7	14,073	12.7	4.9	3.9	5.3	20.0	9.3
Northampton County, PA	14,372	12,087	10,462	47,776	40,553	17.8	7,759	15.8	6.4	5.5	5.6	9.9	14.4
Altoona, PA Metro Area	5,139	4,394	3,781	40,919	34,581	18.3	3,646	13.0	8.2	2.3	4.2	19.5	16.0
Blair County, PA	5,139	4,394	3,781	40,919	34,581	18.3	3,646	13.0	8.2	2.3	4.2	19.5	16.0
Amarillo, TX Metro Area	11,438	9,352	7,183	43,648	37,003	18.0	8,484	10.8	D	4.7	D	D	15.0
Armstrong County, TX	86	77	67	44,078	40,434	9.0	31	1.8	D	D	4.2	7.2	21.6
Carson County, TX	270	239	186	45,244	38,741	16.8	456	D	1.7	D	D	D	4.8
Oldham County, TX	113	88	64	54,690	42,898	27.5	110	D	0.9	D	D	D	14.7
Potter County, TX	5,078	4,150	2,980	41,690	34,184	22.0	5,606	8.8	7.0	5.6	6.0	17.0	17.7
Randall County, TX	5,891	4,798	3,887	45,223	39,585	14.2	2,281	4.1	12.0	3.4	5.2	7.8	10.4
Ames, IA Metro Area	3,764	2,889	2,533	39,204	32,233	21.6	3,233	14.0	4.7	2.1	6.5	7.4	38.9
Story County, IA	3,764	2,889	2,533	39,204	32,233	21.6	3,233	14.0	4.7	2.1	6.5	7.4	38.9
Anchorage, AK Metro Area	23,443	19,972	14,817	58,638	52,124	12.5	16,789	1.1	6.0	3.1	8.3	12.9	27.3
Anchorage Municipality, AK	18,737	16,398	12,236	62,728	55,887	12.2	14,959	1.0	5.6	3.2	8.9	12.7	27.3
Matanuska-Susitna Borough, AK	4,706	3,574	2,580	46,554	39,822	16.9	1,830	2.4	9.7	2.0	4.0	13.8	26.7
Ann Arbor, MI Metro Area	18,447	15,448	13,919	51,400	44,704	15.0	14,801	7.9	4.3	3.2	12.9	11.2	35.1
Washtenaw County, MI	18,447	15,448	13,919	51,400	44,704	15.0	14,801	7.9	4.3	3.2	12.9	11.2	35.1
Anniston-Oxford-Jacksonville, AL Metro Area	3,864	3,633	3,116	33,418	30,677	8.9	2,442	14.5	8.4	2.7	3.1	10.7	32.8
Calhoun County, AL	3,864	3,633	3,116	33,418	30,677	8.9	2,442	14.5	8.4	2.7	3.1	10.7	32.8
Appleton, WI Metro Area	10,559	8,578	7,427	45,314	37,963	19.4	7,751	22.2	6.3	7.0	D	11.1	11.7
Calumet County, WI	2,234	1,807	1,576	44,892	36,868	21.8	820	31.0	6.1	5.3	D	6.9	11.2
Outagamie County, WI	8,325	6,771	5,851	45,429	38,267	18.7	6,931	21.2	6.4	7.2	4.6	11.6	11.7
Asheville, NC Metro Area	17,351	14,035	12,088	38,831	32,988	17.7	10,915	12.6	8.4	3.1	D	D	14.6
Buncombe County, NC	10,379	8,154	6,964	40,994	34,151	20.0	7,642	10.8	7.9	3.4	7.6	20.7	14.0
Haywood County, NC	2,108	1,821	1,536	35,207	30,886	14.0	935	20.7	11.4	3.0	3.7	16.1	16.4
Henderson County, NC	4,231	3,517	3,118	37,558	32,882	14.2	2,116	16.1	9.0	2.5	4.1	14.5	15.5
Madison County, NC	633	543	471	29,965	26,134	14.7	222	8.9	6.3	1.8	D	D	21.3
Athens-Clarke County, GA Metro Area	7,029	5,595	4,901	34,596	28,924	19.6	5,322	9.5	6.2	4.9	D	14.7	30.9
Clarke County, GA	3,636	2,963	2,576	29,343	25,219	16.4	4,239	10.8	6.4	5.1	3.7	16.2	34.7
Madison County, GA	910	767	717	31,988	27,234	17.5	240	4.5	4.9	1.9	D	D	25.7
Oconee County, GA	1,986	1,466	1,265	55,216	44,505	24.1	685	4.0	6.2	5.3	9.2	12.0	12.7
Oglethorpe County, GA	498	401	343	33,480	26,895	24.5	158	4.0	2.4	1.8	1.5	D	17.2
Atlanta-Sandy Springs-Roswell, GA Metro Area	257,510	205,462	183,846	45,092	38,739	16.4	202,116	6.6	6.1	7.2	12.7	8.8	11.4
Barrow County, GA	2,455	1,820	1,593	32,570	26,112	24.7	1,050	11.7	11.9	1.5	D	7.4	16.5
Bartow County, GA	3,479	2,774	2,412	33,856	27,697	22.2	2,220	28.2	6.1	2.0	4.2	7.5	13.3
Butts County, GA	692	594	552	29,320	25,034	17.1	311	14.0	9.0	2.1	D	D	27.2
Carroll County, GA	3,856	3,154	2,666	33,662	28,489	18.2	2,395	16.5	8.2	2.0	D	15.8	18.1
Cherokee County, GA	10,351	7,802	6,846	43,878	36,256	21.0	3,620	7.3	9.0	3.8	7.8	10.0	14.4
Clayton County, GA	7,130	6,400	5,860	26,025	24,634	5.6	8,154	3.8	5.1	1.2	1.3	6.3	11.8
Cobb County, GA	36,400	28,740	27,288	49,101	41,671	17.8	26,783	6.9	6.9	6.5	13.8	9.3	8.7
Coweta County, GA	5,593	4,230	3,439	40,402	33,069	22.2	2,154	14.2	9.3	2.5	4.2	17.0	15.3

[1]Based on resident population estimated on July 1 of the year shown.
[2]Includes other industry categories not shown separately.
D = not shown to avoid disclosure of confidential information.

Table C-3.   Personal Income and Earnings by Industry—*Continued*

	Personal Income												
	Total (million dollars)			Per capita[1] (dollars)			Earnings 2015						
							Percent by selected major industries						
Metropolitan statistical area, division, and component county	2015	2010	2005	2015	2010	Percent change, 2010–2015	Total[2] (million dollars)	Manu-facturing	Retail trade	Finance and insurance	Profes-sional and technical services	Health care and social services	Govern-ment and govern-ment enter-prises
Dawson County, GA	883	690	610	37,879	30,949	22.4	388	9.0	24.0	2.9	D	7.3	14.8
DeKalb County, GA	31,467	25,527	23,342	42,819	36,863	16.2	22,307	4.5	6.8	5.8	8.5	12.2	14.3
Douglas County, GA	4,516	3,767	3,199	32,089	28,400	13.0	2,091	11.0	11.2	3.6	2.8	11.6	16.7
Fayette County, GA	6,019	4,770	4,354	54,361	44,582	21.9	2,508	10.8	8.2	3.3	7.8	15.6	13.9
Forsyth County, GA	11,571	8,121	6,188	54,466	45,945	18.5	5,556	11.0	5.6	3.1	10.6	8.7	8.5
Fulton County, GA	70,716	57,518	50,868	69,977	62,112	12.7	84,298	3.7	4.2	10.4	18.2	7.7	10.4
Gwinnett County, GA	33,240	25,487	24,106	37,106	31,533	17.7	25,928	9.0	7.9	6.8	11.2	6.8	9.0
Haralson County, GA	919	775	660	31,840	26,924	18.3	402	25.8	5.7	3.0	3.0	8.3	21.0
Heard County, GA	327	281	195	28,363	23,717	19.6	161	19.9	1.5	0.7	D	1.9	20.5
Henry County, GA	7,549	6,182	5,077	34,671	30,133	15.1	3,005	8.0	10.6	2.5	3.2	13.2	20.9
Jasper County, GA	446	387	370	32,701	27,852	17.4	130	16.1	3.7	2.7	2.2	D	23.4
Lamar County, GA	541	473	397	29,742	25,883	14.9	211	18.7	5.9	3.0	1.2	5.6	29.5
Meriwether County, GA	666	592	533	31,438	27,120	15.9	261	13.8	5.0	2.7	0.6	D	26.4
Morgan County, GA	753	596	563	41,708	33,303	25.2	362	19.3	7.0	3.8	D	3.2	16.0
Newton County, GA	3,179	2,623	2,185	30,144	26,185	15.1	1,397	25.4	6.8	1.6	D	8.9	19.3
Paulding County, GA	5,026	3,953	3,222	33,011	27,691	19.2	1,251	4.8	10.9	1.7	4.1	9.6	24.5
Pickens County, GA	1,225	1,008	885	40,420	34,202	18.2	496	9.9	7.4	3.5	4.5	25.5	14.6
Pike County, GA	616	505	410	34,324	28,203	21.7	161	11.8	5.4	2.2	D	D	23.6
Rockdale County, GA	2,866	2,499	2,296	32,259	29,258	10.3	2,162	24.5	7.2	3.6	3.8	10.6	12.1
Spalding County, GA	2,005	1,735	1,556	31,305	27,078	15.6	1,171	18.3	7.4	2.5	D	15.4	21.3
Walton County, GA	3,025	2,461	2,172	34,223	29,307	16.8	1,184	14.3	11.3	2.0	4.5	8.0	18.7
Atlantic City-Hammonton, NJ Metro Area	11,982	10,525	8,971	43,695	38,305	14.1	8,590	D	8.1	2.7	5.7	15.5	25.1
Atlantic County, NJ	11,982	10,525	8,971	43,695	38,305	14.1	8,590	D	8.1	2.7	5.7	15.5	25.1
Auburn-Opelika, AL Metro Area	5,278	4,084	3,313	33,622	29,011	15.9	2,985	12.8	6.9	2.9	4.6	6.4	35.0
Lee County, AL	5,278	4,084	3,313	33,622	29,011	15.9	2,985	12.8	6.9	2.9	4.6	6.4	35.0
Augusta-Richmond County, GA-SC Metro Area	21,924	18,638	15,398	37,151	32,896	12.9	15,057	10.2	6.0	3.0	D	11.4	28.5
Burke County, GA	717	651	505	31,527	27,897	13.0	588	6.7	4.1	1.3	4.3	D	13.7
Columbia County, GA	6,374	4,968	3,909	44,250	39,746	11.3	1,924	10.2	11.5	4.7	6.5	11.6	17.5
Lincoln County, GA	251	224	190	32,682	28,068	16.4	71	4.2	5.5	4.0	2.0	2.6	26.0
McDuffie County, GA	691	605	612	32,096	27,727	15.8	341	23.7	9.1	2.0	2.3	D	20.7
Richmond County, GA	6,864	6,124	5,293	34,015	30,478	11.6	7,824	7.7	4.7	2.0	5.2	14.2	40.8
Aiken County, SC	6,200	5,348	4,269	37,389	33,313	12.2	3,960	14.2	5.9	4.6	10.4	7.6	12.1
Edgefield County, SC	827	718	620	31,173	26,616	17.1	349	17.5	5.0	2.1	D	D	31.1
Austin-Round Rock, TX Metro Area	102,072	69,239	51,986	51,014	40,078	27.3	80,171	9.0	5.9	6.3	15.2	8.0	15.0
Bastrop County, TX	2,635	2,094	1,640	32,723	28,172	16.2	1,060	7.1	10.7	2.5	4.2	6.9	22.8
Caldwell County, TX	1,253	991	789	30,925	26,009	18.9	519	5.0	8.7	2.9	3.0	12.2	18.3
Hays County, TX	7,398	5,148	3,653	37,990	32,523	16.8	3,788	8.8	9.9	2.4	6.5	8.7	20.6
Travis County, TX	68,666	45,267	35,046	58,362	43,930	32.9	62,803	8.1	5.1	6.9	17.1	8.0	15.2
Williamson County, TX	22,119	15,740	10,858	43,498	36,906	17.9	12,002	14.0	8.7	4.9	9.3	8.1	11.0
Bakersfield, CA Metro Area	32,953	25,844	20,142	37,355	30,705	21.7	23,895	4.9	6.0	2.0	4.3	8.3	24.0
Kern County, CA	32,953	25,844	20,142	37,355	30,705	21.7	23,895	4.9	6.0	2.0	4.3	8.3	24.0
Baltimore-Columbia-Towson, MD Metro Area	154,626	131,896	110,942	55,275	48,570	13.8	114,056	4.4	4.8	6.2	13.4	12.7	23.3
Anne Arundel County, MD	34,206	28,593	24,761	60,628	53,018	14.4	27,454	5.5	4.8	2.3	12.8	7.3	36.4
Baltimore County, MD	45,210	39,694	34,495	54,395	49,238	10.5	28,948	4.3	6.8	9.9	11.1	13.9	18.7
Carroll County, MD	9,388	8,023	6,608	56,006	47,984	16.7	3,784	7.9	8.4	2.8	10.1	14.1	15.3
Harford County, MD	13,168	11,401	9,487	52,612	46,489	13.2	7,009	5.6	6.2	2.9	12.9	9.5	35.4
Howard County, MD	21,936	18,423	14,586	69,991	63,828	9.7	15,423	4.5	5.0	5.5	27.8	8.0	9.7
Queen Anne's County, MD	2,748	2,339	1,948	56,189	48,910	14.9	956	7.5	9.7	2.7	8.9	5.9	19.1
Baltimore city, MD	27,970	23,423	19,058	44,979	37,707	19.3	30,482	2.7	2.0	7.9	9.7	19.4	21.0
Bangor, ME Metro Area	5,654	5,076	4,355	37,032	32,991	12.2	4,020	4.7	9.4	3.1	3.7	22.3	21.4
Penobscot County, ME	5,654	5,076	4,355	37,032	32,991	12.2	4,020	4.7	9.4	3.1	3.7	22.3	21.4
Barnstable Town, MA Metro Area	13,874	11,308	10,180	64,730	52,369	23.6	7,039	D	9.5	3.4	7.4	16.1	18.7
Barnstable County, MA	13,874	11,308	10,180	64,730	52,369	23.6	7,039	D	9.5	3.4	7.4	16.1	18.7
Baton Rouge, LA Metro Area	36,104	30,177	23,280	43,474	37,519	15.9	27,761	11.9	6.0	D	8.3	10.6	16.9
Ascension Parish, LA	5,431	4,251	2,763	45,469	39,416	15.4	3,475	25.3	6.0	1.5	3.6	5.1	9.1
East Baton Rouge Parish, LA	20,500	17,475	14,361	45,887	39,651	15.7	19,225	7.2	5.7	5.0	10.6	13.1	17.5
East Feliciana Parish, LA	740	668	556	37,578	33,122	13.5	310	7.7	3.4	2.9	2.1	10.4	50.1
Iberville Parish, LA	1,217	1,079	799	36,764	32,342	13.7	1,330	39.8	2.4	1.3	1.8	D	13.7
Livingston Parish, LA	5,249	4,199	3,015	38,095	32,621	16.8	1,601	10.6	12.1	3.0	3.7	7.0	19.7
Pointe Coupee Parish, LA	917	794	601	41,203	34,894	18.1	328	9.1	9.9	5.1	D	7.0	18.4
St. Helena Parish, LA	409	381	265	38,748	34,136	13.5	95	16.2	5.1	D	1.4	5.7	32.7
West Baton Rouge Parish, LA	1,123	898	588	44,043	37,492	17.5	965	24.5	5.7	0.7	D	D	10.1
West Feliciana Parish, LA	518	432	331	33,680	27,639	21.9	432	7.8	4.0	1.3	D	D	34.6
Battle Creek, MI Metro Area	4,964	4,324	3,928	36,958	31,786	16.3	3,842	22.3	4.9	1.7	D	13.8	20.7
Calhoun County, MI	4,964	4,324	3,928	36,958	31,786	16.3	3,842	22.3	4.9	1.7	D	13.8	20.7
Bay City, MI Metro Area	4,003	3,587	3,104	37,884	33,306	13.7	2,168	13.6	7.5	2.7	12.3	18.3	17.3
Bay County, MI	4,003	3,587	3,104	37,884	33,306	13.7	2,168	13.6	7.5	2.7	12.3	18.3	17.3
Beaumont-Port Arthur, TX Metro Area	17,101	13,882	10,916	41,872	34,387	21.8	12,541	24.4	6.2	D	6.6	9.9	12.4
Hardin County, TX	2,352	1,900	1,414	42,096	34,667	21.4	792	8.3	10.3	2.3	4.7	14.0	14.5
Jefferson County, TX	10,809	8,826	7,098	42,505	34,960	21.6	10,001	24.3	5.9	2.5	7.4	10.5	11.8
Newton County, TX	428	337	273	30,625	23,360	31.1	83	8.1	8.4	D	2.9	12.1	34.9
Orange County, TX	3,512	2,819	2,131	41,679	34,378	21.2	1,665	33.5	5.9	2.9	3.3	4.4	13.9
Beckley, WV Metro Area	4,109	3,748	3,134	33,538	30,012	11.7	2,426	2.8	9.5	2.3	4.5	18.7	22.8

[1]Based on resident population estimated on July 1 of the year shown.
[2]Includes other industry categories not shown separately.
D = not shown to avoid disclosure of confidential information.

Table C-3. Personal Income and Earnings by Industry—*Continued*

Metropolitan statistical area, division, and component county	Personal Income Total (million dollars) 2015	2010	2005	Per capita[1] (dollars) 2015	2010	Percent change, 2010–2015	Earnings 2015 Total[2] (million dollars)	Manu-facturing	Retail trade	Finance and insurance	Professional and technical services	Health care and social services	Government and government enterprises
Fayette County, WV	1,371	1,243	1,004	30,462	27,017	12.8	601	3.7	8.7	2.1	3.2	14.7	27.4
Raleigh County, WV	2,738	2,506	2,129	35,324	31,758	11.2	1,825	2.5	9.7	2.4	5.0	20.0	21.3
Bellingham, WA Metro Area	9,024	7,369	5,738	42,511	36,557	16.3	5,880	13.4	8.6	3.1	5.7	12.4	18.8
Whatcom County, WA	9,024	7,369	5,738	42,511	36,557	16.3	5,880	13.4	8.6	3.1	5.7	12.4	18.8
Bend-Redmond, OR Metro Area	7,788	5,415	4,686	44,435	34,304	29.5	5,051	6.1	8.8	4.1	8.1	17.7	12.4
Deschutes County, OR	7,788	5,415	4,686	44,435	34,304	29.5	5,051	6.1	8.8	4.1	8.1	17.7	12.4
Billings, MT Metro Area	7,750	6,080	4,825	46,052	38,151	20.7	5,788	D	D	D	D	D	11.5
Carbon County, MT	448	350	313	43,012	34,798	23.6	157	1.6	5.5	2.9	5.7	8.6	20.1
Golden Valley County, MT	44	32	27	53,667	36,502	47.0	21	D	D	D	D	D	14.3
Yellowstone County, MT	7,258	5,697	4,484	46,213	38,389	20.4	5,610	5.8	7.7	4.7	8.1	16.2	11.2
Binghamton, NY Metro Area	9,771	8,894	7,225	39,714	35,372	12.3	6,487	15.8	6.7	2.8	D	14.8	26.3
Broome County, NY	7,791	7,088	5,759	39,634	35,372	12.0	5,512	11.6	6.9	3.0	4.9	16.5	27.4
Tioga County, NY	1,980	1,806	1,466	40,033	35,369	13.2	975	39.6	5.4	1.4	D	5.1	20.2
Birmingham-Hoover, AL Metro Area	51,059	43,972	38,557	44,568	38,952	14.4	36,393	7.5	5.8	10.4	D	14.7	14.6
Bibb County, AL	657	572	449	29,075	25,003	16.3	249	7.9	6.1	1.6	1.6	D	26.7
Blount County, AL	1,826	1,584	1,301	31,663	27,600	14.7	519	10.9	7.6	2.7	3.2	D	19.9
Chilton County, AL	1,379	1,198	1,020	31,380	27,429	14.4	510	21.6	9.7	3.2	D	D	18.1
Jefferson County, AL	31,512	27,804	24,698	47,718	42,248	12.9	26,737	7.1	5.0	9.7	9.2	16.8	15.7
St. Clair County, AL	2,995	2,472	1,979	34,400	29,497	16.6	1,063	18.9	8.3	2.8	3.9	8.8	15.4
Shelby County, AL	10,271	8,150	7,210	49,212	41,572	18.4	6,294	5.7	6.9	17.3	9.4	7.7	8.0
Walker County, AL	2,420	2,193	1,901	37,056	32,728	13.2	1,021	9.8	12.3	3.2	3.2	D	16.2
Bismarck, ND Metro Area	7,010	4,822	3,440	54,124	41,825	29.4	5,205	D	D	D	D	16.6	19.4
Burleigh County, ND	5,316	3,580	2,560	57,171	43,798	30.5	4,167	3.7	7.4	4.7	8.1	18.9	19.7
Morton County, ND	1,502	1,061	747	49,539	38,487	28.7	848	10.6	7.3	3.8	9.0	8.9	12.0
Oliver County, ND	80	84	57	43,553	45,552	-4.4	90	D	0.4	D	D	D	5.6
Sioux County, ND	112	98	76	25,546	23,512	8.7	100	0.4	D	D	0.6	D	82.4
Blacksburg-Christiansburg-Radford, VA Metro Area	6,247	5,122	4,416	34,370	28,688	19.8	4,249	20.9	5.9	1.5	D	9.0	33.3
Floyd County, VA	543	454	377	34,703	29,558	17.4	162	11.9	5.9	5.3	4.2	11.2	21.1
Giles County, VA	623	541	453	37,295	31,217	19.5	280	29.7	8.0	1.6	4.7	D	15.8
Montgomery County, VA	3,818	3,069	2,566	33,184	27,636	20.1	3,028	15.1	5.6	1.4	7.8	9.0	40.1
Pulaski County, VA	1,262	1,058	1,019	36,770	30,405	20.9	779	42.2	6.6	1.1	D	D	15.7
Radford city, VA	(3)	(3)	(3)	(3)	(3)	(3)	(3)	(3)	(3)	(3)	(3)	(3)	(3)
Bloomington, IL Metro Area	8,409	7,402	5,968	44,397	39,700	11.8	7,015	5.0	5.4	33.9	D	D	15.3
De Witt County, IL	674	622	460	41,486	37,510	10.6	398	8.4	5.8	2.2	D	D	14.9
McLean County, IL	7,735	6,780	5,508	44,670	39,914	11.9	6,617	4.8	5.4	35.8	4.0	9.4	15.4
Bloomington, IN Metro Area	5,829	4,832	4,103	35,203	30,172	16.7	4,146	15.0	5.7	2.9	5.1	D	32.9
Monroe County, IN	5,113	4,197	3,549	35,335	30,291	16.7	3,847	12.7	5.8	2.9	5.4	12.2	34.6
Owen County, IN	716	635	554	34,287	29,414	16.6	299	45.6	4.6	2.7	1.4	D	12.3
Bloomsburg-Berwick, PA Metro Area	3,431	2,960	2,388	40,258	34,554	16.5	2,830	12.2	4.8	5.1	3.3	D	15.6
Columbia County, PA	2,487	2,190	1,806	37,307	32,512	14.7	1,528	20.6	7.5	2.6	3.3	11.0	21.9
Montour County, PA	944	770	583	50,859	42,066	20.9	1,303	2.4	1.7	7.9	3.4	D	8.2
Boise City, ID Metro Area	27,047	20,564	17,588	39,956	33,274	20.1	19,484	12.7	9.2	5.0	7.2	D	14.4
Ada County, ID	19,997	14,951	13,134	46,053	37,998	21.2	15,793	12.4	9.3	5.6	8.1	13.9	14.1
Boise County, ID	260	213	192	36,828	30,386	21.2	73	3.7	5.2	D	D	5.7	34.1
Canyon County, ID	5,863	4,656	3,644	28,258	24,584	14.9	3,224	15.4	9.6	2.7	3.5	9.3	15.3
Gem County, ID	555	451	362	32,963	27,022	22.0	192	2.9	7.8	2.5	2.6	16.9	23.4
Owyhee County, ID	372	294	255	32,867	25,592	28.4	203	4.4	3.7	D	D	D	14.3
Boston-Cambridge-Newton, MA-NH Metro Area	326,046	265,544	216,762	68,292	58,164	17.4	261,620	D	4.2	10.9	17.4	12.5	11.1
Boston, MA Division	*137,843*	*115,115*	*91,016*	*69,458*	*60,780*	*14.3*	*124,752*	*D*	*3.8*	*18.0*	*16.1*	*14.5*	*12.0*
Norfolk County, MA	56,177	44,360	37,674	80,711	65,935	22.4	31,640	7.8	6.2	9.3	12.2	12.5	10.0
Plymouth County, MA	30,252	23,812	20,494	59,273	48,017	23.4	14,478	5.6	7.8	4.8	7.3	13.6	19.0
Suffolk County, MA	51,414	46,942	32,848	66,074	64,725	2.1	78,633	D	2.1	23.9	19.3	15.4	11.6
Cambridge-Newton-Framingham, MA Division	*162,946*	*130,322*	*108,260*	*69,010*	*57,846*	*19.3*	*121,432*	*12.4*	*4.1*	*4.0*	*19.7*	*10.7*	*9.9*
Essex County, MA	46,811	38,689	32,088	60,320	51,887	16.3	26,554	16.2	6.4	4.6	9.5	15.8	13.4
Middlesex County, MA	116,135	91,633	76,172	73,265	60,794	20.5	94,878	11.3	3.4	3.8	22.5	9.3	9.0
Rockingham County-Strafford County, NH Division	*25,257*	*20,108*	*17,485*	*58,928*	*48,041*	*22.7*	*15,437*	*D*	*8.2*	*7.8*	*9.7*	*9.9*	*12.2*
Rockingham County, NH	19,440	15,415	13,614	64,417	52,197	23.4	11,783	10.5	8.4	6.2	11.1	8.9	9.1
Strafford County, NH	5,817	4,692	3,872	45,868	38,081	20.4	3,653	D	7.5	12.8	5.1	13.0	22.1
Boulder, CO Metro Area	19,233	14,655	12,447	60,220	49,513	21.6	14,920	12.1	4.5	3.7	24.2	9.8	15.0
Boulder County, CO	19,233	14,655	12,447	60,220	49,513	21.6	14,920	12.1	4.5	3.7	24.2	9.8	15.0
Bowling Green, KY Metro Area	5,805	4,719	3,904	34,461	29,653	16.2	4,106	D	6.4	D	D	13.4	16.7
Allen County, KY	616	491	418	29,847	24,505	21.8	256	24.5	5.5	2.7	D	D	16.9
Butler County, KY	415	344	283	32,054	27,068	18.4	164	30.0	3.2	2.1	1.1	D	19.6
Edmonson County, KY	355	303	245	29,588	24,878	18.9	87	D	4.0	D	D	D	44.0
Warren County, KY	4,418	3,581	2,958	35,966	31,354	14.7	3,599	18.2	6.7	3.9	4.1	14.1	15.8
Bremerton-Silverdale, WA Metro Area	12,474	10,552	9,261	47,953	41,920	14.4	7,168	2.0	5.6	1.8	6.1	10.2	52.7
Kitsap County, WA	12,474	10,552	9,261	47,953	41,920	14.4	7,168	2.0	5.6	1.8	6.1	10.2	52.7
Bridgeport-Stamford-Norwalk, CT Metro Area	100,856	96,824	67,426	106,382	105,272	1.1	60,699	12.1	5.5	21.4	10.3	8.0	7.1
Fairfield County, CT	100,856	96,824	67,426	106,382	105,272	1.1	60,699	12.1	5.5	21.4	10.3	8.0	7.1
Brownsville-Harlingen, TX Metro Area	11,325	9,437	6,992	26,826	23,152	15.9	7,068	5.3	9.5	2.8	2.7	19.2	26.8
Cameron County, TX	11,325	9,437	6,992	26,826	23,152	15.9	7,068	5.3	9.5	2.8	2.7	19.2	26.8

[1]Based on resident population estimated on July 1 of the year shown.
[2]Includes other industry categories not shown separately.
[3]Radford city included with Montgomery County, VA, in the Blacksburg-Christiansburg-Radford, VA MSA.
D = not shown to avoid disclosure of confidential information.

Table C-3. Personal Income and Earnings by Industry—*Continued*

Metropolitan statistical area, division, and component county	Personal Income												
	Total (million dollars)			Per capita¹ (dollars)		Percent change, 2010–2015	Earnings 2015						
							Total² (million dollars)	Percent by selected major industries					
	2015	2010	2005	2015	2010			Manu-facturing	Retail trade	Finance and insurance	Profes-sional and technical services	Health care and social services	Govern-ment and govern-ment enter-prises
Brunswick, GA Metro Area	4,141	3,575	3,269	35,696	31,771	12.4	2,424	D	7.6	2.7	4.1	7.6	31.7
Brantley County, GA	449	399	348	24,315	21,617	12.5	120	10.0	4.4	1.2	0.7	4.3	34.3
Glynn County, GA	3,328	2,860	2,663	39,814	35,844	11.1	2,209	6.8	7.8	2.8	4.3	8.1	31.4
McIntosh County, GA	365	317	259	26,097	22,147	17.8	95	D	8.9	1.0	2.8	2.0	33.9
Buffalo-Cheektowaga-Niagara Falls, NY Metro Area	51,958	43,954	36,871	45,769	38,706	18.2	36,777	11.9	6.7	6.2	7.0	12.4	22.0
Erie County, NY	43,164	36,372	30,485	46,786	39,575	18.2	32,319	11.3	6.5	6.8	7.4	12.4	21.4
Niagara County, NY	8,794	7,581	6,387	41,355	35,020	18.1	4,458	16.0	8.3	1.7	4.0	12.8	26.9
Burlington, NC Metro Area	5,673	4,803	4,012	35,839	31,686	13.1	3,291	16.3	8.1	3.6	3.4	20.1	11.5
Alamance County, NC	5,673	4,803	4,012	35,839	31,686	13.1	3,291	16.3	8.1	3.6	3.4	20.1	11.5
Burlington-South Burlington, VT Metro Area	11,192	9,163	7,665	51,565	43,315	19.0	8,591	12.1	6.7	4.2	D	D	20.1
Chittenden County, VT	8,837	7,175	5,974	54,756	45,758	19.7	7,367	11.4	6.7	4.6	12.5	15.2	18.6
Franklin County, VT	1,987	1,667	1,415	40,728	34,872	16.8	1,135	17.9	6.9	1.5	D	12.7	30.1
Grand Isle County, VT	368	322	277	53,604	46,248	15.9	89	2.3	8.0	2.4	7.2	D	18.5
California-Lexington Park, MD Metro Area	5,792	4,946	3,654	51,990	46,770	11.2	4,274	0.7	3.8	0.7	23.9	6.3	46.7
St. Mary's County, MD	5,792	4,946	3,654	51,990	46,770	11.2	4,274	0.7	3.8	0.7	23.9	6.3	46.7
Canton-Massillon, OH Metro Area	16,408	13,661	12,215	40,717	33,790	20.5	10,076	20.2	7.0	4.1	4.8	15.6	12.7
Carroll County, OH	999	846	735	35,927	29,342	22.4	443	18.6	6.2	1.0	2.2	6.1	12.4
Stark County, OH	15,409	12,815	11,480	41,072	34,132	20.3	9,633	20.3	7.0	4.3	4.9	16.0	12.7
Cape Coral-Fort Myers, FL Metro Area	31,296	24,273	21,188	44,583	39,117	14.0	16,050	2.6	10.0	3.5	8.8	11.4	18.1
Lee County, FL	31,296	24,273	21,188	44,583	39,117	14.0	16,050	2.6	10.0	3.5	8.8	11.4	18.1
Cape Girardeau, MO-IL Metro Area	3,713	3,197	2,695	38,070	33,148	14.8	2,636	12.4	8.1	D	3.9	D	15.5
Alexander County, IL	210	220	175	31,012	26,728	16.0	112	7.9	2.6	D	0.5	D	46.2
Bollinger County, MO	358	320	274	29,349	25,953	13.1	91	6.8	8.2	3.0	2.4	11.0	24.5
Cape Girardeau County, MO	3,145	2,657	2,246	40,031	35,013	14.3	2,433	12.8	8.4	3.1	4.1	24.6	13.8
Carbondale-Marion, IL Metro Area	4,703	4,254	3,380	37,084	33,542	10.6	3,393	6.6	6.7	3.8	D	17.1	36.2
Jackson County, IL	1,980	1,849	1,527	33,363	30,616	9.0	1,693	2.7	6.1	2.1	3.1	16.6	45.7
Williamson County, IL	2,723	2,405	1,853	40,359	36,202	11.5	1,700	10.4	7.3	5.4	D	17.5	26.7
Carson City, NV Metro Area	2,369	2,315	1,349	43,443	42,076	3.2	2,130	8.6	6.4	2.0	5.9	14.0	38.3
Carson City, NV	2,369	2,315	1,349	43,443	42,076	3.2	2,130	8.6	6.4	2.0	5.9	14.0	38.3
Casper, WY Metro Area	5,645	3,727	2,758	68,692	49,379	39.1	4,135	3.5	5.6	2.1	4.1	10.9	11.0
Natrona County, WY	5,645	3,727	2,758	68,692	49,379	39.1	4,135	3.5	5.6	2.1	4.1	10.9	11.0
Cedar Rapids, IA Metro Area	12,628	10,495	8,326	47,468	40,613	16.9	9,639	21.2	5.5	8.0	5.1	10.6	11.3
Benton County, IA	1,242	1,027	791	48,422	39,424	22.8	444	17.5	7.6	3.9	2.2	D	19.5
Jones County, IA	829	710	548	40,524	34,323	18.1	381	13.6	8.8	3.3	3.0	D	20.5
Linn County, IA	10,557	8,758	6,987	48,003	41,374	16.0	8,813	21.7	5.2	8.4	5.4	11.0	10.5
Chambersburg-Waynesboro, PA Metro Area	6,417	5,389	4,391	41,768	35,942	16.2	3,691	17.9	7.6	2.2	3.9	14.7	16.7
Franklin County, PA	6,417	5,389	4,391	41,768	35,942	16.2	3,691	17.9	7.6	2.2	3.9	14.7	16.7
Champaign-Urbana, IL Metro Area	10,244	8,741	6,793	42,863	37,629	13.9	7,919	6.5	12.2	2.6	5.2	D	34.9
Champaign County, IL	8,823	7,432	5,815	42,243	36,887	14.5	7,319	6.4	12.7	2.5	5.4	12.6	36.4
Ford County, IL	665	606	444	48,382	43,074	12.3	398	9.1	5.0	1.9	1.4	D	11.1
Piatt County, IL	756	702	533	46,140	41,981	9.9	202	6.3	7.1	5.3	4.1	11.7	26.9
Charleston, WV Metro Area	9,274	8,528	7,227	42,039	37,586	11.8	7,525	D	5.6	D	D	D	19.0
Boone County, WV	733	741	566	31,352	30,122	4.1	400	0.7	5.2	1.5	8.6	D	22.0
Clay County, WV	259	236	181	29,045	25,137	15.5	79	D	6.7	D	D	12.3	28.6
Kanawha County, WV	8,283	7,552	6,480	43,980	39,142	12.4	7,046	4.2	5.6	5.8	10.0	18.8	18.7
Charleston-North Charleston, SC Metro Area	32,307	24,045	19,142	43,393	36,022	20.5	23,358	10.1	6.6	5.4	10.3	9.5	23.1
Berkeley County, SC	7,033	5,266	3,979	34,684	29,434	17.8	3,377	14.8	6.4	1.7	19.9	3.4	17.9
Charleston County, SC	19,789	14,443	11,878	50,838	41,141	23.6	18,145	8.3	6.5	6.3	9.1	10.9	24.4
Dorchester County, SC	5,484	4,335	3,285	35,966	31,526	14.1	1,837	19.1	8.0	2.3	4.1	7.4	18.9
Charlotte-Concord-Gastonia, NC-SC Metro Area	109,028	84,662	70,326	44,935	38,073	18.0	88,007	9.0	5.7	11.5	D	D	11.8
Cabarrus County, NC	7,800	6,033	4,860	39,640	33,772	17.4	4,094	8.2	9.3	1.8	3.9	7.0	21.1
Gaston County, NC	7,887	6,983	5,766	36,950	33,886	9.0	4,064	24.6	8.2	2.3	2.8	16.0	13.7
Iredell County, NC	7,549	5,638	4,891	44,442	35,281	26.0	4,920	15.5	7.5	2.2	D	8.9	10.1
Lincoln County, NC	3,142	2,426	1,962	38,774	30,941	25.3	1,259	22.1	7.9	2.2	4.7	5.0	16.7
Mecklenburg County, NC	53,905	41,838	35,376	52,129	45,313	15.0	59,218	5.0	4.8	15.7	11.4	5.8	10.4
Rowan County, NC	4,779	4,030	3,749	34,348	29,139	17.9	2,945	18.5	6.6	1.8	2.9	9.6	20.2
Union County, NC	9,727	7,085	5,290	43,669	35,056	24.6	3,928	19.7	7.3	1.8	5.5	4.7	13.3
Chester County, SC	982	837	794	30,441	25,269	20.5	513	35.0	4.9	1.7	2.2	D	17.4
Lancaster County, SC	3,266	2,313	1,665	38,043	30,051	26.6	1,685	13.8	5.9	2.4	25.7	10.6	12.1
York County, SC	9,992	7,478	5,974	39,778	32,957	20.7	5,381	15.6	7.5	6.3	4.9	10.8	13.4
Charlottesville, VA Metro Area	12,117	9,635	7,873	52,795	43,975	20.1	8,241	3.6	4.6	4.7	10.4	9.7	34.5
Albemarle County, VA	9,183	7,172	5,910	60,294	50,241	20.0	7,311	3.5	4.5	5.1	10.9	10.0	35.4
Buckingham County, VA	468	407	339	27,449	23,787	15.4	201	3.0	5.3	1.0	2.7	10.9	37.8
Fluvanna County, VA	1,040	884	727	39,659	34,312	15.6	277	2.4	3.7	1.5	4.5	D	29.5
Greene County, VA	760	621	423	39,681	33,619	18.0	221	1.7	9.6	1.3	12.1	D	22.4
Nelson County, VA	666	551	474	45,055	36,723	22.7	231	10.2	3.7	2.3	8.9	D	17.9
Charlottesville city, VA	(4)	(4)	(4)	(4)	(4)	(4)	(4)	(4)	(4)	(4)	(4)	(4)	(4)
Chattanooga, TN-GA Metro Area	22,582	18,793	15,552	41,225	35,511	16.1	16,440	14.0	6.2	6.2	D	12.1	16.5
Catoosa County, GA	2,137	1,776	1,520	32,358	27,737	16.7	840	14.1	12.0	3.0	2.3	12.9	16.9
Dade County, GA	489	421	395	30,047	25,356	18.5	198	18.4	5.3	2.7	3.7	8.3	13.0
Walker County, GA	2,026	1,777	1,544	29,772	25,795	15.4	754	31.6	5.7	4.0	D	5.1	21.7

¹Based on resident population estimated on July 1 of the year shown.
²Includes other industry categories not shown separately.
⁴Charlottesville city included with Albemarle County, VA, in the Charlottesville, VA MSA.
D = not shown to avoid disclosure of confidential information.

Table C-3. Personal Income and Earnings by Industry—*Continued*

	Personal Income												
	Total (million dollars)			Per capita[1] (dollars)			Earnings 2015						
								Percent by selected major industries					
Metropolitan statistical area, division, and component county	2015	2010	2005	2015	2010	Percent change, 2010–2015	Total[2] (million dollars)	Manu-facturing	Retail trade	Finance and insurance	Profes-sional and technical services	Health care and social services	Govern-ment and govern-ment enter-prises
Hamilton County, TN	16,451	13,548	11,037	46,460	40,163	15.7	14,075	12.7	5.8	6.7	6.3	12.6	16.0
Marion County, TN	980	868	721	34,388	30,754	11.8	411	26.1	9.0	2.1	D	8.2	17.6
Sequatchie County, TN	498	403	335	33,653	28,508	18.0	162	10.8	7.5	5.3	3.7	8.5	28.2
Cheyenne, WY Metro Area	4,836	3,922	3,134	49,796	42,509	17.1	3,487	3.8	6.6	3.7	4.7	7.7	40.1
Laramie County, WY	4,836	3,922	3,134	49,796	42,509	17.1	3,487	3.8	6.6	3.7	4.7	7.7	40.1
Chicago-Naperville-Elgin, IL-IN-WI Metro Area	**514,662**	**414,871**	**376,685**	**53,886**	**43,803**	**23.0**	**389,395**	**10.2**	**4.9**	**8.5**	**D**	**D**	**12.3**
Chicago-Naperville-Arlington Heights, IL Division	*401,636*	*321,431*	*294,856*	*54,715*	*44,208*	*23.8*	*315,851*	*7.8*	*4.5*	*9.4*	*D*	*9.7*	*11.9*
Cook County, IL	286,603	227,021	211,833	54,714	43,664	25.3	237,056	6.8	4.1	10.5	15.7	9.6	12.3
DuPage County, IL	59,814	48,488	45,662	64,059	52,811	21.3	53,509	9.2	5.0	7.9	13.8	9.5	7.9
Grundy County, IL	2,422	2,149	1,530	47,930	42,874	11.8	1,709	18.9	8.0	1.6	D	8.1	10.7
Kendall County, IL	5,417	4,362	2,979	43,910	37,833	16.1	1,736	15.4	8.1	2.9	5.2	6.4	23.0
McHenry County, IL	15,200	12,764	11,431	49,457	41,291	19.8	6,393	17.5	8.0	3.0	5.4	10.6	16.6
Will County, IL	32,180	26,647	21,422	46,823	39,250	19.3	15,448	11.8	6.6	2.4	6.2	10.7	16.2
Elgin, IL Division	*27,725*	*23,073*	*19,640*	*43,647*	*37,139*	*17.5*	*16,828*	*16.0*	*5.5*	*4.1*	*6.3*	*D*	*19.9*
DeKalb County, IL	3,754	3,247	2,738	35,970	30,874	16.5	2,425	10.8	6.6	3.0	2.2	D	33.2
Kane County, IL	23,971	19,825	16,901	45,156	38,416	17.5	14,403	16.8	5.3	4.2	7.0	10.6	17.6
Gary, IN Division	*29,181*	*24,638*	*21,308*	*41,507*	*34,785*	*19.3*	*17,253*	*21.2*	*6.5*	*2.6*	*D*	*D*	*11.0*
Jasper County, IN	1,395	1,120	937	41,677	33,417	24.7	786	21.7	5.8	1.9	1.6	D	11.1
Lake County, IN	19,464	16,779	14,582	39,896	33,830	17.9	12,466	20.8	6.6	2.6	3.9	15.9	11.3
Newton County, IN	524	438	394	37,437	30,781	21.6	221	16.8	3.1	3.2	D	5.0	15.0
Porter County, IN	7,798	6,301	5,394	46,501	38,291	21.4	3,780	22.5	6.6	2.7	5.0	13.7	9.8
Lake County-Kenosha County, IL-WI Division	*56,121*	*45,729*	*40,882*	*64,333*	*52,507*	*22.5*	*39,463*	*22.6*	*7.1*	*5.0*	*8.4*	*7.0*	*13.1*
Lake County, IL	49,152	39,897	35,719	69,827	56,648	23.3	35,640	23.4	7.1	5.4	9.0	6.3	12.6
Kenosha County, WI	6,969	5,832	5,162	41,373	35,002	18.2	3,823	14.5	7.3	1.6	3.1	13.9	17.8
Chico, CA Metro Area	9,010	7,280	6,167	39,971	33,093	20.8	5,185	5.1	9.0	3.8	5.0	20.1	22.6
Butte County, CA	9,010	7,280	6,167	39,971	33,093	20.8	5,185	5.1	9.0	3.8	5.0	20.1	22.6
Cincinnati, OH-KY-IN Metro Area	101,960	85,152	74,684	47,254	40,207	17.5	75,932	D	5.5	7.0	8.4	12.3	11.6
Dearborn County, IN	2,075	1,753	1,622	41,953	34,985	19.9	817	15.6	8.5	2.8	2.8	8.5	21.6
Ohio County, IN	216	268	248	36,368	43,781	-16.9	74	D	3.0	D	D	3.7	21.5
Union County, IN	242	211	198	33,714	27,993	20.4	81	18.8	7.7	D	2.1	D	25.2
Boone County, KY	5,446	4,415	3,913	42,645	36,988	15.3	4,953	18.4	6.3	4.3	4.1	6.1	8.8
Bracken County, KY	275	246	214	33,058	28,975	14.1	82	D	3.0	1.9	D	6.5	25.5
Campbell County, KY	3,974	3,283	2,840	43,164	36,229	19.1	1,763	12.1	7.4	2.5	6.7	12.4	23.8
Gallatin County, KY	253	192	191	29,322	22,330	31.3	161	D	3.4	1.0	2.9	3.9	14.6
Grant County, KY	795	694	577	32,114	28,102	14.3	278	14.8	11.0	2.0	5.5	D	23.7
Kenton County, KY	8,164	6,936	5,703	49,475	43,347	14.1	4,803	8.7	4.8	9.7	7.1	14.8	15.4
Pendleton County, KY	489	406	343	33,951	27,251	24.6	147	16.0	3.3	1.5	4.3	8.0	23.3
Brown County, OH	1,422	1,265	1,078	32,436	28,193	15.0	491	9.6	6.7	2.2	2.4	D	24.5
Butler County, OH	15,631	12,985	11,435	41,534	35,184	18.0	10,403	19.6	7.2	7.8	3.5	10.4	13.0
Clermont County, OH	9,345	7,422	6,316	46,267	37,543	23.2	4,502	10.1	7.7	6.6	6.2	7.4	11.4
Hamilton County, OH	42,061	35,928	32,535	52,081	44,784	16.3	41,291	11.7	4.3	7.3	11.0	14.5	10.2
Warren County, OH	11,572	9,148	7,411	51,553	42,842	20.3	6,087	16.0	8.0	6.3	7.1	9.3	11.2
Clarksville, TN-KY Metro Area	10,834	9,395	7,328	38,554	35,902	7.4	7,715	8.9	5.4	1.9	2.8	D	50.7
Christian County, KY	2,713	2,399	2,073	37,011	32,351	14.4	4,581	8.2	2.1	1.0	2.1	5.0	68.8
Trigg County, KY	498	457	404	34,991	31,860	9.8	164	16.8	8.9	3.2	2.6	D	24.1
Montgomery County, TN	7,623	6,539	4,851	39,400	37,757	4.4	2,970	9.5	10.4	3.1	4.0	13.4	24.3
Cleveland, TN Metro Area	4,393	3,569	3,001	36,344	30,780	18.1	2,746	23.5	7.3	2.5	2.5	D	12.0
Bradley County, TN	3,874	3,118	2,607	37,216	31,446	18.3	2,601	24.4	7.3	2.5	2.5	D	10.9
Polk County, TN	519	451	394	30,937	26,854	15.2	144	7.8	7.7	2.1	2.2	D	31.1
Cleveland-Elyria, OH Metro Area	98,472	81,783	75,290	47,783	39,401	21.3	74,587	13.7	5.0	6.7	9.1	14.3	14.0
Cuyahoga County, OH	60,919	51,092	47,799	48,506	39,971	21.4	55,821	10.5	4.2	8.1	10.7	15.7	14.0
Geauga County, OH	5,771	4,630	4,329	61,323	49,565	23.7	2,592	20.8	6.6	2.4	5.1	9.4	10.0
Lake County, OH	10,498	8,701	7,951	45,793	37,828	21.1	6,102	28.3	7.1	2.1	4.5	9.8	13.0
Lorain County, OH	12,624	10,385	9,085	41,371	34,448	20.1	6,199	23.4	7.1	3.0	3.8	11.3	17.8
Medina County, OH	8,660	6,974	6,127	49,097	40,422	21.5	3,872	16.3	8.1	2.5	5.0	8.4	12.2
Coeur d'Alene, ID Metro Area	5,804	4,396	3,706	38,605	31,646	22.0	3,201	8.7	10.6	5.1	5.7	12.5	21.0
Kootenai County, ID	5,804	4,396	3,706	38,605	31,646	22.0	3,201	8.7	10.6	5.1	5.7	12.5	21.0
College Station-Bryan, TX Metro Area	8,919	6,823	4,960	35,797	29,734	20.4	6,498	4.7	6.7	2.7	D	D	33.4
Brazos County, TX	7,519	5,694	4,116	34,964	29,098	20.2	5,883	4.8	6.7	2.8	7.2	10.0	35.2
Burleson County, TX	731	583	429	41,880	33,882	23.6	317	6.2	7.2	2.7	D	D	13.0
Robertson County, TX	669	546	415	40,181	32,927	22.0	299	2.8	4.8	2.0	3.1	4.3	18.4
Colorado Springs, CO Metro Area	30,320	24,527	20,175	43,447	37,712	15.2	20,805	D	6.2	4.7	12.5	9.6	32.5
El Paso County, CO	29,262	23,634	19,452	43,385	37,699	15.1	20,381	4.3	6.2	4.8	12.6	9.7	32.9
Teller County, CO	1,057	893	723	45,219	38,085	18.7	425	D	7.2	2.4	8.2	5.5	16.3
Columbia, MO Metro Area	7,402	6,051	4,896	42,302	37,075	14.1	5,880	4.5	7.0	5.8	6.4	11.2	36.3
Boone County, MO	7,402	6,051	4,896	42,302	37,075	14.1	5,880	4.5	7.0	5.8	6.4	11.2	36.3
Columbia, SC Metro Area	32,743	26,305	21,905	40,420	34,176	18.3	24,653	10.8	6.1	6.7	7.3	9.3	25.5
Calhoun County, SC	501	447	411	33,874	29,602	14.4	271	40.8	2.7	0.7	2.0	D	14.5
Fairfield County, SC	765	682	575	33,633	28,604	17.6	883	41.4	2.0	0.4	10.4	D	8.8
Kershaw County, SC	2,364	1,959	1,646	37,163	31,761	17.0	1,127	20.1	8.3	5.3	3.5	6.2	17.2

[1] Based on resident population estimated on July 1 of the year shown.
[2] Includes other industry categories not shown separately.
D = not shown to avoid disclosure of confidential information.

Table C-3.   Personal Income and Earnings by Industry—*Continued*

| | Personal Income | | | | | | Earnings 2015 | | | | | | |
| | Total (million dollars) | | | Per capita[1] (dollars) | | Percent change, 2010–2015 | Total[2] (million dollars) | Percent by selected major industries | | | | | |
Metropolitan statistical area, division, and component county	2015	2010	2005	2015	2010			Manu-facturing	Retail trade	Finance and insurance	Profes-sional and technical services	Health care and social services	Govern-ment and govern-ment enter-prises
Lexington County, SC	11,770	9,064	7,613	41,764	34,416	21.4	7,236	14.6	8.0	3.0	4.5	6.4	19.1
Richland County, SC	16,699	13,578	11,141	41,025	35,196	16.6	14,904	5.5	5.3	9.3	9.0	11.6	30.5
Saluda County, SC	644	574	519	32,113	28,853	11.3	232	34.9	4.2	1.4	1.1	D	21.7
Columbus, GA-AL Metro Area	11,447	9,775	8,619	36,484	32,968	10.7	8,743	D	5.0	D	5.4	D	37.5
Russell County, AL	1,730	1,490	1,171	29,001	27,956	3.7	698	26.0	8.9	4.0	1.4	10.2	21.3
Chattahoochee County, GA	403	353	306	35,448	31,590	12.2	1,562	D	0.2	D	3.9	0.2	91.1
Harris County, GA	1,399	1,158	906	41,900	36,015	16.3	250	16.7	2.2	2.7	D	D	24.6
Marion County, GA	213	175	160	24,273	20,020	21.2	70	19.0	4.9	D	D	6.1	24.9
Muscogee County, GA	7,702	6,599	6,076	38,401	34,527	11.2	6,163	7.4	6.0	16.4	6.4	13.0	26.4
Columbus, IN Metro Area	3,699	2,875	2,360	45,575	37,411	21.8	3,541	48.5	4.0	2.8	4.2	7.1	9.2
Bartholomew County, IN	3,699	2,875	2,360	45,575	37,411	21.8	3,541	48.5	4.0	2.8	4.2	7.1	9.2
Columbus, OH Metro Area	94,148	73,062	62,370	46,570	38,324	21.5	75,364	8.2	5.6	8.3	9.4	10.8	18.2
Delaware County, OH	12,475	9,393	7,786	64,634	53,629	20.5	6,619	8.1	6.4	11.4	11.6	6.9	8.5
Fairfield County, OH	6,230	5,115	4,358	41,145	34,943	17.7	2,413	11.3	9.2	2.2	3.8	16.5	19.0
Franklin County, OH	58,767	45,081	39,067	46,949	38,653	21.5	57,374	6.0	5.1	8.9	9.7	11.5	19.3
Hocking County, OH	959	813	691	33,675	27,596	22.0	368	14.5	7.7	3.1	1.7	8.9	30.2
Licking County, OH	7,093	5,753	4,706	41,581	34,506	20.5	3,388	13.6	9.4	6.7	5.5	11.4	16.0
Madison County, OH	1,620	1,336	1,232	36,730	30,796	19.3	1,043	27.6	6.7	1.0	D	D	21.8
Morrow County, OH	1,199	1,015	864	34,181	29,148	17.3	387	16.3	5.9	1.1	D	D	24.2
Perry County, OH	1,204	990	827	33,469	27,459	21.9	347	12.3	6.4	2.4	2.3	D	25.4
Pickaway County, OH	2,096	1,728	1,366	36,775	30,995	18.6	985	22.1	5.5	1.8	D	8.3	28.4
Union County, OH	2,505	1,839	1,473	46,143	35,075	31.6	2,440	33.5	3.6	1.2	D	3.3	10.5
Corpus Christi, TX Metro Area	19,328	15,231	12,276	42,721	35,586	20.1	14,030	9.9	6.1	2.9	5.9	D	17.8
Aransas County, TX	1,124	855	695	44,321	36,849	20.3	400	1.2	13.0	4.0	8.8	D	14.7
Nueces County, TX	15,417	12,184	9,929	42,859	35,804	19.7	12,215	10.2	5.9	3.0	5.9	12.9	17.1
San Patricio County, TX	2,788	2,191	1,652	41,386	33,985	21.8	1,415	10.3	6.4	1.5	5.1	4.7	24.2
Corvallis, OR Metro Area	3,650	3,039	2,701	41,676	35,519	17.3	2,584	11.2	4.7	2.0	9.0	16.0	31.0
Benton County, OR	3,650	3,039	2,701	41,676	35,519	17.3	2,584	11.2	4.7	2.0	9.0	16.0	31.0
Crestview-Fort Walton Beach-Destin, FL Metro Area	12,149	9,612	8,647	46,340	40,727	13.8	8,028	3.6	8.0	3.0	10.1	7.9	38.2
Okaloosa County, FL	8,984	7,426	6,950	45,222	41,084	10.1	6,569	4.0	6.6	3.4	11.0	7.5	43.7
Walton County, FL	3,165	2,186	1,697	49,839	39,562	26.0	1,460	1.5	14.5	1.5	6.1	9.7	13.5
Cumberland, MD-WV Metro Area	3,683	3,294	2,794	36,836	31,904	15.5	2,180	13.9	7.4	3.0	D	D	24.6
Allegany County, MD	2,699	2,407	2,123	37,214	32,085	16.0	1,735	9.3	7.6	3.4	D	22.3	26.0
Mineral County, WV	984	887	671	35,838	31,423	14.1	446	31.7	7.0	1.5	2.6	D	18.8
Dallas-Fort Worth-Arlington, TX Metro Area	**362,948**	**262,061**	**215,828**	**51,099**	**40,613**	**25.8**	**292,806**	**9.2**	**5.9**	**8.6**	**10.7**	**D**	**10.2**
Dallas-Plano-Irving, TX Division	*248,157*	*176,104*	*147,423*	*52,719*	*41,450*	*27.2*	*213,808*	*8.3*	*5.7*	*9.5*	*12.5*	*9.3*	*9.6*
Collin County, TX	54,420	38,533	31,429	59,532	48,860	21.8	34,535	8.2	7.7	10.3	13.1	9.9	8.8
Dallas County, TX	135,803	95,837	84,108	53,186	40,379	31.7	154,196	7.6	4.9	10.1	13.2	9.1	8.9
Denton County, TX	39,118	27,362	20,757	50,112	41,025	22.1	16,476	7.8	7.7	6.0	9.1	9.9	14.2
Ellis County, TX	6,504	4,938	3,828	39,747	32,840	21.0	3,034	24.5	7.1	2.2	D	6.7	13.6
Hunt County, TX	3,101	2,546	2,149	34,511	29,495	17.0	1,991	36.7	6.0	2.0	3.6	6.7	20.2
Kaufman County, TX	4,370	3,342	2,605	38,106	32,170	18.5	1,765	14.1	8.4	3.0	D	7.3	20.7
Rockwall County, TX	4,841	3,545	2,549	53,285	44,896	18.7	1,811	7.0	9.8	3.4	9.3	16.8	12.2
Fort Worth-Arlington, TX Division	*114,790*	*85,958*	*68,405*	*47,916*	*39,001*	*22.9*	*78,998*	*11.6*	*6.4*	*6.2*	*5.9*	*D*	*11.8*
Hood County, TX	2,610	1,961	1,429	47,088	38,243	23.1	1,171	5.1	8.4	5.5	D	10.1	9.6
Johnson County, TX	6,165	4,902	3,800	38,533	32,405	18.9	2,874	16.5	9.1	2.0	3.1	8.2	14.6
Parker County, TX	6,335	4,592	3,337	50,257	39,137	28.4	2,481	8.6	8.6	2.6	5.0	7.5	12.3
Somervell County, TX	383	299	198	43,880	35,231	24.5	355	1.4	1.7	0.4	4.7	D	13.5
Tarrant County, TX	96,601	72,173	58,158	48,727	39,731	22.6	70,553	11.7	6.2	6.6	6.1	9.6	11.6
Wise County, TX	2,697	2,031	1,481	42,837	34,357	24.7	1,564	10.3	6.4	2.0	D	D	16.1
Dalton, GA Metro Area	4,535	3,645	3,508	31,539	25,609	23.2	3,872	35.3	7.4	1.5	D	D	10.1
Murray County, GA	1,063	911	860	26,855	23,046	16.5	483	40.3	7.2	2.1	D	D	15.9
Whitfield County, GA	3,472	2,733	2,648	33,317	26,595	25.3	3,390	34.6	7.4	1.4	7.8	9.4	9.3
Danville, IL Metro Area	2,825	2,617	2,193	35,630	32,062	11.1	1,776	21.9	6.7	4.2	1.6	9.7	22.5
Vermilion County, IL	2,825	2,617	2,193	35,630	32,062	11.1	1,776	21.9	6.7	4.2	1.6	9.7	22.5
Daphne-Fairhope-Foley, AL Metro Area	8,173	6,612	5,350	40,121	36,090	11.2	3,626	6.9	12.8	3.7	5.2	13.0	14.4
Baldwin County, AL	8,173	6,612	5,350	40,121	36,090	11.2	3,626	6.9	12.8	3.7	5.2	13.0	14.4
Davenport-Moline-Rock Island, IA-IL Metro Area	17,039	15,153	12,733	44,418	39,850	11.5	12,194	15.4	6.2	4.2	D	11.8	16.2
Henry County, IL	2,079	1,843	1,532	42,010	36,531	15.0	871	17.0	7.2	4.9	D	9.7	23.3
Mercer County, IL	642	612	489	40,487	37,262	8.7	174	14.1	7.6	4.7	1.4	13.4	25.6
Rock Island County, IL	5,894	5,488	4,833	40,332	37,171	8.5	5,671	13.2	5.0	4.1	5.2	10.2	20.2
Scott County, IA	8,424	7,211	5,880	48,943	43,504	12.5	5,478	17.5	7.4	4.2	4.6	13.6	10.6
Dayton, OH Metro Area	34,205	28,939	26,349	42,707	36,160	18.1	25,278	12.3	5.4	4.5	8.9	15.3	22.6
Greene County, OH	7,377	6,166	5,462	44,862	38,152	17.6	5,809	4.4	5.2	2.0	15.8	7.0	47.0
Miami County, OH	4,355	3,660	3,120	41,781	35,713	17.0	2,389	29.7	7.6	2.3	3.7	9.2	13.3
Montgomery County, OH	22,474	19,113	17,766	42,223	35,644	18.5	17,080	12.5	5.1	5.7	7.3	19.0	15.6
Decatur, AL Metro Area	5,416	4,806	4,037	35,472	31,228	13.6	3,152	30.4	6.6	3.3	3.9	D	14.9
Lawrence County, AL	1,070	945	777	32,320	27,542	17.3	286	3.8	8.9	4.4	1.6	D	24.9
Morgan County, AL	4,346	3,861	3,260	36,345	32,285	12.6	2,865	33.1	6.4	3.2	4.2	7.6	13.9
Decatur, IL Metro Area	4,762	4,308	3,580	44,383	38,889	14.1	3,727	30.8	5.0	3.2	3.7	12.5	10.7
Macon County, IL	4,762	4,308	3,580	44,383	38,889	14.1	3,727	30.8	5.0	3.2	3.7	12.5	10.7

[1]Based on resident population estimated on July 1 of the year shown.
[2]Includes other industry categories not shown separately.
D = not shown to avoid disclosure of confidential information.

Table C-3. Personal Income and Earnings by Industry—*Continued*

| | Personal Income | | | | | | Earnings 2015 | | | | | | |
| | Total (million dollars) | | | Per capita[1] (dollars) | | | | | Percent by selected major industries | | | | |
Metropolitan statistical area, division, and component county	2015	2010	2005	2015	2010	Percent change, 2010–2015	Total[2] (million dollars)	Manu-facturing	Retail trade	Finance and insurance	Profes-sional and technical services	Health care and social services	Govern-ment and govern-ment enter-prises
Deltona-Daytona Beach-Ormond Beach, FL Metro Area	23,808	19,695	17,317	38,197	33,342	14.6	10,409	7.3	10.2	3.3	6.2	17.9	15.0
Flagler County, FL	4,230	3,181	2,483	40,140	33,114	21.2	1,212	5.6	10.5	3.3	6.6	12.5	18.3
Volusia County, FL	19,577	16,513	14,834	37,802	33,386	13.2	9,197	7.5	10.2	3.3	6.2	18.6	14.6
Denver-Aurora-Lakewood, CO Metro Area	157,532	109,387	98,298	55,975	42,822	30.7	124,486	5.0	4.6	D	13.2	8.3	12.3
Adams County, CO	18,161	13,443	11,510	36,962	30,299	22.0	13,912	7.9	5.7	1.6	4.5	8.4	22.2
Arapahoe County, CO	33,161	22,758	21,998	52,545	39,598	32.7	27,149	2.3	6.0	12.0	14.5	10.6	9.8
Broomfield County, CO	4,757	3,944	2,911	73,107	70,094	4.3	3,721	16.3	4.5	4.5	17.8	2.8	2.6
Clear Creek County, CO	481	393	373	51,710	43,237	19.6	240	D	3.6	D	7.4	D	16.6
Denver County, CO	46,617	28,830	25,654	68,299	47,786	42.9	50,620	3.2	2.5	7.6	13.5	6.6	11.5
Douglas County, CO	21,277	15,279	12,531	65,999	53,243	24.0	10,174	1.8	6.6	8.5	16.6	8.0	7.4
Elbert County, CO	1,223	900	882	49,450	38,954	26.9	249	2.8	6.3	2.5	10.7	2.7	17.0
Gilpin County, CO	237	191	239	40,702	34,953	16.4	291	D	0.4	0.2	D	D	10.0
Jefferson County, CO	30,975	23,133	21,699	54,773	43,189	26.8	17,973	11.7	6.6	4.0	14.5	11.2	14.9
Park County, CO	643	517	501	38,916	31,764	22.5	158	2.3	5.3	1.7	D	1.6	25.0
Des Moines-West Des Moines, IA Metro Area	30,781	24,171	20,088	49,415	42,259	16.9	24,952	5.9	5.6	20.8	7.7	10.4	12.9
Dallas County, IA	4,760	3,260	2,455	59,405	48,876	21.5	2,893	4.2	6.9	43.2	4.7	7.7	7.7
Guthrie County, IA	569	430	374	53,340	39,265	35.8	313	21.7	2.7	6.7	2.8	4.9	15.4
Madison County, IA	698	588	407	44,301	37,387	18.5	239	6.5	7.0	4.9	3.4	6.1	22.8
Polk County, IA	22,593	18,142	15,383	48,306	41,968	15.1	20,844	5.8	5.4	18.6	8.3	10.8	13.3
Warren County, IA	2,159	1,752	1,409	44,410	37,808	17.5	663	5.9	8.8	3.8	4.2	10.7	20.8
Detroit-Warren-Dearborn, MI Metro Area	**201,741**	**162,372**	**163,566**	**46,894**	**37,837**	**23.9**	**148,970**	**14.6**	**5.5**	**5.3**	**D**	**11.9**	**9.9**
Detroit-Dearborn-Livonia, MI Division	*67,756*	*58,536*	*57,978*	*38,512*	*32,248*	*19.4*	*56,498*	*15.0*	*4.5*	*4.3*	*D*	*13.6*	*12.2*
Wayne County, MI	67,756	58,536	57,978	38,512	32,248	19.4	56,498	15.0	4.5	4.3	D	13.6	12.2
Warren-Troy-Farmington Hills, MI Division	*133,986*	*103,836*	*105,588*	*52,694*	*41,935*	*25.7*	*92,471*	*14.4*	*6.1*	*5.9*	*D*	*10.8*	*8.4*
Lapeer County, MI	3,395	2,724	2,596	38,417	30,882	24.4	1,251	24.1	8.2	2.7	3.1	7.0	20.2
Livingston County, MI	9,292	7,133	6,981	49,608	39,403	25.9	3,542	19.3	8.0	4.4	9.2	8.7	11.5
Macomb County, MI	36,191	28,822	29,139	41,847	34,261	22.1	23,585	23.5	6.7	2.1	12.8	10.3	12.9
Oakland County, MI	78,829	59,932	61,827	63,454	49,821	27.4	61,252	10.3	5.7	7.7	20.3	11.0	5.9
St. Clair County, MI	6,278	5,224	5,046	39,268	32,115	22.3	2,841	18.3	7.6	2.8	D	15.5	16.5
Dothan, AL Metro Area	5,464	4,917	4,087	36,879	33,705	9.4	3,248	7.3	9.7	3.3	4.0	D	18.8
Geneva County, AL	861	775	648	32,155	28,934	11.1	312	10.1	6.8	3.1	1.8	4.6	21.3
Henry County, AL	615	536	458	35,727	30,968	15.4	221	14.0	5.1	2.8	11.9	D	15.9
Houston County, AL	3,988	3,606	2,981	38,284	35,427	8.1	2,715	6.4	10.4	3.3	3.6	18.3	18.7
Dover, DE Metro Area	6,625	5,514	4,568	38,178	33,831	12.8	4,339	D	7.4	2.9	4.0	12.3	37.9
Kent County, DE	6,625	5,514	4,568	38,178	33,831	12.8	4,339	D	7.4	2.9	4.0	12.3	37.9
Dubuque, IA Metro Area	4,273	3,453	2,734	43,997	36,767	19.7	3,396	20.0	6.1	8.9	6.3	14.0	8.4
Dubuque County, IA	4,273	3,453	2,734	43,997	36,767	19.7	3,396	20.0	6.1	8.9	6.3	14.0	8.4
Duluth, MN-WI Metro Area	11,610	10,073	8,060	41,523	36,007	15.3	7,920	6.9	6.9	3.6	4.8	20.7	19.6
Carlton County, MN	1,347	1,150	935	37,872	32,478	16.6	784	14.8	5.9	3.7	3.1	10.0	35.7
St. Louis County, MN	8,580	7,471	5,958	42,805	37,327	14.7	6,082	5.1	7.0	3.9	5.4	24.4	17.5
Douglas County, WI	1,683	1,451	1,167	38,603	32,853	17.5	1,054	11.0	6.6	2.1	2.6	7.3	20.1
Durham-Chapel Hill, NC Metro Area	26,250	21,211	16,981	47,513	41,744	13.8	24,634	15.6	3.6	5.6	13.8	15.4	19.9
Chatham County, NC	3,677	3,013	2,283	51,839	44,057	17.7	869	13.0	7.7	2.0	10.0	13.2	16.3
Durham County, NC	13,395	10,750	8,293	44,507	39,684	12.2	17,770	19.9	2.9	6.6	15.9	18.4	9.5
Orange County, NC	7,822	6,455	5,353	55,338	48,156	14.9	5,413	2.0	4.9	3.1	8.8	6.4	54.8
Person County, NC	1,357	1,197	1,052	34,557	30,352	13.9	583	17.8	7.7	2.1	2.7	10.3	17.1
East Stroudsburg, PA Metro Area	6,330	5,396	4,767	38,043	31,756	19.8	3,547	14.6	8.3	1.8	2.3	12.1	26.1
Monroe County, PA	6,330	5,396	4,767	38,043	31,756	19.8	3,547	14.6	8.3	1.8	2.3	12.1	26.1
Eau Claire, WI Metro Area	7,168	5,780	4,638	43,276	35,755	21.0	5,218	14.8	8.4	4.3	4.0	18.9	15.6
Chippewa County, WI	2,701	2,164	1,714	42,518	34,558	23.0	1,623	27.7	9.1	1.5	2.7	9.6	14.6
Eau Claire County, WI	4,467	3,616	2,924	43,747	36,512	19.8	3,595	9.1	8.1	5.6	4.6	23.1	16.1
El Centro, CA Metro Area	6,052	5,052	3,771	33,584	28,911	16.2	4,203	1.7	7.9	1.4	1.8	6.0	38.8
Imperial County, CA	6,052	5,052	3,771	33,584	28,911	16.2	4,203	1.7	7.9	1.4	1.8	6.0	38.8
Elizabethtown-Fort Knox, KY Metro Area	5,596	5,013	3,967	37,656	33,431	12.6	3,833	14.5	6.0	D	3.3	D	42.8
Hardin County, KY	4,148	3,748	2,943	38,972	35,021	11.3	3,434	14.5	5.9	2.7	3.5	6.1	45.1
Larue County, KY	473	396	347	33,232	27,915	19.0	135	16.5	5.0	D	1.4	10.6	24.9
Meade County, KY	974	869	677	34,894	30,235	15.4	264	13.1	8.1	2.5	2.7	D	21.9
Elkhart-Goshen, IN Metro Area	8,115	5,976	5,869	39,882	30,260	31.8	8,045	49.1	4.2	1.7	2.2	7.8	6.0
Elkhart County, IN	8,115	5,976	5,869	39,882	30,260	31.8	8,045	49.1	4.2	1.7	2.2	7.8	6.0
Elmira, NY Metro Area	3,496	3,116	2,568	40,149	35,020	14.6	2,424	16.5	7.2	4.2	2.4	15.6	25.0
Chemung County, NY	3,496	3,116	2,568	40,149	35,020	14.6	2,424	16.5	7.2	4.2	2.4	15.6	25.0
El Paso, TX Metro Area	27,349	22,659	16,585	32,598	28,074	16.1	19,012	D	7.8	D	D	9.9	37.1
El Paso County, TX	27,252	22,589	16,529	32,614	28,108	16.0	18,913	5.9	7.9	2.4	3.5	10.0	37.0
Hudspeth County, TX	97	70	56	28,621	20,145	42.1	98	D	0.7	D	D	1.3	62.7
Enid, OK Metro Area	2,860	2,363	1,791	44,985	38,890	15.7	2,016	7.6	6.3	3.2	6.1	10.5	16.7
Garfield County, OK	2,860	2,363	1,791	44,985	38,890	15.7	2,016	7.6	6.3	3.2	6.1	10.5	16.7
Erie, PA Metro Area	11,240	9,662	8,150	40,425	34,412	17.5	7,787	21.8	6.7	6.4	3.6	17.4	16.0
Erie County, PA	11,240	9,662	8,150	40,425	34,412	17.5	7,787	21.8	6.7	6.4	3.6	17.4	16.0
Eugene, OR Metro Area	14,469	11,740	10,320	39,871	33,355	19.5	9,347	9.8	8.1	4.1	5.2	16.4	18.8
Lane County, OR	14,469	11,740	10,320	39,871	33,355	19.5	9,347	9.8	8.1	4.1	5.2	16.4	18.8

[1]Based on resident population estimated on July 1 of the year shown.
[2]Includes other industry categories not shown separately.
D = not shown to avoid disclosure of confidential information.

Table C-3.   Personal Income and Earnings by Industry—*Continued*

Metropolitan statistical area, division, and component county	Total (million dollars) 2015	2010	2005	Per capita[1] (dollars) 2015	2010	Percent change, 2010–2015	Earnings 2015 Total[2] (million dollars)	Manu-facturing	Retail trade	Finance and insurance	Profes-sional and technical services	Health care and social services	Govern-ment and govern-ment enter-prises
Evansville, IN-KY Metro Area	13,288	11,621	9,821	42,091	37,269	12.9	9,718	20.5	6.2	2.8	5.0	D	9.7
Posey County, IN	1,140	967	808	44,674	37,397	19.5	712	45.0	6.3	1.7	3.9	D	8.3
Vanderburgh County, IN	7,434	6,784	5,717	40,875	37,717	8.4	6,691	16.4	6.4	2.8	5.5	18.5	9.2
Warrick County, IN	3,008	2,419	1,951	48,593	40,422	20.2	1,166	20.0	5.1	4.2	5.5	22.8	9.9
Henderson County, KY	1,706	1,451	1,345	36,766	31,370	17.2	1,150	29.9	6.3	2.5	2.2	11.8	13.5
Fairbanks, AK Metro Area	5,399	4,460	3,308	54,185	45,379	19.4	3,877	1.1	5.5	1.4	3.1	9.4	46.4
Fairbanks North Star Borough, AK	5,399	4,460	3,308	54,185	45,379	19.4	3,877	1.1	5.5	1.4	3.1	9.4	46.4
Fargo, ND-MN Metro Area	11,689	8,356	6,247	49,987	39,900	25.3	9,059	8.6	7.9	7.5	6.2	D	13.7
Clay County, MN	2,504	2,002	1,499	40,177	33,839	18.7	1,234	10.4	7.1	2.0	3.3	D	21.9
Cass County, ND	9,185	6,354	4,748	53,552	42,286	26.6	7,825	8.3	8.0	8.4	6.6	13.9	12.4
Farmington, NM Metro Area	4,485	3,953	3,092	37,777	30,373	24.4	3,227	2.4	8.2	1.7	2.3	11.9	21.2
San Juan County, NM	4,485	3,953	3,092	37,777	30,373	24.4	3,227	2.4	8.2	1.7	2.3	11.9	21.2
Fayetteville, NC Metro Area	13,727	12,106	10,096	36,460	32,932	10.7	12,357	4.6	4.5	1.2	D	D	62.6
Cumberland County, NC	12,180	10,819	9,202	37,611	33,792	11.3	11,916	4.0	4.5	1.2	3.4	5.5	63.8
Hoke County, NC	1,548	1,288	894	29,382	27,129	8.3	440	19.4	4.7	0.9	D	D	31.8
Fayetteville-Springdale-Rogers, AR-MO Metro Area	26,967	17,528	13,731	52,509	37,629	39.5	15,534	9.8	5.8	2.2	5.9	8.8	12.0
Benton County, AR	17,923	10,828	7,918	71,787	48,553	47.9	8,434	6.9	5.1	1.9	7.3	5.8	6.7
Madison County, AR	494	374	348	31,356	23,854	31.4	233	22.7	6.6	1.5	2.2	4.1	13.2
Washington County, AR	7,938	5,813	4,989	35,205	28,492	23.6	6,503	11.6	6.7	2.8	4.4	13.1	18.7
McDonald County, MO	611	513	475	26,988	22,216	21.5	365	36.3	7.4	1.7	0.8	2.9	14.5
Flagstaff, AZ Metro Area	5,705	4,563	3,729	41,018	33,894	21.0	3,786	10.4	6.9	1.3	2.6	15.0	32.5
Coconino County, AZ	5,705	4,563	3,729	41,018	33,894	21.0	3,786	10.4	6.9	1.3	2.6	15.0	32.5
Flint, MI Metro Area	15,042	12,835	12,225	36,612	30,195	21.3	8,530	12.3	9.3	4.5	4.2	18.2	16.2
Genesee County, MI	15,042	12,835	12,225	36,612	30,195	21.3	8,530	12.3	9.3	4.5	4.2	18.2	16.2
Florence, SC Metro Area	7,459	6,426	5,484	36,130	31,241	15.6	5,094	16.6	7.1	9.0	4.7	13.0	19.1
Darlington County, SC	2,275	1,983	1,772	33,680	28,904	16.5	1,281	29.5	5.2	2.1	1.8	10.4	13.1
Florence County, SC	5,184	4,443	3,713	37,322	32,410	15.2	3,814	12.2	7.8	11.3	5.6	13.9	21.1
Florence-Muscle Shoals, AL Metro Area	5,206	4,621	3,856	35,427	31,381	12.9	3,017	19.3	9.1	3.9	2.7	12.8	19.7
Colbert County, AL	1,948	1,731	1,460	35,831	31,755	12.8	1,488	28.0	6.8	3.0	1.5	8.0	20.8
Lauderdale County, AL	3,258	2,890	2,396	35,189	31,161	12.9	1,530	10.8	11.2	4.9	3.9	17.4	18.7
Fond du Lac, WI Metro Area	4,463	3,747	3,179	43,764	36,838	18.8	3,004	25.4	6.3	3.7	2.6	12.7	12.8
Fond du Lac County, WI	4,463	3,747	3,179	43,764	36,838	18.8	3,004	25.4	6.3	3.7	2.6	12.7	12.8
Fort Collins, CO Metro Area	15,117	11,106	9,409	45,318	36,955	22.6	10,041	13.6	6.8	3.2	11.3	8.7	22.1
Larimer County, CO	15,117	11,106	9,409	45,318	36,955	22.6	10,041	13.6	6.8	3.2	11.3	8.7	22.1
Fort Smith, AR-OK Metro Area	9,546	8,240	6,812	34,065	29,357	16.0	6,383	15.8	6.5	2.5	D	13.8	15.7
Crawford County, AR	1,846	1,661	1,297	29,917	26,801	11.6	981	21.7	6.6	2.0	D	6.8	12.4
Sebastian County, AR	4,853	4,083	3,571	37,983	32,462	17.0	4,111	17.9	6.3	2.6	3.4	17.2	11.3
Le Flore County, OK	1,579	1,370	1,077	31,837	27,138	17.3	848	6.4	5.9	2.2	D	D	30.5
Sequoyah County, OK	1,268	1,126	867	30,807	26,524	16.1	442	1.7	9.6	3.3	D	D	35.6
Fort Wayne, IN Metro Area	17,666	14,230	12,561	41,102	34,131	20.4	13,164	19.4	6.2	6.3	D	17.8	9.7
Allen County, IN	15,301	12,212	10,805	41,528	34,313	21.0	11,869	17.3	6.3	6.8	5.0	18.9	9.6
Wells County, IN	1,058	920	801	37,823	33,250	13.8	593	29.3	5.1	2.1	D	11.2	10.6
Whitley County, IN	1,308	1,098	955	39,145	32,924	18.9	702	46.0	5.2	1.9	0.9	6.2	10.3
Fresno, CA Metro Area	37,360	29,472	24,573	38,323	31,607	21.2	24,708	6.6	6.7	3.5	4.2	13.9	22.8
Fresno County, CA	37,360	29,472	24,573	38,323	31,607	21.2	24,708	6.6	6.7	3.5	4.2	13.9	22.8
Gadsden, AL Metro Area	3,513	3,175	2,686	34,086	30,404	12.1	1,897	16.0	8.5	3.8	2.8	22.4	15.0
Etowah County, AL	3,513	3,175	2,686	34,086	30,404	12.1	1,897	16.0	8.5	3.8	2.8	22.4	15.0
Gainesville, FL Metro Area	10,990	9,228	7,827	39,650	34,871	13.7	8,260	3.8	5.5	4.4	6.2	D	38.7
Alachua County, FL	10,450	8,785	7,460	40,199	35,477	13.3	8,053	3.8	5.5	4.4	6.3	17.6	39.0
Gilchrist County, FL	539	443	367	31,356	26,045	20.4	208	1.1	3.5	1.0	1.5	D	28.7
Gainesville, GA Metro Area	7,083	5,472	4,800	36,597	30,401	20.4	5,235	21.1	6.8	3.8	3.4	16.9	11.5
Hall County, GA	7,083	5,472	4,800	36,597	30,401	20.4	5,235	21.1	6.8	3.8	3.4	16.9	11.5
Gettysburg, PA Metro Area	4,606	3,817	3,174	45,023	37,618	19.7	2,095	19.8	6.3	2.3	4.0	D	15.6
Adams County, PA	4,606	3,817	3,174	45,023	37,618	19.7	2,095	19.8	6.3	2.3	4.0	D	15.6
Glens Falls, NY Metro Area	5,343	4,668	3,782	42,101	36,192	16.3	3,398	13.6	8.0	3.3	D	12.8	23.7
Warren County, NY	3,068	2,692	2,161	47,429	40,988	15.7	2,305	10.6	8.9	4.3	5.3	15.4	16.5
Washington County, NY	2,275	1,976	1,621	36,563	31,214	17.1	1,093	19.8	6.3	1.2	D	7.3	38.9
Goldsboro, NC Metro Area	4,444	3,892	3,208	35,801	31,672	13.0	2,750	12.2	7.2	2.5	2.9	12.3	31.4
Wayne County, NC	4,444	3,892	3,208	35,801	31,672	13.0	2,750	12.2	7.2	2.5	2.9	12.3	31.4
Grand Forks, ND-MN Metro Area	4,626	3,714	2,897	45,158	37,664	19.9	3,393	6.8	8.6	3.0	4.0	D	27.0
Polk County, MN	1,355	1,168	893	42,975	36,927	16.4	739	14.9	6.3	2.2	1.9	D	20.6
Grand Forks County, ND	3,271	2,546	2,004	46,129	38,012	21.4	2,653	4.5	9.2	3.2	4.6	16.9	28.8
Grand Island, NE Metro Area	3,460	2,862	2,313	40,671	34,872	16.6	2,563	17.8	7.6	4.0	2.6	10.0	16.3
Hall County, NE	2,348	1,986	1,625	38,072	33,766	12.8	1,925	20.1	8.7	4.3	2.8	11.8	16.8
Hamilton County, NE	454	369	288	49,351	40,497	21.9	266	13.4	5.1	2.8	3.0	D	11.4
Howard County, NE	275	219	184	42,984	34,904	23.1	132	2.0	4.3	2.7	1.7	4.2	25.8
Merrick County, NE	382	288	216	49,110	36,602	34.2	240	13.3	3.3	3.1	1.3	D	12.8
Grand Junction, CO Metro Area	5,772	4,920	3,990	38,863	33,584	15.7	3,667	4.4	7.4	4.4	5.3	16.0	16.9
Mesa County, CO	5,772	4,920	3,990	38,863	33,584	15.7	3,667	4.4	7.4	4.4	5.3	16.0	16.9
Grand Rapids-Wyoming, MI Metro Area	47,121	35,829	32,730	45,371	36,208	25.3	34,699	24.4	5.7	4.8	D	D	9.4
Barry County, MI	2,376	1,901	1,761	40,063	32,181	24.5	843	33.5	4.4	5.4	D	9.0	16.0

[1]Based on resident population estimated on July 1 of the year shown.
[2]Includes other industry categories not shown separately.
D = not shown to avoid disclosure of confidential information.

Table C-3.   Personal Income and Earnings by Industry—*Continued*

Metropolitan statistical area, division, and component county	Total (million dollars) 2015	Total 2010	Total 2005	Per capita¹ (dollars) 2015	Per capita¹ 2010	Percent change, 2010–2015	Total² (million dollars)	Manufacturing	Retail trade	Finance and insurance	Professional and technical services	Health care and social services	Government and government enterprises
Kent County, MI	30,862	23,234	21,151	48,496	38,531	25.9	25,121	20.7	5.9	5.5	7.5	14.9	7.5
Montcalm County, MI	1,952	1,638	1,556	31,015	25,867	19.9	916	20.4	7.9	2.1	1.9	D	21.0
Ottawa County, MI	11,931	9,056	8,263	42,619	34,287	24.3	7,819	35.7	4.7	2.9	4.5	5.7	13.5
Grants Pass, OR Metro Area	3,052	2,477	2,187	36,013	29,896	20.5	1,447	11.0	11.9	3.7	3.4	19.8	13.9
Josephine County, OR	3,052	2,477	2,187	36,013	29,896	20.5	1,447	11.0	11.9	3.7	3.4	19.8	13.9
Great Falls, MT Metro Area	3,460	3,090	2,470	42,053	37,896	11.0	2,324	3.6	9.0	5.6	4.9	17.0	26.9
Cascade County, MT	3,460	3,090	2,470	42,053	37,896	11.0	2,324	3.6	9.0	5.6	4.9	17.0	26.9
Greeley, CO Metro Area	12,202	8,252	6,382	42,787	32,467	31.8	7,910	11.5	5.9	3.2	3.5	6.9	11.1
Weld County, CO	12,202	8,252	6,382	42,787	32,467	31.8	7,910	11.5	5.9	3.2	3.5	6.9	11.1
Green Bay, WI Metro Area	14,454	11,916	10,109	45,665	38,848	17.5	11,517	16.9	4.9	7.8	D	D	12.5
Brown County, WI	12,052	9,895	8,400	46,584	39,817	17.0	10,525	16.4	4.9	8.3	6.2	13.6	12.0
Kewaunee County, WI	873	732	627	42,855	35,634	20.3	453	24.2	4.0	2.6	2.6	D	15.9
Oconto County, WI	1,529	1,289	1,083	40,842	34,206	19.4	539	21.0	6.4	1.9	D	10.6	21.1
Greensboro-High Point, NC Metro Area	29,532	24,702	21,644	39,263	34,068	15.2	22,664	17.1	6.2	6.0	D	11.6	11.7
Guilford County, NC	21,579	17,740	15,463	41,691	36,243	15.0	18,705	14.4	6.1	6.8	6.9	11.9	11.3
Randolph County, NC	4,841	4,152	3,692	33,899	29,256	15.9	2,532	32.1	6.2	2.2	2.1	9.0	12.9
Rockingham County, NC	3,112	2,809	2,489	33,916	29,997	13.1	1,426	25.9	8.3	1.8	D	12.1	15.3
Greenville, NC Metro Area	6,514	5,403	4,297	37,042	32,005	15.7	4,791	9.8	7.1	3.2	3.2	10.0	38.0
Pitt County, NC	6,514	5,403	4,297	37,042	32,005	15.7	4,791	9.8	7.1	3.2	3.2	10.0	38.0
Greenville-Anderson-Mauldin, SC Metro Area	34,306	26,793	22,268	39,213	32,446	20.9	24,672	16.5	6.5	5.5	7.5	D	15.2
Anderson County, SC	6,872	5,681	4,643	35,297	30,335	16.4	3,620	25.4	8.2	2.0	3.0	8.2	20.7
Greenville County, SC	21,215	15,913	13,135	43,132	35,145	22.7	17,766	13.0	6.1	6.8	9.2	9.8	11.8
Laurens County, SC	2,092	1,815	1,642	31,406	27,281	15.1	1,237	39.0	5.1	1.5	3.6	D	16.6
Pickens County, SC	4,127	3,384	2,848	33,911	28,389	19.5	2,050	17.2	8.2	2.4	3.2	8.0	33.9
Gulfport-Biloxi-Pascagoula, MS Metro Area	13,315	12,599	10,836	34,206	33,918	0.8	9,819	17.1	6.0	2.4	5.5	7.4	29.2
Hancock County, MS	1,537	1,462	1,294	33,108	33,145	-0.1	1,014	8.1	4.4	1.5	11.3	4.2	38.6
Harrison County, MS	6,914	6,426	5,727	34,327	34,198	0.4	5,280	4.9	7.3	2.8	4.4	8.3	34.7
Jackson County, MS	4,864	4,711	3,815	34,394	33,785	1.8	3,525	38.0	4.4	2.0	5.3	7.0	18.3
Hagerstown-Martinsburg, MD-WV Metro Area	10,454	8,897	7,081	39,981	35,250	13.4	6,193	9.3	8.9	7.3	3.9	13.8	21.1
Washington County, MD	6,320	5,432	4,477	42,248	36,767	14.9	4,231	11.5	9.9	9.6	3.4	14.0	15.0
Berkeley County, WV	4,135	3,465	2,604	36,950	33,108	11.6	1,962	4.6	6.6	2.3	5.0	13.5	34.1
Hammond, LA Metro Area	4,641	3,976	2,792	36,043	32,725	10.1	2,340	5.6	12.6	3.3	3.7	12.2	27.2
Tangipahoa Parish, LA	4,641	3,976	2,792	36,043	32,725	10.1	2,340	5.6	12.6	3.3	3.7	12.2	27.2
Hanford-Corcoran, CA Metro Area	5,001	4,059	3,416	33,126	26,641	24.3	3,531	9.0	4.4	1.5	1.7	9.3	45.8
Kings County, CA	5,001	4,059	3,416	33,126	26,641	24.3	3,531	9.0	4.4	1.5	1.7	9.3	45.8
Harrisburg-Carlisle, PA Metro Area	27,115	22,340	19,074	47,991	40,600	18.2	23,993	7.0	4.7	7.6	7.6	13.8	21.5
Cumberland County, PA	12,503	10,002	8,607	50,757	42,384	19.8	9,680	5.9	6.0	8.2	9.9	12.0	16.5
Dauphin County, PA	12,790	10,769	9,146	46,851	40,144	16.7	13,794	7.9	3.6	7.3	6.2	15.4	24.9
Perry County, PA	1,822	1,569	1,320	39,884	34,108	16.9	519	5.4	7.8	3.3	3.4	7.2	24.9
Harrisonburg, VA Metro Area	4,681	3,802	3,184	35,700	30,312	17.8	3,798	17.6	6.6	2.4	4.2	11.7	17.7
Rockingham County, VA	4,681	3,802	3,184	35,700	30,312	17.8	3,798	17.6	6.6	2.4	4.2	11.7	17.7
Harrisonburg city, VA	(5)	(5)	(5)	(5)	(5)	(5)	(5)	(5)	(5)	(5)	(5)	(5)	(5)
Hartford-West Hartford-East Hartford, CT Metro Area	71,227	60,861	51,413	58,801	50,127	17.3	57,307	11.5	4.7	15.6	9.1	11.7	15.8
Hartford County, CT	53,070	45,311	38,338	59,240	50,609	17.1	48,300	11.3	4.3	18.0	9.6	11.5	14.1
Middlesex County, CT	10,237	8,719	7,438	62,394	52,643	18.5	5,791	15.9	6.7	3.4	6.9	14.0	17.3
Tolland County, CT	7,921	6,831	5,637	52,311	44,587	17.3	3,216	6.9	7.2	1.8	5.2	10.5	37.8
Hattiesburg, MS Metro Area	5,146	4,317	3,376	34,574	30,127	14.8	3,644	6.8	11.1	D	D	17.0	23.3
Forrest County, MS	2,678	2,303	1,868	35,269	30,713	14.8	2,470	7.6	9.7	2.7	3.1	16.0	28.8
Lamar County, MS	2,122	1,706	1,239	35,014	30,425	15.1	1,025	1.2	15.2	5.0	D	20.7	11.2
Perry County, MS	345	307	269	28,100	25,162	11.7	149	32.3	4.7	D	1.7	9.6	15.9
Hickory-Lenoir-Morganton, NC Metro Area	12,835	10,977	9,917	35,406	30,059	17.8	8,367	27.0	7.5	1.8	D	D	15.3
Alexander County, NC	1,256	1,020	934	33,645	27,376	22.9	532	30.5	4.4	2.2	D	D	19.0
Burke County, NC	2,795	2,450	2,279	31,458	27,020	16.4	1,580	27.6	5.8	1.7	2.3	17.1	24.2
Caldwell County, NC	2,541	2,234	2,091	31,263	26,928	16.1	1,239	23.7	7.4	1.4	2.0	11.7	17.3
Catawba County, NC	6,243	5,273	4,613	40,265	34,176	17.8	5,016	27.3	8.5	1.8	3.9	10.3	11.6
Hilton Head Island-Bluffton-Beaufort, SC Metro Area	9,366	7,152	6,239	45,158	38,074	18.6	5,025	1.2	8.8	3.6	D	9.9	30.6
Beaufort County, SC	8,644	6,605	5,740	48,134	40,541	18.7	4,552	1.0	7.8	3.6	9.0	9.4	32.1
Jasper County, SC	722	547	499	25,951	21,947	18.2	473	3.1	19.1	3.4	D	13.9	15.9
Hinesville, GA Metro Area	2,491	2,137	1,760	31,064	27,626	12.4	2,553	D	2.4	0.8	D	1.9	76.1
Liberty County, GA	2,092	1,838	1,529	33,488	29,328	14.2	2,492	6.3	2.4	0.8	D	1.8	76.7
Long County, GA	399	299	231	22,525	20,359	10.6	61	D	2.7	0.8	0.8	2.0	54.3
Homosassa Springs, FL Metro Area	4,983	4,352	3,636	35,323	30,809	14.7	1,837	1.4	11.8	2.7	5.9	22.7	13.9
Citrus County, FL	4,983	4,352	3,636	35,323	30,809	14.7	1,837	1.4	11.8	2.7	5.9	22.7	13.9
Hot Springs, AR Metro Area	3,604	3,080	2,627	37,090	32,038	15.8	1,905	7.5	10.6	4.0	4.4	22.4	14.3
Garland County, AR	3,604	3,080	2,627	37,090	32,038	15.8	1,905	7.5	10.6	4.0	4.4	22.4	14.3
Houma-Thibodaux, LA Metro Area	9,636	8,232	5,703	45,390	39,532	14.8	7,127	11.1	5.7	1.6	4.7	8.3	10.7
Lafourche Parish, LA	4,513	3,905	2,703	45,899	40,391	13.6	2,833	9.2	4.6	0.8	2.7	6.2	15.6
Terrebonne Parish, LA	5,123	4,327	3,000	44,952	38,788	15.9	4,294	12.4	6.4	2.1	6.0	9.7	7.5

¹Based on resident population estimated on July 1 of the year shown.
²Includes other industry categories not shown separately.
⁵Harrisonburg city included with Rockingham County, VA, in the Harrisonburg, VA MSA.
D = not shown to avoid disclosure of confidential information.

Table C-3.   Personal Income and Earnings by Industry—*Continued*

	Personal Income												
	Total (million dollars)			Per capita[1] (dollars)			Earnings 2015						
								Percent by selected major industries					
Metropolitan statistical area, division, and component county	2015	2010	2005	2015	2010	Percent change, 2010–2015	Total[2] (million dollars)	Manu-facturing	Retail trade	Finance and insurance	Professional and technical services	Health care and social services	Government and government enterprises
Houston-The Woodlands-Sugar Land, TX Metro Area	361,777	264,687	201,478	54,346	44,498	22.1	296,148	10.4	4.7	5.0	D	D	9.5
Austin County, TX	1,515	1,106	830	51,260	38,979	31.5	809	14.1	10.9	3.3	D	4.1	9.8
Brazoria County, TX	15,538	11,502	8,319	44,867	36,574	22.7	8,461	22.5	6.1	1.9	5.2	7.8	13.3
Chambers County, TX	1,929	1,379	946	49,647	38,938	27.5	1,050	29.3	3.3	1.2	4.1	D	12.1
Fort Bend County, TX	40,162	27,330	18,815	56,086	46,276	21.2	14,704	10.5	8.6	3.5	9.1	8.8	10.6
Galveston County, TX	15,464	11,768	8,974	47,991	40,227	19.3	7,307	12.4	6.9	5.3	5.7	6.7	27.6
Harris County, TX	249,989	185,791	145,488	55,088	45,225	21.8	245,728	10.0	4.2	5.3	12.3	6.9	8.6
Liberty County, TX	2,794	2,127	1,874	35,081	28,039	25.1	1,072	9.0	9.5	2.2	D	6.2	22.2
Montgomery County, TX	32,517	22,310	15,238	60,490	48,570	24.5	15,817	6.7	5.9	4.3	9.4	7.0	10.0
Waller County, TX	1,867	1,373	994	38,380	31,603	21.4	1,201	24.8	3.7	1.0	3.8	2.8	19.5
Huntington-Ashland, WV-KY-OH Metro Area	13,070	11,732	9,353	36,146	32,135	12.5	8,154	D	7.0	2.5	4.6	D	17.0
Boyd County, KY	1,737	1,629	1,332	35,941	32,823	9.5	1,619	17.6	6.8	2.2	5.8	21.4	12.6
Greenup County, KY	1,342	1,212	971	37,195	32,854	13.2	523	12.2	6.2	2.3	3.2	24.2	15.6
Lawrence County, OH	2,099	1,879	1,503	34,353	30,097	14.1	717	D	8.4	2.1	2.4	16.9	24.9
Cabell County, WV	3,708	3,288	2,655	38,287	34,121	12.2	3,095	10.7	7.9	3.0	4.8	26.4	16.4
Lincoln County, WV	592	548	439	27,661	25,302	9.3	159	0.2	6.3	1.3	2.9	11.9	28.7
Putnam County, WV	2,383	2,066	1,555	41,923	37,121	12.9	1,444	13.0	6.0	2.8	5.3	8.8	9.8
Wayne County, WV	1,209	1,110	899	29,498	26,148	12.8	597	9.3	4.5	0.9	2.8	D	38.8
Huntsville, AL Metro Area	19,600	16,757	12,770	44,068	39,964	10.3	16,276	12.1	5.4	2.1	22.4	7.2	29.1
Limestone County, AL	3,415	2,783	2,160	37,260	33,470	11.3	1,598	13.1	9.3	1.7	3.6	4.1	33.0
Madison County, AL	16,184	13,973	10,610	45,836	41,570	10.3	14,678	12.0	5.0	2.1	24.4	7.5	28.6
Idaho Falls, ID Metro Area	5,293	4,408	3,572	37,873	32,940	15.0	4,034	6.6	12.9	D	22.4	D	10.5
Bonneville County, ID	4,383	3,613	3,010	39,814	34,513	15.4	2,893	7.5	17.1	3.4	5.7	16.7	12.4
Butte County, ID	84	81	53	33,506	27,821	20.4	781	0.4	0.2	D	93.6	0.6	1.9
Jefferson County, ID	826	714	510	30,407	27,225	11.7	361	12.9	6.6	2.3	2.0	D	14.2
Indianapolis-Carmel-Anderson, IN Metro Area	96,004	77,224	63,266	48,272	40,803	18.3	75,893	11.7	6.3	6.5	D	12.2	11.4
Boone County, IN	3,966	2,885	2,400	62,603	50,756	23.3	1,734	7.5	17.2	3.4	8.3	6.9	12.1
Brown County, IN	620	514	457	41,406	33,837	22.4	168	4.6	8.8	2.1	7.7	D	21.4
Hamilton County, IN	20,023	14,723	11,407	64,654	53,248	21.4	10,501	4.8	6.9	15.4	10.9	10.8	7.5
Hancock County, IN	3,187	2,697	2,277	43,941	38,402	14.4	1,380	16.5	6.2	2.2	17.7	6.5	15.8
Hendricks County, IN	6,857	5,464	4,383	43,345	37,459	15.7	3,399	8.3	11.8	2.1	3.4	7.3	14.9
Johnson County, IN	6,458	5,149	4,366	43,161	36,707	17.6	2,848	14.0	9.4	3.5	4.6	12.8	15.1
Madison County, IN	4,583	3,816	3,575	35,328	28,992	21.9	2,328	22.0	6.3	3.1	2.6	15.3	14.5
Marion County, IN	44,611	37,182	30,021	47,508	41,100	15.6	50,850	12.1	5.2	5.8	9.0	13.2	11.3
Morgan County, IN	2,737	2,341	2,118	39,299	33,843	16.1	922	17.7	8.9	3.0	D	10.6	14.4
Putnam County, IN	1,250	1,056	932	33,264	27,855	19.4	689	23.7	4.9	2.7	1.9	D	17.5
Shelby County, IN	1,713	1,396	1,329	38,511	31,505	22.2	1,075	33.0	5.0	1.4	2.0	6.9	13.6
Iowa City, IA Metro Area	7,879	6,040	4,882	47,324	39,477	19.9	6,473	6.8	5.3	3.1	3.6	7.2	42.9
Johnson County, IA	6,770	5,195	4,212	46,933	39,569	18.6	5,854	6.4	5.3	3.1	3.5	7.4	45.9
Washington County, IA	1,109	844	670	49,859	38,920	28.1	619	10.3	5.3	3.0	4.6	5.5	14.1
Ithaca, NY Metro Area	4,312	3,564	2,912	41,095	35,019	17.4	3,688	7.7	5.2	2.6	7.7	D	13.8
Tompkins County, NY	4,312	3,564	2,912	41,095	35,019	17.4	3,688	7.7	5.2	2.6	7.7	D	13.8
Jackson, MI Metro Area	5,808	4,896	4,428	36,413	30,570	19.1	3,639	19.7	6.3	2.5	4.0	14.8	14.6
Jackson County, MI	5,808	4,896	4,428	36,413	30,570	19.1	3,639	19.7	6.3	2.5	4.0	14.8	14.6
Jackson, MS Metro Area	24,251	20,309	17,348	41,900	35,705	17.4	17,680	7.4	7.4	6.4	6.8	12.8	21.4
Copiah County, MS	897	805	640	31,186	27,371	13.9	405	30.1	6.3	1.9	D	D	18.5
Hinds County, MS	9,312	8,313	7,279	38,337	33,832	13.3	8,701	2.9	5.9	5.5	6.9	15.4	31.1
Madison County, MS	5,997	4,557	3,990	57,964	47,673	21.6	3,855	16.2	8.3	9.1	11.0	8.3	6.8
Rankin County, MS	6,357	5,137	4,133	42,652	36,049	18.3	3,950	6.3	10.1	6.8	4.1	11.1	13.0
Simpson County, MS	927	808	699	34,068	29,371	16.0	379	1.8	7.6	4.4	D	D	19.6
Yazoo County, MS	760	690	608	27,763	24,554	13.1	390	11.9	4.9	4.0	D	D	37.7
Jackson, TN Metro Area	4,781	4,123	3,510	36,870	31,716	16.3	3,875	17.2	8.3	2.5	D	14.3	22.6
Chester County, TN	519	450	365	29,701	26,209	13.3	216	13.0	9.8	2.3	D	D	23.8
Crockett County, TN	525	469	370	35,968	32,162	11.8	278	26.5	20.3	1.4	2.6	D	15.9
Madison County, TN	3,737	3,204	2,775	38,288	32,612	17.4	3,381	16.7	7.2	2.6	3.2	15.0	23.1
Jacksonville, FL Metro Area	64,095	52,177	45,532	44,219	38,676	14.3	44,248	5.6	6.5	11.1	8.7	D	15.4
Baker County, FL	784	689	604	28,588	25,441	12.4	363	1.5	8.0	1.7	1.8	D	40.5
Clay County, FL	7,973	6,469	5,555	39,090	33,792	15.7	2,694	3.0	10.2	2.8	10.3	18.1	16.9
Duval County, FL	37,743	31,732	29,009	41,339	36,651	12.8	35,636	5.7	5.9	12.7	8.5	13.2	14.9
Nassau County, FL	3,897	3,189	2,587	49,675	43,369	14.5	1,289	8.6	7.3	2.2	8.6	9.4	20.3
St. Johns County, FL	13,698	10,098	7,779	60,441	52,798	14.5	4,267	6.2	8.7	6.3	9.1	11.8	14.6
Jacksonville, NC Metro Area	8,189	7,801	5,120	43,952	43,436	1.2	6,077	0.8	4.5	1.2	1.8	3.1	72.2
Onslow County, NC	8,189	7,801	5,120	43,952	43,436	1.2	6,077	0.8	4.5	1.2	1.8	3.1	72.2
Janesville-Beloit, WI Metro Area	6,462	5,380	4,664	40,026	33,577	19.2	4,074	17.2	7.1	2.5	3.0	16.1	15.4
Rock County, WI	6,462	5,380	4,664	40,026	33,577	19.2	4,074	17.2	7.1	2.5	3.0	16.1	15.4
Jefferson City, MO Metro Area	5,970	5,211	4,338	39,497	34,751	13.7	4,620	9.1	5.9	3.9	4.7	8.9	33.1
Callaway County, MO	1,557	1,381	1,133	34,718	31,150	11.5	858	13.6	4.6	1.8	3.2	D	23.4
Cole County, MO	3,290	2,897	2,433	42,884	38,055	12.7	3,219	4.6	6.4	4.8	5.7	10.9	38.5
Moniteau County, MO	529	462	369	33,153	29,593	12.0	241	14.5	5.9	3.2	1.9	D	22.0
Osage County, MO	594	471	402	43,583	33,942	28.4	302	40.5	4.1	2.0	0.6	3.7	12.5
Johnson City, TN Metro Area	7,326	6,327	5,138	36,512	31,800	14.8	4,569	10.9	8.1	4.4	D	D	21.8
Carter County, TN	1,774	1,567	1,323	31,407	27,326	14.9	629	10.1	10.0	3.7	3.7	D	22.3

[1]Based on resident population estimated on July 1 of the year shown.
[2]Includes other industry categories not shown separately.
D = not shown to avoid disclosure of confidential information.

Table C-3. Personal Income and Earnings by Industry—*Continued*

Metropolitan statistical area, division, and component county	Personal Income						Earnings 2015						
	Total (million dollars)			Per capita¹ (dollars)				Percent by selected major industries					
	2015	2010	2005	2015	2010	Percent change, 2010–2015	Total² (million dollars)	Manufacturing	Retail trade	Finance and insurance	Professional and technical services	Health care and social services	Government and government enterprises
Unicoi County, TN	622	556	490	34,826	30,419	14.5	340	37.1	4.1	1.2	D	8.0	15.1
Washington County, TN	4,930	4,204	3,325	39,034	34,085	14.5	3,600	8.5	8.2	4.8	4.4	22.4	22.4
Johnstown, PA Metro Area	5,253	4,668	4,113	38,512	32,540	18.4	3,035	8.7	7.5	5.5	6.3	22.7	18.1
Cambria County, PA	5,253	4,668	4,113	38,512	32,540	18.4	3,035	8.7	7.5	5.5	6.3	22.7	18.1
Jonesboro, AR Metro Area	4,328	3,580	2,895	33,709	29,523	14.2	3,119	13.7	7.7	3.0	3.2	20.7	15.8
Craighead County, AR	3,614	2,899	2,268	34,628	29,976	15.5	2,790	13.8	7.9	3.0	3.4	22.1	15.5
Poinsett County, AR	714	680	627	29,719	27,739	7.1	329	12.8	6.0	2.5	1.0	8.5	18.2
Joplin, MO Metro Area	6,386	5,385	4,479	36,037	30,619	17.7	4,573	20.2	7.8	2.9	2.5	15.4	11.2
Jasper County, MO	4,284	3,563	2,996	36,119	30,263	19.4	3,330	23.0	8.0	3.2	2.9	10.2	11.2
Newton County, MO	2,103	1,822	1,482	35,871	31,339	14.5	1,243	12.8	7.2	1.9	1.5	29.4	11.4
Kahului-Wailuku-Lahaina, HI Metro Area	6,989	5,501	4,690	42,430	35,476	19.6	4,923	1.5	8.2	1.3	3.4	7.2	17.3
Kalawao County, HI	(6)	(6)	(6)	(6)	(6)	(6)	(6)	(6)	(6)	(6)	(6)	(6)	(6)
Maui County, HI	6,989	5,501	4,690	42,430	35,476	19.6	4,923	1.5	8.2	1.3	3.4	7.2	17.3
Kalamazoo-Portage, MI Metro Area	14,004	11,523	10,071	41,760	35,248	18.5	9,335	20.8	5.9	5.7	5.2	14.5	14.7
Kalamazoo County, MI	11,207	9,062	8,005	43,062	36,138	19.2	7,988	22.5	5.9	6.4	4.7	15.9	13.1
Van Buren County, MI	2,796	2,461	2,066	37,247	32,319	15.2	1,347	10.5	6.1	1.5	8.5	6.0	24.2
Kankakee, IL Metro Area	4,108	3,695	3,062	37,049	32,571	13.7	2,554	19.0	6.8	4.1	D	18.0	16.6
Kankakee County, IL	4,108	3,695	3,062	37,049	32,571	13.7	2,554	19.0	6.8	4.1	D	18.0	16.6
Kansas City, MO-KS Metro Area	100,316	82,309	66,355	48,056	40,874	17.6	78,723	9.0	5.7	8.3	D	10.8	14.0
Johnson County, KS	37,739	29,319	22,607	65,050	53,718	21.1	27,638	5.5	5.7	11.9	13.6	10.6	7.1
Leavenworth County, KS	3,131	2,650	2,135	39,477	34,620	14.0	1,967	3.5	3.8	2.8	6.1	4.1	62.9
Linn County, KS	320	286	237	33,533	29,709	12.9	142	5.8	5.6	2.6	3.5	D	25.2
Miami County, KS	1,412	1,187	954	43,387	36,102	20.2	491	7.8	7.3	4.5	4.8	11.9	22.8
Wyandotte County, KS	5,814	4,510	3,565	35,589	28,602	24.4	7,329	26.0	3.9	1.1	5.1	15.2	15.8
Bates County, MO	555	510	433	33,722	29,924	12.7	203	2.5	11.2	6.6	8.3	9.0	29.7
Caldwell County, MO	296	264	227	32,835	27,940	17.5	98	1.6	12.5	3.6	1.6	4.9	28.9
Cass County, MO	4,230	3,535	2,969	41,636	35,439	17.5	1,419	6.8	9.1	3.1	3.6	8.9	20.0
Clay County, MO	10,440	8,851	6,957	44,304	39,758	11.4	7,232	17.8	10.9	2.5	13.7	7.5	14.8
Clinton County, MO	790	665	592	38,313	32,079	19.4	214	5.6	5.9	5.0	D	22.0	27.1
Jackson County, MO	28,568	24,646	20,968	41,545	36,512	13.8	28,313	6.1	4.5	9.4	15.5	11.9	16.0
Lafayette County, MO	1,196	1,068	951	36,573	31,991	14.3	463	10.4	8.5	3.3	5.4	D	23.9
Platte County, MO	4,983	4,078	3,125	51,855	45,455	14.1	2,953	12.3	6.9	4.0	5.4	6.5	11.0
Ray County, MO	843	740	635	36,947	31,512	17.2	261	12.6	8.1	3.2	2.6	D	27.6
Kennewick-Richland, WA Metro Area	11,295	9,589	6,591	40,468	37,510	7.9	8,602	6.2	5.9	1.9	13.6	9.5	17.5
Benton County, WA	8,280	7,166	5,125	43,507	40,598	7.2	6,456	5.3	5.5	2.2	17.6	10.6	16.7
Franklin County, WA	3,015	2,423	1,466	33,955	30,622	10.9	2,146	9.1	7.1	0.8	1.6	6.3	19.8
Killeen-Temple, TX Metro Area	17,343	15,128	10,916	40,237	37,048	8.6	12,157	4.1	5.9	2.2	D	D	48.8
Bell County, TX	13,925	12,098	8,455	41,574	38,654	7.6	10,999	4.1	5.4	2.1	3.0	12.9	50.1
Coryell County, TX	2,441	2,184	1,816	32,334	28,891	11.9	869	2.2	6.5	3.6	D	6.2	41.8
Lampasas County, TX	977	846	645	47,478	42,822	10.9	289	9.8	25.1	2.8	3.5	D	18.3
Kingsport-Bristol-Bristol, TN-VA Metro Area	11,462	10,077	8,349	37,322	32,551	14.7	7,416	24.8	7.1	2.5	D	D	12.8
Hawkins County, TN	1,773	1,575	1,311	31,391	27,687	13.4	712	34.8	5.3	1.5	D	D	18.6
Sullivan County, TN	6,083	5,371	4,394	38,799	34,243	13.3	4,583	25.8	6.9	2.7	3.6	18.3	10.2
Scott County, VA	681	623	540	30,767	26,916	14.3	237	18.9	7.8	2.4	2.4	14.0	27.5
Washington County, VA	2,926	2,510	2,105	40,787	34,498	18.2	1,884	19.4	8.2	2.5	3.3	10.3	15.3
Bristol city, VA	(7)	(7)	(7)	(7)	(7)	(7)	(7)	(7)	(7)	(7)	(7)	(7)	(7)
Kingston, NY Metro Area	8,002	6,913	5,742	44,422	37,897	17.2	4,122	6.1	8.5	2.7	4.3	12.5	32.1
Ulster County, NY	8,002	6,913	5,742	44,422	37,897	17.2	4,122	6.1	8.5	2.7	4.3	12.5	32.1
Knoxville, TN Metro Area	35,206	28,869	24,203	40,870	34,419	18.7	25,548	10.4	7.3	D	10.5	14.9	15.0
Anderson County, TN	2,927	2,576	2,194	38,637	34,277	12.7	2,897	29.1	3.9	3.1	19.3	9.9	12.9
Blount County, TN	4,823	3,928	3,262	37,900	31,893	18.8	3,075	18.8	8.3	4.6	3.7	8.7	15.3
Campbell County, TN	1,232	1,100	955	30,981	27,027	14.6	504	15.2	9.1	3.0	2.4	D	21.6
Grainger County, TN	677	572	477	29,623	25,203	17.5	221	23.6	5.6	D	D	4.1	23.4
Knox County, TN	20,242	16,137	13,589	44,849	37,265	20.4	16,139	5.3	8.0	5.0	7.8	18.3	14.6
Loudon County, TN	2,197	1,782	1,398	42,971	36,554	17.6	941	16.4	7.3	3.9	4.5	8.7	13.8
Morgan County, TN	588	529	432	27,329	24,031	13.7	191	6.9	5.4	2.0	D	11.5	38.8
Roane County, TN	1,975	1,779	1,482	37,441	32,861	13.9	1,422	4.2	4.2	0.8	46.9	D	15.6
Union County, TN	547	466	414	28,611	24,385	17.3	158	15.2	7.9	D	D	D	26.7
Kokomo, IN Metro Area	3,084	2,570	2,576	37,356	31,069	20.2	2,532	47.7	6.0	2.7	1.9	12.2	9.9
Howard County, IN	3,084	2,570	2,576	37,356	31,069	20.2	2,532	47.7	6.0	2.7	1.9	12.2	9.9
La Crosse-Onalaska, WI-MN Metro Area	6,141	5,040	4,131	44,831	37,645	19.1	4,643	11.2	6.0	5.1	3.2	20.6	15.8
Houston County, MN	874	735	648	46,557	38,668	20.4	301	10.1	5.0	2.3	2.7	9.2	20.0
La Crosse County, WI	5,267	4,305	3,484	44,557	37,476	18.9	4,342	11.2	6.1	5.2	3.2	21.4	15.5
Lafayette, LA Metro Area	21,250	17,731	13,048	43,325	37,918	14.3	15,583	8.8	6.8	2.9	7.7	11.7	10.1
Acadia Parish, LA	2,211	1,916	1,485	35,335	30,983	14.0	888	6.9	7.9	2.9	5.2	10.6	16.6
Iberia Parish, LA	2,830	2,563	1,992	38,194	34,986	9.2	2,168	14.3	6.6	2.5	6.7	7.2	11.2
Lafayette Parish, LA	11,884	9,636	7,054	49,496	43,379	14.1	10,674	6.7	6.3	3.1	8.7	13.5	8.4
St. Martin Parish, LA	2,036	1,676	1,143	37,820	32,060	18.0	876	24.1	9.7	1.9	4.2	7.1	12.1
Vermilion Parish, LA	2,289	1,940	1,374	38,226	33,391	14.5	978	6.8	8.7	3.1	4.2	6.5	18.3
Lafayette-West Lafayette, IN Metro Area	7,528	6,173	5,134	35,120	30,546	15.0	5,954	D	5.4	3.3	4.1	12.5	26.1
Benton County, IN	307	297	249	35,402	33,509	5.6	142	16.3	5.2	7.6	1.9	D	19.5
Carroll County, IN	768	661	559	38,695	32,758	18.1	313	D	5.1	2.3	2.1	D	12.8

¹Based on resident population estimated on July 1 of the year shown.
²Includes other industry categories not shown separately.
⁶Kalawao county included with Maui county in the Kahului-Wailuku-Lahaina, HI MSA
⁷Bristol city included with Washington County, VA, in the Kingsport-Bristol-Bristol, TN-VA MSA.
D = not shown to avoid disclosure of confidential information.

Table C-3. Personal Income and Earnings by Industry—*Continued*

	Personal Income												
	Total (million dollars)			Per capita[1] (dollars)			Earnings 2015						
									Percent by selected major industries				
Metropolitan statistical area, division, and component county	2015	2010	2005	2015	2010	Percent change, 2010–2015	Total[2] (million dollars)	Manu-facturing	Retail trade	Finance and insurance	Profes-sional and technical services	Health care and social services	Govern-ment and govern-ment enter-prises
Tippecanoe County, IN	6,453	5,215	4,326	34,725	30,136	15.2	5,499	22.9	5.4	3.2	4.3	13.3	27.0
Lake Charles, LA Metro Area	8,788	6,834	5,472	42,743	34,171	25.1	7,161	17.9	D	2.2	6.1	10.8	11.8
Calcasieu Parish, LA	8,476	6,602	5,287	42,639	34,190	24.7	6,465	19.1	6.9	2.4	6.5	11.9	12.4
Cameron Parish, LA	312	232	185	45,776	33,629	36.1	695	6.8	D	0.1	2.4	0.7	6.1
Lake Havasu City-Kingman, AZ Metro Area	6,041	5,135	4,440	29,505	25,626	15.1	2,646	6.2	11.5	2.8	3.3	20.8	17.8
Mohave County, AZ	6,041	5,135	4,440	29,505	25,626	15.1	2,646	6.2	11.5	2.8	3.3	20.8	17.8
Lakeland-Winter Haven, FL Metro Area	21,923	18,510	16,031	33,723	30,686	9.9	12,438	9.4	8.0	6.0	4.7	14.1	13.6
Polk County, FL	21,923	18,510	16,031	33,723	30,686	9.9	12,438	9.4	8.0	6.0	4.7	14.1	13.6
Lancaster, PA Metro Area	24,146	19,536	17,212	44,995	37,543	19.8	17,033	15.9	7.6	4.1	5.4	13.3	9.1
Lancaster County, PA	24,146	19,536	17,212	44,995	37,543	19.8	17,033	15.9	7.6	4.1	5.4	13.3	9.1
Lansing-East Lansing, MI Metro Area	17,882	15,448	13,688	37,863	33,276	13.8	13,345	11.8	5.2	7.6	D	12.5	27.0
Clinton County, MI	3,130	2,618	2,344	40,446	34,712	16.5	1,047	18.3	8.5	3.7	D	6.5	13.9
Eaton County, MI	4,126	3,541	3,130	37,921	32,859	15.4	2,578	21.1	6.2	13.9	3.0	5.4	14.7
Ingham County, MI	10,626	9,289	8,215	37,142	33,050	12.4	9,720	8.6	4.6	6.4	7.0	15.0	31.6
Laredo, TX Metro Area	8,032	6,408	4,775	29,778	25,497	16.8	5,783	1.0	7.9	2.4	3.2	10.1	26.3
Webb County, TX	8,032	6,408	4,775	29,778	25,497	16.8	5,783	1.0	7.9	2.4	3.2	10.1	26.3
Las Cruces, NM Metro Area	6,907	6,163	4,781	32,233	29,321	9.9	4,295	3.5	6.3	2.6	7.0	15.5	32.0
Doña Ana County, NM	6,907	6,163	4,781	32,233	29,321	9.9	4,295	3.5	6.3	2.6	7.0	15.5	32.0
Las Vegas-Henderson-Paradise, NV Metro Area	85,970	69,292	66,358	40,652	35,473	14.6	59,901	2.5	7.2	3.9	6.5	9.3	15.7
Clark County, NV	85,970	69,292	66,358	40,652	35,473	14.6	59,901	2.5	7.2	3.9	6.5	9.3	15.7
Lawrence, KS Metro Area	4,567	3,703	3,085	38,686	33,286	16.2	2,848	8.5	6.5	2.5	8.7	7.3	35.0
Douglas County, KS	4,567	3,703	3,085	38,686	33,286	16.2	2,848	8.5	6.5	2.5	8.7	7.3	35.0
Lawton, OK Metro Area	4,997	4,632	3,464	38,246	35,209	8.6	3,566	D	5.3	2.5	3.8	5.2	52.6
Comanche County, OK	4,761	4,411	3,278	38,195	35,179	8.6	3,461	8.4	5.4	2.5	3.9	5.2	52.9
Cotton County, OK	236	221	186	39,298	35,832	9.7	105	D	3.6	2.5	1.4	2.6	41.8
Lebanon, PA Metro Area	5,906	4,947	4,098	43,090	37,010	16.4	3,177	17.2	7.7	2.0	2.9	12.3	19.9
Lebanon County, PA	5,906	4,947	4,098	43,090	37,010	16.4	3,177	17.2	7.7	2.0	2.9	12.3	19.9
Lewiston, ID-WA Metro Area	2,486	2,122	1,713	39,999	34,769	15.0	1,595	18.3	9.5	5.9	3.5	D	18.1
Nez Perce County, ID	1,576	1,349	1,103	39,358	34,291	14.8	1,242	21.5	8.5	6.8	3.2	16.3	17.9
Asotin County, WA	910	774	610	41,162	35,635	15.5	353	7.1	12.8	2.7	4.5	D	18.7
Lewiston-Auburn, ME Metro Area	3,979	3,617	3,146	37,106	33,580	10.5	2,791	11.4	7.7	4.9	5.6	21.4	11.8
Androscoggin County, ME.	3,979	3,617	3,146	37,106	33,580	10.5	2,791	11.4	7.7	4.9	5.6	21.4	11.8
Lexington-Fayette, KY Metro Area	21,555	17,439	14,955	43,065	36,832	16.9	17,376	14.7	5.8	3.4	7.5	10.8	21.4
Bourbon County, KY	777	625	584	38,638	31,336	23.3	426	20.9	7.7	3.7	D	D	12.6
Clark County, KY	1,332	1,148	1,018	37,244	32,239	15.5	814	23.0	6.2	2.5	6.9	10.8	11.3
Fayette County, KY	14,227	11,568	9,781	45,238	38,988	16.0	12,855	8.4	5.7	3.9	8.6	12.1	25.0
Jessamine County, KY	1,987	1,572	1,293	38,243	32,275	18.5	942	17.4	11.8	1.6	D	6.4	14.7
Scott County, KY	2,066	1,596	1,326	39,415	33,644	17.2	1,769	50.1	3.0	1.1	2.9	5.5	7.1
Woodford County, KY	1,166	929	954	45,213	37,101	21.9	570	23.7	5.5	2.2	6.3	D	15.8
Lima, OH Metro Area	3,913	3,474	3,035	37,469	32,650	14.8	3,107	25.7	6.5	2.3	2.6	18.5	13.4
Allen County, OH	3,913	3,474	3,035	37,469	32,650	14.8	3,107	25.7	6.5	2.3	2.6	18.5	13.4
Lincoln, NE Metro Area	14,281	11,585	9,717	44,133	38,236	15.4	10,970	8.7	5.9	7.9	7.2	D	21.9
Lancaster County, NE	13,502	10,948	9,199	44,057	38,253	15.2	10,545	8.4	5.9	8.1	7.5	13.2	22.2
Seward County, NE	779	637	518	45,504	37,933	20.0	425	17.7	4.3	3.7	2.1	D	15.7
Little Rock-North Little Rock-Conway, AR Metro Area	30,042	25,660	21,807	41,062	36,531	12.4	22,442	6.2	7.5	6.9	7.9	12.8	23.2
Faulkner County, AR	4,161	3,505	2,573	34,235	30,732	11.4	2,397	8.8	8.0	2.9	12.2	12.0	17.8
Grant County, AR	621	547	442	34,323	30,602	12.2	226	29.4	7.0	1.9	2.2	D	19.2
Lonoke County, AR	2,537	2,192	1,668	35,413	31,903	11.0	747	14.0	8.8	5.4	3.3	9.3	19.5
Perry County, AR	325	300	241	31,935	28,742	11.1	84	2.5	4.2	1.6	2.5	D	22.3
Pulaski County, AR	18,008	15,567	14,248	45,862	40,577	13.0	17,677	5.2	7.0	7.8	7.9	13.1	24.4
Saline County, AR	4,388	3,548	2,635	37,360	32,955	13.4	1,310	6.7	12.7	3.0	4.2	12.4	20.0
Logan, UT-ID Metro Area	4,300	3,481	2,609	32,121	27,589	16.4	3,070	21.7	6.9	3.8	6.9	D	21.3
Franklin County, ID	419	330	268	32,057	25,820	24.2	201	6.6	8.7	2.1	3.2	D	20.2
Cache County, UT	3,881	3,150	2,340	32,128	27,789	15.6	2,868	22.7	6.8	3.9	7.1	9.7	21.3
Longview, TX Metro Area	9,173	7,876	5,925	42,118	36,678	14.8	6,699	10.3	7.3	2.8	D	11.6	9.6
Gregg County, TX	5,791	5,066	3,817	46,664	41,520	12.4	5,261	11.1	8.0	2.6	5.7	12.9	8.1
Rusk County, TX	1,936	1,610	1,212	36,484	30,192	20.8	946	8.8	4.6	3.6	D	7.2	13.8
Upshur County, TX	1,445	1,199	897	35,588	30,459	16.8	493	4.9	5.1	3.3	6.6	6.6	18.3
Longview, WA Metro Area	4,177	3,602	2,657	40,371	35,169	14.8	2,670	21.1	6.4	2.0	2.4	13.9	14.8
Cowlitz County, WA	4,177	3,602	2,657	40,371	35,169	14.8	2,670	21.1	6.4	2.0	2.4	13.9	14.8
Los Angeles-Long Beach-Anaheim, CA Metro Area	**727,377**	**574,299**	**506,680**	**54,526**	**44,714**	**21.9**	**541,541**	**8.5**	**5.7**	**6.4**	**11.9**	**9.3**	**13.9**
Anaheim-Santa Ana-Irvine, CA Division	*183,052*	*149,486*	*139,941*	*57,749*	*49,534*	*16.6*	*137,915*	*11.1*	*5.8*	*9.5*	*13.9*	*8.8*	*10.9*
Orange County, CA	183,052	149,486	139,941	57,749	49,534	16.6	137,915	11.1	5.8	9.5	13.9	8.8	10.9
Los Angeles-Long Beach-Glendale, CA Division	*544,325*	*424,813*	*366,739*	*53,521*	*43,234*	*23.8*	*403,625*	*7.6*	*5.7*	*5.3*	*11.3*	*9.4*	*14.9*
Los Angeles County, CA	544,325	424,813	366,739	53,521	43,234	23.8	403,625	7.6	5.7	5.3	11.3	9.4	14.9
Louisville/Jefferson County, KY-IN Metro Area	56,960	46,329	39,679	44,556	37,428	19.0	42,206	D	5.5	D	7.2	12.1	12.7
Clark County, IN	4,699	3,954	3,015	40,732	35,765	13.9	3,136	18.6	9.9	5.0	2.6	9.8	13.2

[1]Based on resident population estimated on July 1 of the year shown.
[2]Includes other industry categories not shown separately.
D = not shown to avoid disclosure of confidential information

Table C-3.   Personal Income and Earnings by Industry—*Continued*

Metropolitan statistical area, division, and component county	Total (million dollars) 2015	2010	2005	Per capita¹ (dollars) 2015	2010	Percent change, 2010–2015	Earnings 2015 Total² (million dollars)	Manufacturing	Retail trade	Finance and insurance	Professional and technical services	Health care and social services	Government and government enterprises
Floyd County, IN	3,748	2,864	2,549	48,815	38,340	27.3	1,747	23.8	5.6	3.3	5.6	11.9	21.7
Harrison County, IN	1,511	1,299	1,105	38,166	33,003	15.6	555	16.7	7.5	3.8	2.4	D	20.6
Scott County, IN	818	662	591	34,442	27,385	25.8	383	34.6	7.8	2.3	2.1	D	15.3
Washington County, IN	991	789	684	35,615	27,881	27.7	387	23.8	7.2	2.7	1.8	8.4	15.5
Bullitt County, KY	2,862	2,341	1,826	36,362	31,423	15.7	1,133	16.5	4.4	1.7	2.9	4.7	15.0
Henry County, KY	549	461	409	35,170	29,947	17.4	166	18.3	4.6	D	D	D	26.8
Jefferson County, KY	35,476	28,910	25,552	46,457	38,950	19.3	32,611	12.8	5.0	10.4	8.1	13.0	11.5
Oldham County, KY	3,482	2,755	2,167	53,671	45,594	17.7	1,000	6.8	5.2	11.6	9.1	12.7	19.7
Shelby County, KY	1,808	1,459	1,227	39,613	34,500	14.8	895	29.8	7.7	2.9	D	7.4	14.0
Spencer County, KY	722	586	416	40,375	34,255	17.9	121	D	8.5	4.7	5.5	10.6	28.6
Trimble County, KY	295	250	140	33,644	28,388	18.5	70	D	2.4	4.7	2.5	D	27.0
Lubbock, TX Metro Area	11,946	9,679	7,587	38,392	33,125	15.9	8,528	D	9.0	D	4.5	15.6	23.7
Crosby County, TX	196	223	199	32,805	36,943	-11.2	84	D	13.6	D	D	7.3	25.9
Lubbock County, TX	11,546	9,238	7,197	38,557	32,963	17.0	8,348	3.3	9.1	5.7	4.6	15.8	23.6
Lynn County, TX	204	218	191	35,607	36,890	-3.5	96	3.3	2.2	4.4	D	1.7	27.9
Lynchburg, VA Metro Area	9,646	8,308	6,857	37,107	32,829	13.0	5,927	18.5	6.8	4.2	8.1	14.7	13.2
Amherst County, VA	1,084	963	835	33,981	29,731	14.3	477	20.6	7.6	1.4	2.3	D	30.1
Appomattox County, VA	538	462	382	34,915	30,708	13.7	160	3.4	14.5	1.5	4.3	D	27.2
Bedford County, VA	3,227	2,714	2,266	41,514	36,182	14.7	1,123	12.9	7.0	3.0	7.3	10.7	14.5
Campbell County, VA	4,797	4,169	3,374	35,559	31,916	11.4	4,168	20.3	6.4	5.0	9.1	16.8	10.4
Lynchburg city, VA	(8)	(8)	(8)	(8)	(8)	(8)	(8)	(8)	(8)	(8)	(8)	(8)	(8)
Macon, GA Metro Area	8,622	7,585	6,626	37,470	32,659	14.7	6,076	D	D	9.8	6.5	19.7	13.8
Bibb County, GA	5,900	5,281	4,712	38,379	33,943	13.1	5,188	7.3	7.9	11.0	7.2	21.3	11.6
Crawford County, GA	385	338	292	31,046	26,783	15.9	94	2.3	3.4	D	4.5	6.1	21.7
Jones County, GA	959	849	683	33,643	29,662	13.4	243	0.9	4.9	3.5	D	D	25.2
Monroe County, GA	1,085	870	722	40,025	32,879	21.7	462	2.0	4.1	2.3	D	D	29.9
Twiggs County, GA	294	247	216	35,057	27,543	27.3	88	D	D	D	D	D	17.5
Madera, CA Metro Area	5,450	4,270	3,431	35,165	28,252	24.5	3,628	7.6	4.8	1.0	1.4	13.9	21.4
Madera County, CA	5,450	4,270	3,431	35,165	28,252	24.5	3,628	7.6	4.8	1.0	1.4	13.9	21.4
Madison, WI Metro Area	33,578	25,998	22,624	52,352	42,862	22.1	27,222	9.8	6.1	7.0	D	D	22.0
Columbia County, WI	2,687	2,150	1,847	47,346	37,810	25.2	1,506	27.0	5.7	1.9	3.1	10.2	15.2
Dane County, WI	28,122	21,609	18,825	53,705	44,174	21.6	24,049	8.0	5.3	7.6	9.5	9.2	23.1
Green County, WI	1,724	1,401	1,200	46,367	38,023	21.9	1,001	25.7	12.0	2.4	D	12.9	12.8
Iowa County, WI	1,045	838	752	43,877	35,416	23.9	666	10.7	28.7	1.9	1.9	D	12.9
Manchester-Nashua, NH Metro Area	23,254	19,344	16,858	57,180	48,238	18.5	16,836	14.2	8.0	8.9	11.4	11.3	10.3
Hillsborough County, NH	23,254	19,344	16,858	57,180	48,238	18.5	16,836	14.2	8.0	8.9	11.4	11.3	10.3
Manhattan, KS Metro Area	3,987	3,538	2,426	40,455	37,917	6.7	2,349	7.8	6.6	3.8	4.7	10.4	34.9
Pottawatomie County, KS	1,090	933	598	46,772	42,978	8.8	557	25.3	9.2	2.4	2.3	8.4	10.8
Riley County, KS	2,897	2,605	1,828	38,499	36,382	5.8	1,792	2.4	5.8	4.2	5.5	11.0	42.3
Mankato-North Mankato, MN Metro Area	4,329	3,328	2,953	43,665	34,368	27.1	3,371	18.1	7.0	3.1	D	D	16.1
Blue Earth County, MN	2,840	2,131	1,936	43,168	33,252	29.8	2,462	15.5	8.1	3.2	4.6	19.3	14.3
Nicollet County, MN	1,489	1,197	1,017	44,646	36,552	22.1	909	24.9	4.2	2.8	D	D	20.9
Mansfield, OH Metro Area	4,331	3,765	3,536	35,588	30,317	17.4	2,825	21.9	8.0	2.7	2.6	14.2	18.2
Richland County, OH	4,331	3,765	3,536	35,588	30,317	17.4	2,825	21.9	8.0	2.7	2.6	14.2	18.2
McAllen-Edinburg-Mission, TX Metro Area	20,703	16,921	12,094	24,579	21,718	13.2	13,688	2.8	10.6	3.2	2.9	17.8	25.3
Hidalgo County, TX	20,703	16,921	12,094	24,579	21,718	13.2	13,688	2.8	10.6	3.2	2.9	17.8	25.3
Medford, OR Metro Area	8,651	6,708	5,984	40,698	32,978	23.4	5,207	9.0	10.5	3.6	4.7	19.3	14.6
Jackson County, OR	8,651	6,708	5,984	40,698	32,978	23.4	5,207	9.0	10.5	3.6	4.7	19.3	14.6
Memphis, TN-MS-AR Metro Area	56,856	48,938	43,478	42,300	36,895	14.6	43,567	10.6	D	5.1	5.0	13.1	14.1
Crittenden County, AR	1,672	1,476	1,231	34,148	28,962	17.9	984	12.0	6.6	1.5	2.0	10.8	15.2
Benton County, MS	225	195	166	27,483	22,447	22.4	57	12.0	D	1.3	D	D	35.7
DeSoto County, MS	6,305	5,132	4,135	36,375	31,722	14.7	2,898	8.4	10.6	2.3	2.7	11.9	13.1
Marshall County, MS	1,068	927	773	29,738	24,988	19.0	414	10.3	7.2	3.6	1.1	D	15.7
Tate County, MS	905	795	680	31,984	27,437	16.6	304	7.4	10.0	3.1	3.0	D	27.2
Tunica County, MS	311	283	248	30,052	26,362	14.0	390	5.2	2.6	0.9	0.9	2.2	10.3
Fayette County, TN	1,866	1,567	1,191	47,649	40,806	16.8	645	30.9	5.8	2.6	D	6.8	11.9
Shelby County, TN	42,356	36,712	33,519	45,153	39,534	14.2	37,213	10.5	6.4	5.6	5.4	13.6	13.8
Tipton County, TN	2,148	1,851	1,536	34,721	30,267	14.7	663	14.1	7.3	2.5	D	D	24.5
Merced, CA Metro Area	9,714	7,240	6,116	36,185	28,191	28.4	5,729	11.1	5.7	1.4	1.7	8.7	26.3
Merced County, CA	9,714	7,240	6,116	36,185	28,191	28.4	5,729	11.1	5.7	1.4	1.7	8.7	26.3
Miami-Fort Lauderdale-West Palm Beach, FL Metro Area	**299,528**	**240,662**	**219,732**	**49,819**	**43,086**	**15.6**	**184,869**	**3.3**	**7.7**	**7.7**	**10.8**	**11.6**	**13.4**
Fort Lauderdale-Pompano Beach-Deerfield Beach, FL Division	85,167	71,381	66,895	44,909	40,713	10.3	55,971	3.6	8.5	6.8	10.2	10.2	14.2
Broward County, FL	85,167	71,381	66,895	44,909	40,713	10.3	55,971	3.6	8.5	6.8	10.2	10.2	14.2
Miami-Miami Beach-Kendall, FL Division	*116,553*	*95,717*	*81,989*	*43,278*	*38,162*	*13.4*	*84,718*	*3.0*	*7.3*	*8.1*	*10.5*	*11.5*	*13.9*
Miami-Dade County, FL	116,553	95,717	81,989	43,278	38,162	13.4	84,718	3.0	7.3	8.1	10.5	11.5	13.9
West Palm Beach-Boca Raton-Delray Beach, FL Division	*97,807*	*73,564*	*70,847*	*68,743*	*55,555*	*23.7*	*44,179*	*3.6*	*7.4*	*8.1*	*12.0*	*13.3*	*11.4*
Palm Beach County, FL	97,807	73,564	70,847	68,743	55,555	23.7	44,179	3.6	7.4	8.1	12.0	13.3	11.4
Michigan City-La Porte, IN Metro Area	4,194	3,528	3,038	37,827	31,654	19.5	2,407	20.8	6.7	2.7	2.9	13.9	15.1
LaPorte County, IN	4,194	3,528	3,038	37,827	31,654	19.5	2,407	20.8	6.7	2.7	2.9	13.9	15.1

¹Based on resident population estimated on July 1 of the year shown.
²Includes other industry categories not shown separately.
⁸Lynchburg city included with Campbell County, VA, in the Lynchburg, VA MSA.
D = not shown to avoid disclosure of confidential information.

Table C-3. Personal Income and Earnings by Industry—*Continued*

	Personal Income											
	Total (million dollars)			Per capita[1] (dollars)			Earnings 2015						
								Percent by selected major industries					
Metropolitan statistical area, division, and component county	2015	2010	2005	2015	2010	Percent change, 2010–2015	Total[2] (million dollars)	Manu-facturing	Retail trade	Finance and insurance	Profes-sional and technical services	Health care and social services	Govern-ment and govern-ment enter-prises
Midland, MI Metro Area	3,760	3,563	3,098	44,954	42,588	5.6	2,449	8.8	5.1	2.7	4.2	14.3	9.1
Midland County, MI	3,760	3,563	3,098	44,954	42,588	5.6	2,449	8.8	5.1	2.7	4.2	14.3	9.1
Midland, TX Metro Area	17,458	10,005	7,621	104,714	70,557	48.4	15,196	D	2.8	D	3.4	2.9	4.4
Martin County, TX	289	207	138	51,211	43,056	18.9	161	D	5.3	D	1.4	3.0	19.0
Midland County, TX	17,169	9,798	7,484	106,588	71,524	49.0	15,035	2.3	2.8	4.4	3.5	2.9	4.3
Milwaukee-Waukesha-West Allis, WI Metro Area..	79,861	67,189	58,931	50,681	43,161	17.4	61,260	16.2	5.5	8.3	8.2	13.1	11.0
Milwaukee County, WI	41,202	35,250	30,813	43,020	37,171	15.7	36,329	12.3	4.6	9.0	8.5	15.1	13.2
Ozaukee County, WI	6,454	5,381	4,743	73,462	62,306	17.9	2,900	24.8	5.6	8.1	10.0	13.3	9.2
Washington County, WI	6,832	5,696	4,974	51,110	43,162	18.4	3,611	29.3	6.4	5.7	3.1	10.6	10.3
Waukesha County, WI	25,373	20,862	18,401	63,995	53,482	19.7	18,421	19.8	7.2	7.5	8.3	9.7	7.0
Minneapolis-St. Paul-Bloomington, MN-WI Metro	194,372	153,074	135,476	55,148	45,618	20.9	152,042	11.7	5.1	10.0	D	10.5	12.0
Anoka County, MN	15,678	12,545	11,455	45,556	37,848	20.4	8,563	25.6	6.1	2.8	5.2	11.8	12.5
Carver County, MN	6,249	4,643	3,700	63,291	50,800	24.6	3,060	26.3	4.0	2.6	6.0	10.7	10.3
Chisago County, MN	2,306	1,870	1,599	42,475	34,674	22.5	921	22.0	6.9	1.4	2.1	21.1	16.7
Dakota County, MN	22,273	17,690	16,277	53,710	44,315	21.2	13,842	13.1	7.5	9.6	6.7	7.8	11.2
Hennepin County, MN	79,787	62,494	55,558	65,231	54,143	20.5	81,181	8.7	4.5	13.7	14.8	9.7	9.3
Isanti County, MN	1,495	1,248	1,054	38,905	32,950	18.1	638	16.8	8.8	2.5	D	D	18.3
Le Sueur County, MN	1,223	959	803	44,197	34,623	27.7	563	33.9	4.7	2.9	2.4	4.1	12.2
Mille Lacs County, MN	957	804	662	37,095	30,812	20.4	480	9.0	6.1	2.8	3.1	D	36.4
Ramsey County, MN	26,076	20,983	19,404	48,457	41,190	17.6	26,877	10.7	4.2	6.6	6.5	12.9	17.4
Scott County, MN	7,460	5,721	4,599	52,660	43,830	20.1	3,349	18.5	5.4	1.5	7.6	7.9	17.9
Sherburne County, MN	3,804	3,054	2,566	41,482	34,395	20.6	1,613	14.4	7.3	1.6	3.0	10.4	17.4
Sibley County, MN	652	563	472	43,865	36,948	18.7	262	8.2	2.5	1.8	2.0	D	15.1
Washington County, MN	14,634	11,269	9,717	58,163	47,153	23.3	5,383	12.5	8.0	6.2	7.2	13.8	13.8
Wright County, MN	5,791	4,531	3,682	44,103	36,212	21.8	2,611	15.5	7.7	1.9	2.5	11.2	13.7
Pierce County, WI	1,752	1,412	1,212	42,855	34,351	24.8	683	13.3	4.1	2.2	2.8	D	35.6
St. Croix County, WI	4,235	3,287	2,716	48,392	38,934	24.3	2,016	21.3	7.5	3.5	6.0	12.2	14.3
Missoula, MT Metro Area	4,659	3,682	3,071	40,803	33,642	21.3	3,390	3.0	8.6	4.8	7.6	18.3	19.4
Missoula County, MT	4,659	3,682	3,071	40,803	33,642	21.3	3,390	3.0	8.6	4.8	7.6	18.3	19.4
Mobile, AL Metro Area	14,684	13,138	10,766	35,348	31,785	11.2	11,129	15.9	6.6	4.7	7.6	12.2	15.3
Mobile County, AL	14,684	13,138	10,766	35,348	31,785	11.2	11,129	15.9	6.6	4.7	7.6	12.2	15.3
Modesto, CA Metro Area	21,237	16,449	14,477	39,445	31,918	23.6	12,950	13.3	7.6	2.1	3.4	16.2	18.2
Stanislaus County, CA	21,237	16,449	14,477	39,445	31,918	23.6	12,950	13.3	7.6	2.1	3.4	16.2	18.2
Monroe, LA Metro Area	6,491	5,721	4,681	36,214	32,358	11.9	4,377	D	7.4	5.5	D	18.2	16.0
Ouachita Parish, LA	5,706	5,053	4,091	36,396	32,819	10.9	4,092	9.5	7.4	5.7	5.7	18.9	16.0
Union Parish, LA	785	668	589	34,941	29,245	19.5	285	D	7.5	2.7	D	8.1	16.2
Monroe, MI Metro Area	6,238	5,164	4,907	41,707	33,989	22.7	2,819	16.1	6.6	1.9	7.3	9.8	12.6
Monroe County, MI	6,238	5,164	4,907	41,707	33,989	22.7	2,819	16.1	6.6	1.9	7.3	9.8	12.6
Montgomery, AL Metro Area	14,713	13,053	11,309	39,362	34,797	13.1	10,324	12.3	6.1	D	D	11.0	29.0
Autauga County, AL	2,091	1,829	1,421	37,773	33,452	12.9	610	18.1	8.5	3.2	2.5	10.1	19.5
Elmore County, AL	3,060	2,698	2,097	37,561	33,954	10.6	1,015	16.5	10.7	2.9	4.1	9.6	23.9
Lowndes County, AL	394	350	281	37,720	31,030	21.6	199	38.1	2.0	D	D	2.2	14.7
Montgomery County, AL	9,168	8,177	7,511	40,474	35,593	13.7	8,499	10.8	5.5	5.1	8.0	11.5	30.7
Morgantown, WV Metro Area	5,442	4,429	3,386	39,383	33,979	15.9	4,374	9.8	5.4	1.6	D	D	26.6
Monongalia County, WV	4,318	3,463	2,533	41,429	35,781	15.8	3,916	10.2	5.3	1.5	7.7	19.5	25.2
Preston County, WV	1,123	966	853	33,100	28,782	15.0	458	7.0	6.7	2.1	D	D	38.4
Morristown, TN Metro Area	3,903	3,268	2,718	33,463	28,623	16.9	2,518	27.6	8.0	1.8	2.1	D	13.7
Hamblen County, TN	2,200	1,844	1,586	34,696	29,478	17.7	1,729	33.0	8.4	1.8	1.9	12.8	12.6
Jefferson County, TN	1,703	1,424	1,132	31,994	27,587	16.0	789	15.9	7.1	1.9	2.7	D	16.1
Mount Vernon-Anacortes, WA Metro Area	5,419	4,405	3,601	44,470	37,651	18.1	3,351	15.5	8.5	3.4	4.8	8.0	23.2
Skagit County, WA	5,419	4,405	3,601	44,470	37,651	18.1	3,351	15.5	8.5	3.4	4.8	8.0	23.2
Muncie, IN Metro Area	3,844	3,289	3,054	32,896	27,950	17.7	2,569	11.0	8.1	4.3	5.0	19.1	22.8
Delaware County, IN	3,844	3,289	3,054	32,896	27,950	17.7	2,569	11.0	8.1	4.3	5.0	19.1	22.8
Muskegon, MI Metro Area	5,979	4,918	4,396	34,604	28,605	21.0	3,633	27.2	9.6	2.1	2.6	17.1	14.0
Muskegon County, MI	5,979	4,918	4,396	34,604	28,605	21.0	3,633	27.2	9.6	2.1	2.6	17.1	14.0
Myrtle Beach-Conway-North Myrtle Beach, SC-NC Metro Area	14,608	11,162	9,095	33,818	29,474	14.7	7,952	3.2	11.4	5.0	D	11.8	16.5
Brunswick County, NC	4,457	3,405	2,722	36,307	31,476	15.3	1,827	4.6	8.4	2.3	D	11.2	16.9
Horry County, SC	10,151	7,757	6,372	32,830	28,674	14.5	6,125	2.8	12.3	5.9	4.8	12.0	16.4
Napa, CA Metro Area	8,759	6,347	5,861	61,483	46,396	32.5	6,655	22.9	5.1	3.1	5.6	9.0	14.9
Napa County, CA	8,759	6,347	5,861	61,483	46,396	32.5	6,655	22.9	5.1	3.1	5.6	9.0	14.9
Naples-Immokalee-Marco Island, FL Metro Area..	28,039	20,547	18,403	78,473	63,677	23.2	9,736	3.1	9.0	6.6	10.9	11.6	9.9
Collier County, FL	28,039	20,547	18,403	78,473	63,677	23.2	9,736	3.1	9.0	6.6	10.9	11.6	9.9
Nashville-Davidson--Murfreesboro--Franklin, TN Metro Area	92,680	69,687	54,830	50,635	41,580	21.8	76,850	7.5	6.4	6.1	9.8	20.8	9.7
Cannon County, TN	462	384	352	33,416	27,852	20.0	134	10.6	5.3	D	2.4	D	23.7
Cheatham County, TN	1,517	1,224	1,131	38,177	31,288	22.0	605	22.8	6.1	1.5	D	5.7	15.2
Davidson County, TN	37,618	29,837	23,267	55,411	47,501	16.7	41,576	3.2	5.9	6.3	11.9	22.8	8.7
Dickson County, TN	1,851	1,511	1,229	35,952	30,397	18.3	987	20.7	8.5	3.1	2.2	14.6	14.8
Hickman County, TN	712	595	510	29,238	24,113	21.3	253	11.0	7.0	1.3	2.1	D	25.8
Macon County, TN	715	573	523	30,845	25,754	19.8	299	12.1	11.1	4.7	2.2	D	20.0

[1]Based on resident population estimated on July 1 of the year shown.
[2]Includes other industry categories not shown separately.
D = not shown to avoid disclosure of confidential information.

Table C-3.   Personal Income and Earnings by Industry—*Continued*

| Metropolitan statistical area, division, and component county | Total (million dollars) | | | Per capita¹ (dollars) | | | Earnings 2015 | | | | | | |
| | | | | | | | | Percent by selected major industries | | | | | |
	2015	2010	2005	2015	2010	Percent change, 2010–2015	Total² (million dollars)	Manu-facturing	Retail trade	Finance and insurance	Profes-sional and technical services	Health care and social services	Govern-ment and govern-ment enter-prises
Maury County, TN	3,330	2,560	2,133	37,947	31,524	20.4	2,025	17.1	6.6	6.4	3.3	10.6	19.8
Robertson County, TN	2,582	2,091	1,805	37,661	31,523	19.5	1,382	30.5	6.6	2.0	D	6.4	15.2
Rutherford County, TN	11,244	8,207	6,800	37,654	31,112	21.0	8,331	25.7	6.7	3.9	3.2	10.1	14.8
Smith County, TN	679	559	448	35,182	29,202	20.5	340	22.7	7.9	3.1	1.9	7.5	17.2
Sumner County, TN	7,581	5,747	4,679	43,079	35,632	20.9	3,637	12.7	7.9	3.2	7.2	13.5	12.6
Trousdale County, TN	281	227	184	34,954	28,896	21.0	100	11.4	8.1	D	3.8	D	26.5
Williamson County, TN	18,504	12,014	8,356	87,419	65,267	33.9	14,441	1.4	5.9	9.1	12.2	29.7	4.9
Wilson County, TN	5,602	4,158	3,414	43,458	36,278	19.8	2,741	11.3	12.5	2.8	5.0	8.8	11.2
New Bern, NC Metro Area	5,047	4,562	3,734	39,975	35,887	11.4	3,355	7.6	5.4	1.7	4.3	9.1	50.1
Craven County, NC	4,195	3,788	3,077	40,555	36,447	11.3	3,083	8.0	5.2	1.0	4.5	0.0	52.1
Jones County, NC	370	326	292	36,906	32,373	14.0	114	1.5	3.1	0.8	1.8	D	27.3
Pamlico County, NC	482	447	365	37,682	34,142	10.4	158	4.4	11.4	1.7	4.0	D	29.2
New Haven-Milford, CT Metro Area	44,551	38,416	34,037	51,835	44,494	16.5	29,461	8.8	6.3	4.1	8.8	15.3	15.3
New Haven County, CT	44,551	38,416	34,037	51,835	44,494	16.5	29,461	8.8	6.3	4.1	8.8	15.3	15.3
New Orleans-Metairie, LA Metro Area	60,404	50,308	43,076	47,830	42,077	13.7	44,275	7.5	D	4.7	9.6	10.4	13.7
Jefferson Parish, LA	20,471	18,189	15,092	46,922	42,033	11.6	14,496	4.9	7.9	6.5	8.4	14.2	10.0
Orleans Parish, LA	18,189	14,531	14,452	46,684	41,769	11.8	15,433	2.2	3.9	4.8	14.8	9.9	18.8
Plaquemines Parish, LA	1,084	973	746	46,136	42,074	9.7	1,439	15.8	D	0.6	D	D	13.4
St. Bernard Parish, LA	1,329	1,108	1,395	29,279	30,112	-2.8	764	29.6	6.3	1.2	1.7	D	17.6
St. Charles Parish, LA	2,305	2,000	1,686	45,347	39,557	14.6	2,501	29.6	3.0	0.9	6.2	3.0	9.1
St. James Parish, LA	920	845	575	42,678	38,421	11.1	812	46.4	2.2	1.1	D	1.5	11.8
St. John the Baptist Parish, LA	1,703	1,546	1,143	39,031	33,894	15.2	1,231	32.2	5.3	1.9	2.1	3.9	11.5
St. Tammany Parish, LA	14,312	11,023	8,086	57,229	46,995	21.8	7,598	3.8	7.1	3.9	7.0	11.0	12.4
New York-Newark-Jersey City, NY-NJ-PA Metro Area	**1,303,530**	**1,045,891**	**899,710**	**64,588**	**53,359**	**21.0**	**966,007**	**D**	**4.9**	**15.3**	**13.1**	**10.3**	**14.0**
Dutchess County-Putnam County, NY Division	*20,328*	*17,453*	*15,567*	*51,490*	*43,903*	*17.3*	*10,427*	*11.6*	*6.6*	*2.6*	*5.7*	*15.8*	*24.8*
Dutchess County, NY	14,469	12,444	11,012	48,921	41,793	17.1	8,354	13.1	7.0	2.6	5.3	15.7	24.5
Putnam County, NY	5,859	5,010	4,555	59,160	50,199	17.9	2,073	5.7	5.0	2.6	7.3	16.2	26.0
Nassau County-Suffolk County, NY Division	*195,181*	*162,097*	*140,607*	*68,175*	*57,142*	*19.3*	*111,833*	*5.6*	*7.5*	*7.0*	*9.2*	*14.8*	*19.5*
Nassau County, NY	105,861	86,937	76,697	77,762	64,787	20.0	56,924	3.1	8.2	6.6	9.8	17.8	17.4
Suffolk County, NY	89,321	75,160	63,911	59,484	50,278	18.3	54,908	8.3	6.7	7.3	8.6	11.7	21.6
Newark, NJ-PA Division	*173,752*	*145,466*	*127,131*	*69,183*	*58,826*	*17.6*	*121,638*	*D*	*4.6*	*8.3*	*14.9*	*9.4*	*13.8*
Essex County, NJ	47,870	40,697	35,932	60,030	51,870	15.7	33,223	4.5	3.3	11.0	11.1	10.7	22.0
Hunterdon County, NJ	10,134	9,074	8,068	80,759	71,259	13.3	4,781	4.1	7.2	10.2	16.0	10.0	15.1
Morris County, NJ	43,248	36,700	30,682	86,582	74,473	16.3	34,504	7.6	4.6	8.4	19.2	9.0	9.0
Somerset County, NJ	28,850	22,565	19,214	86,468	69,608	24.2	23,270	15.9	4.8	8.2	14.7	6.4	7.1
Sussex County, NJ	7,973	7,029	6,623	55,497	47,236	17.5	2,960	5.7	8.3	2.4	7.6	14.0	22.4
Union County, NJ	33,396	27,437	24,889	60,089	51,020	17.8	22,230	11.1	5.1	4.7	14.9	10.4	14.0
Pike County, PA	2,279	1,965	1,723	40,738	34,266	18.9	670	D	9.3	2.0	4.2	8.5	29.2
New York-Jersey City-White Plains, NY-NJ Division	*914,269*	*720,874*	*616,405*	*63,433*	*51,884*	*22.3*	*722,109*	*2.9*	*4.5*	*18.0*	*13.5*	*9.7*	*13.0*
Bergen County, NJ	71,184	59,922	52,215	75,849	66,073	14.8	44,938	6.6	6.5	4.7	12.1	13.7	9.9
Hudson County, NJ	36,404	28,375	22,835	53,945	44,593	21.0	27,724	2.4	4.7	24.2	9.3	5.9	15.5
Middlesex County, NJ	44,961	38,330	32,254	53,467	47,248	13.2	36,885	8.2	5.3	5.9	14.8	9.0	14.0
Monmouth County, NJ	43,639	36,422	32,956	69,410	57,750	20.2	21,410	3.6	7.5	6.5	13.2	15.2	14.7
Ocean County, NJ	27,145	22,986	20,226	46,109	39,793	15.9	11,562	3.1	10.2	2.7	7.1	18.1	21.5
Passaic County, NJ	24,110	20,312	17,820	47,189	40,440	16.7	14,407	17.0	7.3	3.2	6.3	12.1	18.6
Bronx County, NY	47,217	41,031	33,530	32,442	29,556	9.8	23,252	1.7	6.2	1.2	1.6	25.8	27.6
Kings County, NY	112,703	88,905	73,224	42,743	35,416	20.7	47,317	2.4	7.2	3.9	5.8	20.9	22.0
New York County, NY	257,710	180,535	152,783	156,708	113,643	37.9	370,152	0.8	2.7	29.2	18.3	4.9	7.9
Orange County, NY	17,566	14,815	12,756	46,513	39,674	17.2	9,892	6.0	9.0	2.4	5.7	14.0	31.5
Queens County, NY	98,919	81,957	71,302	42,288	36,661	15.3	50,982	2.8	5.8	4.0	2.9	14.2	20.5
Richmond County, NY	23,804	20,205	17,580	50,161	43,022	16.6	8,455	0.9	7.2	2.0	4.2	22.5	22.9
Rockland County, NY	17,879	15,043	12,976	54,838	48,140	13.9	10,026	12.3	6.4	2.5	7.8	13.9	21.0
Westchester County, NY	91,029	72,034	63,946	93,229	75,775	23.0	45,106	5.5	5.1	8.9	12.2	12.9	17.0
Niles-Benton Harbor, MI Metro Area	6,485	5,668	4,950	41,939	36,148	16.0	4,132	31.9	5.3	3.0	3.2	11.2	13.6
Berrien County, MI	6,485	5,668	4,950	41,939	36,148	16.0	4,132	31.9	5.3	3.0	3.2	11.2	13.6
North Port-Sarasota-Bradenton, FL Metro Area	38,553	29,736	29,523	50,139	42,277	18.6	17,816	6.3	9.1	5.2	9.8	15.8	10.8
Manatee County, FL	15,669	12,273	11,863	43,121	37,946	13.6	7,230	7.9	9.2	3.5	6.8	13.9	11.9
Sarasota County, FL	22,884	17,464	17,660	56,426	45,964	22.8	10,586	5.2	9.1	6.3	11.8	17.1	10.0
Norwich-New London, CT Metro Area	14,272	12,576	11,078	52,498	45,888	14.4	9,881	18.1	6.0	1.8	7.0	11.3	27.8
New London County, CT	14,272	12,576	11,078	52,498	45,888	14.4	9,881	18.1	6.0	1.8	7.0	11.3	27.8
Ocala, FL Metro Area	11,602	10,036	8,574	33,800	30,281	11.6	5,289	9.1	11.1	3.7	5.1	19.8	16.1
Marion County, FL	11,602	10,036	8,574	33,800	30,281	11.6	5,289	9.1	11.1	3.7	5.1	19.8	16.1
Ocean City, NJ Metro Area	5,050	4,318	4,113	53,309	44,399	20.1	2,618	D	9.7	2.9	4.5	10.9	27.9
Cape May County, NJ	5,050	4,318	4,113	53,309	44,399	20.1	2,618	D	9.7	2.9	4.5	10.9	27.9
Odessa, TX Metro Area	7,303	4,804	3,243	45,806	35,047	30.7	6,104	9.3	7.0	1.6	3.3	5.1	10.8
Ector County, TX	7,303	4,804	3,243	45,806	35,047	30.7	6,104	9.3	7.0	1.6	3.3	5.1	10.8
Ogden-Clearfield, UT Metro Area	24,564	19,165	15,559	38,212	31,953	19.6	14,885	15.2	6.9	3.7	D	D	25.1
Box Elder County, UT	1,728	1,389	1,100	33,161	27,686	19.8	1,091	37.3	5.1	1.5	D	6.3	13.1
Davis County, UT	13,442	10,178	8,398	40,000	33,053	21.0	7,884	11.2	6.9	2.7	8.9	7.4	29.3

¹Based on resident population estimated on July 1 of the year shown.
²Includes other industry categories not shown separately.
D = not shown to avoid disclosure of confidential information.

Table C-3. Personal Income and Earnings by Industry—*Continued*

| | Personal Income Total (million dollars) | | | Per capita[1] (dollars) | | Percent change, 2010–2015 | Earnings 2015 Total[2] (million dollars) | Percent by selected major industries | | | | | |
Metropolitan statistical area, division, and component county	2015	2010	2005	2015	2010			Manu-facturing	Retail trade	Finance and insurance	Profes-sional and technical services	Health care and social services	Govern-ment and govern-ment enter-prises
Morgan County, UT	497	352	234	44,916	36,996	21.4	142	10.5	5.7	6.3	6.2	D	16.3
Weber County, UT	8,898	7,246	5,828	36,522	31,208	17.0	5,768	16.7	7.3	5.4	4.8	12.7	21.8
Oklahoma City, OK Metro Area	62,592	48,744	39,025	46,076	38,749	18.9	47,018	5.8	6.2	4.5	D	11.6	19.7
Canadian County, OK	5,812	4,177	2,925	43,573	35,902	21.4	2,256	14.1	6.7	2.5	3.6	6.1	16.3
Cleveland County, OK	11,724	9,249	7,079	42,716	36,000	18.7	5,428	5.2	8.7	2.9	7.0	8.8	28.7
Grady County, OK	2,114	1,667	1,275	38,678	31,770	21.7	856	9.5	7.5	3.0	4.4	6.9	17.2
Lincoln County, OK	1,226	945	730	34,985	27,529	27.1	464	7.2	8.0	7.7	1.9	6.0	18.6
Logan County, OK	1,796	1,371	1,007	39,036	32,602	19.7	472	4.9	9.3	3.9	D	10.6	15.3
McClain County, OK	1,618	1,215	842	42,507	34,985	21.5	569	2.7	9.5	3.1	4.4	6.9	16.9
Oklahoma County, OK	38,303	30,120	25,165	49,304	41,770	18.0	36,973	5.3	5.6	4.9	6.7	12.7	18.7
Olympia-Tumwater, WA Metro Area	11,901	10,054	8,127	44,155	39,730	11.1	7,536	3.1	6.3	3.0	5.2	12.7	39.3
Thurston County, WA	11,901	10,054	8,127	44,155	39,730	11.1	7,536	3.1	6.3	3.0	5.2	12.7	39.3
Omaha-Council Bluffs, NE-IA Metro Area	47,178	38,474	30,955	51,543	44,317	16.3	36,578	6.3	5.0	8.2	D	10.8	13.7
Harrison County, IA	591	530	454	41,425	35,512	16.7	248	9.4	8.3	3.7	3.1	D	18.7
Mills County, IA	731	641	547	49,265	42,579	15.7	280	12.6	3.9	3.0	D	D	35.8
Pottawattamie County, IA	3,917	3,144	2,750	41,819	33,669	24.2	2,400	17.3	7.7	2.2	3.2	12.6	15.1
Cass County, NE	1,168	972	844	45,775	38,457	19.0	383	9.9	6.3	3.4	3.0	4.6	19.5
Douglas County, NE	30,920	25,251	19,949	56,212	48,684	15.5	27,371	5.4	4.6	9.4	8.4	11.9	10.7
Sarpy County, NE	7,874	6,330	5,086	44,819	39,623	13.1	4,836	3.9	5.4	6.7	7.2	5.1	26.3
Saunders County, NE	967	765	627	46,035	36,660	25.6	402	6.3	5.4	3.7	4.6	D	20.5
Washington County, NE	1,009	843	700	49,835	41,562	19.9	659	18.2	9.7	3.1	1.8	D	22.9
Orlando-Kissimmee-Sanford, FL Metro Area	92,221	71,097	62,324	38,632	33,230	16.3	71,727	4.7	7.4	5.6	9.5	11.5	11.4
Lake County, FL	12,285	9,632	8,274	37,698	32,337	16.6	4,925	4.2	11.7	3.1	4.4	19.7	16.6
Orange County, FL	50,998	38,854	33,176	39,591	33,821	17.1	50,856	5.1	6.1	5.5	10.5	10.6	10.7
Osceola County, FL	9,691	7,102	5,692	29,911	26,319	13.6	4,729	1.6	10.3	1.6	3.5	15.4	17.2
Seminole County, FL	19,246	15,510	15,182	42,851	36,660	16.9	11,216	4.0	10.0	9.3	10.0	10.4	9.8
Oshkosh-Neenah, WI Metro Area	7,189	6,155	5,335	42,399	36,845	15.1	6,357	29.1	4.8	4.6	5.3	9.6	12.5
Winnebago County, WI	7,189	6,155	5,335	42,399	36,845	15.1	6,357	29.1	4.8	4.6	5.3	9.6	12.5
Owensboro, KY Metro Area	4,658	4,039	3,205	39,657	35,191	12.7	3,125	22.2	6.7	D	D	D	12.1
Daviess County, KY	3,973	3,372	2,721	40,032	34,871	14.8	2,573	16.2	7.6	7.2	3.3	19.6	12.8
Hancock County, KY	333	355	200	38,284	41,501	-7.8	413	65.0	0.9	1.2	0.5	D	5.9
McLean County, KY	352	312	283	37,007	32,766	12.9	139	7.2	6.3	D	D	D	17.5
Oxnard-Thousand Oaks-Ventura, CA Metro Area	46,060	37,605	33,794	54,155	45,566	18.8	27,491	15.3	7.4	5.8	7.6	9.1	17.0
Ventura County, CA	46,060	37,605	33,794	54,155	45,566	18.8	27,491	15.3	7.4	5.8	7.6	9.1	17.0
Palm Bay-Melbourne-Titusville, FL Metro Area	23,014	20,021	17,759	40,511	36,806	10.1	13,362	16.2	7.6	2.9	9.8	13.9	16.9
Brevard County, FL	23,014	20,021	17,759	40,511	36,806	10.1	13,362	16.2	7.6	2.9	9.8	13.9	16.9
Panama City, FL Metro Area	7,692	6,617	5,721	38,947	35,755	8.9	4,945	5.5	8.7	3.1	6.9	D	26.6
Bay County, FL	7,214	6,202	5,356	39,717	36,648	8.4	4,739	5.6	8.7	3.1	6.9	13.5	26.3
Gulf County, FL	478	414	365	30,125	26,199	15.0	206	2.6	7.5	2.6	6.2	D	33.2
Parkersburg-Vienna, WV Metro Area	3,568	2,987	2,514	38,642	32,199	20.0	2,344	D	9.0	D	3.1	14.8	20.1
Wirt County, WV	172	137	109	29,315	23,932	22.5	35	D	7.8	D	2.4	11.1	36.7
Wood County, WV	3,396	2,849	2,405	39,276	32,745	19.9	2,309	10.8	9.0	4.9	3.2	14.9	19.9
Pensacola-Ferry Pass-Brent, FL Metro Area	18,667	15,793	13,481	39,048	35,010	11.5	11,029	4.4	7.3	5.9	7.4	15.1	27.8
Escambia County, FL	11,945	10,261	8,808	38,408	34,415	11.6	8,781	5.0	7.0	6.6	7.2	15.8	28.3
Santa Rosa County, FL	6,722	5,532	4,673	40,240	36,169	11.3	2,248	2.3	8.3	3.2	8.4	12.5	25.9
Peoria, IL Metro Area	17,061	15,060	12,344	45,132	39,741	13.6	12,714	23.8	5.1	D	D	14.0	11.5
Marshall County, IL	484	435	386	40,408	34,450	17.3	181	34.0	3.5	4.0	2.1	6.1	16.3
Peoria County, IL	8,767	7,781	6,248	47,076	41,786	12.7	7,209	11.0	4.8	5.1	15.6	20.5	11.3
Stark County, IL	204	195	166	35,185	32,671	7.7	80	22.6	7.8	D	D	5.9	23.5
Tazewell County, IL	5,759	5,083	4,319	42,719	37,522	13.9	4,543	44.4	5.3	3.3	2.6	5.2	10.7
Woodford County, IL	1,848	1,565	1,223	47,111	40,485	16.4	700	19.5	6.6	2.8	2.5	7.9	16.0
Philadelphia-Camden-Wilmington, PA-NJ-DE-MD Metro Area	**347,032**	**288,083**	**244,915**	**57,173**	**48,243**	**18.5**	**249,636**	**D**	**5.2**	**8.1**	**D**	**13.0**	**12.6**
Camden, NJ Division	*63,656*	*55,042*	*47,420*	*50,818*	*43,980*	*15.5*	*38,670*	*8.0*	*7.9*	*6.0*	*D*	*14.8*	*19.6*
Burlington County, NJ	24,865	21,557	18,594	55,227	47,987	15.1	16,663	8.5	7.4	9.8	9.4	13.2	18.4
Camden County, NJ	24,567	21,345	18,796	48,084	41,561	15.7	14,848	7.0	7.2	3.6	9.0	18.9	19.4
Gloucester County, NJ	14,224	12,140	10,030	48,799	42,050	16.0	7,159	9.1	10.7	2.1	D	10.3	23.1
Montgomery County-Bucks County-Chester County, PA Division	*136,840*	*112,664*	*100,034*	*69,725*	*58,482*	*19.2*	*88,666*	*9.9*	*6.4*	*7.3*	*16.7*	*11.9*	*8.4*
Bucks County, PA	40,343	33,010	28,596	64,306	52,775	21.8	20,193	11.1	7.2	4.4	9.9	14.6	10.4
Chester County, PA	38,078	30,831	27,388	73,803	61,669	19.7	25,629	8.1	7.1	11.0	17.1	8.4	8.2
Montgomery County, PA	58,418	48,823	44,050	71,306	60,948	17.0	42,845	10.4	5.7	6.5	19.7	12.9	7.5
Philadelphia, PA Division	110,472	89,715	69,385	51,832	42,979	20.6	93,473	3.8	3.0	7.3	11.1	13.5	13.4
Delaware County, PA	32,568	27,285	23,723	57,756	48,805	18.3	18,668	9.5	5.0	9.6	9.5	13.6	11.4
Philadelphia County, PA	77,904	62,430	45,663	49,701	40,848	21.7	74,805	2.4	2.5	6.7	11.5	13.5	13.9
Wilmington, DE-MD-NJ Division	*36,064*	*30,662*	*28,076*	*49,858*	*43,426*	*14.8*	*28,827*	*D*	*4.9*	*15.7*	*13.4*	*12.6*	*13.6*
New Castle County, DE	28,780	24,217	22,591	51,690	44,937	15.0	24,947	D	4.9	17.9	15.0	13.0	12.2
Cecil County, MD	4,441	3,800	3,278	43,374	37,559	15.5	2,137	20.7	6.1	1.3	D	10.2	24.4
Salem County, NJ	2,843	2,646	2,207	44,304	40,086	10.5	1,744	13.7	4.3	1.7	D	10.2	20.1
Phoenix-Mesa-Scottsdale, AZ Metro Area	186,693	146,616	131,424	40,811	34,867	17.0	134,303	8.1	7.8	8.8	8.6	12.0	12.9
Maricopa County, AZ	175,438	137,837	125,668	42,092	36,030	16.8	130,501	8.2	7.9	9.1	8.8	12.1	12.3

[1]Based on resident population estimated on July 1 of the year shown.
[2]Includes other industry categories not shown separately.
D = not shown to avoid disclosure of confidential information.

Table C-3. Personal Income and Earnings by Industry—*Continued*

	Personal Income											
	Total (million dollars)			Per capita[1] (dollars)			Earnings 2015					
								Percent by selected major industries				
Metropolitan statistical area, division, and component county	2015	2010	2005	2015	2010	Percent change, 2010–2015	Total[2] (million dollars)	Manu-facturing	Retail trade	Finance and insurance	Profes-sional and technical services	Health care and social services	Govern-ment and govern-ment enter-prises
---	---	---	---	---	---	---	---	---	---	---	---	---	---
Pinal County, AZ	11,255	8,779	5,756	27,682	23,140	19.6	3,801	5.8	6.6	1.7	2.7	6.4	34.9
Pine Bluff, AR Metro Area	2,940	2,766	2,484	31,377	27,638	13.5	1,928	17.3	5.5	D	1.8	D	29.5
Cleveland County, AR	291	247	236	34,987	28,456	23.0	78	4.5	2.0	D	D	5.2	20.6
Jefferson County, AR	2,304	2,221	1,980	32,189	28,718	12.1	1,665	18.8	6.0	3.7	2.0	14.4	29.3
Lincoln County, AR	346	298	268	25,003	21,201	17.9	185	8.3	3.3	1.9	D	D	35.6
Pittsburgh, PA Metro Area	119,432	100,644	85,254	50,756	42,700	18.9	88,054	7.9	5.4	6.8	10.5	13.9	11.2
Allegheny County, PA	66,556	56,414	48,470	54,090	46,093	17.3	58,201	5.2	4.7	8.9	13.0	14.6	10.0
Armstrong County, PA	2,780	2,417	2,022	41,456	35,100	18.1	1,234	11.2	6.1	2.1	2.4	13.0	15.9
Beaver County, PA	7,321	6,276	5,253	43,355	36,785	17.9	3,473	14.0	7.0	2.3	5.8	16.1	15.9
Butler County, PA	9,675	7,837	6,285	51,790	42,568	21.7	6,296	15.9	6.6	3.1	6.1	11.3	13.9
Fayette County, PA	5,159	4,501	3,750	38,609	32,984	17.1	2,431	9.7	8.5	1.6	2.9	15.4	20.0
Washington County, PA	11,201	8,772	7,028	53,783	42,198	27.5	7,779	9.4	4.8	2.4	5.8	10.3	9.3
Westmoreland County, PA	16,739	14,426	12,447	46,764	39,512	18.4	8,641	15.1	8.2	2.9	6.1	12.8	13.6
Pittsfield, MA Metro Area	6,482	5,412	4,774	50,712	41,228	23.0	4,030	9.9	7.9	4.6	7.5	19.0	15.0
Berkshire County, MA	6,482	5,412	4,774	50,712	41,228	23.0	4,030	9.9	7.9	4.6	7.5	19.0	15.0
Pocatello, ID Metro Area	2,792	2,381	2,071	33,344	28,684	16.2	1,784	7.8	8.1	6.3	4.2	15.4	25.5
Bannock County, ID	2,792	2,381	2,071	33,344	28,684	16.2	1,784	7.8	8.1	6.3	4.2	15.4	25.5
Portland-South Portland, ME Metro Area	25,918	21,988	19,113	49,246	42,787	15.1	18,267	D	6.8	7.8	9.1	14.9	16.0
Cumberland County, ME	15,165	12,830	11,050	52,298	45,582	14.7	12,407	6.2	6.5	10.3	10.9	17.0	11.9
Sagadahoc County, ME	1,606	1,376	1,177	45,702	39,054	17.0	1,125	D	5.6	2.1	6.6	5.0	11.6
York County, ME	9,146	7,782	6,886	45,466	39,465	15.2	4,734	10.8	7.8	2.6	5.2	11.7	27.7
Portland-Vancouver-Hillsboro, OR-WA Metro Area	115,691	88,151	74,697	48,422	39,486	22.6	86,340	13.6	5.8	5.2	D	D	13.2
Clackamas County, OR	19,901	15,759	14,071	49,565	41,812	18.5	10,848	13.5	7.5	5.3	9.6	13.3	10.2
Columbia County, OR	1,927	1,586	1,350	38,845	32,132	20.9	622	17.4	7.8	3.2	D	8.8	20.5
Multnomah County, OR	38,906	29,573	24,441	49,230	40,109	22.7	37,242	7.0	5.2	6.3	12.4	11.5	17.0
Washington County, OR	29,813	21,771	18,409	51,909	40,950	26.8	24,757	24.7	5.4	4.1	6.6	8.2	6.6
Yamhill County, OR	3,996	3,194	2,790	38,920	32,163	21.0	2,152	21.5	6.1	3.2	4.1	12.4	13.9
Clark County, WA	20,710	15,911	13,337	45,070	37,280	20.9	10,591	9.0	6.9	4.4	8.1	13.2	17.6
Skamania County, WA	439	356	300	38,725	32,095	20.7	128	14.2	4.1	0.8	5.7	D	32.2
Port St. Lucie, FL Metro Area	21,763	16,523	14,950	47,847	38,855	23.1	8,301	5.2	9.9	3.4	7.6	17.5	15.4
Martin County, FL	11,127	8,091	7,889	71,197	55,051	29.3	4,046	6.2	9.8	4.7	9.5	18.7	9.7
St. Lucie County, FL	10,636	8,432	7,060	35,625	30,300	17.6	4,255	4.3	10.0	2.3	5.7	16.3	20.8
Prescott, AZ Metro Area	7,900	6,141	5,387	35,545	29,088	22.2	3,512	5.5	9.5	2.0	4.6	15.1	19.7
Yavapai County, AZ	7,900	6,141	5,387	35,545	29,088	22.2	3,512	5.5	9.5	2.0	4.6	15.1	19.7
Providence-Warwick, RI-MA Metro Area	79,722	67,310	58,350	49,423	42,006	17.7	51,078	D	6.8	6.4	6.8	14.5	16.7
Bristol County, MA	26,888	22,287	18,915	48,294	40,583	19.0	15,620	D	7.9	2.4	5.1	15.0	15.7
Bristol County, RI	3,390	2,993	2,576	69,066	60,025	15.1	1,016	D	5.1	3.9	7.4	11.4	18.2
Kent County, RI	8,862	7,482	6,734	53,776	45,060	19.3	5,058	11.0	8.9	6.7	8.0	13.8	13.4
Newport County, RI	5,083	4,055	3,833	61,666	48,767	26.5	3,317	D	7.3	3.2	9.9	6.9	35.1
Providence County, RI	28,126	24,266	20,741	44,399	38,696	14.7	22,032	6.9	4.8	10.5	7.5	16.3	14.4
Washington County, RI	7,373	6,228	5,550	58,274	49,008	18.9	4,035	17.0	10.4	2.5	5.4	11.2	21.4
Provo-Orem, UT Metro Area	20,050	13,733	10,567	34,227	25,898	32.2	13,730	10.1	10.0	D	10.1	D	11.9
Juab County, UT	331	250	205	31,206	24,413	27.8	191	23.7	3.6	D	4.6	D	18.3
UT County, UT	19,720	13,483	10,361	34,283	25,928	32.2	13,539	9.9	10.1	3.2	10.2	9.0	11.8
Pueblo, CO Metro Area	5,698	4,678	3,992	34,831	29,326	18.8	3,401	9.4	8.1	2.2	5.4	20.5	21.5
Pueblo County, CO	5,698	4,678	3,992	34,831	29,326	18.8	3,401	9.4	8.1	2.2	5.4	20.5	21.5
Punta Gorda, FL Metro Area	6,534	5,153	4,723	37,745	32,216	17.2	2,565	1.8	12.3	3.5	6.4	22.2	15.3
Charlotte County, FL	6,534	5,153	4,723	37,745	32,216	17.2	2,565	1.8	12.3	3.5	6.4	22.2	15.3
Racine, WI Metro Area	8,483	7,365	6,549	43,486	37,682	15.4	4,982	34.1	5.5	3.4	3.2	12.3	14.3
Racine County, WI	8,483	7,365	6,549	43,486	37,682	15.4	4,982	34.1	5.5	3.4	3.2	12.3	14.3
Raleigh, NC Metro Area	61,655	48,483	36,895	48,411	42,624	13.6	43,513	8.8	6.1	5.3	D	9.2	14.7
Franklin County, NC	2,029	1,680	1,408	31,852	27,615	15.3	768	22.4	5.5	1.8	D	7.7	17.7
Johnston County, NC	6,597	5,370	4,261	35,533	31,654	12.3	2,766	18.9	8.9	1.9	3.4	7.0	18.8
Wake County, NC	53,029	41,433	31,225	51,776	45,683	13.3	39,979	7.9	5.9	5.6	15.4	9.3	14.3
Rapid City, SD Metro Area	6,454	5,340	4,337	44,775	39,533	13.3	4,274	4.0	8.1	5.3	D	D	23.3
Custer County, SD	358	278	241	42,405	33,567	26.3	141	1.5	5.7	2.6	D	D	30.0
Meade County, SD	1,043	881	750	38,645	34,558	11.8	515	3.7	7.2	2.9	3.3	4.7	38.9
Pennington County, SD	5,053	4,181	3,346	46,480	41,273	12.6	3,618	4.1	8.3	5.7	5.4	19.9	20.8
Reading, PA Metro Area	18,609	15,686	13,015	44,813	38,074	17.7	12,157	19.1	6.0	3.1	6.2	13.8	13.5
Berks County, PA	18,609	15,686	13,015	44,813	38,074	17.7	12,157	19.1	6.0	3.1	6.2	13.8	13.5
Redding, CA Metro Area	7,340	6,061	5,262	40,882	34,181	19.6	4,183	3.7	9.8	3.7	5.2	19.4	24.7
Shasta County, CA	7,340	6,061	5,262	40,882	34,181	19.6	4,183	3.7	9.8	3.7	5.2	19.4	24.7
Reno, NV Metro Area	21,429	17,982	17,706	47,526	42,200	12.6	13,665	7.0	D	D	D	D	17.8
Storey County, NV	164	140	132	41,027	35,084	16.9	335	20.8	D	D	D	D	9.2
Washoe County, NV	21,265	17,842	17,575	47,584	42,267	12.6	13,330	6.7	6.8	5.0	9.8	12.0	18.1
Richmond, VA Metro Area	64,152	51,533	44,583	50,460	42,580	18.5	48,286	D	5.2	9.8	10.2	11.6	18.7
Amelia County, VA	523	434	366	40,511	34,094	18.8	182	11.0	7.7	1.2	2.0	D	15.6
Caroline County, VA	1,140	979	735	38,035	34,172	11.3	334	5.6	4.6	1.0	D	D	35.0
Charles City County, VA	296	254	238	42,002	34,894	20.4	109	15.8	2.6	D	D	D	17.3

[1] Based on resident population estimated on July 1 of the year shown.
[2] Includes other industry categories not shown separately.
D = not shown to avoid disclosure of confidential information.

Table C-3. Personal Income and Earnings by Industry—*Continued*

	Personal Income						Earnings 2015						
	Total (million dollars)			Per capita[1] (dollars)				Percent by selected major industries					
Metropolitan statistical area, division, and component county	2015	2010	2005	2015	2010	Percent change, 2010–2015	Total[2] (million dollars)	Manufacturing	Retail trade	Finance and insurance	Professional and technical services	Health care and social services	Government and government enterprises
Chesterfield County, VA	16,285	13,445	11,466	48,513	42,372	14.5	8,694	9.2	8.3	5.2	9.2	10.4	16.4
Dinwiddie County, VA	2,970	2,661	2,284	38,010	34,164	11.3	1,699	9.1	9.6	3.4	2.5	D	23.2
Goochland County, VA	1,875	1,496	1,378	84,253	68,794	22.5	1,695	2.1	1.3	D	3.2	1.7	4.9
Hanover County, VA	5,571	4,458	3,749	53,971	44,612	21.0	3,184	7.0	9.1	2.0	5.6	11.8	9.4
Henrico County, VA	19,006	14,346	12,507	58,452	46,634	25.3	16,026	3.3	5.5	13.8	10.8	13.7	8.3
King William County, VA	694	586	522	42,633	36,644	16.3	245	28.6	14.3	2.4	4.4	D	17.6
New Kent County, VA	1,119	791	607	54,876	42,643	28.7	256	3.5	6.1	1.5	5.0	10.1	22.5
Powhatan County, VA	1,376	1,108	936	49,105	39,415	24.6	442	3.3	6.1	2.4	9.9	4.6	30.1
Prince George County, VA	2,240	1,888	1,537	37,178	32,391	14.8	2,527	11.7	2.0	0.5	3.3	4.2	63.1
Sussex County, VA	339	320	286	28,943	26,664	8.5	206	2.3	6.4	0.8	D	D	38.8
Colonial Heights city, VA	(9)	(9)	(9)	(9)	(9)	(9)	(9)	(9)	(9)	(9)	(9)	(9)	(9)
Hopewell city, VA	(10)	(10)	(10)	(10)	(10)	(10)	(10)	(10)	(10)	(10)	(10)	(10)	(10)
Petersburg city, VA	(9)	(9)	(9)	(9)	(9)	(9)	(9)	(9)	(9)	(9)	(9)	(9)	(9)
Richmond city, VA	10,717	8,767	7,971	48,652	42,945	13.3	12,686	D	2.3	8.0	15.5	12.2	27.0
Riverside-San Bernardino-Ontario, CA Metro Area	159,429	126,656	111,588	35,514	29,844	19.0	94,676	7.3	8.0	2.5	4.0	11.6	24.3
Riverside County, CA	84,026	66,905	57,670	35,589	30,380	17.1	46,252	6.5	8.5	2.4	4.1	10.8	24.2
San Bernardino County, CA	75,403	59,752	53,918	35,431	29,266	21.1	48,424	8.0	7.5	2.6	3.9	12.3	24.4
Roanoke, VA Metro Area	13,653	11,646	9,938	43,405	37,729	15.0	10,005	13.8	D	5.4	6.5	16.0	14.4
Botetourt County, VA	1,561	1,305	1,130	46,811	39,330	19.0	625	20.3	D	1.7	2.8	6.2	13.2
Craig County, VA	181	153	125	34,690	29,539	17.4	42	D	6.2	2.9	3.8	D	30.3
Franklin County, VA	2,063	1,762	1,531	36,668	31,348	17.0	783	18.1	8.3	2.0	3.6	D	16.3
Roanoke County, VA	5,758	4,913	4,316	48,047	41,874	14.7	4,103	20.5	6.0	5.5	7.0	D	15.5
Roanoke city, VA	4,091	3,513	2,835	40,947	36,300	12.8	4,452	D	6.5	6.6	7.2	20.2	13.0
Salem city, VA	(11)	(11)	(11)	(11)	(11)	(11)	(11)	(11)	(11)	(11)	(11)	(11)	(11)
Rochester, MN Metro Area	10,454	8,796	7,038	48,881	42,459	15.1	8,314	12.3	5.1	1.9	2.4	44.8	9.6
Dodge County, MN	877	745	614	43,069	36,982	16.5	425	25.3	3.0	1.7	2.4	2.1	15.9
Fillmore County, MN	938	735	621	45,036	35,280	27.7	473	33.7	5.1	3.2	1.8	D	13.2
Olmsted County, MN	7,702	6,529	5,103	50,858	45,178	12.6	6,982	9.4	5.2	1.8	2.5	52.3	8.6
Wabasha County, MN	937	787	700	44,126	36,318	21.5	435	21.8	4.7	2.9	1.6	D	14.1
Rochester, NY Metro Area	49,852	42,717	35,708	46,076	39,542	16.5	36,131	13.4	5.6	4.3	7.9	12.9	17.9
Livingston County, NY	2,456	2,137	1,775	37,955	32,753	15.9	1,256	10.7	6.4	1.3	2.0	8.7	38.2
Monroe County, NY	35,971	30,938	25,997	47,986	41,534	15.5	27,831	12.8	5.2	4.9	9.4	13.9	15.3
Ontario County, NY	5,248	4,266	3,454	47,900	39,421	21.5	3,770	13.0	7.9	2.8	3.8	11.2	19.0
Orleans County, NY	1,469	1,301	1,119	35,324	30,370	16.3	879	18.5	4.7	3.4	D	D	40.1
Wayne County, NY	3,797	3,282	2,700	41,524	35,009	18.6	1,950	22.4	6.2	1.7	2.3	7.2	29.1
Yates County, NY	911	793	663	36,371	31,265	16.3	446	14.6	7.1	1.6	D	D	21.3
Rockford, IL Metro Area	13,516	11,741	10,091	39,674	33,619	18.0	9,370	26.8	6.6	4.9	3.5	15.3	12.9
Boone County, IL	2,217	1,876	1,484	41,376	34,653	19.4	1,157	50.6	4.4	1.2	1.9	3.7	12.3
Winnebago County, IL	11,298	9,865	8,607	39,357	33,429	17.7	8,213	23.4	6.9	5.4	3.8	17.0	13.0
Rocky Mount, NC Metro Area	5,398	4,861	4,104	36,459	31,888	14.3	3,275	22.5	8.5	2.6	3.4	D	17.8
Edgecombe County, NC	1,737	1,598	1,431	32,084	28,232	13.6	851	18.4	10.7	1.4	1.5	D	26.8
Nash County, NC	3,661	3,263	2,673	38,982	34,047	14.5	2,424	23.9	7.7	3.0	4.0	9.0	14.6
Rome, GA Metro Area	3,383	2,931	2,619	35,054	30,395	15.3	2,397	16.9	7.0	3.0	D	24.2	13.5
Floyd County, GA	3,383	2,931	2,619	35,054	30,395	15.3	2,397	16.9	7.0	3.0	D	24.2	13.5
Sacramento--Roseville--Arden-Arcade, CA Metro Area	112,889	87,912	76,666	49,639	40,804	21.7	80,780	4.5	5.6	5.5	8.7	11.7	33.6
El Dorado County, CA	10,909	8,683	7,546	59,145	47,935	23.4	4,131	5.0	6.6	10.1	6.9	11.4	21.0
Placer County, CA	21,659	16,605	14,424	57,696	47,412	21.7	12,069	5.8	8.4	8.8	7.8	16.5	13.4
Sacramento County, CA	69,870	54,666	48,170	46,539	38,443	21.1	55,689	4.0	5.1	5.1	9.6	11.5	37.3
Yolo County, CA	10,451	7,958	6,527	49,063	39,567	24.0	8,892	5.5	4.5	1.3	5.3	6.4	43.4
Saginaw, MI Metro Area	6,849	6,103	5,608	35,429	30,527	16.1	5,018	19.2	7.3	4.3	4.4	19.0	14.2
Saginaw County, MI	6,849	6,103	5,608	35,429	30,527	16.1	5,018	19.2	7.3	4.3	4.4	19.0	14.2
St. Cloud, MN Metro Area	8,054	6,451	5,363	41,429	34,090	21.5	6,374	14.2	7.1	4.2	3.6	17.1	14.1
Benton County, MN	1,543	1,277	1,154	38,845	33,184	17.1	964	22.3	6.1	1.6	2.1	8.8	10.4
Stearns County, MN	6,512	5,174	4,209	42,092	34,321	22.6	5,410	12.8	7.3	4.6	3.8	18.5	14.7
St. George, UT Metro Area	4,881	3,508	2,841	31,368	25,343	23.8	2,928	5.5	9.7	3.3	5.8	17.0	15.3
Washington County, UT	4,881	3,508	2,841	31,368	25,343	23.8	2,928	5.5	9.7	3.3	5.8	17.0	15.3
St. Joseph, MO-KS Metro Area	4,516	3,960	3,345	35,589	31,120	14.4	3,299	D	6.3	4.5	D	14.1	16.2
Doniphan County, KS	262	241	192	33,621	30,316	10.9	126	19.2	3.1	3.6	1.4	6.0	31.2
Andrew County, MO	680	611	494	39,302	35,269	11.4	137	1.9	8.8	2.8	D	D	26.0
Buchanan County, MO	3,266	2,811	2,423	36,650	31,547	16.2	2,879	26.3	6.2	4.4	4.2	15.0	13.7
DeKalb County, MO	308	297	236	24,284	23,079	5.2	157	D	9.0	8.6	0.8	D	42.0
St. Louis, MO-IL Metro Area	137,702	118,065	102,431	48,977	42,317	15.7	98,802	10.8	5.5	D	9.2	12.5	12.7
Bond County, IL	568	523	469	33,534	29,441	13.9	307	23.4	3.1	2.4	1.3	D	24.8
Calhoun County, IL	176	172	140	36,000	33,789	6.5	40	3.2	8.6	D	D	D	36.2
Clinton County, IL	1,561	1,374	1,145	41,300	36,318	13.7	657	8.7	8.7	D	2.9	11.0	23.0
Jersey County, IL	821	775	658	36,696	33,766	8.7	262	2.8	10.7	3.9	8.1	D	30.7
Macoupin County, IL	1,664	1,569	1,369	36,145	32,839	10.1	559	8.7	9.6	3.9	D	D	24.1
Madison County, IL	11,173	9,865	8,344	41,970	36,620	14.6	6,313	17.2	6.9	3.4	6.8	11.4	17.2

[1] Based on resident population estimated on July 1 of the year shown.
[2] Includes other industry categories not shown separately.
[9] Colonial Heights and Petersburg cities included with Dinwiddie County, VA, in the Richmond, VA MSA.
[10] Hopewell city included with Prince George County, VA, in the Richmond, VA MSA.
[11] Salem city included with Roanoke County, VA, in the Roanoke, VA MSA.
D = not shown to avoid disclosure of confidential information.

Table C-3. Personal Income and Earnings by Industry—*Continued*

Metropolitan statistical area, division, and component county	Total (million dollars) 2015	2010	2005	Per capita[1] (dollars) 2015	2010	Percent change, 2010–2015	Total[2] (million dollars)	Manu-facturing	Retail trade	Finance and insurance	Profes-sional and technical services	Health care and social services	Govern-ment and govern-ment enter-prises
Monroe County, IL	1,737	1,461	1,146	51,277	44,258	15.9	498	4.9	8.8	6.1	11.4	6.9	17.7
St. Clair County, IL	10,750	9,781	8,241	40,711	36,177	12.5	6,520	6.1	6.6	3.0	7.7	12.8	31.6
Franklin County, MO	3,965	3,401	2,997	38,714	33,505	15.5	2,177	27.6	6.9	3.3	4.0	11.5	11.9
Jefferson County, MO	8,458	7,151	6,052	37,740	32,632	15.7	2,753	10.7	8.4	3.3	3.1	11.3	19.2
Lincoln County, MO	1,930	1,603	1,326	35,292	30,417	16.0	673	16.4	7.8	3.1	D	7.3	19.4
St. Charles County, MO	18,154	14,415	12,561	47,082	39,839	18.2	8,992	14.6	8.3	6.6	5.2	9.5	11.7
St. Louis County, MO	62,403	53,717	47,868	62,194	53,782	15.6	49,101	9.6	5.7	9.5	9.8	12.3	8.1
Warren County, MO	1,197	1,013	832	35,729	31,082	15.0	400	24.6	6.5	3.0	2.9	D	17.8
St. Louis City, MO	13,143	11,246	9,281	41,632	35,222	18.2	19,549	9.6	1.6	8.0	13.0	15.4	14.6
Salem, OR Metro Area	15,223	12,085	10,147	37,121	30,866	20.3	10,093	6.7	6.8	3.2	4.0	15.3	30.0
Marion County, OR	12,302	9,727	8,157	37,199	30,787	20.8	9,025	6.2	7.0	3.3	4.1	15.7	30.2
Polk County, OR	2,921	2,358	1,991	36,797	31,196	18.0	1,068	10.9	4.9	1.7	3.2	12.1	29.1
Salinas, CA Metro Area	21,624	17,247	14,856	49,836	41,418	20.3	15,011	2.6	5.3	1.8	4.4	7.5	24.5
Monterey County, CA	21,624	17,247	14,856	49,836	41,418	20.3	15,011	2.6	5.3	1.8	4.4	7.5	24.5
Salisbury, MD-DE Metro Area	17,115	13,594	11,566	43,296	36,272	19.4	9,779	8.2	D	D	4.1	15.6	16.5
Sussex County, DE	9,653	7,241	6,199	44,767	36,591	22.3	4,986	10.7	9.4	2.6	4.3	15.4	11.8
Somerset County, MD	765	672	577	29,684	25,378	17.0	502	3.4	D	D	2.2	12.4	45.4
Wicomico County, MD	3,974	3,397	2,857	38,816	34,331	13.1	2,875	7.5	9.5	3.3	4.0	19.6	18.4
Worcester County, MD	2,724	2,284	1,932	52,847	44,379	19.1	1,416	2.6	9.5	2.5	4.6	9.0	18.9
Salt Lake City, UT Metro Area	51,558	38,770	31,965	44,057	35,513	24.1	48,332	8.9	7.5	8.9	D	7.7	15.6
Salt Lake County, UT	49,488	37,101	30,670	44,692	35,909	24.5	47,422	8.8	7.5	9.1	10.5	7.7	15.3
Tooele County, UT	2,070	1,669	1,294	32,890	28,525	15.3	911	13.2	5.6	1.3	D	6.8	29.6
San Angelo, TX Metro Area	5,274	4,100	3,269	44,072	36,515	20.7	3,375	D	7.3	D	D	D	21.6
Irion County, TX	108	69	48	69,555	43,051	61.6	76	D	1.5	D	D	D	8.1
Tom Green County, TX	5,166	4,031	3,221	43,737	36,420	20.1	3,299	10.1	7.4	4.5	3.8	14.0	21.9
San Antonio-New Braunfels, TX Metro Area	103,790	76,786	59,411	43,535	35,661	22.1	73,724	4.4	6.5	8.9	6.6	10.6	20.3
Atascosa County, TX	1,862	1,289	915	38,437	28,661	34.1	917	3.6	7.8	1.8	3.1	6.8	15.0
Bandera County, TX	890	673	574	41,827	32,738	27.8	229	1.0	6.3	2.7	6.2	D	17.1
Bexar County, TX	81,038	60,709	48,013	42,702	35,235	21.2	64,571	3.7	6.1	9.8	6.7	10.9	21.1
Comal County, TX	6,931	4,796	3,371	53,710	43,875	22.4	3,386	6.0	10.4	2.5	6.0	10.5	10.8
Guadalupe County, TX	6,217	4,489	3,210	41,103	33,861	21.4	2,278	22.8	7.6	2.0	3.4	6.3	16.6
Kendall County, TX	3,055	2,037	1,276	75,638	60,538	24.9	1,238	5.2	13.8	5.2	11.6	8.0	9.3
Medina County, TX	1,777	1,354	1,019	36,697	29,359	25.0	584	1.1	8.3	3.6	4.7	D	27.6
Wilson County, TX	2,021	1,440	1,034	42,537	33,426	27.3	521	4.2	9.9	1.9	4.7	6.9	24.0
San Diego-Carlsbad, CA Metro Area	175,859	136,576	123,685	53,298	43,995	21.1	128,209	8.8	5.3	4.2	15.2	8.6	24.2
San Diego County, CA	175,859	136,576	123,685	53,298	43,995	21.1	128,209	8.8	5.3	4.2	15.2	8.6	24.2
San Francisco-Oakland-Hayward, CA Metro Area	**368,795**	**264,061**	**235,798**	**79,206**	**60,768**	**30.3**	**275,320**	**6.2**	**4.8**	**7.6**	**20.0**	**8.2**	**12.9**
Oakland-Hayward-Berkeley, CA Division	*176,127*	*128,788*	*119,209*	*63,700*	*50,177*	*27.0*	*110,681*	*9.5*	*5.6*	*4.0*	*13.9*	*11.7*	*15.5*
Alameda County, CA	101,370	72,194	64,774	61,879	47,692	29.7	75,602	11.0	5.4	2.1	15.1	10.5	16.6
Contra Costa County, CA	74,757	56,594	54,436	66,348	53,750	23.4	35,079	6.4	6.1	8.0	11.4	14.2	13.2
San Francisco-Redwood City-South San Francisco, CA Division	*164,175*	*114,223*	*95,788*	*100,724*	*74,862*	*34.5*	*151,223*	*3.9*	*4.1*	*10.4*	*24.8*	*5.4*	*11.0*
San Francisco County, CA	89,533	61,333	50,327	103,529	76,114	36.0	95,904	1.4	4.1	12.3	26.6	4.9	13.7
San Mateo County, CA	74,641	52,890	45,461	97,553	73,460	32.8	55,319	8.3	4.1	7.0	21.5	6.1	6.3
San Rafael, CA Division	*28,493*	*21,050*	*20,801*	*109,076*	*83,232*	*31.1*	*13,416*	*4.7*	*6.6*	*6.5*	*15.7*	*10.7*	*12.8*
Marin County, CA	28,493	21,050	20,801	109,076	83,232	31.1	13,416	4.7	6.6	6.5	15.7	10.7	12.8
San Jose-Sunnyvale-Santa Clara, CA Metro Area	161,295	111,306	89,936	81,592	60,414	35.1	153,129	21.4	3.9	2.7	D	6.4	6.6
San Benito County, CA	2,566	1,975	1,866	43,643	35,556	22.7	1,211	13.4	12.4	1.8	D	4.4	22.1
Santa Clara County, CA	158,729	109,331	88,069	82,756	61,186	35.3	151,918	21.5	3.8	2.7	19.3	6.4	6.5
San Luis Obispo-Paso Robles-Arroyo Grande, CA Metro Area	14,034	10,779	9,266	49,873	39,935	24.9	8,636	6.5	8.7	2.6	7.2	10.9	21.6
San Luis Obispo County, CA	14,034	10,779	9,266	49,873	39,935	24.9	8,636	6.5	8.7	2.6	7.2	10.9	21.6
Santa Cruz-Watsonville, CA Metro Area	15,697	12,565	10,643	57,257	47,729	20.0	8,698	7.1	7.1	2.6	7.6	12.6	19.0
Santa Cruz County, CA	15,697	12,565	10,643	57,257	47,729	20.0	8,698	7.1	7.1	2.6	7.6	12.6	19.0
Santa Fe, NM Metro Area	7,536	6,145	5,224	50,684	42,540	19.1	4,152	1.2	8.5	6.5	9.3	14.0	29.6
Santa Fe County, NM	7,536	6,145	5,224	50,684	42,540	19.1	4,152	1.2	8.5	6.5	9.3	14.0	29.6
Santa Maria-Santa Barbara, CA Metro Area	24,208	19,181	17,212	54,428	45,198	20.4	16,579	7.3	6.0	2.7	9.4	10.6	20.8
Santa Barbara County, CA	24,208	19,181	17,212	54,428	45,198	20.4	16,579	7.3	6.0	2.7	9.4	10.6	20.8
Santa Rosa, CA Metro Area	26,875	20,627	18,993	53,520	42,548	25.8	16,720	13.5	7.5	3.3	7.7	12.9	14.6
Sonoma County, CA	26,875	20,627	18,993	53,520	42,548	25.8	16,720	13.5	7.5	3.3	7.7	12.9	14.6
Savannah, GA Metro Area	15,894	13,047	10,447	41,915	37,411	12.0	11,054	17.1	6.5	3.2	D	13.0	18.5
Bryan County, GA	1,667	1,264	954	47,448	41,562	14.2	433	6.7	7.6	3.5	D	D	26.0
Chatham County, GA	12,085	10,074	8,173	42,115	37,886	11.2	10,028	17.4	6.4	3.2	4.4	13.7	17.7
Effingham County, GA	2,142	1,710	1,319	37,507	32,597	15.1	593	20.2	6.9	1.6	6.0	D	27.7
Scranton--Wilkes-Barre--Hazleton, PA Metro Area	23,167	20,492	17,411	41,505	36,350	14.2	15,271	11.5	7.1	5.6	4.9	D	15.3
Lackawanna County, PA	9,041	8,106	6,827	42,662	37,789	12.9	5,853	10.0	7.1	6.8	6.0	18.1	14.3
Luzerne County, PA	12,976	11,469	9,801	40,746	35,729	14.0	8,672	11.2	7.2	5.2	4.4	15.8	16.3
Wyoming County, PA	1,150	917	782	41,369	32,477	27.4	746	26.6	6.0	1.7	3.3	D	11.0
Seattle-Tacoma-Bellevue, WA Metro Area	**227,827**	**166,156**	**142,180**	**61,021**	**48,180**	**26.7**	**178,208**	**11.3**	**7.6**	**4.3**	**10.3**	**9.1**	**15.0**
Seattle-Bellevue-Everett, WA Division	*190,187*	*135,899*	*116,809*	*65,817*	*51,221*	*28.5*	*154,579*	*12.2*	*7.8*	*4.4*	*11.3*	*8.0*	*12.4*

[1]Based on resident population estimated on July 1 of the year shown.
[2]Includes other industry categories not shown separately.
D = not shown to avoid disclosure of confidential information.

Table C-3. Personal Income and Earnings by Industry—*Continued*

Metropolitan statistical area, division, and component county	Total (million dollars) 2015	2010	2005	Per capita[1] (dollars) 2015	2010	Percent change, 2010–2015	Earnings 2015 Total[2] (million dollars)	Manu-facturing	Retail trade	Finance and insurance	Profes-sional and technical services	Health care and social services	Govern-ment and govern-ment enter-prises
King County, WA	153,554	107,552	94,050	72,530	55,505	30.7	131,339	8.8	8.0	4.5	12.3	7.9	12.0
Snohomish County, WA	36,633	28,347	22,759	47,421	39,618	19.7	23,240	31.1	6.6	4.0	5.5	8.3	14.5
Tacoma-Lakewood, WA Division	*37,640*	*30,257*	*25,371*	*44,600*	*38,038*	*17.3*	*23,629*	*5.9*	*6.5*	*3.4*	*3.9*	*16.0*	*32.2*
Pierce County, WA	37,640	30,257	25,371	44,600	38,038	17.3	23,629	5.9	6.5	3.4	3.9	16.0	32.2
Sebastian-Vero Beach, FL Metro Area	10,055	7,419	6,875	67,978	53,668	26.7	3,274	4.1	9.6	4.9	11.4	16.9	10.6
Indian River County, FL	10,055	7,419	6,875	67,978	53,668	26.7	3,274	4.1	9.6	4.9	11.4	16.9	10.6
Sebring, FL Metro Area	3,179	2,850	2,386	31,949	28,881	10.6	1,413	2.4	10.6	2.6	3.0	22.5	16.8
Highlands County, FL	3,179	2,850	2,386	31,949	28,881	10.6	1,413	2.4	10.6	2.6	3.0	22.5	16.8
Sheboygan, WI Metro Area	5,304	4,452	3,911	45,896	38,555	19.0	3,892	39.8	5.5	5.6	2.5	11.8	9.9
Sheboygan County, WI	5,304	4,452	3,911	45,896	38,555	19.0	3,892	39.8	5.5	5.6	2.5	11.8	9.9
Sherman-Denison, TX Metro Area	4,916	3,875	3,150	39,181	32,016	22.4	2,736	15.8	8.3	6.3	3.6	18.5	13.4
Grayson County, TX	4,916	3,875	3,150	39,181	32,016	22.4	2,736	15.8	8.3	6.3	3.6	18.5	13.4
Shreveport-Bossier City, LA Metro Area	20,127	16,764	13,145	45,360	37,998	19.4	14,026	D	7.0	2.8	3.9	14.4	18.6
Bossier Parish, LA	5,329	4,318	3,258	42,574	36,714	16.0	3,367	4.3	9.8	2.3	2.7	7.5	30.2
Caddo Parish, LA	12,342	10,216	8,189	49,080	39,953	22.8	9,460	5.5	5.9	3.0	4.5	17.3	14.5
De Soto Parish, LA	1,017	892	641	37,595	33,414	12.5	492	D	5.6	1.9	1.5	D	20.4
Webster Parish, LA	1,439	1,339	1,057	35,944	32,494	10.6	706	13.7	9.2	2.8	2.7	D	16.5
Sierra Vista-Douglas, AZ Metro Area	4,821	4,607	3,574	38,133	34,954	9.1	2,651	1.1	5.8	1.9	7.1	7.7	50.9
Cochise County, AZ	4,821	4,607	3,574	38,133	34,954	9.1	2,651	1.1	5.8	1.9	7.1	7.7	50.9
Sioux City, IA-NE-SD Metro Area	7,864	6,804	5,671	46,514	40,301	15.4	5,806	D	6.1	4.1	2.9	11.6	11.6
Plymouth County, IA	1,356	1,041	869	54,663	41,697	31.1	886	20.9	4.0	2.8	D	4.1	9.9
Woodbury County, IA	4,172	3,640	3,426	40,591	35,557	14.2	3,248	10.9	7.9	2.9	3.2	14.8	14.1
Dakota County, NE	747	611	484	35,931	29,028	23.8	716	39.1	4.2	7.6	D	3.7	10.0
Dixon County, NE	267	204	161	46,080	34,202	34.7	143	D	0.7	1.4	D	2.2	12.7
Union County, SD	1,323	1,308	732	88,707	90,297	-1.8	813	16.0	3.7	7.6	5.3	15.2	5.0
Sioux Falls, SD Metro Area	13,542	10,519	7,787	53,769	45,895	17.2	10,923	D	7.2	D	D	D	8.6
Lincoln County, SD	3,342	2,258	1,417	63,242	49,982	26.5	1,705	19.1	6.7	12.7	D	12.5	5.1
McCook County, SD	259	222	171	46,234	39,632	16.7	129	D	4.4	3.9	3.2	8.0	10.4
Minnehaha County, SD	9,401	7,708	5,887	50,760	45,322	12.0	8,733	7.5	7.6	15.8	6.5	19.7	9.4
Turner County, SD	540	331	312	65,784	39,670	65.8	355	43.7	1.5	D	1.5	D	5.0
South Bend-Mishawaka, IN-MI Metro Area	13,560	10,788	9,944	42,362	33,819	25.3	8,862	15.8	5.8	3.9	7.5	D	10.0
St. Joseph County, IN	11,554	9,144	8,415	43,040	34,274	25.6	8,312	15.4	5.8	4.0	7.8	14.9	9.2
Cass County, MI	2,006	1,644	1,529	38,838	31,493	23.3	551	22.2	5.3	3.1	3.8	D	22.3
Spartanburg, SC Metro Area	12,338	9,814	8,340	37,954	31,286	21.3	8,898	24.4	6.5	4.0	4.2	D	16.6
Spartanburg County, SC	11,501	9,063	7,652	38,686	31,824	21.6	8,512	24.4	6.5	4.0	4.4	6.9	16.1
Union County, SC	836	751	688	30,115	25,985	15.9	385	25.2	7.2	2.9	1.4	D	25.9
Spokane-Spokane Valley, WA Metro Area	21,775	18,155	14,469	39,748	34,347	15.7	14,906	7.7	7.1	6.3	5.8	D	20.6
Pend Oreille County, WA	460	403	290	35,151	31,082	13.1	212	10.1	3.2	0.9	2.3	D	48.1
Spokane County, WA	19,796	16,476	13,186	40,322	34,898	15.5	14,067	7.4	7.2	6.6	6.0	17.3	19.9
Stevens County, WA	1,519	1,276	993	34,694	29,344	18.2	627	13.8	6.5	1.6	3.1	13.4	27.9
Springfield, IL Metro Area	9,204	8,153	6,785	43,590	38,731	12.5	6,903	3.3	6.2	7.0	7.0	D	25.6
Menard County, IL	499	469	382	40,081	36,892	8.6	116	1.5	6.4	6.0	6.2	D	31.7
Sangamon County, IL	8,706	7,684	6,403	43,810	38,849	12.8	6,787	3.3	6.2	7.0	7.0	19.6	25.5
Springfield, MA Metro Area	29,295	24,253	20,631	46,354	38,904	19.1	18,712	8.7	6.2	6.6	4.6	18.1	22.8
Hampden County, MA	21,754	18,097	15,348	46,216	38,989	18.5	14,082	10.0	6.2	8.1	4.3	20.0	19.8
Hampshire County, MA	7,541	6,157	5,283	46,756	38,654	21.0	4,630	4.7	6.3	2.2	5.5	12.2	32.0
Springfield, MO Metro Area	16,808	13,940	12,078	36,824	31,870	15.5	11,936	8.5	7.9	4.9	7.1	17.3	14.2
Christian County, MO	2,971	2,348	1,826	35,675	30,160	18.3	946	7.5	8.9	3.7	5.0	7.0	18.1
Dallas County, MO	489	417	384	29,822	24,913	19.7	150	5.1	10.8	3.9	1.3	D	21.6
Greene County, MO	11,220	9,434	8,396	38,947	34,257	13.7	9,958	8.6	7.7	5.2	7.8	19.2	12.7
Polk County, MO	948	781	676	30,365	25,073	21.1	465	2.7	7.3	2.5	D	10.7	32.2
Webster County, MO	1,181	960	795	31,503	26,475	19.0	418	15.5	9.2	2.9	D	D	18.4
Springfield, OH Metro Area	5,055	4,434	3,939	37,183	32,074	15.9	2,738	16.5	6.9	7.0	2.7	14.6	16.2
Clark County, OH	5,055	4,434	3,939	37,183	32,074	15.9	2,738	16.5	6.9	7.0	2.7	14.6	16.2
State College, PA Metro Area	6,639	5,415	4,469	41,344	35,108	17.8	5,883	4.7	4.5	1.9	5.8	9.7	49.5
Centre County, PA	6,639	5,415	4,469	41,344	35,108	17.8	5,883	4.7	4.5	1.9	5.8	9.7	49.5
Staunton-Waynesboro, VA Metro Area	4,809	4,181	3,423	40,000	35,331	13.2	2,868	17.6	6.8	2.2	3.3	D	17.4
Augusta County, VA	4,809	4,181	3,423	40,000	35,331	13.2	2,868	17.6	6.8	2.2	3.3	D	17.4
Staunton city, VA	(12)	(12)	(12)	(12)	(12)	(12)	(12)	(12)	(12)	(12)	(12)	(12)	(12)
Waynesboro city, VA	(12)	(12)	(12)	(12)	(12)	(12)	(12)	(12)	(12)	(12)	(12)	(12)	(12)
Stockton-Lodi, CA Metro Area	28,151	22,214	19,484	38,769	32,314	20.0	16,517	8.1	7.0	2.6	3.0	12.2	22.0
San Joaquin County, CA	28,151	22,214	19,484	38,769	32,314	20.0	16,517	8.1	7.0	2.6	3.0	12.2	22.0
Sumter, SC Metro Area	3,959	3,250	2,787	36,834	30,213	21.9	2,576	15.5	5.9	1.9	3.2	11.2	36.3
Sumter County, SC	3,959	3,250	2,787	36,834	30,213	21.9	2,576	15.5	5.9	1.9	3.2	11.2	36.3
Syracuse, NY Metro Area	29,258	25,050	20,968	44,299	37,781	17.3	21,444	10.0	6.6	5.3	D	D	21.9
Madison County, NY	2,827	2,467	2,050	39,352	33,598	17.1	1,341	13.3	7.9	2.7	4.4	D	24.5
Onondaga County, NY	22,034	18,692	15,771	47,034	39,986	17.6	17,886	9.5	6.4	5.9	9.1	13.0	20.5
Oswego County, NY	4,397	3,891	3,147	36,593	31,857	14.9	2,217	11.4	7.4	1.8	D	10.7	31.2
Tallahassee, FL Metro Area	14,258	12,697	10,843	37,728	34,372	9.8	10,331	2.1	6.1	4.1	11.6	D	38.1
Gadsden County, FL	1,396	1,310	1,166	30,334	27,401	10.7	670	8.0	5.4	1.1	1.1	3.9	36.2

[1]Based on resident population estimated on July 1 of the year shown.
[2]Includes other industry categories not shown separately.

Table C-3.   Personal Income and Earnings by Industry—Continued

| | Total (million dollars) | | | Per capita[1] (dollars) | | | Earnings 2015 | | | | | | |
| | | | | | | | | Percent by selected major industries | | | | | |
Metropolitan statistical area, division, and component county	2015	2010	2005	2015	2010	Percent change, 2010–2015	Total[2] (million dollars)	Manu-facturing	Retail trade	Finance and insurance	Profes-sional and technical services	Health care and social services	Govern-ment and govern-ment enter-prises
Jefferson County, FL	515	461	399	36,596	31,279	17.0	154	0.6	5.6	1.3	4.8	D	25.2
Leon County, FL	11,356	10,044	8,615	39,670	36,387	9.0	9,201	1.2	6.1	4.4	12.6	13.0	38.6
Wakulla County, FL	990	882	662	31,405	28,617	9.7	306	16.1	7.3	1.4	7.2	5.2	32.5
Tampa-St. Petersburg-Clearwater, FL Metro Area.	127,958	107,636	92,138	43,008	38,597	11.4	85,385	5.6	8.1	9.0	11.6	13.4	13.4
Hernando County, FL	6,007	5,250	4,391	33,666	30,350	10.9	2,116	5.6	11.8	2.6	4.6	22.2	18.2
Hillsborough County, FL	58,596	48,852	40,217	43,435	39,594	9.7	49,212	3.9	7.3	10.7	13.1	11.1	13.6
Pasco County, FL	18,018	14,919	11,905	36,187	32,052	12.9	6,348	3.4	14.0	2.9	5.9	20.2	16.7
Pinellas County, FL	45,337	38,615	35,626	47,731	42,136	13.3	27,710	9.2	7.9	7.8	10.8	15.4	11.9
Terre Haute, IN Metro Area	5,882	5,273	4,501	34,396	30,605	12.4	3,841	19.2	6.8	D	D	D	18.2
Clay County, IN	909	802	712	34,300	29,851	14.9	404	41.2	7.0	2.2	D	D	14.9
Sullivan County, IN	660	607	499	31,546	28,369	11.2	342	11.6	5.1	2.2	2.0	3.9	27.1
Vermillion County, IN	545	512	433	34,742	31,735	9.5	280	25.2	7.1	D	D	10.3	11.5
Vigo County, IN	3,768	3,352	2,858	34,922	31,068	12.4	2,816	16.3	7.0	3.6	3.3	18.6	18.2
Texarkana, TX-AR Metro Area	5,246	4,756	3,905	35,026	31,845	10.0	3,449	11.8	7.9	4.8	D	D	24.7
Little River County, AR	408	379	296	32,686	28,861	13.3	258	49.9	4.5	1.4	1.1	2.3	15.5
Miller County, AR	1,377	1,236	1,053	31,350	28,394	10.4	758	24.3	5.3	2.4	D	D	15.1
Bowie County, TX	3,462	3,141	2,556	37,066	33,889	9.4	2,432	3.9	9.1	5.9	3.0	18.7	28.7
The Villages, FL Metro Area	4,638	2,813	1,666	39,012	29,833	30.8	1,543	4.3	8.8	4.1	D	13.3	22.7
Sumter County, FL	4,638	2,813	1,666	39,012	29,833	30.8	1,543	4.3	8.8	4.1	D	13.3	22.7
Toledo, OH Metro Area	25,503	21,560	19,360	42,087	35,337	19.1	19,683	19.1	6.0	3.0	D	D	15.9
Fulton County, OH	1,719	1,442	1,333	40,414	33,836	19.4	1,126	37.0	5.7	1.4	D	D	13.0
Lucas County, OH	18,247	15,391	14,174	42,075	34,854	20.7	14,440	15.8	6.3	3.5	6.1	16.8	15.7
Wood County, OH	5,537	4,728	3,853	42,679	37,539	13.7	4,116	25.8	5.1	1.9	4.1	6.8	17.5
Topeka, KS Metro Area	9,905	8,572	7,044	42,365	36,591	15.8	6,947	7.0	5.0	9.4	D	14.5	24.3
Jackson County, KS	500	435	385	37,478	32,329	15.9	206	6.8	6.5	4.0	2.0	D	47.3
Jefferson County, KS	755	660	516	39,884	34,505	15.6	230	4.9	3.5	D	D	D	23.3
Osage County, KS	601	533	424	37,926	32,730	15.9	151	4.8	6.7	4.4	3.9	9.4	33.7
Shawnee County, KS	7,724	6,665	5,525	43,216	37,371	15.6	6,283	7.0	5.0	10.0	8.1	15.2	23.4
Wabaunsee County, KS	325	278	193	46,762	39,577	18.2	77	12.9	2.0	D	2.7	D	25.9
Trenton, NJ Metro Area	23,490	19,548	17,386	63,247	53,125	19.1	21,001	4.2	4.0	10.0	18.3	8.9	19.5
Mercer County, NJ	23,490	19,548	17,386	63,247	53,125	19.1	21,001	4.2	4.0	10.0	18.3	8.9	19.5
Tucson, AZ Metro Area	38,922	33,362	28,572	38,536	33,978	13.4	23,659	9.9	6.6	3.9	7.7	14.7	25.2
Pima County, AZ	38,922	33,362	28,572	38,536	33,978	13.4	23,659	9.9	6.6	3.9	7.7	14.7	25.2
Tulsa, OK Metro Area	56,631	37,105	31,434	57,727	39,474	46.2	43,494	9.7	4.7	D	5.5	8.6	7.4
Creek County, OK	2,701	2,276	1,764	38,096	32,419	17.5	1,230	22.6	5.6	2.7	D	9.5	15.2
Okmulgee County, OK	1,253	1,091	887	31,985	27,189	17.6	560	18.5	8.3	3.3	2.7	D	34.8
Osage County, OK	1,599	1,322	1,120	33,397	27,870	19.8	538	6.5	3.6	1.7	2.1	D	26.8
Pawnee County, OK	557	482	381	33,897	29,050	16.7	226	2.9	7.4	D	11.5	7.9	27.8
Rogers County, OK	3,739	2,937	2,140	41,178	33,756	22.0	1,891	22.4	6.2	1.7	D	6.7	20.8
Tulsa County, OK	44,001	26,740	23,463	68,833	44,184	55.8	38,390	8.4	4.5	3.1	5.8	8.8	5.6
Wagoner County, OK	2,780	2,257	1,678	36,313	30,738	18.1	659	23.7	6.5	2.4	D	D	15.9
Tuscaloosa, AL Metro Area	8,499	7,278	6,089	35,424	31,584	12.2	6,131	19.1	5.7	D	D	7.3	27.4
Hale County, AL	523	465	392	34,726	29,583	17.4	191	16.7	4.5	2.1	0.9	D	23.0
Pickens County, AL	629	577	525	30,139	29,248	3.0	233	18.3	4.9	D	D	D	32.8
Tuscaloosa County, AL	7,346	6,236	5,172	36,016	31,982	12.6	5,708	19.2	5.7	2.7	4.5	7.3	27.3
Tyler, TX Metro Area	11,197	8,676	6,496	50,224	41,224	21.8	8,656	6.8	10.4	4.0	4.6	16.5	9.6
Smith County, TX	11,197	8,676	6,496	50,224	41,224	21.8	8,656	6.8	10.4	4.0	4.6	16.5	9.6
Urban Honolulu, HI Metro Area	52,055	43,244	35,681	52,122	45,216	15.3	38,509	1.9	5.5	3.3	6.2	10.2	33.7
Honolulu County, HI	52,055	43,244	35,681	52,122	45,216	15.3	38,509	1.9	5.5	3.3	6.2	10.2	33.7
Utica-Rome, NY Metro Area	11,572	10,555	8,553	39,146	35,268	11.0	7,509	9.7	6.0	6.3	4.5	15.6	32.3
Herkimer County, NY	2,345	2,104	1,730	37,163	32,656	13.8	1,014	15.5	7.7	1.5	1.8	9.2	30.9
Oneida County, NY	9,227	8,450	6,824	39,684	35,984	10.3	6,496	8.8	5.7	7.1	4.9	16.6	32.5
Valdosta, GA Metro Area	4,592	4,028	3,316	32,138	28,754	11.8	3,121	8.3	D	D	D	D	35.0
Brooks County, GA	505	451	392	32,246	27,701	16.4	185	6.3	5.0	2.7	1.3	8.3	18.3
Echols County, GA	96	80	75	23,721	19,787	19.9	32	2.9	D	D	D	D	26.9
Lanier County, GA	246	214	160	23,847	21,206	12.5	70	8.5	4.9	D	1.5	2.5	46.0
Lowndes County, GA	3,745	3,283	2,689	33,182	29,934	10.9	2,834	8.5	7.4	2.4	3.9	9.6	35.9
Vallejo-Fairfield, CA Metro Area	19,408	15,455	14,055	44,504	37,324	19.2	11,283	13.2	6.7	2.9	3.5	16.6	25.1
Solano County, CA	19,408	15,455	14,055	44,504	37,324	19.2	11,283	13.2	6.7	2.9	3.5	16.6	25.1
Victoria, TX Metro Area	4,696	3,418	2,903	47,005	36,327	29.4	3,042	8.8	7.8	D	3.9	13.5	13.4
Goliad County, TX	345	220	197	45,825	30,466	50.4	95	3.5	4.1	D	8.8	5.1	24.8
Victoria County, TX	4,351	3,198	2,706	47,101	36,814	27.9	2,947	8.9	7.9	2.7	3.8	13.8	13.1
Vineland-Bridgeton, NJ Metro Area	5,650	5,184	4,344	36,253	32,987	9.9	4,060	14.6	7.3	1.8	D	15.5	28.5
Cumberland County, NJ	5,650	5,184	4,344	36,253	32,987	9.9	4,060	14.6	7.3	1.8	D	15.5	28.5
Virginia Beach-Norfolk-Newport News, VA-NC Metro Area	80,034	68,253	58,718	46,400	40,627	14.2	56,429	D	5.4	D	8.0	9.9	36.1
Currituck County, NC	1,037	835	708	41,035	35,280	16.3	385	0.8	11.4	2.0	D	D	17.6
Gates County, NC	382	368	302	33,458	30,287	10.5	80	D	6.2	D	3.2	D	32.9
Gloucester County, VA	1,661	1,468	1,228	44,728	39,754	12.5	478	2.0	12.5	2.9	D	15.3	27.6
Isle of Wight County, VA	1,839	1,600	1,296	50,643	45,304	11.8	699	26.7	3.6	2.3	D	D	12.8
James City County, VA	5,160	4,197	3,082	58,504	51,538	13.5	2,404	6.5	8.4	3.1	7.9	11.2	23.9

[1]Based on resident population estimated on July 1 of the year shown.
[2]Includes other industry categories not shown separately.

Table C-3. Personal Income and Earnings by Industry—*Continued*

| | Personal Income | | | | | | Earnings 2015 | | | | | | |
| | Total (million dollars) | | | Per capita[1] (dollars) | | | | Percent by selected major industries | | | | | |
Metropolitan statistical area, division, and component county	2015	2010	2005	2015	2010	Percent change, 2010–2015	Total[2] (million dollars)	Manu-facturing	Retail trade	Finance and insurance	Profes-sional and technical services	Health care and social services	Govern-ment and govern-ment enter-prises
Mathews County, VA	450	393	361	50,774	43,811	15.9	89	4.6	6.2	1.9	6.0	D	24.2
York County, VA	4,403	3,743	3,037	55,111	48,390	13.9	1,466	2.3	8.6	1.7	D	D	30.5
Chesapeake city, VA	11,011	9,404	7,783	46,769	42,070	11.2	5,865	5.8	9.0	4.4	11.0	7.5	18.5
Hampton city, VA	5,562	4,933	4,457	40,759	35,892	13.6	4,224	3.6	5.5	1.4	10.6	9.8	48.4
Newport News city, VA	7,378	6,360	5,277	40,453	35,158	15.1	7,796	31.0	4.2	1.5	5.8	9.9	24.7
Norfolk city, VA	9,530	8,380	8,110	38,676	34,501	12.1	14,377	3.1	2.7	4.1	5.9	9.7	51.9
Poquoson city, VA	(13)	(13)	(13)	(13)	(13)	(13)	(13)	(13)	(13)	(13)	(13)	(13)	(13)
Portsmouth city, VA	3,781	3,313	2,838	39,301	34,701	13.3	3,953	2.5	2.4	0.8	3.2	10.4	60.7
Suffolk city, VA	4,191	3,585	2,637	47,533	42,234	12.5	2,014	8.1	5.8	1.8	16.6	12.8	26.6
Virginia Beach city, VA	23,649	19,674	17,603	52,235	44,812	16.6	12,598	3.1	6.9	6.4	9.9	11.4	28.1
Williamsburg city, VA	(14)	(14)	(14)	(14)	(14)	(14)	(14)	(14)	(14)	(14)	(14)	(14)	(14)
Visalia-Porterville, CA Metro Area	16,809	13,264	10,555	36,551	29,936	22.1	10,352	8.3	6.9	2.1	2.2	6.6	24.5
Tulare County, CA	16,809	13,264	10,555	36,551	29,936	22.1	10,352	8.3	6.9	2.1	2.2	6.6	24.5
Waco, TX Metro Area	9,702	7,888	6,494	36,917	31,076	18.8	7,010	18.2	6.1	D	4.3	10.5	16.1
Falls County, TX	549	476	391	31,999	26,605	20.3	215	3.7	6.7	D	3.2	8.9	38.0
McLennan County, TX	9,154	7,412	6,103	37,260	31,415	18.6	6,795	18.7	6.1	5.9	4.4	10.5	15.4
Walla Walla, WA Metro Area	2,721	2,220	1,689	42,333	35,228	20.2	1,870	13.5	4.7	2.5	D	14.3	23.2
Columbia County, WA	192	161	116	48,769	39,323	24.0	110	2.2	3.0	1.3	1.0	6.3	30.0
Walla Walla County, WA	2,529	2,059	1,573	41,912	34,942	19.9	1,760	14.2	4.8	2.6	D	14.8	22.8
Warner Robins, GA Metro Area	7,120	6,101	4,917	37,841	33,814	11.9	4,763	D	5.4	D	6.4	D	52.4
Houston County, GA	5,881	5,023	4,049	39,199	35,687	9.8	4,088	7.6	5.1	1.6	7.2	6.2	57.5
Peach County, GA	936	801	622	35,027	28,865	21.3	522	32.9	7.2	1.4	1.1	5.0	21.8
Pulaski County, GA	303	277	247	26,551	23,216	14.4	153	D	6.1	D	2.5	D	21.5
Washington-Arlington-Alexandria, DC-VA-MD-WV Metro Area	**395,632**	**329,497**	**272,340**	**64,882**	**58,148**	**11.6**	**326,298**	**1.7**	**D**	**D**	**D**	**6.8**	**27.6**
Silver Spring-Frederick-Rockville, MD Division	*93,413*	*80,648*	*68,158*	*72,670*	*66,631*	*9.1*	*62,526*	*3.6*	*D*	*D*	*D*	*9.1*	*20.9*
Frederick County, MD	13,467	11,499	9,234	54,893	49,099	11.8	7,571	5.7	D	D	D	10.0	19.8
Montgomery County, MD	79,946	69,149	58,924	76,863	70,837	8.5	54,956	3.3	4.3	6.5	18.3	8.9	21.1
Washington-Arlington-Alexandria, DC-VA-MD-WV Division	*302,219*	*248,849*	*204,183*	*62,802*	*55,844*	*12.5*	*263,772*	*1.2*	*D*	*D*	*D*	*6.3*	*29.2*
District of Columbia, DC	49,276	37,437	30,551	73,302	61,866	18.5	91,938	0.2	1.0	3.4	23.9	5.7	39.0
Calvert County, MD	5,075	4,446	3,554	56,018	49,980	12.1	1,687	2.6	6.3	1.6	6.9	13.9	19.5
Charles County, MD	8,151	7,025	5,514	52,212	47,741	9.4	2,882	1.5	13.1	2.1	7.1	10.2	31.9
Prince George's County, MD	40,807	35,381	29,499	44,866	40,860	9.8	25,496	2.3	6.2	1.8	10.1	8.0	38.9
Arlington County, VA	19,745	16,592	13,390	86,161	79,226	8.8	21,364	0.6	1.7	4.2	30.4	3.4	30.8
Clarke County, VA	810	700	571	56,372	49,836	13.1	270	13.3	2.8	2.9	16.3	D	14.6
Culpeper County, VA	2,062	1,707	1,362	41,724	36,439	14.5	999	9.2	9.0	1.9	7.5	12.9	20.8
Fairfax County, VA	88,419	73,999	65,872	74,923	65,960	13.6	73,142	0.6	4.0	5.3	34.4	6.2	16.6
Fauquier County, VA	4,249	3,593	3,225	61,780	54,871	12.6	1,630	3.2	7.7	3.0	15.6	10.7	20.7
Loudoun County, VA	26,255	19,875	12,876	69,895	62,976	11.0	13,879	5.6	5.0	3.0	21.8	5.9	13.7
Prince William County, VA	25,621	21,376	16,568	50,315	46,562	8.1	11,719	3.4	D	2.0	D	D	28.7
Rappahannock County, VA	421	364	295	57,071	48,462	17.8	147	3.0	3.8	1.1	10.7	2.2	13.4
Spotsylvania County, VA	7,359	6,111	4,998	46,401	41,462	11.9	3,524	D	12.4	3.1	10.3	19.4	17.5
Stafford County, VA	7,110	6,037	4,452	50,067	46,494	7.7	3,099	1.3	5.5	D	11.4	5.9	35.2
Warren County, VA	1,634	1,380	1,121	41,815	36,785	13.7	705	11.1	7.1	3.1	4.2	11.1	17.6
Alexandria city, VA	12,693	10,725	8,668	82,683	76,153	8.6	10,308	D	4.6	3.8	26.0	4.5	31.5
Fairfax city, VA	(15)	(15)	(15)	(15)	(15)	(15)	(15)	(15)	(15)	(15)	(15)	(15)	(15)
Falls Church city, VA	(15)	(15)	(15)	(15)	(15)	(15)	(15)	(15)	(15)	(15)	(15)	(15)	(15)
Fredericksburg city, VA	(16)	(16)	(16)	(16)	(16)	(16)	(16)	(16)	(16)	(16)	(16)	(16)	(16)
Manassas city, VA	(17)	(17)	(17)	(17)	(17)	(17)	(17)	(17)	(17)	(17)	(17)	(17)	(17)
Manassas Park city, VA	(17)	(17)	(17)	(17)	(17)	(17)	(17)	(17)	(17)	(17)	(17)	(17)	(17)
Jefferson County, WV	2,532	2,104	1,665	44,834	39,240	14.3	984	4.7	5.6	2.2	8.8	6.1	30.7
Waterloo-Cedar Falls, IA Metro Area	7,077	6,025	4,968	41,478	35,879	15.6	5,383	23.7	6.4	D	D	12.4	16.1
Black Hawk County, IA	5,375	4,564	3,810	40,273	34,791	15.8	4,505	25.2	6.6	4.7	4.4	13.1	15.9
Bremer County, IA	1,103	934	737	44,610	38,472	16.0	610	19.4	5.8	13.2	2.4	D	18.7
Grundy County, IA	599	527	421	48,180	42,276	14.0	269	7.7	4.1	D	D	D	13.0
Watertown-Fort Drum, NY Metro Area	5,078	4,821	3,542	43,170	41,359	4.4	3,923	4.5	5.9	1.3	1.8	9.7	59.3
Jefferson County, NY	5,078	4,821	3,542	43,170	41,359	4.4	3,923	4.5	5.9	1.3	1.8	9.7	59.3
Wausau, WI Metro Area	5,967	5,057	4,414	43,921	37,717	16.4	4,628	22.2	7.2	8.3	4.7	15.8	11.5
Marathon County, WI	5,967	5,057	4,414	43,921	37,717	16.4	4,628	22.2	7.2	8.3	4.7	15.8	11.5
Weirton-Steubenville, WV-OH Metro Area	4,402	3,812	3,241	36,529	30,669	19.1	2,232	18.3	7.1	2.2	D	17.6	13.7
Jefferson County, OH	2,391	2,080	1,790	35,496	29,886	18.8	1,218	7.3	8.1	1.9	D	D	15.5
Brooke County, WV	870	735	636	37,261	30,629	21.7	474	25.8	7.5	1.4	1.7	D	10.0
Hancock County, WV	1,142	996	814	38,290	32,480	17.9	540	36.4	4.4	3.8	4.5	7.6	13.0
Wenatchee, WA Metro Area	4,860	3,760	2,946	41,836	33,786	23.8	3,127	5.6	7.9	1.8	4.0	14.6	21.0
Chelan County, WA	3,389	2,591	2,053	44,797	35,616	25.8	2,481	5.9	7.7	1.9	3.3	17.0	19.9

[1]Based on resident population estimated on July 1 of the year shown.
[2]Includes other industry categories not shown separately.
[13]Poquoson city included with York County, VA, in the Virginia Beach-Norfolk-Newport News, VA-NC MSA.
[14]Williamsburg city included with James City County, VA, in the Virginia Beach-Norfolk-Newport News, VA-NC MSA.

Table C-3. Personal Income and Earnings by Industry—*Continued*

Metropolitan statistical area, division, and component county	Total (million dollars) 2015	2010	2005	Per capita[1] (dollars) 2015	2010	Percent change, 2010–2015	Earnings 2015 Total[2] (million dollars)	Manu-facturing	Retail trade	Finance and insurance	Profes-sional and technical services	Health care and social services	Govern-ment and govern-ment enter-prises
Douglas County, WA	1,472	1,169	893	36,310	30,334	19.7	647	4.5	8.7	1.5	6.4	5.2	25.4
Wheeling, WV-OH Metro Area	5,854	4,870	4,428	40,594	32,937	23.2	3,873	6.0	8.1	3.6	D	D	13.7
Belmont County, OH	2,586	2,151	1,840	37,393	30,586	22.3	1,419	4.0	10.0	3.4	D	12.5	16.0
Marshall County, WV	1,171	935	813	36,617	28,284	29.5	752	14.4	6.0	1.5	D	D	12.7
Ohio County, WV	2,097	1,784	1,774	48,687	40,114	21.4	1,702	4.0	7.5	4.7	7.7	23.6	12.3
Wichita, KS Metro Area	31,148	24,143	19,575	48,321	38,207	26.5	21,617	22.5	5.7	3.0	4.8	11.2	12.9
Butler County, KS	2,823	2,387	1,891	42,301	36,211	16.8	1,244	14.5	5.8	2.9	3.6	12.1	22.5
Harvey County, KS	1,346	1,171	963	38,369	33,708	13.8	850	28.1	6.3	2.8	3.1	D	11.8
Kingman County, KS	314	270	238	40,881	34,398	18.8	154	16.1	4.3	6.8	3.3	10.4	15.9
Sedgwick County, KS	25,808	19,509	15,794	50,448	39,072	29.1	18,952	23.0	5.7	3.0	5.1	11.0	12.1
Sumner County, KS	857	807	690	36,407	33,474	8.8	417	17.8	6.1	3.8	2.6	D	21.1
Wichita Falls, TX Metro Area	6,393	5,607	4,572	42,398	36,973	14.7	4,206	9.0	7.4	3.7	D	D	24.2
Archer County, TX	432	351	280	49,597	38,490	28.9	181	4.8	6.8	1.3	5.4	2.6	15.3
Clay County, TX	436	379	286	42,079	35,306	19.2	120	5.2	6.9	2.7	D	D	21.7
Wichita County, TX	5,525	4,877	4,006	41,947	37,003	13.4	3,904	9.3	7.4	3.8	2.8	13.0	24.7
Williamsport, PA Metro Area	4,778	3,962	3,326	41,171	34,091	20.8	3,389	15.8	6.4	3.1	3.8	15.2	18.6
Lycoming County, PA	4,778	3,962	3,326	41,171	34,091	20.8	3,389	15.8	6.4	3.1	3.8	15.2	18.6
Wilmington, NC Metro Area	10,819	8,586	7,489	38,922	33,586	15.9	7,251	5.8	8.4	4.1	D	10.9	20.2
New Hanover County, NC	8,922	7,032	6,238	40,487	34,588	17.1	6,596	5.8	8.5	4.4	11.2	11.2	19.9
Pender County, NC	1,898	1,555	1,251	32,937	29,095	10.9	654	6.0	7.4	1.2	D	7.8	23.4
Winchester, VA-WV Metro Area	5,680	4,696	3,840	42,436	36,490	16.3	3,744	13.4	8.6	4.7	D	D	18.1
Frederick County, VA	4,957	4,048	3,338	44,871	38,642	16.1	3,526	14.0	8.6	4.7	D	17.2	17.4
Winchester city, VA	(18)	(18)	(18)	(18)	(18)	(18)	(18)	(18)	(18)	(18)	(18)	(18)	(18)
Hampshire County, WV	722	648	503	30,920	27,077	14.2	217	3.7	8.4	3.9	2.7	D	30.0
Winston-Salem, NC Metro Area	26,516	22,644	19,686	40,217	35,304	13.9	17,180	13.1	6.8	7.2	D	D	10.7
Davidson County, North Carolina	5,774	4,957	4,377	35,073	30,431	15.3	2,500	22.3	6.7	1.7	2.8	8.5	14.3
Davie County, North Carolina	1,759	1,487	1,259	42,136	36,015	17.0	634	21.5	7.5	2.5	D	D	13.9
Forsyth County, North Carolina	16,185	13,728	11,919	43,859	39,058	12.3	13,126	10.4	6.8	8.8	7.3	17.1	9.3
Stokes County, North Carolina	1,521	1,338	1,133	32,811	28,276	16.0	390	12.7	7.3	2.1	3.6	12.5	24.0
Yadkin County, North Carolina	1,278	1,134	997	33,995	29,514	15.2	529	24.3	6.0	1.9	2.1	5.7	14.9
Worcester, MA-CT Metro Area	47,102	39,330	33,043	50,348	42,800	17.6	28,180	13.2	6.2	5.5	8.2	15.9	17.3
Windham County, CT	5,032	4,426	3,758	43,167	37,325	15.7	2,569	18.2	8.2	1.7	4.0	14.3	20.9
Worcester County, MA	42,070	34,904	29,284	51,370	43,611	17.8	25,611	12.7	6.0	5.9	8.6	16.0	16.9
Yakima, WA Metro Area	9,587	7,813	5,896	38,527	31,981	20.5	6,301	8.0	6.5	1.9	2.2	13.2	18.2
Yakima County, WA	9,587	7,813	5,896	38,527	31,981	20.5	6,301	8.0	6.5	1.9	2.2	13.2	18.2
York-Hanover, PA Metro Area	19,774	17,614	14,740	44,651	40,442	10.4	11,588	19.5	6.3	2.8	4.5	13.7	14.2
York County, PA	19,774	17,614	14,740	44,651	40,442	10.4	11,588	19.5	6.3	2.8	4.5	13.7	14.2
Youngstown-Warren-Boardman, OH-PA Metro Area	21,145	18,519	17,262	38,454	32,784	17.3	13,085	17.8	7.8	3.0	3.3	16.2	15.2
Mahoning County, OH	9,321	8,249	7,720	40,192	34,602	16.2	5,799	10.2	7.7	3.1	4.5	17.7	16.9
Trumbull County, OH	7,504	6,509	6,211	36,831	31,018	18.7	4,412	25.3	7.9	2.2	2.3	12.9	14.4
Mercer County, PA	4,320	3,761	3,331	37,820	32,248	17.3	2,874	21.6	7.8	4.2	2.2	18.1	13.1
Yuba City, CA Metro Area	6,704	5,557	4,332	39,216	33,243	18.0	3,689	4.3	6.5	1.8	2.7	12.6	35.0
Sutter County, CA	3,908	3,283	2,582	40,514	34,629	17.0	2,026	5.3	9.0	2.7	2.7	13.0	18.6
Yuba County, CA	2,796	2,274	1,750	37,535	31,428	19.4	1,663	3.1	3.5	0.7	2.7	12.1	55.1
Yuma, AZ Metro Area	6,450	5,331	4,289	31,574	27,049	16.7	4,351	2.7	7.5	1.7	4.1	10.2	29.7
Yuma County, AZ	6,450	5,331	4,289	31,574	27,049	16.7	4,351	2.7	7.5	1.7	4.1	10.2	29.7

[1]Based on resident population estimated on July 1 of the year shown.
[2]Includes other industry categories not shown separately.
[18]Winchester city included with Frederick County, VA, in the Winchester, VA-WV MSA.
D = not shown to avoid disclosure of confidential information.

Table C-4. Labor Force and Private Business Establishments and Employment

Metropolitan statistical area, division, and component county	Civilian labor force								Private nonfarm businesses				
	Total			Percent change		Unemployment rate[1]			Establishments		Employment[2]		Annual payroll per employee 2014 (dollars)
	2015	2010	2005	2005–2010	2010–2015	2015	2010	2005	2014	Change 2010–2014	2014	Change 2010–2014	
Abilene, TX Metro Area	75,160	76,448	80,081	-4.5	-1.7	3.9	7.0	4.2	3,858	-1.1	57,611	3.2	34,636
Callahan County, TX	5,781	6,002	6,993	-14.2	-3.7	4.3	7.3	4.1	209	-9.1	1,439	-5.1	35,006
Jones County, TX	5,725	6,161	7,869	-21.7	-7.1	5.5	8.8	5.4	275	-8.3	2,583	1.4	37,877
Taylor County, TX	63,654	64,285	65,219	-1.4		3.7	6.8	4.1	3,374	0.1	53,589	3.5	34,470
Akron, OH Metro Area	359,928	372,207	380,527	-2.2	-3.3	4.9	10.5	5.9	16,419	-0.9	291,083	7.7	43,821
Portage County, OH	87,007	90,710	89,469	1.4	-4.1	4.9	10.3	5.8	3,001	1.1	44,531	9.3	37,860
Summit County, OH	272,921	281,497	291,058	-3.3	-3.0	4.9	10.6	5.9	13,418	-1.4	246,552	7.4	44,898
Albany, GA Metro Area	65,508	70,765	74,349	-4.8	-7.4	7.0	11.8	5.7	3,169	-4.9	46,393	3.8	35,100
Baker County, GA	1,143	1,232	1,791	-31.2	-7.2	7.3	12.1	5.2	25	4.2	217	-7.7	38,894
Dougherty County, GA	37,924	41,490	41,217	0.7	-8.6	7.7	12.6	6.3	2,337	-4.8	37,973	2.1	35,558
Lee County, GA	13,986	14,345	16,403	-12.5	-2.5	5.3	9.0	4.0	371	-0.5	3,930	22.0	36,213
Terrell County, GA	3,600	3,917	4,586	-14.6	-8.1	7.4	12.2	6.9	163	-9.4	1,758	9.8	30,863
Worth County, GA	8,855	9,781	10,352	-5.5	-9.5	6.4	12.1	5.5	273	-9.0	2,515	2.9	29,087
Albany, OR Metro Area	54,608	57,072	51,945	9.9	-4.3	6.9	12.8	7.5	2,441	-0.1	33,472	5.6	37,011
Linn County, OR	54,608	57,072	51,945	9.9	-4.3	6.9	12.8	7.5	2,441	-0.1	33,472	5.6	37,011
Albany-Schenectady-Troy, NY Metro Area	449,051	459,102	454,313	1.1	-2.2	4.5	7.3	4.0	21,201	0.7	340,468	5.3	44,749
Albany County, NY	158,773	161,511	159,258	1.4	-1.7	4.4	7.0	3.9	9,398	-0.7	175,816	4.7	45,911
Rensselaer County, NY	81,816	84,603	83,813	0.9	-3.3	4.7	7.8	4.2	2,962	-0.6	42,702	3.1	44,213
Saratoga County, NY	116,864	118,048	119,981	-1.6		4.2	6.9	3.6	5,198	4.8	67,946	11.2	43,889
Schenectady County, NY	76,734	79,016	75,405	4.8	-2.9	4.8	7.6	4.2	3,073	-0.9	48,689	2.6	43,492
Schoharie County, NY	14,864	15,924	15,856	0.4	-6.7	5.8	8.9	5.0	570	2.5	5,315	-2.8	33,129
Albuquerque, NM Metro Area	413,907	424,972	394,236	7.8	-2.6	6.2	8.0	4.8	18,571	-0.6	279,897	0.0	38,285
Bernalillo County, NM	318,387	326,799	305,757	6.9	-2.6	5.9	7.7	4.7	15,771	-1.1	244,760	0.7	39,040
Sandoval County, NM	60,693	60,922	50,173	21.4	-0.4	6.7	8.4	5.2	1,671	3.7	23,029	-5.6	36,526
Torrance County, NM	5,449	6,041	7,606	-20.6	-9.8	9.0	11.5	5.5	225	-3.4	1,912	6.4	26,696
Valencia County, NM	29,378	31,210	30,700	1.7	-5.9	7.5	9.6	5.3	904	0.4	10,196	-4.7	26,303
Alexandria, LA Metro Area	67,099	67,410	67,767	-0.5	-0.5	6.5	7.7	6.2	3,320	-3.7	49,751	1.8	36,990
Grant Parish, LA	8,522	8,590	8,558	0.4	-0.8	7.2	8.5	6.3	171	-9.0	1,801	8.3	33,473
Rapides Parish, LA	58,577	58,820	59,209	-0.7	-0.4	6.4	7.6	6.2	3,149	-3.4	47,950	1.5	37,122
Allentown-Bethlehem-Easton, PA-NJ Metro Area	429,733	419,501	407,310	3.0	2.4	5.2	9.2	4.9	18,280	-0.1	308,398	8.5	46,208
Warren County, NJ	57,209	58,563	58,567	0.0	-2.3	5.2	9.9	4.0	2,455	-3.1	27,906	-0.4	44,715
Carbon County, PA	31,667	31,799	30,223	5.2	-0.4	5.8	10.6	6.0	1,140	1.1	13,372	0.4	29,067
Lehigh County, PA	184,342	177,231	170,760	3.8	4.0	5.2	9.2	4.9	8,448	0.5	169,299	10.5	50,384
Northampton County, PA	156,515	151,908	147,760	2.8	3.0	5.1	8.8	5.0	6,237	0.1	97,821	9.1	41,751
Altoona, PA Metro Area	61,018	61,777	64,786	-4.6	-1.2	5.0	8.0	5.2	3,174	-1.3	50,319	-0.3	34,164
Blair County, PA	61,018	61,777	64,786	-4.6	-1.2	5.0	8.0	5.2	3,174	-1.3	50,319	-0.3	34,164
Amarillo, TX Metro Area	130,021	129,609	127,588	1.6	0.3	3.1	5.7	4.0	6,279	4.1	94,941	D	37,165
Armstrong County, TX	988	1,012	1,123	-9.9	-2.4	2.7	4.9	3.9	38	22.6	323	75.5	24,700
Carson County, TX	3,114	3,353	3,489	-3.9	-7.1	3.2	5.4	3.9	118	8.3	661	-83.8	46,581
Oldham County, TX	922	961	1,058	-9.2	-4.1	3.0	4.6	3.8	41	17.1	568	D	30,246
Potter County, TX	56,556	58,038	56,544	2.6	-2.6	3.4	6.3	4.6	3,618	1.3	61,359	4.4	38,461
Randall County, TX	68,441	66,245	65,374	1.3	3.3	2.9	5.2	3.5	2,464	7.7	32,030	25.3	34,737
Ames, IA Metro Area	57,365	53,344	46,922	13.7	7.5	2.4	4.2	3.0	2,003	-1.4	31,660	12.6	38,315
Story County, IA	57,365	53,344	46,922	13.7	7.5	2.4	4.2	3.0	2,003	-1.4	31,660	12.6	38,315
Anchorage, AK Metro Area	203,081	200,237	185,756	7.8	1.4	5.6	7.2	5.9	10,799	3.6	164,797	2.9	60,378
Anchorage Municipality, AK	158,216	157,923	149,028	6.0	0.2	5.0	6.6	5.5	8,710	2.8	147,597	1.7	61,811
Matanuska-Susitna Borough, AK	44,865	42,314	36,728	15.2	6.0	7.8	9.4	7.6	2,089	6.9	17,200	14.2	48,087
Ann Arbor, MI Metro Area	189,852	182,801	189,926	-3.8	3.9	3.5	8.1	4.5	8,049	1.8	142,761	7.7	51,755
Washtenaw County, MI	189,852	182,801	189,926	-3.8	3.9	3.5	8.1	4.5	8,049	1.8	142,761	7.7	51,755
Anniston-Oxford-Jacksonville, AL Metro Area	46,051	51,559	53,955	-4.4	-10.7	7.0	11.4	4.5	2,309	-4.9	35,096	-5.0	32,401
Calhoun County, AL	46,051	51,559	53,955	-4.4	-10.7	7.0	11.4	4.5	2,309	-4.9	35,096	-5.0	32,401
Appleton, WI Metro Area	129,446	127,899	119,949	6.6	1.2	3.9	7.8	4.4	5,795	-0.4	110,641	8.6	42,867
Calumet County, WI	27,488	27,304	25,092	8.8	0.7	3.6	6.9	4.1	881	2.4	12,758	10.1	38,686
Outagamie County, WI	101,958	100,595	94,857	6.0	1.4	4.0	8.1	4.5	4,914	-0.9	97,883	8.5	43,412
Asheville, NC Metro Area	219,079	209,299	198,283	5.6	4.7	4.6	9.0	4.4	11,745	2.1	156,217	10.1	36,307
Buncombe County, NC	130,911	123,877	115,125	7.6	5.7	4.3	8.5	4.4	7,607	5.7	107,803	12.6	37,541
Haywood County, NC	27,858	27,643	27,125	1.9	0.8	5.2	10.3	4.5	1,340	-5.2	14,235	1.9	31,293
Henderson County, NC	50,697	48,376	46,267	4.6	4.8	4.7	9.1	4.2	2,502	-2.9	31,089	6.2	35,527
Madison County, NC	9,613	9,403	9,766	-3.7	2.2	5.7	10.4	5.1	296	-5.7	3,090	8.6	24,194
Athens-Clarke County, GA Metro Area	93,471	93,927	99,200	-5.3	-0.5	5.5	9.1	4.3	4,475	1.9	58,608	9.1	35,041
Clarke County, GA	56,558	56,637	59,066	-4.1	-0.1	5.9	9.3	4.5	2,940	1.5	45,676	7.2	35,532
Madison County, GA	12,752	13,374	15,469	-13.5	-4.7	5.4	10.4	4.4	359	-1.6	2,009	-5.4	27,303
Oconee County, GA	17,430	16,837	17,109	-1.6	3.5	4.3	7.1	3.5	1,010	7.1	9,792	24.0	35,349
Oglethorpe County, GA	6,731	7,079	7,556	-6.3	-4.9	5.3	9.6	4.6	166	-10.3	1,131	3.8	26,328
Atlanta-Sandy Springs-Roswell, GA Metro Area	2,836,326	2,720,049	2,584,602	5.2	4.3	5.6	10.3	5.4	134,212	3.5	2,178,578	8.5	52,454
Barrow County, GA	35,577	34,670	30,504	13.7	2.6	5.2	10.8	4.8	1,105	8.3	14,973	17.3	31,936
Bartow County, GA	47,007	47,837	44,608	7.2	-1.7	5.7	12.2	5.8	1,884	2.7	29,469	11.4	39,633
Butts County, GA	10,154	10,491	9,107	15.2	-3.2	6.4	11.5	6.1	358	2.0	4,014	6.0	31,278
Carroll County, GA	52,274	51,817	50,679	2.2	0.9	6.6	11.7	5.5	1,978	-0.2	32,496	10.4	37,452
Cherokee County, GA	119,452	112,578	99,737	12.9	6.1	4.6	8.8	4.2	4,971	9.8	45,667	22.3	33,905
Clayton County, GA	125,051	125,156	136,125	-8.1	-0.1	7.5	13.5	6.9	3,757	-4.4	70,883	0.2	36,160
Cobb County, GA	398,123	380,297	369,291	3.0	4.7	5.0	9.3	4.8	19,336	2.0	318,225	5.5	53,882
Coweta County, GA	67,350	64,319	55,824	15.2	4.7	5.2	9.7	4.9	2,193	7.7	30,700	18.3	34,990
Dawson County, GA	10,918	10,966	10,287	6.6	-0.4	5.0	10.9	4.3	603	-0.5	6,241	7.1	23,490
DeKalb County, GA	371,671	363,001	368,282	-1.4	2.4	5.9	10.8	6.1	16,300	1.5	262,339	3.9	50,888
Douglas County, GA	68,274	66,575	59,500	11.9	2.6	6.2	11.2	5.7	2,438	-1.9	34,833	4.6	31,599
Fayette County, GA	54,393	52,927	53,172	-0.5	2.8	5.1	8.2	4.6	3,235	3.5	38,978	7.7	36,901

[1]Civilian employment as a percent of the civilian labor force.
[2]For the pay period including March 12 of the year shown.
D = not shown to avoid disclosure of confidential information.

Table C-4. Labor Force and Private Business Establishments and Employment—*Continued*

| Metropolitan statistical area, division, and component county | Civilian labor force | | | | | | | | Private nonfarm businesses | | | | Annual payroll per employee 2014 (dollars) |
| | Total | | | Percent change | | Unemployment rate[1] | | | Establishments | | Employment[2] | | |
	2015	2010	2005	2005–2010	2010–2015	2015	2010	2005	2014	Change 2010–2014	2014	Change 2010–2014	
Forsyth County, GA	101,774	88,343	75,083	17.7	15.2	4.4	8.0	3.8	5,796	14.5	66,853	20.3	45,329
Fulton County, GA	514,221	485,002	457,326	6.1	6.0	5.8	10.5	5.8	34,622	5.0	739,045	8.5	66,720
Gwinnett County, GA	449,411	418,368	398,300	5.0	7.4	5.1	9.2	4.7	22,012	4.2	311,031	10.5	46,874
Haralson County, GA	11,926	12,385	12,834	-3.5	-3.7	6.3	12.3	5.4	433	1.4	5,050	3.4	37,510
Heard County, GA	4,999	5,249	4,936	6.3	-4.8	6.2	12.1	5.8	123	2.5	1,188	14.7	44,227
Henry County, GA	104,569	101,141	88,594	14.2	3.4	6.0	10.3	5.3	3,411	4.9	48,299	18.9	32,049
Jasper County, GA	6,431	6,873	6,231	10.3	-6.4	5.4	11.7	5.1	148	-9.2	1,394	3.3	27,369
Lamar County, GA	7,787	8,160	7,764	5.1	-4.6	7.6	14.2	6.1	217	-9.2	2,591	10.2	30,175
Meriwether County, GA	8,781	9,336	9,814	-4.9	-5.9	7.8	13.7	7.2	296	-4.5	3,380	5.6	32,031
Morgan County, GA	8,486	8,630	8,932	-3.4	-1.7	5.4	10.4	4.6	451	0.0	5,355	-3.8	34,675
Newton County, GA	48,245	47,977	42,367	13.2	0.6	6.6	12.7	6.0	1,299	-3.9	17,441	8.0	36,690
Paulding County, GA	75,712	73,735	58,563	25.9	2.7	5.1	10.0	4.7	1,758	9.9	16,510	14.3	28,854
Pickens County, GA	13,920	14,045	14,232	-1.3	-0.9	5.2	11.0	4.2	645	-1.1	6,017	11.0	33,970
Pike County, GA	8,260	8,505	7,706	10.4	-2.9	5.6	10.7	5.7	241	-0.4	1,552	6.1	30,974
Hockdale County, GA	42,292	41,960	39,089	7.3	0.8	6.4	11.3	5.8	1,939	-4.8	31,313	18.2	42,469
Spalding County, GA	27,415	28,669	28,138	1.9	-4.4	7.8	14.9	7.3	1,120	-3.9	16,898	3.6	32,963
Walton County, GA	41,853	41,037	37,577	9.2	2.0	5.3	10.6	4.8	1,543	1.8	15,843	7.3	34,372
Atlantic City-Hammonton, NJ Metro Area	127,666	140,600	136,314	3.1	-9.2	9.4	12.3	5.4	6,365	-1.8	110,726	-2.5	35,949
Atlantic County, NJ	127,666	140,600	136,314	3.1	-9.2	9.4	12.3	5.4	6,365	-1.8	110,726	-2.5	35,949
Auburn-Opelika, AL Metro Area	71,548	66,764	63,530	5.1	7.2	5.1	9.0	3.7	2,576	9.5	39,528	13.2	30,971
Lee County, AL	71,548	66,764	63,530	5.1	7.2	5.1	9.0	3.7	2,576	9.5	39,528	13.2	30,971
Augusta-Richmond County, GA-SC Metro Area	256,201	255,682	256,395	-0.3	0.2	6.3	9.7	6.1	10,318	-1.6	179,942	5.1	40,704
Burke County, GA	9,131	9,791	10,078	-2.8	-6.7	8.0	12.2	7.6	291	-4.0	5,189	7.3	59,415
Columbia County, GA	66,525	61,522	56,828	8.3	8.1	5.0	7.3	4.6	2,143	0.5	26,600	1.2	33,377
Lincoln County, GA	3,347	3,679	3,615	1.8	-9.0	6.6	11.5	7.1	130	-12.2	839	-10.7	26,820
McDuffie County, GA	8,727	9,447	10,635	-11.2	-7.6	8.2	13.2	7.0	432	-2.7	6,094	-1.3	31,296
Richmond County, GA	84,209	87,887	89,801	-2.1	-4.2	7.3	11.0	6.8	4,322	-0.9	87,631	8.8	40,182
Aiken County, SC	73,562	72,370	74,270	-2.6	1.6	5.9	9.3	5.9	2,690	-2.5	48,978	1.6	45,561
Edgefield County, SC	10,700	10,986	11,168	-1.6	-2.6	6.4	9.9	7.2	310	-8.0	4,611	6.8	35,219
Austin-Round Rock, TX Metro Area	1,069,773	930,551	798,312	16.6	15.0	3.4	7.0	4.5	46,884	13.8	745,697	16.4	51,744
Bastrop County, TX	37,336	35,289	33,653	4.9	5.8	3.9	8.2	5.1	1,175	16.3	12,475	14.1	33,362
Caldwell County, TX	17,557	16,661	15,967	4.3	5.4	4.3	8.6	5.3	580	8.8	6,116	14.1	32,288
Hays County, TX	96,012	80,387	67,038	19.9	19.4	3.4	7.0	4.5	3,660	14.8	46,675	24.5	32,438
Travis County, TX	658,215	575,630	502,123	14.6	14.3	3.3	6.8	4.5	32,217	13.3	544,038	15.6	55,270
Williamson County, TX	260,653	222,584	179,531	24.0	17.1	3.5	7.2	4.6	9,252	14.9	136,393	17.2	46,840
Bakersfield, CA Metro Area	393,764	371,515	326,748	13.7	6.0	10.2	15.7	8.4	12,480	4.7	192,765	10.2	44,382
Kern County, CA	393,764	371,515	326,748	13.7	6.0	10.2	15.7	8.4	12,480	4.7	192,765	10.2	44,382
Baltimore-Columbia-Towson, MD Metro Area	1,472,177	1,425,226	1,366,365	4.3	3.3	5.4	8.1	4.4	66,213	1.6	1,123,100	6.0	51,574
Anne Arundel County, MD	300,068	286,058	274,457	4.2	4.9	4.5	6.9	3.5	13,881	2.6	222,781	11.3	51,953
Baltimore County, MD	444,854	431,512	419,256	2.9	3.1	5.4	8.3	4.3	19,869	0.3	310,382	-0.1	46,347
Carroll County, MD	93,569	92,595	91,900	0.8	1.1	4.3	6.8	3.3	4,215	1.1	49,797	5.1	36,852
Harford County, MD	136,343	132,786	129,191	2.8	2.7	5.0	7.8	3.9	5,377	1.1	70,062	6.7	40,008
Howard County, MD	175,167	160,630	154,170	4.2	9.0	3.9	5.6	3.1	9,139	6.5	168,040	11.3	59,789
Queen Anne's County, MD	26,694	26,141	25,037	4.4	2.1	4.6	7.3	3.5	1,355	-0.7	11,634	8.7	33,516
Baltimore city, MD	295,482	295,504	272,354	8.5	0.0	7.7	11.2	6.9	12,377	0.5	290,404	6.0	58,155
Bangor, ME Metro Area	76,643	79,110	77,286	2.4	-3.1	4.8	8.6	5.1	4,138	-1.3	57,535	-0.1	35,192
Penobscot County, ME	76,643	79,110	77,286	2.4	-3.1	4.8	8.6	5.1	4,138	-1.3	57,535	-0.1	35,192
Barnstable Town, MA Metro Area	111,332	111,013	122,143	-9.1	0.3	6.3	9.9	4.9	8,390	2.1	72,254	5.0	43,378
Barnstable County, MA	111,332	111,013	122,143	-9.1	0.3	6.3	9.9	4.9	8,390	2.1	72,254	5.0	43,378
Baton Rouge, LA Metro Area	421,898	390,669	362,526	7.8	8.0	5.4	7.8	7.0	17,862	0.6	338,772	9.5	48,572
Ascension Parish, LA	60,925	53,392	45,815	16.5	14.1	5.0	7.5	6.5	2,133	8.2	36,244	19.4	51,235
East Baton Rouge Parish, LA	236,689	221,984	212,877	4.3	6.6	5.3	7.6	6.9	12,063		249,880	8.6	49,014
East Feliciana Parish, LA	8,327	8,103	8,204	-1.2	2.8	5.8	8.3	6.8	249	-6.0	3,381	-8.6	36,866
Iberville Parish, LA	14,610	14,031	12,609	11.3	4.1	7.1	10.0	9.0	523	-1.5	10,289	10.9	65,800
Livingston Parish, LA	67,857	61,281	53,346	14.9	10.7	5.1	7.5	5.9	1,694	5.8	19,878	14.3	33,905
Pointe Coupee Parish, LA	10,276	10,001	9,917	0.8	2.7	6.5	8.7	8.9	359	-6.3	4,244		37,648
St. Helena Parish, LA	4,585	4,716	4,370	7.9	-2.8	8.9	13.1	14.1	112	-6.7	1,208	6.5	30,193
West Baton Rouge Parish, LA	13,169	11,924	10,456	14.0	10.4	5.6	7.9	7.0	542	8.4	10,980	3.7	48,378
West Feliciana Parish, LA	5,460	5,237	4,932	6.2	4.3	5.2	6.7	8.1	187	-3.6	2,668	7.2	55,154
Battle Creek, MI Metro Area	64,682	64,996	71,724	-9.4	-0.5	4.9	11.7	6.7	2,617	-2.4	D	D	D
Calhoun County, MI	64,682	64,996	71,724	-9.4	-0.5	4.9	11.7	6.7	2,617	-2.4	D	D	D
Bay City, MI Metro Area	52,570	54,666	55,557	-1.6	-3.8	5.5	11.6	7.1	2,234	-2.5	30,512	4.0	37,420
Bay County, MI	52,570	54,666	55,557	-1.6	-3.8	5.5	11.6	7.1	2,234	-2.5	30,512	4.0	37,420
Beaumont-Port Arthur, TX Metro Area	176,632	183,461	182,725	0.4	-3.7	6.7	11.3	7.7	7,908	-1.9	129,190	1.2	49,603
Hardin County, TX	25,221	25,839	24,619	5.0	-2.4	5.6	9.9	6.6	820	5.3	8,894	6.9	38,853
Jefferson County, TX	108,580	113,217	111,553	1.5	-4.1	7.0	11.3	7.8	5,606	-2.7	100,209	1.4	50,649
Newton County, TX	5,497	5,939	5,771	2.9	-7.4	7.5	12.7	9.2	126	-6.7	1,036	-15.9	26,403
Orange County, TX	37,334	38,466	40,782	-5.7	-2.9	6.5	11.7	8.0	1,356	-2.0	19,051	-1.3	50,380
Beckley, WV Metro Area	47,037	50,037	49,913	0.2	-6.0	7.8	8.8	5.1	2,608	-4.2	38,372	1.6	38,841
Fayette County, WV	16,354	17,567	17,747		-6.9	8.5	10.0	5.8	754	-7.6	9,744	11.9	44,942
Raleigh County, WV	30,683	32,470	32,166	0.9	-5.5	7.3	8.1	4.7	1,854	-2.8	28,628	-1.4	36,764
Bellingham, WA Metro Area	102,918	104,359	102,524	1.8	-1.4	5.9	9.5	5.3	6,279	0.6	71,947	6.7	40,068
Whatcom County, WA	102,918	104,359	102,524	1.8	-1.4	5.9	9.5	5.3	6,279	0.6	71,947	6.7	40,068
Bend-Redmond, OR Metro Area	84,185	81,238	74,532	9.0	3.6	6.0	13.8	5.7	6,260	7.8	56,454	9.6	37,978
Deschutes County, OR	84,185	81,238	74,532	9.0	3.6	6.0	13.8	5.7	6,260	7.8	56,454	9.6	37,978
Billings, MT Metro Area	87,832	82,163	84,503	-2.8	6.9	3.3	5.9	3.6	5,965	D	D	D	D
Carbon County, MT	5,543	5,330	5,387	-1.1	4.0	3.6	6.4	3.8	407	4.1	2,158	1.4	26,995
Golden Valley County, MT	401	418	537	-22.2	-4.1	4.2	6.7	4.8	15	D	D	D	D

[1]Civilian employment as a percent of the civilian labor force.
[2]For the pay period including March 12 of the year shown.
D = not shown to avoid disclosure of confidential information.

Table C-4. Labor Force and Private Business Establishments and Employment—*Continued*

Metropolitan statistical area, division, and component county	Civilian labor force								Private nonfarm businesses				
	Total			Percent change		Unemployment rate[1]			Establishments		Employment[2]		Annual payroll per employee 2014 (dollars)
	2015	2010	2005	2005–2010	2010–2015	2015	2010	2005	2014	Change 2010–2014	2014	Change 2010–2014	
Yellowstone County, MT	81,888	76,415	78,579	-2.8	7.2	3.3	5.9	3.5	5,543	0.7	68,776	2.4	42,056
Binghamton, NY Metro Area	110,454	124,412	122,597	1.5	-11.2	6.0	8.6	4.8	5,075	-0.8	82,583	-2.0	39,669
Broome County, NY	86,925	97,844	96,287	1.6	-11.2	6.0	8.7	4.9	4,261	-1.1	71,889	-0.7	38,175
Tioga County, NY	23,529	26,568	26,310	1.0	-11.4	5.6	8.0	4.7	814	0.9	10,694	-10.1	49,711
Birmingham-Hoover, AL Metro Area	531,231	539,753	530,561	1.7	-1.6	5.5	9.8	4.1	25,260	-1.7	445,333	2.6	46,829
Bibb County, AL	8,490	8,934	8,861	0.8	-5.0	6.6	11.4	4.5	274	-6.5	3,424	17.0	35,006
Blount County, AL	24,352	24,906	26,446	-5.8	-2.2	5.4	9.8	3.6	656	-6.4	6,446	0.2	29,543
Chilton County, AL	19,021	19,462	19,674	-1.1	-2.3	5.7	10.3	3.9	721	-1.9	7,259	7.4	31,088
Jefferson County, AL	309,229	318,520	317,359	0.4	-2.9	5.8	10.3	4.4	16,213	-2.4	318,416	0.9	48,725
St. Clair County, AL	38,172	38,280	33,750	13.4	-0.3	5.2	10.1	4.0	1,257	3.8	15,609	21.3	32,295
Shelby County, AL	106,491	102,372	94,699	8.1	4.0	4.2	7.1	3.1	4,891	1.5	79,232	6.9	47,679
Walker County, AL	25,476	27,229	29,772	-8.4	-6.6	7.2	12.7	4.4	1,248	-5.1	14,947	-3.2	34,919
Bismarck, ND Metro Area	67,337	64,565	61,247	5.4	4.3	2.6	3.9	3.1	3,912	D	58,623	D	46,428
Burleigh County, ND	48,739	46,337	44,286	4.6	5.2	2.3	3.6	2.8	3,016	12.1	47,295	10.1	46,193
Morton County, ND	16,361	15,993	14,527	10.1	2.3	3.0	4.6	3.6	829	12.8	9,661	12.0	47,310
Oliver County, ND	902	927	1,097	-15.5	-2.7	5.7	5.7	4.7	41	2.5	653	D	80,493
Sioux County, ND	1,335	1,308	1,337	-2.2	2.1	4.2	5.1	6.8	26	D	1,014	D	27,069
Blacksburg-Christiansburg-Radford, VA Metro Area	91,365	88,695	83,789	5.9	3.0	4.6	8.3	4.1	3,475	-2.9	49,430	6.8	36,092
Floyd County, VA	8,340	8,134	7,094	14.7	2.5	4.0	7.0	3.7	320	4.6	2,090	6.4	27,941
Giles County, VA	8,069	8,302	8,352	-0.6	-2.8	5.1	9.6	5.2	287	-5.9	3,669	-2.2	39,939
Montgomery County, VA	50,008	47,497	43,120	10.2	5.3	4.3	7.1	3.6	1,936	-2.7	27,917	7.2	35,873
Pulaski County, VA	16,461	16,975	17,995	-5.7	-3.0	5.0	11.1	4.5	629	-3.8	11,384	9.5	37,185
Radford city, VA	8,487	7,787	7,228	7.7	9.0	5.6	9.3	4.6	303	-6.2	4,370	5.8	35,317
Bloomington, IL Metro Area	99,036	104,944	95,546	9.8	-5.6	4.9	7.2	4.2	4,035		81,138	0.6	50,571
De Witt County, IL	7,926	8,805	8,381	5.1	-10.0	5.6	8.6	5.4	382	2.1	4,459	-2.6	48,563
McLean County, IL	91,110	96,139	87,165	10.3	-5.2	4.9	7.1	4.1	3,653	-1.3	76,679	0.8	50,688
Bloomington, IN Metro Area	76,540	78,053	78,446	-0.5	-1.9	5.0	8.4	5.1	3,173	-3.6	51,752	1.8	36,746
Monroe County, IN	67,158	67,737	66,680	1.6	-0.9	4.9	7.9	4.8	2,892	-3.3	48,821	4.1	37,194
Owen County, IN	9,382	10,316	11,766	-12.3	-9.1	6.2	11.5	6.3	281	-6.3	2,931	-25.0	29,290
Bloomsburg-Berwick, PA Metro Area	43,034	43,840	42,998	2.0	-1.8	5.2	8.8	5.5	1,842	-0.5	37,443	9.6	46,596
Columbia County, PA	33,867	34,756	34,035	2.1	-2.6	5.5	9.3	5.8	1,392	-3.0	22,893	6.2	34,693
Montour County, PA	9,167	9,084	8,963	1.3	0.9	4.2	6.7	4.4	450	8.2	14,550	15.3	65,324
Boise City, ID Metro Area	324,068	297,428	281,557	5.6	9.0	4.0	9.2	3.7	16,914	2.8	234,236	11.7	42,383
Ada County, ID	217,281	196,922	187,127	5.2	10.3	3.6	8.3	3.3	12,507	2.4	182,706	11.4	45,580
Boise County, ID	3,006	3,048	3,683	-17.2	-1.4	6.2	10.6	4.5	149	3.5	549	4.2	22,761
Canyon County, ID	90,816	84,728	78,790	7.5	7.2	4.9	11.3	4.4	3,723	4.5	47,157	14.2	31,291
Gem County, ID	7,661	7,680	7,238	6.1	-0.2	5.1	11.4	4.8	351	-0.8	2,299	3.2	27,180
Owyhee County, ID	5,304	5,050	4,719	7.0	5.0	4.6	4.2	2.5	184	4.0	1,525	-4.9	32,396
Boston-Cambridge-Newton, MA-NH Metro Area	2,564,753	2,474,337	2,369,644	4.4	3.7	4.4	7.5	4.5	125,686	2.9	2,363,791	6.2	64,950
Boston, MA Division	*1,052,776*	*1,014,231*	*946,385*	*7.2*	*3.8*	*4.7*	*7.9*	*4.8*	*52,152*	*3.6*	*1,068,953*	*5.9*	*179,383*
Norfolk County, MA	368,331	358,048	355,881	0.6	2.9	4.3	7.4	4.2	19,637	3.2	334,197	8.6	54,163
Plymouth County, MA	267,574	262,396	258,416	1.5	2.0	5.2	9.0	4.9	12,020	2.0	162,524	11.7	45,429
Suffolk County, MA	416,871	393,787	332,082	18.6	5.9	4.6	7.7	5.3	20,495	5.0	572,232	2.9	79,791
Cambridge-Newton-Framingham, MA Division	*1,263,377*	*1,218,157*	*1,185,870*	*2.7*	*3.7*	*4.4*	*7.5*	*4.4*	*61,463*	*2.6*	*1,129,471*	*7.1*	*66,078*
Essex County, MA	405,706	392,548	375,771	4.5	3.4	5.2	8.7	5.3	18,332	2.5	281,447	7.0	49,686
Middlesex County, MA	857,671	825,609	810,099	1.9	3.9	4.0	6.9	4.1	43,131	2.7	848,024	7.1	71,518
Rockingham County-Strafford County, NH Division	*248,600*	*241,949*	*237,389*	*1.9*	*2.7*	*3.5*	*5.9*	*3.9*	*12,071*	*0.9*	*165,367*	*2.9*	*46,880*
Rockingham County, NH	177,897	172,375	170,876	0.9	3.2	3.6	6.0	4.1	9,490	0.4	129,125	3.3	47,290
Strafford County, NH	70,703	69,574	66,513	4.6	1.6	3.1	5.7	3.4	2,581	2.6	36,242	1.5	45,422
Boulder, CO Metro Area	176,726	170,293	168,036	1.3	3.8	3.2	7.0	4.4	11,932	4.3	145,558	9.2	61,265
Boulder County, CO	176,726	170,293	168,036	1.3	3.8	3.2	7.0	4.4	11,932	4.3	145,558	9.2	61,265
Bowling Green, KY Metro Area	75,913	77,926	74,979	3.9	-2.6	4.9	10.0	5.4	3,502	7.6	55,872	8.3	36,500
Allen County, KY	8,472	9,126	8,586	6.3	-7.2	5.0	11.7	6.5	241	1.7	3,375	19.3	28,451
Butler County, KY	5,016	5,457	5,719	-4.6	-8.1	6.0	12.0	7.1	196	3.7	1,991	19.1	30,273
Edmonson County, KY	4,641	5,122	5,408	-5.3	-9.4	7.1	13.3	7.1	131	-0.8	816	3.8	27,134
Warren County, KY	57,784	58,221	55,266	5.3	-0.8	4.6	9.2	4.9	2,934	8.7	49,690	7.3	37,450
Bremerton-Silverdale, WA Metro Area	115,211	120,592	120,999	-0.3	-4.5	5.5	8.6	5.3	5,607	-0.9	55,893	-0.6	36,477
Kitsap County, WA	115,211	120,592	120,999	-0.3	-4.5	5.5	8.6	5.3	5,607	-0.9	55,893	-0.6	36,477
Bridgeport-Stamford-Norwalk, CT Metro Area	479,044	474,646	451,803	5.1	0.9	5.3	8.4	4.4	27,022	0.0	408,854	3.8	77,935
Fairfield County, CT	479,044	474,646	451,803	5.1	0.9	5.3	8.4	4.4	27,022	0.0	408,854	3.8	77,935
Brownsville-Harlingen, TX Metro Area	164,295	162,316	140,218	15.8	1.2	7.1	11.2	7.6	6,312	-0.2	100,798	2.0	26,393
Cameron County, TX	164,295	162,316	140,218	15.8	1.2	7.1	11.2	7.6	6,312	-0.2	100,798	2.0	26,393
Brunswick, GA Metro Area	50,101	52,097	51,706	0.8	-3.8	6.2	10.5	4.7	2,807	-1.9	33,005	2.4	33,113
Brantley County, GA	6,918	7,468	7,559	-1.2	-7.4	7.3	12.7	5.4	180	1.7	1,240	-5.2	29,205
Glynn County, GA	37,236	38,340	38,916	-1.5	-2.9	6.0	10.0	4.5	2,452	-1.5	30,438	2.6	33,745
McIntosh County, GA	5,947	6,289	5,231	20.2	-5.4	6.4	10.6	5.4	175	-9.8	1,327	6.6	22,265
Buffalo-Cheektowaga-Niagara Falls, NY Metro Area	550,798	573,522	583,969	-1.8	-4.0	5.6	8.6	5.3	27,077	0.7	474,220	4.1	41,553
Erie County, NY	449,176	465,675	472,255	-1.4	-3.5	5.4	8.3	5.2	22,565	0.8	414,626	4.3	42,570
Niagara County, NY	101,622	107,847	111,714	-3.5	-5.8	6.2	9.6	5.5	4,512	0.1	59,594	2.2	34,481
Burlington, NC Metro Area	77,083	76,792	68,710	11.8	0.4	5.3	10.9	6.0	3,138	-2.1	51,102	5.9	35,395
Alamance County, NC	77,083	76,792	68,710	11.8	0.4	5.3	10.9	6.0	3,138	-2.1	51,102	5.9	35,395
Burlington-South Burlington, VT Metro Area	126,711	126,352	117,420	7.6	0.3	3.0	5.1	3.3	6,739	0.3	99,680	1.8	43,109
Chittenden County, VT	95,254	94,524	87,236	8.4	0.8	2.7	4.8	3.1	5,552	0.9	86,656	1.5	44,001
Franklin County, VT	27,404	27,696	25,936	6.8	-1.1	3.7	5.7	3.8	1,009	-1.4	12,403	3.7	37,316
Grand Isle County, VT	4,053	4,132	4,248	-2.7	-1.9	4.1	6.9	5.0	178	-7.8	621	-1.1	34,443

[1] Civilian employment as a percent of the civilian labor force.
[2] For the pay period including March 12 of the year shown.

Table C-4. Labor Force and Private Business Establishments and Employment—*Continued*

Metropolitan statistical area, division, and component county	Civilian labor force								Private nonfarm businesses				
	Total			Percent change		Unemployment rate[1]			Establishments		Employment[2]		Annual payroll per employee 2014 (dollars)
	2015	2010	2005	2005–2010	2010–2015	2015	2010	2005	2014	Change 2010–2014	2014	Change 2010–2014	
California-Lexington Park, MD Metro Area	54,498	53,617	49,151	9.1	1.6	5.0	6.5	3.5	1,925	0.8	28,959	-0.1	49,587
St. Mary's County, MD	54,498	53,617	49,151	9.1	1.6	5.0	6.5	3.5	1,925	0.8	28,959	-0.1	49,587
Canton-Massillon, OH Metro Area	200,293	206,242	204,520	0.8	-2.9	5.3	11.4	6.6	8,684	-2.5	143,440	4.2	37,039
Carroll County, OH	13,521	14,373	14,150	1.6	-5.9	5.9	13.0	6.9	472	0.4	5,137	5.9	31,629
Stark County, OH	186,772	191,869	190,370	0.8	-2.7	5.3	11.3	6.6	8,212	-2.7	138,303	4.2	37,240
Cape Coral-Fort Myers, FL Metro Area	319,967	283,236	272,752	3.8	13.0	5.0	12.5	3.2	16,857	8.3	193,523	15.8	36,496
Lee County, FL	319,967	283,236	272,752	3.8	13.0	5.0	12.5	3.2	16,857	8.3	193,523	15.8	36,496
Cape Girardeau, MO-IL Metro Area	49,351	49,844	47,208	5.6		4.7	7.9	5.0	2,697	-13.7	40,531	-0.6	34,890
Alexander County, IL	2,516	2,972	3,319	-10.5	-15.3	8.6	11.8	8.6	96	-22.0	1,075	-14.6	35,695
Bollinger County, MO	5,725	5,842	5,856	-0.2	-2.0	5.6	10.1	6.2	202	-1.9	1,371	-1.4	25,759
Cape Girardeau County, MO	41,110	41,030	38,033	7.9	0.2	4.3	7.3	4.5	2,399	-14.2	38,085	-0.1	35,196
Carbondale-Marion, IL Metro Area	60,747	62,395	64,840	-3.8	-2.6	6.0	9.0	5.0	2,923	-1.7	39,025	-0.7	34,401
Jackson County, IL	28,905	29,856	31,477	-5.1	-3.2	5.6	8.2	4.6	1,312	-3.7	16,534	-4.0	32,017
Williamson County, IL	31,842	32,539	33,363	-2.5	-2.1	6.2	9.7	5.3	1,611	0.0	22,491	1.8	36,154
Carson City, NV Metro Area	25,103	26,700	27,201	-1.8	-6.0	7.3	13.5	4.5	1,930	-9.9	20,718	-1.8	42,823
Carson City, NV	25,103	26,700	27,201	-1.8	-6.0	7.3	13.5	4.5	1,930	-9.9	20,718	-1.8	42,823
Casper, WY Metro Area	42,894	39,894	39,124	2.0	7.5	4.8	7.0	3.4	2,982	2.4	36,040	10.4	49,012
Natrona County, WY	42,894	39,894	39,124	2.0	7.5	4.8	7.0	3.4	2,982	2.4	36,040	10.4	49,012
Cedar Rapids, IA Metro Area	144,526	145,562	138,103	5.4	-0.7	3.8	6.0	4.4	6,445	-0.1	125,754	3.5	45,554
Benton County, IA	13,868	14,331	14,432	-0.7	-3.2	3.8	6.2	4.7	564	-1.4	4,477	3.4	33,665
Jones County, IA	10,843	11,108	10,423	6.6	-2.4	4.1	6.4	4.8	490	-4.1	4,872	7.9	31,337
Linn County, IA	119,815	120,123	113,248	6.1	-0.3	3.7	6.0	4.3	5,391	0.4	116,405	3.3	46,606
Chambersburg-Waynesboro, PA Metro Area	77,739	75,708	76,938	-1.6	2.7	4.8	8.5	3.4	3,017	-0.4	48,464	4.7	36,461
Franklin County, PA	77,739	75,708	76,938	-1.6	2.7	4.8	8.5	3.4	3,017	-0.4	48,464	4.7	36,461
Champaign-Urbana, IL Metro Area	119,357	125,440	117,505	6.8	-4.8	5.2	8.2	4.1	4,844	-1.4	75,108	0.0	37,883
Champaign County, IL	104,416	108,978	101,124	7.8	-4.2	5.2	8.2	4.1	4,135	-1.1	68,541	0.2	38,320
Ford County, IL	6,521	7,292	7,262	0.4	-10.6	5.4	9.4	4.8	378	-0.5	4,270	3.8	33,157
Piatt County, IL	8,420	9,170	9,119	0.6	-8.2	5.1	7.8	4.0	331	-6.5	2,297	-11.1	33,625
Charleston, WV Metro Area	99,054	105,062	103,457	1.6	-5.7	6.4	7.7	4.9	5,451	-7.7	93,147	-5.4	41,727
Boone County, WV	8,332	8,812	9,294	-5.2	-5.4	9.6	8.8	4.6	284	-10.1	5,485	-24.3	52,053
Clay County, WV	3,297	3,647	3,484	4.7	-9.6	11.2	14.1	7.8	90	-18.9	880	-39.1	29,825
Kanawha County, WV	87,425	92,603	90,679	2.1	-5.6	6.0	7.4	4.9	5,077	-7.4	86,782	-3.3	41,195
Charleston-North Charleston, SC Metro Area	361,515	327,157	295,680	10.6	10.5	5.1	9.3	5.4	17,270	5.3	256,192	12.1	41,597
Berkeley County, SC	92,754	82,742	71,630	15.5	12.1	5.5	10.0	5.3	2,760	5.2	40,857	9.3	44,511
Charleston County, SC	196,913	178,851	167,313	6.9	10.1	4.8	8.8	5.4	12,358	6.3	190,684	12.9	41,944
Dorchester County, SC	71,848	65,564	56,737	15.6	9.6	5.4	9.5	5.3	2,152	-0.1	24,651	10.2	34,079
Charlotte-Concord-Gastonia, NC-SC Metro Area	1,235,300	1,140,626	1,000,379	14.0	8.3	5.5	11.7	5.4	56,408	4.1	954,262	11.8	50,169
Cabarrus County, NC	96,803	89,005	77,153	15.4	8.8	5.2	11.5	4.6	4,057	3.8	58,214	4.2	36,157
Gaston County, NC	103,234	101,200	96,079	5.3	2.0	6.0	13.5	6.1	3,917	-0.5	62,250	8.1	36,632
Iredell County, NC	81,897	78,633	72,392	8.6	4.2	5.5	12.9	5.0	4,432	4.3	61,861	9.7	42,682
Lincoln County, NC	40,637	39,965	36,213	10.4	1.7	5.4	12.7	5.6	1,539	1.1	17,312	5.8	33,827
Mecklenburg County, NC	562,314	502,180	426,529	17.7	12.0	5.4	10.7	5.0	29,301	5.1	569,552	13.2	57,801
Rowan County, NC	63,805	64,298	67,803	-5.2	-0.8	6.0	14.1	5.4	2,527	-1.6	42,623	9.6	40,903
Union County, NC	111,919	101,105	82,302	22.8	10.7	4.8	10.0	4.5	4,215	7.6	50,005	17.6	37,913
Chester County, SC	13,621	14,684	15,896	-7.6	-7.2	8.3	19.3	9.2	531	-0.9	6,610	8.1	38,683
Lancaster County, SC	35,971	33,942	29,727	14.2	6.0	6.3	14.7	8.4	1,256	4.8	16,637	27.9	41,039
York County, SC	125,099	115,614	96,285	20.1	8.2	5.5	12.1	6.6	4,633	4.1	69,198	7.8	39,955
Charlottesville, VA Metro Area	116,114	111,065	103,869	6.9	4.5	3.9	6.5	3.2	6,005	2.0	80,519	5.4	46,304
Albemarle County, VA	54,361	50,987	47,414	7.5	6.6	3.9	6.0	2.9	2,625	4.4	38,494	6.0	47,376
Buckingham County, VA	6,371	6,568	6,783	-3.2	-3.0	5.8	10.7	4.4	257	1.6	1,900	5.7	34,533
Fluvanna County, VA	13,353	13,078	12,793	2.2	2.1	3.7	6.3	3.1	396		2,493	-4.5	32,946
Greene County, VA	9,974	9,655	9,658	0.0	3.3	3.7	6.7	2.9	328	1.2	2,413	10.6	29,075
Nelson County, VA	7,442	7,574	7,424	2.0	-1.7	4.0	7.1	3.3	370	-4.1	3,174	4.8	26,421
Charlottesville city, VA	24,613	23,203	19,797	17.2	6.1	3.7	6.1	3.8	2,029	0.8	32,045	5.1	50,021
Chattanooga, TN-GA Metro Area	253,594	258,365	251,219	2.8	-1.8	5.6	8.8	4.8	11,112	-0.2	213,139	9.7	38,087
Catoosa County, GA	31,304	31,351	34,815	-9.9	-0.1	5.1	8.6	4.4	886	-4.2	11,670	-4.7	31,351
Dade County, GA	7,948	8,348	8,433		-4.8	5.4	8.7	4.8	203	-6.0	2,681	16.1	32,891
Walker County, GA	29,580	30,980	32,829	-5.6	-4.5	5.8	10.3	5.0	679	-5.0	10,408	3.3	31,298
Hamilton County, TN	167,197	169,043	156,630	7.9	-1.1	5.5	8.3	4.7	8,740	1.0	180,791	11.2	39,303
Marion County, TN	11,768	12,542	12,720	-1.4	-6.2	6.9	11.1	6.2	423	-4.3	5,637	7.0	32,040
Sequatchie County, TN	5,797	6,101	5,792	5.3	-5.0	6.7	12.1	5.7	181	-2.2	1,952	6.3	26,456
Cheyenne, WY Metro Area	48,910	46,182	41,359	11.7	5.9	3.9	6.7	4.1	3,056	13.1	34,481	12.1	40,859
Laramie County, WY	48,910	46,182	41,359	11.7	5.9	3.9	6.7	4.1	3,056	13.1	34,481	12.1	40,859
Chicago-Naperville-Elgin, IL-IN-WI Metro Area	**4,888,023**	**4,872,834**	**4,698,563**	**3.7**	**0.3**	**5.8**	**10.6**	**5.9**	**241,284**	**1.9**	**4,079,228**	**7.4**	**55,126**
Chicago-Naperville-Arlington Heights, IL Division	*3,772,665*	*3,759,447*	*3,628,915*	*3.6*	*0.4*	*5.9*	*10.6*	*6.0*	*190,016*	*2.3*	*3,258,595*	*7.7*	*55,732*
Cook County, IL	2,649,758	2,643,788	2,548,067	3.8	0.2	6.1	10.9	6.4	130,833	2.3	2,335,270	7.6	57,499
DuPage County, IL	511,043	502,833	512,686	-1.9	1.6	4.7	8.9	4.7	33,668	1.6	595,352	7.4	56,356
Grundy County, IL	25,400	25,934	23,302	11.3	-2.1	6.8	13.2	7.1	1,060	-1.3	14,994	0.1	56,058
Kendall County, IL	65,148	62,424	44,205	41.2	4.4	5.1	10.2	5.0	2,063	7.1	22,115	9.9	32,720
McHenry County, IL	165,699	168,802	166,361	1.5	-1.8	5.3	10.5	5.1	7,827	0.1	84,791	4.4	41,865
Will County, IL	355,617	355,666	334,294	6.4	0.0	6.0	11.1	5.8	14,565	5.2	206,073	12.0	42,053
Elgin, IL Division	*322,262*	*323,571*	*302,944*	*6.8*	*-0.4*	*5.8*	*10.9*	*5.5*	*14,266*	*0.7*	*209,420*	*7.0*	*41,293*
DeKalb County, IL	55,407	56,366	53,459	5.4	-1.7	5.6	10.5	5.1	1,921	-2.2	25,404	0.3	37,434
Kane County, IL	266,855	267,205	249,485	7.1	-0.1	5.8	11.0	5.5	12,345	1.2	184,016	8.0	41,826
Gary, IN Division	*337,557*	*333,944*	*328,821*	*1.6*	*1.1*	*6.4*	*10.5*	*5.8*	*14,319*	*-1.1*	*231,148*	*3.0*	*42,370*
Jasper County, IN	16,311	16,140	15,224	6.0	1.1	5.8	10.4	5.7	736	-0.7	8,881	3.4	34,378

[1]Civilian employment as a percent of the civilian labor force.
[2]For the pay period including March 12 of the year shown.

Table C-4. Labor Force and Private Business Establishments and Employment—*Continued*

Metropolitan statistical area, division, and component county	Civilian labor force								Private nonfarm businesses				
	Total			Percent change		Unemployment rate[1]			Establishments		Employment[2]		Annual payroll per employee 2014 (dollars)
	2015	2010	2005	2005–2010	2010–2015	2015	2010	2005	2014	Change 2010–2014	2014	Change 2010–2014	
Lake County, IN	230,072	229,128	225,412	1.6	0.4	6.8	10.8	6.2	9,852	-1.4	167,974	2.0	42,616
Newton County, IN	7,013	7,075	7,083	-0.1	-0.9	5.7	11.3	5.4	255	-10.5	2,312	-8.1	32,878
Porter County, IN	84,161	81,601	81,102	0.6	3.1	5.4	9.5	4.8	3,476	0.7	51,981	7.1	43,360
Lake County-Kenosha County, IL-WI Division	*455,539*	*455,872*	*437,883*	*4.1*	*-0.1*	*5.4*	*9.9*	*4.8*	*22,683*	*1.2*	*380,065*	*7.5*	*65,307*
Lake County, IL	368,107	369,999	355,521	4.1	-0.5	5.5	9.8	4.6	19,623	1.2	330,815	7.6	69,349
Kenosha County, WI	87,432	85,873	82,362	4.3	1.8	5.2	10.3	5.6	3,060	1.5	49,250	7.1	38,153
Chico, CA Metro Area	101,731	102,568	98,309	4.3	-0.8	7.2	13.9	6.7	4,637	-1.6	57,562	6.8	35,059
Butte County, CA	101,731	102,568	98,309	4.3	-0.8	7.2	13.9	6.7	4,637	-1.6	57,562	6.8	35,059
Cincinnati, OH-KY-IN Metro Area	1,072,143	1,095,962	1,088,914	0.6	-2.2	4.5	9.9	5.4	45,633	-0.4	896,336	2.9	48,203
Dearborn County, IN	25,302	25,524	26,428	-3.4	-0.9	5.1	10.9	5.7	911	-5.9	12,459	-9.0	34,291
Ohio County, IN	3,236	3,263	3,152	3.5	-0.8	5.4	11.1	5.3	86	3.6	1,146	-9.7	24,040
Union County, IN	3,603	3,729	3,874	-3.7	-3.4	4.4	10.3	5.6	108	-12.9	899	4.8	28,788
Boone County, KY	63,598	63,271	59,889	5.6	0.5	4.2	8.9	4.8	3,014	6.9	74,617	21.0	41,934
Bracken County, KY	3,686	3,982	4,422	-10.0	-7.4	6.4	11.4	6.3	94	-4.1	877	2.8	30,715
Campbell County, KY	46,674	48,713	45,946	6.0	-4.2	4.2	9.1	5.4	1,646	1.7	23,641	-1.1	34,760
Gallatin County, KY	3,745	4,076	4,053	0.6	-8.1	5.3	12.3	5.9	86	-3.4	764	-1.8	23,147
Grant County, KY	10,906	11,684	12,592	-7.2	-6.7	5.4	11.8	5.5	366	-6.9	3,642	-9.1	31,524
Kenton County, KY	81,007	83,798	84,011	-0.3	-3.3	4.6	9.8	5.0	3,072	-1.5	51,652	-24.8	44,843
Pendleton County, KY	6,573	7,387	7,494	-1.4	-11.0	5.5	12.3	5.7	182	-1.6	1,725	7.9	33,790
Brown County, OH	19,681	21,125	22,047	-4.2	-6.8	6.2	13.3	7.0	528	-2.4	6,139	-0.7	29,092
Butler County, OH	187,121	190,738	186,502	2.3	-1.9	4.6	10.0	5.4	7,002	0.8	126,095	4.9	42,381
Clermont County, OH	102,877	104,819	104,576	0.2	-1.9	4.5	10.4	5.5	3,524	-0.8	48,803	9.3	42,384
Hamilton County, OH	402,663	413,738	419,952	-1.5	-2.7	4.5	9.9	5.6	20,954	-2.0	468,724	4.1	53,390
Warren County, OH	111,471	110,115	103,976	5.9	1.2	4.1	9.0	4.9	4,060	3.8	75,153	4.1	48,225
Clarksville, TN-KY Metro Area	108,713	109,371	98,089	11.5	-0.6	6.1	9.6	5.6	4,276	3.2	66,687	2.3	32,249
Christian County, KY	24,962	27,294	26,460	3.2	-8.5	6.4	11.7	7.0	1,318	-2.2	22,984	-5.0	34,653
Trigg County, KY	5,623	6,440	6,469	-0.4	-12.7	5.9	14.1	6.6	230	-5.7	2,221	-5.4	27,688
Montgomery County, TN	78,128	75,637	65,160	16.1	3.3	6.0	8.5	4.9	2,728	7.0	41,482	7.3	31,161
Cleveland, TN Metro Area	56,372	53,784	53,462	0.6	4.8	5.6	9.6	5.3	2,104	0.0	40,238	10.4	36,445
Bradley County, TN	49,042	46,448	46,242	0.4	5.6	5.4	9.4	5.3	1,897	0.9	38,779	11.0	36,783
Polk County, TN	7,330	7,336	7,220	1.6	-0.1	6.8	11.2	5.9	207	-6.8	1,459	-2.8	27,467
Cleveland-Elyria, OH Metro Area	1,025,539	1,052,045	1,078,484	-2.5	-2.5	4.8	8.4	5.1	51,260	-1.7	914,102	5.1	47,462
Cuyahoga County, OH	610,001	631,675	654,861	-3.5	-3.4	5.0	8.5	5.4	33,016	-1.9	664,773	5.6	49,827
Geauga County, OH	48,751	48,975	50,378	-2.8	-0.5	4.0	6.9	4.3	2,744	0.1	28,158	-5.6	41,401
Lake County, OH	123,388	126,272	129,690	-2.6	-2.3	4.4	7.9	4.6	5,996	-2.3	86,124	3.9	43,223
Lorain County, OH	149,186	151,082	151,819	-0.5	-1.3	5.4	9.1	5.2	5,518	-1.9	84,068	7.2	39,785
Medina County, OH	94,213	94,041	91,736	2.5	0.2	4.0	7.4	4.4	3,986	0.3	50,979	3.3	39,792
Coeur d'Alene, ID Metro Area	71,896	68,851	67,178	2.5	4.4	5.0	10.9	4.5	4,366	-1.4	46,988	8.2	35,334
Kootenai County, ID	71,896	68,851	67,178	2.5	4.4	5.0	10.9	4.5	4,366	-1.4	46,988	8.2	35,334
College Station-Bryan, TX Metro Area	120,844	115,448	102,867	12.2	4.7	3.5	6.6	4.3	4,698	8.1	67,251	13.9	34,795
Brazos County, TX	105,943	100,017	86,694	15.4	5.9	3.4	6.3	4.2	4,094	8.7	61,500	14.0	33,988
Burleson County, TX	7,695	7,870	8,615	-8.6	-2.2	4.4	7.9	4.1	333	8.8	3,063	22.0	40,179
Robertson County, TX	7,206	7,561	7,558	0.0	-4.7	4.8	9.2	5.0	271	-1.5	2,688	3.1	47,112
Colorado Springs, CO Metro Area	319,535	318,662	301,904	5.6	0.3	4.6	9.3	5.3	16,965	2.5	229,344	5.2	43,139
El Paso County, CO	307,936	306,308	289,307	5.9	0.5	4.6	9.3	5.3	16,292	2.8	224,066	5.3	43,386
Teller County, CO	11,599	12,354	12,597	-1.9	-6.1	4.4	9.4	4.9	673	-3.3	5,278	1.5	32,649
Columbia, MO Metro Area	100,284	92,559	85,727	8.0	8.3	3.5	6.5	3.6	4,517	4.2	73,688	10.1	36,482
Boone County, MO	100,284	92,559	85,727	8.0	8.3	3.5	6.5	3.6	4,517	4.2	73,688	10.1	36,482
Columbia, SC Metro Area	396,021	372,416	355,320	4.8	6.3	5.5	9.3	5.7	16,848	-1.5	279,659	3.3	39,734
Calhoun County, SC	6,966	7,044	7,091	-0.7	-1.1	7.0	12.3	7.3	239	-1.6	3,422	12.9	42,221
Fairfield County, SC	10,167	10,672	11,316	-5.7	-4.7	8.0	14.6	7.8	286	-10.1	5,181	13.8	57,626
Kershaw County, SC	28,889	28,137	28,995	-3.0	2.7	6.0	11.5	6.5	1,103	-3.3	15,335	16.4	35,114
Lexington County, SC	144,101	132,940	127,602	4.2	8.4	4.8	8.2	4.9	6,212	2.4	94,192	8.0	36,060
Richland County, SC	197,036	184,939	171,046	8.1	6.5	5.7	9.4	5.9	8,761	-3.4	157,927	-0.7	41,979
Saluda County, SC	8,862	8,684	9,270	-6.3	2.0	5.2	10.0	6.6	247	-5.4	3,602	0.1	28,935
Columbus, GA-AL Metro Area	124,454	127,888	127,552	0.3	-2.7	6.9	10.0	6.0	5,621	-1.7	97,888	3.9	35,995
Russell County, AL	24,283	23,814	21,501	10.8	2.0	6.0	10.9	6.0	780	-6.9	11,097	4.5	32,508
Chattahoochee County, GA	2,199	2,218	2,657	-16.5	-0.9	8.8	10.9	10.6	100	49.3	1,444	130.3	39,691
Harris County, GA	15,480	16,415	15,281	7.4	-5.7	5.2	7.7	4.2	399	0.3	4,475	33.2	24,777
Marion County, GA	3,454	3,723	3,410	9.2	-7.2	8.2	10.7	5.3	76	0.0	1,397	18.2	25,299
Muscogee County, GA	79,038	81,718	84,703	-3.5	-3.3	7.4	10.1	6.2	4,266	-1.7	79,475	1.4	37,234
Columbus, IN Metro Area	43,649	38,387	37,388	2.7	13.7	3.6	9.5	4.8	1,796	-3.2	44,983	16.3	46,552
Bartholomew County, IN	43,649	38,387	37,388	2.7	13.7	3.6	9.5	4.8	1,796	-3.2	44,983	16.3	46,552
Columbus, OH Metro Area	1,038,547	1,004,299	956,304	5.0	3.4	4.1	9.0	5.5	40,850	1.6	826,924	8.9	47,360
Delaware County, OH	101,620	94,233	83,514	12.8	7.8	3.5	7.2	4.4	4,230	11.3	76,684	15.8	49,958
Fairfield County, OH	75,367	74,265	73,172	1.5	1.5	4.3	9.2	5.5	2,613	2.0	34,460	6.3	32,568
Franklin County, OH	654,086	626,837	601,304	4.2	4.3	4.1	8.9	5.4	27,388	1.0	608,429	8.6	48,826
Hocking County, OH	13,284	14,036	13,850	1.3	-5.4	5.5	11.7	7.7	467	-2.9	4,925	-0.9	28,733
Licking County, OH	87,474	87,551	81,708	7.2	-0.1	4.4	9.6	5.9	2,897	-0.9	47,805	3.4	38,130
Madison County, OH	20,682	20,665	19,828	4.2	0.1	4.0	9.0	6.0	681	-2.6	11,831	16.4	39,270
Morrow County, OH	16,936	17,309	17,738	-2.4	-2.2	5.0	11.4	6.4	381	0.3	3,646	-0.5	32,725
Perry County, OH	15,953	16,646	16,652	0.0	-4.2	6.5	13.4	8.4	419	-1.2	3,758	-1.9	30,073
Pickaway County, OH	26,024	26,100	24,055	8.5	-0.3	4.7	10.6	7.2	777	-2.4	11,129	6.9	39,032
Union County, OH	27,121	26,657	24,483	8.9	1.7	3.8	8.4	5.1	997	-0.5	24,257	16.5	57,999
Corpus Christi, TX Metro Area	207,775	202,622	197,063	2.8	2.5	5.2	8.5	5.6	9,463	2.2	159,813	12.6	41,538
Aransas County, TX	10,092	9,686	10,964	-11.7	4.2	5.1	9.2	5.5	503	6.8	4,131	4.0	27,429
Nueces County, TX	167,125	162,502	156,542	3.8	2.8	4.9	8.1	5.4	7,903	1.8	139,655	11.4	41,679

[1] Civilian employment as a percent of the civilian labor force.
[2] For the pay period including March 12 of the year shown.

Table C-4.   Labor Force and Private Business Establishments and Employment—*Continued*

Metropolitan statistical area, division, and component county	Civilian labor force								Private nonfarm businesses				
	Total			Percent change		Unemployment rate[1]			Establishments		Employment[2]		Annual payroll per employee 2014 (dollars)
	2015	2010	2005	2005–2010	2010–2015	2015	2010	2005	2014	Change 2010–2014	2014	Change 2010–2014	
San Patricio County, TX	30,558	30,434	29,557	3.0	0.4	6.5	10.5	6.9	1,057	3.0	16,027	26.7	43,941
Corvallis, OR Metro Area	45,171	45,075	41,922	7.5	0.2	4.3	7.1	4.9	2,103	2.1	24,947	1.7	41,071
Benton County, OR	45,171	45,075	41,922	7.5	0.2	4.3	7.1	4.9	2,103	2.1	24,947	1.7	41,071
Crestview-Fort Walton Beach-Destin, FL Metro Area	119,866	115,030	124,514	-7.6	4.2	4.5	8.6	2.8	7,071	5.9	75,717	4.9	34,933
Okaloosa County, FL	92,220	89,046	96,570	-7.8	3.6	4.5	8.4	2.8	5,146	3.0	57,515	1.4	35,905
Walton County, FL	27,646	25,984	27,944	-7.0	6.4	4.6	9.4	2.8	1,925	14.4	18,202	18.0	31,859
Cumberland, MD-WV Metro Area	44,385	46,779	48,703	-4.0	-5.1	7.1	9.3	5.9	2,030	-5.1	30,983	2.8	33,876
Allegany County, MD	32,732	34,417	35,318	-2.6	-4.9	7.1	9.3	6.1	1,575	-5.7	24,909	4.9	32,542
Mineral County, WV	11,653	12,362	13,385	-7.6	-5.7	7.3	9.3	5.3	455	-3.0	6,074	-4.8	39,343
Dallas-Fort Worth-Arlington, TX Metro Area	**3,584,196**	**3,300,763**	**3,024,615**	**9.1**	**8.6**	**4.1**	**8.1**	**5.2**	**152,400**	**7.5**	**2,869,738**	**13.7**	**53,071**
Dallas-Plano-Irving, TX Division	*2,400,143*	*2,192,401*	*2,004,189*	*9.4*	*9.5*	*4.0*	*8.0*	*5.3*	*104,914*	*7.6*	*2,011,934*	*13.8*	*55,762*
Collin County, TX	484,121	425,252	367,439	15.7	13.8	3.6	7.2	4.7	20,610	16.3	354,722	22.9	58,561
Dallas County, TX	1,274,040	1,194,015	1,142,456	4.5	6.7	4.3	8.6	5.7	63,485	3.6	1,361,547	10.6	58,281
Denton County, TX	423,135	369,088	314,097	17.5	14.6	3.6	7.1	4.6	13,062	15.2	191,536	22.8	42,296
Ellis County, TX	80,632	75,674	66,297	14.1	6.6	4.0	8.0	5.3	2,643	8.1	37,683	19.7	37,022
Hunt County, TX	39,186	38,126	38,516		2.8	4.7	8.9	5.5	1,379	-0.4	21,599	-0.3	47,013
Kaufman County, TX	54,638	50,807	43,006	18.1	7.5	4.1	8.5	5.5	1,773	7.2	22,813	12.3	34,218
Rockwall County, TX	44,391	39,439	32,378	21.8	12.6	3.8	7.4	4.7	1,962	18.1	22,034	17.4	35,043
Fort Worth-Arlington, TX Division	*1,184,053*	*1,108,362*	*1,020,426*	*8.6*	*6.8*	*4.2*	*8.2*	*5.1*	*47,486*	*7.1*	*857,804*	*13.4*	*46,758*
Hood County, TX	24,367	23,352	22,525	3.7	4.3	4.5	8.5	5.2	1,241	2.9	13,536	13.2	40,363
Johnson County, TX	74,614	71,940	72,108	-0.2	3.7	4.4	8.7	4.9	2,686	5.6	36,399	15.3	40,358
Parker County, TX	59,407	56,408	50,654	11.4	5.3	4.2	7.6	4.8	2,447	11.5	28,284	25.6	41,032
Somervell County, TX	4,173	4,043	3,686	9.7	3.2	5.0	8.0	5.4	195	-3.5	3,640	20.8	54,589
Tarrant County, TX	992,840	924,951	843,857	9.6	7.3	4.2	8.1	5.1	39,633	7.1	756,293	12.5	47,317
Wise County, TX	28,652	27,668	27,596	0.3	3.6	4.6	8.7	4.7	1,284	8.9	19,652	27.2	48,284
Dalton, GA Metro Area	60,505	64,820	66,501	-2.5	-6.7	6.6	12.4	4.8	2,541	-5.7	54,075	-3.6	38,113
Murray County, GA	15,810	17,181	20,981	-18.1	-8.0	7.4	13.8	4.6	374	-10.3	7,314	-11.5	32,839
Whitfield County, GA	44,695	47,639	45,520	4.7	-6.2	6.3	11.9	4.8	2,167	-4.8	46,761	-2.3	38,937
Danville, IL Metro Area	35,642	37,973	37,822	0.4	-6.1	7.1	11.4	6.3	1,451	-5.7	24,259	-0.1	38,805
Vermilion County, IL	35,642	37,973	37,822	0.4	-6.1	7.1	11.4	6.3	1,451	-5.7	24,259	-0.1	38,805
Daphne-Fairhope-Foley, AL Metro Area	87,316	83,459	76,804	8.7	4.6	5.5	10.0	4.0	4,969	6.5	56,531	10.5	30,943
Baldwin County, AL	87,316	83,459	76,804	8.7	4.6	5.5	10.0	4.0	4,969	6.5	56,531	10.5	30,943
Davenport-Moline-Rock Island, IA-IL Metro Area	192,696	198,838	202,279	-1.7	-3.1	5.6	8.2	4.5	8,960	-2.4	159,530	3.4	43,192
Henry County, IL	25,147	26,722	27,308	-2.1	-5.9	6.2	9.1	4.5	1,075	-4.9	13,146	0.6	35,197
Mercer County, IL	8,228	8,954	8,911	0.5	-8.1	6.2	10.0	5.5	274	-9.0	2,391	2.3	32,903
Rock Island County, IL	72,188	76,282	77,924	-2.1	-5.4	6.5	9.5	4.6	3,258	-2.7	62,827	2.5	50,761
Scott County, IA	87,133	86,880	88,136	1.4	0.3	4.6	6.7	4.4	4,353		81,166	4.6	38,932
Dayton, OH Metro Area	381,765	401,835	404,463	-0.6	-5.0	4.8	11.0	6.2	16,598	-0.9	310,429	3.7	42,421
Greene County, OH	80,098	82,080	77,375	6.1	-2.4	4.4	9.5	5.7	3,042	2.0	49,576	2.3	38,843
Miami County, OH	52,238	54,400	54,855	-0.8	-4.0	4.4	11.1	5.8	2,099	-1.4	35,171	6.5	37,928
Montgomery County, OH	249,429	265,355	272,233	-2.5	-6.0	5.0	11.4	6.5	11,457	-1.6	225,682	3.6	43,907
Decatur, AL Metro Area	68,970	72,718	71,679	1.4	-5.2	6.2	11.1	4.8	2,963	-4.7	46,068	0.2	40,103
Lawrence County, AL	13,864	14,901	15,979	-6.7	-7.0	7.7	12.6	5.6	395	-4.6	3,544	-19.4	30,508
Morgan County, AL	55,106	57,817	55,700	3.8	-4.7	5.8	10.8	4.5	2,568	-4.7	42,524	2.3	40,903
Decatur, IL Metro Area	50,593	55,189	52,836	4.5	-8.3	7.1	11.2	6.1	2,434	-3.0	46,164	-0.4	41,208
Macon County, IL	50,593	55,189	52,836	4.5	-8.3	7.1	11.2	6.1	2,434	-3.0	46,164	-0.4	41,208
Deltona-Daytona Beach-Ormond Beach, FL Metro Area	282,822	279,521	274,669	1.8	1.2	5.8	12.3	3.8	14,071	4.1	153,420	7.8	33,286
Flagler County, FL	43,502	41,338	29,981	37.9	5.2	6.2	12.4	4.4	1,928	10.6	17,207	16.3	29,406
Volusia County, FL	239,320	238,183	244,688	-2.7	0.5	5.7	12.3	3.7	12,143	3.1	136,213	6.8	33,777
Denver-Aurora-Lakewood, CO Metro Area	1,504,945	1,423,355	1,314,305	8.3	5.7	3.7	8.7	5.1	78,126	6.1	1,174,056	13.1	55,128
Adams County, CO	247,538	234,221	209,927	11.6	5.7	4.3	10.0	5.7	8,833	8.1	147,456	13.6	46,234
Arapahoe County, CO	334,800	316,886	298,738	6.1	5.7	3.7	8.6	5.1	17,628	5.1	267,580	13.4	57,940
Broomfield County, CO	34,673	31,538	24,506	28.7	9.9	3.3	7.4	4.8	1,861	8.4	39,556	22.7	67,049
Clear Creek County, CO	5,591	5,623	5,837	-3.7	-0.6	3.7	8.1	4.7	329	-4.1	2,624	3.5	40,782
Denver County, CO	373,109	347,590	302,009	15.1	7.3	3.7	9.1	5.7	23,558	6.8	414,818	12.6	59,225
Douglas County, CO	171,569	157,522	142,904	10.2	8.9	3.1	7.0	4.1	8,355	12.1	99,978	28.3	55,225
Elbert County, CO	13,242	12,755	12,895	-1.1	3.8	3.1	8.1	4.5	581	14.8	2,400	19.5	38,643
Gilpin County, CO	3,483	3,327	3,337	-0.3	4.7	3.1	8.0	4.8	119	9.2	4,658	5.5	35,125
Jefferson County, CO	311,470	304,252	304,514	-0.1	2.4	3.5	8.4	4.9	16,436	2.1	193,767	5.5	47,781
Park County, CO	9,470	9,641	9,638	0.0	-1.8	3.4	8.1	4.7	426	-5.1	1,219	0.2	32,692
Des Moines-West Des Moines, IA Metro Area	339,509	322,912	296,276	9.0	5.1	3.5	5.8	3.9	15,320	3.0	297,427	7.4	47,757
Dallas County, IA	42,930	37,296	29,439	26.7	15.1	2.8	4.6	3.4	1,762	15.9	35,151	21.0	47,896
Guthrie County, IA	5,728	5,852	6,116	-4.3	-2.1	3.6	6.5	4.2	313	-3.1	2,495	-6.8	35,074
Madison County, IA	8,292	8,460	8,141	3.9	-2.0	3.8	6.4	4.5	367	0.8	2,472	-6.0	32,239
Polk County, IA	255,763	244,947	227,980	7.4	4.4	3.6	6.0	4.0	12,078	1.5	249,489	6.3	48,583
Warren County, IA	26,796	26,357	24,600	7.1	1.7	3.3	5.6	3.7	800	3.2	7,820	-1.9	29,737
Detroit-Warren-Dearborn, MI Metro Area	**1,998,430**	**2,058,555**	**2,209,029**	**-6.8**	**-2.9**	**6.2**	**13.9**	**7.0**	**97,940**	**0.7**	**1,658,435**	**10.5**	**51,618**
Detroit-Dearborn-Livonia, MI Division	*750,854*	*802,754*	*910,762*	*-11.9*	*-6.5*	*7.3*	*15.5*	*8.3*	*31,877*	*-2.1*	*605,093*	*6.6*	*51,004*
Wayne County, MI	750,854	802,754	910,762	-11.9	-6.5	7.3	15.5	8.3	31,877	-2.1	605,093	6.6	51,004
Warren-Troy-Farmington Hills, MI Division	*1,247,576*	*1,255,801*	*1,298,267*	*-3.3*	*-0.7*	*5.6*	*12.9*	*6.0*	*66,063*	*2.2*	*1,053,342*	*12.9*	*51,971*
Lapeer County, MI	39,322	41,335	45,788	-9.7	-4.9	7.5	16.3	7.5	1,601	1.5	17,580	19.8	33,509
Livingston County, MI	94,748	94,112	96,140	-2.1	0.7	4.9	11.2	5.2	4,173	3.6	48,727	12.0	37,521
Macomb County, MI	415,825	420,803	428,038	-1.7	-1.2	6.1	13.9	6.6	18,641	5.0	285,162	12.9	46,051
Oakland County, MI	625,346	621,876	642,576	-3.2	0.6	5.0	11.8	5.5	38,592	1.2	661,188	13.2	56,878
St. Clair County, MI	72,335	77,675	85,725	-9.4	-6.9	7.1	16.4	7.7	3,056	-3.6	40,685	6.1	39,011

[1]Civilian employment as a percent of the civilian labor force.
[2]For the pay period including March 12 of the year shown.

Table C-4. Labor Force and Private Business Establishments and Employment—*Continued*

Metropolitan statistical area, division, and component county	Civilian labor force								Private nonfarm businesses				
	Total			Percent change		Unemployment rate[1]			Establishments		Employment[2]		Annual payroll per employee 2014 (dollars)
	2015	2010	2005	2005–2010	2010–2015	2015	2010	2005	2014	Change 2010–2014	2014	Change 2010–2014	
Dothan, AL Metro Area	62,284	65,232	65,199	0.1	-4.5	6.2	9.6	3.9	3,394	-2.6	48,817	-1.7	35,668
Geneva County, AL	10,806	11,559	11,628	-0.6	-6.5	5.9	10.4	3.9	402	-4.7	3,667	-7.4	28,866
Henry County, AL	6,735	7,259	7,469	-2.8	-7.2	6.8	10.9	4.3	290	-3.0	2,584	-6.4	34,791
Houston County, AL	44,743	46,414	46,102	0.7	-3.6	6.2	9.1	3.8	2,702	-2.3	42,566	-0.9	36,307
Dover, DE Metro Area	76,887	72,689	72,015	0.9	5.8	5.4	8.9	3.6	3,263	2.0	49,311	6.3	38,583
Kent County, DE	76,887	72,689	72,015	0.9	5.8	5.4	8.9	3.6	3,263	2.0	49,311	6.3	38,583
Dubuque, IA Metro Area	55,729	54,224	50,793	6.8	2.8	3.6	5.8	4.3	2,779	1.5	53,990	6.7	39,439
Dubuque County, IA	55,729	54,224	50,793	6.8	2.8	3.6	5.8	4.3	2,779	1.5	53,990	6.7	39,439
Duluth, MN-WI Metro Area	142,600	144,905	141,059	2.7	-1.6	5.0	8.2	5.2	7,001	-4.0	108,003	2.4	39,658
Carlton County, MN	17,511	17,794	17,021	4.5	-1.6	5.0	8.4	5.8	701	-2.0	8,171	1.9	37,039
St. Louis County, MN	101,814	103,374	101,353	2.0	-1.5	5.0	8.1	5.0	5,282	-4.1	86,432	3.3	40,007
Douglas County, WI	23,275	23,737	22,685	4.6	-1.9	5.1	8.3	5.3	1,018	-5.0	13,400	-2.5	39,009
Durham-Chapel Hill, NC Metro Area	281,198	262,690	244,489	7.4	7.0	5.0	8.1	4.3	12,116	3.7	233,692	7.9	56,330
Chatham County, NC	32,900	30,655	30,758	-0.3	7.3	4.8	8.6	4.0	1,338	5.9	13,040	-2.1	31,065
Durham County, NC	155,994	143,385	129,938	10.3	8.8	5.0	8.2	4.3	6,948	4.7	171,271	9.8	62,996
Orange County, NC	74,172	69,949	65,060	7.5	6.0	4.6	6.6	3.7	3,170	2.7	41,624	6.1	40,925
Person County, NC	18,132	18,701	18,733	-0.2	-3.0	6.7	12.4	6.4	660	-5.8	7,757	-4.3	34,292
East Stroudsburg, PA Metro Area	80,651	82,741	77,999	6.1	-2.5	6.3	9.7	5.5	3,350	-1.7	45,985	2.7	37,576
Monroe County, PA	80,651	82,741	77,999	6.1	-2.5	6.3	9.7	5.5	3,350	-1.7	45,985	2.7	37,576
Eau Claire, WI Metro Area	91,409	90,289	86,404	4.5	1.2	4.2	7.5	4.6	4,248	2.0	71,423	5.6	36,460
Chippewa County, WI	33,273	33,182	32,640	1.7	0.3	4.8	8.4	5.4	1,569	3.8	21,488	9.7	36,146
Eau Claire County, WI	58,136	57,107	53,764	6.2	1.8	3.9	7.0	4.1	2,679	0.9	49,935	4.0	36,595
El Centro, CA Metro Area	78,910	78,665	60,592	29.8	0.3	24.0	28.8	16.0	2,465	4.1	32,849	12.4	30,535
Imperial County, CA	78,910	78,665	60,592	29.8	0.3	24.0	28.8	16.0	2,465	4.1	32,849	12.4	30,535
Elizabethtown-Fort Knox, KY Metro Area	63,537	65,301	65,279	0.0	-2.7	5.2	10.2	6.1	2,904	3.5	40,169	6.7	34,145
Hardin County, KY	45,953	46,901	46,216	1.5	-2.0	5.1	9.7	5.8	2,313	3.4	34,714	7.4	34,643
Larue County, KY	5,665	6,062	6,884	-11.9	-6.5	5.3	11.3	6.3	220	-4.8	1,847	-14.2	28,476
Meade County, KY	11,919	12,338	12,179	1.3	-3.4	5.6	11.8	7.0	371	9.8	3,608	14.1	32,262
Elkhart-Goshen, IN Metro Area	104,616	94,498	101,915	-7.3	10.7	3.8	13.3	4.6	4,825	-1.3	117,990	25.1	41,671
Elkhart County, IN	104,616	94,498	101,915	-7.3	10.7	3.8	13.3	4.6	4,825	-1.3	117,990	25.1	41,671
Elmira, NY Metro Area	37,960	41,594	40,595	2.5	-8.7	5.9	8.4	5.3	1,810	-2.5	31,795	-2.6	39,287
Chemung County, NY	37,960	41,594	40,595	2.5	-8.7	5.9	8.4	5.3	1,810	-2.5	31,795	-2.6	39,287
El Paso, TX Metro Area	344,725	342,254	291,338	17.5	0.7	5.2	9.2	7.0	13,907	3.9	223,804	8.0	31,170
El Paso County, TX	343,495	340,841	290,010	17.5	0.8	5.2	9.2	7.0	13,875	3.9	223,489	8.0	31,164
Hudspeth County, TX	1,230	1,413	1,328	6.4	-13.0	5.8	7.9	6.9	32	-5.9	315	-2.2	34,730
Enid, OK Metro Area	29,973	28,519	28,304	0.8	5.1	3.9	5.5	3.6	1,700	3.3	22,785	2.4	38,262
Garfield County, OK	29,973	28,519	28,304	0.8	5.1	3.9	5.5	3.6	1,700	3.3	22,785	2.4	38,262
Erie, PA Metro Area	134,873	136,354	140,605	-3.0	-1.1	5.3	9.3	5.4	6,176	-1.8	112,761	1.0	37,759
Erie County, PA	134,873	136,354	140,605	-3.0	-1.1	5.3	9.3	5.4	6,176	-1.8	112,761	1.0	37,759
Eugene, OR Metro Area	171,388	178,303	173,600	2.7	-3.9	5.9	11.0	6.1	9,558	-0.4	120,985	8.3	37,163
Lane County, OR	171,388	178,303	173,600	2.7	-3.9	5.9	11.0	6.1	9,558	-0.4	120,985	8.3	37,163
Evansville, IN-KY Metro Area	158,056	159,288	159,088	0.1	-0.8	4.3	8.9	5.1	7,539	-0.8	140,148	-1.9	41,115
Posey County, IN	13,326	13,494	13,870	-2.7	-1.2	3.9	7.8	4.9	480	-5.9	8,296		56,068
Vanderburgh County, IN	92,371	92,127	91,447	0.7	0.3	4.2	8.9	5.2	4,938	-0.6	101,712	-3.8	40,239
Warrick County, IN	31,398	30,817	30,602	0.7	1.9	4.1	8.0	4.7	1,116	3.3	13,640	8.4	42,589
Henderson County, KY	20,961	22,850	23,169	-1.4	-8.3	5.0	10.3	5.4	1,005	-3.1	16,500	1.5	37,781
Fairbanks, AK Metro Area	46,486	48,285	45,247	6.7	-3.7	5.4	6.6	5.8	2,471	1.1	27,435	1.0	50,978
Fairbanks North Star Borough, AK	46,486	48,285	45,247	6.7	-3.7	5.4	6.6	5.8	2,471	1.1	27,435	1.0	50,978
Fargo, ND-MN Metro Area	130,873	122,707	113,083	8.5	6.7	2.4	4.1	2.9	6,559	4.2	117,483	8.4	41,941
Clay County, MN	35,850	33,883	30,853	9.8	5.8	3.1	5.5	3.4	1,238	-2.9	17,236	2.8	30,332
Cass County, ND	95,023	88,824	82,230	8.0	7.0	2.2	3.5	2.7	5,321	6.0	100,247	9.4	43,937
Farmington, NM Metro Area	55,257	54,896	54,461	0.8	0.7	7.0	9.4	5.3	2,793	-1.1	39,206	3.4	47,002
San Juan County, NM	55,257	54,896	54,461	0.8	0.7	7.0	9.4	5.3	2,793	-1.1	39,206	3.4	47,002
Fayetteville, NC Metro Area	145,827	149,647	145,555	2.8	-2.6	7.5	10.1	5.5	6,106	-0.1	97,552		32,869
Cumberland County, NC	126,488	131,073	127,153	3.1	-3.5	7.4	10.1	5.4	5,689	-0.3	92,537	-0.5	33,281
Hoke County, NC	19,339	18,574	18,402	0.9	4.1	8.1	10.1	5.8	417	2.7	5,015	-9.5	25,269
Fayetteville-Springdale-Rogers, AR-MO Metro Area	253,105	227,616	220,833	3.1	11.2	3.8	6.7	3.4	11,125	4.5	193,752	9.9	48,165
Benton County, AR	120,331	107,121	100,203	6.9	12.3	3.9	6.6	3.2	5,624	5.8	103,273	13.4	57,324
Madison County, AR	7,176	7,270	7,835	-7.2	-1.3	3.9	7.1	3.7	188	2.2	2,461	7.8	28,286
Washington County, AR	114,790	102,865	100,890	2.0	11.6	3.6	6.5	3.4	5,017	3.8	82,559	6.2	38,528
McDonald County, MO	10,808	10,360	11,905	-13.0	4.3	4.6	9.2	4.3	296	-6.0	5,459	4.1	29,583
Flagstaff, AZ Metro Area	73,041	72,846	67,883	7.3	0.3	6.6	9.9	4.9	3,522	-1.5	47,538	9.5	37,071
Coconino County, AZ	73,041	72,846	67,883	7.3	0.3	6.6	9.9	4.9	3,522	-1.5	47,538	9.5	37,071
Flint, MI Metro Area	182,886	188,190	212,686	-11.5	-2.8	5.8	14.0	7.9	7,716	-2.4	115,459	4.6	38,750
Genesee County, MI	182,886	188,190	212,686	-11.5	-2.8	5.8	14.0	7.9	7,716	-2.4	115,459	4.6	38,750
Florence, SC Metro Area	95,466	94,766	92,386	2.6	0.7	6.8	11.9	8.8	4,142	-3.9	73,195	4.2	37,940
Darlington County, SC	30,054	30,591	30,588	0.0	-1.8	7.4	13.2	8.7	1,098	-2.8	17,552	-3.5	43,543
Florence County, SC	65,412	64,175	61,798	3.8	1.9	6.6	11.3	8.9	3,044	-4.2	55,643	6.9	36,173
Florence-Muscle Shoals, AL Metro Area	66,300	67,824	67,023	1.2	-2.2	7.3	10.6	5.2	3,197	-2.4	46,611	5.5	32,503
Colbert County, AL	23,586	24,228	24,960	-2.9	-2.6	7.9	11.5	5.4	1,223	-4.8	20,152	7.8	38,015
Lauderdale County, AL	42,714	43,596	42,063	3.6	-2.0	6.9	10.1	5.1	1,974		26,459	3.8	28,305
Fond du Lac, WI Metro Area	57,286	56,516	55,868	1.2	1.4	4.1	8.5	4.6	2,339	-4.1	42,213	9.0	37,447
Fond du Lac County, WI	57,286	56,516	55,868	1.2	1.4	4.1	8.5	4.6	2,339	-4.1	42,213	9.0	37,447
Fort Collins, CO Metro Area	180,306	170,001	165,944	2.4	6.1	3.3	7.6	4.4	10,031	7.0	116,753	14.5	44,612
Larimer County, CO	180,306	170,001	165,944	2.4	6.1	3.3	7.6	4.4	10,031	7.0	116,753	14.5	44,612

[1]Civilian employment as a percent of the civilian labor force.
[2]For the pay period including March 12 of the year shown.

Table C-4. Labor Force and Private Business Establishments and Employment—*Continued*

Metropolitan statistical area, division, and component county	Civilian labor force Total 2015	2010	2005	Percent change 2005–2010	2010–2015	Unemployment rate[1] 2015	2010	2005	Private nonfarm businesses Establishments 2014	Change 2010–2014	Employment[2] 2014	Change 2010–2014	Annual payroll per employee 2014 (dollars)
Fort Smith, AR-OK Metro Area	121,212	126,732	126,475	0.2	-4.4	5.5	8.5	4.6	5,829	-2.8	96,280	-3.8	35,992
Crawford County, AR	26,897	28,323	27,438	3.2	-5.0	5.4	8.2	4.4	1,041	-5.7	19,684	-9.0	32,594
Sebastian County, AR	57,390	59,543	59,664	-0.2	-3.6	5.0	8.0	4.3	3,392	-3.5	61,320	-4.3	38,953
Le Flore County, OK	19,892	20,766	21,322	-2.6	-4.2	6.7	9.4	5.1	814	3.0	8,409	5.4	31,925
Sequoyah County, OK	17,033	18,100	18,051	0.3	-5.9	6.1	9.6	5.5	582		6,867	7.4	24,270
Fort Wayne, IN Metro Area	210,126	207,683	211,446	-1.8	1.2	4.5	10.7	5.2	10,382	-0.7	187,136	6.3	39,657
Allen County, IN	178,779	175,943	178,905	-1.7	1.6	4.5	10.7	5.3	9,070	-0.7	166,360	6.1	40,070
Wells County, IN	14,140	14,137	14,861	-4.9	0.0	3.9	9.8	4.8	632	-0.3	10,268	9.4	34,405
Whitley County, IN	17,207	17,603	17,680	-0.4	-2.2	4.1	11.5	5.1	680	0.0	10,508	6.3	38,250
Fresno, CA Metro Area	444,168	439,593	407,163	8.0	1.0	10.2	16.7	9.0	16,119	2.1	244,494	8.6	39,371
Fresno County, CA	444,168	439,593	407,163	8.0	1.0	10.2	16.7	9.0	16,119	2.1	244,494	8.6	39,371
Gadsden, AL Metro Area	43,203	44,000	46,762	-5.9	-1.8	6.1	10.9	4.7	1,995	-1.8	28,573	-3.1	32,723
Etowah County, AL	43,203	44,000	46,762	-5.9	-1.8	6.1	10.9	4.7	1,995	-1.8	28,573	-3.1	32,723
Gainesville, FL Metro Area	136,632	135,244	131,039	3.2	1.0	4.6	8.2	2.9	6,155	2.7	86,989	4.9	38,263
Alachua County, FL	130,067	128,370	123,550	3.9	1.3	4.5	8.0	2.9	5,938	2.6	85,536	4.9	38,877
Gilchrist County, FL	6,565	6,874	7,489	-8.2	-4.5	5.5	10.8	3.2	217	3.3	1,453	2.4	31,509
Gainesville, GA Metro Area	92,277	86,546	82,801	4.5	6.6	4.7	9.6	4.5	4,040	2.3	66,547	15.1	42,564
Hall County, GA	92,277	86,546	82,801	4.5	6.6	4.7	9.6	4.5	4,040	2.3	66,547	15.1	42,564
Gettysburg, PA Metro Area	55,038	54,588	54,495	0.2	0.8	4.1	7.7	3.6	1,930	0.9	28,076	2.1	35,648
Adams County, PA	55,038	54,588	54,495	0.2	0.8	4.1	7.7	3.6	1,930	0.9	28,076	2.1	35,648
Glens Falls, NY Metro Area	61,203	64,387	67,615	-4.8	-4.9	5.4	8.6	4.5	3,355	-2.8	41,649	2.5	38,352
Warren County, NY	32,442	34,154	35,471	-3.7	-5.0	5.6	9.0	4.6	2,306	-2.8	31,200	0.2	38,815
Washington County, NY	28,761	30,233	32,144	-5.9	-4.9	5.1	8.2	4.5	1,049	-2.9	10,449	9.9	36,968
Goldsboro, NC Metro Area	53,947	54,798	51,135	7.2	-1.6	6.1	9.2	5.2	2,145	-3.4	33,742	-0.2	33,048
Wayne County, NC	53,947	54,798	51,135	7.2	-1.6	6.1	9.2	5.2	2,145	-3.4	33,742	-0.2	33,048
Grand Forks, ND-MN Metro Area	54,843	55,022	54,988	0.1	-0.3	3.0	4.5	3.6	2,697	3.3	42,548	4.3	35,834
Polk County, MN	17,443	17,156	16,899	1.5	1.7	4.2	6.6	4.5	786	1.9	9,524	-2.2	33,985
Grand Forks County, ND	37,400	37,866	38,089	-0.6	-1.2	2.4	3.5	3.2	1,911	3.9	33,024	6.3	36,367
Grand Island, NE Metro Area	43,894	43,870	43,547	0.7	0.1	3.8	4.5	3.6	2,518	0.7	35,599	1.8	35,457
Hall County, NE	31,826	31,519	30,130	4.6	1.0	3.9	4.6	3.8	1,822	-0.3	30,308	1.6	35,253
Hamilton County, NE	4,692	4,806	5,439	-11.6	-2.4	2.9	3.8	2.7	304	1.0	2,676	3.2	38,468
Howard County, NE	3,319	3,346	3,688	-9.3	-0.8	3.6	4.4	3.6	152	7.0	985	7.5	28,048
Merrick County, NE	4,057	4,199	4,290	-2.1	-3.4	3.7	4.5	3.7	240	4.3	1,630	-0.2	38,799
Grand Junction, CO Metro Area	72,039	76,113	70,811	7.5	-5.4	5.5	11.0	4.9	4,427	-4.7	50,695	2.4	42,259
Mesa County, CO	72,039	76,113	70,811	7.5	-5.4	5.5	11.0	4.9	4,427	-4.7	50,695	2.4	42,259
Grand Rapids-Wyoming, MI Metro Area	555,088	513,987	518,245	-0.8	8.0	3.7	10.4	5.8	23,512	2.4	457,413	14.8	41,841
Barry County, MI	30,639	29,360	30,891	-5.0	4.4	4.1	10.4	5.2	853	-4.4	9,582	6.8	37,638
Kent County, MI	343,743	316,233	321,655	-1.7	8.7	3.6	10.1	5.8	15,749	2.6	332,683	14.3	42,998
Montcalm County, MI	28,038	27,809	29,471	-5.6	0.8	5.4	14.1	8.7	1,005	-3.3	11,869	1.9	32,692
Ottawa County, MI	152,668	140,585	136,228	3.2	8.6	3.5	10.3	5.2	5,905	3.9	103,279	18.7	39,558
Grants Pass, OR Metro Area	33,162	34,491	34,300	0.6	-3.9	7.9	14.0	7.3	1,906	-5.4	20,344	6.0	32,096
Josephine County, OR	33,162	34,491	34,300	0.6	-3.9	7.9	14.0	7.3	1,906	-5.4	20,344	6.0	32,096
Great Falls, MT Metro Area	38,888	38,447	38,950	-1.3	1.1	4.0	6.4	4.3	2,420	-1.4	29,900	-1.3	32,847
Cascade County, MT	38,888	38,447	38,950	-1.3	1.1	4.0	6.4	4.3	2,420	-1.4	29,900	-1.3	32,847
Greeley, CO Metro Area	147,984	131,910	111,087	18.7	12.2	3.8	9.2	5.5	5,637	9.2	77,367	19.7	47,142
Weld County, CO	147,984	131,910	111,087	18.7	12.2	3.8	9.2	5.5	5,637	9.2	77,367	19.7	47,142
Green Bay, WI Metro Area	170,742	169,659	167,690	1.2	0.6	4.2	8.3	4.6	7,581	-0.5	153,096	6.6	43,137
Brown County, WI	139,236	137,150	135,667	1.1	1.5	4.1	7.9	4.5	6,349	-0.4	140,949	7.3	43,834
Kewaunee County, WI	11,014	11,178	11,800	-5.3	-1.5	4.1	8.2	4.5	455	-4.8	5,179	-5.5	39,219
Oconto County, WI	20,492	21,331	20,223	5.5	-3.9	5.2	10.7	5.7	777	1.2	6,968	3.4	31,955
Greensboro-High Point, NC Metro Area	364,824	365,556	360,977	1.3	-0.2	5.9	11.5	5.2	17,400	-0.9	316,549	6.8	41,010
Guilford County, NC	256,090	251,966	240,605	4.7	1.6	5.9	11.1	5.1	13,205	-0.5	254,674	7.5	42,951
Randolph County, NC	67,250	69,387	74,686	-7.1	-3.1	5.7	12.0	4.8	2,507	-3.1	39,739	7.8	32,403
Rockingham County, NC	41,484	44,203	45,686	-3.2	-6.2	6.6	13.2	6.6	1,688	-1.4	22,136	-2.2	34,128
Greenville, NC Metro Area	87,628	85,902	73,488	16.9	2.0	6.1	10.2	5.8	3,533		57,990	2.9	35,563
Pitt County, NC	87,628	85,902	73,488	16.9	2.0	6.1	10.2	5.8	3,533		57,990	2.9	35,563
Greenville-Anderson-Mauldin, SC Metro Area	415,467	390,078	384,213	1.5	6.5	5.3	10.4	6.2	18,851	0.7	318,675	7.2	38,967
Anderson County, SC	88,383	85,236	83,943	1.5	3.7	5.4	11.6	7.4	3,623	-1.6	55,098	9.1	36,301
Greenville County, SC	240,641	220,215	209,830	4.9	9.3	5.0	9.6	5.5	12,315	2.0	218,473	5.7	41,080
Laurens County, SC	30,497	30,191	33,202	-9.1	1.0	6.5	12.3	6.7	929	-1.6	16,112	2.1	37,155
Pickens County, SC	55,946	54,436	57,238	-4.9	2.8	5.8	10.9	6.5	1,984	-2.1	28,992	19.5	29,121
Gulfport-Biloxi-Pascagoula, MS Metro Area	163,808	172,825	176,008	-1.8	-5.2	6.5	9.1	10.5	7,039	-2.2	123,516	-3.2	39,845
Hancock County, MS	18,688	19,652	21,028	-6.5	-4.9	6.6	9.0	10.8	686	-3.1	9,378	-7.0	40,670
Harrison County, MS	85,601	88,743	92,740	-4.3	-3.5	6.1	8.8	10.8	4,120	-2.0	70,791	2.3	36,018
Jackson County, MS	59,519	64,430	62,240	3.5	-7.6	7.2	9.5	9.9	2,233	-2.3	43,347	-10.3	45,916
Hagerstown-Martinsburg, MD-WV Metro Area	128,895	126,822	111,364	13.9	1.6	5.5	9.2	4.2	5,012	-1.3	83,845	10.5	36,270
Washington County, MD	76,345	75,802	67,796	11.8	0.7	5.8	9.6	4.4	3,435	-1.5	59,656	8.0	36,263
Berkeley County, WV	52,550	51,020	43,568	17.1	3.0	5.0	8.6	4.0	1,577	-0.7	24,189	17.1	36,285
Hammond, LA Metro Area	54,029	53,664	50,534	6.2	0.7	7.2	9.7	9.5	2,307	2.8	34,530	8.3	35,458
Tangipahoa Parish, LA	54,029	53,664	50,534	6.2	0.7	7.2	9.7	9.5	2,307	2.8	34,530	8.3	35,458
Hanford-Corcoran, CA Metro Area	58,354	59,440	53,840	10.4	-1.8	10.5	16.1	9.4	1,589	-1.5	23,624	4.7	35,626
Kings County, CA	58,354	59,440	53,840	10.4	-1.8	10.5	16.1	9.4	1,589	-1.5	23,624	4.7	35,626
Harrisburg-Carlisle, PA Metro Area	293,252	289,988	277,860	4.4	1.1	4.2	7.5	4.0	13,300	-0.8	263,396	1.5	45,504
Cumberland County, PA	127,912	124,442	119,810	3.9	2.8	3.9	6.8	3.7	5,805	1.4	115,978	3.9	43,271
Dauphin County, PA	141,108	140,559	133,946	4.9	0.4	4.5	8.0	4.3	6,718	-2.5	141,108	-0.3	48,229
Perry County, PA	24,232	24,987	24,104	3.7	-3.0	4.3	8.1	4.2	777	-2.4	6,310	2.8	25,611

[1] Civilian employment as a percent of the civilian labor force.
[2] For the pay period including March 12 of the year shown.

Table C-4.   Labor Force and Private Business Establishments and Employment—*Continued*

Metropolitan statistical area, division, and component county	Civilian labor force								Private nonfarm businesses				
	Total			Percent change		Unemployment rate[1]			Establishments		Employment[2]		Annual payroll per employee 2014 (dollars)
	2015	2010	2005	2005–2010	2010–2015	2015	2010	2005	2014	Change 2010–2014	2014	Change 2010–2014	
Harrisonburg, VA Metro Area	64,253	63,538	61,197	3.8	1.1	4.6	7.3	3.3	2,968	-0.7	50,872	0.6	35,606
Rockingham County, VA	40,219	40,373	40,244	0.3	-0.4	4.1	6.7	3.0	1,404	-0.3	26,754	10.3	40,306
Harrisonburg city, VA	24,034	23,165	20,953	10.6	3.8	5.3	8.3	3.9	1,564	-1.1	24,118	-8.3	30,393
Hartford-West Hartford-East Hartford, CT Metro Area	649,443	657,562	607,993	8.2	-1.2	5.6	9.0	5.0	29,110	-1.5	536,262	1.3	55,932
Hartford County, CT	472,790	478,512	437,887	9.3	-1.2	5.9	9.5	5.3	22,531	-1.4	442,655	0.1	58,639
Middlesex County, CT	92,074	93,050	89,289	4.2		4.8	7.8	4.3	4,161	-1.4	61,384	6.2	46,713
Tolland County, CT	84,579	86,000	80,817	6.4	-1.7	4.8	7.7	4.2	2,418	-2.7	32,223	10.5	36,317
Hattiesburg, MS Metro Area	66,575	66,379	63,099	5.2	0.3	5.8	9.0	6.1	3,291	-0.8	49,475	1.3	35,236
Forrest County, MS	33,321	34,088	35,646	-4.4	-2.3	6.4	9.8	6.2	1,848	-0.1	31,621	1.6	37,565
Lamar County, MS	28,918	27,653	22,323	23.9	4.6	4.9	7.2	5.3	1,298	-0.7	16,298	1.8	29,527
Perry County, MS	4,336	4,638	5,130	-9.6	-6.5	8.0	13.7	8.2	145	-8.8	1,556	-7.3	47,700
Hickory-Lenoir-Morganton, NC Metro Area	167,395	176,027	176,216	-0.1	-4.9	5.7	13.4	6.6	7,325	-4.1	124,874	3.6	36,015
Alexander County, NC	17,546	18,257	18,234	0.1	-3.9	5.0	13.1	5.4	557	-5.3	7,141	7.0	28,579
Burke County, NC	39,574	41,680	41,432	0.6	-5.1	5.7	12.9	6.3	1,439	-1.2	22,385	7.4	32,395
Caldwell County, NC	35,501	38,206	39,683	-3.7	-7.1	6.3	14.8	8.1	1,306	-7.4	17,114	-7.7	31,324
Catawba County, NC	74,774	77,884	76,867	1.3	-4.0	5.6	13.1	6.2	4,023	-3.8	78,234	5.0	38,755
Hilton Head Island-Bluffton-Beaufort, SC Metro Area	83,077	76,235	71,681	6.4	9.0	5.4	8.8	4.9	5,516	4.6	58,645	10.9	33,538
Beaufort County, SC	71,344	65,338	61,574	6.1	9.2	5.4	8.7	4.9	4,940	4.7	52,003	10.2	33,384
Jasper County, SC	11,733	10,897	10,107	7.8	7.7	5.1	9.8	5.2	576	3.4	6,642	16.5	34,740
Hinesville, GA Metro Area	32,006	33,158	28,663	15.7	-3.5	6.2	8.9	5.5	886	0.0	12,444	5.5	37,583
Liberty County, GA	25,338	26,927	22,914	17.5	-5.9	6.3	9.0	5.9	820	0.7	12,182	6.3	37,912
Long County, GA	6,668	6,231	5,749	8.4	7.0	5.9	8.4	4.0	66	-8.3	262	-21.1	22,260
Homosassa Springs, FL Metro Area	47,739	52,847	51,324	3.0	-9.7	7.4	13.7	4.3	2,632	-1.3	26,262	5.0	33,183
Citrus County, FL	47,739	52,847	51,324	3.0	-9.7	7.4	13.7	4.3	2,632	-1.3	26,262	5.0	33,183
Hot Springs, AR Metro Area	40,046	41,563	41,936	-0.9	-3.6	5.7	8.5	5.7	2,648	-2.0	32,870	7.6	30,879
Garland County, AR	40,046	41,563	41,936	-0.9	-3.6	5.7	8.5	5.7	2,648	-2.0	32,870	7.6	30,879
Houma-Thibodaux, LA Metro Area	99,998	95,980	96,374	-0.4	4.2	5.6	6.3	6.3	4,825	-0.2	83,844	9.9	50,966
Lafourche Parish, LA	46,863	45,070	45,371	-0.7	4.0	5.3	6.1	6.0	1,805	-6.1	28,854	5.6	50,886
Terrebonne Parish, LA	53,135	50,910	51,003	-0.2	4.4	5.9	6.5	6.5	3,020	3.8	54,990	12.2	51,007
Houston-The Woodlands-Sugar Land, TX Metro Are	3,252,943	2,970,263	2,592,941	14.6	9.5	4.6	8.3	5.6	132,729	8.5	2,507,620	15.3	61,983
Austin County, TX	14,154	13,920	12,797	8.8	1.7	4.6	8.0	4.5	609	5.9	7,722	-18.2	39,748
Brazoria County, TX	167,023	155,221	133,540	16.2	7.6	4.6	8.5	5.7	5,153	7.0	83,160	18.3	48,165
Chambers County, TX	17,895	16,607	13,984	18.8	7.8	5.3	9.7	6.2	558	13.2	10,174	24.4	61,225
Fort Bend County, TX	348,961	298,162	235,000	26.9	17.0	4.3	7.6	5.2	11,358	23.1	145,249	26.4	45,583
Galveston County, TX	157,727	147,321	137,734	7.0	7.1	5.0	9.1	5.7	5,479	7.1	79,740	2.7	40,235
Harris County, TX	2,239,426	2,064,026	1,823,699	13.2	8.5	4.6	8.3	5.7	97,513	6.5	2,012,118	14.7	65,271
Liberty County, TX	31,068	30,614	31,272	-2.1	1.5	6.9	11.7	6.8	1,060	1.0	13,274	16.4	40,889
Montgomery County, TX	255,338	224,426	189,082	18.7	13.8	4.3	7.5	4.7	10,282	15.7	144,894	20.1	56,929
Waller County, TX	21,351	19,960	15,833	26.1	7.0	4.8	8.6	5.5	717	9.8	11,289	28.0	47,948
Huntington-Ashland, WV-KY-OH Metro Area	147,778	157,968	164,800	-4.1	-6.5	6.3	9.0	5.4	7,097	-2.2	112,452	1.6	39,436
Boyd County, KY	18,211	20,421	22,989	-11.2	-10.8	7.0	10.2	5.9	1,365	-2.7	22,464	-7.3	43,502
Greenup County, KY	13,626	15,351	17,203	-10.8	-11.2	7.8	11.5	6.4	522	4.8	5,039	1.9	35,259
Lawrence County, OH	25,336	27,703	28,685	-3.4	-8.5	5.8	10.3	6.2	811	-2.9	10,277	1.0	33,220
Cabell County, WV	41,710	43,292	44,041	-1.7	-3.7	5.4	7.2	4.5	2,456	-3.3	47,298	3.5	37,059
Lincoln County, WV	7,459	7,873	7,837	0.5	-5.3	9.7	11.7	6.4	200	-6.5	1,963	-5.6	32,356
Putnam County, WV	25,693	26,390	26,468	-0.3	-2.6	5.5	7.6	4.6	1,224	2.3	18,208	13.9	44,930
Wayne County, WV	15,743	16,938	17,577	-3.6	-7.1	7.0	8.5	5.2	519	-9.4	7,203	-5.1	42,203
Huntsville, AL Metro Area	209,345	208,154	193,890	7.4	0.6	5.5	8.6	3.7	9,451	1.0	170,407	3.0	46,959
Limestone County, AL	39,607	38,321	35,123	9.1	3.4	5.5	9.6	4.4	1,301	3.1	16,004	15.6	33,837
Madison County, AL	169,738	169,833	158,767	7.0	-0.1	5.5	8.3	3.6	8,150	0.7	154,403	1.9	48,319
Idaho Falls, ID Metro Area	65,172	63,055	61,167	3.1	3.4	3.4	7.0	3.1	3,830	3.0	D	D	D
Bonneville County, ID	51,227	49,093	49,007	0.2	4.3	3.4	7.0	3.0	3,314	3.0	44,285	3.8	38,874
Butte County, ID	1,335	1,352	1,397	-3.2	-1.3	4.3	7.2	4.3	63	-11.3	D	D	D
Jefferson County, ID	12,610	12,610	10,763	17.2	0.0	3.4	7.1	3.3	453	4.6	3,930	15.9	30,279
Indianapolis-Carmel-Anderson, IN Metro Area	1,008,205	950,612	941,192	1.0	6.1	4.5	9.6	5.0	45,350	1.5	854,861	10.0	46,172
Boone County, IN	32,959	29,395	27,178	8.2	12.1	3.7	7.6	4.1	1,445	8.2	20,809	23.3	34,922
Brown County, IN	7,482	7,566	8,002	-5.4	-1.1	4.7	10.4	5.7	353	-2.8	2,081	-5.3	23,258
Hamilton County, IN	164,518	144,863	130,720	10.8	13.6	3.4	6.7	3.5	8,274	11.9	122,263	22.7	50,621
Hancock County, IN	37,332	35,810	34,425	4.0	4.3	4.2	9.3	4.3	1,369	-0.1	19,717	24.9	38,581
Hendricks County, IN	82,290	74,719	69,433	7.6	10.1	3.8	7.9	4.1	3,027	6.2	52,733	15.1	34,839
Johnson County, IN	77,004	71,599	70,047	2.2	7.5	4.0	8.8	4.4	3,065	4.4	43,929	17.5	35,408
Madison County, IN	58,737	59,407	63,209	-6.0	-1.1	5.6	12.1	6.6	2,242	-4.3	34,727	1.8	32,958
Marion County, IN	472,929	452,839	459,492	-1.4	4.4	5.0	10.5	5.6	22,808	-1.9	520,458	6.4	49,679
Morgan County, IN	35,614	35,026	37,206	-5.9	1.7	4.6	10.4	5.0	1,158	-3.7	12,464	11.4	32,841
Putnam County, IN	16,520	16,674	17,804	-6.3	-0.9	5.1	11.6	6.7	691	-0.6	10,900	5.7	30,701
Shelby County, IN	22,820	22,714	23,676	-4.1	0.5	4.4	11.0	5.0	918	0.5	14,780	2.8	41,196
Iowa City, IA Metro Area	96,342	91,689	86,066	6.5	5.1	2.7	4.3	3.2	3,922	4.7	67,175	4.5	38,955
Johnson County, IA	83,891	79,267	73,815	7.4	5.8	2.6	4.2	3.1	3,218	5.8	60,242	4.5	39,861
Washington County, IA	12,451	12,422	12,251	1.4	0.2	3.1	5.1	3.7	704	0.1	6,933	5.3	31,079
Ithaca, NY Metro Area	55,371	54,767	54,600	0.3	1.1	4.1	6.2	3.6	2,361	1.8	47,972	5.5	36,842
Tompkins County, NY	55,371	54,767	54,600	0.3	1.1	4.1	6.2	3.6	2,361	1.8	47,972	5.5	36,842
Jackson, MI Metro Area	73,043	74,673	78,307	-4.6	-2.2	5.1	12.2	6.8	2,905	-3.7	48,179	7.8	43,784
Jackson County, MI	73,043	74,673	78,307	-4.6	-2.2	5.1	12.2	6.8	2,905	-3.7	48,179	7.8	43,784
Jackson, MS Metro Area	267,233	266,750	272,411	-2.1	0.2	5.4	8.7	5.9	13,095	-1.2	214,422	5.8	40,173

[1]Civilian employment as a percent of the civilian labor force.
[2]For the pay period including March 12 of the year shown.

Table C-4. Labor Force and Private Business Establishments and Employment—*Continued*

Metropolitan statistical area, division, and component county	Civilian labor force								Private nonfarm businesses				Annual payroll per employee 2014 (dollars)
	Total			Percent change		Unemployment rate[1]			Establishments		Employment[2]		
	2015	2010	2005	2005–2010	2010–2015	2015	2010	2005	2014	Change 2010–2014	2014	Change 2010–2014	
Copiah County, MS	11,387	11,993	12,489	-4.0	-5.1	7.3	11.4	8.0	436	3.6	5,514	-5.9	28,237
Hinds County, MS	110,730	113,889	122,092	-6.7	-2.8	6.1	9.8	6.5	5,379	-6.8	98,269	3.3	43,281
Madison County, MS	51,290	48,716	44,044	10.6	5.3	4.6	7.4	5.1	2,972	5.4	46,526	9.3	41,014
Rankin County, MS	73,278	70,856	71,680	-1.1	3.4	4.2	6.9	4.5	3,484	1.8	54,164	9.1	36,850
Simpson County, MS	11,107	11,375	11,967	-4.9	-2.4	5.9	9.4	6.0	423	2.4	5,915	5.4	27,271
Yazoo County, MS	9,441	9,921	10,139	-2.2	-4.8	8.2	12.3	9.6	401	-1.5	4,034	5.5	34,598
Jackson, TN Metro Area	61,636	63,842	60,322	5.8	-3.5	6.1	10.2	5.9	3,006	-0.9	56,058	4.4	35,752
Chester County, TN	8,159	8,363	7,533	11.0	-2.4	6.1	10.0	6.0	234	-3.3	2,995	6.6	25,793
Crockett County, TN	6,833	7,278	6,390	13.9	-6.1	6.6	11.6	7.8	223	0.0	2,452	24.2	34,632
Madison County, TN	46,644	48,201	46,399	3.9	-3.2	6.1	10.0	5.6	2,549	-0.7	50,611	3.5	36,396
Jacksonville, FL Metro Area	724,881	697,120	635,531	9.7	4.0	5.2	10.7	3.8	35,227	3.4	528,075	9.5	45,129
Baker County, FL	11,335	11,552	11,112	4.0	-1.9	5.4	11.3	3.2	395	10.0	5,252	-0.2	31,904
Clay County, FL	99,182	95,867	86,643	10.6	3.5	4.9	9.9	3.4	3,657	4.0	37,630	3.5	31,341
Duval County, FL	465,537	454,798	421,549	7.9	2.4	5.7	11.4	4.0	23,987	1.3	417,182	9.0	48,071
Nassau County, FL	36,696	35,799	32,720	9.4	2.5	5.0	10.6	3.3	1,689	5.9	16,169	11.8	34,835
St. Johns County, FL	112,131	99,104	83,507	18.7	13.1	3.9	8.7	3.1	5,499	11.5	51,842	18.9	36,013
Jacksonville, NC Metro Area	63,959	63,331	55,996	13.1	1.0	6.0	8.3	5.3	2,757	2.4	34,547	3.9	27,394
Onslow County, NC	63,959	63,331	55,996	13.1	1.0	6.0	8.3	5.3	2,757	2.4	34,547	3.9	27,394
Janesville-Beloit, WI Metro Area	83,596	82,698	83,193	-0.6	1.1	5.2	11.3	5.8	3,236	-1.7	54,808	7.1	40,706
Rock County, WI	83,596	82,698	83,193	-0.6	1.1	5.2	11.3	5.8	3,236	-1.7	54,808	7.1	40,706
Jefferson City, MO Metro Area	76,650	77,926	77,810	0.1	-1.6	4.3	7.4	4.4	3,619	0.6	50,402	0.7	37,138
Callaway County, MO	21,967	22,377	22,596		-1.8	4.7	8.3	4.7	761	0.0	11,839	5.8	37,832
Cole County, MO	39,909	40,685	40,148	1.3	-1.9	4.0	6.9	4.1	2,257	0.9	32,848	-1.7	37,970
Moniteau County, MO	7,463	7,397	7,564	-2.2	0.9	4.9	8.4	5.1	329	-1.2	2,701	3.0	30,932
Osage County, MO	7,311	7,467	7,502	-0.5	-2.1	3.7	6.9	4.7	272	1.1	3,014	7.5	30,902
Johnson City, TN Metro Area	88,392	94,817	94,637	0.2	-6.8	6.2	9.6	5.3	3,758	-2.0	63,725	2.2	35,332
Carter County, TN	23,656	26,226	28,740	-8.7	-9.8	6.6	10.9	5.8	702	-4.0	9,085	0.5	26,955
Unicoi County, TN	7,059	7,919	8,144	-2.8	-10.9	8.1	11.9	6.2	247	-3.5	3,656	-10.0	39,326
Washington County, TN	57,677	60,672	57,753	5.1	-4.9	5.7	8.7	4.9	2,809	-1.4	50,984	3.5	36,539
Johnstown, PA Metro Area	62,363	66,747	67,122	-0.6	-6.6	6.4	9.4	6.1	3,286	-4.4	47,647	-5.7	34,546
Cambria County, PA	62,363	66,747	67,122	-0.6	-6.6	6.4	9.4	6.1	3,286	-4.4	47,647	-5.7	34,546
Jonesboro, AR Metro Area	60,852	58,533	56,567	3.5	4.0	4.8	7.8	5.1	2,797	1.1	43,048	8.8	34,336
Craighead County, AR	50,611	47,796	45,084	6.0	5.9	4.6	7.4	4.8	2,431	1.2	39,394	9.4	34,817
Poinsett County, AR	10,241	10,737	11,483	-6.5	-4.6	5.7	9.3	6.6	366	0.8	3,654	3.5	29,141
Joplin, MO Metro Area	87,769	87,785	82,311	6.7	0.0	4.3	8.6	4.9	3,980	-6.2	68,025	-6.9	36,352
Jasper County, MO	58,752	59,026	54,567	8.2	-0.5	4.2	8.5	4.8	2,790	-6.1	47,215	-13.3	37,303
Newton County, MO	29,017	28,759	27,744	3.7	0.9	4.5	9.0	5.0	1,190	-6.6	20,810	11.5	34,194
Kahului-Wailuku-Lahaina, HI Metro Area	84,233	78,966	74,992	5.3	6.7	3.8	8.5	2.7	4,500	D	D	D	D
Kalawao County, HI	NA	NA	NA	NA	NA	NA	NA	NA	NA	NA	NA	NA	NA
Maui County, HI	84,233	78,966	74,992	5.3	6.7	3.8	8.5	2.7	4,499	3.9	63,429	10.6	36,254
Kalamazoo-Portage, MI Metro Area	165,663	167,416	173,449	-3.5		4.5	10.8	5.7	6,783	-2.5	119,742	0.8	44,193
Kalamazoo County, MI	129,993	129,632	132,576	-2.2	0.3	4.1	10.0	5.2	5,511	-2.1	103,748	1.0	45,202
Van Buren County, MI	35,670	37,784	40,873	-7.6	-5.6	6.0	13.5	7.0	1,272	-4.1	15,994	-0.4	37,653
Kankakee, IL Metro Area	55,211	57,454	52,672	9.1	-3.9	6.8	12.3	6.4	2,360	0.1	36,792	4.4	36,103
Kankakee County, IL	55,211	57,454	52,672	9.1	-3.9	6.8	12.3	6.4	2,360	0.1	36,792	4.4	36,103
Kansas City, MO-KS Metro Area	1,121,621	1,082,274	1,013,562	6.8	3.6	4.8	8.7	5.6	51,485	3.9	908,323	6.7	48,213
Johnson County, KS	325,010	307,190	290,970	5.6	5.8	3.4	6.1	4.6	17,423	3.3	322,765	9.7	52,000
Leavenworth County, KS	35,436	34,342	33,105	3.7	3.2	4.5	7.6	6.1	1,221	3.0	14,022	5.3	34,937
Linn County, KS	4,358	4,534	4,897	-7.4	-3.9	6.4	11.2	7.2	193	7.8	1,225	6.3	45,683
Miami County, KS	17,076	17,111	16,335	4.8	-0.2	4.3	7.6	5.1	713	-0.7	6,671	2.2	35,478
Wyandotte County, KS	76,236	74,994	73,559	2.0	1.7	6.1	10.1	8.7	3,072	2.6	68,001	7.4	45,659
Bates County, MO	8,362	8,397	7,936	5.8	-0.4	6.0	11.0	6.4	349	-0.6	2,783	-1.8	28,202
Caldwell County, MO	4,480	4,560	4,406	3.5	-1.8	4.5	9.6	6.0	144	-12.7	864	9.9	33,022
Cass County, MO	54,463	53,355	48,720	9.5	2.1	4.8	9.6	5.1	1,846	-0.5	19,588	10.1	30,421
Clay County, MO	133,448	125,001	111,211	12.4	6.8	4.5	8.4	4.6	4,846	2.0	93,216	12.7	48,360
Clinton County, MO	11,026	11,071	10,328	7.2	-0.4	4.9	9.7	5.4	364	-4.5	2,792	-9.5	30,370
Jackson County, MO	367,142	361,018	336,286	7.4	1.7	5.9	10.7	6.4	17,961	6.9	328,883	3.6	48,885
Lafayette County, MO	17,474	17,549	16,710	5.0	-0.4	4.8	9.8	5.5	692	-5.2	6,083	-2.7	28,800
Platte County, MO	55,677	51,580	47,312	9.0	7.9	4.2	7.7	4.5	2,310	5.4	38,472	-1.1	38,616
Ray County, MO	11,433	11,572	11,787	-1.8	-1.2	5.4	10.3	5.4	351	-9.3	2,958	1.5	29,714
Kennewick-Richland, WA Metro Area	130,602	132,506	114,306	15.9	-1.4	6.8	8.1	6.4	5,533	5.4	79,211	5.8	46,545
Benton County, WA	91,650	94,385	85,027	11.0	-2.9	6.6	7.8	6.0	4,088	4.7	60,614	4.0	48,838
Franklin County, WA	38,952	38,121	29,279	30.2	2.2	7.5	8.9	7.4	1,445	7.4	18,597	12.1	39,071
Killeen-Temple, TX Metro Area	169,589	166,193	149,377	11.3	2.0	4.7	7.6	5.2	6,022	1.8	101,153	6.7	36,130
Bell County, TX	135,742	131,835	114,094	15.5	3.0	4.7	7.7	5.0	4,925	3.2	87,549	7.7	37,665
Coryell County, TX	24,857	25,338	25,361	-0.1	-1.9	4.8	7.5	6.2	706	-6.5	9,974	0.4	24,930
Lampasas County, TX	8,990	9,020	9,922	-9.1	-0.3	4.4	7.1	4.3	391	0.3	3,630	2.4	29,885
Kingsport-Bristol-Bristol, TN-VA Metro Area	137,222	144,661	140,267	3.1	-5.1	5.7	9.1	5.3	5,988	-1.7	104,930	2.0	40,241
Hawkins County, TN	23,592	25,559	25,347	0.8	-7.7	6.5	10.9	6.2	583	-5.2	9,544	11.0	34,926
Sullivan County, TN	69,138	73,637	71,480	3.0	-6.1	5.9	9.0	5.2	3,310	-1.5	64,500	1.9	42,941
Scott County, VA	9,676	10,072	9,769	3.1	-3.9	5.1	8.5	5.3	288	-3.7	3,522	3.6	32,104
Washington County, VA	27,234	27,416	25,934	5.7	-0.7	4.8	7.9	4.5	1,179	-2.0	18,185	7.6	39,316
Bristol city, VA	7,582	7,977	7,737	3.1	-5.0	5.3	8.8	5.5	628	2.1	9,179	-14.1	31,754
Kingston, NY Metro Area	88,438	93,606	91,816	1.9	-5.5	4.9	7.8	4.3	4,727	0.4	45,384	0.7	33,688
Ulster County, NY	88,438	93,606	91,816	1.9	-5.5	4.9	7.8	4.3	4,727	0.4	45,384	0.7	33,688
Knoxville, TN Metro Area	405,227	415,146	398,020	4.3	-2.4	5.4	8.5	4.7	17,489	-1.6	319,576	4.3	41,536

[1]Civilian employment as a percent of the civilian labor force.
[2]For the pay period including March 12 of the year shown.
D = not shown to avoid disclosure of confidential information.
NA = Not available or Not applicable.

Table C-4.   Labor Force and Private Business Establishments and Employment—*Continued*

Metropolitan statistical area, division, and component county	Civilian labor force								Private nonfarm businesses				
	Total			Percent change		Unemployment rate[1]			Establishments		Employment[2]		Annual payroll per employee 2014 (dollars)
	2015	2010	2005	2005–2010	2010–2015	2015	2010	2005	2014	Change 2010–2014	2014	Change 2010–2014	
Anderson County, TN	33,411	34,926	34,488	1.3	-4.3	6.0	9.3	5.1	1,503	-6.8	37,860	-9.1	57,466
Blount County, TN	59,500	61,408	59,009	4.1	-3.1	5.3	9.1	4.7	2,248	-1.1	41,175	8.3	43,135
Campbell County, TN	14,792	16,131	16,672	-3.2	-8.3	8.1	12.5	6.0	588	2.3	7,311	6.3	28,198
Grainger County, TN	9,216	10,040	10,042	0.0	-8.2	6.8	12.7	6.0	223	0.9	2,318	15.0	29,541
Knox County, TN	228,557	229,800	213,735	7.5	-0.5	4.8	7.4	4.2	10,949	-1.3	207,005	6.5	39,897
Loudon County, TN	21,930	22,352	21,651	3.2	-1.9	5.7	9.3	4.7	896	1.8	12,205	3.6	37,189
Morgan County, TN	7,829	8,403	8,118	3.5	-6.8	7.6	11.4	7.5	160	-5.3	1,600	0.1	31,583
Roane County, TN	22,729	24,323	25,587	-4.9	-6.6	6.6	9.2	5.8	732	-1.7	8,517	0.0	28,487
Union County, TN	7,263	7,763	8,718	-11.0	-6.4	6.9	10.8	5.6	190	-6.4	1,585	-6.5	26,408
Kokomo, IN Metro Area	36,934	35,806	39,174	-8.6	3.2	5.0	12.6	6.6	1,742	-3.9	31,758	11.8	42,203
Howard County, IN	36,934	35,806	39,174	-8.6	3.2	5.0	12.6	6.6	1,742	-3.9	31,758	11.8	42,203
La Crosse-Onalaska, WI-MN Metro Area	77,256	76,423	72,515	5.4	1.1	3.9	6.8	4.1	3,440	1.8	65,254	6.8	37,218
Houston County, MN	10,528	10,830	11,082	-2.3	-2.8	3.8	7.7	4.5	432	-4.2	4,025	0.0	28,036
La Crosse County, WI	66,728	65,593	61,433	6.8	1.7	3.9	6.6	4.0	3,008	2.7	61,229	7.2	37,822
Lafayette, LA Metro Area	228,600	221,628	208,275	6.4	3.1	6.3	7.0	5.7	13,350	5.4	198,883	11.3	46,758
Acadia Parish, LA	26,186	26,130	25,409	2.8	0.2	6.7	7.3	6.1	1,131	2.0	13,425	5.6	34,112
Iberia Parish, LA	32,226	32,240	32,671	-1.3	0.0	7.9	8.6	6.7	1,710	-1.4	30,483	6.9	51,309
Lafayette Parish, LA	119,830	113,571	104,121	9.1	5.5	5.6	6.2	5.2	8,492	7.2	131,883	13.3	47,814
St. Martin Parish, LA	24,235	24,050	22,687	6.0	0.8	6.7	8.0	6.0	970	9.7	12,576	14.7	44,676
Vermilion Parish, LA	26,123	25,637	23,387	9.6	1.9	6.8	7.3	6.0	1,047	2.2	10,516	4.6	38,952
Lafayette-West Lafayette, IN Metro Area	107,381	101,447	94,494	7.4	5.8	4.2	9.0	4.9	3,975	0.5	69,505	7.9	39,111
Benton County, IN	4,627	4,662	4,599	1.4	-0.8	4.4	9.2	5.3	184	-10.2	1,391	-9.9	34,463
Carroll County, IN	10,141	10,254	10,515	-2.5	-1.1	4.3	9.9	5.2	376	-5.5	4,379	3.3	34,215
Tippecanoe County, IN	92,613	86,531	79,380	9.0	7.0	4.2	8.9	4.9	3,415	1.9	63,735	8.7	39,549
Lake Charles, LA Metro Area	102,160	91,195	95,465	-4.5	12.0	5.3	8.0	7.4	4,532	3.3	73,507	7.1	42,795
Calcasieu Parish, LA	98,561	87,896	91,004	-3.4	12.1	5.4	8.0	7.5	4,376	3.2	72,192	7.7	42,630
Cameron Parish, LA	3,599	3,299	4,461	-26.0	9.1	4.6	6.3	5.8	156	4.7	1,315	-16.6	51,897
Lake Havasu City-Kingman, AZ Metro Area	79,310	82,726	89,079	-7.1	-4.1	8.0	13.0	4.3	3,630	-2.2	40,695	2.5	32,841
Mohave County, AZ	79,310	82,726	89,079	-7.1	-4.1	8.0	13.0	4.3	3,630	-2.2	40,695	2.5	32,841
Lakeland-Winter Haven, FL Metro Area	279,903	278,479	258,158	7.9	0.5	6.2	12.1	4.1	11,021	0.7	171,305	7.6	38,285
Polk County, FL	279,903	278,479	258,158	7.9	0.5	6.2	12.1	4.1	11,021	0.7	171,305	7.6	38,285
Lancaster, PA Metro Area	275,869	268,001	267,575	0.2	2.9	4.0	7.5	3.7	12,414	3.1	220,898	6.6	40,430
Lancaster County, PA	275,869	268,001	267,575	0.2	2.9	4.0	7.5	3.7	12,414	3.1	220,898	6.6	40,430
Lansing-East Lansing, MI Metro Area	242,918	245,259	248,085	-1.1		4.3	9.8	6.0	9,486	-0.7	160,216	5.8	41,704
Clinton County, MI	40,104	39,637	37,266	6.4	1.2	3.7	8.4	5.4	1,315	5.6	15,320	2.2	36,793
Eaton County, MI	56,313	57,180	58,653	-2.5	-1.5	4.2	9.6	5.5	2,053	-0.4	39,526	5.5	41,253
Ingham County, MI	146,501	148,442	152,166	-2.4	-1.3	4.4	10.3	6.4	6,118	-2.1	105,370	6.5	42,587
Laredo, TX Metro Area	112,415	105,016	85,624	22.6	7.0	4.7	8.2	6.0	5,123	8.8	73,755	16.1	29,105
Webb County, TX	112,415	105,016	85,624	22.6	7.0	4.7	8.2	6.0	5,123	8.8	73,755	16.1	29,105
Las Cruces, NM Metro Area	93,179	93,661	85,089	10.1	-0.5	7.4	7.7	5.6	3,546	-1.8	50,861	1.5	31,337
Doña Ana County, NM	93,179	93,661	85,089	10.1	-0.5	7.4	7.7	5.6	3,546	-1.8	50,861	1.5	31,337
Las Vegas-Henderson-Paradise, NV Metro Area	1,047,528	984,004	869,251	13.2	6.5	6.8	13.8	4.1	42,031	6.1	797,871	9.0	38,977
Clark County, NV	1,047,528	984,004	869,251	13.2	6.5	6.8	13.8	4.1	42,031	6.1	797,871	9.0	38,977
Lawrence, KS Metro Area	65,273	64,379	63,186	1.9	1.4	3.7	5.9	4.0	2,675	1.8	38,850	3.9	30,424
Douglas County, KS	65,273	64,379	63,186	1.9	1.4	3.7	5.9	4.0	2,675	1.8	38,850	3.9	30,424
Lawton, OK Metro Area	53,127	54,506	48,573	12.2	-2.5	4.2	5.8	4.5	2,237	-2.7	33,026	-2.9	33,332
Comanche County, OK	50,169	51,497	45,272	13.8	-2.6	4.2	5.8	4.5	2,162	-2.6	31,938	-2.3	33,382
Cotton County, OK	2,958	3,009	3,301	-8.8	-1.7	4.0	6.7	3.7	75	-7.4	1,088	-17.6	31,878
Lebanon, PA Metro Area	70,133	70,059	70,117	-0.1	0.1	4.4	7.5	3.6	2,641	0.0	44,254	1.9	35,898
Lebanon County, PA	70,133	70,059	70,117	-0.1	0.1	4.4	7.5	3.6	2,641	0.0	44,254	1.9	35,898
Lewiston, ID-WA Metro Area	30,473	30,420	29,869	1.8	0.2	4.0	7.6	5.0	1,546	-1.8	21,337	2.1	36,269
Nez Perce County, ID	20,746	20,086	19,352	3.8	3.3	3.7	6.7	4.4	1,106	-3.2	16,724	2.1	37,077
Asotin County, WA	9,727	10,334	10,517	-1.7	-5.9	4.7	9.4	6.3	440	1.9	4,613	1.9	33,338
Lewiston-Auburn, ME Metro Area	54,566	55,912	57,033	-2.0	-2.4	4.1	8.6	4.9	2,667	-3.6	44,283	1.1	37,968
Androscoggin County, ME	54,566	55,912	57,033	-2.0	-2.4	4.1	8.6	4.9	2,667	-3.6	44,283	1.1	37,968
Lexington-Fayette, KY Metro Area	254,913	255,705	229,055	11.6	-0.3	4.1	7.9	4.6	12,195	3.3	216,411	8.2	40,954
Bourbon County, KY	9,552	10,064	9,810	2.6	-5.1	4.9	9.1	5.4	389	-0.3	5,111	-15.0	41,690
Clark County, KY	16,684	17,775	17,061	4.2	-6.1	5.3	10.8	5.5	735	-3.5	11,725	9.8	35,158
Fayette County, KY	164,121	163,286	146,365	11.6	0.5	3.9	7.4	4.5	8,565	3.9	154,990	8.2	40,941
Jessamine County, KY	24,442	24,710	21,888	12.9	-1.1	4.3	8.5	4.7	1,068	3.6	14,744	5.9	33,007
Scott County, KY	26,050	25,429	20,631	23.3	2.4	4.1	8.7	4.9	895	6.4	23,284	22.2	49,018
Woodford County, KY	14,064	14,441	13,300	8.6	-2.6	3.6	7.3	4.2	543	0.9	6,557	-5.8	40,286
Lima, OH Metro Area	48,106	52,009	52,706	-1.3	-7.5	4.8	10.7	6.2	2,436	-4.4	44,435	-4.5	39,321
Allen County, OH	48,106	52,009	52,706	-1.3	-7.5	4.8	10.7	6.2	2,436	-4.4	44,435	-4.5	39,321
Lincoln, NE Metro Area	177,288	171,332	165,264	3.7	3.5	2.6	4.2	3.5	8,556	4.1	134,985	3.6	38,803
Lancaster County, NE	168,402	162,567	156,012	4.2	3.6	2.6	4.2	3.5	8,111	4.3	129,360	3.3	39,132
Seward County, NE	8,886	8,765	9,252	-5.3	1.4	2.9	4.0	3.2	445	0.7	5,625	10.9	31,230
Little Rock-North Little Rock-Conway, AR Metro Area	346,926	347,828	334,366	4.0	-0.3	4.7	7.2	4.7	17,632	0.2	274,359	-0.5	41,414
Faulkner County, AR	59,655	58,711	52,018	12.9	1.6	4.8	7.2	4.4	2,452	5.4	36,081	6.0	40,431
Grant County, AR	8,291	8,567	8,663	-1.1	-3.2	4.7	7.1	4.9	272	2.3	2,990	0.0	31,913
Lonoke County, AR	33,019	33,287	30,788	8.1	-0.8	4.3	6.8	4.5	995	-0.6	10,072	-4.6	30,592
Perry County, AR	4,233	4,560	4,966	-8.2	-7.2	6.3	8.9	5.1	107	-5.3	802	-14.0	27,776
Pulaski County, AR	186,455	189,321	190,594	-0.7	-1.5	4.7	7.3	4.8	11,993	-1.1	204,699	-2.1	43,398
Saline County, AR	55,273	53,382	47,337	12.8	3.5	4.2	6.7	4.3	1,813	2.5	19,715	8.1	30,143
Logan, UT-ID Metro Area	66,786	63,443	63,440	0.0	5.3	3.0	6.0	3.2	3,380	0.8	41,306	5.8	31,484
Franklin County, ID	6,556	6,194	6,218	-0.4	5.8	3.1	5.3	3.2	271	-7.2	1,980	2.5	28,484

[1]Civilian employment as a percent of the civilian labor force.
[2]For the pay period including March 12 of the year shown.

Table C-4. Labor Force and Private Business Establishments and Employment—*Continued*

Metropolitan statistical area, division, and component county	Civilian labor force								Private nonfarm businesses				Annual payroll per employee 2014 (dollars)
	Total			Percent change		Unemployment rate[1]			Establishments		Employment[2]		
	2015	2010	2005	2005–2010	2010–2015	2015	2010	2005	2014	Change 2010–2014	2014	Change 2010–2014	
Cache County, UT	60,230	57,249	57,222	0.0	5.2	3.0	6.1	3.2	3,109	1.6	39,326	5.9	31,635
Longview, TX Metro Area	100,907	102,607	101,999	0.6	-1.7	5.0	8.1	5.0	5,408	2.2	84,869	8.6	42,496
Gregg County, TX	59,424	60,363	60,526	-0.3	-1.6	5.0	7.9	4.9	4,096	2.1	68,188	7.7	42,836
Rusk County, TX	23,436	23,961	22,712	5.5	-2.2	4.7	7.8	5.2	836	3.1	12,059	14.0	44,121
Upshur County, TX	18,047	18,283	18,761	-2.5	-1.3	5.3	8.8	5.0	476	1.3	4,622	9.6	33,240
Longview, WA Metro Area	44,276	46,432	42,978	8.0	-4.6	7.6	12.9	7.6	2,119	-3.9	30,038	3.2	45,831
Cowlitz County, WA	44,276	46,432	42,978	8.0	-4.6	7.6	12.9	7.6	2,119	-3.9	30,038	3.2	45,831
Los Angeles-Long Beach-Anaheim, CA Metro Area	**6,608,778**	**6,454,562**	**6,367,520**	**1.4**	**2.4**	**6.2**	**11.8**	**5.0**	**349,938**	**5.7**	**5,354,029**	**10.3**	**52,338**
Anaheim-Santa Ana-Irvine, CA Division	*1,597,071*	*1,537,187*	*1,585,916*	*-3.1*	*3.9*	*4.5*	*9.7*	*3.7*	*90,956*	*5.1*	*1,421,125*	*11.7*	*54,141*
Orange County, CA	1,597,071	1,537,187	1,585,916	-3.1	3.9	4.5	9.7	3.7	90,956	5.1	1,421,125	11.7	54,141
Los Angeles-Long Beach-Glendale, CA Division	*5,011,707*	*4,917,375*	*4,781,604*	*2.8*	*1.9*	*6.7*	*12.5*	*5.4*	*258,982*	*5.9*	*3,932,904*	*9.9*	*51,686*
Los Angeles County, CA	5,011,707	4,917,375	4,781,604	2.8	1.9	6.7	12.5	5.4	258,982	5.9	3,932,904	9.9	51,686
Louisville/Jefferson County, KY-IN Metro Area	623,267	626,312	590,223	6.1	-0.5	4.7	9.9	5.8	28,932	-0.3	540,954	7.0	43,131
Clark County, IN	58,764	55,317	53,370	3.6	6.2	4.5	9.5	5.2	2,400	0.3	45,829	12.5	35,400
Floyd County, IN	39,918	37,858	37,486	1.0	5.4	4.2	8.9	5.2	1,761	0.5	25,577	-0.6	37,363
Harrison County, IN	19,418	18,990	19,628	-3.3	2.3	4.5	9.9	6.3	651	-2.8	9,053	-0.5	29,574
Scott County, IN	10,344	10,590	11,393	-7.0	-2.3	5.4	13.2	6.2	407	-4.2	5,889	6.3	32,264
Washington County, IN	13,645	13,806	14,013	-1.5	-1.2	5.1	12.2	6.2	437	-4.2	4,546	4.7	29,896
Bullitt County, KY	38,493	38,803	35,870	8.2	-0.8	4.7	10.6	5.7	1,073	0.8	17,185	23.2	31,922
Henry County, KY	7,526	7,834	7,904	-0.9	-3.9	4.8	9.9	5.7	212	-2.8	1,926	4.4	30,604
Jefferson County, KY	370,336	378,722	351,726	7.7	-2.2	4.9	10.0	5.9	19,558	-0.4	404,871	6.3	45,943
Oldham County, KY	29,834	29,248	26,226	11.5	2.0	4.0	7.5	4.8	1,211	-1.6	11,709	14.1	34,807
Shelby County, KY	22,186	21,851	20,059	8.9	1.5	4.1	8.9	5.2	939	4.9	12,624	11.4	38,460
Spencer County, KY	9,009	9,205	8,190	12.4	-2.1	4.4	9.9	5.3	205	-1.9	1,156	4.7	23,954
Trimble County, KY	3,794	4,088	4,358	-6.2	-7.2	5.8	12.9	6.4	78	-7.1	639	3.9	50,798
Lubbock, TX Metro Area	153,745	149,359	143,067	4.4	2.9	3.5	6.3	4.1	7,196	2.0	112,158	7.0	34,290
Crosby County, TX	2,643	2,951	2,923	1.0	-10.4	4.4	8.0	5.4	98	-8.4	622	-24.9	37,921
Lubbock County, TX	148,287	143,339	137,313	4.4	3.5	3.4	6.3	4.1	7,015	2.4	110,878	7.3	34,247
Lynn County, TX	2,815	3,069	2,831	8.4	-8.3	4.0	6.6	5.8	83	-11.7	658	-4.6	38,040
Lynchburg, VA Metro Area	123,006	126,345	116,542	8.4	-2.6	4.9	7.8	4.1	5,871	-2.2	95,088	1.2	38,967
Amherst County, VA	15,544	16,352	15,320	6.7	-4.9	4.8	8.1	4.1	571	-5.0	6,375	-4.8	31,001
Appomattox County, VA	7,067	7,343	6,824	7.6	-3.8	4.9	8.6	4.7	285	-4.0	2,311	-4.0	24,099
Bedford County, VA	38,173	39,053	36,472	7.1	-2.3	4.4	7.0	3.5	1,670	-4.2	15,672	-4.5	35,089
Campbell County, VA	26,482	27,756	26,677	4.0	-4.6	4.8	7.7	4.0	1,154	0.5	13,945	3.1	38,011
Lynchburg city, VA	35,740	35,841	31,249	14.7	-0.3	5.6	8.5	4.6	2,191	-1.1	56,785	3.3	41,772
Macon, GA Metro Area	103,239	105,508	110,115	-4.2	-2.2	6.3	11.3	5.6	5,122	-3.1	D	D	D
Bibb County, GA	68,327	70,225	72,845	-3.6	-2.7	6.6	11.6	5.8	4,116	-3.8	72,701	3.0	36,965
Crawford County, GA	5,597	5,769	6,269	-8.0	-3.0	6.1	11.4	5.9	100	2.0	549	6.2	33,124
Jones County, GA	13,666	13,698	13,664	0.2	-0.2	5.3	9.7	4.9	324	-4.1	2,529	1.6	30,715
Monroe County, GA	12,692	12,551	12,689	-1.1	1.1	5.6	10.2	5.1	511	3.0	6,678	12.2	30,292
Twiggs County, GA	2,957	3,265	4,648	-29.8	-9.4	9.1	15.5	6.9	71	-7.8	D	D	D
Madera, CA Metro Area	60,566	61,607	61,881	-0.4	-1.7	10.5	16.6	7.9	1,918	0.4	25,722	5.0	38,910
Madera County, CA	60,566	61,607	61,881	-0.4	-1.7	10.5	16.6	7.9	1,918	0.4	25,722	5.0	38,910
Madison, WI Metro Area	376,678	360,360	351,442	2.5	4.5	3.4	6.4	3.4	16,492	2.6	308,317	8.7	47,474
Columbia County, WI	31,626	32,090	31,579	1.6	-1.4	4.4	8.5	4.4	1,401	0.5	18,969	-0.2	34,644
Dane County, WI	309,956	293,224	285,593	2.7	5.7	3.2	5.9	3.1	13,590	3.1	267,697	9.7	49,189
Green County, WI	21,252	21,274	20,008	6.3	-0.1	3.8	8.0	4.4	943	-0.1	13,024	11.1	37,132
Iowa County, WI	13,844	13,772	14,262	-3.4	0.5	4.2	8.2	4.2	558	0.9	8,627	-1.2	38,089
Manchester-Nashua, NH Metro Area	228,523	226,154	226,188	0.0	1.0	3.6	6.2	3.6	10,889	0.6	180,527	1.7	53,691
Hillsborough County, NH	228,523	226,154	226,188	0.0	1.0	3.6	6.2	3.6	10,889	0.6	180,527	1.7	53,691
Manhattan, KS Metro Area	50,089	47,981	44,806	7.1	4.4	3.3	5.1	3.8	2,176	2.9	28,976	0.6	31,129
Pottawatomie County, KS	12,407	11,890	10,813	10.0	4.3	3.5	5.2	4.1	568	-0.5	8,314	11.5	37,287
Riley County, KS	37,682	36,091	33,993	6.2	4.4	3.3	5.0	3.7	1,608	4.2	20,662	-3.2	28,651
Mankato-North Mankato, MN Metro Area	59,195	57,896	54,322	6.6	2.2	2.9	6.3	3.3	2,573	1.0	47,621	5.1	35,730
Blue Earth County, MN	39,068	38,114	35,479	7.4	2.5	3.0	6.4	3.3	1,940	1.9	35,284	3.7	34,822
Nicollet County, MN	20,127	19,782	18,843	5.0	1.7	2.7	6.1	3.2	633	-1.7	12,337	9.4	38,325
Mansfield, OH Metro Area	53,647	59,079	62,761	-5.9	-9.2	5.6	12.1	6.7	2,613	-4.5	43,022	1.2	33,678
Richland County, OH	53,647	59,079	62,761	-5.9	-9.2	5.6	12.1	6.7	2,613	-4.5	43,022	1.2	33,678
McAllen-Edinburg-Mission, TX Metro Area	331,632	318,302	260,575	22.2	4.2	7.9	11.8	7.9	11,780	6.7	181,601	8.7	27,389
Hidalgo County, TX	331,632	318,302	260,575	22.2	4.2	7.9	11.8	7.9	11,780	6.7	181,601	8.7	27,389
Medford, OR Metro Area	97,648	100,968	98,727	2.3	-3.3	6.9	12.5	6.2	5,951	2.9	67,428	5.4	36,285
Jackson County, OR	97,648	100,968	98,727	2.3	-3.3	6.9	12.5	6.2	5,951	2.9	67,428	5.4	36,285
Memphis, TN-MS-AR Metro Area	614,498	635,580	600,070	5.9	-3.3	6.5	9.7	6.1	25,224	-2.3	523,501	2.6	45,119
Crittenden County, AR	21,593	22,819	22,513	1.4	-5.4	6.4	10.5	6.5	844	-3.2	13,528	1.8	31,145
Benton County, MS	3,041	3,269	2,987	9.4	-7.0	8.0	12.4	9.9	58	-1.7	937	10.2	26,763
DeSoto County, MS	83,862	79,618	71,502	11.4	5.3	4.9	7.5	4.1	2,681	6.3	47,635	17.0	31,662
Marshall County, MS	14,663	15,502	15,345	1.0	-5.4	7.3	12.1	8.5	412	-3.5	6,626	6.6	29,262
Tate County, MS	12,024	12,629	11,896	6.2	-4.8	7.2	10.8	6.5	356	-5.1	3,840	-1.1	29,330
Tunica County, MS	4,789	5,030	4,505	11.7	-4.8	9.2	13.7	10.2	223	2.3	9,139	-19.2	27,445
Fayette County, TN	17,768	18,830	15,955	18.0	-5.6	6.4	9.9	6.8	581	5.6	6,555	7.6	39,878
Shelby County, TN	429,430	448,829	428,931	4.6	-4.3	6.6	9.8	6.2	19,372	-3.3	426,313	1.6	48,264
Tipton County, TN	27,328	29,054	26,436	9.9	-5.9	7.3	11.3	6.4	697	-7.1	8,928	9.0	30,301
Merced, CA Metro Area	115,086	113,579	98,738	15.0	1.3	11.4	18.0	10.0	2,903	0.7	42,083	8.3	36,124
Merced County, CA	115,086	113,579	98,738	15.0	1.3	11.4	18.0	10.0	2,903	0.7	42,083	8.3	36,124
Miami-Fort Lauderdale-West Palm Beach, FL Metro Area	**3,020,429**	**2,807,697**	**2,710,277**	**3.6**	**7.6**	**5.5**	**10.8**	**3.6**	**184,069**	**7.9**	**2,052,560**	**12.7**	**45,270**

[1] Civilian employment as a percent of the civilian labor force.
[2] For the pay period including March 12 of the year shown.

Table C-4. Labor Force and Private Business Establishments and Employment—*Continued*

Metropolitan statistical area, division, and component county	Civilian labor force								Private nonfarm businesses				
	Total			Percent change		Unemployment rate[1]			Establishments		Employment[2]		Annual payroll per employee 2014 (dollars)
	2015	2010	2005	2005–2010	2010–2015	2015	2010	2005	2014	Change 2010–2014	2014	Change 2010–2014	
Fort Lauderdale-Pompano Beach-Deerfield Beach, FL Division	992,392	936,563	957,619	-2.2	6.0	5.0	10.2	3.7	58,549	5.4	647,907	9.2	44,523
Broward County, FL	992,392	936,563	957,619	-2.2	6.0	5.0	10.2	3.7	58,549	5.4	647,907	9.2	44,523
Miami-Miami Beach-Kendall, FL Division	*1,334,402*	*1,225,397*	*1,147,797*	*6.8*	*8.9*	*6.1*	*11.1*	*3.2*	*80,197*	*9.2*	*919,859*	*14.7*	*45,318*
Miami-Dade County, FL	1,334,402	1,225,397	1,147,797	6.8	8.9	6.1	11.1	3.2	80,197	9.2	919,859	14.7	45,318
West Palm Beach-Boca Raton-Delray Beach, FL Division	*693,635*	*645,737*	*604,861*	*6.8*	*7.4*	*5.0*	*11.0*	*4.3*	*45,323*	*8.7*	*484,794*	*14.0*	*46,177*
Palm Beach County, FL	693,635	645,737	604,861	6.8	7.4	5.0	11.0	4.3	45,323	8.7	484,794	14.0	46,177
Michigan City-La Porte, IN Metro Area	48,522	51,336	53,070	-3.3	-5.5	6.3	12.0	6.1	2,290	-7.6	33,509	-1.6	35,998
LaPorte County, IN	48,522	51,336	53,070	-3.3	-5.5	6.3	12.0	6.1	2,290	-7.6	33,509	-1.6	35,998
Midland, MI Metro Area	41,702	41,219	41,907	-1.6	1.2	4.7	9.8	5.9	1,908	4.6	34,973	3.6	65,880
Midland County, MI	41,702	41,219	41,907	-1.6	1.2	4.7	9.8	5.9	1,908	4.6	34,973	3.6	65,880
Midland, TX Metro Area	91,038	73,527	68,430	7.4	23.8	3.5	5.9	3.7	5,250	12.6	88,906	46.8	68,087
Martin County, TX	2,582	2,196	2,113	3.9	17.6	3.5	6.0	4.4	103	9.6	1,168	46.7	52,638
Midland County, TX	88,456	71,331	66,317	7.6	24.0	3.5	5.9	3.7	5,147	12.7	87,738	46.8	68,293
Milwaukee-Waukesha-West Allis, WI Metro Area	822,946	817,477	782,820	4.4	0.7	5.0	8.9	5.0	37,739	-1.8	764,662	3.7	48,997
Milwaukee County, WI	477,696	476,449	451,298	5.6	0.3	5.8	10.0	5.7	19,407	-3.0	447,390	0.7	50,539
Ozaukee County, WI	48,136	47,416	47,669	-0.5	1.5	3.7	7.1	3.7	2,752	0.2	38,167	10.2	42,651
Washington County, WI	75,988	75,603	71,985	5.0	0.5	3.8	8.1	4.2	3,189	1.5	50,892	12.2	40,372
Waukesha County, WI	221,126	218,009	211,868	2.9	1.4	3.8	7.3	3.8	12,391		228,213	7.1	48,960
Minneapolis-St. Paul-Bloomington, MN-WI Metro	1,938,857	1,870,769	1,845,419	1.4	3.6	3.4	7.3	3.8	93,843	2.5	1,753,004	10.3	54,146
Anoka County, MN	191,057	187,355	189,702	-1.2	2.0	3.6	8.0	3.9	7,420	1.5	113,460	10.3	52,886
Carver County, MN	55,104	51,621	48,068	7.4	6.7	3.2	6.7	3.4	2,485	6.5	39,102	17.4	48,156
Chisago County, MN	28,963	29,314	27,047	8.4	-1.2	4.2	8.9	4.8	1,206	-2.9	13,019	0.8	40,731
Dakota County, MN	234,087	227,259	227,941	-0.3	3.0	3.3	7.0	3.6	10,343	4.6	178,419	11.2	48,428
Hennepin County, MN	679,549	650,891	652,568	-0.3	4.4	3.3	7.0	3.7	39,606	1.7	875,851	11.4	59,473
Isanti County, MN	20,445	20,561	21,044	-2.3	-0.6	4.3	9.6	4.8	820	6.5	8,935	8.5	35,128
Le Sueur County, MN	15,770	15,715	14,186	10.8	0.3	4.7	8.9	5.4	697	0.9	6,980	14.6	40,083
Mille Lacs County, MN	12,827	13,152	11,974	9.8	-2.5	5.8	11.1	6.7	669	2.6	8,097	5.3	29,887
Ramsey County, MN	280,408	270,063	271,356	-0.5	3.8	3.5	7.5	3.9	13,280	0.5	298,467	5.0	54,539
Scott County, MN	79,078	74,151	69,821	6.2	6.6	3.1	6.9	3.5	3,252	5.8	41,373	10.1	49,208
Sherburne County, MN	49,794	48,989	46,529	5.3	1.6	4.0	8.4	4.3	1,970	3.8	21,232	9.8	40,935
Sibley County, MN	8,633	8,506	8,874	-4.1	1.5	4.1	7.9	4.2	351	-5.9	3,333	4.0	33,830
Washington County, MN	137,668	132,046	125,591	5.1	4.3	3.2	6.7	3.5	5,587	5.1	73,717	12.1	40,578
Wright County, MN	72,145	70,095	62,757	11.7	2.9	3.7	8.0	4.3	3,209	7.1	35,850	15.7	38,781
Pierce County, WI	24,426	23,984	23,337	2.8	1.8	3.9	7.0	4.1	781	0.1	6,695	13.0	32,515
St. Croix County, WI	48,903	47,067	44,624	5.5	3.9	3.8	7.6	4.6	2,167	4.8	28,474	17.1	36,639
Missoula, MT Metro Area	61,143	58,536	57,899	1.1	4.5	3.9	7.3	3.9	4,225	1.3	49,006	6.0	34,273
Missoula County, MT	61,143	58,536	57,899	1.1	4.5	3.9	7.3	3.9	4,225	1.3	49,006	6.0	34,273
Mobile, AL Metro Area	183,097	192,730	180,384	6.8	-5.0	7.0	11.3	5.0	8,492	-3.8	142,481	-4.1	39,654
Mobile County, AL	183,097	192,730	180,384	6.8	-5.0	7.0	11.3	5.0	8,492	-3.8	142,481	-4.1	39,654
Modesto, CA Metro Area	242,710	243,274	226,627	7.3	-0.2	9.5	16.9	8.4	8,544	2.1	132,417	8.9	41,277
Stanislaus County, CA	242,710	243,274	226,627	7.3	-0.2	9.5	16.9	8.4	8,544	2.1	132,417	8.9	41,277
Monroe, LA Metro Area	81,813	80,403	82,886	-3.0	1.8	6.6	8.5	6.1	4,552	0.3	66,676	1.9	35,146
Ouachita Parish, LA	72,395	70,729	72,428	-2.3	2.4	6.6	8.3	6.1	4,220	0.5	62,579	1.9	35,553
Union Parish, LA	9,418	9,674	10,458	-7.5	-2.6	7.0	10.4	6.2	332	-1.8	4,097	1.7	28,923
Monroe, MI Metro Area	76,732	75,640	77,855	-2.8	1.4	4.4	11.7	6.2	2,260	-5.2	36,169	4.3	42,856
Monroe County, MI	76,732	75,640	77,855	-2.8	1.4	4.4	11.7	6.2	2,260	-5.2	36,169	4.3	42,856
Montgomery, AL Metro Area	168,786	175,499	168,497	4.2	-3.8	5.9	9.8	4.4	7,626	-1.5	130,334	2.6	38,501
Autauga County, AL	25,308	25,713	23,949	7.4	-1.6	5.2	8.9	3.8	817	-6.2	10,202	0.3	29,519
Elmore County, AL	36,075	36,683	34,448	6.5	-1.7	5.1	9.1	3.7	1,142	2.8	14,684	6.7	31,789
Lowndes County, AL	3,824	4,350	4,952	-12.2	-12.1	11.6	18.5	8.0	100	-20.0	2,135	1.1	57,612
Montgomery County, AL	103,579	108,753	105,148	3.4	-4.8	6.2	10.0	4.6	5,567	-1.2	103,313	2.3	39,946
Morgantown, WV Metro Area	65,696	63,289	58,509	8.2	3.8	5.0	6.2	3.9	2,819	2.8	49,376	11.2	40,111
Monongalia County, WV	50,908	48,354	44,216	9.4	5.3	4.7	5.6	3.7	2,296	5.3	44,406	11.4	40,820
Preston County, WV	14,788	14,935	14,293	4.5		6.2	8.4	4.8	523	-7.1	4,970	9.0	33,779
Morristown, TN Metro Area	49,733	52,817	52,907	-0.2	-5.8	6.4	11.5	5.9	1,923	-3.0	37,218	0.9	34,497
Hamblen County, TN	26,510	28,403	29,400	-3.4	-6.7	6.3	11.6	5.8	1,265	-3.7	26,816	-0.2	34,720
Jefferson County, TN	23,223	24,414	23,507	3.9	-4.9	6.5	11.5	5.9	658	-1.6	10,402	3.8	33,921
Mount Vernon-Anacortes, WA Metro Area	56,856	59,114	56,282	5.0	-3.8	6.7	10.9	6.2	3,361	-2.1	39,626	4.2	41,971
Skagit County, WA	56,856	59,114	56,282	5.0	-3.8	6.7	10.9	6.2	3,361	-2.1	39,626	4.2	41,971
Muncie, IN Metro Area	54,475	54,724	56,113	-2.5	-0.5	5.7	11.6	6.9	2,322	-4.8	38,419	7.0	34,199
Delaware County, IN	54,475	54,724	56,113	-2.5	-0.5	5.7	11.6	6.9	2,322	-4.8	38,419	7.0	34,199
Muskegon, MI Metro Area	77,763	77,712	90,054	-13.7	0.1	5.6	14.5	7.0	3,153	-6.7	52,027	9.1	38,614
Muskegon County, MI	77,763	77,712	90,054	-13.7	0.1	5.6	14.5	7.0	3,153	-6.7	52,027	9.1	38,614
Myrtle Beach-Conway-North Myrtle Beach, SC-NC Metro Area	184,985	177,470	164,187	8.1	4.2	7.1	12.3	5.6	10,592	0.6	123,205	6.9	29,775
Brunswick County, NC	48,509	46,521	42,827	8.6	4.3	7.2	12.5	5.0	2,298	0.5	23,815	3.8	33,717
Horry County, SC	136,476	130,949	121,360	7.9	4.2	7.0	12.3	5.7	8,294	0.6	99,390	7.6	28,830
Napa, CA Metro Area	74,752	70,216	71,328	-1.6	6.5	4.6	10.3	4.4	4,075	3.3	60,882	10.8	48,174
Napa County, CA	74,752	70,216	71,328	-1.6	6.5	4.6	10.3	4.4	4,075	3.3	60,882	10.8	48,174
Naples-Immokalee-Marco Island, FL Metro Area	162,124	145,349	145,136	0.1	11.5	5.2	11.6	3.5	11,003	11.6	114,225	12.6	41,057
Collier County, FL	162,124	145,349	145,136	0.1	11.5	5.2	11.6	3.5	11,003	11.6	114,225	12.6	41,057
Nashville-Davidson--Murfreesboro--Franklin, TN Metro Area	934,338	878,273	779,926	12.6	6.4	4.6	8.6	4.6	40,484	3.1	774,736	14.6	47,211
Cannon County, TN	5,910	6,082	6,377	-4.6	-2.8	5.8	11.1	5.3	174	6.1	1,474	7.0	32,554
Cheatham County, TN	20,182	20,210	20,229	-0.1	-0.1	4.9	9.0	4.4	551	1.8	5,842	5.1	37,395

[1]Civilian employment as a percent of the civilian labor force.
[2]For the pay period including March 12 of the year shown.
D = not shown to avoid disclosure of confidential information.

Table C-4.   Labor Force and Private Business Establishments and Employment—*Continued*

Metropolitan statistical area, division, and component county	Civilian labor force								Private nonfarm businesses				Annual payroll per employee 2014 (dollars)
	Total			Percent change		Unemployment rate[1]			Establishments		Employment[2]		
	2015	2010	2005	2005–2010	2010–2015	2015	2010	2005	2014	Change 2010–2014	2014	Change 2010–2014	
Davidson County, TN	364,254	342,404	301,917	13.4	6.4	4.5	8.2	4.5	18,619	2.7	418,413	12.9	49,319
Dickson County, TN	24,053	23,958	22,668	5.7	0.4	5.6	10.2	5.0	904	-2.1	13,153	10.9	33,878
Hickman County, TN	10,487	10,980	10,122	8.5	-4.5	5.7	11.1	6.2	249	-7.1	2,268	-1.6	32,316
Macon County, TN	10,034	10,245	10,453	-2.0	-2.1	5.3	11.2	5.7	324	-5.5	3,311	0.9	29,619
Maury County, TN	41,959	41,469	35,653	16.3	1.2	5.3	12.3	6.0	1,677	1.9	24,546	6.7	39,393
Robertson County, TN	34,102	33,768	31,473	7.3	1.0	4.9	9.2	4.9	1,095	3.3	17,776	13.7	36,165
Rutherford County, TN	152,997	140,219	117,742	19.1	9.1	4.6	8.9	4.2	4,758	5.8	101,022	22.4	40,695
Smith County, TN	8,494	8,934	9,047	-1.2	-4.9	5.7	12.3	6.0	262	-7.4	3,787	11.3	35,743
Sumner County, TN	88,328	83,250	75,319	10.5	6.1	4.7	8.9	4.6	2,987	3.9	42,382	18.3	38,933
Trousdale County, TN	3,722	3,742	3,671	1.9	-0.5	5.9	10.8	6.6	115	-8.7	1,033	-4.3	25,905
Williamson County, TN	105,943	94,495	81,057	16.6	12.1	4.1	6.6	3.8	6,333	4.4	104,390	15.4	59,158
Wilson County, TN	63,873	58,517	54,198	8.0	9.2	4.7	8.4	4.6	2,436	3.7	35,339	21.2	38,152
New Bern, NC Metro Area	51,352	52,370	51,421	1.8	-1.9	6.1	10.7	4.7	2,521	-6.9	30,794	-0.9	35,821
Craven County, NC	41,439	42,272	40,795	3.6	-2.0	6.1	10.7	4.7	2,133	-7.5	27,477	-2.5	36,700
Jones County, NC	4,547	4,597	4,935	-6.8	-1.1	5.8	11.2	4.9	126	-14.9	778	-21.8	32,886
Pamlico County, NC	5,366	5,501	5,691	-3.3	-2.5	6.1	10.2	4.5	262	2.7	2,539	33.6	27,208
New Haven-Milford, CT Metro Area	454,396	462,233	429,962	7.5	-1.7	6.1	10.0	5.3	19,467	-0.7	338,587	5.5	49,068
New Haven County, CT	454,396	462,233	429,962	7.5	-1.7	6.1	10.0	5.3	19,467	-0.7	338,587	5.5	49,068
New Orleans-Metairie, LA Metro Area	603,674	570,730	9,021	6,226.7	5.8	6.0	7.7	10.6	30,049	2.2	490,361	8.3	47,137
Jefferson Parish, LA	220,629	216,258	NA	NA	2.0	5.7	7.4	NA	11,648	-1.3	182,695	2.1	44,201
Orleans Parish, LA	180,778	162,592	NA	NA	11.2	6.5	8.7	NA	8,853	4.9	169,860	14.0	48,374
Plaquemines Parish, LA	10,373	10,028	NA	NA	3.4	5.5	6.1	NA	699	0.3	11,741	16.5	66,845
St. Bernard Parish, LA	19,424	15,951	NA	NA	21.8	6.6	8.3	NA	677	6.1	7,804	15.9	41,699
St. Charles Parish, LA	25,750	25,481	NA	NA	1.1	5.7	7.4	NA	968	1.6	20,810	4.0	65,218
St. James Parish, LA	9,895	10,130	9,021	12.3	-2.3	8.3	11.7	10.6	318	0.3	6,244	-8.9	66,840
St. John the Baptist Parish, LA	20,553	21,535	NA	NA	-4.6	7.3	10.6	NA	695	-5.2	14,825	5.4	49,082
St. Tammany Parish, LA	116,272	108,755	NA	NA	6.9	5.3	6.3	NA	6,191	6.1	76,382	13.7	42,023
New York-Newark-Jersey City, NY-NJ-PA Metro Area	**10,073,374**	**9,812,850**	**9,505,717**	**3.2**	**2.7**	**5.3**	**8.9**	**4.9**	**569,055**	**3.5**	**8,040,243**	**7.6**	**67,740**
Dutchess County-Putnam County, NY Division	*194,132*	*201,790*	*203,076*	*-0.6*	*-3.8*	*4.5*	*7.6*	*3.9*	*10,352*	*0.0*	*114,736*	*-2.0*	*45,094*
Dutchess County, NY	143,390	149,196	147,009	1.5	-3.9	4.6	7.7	3.9	7,478	0.5	93,981	-2.5	45,714
Putnam County, NY	50,742	52,594	56,067	-6.2	-3.5	4.3	7.2	3.7	2,874	-1.1	20,755	0.3	42,288
Nassau County-Suffolk County, NY Division	*1,472,173*	*1,469,298*	*1,467,327*	*0.1*	*0.2*	*4.6*	*7.5*	*4.1*	*96,654*	*1.9*	*1,107,585*	*6.2*	*51,042*
Nassau County, NY	695,815	691,435	689,655	0.3	0.6	4.3	7.1	4.0	47,823	1.5	545,065	6.6	50,668
Suffolk County, NY	776,358	777,863	777,672	0.0	-0.2	4.8	7.7	4.2	48,831	2.3	562,520	5.8	51,403
Newark, NJ-PA Division	*1,262,102*	*1,277,890*	*1,247,158*	*2.5*	*-1.2*	*5.5*	*9.1*	*4.4*	*67,109*	*-0.5*	*1,045,550*	*1.7*	*66,466*
Essex County, NJ	375,624	382,570	360,801	6.0	-1.8	6.7	10.8	5.6	18,751	-2.0	289,817	-1.7	58,560
Hunterdon County, NJ	66,112	68,378	71,103	-3.8	-3.3	4.1	7.4	3.1	3,865	-0.8	44,220	0.6	69,906
Morris County, NJ	263,272	265,178	267,019	-0.7	-0.7	4.2	7.4	3.3	16,771	0.0	286,394	4.1	74,003
Somerset County, NJ	174,497	173,704	174,544	-0.5	0.5	4.4	7.6	3.4	9,914	1.8	184,296	6.6	80,078
Sussex County, NJ	77,573	82,355	82,976	-0.7	-5.8	5.2	9.4	3.9	3,254	-3.4	30,254	-3.1	39,557
Union County, NJ	279,864	279,537	264,877	5.5	0.1	5.9	9.5	4.8	13,668	0.3	202,369	0.1	59,632
Pike County, PA	25,160	26,168	25,838	1.3	-3.9	6.3	9.7	5.9	886	-0.1	8,200	8.3	26,043
New York-Jersey City-White Plains, NY-NJ Division	*7,144,967*	*6,863,872*	*6,588,156*	*4.2*	*4.1*	*5.4*	*9.2*	*5.2*	*394,940*	*4.6*	*5,772,372*	*9.2*	*71,625*
Bergen County, NJ	485,316	478,553	465,823	2.7	1.4	4.6	8.0	3.7	31,573	0.8	439,344	7.7	60,451
Hudson County, NJ	362,265	352,624	287,475	22.7	2.7	5.3	9.6	5.5	13,149	4.2	209,244	2.5	69,155
Middlesex County, NJ	440,343	424,333	414,728	2.3	3.8	5.0	8.9	4.2	21,560	1.9	383,660	6.7	60,935
Monmouth County, NJ	331,623	330,310	323,151	2.2	0.4	5.0	8.7	4.1	18,997	0.8	228,837	5.6	48,278
Ocean County, NJ	268,585	264,522	248,890	6.3	1.5	6.0	10.3	4.7	12,552	6.1	134,831	8.4	36,189
Passaic County, NJ	249,659	253,177	234,831	7.8	-1.4	6.9	11.4	5.5	11,941	2.5	150,645	4.9	44,723
Bronx County, NY	615,993	582,287	507,229	14.8	5.8	7.7	12.0	7.6	17,466	6.8	246,446	8.0	43,552
Kings County, NY	1,242,931	1,163,502	1,070,528	8.7	6.8	5.9	9.9	6.2	54,723	13.5	562,928	15.0	38,761
New York County, NY	931,558	881,204	902,717	-2.4	5.7	4.8	8.6	5.1	105,998	2.2	2,188,523	11.2	106,194
Orange County, NY	178,292	181,295	177,596	2.1	-1.7	4.7	8.0	4.2	9,189	-0.3	112,409	9.1	37,071
Queens County, NY	1,181,681	1,106,461	1,090,028	1.5	6.8	5.0	8.6	5.2	47,510	9.7	537,442	11.0	45,285
Richmond County, NY	225,115	216,950	231,455	-6.3	3.8	5.8	9.4	5.3	9,044	6.5	96,645	5.9	37,971
Rockland County, NY	152,086	149,978	151,221	-0.8	1.4	4.6	7.5	4.0	9,546	3.6	103,615	6.9	44,934
Westchester County, NY	479,520	478,676	482,484	-0.8	0.2	4.6	7.4	4.0	31,692	0.4	377,803	2.8	65,072
Niles-Benton Harbor, MI Metro Area	74,150	76,628	79,071	-3.1	-3.2	5.0	12.0	6.9	3,543	-3.6	53,366	7.8	42,584
Berrien County, MI	74,150	76,628	79,071	-3.1	-3.2	5.0	12.0	6.9	3,543	-3.6	53,366	7.8	42,584
North Port-Sarasota-Bradenton, FL Metro Area	343,357	314,794	313,922	0.3	9.1	5.0	11.5	3.4	21,306	7.2	221,630	11.9	37,440
Manatee County, FL	164,480	147,572	144,617	2.0	11.5	5.0	11.4	3.5	8,244	9.9	89,428	12.6	35,296
Sarasota County, FL	178,877	167,222	169,305	-1.2	7.0	5.0	11.6	3.4	13,062	5.5	132,202	11.5	38,890
Norwich-New London, CT Metro Area	136,630	144,517	144,132	0.3	-5.5	5.8	8.9	4.5	5,732		102,281	-4.4	47,734
New London County, CT	136,630	144,517	144,132	0.3	-5.5	5.8	8.9	4.5	5,732		102,281	-4.4	47,734
Ocala, FL Metro Area	131,147	132,351	127,862	3.5	-0.9	6.4	13.6	3.8	6,842	1.0	76,032	2.8	34,011
Marion County, FL	131,147	132,351	127,862	3.5	-0.9	6.4	13.6	3.8	6,842	1.0	76,032	2.8	34,011
Ocean City, NJ Metro Area	48,896	50,032	57,700	-13.3	-2.3	10.9	14.0	6.6	3,788	-1.7	25,547	4.4	38,581
Cape May County, NJ	48,896	50,032	57,700	-13.3	-2.3	10.9	14.0	6.6	3,788	-1.7	25,547	4.4	38,581
Odessa, TX Metro Area	79,869	68,186	62,285	9.5	17.1	4.6	8.3	4.5	3,686	13.9	63,283	29.2	55,926
Ector County, TX	79,869	68,186	62,285	9.5	17.1	4.6	8.3	4.5	3,686	13.9	63,283	29.2	55,926
Ogden-Clearfield, UT Metro Area	307,072	288,136	270,310	6.6	6.6	3.6	7.8	4.2	12,946	4.5	173,052	9.5	37,174
Box Elder County, UT	24,184	23,644	22,413	5.5	2.3	3.6	8.5	4.3	1,038	0.7	16,753	4.3	47,020
Davis County, UT	160,089	146,959	135,870	8.2	8.9	3.3	7.0	3.9	6,667	7.6	77,365	8.3	36,496
Morgan County, UT	4,820	4,274	3,818	11.9	12.8	3.1	6.9	4.2	236	5.4	1,498	5.2	40,272
Weber County, UT	117,979	113,259	108,209	4.7	4.2	4.0	8.8	4.6	5,005	1.3	77,436	11.9	35,662
Oklahoma City, OK Metro Area	668,199	623,505	573,874	8.6	7.2	3.7	5.9	4.3	34,769	5.4	502,066	10.9	44,102

[1]Civilian employment as a percent of the civilian labor force.
[2]For the pay period including March 12 of the year shown.

Table C-4. Labor Force and Private Business Establishments and Employment—*Continued*

	Civilian labor force								Private nonfarm businesses				
	Total			Percent change		Unemployment rate[1]			Establishments		Employment[2]		Annual payroll per employee 2014 (dollars)
Metropolitan statistical area, division, and component county	2015	2010	2005	2005–2010	2010–2015	2015	2010	2005	2014	Change 2010–2014	2014	Change 2010–2014	
Canadian County, OK	67,910	60,083	51,178	17.4	13.0	3.5	5.2	3.7	2,531	11.9	27,420	21.6	40,052
Cleveland County, OK	139,063	131,125	118,305	10.8	6.1	3.4	5.3	3.8	5,621	5.6	70,651	8.9	33,949
Grady County, OK	26,420	25,401	23,447	8.3	4.0	4.3	6.5	4.5	1,119	6.0	11,998	16.4	33,216
Lincoln County, OK	16,037	15,657	14,775	6.0	2.4	4.5	6.5	4.8	564	-1.2	5,807	9.5	35,313
Logan County, OK	21,624	19,805	18,151	9.1	9.2	3.7	5.7	3.9	799	11.4	6,310	9.2	29,090
McClain County, OK	18,803	17,180	14,736	16.6	9.4	3.6	5.6	4.2	845	11.8	7,514	8.7	34,786
Oklahoma County, OK	378,342	354,254	333,282	6.3	6.8	3.8	6.1	4.6	23,290	4.4	372,366	10.5	47,257
Olympia-Tumwater, WA Metro Area	125,603	126,948	121,951	4.1	-1.1	5.9	9.0	5.3	5,923	1.7	66,373	4.3	38,578
Thurston County, WA	125,603	126,948	121,951	4.1	-1.1	5.9	9.0	5.3	5,923	1.7	66,373	4.3	38,578
Omaha-Council Bluffs, NE-IA Metro Area	477,954	465,973	440,297	5.8	2.6	3.2	5.1	4.3	22,855	2.5	402,263	0.9	45,594
Harrison County, IA	7,650	8,001	8,066	-0.8	-4.4	3.3	5.6	4.7	364	4.6	3,070	3.9	32,957
Mills County, IA	7,496	7,610	8,177	-6.9	-1.5	4.0	5.2	4.1	297	2.4	2,276	7.2	32,160
Pottawattamie County, IA	49,267	50,344	48,658	3.5	-2.1	3.6	5.8	4.9	1,981	-0.9	31,202	1.2	33,460
Cass County, NE	13,283	13,404	14,017	-4.4	-0.9	3.3	5.6	4.1	536	0.8	3,530	6.5	34,995
Douglas County, NE	287,805	279,280	266,086	5.0	3.1	3.3	5.1	4.5	15,136	1.2	305,146	-1.7	48,113
Sarpy County, NE	90,294	84,923	72,972	16.4	6.3	2.8	4.4	3.4	3,442	10.1	46,905	18.4	40,552
Saunders County, NE	11,045	11,179	11,153	0.2	-1.2	3.0	4.8	3.9	535	7.2	3,732	7.1	31,444
Washington County, NE	11,114	11,232	11,168	0.6	-1.1	3.0	4.6	3.3	564	5.0	6,402	4.7	46,538
Orlando-Kissimmee-Sanford, FL Metro Area	1,223,514	1,137,389	1,015,778	12.0	7.6	5.0	11.1	3.6	58,984	7.1	959,387	12.1	40,349
Lake County, FL	140,471	134,021	118,339	13.3	4.8	5.4	11.8	3.8	6,649	6.0	73,167	11.4	31,987
Orange County, FL	688,018	635,299	553,951	14.7	8.3	4.9	10.8	3.6	34,229	8.6	659,812	11.7	42,217
Osceola County, FL	155,082	137,372	116,456	18.0	12.9	5.7	12.5	3.8	5,340	10.8	69,236	16.4	30,078
Seminole County, FL	239,943	230,697	227,032	1.6	4.0	4.8	10.6	3.4	12,766	2.5	157,172	12.5	40,926
Oshkosh-Neenah, WI Metro Area	91,499	92,449	91,185	1.4		4.3	7.8	4.4	3,490	-3.1	81,908	-1.8	47,458
Winnebago County, WI	91,499	92,449	91,185	1.4		4.3	7.8	4.4	3,490	-3.1	81,908	-1.8	47,458
Owensboro, KY Metro Area	52,664	55,465	55,137	0.6	-5.1	4.7	9.4	6.0	2,533	-1.3	46,605	4.6	37,398
Daviess County, KY	44,609	46,881	46,341	1.2	-4.8	4.7	9.3	5.8	2,241	-1.2	41,934	4.3	35,064
Hancock County, KY	3,868	4,060	4,154	-2.3	-4.7	5.1	10.3	6.2	126	-4.5	3,553	10.2	65,973
McLean County, KY	4,187	4,524	4,642	-2.5	-7.4	5.0	10.2	7.2	166	0.6	1,118	1.4	34,121
Oxnard-Thousand Oaks-Ventura, CA Metro Area	429,784	430,010	415,958	3.4	-0.1	5.7	10.8	4.7	20,251	3.3	251,566	6.8	50,984
Ventura County, CA	429,784	430,010	415,958	3.4	-0.1	5.7	10.8	4.7	20,251	3.3	251,566	6.8	50,984
Palm Bay-Melbourne-Titusville, FL Metro Area	257,684	265,643	260,435	2.0	-3.0	5.9	11.3	3.6	13,348	2.8	166,056	1.3	40,976
Brevard County, FL	257,684	265,643	260,435	2.0	-3.0	5.9	11.3	3.6	13,348	2.8	166,056	1.3	40,976
Panama City, FL Metro Area	93,702	92,304	88,727	4.0	1.5	5.4	10.5	3.5	4,744	-0.7	62,727	11.3	32,839
Bay County, FL	87,575	86,072	82,406	4.4	1.7	5.4	10.5	3.6	4,461	-0.4	60,513	11.2	32,822
Gulf County, FL	6,127	6,232	6,321	-1.4	-1.7	5.1	10.3	3.3	283	-5.0	2,214	13.5	33,319
Parkersburg-Vienna, WV Metro Area	39,832	41,640	43,449	-4.2	-4.3	6.5	9.1	5.6	2,111	-3.6	33,284	0.7	34,673
Wirt County, WV	2,278	2,292	2,505	-8.5	-0.6	10.3	12.5	7.4	52	-25.7	386	0.0	21,262
Wood County, WV	37,554	39,348	40,944	-3.9	-4.6	6.2	8.9	5.5	2,059	-2.8	32,898	0.7	34,831
Pensacola-Ferry Pass-Brent, FL Metro Area	213,181	211,246	203,128	4.0	0.9	5.3	9.8	3.8	9,185	1.1	122,512	5.7	36,869
Escambia County, FL	139,644	139,913	135,677	3.1	-0.2	5.6	10.1	3.9	6,657	0.6	99,633	4.5	37,639
Santa Rosa County, FL	73,537	71,333	67,451	5.8	3.1	4.8	9.3	3.6	2,528	2.6	22,879	11.1	33,519
Peoria, IL Metro Area	186,547	197,473	191,072	3.4	-5.5	6.5	10.0	4.7	8,465	-3.4	161,541	0.0	49,831
Marshall County, IL	5,742	6,423	7,115	-9.7	-10.6	6.7	10.2	4.4	270	-3.6	2,914	-1.7	36,160
Peoria County, IL	90,864	96,018	92,082	4.3	-5.4	6.9	10.5	4.9	4,519	-4.4	104,510	-1.5	55,678
Stark County, IL	2,781	3,021	2,833	6.6	-7.9	6.6	9.5	5.5	118	-2.5	982	8.4	38,701
Tazewell County, IL	67,541	71,662	69,006	3.8	-5.8	6.3	9.9	4.6	2,803	-1.6	44,318	1.6	39,540
Woodford County, IL	19,619	20,349	20,036	1.6	-3.6	5.1	7.7	3.7	755	-4.7	8,817	9.1	38,004
Philadelphia-Camden-Wilmington, PA-NJ-DE-MD Metro Area	**3,059,036**	**3,020,334**	**2,916,385**	**3.6**	**1.3**	**5.3**	**8.8**	**4.7**	**145,269**	**0.4**	**2,550,162**	**5.3**	**54,865**
Camden, NJ Division	*637,382*	*653,792*	*648,744*	*0.8*	*-2.5*	*5.8*	*10.1*	*4.4*	*27,817*	*-0.6*	*439,174*	*3.2*	*46,953*
Burlington County, NJ	232,359	236,856	237,927	-0.5	-1.9	5.2	9.0	3.9	10,531	1.3	180,008	3.7	51,690
Camden County, NJ	255,354	264,513	262,726	0.7	-3.5	6.3	10.9	4.8	11,402	-3.0	170,942	1.8	45,420
Gloucester County, NJ	149,669	152,423	148,091	2.9	-1.8	5.9	10.3	4.4	5,884	0.7	88,224	4.9	40,257
Montgomery County-Bucks County-Chester County, PA Division	*1,056,108*	*1,037,023*	*1,020,158*	*1.7*	*1.8*	*4.1*	*7.0*	*3.9*	*58,960*	*0.9*	*984,156*	*6.2*	*57,244*
Bucks County, PA	338,412	337,133	341,282	-1.2	0.4	4.5	7.6	4.1	18,952	0.7	244,396	1.2	44,020
Chester County, PA	276,442	269,526	256,305	5.2	2.6	3.7	6.2	3.6	14,024	1.7	244,291	8.8	66,713
Montgomery County, PA	441,254	430,364	422,571	1.8	2.5	4.0	6.9	3.9	25,984	0.7	495,469	7.6	59,099
Philadelphia, PA Division	*988,102*	*973,948*	*896,383*	*8.7*	*1.5*	*6.2*	*9.8*	*6.0*	*40,070*	*0.9*	*809,220*	*4.8*	*54,763*
Delaware County, PA	291,908	286,173	279,252	2.5	2.0	4.7	8.0	4.6	12,675	-0.8	214,886	6.6	55,232
Philadelphia County, PA	696,194	687,775	617,131	11.4	1.2	6.9	10.6	6.7	27,395	1.7	594,334	4.2	54,594
Wilmington, DE-MD-NJ Division	*377,444*	*355,571*	*351,100*	*1.3*	*6.2*	*5.1*	*8.8*	*4.5*	*18,422*	*-1.1*	*317,612*	*7.0*	*58,695*
New Castle County, DE	292,754	271,492	270,152	0.5	7.8	4.7	8.3	4.4	15,504		274,816	7.7	60,116
Cecil County, MD	53,245	51,979	49,714	4.6	2.4	6.0	9.5	4.6	1,771	-0.7	24,487	3.9	44,109
Salem County, NJ	31,445	32,100	31,234	2.8	-2.0	7.1	11.7	4.9	1,147	-3.9	18,309	0.6	56,870
Phoenix-Mesa-Scottsdale, AZ Metro Area	2,165,131	2,073,297	1,943,498	6.7	4.4	5.3	9.6	4.1	90,849	3.6	1,574,007	8.3	45,952
Maricopa County, AZ	2,007,847	1,919,590	1,856,076	3.4	4.6	5.2	9.5	4.0	87,501	3.5	1,527,799	8.2	46,311
Pinal County, AZ	157,284	153,707	87,422	75.8	2.3	6.3	10.7	5.6	3,348	4.5	46,208	11.3	34,063
Pine Bluff, AR Metro Area	36,709	42,560	46,561	-8.6	-13.7	7.0	10.1	7.4	1,590	-6.5	22,935	-10.7	34,471
Cleveland County, AR	3,416	3,888	4,273	-9.0	-12.1	5.8	8.4	5.9	79	-2.5	644	39.7	29,489
Jefferson County, AR	29,115	33,973	37,037	-8.3	-14.3	7.2	10.4	7.6	1,358	-7.0	20,829	-12.0	34,690
Lincoln County, AR	4,178	4,699	5,251	-10.5	-11.1	6.3	9.4	7.6	153	-4.4	1,462	-5.9	33,558
Pittsburgh, PA Metro Area	1,213,284	1,201,150	1,196,815	0.4	1.0	5.1	8.0	5.2	59,644	0.7	1,092,675	6.0	47,493
Allegheny County, PA	647,803	636,060	628,051	1.3	1.8	4.8	7.6	5.0	33,614	0.8	703,336	6.2	50,164
Armstrong County, PA	33,342	33,635	32,901	2.2	-0.9	6.4	9.1	6.1	1,320	3.7	14,409	8.3	34,813
Beaver County, PA	85,989	85,607	89,335	-4.2	0.4	5.9	8.6	5.6	3,445	-0.4	50,618	5.6	37,921

[1] Civilian employment as a percent of the civilian labor force.
[2] For the pay period including March 12 of the year shown.

Table C-4. Labor Force and Private Business Establishments and Employment—*Continued*

Metropolitan statistical area, division, and component county	Civilian labor force Total 2015	2010	2005	Percent change 2005–2010	2010–2015	Unemployment rate[1] 2015	2010	2005	Private nonfarm businesses Establishments 2014	Change 2010–2014	Employment[2] 2014	Change 2010–2014	Annual payroll per employee 2014 (dollars)
Butler County, PA	97,620	95,776	94,848	1.0	1.9	4.6	7.4	4.8	4,815	3.7	80,370	8.7	44,693
Fayette County, PA	58,480	59,531	65,225	-8.7	-1.8	7.2	10.7	7.0	2,676	-2.4	36,687	1.3	33,424
Washington County, PA	106,529	105,274	102,273	2.9	1.2	5.4	8.1	5.5	5,091	1.3	83,500	5.9	52,617
Westmoreland County, PA	183,521	185,267	184,182	0.6	-0.9	5.2	8.2	5.3	8,683	-0.8	123,755	4.4	40,236
Pittsfield, MA Metro Area	65,608	68,212	72,664	-6.1	-3.8	5.6	8.7	4.4	3,900	-3.2	52,802	-1.7	41,507
Berkshire County, MA	65,608	68,212	72,664	-6.1	-3.8	5.6	8.7	4.4	3,900	-3.2	52,802	-1.7	41,507
Pocatello, ID Metro Area	42,141	41,091	40,549	1.3	2.6	4.0	8.0	3.9	1,943	-3.7	25,273	1.5	30,274
Bannock County, ID	42,141	41,091	40,549	1.3	2.6	4.0	8.0	3.9	1,943	-3.7	25,273	1.5	30,274
Portland-South Portland, ME Metro Area	283,514	283,853	285,935	-0.7	-0.1	3.6	7.1	3.9	17,349	0.1	225,199	3.2	44,096
Cumberland County, ME	156,529	156,068	155,620	0.3	0.3	3.4	6.6	3.6	10,926	0.2	160,331	3.9	45,996
Sagadahoc County, ME	18,790	19,193	18,535	3.6	-2.1	3.5	6.5	4.4	923	-2.7	13,169	-1.4	46,781
York County, ME	108,195	108,592	111,780	-2.9	-0.4	3.9	8.0	4.2	5,500	0.3	51,699	2.4	37,519
Portland-Vancouver-Hillsboro, OR-WA Metro Area	1,224,063	1,207,037	1,093,793	10.4	1.3	5.3	10.2	5.0	65,127	4.3	941,033	8.1	51,527
Clackamas County, OR	204,481	202,654	190,177	6.6	0.9	5.2	10.1	5.5	11,244	4.6	134,580	-2.1	45,088
Columbia County, OR	22,896	23,649	23,209	1.9	-3.2	7.2	12.9	7.3	897	-5.8	7,886	14.0	30,264
Multnomah County, OR	427,659	418,838	360,354	16.2	2.1	5.0	9.6	6.1	25,872	5.0	401,261	8.4	50,787
Washington County, OR	299,458	289,670	268,325	8.0	3.4	4.8	9.0	5.2	14,688	3.8	249,517	13.7	60,979
Yamhill County, OR	51,073	51,226	44,039	16.3	-0.3	5.3	10.4	6.1	2,347	2.7	26,478	-4.5	38,675
Clark County, WA	213,480	216,621	202,656	6.9	-1.4	6.4	12.9	6.7	9,881	4.0	119,895	11.3	46,045
Skamania County, WA	5,016	5,179	5,033	2.9	-3.1	7.3	12.8	7.9	198	4.2	1,416	12.3	30,258
Port St. Lucie, FL Metro Area	201,248	195,326	177,600	10.0	3.0	5.9	12.7	4.5	10,324	4.7	107,781	8.9	35,951
Martin County, FL	69,915	66,636	64,652	3.1	4.9	5.2	10.8	4.0	5,201	4.4	51,673	9.8	38,319
St. Lucie County, FL	131,333	128,690	112,948	13.9	2.1	6.2	13.8	4.8	5,123	5.0	56,108	8.1	33,770
Prescott, AZ Metro Area	97,545	96,533	91,442	5.6	1.0	5.6	10.7	4.4	5,647	0.1	55,932	10.0	33,444
Yavapai County, AZ	97,545	96,533	91,442	5.6	1.0	5.6	10.7	4.4	5,647	0.1	55,932	10.0	33,444
Providence-Warwick, RI-MA Metro Area	842,619	853,201	853,565	0.0	-1.2	6.1	11.0	5.4	40,615	-1.5	610,632	3.4	45,117
Bristol County, MA	288,062	286,497	287,829	-0.5	0.5	6.3	10.5	6.0	12,703	-0.8	192,140	-0.3	42,889
Bristol County, RI	26,254	27,032	28,254	-4.3	-2.9	5.1	9.6	4.3	1,227	-0.2	14,219	8.2	31,531
Kent County, RI	91,172	94,148	96,472	-2.4	-3.2	5.5	11.1	4.8	4,668	-3.1	68,240	-0.9	42,115
Newport County, RI	44,108	45,159	44,632	1.2	-2.3	5.2	9.7	4.6	2,715	-1.6	30,089	4.8	46,039
Providence County, RI	323,300	328,845	323,279	1.7	-1.7	6.4	11.9	5.4	15,563	-1.7	263,991	6.6	48,184
Washington County, RI	69,723	71,520	73,099	-2.2	-2.5	5.5	9.9	4.1	3,739	-1.4	41,953	6.8	44,846
Provo-Orem, UT Metro Area	271,088	234,432	209,058	12.1	15.6	3.2	7.5	3.9	11,926	10.4	180,449	16.4	38,960
Juab County, UT	5,010	4,612	3,916	17.8	8.6	3.9	9.1	4.8	191	4.9	2,097	-0.6	33,190
UT County, UT	266,078	229,820	205,142	12.0	15.8	3.2	7.4	3.9	11,735	10.4	178,352	16.6	39,027
Pueblo, CO Metro Area	71,996	74,396	69,326	7.3	-3.2	5.7	10.4	6.8	3,014	-4.5	47,148	0.6	37,269
Pueblo County, CO	71,996	74,396	69,326	7.3	3.2	5.7	10.4	6.8	3,014	-4.5	47,148	0.6	37,269
Punta Gorda, FL Metro Area	67,559	66,293	66,088	0.3	1.9	5.9	12.7	4.0	3,704	5.1	35,818	-3.0	31,235
Charlotte County, FL	67,559	66,293	66,088	0.3	1.9	5.9	12.7	4.0	3,704	5.1	35,818	-3.0	31,235
Racine, WI Metro Area	99,446	100,313	98,509	1.8	-0.9	5.7	10.2	5.9	3,986	-1.6	68,267	6.4	44,849
Racine County, WI	99,446	100,313	98,509	1.8	-0.9	5.7	10.2	5.9	3,986	-1.6	68,267	6.4	44,849
Raleigh, NC Metro Area	656,759	590,114	500,724	17.9	11.3	4.8	8.6	4.2	30,759	6.3	472,872	15.2	49,692
Franklin County, NC	29,044	27,950	25,987	7.6	3.9	5.9	10.9	4.8	940	2.1	9,495	2.2	41,091
Johnston County, NC	88,283	81,686	70,876	15.3	8.1	5.2	9.9	4.5	3,064		38,094	6.4	34,397
Wake County, NC	539,432	480,478	403,861	19.0	12.3	4.7	8.3	4.1	26,755	7.4	425,283	16.3	51,254
Rapid City, SD Metro Area	71,553	70,045	70,122	-0.1	2.2	3.3	5.3	3.7	4,705	4.6	54,622	9.6	36,734
Custer County, SD	3,974	4,069	4,800	-15.2	-2.3	4.3	5.8	3.9	271	-0.4	1,303	-0.1	36,195
Meade County, SD	13,345	13,146	12,738	3.2	1.5	3.2	5.3	3.8	697	3.9	5,271	5.2	43,893
Pennington County, SD	54,234	52,830	52,584	0.5	2.7	3.2	5.2	3.6	3,737	5.1	48,048	10.4	35,963
Reading, PA Metro Area	213,249	210,138	198,712	5.8	1.5	4.8	8.7	4.9	8,274	-0.1	149,151	4.6	43,764
Berks County, PA	213,249	210,138	198,712	5.8	1.5	4.8	8.7	4.9	8,274	-0.1	149,151	4.6	43,764
Redding, CA Metro Area	74,858	78,503	81,748	-4.0	-4.6	7.8	16.8	7.2	4,114	-4.8	47,366	1.3	36,912
Shasta County, CA	74,858	78,503	81,748	-4.0	-4.6	7.8	16.8	7.2	4,114	-4.8	47,366	1.3	36,912
Reno, NV Metro Area	230,111	222,838	210,769	5.7	3.3	6.3	13.0	3.9	11,742	-0.5	173,723	4.8	42,708
Storey County, NV	1,884	2,013	2,266	-11.2	-6.4	7.3	16.7	4.3	87	1.2	588	58.5	28,452
Washoe County, NV	228,227	220,825	208,503	5.9	3.4	6.2	12.9	3.9	11,655	-0.5	173,135	4.7	42,756
Richmond, VA Metro Area	661,671	628,685	592,935	6.0	5.2	4.6	8.0	3.8	30,695	1.5	D	D	D
Amelia County, VA	6,272	6,227	6,317	-1.4	0.7	4.4	8.5	3.5	266	-7.0	1,815	-2.7	29,878
Caroline County, VA	14,882	14,342	12,862	11.5	3.8	5.1	9.6	3.8	386	0.5	3,699	-2.1	34,260
Charles City County, VA	3,769	3,901	3,757	3.8	-3.4	5.2	9.6	4.4	144	3.6	1,547	30.7	36,767
Chesterfield County, VA	179,333	168,602	158,613	6.3	6.4	4.3	7.3	3.2	7,052	3.8	106,893	11.2	42,179
Dinwiddie County, VA	13,536	13,566	12,594	7.7	-0.2	5.3	8.8	4.1	346	-5.7	4,312	4.6	43,869
Goochland County, VA	10,640	10,483	10,343	1.4	1.5	4.1	7.2	3.0	633	1.4	D	D	D
Hanover County, VA	56,478	54,430	53,511	1.7	3.8	3.9	6.6	3.0	3,066	1.7	43,788	11.2	37,186
Henrico County, VA	178,200	167,701	156,494	7.2	6.3	4.3	7.3	3.4	9,002	3.5	164,343	5.9	49,903
King William County, VA	8,810	8,656	7,911	9.4	1.8	4.2	7.5	3.5	305	-8.7	2,911	2.0	48,318
New Kent County, VA	11,200	10,294	8,789	17.1	8.8	3.8	7.2	3.3	347	3.6	2,950	15.2	30,031
Powhatan County, VA	13,816	13,510	13,506	0.0	2.3	3.9	7.1	2.9	660	2.3	4,758	21.5	34,565
Prince George County, VA	14,909	13,962	15,026	-7.1	6.8	5.3	8.1	3.9	472	7.5	9,319	46.7	32,728
Sussex County, VA	4,156	4,281	4,408	-2.9	-2.9	6.8	11.4	5.9	179	-7.3	2,045	-7.4	31,285
Colonial Heights city, VA	8,772	8,533	9,059	-5.8	2.8	4.7	8.3	4.1	656	-6.6	9,633	0.7	24,199
Hopewell city, VA	9,703	9,864	10,276	-4.0	-1.6	7.5	11.6	5.8	419	-9.7	6,699	2.1	53,019
Petersburg city, VA	13,811	13,877	13,965	-0.6	-0.5	9.0	14.0	7.4	716	-3.2	14,120	16.5	34,668
Richmond city, VA	113,384	106,456	95,504	11.5	6.5	5.2	9.5	5.4	6,046	-0.4	121,294	9.7	53,738
Riverside-San Bernardino-Ontario, CA Metro Area	1,961,819	1,866,722	1,704,048	9.5	5.1	6.6	13.7	5.3	68,525	5.4	1,069,244	11.7	38,446
Riverside County, CA	1,035,178	976,444	852,578	14.5	6.0	6.7	13.8	5.4	35,595	6.1	514,885	12.8	36,793

[1]Civilian employment as a percent of the civilian labor force.
[2]For the pay period including March 12 of the year shown.

Table C-4. Labor Force and Private Business Establishments and Employment—*Continued*

Metropolitan statistical area, division, and component county	Civilian labor force								Private nonfarm businesses				
	Total			Percent change		Unemployment rate[1]			Establishments		Employment[2]		Annual payroll per employee 2014 (dollars)
	2015	2010	2005	2005–2010	2010–2015	2015	2010	2005	2014	Change 2010–2014	2014	Change 2010–2014	
San Bernardino County, CA	926,641	890,278	851,470	4.6	4.1	6.5	13.5	5.2	32,930	4.6	554,359	10.6	39,981
Roanoke, VA Metro Area	158,927	159,127	149,437	6.5	-0.1	4.4	7.6	3.5	8,065	-1.5	135,834	2.7	39,598
Botetourt County, VA	17,546	17,700	17,017	4.0	-0.9	4.2	6.4	3.0	719	-3.2	9,939	13.4	39,454
Craig County, VA	2,431	2,441	2,500	-2.4	-0.4	5.5	7.9	3.9	59	0.0	345	-10.9	27,136
Franklin County, VA	26,923	27,622	25,337	9.0	-2.5	4.6	8.7	3.7	1,178	4.2	12,513	12.9	27,024
Roanoke County, VA	49,551	49,258	46,636	5.6	0.6	3.9	6.3	3.0	2,013	-4.2	28,109	-7.5	37,007
Roanoke city, VA	49,475	49,317	45,225	9.0	0.3	4.9	8.7	4.2	3,133	-1.8	66,295	5.2	41,479
Salem city, VA	13,001	12,789	12,722	0.5	1.7	4.4	6.9	3.2	963	-0.1	18,633	0.0	45,568
Rochester, MN Metro Area	118,535	115,857	113,329	2.2	2.3	3.2	6.3	3.6	5,140	2.3	98,888	8.9	46,569
Dodge County, MN	11,481	11,307	11,172	1.2	1.5	3.7	6.9	3.9	440	4.5	4,265	5.1	44,912
Fillmore County, MN	11,416	11,246	11,274	-0.2	1.5	4.1	7.5	4.2	598	-4.2	4,620	-6.8	30,961
Olmsted County, MN	83,552	81,197	78,290	3.7	2.9	3.0	5.9	3.5	3,539	4.2	83,892	10.3	48,508
Wabasha County, MN	12,086	12,107	12,593	-3.9	-0.2	3.6	7.1	4.1	563	-3.3	6,111	6.6	32,897
Rochester, NY Metro Area	525,622	546,181	547,998	-0.3	-3.8	5.2	8.1	4.6	24,531	1.8	433,909	3.3	42,254
Livingston County, NY	31,149	32,754	32,873	-0.4	-4.9	5.4	8.1	5.0	1,239	-1.2	13,183	3.9	32,520
Monroe County, NY	365,058	378,251	376,359	0.5	-3.5	5.2	8.0	4.5	17,499	2.4	343,350	3.4	43,383
Ontario County, NY	55,067	56,368	56,825	-0.8	-2.3	4.8	7.4	4.5	2,878	3.0	44,462	4.6	41,676
Orleans County, NY	18,026	19,149	19,959	-4.1	-5.9	6.5	9.6	5.6	655	-2.4	7,918	-3.5	32,691
Wayne County, NY	44,518	47,429	48,987	-3.2	-6.1	5.4	8.9	4.9	1,720	-0.8	19,905	1.1	37,492
Yates County, NY	11,804	12,230	12,995	-5.9	-3.5	5.0	7.4	4.3	540	-1.8	5,091	0.7	29,816
Rockford, IL Metro Area	168,616	177,527	165,009	7.6	-5.0	7.0	14.0	6.4	7,309	-2.6	132,384	4.8	41,191
Boone County, IL	26,362	27,437	24,516	11.9	-3.9	6.6	13.8	6.6	838	-2.0	14,682	29.2	44,061
Winnebago County, IL	142,254	150,090	140,493	6.8	-5.2	7.1	14.0	6.3	6,471	-2.7	117,702	2.4	40,833
Rocky Mount, NC Metro Area	67,015	72,942	68,411	6.6	-8.1	8.1	13.7	6.9	2,787	-7.1	47,893	-3.4	36,256
Edgecombe County, NC	23,078	25,497	24,224	5.3	-9.5	9.6	15.7	8.4	737	-8.4	12,307	-13.2	32,081
Nash County, NC	43,937	47,445	44,187	7.4	-7.4	7.3	12.6	6.0	2,050	-6.6	35,586	0.6	37,700
Rome, GA Metro Area	42,787	45,087	50,139	-10.1	-5.1	6.6	11.8	5.2	1,942	-2.0	33,947	0.0	36,412
Floyd County, GA	42,787	45,087	50,139	-10.1	-5.1	6.6	11.8	5.2	1,942	-2.0	33,947	0.0	36,412
Sacramento--Roseville--Arden-Arcade, CA Metro Area	1,060,164	1,049,782	1,011,984	3.7	1.0	5.9	12.4	4.9	46,077	3.5	669,449	7.8	48,982
El Dorado County, CA	89,121	91,129	91,050	0.1	-2.2	5.7	12.2	4.8	4,317	1.3	42,457	3.5	41,379
Placer County, CA	178,176	173,338	164,249	5.5	2.8	5.0	11.6	4.3	9,880	6.1	131,786	11.4	49,662
Sacramento County, CA	688,999	683,127	664,327	2.8	0.9	6.0	12.6	4.9	27,976	3.1	435,440	7.7	50,049
Yolo County, CA	103,868	102,188	92,358	10.6	1.6	6.4	12.1	5.5	3,904	2.6	59,766	3.9	45,114
Saginaw, MI Metro Area	89,015	90,722	98,365	-7.8	-1.9	5.5	12.2	8.0	4,368	-2.8	77,998	5.4	37,606
Saginaw County, MI	89,015	90,722	98,365	-7.8	-1.9	5.5	12.2	8.0	4,368	-2.8	77,998	5.4	37,606
St. Cloud, MN Metro Area	110,552	106,774	102,805	3.9	3.5	3.8	7.5	4.4	5,288	1.0	95,502	6.9	39,792
Benton County, MN	21,867	21,100	22,165	-4.8	3.6	4.4	8.7	4.7	925	2.2	16,813	20.3	35,290
Stearns County, MN	88,685	85,674	80,640	6.2	3.5	3.6	7.2	4.3	4,363	0.7	78,689	4.4	40,753
St. George, UT Metro Area	63,906	56,776	56,944	-0.3	12.6	4.0	10.5	4.0	4,381	14.8	42,838	19.0	31,273
Washington County, UT	63,906	56,776	56,944	-0.3	12.6	4.0	10.5	4.0	4,381	14.8	42,838	19.0	31,273
St. Joseph, MO-KS Metro Area	66,285	66,123	64,845	2.0	0.2	4.5	9.0	5.8	2,959	-9.2	47,077	-3.4	39,212
Doniphan County, KS	4,339	4,540	4,436	2.3	-4.4	4.4	8.8	6.3	156	-4.3	1,447	24.5	33,064
Andrew County, MO	10,011	9,898	9,805	0.9	1.1	4.2	8.3	5.2	292	-14.6	1,734	-1.4	27,765
Buchanan County, MO	46,861	46,660	45,542	2.5	0.4	4.6	9.2	5.8	2,294	-9.1	41,950	-4.5	40,252
DeKalb County, MO	5,074	5,025	5,062	-0.7	1.0	4.7	8.8	5.9	217	-5.7	1,946	3.5	31,565
St. Louis, MO-IL Metro Area	1,481,428	1,478,074	1,426,498	3.6	0.2	5.1	9.6	5.5	73,306	4.7	1,201,903	3.0	47,994
Bond County, IL	7,944	8,526	8,460	0.8	-6.8	5.3	9.9	5.4	304	-6.5	3,749	-2.7	31,662
Calhoun County, IL	2,375	2,503	2,552	-1.9	-5.1	6.8	10.2	6.1	87	-10.3	590	-2.3	21,997
Clinton County, IL	20,159	20,546	18,508	11.0	-1.9	4.5	7.3	4.7	855	-1.7	8,652	-2.3	30,349
Jersey County, IL	11,195	11,610	11,464	1.3	-3.6	6.3	9.1	5.3	423	-6.8	4,673	-1.5	26,370
Macoupin County, IL	23,302	24,784	24,383	1.6	-6.0	6.3	10.3	5.7	886	-7.0	8,498	-4.1	31,755
Madison County, IL	133,510	138,751	134,905	2.9	-3.8	6.1	9.8	5.5	5,806	-2.7	83,211	-0.9	41,292
Monroe County, IL	18,055	18,008	17,252	4.4	0.3	4.4	7.3	4.2	796	1.4	8,227	12.0	32,882
St. Clair County, IL	127,292	133,106	121,152	9.9	-4.4	6.6	10.3	6.3	5,217	-4.4	76,601	-2.5	36,607
Franklin County, MO	53,129	53,456	52,490	1.8	-0.6	5.0	11.3	5.8	2,572	-2.0	33,891	10.2	35,855
Jefferson County, MO	118,670	117,544	115,830	1.5	1.0	4.8	10.4	5.4	4,076	0.3	41,053	3.9	33,403
Lincoln County, MO	27,135	26,706	24,529	8.9	1.6	5.2	11.8	5.5	884	-1.8	8,230	5.1	34,330
St. Charles County, MO	217,392	205,228	186,254	10.2	5.9	3.9	8.2	4.2	8,170	2.6	124,616	10.5	39,528
St. Louis County, MO	540,801	535,129	535,866	-0.1	1.1	4.6	8.9	5.2	31,779	6.9	570,809	4.9	53,509
Warren County, MO	17,468	17,262	15,347	12.5	1.2	4.8	11.0	5.4	575	1.4	5,951	2.4	34,015
St. Louis city, MO	163,001	164,915	157,506	4.7	-1.2	6.1	11.5	8.1	10,876	17.8	223,152	-2.6	53,084
Salem, OR Metro Area	188,784	191,735	183,380	4.6	-1.5	6.0	10.9	6.3	9,096	1.1	111,414	4.0	35,048
Marion County, OR	152,400	155,350	147,824	5.1	-1.9	6.1	11.2	6.5	7,734	0.9	98,245	2.2	35,466
Polk County, OR	36,384	36,385	35,556	2.3	0.0	5.7	9.7	5.6	1,362	2.7	13,169	19.6	31,926
Salinas, CA Metro Area	221,383	215,788	206,565	4.5	2.6	8.1	12.7	7.3	8,420	1.0	102,790	6.6	42,780
Monterey County, CA	221,383	215,788	206,565	4.5	2.6	8.1	12.7	7.3	8,420	1.0	102,790	6.6	42,780
Salisbury, MD-DE Metro Area	184,118	177,111	181,096	-2.2	4.0	6.4	9.8	4.4	10,364	-0.3	121,303	7.6	35,308
Sussex County, DE	97,831	90,239	90,242	0.0	8.4	5.0	8.5	3.7	5,340	-0.4	63,078	11.0	34,561
Somerset County, MD	9,438	9,944	11,436	-13.0	-5.1	8.3	11.9	6.0	357	-6.8	3,792	0.9	33,906
Wicomico County, MD	50,820	50,455	51,702	-2.4	0.7	6.8	9.7	4.2	2,534	0.2	36,723	3.5	37,941
Worcester County, MD	26,029	26,473	27,716	-4.5	-1.7	10.6	13.3	6.6	2,133	0.5	17,710	6.2	32,811
Salt Lake City, UT Metro Area	616,414	575,832	542,619	6.1	7.0	3.4	7.7	4.0	31,072	5.2	560,004	11.3	46,890
Salt Lake County, UT	587,026	548,378	517,454	6.0	7.0	3.3	7.7	4.0	30,279	5.2	549,047	11.4	47,058
Tooele County, UT	29,388	27,454	25,165	9.1	7.0	4.1	8.3	4.4	793	6.6	10,957	5.2	38,452
San Angelo, TX Metro Area	55,306	53,468	52,796	1.3	3.4	4.1	6.5	4.3	2,850	8.1	40,957	12.6	37,415

[1] Civilian employment as a percent of the civilian labor force.
[2] For the pay period including March 12 of the year shown.

Table C-4. Labor Force and Private Business Establishments and Employment—*Continued*

Metropolitan statistical area, division, and component county	Civilian labor force								Private nonfarm businesses				
	Total			Percent change		Unemployment rate[1]			Establishments		Employment[2]		Annual payroll per employee 2014 (dollars)
	2015	2010	2005	2005–2010	2010–2015	2015	2010	2005	2014	Change 2010–2014	2014	Change 2010–2014	
Irion County, TX	821	873	957	-8.8	-6.0	3.7	5.3	3.6	65	38.3	609	119.1	71,015
Tom Green County, TX	54,485	52,595	51,839	1.5	3.6	4.1	6.6	4.3	2,785	7.5	40,348	11.8	36,908
San Antonio-New Braunfels, TX Metro Area	1,099,596	1,017,400	894,737	13.7	8.1	3.8	7.2	5.0	43,171	7.1	798,637	11.2	42,566
Atascosa County, TX	20,621	19,631	19,011	3.3	5.0	4.8	8.2	5.2	757	20.3	11,462	76.9	50,787
Bandera County, TX	9,180	9,176	9,665	-5.1	0.0	4.0	7.8	4.5	355	-1.4	2,956	47.1	28,513
Bexar County, TX	874,901	812,516	714,126	13.8	7.7	3.8	7.3	5.1	34,489	6.1	688,074	9.4	43,105
Comal County, TX	60,421	53,489	48,830	9.5	13.0	3.7	7.0	4.5	3,150	12.3	41,385	17.1	38,373
Guadalupe County, TX	72,288	64,924	51,700	25.6	11.3	3.6	6.7	4.6	1,927	8.3	30,511	21.0	40,143
Kendall County, TX	18,785	16,412	14,298	14.8	14.5	3.3	6.2	4.2	1,150	5.5	11,127	10.2	39,134
Medina County, TX	20,564	20,017	19,420	3.1	2.7	4.4	7.5	4.9	702	9.9	6,946	31.1	31,913
Wilson County, TX	22,836	21,235	17,687	20.1	7.5	3.8	6.8	4.8	641	21.6	6,176	29.3	32,330
San Diego-Carlsbad, CA Metro Area	1,563,836	1,515,198	1,489,799	1.7	3.2	5.2	10.8	4.3	79,958	5.5	1,202,583	9.2	51,349
San Diego County, CA	1,563,836	1,515,198	1,489,799	1.7	3.2	5.2	10.8	4.3	79,958	5.5	1,202,583	9.2	51,349
San Francisco-Oakland-Hayward, CA Metro Area	**2,505,850**	**2,320,104**	**2,146,852**	**8.1**	**8.0**	**4.3**	**9.9**	**4.8**	**124,273**	**5.6**	**1,969,853**	**11.4**	**79,655**
Oakland-Hayward-Berkeley, CA Division	*1,374,757*	*1,308,069*	*1,244,122*	*5.1*	*5.1*	*4.8*	*10.9*	*5.0*	*60,630*	*4.6*	*929,824*	*8.6*	*63,417*
Alameda County, CA	824,809	782,522	734,258	6.6	5.4	4.7	10.9	5.1	37,901	5.2	622,942	10.7	63,430
Contra Costa County, CA	549,948	525,547	509,864	3.1	4.6	5.0	11.0	4.8	22,729	3.8	306,882	4.6	63,390
San Francisco-Redwood City-South San Francisco, CA Division	*989,970*	*879,023*	*773,635*	*13.6*	*12.6*	*3.5*	*8.7*	*4.6*	*53,842*	*7.1*	*940,445*	*14.8*	*97,959*
San Francisco County, CA	548,004	486,019	413,337	17.6	12.8	3.6	8.9	5.0	33,189	8.5	573,297	16.8	92,332
San Mateo County, CA	441,966	393,004	360,298	9.1	12.5	3.4	8.4	4.2	20,653	5.0	367,148	11.8	106,747
San Rafael, CA Division	*141,123*	*133,012*	*129,095*	*3.0*	*6.1*	*3.5*	*7.9*	*3.9*	*9,801*	*2.9*	*99,584*	*7.4*	*58,405*
Marin County, CA	141,123	133,012	129,095	3.0	6.1	3.5	7.9	3.9	9,801	2.9	99,584	7.4	58,405
San Jose-Sunnyvale-Santa Clara, CA Metro Area	1,048,170	954,431	839,860	13.6	9.8	4.3	10.5	5.4	47,951	6.5	973,967	13.6	104,438
San Benito County, CA	29,763	27,906	24,499	13.9	6.7	7.6	15.1	8.1	932	2.2	10,868	8.9	40,152
Santa Clara County, CA	1,018,407	926,525	815,361	13.6	9.9	4.2	10.4	5.3	47,019	6.6	963,099	13.7	105,163
San Luis Obispo-Paso Robles-Arroyo Grande, CA Metro Area	143,293	133,651	131,479	1.7	7.2	4.6	10.1	4.3	8,028	3.2	89,509	11.1	39,213
San Luis Obispo County, CA	143,293	133,651	131,479	1.7	7.2	4.6	10.1	4.3	8,028	3.2	89,509	11.1	39,213
Santa Cruz-Watsonville, CA Metro Area	144,248	141,717	142,992	-0.9	1.8	7.5	13.3	6.3	6,830	0.7	72,301	6.2	43,481
Santa Cruz County, CA	144,248	141,717	142,992	-0.9	1.8	7.5	13.3	6.3	6,830	0.7	72,301	6.2	43,481
Santa Fe, NM Metro Area	71,658	73,760	76,704	-3.8	-2.8	5.4	6.8	4.1	4,711	-1.4	45,219	2.5	39,456
Santa Fe County, NM	71,658	73,760	76,704	-3.8	-2.8	5.4	6.8	4.1	4,711	-1.4	45,219	2.5	39,456
Santa Maria-Santa Barbara, CA Metro Area	220,001	212,267	213,206	-0.4	3.6	5.3	9.7	4.3	11,296	0.8	141,785	5.4	48,152
Santa Barbara County, CA	220,001	212,267	213,206	-0.4	3.6	5.3	9.7	4.3	11,296	0.8	141,785	5.4	48,152
Santa Rosa, CA Metro Area	260,344	244,634	253,410	-3.5	6.4	4.5	10.8	4.4	13,523	2.6	158,918	11.1	46,494
Sonoma County, CA	260,344	244,634	253,410	-3.5	6.4	4.5	10.8	4.4	13,523	2.6	158,918	11.1	46,494
Savannah, GA Metro Area	175,755	167,555	165,458	1.3	4.9	5.6	9.8	4.4	8,717	4.0	139,798	11.1	40,534
Bryan County, GA	15,784	14,455	15,280	-5.4	9.2	5.2	9.6	4.0	622	6.5	5,550	1.5	28,778
Chatham County, GA	133,265	127,323	124,569	2.2	4.7	5.7	9.9	4.6	7,416	4.5	126,850	11.7	41,205
Effingham County, GA	26,706	25,777	25,609	0.7	3.6	5.0	9.6	4.0	679	-2.6	7,398	9.4	37,842
Scranton--Wilkes-Barre--Hazleton, PA Metro Are .	278,915	281,080	277,022	1.5	-0.8	6.0	9.5	5.6	13,208		238,759	5.5	37,518
Lackawanna County, PA	106,388	106,987	105,324	1.6	-0.6	5.7	9.0	5.3	5,372	0.0	96,324	0.6	34,879
Luzerne County, PA	158,303	159,759	157,434	1.5	-0.9	6.3	10.0	5.8	7,169	-2.1	131,081	7.2	37,339
Wyoming County, PA	14,224	14,334	14,264	0.5	-0.8	5.9	8.8	5.2	667	3.1	11,354	38.8	61,978
Seattle-Tacoma-Bellevue, WA Metro Area	**1,971,002**	**1,888,261**	**1,727,043**	**9.3**	**4.4**	**4.9**	**9.7**	**4.8**	**99,432**	**2.7**	**1,574,478**	**9.7**	**63,666**
Seattle-Bellevue-Everett, WA Division	*1,579,039*	*1,492,417*	*1,357,888*	*9.9*	*5.8*	*4.5*	*9.4*	*4.5*	*82,823*	*3.3*	*1,333,184*	*10.0*	*67,592*
King County, WA	1,177,297	1,105,906	1,011,681	9.3	6.5	4.4	9.0	4.4	65,314	3.4	1,096,927	9.8	71,501
Snohomish County, WA	401,742	386,511	346,207	11.6	3.9	4.8	10.7	4.8	17,509	2.8	236,257	11.0	49,447
Tacoma-Lakewood, WA Division	*391,963*	*395,844*	*369,155*	*7.2*		*6.3*	*10.4*	*6.1*	*16,609*	*0.1*	*241,294*	*7.9*	*41,974*
Pierce County, WA	391,963	395,844	369,155	7.2		6.3	10.4	6.1	16,609	0.1	241,294	7.9	41,974
Sebastian-Vero Beach, FL Metro Area	61,307	61,384	59,484	3.2	-0.1	6.8	13.9	4.8	4,058	4.9	40,165	7.7	36,170
Indian River County, FL	61,307	61,384	59,484	3.2	-0.1	6.8	13.9	4.8	4,058	4.9	40,165	7.7	36,170
Sebring, FL Metro Area	35,272	37,247	39,983	-6.8	-5.3	7.4	12.5	4.2	1,833	-7.4	19,520	3.7	29,723
Highlands County, FL	35,272	37,247	39,983	-6.8	-5.3	7.4	12.5	4.2	1,833	-7.4	19,520	3.7	29,723
Sheboygan, WI Metro Area	61,368	62,238	64,550	-3.6	-1.4	3.8	9.3	4.0	2,635	-1.7	51,649	2.1	40,435
Sheboygan County, WI	61,368	62,238	64,550	-3.6	-1.4	3.8	9.3	4.0	2,635	-1.7	51,649	2.1	40,435
Sherman-Denison, TX Metro Area	60,503	59,489	56,416	5.4	1.7	4.0	8.2	5.4	2,517	-0.2	39,698	2.2	33,629
Grayson County, TX	60,503	59,489	56,416	5.4	1.7	4.0	8.2	5.4	2,517	-0.2	39,698	2.2	33,629
Shreveport-Bossier City, LA Metro Area	195,684	201,600	199,914	0.8	-2.9	6.8	7.8	6.0	9,980	0.0	160,556	2.1	37,132
Bossier Parish, LA	58,126	56,576	51,496	9.9	2.7	5.6	6.1	5.4	2,446	1.7	37,056	5.2	31,572
Caddo Parish, LA	110,757	116,799	117,535	-0.6	-5.2	7.1	8.1	6.1	6,310	-0.7	106,795	0.1	38,286
De Soto Parish, LA	11,111	11,394	11,419	-0.2	-2.5	7.9	8.8	6.9	422	5.8	5,583	26.4	51,033
Webster Parish, LA	15,690	16,831	19,464	-13.5	-6.8	8.7	10.4	6.4	802	-2.4	11,122	2.6	37,593
Sierra Vista-Douglas, AZ Metro Area	50,040	57,023	55,774	2.2	-12.2	7.4	9.3	4.8	2,222	-6.2	26,487	-8.8	33,577
Cochise County, AZ	50,040	57,023	55,774	2.2	-12.2	7.4	9.3	4.8	2,222	-6.2	26,487	-8.8	33,577
Sioux City, IA-NE-SD Metro Area	92,977	92,723	88,637	4.6	0.3	3.5	6.2	4.5	4,394	-1.9	76,646	2.0	36,250
Plymouth County, IA	14,833	14,568	14,087	3.4	1.8	2.8	4.5	3.5	693	-1.4	9,898	6.4	38,537
Woodbury County, IA	55,883	55,997	53,329	5.0	-0.2	3.7	6.6	4.8	2,672	-3.0	46,158	-0.7	33,310
Dakota County, NE	11,070	11,299	10,531	7.3	-2.0	3.5	7.3	4.7	430	-0.2	10,773	6.9	37,982
Dixon County, NE	3,089	3,115	3,144	-0.9	-0.8	3.3	4.8	3.9	104	-8.0	1,079	2.5	31,767
Union County, SD	8,102	7,744	7,546	2.6	4.6	3.4	5.8	4.0	495	4.0	8,738	6.0	47,610
Sioux Falls, SD Metro Area	144,580	133,561	120,564	10.8	8.3	2.6	4.8	3.4	7,302	3.9	133,393	8.7	42,117
Lincoln County, SD	30,133	26,312	19,303	36.3	14.5	2.3	3.9	3.0	1,329	18.4	14,621	33.5	40,086
McCook County, SD	3,199	3,241	2,962	9.4	-1.3	2.4	4.9	3.4	184	5.1	1,039	16.6	26,158

[1]Civilian employment as a percent of the civilian labor force.
[2]For the pay period including March 12 of the year shown.

Table C-4. Labor Force and Private Business Establishments and Employment—*Continued*

Metropolitan statistical area, division, and component county	Civilian labor force								Private nonfarm businesses				
	Total			Percent change		Unemployment rate[1]			Establishments		Employment[2]		Annual payroll per employee 2014 (dollars)
	2015	2010	2005	2005–2010	2010–2015	2015	2010	2005	2014	Change 2010–2014	2014	Change 2010–2014	
Minnehaha County, SD	106,517	99,159	93,785	5.7	7.4	2.7	5.0	3.5	5,523	0.8	116,138	6.4	42,659
Turner County, SD	4,731	4,849	4,514	7.4	-2.4	2.7	4.6	3.7	266	5.6	1,595	-8.4	31,684
South Bend-Mishawaka, IN-MI Metro Area	155,200	155,046	161,819	-4.2	0.1	5.0	11.5	5.3	6,465	-3.8	123,813	5.5	37,409
St. Joseph County, IN	130,912	130,463	134,160	-2.8	0.3	5.0	11.6	5.3	5,740	-3.7	116,701	5.7	37,750
Cass County, MI	24,288	24,583	27,659	-11.1	-1.2	4.8	11.4	5.1	725	-4.9	7,112	3.3	31,821
Spartanburg, SC Metro Area	150,795	144,213	144,362	-0.1	4.6	5.9	12.3	7.8	6,575	-3.6	128,014	11.7	41,466
Spartanburg County, SC	139,121	131,821	131,691	0.1	5.5	5.7	11.8	7.5	6,146	-3.0	121,579	12.2	42,085
Union County, SC	11,674	12,392	12,671	-2.2	-5.8	7.8	17.7	10.8	429	-10.6	6,435	2.8	29,764
Spokane-Spokane Valley, WA Metro Area	250,194	262,377	247,213	6.1	-4.6	6.6	10.4	6.1	13,449	-0.4	184,736	1.7	41,796
Pend Oreille County, WA	4,624	5,148	5,067	1.6	-10.2	9.5	15.3	8.4	217	-6.9	1,581	-1.4	40,980
Spokane County, WA	227,976	238,125	224,140	6.2	-4.3	6.4	10.1	5.9	12,389	0.2	176,491	2.0	42,011
Stevens County, WA	17,594	19,104	18,006	6.1	-7.9	8.8	13.1	8.0	843	-6.4	6,664	-6.7	36,302
Springfield, IL Metro Area	111,709	115,875	112,103	3.4	-3.6	5.2	7.7	4.5	5,233	-2.5	84,441	1.5	39,832
Menard County, IL	6,767	7,148	6,982	2.4	-5.3	4.8	7.5	4.4	209	-7.1	1,230	-13.7	32,093
Sangamon County, IL	104,942	108,727	105,121	3.4	-3.5	5.3	7.7	4.5	5,024	-2.3	83,211	1.8	39,946
Springfield, MA Metro Area	307,893	306,283	311,982	-1.8	0.5	6.1	9.4	5.3	13,217	-0.2	225,499	3.0	40,835
Hampden County, MA	221,258	220,857	224,160	-1.5	0.2	6.8	10.4	5.8	9,669	-0.4	166,806	1.8	43,719
Hampshire County, MA	86,635	85,426	87,822	-2.7	1.4	4.4	6.8	4.0	3,548	0.2	58,693	6.4	32,639
Springfield, MO Metro Area	233,488	223,668	212,489	5.3	4.4	4.3	8.8	4.3	11,601	3.4	175,052	7.1	36,665
Christian County, MO	43,444	40,861	37,337	9.4	6.3	4.2	8.4	4.3	1,678	4.5	14,130	14.1	28,606
Dallas County, MO	7,132	7,285	7,448	-2.2	-2.1	6.2	12.6	5.4	273	7.9	2,384	-3.3	18,422
Greene County, MO	151,650	144,734	137,034	5.6	4.8	4.1	8.3	4.2	8,434	3.6	146,256	6.9	37,953
Polk County, MO	14,499	14,405	13,964	3.2	0.7	5.2	10.3	4.9	576	0.2	7,338	7.3	37,455
Webster County, MO	16,763	16,383	16,706	-1.9	2.3	5.0	10.5	4.7	640	-0.8	4,944	1.5	29,240
Springfield, OH Metro Area	64,200	68,266	70,529	-3.2	-6.0	5.0	11.0	6.5	2,321	-5.2	40,253	-1.1	34,746
Clark County, OH	64,200	68,266	70,529	-3.2	-6.0	5.0	11.0	6.5	2,321	-5.2	40,253	-1.1	34,746
State College, PA Metro Area	77,888	77,335	72,388	6.8	0.7	3.8	5.9	4.0	3,290	3.2	45,984	6.8	37,296
Centre County, PA	77,888	77,335	72,388	6.8	0.7	3.8	5.9	4.0	3,290	3.2	45,984	6.8	37,296
Staunton-Waynesboro, VA Metro Area	58,831	59,146	57,325	3.2	-0.5	4.3	7.6	3.2	2,779	-0.6	39,094	3.2	34,947
Augusta County, VA	36,792	37,130	36,267	2.4	-0.9	4.1	7.1	3.1	1,415	1.8	19,027	2.7	39,438
Staunton city, VA	11,992	11,846	11,231	5.5	1.2	4.4	7.8	3.3	761	-2.3	10,609	4.9	28,011
Waynesboro city, VA	10,047	10,170	9,827	3.5	-1.2	4.7	9.0	3.8	603	-4.0	9,458	2.4	33,693
Stockton-Lodi, CA Metro Area	316,903	311,437	283,588	9.8	1.8	8.9	16.5	7.9	10,825	0.0	168,367	4.8	41,079
San Joaquin County, CA	316,903	311,437	283,588	9.8	1.8	8.9	16.5	7.9	10,825	0.0	168,367	4.8	41,079
Sumter, SC Metro Area	44,413	44,420	46,446	-4.4	0.0	6.9	12.5	8.5	1,777	-2.4	31,005	12.3	33,070
Sumter County, SC	44,413	44,420	46,446	-4.4	0.0	6.9	12.5	8.5	1,777	-2.4	31,005	12.3	33,070
Syracuse, NY Metro Area	312,827	331,466	330,039	0.4	-5.6	5.4	8.5	4.9	15,392	0.7	258,096	2.3	41,677
Madison County, NY	33,434	35,586	36,109	-1.4	-6.0	5.7	8.3	5.1	1,430	0.9	17,019	-1.2	33,569
Onondaga County, NY	224,505	236,994	233,689	1.4	-5.3	5.0	8.0	4.5	11,809	0.5	217,506	2.8	42,467
Oswego County, NY	54,888	58,886	60,241	-2.2	-6.8	7.2	10.6	6.2	2,153	2.0	23,571	0.9	40,247
Tallahassee, FL Metro Area	186,294	190,683	179,409	6.3	-2.3	5.2	8.4	3.2	8,771	1.0	108,416	4.6	38,235
Gadsden County, FL	18,463	20,080	20,488	-2.0	-8.1	7.0	11.8	3.9	636	-1.5	8,523	-3.9	35,848
Jefferson County, FL	5,424	6,042	6,814	-11.3	-10.2	5.8	9.9	3.2	245	-5.4	1,574	-5.9	28,686
Leon County, FL	148,346	149,972	137,708	8.9	-1.1	5.0	7.9	3.2	7,471	1.4	95,086	5.8	38,945
Wakulla County, FL	14,061	14,589	14,399	1.3	-3.6	4.6	8.4	2.8	419	0.5	3,233	2.5	28,270
Tampa-St. Petersburg-Clearwater, FL Metro Area	1,447,077	1,384,699	1,258,615	10.0	4.5	5.1	11.1	4.0	72,931	5.1	1,038,508	11.4	43,281
Hernando County, FL	66,609	66,470	57,093	16.4	0.2	6.8	13.5	4.9	3,004	2.5	30,578	7.3	30,465
Hillsborough County, FL	689,463	645,687	570,252	13.2	6.8	5.0	10.7	3.8	34,020	6.8	557,545	13.9	46,405
Pasco County, FL	214,802	207,364	177,737	16.7	3.6	5.8	11.9	4.4	8,884	6.7	87,322	15.9	32,924
Pinellas County, FL	476,203	465,178	453,533	2.6	2.4	4.9	10.8	3.9	27,023	2.9	363,063	7.1	42,054
Terre Haute, IN Metro Area	77,277	81,204	80,637	0.7	-4.8	6.1	11.2	7.0	3,563	-4.8	59,126	1.1	36,265
Clay County, IN	12,370	13,180	13,314		-6.1	5.3	11.1	7.0	468	-6.4	5,864	17.1	29,549
Sullivan County, IN	8,688	9,085	9,294	-2.2	-4.4	6.2	10.1	7.5	343	-2.8	4,421	26.5	43,988
Vermillion County, IN	7,211	7,810	8,131	-3.9	-7.7	7.1	12.9	7.4	265	-7.7	3,119	-21.3	50,552
Vigo County, IN	49,008	51,129	49,898	2.5	-4.1	6.1	11.2	6.8	2,487	-4.4	45,722	-0.6	35,405
Texarkana, TX-AR Metro Area	64,636	68,991	68,421	0.8	-6.3	5.0	7.6	5.2	3,075	0.3	46,704	4.4	34,722
Little River County, AR	5,626	6,220	6,529	-4.7	-9.5	5.7	7.7	4.7	163	-3.6	2,704	-6.7	48,791
Miller County, AR	19,710	20,560	19,724	4.2	-4.1	5.2	5.8	4.8	725	1.1	11,550	2.9	36,321
Bowie County, TX	39,300	42,211	42,168	0.1	-6.9	4.8	8.4	5.4	2,187	0.3	32,450	6.0	32,981
The Villages, FL Metro Area	28,583	25,310	25,555		12.9	7.5	13.3	3.4	1,334	17.3	18,994	33.2	36,689
Sumter County, FL	28,583	25,310	25,555		12.9	7.5	13.3	3.4	1,334	17.3	18,994	33.2	36,689
Toledo, OH Metro Area	301,153	309,116	315,736	-2.1	-2.6	5.0	11.2	6.7	13,313	-2.5	262,741	5.4	40,560
Fulton County, OH	22,444	23,144	23,151	0.0	-3.0	4.9	11.8	6.3	935	-3.8	14,491	-2.3	40,323
Lucas County, OH	209,263	217,424	224,694	-3.2	-3.8	5.3	11.5	7.0	9,627	-3.2	197,169	4.7	40,240
Wood County, OH	69,446	68,548	67,891	1.0	1.3	4.3	9.9	5.8	2,751	0.8	51,081	10.9	41,860
Topeka, KS Metro Area	121,135	124,269	123,539	0.6	-2.5	4.3	7.1	5.5	5,166	-4.3	85,311	-0.9	39,718
Jackson County, KS	7,389	7,509	7,157	4.9	-1.6	3.7	6.2	5.8	254	-5.9	2,933	-0.8	27,587
Jefferson County, KS	10,205	10,671	10,146	5.2	-4.4	4.2	7.5	5.2	303	-5.6	2,285	-3.4	36,988
Osage County, KS	8,147	8,618	9,123	-5.5	-5.5	5.0	8.3	6.2	265	-1.9	2,686	-18.3	20,023
Shawnee County, KS	91,606	93,584	93,338	0.3	-2.1	4.3	7.0	5.5	4,218	-4.4	76,525	0.0	41,108
Wabaunsee County, KS	3,788	3,887	3,775	3.0	-2.5	3.9	6.5	4.5	126	0.8	882	-7.2	26,541
Trenton, NJ Metro Area	199,062	192,625	193,721	-0.6	3.3	4.8	8.4	3.9	9,627	-1.3	182,255	3.7	66,109
Mercer County, NJ	199,062	192,625	193,721	-0.6	3.3	4.8	8.4	3.9	9,627	-1.3	182,255	3.7	66,109
Tucson, AZ Metro Area	464,150	478,743	441,581	8.4	-3.0	5.6	9.3	4.5	19,931	-1.9	303,841	0.9	38,734
Pima County, AZ	464,150	478,743	441,581	8.4	-3.0	5.6	9.3	4.5	19,931	-1.9	303,841	0.9	38,734
Tulsa, OK Metro Area	476,532	462,935	442,814	4.5	2.9	4.2	7.3	4.4	24,173	0.4	398,738	8.4	46,699
Creek County, OK	31,702	31,807	32,063	-0.8	-0.3	4.8	8.6	5.7	1,389	-1.4	16,906	15.4	40,068

[1]Civilian employment as a percent of the civilian labor force.
[2]For the pay period including March 12 of the year shown.

Table C-4. Labor Force and Private Business Establishments and Employment—*Continued*

Metropolitan statistical area, division, and component county	Civilian labor force								Private nonfarm businesses				
	Total			Percent change		Unemployment rate[1]			Establishments		Employment[2]		Annual payroll per employee 2014 (dollars)
	2015	2010	2005	2005–2010	2010–2015	2015	2010	2005	2014	Change 2010–2014	2014	Change 2010–2014	
Okmulgee County, OK	16,414	16,887	16,816	0.4	-2.8	6.4	9.8	6.3	694	-0.9	7,525	0.1	28,673
Osage County, OK	21,581	21,250	20,773	2.3	1.6	5.1	7.8	4.8	598	-2.4	5,911	3.6	32,480
Pawnee County, OK	7,566	7,675	7,798	-1.6	-1.4	5.6	9.1	5.0	259	-10.4	2,978	20.9	38,340
Rogers County, OK	44,818	43,377	39,849	8.9	3.3	4.2	6.9	4.0	1,715	4.4	27,270	17.2	47,349
Tulsa County, OK	318,047	306,671	293,516	4.5	3.7	4.0	7.0	4.1	18,606	0.5	329,662	7.6	48,002
Wagoner County, OK	36,404	35,268	31,999	10.2	3.2	4.0	6.8	4.1	912	0.4	8,486	8.3	36,024
Tuscaloosa, AL Metro Area	111,973	108,059	99,823	8.3	3.6	5.7	9.8	4.0	4,454	-0.9	78,365	4.9	39,666
Hale County, AL	6,102	6,445	7,053	-8.6	-5.3	7.8	15.1	5.4	198	3.1	1,833	-13.9	34,183
Pickens County, AL	7,820	7,699	7,960	-3.3	1.6	6.8	13.1	5.4	271	-6.2	2,746	-2.1	30,515
Tuscaloosa County, AL	98,051	93,915	84,810	10.7	4.4	5.5	9.2	3.7	3,985	-0.7	73,786	5.7	40,143
Tyler, TX Metro Area	102,736	101,151	95,360	6.1	1.6	4.5	7.9	5.0	5,734	5.4	90,521	6.2	41,087
Smith County, TX	102,736	101,151	95,360	6.1	1.6	4.5	7.9	5.0	5,734	5.4	90,521	6.2	41,087
Urban Honolulu, HI Metro Area	468,885	446,189	439,257	1.6	5.1	3.4	6.0	2.8	21,195	-1.8	354,302	5.5	42,317
Honolulu County, HI	468,885	446,189	439,257	1.6	5.1	3.4	6.0	2.8	21,195	-1.8	354,302	5.5	42,317
Utica-Rome, NY Metro Area	131,965	143,800	142,904	0.6	-8.2	5.6	7.8	4.9	6,035	-0.6	101,751	2.0	35,775
Herkimer County, NY	28,914	31,552	31,671	-0.4	-8.4	6.3	8.6	5.3	1,127	-3.5	12,379	3.3	32,500
Oneida County, NY	103,051	112,248	111,233	0.9	-8.2	5.4	7.6	4.8	4,908	0.1	89,372	1.8	36,229
Valdosta, GA Metro Area	62,718	64,076	64,829	-1.2	-2.1	6.0	9.6	4.0	3,025	0.2	42,666	D	30,315
Brooks County, GA	6,740	7,309	8,289	-11.8	-7.8	5.9	9.6	4.3	201	1.0	1,999	0.2	31,612
Echols County, GA	1,840	1,876	2,314	-18.9	-1.9	4.7	8.2	3.4	26	44.4	108	D	36,204
Lanier County, GA	3,783	3,872	3,810	1.6	-2.3	6.6	10.5	4.0	98	-11.7	817	-11.6	21,411
Lowndes County, GA	50,355	51,019	50,416	1.2	-1.3	5.9	9.6	4.0	2,700	0.4	39,742	6.7	30,417
Vallejo-Fairfield, CA Metro Area	206,604	202,407	208,486	-2.9	2.1	6.1	12.6	5.3	6,745	0.0	105,212	7.3	47,326
Solano County, CA	206,604	202,407	208,486	-2.9	2.1	6.1	12.6	5.3	6,745	0.0	105,212	7.3	47,326
Victoria, TX Metro Area	49,508	46,435	47,296	-1.8	6.6	4.2	7.6	4.5	2,524	6.7	35,847	14.2	44,844
Goliad County, TX	3,550	3,356	3,397	-1.2	5.8	4.4	7.4	4.8	124	12.7	760	-3.9	40,114
Victoria County, TX	45,958	43,079	43,899	-1.9	6.7	4.1	7.7	4.5	2,400	6.4	35,087	14.7	44,947
Vineland-Bridgeton, NJ Metro Area	67,387	72,379	69,082	4.8	-6.9	8.7	13.0	6.4	2,883	-2.9	44,491	-1.2	37,406
Cumberland County, NJ	67,387	72,379	69,082	4.8	-6.9	8.7	13.0	6.4	2,883	-2.9	44,491	-1.2	37,406
Virginia Beach-Norfolk-Newport News,													
VA-NC Metro Area	839,466	833,871	792,283	5.2	0.7	4.9	7.6	4.0	36,925	-1.9	597,243	0.7	40,597
Currituck County, NC	12,758	12,187	12,065	1.0	4.7	5.9	8.9	3.0	608	4.1	4,648	20.1	35,794
Gates County, NC	5,225	5,459	4,918	11.0	-4.3	5.5	8.0	4.1	117	-10.0	789	-10.7	23,773
Gloucester County, VA	19,306	19,553	19,798	-1.2	-1.3	4.1	6.8	3.1	861	-3.8	7,128	-2.5	26,849
Isle of Wight County, VA	18,858	18,800	17,369	8.2	0.3	4.6	7.1	3.7	637	-0.6	7,236	-25.5	42,925
James City County, VA	34,406	32,243	28,790	12.0	6.7	4.3	6.3	3.2	1,669	1.9	26,468	15.9	36,150
Mathews County, VA	4,106	4,224	4,396	-3.9	-2.8	4.2	6.3	3.0	176	-1.7	1,081	11.3	22,286
York County, VA	31,651	31,289	30,554	2.4	1.2	4.3	6.1	3.1	1,394	-3.9	17,151	-1.2	31,973
Chesapeake city, VA	116,597	113,319	111,678	1.5	2.9	4.5	7.2	3.6	5,302	-1.5	87,289	5.4	39,723
Hampton city, VA	65,159	66,666	66,763	-0.1	-2.3	6.0	9.0	4.5	2,350	-2.5	39,893	-4.7	39,674
Newport News city, VA	90,051	90,663	86,290	5.1	-0.7	5.4	8.3	4.5	3,737	-0.6	88,776	3.7	48,555
Norfolk city, VA	111,318	112,449	96,113	17.0		5.6	8.8	5.1	5,349	-8.4	107,411	-6.5	44,651
Poquoson city, VA	6,263	6,395	6,161	3.8	-2.1	3.8	6.1	2.9	204	-8.1	1,281	-11.9	25,415
Portsmouth city, VA	44,656	45,461	44,821	1.4	-1.8	6.2	9.6	5.4	1,658	-6.2	27,251	-4.1	37,968
Suffolk city, VA	42,106	41,753	37,792	10.5	0.8	5.0	7.6	4.0	1,520	1.5	20,546	-0.7	38,370
Virginia Beach city, VA	230,434	226,894	220,002	3.1	1.6	4.3	6.5	3.4	10,815	0.5	151,195	4.5	38,110
Williamsburg city, VA	6,572	6,516	4,773	36.5	0.9	6.3	10.1	7.3	528	10.0	9,100	-7.1	28,092
Visalia-Porterville, CA Metro Area	203,392	203,021	183,305	10.8	0.2	11.7	17.2	9.4	6,165	0.5	90,454	5.9	36,632
Tulare County, CA	203,392	203,021	183,305	10.8	0.2	11.7	17.2	9.4	6,165	0.5	90,454	5.9	36,632
Waco, TX Metro Area	118,946	120,142	119,278	0.7		4.1	7.4	5.1	5,248	1.9	101,733	4.9	35,218
Falls County, TX	6,454	7,242	7,276	-0.5	-10.9	4.3	8.5	6.2	212	-9.0	1,729	-5.6	28,260
McLennan County, TX	112,492	112,900	112,002	0.8	-0.4	4.1	7.4	5.0	5,036	2.4	100,004	5.1	35,338
Walla Walla, WA Metro Area	29,878	32,489	30,619	6.1	-8.0	5.8	8.1	6.2	1,494	-0.9	19,755	-3.3	36,392
Columbia County, WA	1,721	1,959	1,636	19.7	-12.1	6.4	9.4	8.1	130	3.2	781	5.4	34,905
Walla Walla County, WA	28,157	30,530	28,983	5.3	-7.8	5.8	8.0	6.1	1,364	-1.3	18,974	-3.6	36,453
Warner Robins, GA Metro Area	80,533	84,547	78,315	8.0	-4.7	6.1	9.1	5.1	3,014	0.6	43,911	5.2	32,971
Houston County, GA	65,143	67,099	62,594	7.2	-2.9	5.8	8.5	4.8	2,391	3.9	35,678	6.0	32,248
Peach County, GA	11,354	12,918	11,353	13.8	-12.1	7.9	12.1	6.7	456	-8.1	6,114	-1.2	37,147
Pulaski County, GA	4,036	4,530	4,368	3.7	-10.9	6.5	9.2	5.7	167	-16.1	2,119	12.8	33,104
Washington-Arlington-Alexandria, DC-VA-MD-WV Metro Area	**3,287,741**	**3,150,741**	**2,904,466**	**8.5**	**4.3**	**4.4**	**6.3**	**3.5**	**147,986**	**4.1**	**2,545,212**	**6.8**	**63,121**
Silver Spring-Frederick-Rockville, MD Division	*678,582*	*660,456*	*624,759*	*5.7*	*2.7*	*4.1*	*5.9*	*3.1*	*33,088*	*2.7*	*515,716*	*7.2*	*61,209*
Frederick County, MD	129,295	127,907	120,349	6.3	1.1	4.5	6.9	3.1	5,975	3.1	86,414	6.7	46,165
Montgomery County, MD	549,287	532,549	504,410	5.6	3.1	4.0	5.6	3.1	27,113	2.6	429,302	7.3	64,237
Washington-Arlington-Alexandria, DC-VA-MD-WV Division	*2,609,159*	*2,490,285*	*2,279,707*	*9.2*	*4.8*	*4.5*	*6.5*	*3.6*	*114,898*	*4.5*	*2,029,496*	*6.7*	*63,607*
District of Columbia, DC	388,388	346,065	315,616	9.6	12.2	6.9	9.4	6.4	22,210	3.3	495,453	7.0	74,585
Calvert County, MD	47,681	47,829	46,014	3.9	-0.3	4.6	6.9	3.4	1,671	-2.8	17,579	2.4	41,686
Charles County, MD	80,945	78,219	72,704	7.6	3.5	5.1	6.9	3.4	2,618	-1.9	32,571	3.6	36,389
Prince George's County, MD	490,697	479,606	442,341	8.4	2.3	5.3	7.5	4.5	14,459	1.5	250,865	5.4	46,320
Arlington County, VA	145,058	137,368	123,328	11.4	5.6	2.8	4.1	2.3	6,347	5.4	132,820	5.2	76,071
Clarke County, VA	7,574	7,695	7,738	-0.6	-1.6	4.0	6.7	2.6	357	-9.8	2,872	-11.3	43,222
Culpeper County, VA	23,328	23,262	19,022	22.3	0.3	4.3	7.2	3.3	970	2.4	12,561	8.4	39,620
Fairfax County, VA	620,408	610,520	568,187	7.5	1.6	3.6	5.1	2.6	30,139	4.7	581,452	4.0	74,232
Fauquier County, VA	35,985	35,763	35,413	1.0	0.6	3.9	6.2	2.7	1,784	-0.1	17,262	6.9	41,562
Loudoun County, VA	196,323	175,439	147,280	19.1	11.9	3.6	5.1	2.4	9,486	17.5	136,232	16.1	57,381
Prince William County, VA	231,924	218,394	189,649	15.2	6.2	4.1	6.1	2.7	7,660	9.9	96,572	15.8	39,987
Rappahannock County, VA	3,781	4,025	4,112	-2.1	-6.1	4.1	6.3	2.6	184	0.0	1,043	13.1	32,821

[1]Civilian employment as a percent of the civilian labor force.
[2]For the pay period including March 12 of the year shown.

Table C-4.   Labor Force and Private Business Establishments and Employment—*Continued*

| Metropolitan statistical area, division, and component county | Civilian labor force | | | | | | | | Private nonfarm businesses | | | | |
| | Total | | | Percent change | | Unemployment rate[1] | | | Establishments | | Employment[2] | | Annual payroll per employee 2014 (dollars) |
	2015	2010	2005	2005–2010	2010–2015	2015	2010	2005	2014	Change 2010–2014	2014	Change 2010–2014	
Spotsylvania County, VA	64,130	63,357	61,880	2.4	1.2	4.6	7.0	2.7	2,379	3.7	30,013	16.8	37,055
Stafford County, VA	66,721	63,904	61,558	3.8	4.4	4.5	6.5	2.7	2,180	5.8	30,776	9.0	40,523
Warren County, VA	19,866	20,103	18,604	8.1	-1.2	4.7	8.1	3.1	777	-2.9	10,046	9.9	33,287
Alexandria city, VA	93,782	90,361	84,746	6.6	3.8	3.3	4.9	2.6	4,668	4.0	83,447	5.9	59,216
Fairfax city, VA	13,242	12,663	12,777	-0.9	4.6	3.4	5.4	2.7	2,232	-3.0	31,057	11.8	52,477
Falls Church city, VA	7,797	7,382	6,428	14.8	5.6	3.0	4.9	3.4	851	6.0	9,166	-2.2	46,939
Fredericksburg city, VA	13,679	12,423	11,225	10.7	10.1	5.3	9.0	4.5	1,333	0.4	20,511	-0.2	39,509
Manassas city, VA	22,087	20,972	20,522	2.2	5.3	4.1	7.0	2.9	1,439	2.1	21,039	-5.4	58,483
Manassas Park city, VA	8,166	8,066	6,519	23.7	1.2	4.2	6.2	2.5	322	14.2	3,102	4.1	45,057
Jefferson County, WV	27,597	26,869	24,044	11.7	2.7	4.1	6.7	3.3	832	-3.4	13,462	37.4	31,271
Waterloo-Cedar Falls, IA Metro Area	91,256	91,608	92,114	-0.5	-0.4	4.3	6.0	4.2	4,126	-0.1	81,935	8.9	37,566
Black Hawk County, IA	70,499	70,989	71,506	-0.7	-0.7	4.5	6.2	4.3	3,209	-0.6	69,526	8.2	37,110
Bremer County, IA	14,029	13,864	13,732	1.0	1.2	3.4	4.9	3.7	603	-0.8	9,090	10.4	39,433
Grundy County, IA	6,728	6,755	6,876	-1.8	-0.4	3.7	5.7	3.8	314	6.1	3,319	21.7	42,010
Watertown-Fort Drum, NY Metro Area	46,610	50,310	47,105	6.8	-7.4	6.7	9.3	6.1	2,435	-2.5	29,831	-0.5	34,441
Jefferson County, NY	46,610	50,310	47,105	6.8	-7.4	6.7	9.3	6.1	2,435	-2.5	29,831	-0.5	34,441
Wausau, WI Metro Area	73,833	73,520	74,364	-1.1	0.4	4.1	9.3	4.1	3,243	-4.5	62,652	6.4	40,387
Marathon County, WI	73,833	73,520	74,364	-1.1	0.4	4.1	9.3	4.1	3,243	-4.5	62,652	6.4	40,387
Weirton-Steubenville, WV-OH Metro Area	52,809	58,426	57,537	1.5	-9.6	7.5	13.3	7.6	2,245	-4.9	36,182	-2.6	34,364
Jefferson County, OH	29,552	33,335	31,747	5.0	-11.3	7.4	14.5	7.7	1,272	-5.4	19,023	-1.6	34,257
Brooke County, WV	10,151	10,917	11,095	-1.6	-7.0	7.3	11.4	7.3	394	-1.7	7,204	-8.6	36,816
Hancock County, WV	13,106	14,174	14,695	-3.5	-7.5	7.8	12.1	7.4	579	-6.0	9,955	0.2	32,794
Wenatchee, WA Metro Area	62,791	61,977	59,416	4.3	1.3	5.7	9.2	6.0	3,136	1.0	32,937	2.6	40,072
Chelan County, WA	42,983	42,201	39,450	7.0	1.9	5.5	8.9	6.2	2,441	0.7	26,785	2.8	41,744
Douglas County, WA	19,808	19,776	19,966	0.2		6.3	9.7	5.7	695	1.9	6,152	2.0	32,789
Wheeling, WV-OH Metro Area	66,273	69,968	68,509	2.1	-5.3	6.6	9.9	5.9	3,406	-1.5	56,037	3.5	36,529
Belmont County, OH	31,298	33,462	32,494	3.0	-6.5	6.3	11.3	6.6	1,471	-1.5	19,256	3.7	33,301
Marshall County, WV	14,218	14,680	15,048	-2.4	-3.1	8.4	9.7	5.8	509	3.2	9,456	15.9	44,093
Ohio County, WV	20,757	21,826	20,967	4.1	-4.9	5.6	7.9	4.9	1,426	-3.2	27,325	-0.3	36,185
Wichita, KS Metro Area	312,386	319,316	311,614	2.5	-2.2	4.7	8.6	5.4	14,605	-2.2	261,043	1.3	43,616
Butler County, KS	32,125	33,009	32,038	3.0	-2.7	4.3	7.8	5.5	1,298	0.9	13,420	1.1	33,038
Harvey County, KS	17,264	17,774	18,030	-1.4	-2.9	3.9	7.2	4.5	762	-6.5	13,741	9.8	35,939
Kingman County, KS	3,688	3,862	4,332	-10.8	-4.5	4.4	6.9	4.2	210	-3.2	1,837	-5.9	33,633
Sedgwick County, KS	248,120	252,713	244,942	3.2	-1.8	4.8	8.8	5.5	11,852	-2.2	227,564	1.0	45,001
Sumner County, KS	11,189	11,958	12,272	-2.6	-6.4	4.5	8.9	5.9	483	-1.8	4,481	-1.8	32,645
Wichita Falls, TX Metro Area	64,860	69,420	74,253	-6.5	-6.6	4.3	7.7	4.5	3,495		48,534	2.5	34,410
Archer County, TX	4,180	4,601	5,289	-13.0	-9.2	4.4	6.7	3.5	201	9.2	1,539	23.0	40,561
Clay County, TX	4,935	5,539	6,476	-14.5	-10.9	4.4	7.5	3.8	129	0.8	812	-16.3	27,441
Wichita County, TX	55,745	59,280	62,488	-5.1	-6.0	4.3	7.8	4.7	3,165	-1.7	46,183	2.3	34,328
Williamsport, PA Metro Area	60,975	59,483	59,297	0.3	2.5	5.9	8.9	5.4	2,826	-0.9	46,628	5.1	38,027
Lycoming County, PA	60,975	59,483	59,297	0.3	2.5	5.9	8.9	5.4	2,826	-0.9	46,628	5.1	38,027
Wilmington, NC Metro Area	139,010	132,004	119,805	10.2	5.3	5.5	10.0	4.2	7,902	3.9	95,866	7.8	39,193
New Hanover County, NC	113,185	107,563	97,891	9.9	5.2	5.3	9.7	4.1	6,922	3.4	87,723	7.4	39,911
Pender County, NC	25,825	24,441	21,914	11.5	5.7	6.1	11.4	4.8	980	8.3	8,143	13.1	31,457
Winchester, VA-WV Metro Area	68,991	65,434	61,426	6.5	5.4	4.3	7.9	3.1	3,136	2.1	49,104	10.5	38,652
Frederick County, VA	44,758	41,981	38,283	9.7	6.6	4.0	7.5	2.8	1,488	4.2	22,730	11.2	39,076
Winchester city, VA	14,519	13,688	13,740	-0.4	6.1	4.3	8.3	3.1	1,319	1.0	23,756	11.3	39,460
Hampshire County, WV	9,714	9,765	9,403	3.8	-0.5	5.5	9.1	4.1	329	-2.1	2,618	-1.2	27,647
Winston-Salem, NC Metro Area	317,805	314,873	309,332	1.8	0.9	5.5	10.9	5.0	12,966	-1.1	224,191	6.2	43,631
Davidson County, North Carolina	79,038	80,608	78,306	2.9	-1.9	5.5	12.3	6.0	2,723	-1.7	44,818	33.5	37,161
Davie County, North Carolina	19,841	20,255	19,826	2.2	-2.0	5.0	11.8	4.2	796	0.5	8,359	4.5	31,724
Forsyth County, North Carolina	179,226	172,972	168,092	2.9	3.6	5.5	10.1	4.7	8,247	-0.8	156,618	0.3	47,309
Stokes County, North Carolina	21,991	22,843	23,944	-4.6	-3.7	5.4	11.4	5.0	619	1.6	5,377	-2.1	31,077
Yadkin County, North Carolina	17,709	18,195	19,164	-5.1	-2.7	5.0	11.0	4.6	581	-6.7	9,019	14.1	30,449
Worcester, MA-CT Metro Area	488,301	484,955	459,459	5.5	0.7	5.4	9.1	5.3	19,713	-0.3	313,932	6.3	45,951
Windham County, CT	63,011	64,570	60,903	6.0	-2.4	6.2	10.2	5.5	2,052	-4.5	30,180	6.8	38,952
Worcester County, MA	425,290	420,385	398,556	5.5	1.2	5.3	8.9	5.2	17,661	0.2	283,752	6.2	46,696
Yakima, WA Metro Area	122,052	122,141	117,560	3.9	-0.1	8.0	10.6	7.8	4,653	-0.7	63,154	1.2	37,673
Yakima County, WA	122,052	122,141	117,560	3.9	-0.1	8.0	10.6	7.8	4,653	-0.7	63,154	1.2	37,673
York-Hanover, PA Metro Area	232,848	230,390	218,916	5.2	1.1	4.6	8.4	4.2	8,611	0.4	159,950	5.1	40,057
York County, PA	232,848	230,390	218,916	5.2	1.1	4.6	8.4	4.2	8,611	0.4	159,950	5.1	40,057
Youngstown-Warren-Boardman, OH-PA Metro Area	251,809	268,560	281,253	-4.5	-6.2	6.1	11.8	6.9	12,447	-3.1	202,884	2.9	36,650
Mahoning County, OH	107,101	115,100	119,944	-4.0	-6.9	6.1	11.7	7.1	5,559	-4.1	88,782	6.5	35,764
Trumbull County, OH	91,662	99,834	105,645	-5.5	-8.2	6.5	13.2	7.0	4,094	-4.1	68,435	-3.0	39,405
Mercer County, PA	53,046	53,626	55,664	-3.7	-1.1	5.3	9.5	6.3	2,794	0.4	45,667	5.4	34,244
Yuba City, CA Metro Area	72,961	75,029	65,683	14.2	-2.8	10.2	18.1	9.4	2,498		29,333	1.4	37,584
Sutter County, CA	44,824	45,965	39,999	14.9	-2.5	10.8	18.4	9.6	1,692	-0.8	20,096	1.8	38,199
Yuba County, CA	28,137	29,064	25,684	13.2	-3.2	9.2	17.8	9.0	806	-1.6	9,237	0.4	36,248
Yuma, AZ Metro Area	93,702	92,816	76,067	22.0	1.0	21.8	25.1	15.9	2,907	-1.3	41,082	1.1	31,011
Yuma County, AZ	93,702	92,816	76,067	22.0	1.0	21.8	25.1	15.9	2,907	-1.3	41,082	1.1	31,011

[1]Civilian employment as a percent of the civilian labor force.
[2]For the pay period including March 12 of the year shown.

PART D

MICROPOLITAN AREAS

Page

283   Population and Personal Income

Table D-1.   Population and Personal Income

Micropolitan statistical area component counties	Population							Personal Income				
	2015 estimate (July 1)	2010 census estimates base (April 1)[1]	2000 census estimates base (April 1)[1]	Net change		Percent change		Total (million dollars)		Percent change, 2010–2015	Per capita[4]	
				2010–2015[2]	2000–2010[3]	2010–2015[2]	2000–2010[3]	2015	2010		2015	2010
Aberdeen, SD Micro Area	42,784	40,602	39,835	2,182	767	5.4	1.9	2,131.3	1,693.2	25.9	49,816	41,578
Brown County, SD	38,785	36,531	35,468	2,254	1,063	6.2	3.0	1,939.3	1,533.2	26.5	50,001	41,832
Edmunds County, SD	3,999	4,071	4,367	-72	-296	-1.8	-6.8	192.1	160.0	20.1	48,026	39,286
Aberdeen, WA Micro Area	71,122	72,797	67,141	-1,675	5,656	-2.3	8.4	2,533.7	2,205.0	14.9	35,625	30,265
Grays Harbor County, WA	71,122	72,797	67,141	-1,675	5,656	-2.3	8.4	2,533.7	2,205.0	14.9	35,625	30,265
Ada, OK Micro Area	38,194	37,492	35,146	702	2,346	1.9	6.7	1,534.6	1,272.3	20.6	40,180	33,838
Pontotoc County, OK	38,194	37,492	35,146	702	2,346	1.9	6.7	1,534.6	1,272.3	20.6	40,180	33,838
Adrian, MI Micro Area	98,573	99,892	98,970	-1,319	922	-1.3	0.9	3,514.3	2,992.7	17.4	35,652	30,036
Lenawee County, MI	98,573	99,892	98,970	-1,319	922	-1.3	0.9	3,514.3	2,992.7	17.4	35,652	30,036
Alamogordo, NM Micro Area	64,362	63,799	62,195	563	1,604	0.9	2.6	2,192.1	2,022.5	8.4	34,058	31,427
Otero County, NM	64,362	63,799	62,195	563	1,604	0.9	2.6	2,192.1	2,022.5	8.4	34,058	31,427
Albemarle, NC Micro Area	60,714	60,585	58,092	129	2,493	0.2	4.3	2,068.1	1,737.4	19.0	34,063	28,692
Stanly County, NC	60,714	60,585	58,092	129	2,493	0.2	4.3	2,068.1	1,737.4	19.0	34,063	28,692
Albert Lea, MN Micro Area	30,613	31,255	32,584	-642	-1,329	-2.1	-4.1	1,266.5	1,085.0	16.7	41,371	34,764
Freeborn County, MN	30,613	31,255	32,584	-642	-1,329	-2.1	-4.1	1,266.5	1,085.0	16.7	41,371	34,764
Albertville, AL Micro Area	94,725	93,019	82,303	1,706	10,716	1.8	13.0	3,125.6	2,762.1	13.2	32,996	29,654
Marshall County, AL	94,725	93,019	82,303	1,706	10,716	1.8	13.0	3,125.6	2,762.1	13.2	32,996	29,654
Alexander City, AL Micro Area	40,844	41,618	41,771	-774	-153	-1.9	-0.4	1,468.0	1,348.9	8.8	35,942	32,502
Tallapoosa County, AL	40,844	41,618	41,771	-774	-153	-1.9	-0.4	1,468.0	1,348.9	8.8	35,942	32,502
Alexandria, MN Micro Area	37,075	36,009	32,808	1,066	3,201	3.0	9.8	1,738.9	1,461.1	19.0	46,902	40,590
Douglas County, MN	37,075	36,009	32,808	1,066	3,201	3.0	9.8	1,738.9	1,461.1	19.0	46,902	40,590
Alice, TX Micro Area	41,382	40,838	39,344	544	1,494	1.3	3.8	1,752.9	1,349.1	29.9	42,359	32,993
Jim Wells County, TX	41,382	40,838	39,344	544	1,494	1.3	3.8	1,752.9	1,349.1	29.9	42,359	32,993
Alma, MI Micro Area	41,540	42,476	42,289	-936	187	-2.2	0.4	1,394.5	1,223.9	13.9	33,571	28,850
Gratiot County, MI	41,540	42,476	42,289	-936	187	-2.2	0.4	1,394.5	1,223.9	13.9	33,571	28,850
Alpena, MI Micro Area	28,803	29,598	31,297	-795	-1,699	-2.7	-5.4	1,050.4	936.9	12.1	36,467	31,717
Alpena County, MI	28,803	29,598	31,297	-795	-1,699	-2.7	-5.4	1,050.4	936.9	12.1	36,467	31,717
Altus, OK Micro Area	25,574	26,446	28,439	-872	-1,993	-3.3	-7.0	968.2	903.8	7.1	37,858	34,150
Jackson County, OK	25,574	26,446	28,439	-872	-1,993	-3.3	-7.0	968.2	903.8	7.1	37,858	34,150
Americus, GA Micro Area	35,947	37,827	36,988	-1,880	839	-5.0	2.3	1,094.1	1,006.4	8.7	30,435	26,672
Schley County, GA	5,168	5,010	3,760	158	1,250	3.2	33.2	142.1	123.7	14.9	27,488	24,666
Sumter County, GA	30,779	32,817	33,228	-2,038	-411	-6.2	-1.2	952.0	882.8	7.8	30,930	26,980
Amsterdam, NY Micro Area	49,642	50,257	49,637	-615	620	-1.2	1.2	1,929.7	1,747.9	10.4	38,872	34,760
Montgomery County, NY	49,642	50,257	49,637	-615	620	-1.2	1.2	1,929.7	1,747.9	10.4	38,872	34,760
Andrews, TX Micro Area	18,105	14,786	13,002	3,319	1,784	22.4	13.7	947.2	548.5	72.7	52,319	36,973
Andrews County, TX	18,105	14,786	13,002	3,319	1,784	22.4	13.7	947.2	548.5	72.7	52,319	36,973
Angola, IN Micro Area	34,372	34,183	33,233	189	950	0.6	2.9	1,293.7	1,038.4	24.6	37,638	30,420
Steuben County, IN	34,372	34,183	33,233	189	950	0.6	2.9	1,293.7	1,038.4	24.6	37,638	30,420
Arcadia, FL Micro Area	35,458	34,862	32,204	596	2,658	1.7	8.3	834.1	765.9	8.9	23,522	21,933
DeSoto County, FL	35,458	34,862	32,204	596	2,658	1.7	8.3	834.1	765.9	8.9	23,522	21,933
Ardmore, OK Micro Area	48,689	47,726	45,614	963	2,112	2.0	4.6	2,124.3	1,657.2	28.2	43,630	34,677
Carter County, OK	48,689	47,726	45,614	963	2,112	2.0	4.6	2,124.3	1,657.2	28.2	43,630	34,677
Arkadelphia, AR Micro Area	22,633	22,995	23,541	-362	-546	-1.6	-2.3	702.1	621.6	12.9	31,021	27,090
Clark County, AR	22,633	22,995	23,541	-362	-546	-1.6	-2.3	702.1	621.6	12.9	31,021	27,090
Arkansas City-Winfield, KS Micro Area	35,788	36,311	36,307	-523	4	-1.4	0.0	1,337.8	1,129.9	18.4	37,381	31,127
Cowley County, KS	35,788	36,311	36,307	-523	4	-1.4	0.0	1,337.8	1,129.9	18.4	37,381	31,127
Ashland, OH Micro Area	53,213	53,139	52,516	74	623	0.1	1.2	1,842.0	1,562.8	17.9	34,615	29,311
Ashland County, OH	53,213	53,139	52,516	74	623	0.1	1.2	1,842.0	1,562.8	17.9	34,615	29,311
Ashtabula, OH Micro Area	98,632	101,497	102,681	-2,865	-1,184	-2.8	-1.2	3,444.0	2,989.6	15.2	34,918	29,484
Ashtabula County, OH	98,632	101,497	102,681	-2,865	-1,184	-2.8	-1.2	3,444.0	2,989.6	15.2	34,918	29,484
Astoria, OR Micro Area	37,831	37,037	35,634	794	1,403	2.1	3.9	1,523.7	1,246.3	22.3	40,278	33,605
Clatsop County, OR	37,831	37,037	35,634	794	1,403	2.1	3.9	1,523.7	1,246.3	22.3	40,278	33,605
Atchison, KS Micro Area	16,398	16,924	16,787	-526	137	-3.1	0.8	552.5	499.3	10.7	33,694	29,597
Atchison County, KS	16,398	16,924	16,787	-526	137	-3.1	0.8	552.5	499.3	10.7	33,694	29,597
Athens, OH Micro Area	65,886	64,773	62,193	1,113	2,580	1.7	4.1	2,082.9	1,786.5	16.6	31,613	27,390
Athens County, OH	65,886	64,773	62,193	1,113	2,580	1.7	4.1	2,082.9	1,786.5	16.6	31,613	27,390
Athens, TN Micro Area	52,639	52,266	49,011	373	3,255	0.7	6.6	1,738.2	1,486.1	17.0	33,020	28,478
McMinn County, TN	52,639	52,266	49,011	373	3,255	0.7	6.6	1,738.2	1,486.1	17.0	33,020	28,478
Athens, TX Micro Area	79,545	78,536	73,105	1,009	5,431	1.3	7.4	2,920.1	2,360.1	23.7	36,711	30,006
Henderson County, TX	79,545	78,536	73,105	1,009	5,431	1.3	7.4	2,920.1	2,360.1	23.7	36,711	30,006
Atmore, AL Micro Area	37,789	38,319	38,452	-530	-133	-1.4	-0.3	1,146.6	1,012.7	13.2	30,342	26,435
Escambia County, AL	37,789	38,319	38,452	-530	-133	-1.4	-0.3	1,146.6	1,012.7	13.2	30,342	26,435
Auburn, IN Micro Area	42,589	42,223	40,303	366	1,920	0.9	4.8	1,616.0	1,318.5	22.6	37,945	31,176
DeKalb County, IN	42,589	42,223	40,303	366	1,920	0.9	4.8	1,616.0	1,318.5	22.6	37,945	31,176
Auburn, NY Micro Area	78,288	80,020	81,910	-1,732	-1,890	-2.2	-2.3	2,995.0	2,594.5	15.4	38,257	32,489
Cayuga County, NY	78,288	80,020	81,910	-1,732	-1,890	-2.2	-2.3	2,995.0	2,594.5	15.4	38,257	32,489
Augusta-Waterville, ME Micro Area	119,980	122,151	117,074	-2,171	5,077	-1.8	4.3	4,985.6	4,553.4	9.5	41,554	37,291
Kennebec County, ME	119,980	122,151	117,074	-2,171	5,077	-1.8	4.3	4,985.6	4,553.4	9.5	41,554	37,291
Austin, MN Micro Area	39,116	39,163	38,604	-47	559	-0.1	1.4	1,657.1	1,422.7	16.5	42,364	36,302
Mower County, MN	39,116	39,163	38,604	-47	559	-0.1	1.4	1,657.1	1,422.7	16.5	42,364	36,302
Bainbridge, GA Micro Area	27,174	27,842	28,252	-668	-410	-2.4	-1.5	912.0	827.7	10.2	33,563	29,764
Decatur County, GA	27,174	27,842	28,252	-668	-410	-2.4	-1.5	912.0	827.7	10.2	33,563	29,764
Baraboo, WI Micro Area	63,642	61,976	55,187	1,666	6,789	2.7	12.3	2,785.2	2,210.5	26.0	43,763	35,636
Sauk County, WI	63,642	61,976	55,187	1,666	6,789	2.7	12.3	2,785.2	2,210.5	26.0	43,763	35,636

[1]The April 1, 2000 and 2010 population estimates bases reflect modifications to the census populations as documented in the Count Question Resolution program and geographic program revisions.
[2]Based on the April 1, 2010 estimates base and the July 1, 2015 estimates.
[3]Based on the April 1, 2000 and April 1, 2010 estimates bases.
[4]Based on the July 1 population estimate of the year shown.

Table D-1. Population and Personal Income—Continued

Micropolitan statistical area component counties	2015 estimate (July 1)	2010 census estimates base (April 1)[1]	2000 census estimates base (April 1)[1]	Net change 2010–2015[2]	Net change 2000–2010[3]	Percent change 2010–2015[2]	Percent change 2000–2010[3]	Total (million dollars) 2015	Total (million dollars) 2010	Percent change, 2010–2015	Per capita[4] 2015	Per capita[4] 2010
Bardstown, KY Micro Area	45,126	43,437	37,487	1,689	5,950	3.9	15.9	1,710.6	1,381.2	23.8	37,908	31,674
Nelson County, KY	45,126	43,437	37,487	1,689	5,950	3.9	15.9	1,710.6	1,381.2	23.8	37,908	31,674
Barre, VT Micro Area	58,612	59,526	58,034	-914	1,492	-1.5	2.6	3,079.6	2,608.5	18.1	52,541	43,789
Washington County, VT	58,612	59,526	58,034	-914	1,492	-1.5	2.6	3,079.6	2,608.5	18.1	52,541	43,789
Bartlesville, OK Micro Area	52,021	50,977	49,015	1,044	1,962	2.0	4.0	3,024.9	2,547.2	18.8	58,148	49,883
Washington County, OK	52,021	50,977	49,015	1,044	1,962	2.0	4.0	3,024.9	2,547.2	18.8	58,148	49,883
Bastrop, LA Micro Area	26,395	27,979	31,037	-1,584	-3,058	-5.7	-9.9	889.9	836.2	6.4	33,714	29,978
Morehouse Parish, LA	26,395	27,979	31,037	-1,584	-3,058	-5.7	-9.9	889.9	836.2	6.4	33,714	29,978
Batavia, NY Micro Area	58,937	60,033	60,548	-1,096	-515	-1.8	-0.9	2,388.8	2,084.2	14.6	40,532	34,719
Genesee County, NY	58,937	60,033	60,548	-1,096	-515	-1.8	-0.9	2,388.8	2,084.2	14.6	40,532	34,719
Batesville, AR Micro Area	37,052	36,647	34,246	405	2,401	1.1	7.0	1,205.7	1,070.0	12.7	32,542	29,070
Independence County, AR	37,052	36,647	34,246	405	2,401	1.1	7.0	1,205.7	1,070.0	12.7	32,542	29,070
Bay City, TX Micro Area	36,770	36,702	37,919	68	-1,217	0.2	-3.2	1,452.2	1,130.5	28.5	39,493	30,800
Matagorda County, TX	36,770	36,702	37,919	68	-1,217	0.2	-3.2	1,452.2	1,130.5	28.5	39,493	30,800
Beatrice, NE Micro Area	21,900	22,311	22,992	-411	-681	-1.8	-3.0	995.3	861.2	15.6	45,448	38,627
Gage County, NE	21,900	22,311	22,992	-411	-681	-1.8	-3.0	995.3	861.2	15.6	45,448	38,627
Beaver Dam, WI Micro Area	88,502	88,761	85,851	-259	2,910	-0.3	3.4	3,633.5	3,090.0	17.6	41,055	34,851
Dodge County, WI	88,502	88,761	85,851	-259	2,910	-0.3	3.4	3,633.5	3,090.0	17.6	41,055	34,851
Bedford, IN Micro Area	45,495	46,129	45,912	-634	217	-1.4	0.5	1,640.5	1,408.7	16.5	36,058	30,542
Lawrence County, IN	45,495	46,129	45,912	-634	217	-1.4	0.5	1,640.5	1,408.7	16.5	36,058	30,542
Beeville, TX Micro Area	32,874	31,861	32,347	1,013	-486	3.2	-1.5	934.4	785.5	19.0	28,423	24,634
Bee County, TX	32,874	31,861	32,347	1,013	-486	3.2	-1.5	934.4	785.5	19.0	28,423	24,634
Bellefontaine, OH Micro Area	45,386	45,858	46,002	-472	-144	-1.0	-0.3	1,749.2	1,455.1	20.2	38,540	31,792
Logan County, OH	45,386	45,858	46,002	-472	-144	-1.0	-0.3	1,749.2	1,455.1	20.2	38,540	31,792
Bemidji, MN Micro Area	45,672	44,442	39,638	1,230	4,804	2.8	12.1	1,659.2	1,361.6	21.9	36,329	30,542
Beltrami County, MN	45,672	44,442	39,638	1,230	4,804	2.8	12.1	1,659.2	1,361.6	21.9	36,329	30,542
Bennettsville, SC Micro Area	27,494	28,933	28,820	-1,439	113	-5.0	0.4	691.8	617.3	12.1	25,161	21,361
Marlboro County, SC	27,494	28,933	28,820	-1,439	113	-5.0	0.4	691.8	617.3	12.1	25,161	21,361
Bennington, VT Micro Area	36,317	37,125	36,969	-808	156	-2.2	0.4	1,732.3	1,481.0	17.0	47,700	39,913
Bennington County, VT	36,317	37,125	36,969	-808	156	-2.2	0.4	1,732.3	1,481.0	17.0	47,700	39,913
Berlin, NH-VT Micro Area	37,375	39,358	39,539	-1,983	-181	-5.0	-0.5	1,498.6	1,332.4	12.5	40,097	33,919
Coos County, NH	31,212	33,052	33,089	-1,840	-37	-5.6	-0.1	1,286.0	1,138.4	13.0	41,203	34,519
Essex County, VT	6,163	6,306	6,450	-143	-144	-2.3	-2.2	212.6	194.0	9.6	34,497	30,779
Big Rapids, MI Micro Area	43,067	42,798	40,547	269	2,251	0.6	5.6	1,277.9	1,092.9	16.9	29,673	25,510
Mecosta County, MI	43,067	42,798	40,547	269	2,251	0.6	5.6	1,277.9	1,092.9	16.9	29,673	25,510
Big Spring, TX Micro Area	38,521	36,238	35,043	2,283	1,195	6.3	3.4	1,391.5	1,075.5	29.4	36,123	29,677
Glasscock County, TX	1,315	1,226	1,413	89	-187	7.3	-13.2	103.3	59.3	74.1	78,529	48,181
Howard County, TX	37,206	35,012	33,630	2,194	1,382	6.3	4.1	1,288.2	1,016.2	26.8	34,624	29,026
Big Stone Gap, VA Micro Area	58,772	61,319	62,478	-2,547	-1,159	-4.2	-1.9	1,732.2	1,819.5	-4.8	29,472	29,607
Dickenson County, VA	15,115	15,892	16,380	-777	-488	-4.9	-3.0	429.9	452.0	-4.9	28,443	28,484
Wise County, VA	39,718	41,476	42,153	-1,758	-677	-4.2	-1.6	1,302.2	1,367.4	-4.8	29,829	29,997
Norton city, VA	3,939	3,951	3,945	-12	6	-0.3	0.2	(5)	(5)	(5)	(5)	(5)
Blackfoot, ID Micro Area	44,990	45,607	41,737	-617	3,870	-1.4	9.3	1,503.6	1,322.9	13.7	33,422	28,905
Bingham County, ID	44,990	45,607	41,737	-617	3,870	-1.4	9.3	1,503.6	1,322.9	13.7	33,422	28,905
Bluefield, WV-VA Micro Area	104,063	107,345	107,577	-3,282	-232	-3.1	-0.2	3,545.1	3,391.3	4.5	34,067	31,560
Tazewell County, VA	42,899	45,078	44,599	-2,179	479	-4.8	1.1	1,463.7	1,414.5	3.5	34,121	31,330
Mercer County, WV	61,164	62,267	62,978	-1,103	-711	-1.8	-1.1	2,081.3	1,976.9	5.3	34,029	31,726
Blytheville, AR Micro Area	43,738	46,480	51,999	-2,742	-5,519	-5.9	-10.6	1,362.5	1,339.1	1.7	31,150	28,867
Mississippi County, AR	43,738	46,480	51,999	-2,742	-5,519	-5.9	-10.6	1,362.5	1,339.1	1.7	31,150	28,867
Bogalusa, LA Micro Area	46,371	47,171	43,943	-800	3,228	-1.7	7.3	1,486.7	1,319.8	12.6	32,062	28,022
Washington Parish, LA	46,371	47,171	43,943	-800	3,228	-1.7	7.3	1,486.7	1,319.8	12.6	32,062	28,022
Bonham, TX Micro Area	33,693	33,915	31,225	-222	2,690	-0.7	8.6	1,194.4	936.9	27.5	35,449	27,629
Fannin County, TX	33,693	33,915	31,225	-222	2,690	-0.7	8.6	1,194.4	936.9	27.5	35,449	27,629
Boone, IA Micro Area	26,643	26,306	26,206	337	100	1.3	0.4	1,228.9	1,017.0	20.8	46,124	38,702
Boone County, IA	26,643	26,306	26,206	337	100	1.3	0.4	1,228.9	1,017.0	20.8	46,124	38,702
Boone, NC Micro Area	52,906	51,079	42,684	1,827	8,395	3.6	19.7	1,751.4	1,486.1	17.9	33,103	29,149
Watauga County, NC	52,906	51,079	42,684	1,827	8,395	3.6	19.7	1,751.4	1,486.1	17.9	33,103	29,149
Borger, TX Micro Area	21,734	22,249	23,864	-515	-1,615	-2.3	-6.8	897.1	762.9	17.6	41,275	34,359
Hutchinson County, TX	21,734	22,249	23,864	-515	-1,615	-2.3	-6.8	897.1	762.9	17.6	41,275	34,359
Bozeman, MT Micro Area	100,739	89,513	67,837	11,226	21,676	12.5	32.0	4,667.9	3,247.1	43.8	46,337	36,230
Gallatin County, MT	100,739	89,513	67,837	11,226	21,676	12.5	32.0	4,667.9	3,247.1	43.8	46,337	36,230
Bradford, PA Micro Area	42,412	43,450	45,908	-1,038	-2,458	-2.4	-5.4	1,708.8	1,437.8	18.8	40,291	33,161
McKean County, PA	42,412	43,450	45,908	-1,038	-2,458	-2.4	-5.4	1,708.8	1,437.8	18.8	40,291	33,161
Brainerd, MN Micro Area	92,134	91,067	82,133	1,067	8,934	1.2	10.9	3,766.6	3,089.6	21.9	40,882	33,849
Cass County, MN	28,706	28,567	27,148	139	1,419	0.5	5.2	1,184.5	986.6	20.1	41,263	34,437
Crow Wing County, MN	63,428	62,500	54,985	928	7,515	1.5	13.7	2,582.2	2,102.9	22.8	40,710	33,580
Branson, MO Micro Area	85,535	83,880	68,281	1,655	15,599	2.0	22.8	2,808.6	2,377.4	18.1	32,836	28,308
Stone County, MO	30,943	32,208	28,505	-1,265	3,703	-3.9	13.0	1,041.8	872.3	19.4	33,669	27,209
Taney County, MO	54,592	51,672	39,776	2,920	11,896	5.7	29.9	1,766.8	1,505.1	17.4	32,363	28,986
Breckenridge, CO Micro Area	30,257	27,994	23,560	2,263	4,434	8.1	18.8	1,652.5	1,173.9	40.8	54,615	41,827
Summit County, CO	30,257	27,994	23,560	2,263	4,434	8.1	18.8	1,652.5	1,173.9	40.8	54,615	41,827
Brenham, TX Micro Area	34,765	33,708	30,412	1,057	3,296	3.1	10.8	1,775.8	1,428.3	24.3	51,080	42,350
Washington County, TX	34,765	33,708	30,412	1,057	3,296	3.1	10.8	1,775.8	1,428.3	24.3	51,080	42,350
Brevard, NC Micro Area	33,211	33,090	29,316	121	3,774	0.4	12.9	1,178.6	974.1	21.0	35,487	29,461
Transylvania County, NC	33,211	33,090	29,316	121	3,774	0.4	12.9	1,178.6	974.1	21.0	35,487	29,461

[1] The April 1, 2000 and 2010 population estimates bases reflect modifications to the census populations as documented in the Count Question Resolution program and geographic program revisions.
[2] Based on the April 1, 2010 estimates base and the July 1, 2015 estimates.
[3] Based on the April 1, 2000 and April 1, 2010 estimates bases.
[4] Based on the July 1 population estimate of the year shown.
[5] Norton city is included with Wise county.

Table D-1. Population and Personal Income—*Continued*

Micropolitan statistical area component counties	2015 estimate (July 1)	2010 census estimates base (April 1)[1]	2000 census estimates base (April 1)[1]	Net change 2010–2015[2]	Net change 2000–2010[3]	Percent change 2010–2015[2]	Percent change 2000–2010[3]	Total (million dollars) 2015	Total (million dollars) 2010	Percent change, 2010–2015	Per capita[4] 2015	Per capita[4] 2010
Brookhaven, MS Micro Area	34,649	34,869	33,191	-220	1,678	-0.6	5.1	1,241.6	1,062.6	16.8	35,834	30,468
Lincoln County, MS	34,649	34,869	33,191	-220	1,678	-0.6	5.1	1,241.6	1,062.6	16.8	35,834	30,468
Brookings, OR Micro Area	22,483	22,364	21,147	119	1,217	0.5	5.8	870.2	732.5	18.8	38,707	32,743
Curry County, OR	22,483	22,364	21,147	119	1,217	0.5	5.8	870.2	732.5	18.8	38,707	32,743
Brookings, SD Micro Area	33,897	31,965	28,233	1,932	3,732	6.0	13.2	1,485.2	1,136.8	30.6	43,815	35,507
Brookings County, SD	33,897	31,965	28,233	1,932	3,732	6.0	13.2	1,485.2	1,136.8	30.6	43,815	35,507
Brownsville, TN Micro Area	18,023	18,787	19,790	-764	-1,003	-4.1	-5.1	514.5	498.7	3.2	28,546	26,570
Haywood County, TN	18,023	18,787	19,790	-764	-1,003	-4.1	-5.1	514.5	498.7	3.2	28,546	26,570
Brownwood, TX Micro Area	37,896	38,106	37,668	-210	438	-0.6	1.2	1,285.3	1,091.0	17.8	33,917	28,622
Brown County, TX	37,896	38,106	37,668	-210	438	-0.6	1.2	1,285.3	1,091.0	17.8	33,917	28,622
Bucyrus, OH Micro Area	42,306	43,784	46,909	-1,478	-3,125	-3.4	-6.7	1,466.9	1,317.1	11.4	34,675	30,093
Crawford County, OH	42,306	43,784	46,909	-1,478	-3,125	-3.4	-6.7	1,466.9	1,317.1	11.4	34,675	30,093
Burley, ID Micro Area	43,967	43,021	41,554	946	1,467	2.2	3.5	1,776.2	1,331.9	33.4	40,399	30,852
Cassia County, ID	23,506	22,958	21,399	548	1,559	2.4	7.3	1,006.6	752.1	33.8	42,823	32,574
Minidoka County, ID	20,461	20,063	20,155	398	-92	2.0	-0.5	769.6	579.8	32.7	37,614	28,873
Burlington, IA-IL Micro Area	47,050	47,653	50,535	-603	-2,882	-1.3	-5.7	2,209.5	1,658.5	33.2	46,962	34,851
Henderson County, IL	6,995	7,328	8,176	-333	-848	-4.5	-10.4	256.4	233.6	9.8	36,661	31,854
Des Moines County, IA	40,055	40,325	42,359	-270	-2,034	-0.7	-4.8	1,953.1	1,424.9	37.1	48,760	35,397
Butte-Silver Bow, MT Micro Area	34,622	34,209	34,625	413	-416	1.2	-1.2	1,535.7	1,439.0	6.7	44,355	42,039
Silver Bow County, MT	34,622	34,209	34,625	413	-416	1.2	-1.2	1,535.7	1,439.0	6.7	44,355	42,039
Cadillac, MI Micro Area	47,906	47,584	44,948	322	2,636	0.7	5.9	1,552.5	1,318.5	17.7	32,407	27,717
Missaukee County, MI	14,903	14,849	14,473	54	376	0.4	2.6	463.6	396.7	16.9	31,109	26,776
Wexford County, MI	33,003	32,735	30,475	268	2,260	0.8	7.4	1,088.9	921.9	18.1	32,993	28,142
Calhoun, GA Micro Area	56,574	55,186	44,090	1,388	11,096	2.5	25.2	1,780.0	1,452.2	22.6	31,463	26,304
Gordon County, GA	56,574	55,186	44,090	1,388	11,096	2.5	25.2	1,780.0	1,452.2	22.6	31,463	26,304
Cambridge, MD Micro Area	32,384	32,618	30,671	-234	1,947	-0.7	6.3	1,345.7	1,158.8	16.1	41,553	35,486
Dorchester County, MD	32,384	32,618	30,671	-234	1,947	-0.7	6.3	1,345.7	1,158.8	16.1	41,553	35,486
Cambridge, OH Micro Area	39,258	40,087	40,813	-829	-726	-2.1	-1.8	1,457.3	1,160.9	25.5	37,121	28,923
Guernsey County, OH	39,258	40,087	40,813	-829	-726	-2.1	-1.8	1,457.3	1,160.9	25.5	37,121	28,923
Camden, AR Micro Area	29,587	31,489	34,507	-1,902	-3,018	-6.0	-8.7	977.5	922.4	6.0	33,038	29,363
Calhoun County, AR	5,229	5,368	5,731	-139	-363	-2.6	-6.3	160.9	137.4	17.1	30,770	25,733
Ouachita County, AR	24,358	26,121	28,776	-1,763	-2,655	-6.7	-9.2	816.6	785.0	4.0	33,525	30,105
Campbellsville, KY Micro Area	25,420	24,512	22,889	908	1,623	3.7	7.1	846.7	695.3	21.8	33,309	28,308
Taylor County, KY	25,420	24,512	22,889	908	1,623	3.7	7.1	846.7	695.3	21.8	33,309	28,308
Cañon City, CO Micro Area	46,692	46,824	46,140	-132	684	-0.3	1.5	1,443.8	1,192.6	21.1	30,921	25,453
Fremont County, CO	46,692	46,824	46,140	-132	684	-0.3	1.5	1,443.8	1,192.6	21.1	30,921	25,453
Canton, IL Micro Area	35,699	37,069	38,244	-1,370	-1,175	-3.7	-3.1	1,194.5	1,160.4	2.9	33,461	31,317
Fulton County, IL	35,699	37,069	38,244	-1,370	-1,175	-3.7	-3.1	1,194.5	1,160.4	2.9	33,461	31,317
Carlsbad-Artesia, NM Micro Area	57,578	53,829	51,633	3,749	2,196	7.0	4.3	3,086.7	2,324.8	32.8	53,609	43,127
Eddy County, NM	57,578	53,829	51,633	3,749	2,196	7.0	4.3	3,086.7	2,324.8	32.8	53,609	43,127
Carroll, IA Micro Area	20,498	20,816	21,433	-318	-617	-1.5	-2.9	1,023.1	833.6	22.7	49,914	40,022
Carroll County, IA	20,498	20,816	21,433	-318	-617	-1.5	-2.9	1,023.1	833.6	22.7	49,914	40,022
Cedar City, UT Micro Area	48,368	46,163	33,793	2,205	12,370	4.8	36.6	1,307.7	1,015.8	28.7	27,037	21,954
Iron County, UT	48,368	46,163	33,793	2,205	12,370	4.8	36.6	1,307.7	1,015.8	28.7	27,037	21,954
Cedartown, GA Micro Area	41,524	41,475	38,102	49	3,373	0.1	8.9	1,213.2	1,066.9	13.7	29,216	25,686
Polk County, GA	41,524	41,475	38,102	49	3,373	0.1	8.9	1,213.2	1,066.9	13.7	29,216	25,686
Celina, OH Micro Area	40,968	40,814	40,936	154	-122	0.4	-0.3	1,850.4	1,489.3	24.2	45,167	36,518
Mercer County, OH	40,968	40,814	40,936	154	-122	0.4	-0.3	1,850.4	1,489.3	24.2	45,167	36,518
Central City, KY Micro Area	31,183	31,499	31,845	-316	-346	-1.0	-1.1	981.4	853.0	15.0	31,472	26,962
Muhlenberg County, KY	31,183	31,499	31,845	-316	-346	-1.0	-1.1	981.4	853.0	15.0	31,472	26,962
Centralia, IL Micro Area	38,339	39,437	41,678	-1,098	-2,241	-2.8	-5.4	1,481.5	1,337.8	10.7	38,643	33,913
Marion County, IL	38,339	39,437	41,678	-1,098	-2,241	-2.8	-5.4	1,481.5	1,337.8	10.7	38,643	33,913
Centralia, WA Micro Area	75,882	75,455	68,585	427	6,870	0.6	10.0	2,844.5	2,430.6	17.0	37,486	32,187
Lewis County, WA	75,882	75,455	68,585	427	6,870	0.6	10.0	2,844.5	2,430.6	17.0	37,486	32,187
Charleston-Mattoon, IL Micro Area	63,419	64,921	64,521	-1,502	400	-2.3	0.6	2,309.5	2,061.5	12.0	36,417	31,743
Coles County, IL	52,521	53,873	53,210	-1,352	663	-2.5	1.2	1,907.8	1,695.6	12.5	36,325	31,461
Cumberland County, IL	10,898	11,048	11,311	-150	-263	-1.4	-2.3	401.7	365.9	9.8	36,864	33,121
Chillicothe, OH Micro Area	77,170	78,064	73,382	-894	4,682	-1.1	6.4	2,628.5	2,246.2	17.0	34,061	28,760
Ross County, OH	77,170	78,064	73,382	-894	4,682	-1.1	6.4	2,628.5	2,246.2	17.0	34,061	28,760
Claremont-Lebanon, NH VT Micro Area	216,923	218,458	207,897	-1,535	10,561	-0.7	5.1	11,287.0	9,332.3	20.9	52,032	42,725
Grafton County, NH	89,320	89,114	81,764	206	7,350	0.2	9.0	5,018.2	4,076.6	23.1	56,182	45,751
Sullivan County, NH	42,967	43,742	40,435	-775	3,307	-1.8	8.2	2,099.7	1,702.1	23.4	48,868	38,907
Orange County, VT	28,899	28,936	28,314	-37	622	-0.1	2.2	1,237.9	1,063.4	16.4	42,836	36,731
Windsor County, VT	55,737	56,666	57,384	-929	-718	-1.6	-1.3	2,931.1	2,490.2	17.7	52,588	43,978
Clarksburg, WV Micro Area	93,802	94,196	92,061	-394	2,135	-0.4	2.3	3,824.8	3,178.2	20.3	40,775	33,687
Doddridge County, WV	8,176	8,198	7,366	-22	832	-0.3	11.3	220.5	138.5	59.3	26,971	16,898
Harrison County, WV	68,714	69,108	68,635	-394	473	-0.6	0.7	3,016.4	2,553.8	18.1	43,898	36,870
Taylor County, WV	16,912	16,890	16,060	22	830	0.1	5.2	587.9	486.0	21.0	34,761	28,778
Clarksdale, MS Micro Area	24,620	26,145	30,617	-1,525	-4,472	-5.8	-14.6	739.3	726.3	1.8	30,030	27,804
Coahoma County, MS	24,620	26,145	30,617	-1,525	-4,472	-5.8	-14.6	739.3	726.3	1.8	30,030	27,804
Clearlake, CA Micro Area	64,591	64,665	58,331	-74	6,334	-0.1	10.9	2,442.0	1,972.3	23.8	37,807	30,463
Lake County, CA	64,591	64,665	58,331	-74	6,334	-0.1	10.9	2,442.0	1,972.3	23.8	37,807	30,463
Cleveland, MS Micro Area	33,322	34,148	40,619	-826	-6,471	-2.4	-15.9	1,143.7	1,004.8	13.8	34,322	29,474
Bolivar County, MS	33,322	34,148	40,619	-826	-6,471	-2.4	-15.9	1,143.7	1,004.8	13.8	34,322	29,474
Clewiston, FL Micro Area	39,119	39,140	36,184	-21	2,956	-0.1	8.2	1,166.6	1,022.7	14.1	29,822	26,195
Hendry County, FL	39,119	39,140	36,184	-21	2,956	-0.1	8.2	1,166.6	1,022.7	14.1	29,822	26,195

[1]The April 1, 2000 and 2010 population estimates bases reflect modifications to the census populations as documented in the Count Question Resolution program and geographic program revisions.
[2]Based on the April 1, 2010 estimates base and the July 1, 2015 estimates.
[3]Based on the April 1, 2000 and April 1, 2010 estimates bases.
[4]Based on the July 1 population estimate of the year shown.

Table D-1. Population and Personal Income—*Continued*

	Population								Personal Income				
		2010 census estimates base (April 1)[1]	2000 census estimates base (April 1)[1]	Net change		Percent change			Total (million dollars)		Percent change, 2010–2015	Per capita[4]	
Micropolitan statistical area component counties	2015 estimate (July 1)			2010–2015[2]	2000–2010[3]	2010–2015[2]	2000–2010[3]		2015	2010		2015	2010
Clinton, IA Micro Area	47,768	49,116	50,159	-1,348	-1,043	-2.7	-2.1		1,918.4	1,726.9	11.1	40,161	35,164
Clinton County, IA	47,768	49,116	50,159	-1,348	-1,043	-2.7	-2.1		1,918.4	1,726.9	11.1	40,161	35,164
Clovis, NM Micro Area	50,398	48,376	45,050	2,022	3,326	4.2	7.4		2,100.8	1,772.7	18.5	41,684	36,209
Curry County, NM	50,398	48,376	45,050	2,022	3,326	4.2	7.4		2,100.8	1,772.7	18.5	41,684	36,209
Coffeyville, KS Micro Area	33,314	35,471	36,267	-2,157	-796	-6.1	-2.2		1,257.7	1,146.0	9.7	37,751	32,390
Montgomery County, KS	33,314	35,471	36,267	-2,157	-796	-6.1	-2.2		1,257.7	1,146.0	9.7	37,751	32,390
Coldwater, MI Micro Area	43,664	45,248	45,781	-1,584	-533	-3.5	-1.2		1,410.0	1,212.8	16.3	32,293	26,848
Branch County, MI	43,664	45,248	45,781	-1,584	-533	-3.5	-1.2		1,410.0	1,212.8	16.3	32,293	26,848
Columbus, MS Micro Area	59,710	59,779	61,596	-69	-1,817	-0.1	-2.9		2,196.9	1,893.6	16.0	36,793	31,665
Lowndes County, MS	59,710	59,779	61,596	-69	-1,817	-0.1	-2.9		2,196.9	1,893.6	16.0	36,793	31,665
Columbus, NE Micro Area	32,847	32,237	31,574	610	663	1.9	2.1		1,484.5	1,186.9	25.1	45,193	36,747
Platte County, NE	32,847	32,237	31,574	610	663	1.9	2.1		1,484.5	1,186.9	25.1	45,193	36,747
Concord, NH Micro Area	147,994	146,442	136,264	1,552	10,178	1.1	7.5		7,875.2	7,886.1	-0.1	53,213	53,856
Merrimack County, NH	147,994	146,442	136,264	1,552	10,178	1.1	7.5		7,875.2	7,886.1	-0.1	53,213	53,856
Connersville, IN Micro Area	23,434	24,302	25,591	-868	-1,289	-3.6	-5.0		830.8	707.4	17.4	35,453	29,071
Fayette County, IN	23,434	24,302	25,591	-868	-1,289	-3.6	-5.0		830.8	707.4	17.4	35,453	29,071
Cookeville, TN Micro Area	108,191	106,059	93,426	2,132	12,633	2.0	13.5		3,688.2	3,136.7	17.6	34,089	29,516
Jackson County, TN	11,509	11,614	10,987	-105	627	-0.9	5.7		325.2	288.3	12.8	28,256	24,906
Overton County, TN	22,129	22,078	20,124	51	1,954	0.2	9.7		663.0	564.4	17.5	29,962	25,548
Putnam County, TN	74,553	72,367	62,315	2,186	10,052	3.0	16.1		2,699.9	2,284.0	18.2	36,215	31,459
Coos Bay, OR Micro Area	63,121	63,043	62,795	78	248	0.1	0.4		2,428.6	1,996.2	21.7	38,475	31,678
Coos County, OR	63,121	63,043	62,795	78	248	0.1	0.4		2,428.6	1,996.2	21.7	38,475	31,678
Cordele, GA Micro Area	22,881	23,439	22,020	-558	1,419	-2.4	6.4		620.5	557.9	11.2	27,120	23,838
Crisp County, GA	22,881	23,439	22,020	-558	1,419	-2.4	6.4		620.5	557.9	11.2	27,120	23,838
Corinth, MS Micro Area	37,388	37,057	34,519	331	2,538	0.9	7.4		1,145.3	981.2	16.7	30,633	26,441
Alcorn County, MS	37,388	37,057	34,519	331	2,538	0.9	7.4		1,145.3	981.2	16.7	30,633	26,441
Cornelia, GA Micro Area	43,996	43,041	35,884	955	7,157	2.2	19.9		1,302.4	1,098.0	18.6	29,603	25,488
Habersham County, GA	43,996	43,041	35,884	955	7,157	2.2	19.9		1,302.4	1,098.0	18.6	29,603	25,488
Corning, NY Micro Area	97,631	98,994	98,681	-1,363	313	-1.4	0.3		3,928.9	3,506.6	12.0	40,243	35,423
Steuben County, NY	97,631	98,994	98,681	-1,363	313	-1.4	0.3		3,928.9	3,506.6	12.0	40,243	35,423
Corsicana, TX Micro Area	48,323	47,831	45,113	492	2,718	1.0	6.0		1,729.6	1,446.8	19.5	35,792	30,235
Navarro County, TX	48,323	47,831	45,113	492	2,718	1.0	6.0		1,729.6	1,446.8	19.5	35,792	30,235
Cortland, NY Micro Area	48,494	49,306	48,704	-812	602	-1.6	1.2		1,807.1	1,560.7	15.8	37,265	31,679
Cortland County, NY	48,494	49,306	48,704	-812	602	-1.6	1.2		1,807.1	1,560.7	15.8	37,265	31,679
Coshocton, OH Micro Area	36,569	36,901	36,654	-332	247	-0.9	0.7		1,283.8	1,023.1	25.5	35,107	27,704
Coshocton County, OH	36,569	36,901	36,654	-332	247	-0.9	0.7		1,283.8	1,023.1	25.5	35,107	27,704
Craig, CO Micro Area	12,937	13,795	13,178	-858	617	-6.2	4.7		502.9	440.3	14.2	38,875	31,880
Moffat County, CO	12,937	13,795	13,178	-858	617	-6.2	4.7		502.9	440.3	14.2	38,875	31,880
Crawfordsville, IN Micro Area	38,227	38,126	37,629	101	497	0.3	1.3		1,456.1	1,270.5	14.6	38,092	33,358
Montgomery County, IN	38,227	38,126	37,629	101	497	0.3	1.3		1,456.1	1,270.5	14.6	38,092	33,358
Crescent City, CA Micro Area	27,254	28,610	27,505	-1,356	1,105	-4.7	4.0		902.9	767.6	17.6	33,129	26,870
Del Norte County, CA	27,254	28,610	27,505	-1,356	1,105	-4.7	4.0		902.9	767.6	17.6	33,129	26,870
Crossville, TN Micro Area	58,229	56,050	46,781	2,179	9,269	3.9	19.8		1,978.2	1,646.1	20.2	33,973	29,292
Cumberland County, TN	58,229	56,050	46,781	2,179	9,269	3.9	19.8		1,978.2	1,646.1	20.2	33,973	29,292
Cullman, AL Micro Area	82,005	80,410	77,426	1,595	2,984	2.0	3.9		2,945.9	2,450.7	20.2	35,923	30,454
Cullman County, AL	82,005	80,410	77,426	1,595	2,984	2.0	3.9		2,945.9	2,450.7	20.2	35,923	30,454
Cullowhee, NC Micro Area	41,265	40,271	33,103	994	7,168	2.5	21.7		1,328.8	1,072.8	23.9	32,202	26,590
Jackson County, NC	41,265	40,271	33,103	994	7,168	2.5	21.7		1,328.8	1,072.8	23.9	32,202	26,590
Danville, KY Micro Area	54,272	53,174	51,001	1,098	2,173	2.1	4.3		1,747.6	1,482.4	17.9	32,201	27,766
Boyle County, KY	29,809	28,420	27,676	1,389	744	4.9	2.7		1,033.2	870.6	18.7	34,660	30,401
Lincoln County, KY	24,463	24,754	23,325	-291	1,429	-1.2	6.1		714.4	611.8	16.8	29,204	24,719
Danville, VA Micro Area	104,276	106,563	110,102	-2,287	-3,539	-2.1	-3.2		3,557.8	3,071.0	15.9	34,119	28,829
Pittsylvania County, VA	62,194	63,504	61,790	-1,310	1,714	-2.1	2.8		3,557.8	3,071.0	15.9	34,119	28,829
Danville city, VA	42,082	43,059	48,312	-977	-5,253	-2.3	-10.9		(6)	(6)	(6)	(6)	(6)
Dayton, TN Micro Area	32,526	31,809	28,398	717	3,411	2.3	12.0		1,059.5	880.7	20.3	32,573	27,639
Rhea County, TN	32,526	31,809	28,398	717	3,411	2.3	12.0		1,059.5	880.7	20.3	32,573	27,639
Decatur, IN Micro Area	34,980	34,387	33,605	593	782	1.7	2.3		1,220.3	959.4	27.2	34,885	27,846
Adams County, IN	34,980	34,387	33,605	593	782	1.7	2.3		1,220.3	959.4	27.2	34,885	27,846
Defiance, OH Micro Area	38,352	39,035	39,502	-683	-467	-1.7	-1.2		1,385.6	1,196.4	15.8	36,128	30,589
Defiance County, OH	38,352	39,035	39,502	-683	-467	-1.7	-1.2		1,385.6	1,196.4	15.8	36,128	30,589
Del Rio, TX Micro Area	48,988	48,879	44,834	109	4,045	0.2	9.0		1,670.5	1,450.2	15.2	34,100	29,589
Val Verde County, TX	48,988	48,879	44,834	109	4,045	0.2	9.0		1,670.5	1,450.2	15.2	34,100	29,589
Deming, NM Micro Area	24,518	25,095	24,986	-577	109	-2.3	0.4		732.0	677.5	8.0	29,854	26,984
Luna County, NM	24,518	25,095	24,986	-577	109	-2.3	0.4		732.0	677.5	8.0	29,854	26,984
DeRidder, LA Micro Area	36,462	35,654	32,948	808	2,706	2.3	8.2		1,461.7	1,258.5	16.1	40,088	35,110
Beauregard Parish, LA	36,462	35,654	32,948	808	2,706	2.3	8.2		1,461.7	1,258.5	16.1	40,088	35,110
Dickinson, ND Micro Area	32,154	24,199	22,635	7,955	1,564	32.9	6.9		2,754.9	1,257.3	119.1	85,677	51,632
Stark County, ND	32,154	24,199	22,635	7,955	1,564	32.9	6.9		2,754.9	1,257.3	119.1	85,677	51,632
Dixon, IL Micro Area	34,584	36,031	36,062	-1,447	-31	-4.0	-0.1		1,310.6	1,177.3	11.3	37,895	32,767
Lee County, IL	34,584	36,031	36,062	-1,447	-31	-4.0	-0.1		1,310.6	1,177.3	11.3	37,895	32,767
Dodge City, KS Micro Area	34,536	33,848	32,452	688	1,396	2.0	4.3		1,162.6	1,070.2	8.6	33,663	31,439
Ford County, KS	34,536	33,848	32,452	688	1,396	2.0	4.3		1,162.6	1,070.2	8.6	33,663	31,439
Douglas, GA Micro Area	43,108	42,356	37,421	752	4,935	1.8	13.2		1,226.2	1,051.4	16.6	28,445	24,610
Coffee County, GA	43,108	42,356	37,421	752	4,935	1.8	13.2		1,226.2	1,051.4	16.6	28,445	24,610
Dublin, GA Micro Area	57,387	58,418	53,387	-1,031	5,031	-1.8	9.4		1,776.7	1,615.5	10.0	30,960	27,670

[1]The April 1, 2000 and 2010 population estimates bases reflect modifications to the census populations as documented in the Count Question Resolution program and geographic program revisions.
[2]Based on the April 1, 2010 estimates base and the July 1, 2015 estimates.
[3]Based on the April 1, 2000 and April 1, 2010 estimates bases.
[4]Based on the July 1 population estimate of the year shown.

Table D-1. Population and Personal Income—*Continued*

Micropolitan statistical area component counties	Population							Personal Income				
	2015 estimate (July 1)	2010 census estimates base (April 1)[1]	2000 census estimates base (April 1)[1]	Net change		Percent change		Total (million dollars)		Percent change, 2010–2015	Per capita[4]	
				2010–2015[2]	2000–2010[3]	2010–2015[2]	2000–2010[3]	2015	2010		2015	2010
Johnson County, GA	9,656	9,984	8,526	-328	1,458	-3.3	17.1	226.6	201.6	12.4	23,464	20,194
Laurens County, GA	47,731	48,434	44,861	-703	3,573	-1.5	8.0	1,550.1	1,413.9	9.6	32,477	29,212
DuBois, PA Micro Area	80,994	81,644	83,529	-650	-1,885	-0.8	-2.3	3,205.6	2,840.4	12.9	39,578	34,816
Clearfield County, PA	80,994	81,644	83,529	-650	-1,885	-0.8	-2.3	3,205.6	2,840.4	12.9	39,578	34,816
Dumas, TX Micro Area	22,255	21,904	20,123	351	1,781	1.6	8.9	858.6	635.2	35.2	38,581	28,870
Moore County, TX	22,255	21,904	20,123	351	1,781	1.6	8.9	858.6	635.2	35.2	38,581	28,870
Duncan, OK Micro Area	44,581	45,048	43,204	-467	1,844	-1.0	4.3	2,084.2	1,648.2	26.5	46,750	36,541
Stephens County, OK	44,581	45,048	43,204	-467	1,844	-1.0	4.3	2,084.2	1,648.2	26.5	46,750	36,541
Dunn, NC Micro Area	128,140	114,678	90,978	13,462	23,700	11.7	26.1	3,988.9	3,323.8	20.0	31,129	28,721
Harnett County, NC	128,140	114,678	90,978	13,462	23,700	11.7	26.1	3,988.9	3,323.8	20.0	31,129	28,721
Durango, CO Micro Area	54,688	51,334	43,957	3,354	7,377	6.5	16.8	2,815.1	2,083.2	35.1	51,475	40,552
La Plata County, CO	54,688	51,334	43,957	3,354	7,377	6.5	16.8	2,815.1	2,083.2	35.1	51,475	40,552
Durant, OK Micro Area	44,884	42,416	36,524	2,468	5,892	5.8	16.1	1,393.1	1,125.2	23.8	31,039	26,397
Bryan County, OK	44,884	42,416	36,524	2,468	5,892	5.8	16.1	1,393.1	1,125.2	23.8	31,039	26,397
Dyersburg, TN Micro Area	37,893	38,337	37,284	-444	1,053	-1.2	2.8	1,445.7	1,268.2	14.0	38,153	33,094
Dyer County, TN	37,893	38,337	37,284	-444	1,053	-1.2	2.8	1,445.7	1,268.2	14.0	38,153	33,094
Eagle Pass, TX Micro Area	57,706	54,258	47,285	3,448	6,973	6.4	14.7	1,557.0	1,259.8	23.6	26,982	23,122
Maverick County, TX	57,706	54,258	47,285	3,448	6,973	6.4	14.7	1,557.0	1,259.8	23.6	26,982	23,122
Easton, MD Micro Area	37,512	37,782	33,806	-270	3,976	-0.7	11.8	2,430.9	2,165.4	12.3	64,804	57,157
Talbot County, MD	37,512	37,782	33,806	-270	3,976	-0.7	11.8	2,430.9	2,165.4	12.3	64,804	57,157
Edwards, CO Micro Area	53,605	52,197	41,623	1,408	10,574	2.7	25.4	3,297.9	2,223.2	48.3	61,522	42,684
Eagle County, CO	53,605	52,197	41,623	1,408	10,574	2.7	25.4	3,297.9	2,223.2	48.3	61,522	42,684
Effingham, IL Micro Area	34,371	34,242	34,267	129	-25	0.4	-0.1	1,466.2	1,319.2	11.1	42,657	38,546
Effingham County, IL	34,371	34,242	34,267	129	-25	0.4	-0.1	1,466.2	1,319.2	11.1	42,657	38,546
El Campo, TX Micro Area	41,486	41,280	41,191	206	89	0.5	0.2	1,720.0	1,381.7	24.5	41,460	33,446
Wharton County, TX	41,486	41,280	41,191	206	89	0.5	0.2	1,720.0	1,381.7	24.5	41,460	33,446
El Dorado, AR Micro Area	40,144	41,639	45,633	-1,495	-3,994	-3.6	-8.8	1,772.4	1,574.4	12.6	44,151	37,886
Union County, AR	40,144	41,639	45,633	-1,495	-3,994	-3.6	-8.8	1,772.4	1,574.4	12.6	44,151	37,886
Elizabeth City, NC Micro Area	63,578	64,094	53,143	-516	10,951	-0.8	20.6	2,343.2	2,119.2	10.6	36,856	33,015
Camden County, NC	10,309	9,980	6,884	329	3,096	3.3	45.0	426.3	375.1	13.7	41,351	37,573
Pasquotank County, NC	39,829	40,661	34,890	-832	5,771	-2.0	16.5	1,415.9	1,295.1	9.3	35,550	31,804
Perquimans County, NC	13,440	13,453	11,369	-13	2,084	-0.1	18.3	501.0	449.0	11.6	37,279	33,298
Elk City, OK Micro Area	23,768	22,119	19,807	1,649	2,312	7.5	11.7	949.3	686.5	38.3	39,940	31,127
Beckham County, OK	23,768	22,119	19,807	1,649	2,312	7.5	11.7	949.3	686.5	38.3	39,940	31,127
Elkins, WV Micro Area	29,126	29,405	28,274	-279	1,131	-0.9	4.0	968.3	842.4	14.9	33,244	28,684
Randolph County, WV	29,126	29,405	28,274	-279	1,131	-0.9	4.0	968.3	842.4	14.9	33,244	28,684
Elko, NV Micro Area	53,951	50,929	46,938	3,022	3,991	5.9	8.5	2,349.7	2,049.6	14.6	43,552	40,133
Elko County, NV	51,935	48,942	45,287	2,993	3,655	6.1	8.1	2,274.3	1,985.1	14.6	43,791	40,450
Eureka County, NV	2,016	1,987	1,651	29	336	1.5	20.4	75.4	64.4	17.0	37,396	32,330
Ellensburg, WA Micro Area	43,269	40,909	33,369	2,360	7,540	5.8	22.6	1,694.3	1,370.7	23.6	39,157	33,421
Kittitas County, WA	43,269	40,909	33,369	2,360	7,540	5.8	22.6	1,694.3	1,370.7	23.6	39,157	33,421
Emporia, KS Micro Area	33,339	33,690	35,934	-351	-2,244	-1.0	-6.2	1,118.3	992.1	12.7	33,543	29,491
Lyon County, KS	33,339	33,690	35,934	-351	-2,244	-1.0	-6.2	1,118.3	992.1	12.7	33,543	29,491
Enterprise, AL Micro Area	51,211	49,948	43,639	1,263	6,309	2.5	14.5	1,993.6	1,769.8	12.6	38,929	35,272
Coffee County, AL	51,211	49,948	43,639	1,263	6,309	2.5	14.5	1,993.6	1,769.8	12.6	38,929	35,272
Escanaba, MI Micro Area	36,377	37,069	38,528	-692	-1,459	-1.9	-3.8	1,321.2	1,189.0	11.1	36,319	32,074
Delta County, MI	36,377	37,069	38,528	-692	-1,459	-1.9	-3.8	1,321.2	1,189.0	11.1	36,319	32,074
Española, NM Micro Area	39,465	40,247	41,171	-782	-924	-1.9	-2.2	1,272.9	1,200.0	6.1	32,254	29,771
Rio Arriba County, NM	39,465	40,247	41,171	-782	-924	-1.9	-2.2	1,272.9	1,200.0	6.1	32,254	29,771
Eufaula, AL-GA Micro Area	28,791	29,970	31,638	-1,179	-1,668	-3.9	-5.3	895.4	821.4	9.0	31,101	27,519
Barbour County, AL	26,489	27,457	29,042	-968	-1,585	-3.5	-5.5	832.9	763.4	9.1	31,443	27,923
Quitman County, GA	2,302	2,513	2,596	-211	-83	-8.4	-3.2	62.5	57.9	8.0	27,169	23,109
Eureka-Arcata-Fortuna, CA Micro Area	135,727	134,623	126,508	1,104	8,115	0.8	6.4	5,636.1	4,783.3	17.8	41,525	35,425
Humboldt County, CA	135,727	134,623	126,508	1,104	8,115	0.8	6.4	5,636.1	4,783.3	17.8	41,525	35,425
Evanston, WY Micro Area	20,822	21,118	19,745	-296	1,373	-1.4	7.0	853.8	822.9	3.8	41,005	38,998
Uinta County, WY	20,822	21,118	19,745	-296	1,373	-1.4	7.0	853.8	822.9	3.8	41,005	38,998
Fairfield, IA Micro Area	17,555	16,843	16,180	712	663	4.2	4.1	703.6	551.0	27.7	40,079	32,750
Jefferson County, IA	17,555	16,843	16,180	712	663	4.2	4.1	703.6	551.0	27.7	40,079	32,750
Fairmont, MN Micro Area	20,022	20,840	21,807	-818	-967	-3.9	-4.4	945.7	825.8	14.5	47,232	39,666
Martin County, MN	20,022	20,840	21,807	-818	-967	-3.9	-4.4	945.7	825.8	14.5	47,232	39,666
Fairmont, WV Micro Area	56,925	56,418	56,603	507	-185	0.9	-0.3	2,220.5	1,952.9	13.7	39,007	34,555
Marion County, WV	56,925	56,418	56,603	507	-185	0.9	-0.3	2,220.5	1,952.9	13.7	39,007	34,555
Fallon, NV Micro Area	24,200	24,877	23,984	-677	893	-2.7	3.7	892.4	803.1	11.1	36,876	32,378
Churchill County, NV	24,200	24,877	23,984	-677	893	-2.7	3.7	892.4	803.1	11.1	36,876	32,378
Faribault-Northfield, MN Micro Area	65,400	64,144	56,663	1,256	7,481	2.0	13.2	2,585.4	2,123.4	21.8	39,532	33,053
Rice County, MN	65,400	64,144	56,663	1,256	7,481	2.0	13.2	2,585.4	2,123.4	21.8	39,532	33,053
Farmington, MO Micro Area	66,520	65,365	55,643	1,155	9,722	1.8	17.5	2,027.0	1,766.0	14.8	30,471	26,945
St. Francois County, MO	66,520	65,365	55,643	1,155	9,722	1.8	17.5	2,027.0	1,766.0	14.8	30,471	26,945
Fergus Falls, MN Micro Area	57,716	57,303	57,083	413	220	0.7	0.4	2,447.8	1,992.7	22.8	42,411	34,788
Otter Tail County, MN	57,716	57,303	57,083	413	220	0.7	0.4	2,447.8	1,992.7	22.8	42,411	34,788
Fernley, NV Micro Area	52,585	51,980	34,503	605	17,477	1.2	50.7	1,725.9	1,457.7	18.4	32,822	27,995
Lyon County, NV	52,585	51,980	34,503	605	17,477	1.2	50.7	1,725.9	1,457.7	18.4	32,822	27,995
Findlay, OH Micro Area	75,573	74,782	71,303	791	3,479	1.1	4.9	3,695.2	2,690.8	37.3	48,896	36,031
Hancock County, OH	75,573	74,782	71,303	791	3,479	1.1	4.9	3,695.2	2,690.8	37.3	48,896	36,031
Fitzgerald, GA Micro Area	17,403	17,634	17,498	-231	136	-1.3	0.8	476.2	433.4	9.9	27,364	24,581
Ben Hill County, GA	17,403	17,634	17,498	-231	136	-1.3	0.8	476.2	433.4	9.9	27,364	24,581

[1]The April 1, 2000 and 2010 population estimates bases reflect modifications to the census populations as documented in the Count Question Resolution program and geographic program revisions.
[2]Based on the April 1, 2010 estimates base and the July 1, 2015 estimates.
[3]Based on the April 1, 2000 and April 1, 2010 estimates bases.
[4]Based on the July 1 population estimate of the year shown.

Table D-1. Population and Personal Income—*Continued*

Micropolitan statistical area component counties	Population							Personal Income				
	2015 estimate (July 1)	2010 census estimates base (April 1)[1]	2000 census estimates base (April 1)[1]	Net change		Percent change		Total (million dollars)		Percent change, 2010–2015	Per capita[4]	
				2010–2015[2]	2000–2010[3]	2010–2015[2]	2000–2010[3]	2015	2010		2015	2010
Forest City, NC Micro Area	66,390	67,809	62,923	-1,419	4,886	-2.1	7.8	1,934.7	1,713.1	12.9	29,142	25,287
Rutherford County, NC	66,390	67,809	62,923	-1,419	4,886	-2.1	7.8	1,934.7	1,713.1	12.9	29,142	25,287
Forrest City, AR Micro Area	26,589	28,258	29,330	-1,669	-1,072	-5.9	-3.7	696.0	644.7	8.0	26,176	22,875
St. Francis County, AR	26,589	28,258	29,330	-1,669	-1,072	-5.9	-3.7	696.0	644.7	8.0	26,176	22,875
Fort Dodge, IA Micro Area	37,071	38,013	40,230	-942	-2,217	-2.5	-5.5	1,606.2	1,302.8	23.3	43,327	34,397
Webster County, IA	37,071	38,013	40,230	-942	-2,217	-2.5	-5.5	1,606.2	1,302.8	23.3	43,327	34,397
Fort Leonard Wood, MO Micro Area	53,221	52,274	41,170	947	11,104	1.8	27.0	2,078.7	2,046.1	1.6	39,057	38,719
Pulaski County, MO	53,221	52,274	41,170	947	11,104	1.8	27.0	2,078.7	2,046.1	1.6	39,057	38,719
Fort Madison-Keokuk, IA-IL-MO Micro Area	60,433	62,095	65,649	-1,662	-3,554	-2.7	-5.4	2,339.1	1,999.6	17.0	38,706	32,227
Hancock County, IL	18,543	19,104	20,171	-561	-1,067	-2.9	-5.3	730.1	675.3	8.1	39,374	35,385
Lee County, IA	35,089	35,862	38,062	-773	-2,200	-2.2	-5.8	1,388.5	1,125.8	23.3	39,570	31,415
Clark County, MO	6,801	7,129	7,416	-328	-287	-4.6	-3.9	220.5	198.4	11.1	32,425	27,846
Fort Morgan, CO Micro Area	28,360	28,159	27,172	201	987	0.7	3.6	1,135.0	854.0	32.9	40,020	30,313
Morgan County, CO	28,360	28,159	27,172	201	987	0.7	3.6	1,135.0	854.0	32.9	40,020	30,313
Fort Payne, AL Micro Area	71,130	71,115	64,436	15	6,679	0.0	10.4	2,106.9	1,913.1	10.1	29,621	26,892
DeKalb County, AL	71,130	71,115	64,436	15	6,679	0.0	10.4	2,106.9	1,913.1	10.1	29,621	26,892
Fort Polk South, LA Micro Area	50,803	52,334	52,539	-1,531	-205	-2.9	-0.4	1,965.2	1,863.5	5.5	38,683	35,332
Vernon Parish, LA	50,803	52,334	52,539	-1,531	-205	-2.9	-0.4	1,965.2	1,863.5	5.5	38,683	35,332
Frankfort, IN Micro Area	32,609	33,219	33,879	-610	-660	-1.8	-1.9	1,130.7	992.3	14.0	34,675	29,885
Clinton County, IN	32,609	33,219	33,879	-610	-660	-1.8	-1.9	1,130.7	992.3	14.0	34,675	29,885
Frankfort, KY Micro Area	72,354	70,706	66,796	1,648	3,910	2.3	5.9	2,788.8	2,359.5	18.2	38,544	33,344
Anderson County, KY	21,979	21,421	19,093	558	2,328	2.6	12.2	809.6	682.9	18.6	36,834	31,833
Franklin County, KY	50,375	49,285	47,703	1,090	1,582	2.2	3.3	1,979.2	1,676.6	18.0	39,290	34,001
Fredericksburg, TX Micro Area	25,963	24,837	20,806	1,126	4,031	4.5	19.4	1,413.4	1,042.3	35.6	54,441	41,899
Gillespie County, TX	25,963	24,837	20,806	1,126	4,031	4.5	19.4	1,413.4	1,042.3	35.6	54,441	41,899
Freeport, IL Micro Area	45,749	47,711	48,995	-1,962	-1,284	-4.1	-2.6	1,773.5	1,599.4	10.9	38,766	33,562
Stephenson County, IL	45,749	47,711	48,995	-1,962	-1,284	-4.1	-2.6	1,773.5	1,599.4	10.9	38,766	33,562
Fremont, NE Micro Area	36,706	36,685	36,150	21	535	0.1	1.5	1,537.1	1,310.5	17.3	41,875	35,746
Dodge County, NE	36,706	36,685	36,150	21	535	0.1	1.5	1,537.1	1,310.5	17.3	41,875	35,746
Fremont, OH Micro Area	59,679	60,944	61,797	-1,265	-853	-2.1	-1.4	2,253.8	1,980.0	13.8	37,765	32,526
Sandusky County, OH	59,679	60,944	61,797	-1,265	-853	-2.1	-1.4	2,253.8	1,980.0	13.8	37,765	32,526
Gaffney, SC Micro Area	56,194	55,467	52,532	727	2,935	1.3	5.6	1,651.8	1,493.6	10.6	29,394	26,897
Cherokee County, SC	56,194	55,467	52,532	727	2,935	1.3	5.6	1,651.8	1,493.6	10.6	29,394	26,897
Gainesville, TX Micro Area	39,229	38,437	36,370	792	2,067	2.1	5.7	2,093.1	1,464.6	42.9	53,355	38,085
Cooke County, TX	39,229	38,437	36,370	792	2,067	2.1	5.7	2,093.1	1,464.6	42.9	53,355	38,085
Galesburg, IL Micro Area	51,441	52,919	55,842	-1,478	-2,923	-2.8	-5.2	1,941.8	1,810.8	7.2	37,748	34,210
Knox County, IL	51,441	52,919	55,842	-1,478	-2,923	-2.8	-5.2	1,941.8	1,810.8	7.2	37,748	34,210
Gallup, NM Micro Area	76,708	71,491	74,795	5,217	-3,304	7.3	-4.4	1,890.1	1,719.0	10.0	24,640	23,957
McKinley County, NM	76,708	71,491	74,795	5,217	-3,304	7.3	-4.4	1,890.1	1,719.0	10.0	24,640	23,957
Garden City, KS Micro Area	41,074	40,753	45,042	321	-4,289	0.8	-9.5	1,710.9	1,451.6	17.9	41,655	35,450
Finney County, KS	37,118	36,776	40,517	342	-3,741	0.9	-9.2	1,493.2	1,273.6	17.2	40,227	34,461
Kearny County, KS	3,956	3,977	4,525	-21	-548	-0.5	-12.1	217.8	178.0	22.4	55,054	44,609
Gardnerville Ranchos, NV Micro Area	47,710	46,997	41,245	713	5,752	1.5	13.9	2,860.4	2,373.3	20.5	59,953	50,467
Douglas County, NV	47,710	46,997	41,245	713	5,752	1.5	13.9	2,860.4	2,373.3	20.5	59,953	50,467
Georgetown, SC Micro Area	61,298	60,158	55,823	1,140	4,335	1.9	7.8	2,445.1	2,088.2	17.1	39,888	34,725
Georgetown County, SC	61,298	60,158	55,823	1,140	4,335	1.9	7.8	2,445.1	2,088.2	17.1	39,888	34,725
Gillette, WY Micro Area	49,220	46,133	33,705	3,087	12,428	6.7	36.9	2,690.0	2,282.3	17.9	54,653	49,354
Campbell County, WY	49,220	46,133	33,705	3,087	12,428	6.7	36.9	2,690.0	2,282.3	17.9	54,653	49,354
Glasgow, KY Micro Area	53,479	52,272	48,070	1,207	4,202	2.3	8.7	1,835.9	1,449.0	26.7	34,330	27,735
Barren County, KY	43,570	42,173	38,045	1,397	4,128	3.3	10.9	1,540.7	1,206.3	27.7	35,361	28,638
Metcalfe County, KY	9,909	10,099	10,025	-190	74	-1.9	0.7	295.2	242.7	21.7	29,794	23,980
Glenwood Springs, CO Micro Area	75,882	73,537	58,675	2,345	14,862	3.2	25.3	5,180.6	3,550.4	45.9	68,272	48,470
Garfield County, CO	58,095	56,389	43,786	1,706	12,603	3.0	28.8	2,937.0	2,041.1	43.9	50,556	36,387
Pitkin County, CO	17,787	17,148	14,889	639	2,259	3.7	15.2	2,243.6	1,509.3	48.6	126,137	87,976
Gloversville, NY Micro Area	53,992	55,524	55,053	-1,532	471	-2.8	0.9	2,092.7	1,870.5	11.9	38,760	33,723
Fulton County, NY	53,992	55,524	55,053	-1,532	471	-2.8	0.9	2,092.7	1,870.5	11.9	38,760	33,723
Grand Rapids, MN Micro Area	45,435	45,058	43,909	377	1,149	0.8	2.6	1,714.4	1,436.1	19.4	37,733	31,904
Itasca County, MN	45,435	45,058	43,909	377	1,149	0.8	2.6	1,714.4	1,436.1	19.4	37,733	31,904
Grants, NM Micro Area	27,329	27,213	25,588	116	1,625	0.4	6.4	723.1	635.4	13.8	26,459	23,265
Cibola County, NM	27,329	27,213	25,588	116	1,625	0.4	6.4	723.1	635.4	13.8	26,459	23,265
Great Bend, KS Micro Area	27,103	27,674	28,200	-571	-526	-2.1	-1.9	1,306.2	1,073.5	21.7	48,193	38,779
Barton County, KS	27,103	27,674	28,200	-571	-526	-2.1	-1.9	1,306.2	1,073.5	21.7	48,193	38,779
Greeneville, TN Micro Area	68,580	68,831	62,911	-251	5,920	-0.4	9.4	2,580.1	2,235.9	15.4	37,622	32,483
Greene County, TN	68,580	68,831	62,911	-251	5,920	-0.4	9.4	2,580.1	2,235.9	15.4	37,622	32,483
Greenfield Town, MA Micro Area	70,601	71,372	71,540	-771	-168	-1.1	-0.2	3,419.1	2,885.5	18.5	48,428	40,464
Franklin County, MA	70,601	71,372	71,540	-771	-168	-1.1	-0.2	3,419.1	2,885.5	18.5	48,428	40,464
Greensburg, IN Micro Area	26,521	25,740	24,559	781	1,181	3.0	4.8	1,010.3	849.0	19.0	38,095	32,920
Decatur County, IN	26,521	25,740	24,559	781	1,181	3.0	4.8	1,010.3	849.0	19.0	38,095	32,920
Greenville, MS Micro Area	48,130	51,135	63,035	-3,005	-11,900	-5.9	-18.9	1,605.4	1,511.6	6.2	33,356	29,595
Washington County, MS	48,130	51,135	63,035	-3,005	-11,900	-5.9	-18.9	1,605.4	1,511.6	6.2	33,356	29,595
Greenville, OH Micro Area	52,076	52,959	53,313	-883	-354	-1.7	-0.7	1,997.7	1,701.3	17.4	38,360	32,123
Darke County, OH	52,076	52,959	53,313	-883	-354	-1.7	-0.7	1,997.7	1,701.3	17.4	38,360	32,123
Greenwood, MS Micro Area	41,242	42,914	48,702	-1,672	-5,788	-3.9	-11.9	1,283.2	1,210.7	6.0	31,115	28,212
Carroll County, MS	10,243	10,597	10,751	-354	-154	-3.3	-1.4	335.9	287.5	16.8	32,788	27,174
Leflore County, MS	30,999	32,317	37,951	-1,318	-5,634	-4.1	-14.8	947.4	923.2	2.6	30,562	28,552
Greenwood, SC Micro Area	94,770	95,077	92,462	-307	2,615	-0.3	2.8	3,114.8	2,745.2	13.5	32,867	28,876
Abbeville County, SC	24,932	25,416	26,153	-484	-737	-1.9	-2.8	759.6	667.5	13.8	30,468	26,343

[1]The April 1, 2000 and 2010 population estimates bases reflect modifications to the census populations as documented in the Count Question Resolution program and geographic program revisions.
[2]Based on the April 1, 2010 estimates base and the July 1, 2015 estimates.
[3]Based on the April 1, 2000 and April 1, 2010 estimates bases.
[4]Based on the July 1 population estimate of the year shown.

Table D-1.   Population and Personal Income—*Continued*

Micropolitan statistical area component counties	Population							Personal Income				
	2015 estimate (July 1)	2010 census estimates base (April 1)[1]	2000 census estimates base (April 1)[1]	Net change 2010–2015[2]	Net change 2000–2010[3]	Percent change 2010–2015[2]	Percent change 2000–2010[3]	Total (million dollars) 2015	Total (million dollars) 2010	Percent change, 2010–2015	Per capita[4] 2015	Per capita[4] 2010
Greenwood County, SC	69,838	69,661	66,309	177	3,352	0.3	5.1	2,355.2	2,077.7	13.4	33,723	29,796
Grenada, MS Micro Area	21,578	21,906	23,273	-328	-1,367	-1.5	-5.9	751.3	663.5	13.2	34,819	30,359
Grenada County, MS	21,578	21,906	23,273	-328	-1,367	-1.5	-5.9	751.3	663.5	13.2	34,819	30,359
Guymon, OK Micro Area	21,489	20,640	20,098	849	542	4.1	2.7	987.7	693.5	42.4	45,962	33,342
Texas County, OK	21,489	20,640	20,098	849	542	4.1	2.7	987.7	693.5	42.4	45,962	33,342
Hailey, ID Micro Area	27,955	27,701	24,025	254	3,676	0.9	15.3	2,122.5	1,470.0	44.4	75,925	53,206
Blaine County, ID	21,592	21,378	18,994	214	2,384	1.0	12.6	1,889.2	1,286.8	46.8	87,496	60,411
Camas County, ID	1,066	1,117	981	-51	136	-4.6	13.9	42.0	29.5	42.4	39,431	26,566
Lincoln County, ID	5,297	5,206	4,050	91	1,156	1.7	28.5	191.2	153.6	24.5	36,100	29,453
Hannibal, MO Micro Area	39,076	38,948	37,899	128	1,049	0.3	2.8	1,417.8	1,292.9	9.7	36,283	33,171
Marion County, MO	28,880	28,781	28,267	99	514	0.3	1.8	1,053.4	951.3	10.7	36,477	33,048
Ralls County, MO	10,196	10,167	9,632	29	535	0.3	5.6	364.3	341.6	6.7	35,733	33,517
Harrison, AR Micro Area	45,135	45,233	42,543	-98	2,690	-0.2	6.3	1,407.6	1,218.2	15.5	31,187	26,936
Boone County, AR	37,222	36,903	33,940	319	2,963	0.9	8.7	1,197.3	1,031.1	16.1	32,166	27,945
Newton County, AR	7,913	8,330	8,603	-417	-273	-5.0	-3.2	210.4	187.1	12.4	26,583	22,464
Hastings, NE Micro Area	31,587	31,364	31,150	223	214	0.7	0.7	1,401.9	1,130.5	24.0	44,381	36,074
Adams County, NE	31,587	31,364	31,150	223	214	0.7	0.7	1,401.9	1,130.5	24.0	44,381	36,074
Hays, KS Micro Area	29,029	28,452	27,506	577	946	2.0	3.4	1,330.8	1,096.0	21.4	45,843	38,530
Ellis County, KS	29,029	28,452	27,506	577	946	2.0	3.4	1,330.8	1,096.0	21.4	45,843	38,530
Heber, UT Micro Area	29,161	23,525	15,206	5,636	8,319	24.0	54.7	1,186.0	749.7	58.2	40,670	31,714
Wasatch County, UT	29,161	23,525	15,206	5,636	8,319	24.0	54.7	1,186.0	749.7	58.2	40,670	31,714
Helena, MT Micro Area	78,063	74,798	65,750	3,265	9,048	4.4	13.8	3,437.8	3,265.9	5.3	44,039	43,546
Jefferson County, MT	11,645	11,403	10,034	242	1,369	2.1	13.6	505.3	421.6	19.9	43,394	37,006
Lewis and Clark County, MT	66,418	63,395	55,716	3,023	7,679	4.8	13.8	2,932.5	2,844.3	3.1	44,153	44,718
Helena-West Helena, AR Micro Area	19,513	21,757	26,438	-2,244	-4,681	-10.3	-17.7	619.0	586.2	5.6	31,720	27,052
Phillips County, AR	19,513	21,757	26,438	-2,244	-4,681	-10.3	-17.7	619.0	586.2	5.6	31,720	27,052
Henderson, NC Micro Area	44,568	45,419	42,946	-851	2,473	-1.9	5.8	1,416.9	1,350.6	4.9	31,792	29,814
Vance County, NC	44,568	45,419	42,946	-851	2,473	-1.9	5.8	1,416.9	1,350.6	4.9	31,792	29,814
Hereford, TX Micro Area	18,952	19,372	18,565	-420	807	-2.2	4.3	917.8	628.3	46.1	48,426	32,308
Deaf Smith County, TX	18,952	19,372	18,565	-420	807	-2.2	4.3	917.8	628.3	46.1	48,426	32,308
Hermiston-Pendleton, OR Micro Area	87,721	87,062	81,551	659	5,511	0.8	6.8	3,283.9	2,647.5	24.0	37,435	30,332
Morrow County, OR	11,190	11,173	10,995	17	178	0.2	1.6	495.5	356.9	38.8	44,281	31,857
Umatilla County, OR	76,531	75,889	70,556	642	5,333	0.8	7.6	2,788.3	2,290.6	21.7	36,434	30,108
Hillsdale, MI Micro Area	45,941	46,688	46,540	-747	148	-1.6	0.3	1,505.8	1,330.4	13.2	32,778	28,537
Hillsdale County, MI	45,941	46,688	46,540	-747	148	-1.6	0.3	1,505.8	1,330.4	13.2	32,778	28,537
Hilo, HI Micro Area	196,428	185,079	148,641	11,349	36,438	6.1	24.5	7,067.3	5,807.1	21.7	35,979	31,334
Hawaii County, HI	196,428	185,079	148,641	11,349	36,438	6.1	24.5	7,067.3	5,807.1	21.7	35,979	31,334
Hobbs, NM Micro Area	71,180	64,727	55,528	6,453	9,199	10.0	16.6	2,491.2	2,082.7	19.6	34,998	32,228
Lea County, NM	71,180	64,727	55,528	6,453	9,199	10.0	16.6	2,491.2	2,082.7	19.6	34,998	32,228
Holland, MI Micro Area	114,625	111,408	105,631	3,217	5,777	2.9	5.5	4,538.9	3,645.6	24.5	39,598	32,695
Allegan County, MI	114,625	111,408	105,631	3,217	5,777	2.9	5.5	4,538.9	3,645.6	24.5	39,598	32,695
Hood River, OR Micro Area	23,137	22,346	20,407	791	1,939	3.5	9.5	1,061.0	780.7	35.9	45,856	34,789
Hood River County, OR	23,137	22,346	20,407	791	1,939	3.5	9.5	1,061.0	780.7	35.9	45,856	34,789
Hope, AR Micro Area	30,642	31,606	33,537	-964	-1,931	-3.1	-5.8	932.0	823.4	13.2	30,417	26,076
Hempstead County, AR	22,084	22,609	23,597	-525	-988	-2.3	-4.2	653.5	568.9	14.9	29,591	25,172
Nevada County, AR	8,558	8,997	9,940	-439	-943	-4.9	-9.5	278.5	254.4	9.5	32,548	28,352
Houghton, MI Micro Area	38,548	38,784	38,309	-236	475	-0.6	1.2	1,283.5	1,113.2	15.3	33,297	28,646
Houghton County, MI	36,380	36,628	36,013	-248	615	-0.7	1.7	1,199.4	1,040.6	15.3	32,968	28,343
Keweenaw County, MI	2,168	2,156	2,296	12	-140	0.6	-6.1	84.2	72.5	16.1	38,827	33,830
Hudson, NY Micro Area	61,509	63,096	63,074	-1,587	22	-2.5	0.0	3,121.0	2,625.8	18.9	50,741	41,666
Columbia County, NY	61,509	63,096	63,074	-1,587	22	-2.5	0.0	3,121.0	2,625.8	18.9	50,741	41,666
Huntingdon, PA Micro Area	45,668	46,027	45,613	-359	414	-0.8	0.9	1,652.9	1,427.4	15.8	36,195	31,021
Huntingdon County, PA	45,668	46,027	45,613	-359	414	-0.8	0.9	1,652.9	1,427.4	15.8	36,195	31,021
Huntington, IN Micro Area	36,630	37,124	38,078	-494	-954	-1.3	-2.5	1,363.5	1,172.1	16.3	37,225	31,579
Huntington County, IN	36,630	37,124	38,078	-494	-954	-1.3	-2.5	1,363.5	1,172.1	16.3	37,225	31,579
Huntsville, TX Micro Area	85,101	82,536	75,505	2,565	7,031	3.1	9.3	2,329.1	1,887.1	23.4	27,369	22,757
Trinity County, TX	14,402	14,675	13,748	-273	927	-1.9	6.7	486.6	404.0	20.4	33,789	27,467
Walker County, TX	70,699	67,861	61,757	2,838	6,104	4.2	9.9	1,842.5	1,483.1	24.2	26,061	21,741
Huron, SD Micro Area	18,372	17,398	17,027	974	371	5.6	2.2	920.2	684.3	34.5	50,086	39,279
Beadle County, SD	18,372	17,398	17,027	974	371	5.6	2.2	920.2	684.3	34.5	50,086	39,279
Hutchinson, KS Micro Area	63,718	64,511	64,793	-793	-282	-1.2	-0.4	2,387.4	2,176.8	9.7	37,469	33,713
Reno County, KS	63,718	64,511	64,793	-793	-282	-1.2	-0.4	2,387.4	2,176.8	9.7	37,469	33,713
Hutchinson, MN Micro Area	35,932	36,651	34,906	-719	1,745	-2.0	5.0	1,562.5	1,285.3	21.6	43,484	35,112
McLeod County, MN	35,932	36,651	34,906	-719	1,745	-2.0	5.0	1,562.5	1,285.3	21.6	43,484	35,112
Indiana, PA Micro Area	86,966	88,893	89,593	-1,927	-700	-2.2	-0.8	3,131.9	2,781.1	12.6	36,013	31,301
Indiana County, PA	86,966	88,893	89,593	-1,927	-700	-2.2	-0.8	3,131.9	2,781.1	12.6	36,013	31,301
Indianola, MS Micro Area	27,005	29,450	34,382	-2,445	-4,932	-8.3	-14.3	732.8	718.1	2.0	27,136	24,751
Sunflower County, MS	27,005	29,450	34,382	-2,445	-4,932	-8.3	-14.3	732.8	718.1	2.0	27,136	24,751
Ionia, MI Micro Area	64,223	63,905	61,539	318	2,366	0.5	3.8	2,027.0	1,683.4	20.4	31,562	26,358
Ionia County, MI	64,223	63,905	61,539	318	2,366	0.5	3.8	2,027.0	1,683.4	20.4	31,562	26,358
Iron Mountain, MI-WI Micro Area	30,252	30,591	32,553	-339	-1,962	-1.1	-6.0	1,310.3	1,105.8	18.5	43,311	36,207
Dickinson County, MI	25,788	26,168	27,474	-380	-1,306	-1.5	-4.8	1,101.4	939.5	17.2	42,709	35,936
Florence County, WI	4,464	4,423	5,079	41	-656	0.9	-12.9	208.9	166.3	25.6	46,793	37,818
Jackson, OH Micro Area	32,596	33,225	32,653	-629	572	-1.9	1.8	1,083.1	963.2	12.4	33,227	28,947
Jackson County, OH	32,596	33,225	32,653	-629	572	-1.9	1.8	1,083.1	963.2	12.4	33,227	28,947
Jackson, WY-ID Micro Area	33,689	31,464	24,263	2,225	7,201	7.1	29.7	4,833.9	3,315.4	45.8	143,486	105,404
Teton County, ID	10,564	10,170	6,006	394	4,164	3.9	69.3	327.7	240.2	36.4	31,023	23,649

[1]The April 1, 2000 and 2010 population estimates bases reflect modifications to the census populations as documented in the Count Question Resolution program and geographic program revisions.
[2]Based on the April 1, 2010 estimates base and the July 1, 2015 estimates.
[3]Based on the April 1, 2000 and April 1, 2010 estimates bases.
[4]Based on the July 1 population estimate of the year shown.

Table D-1.　Population and Personal Income—*Continued*

Micropolitan statistical area component counties	2015 estimate (July 1)	2010 census estimates base (April 1)[1]	2000 census estimates base (April 1)[1]	Net change 2010–2015[2]	Net change 2000–2010[3]	Percent change 2010–2015[2]	Percent change 2000–2010[3]	Total (million dollars) 2015	Total (million dollars) 2010	Percent change, 2010–2015	Per capita[4] 2015	Per capita[4] 2010
Teton County, WY	23,125	21,294	18,257	1,831	3,037	8.6	16.6	4,506.2	3,075.2	46.5	194,861	144,395
Jacksonville, IL Micro Area	39,920	40,906	42,166	-986	-1,260	-2.4	-3.0	1,417.7	1,376.4	3.0	35,514	33,690
Morgan County, IL	34,828	35,551	36,627	-723	-1,076	-2.0	-2.9	1,245.3	1,201.8	3.6	35,757	33,837
Scott County, IL	5,092	5,355	5,539	-263	-184	-4.9	-3.3	172.4	174.5	-1.2	33,852	32,713
Jacksonville, TX Micro Area	51,542	50,836	46,716	706	4,120	1.4	8.8	1,663.5	1,397.2	19.1	32,274	27,443
Cherokee County, TX	51,542	50,836	46,716	706	4,120	1.4	8.8	1,663.5	1,397.2	19.1	32,274	27,443
Jamestown, ND Micro Area	21,103	21,100	21,912	3	-812	0.0	-3.7	993.4	847.2	17.3	47,076	40,104
Stutsman County, ND	21,103	21,100	21,912	3	-812	0.0	-3.7	993.4	847.2	17.3	47,076	40,104
Jamestown-Dunkirk-Fredonia, NY Micro Area	130,779	134,894	139,698	-4,115	-4,804	-3.1	-3.4	4,767.4	4,195.2	13.6	36,454	31,133
Chautauqua County, NY	130,779	134,894	139,698	-4,115	-4,804	-3.1	-3.4	4,767.4	4,195.2	13.6	36,454	31,133
Jasper, IN Micro Area	55,055	54,733	52,703	322	2,030	0.6	3.9	2,611.7	2,051.7	27.3	47,437	37,469
Dubois County, IN	42,461	41,889	39,868	572	2,021	1.4	5.1	2,163.1	1,661.4	30.2	50,943	39,646
Pike County, IN	12,594	12,844	12,835	-250	9	-1.9	0.1	448.6	390.3	14.9	35,617	30,370
Jefferson, GA Micro Area	63,360	60,485	41,612	2,875	18,873	4.8	45.4	2,224.5	1,736.1	28.1	35,110	28,578
Jackson County, GA	63,360	60,485	41,612	2,875	18,873	4.8	45.4	2,224.5	1,736.1	28.1	35,110	28,578
Jennings, LA Micro Area	31,439	31,594	31,432	-155	162	-0.5	0.5	1,218.0	988.1	23.3	38,743	31,243
Jefferson Davis Parish, LA	31,439	31,594	31,432	-155	162	-0.5	0.5	1,218.0	988.1	23.3	38,743	31,243
Jesup, GA Micro Area	29,534	30,099	26,571	-565	3,528	-1.9	13.3	934.8	852.3	9.7	31,651	28,322
Wayne County, GA	29,534	30,099	26,571	-565	3,528	-1.9	13.3	934.8	852.3	9.7	31,651	28,322
Junction City, KS Micro Area	37,030	34,362	27,849	2,668	6,513	7.8	23.4	1,587.7	1,394.5	13.9	42,875	39,520
Geary County, KS	37,030	34,362	27,849	2,668	6,513	7.8	23.4	1,587.7	1,394.5	13.9	42,875	39,520
Juneau, AK Micro Area	32,756	31,275	30,704	1,481	571	4.7	1.9	2,053.6	1,694.3	21.2	62,694	53,978
Juneau City and Borough, AK	32,756	31,275	30,704	1,481	571	4.7	1.9	2,053.6	1,694.3	21.2	62,694	53,978
Kalispell, MT Micro Area	96,165	90,928	74,507	5,237	16,421	5.8	22.0	3,885.7	3,129.9	24.1	40,407	34,444
Flathead County, MT	96,165	90,928	74,507	5,237	16,421	5.8	22.0	3,885.7	3,129.9	24.1	40,407	34,444
Kapaa, HI Micro Area	71,735	67,090	58,460	4,645	8,630	6.9	14.8	3,017.9	2,356.5	28.1	42,070	35,063
Kauai County, HI	71,735	67,090	58,460	4,645	8,630	6.9	14.8	3,017.9	2,356.5	28.1	42,070	35,063
Kearney, NE Micro Area	55,448	52,591	49,119	2,857	3,472	5.4	7.1	2,967.8	2,022.8	46.7	53,524	38,411
Buffalo County, NE	48,863	46,102	42,232	2,761	3,870	6.0	9.2	2,250.2	1,738.5	29.4	46,051	37,649
Kearney County, NE	6,585	6,489	6,887	96	-398	1.5	-5.8	717.6	284.3	152.4	108,975	43,836
Keene, NH Micro Area	75,909	77,117	73,811	-1,208	3,306	-1.6	4.5	3,715.2	3,142.1	18.2	48,942	40,839
Cheshire County, NH	75,909	77,117	73,811	-1,208	3,306	-1.6	4.5	3,715.2	3,142.1	18.2	48,942	40,839
Kendallville, IN Micro Area	47,733	47,536	46,468	197	1,068	0.4	2.3	1,698.2	1,329.5	27.7	35,578	28,003
Noble County, IN	47,733	47,536	46,468	197	1,068	0.4	2.3	1,698.2	1,329.5	27.7	35,578	28,003
Kennett, MO Micro Area	30,895	31,953	33,184	-1,058	-1,231	-3.3	-3.7	983.4	955.8	2.9	31,831	29,920
Dunklin County, MO	30,895	31,953	33,184	-1,058	-1,231	-3.3	-3.7	983.4	955.8	2.9	31,831	29,920
Kerrville, TX Micro Area	50,955	49,625	43,646	1,330	5,979	2.7	13.7	2,332.2	1,888.1	23.5	45,770	38,029
Kerr County, TX	50,955	49,625	43,646	1,330	5,979	2.7	13.7	2,332.2	1,888.1	23.5	45,770	38,029
Ketchikan, AK Micro Area	13,709	13,479	14,074	230	-595	1.7	-4.2	866.9	724.9	19.6	63,235	53,595
Ketchikan Gateway Borough, AK	13,709	13,479	14,074	230	-595	1.7	-4.2	866.9	724.9	19.6	63,235	53,595
Key West, FL Micro Area	77,482	73,090	79,602	4,392	-6,512	6.0	-8.2	5,765.4	4,565.4	26.3	74,409	62,358
Monroe County, FL	77,482	73,090	79,602	4,392	-6,512	6.0	-8.2	5,765.4	4,565.4	26.3	74,409	62,358
Kill Devil Hills, NC Micro Area	39,733	38,327	34,102	1,406	4,225	3.7	12.4	1,857.5	1,467.2	26.6	46,749	38,210
Dare County, NC	35,663	33,920	29,959	1,743	3,961	5.1	13.2	1,733.3	1,366.4	26.9	48,602	40,204
Tyrrell County, NC	4,070	4,407	4,143	-337	264	-7.6	6.4	124.2	100.8	23.2	30,514	22,848
Kingsville, TX Micro Area	32,264	32,477	32,024	-213	453	-0.7	1.4	1,196.4	941.7	27.1	37,082	28,996
Kenedy County, TX	407	416	414	-9	2	-2.2	0.5	27.6	12.2	125.9	67,830	29,234
Kleberg County, TX	31,857	32,061	31,610	-204	451	-0.6	1.4	1,168.8	929.5	25.8	36,689	28,993
Kinston, NC Micro Area	58,106	59,495	59,636	-1,389	-141	-2.3	-0.2	2,175.6	1,913.3	13.7	37,442	32,183
Lenoir County, NC	58,106	59,495	59,636	-1,389	-141	-2.3	-0.2	2,175.6	1,913.3	13.7	37,442	32,183
Kirksville, MO Micro Area	29,814	30,038	29,141	-224	897	-0.7	3.1	882.9	807.0	9.4	29,612	26,850
Adair County, MO	25,378	25,607	24,968	-229	639	-0.9	2.6	766.1	691.6	10.8	30,188	27,002
Schuyler County, MO	4,436	4,431	4,173	5	258	0.1	6.2	116.8	115.3	1.2	26,321	25,971
Klamath Falls, OR Micro Area	66,016	66,380	63,771	-364	2,609	-0.5	4.1	2,324.8	1,951.7	19.1	35,216	29,423
Klamath County, OR	66,016	66,380	63,771	-364	2,609	-0.5	4.1	2,324.8	1,951.7	19.1	35,216	29,423
Laconia, NH Micro Area	60,641	60,092	56,268	549	3,824	0.9	6.8	3,344.9	2,645.3	26.4	55,160	44,001
Belknap County, NH	60,641	60,092	56,268	549	3,824	0.9	6.8	3,344.9	2,645.3	26.4	55,160	44,001
La Grande, OR Micro Area	25,790	25,744	24,522	46	1,222	0.2	5.0	935.4	777.1	20.4	36,268	30,188
Union County, OR	25,790	25,744	24,522	46	1,222	0.2	5.0	935.4	777.1	20.4	36,268	30,188
LaGrange, GA Micro Area	69,763	67,044	58,753	2,719	8,291	4.1	14.1	2,367.8	1,979.3	19.6	33,940	29,503
Troup County, GA	69,763	67,044	58,753	2,719	8,291	4.1	14.1	2,367.8	1,979.3	19.6	33,940	29,503
Lake City, FL Micro Area	68,348	67,532	56,413	816	11,119	1.2	19.7	2,212.2	1,909.9	15.8	32,366	28,265
Columbia County, FL	68,348	67,532	56,413	816	11,119	1.2	19.7	2,212.2	1,909.9	15.8	32,366	28,265
Lamesa, TX Micro Area	13,520	13,833	14,987	-313	-1,154	-2.3	-7.7	467.3	439.0	6.4	34,562	31,731
Dawson County, TX	13,520	13,833	14,987	-313	-1,154	-2.3	-7.7	467.3	439.0	6.4	34,562	31,731
Laramie, WY Micro Area	37,956	36,299	32,029	1,657	4,270	4.6	13.3	1,482.3	1,214.5	22.0	39,052	33,341
Albany County, WY	37,956	36,299	32,029	1,657	4,270	4.6	13.3	1,482.3	1,214.5	22.0	39,052	33,341
Las Vegas, NM Micro Area	27,967	29,393	30,089	-1,426	-696	-4.9	-2.3	907.8	825.1	10.0	32,461	28,063
San Miguel County, NM	27,967	29,393	30,089	-1,426	-696	-4.9	-2.3	907.8	825.1	10.0	32,461	28,063
Laurel, MS Micro Area	84,784	84,823	83,103	-39	1,720	0.0	2.1	3,114.4	2,672.1	16.6	36,734	31,510
Jasper County, MS	16,569	17,062	18,148	-493	-1,086	-2.9	-6.0	570.1	492.3	15.8	34,409	28,979
Jones County, MS	68,215	67,761	64,955	454	2,806	0.7	4.3	2,544.3	2,179.8	16.7	37,299	32,144
Laurinburg, NC Micro Area	35,509	36,157	35,952	-648	205	-1.8	0.6	1,087.4	1,051.4	3.4	30,625	29,139
Scotland County, NC	35,509	36,157	35,952	-648	205	-1.8	0.6	1,087.4	1,051.4	3.4	30,625	29,139
Lawrenceburg, TN Micro Area	42,564	41,869	39,910	695	1,959	1.7	4.9	1,358.6	1,137.1	19.5	31,919	27,071
Lawrence County, TN	42,564	41,869	39,910	695	1,959	1.7	4.9	1,358.6	1,137.1	19.5	31,919	27,071

[1]The April 1, 2000 and 2010 population estimates bases reflect modifications to the census populations as documented in the Count Question Resolution program and geographic program revisions.
[2]Based on the April 1, 2010 estimates base and the July 1, 2015 estimates.
[3]Based on the April 1, 2000 and April 1, 2010 estimates bases.
[4]Based on the July 1 population estimate of the year shown.

Table D-1.   Population and Personal Income—*Continued*

Micropolitan statistical area component counties	2015 estimate (July 1)	2010 census estimates base (April 1)[1]	2000 census estimates base (April 1)[1]	Net change 2010–2015[2]	Net change 2000–2010[3]	Percent change 2010–2015[2]	Percent change 2000–2010[3]	Total (million dollars) 2015	Total (million dollars) 2010	Percent change, 2010–2015	Per capita[4] 2015	Per capita[4] 2010
Lebanon, MO Micro Area	35,473	35,571	32,532	-98	3,039	-0.3	9.3	1,139.8	967.2	17.8	32,131	27,125
Laclede County, MO	35,473	35,571	32,532	-98	3,039	-0.3	9.3	1,139.8	967.2	17.8	32,131	27,125
Levelland, TX Micro Area	23,433	22,935	22,719	498	216	2.2	1.0	963.0	820.8	17.3	41,096	35,908
Hockley County, TX	23,433	22,935	22,719	498	216	2.2	1.0	963.0	820.8	17.3	41,096	35,908
Lewisburg, PA Micro Area	44,954	44,949	41,583	5	3,366	0.0	8.1	1,635.9	1,369.3	19.5	36,391	30,446
Union County, PA	44,954	44,949	41,583	5	3,366	0.0	8.1	1,635.9	1,369.3	19.5	36,391	30,446
Lewisburg, TN Micro Area	31,552	30,617	26,761	935	3,856	3.1	14.4	1,057.4	835.2	26.6	33,513	27,218
Marshall County, TN	31,552	30,617	26,761	935	3,856	3.1	14.4	1,057.4	835.2	26.6	33,513	27,218
Lewistown, PA Micro Area	46,500	46,683	46,471	-183	212	-0.4	0.5	1,633.9	1,389.5	17.6	35,139	29,782
Mifflin County, PA	46,500	46,683	46,471	-183	212	-0.4	0.5	1,633.9	1,389.5	17.6	35,139	29,782
Lexington, NE Micro Area	25,859	26,370	26,513	-511	-143	-1.9	-0.5	1,018.1	803.1	26.8	39,372	30,447
Dawson County, NE	23,886	24,326	24,370	-440	-44	-1.8	-0.2	921.8	720.0	28.0	38,590	29,589
Gosper County, NE	1,973	2,044	2,143	-71	-99	-3.5	-4.6	96.4	83.1	16.0	48,840	40,657
Liberal, KS Micro Area	23,152	22,952	22,517	200	435	0.9	1.9	813.2	664.4	22.4	35,123	28,908
Seward County, KS	23,152	22,952	22,517	200	435	0.9	1.9	813.2	664.4	22.4	35,123	28,908
Lincoln, IL Micro Area	29,494	30,305	31,199	-811	-894	-2.7	-2.9	995.3	908.7	9.5	33,746	30,017
Logan County, IL	29,494	30,305	31,199	-811	-894	-2.7	-2.9	995.3	908.7	9.5	33,746	30,017
Lock Haven, PA Micro Area	39,441	39,241	37,879	200	1,362	0.5	3.6	1,443.0	1,155.7	24.9	36,586	29,450
Clinton County, PA	39,441	39,241	37,879	200	1,362	0.5	3.6	1,443.0	1,155.7	24.9	36,586	29,450
Logan, WV Micro Area	34,707	36,745	37,705	-2,038	-960	-5.5	-2.5	1,164.3	1,160.3	0.3	33,546	31,593
Logan County, WV	34,707	36,745	37,705	-2,038	-960	-5.5	-2.5	1,164.3	1,160.3	0.3	33,546	31,593
Logansport, IN Micro Area	37,979	38,966	40,924	-987	-1,958	-2.5	-4.8	1,326.1	1,163.6	14.0	34,916	29,855
Cass County, IN	37,979	38,966	40,924	-987	-1,958	-2.5	-4.8	1,326.1	1,163.6	14.0	34,916	29,855
London, KY Micro Area	127,953	126,369	120,326	1,584	6,043	1.3	5.0	3,951.8	3,468.0	13.9	30,885	27,395
Knox County, KY	31,730	31,883	31,739	-153	144	-0.5	0.5	853.8	764.7	11.7	26,907	24,002
Laurel County, KY	60,094	58,849	52,712	1,245	6,137	2.1	11.6	1,938.3	1,683.7	15.1	32,254	28,544
Whitley County, KY	36,129	35,637	35,875	492	-238	1.4	-0.7	1,159.7	1,019.6	13.7	32,100	28,522
Los Alamos, NM Micro Area	17,785	17,950	18,347	-165	-397	-0.9	-2.2	1,161.7	1,089.2	6.7	65,317	60,469
Los Alamos County, NM	17,785	17,950	18,347	-165	-397	-0.9	-2.2	1,161.7	1,089.2	6.7	65,317	60,469
Ludington, MI Micro Area	28,783	28,705	28,283	78	422	0.3	1.5	1,066.3	907.6	17.5	37,046	31,589
Mason County, MI	28,783	28,705	28,283	78	422	0.3	1.5	1,066.3	907.6	17.5	37,046	31,589
Lufkin, TX Micro Area	88,255	86,771	80,123	1,484	6,648	1.7	8.3	3,470.9	2,734.4	26.9	39,328	31,460
Angelina County, TX	88,255	86,771	80,123	1,484	6,648	1.7	8.3	3,470.9	2,734.4	26.9	39,328	31,460
Lumberton, NC Micro Area	134,197	134,168	123,170	29	10,998	0.0	8.9	3,688.7	3,311.9	11.4	27,487	24,645
Robeson County, NC	134,197	134,168	123,170	29	10,998	0.0	8.9	3,688.7	3,311.9	11.4	27,487	24,645
Macomb, IL Micro Area	31,333	32,612	32,906	-1,279	-294	-3.9	-0.9	1,063.2	1,027.1	3.5	33,934	31,498
McDonough County, IL	31,333	32,612	32,906	-1,279	-294	-3.9	-0.9	1,063.2	1,027.1	3.5	33,934	31,498
Madison, IN Micro Area	32,416	32,428	31,712	-12	716	0.0	2.3	1,249.2	1,051.9	18.8	38,536	32,443
Jefferson County, IN	32,416	32,428	31,712	-12	716	0.0	2.3	1,249.2	1,051.9	18.8	38,536	32,443
Madisonville, KY Micro Area	46,222	46,920	46,519	-698	401	-1.5	0.9	1,687.9	1,460.1	15.6	36,518	31,156
Hopkins County, KY	46,222	46,920	46,519	-698	401	-1.5	0.9	1,687.9	1,460.1	15.6	36,518	31,156
Magnolia, AR Micro Area	24,114	24,552	25,612	-438	-1,060	-1.8	-4.1	810.2	716.5	13.1	33,601	28,954
Columbia County, AR	24,114	24,552	25,612	-438	-1,060	-1.8	-4.1	810.2	716.5	13.1	33,601	28,954
Malone, NY Micro Area	50,660	51,606	51,110	-946	496	-1.8	1.0	1,829.5	1,641.4	11.5	36,113	31,793
Franklin County, NY	50,660	51,606	51,110	-946	496	-1.8	1.0	1,829.5	1,641.4	11.5	36,113	31,793
Malvern, AR Micro Area	33,426	32,923	30,413	503	2,510	1.5	8.3	976.9	842.6	15.9	29,226	25,436
Hot Spring County, AR	33,426	32,923	30,413	503	2,510	1.5	8.3	976.9	842.6	15.9	29,226	25,436
Manitowoc, WI Micro Area	79,806	81,442	82,907	-1,636	-1,465	-2.0	-1.8	3,575.6	3,115.5	14.8	44,803	38,321
Manitowoc County, WI	79,806	81,442	82,907	-1,636	-1,465	-2.0	-1.8	3,575.6	3,115.5	14.8	44,803	38,321
Marietta, OH Micro Area	61,112	61,778	63,242	-666	-1,464	-1.1	-2.3	2,355.7	1,933.8	21.8	38,548	31,337
Washington County, OH	61,112	61,778	63,242	-666	-1,464	-1.1	-2.3	2,355.7	1,933.8	21.8	38,548	31,337
Marinette, WI-MI Micro Area	64,432	65,778	68,715	-1,346	-2,937	-2.0	-4.3	2,526.0	2,171.9	16.3	39,205	33,078
Menominee County, MI	23,548	24,029	25,323	-481	-1,294	-2.0	-5.1	903.7	775.2	16.6	38,377	32,333
Marinette County, WI	40,884	41,749	43,392	-865	-1,643	-2.1	-3.8	1,622.3	1,396.7	16.2	39,681	33,506
Marion, IN Micro Area	67,979	70,063	73,410	-2,084	-3,347	-3.0	-4.6	2,495.8	2,137.7	16.8	36,715	30,567
Grant County, IN	67,979	70,063	73,410	-2,084	-3,347	-3.0	-4.6	2,495.8	2,137.7	16.8	36,715	30,567
Marion, NC Micro Area	44,989	44,996	42,134	-7	2,862	0.0	6.8	1,380.4	1,169.9	18.0	30,683	25,957
McDowell County, NC	44,989	44,996	42,134	-7	2,862	0.0	6.8	1,380.4	1,169.9	18.0	30,683	25,957
Marion, OH Micro Area	65,355	66,501	66,198	-1,146	303	-1.7	0.5	2,152.4	1,931.3	11.5	32,935	29,063
Marion County, OH	65,355	66,501	66,198	-1,146	303	-1.7	0.5	2,152.4	1,931.3	11.5	32,935	29,063
Marquette, MI Micro Area	67,215	67,077	64,634	138	2,443	0.2	3.8	2,472.7	2,197.7	12.5	36,788	32,748
Marquette County, MI	67,215	67,077	64,634	138	2,443	0.2	3.8	2,472.7	2,197.7	12.5	36,788	32,748
Marshall, MN Micro Area	25,673	25,857	25,437	-184	420	-0.7	1.7	1,176.0	991.5	18.6	45,806	38,341
Lyon County, MN	25,673	25,857	25,437	-184	420	-0.7	1.7	1,176.0	991.5	18.6	45,806	38,341
Marshall, MO Micro Area	23,258	23,370	23,764	-112	-394	-0.5	-1.7	853.7	765.6	11.5	36,705	32,714
Saline County, MO	23,258	23,370	23,764	-112	-394	-0.5	-1.7	853.7	765.6	11.5	36,705	32,714
Marshall, TX Micro Area	66,746	65,629	62,096	1,117	3,533	1.7	5.7	2,705.9	2,276.4	18.9	40,540	34,646
Harrison County, TX	66,746	65,629	62,096	1,117	3,533	1.7	5.7	2,705.9	2,276.4	18.9	40,540	34,646
Marshalltown, IA Micro Area	40,746	40,648	39,332	98	1,316	0.2	3.3	1,608.6	1,369.6	17.4	39,478	33,655
Marshall County, IA	40,746	40,648	39,332	98	1,316	0.2	3.3	1,608.6	1,369.6	17.4	39,478	33,655
Martin, TN Micro Area	33,960	35,021	34,917	-1,061	104	-3.0	0.3	1,106.2	1,008.2	9.7	32,575	28,780
Weakley County, TN	33,960	35,021	34,917	-1,061	104	-3.0	0.3	1,106.2	1,008.2	9.7	32,575	28,780
Martinsville, VA Micro Area	65,526	67,964	73,362	-2,438	-5,398	-3.6	-7.4	2,291.3	2,049.1	11.8	34,968	30,203
Henry County, VA	51,881	54,143	57,944	-2,262	-3,801	-4.2	-6.6	2,291.3	2,049.1	11.8	34,968	30,203
Martinsville city, VA	13,645	13,821	15,418	-176	-1,597	-1.3	-10.4	(7)	(7)	(7)	(7)	(7)
Maryville, MO Micro Area	22,810	23,370	21,913	-560	1,457	-2.4	6.6	652.0	636.2	2.5	28,586	27,214

[1] The April 1, 2000 and 2010 population estimates bases reflect modifications to the census populations as documented in the Count Question Resolution program and geographic program revisions.
[2] Based on the April 1, 2010 estimates base and the July 1, 2015 estimates.
[3] Based on the April 1, 2000 and April 1, 2010 estimates bases.
[4] Based on the July 1 population estimate of the year shown.
[7] Martinsville city is included with Henry county.

Table D-1. Population and Personal Income—Continued

Micropolitan statistical area component counties	Population 2015 estimate (July 1)	2010 census estimates base (April 1)[1]	2000 census estimates base (April 1)[1]	Net change 2010–2015[2]	Net change 2000–2010[3]	Percent change 2010–2015[2]	Percent change 2000–2010[3]	Personal Income Total (million dollars) 2015	Total (million dollars) 2010	Percent change, 2010–2015	Per capita[4] 2015	Per capita[4] 2010
Nodaway County, MO	22,810	23,370	21,913	-560	1,457	-2.4	6.6	652.0	636.2	2.5	28,586	27,214
Mason City, IA Micro Area	50,586	51,749	54,358	-1,163	-2,609	-2.2	-4.8	2,821.4	1,978.5	42.6	55,773	38,271
Cerro Gordo County, IA	43,017	44,151	46,454	-1,134	-2,303	-2.6	-5.0	2,438.1	1,710.9	42.5	56,676	38,784
Worth County, IA	7,569	7,598	7,904	-29	-306	-0.4	-3.9	383.3	267.6	43.2	50,642	35,289
Mayfield, KY Micro Area	37,421	37,121	37,024	300	97	0.8	0.3	1,317.4	1,120.1	17.6	35,204	30,092
Graves County, KY	37,421	37,121	37,024	300	97	0.8	0.3	1,317.4	1,120.1	17.6	35,204	30,092
Maysville, KY Micro Area	17,099	17,490	16,812	-391	678	-2.2	4.0	629.9	544.3	15.7	36,840	31,106
Mason County, KY	17,099	17,490	16,812	-391	678	-2.2	4.0	629.9	544.3	15.7	36,840	31,106
McAlester, OK Micro Area	44,610	45,837	43,944	-1,227	1,893	-2.7	4.3	1,586.2	1,462.1	8.5	35,556	31,949
Pittsburg County, OK	44,610	45,837	43,944	-1,227	1,893	-2.7	4.3	1,586.2	1,462.1	8.5	35,556	31,949
McComb, MS Micro Area	52,530	53,535	52,522	-1,005	1,013	-1.9	1.9	1,605.1	1,422.5	12.8	30,557	26,564
Amite County, MS	12,574	13,128	13,565	-554	-437	-4.2	-3.2	389.2	335.9	15.9	30,950	25,620
Pike County, MS	39,956	40,407	38,957	-451	1,450	-1.1	3.7	1,216.0	1,086.6	11.9	30,433	26,870
McMinnville, TN Micro Area	40,435	39,840	38,275	595	1,565	1.5	4.1	1,299.4	1,087.0	19.5	32,135	27,267
Warren County, TN	40,435	39,840	38,275	595	1,565	1.5	4.1	1,299.4	1,087.0	19.5	32,135	27,267
McPherson, KS Micro Area	28,941	29,180	29,560	-239	-380	-0.8	-1.3	1,418.5	1,170.8	21.2	49,015	40,178
McPherson County, KS	28,941	29,180	29,560	-239	-380	-0.8	-1.3	1,418.5	1,170.8	21.2	49,015	40,178
Meadville, PA Micro Area	86,484	88,765	90,352	-2,281	-1,587	-2.6	-1.8	3,197.1	2,765.6	15.6	36,967	31,183
Crawford County, PA	86,484	88,765	90,352	-2,281	-1,587	-2.6	-1.8	3,197.1	2,765.6	15.6	36,967	31,183
Menomonie, WI Micro Area	44,497	43,857	39,853	640	4,004	1.5	10.0	1,616.0	1,333.1	21.2	36,316	30,378
Dunn County, WI	44,497	43,857	39,853	640	4,004	1.5	10.0	1,616.0	1,333.1	21.2	36,316	30,378
Meridian, MS Micro Area	104,499	107,454	106,411	-2,955	1,043	-2.8	1.0	3,593.1	3,183.1	12.9	34,384	29,589
Clarke County, MS	16,006	16,732	17,796	-726	-1,064	-4.3	-6.0	572.7	493.9	15.9	35,778	29,563
Kemper County, MS	9,969	10,461	10,447	-492	14	-4.7	0.1	274.9	236.8	16.1	27,575	22,639
Lauderdale County, MS	78,524	80,261	78,168	-1,737	2,093	-2.2	2.7	2,745.5	2,452.4	12.0	34,964	30,499
Merrill, WI Micro Area	27,980	28,743	29,625	-763	-882	-2.7	-3.0	1,116.8	1,009.8	10.6	39,916	35,106
Lincoln County, WI	27,980	28,743	29,625	-763	-882	-2.7	-3.0	1,116.8	1,009.8	10.6	39,916	35,106
Mexico, MO Micro Area	26,096	25,529	25,857	567	-328	2.2	-1.3	949.7	814.0	16.7	36,391	31,972
Audrain County, MO	26,096	25,529	25,857	567	-328	2.2	-1.3	949.7	814.0	16.7	36,391	31,972
Miami, OK Micro Area	31,981	31,848	33,164	133	-1,316	0.4	-4.0	1,098.0	952.3	15.3	34,331	29,908
Ottawa County, OK	31,981	31,848	33,164	133	-1,316	0.4	-4.0	1,098.0	952.3	15.3	34,331	29,908
Middlesborough, KY Micro Area	27,337	28,691	30,049	-1,354	-1,358	-4.7	-4.5	793.9	739.7	7.3	29,042	25,766
Bell County, KY	27,337	28,691	30,049	-1,354	-1,358	-4.7	-4.5	793.9	739.7	7.3	29,042	25,766
Milledgeville, GA Micro Area	54,010	55,237	54,699	-1,227	538	-2.2	1.0	1,533.2	1,375.4	11.5	28,387	24,953
Baldwin County, GA	45,459	45,835	44,616	-376	1,219	-0.8	2.7	1,314.2	1,182.3	11.2	28,910	25,870
Hancock County, GA	8,551	9,402	10,083	-851	-681	-9.1	-6.8	219.0	193.1	13.4	25,607	20,503
Mineral Wells, TX Micro Area	27,895	28,111	27,015	-216	1,096	-0.8	4.1	1,064.8	873.5	21.9	38,171	31,128
Palo Pinto County, TX	27,895	28,111	27,015	-216	1,096	-0.8	4.1	1,064.8	873.5	21.9	38,171	31,128
Minot, ND Micro Area	79,814	69,540	67,394	10,274	2,146	14.8	3.2	4,413.7	3,073.2	43.6	55,300	43,911
McHenry County, ND	5,968	5,395	5,983	573	-588	10.6	-9.8	301.4	239.5	25.8	50,497	44,377
Renville County, ND	2,571	2,470	2,612	101	-142	4.1	-5.4	131.4	122.3	7.5	51,125	49,382
Ward County, ND	71,275	61,675	58,799	9,600	2,876	15.6	4.9	3,980.9	2,711.4	46.8	55,852	43,652
Mitchell, SD Micro Area	23,243	22,835	21,887	408	948	1.8	4.3	1,213.2	944.9	28.4	52,197	41,373
Davison County, SD	19,858	19,504	18,743	354	761	1.8	4.1	995.5	768.7	29.5	50,132	39,411
Hanson County, SD	3,385	3,331	3,144	54	187	1.6	5.9	217.7	176.2	23.5	64,310	52,855
Moberly, MO Micro Area	25,104	25,414	24,663	-310	751	-1.2	3.0	910.0	752.1	21.0	36,247	29,563
Randolph County, MO	25,104	25,414	24,663	-310	751	-1.2	3.0	910.0	752.1	21.0	36,247	29,563
Montrose, CO Micro Area	40,946	41,278	33,438	-332	7,840	-0.8	23.4	1,415.1	1,203.6	17.6	34,559	29,218
Montrose County, CO	40,946	41,278	33,438	-332	7,840	-0.8	23.4	1,415.1	1,203.6	17.6	34,559	29,218
Morehead City, NC Micro Area	68,879	66,469	59,334	2,410	7,135	3.6	12.0	3,044.4	2,608.3	16.7	44,199	39,107
Carteret County, NC	68,879	66,469	59,334	2,410	7,135	3.6	12.0	3,044.4	2,608.3	16.7	44,199	39,107
Morgan City, LA Micro Area	52,810	54,650	53,539	-1,840	1,111	-3.4	2.1	2,020.4	1,930.8	4.6	38,257	35,400
St. Mary Parish, LA	52,810	54,650	53,539	-1,840	1,111	-3.4	2.1	2,020.4	1,930.8	4.6	38,257	35,400
Moscow, ID Micro Area	38,778	37,244	34,925	1,534	2,319	4.1	6.6	1,412.5	1,202.3	17.5	36,425	32,253
Latah County, ID	38,778	37,244	34,925	1,534	2,319	4.1	6.6	1,412.5	1,202.3	17.5	36,425	32,253
Moses Lake, WA Micro Area	93,259	89,120	74,714	4,139	14,406	4.6	19.3	3,551.4	2,745.4	29.4	38,081	30,631
Grant County, WA	93,259	89,120	74,714	4,139	14,406	4.6	19.3	3,551.4	2,745.4	29.4	38,081	30,631
Moultrie, GA Micro Area	45,844	45,498	42,050	346	3,448	0.8	8.2	1,357.1	1,210.1	12.1	29,603	26,514
Colquitt County, GA	45,844	45,498	42,050	346	3,448	0.8	8.2	1,357.1	1,210.1	12.1	29,603	26,514
Mountain Home, AR Micro Area	41,053	41,513	38,365	-460	3,148	-1.1	8.2	1,426.6	1,203.0	18.6	34,751	28,962
Baxter County, AR	41,053	41,513	38,365	-460	3,148	-1.1	8.2	1,426.6	1,203.0	18.6	34,751	28,962
Mountain Home, ID Micro Area	25,876	27,038	29,116	-1,162	-2,078	-4.3	-7.1	901.8	757.7	19.0	34,851	27,940
Elmore County, ID	25,876	27,038	29,116	-1,162	-2,078	-4.3	-7.1	901.8	757.7	19.0	34,851	27,940
Mount Airy, NC Micro Area	72,743	73,673	71,208	-930	2,465	-1.3	3.5	2,518.9	2,155.0	16.9	34,628	29,244
Surry County, NC	72,743	73,673	71,208	-930	2,465	-1.3	3.5	2,518.9	2,155.0	16.9	34,628	29,244
Mount Pleasant, MI Micro Area	70,698	70,311	63,336	387	6,975	0.6	11.0	2,255.3	1,894.7	19.0	31,900	26,947
Isabella County, MI	70,698	70,311	63,336	387	6,975	0.6	11.0	2,255.3	1,894.7	19.0	31,900	26,947
Mount Pleasant, TX Micro Area	32,623	32,334	28,118	289	4,216	0.9	15.0	1,068.7	896.1	19.3	32,760	27,657
Titus County, TX	32,623	32,334	28,118	289	4,216	0.9	15.0	1,068.7	896.1	19.3	32,760	27,657
Mount Sterling, KY Micro Area	46,194	44,396	40,174	1,798	4,222	4.0	10.5	1,466.2	1,195.7	22.6	31,741	26,857
Bath County, KY	12,228	11,591	11,099	637	492	5.5	4.4	355.5	288.5	23.3	29,076	24,839
Menifee County, KY	6,358	6,306	6,539	52	-233	0.8	-3.6	185.6	155.0	19.8	29,196	24,377
Montgomery County, KY	27,608	26,499	22,536	1,109	3,963	4.2	17.6	925.1	752.3	23.0	33,507	28,334
Mount Vernon, IL Micro Area	38,353	38,825	40,051	-472	-1,226	-1.2	-3.1	1,399.6	1,251.7	11.8	36,493	32,292
Jefferson County, IL	38,353	38,825	40,051	-472	-1,226	-1.2	-3.1	1,399.6	1,251.7	11.8	36,493	32,292
Mount Vernon, OH Micro Area	61,061	60,930	54,482	131	6,448	0.2	11.8	2,402.4	1,893.8	26.9	39,345	31,002
Knox County, OH	61,061	60,930	54,482	131	6,448	0.2	11.8	2,402.4	1,893.8	26.9	39,345	31,002

[1]The April 1, 2000 and 2010 population estimates bases reflect modifications to the census populations as documented in the Count Question Resolution program and geographic program revisions.
[2]Based on the April 1, 2010 estimates base and the July 1, 2015 estimates.
[3]Based on the April 1, 2000 and April 1, 2010 estimates bases.
[4]Based on the July 1 population estimate of the year shown.

Table D-1. Population and Personal Income—*Continued*

Micropolitan statistical area component counties	2015 estimate (July 1)	2010 census estimates base (April 1)[1]	2000 census estimates base (April 1)[1]	Net change 2010–2015[2]	Net change 2000–2010[3]	Percent change 2010–2015[2]	Percent change 2000–2010[3]	Total (million dollars) 2015	Total (million dollars) 2010	Percent change, 2010–2015	Per capita[4] 2015	Per capita[4] 2010
Murray, KY Micro Area	38,343	37,191	34,182	1,152	3,009	3.1	8.8	1,280.2	1,142.1	12.1	33,387	30,566
Calloway County, KY	38,343	37,191	34,182	1,152	3,009	3.1	8.8	1,280.2	1,142.1	12.1	33,387	30,566
Muscatine, IA Micro Area	43,011	42,749	41,723	262	1,026	0.6	2.5	1,860.8	1,548.8	20.1	43,264	36,241
Muscatine County, IA	43,011	42,749	41,723	262	1,026	0.6	2.5	1,860.8	1,548.8	20.1	43,264	36,241
Muskogee, OK Micro Area	69,699	70,988	69,471	-1,289	1,517	-1.8	2.2	2,369.1	2,116.0	12.0	33,990	29,760
Muskogee County, OK	69,699	70,988	69,471	-1,289	1,517	-1.8	2.2	2,369.1	2,116.0	12.0	33,990	29,760
Nacogdoches, TX Micro Area	65,664	64,524	59,197	1,140	5,327	1.8	9.0	2,249.5	1,961.7	14.7	34,258	30,336
Nacogdoches County, TX	65,664	64,524	59,197	1,140	5,327	1.8	9.0	2,249.5	1,961.7	14.7	34,258	30,336
Natchez, MS-LA Micro Area	51,396	53,119	54,560	-1,723	-1,441	-3.2	-2.6	1,720.1	1,615.5	6.5	33,468	30,257
Concordia Parish, LA	20,142	20,822	20,221	-680	601	-3.3	3.0	630.6	677.6	-6.9	31,309	32,530
Adams County, MS	31,254	32,297	34,339	-1,043	-2,042	-3.2	-5.9	1,089.5	937.8	16.2	34,860	28,803
Natchitoches, LA Micro Area	39,179	39,566	39,077	-387	489	-1.0	1.3	1,368.8	1,238.8	10.5	34,937	31,342
Natchitoches Parish, LA	39,179	39,566	39,077	-387	489	-1.0	1.3	1,368.8	1,238.8	10.5	34,937	31,342
Newberry, SC Micro Area	38,012	37,508	35,979	504	1,529	1.3	4.2	1,317.5	1,123.0	17.3	34,660	29,883
Newberry County, SC	38,012	37,508	35,979	504	1,529	1.3	4.2	1,317.5	1,123.0	17.3	34,660	29,883
New Castle, IN Micro Area	48,985	49,462	48,511	-477	951	-1.0	2.0	1,645.3	1,427.4	15.3	33,589	28,844
Henry County, IN	48,985	49,462	48,511	-477	951	-1.0	2.0	1,645.3	1,427.4	15.3	33,589	28,844
New Castle, PA Micro Area	88,082	91,140	94,567	-3,058	-3,427	-3.4	-3.6	3,513.9	3,098.5	13.4	39,893	34,060
Lawrence County, PA	88,082	91,140	94,567	-3,058	-3,427	-3.4	-3.6	3,513.9	3,098.5	13.4	39,893	34,060
New Philadelphia-Dover, OH Micro Area	92,916	92,582	90,919	334	1,663	0.4	1.8	3,706.7	2,951.9	25.6	39,893	31,893
Tuscarawas County, OH	92,916	92,582	90,919	334	1,663	0.4	1.8	3,706.7	2,951.9	25.6	39,893	31,893
Newport, OR Micro Area	47,038	46,032	44,481	1,006	1,551	2.2	3.5	1,833.0	1,522.8	20.4	38,968	33,112
Lincoln County, OR	47,038	46,032	44,481	1,006	1,551	2.2	3.5	1,833.0	1,522.8	20.4	38,968	33,112
Newport, TN Micro Area	35,162	35,662	33,548	-500	2,114	-1.4	6.3	1,026.9	901.5	13.9	29,206	25,279
Cocke County, TN	35,162	35,662	33,548	-500	2,114	-1.4	6.3	1,026.9	901.5	13.9	29,206	25,279
Newton, IA Micro Area	36,827	36,842	37,229	-15	-387	0.0	-1.0	1,437.9	1,226.6	17.2	39,044	33,317
Jasper County, IA	36,827	36,842	37,229	-15	-387	0.0	-1.0	1,437.9	1,226.6	17.2	39,044	33,317
New Ulm, MN Micro Area	25,313	25,893	26,916	-580	-1,023	-2.2	-3.8	1,207.1	996.8	21.1	47,688	38,550
Brown County, MN	25,313	25,893	26,916	-580	-1,023	-2.2	-3.8	1,207.1	996.8	21.1	47,688	38,550
Nogales, AZ Micro Area	46,461	47,420	38,381	-959	9,039	-2.0	23.6	1,563.2	1,427.8	9.5	33,646	30,115
Santa Cruz County, AZ	46,461	47,420	38,381	-959	9,039	-2.0	23.6	1,563.2	1,427.8	9.5	33,646	30,115
Norfolk, NE Micro Area	48,184	48,271	49,550	-87	-1,279	-0.2	-2.6	2,304.4	1,762.1	30.8	47,825	36,466
Madison County, NE	35,039	34,876	35,254	163	-378	0.5	-1.1	1,573.8	1,280.0	23.0	44,915	36,639
Pierce County, NE	7,208	7,266	7,843	-58	-577	-0.8	-7.4	462.0	269.6	71.4	64,100	37,168
Stanton County, NE	5,937	6,129	6,453	-192	-324	-3.1	-5.0	268.6	212.5	26.4	45,243	34,645
North Platte, NE Micro Area	36,908	37,590	35,937	-682	1,653	-1.8	4.6	1,771.2	1,381.1	28.2	47,989	36,762
Lincoln County, NE	35,656	36,288	34,630	-632	1,658	-1.7	4.8	1,704.9	1,337.4	27.5	47,816	36,881
Logan County, NE	777	763	774	14	-11	1.8	-1.4	38.1	27.4	39.1	48,979	35,536
McPherson County, NE	475	539	533	-64	6	-11.9	1.1	28.2	16.4	72.2	59,379	30,497
North Vernon, IN Micro Area	27,897	28,525	27,561	-628	964	-2.2	3.5	968.9	794.9	21.9	34,730	27,916
Jennings County, IN	27,897	28,525	27,561	-628	964	-2.2	3.5	968.9	794.9	21.9	34,730	27,916
North Wilkesboro, NC Micro Area	68,502	69,340	65,630	-838	3,710	-1.2	5.7	2,222.8	1,927.1	15.3	32,449	27,837
Wilkes County, NC	68,502	69,340	65,630	-838	3,710	-1.2	5.7	2,222.8	1,927.1	15.3	32,449	27,837
Norwalk, OH Micro Area	58,469	59,626	59,447	-1,157	179	-1.9	0.3	2,131.4	1,854.0	15.0	36,453	31,119
Huron County, OH	58,469	59,626	59,447	-1,157	179	-1.9	0.3	2,131.4	1,854.0	15.0	36,453	31,119
Oak Harbor, WA Micro Area	80,593	78,506	71,571	2,087	6,935	2.7	9.7	3,873.3	3,133.5	23.6	48,060	39,810
Island County, WA	80,593	78,506	71,571	2,087	6,935	2.7	9.7	3,873.3	3,133.5	23.6	48,060	39,810
Ogdensburg-Massena, NY Micro Area	111,007	111,941	111,922	-934	19	-0.8	0.0	3,761.1	3,323.6	13.2	33,882	29,722
St. Lawrence County, NY	111,007	111,941	111,922	-934	19	-0.8	0.0	3,761.1	3,323.6	13.2	33,882	29,722
Oil City, PA Micro Area	53,119	54,983	57,500	-1,864	-2,517	-3.4	-4.4	2,029.4	1,856.2	9.3	38,205	33,770
Venango County, PA	53,119	54,983	57,500	-1,864	-2,517	-3.4	-4.4	2,029.4	1,856.2	9.3	38,205	33,770
Okeechobee, FL Micro Area	39,469	39,996	35,869	-527	4,127	-1.3	11.5	1,172.0	969.8	20.9	29,695	24,229
Okeechobee County, FL	39,469	39,996	35,869	-527	4,127	-1.3	11.5	1,172.0	969.8	20.9	29,695	24,229
Olean, NY Micro Area	77,922	80,354	83,874	-2,432	-3,520	-3.0	-4.2	2,889.3	2,658.6	8.7	37,080	33,125
Cattaraugus County, NY	77,922	80,354	83,874	-2,432	-3,520	-3.0	-4.2	2,889.3	2,658.6	8.7	37,080	33,125
Oneonta, NY Micro Area	60,636	62,249	61,692	-1,613	557	-2.6	0.9	2,321.9	2,039.8	13.8	38,293	32,792
Otsego County, NY	60,636	62,249	61,692	-1,613	557	-2.6	0.9	2,321.9	2,039.8	13.8	38,293	32,792
Ontario, OR-ID Micro Area	53,276	53,935	52,202	-659	1,733	-1.2	3.3	1,721.5	1,400.1	23.0	32,313	25,936
Payette County, ID	22,896	22,623	20,584	273	2,039	1.2	9.9	802.4	678.2	18.3	35,045	29,960
Malheur County, OR	30,380	31,312	31,618	-932	-306	-3.0	-1.0	919.1	721.9	27.3	30,255	23,030
Opelousas, LA Micro Area	83,848	83,384	87,662	464	-4,278	0.6	-4.9	3,187.2	2,753.7	15.7	38,012	32,982
St. Landry Parish, LA	83,848	83,384	87,662	464	-4,278	0.6	-4.9	3,187.2	2,753.7	15.7	38,012	32,982
Orangeburg, SC Micro Area	89,208	92,495	91,511	-3,287	984	-3.6	1.1	2,727.8	2,470.7	10.4	30,578	26,770
Orangeburg County, SC	89,208	92,495	91,511	-3,287	984	-3.6	1.1	2,727.8	2,470.7	10.4	30,578	26,770
Oskaloosa, IA Micro Area	22,324	22,381	22,319	-57	62	-0.3	0.3	862.9	725.1	19.0	38,653	32,371
Mahaska County, IA	22,324	22,381	22,319	-57	62	-0.3	0.3	862.9	725.1	19.0	38,653	32,371
Othello, WA Micro Area	19,254	18,728	16,426	526	2,302	2.8	14.0	807.9	594.3	35.9	41,962	31,596
Adams County, WA	19,254	18,728	16,426	526	2,302	2.8	14.0	807.9	594.3	35.9	41,962	31,596
Ottawa, KS Micro Area	25,609	25,996	24,784	-387	1,212	-1.5	4.9	969.9	830.0	16.9	37,872	31,908
Franklin County, KS	25,609	25,996	24,784	-387	1,212	-1.5	4.9	969.9	830.0	16.9	37,872	31,908
Ottawa-Peru, IL Micro Area	150,564	154,906	153,172	-4,342	1,734	-2.8	1.1	5,994.6	5,358.6	11.9	39,814	34,627
Bureau County, IL	33,587	34,978	35,496	-1,391	-518	-4.0	-1.5	1,291.3	1,184.6	9.0	38,446	33,923
LaSalle County, IL	111,333	113,922	111,599	-2,589	2,323	-2.3	2.1	4,406.8	3,950.5	11.5	39,582	34,704
Putnam County, IL	5,644	6,006	6,077	-362	-71	-6.0	-1.2	296.5	223.5	32.7	52,533	37,256
Ottumwa, IA Micro Area	43,942	44,378	44,608	-436	-230	-1.0	-0.5	1,589.6	1,370.9	16.0	36,175	30,865
Davis County, IA	8,769	8,753	8,541	16	212	0.2	2.5	315.9	258.0	22.5	36,029	29,416
Wapello County, IA	35,173	35,625	36,067	-452	-442	-1.3	-1.2	1,273.6	1,112.9	14.4	36,211	31,221

[1]The April 1, 2000 and 2010 population estimates bases reflect modifications to the census populations as documented in the Count Question Resolution program and geographic program revisions.
[2]Based on the April 1, 2010 estimates base and the July 1, 2015 estimates.
[3]Based on the April 1, 2000 and April 1, 2010 estimates bases.
[4]Based on the July 1 population estimate of the year shown.

Table D-1. Population and Personal Income—*Continued*

Micropolitan statistical area component counties	Population 2015 estimate (July 1)	2010 census estimates base (April 1)[1]	2000 census estimates base (April 1)[1]	Net change 2010–2015[2]	Net change 2000–2010[3]	Percent change 2010–2015[2]	Percent change 2000–2010[3]	Personal Income Total (million dollars) 2015	Total 2010	Percent change, 2010–2015	Per capita[4] 2015	Per capita 2010
Owatonna, MN Micro Area	36,755	36,576	33,684	179	2,892	0.5	8.6	1,569.9	1,347.9	16.5	42,712	36,922
Steele County, MN	36,755	36,576	33,684	179	2,892	0.5	8.6	1,569.9	1,347.9	16.5	42,712	36,922
Owosso, MI Micro Area	68,619	70,648	71,695	-2,029	-1,047	-2.9	-1.5	2,407.0	2,086.5	15.4	35,078	29,553
Shiawassee County, MI	68,619	70,648	71,695	-2,029	-1,047	-2.9	-1.5	2,407.0	2,086.5	15.4	35,078	29,553
Oxford, MS Micro Area	53,154	47,359	38,687	5,795	8,672	12.2	22.4	1,878.6	1,442.5	30.2	35,342	30,329
Lafayette County, MS	53,154	47,359	38,687	5,795	8,672	12.2	22.4	1,878.6	1,442.5	30.2	35,342	30,329
Oxford, NC Micro Area	58,674	57,532	48,486	1,142	9,046	2.0	18.7	1,990.2	1,723.0	15.5	33,919	29,887
Granville County, NC	58,674	57,532	48,486	1,142	9,046	2.0	18.7	1,990.2	1,723.0	15.5	33,919	29,887
Ozark, AL Micro Area	49,565	50,251	49,120	-686	1,131	-1.4	2.3	1,690.5	1,650.8	2.4	34,107	32,782
Dale County, AL	49,565	50,251	49,120	-686	1,131	-1.4	2.3	1,690.5	1,650.8	2.4	34,107	32,782
Paducah, KY-IL Micro Area	97,312	98,760	98,773	-1,448	-13	-1.5	0.0	4,024.9	3,475.3	15.8	41,361	35,199
Massac County, IL	14,766	15,429	15,163	-663	266	-4.3	1.8	514.3	474.6	8.4	34,828	30,800
Ballard County, KY	8,212	8,247	8,293	-35	-46	-0.4	-0.6	293.3	249.9	17.4	35,717	30,263
Livingston County, KY	9,316	9,519	9,806	-203	-287	-2.1	-2.9	328.7	291.9	12.6	35,284	30,609
McCracken County, KY	65,018	65,565	65,511	-547	54	-0.8	0.1	2,888.6	2,458.9	17.5	44,428	37,523
Pahrump, NV Micro Area	42,477	43,945	32,522	-1,468	11,423	-3.3	35.1	1,481.2	1,452.5	2.0	34,871	33,119
Nye County, NV	42,477	43,945	32,522	-1,468	11,423	-3.3	35.1	1,481.2	1,452.5	2.0	34,871	33,119
Palatka, FL Micro Area	72,023	74,364	70,418	-2,341	3,946	-3.1	5.6	2,052.7	1,947.5	5.4	28,501	26,233
Putnam County, FL	72,023	74,364	70,418	-2,341	3,946	-3.1	5.6	2,052.7	1,947.5	5.4	28,501	26,233
Palestine, TX Micro Area	57,580	58,458	55,114	-878	3,344	-1.5	6.1	1,824.5	1,542.3	18.3	31,686	26,371
Anderson County, TX	57,580	58,458	55,114	-878	3,344	-1.5	6.1	1,824.5	1,542.3	18.3	31,686	26,371
Pampa, TX Micro Area	23,210	22,535	22,742	675	-207	3.0	-0.9	1,091.4	851.8	28.1	47,024	37,929
Gray County, TX	23,210	22,535	22,742	675	-207	3.0	-0.9	1,091.4	851.8	28.1	47,024	37,929
Paragould, AR Micro Area	44,196	42,090	37,383	2,106	4,707	5.0	12.6	1,396.0	1,164.7	19.9	31,588	27,607
Greene County, AR	44,196	42,090	37,383	2,106	4,707	5.0	12.6	1,396.0	1,164.7	19.9	31,588	27,607
Paris, TN Micro Area	32,147	32,330	31,112	-183	1,218	-0.6	3.9	1,218.1	1,003.1	21.4	37,891	30,977
Henry County, TN	32,147	32,330	31,112	-183	1,218	-0.6	3.9	1,218.1	1,003.1	21.4	37,891	30,977
Paris, TX Micro Area	49,440	49,789	48,491	-349	1,298	-0.7	2.7	1,857.9	1,621.0	14.6	37,578	32,541
Lamar County, TX	49,440	49,789	48,491	-349	1,298	-0.7	2.7	1,857.9	1,621.0	14.6	37,578	32,541
Parsons, KS Micro Area	20,803	21,607	22,821	-804	-1,214	-3.7	-5.3	837.3	733.4	14.2	40,251	34,043
Labette County, KS	20,803	21,607	22,821	-804	-1,214	-3.7	-5.3	837.3	733.4	14.2	40,251	34,043
Payson, AZ Micro Area	53,159	53,597	51,298	-438	2,299	-0.8	4.5	1,917.2	1,630.7	17.6	36,066	30,455
Gila County, AZ	53,159	53,597	51,298	-438	2,299	-0.8	4.5	1,917.2	1,630.7	17.6	36,066	30,455
Pecos, TX Micro Area	14,732	13,783	13,141	949	642	6.9	4.9	452.2	305.1	48.2	30,692	22,083
Reeves County, TX	14,732	13,783	13,141	949	642	6.9	4.9	452.2	305.1	48.2	30,692	22,083
Pella, IA Micro Area	33,294	33,309	32,048	-15	1,261	0.0	3.9	1,388.9	1,154.0	20.4	41,716	34,726
Marion County, IA	33,294	33,309	32,048	-15	1,261	0.0	3.9	1,388.9	1,154.0	20.4	41,716	34,726
Peru, IN Micro Area	35,862	36,903	36,085	-1,041	818	-2.8	2.3	1,115.2	940.2	18.6	31,097	25,551
Miami County, IN	35,862	36,903	36,085	-1,041	818	-2.8	2.3	1,115.2	940.2	18.6	31,097	25,551
Picayune, MS Micro Area	55,191	55,747	48,518	-556	7,229	-1.0	14.9	1,864.3	1,729.9	7.8	33,778	31,044
Pearl River County, MS	55,191	55,747	48,518	-556	7,229	-1.0	14.9	1,864.3	1,729.9	7.8	33,778	31,044
Pierre, SD Micro Area	21,935	21,361	20,808	574	553	2.7	2.7	1,137.9	1,009.3	12.7	51,874	47,132
Hughes County, SD	17,555	17,022	16,483	533	539	3.1	3.3	861.7	764.4	12.7	49,087	44,801
Stanley County, SD	2,954	2,966	2,772	-12	194	-0.4	7.0	190.6	137.1	39.0	64,515	46,113
Sully County, SD	1,426	1,373	1,553	53	-180	3.9	-11.6	85.6	107.8	-20.6	60,007	78,162
Pinehurst-Southern Pines, NC Micro Area	94,352	88,247	74,772	6,105	13,475	6.9	18.0	4,125.5	3,419.7	20.6	43,725	38,594
Moore County, NC	94,352	88,247	74,772	6,105	13,475	6.9	18.0	4,125.5	3,419.7	20.6	43,725	38,594
Pittsburg, KS Micro Area	39,217	39,134	38,248	83	886	0.2	2.3	1,343.6	1,219.5	10.2	34,260	31,127
Crawford County, KS	39,217	39,134	38,248	83	886	0.2	2.3	1,343.6	1,219.5	10.2	34,260	31,127
Plainview, TX Micro Area	34,360	36,273	36,605	-1,913	-332	-5.3	-0.9	1,077.8	1,112.2	-3.1	31,367	30,601
Hale County, TX	34,360	36,273	36,605	-1,913	-332	-5.3	-0.9	1,077.8	1,112.2	-3.1	31,367	30,601
Platteville, WI Micro Area	52,250	51,208	49,590	1,042	1,618	2.0	3.3	2,007.1	1,702.6	17.9	38,413	33,251
Grant County, WI	52,250	51,208	49,590	1,042	1,618	2.0	3.3	2,007.1	1,702.6	17.9	38,413	33,251
Plattsburgh, NY Micro Area	81,251	82,131	79,882	-880	2,249	-1.1	2.8	3,270.6	2,888.5	13.2	40,253	35,196
Clinton County, NY	81,251	82,131	79,882	-880	2,249	-1.1	2.8	3,270.6	2,888.5	13.2	40,253	35,196
Plymouth, IN Micro Area	46,857	47,047	45,126	-190	1,921	-0.4	4.3	1,731.7	1,452.4	19.2	36,958	30,897
Marshall County, IN	46,857	47,047	45,126	-190	1,921	-0.4	4.3	1,731.7	1,452.4	19.2	36,958	30,897
Point Pleasant, WV-OH Micro Area	57,179	58,260	57,010	-1,081	1,250	-1.9	2.2	1,862.3	1,696.7	9.8	32,570	29,036
Gallia County, OH	30,142	30,934	31,058	-792	-124	-2.6	-0.4	1,058.9	956.9	10.7	35,129	30,783
Mason County, WV	27,037	27,326	25,952	-289	1,374	-1.1	5.3	803.4	739.8	8.6	29,716	27,050
Ponca City, OK Micro Area	45,366	46,562	48,086	-1,196	-1,524	-2.6	-3.2	1,744.0	1,546.0	12.8	38,443	33,299
Kay County, OK	45,366	46,562	48,086	-1,196	-1,524	-2.6	-3.2	1,744.0	1,546.0	12.8	38,443	33,299
Pontiac, IL Micro Area	36,671	38,950	39,734	-2,279	-784	-5.9	-2.0	1,463.5	1,385.1	5.7	39,910	35,634
Livingston County, IL	36,671	38,950	39,734	-2,279	-784	-5.9	-2.0	1,463.5	1,385.1	5.7	39,910	35,634
Poplar Bluff, MO Micro Area	42,951	42,794	40,864	157	1,930	0.4	4.7	1,426.5	1,344.1	6.1	33,212	31,408
Butler County, MO	42,951	42,794	40,864	157	1,930	0.4	4.7	1,426.5	1,344.1	6.1	33,212	31,408
Portales, NM Micro Area	19,120	19,846	18,022	-726	1,824	-3.7	10.1	696.3	619.8	12.3	36,417	30,968
Roosevelt County, NM	19,120	19,846	18,022	-726	1,824	-3.7	10.1	696.3	619.8	12.3	36,417	30,968
Port Angeles, WA Micro Area	73,486	71,404	64,183	2,082	7,221	2.9	11.3	2,920.2	2,465.3	18.4	39,738	34,464
Clallam County, WA	73,486	71,404	64,183	2,082	7,221	2.9	11.3	2,920.2	2,465.3	18.4	39,738	34,464
Port Clinton, OH Micro Area	40,877	41,434	40,974	-557	460	-1.3	1.1	1,838.6	1,596.3	15.2	44,978	38,565
Ottawa County, OH	40,877	41,434	40,974	-557	460	-1.3	1.1	1,838.6	1,596.3	15.2	44,978	38,565
Port Lavaca, TX Micro Area	21,895	21,381	20,645	514	736	2.4	3.6	845.5	642.1	31.7	38,618	30,105
Calhoun County, TX	21,895	21,381	20,645	514	736	2.4	3.6	845.5	642.1	31.7	38,618	30,105

[1]The April 1, 2000 and 2010 population estimates bases reflect modifications to the census populations as documented in the Count Question Resolution program and geographic program revisions.
[2]Based on the April 1, 2010 estimates base and the July 1, 2015 estimates.
[3]Based on the April 1, 2000 and April 1, 2010 estimates bases.
[4]Based on the July 1 population estimate of the year shown.

Table D-1. Population and Personal Income—*Continued*

Micropolitan statistical area component counties	2015 estimate (July 1)	2010 census estimates base (April 1)[1]	2000 census estimates base (April 1)[1]	Net change 2010–2015[2]	Net change 2000–2010[3]	Percent change 2010–2015[2]	Percent change 2000–2010[3]	Total (million dollars) 2015	Total (million dollars) 2010	Percent change, 2010–2015	Per capita[4] 2015	Per capita[4] 2010
Portsmouth, OH Micro Area	76,825	79,499	79,215	-2,674	284	-3.4	0.4	2,521.9	2,258.5	11.7	32,826	28,399
Scioto County, OH	76,825	79,499	79,215	-2,674	284	-3.4	0.4	2,521.9	2,258.5	11.7	32,826	28,399
Pottsville, PA Micro Area	144,590	148,289	150,263	-3,699	-1,974	-2.5	-1.3	5,716.9	5,069.6	12.8	39,539	34,205
Schuylkill County, PA	144,590	148,289	150,263	-3,699	-1,974	-2.5	-1.3	5,716.9	5,069.6	12.8	39,539	34,205
Price, UT Micro Area	20,479	21,403	20,531	-924	872	-4.3	4.2	704.3	661.8	6.4	34,392	30,896
Carbon County, UT	20,479	21,403	20,531	-924	872	-4.3	4.2	704.3	661.8	6.4	34,392	30,896
Prineville, OR Micro Area	21,630	20,978	19,175	652	1,803	3.1	9.4	782.0	588.8	32.8	36,153	28,174
Crook County, OR	21,630	20,978	19,175	652	1,803	3.1	9.4	782.0	588.8	32.8	36,153	28,174
Pullman, WA Micro Area	48,177	44,776	40,742	3,401	4,034	7.6	9.9	1,726.4	1,387.9	24.4	35,834	30,983
Whitman County, WA	48,177	44,776	40,742	3,401	4,034	7.6	9.9	1,726.4	1,387.9	24.4	35,834	30,983
Quincy, IL-MO Micro Area	77,220	77,314	78,748	-94	-1,434	-0.1	-1.8	3,089.8	2,739.3	12.8	40,012	35,413
Adams County, IL	67,013	67,103	68,261	-90	-1,158	-0.1	-1.7	2,772.3	2,455.7	12.9	41,369	36,567
Lewis County, MO	10,207	10,211	10,487	-4	-276	0.0	-2.6	317.5	283.6	11.9	31,103	27,809
Raymondville, TX Micro Area	21,903	22,134	20,079	-231	2,055	-1.0	10.2	615.0	504.1	22.0	28,078	22,708
Willacy County, TX	21,903	22,134	20,079	-231	2,055	-1.0	10.2	615.0	504.1	22.0	28,078	22,708
Red Bluff, CA Micro Area	63,308	63,461	56,060	-153	7,401	-0.2	13.2	2,269.6	1,799.2	26.1	35,850	28,293
Tehama County, CA	63,308	63,461	56,060	-153	7,401	-0.2	13.2	2,269.6	1,799.2	26.1	35,850	28,293
Red Wing, MN Micro Area	46,435	46,183	44,139	252	2,044	0.5	4.6	2,248.7	1,817.4	23.7	48,427	39,339
Goodhue County, MN	46,435	46,183	44,139	252	2,044	0.5	4.6	2,248.7	1,817.4	23.7	48,427	39,339
Rexburg, ID Micro Area	51,092	50,778	39,304	314	11,474	0.6	29.2	1,344.2	1,044.1	28.7	26,309	20,540
Fremont County, ID	12,819	13,242	11,813	-423	1,429	-3.2	12.1	446.5	345.8	29.1	34,828	26,113
Madison County, ID	38,273	37,536	27,491	737	10,045	2.0	36.5	897.7	698.3	28.6	23,456	18,577
Richmond, IN Micro Area	67,001	69,003	71,087	-2,002	-2,084	-2.9	-2.9	2,445.2	2,093.9	16.8	36,494	30,391
Wayne County, IN	67,001	69,003	71,087	-2,002	-2,084	-2.9	-2.9	2,445.2	2,093.9	16.8	36,494	30,391
Richmond-Berea, KY Micro Area	104,766	99,972	87,462	4,794	12,510	4.8	14.3	3,462.1	2,831.6	22.3	33,046	28,242
Madison County, KY	87,824	82,916	70,916	4,908	12,000	5.9	16.9	2,968.5	2,415.5	22.9	33,800	29,034
Rockcastle County, KY	16,942	17,056	16,546	-114	510	-0.7	3.1	493.7	416.1	18.6	29,138	24,382
Rio Grande City, TX Micro Area	63,795	60,968	53,573	2,827	7,395	4.6	13.8	1,565.6	1,303.5	20.1	24,540	21,309
Starr County, TX	63,795	60,968	53,573	2,827	7,395	4.6	13.8	1,565.6	1,303.5	20.1	24,540	21,309
Riverton, WY Micro Area	40,315	40,123	35,805	192	4,318	0.5	12.1	1,653.7	1,421.3	16.4	41,019	35,337
Fremont County, WY	40,315	40,123	35,805	192	4,318	0.5	12.1	1,653.7	1,421.3	16.4	41,019	35,337
Roanoke Rapids, NC Micro Area	72,882	76,789	79,495	-3,907	-2,706	-5.1	-3.4	2,360.9	2,179.4	8.3	32,393	28,479
Halifax County, NC	52,456	54,691	57,444	-2,235	-2,753	-4.1	-4.8	1,728.2	1,591.3	8.6	32,947	29,181
Northampton County, NC	20,426	22,098	22,051	-1,672	47	-7.6	0.2	632.6	588.1	7.6	30,971	26,739
Rochelle, IL Micro Area	51,659	53,497	51,001	-1,838	2,496	-3.4	4.9	2,102.4	1,871.1	12.4	40,698	35,014
Ogle County, IL	51,659	53,497	51,001	-1,838	2,496	-3.4	4.9	2,102.4	1,871.1	12.4	40,698	35,014
Rockingham, NC Micro Area	45,437	46,639	46,597	-1,202	42	-2.6	0.1	1,425.0	1,275.6	11.7	31,361	27,357
Richmond County, NC	45,437	46,639	46,597	-1,202	42	-2.6	0.1	1,425.0	1,275.6	11.7	31,361	27,357
Rock Springs, WY Micro Area	44,626	43,806	37,620	820	6,186	1.9	16.4	2,172.4	1,855.5	17.1	48,681	42,563
Sweetwater County, WY	44,626	43,806	37,620	820	6,186	1.9	16.4	2,172.4	1,855.5	17.1	48,681	42,563
Rolla, MO Micro Area	44,794	45,154	39,826	-360	5,328	-0.8	13.4	1,496.3	1,315.3	13.8	33,403	29,028
Phelps County, MO	44,794	45,154	39,826	-360	5,328	-0.8	13.4	1,496.3	1,315.3	13.8	33,403	29,028
Roseburg, OR Micro Area	107,685	107,667	100,375	18	7,292	0.0	7.3	3,874.2	3,295.3	17.6	35,977	30,608
Douglas County, OR	107,685	107,667	100,375	18	7,292	0.0	7.3	3,874.2	3,295.3	17.6	35,977	30,608
Roswell, NM Micro Area	65,764	65,645	61,373	119	4,272	0.2	7.0	2,398.1	2,030.4	18.1	36,466	30,883
Chaves County, NM	65,764	65,645	61,373	119	4,272	0.2	7.0	2,398.1	2,030.4	18.1	36,466	30,883
Ruidoso, NM Micro Area	19,420	20,497	19,374	-1,077	1,123	-5.3	5.8	768.8	634.4	21.2	39,585	31,001
Lincoln County, NM	19,420	20,497	19,374	-1,077	1,123	-5.3	5.8	768.8	634.4	21.2	39,585	31,001
Russellville, AR Micro Area	85,103	83,939	75,619	1,164	8,320	1.4	11.0	2,732.8	2,315.0	18.0	32,112	27,473
Pope County, AR	63,390	61,754	54,492	1,636	7,262	2.6	13.3	2,071.9	1,769.4	17.1	32,684	28,489
Yell County, AR	21,713	22,185	21,127	-472	1,058	-2.1	5.0	661.0	545.6	21.1	30,441	24,625
Ruston, LA Micro Area	47,774	46,735	42,503	1,039	4,232	2.2	10.0	1,702.1	1,421.0	19.8	35,628	30,321
Lincoln Parish, LA	47,774	46,735	42,503	1,039	4,232	2.2	10.0	1,702.1	1,421.0	19.8	35,628	30,321
Rutland, VT Micro Area	59,736	61,646	63,386	-1,910	-1,740	-3.1	-2.7	2,849.0	2,485.1	14.6	47,694	40,352
Rutland County, VT	59,736	61,646	63,386	-1,910	-1,740	-3.1	-2.7	2,849.0	2,485.1	14.6	47,694	40,352
Safford, AZ Micro Area	37,666	37,220	33,475	446	3,745	1.2	11.2	1,119.9	903.3	24.0	29,731	24,324
Graham County, AZ	37,666	37,220	33,475	446	3,745	1.2	11.2	1,119.9	903.3	24.0	29,731	24,324
St. Marys, GA Micro Area	52,102	50,513	43,658	1,589	6,855	3.1	15.7	1,706.6	1,456.4	17.2	32,754	28,743
Camden County, GA	52,102	50,513	43,658	1,589	6,855	3.1	15.7	1,706.6	1,456.4	17.2	32,754	28,743
St. Marys, PA Micro Area	30,872	31,946	35,114	-1,074	-3,168	-3.4	-9.0	1,346.8	1,228.8	9.6	43,625	38,569
Elk County, PA	30,872	31,946	35,114	-1,074	-3,168	-3.4	-9.0	1,346.8	1,228.8	9.6	43,625	38,569
Salem, OH Micro Area	104,806	107,841	112,050	-3,035	-4,209	-2.8	-3.8	3,701.1	3,172.5	16.7	35,314	29,412
Columbiana County, OH	104,806	107,841	112,050	-3,035	-4,209	-2.8	-3.8	3,701.1	3,172.5	16.7	35,314	29,412
Salina, KS Micro Area	61,666	61,697	59,763	-31	1,934	-0.1	3.2	2,607.9	2,273.9	14.7	42,290	36,753
Ottawa County, KS	5,975	6,091	6,164	-116	-73	-1.9	-1.2	222.9	208.4	7.0	37,312	34,186
Saline County, KS	55,691	55,606	53,599	85	2,007	0.2	3.7	2,384.9	2,065.5	15.5	42,824	37,034
Sandpoint, ID Micro Area	41,859	40,877	36,809	982	4,068	2.4	11.1	1,449.7	1,201.5	20.7	34,634	29,365
Bonner County, ID	41,859	40,877	36,809	982	4,068	2.4	11.1	1,449.7	1,201.5	20.7	34,634	29,365
Sandusky, OH Micro Area	75,550	77,079	79,623	-1,529	-2,544	-2.0	-3.2	3,723.3	3,490.5	6.7	49,283	45,311
Erie County, OH	75,550	77,079	79,623	-1,529	-2,544	-2.0	-3.2	3,723.3	3,490.5	6.7	49,283	45,311
Sanford, NC Micro Area	59,660	57,866	49,196	1,794	8,670	3.1	17.6	2,127.2	1,803.3	18.0	35,655	31,151
Lee County, NC	59,660	57,866	49,196	1,794	8,670	3.1	17.6	2,127.2	1,803.3	18.0	35,655	31,151
Sault Ste. Marie, MI Micro Area	38,033	38,673	38,543	-640	130	-1.7	0.3	1,192.6	1,081.4	10.3	31,358	28,016
Chippewa County, MI	38,033	38,673	38,543	-640	130	-1.7	0.3	1,192.6	1,081.4	10.3	31,358	28,016
Sayre, PA Micro Area	61,281	62,622	62,747	-1,341	-125	-2.1	-0.2	2,410.1	1,985.6	21.4	39,329	31,712
Bradford County, PA	61,281	62,622	62,747	-1,341	-125	-2.1	-0.2	2,410.1	1,985.6	21.4	39,329	31,712

[1]The April 1, 2000 and 2010 population estimates bases reflect modifications to the census populations as documented in the Count Question Resolution program and geographic program revisions.
[2]Based on the April 1, 2010 estimates base and the July 1, 2015 estimates.
[3]Based on the April 1, 2000 and April 1, 2010 estimates bases.
[4]Based on the July 1 population estimate of the year shown.

Table D-1.   Population and Personal Income—*Continued*

Micropolitan statistical area component counties	Population							Personal Income					
	2015 estimate (July 1)	2010 census estimates base (April 1)[1]	2000 census estimates base (April 1)[1]	Net change		Percent change		Total (million dollars)		Percent change, 2010–2015	Per capita[4]	
				2010–2015[2]	2000–2010[3]	2010–2015[2]	2000–2010[3]	2015	2010		2015	2010
Scottsbluff, NE Micro Area	38,309	38,971	39,242	-662	-271	-1.7	-0.7	1,619.1	1,325.5	22.1	42,264	33,915
Banner County, NE	788	690	815	98	-125	14.2	-15.3	54.1	31.1	73.9	68,652	44,641
Scotts Bluff County, NE	36,261	36,970	36,952	-709	18	-1.9	0.0	1,486.1	1,248.1	19.1	40,984	33,664
Sioux County, NE	1,260	1,311	1,475	-51	-164	-3.9	-11.1	78.9	46.4	70.1	62,599	35,321
Scottsboro, AL Micro Area	52,419	53,226	53,871	-807	-645	-1.5	-1.2	1,778.6	1,566.7	13.5	33,930	29,460
Jackson County, AL	52,419	53,226	53,871	-807	-645	-1.5	-1.2	1,778.6	1,566.7	13.5	33,930	29,460
Searcy, AR Micro Area	79,161	77,076	67,164	2,085	9,912	2.7	14.8	2,564.7	2,265.4	13.2	32,398	29,294
White County, AR	79,161	77,076	67,164	2,085	9,912	2.7	14.8	2,564.7	2,265.4	13.2	32,398	29,294
Sedalia, MO Micro Area	42,255	42,201	39,418	54	2,783	0.1	7.1	1,491.3	1,310.8	13.8	35,292	31,013
Pettis County, MO	42,255	42,201	39,418	54	2,783	0.1	7.1	1,491.3	1,310.8	13.8	35,292	31,013
Selinsgrove, PA Micro Area	40,444	39,709	37,506	735	2,203	1.9	5.9	1,557.9	1,303.0	19.6	38,519	32,785
Snyder County, PA	40,444	39,709	37,506	735	2,203	1.9	5.9	1,557.9	1,303.0	19.6	38,519	32,785
Selma, AL Micro Area	41,131	43,820	46,361	-2,689	-2,541	-6.1	-5.5	1,299.5	1,234.0	5.3	31,595	28,172
Dallas County, AL	41,131	43,820	46,361	-2,689	-2,541	-6.1	-5.5	1,299.5	1,234.0	5.3	31,595	28,172
Seneca, SC Micro Area	75,713	74,275	66,199	1,438	8,076	1.9	12.2	2,859.0	2,366.5	20.8	37,761	31,826
Oconee County, SC	75,713	74,275	66,199	1,438	8,076	1.9	12.2	2,859.0	2,366.5	20.8	37,761	31,826
Seneca Falls, NY Micro Area	34,833	35,244	33,319	-411	1,925	-1.2	5.8	1,235.6	1,092.7	13.1	35,472	31,004
Seneca County, NY	34,833	35,244	33,319	-411	1,925	-1.2	5.8	1,235.6	1,092.7	13.1	35,472	31,004
Sevierville, TN Micro Area	95,946	89,876	71,200	6,070	18,676	6.8	26.2	3,328.7	2,637.3	26.2	34,693	29,261
Sevier County, TN	95,946	89,876	71,200	6,070	18,676	6.8	26.2	3,328.7	2,637.3	26.2	34,693	29,261
Seymour, IN Micro Area	44,069	42,380	41,397	1,689	983	4.0	2.4	1,747.1	1,465.7	19.2	39,645	34,424
Jackson County, IN	44,069	42,380	41,397	1,689	983	4.0	2.4	1,747.1	1,465.7	19.2	39,645	34,424
Shawano, WI Micro Area	45,877	46,187	45,230	-310	957	-0.7	2.1	1,658.7	1,430.6	15.9	36,155	30,966
Menominee County, WI	4,573	4,232	4,554	341	-322	8.1	-7.1	123.5	104.2	18.5	27,013	24,436
Shawano County, WI	41,304	41,955	40,676	-651	1,279	-1.6	3.1	1,535.1	1,326.4	15.7	37,167	31,630
Shawnee, OK Micro Area	71,875	69,442	65,505	2,433	3,937	3.5	6.0	2,587.5	2,387.5	8.4	35,999	34,277
Pottawatomie County, OK	71,875	69,442	65,505	2,433	3,937	3.5	6.0	2,587.5	2,387.5	8.4	35,999	34,277
Shelby, NC Micro Area	96,879	98,083	96,129	-1,204	1,954	-1.2	2.0	3,266.0	2,827.6	15.5	33,712	28,857
Cleveland County, NC	96,879	98,083	96,129	-1,204	1,954	-1.2	2.0	3,266.0	2,827.6	15.5	33,712	28,857
Shelbyville, TN Micro Area	47,183	45,058	37,608	2,125	7,450	4.7	19.8	1,633.4	1,246.8	31.0	34,618	27,644
Bedford County, TN	47,183	45,058	37,608	2,125	7,450	4.7	19.8	1,633.4	1,246.8	31.0	34,618	27,644
Shelton, WA Micro Area	61,023	60,699	49,443	324	11,256	0.5	22.8	2,234.9	1,956.0	14.3	36,623	32,196
Mason County, WA	61,023	60,699	49,443	324	11,256	0.5	22.8	2,234.9	1,956.0	14.3	36,623	32,196
Sheridan, WY Micro Area	30,009	29,116	26,563	893	2,553	3.1	9.6	1,653.2	1,471.4	12.4	55,089	50,484
Sheridan County, WY	30,009	29,116	26,563	893	2,553	3.1	9.6	1,653.2	1,471.4	12.4	55,089	50,484
Show Low, AZ Micro Area	108,277	107,491	97,452	786	10,039	0.7	10.3	3,154.3	2,663.9	18.4	29,132	24,731
Navajo County, AZ	108,277	107,491	97,452	786	10,039	0.7	10.3	3,154.3	2,663.9	18.4	29,132	24,731
Sidney, OH Micro Area	48,901	49,423	48,292	-522	1,131	-1.1	2.3	2,051.0	1,628.7	25.9	41,942	33,028
Shelby County, OH	48,901	49,423	48,292	-522	1,131	-1.1	2.3	2,051.0	1,628.7	25.9	41,942	33,028
Sikeston, MO Micro Area	39,008	39,187	40,437	-179	-1,250	-0.5	-3.1	1,430.4	1,293.4	10.6	36,669	32,960
Scott County, MO	39,008	39,187	40,437	-179	-1,250	-0.5	-3.1	1,430.4	1,293.4	10.6	36,669	32,960
Silver City, NM Micro Area	28,609	29,514	31,004	-905	-1,490	-3.1	-4.8	1,024.9	885.0	15.8	35,824	30,103
Grant County, NM	28,609	29,514	31,004	-905	-1,490	-3.1	-4.8	1,024.9	885.0	15.8	35,824	30,103
Snyder, TX Micro Area	17,615	16,921	16,366	694	555	4.1	3.4	889.4	628.7	41.5	50,489	37,114
Scurry County, TX	17,615	16,921	16,366	694	555	4.1	3.4	889.4	628.7	41.5	50,489	37,114
Somerset, KY Micro Area	63,782	63,063	56,281	719	6,782	1.1	12.1	2,284.8	1,911.9	19.5	35,823	30,248
Pulaski County, KY	63,782	63,063	56,281	719	6,782	1.1	12.1	2,284.8	1,911.9	19.5	35,823	30,248
Somerset, PA Micro Area	75,522	77,748	80,047	-2,226	-2,299	-2.9	-2.9	2,769.5	2,620.1	5.7	36,671	33,695
Somerset County, PA	75,522	77,748	80,047	-2,226	-2,299	-2.9	-2.9	2,769.5	2,620.1	5.7	36,671	33,695
Sonora, CA Micro Area	53,709	55,365	54,522	-1,656	843	-3.0	1.5	2,243.4	1,871.2	19.9	41,770	33,908
Tuolumne County, CA	53,709	55,365	54,522	-1,656	843	-3.0	1.5	2,243.4	1,871.2	19.9	41,770	33,908
Spearfish, SD Micro Area	24,827	24,097	21,805	730	2,292	3.0	10.5	1,092.0	897.5	21.7	43,984	37,093
Lawrence County, SD	24,827	24,097	21,805	730	2,292	3.0	10.5	1,092.0	897.5	21.7	43,984	37,093
Spencer, IA Micro Area	16,507	16,667	17,369	-160	-702	-1.0	-4.0	815.9	653.1	24.9	49,426	39,264
Clay County, IA	16,507	16,667	17,369	-160	-702	-1.0	-4.0	815.9	653.1	24.9	49,426	39,264
Spirit Lake, IA Micro Area	17,111	16,667	16,429	444	238	2.7	1.4	926.7	723.8	28.0	54,156	43,422
Dickinson County, IA	17,111	16,667	16,429	444	238	2.7	1.4	926.7	723.8	28.0	54,156	43,422
Starkville, MS Micro Area	49,800	47,671	42,920	2,129	4,751	4.5	11.1	1,516.2	1,279.8	18.5	30,445	26,823
Oktibbeha County, MS	49,800	47,671	42,920	2,129	4,751	4.5	11.1	1,516.2	1,279.8	18.5	30,445	26,823
Statesboro, GA Micro Area	72,651	70,217	55,961	2,434	14,256	3.5	25.5	2,125.6	1,837.0	15.7	29,258	26,005
Bulloch County, GA	72,651	70,217	55,961	2,434	14,256	3.5	25.5	2,125.6	1,837.0	15.7	29,258	26,005
Steamboat Springs, CO Micro Area	24,130	23,506	19,679	624	3,827	2.7	19.4	1,586.2	1,168.9	35.7	65,734	49,847
Routt County, CO	24,130	23,506	19,679	624	3,827	2.7	19.4	1,586.2	1,168.9	35.7	65,734	49,847
Stephenville, TX Micro Area	41,122	37,890	32,981	3,232	4,909	8.5	14.9	1,363.0	1,055.8	29.1	33,144	27,867
Erath County, TX	41,122	37,890	32,981	3,232	4,909	8.5	14.9	1,363.0	1,055.8	29.1	33,144	27,867
Sterling, CO Micro Area	22,036	22,709	20,566	-673	2,143	-3.0	10.4	1,074.4	760.5	41.3	48,755	34,367
Logan County, CO	22,036	22,709	20,566	-673	2,143	-3.0	10.4	1,074.4	760.5	41.3	48,755	34,367
Sterling, IL Micro Area	57,079	58,498	60,662	-1,419	-2,164	-2.4	-3.6	2,253.6	2,039.7	10.5	39,483	34,868
Whiteside County, IL	57,079	58,498	60,662	-1,419	-2,164	-2.4	-3.6	2,253.6	2,039.7	10.5	39,483	34,868
Stevens Point, WI Micro Area	70,408	70,019	67,181	389	2,838	0.6	4.2	2,917.3	2,460.9	18.5	41,434	35,158
Portage County, WI	70,408	70,019	67,181	389	2,838	0.6	4.2	2,917.3	2,460.9	18.5	41,434	35,158
Stillwater, OK Micro Area	80,850	77,350	68,201	3,500	9,149	4.5	13.4	2,971.8	2,366.9	25.6	36,757	30,562
Payne County, OK	80,850	77,350	68,201	3,500	9,149	4.5	13.4	2,971.8	2,366.9	25.6	36,757	30,562
Storm Lake, IA Micro Area	20,493	20,260	20,415	233	-155	1.2	-0.8	975.8	765.8	27.4	47,617	37,678
Buena Vista County, IA	20,493	20,260	20,415	233	-155	1.2	-0.8	975.8	765.8	27.4	47,617	37,678
Sturgis, MI Micro Area	61,018	61,295	62,411	-277	-1,116	-0.5	-1.8	2,087.7	1,798.2	16.1	34,215	29,340
St. Joseph County, MI	61,018	61,295	62,411	-277	-1,116	-0.5	-1.8	2,087.7	1,798.2	16.1	34,215	29,340

[1]The April 1, 2000 and 2010 population estimates bases reflect modifications to the census populations as documented in the Count Question Resolution program and geographic program revisions.
[2]Based on the April 1, 2010 estimates base and the July 1, 2015 estimates.
[3]Based on the April 1, 2000 and April 1, 2010 estimates bases.
[4]Based on the July 1 population estimate of the year shown.

Table D-1. Population and Personal Income—*Continued*

Micropolitan statistical area component counties	2015 estimate (July 1)	2010 census estimates base (April 1)[1]	2000 census estimates base (April 1)[1]	Net change 2010–2015[2]	Net change 2000–2010[3]	Percent change 2010–2015[2]	Percent change 2000–2010[3]	Total (million dollars) 2015	Total (million dollars) 2010	Percent change, 2010–2015	Per capita[4] 2015	Per capita[4] 2010
Sulphur Springs, TX Micro Area	36,223	35,161	31,960	1,062	3,201	3.0	10.0	1,340.6	1,070.1	25.3	37,009	30,398
Hopkins County, TX	36,223	35,161	31,960	1,062	3,201	3.0	10.0	1,340.6	1,070.1	25.3	37,009	30,398
Summerville, GA Micro Area	24,922	26,015	25,423	-1,093	592	-4.2	2.3	704.6	624.8	12.8	28,274	24,070
Chattooga County, GA	24,922	26,015	25,423	-1,093	592	-4.2	2.3	704.6	624.8	12.8	28,274	24,070
Summit Park, UT Micro Area	39,633	36,327	29,746	3,306	6,581	9.1	22.1	3,889.1	2,500.1	55.6	98,128	68,473
Summit County, UT	39,633	36,327	29,746	3,306	6,581	9.1	22.1	3,889.1	2,500.1	55.6	98,128	68,473
Sunbury, PA Micro Area	93,246	94,514	94,867	-1,268	-353	-1.3	-0.4	3,514.3	3,087.9	13.8	37,689	32,728
Northumberland County, PA	93,246	94,514	94,867	-1,268	-353	-1.3	-0.4	3,514.3	3,087.9	13.8	37,689	32,728
Susanville, CA Micro Area	31,345	34,895	33,828	-3,550	1,067	-10.2	3.2	1,085.5	973.6	11.5	34,630	27,946
Lassen County, CA	31,345	34,895	33,828	-3,550	1,067	-10.2	3.2	1,085.5	973.6	11.5	34,630	27,946
Sweetwater, TX Micro Area	15,107	15,217	15,805	-110	-588	-0.7	-3.7	562.3	469.8	19.7	37,222	30,813
Nolan County, TX	15,107	15,217	15,805	-110	-588	-0.7	-3.7	562.3	469.8	19.7	37,222	30,813
Tahlequah, OK Micro Area	48,447	46,985	42,475	1,462	4,510	3.1	10.6	1,411.1	1,199.6	17.6	29,127	25,459
Cherokee County, OK	48,447	46,985	42,475	1,462	4,510	3.1	10.6	1,411.1	1,199.6	17.6	29,127	25,459
Talladega-Sylacauga, AL Micro Area	91,586	94,049	92,576	-2,463	1,473	-2.6	1.6	2,879.0	2,551.1	12.9	31,435	27,188
Coosa County, AL	10,724	11,758	11,842	-1,034	-84	-8.8	-0.7	307.3	278.5	10.3	28,651	23,683
Talladega County, AL	80,862	82,291	80,734	-1,429	1,557	-1.7	1.9	2,571.8	2,272.6	13.2	31,805	27,691
Taos, NM Micro Area	32,907	32,940	29,981	-33	2,959	-0.1	9.9	1,136.4	945.4	20.2	34,535	28,733
Taos County, NM	32,907	32,940	29,981	-33	2,959	-0.1	9.9	1,136.4	945.4	20.2	34,535	28,733
Taylorville, IL Micro Area	33,642	34,800	35,380	-1,158	-580	-3.3	-1.6	1,223.3	1,193.6	2.5	36,363	34,313
Christian County, IL	33,642	34,800	35,380	-1,158	-580	-3.3	-1.6	1,223.3	1,193.6	2.5	36,363	34,313
The Dalles, OR Micro Area	25,775	25,213	23,797	562	1,416	2.2	6.0	1,056.5	842.6	25.4	40,989	33,344
Wasco County, OR	25,775	25,213	23,797	562	1,416	2.2	6.0	1,056.5	842.6	25.4	40,989	33,344
Thomaston, GA Micro Area	26,368	27,153	27,761	-785	-608	-2.9	-2.2	826.1	728.0	13.5	31,330	26,899
Upson County, GA	26,368	27,153	27,761	-785	-608	-2.9	-2.2	826.1	728.0	13.5	31,330	26,899
Thomasville, GA Micro Area	45,063	44,719	42,791	344	1,928	0.8	4.5	1,738.3	1,493.0	16.4	38,574	33,359
Thomas County, GA	45,063	44,719	42,791	344	1,928	0.8	4.5	1,738.3	1,493.0	16.4	38,574	33,359
Tiffin, OH Micro Area	55,610	56,745	58,663	-1,135	-1,918	-2.0	-3.3	2,090.5	1,690.5	23.7	37,592	29,852
Seneca County, OH	55,610	56,745	58,663	-1,135	-1,918	-2.0	-3.3	2,090.5	1,690.5	23.7	37,592	29,852
Tifton, GA Micro Area	40,764	40,122	38,376	642	1,746	1.6	4.5	1,523.1	1,186.3	28.4	37,363	29,479
Tift County, GA	40,764	40,122	38,376	642	1,746	1.6	4.5	1,523.1	1,186.3	28.4	37,363	29,479
Toccoa, GA Micro Area	25,586	26,172	25,442	-586	730	-2.2	2.9	867.4	722.3	20.1	33,902	27,622
Stephens County, GA	25,586	26,172	25,442	-586	730	-2.2	2.9	867.4	722.3	20.1	33,902	27,622
Torrington, CT Micro Area	183,603	189,927	182,183	-6,324	7,744	-3.3	4.3	10,771.0	9,301.5	15.8	58,665	49,014
Litchfield County, CT	183,603	189,927	182,183	-6,324	7,744	-3.3	4.3	10,771.0	9,301.5	15.8	58,665	49,014
Traverse City, MI Micro Area	148,334	143,372	131,331	4,962	12,041	3.5	9.2	6,544.2	4,953.8	32.1	44,118	34,566
Benzie County, MI	17,457	17,525	15,986	-68	1,539	-0.4	9.6	655.6	529.3	23.9	37,557	30,234
Grand Traverse County, MI	91,636	86,986	77,655	4,650	9,331	5.3	12.0	4,020.6	3,101.2	29.6	43,876	35,661
Kalkaska County, MI	17,260	17,153	16,565	107	588	0.6	3.5	562.4	444.0	26.7	32,581	25,923
Leelanau County, MI	21,981	21,708	21,125	273	583	1.3	2.8	1,305.6	879.3	48.5	59,396	40,491
Troy, AL Micro Area	33,046	32,899	29,688	147	3,211	0.4	10.8	1,167.3	1,056.0	10.5	35,323	32,040
Pike County, AL	33,046	32,899	29,688	147	3,211	0.4	10.8	1,167.3	1,056.0	10.5	35,323	32,040
Truckee-Grass Valley, CA Micro Area	98,877	98,748	92,055	129	6,693	0.1	7.3	5,470.4	4,462.2	22.6	55,325	45,174
Nevada County, CA	98,877	98,748	92,055	129	6,693	0.1	7.3	5,470.4	4,462.2	22.6	55,325	45,174
Tullahoma-Manchester, TN Micro Area	102,048	100,209	93,008	1,839	7,201	1.8	7.7	3,714.3	3,083.3	20.5	36,397	30,805
Coffee County, TN	54,277	52,795	48,052	1,482	4,743	2.8	9.9	1,990.8	1,656.1	20.2	36,679	31,378
Franklin County, TN	41,449	41,052	39,258	397	1,794	1.0	4.6	1,482.1	1,235.4	20.0	35,757	30,163
Moore County, TN	6,322	6,362	5,698	-40	664	-0.6	11.7	241.4	191.9	25.8	38,179	30,187
Tupelo, MS Micro Area	139,817	136,268	125,249	3,549	11,019	2.6	8.8	4,872.5	4,077.6	19.5	34,849	29,903
Itawamba County, MS	23,609	23,401	22,774	208	627	0.9	2.8	754.4	644.1	17.1	31,954	27,512
Lee County, MS	85,300	82,910	75,664	2,390	7,246	2.9	9.6	3,192.4	2,651.0	20.4	37,426	31,975
Pontotoc County, MS	30,908	29,957	26,811	951	3,146	3.2	11.7	925.7	782.5	18.3	29,950	26,047
Twin Falls, ID Micro Area	105,189	99,604	82,687	5,585	16,917	5.6	20.5	3,743.3	2,941.6	27.3	35,586	29,415
Jerome County, ID	22,814	22,374	18,401	440	3,973	2.0	21.6	853.7	644.8	32.4	37,418	28,709
Twin Falls County, ID	82,375	77,230	64,286	5,145	12,944	6.7	20.1	2,889.6	2,296.8	25.8	35,079	29,620
Ukiah, CA Micro Area	87,649	87,840	86,253	-191	1,587	-0.2	1.8	3,842.9	3,259.7	17.9	43,845	37,122
Mendocino County, CA	87,649	87,840	86,253	-191	1,587	-0.2	1.8	3,842.9	3,259.7	17.9	43,845	37,122
Union City, TN-KY Micro Area	36,877	38,620	40,225	-1,743	-1,605	-4.5	-4.0	1,288.7	1,193.2	8.0	34,945	30,887
Fulton County, KY	6,238	6,813	7,755	-575	-942	-8.4	-12.1	194.9	179.1	8.8	31,244	26,288
Obion County, TN	30,639	31,807	32,470	-1,168	-663	-3.7	-2.0	1,093.8	1,014.1	7.9	35,699	31,872
Urbana, OH Micro Area	38,987	40,097	38,904	-1,110	1,193	-2.8	3.1	1,452.5	1,231.9	17.9	37,256	30,753
Champaign County, OH	38,987	40,097	38,904	-1,110	1,193	-2.8	3.1	1,452.5	1,231.9	17.9	37,256	30,753
Uvalde, TX Micro Area	27,245	26,405	25,919	840	486	3.2	1.9	1,062.9	790.8	34.4	39,013	29,900
Uvalde County, TX	27,245	26,405	25,919	840	486	3.2	1.9	1,062.9	790.8	34.4	39,013	29,900
Valley, AL Micro Area	34,123	34,170	36,600	-47	-2,430	-0.1	-6.6	1,067.4	931.9	14.5	31,282	27,330
Chambers County, AL	34,123	34,170	36,600	-47	-2,430	-0.1	-6.6	1,067.4	931.9	14.5	31,282	27,330
Van Wert, OH Micro Area	28,562	28,744	29,654	-182	-910	-0.6	-3.1	1,044.1	914.7	14.1	36,556	31,910
Van Wert County, OH	28,562	28,744	29,654	-182	-910	-0.6	-3.1	1,044.1	914.7	14.1	36,556	31,910
Vermillion, SD Micro Area	13,964	13,864	13,538	100	326	0.7	2.4	503.0	434.4	15.8	36,022	31,399
Clay County, SD	13,964	13,864	13,538	100	326	0.7	2.4	503.0	434.4	15.8	36,022	31,399
Vernal, UT Micro Area	37,928	32,584	25,174	5,344	7,410	16.4	29.4	1,196.6	991.9	20.6	31,549	30,572
Uintah County, UT	37,928	32,584	25,174	5,344	7,410	16.4	29.4	1,196.6	991.9	20.6	31,549	30,572
Vernon, TX Micro Area	13,027	13,535	14,679	-508	-1,144	-3.8	-7.8	493.3	453.3	8.8	37,869	33,573
Wilbarger County, TX	13,027	13,535	14,679	-508	-1,144	-3.8	-7.8	493.3	453.3	8.8	37,869	33,573
Vicksburg, MS Micro Area	56,635	58,371	61,505	-1,736	-3,134	-3.0	-5.1	1,986.4	1,880.3	5.6	35,073	32,205
Claiborne County, MS	9,150	9,598	11,837	-448	-2,239	-4.7	-18.9	279.2	265.0	5.3	30,516	27,693
Warren County, MS	47,485	48,773	49,668	-1,288	-895	-2.6	-1.8	1,707.1	1,615.3	5.7	35,951	33,090

[1]The April 1, 2000 and 2010 population estimates bases reflect modifications to the census populations as documented in the Count Question Resolution program and geographic program revisions.
[2]Based on the April 1, 2010 estimates base and the July 1, 2015 estimates.
[3]Based on the April 1, 2000 and April 1, 2010 estimates bases.
[4]Based on the July 1 population estimate of the year shown.

Table D-1.   Population and Personal Income—*Continued*

Micropolitan statistical area component counties	2015 estimate (July 1)	2010 census estimates base (April 1)[1]	2000 census estimates base (April 1)[1]	Net change 2010–2015[2]	Net change 2000–2010[3]	Percent change 2010–2015[2]	Percent change 2000–2010[3]	Total (million dollars) 2015	Total (million dollars) 2010	Percent change, 2010–2015	Per capita[4] 2015	Per capita[4] 2010
Vidalia, GA Micro Area	36,192	36,346	34,367	-154	1,979	-0.4	5.8	1,143.4	1,013.4	12.8	31,593	27,844
Montgomery County, GA	8,951	9,123	8,234	-172	889	-1.9	10.8	245.2	225.6	8.7	27,392	24,816
Toombs County, GA	27,241	27,223	26,133	18	1,090	0.1	4.2	898.2	787.8	14.0	32,973	28,852
Vincennes, IN Micro Area	37,927	38,440	39,263	-513	-823	-1.3	-2.1	1,563.9	1,330.9	17.5	41,234	34,669
Knox County, IN	37,927	38,440	39,263	-513	-823	-1.3	-2.1	1,563.9	1,330.9	17.5	41,234	34,669
Vineyard Haven, MA Micro Area	17,299	16,535	15,001	764	1,534	4.6	10.2	1,362.2	1,049.5	29.8	78,745	63,384
Dukes County, MA	17,299	16,535	15,001	764	1,534	4.6	10.2	1,362.2	1,049.5	29.8	78,745	63,384
Wabash, IN Micro Area	32,138	32,888	34,968	-750	-2,080	-2.3	-5.9	1,267.7	1,029.6	23.1	39,447	31,338
Wabash County, IN	32,138	32,888	34,968	-750	-2,080	-2.3	-5.9	1,267.7	1,029.6	23.1	39,447	31,338
Wahpeton, ND-MN Micro Area	22,798	22,897	25,127	-99	-2,230	-0.4	-8.9	1,073.6	969.7	10.7	47,093	42,330
Wilkin County, MN	6,396	6,576	7,135	-180	-559	-2.7	-7.8	327.6	307.9	6.4	51,214	46,802
Richland County, ND	16,402	16,321	17,992	81	-1,671	0.5	-9.3	746.1	661.8	12.7	45,487	40,529
Wapakoneta, OH Micro Area	45,876	45,949	46,230	-73	-281	-0.2	-0.6	1,960.5	1,621.3	20.9	42,736	35,297
Auglaize County, OH	45,876	45,949	46,230	-73	-281	-0.2	-0.6	1,960.5	1,621.3	20.9	42,736	35,297
Warren, PA Micro Area	40,396	41,815	43,784	-1,419	-1,969	-3.4	-4.5	1,686.3	1,416.6	19.0	41,745	33,927
Warren County, PA	40,396	41,815	43,784	-1,419	-1,969	-3.4	-4.5	1,686.3	1,416.6	19.0	41,745	33,927
Warrensburg, MO Micro Area	53,951	52,595	48,270	1,356	4,325	2.6	9.0	1,765.2	1,508.9	17.0	32,718	28,618
Johnson County, MO	53,951	52,595	48,270	1,356	4,325	2.6	9.0	1,765.2	1,508.9	17.0	32,718	28,618
Warsaw, IN Micro Area	78,620	77,356	74,053	1,264	3,303	1.6	4.5	3,527.2	2,614.2	34.9	44,864	33,801
Kosciusko County, IN	78,620	77,356	74,053	1,264	3,303	1.6	4.5	3,527.2	2,614.2	34.9	44,864	33,801
Washington, IN Micro Area	32,906	31,654	29,815	1,252	1,839	4.0	6.2	1,255.9	1,003.7	25.1	38,167	31,617
Daviess County, IN	32,906	31,654	29,815	1,252	1,839	4.0	6.2	1,255.9	1,003.7	25.1	38,167	31,617
Washington, NC Micro Area	47,651	47,773	44,916	-122	2,857	-0.3	6.4	1,799.9	1,575.6	14.2	37,773	32,975
Beaufort County, NC	47,651	47,773	44,916	-122	2,857	-0.3	6.4	1,799.9	1,575.6	14.2	37,773	32,975
Washington Court House, OH Micro Area	28,679	29,030	28,474	-351	556	-1.2	2.0	992.0	847.0	17.1	34,591	29,190
Fayette County, OH	28,679	29,030	28,474	-351	556	-1.2	2.0	992.0	847.0	17.1	34,591	29,190
Watertown, SD Micro Area	27,939	27,227	25,909	712	1,318	2.6	5.1	1,196.3	1,025.3	16.7	42,820	37,664
Codington County, SD	27,939	27,227	25,909	712	1,318	2.6	5.1	1,196.3	1,025.3	16.7	42,820	37,664
Watertown-Fort Atkinson, WI Micro Area	84,559	83,681	75,855	878	7,826	1.0	10.3	3,446.7	2,943.6	17.1	40,761	35,174
Jefferson County, WI	84,559	83,681	75,855	878	7,826	1.0	10.3	3,446.7	2,943.6	17.1	40,761	35,174
Wauchula, FL Micro Area	27,502	27,731	26,854	-229	877	-0.8	3.3	703.8	627.3	12.2	25,591	22,617
Hardee County, FL	27,502	27,731	26,854	-229	877	-0.8	3.3	703.8	627.3	12.2	25,591	22,617
Waycross, GA Micro Area	54,473	55,064	51,121	-591	3,943	-1.1	7.7	1,681.1	1,522.8	10.4	30,862	27,596
Pierce County, GA	19,103	18,758	15,624	345	3,134	1.8	20.1	599.2	536.6	11.7	31,369	28,530
Ware County, GA	35,370	36,306	35,497	-936	809	-2.6	2.3	1,081.9	986.1	9.7	30,587	27,113
Weatherford, OK Micro Area	29,744	27,469	26,147	2,275	1,322	8.3	5.1	1,160.4	920.0	26.1	39,014	33,467
Custer County, OK	29,744	27,469	26,147	2,275	1,322	8.3	5.1	1,160.4	920.0	26.1	39,014	33,467
West Plains, MO Micro Area	40,117	40,400	37,273	-283	3,127	-0.7	8.4	1,270.8	1,105.2	15.0	31,677	27,241
Howell County, MO	40,117	40,400	37,273	-283	3,127	-0.7	8.4	1,270.8	1,105.2	15.0	31,677	27,241
West Point, MS Micro Area	20,048	20,634	21,984	-586	-1,350	-2.8	-6.1	692.1	601.4	15.1	34,522	29,268
Clay County, MS	20,048	20,634	21,984	-586	-1,350	-2.8	-6.1	692.1	601.4	15.1	34,522	29,268
Whitewater-Elkhorn, WI Micro Area	102,804	102,228	91,895	576	10,333	0.6	11.2	4,363.6	3,575.6	22.0	42,446	34,990
Walworth County, WI	102,804	102,228	91,895	576	10,333	0.6	11.2	4,363.6	3,575.6	22.0	42,446	34,990
Williston, ND Micro Area	35,294	22,398	19,754	12,896	2,644	57.6	13.4	3,587.5	1,401.7	155.9	101,645	62,059
Williams County, ND	35,294	22,398	19,754	12,896	2,644	57.6	13.4	3,587.5	1,401.7	155.9	101,645	62,059
Willmar, MN Micro Area	42,542	42,239	41,193	303	1,046	0.7	2.5	2,087.1	1,690.1	23.5	49,060	40,006
Kandiyohi County, MN	42,542	42,239	41,193	303	1,046	0.7	2.5	2,087.1	1,690.1	23.5	49,060	40,006
Wilmington, OH Micro Area	41,917	42,037	40,473	-120	1,564	-0.3	3.9	1,632.6	1,482.9	10.1	38,947	35,390
Clinton County, OH	41,917	42,037	40,473	-120	1,564	-0.3	3.9	1,632.6	1,482.9	10.1	38,947	35,390
Wilson, NC Micro Area	81,714	81,234	73,810	480	7,424	0.6	10.1	3,073.8	2,721.9	12.9	37,617	33,502
Wilson County, NC	81,714	81,234	73,810	480	7,424	0.6	10.1	3,073.8	2,721.9	12.9	37,617	33,502
Winnemucca, NV Micro Area	17,019	16,525	16,081	494	444	3.0	2.8	752.2	680.0	10.6	44,198	40,986
Humboldt County, NV	17,019	16,525	16,081	494	444	3.0	2.8	752.2	680.0	10.6	44,198	40,986
Winona, MN Micro Area	50,885	51,461	49,996	-576	1,465	-1.1	2.9	2,189.8	1,773.5	23.5	43,034	34,492
Winona County, MN	50,885	51,461	49,996	-576	1,465	-1.1	2.9	2,189.8	1,773.5	23.5	43,034	34,492
Wisconsin Rapids-Marshfield, WI Micro Area	73,435	74,749	75,500	-1,314	-751	-1.8	-1.0	3,075.7	2,756.9	11.6	41,883	36,854
Wood County, WI	73,435	74,749	75,500	-1,314	-751	-1.8	-1.0	3,075.7	2,756.9	11.6	41,883	36,854
Woodward, OK Micro Area	21,559	20,081	18,489	1,478	1,592	7.4	8.6	1,014.7	672.1	51.0	47,068	33,643
Woodward County, OK	21,559	20,081	18,489	1,478	1,592	7.4	8.6	1,014.7	672.1	51.0	47,068	33,643
Wooster, OH Micro Area	116,063	114,514	111,562	1,549	2,952	1.4	2.6	4,467.2	3,605.8	23.9	38,489	31,508
Wayne County, OH	116,063	114,514	111,562	1,549	2,952	1.4	2.6	4,467.2	3,605.8	23.9	38,489	31,508
Worthington, MN Micro Area	21,770	21,378	20,832	392	546	1.8	2.6	966.2	765.6	26.2	44,383	35,780
Nobles County, MN	21,770	21,378	20,832	392	546	1.8	2.6	966.2	765.6	26.2	44,383	35,780
Yankton, SD Micro Area	22,702	22,438	21,657	264	781	1.2	3.6	1,020.5	882.6	15.6	44,953	39,309
Yankton County, SD	22,702	22,438	21,657	264	781	1.2	3.6	1,020.5	882.6	15.6	44,953	39,309
Zanesville, OH Micro Area	86,290	86,074	84,549	216	1,525	0.3	1.8	3,266.5	2,640.8	23.7	37,855	30,634
Muskingum County, OH	86,290	86,074	84,549	216	1,525	0.3	1.8	3,266.5	2,640.8	23.7	37,855	30,634
Zapata, TX Micro Area	14,374	14,018	12,081	356	1,937	2.5	16.0	397.1	328.4	20.9	27,625	23,330
Zapata County, TX	14,374	14,018	12,081	356	1,937	2.5	16.0	397.1	328.4	20.9	27,625	23,330

[1]The April 1, 2000 and 2010 population estimates bases reflect modifications to the census populations as documented in the Count Question Resolution program and geographic program revisions.
[2]Based on the April 1, 2010 estimates base and the July 1, 2015 estimates.
[3]Based on the April 1, 2000 and April 1, 2010 estimates bases.
[4]Based on the July 1 population estimate of the year shown.

APPENDIXES

Page

301   **APPENDIX A.**
        SOURCE NOTES AND EXPLANATIONS

371   **APPENDIX B.**
        LIMITATIONS OF THE DATA AND METHODOLOGY

383   **APPENDIX C.**
        GEOGRAPHIC CONCEPTS

437   **APPENDIX D.**
        GUIDE TO STATE STATISTICAL ABSTRACTS AND STATE INFORMATION

APPENDIX A
SOURCE NOTES AND EXPLANATIONS

This appendix presents General Notes on population and economic and government censuses followed by source notes and explanations of the data items presented in table sets A through D of this publication. These table sets vary in both geographic and data coverage.

Each table set begins with the table number and title, followed by the source citation for these items, and related definitions and other explanatory text on the source.

GENERAL NOTES

Population

Decennial censuses. The population statistics for 2010 and earlier are based on results from the censuses of population and housing, conducted by the U.S. Census Bureau as of April 1 in each of those years. As provided by Article 1, Section 2, of the U.S. Constitution, adopted in 1787, a census has been taken every 10 years since 1790. The original purposes of the census were to apportion the seats in the U.S. House of Representatives based on the population of each state and to derive an equitable tax on each state for the payment of the Revolutionary War debt. Through the years, the nation's needs and interests have become more complex, and the content of the decennial census has changed accordingly. At present, census data not only are used to apportion seats in the House and to aid legislators in the realignment of legislative district boundaries but are also used in the distribution of billions of federal dollars each year and are vital to state and local governments and to private firms for such functions as market analysis, site selection, and environmental impact studies.

The decennial censuses prior to 2010 used both short- and long-form questionnaires to gather information. The short form asked a limited number of basic questions. These questions were asked of all people and housing units and are often referred to as 100 percent questions because they were asked of the entire population. In 2010, these became the only questions because the long-form questionnaire has been replaced by the American Community Survey. The population items include sex, age, race, Hispanic or Latino, household relationship, and group quarters. Housing items include occupancy status, vacancy status, tenure (owner occupied or renter

occupied), and mortgage status. The long form of the earlier censuses asked more detailed information on a sample basis and included the 100 percent questions as well as questions on education, employment, income, ancestry, homeowner costs, units in a structure, number of rooms, etc. For information about the 2010 census, see www.census.gov/2010census/. For information about the 2000 census, see www.census.gov/main/www/cen2000.html.

Persons enumerated in the census were counted as inhabitants of their usual place of residence, which generally means the place where a person lives and sleeps most of the time. This place is not necessarily the same as the legal residence, voting residence, or domicile. In the vast majority of cases, however, the use of these different bases of classification would produce substantially the same statistics, although appreciable differences may exist for a few areas.

The implementation of this usual-residence practice has resulted in the establishment of residence rules for certain categories of persons whose usual place of residence is not immediately apparent (e.g., college students were counted at their college residence). As in the above example, persons were not always counted as residents of the place where they happened to be staying on census day. However, persons without a usual place of residence were counted where they were enumerated.

For links to information on procedures and concepts used for the 2010 Census of Population and Housing, as well as a facsimile of the questionnaires and descriptions of the data products resulting from the census, see U.S. Census Bureau, see www.census.gov/2010census/data/.

Population estimates. The U.S. Census Bureau annually produces estimates of resident population for each state and county using a component of population change method at the county level. To produce the state population estimates, all county populations within each state are summed.

The Census Bureau develops county population estimates with a component of population change method in which they use administrative records and other data to estimate the household and group quarters population.

For the household population, the components of population change are births, deaths, net domestic migration, and net international migration. The Census Bureau measures change in the nonhousehold, or group quarters, population by the net change in the population living in group quarters facilities.

A major assumption underlying this approach is that changes in selected administrative and other data sources closely approximate the components of population change. Therefore, Census Bureau demographers separately estimate each component of population change based on administrative records, including registered births and deaths, federal income tax returns, medicare enrollees, and military movement. The Census Bureau also separately estimates net international migration using information from the American Community Survey (ACS), the decennial census, and other data sources.

Most administrative record data sources lag the current estimate year by as much as 2 years. As a result, the Census Bureau projects the data for the current year based on past years' data. As updated data become available, the Census Bureau revises the projected input data so that each vintage's estimates are always based on the most recent data available.

The Census Bureau produces the estimate of each county's population, starting with the base population from either the 2010 census (for the July 1, 2010, estimates) or the revised population estimate for the prior year (for the July 1, 2011, and later estimates). The Census Bureau then adds or subtracts the demographic components of population change calculated for that time period. The Census Bureau will then add the estimates of net domestic migration, net international migration and the net change in the group quarters population.

State and county estimates may also incorporate other changes due to corrections made since the 2010 census. The corrections occur outside the component estimation framework and are the result of successful local challenges or special censuses.

The results of the 2010 census are used as the base population for subsequent annual population estimates. The enumerated resident population in the 2010 census is the starting point for the post-2010 population estimates. The Census Bureau will modify this enumerated population in two ways to produce the April 1, 2010, population estimates base. First, they reconcile the Census 2010 race categories with the race categories that appear in their administrative records data by recoding the "Some other race" 2010 census responses to one or more of the five 1997 Office of Management and Budget (OMB) race categories: White, Black or African American, American

Indian and Alaska Native, Asian, and Native Hawaiian and Other Pacific Islander. Second, they update the population estimates base to reflect changes to the 2010 census population due to the Count Question Resolution program, legal boundary updates and other geographic program revisions.

The birth and death components are estimated using data from two sources. Where possible, members of the Federal State Cooperative Program for Population Estimates (FSCPE) provide summary data on all registered births and deaths to residents of their respective states and counties from 2010 to the most recent calendar year. The National Center for Health Statistics (NCHS) also provides birth and death data, but these data are not as current as those available from members of the FSCPE. However, the NCHS data include individual record data on each registered birth and death by state, county, month, sex, race, Hispanic origin, and age (for deaths). Where FSCPE vital data are not available, only NCHS data is used.

County birth totals from FSCPE and NCHS sources are controlled to the national NCHS birth total for the corresponding year. Then the county-level sex, race, and Hispanic origin distribution of NCHS births for that year is applied to these totals to derive births for each demographic group for all U.S. counties. Estimates of annual deaths for demographic groups are calculated in similar fashion. The Census Bureau reconciles county death totals from the two data sources to the NCHS national death total for the corresponding year and assigns the county-level age, sex, race, and Hispanic origin distribution of NCHS deaths for that year. Since they produce estimates for July 1 of each year, the Census Bureau uses the NCHS month-of-occurrence information to derive births and deaths for the July 1 to June 30 period for each year.

The Census Bureau produces separate population estimates for the populations under 18, age 18 to 64 and age 65 and over, mainly because different data are used to measure the domestic migration of these three populations. To determine the net domestic migration for the population under the age of 65, the Census Bureau uses data derived from federal income tax returns supplied by the Internal Revenue Service (IRS). The data used is limited to filers and their dependents under 65.

To calculate net domestic migration rates the Census Bureau will subtract the out-migrants from the in-migrants for each county to produce the number of net migrants. Then, they will divide the number of IRS-based net migrants in each county by the number of individuals represented on the tax returns in the first year in each county.

To determine the net migration for the age of 65 and over, the Census Bureau uses medicare enrollment data from the Centers for Medicare and Medicaid (CMS.)

International migration is considered any change of residence across the borders of the United States (50 states and District of Columbia). The net international migration component of the population estimates combines four parts: (a) net international migration of the foreign born, (b) net migration between the United States and Puerto Rico, (c) net migration of natives to and from the United States, and (d) net movement of the Armed Forces population between the United States and overseas.

Net international migration of the foreign-born population is estimated in two parts, immigration and emigration. The estimate of immigration utilizes information from the American Community Survey (ACS) on the reported residence of the foreign-born population in the prior year. The foreign born who reported being abroad in the year prior to the survey are considered immigrants.

Group quarters population data are used from two sources to estimate the change in the group quarters (GQ) populations: (1) Census 2010 group quarters population by single year of age and facility type (i.e., correctional institutions, juvenile facilities, nursing homes, other institutional facilities, university dormitories, military barracks, other non-institutional facilities) for each sub-county area (e.g., cities and towns) and (2) a time series of individual GQ records from the Group Quarters Report (GQR) prepared by the FSCPE members.

For further elaboration and explanation regarding Census Bureau methodology for population estimates, including information on net international migration, group quarters population, and estimations of the county populations, see https://www.census.gov/programs-surveys/popest/technical-documentation/methodology.html.

American Community Survey

The American Community Survey (ACS) is a nationwide survey designed to provide communities with a fresh look at how they are changing. It was designed to eliminate the need for the long form in the 2010 census. The ACS collects information from U.S. households similar to what was collected on the 2000 census long form, such as income, commute time to work, home value, veteran status, and other important data. As with the official U.S. census, information about individuals will remain confidential.

The ACS collects and produces population and housing information every year instead of every 10 years. About three million households are surveyed each year.

Collecting data every year reduces the cost of the official decennial census and provides more up-to-date information throughout the decade about trends in the U.S. population at the local community level. The ACS began in 1996 and has expanded each subsequent year.

Each year, 1-year estimates are available for geographic areas with a population of 65,000 or more. This includes the nation, all states and the District of Columbia, all congressional districts, approximately 800 counties, and 500 metropolitan and micropolitan statistical areas, among others. Between 2008 and 2012, the ACS released 3-year estimates for geographic areas with a population of 20,000 or more, including the nation, all states and the District of Columbia, all congressional districts, approximately 1,800 counties, and 900 metropolitan and micropolitan statistical areas, among others. When these 3-year estimates were discontinued, they were replaced by 1-year Supplemental Estimates with less detail than the regular 1-year estimates, but providing data for geographic areas with 20,000 to 65,000 residents. For areas with a population less than 20,000, 5-year estimates are available. The first 5-year estimates, based on the ACS data collected from 2005 through 2009, were released in 2010. Since then, 5-year estimates are released every year.

More information on the American Community Survey can be found at www.census.gov/acs/www.

Economic Censuses

The economic census is the major source of facts about the structure and functioning of the nation's economy. It provides essential information for government, business, industry, and the general public. It furnishes an important part of the framework for such composite measures as the gross domestic product estimates, input/output measures, production and price indexes, and other statistical series that measure short-term changes in economic conditions. Title 13 of the U.S. Code (Sections 131, 191, and 224) directs the Census Bureau to take the economic census every 5 years, covering years ending in "2" and "7." The economic censuses form an integrated program at 5-year intervals since 1967 and before that for 1963, 1958, and 1954. Prior to that time, the individual censuses were taken separately at varying intervals. Beginning with the 1997 Economic Census data, the census presents data based on the North American Industry Classification System.

The economic censuses are collected on an establishment basis. An establishment is generally a single physical location where business is conducted or where services or industrial operations are performed (e.g., factory, mill, store, hotel, movie theater, mine, farm, airline terminal, sales office, warehouse, or central administrative office). A company operating at more than one location is required to file a separate report for each store, factory, shop, or other location. Each establishment is assigned a separate industry classification based on its primary activity and not that of its parent company. Establishments responding to the establishment survey are classified into industries on the basis of their principal product or activity (determined by annual sales volume) in accordance with the *North American Industry Classification System—United States, 2007* manual available at https://www.census.gov/cgi-bin/sssd/naics/naicsrch?chart=2007.

More detailed information about the scope, coverage, classification system, data items, and publications for each of the economic censuses and related surveys can be found at https://www.census.gov/econ/.

Data from the 2007 and 2012 Economic Censuses were released through the Census Bureau's American Fact-Finder, the Census Bureau's online system for access and dissemination of data.

North American Industry Classification System (NAICS) Sector

The North American Industry Classification System (NAICS) was developed under the direction and guidance of the Office of Management and Budget (OMB) as the standard for use by federal statistical agencies in classifying business establishments for the collection, tabulation, presentation, and analysis of statistical data describing the U.S. economy. Use of the standard provides uniformity and comparability in the presentation of these statistical data. NAICS is based on a production-oriented concept, meaning that it groups establishments into industries according to similarity in the processes used to produce goods or services. Previous census data were presented based on the Standard Industrial Classification (SIC) system developed in 1937. Due to this change, comparability between census years and data found in previous books will be limited.

There are 20 NAICS sectors, which are further subdivided into subsectors (three-digit codes), industry groups (four-digit codes), and, as implemented in the United States, industries (five- and six-digit codes). For more information regarding the classifications see https://www.census.gov/cgi-bin/sssd/naics/naicsrch?chart=2017.

The **Agriculture, Forestry, Fishing, and Hunting** (NAICS 11) sector comprises establishments primarily engaged in growing crops, raising animals, harvesting timber, and harvesting fish and other animals from a farm, ranch, or their natural habitats.

The establishments in this sector are often described as farms, ranches, dairies, greenhouses, nurseries, orchards,

or hatcheries. A farm may consist of a single tract of land or a number of separate tracts, which may be held under different tenures. For example, one tract may be owned by the farm operator and another rented. It may be operated by the operator alone or with the assistance of members of the household or hired employees, or it may be operated by a partnership, corporation, or other type of organization. When a landowner has one or more tenants, renters, croppers, or managers, the land operated by each is considered a farm. The sector distinguishes two basic activities: agricultural production and agricultural support activities. Agricultural production includes establishments performing the complete farm or ranch operation, such as farm owner-operators, tenant farm operators, and sharecroppers. Agricultural support activities include establishments that perform one or more activities associated with farm operation, such as soil preparation, planting, harvesting, and management, on a contract or fee basis.

Excluded from the Agriculture, Forestry, Fishing, and Hunting sector are establishments primarily engaged in agricultural research and establishments primarily engaged in administering programs for regulating and conserving land, mineral, wildlife, and forest use. These establishments are classified in Industry 54171, Research and Development in the Physical, Engineering, and Life Sciences; and Industry 92412, Administration of Conservation Programs, respectively.

For information on the subsectors of Agriculture, Forestry, Fishing, and Hunting (NAICS 11), see www.census.gov/eos/www/naics/.

The **Mining, Quarrying, and Oil and Gas Extraction** sector (NAICS 21) comprises establishments that extract naturally occurring mineral solids, such as coal and ores; liquid minerals, such as crude petroleum; and gases, such as natural gas. The term mining is used in the broad sense to include quarrying, well operations, beneficiating (e.g., crushing, screening, washing, and flotation), and other preparation customarily performed at the mine site or as a part of mining activity.

The Mining, Quarrying, and Oil and Gas Extraction sector distinguishes two basic activities: mine operation and mining support activities. Mine operation includes establishments operating mines, quarries, or oil and gas wells on their own account or for others on a contract or fee basis. Mining support activities include establishments that perform exploration (except geophysical surveying) and/ or other mining services on a contract or fee basis (except mine site preparation and construction of oil/gas pipelines).

Establishments in the Mining, Quarrying, and Oil and Gas Extraction sector are grouped and classified according to the natural resource mined or to be mined. Industries include establishments that develop the mine site, extract the natural resources, and/or those that beneficiate (i.e., prepare) the mineral mined. Beneficiation is the process whereby the extracted material is reduced to particles that can be separated into mineral and waste, the former suitable for further processing or direct use. The operations that take place in beneficiation are primarily mechanical, such as grinding, washing, magnetic separation, and centrifugal separation. In contrast, manufacturing operations primarily use chemical and electrochemical processes, such as electrolysis and distillation. However, some treatments, such as heat treatments, take place in both the beneficiation and the manufacturing (i.e., smelting/refining) stages. The range of preparation activities varies by mineral and the purity of any given ore deposit. While some minerals, such as petroleum and natural gas, require little or no preparation, others are washed and screened, while yet others, such as gold and silver, can be transformed into bullion before leaving the mine site.

Mining, beneficiating, and manufacturing activities often occur in a single location. Separate receipts will be collected for these activities whenever possible. When receipts cannot be broken out between mining and manufacturing, establishments that mine or quarry nonmetallic minerals, and then beneficiate the nonmetallic minerals into more finished manufactured products are classified based on the primary activity of the establishment. A mine that manufactures a small amount of finished products will be classified in Sector 21, Mining, Quarrying, and Oil and Gas Extraction. An establishment that mines whose primary output is a more finished manufactured product will be classified in Sector 31–33, Manufacturing.

For information on the subsectors of Mining, Quarrying, and Oil and Gas Extraction (NAICS 21), see www.census.gov/eos/www/naics/.

The **Utilities** sector (NAICS 22) comprises establishments engaged in the provision of the following utility services: electric power, natural gas, steam supply, water supply, and sewage removal. Within this sector, the specific activities associated with the utility services provided vary by utility: electric power includes generation, transmission, and distribution; natural gas includes distribution; steam supply includes provision and/or distribution; water supply includes treatment and distribution; and sewage removal includes collection, treatment, and disposal of waste through sewer systems and sewage treatment facilities.

Excluded from this sector are establishments primarily engaged in waste management services classified in Subsector 562, Waste Management and Remediation Services. These establishments also collect, treat, and dispose of waste materials; however, they do not use sewer systems or sewage treatment facilities.

For information on the subsectors of Utilities (NAICS 22), see www.census.gov/eos/www/naics/.

The **Construction** sector (NAICS 23) comprises establishments primarily engaged in the construction of buildings or engineering projects (e.g., highways and utility systems). Establishments primarily engaged in the preparation of sites for new construction and establishments primarily engaged in subdividing land for sale as building sites also are included in this sector.

Construction work done may include new work, additions, alterations, or maintenance and repairs. Activities of these establishments generally are managed at a fixed place of business, but they usually perform construction activities at multiple project sites. Production responsibilities for establishments in this sector are usually specified in (1) contracts with the owners of construction projects (prime contracts) or (2) contracts with other construction establishments (subcontracts).

Establishments primarily engaged in contracts that include responsibility for all aspects of individual construction projects are commonly known as general contractors, but also may be known as design-builders, construction managers, turnkey contractors, or (in cases where two or more establishments jointly secure a general contract) joint-venture contractors. Construction managers that provide oversight and scheduling only (i.e., agency) as well as construction managers that are responsible for the entire project (i.e., at risk) are included as general contractor type establishments. Establishments of the "general contractor type" frequently arrange construction of separate parts of their projects through subcontracts with other construction establishments.

Establishments primarily engaged in activities to produce a specific component (e.g., masonry, painting, and electrical work) of a construction project are commonly known as specialty trade contractors. Activities of specialty trade contractors are usually subcontracted from other construction establishments, but especially in remodeling and repair construction, the work may be done directly for the owner of the property.

Establishments primarily engaged in activities to construct buildings to be sold on sites that they own are known as operative builders, but also may be known as speculative builders or merchant builders. Operative builders produce buildings in a manner similar to general contractors, but their production processes also include site acquisition and securing of financial backing.

Operative builders are most often associated with the construction of residential buildings. Like general contractors, they may subcontract all or part of the actual construction work on their buildings.

There are substantial differences in the types of equipment, work force skills, and other inputs required by establishments in this sector. To highlight these differences and variations in the underlying production functions, this sector is divided into three subsectors.

Subsector 236, Construction of Buildings, comprises establishments of the general contractor type and operative builders involved in the construction of buildings. Subsector 237, Heavy and Civil Engineering Construction, comprises establishments involved in the construction of engineering projects. Subsector 238, Specialty Trade Contractors, comprises establishments engaged in specialty trade activities generally needed in the construction of all types of buildings. Force account construction is construction work performed by an enterprise primarily engaged in some business other than construction for its own account and use, using employees of the enterprise. This activity is not included in the construction sector unless the construction work performed is the primary activity of a separate establishment of the enterprise. The installation and the ongoing repair and maintenance of telecommunications and utility networks are excluded from construction when the establishments performing the work are not independent contractors. Although a growing proportion of this work is subcontracted to independent contractors in the Construction Sector, the operating units of telecommunications and utility companies performing this work are included with the telecommunications or utility activities.

For information on the subsectors of Construction (NAICS 23), see www.census.gov/eos/www/naics/.

The **Manufacturing** sector (NAICS 31–33) comprises establishments engaged in the mechanical, physical, or chemical transformation of materials, substances, or components into new products. The assembling of component parts of manufactured products is considered manufacturing, except in cases where the activity is appropriately classified in Sector 23, Construction.

Establishments in the Manufacturing sector are often described as plants, factories, or mills and characteristically use power-driven machines and materials-handling equipment. However, establishments that transform materials or substances into new products by hand or in the workers home and those engaged in selling to the general public products made on the same premises from which they are sold, such as bakeries, candy stores, and custom tailors, may also be included in this sector.

Manufacturing establishments may process materials or may contract with other establishments to process their materials for them. Both types of establishments are included in manufacturing.

The materials, substances, or components transformed by manufacturing establishments are raw materials that are products of agriculture, forestry, fishing, mining, or quarrying as well as products of other manufacturing establishments. The materials used may be purchased directly from producers, obtained through customary trade channels, or secured without recourse to the market by transferring the product from one establishment to another, under the same ownership.

The new product of a manufacturing establishment may be finished in the sense that it is ready for utilization or consumption, or it may be semifinished to become an input for an establishment engaged in further manufacturing. For example, the product of the alumina refinery is the input used in the primary production of aluminum; primary aluminum is the input to an aluminum wire drawing plant; and aluminum wire is the input for a fabricated wire product manufacturing establishment.

The subsectors in the Manufacturing sector generally reflect distinct production processes related to material inputs, production equipment, and employee skills. In the machinery area, where assembling is a key activity, parts and accessories for manufactured products are classified in the industry of the finished manufactured item when they are made for separate sale. For example, a replacement refrigerator door would be classified with refrigerators and an attachment for a piece of metal working machinery would be classified with metal working machinery. However, components, input from other manufacturing establishments, are classified based on the production function of the component manufacturer. For example, electronic components are classified in Subsector 334, Computer and Electronic Product Manufacturing and stampings are classified in Subsector 332, Fabricated Metal Product Manufacturing.

Manufacturing establishments often perform one or more activities that are classified outside the Manufacturing sector of NAICS. For instance, almost all manufacturing has some captive research and development or administrative operations, such as accounting, payroll, or management. These captive services are treated the same as captive manufacturing activities. When the services are provided by separate establishments, they are classified to the NAICS sector where such services are primary, not in manufacturing.

The boundaries of manufacturing and the other sectors of the classification system can be somewhat blurry. The establishments in the manufacturing sector are engaged in the transformation of materials into new products. Their output is a new product. However, the definition of what constitutes a new product can be somewhat subjective. As clarification, the following activities are considered manufacturing in NAICS: Milk bottling and pasteurizing; Grinding of lenses to prescription; Water bottling and processing; Wood preserving; Fresh fish packaging (oyster shucking, electroplating, plating, metal heat fish filleting); Treating and polishing for the trade; Apparel jobbing (assigning of materials lapidary work for the trade, to contract factories or shops for fabricating signs and advertising displays, fabrication or other contract operations); Rebuilding or remanufacturing as well as contracting on materials owned by others; Machinery (i.e., automotive parts); Printing and related activities; Ship repair and renovation; Ready-mixed concrete production; Machine shops; Leather converting; and Tire retreading.

Conversely, there are activities that are sometimes considered manufacturing, but which for NAICS are classified in another sector (i.e., not classified as manufacturing). They include: (1) Logging, classified in Sector 11, Agriculture, Forestry, Fishing, and Hunting, is considered a harvesting operation; (2) The beneficiating of ores and other minerals, classified in Sector 21, Mining, Quarrying, and Oil and Gas Extraction, is considered part of the activity of mining; (3) The construction of structures and fabricating operations performed at the site of construction by contractors, is classified in Sector 23, Construction; (4) Establishments engaged in breaking of bulk and redistribution in smaller lots, including packaging, repackaging, or bottling products, such as liquors or chemicals; the customized assembly of computers; sorting of scrap; mixing paints to customer order; and cutting metals to customer order, classified in Sector 42, Wholesale Trade or Sector 44–45, Retail Trade, produce a modified version of the same product, not a new product; and (5) Publishing and the combined activity of publishing and printing, classified in Sector 51, Information, perform the transformation of information into a product whereas the value of the product to the consumer lies in the information content, not in the format in which it is distributed (i.e., the book or CD-ROM).

For information on the subsectors of Manufacturing (NAICS 31–33), see https://www.census.gov/eos/www/naics/.

The **Wholesale Trade** sector (NAICS 42) comprises establishments engaged in wholesaling merchandise, generally without transformation, and rendering services incidental to the sale of merchandise. The merchandise described in this sector includes the outputs of agriculture, mining, manufacturing, and certain information industries, such as publishing.

The wholesaling process is an intermediate step in the distribution of merchandise. Wholesalers are organized to sell or arrange the purchase or sale of (a) goods for resale (i.e., goods sold to other wholesalers or retailers), (b) capital or durable nonconsumer goods, and (c) raw and intermediate materials and supplies used in production.

Wholesalers sell merchandise to other businesses and normally operate from a warehouse or office. These warehouses and offices are characterized by having little or no display of merchandise. In addition, neither the design nor the location of the premises is intended to solicit walk-in traffic. Wholesalers do not normally use advertising directed to the general public. Customers are generally reached initially via telephone, in-person marketing, or by specialized advertising that may include Internet and other electronic means. Follow-up orders are either vendor-initiated or client-initiated, generally based on previous sales, and typically exhibit strong ties between sellers and buyers. In fact, transactions are often conducted between wholesalers and clients that have long-standing business relationships.

This sector comprises two main types of wholesalers: merchant wholesalers that sell goods on their own account and business-to-business electronic markets, agents, and brokers that arrange sales and purchases for others generally for a commission or fee.

1. Establishments that sell goods on their own account are known as wholesale merchants, distributors, jobbers, drop shippers, and import/export merchants. Also included as wholesale merchants are sales offices and sales branches (but not retail stores) maintained by manufacturing, refining, or mining enterprises apart from their plants or mines for the purpose of marketing their products. Merchant wholesale establishments typically maintain their own warehouse where they receive and handle goods for their customers. Goods are generally sold without transformation, but may include integral functions, such as sorting, packaging, labeling, and other marketing services.

2. Establishments arranging for the purchase or sale of goods owned by others or purchasing goods, generally on a commission basis are known as business-to-business electronic markets, agents and brokers, commission merchants, import/export agents and brokers, auction companies, and manufacturers representatives. These establishments operate from offices and generally do not own or handle the goods they sell.

Some wholesale establishments may be connected with a single manufacturer and promote and sell the particular manufacturers' products to a wide range of other wholesalers or retailers. Other wholesalers may be connected to a retail chain, or limited number of retail chains, and only provide a variety of products needed by that particular retail operation(s). These wholesalers may obtain the products from a wide range of manufacturers. Still other wholesalers may not take title to the goods, but act as agents and brokers for a commission.

Although, in general, wholesaling normally denotes sales in large volumes, durable nonconsumer goods may be sold in single units. Sales of capital or durable nonconsumer goods used in the production of goods and services, such as farm machinery, medium and heavy-duty trucks, and industrial machinery, are always included in Wholesale trade. For information on the subsectors of Wholesale Trade sector (NAICS 42), see www.census.gov/eos/www/naics/.

The **Retail Trade** sector (NAICS 44–45) comprises establishments engaged in retailing merchandise, generally without transformation, and rendering services incidental to the sale of merchandise.

The retailing process is the final step in the distribution of merchandise; retailers are, therefore, organized to sell merchandise in small quantities to the general public. This sector comprises two main types of retailers: store and nonstore retailers.

Store retailers operate fixed point-of-sale locations, located and designed to attract a high volume of walk-in customers. In general, retail stores have extensive displays of merchandise and use mass-media advertising to attract customers. They typically sell merchandise to the general public for personal or household consumption, but some also serve business and institutional clients. These include establishments, such as office supply stores, computer and software stores, building materials dealers, plumbing supply stores, and electrical supply stores. Catalog showrooms, gasoline stations, automotive dealers, and mobile home dealers are treated as store retailers.

In addition to retailing merchandise, some types of store retailers are also engaged in the provision of after-sales services, such as repair and installation. For example, new automobile dealers, electronics and appliance stores, and musical instrument and supplies stores often provide repair services. As a general rule, establishments engaged in retailing merchandise and providing after-sales services are classified in this sector.

The first 11 subsectors of retail trade are store retailers. The establishments are grouped into industries and industry groups typically based on one or more of the following criteria:

1. The merchandise line or lines carried by the store; for example, specialty stores are distinguished from general-line stores.

2. The usual trade designation of the establishments. This criterion applies in cases where a store type is well recognized by the industry and the public, but difficult to define strictly in terms of merchandise lines carried; for example, pharmacies, hardware stores, and department stores.

3. Capital requirements in terms of display equipment; for example, food stores have equipment requirements not found in other retail industries.

4. Human resource requirements in terms of expertise; for example, the staff of an automobile dealer requires knowledge in financing, registering, and licensing issues that are not necessary in other retail industries.

Nonstore retailers, like store retailers, are organized to serve the general public, but their retailing methods differ. The establishments of this subsector reach customers and market merchandise with methods, such as the broadcasting of "infomercials," the broadcasting and publishing of direct-response advertising, the publishing of paper and electronic catalogs, door-to-door solicitation, in-home demonstration, selling from portable stalls (street vendors, except food), and distribution through vending machines. Establishments engaged in the direct sale (nonstore) of products, such as home heating oil dealers and home delivery newspaper routes are included here.

The buying of goods for resale is a characteristic of retail trade establishments that particularly distinguishes them from establishments in the agriculture, manufacturing, and construction industries. For example, farms that sell their products at or from the point of production are not classified in retail, but rather in agriculture. Similarly, establishments that both manufacture and sell their products to the general public are not classified in retail, but rather in manufacturing. However, establishments that engage in processing activities incidental to retailing are classified in retail. This includes establishments, such as optical goods stores that do in-store grinding of lenses, and meat and seafood markets.

Wholesalers also engage in the buying of goods for resale, but they are not usually organized to serve the general public. They typically operate from a warehouse or office and neither the design nor the location of these premises is intended to solicit a high volume of walk-in traffic. Wholesalers supply institutional, industrial, wholesale, and retail clients; their operations are, therefore, generally organized to purchase, sell, and deliver merchandise in larger quantities. However, dealers of durable nonconsumer goods, such as farm machinery and heavy-duty trucks, are included in wholesale trade even if they often sell these products in single units.

For information on the subsectors of Retail Trade (NAICS 44–45), see www.census.gov/eos/www/naics/.

The **Transportation and Warehousing** sector (NAICS 48–49) includes industries providing transportation of passengers and cargo, warehousing and storage for goods, scenic and sightseeing transportation, and support activities related to modes of transportation. Establishments in these industries use transportation equipment or transportation related facilities as a productive asset. The type of equipment depends on the mode of transportation. The modes of transportation are air, rail, water, road, and pipeline.

The Transportation and Warehousing sector distinguishes three basic types of activities: subsectors for each mode of transportation, a subsector for warehousing and storage, and a subsector for establishments providing support activities for transportation. In addition, there are subsectors for establishments that provide passenger transportation for scenic and sightseeing purposes, postal services, and courier services.

A separate subsector for support activities is established in the sector because, first, support activities for transportation are inherently multimodal, such as freight transportation arrangement, or have multimodal aspects. Secondly, there are production process similarities among the support activity industries.

One of the support activities identified in the support activity subsector is the routine repair and maintenance of transportation equipment (e.g., aircraft at an airport, railroad rolling stock at a railroad terminal, or ships at a harbor or port facility). Such establishments do not perform complete overhauling or rebuilding of transportation equipment (i.e., periodic restoration of transportation equipment to original design specifications) or transportation equipment conversion (i.e., major modification to systems). An establishment that primarily performs factory (or shipyard) overhauls, rebuilding, or conversions of aircraft, railroad rolling stock, or a ship is classified in Subsector 336, Transportation Equipment Manufacturing, according to the type of equipment.

Many of the establishments in this sector often operate on networks, with physical facilities, labor forces, and equipment spread over an extensive geographic area.

Warehousing establishments in this sector are distinguished from merchant wholesaling in that the warehouse establishments do not sell the goods.

Excluded from this sector are establishments primarily engaged in providing travel agent services that support transportation and other establishments, such as hotels, businesses, and government agencies. These establishments are classified in Sector 56, Administrative and Support and Waste Management and Remediation Services. Also, establishments primarily engaged in providing rental and leasing of transportation equipment without operator are classified in Subsector 532, Rental and Leasing Services.

For information on the subsectors of Transportation and Warehousing sector (NAICS 48–49), see www.census.gov/eos/www/naics/.

The **Information** sector (NAICS 51) comprises establishments engaged in the following processes: (a) producing and distributing information and cultural products, (b) providing the means to transmit or distribute these products as well as data or communications, and (c) processing data.

The main components of this sector are the publishing industries, including software publishing, and both traditional publishing and publishing exclusively on the internet; the motion picture and sound recording industries; the broadcasting industries, including traditional broadcasting and those broadcasting exclusively over the internet; the telecommunications industries; web search portals, data processing industries, and the information services industries.

The expressions "information age" and "global information economy" are used with considerable frequency today. The general idea of an "information economy" includes both the notion of industries primarily producing, processing, and distributing information, as well as the idea that every industry is using available information and information technology to reorganize and make themselves more productive.

For the purposes of NAICS, it is the transformation of information into a commodity that is produced and distributed by a number of growing industries that is at issue. The Information sector groups three types of establishments: (1) those engaged in producing and distributing information and cultural products; (2) those that provide the means to transmit or distribute these products as well as data or communications; and (3) those that process data. Cultural products are those that directly express attitudes, opinions, ideas, values, and artistic creativity; provide entertainment; or offer information and analysis concerning the past and present. Included in this definition are popular, mass-produced products as well as cultural products that normally have a more limited audience, such as poetry books, literary magazines, or classical records.

The unique characteristics of information and cultural products, and of the processes involved in their production and distribution, distinguish the Information sector from the goods-producing and service-producing sectors. Some of these characteristics are:

1. Unlike traditional goods, an "information or cultural product," such as a newspaper online or television program, does not necessarily have tangible qualities, nor is it necessarily associated with a particular form. A movie can be shown at a movie theater, on a television broadcast, through video-on-demand, or rented at a local video store. A sound recording can be aired on radio, embedded in multimedia products, or sold at a record store.

2. Unlike traditional services, the delivery of these products does not require direct contact between the supplier and the consumer.

3. The value of these products to the consumer lies in their informational, educational, cultural, or entertainment content, not in the format in which they are distributed. Most of these products are protected from unlawful reproduction by copyright laws.

4. The intangible property aspect of information and cultural products makes the processes involved in their production and distribution very different from goods and services. Only those possessing the rights to these works are authorized to reproduce, alter, improve, and distribute them. Acquiring and using these rights often involves significant costs. In addition, technology is revolutionizing the distribution of these products. It is possible to distribute them in a physical form, via broadcast, or online.

5. Distributors of information and cultural products can easily add value to the products they distribute. For instance, broadcasters add advertising not contained in the original product. This capacity means that unlike traditional distributors, they derive revenue not from sale of the distributed product to the final consumer, but from those who pay for the privilege of adding information to the original product. Similarly, a directory and mailing list publisher can acquire the rights to thousands of previously published newspaper and periodical articles and add new value by providing search and software and organizing the information in a way that facilitates research and retrieval. These products often command a much higher price than the original information.

The distribution modes for information commodities may either eliminate the necessity for traditional manufacture, or reverse the conventional order of manufacture-distribute.

A newspaper distributed online, for example, can be printed locally or by the final consumer. Similarly, it is anticipated that packaged software, which at the time of the 2007 economic census was mainly bought through the traditional retail channels, is now available mainly online. The NAICS Information sector is designed to make such economic changes transparent as they occur, or to facilitate designing surveys that will monitor the new phenomena and provide data to analyze the changes.

Many of the industries in the NAICS Information sector are engaged in producing products protected by copyright law or in distributing them (other than distribution by traditional wholesale and retail methods). Examples are traditional publishing industries, software and directory and mailing list publishing industries, and film and sound industries. Broadcasting and telecommunications industries and information providers and processors are also included in the Information sector because their technologies are so closely linked to other industries in the Information sector.

For information on the subsectors of Information sector (NAICS 51), see www.census.gov/eos/www/naics/.

The **Finance and Insurance** sector (NAICS 52) comprises establishments primarily engaged in financial transactions (transactions involving the creation, liquidation, or change in ownership of financial assets) and/or in facilitating financial transactions. Three principal types of activities are identified:

1. Raising funds by taking deposits and/or issuing securities and, in the process, incurring liabilities. Establishments engaged in this activity use raised funds to acquire financial assets by making loans and/ or purchasing securities. Putting themselves at risk, they channel funds from lenders to borrowers and transform or repackage the funds with respect to maturity, scale, and risk. This activity is known as financial intermediation.

2. Pooling of risk by underwriting insurance and annuities. Establishments engaged in this activity collect fees, insurance premiums, or annuity considerations; build up reserves; invest those reserves; and make contractual payments. Fees are based on the expected incidence of the insured risk and the expected return on investment.

3. Providing specialized services facilitating or supporting financial intermediation, insurance, and employee benefit programs.

In addition, monetary authorities charged with monetary control are included in this sector.

The subsectors, industry groups, and industries within the NAICS Finance and Insurance sector are defined on the basis of their unique production processes. As with all industries, the production processes are distinguished by their use of specialized human resources and specialized physical capital. In addition, the way in which these establishments acquire and allocate financial capital, their source of funds, and the use of those funds provides a third basis for distinguishing characteristics of the production process. For instance, the production process in raising funds through deposit taking is different from the process of raising funds in bond or money markets. The process of making loans to individuals also requires different production processes than does the creation of investment pools or the underwriting of securities.

Most of the Finance and Insurance subsectors contain one or more industry groups of (1) intermediaries with similar patterns of raising and using funds and (2) establishments engaged in activities that facilitate, or are otherwise related to, that type of financial or insurance intermediation. Industries within this sector are defined in terms of activities for which a production process can be specified, and many of these activities are not exclusive to a particular type of financial institution. To deal with the varied activities taking place within existing financial institutions, the approach is to split these institutions into components performing specialized services. This requires defining the units engaged in providing those services and developing procedures that allow for their delineation. These units are the equivalents for finance and insurance of the establishments defined for other industries.

The output of many financial services, as well as the inputs and the processes by which they are combined, cannot be observed at a single location and can only be defined at a higher level of the organizational structure of the enterprise. Additionally, a number of independent activities that represent separate and distinct production processes may take place at a single location belonging to a multilocation financial firm. Activities are more likely to be homogeneous with respect to production characteristics than are locations, at least in financial services. The classification defines activities broadly enough that it can be used both by those classifying by location and by those employing a more top-down approach to the delineation of the establishment.

Establishments engaged in activities that facilitate, or are otherwise related to, the various types of intermediation have been included in individual subsectors, rather than in a separate subsector dedicated to services alone because these services are performed by intermediaries, as well as by specialist establishments, the extent to which the activity of the intermediaries can be separately identified is not clear.

The Finance and Insurance sector has been defined to encompass establishments primarily engaged in financial transactions; that is, transactions involving the creation, liquidation, change in ownership of financial assets; or in facilitating financial transactions. Financial industries are extensive users of electronic means for facilitating the verification of financial balances, authorizing transactions, transferring funds to and from transactors accounts, notifying banks (or credit card issuers) of the individual transactions, and providing daily summaries. Since these transaction-processing activities are integral to the production of finance and insurance services, establishments that principally provide a financial transaction processing service are classified to this sector, rather than to the data processing industry in the Information sector.

Legal entities that hold portfolios of assets on behalf of others are significant and data on them are required for a variety of purposes. Thus for NAICS, these funds, trusts, and other financial vehicles are the fifth subsector of the Finance and Insurance sector. These entities earn interest, dividends, and other property income, but have little or no employment and no revenue from the sale of services. Separate establishments and employees devoted to the management of funds are classified in Industry Group 5239, Other Financial Investment Activities.

For information on the subsectors of **Finance and Insurance** sector (NAICS 52), see www.census.gov/eos/www/naics/.

The **Real Estate and Rental and Leasing** sector (NAICS 53) comprises establishments primarily engaged in renting, leasing, or otherwise allowing the use of tangible or intangible assets, and establishments providing related services. The major portion of this sector comprises establishments that rent, lease, or otherwise allow the use of their own assets by others. The assets may be tangible, as is the case of real estate and equipment, or intangible, as is the case with patents and trademarks.

This sector also includes establishments primarily engaged in managing real estate for others, selling, renting and/or buying real estate for others, and appraising real estate. These activities are closely related to this sector's main activity, and it was felt that from a production basis they would best be included here. In addition, a substantial proportion of property management is self-performed by lessors.

The main components of this sector are the real estate lessors industries (including equity real estate investment trusts (REITs)); equipment lessors industries (including motor vehicles, computers, and consumer goods); and lessors of nonfinancial intangible assets (except copyrighted works).

Excluded from this sector are establishments primarily engaged in renting or leasing equipment with operators. Establishments renting or leasing equipment with operators are classified in various subsectors of NAICS depending on the nature of the services provided (e.g., transportation, construction, agriculture). These activities are excluded from this sector because the client is paying for the expertise and knowledge of the equipment operator, in addition to the rental of the equipment. In many cases, such as the rental of heavy construction equipment, the operator is essential to operate the equipment.

For information on the subsectors of Real Estate and Rental and Leasing sector (NAICS 53), see www.census. gov/eos/www/naics/.

The **Professional, Scientific, and Technical Services** sector (NAICS 54) comprises establishments that specialize in performing professional, scientific, and technical activities for others. These activities require a high degree of expertise and training. The establishments in this sector specialize according to expertise and provide these services to clients in a variety of industries and, in some cases, to households. Activities performed include: legal advice and representation; accounting, bookkeeping, and payroll services; architectural, engineering, and specialized design services; computer services; consulting services; research services; advertising services; photographic services; translation and interpretation services; veterinary services; and other professional, scientific, and technical services.

This sector excludes establishments primarily engaged in providing a range of day-to-day office administrative services, such as financial planning, billing and recordkeeping, personnel, and physical distribution and logistics. These establishments are classified in Sector 56, Administrative and Support and Waste Management and Remediation Services.

For information on the subsectors of Professional, Scientific, and Technical Services sector (NAICS 54) see www. census.gov/eos/www/naics/.

The **Management of Companies and Enterprises** sector (NAICS 55) comprises (1) establishments that hold the securities of (or other equity interests in) companies and enterprises for the purpose of owning a controlling interest or influencing management decisions or (2) establishments (except government establishments) that administer, oversee, and manage establishments of the company or enterprise and that normally undertake the

strategic or organizational planning and decision-making role of the company or enterprise. Establishments that administer, oversee, and manage may hold the securities of the company or enterprise.

Establishments in this sector perform essential activities that are often undertaken, in-house, by establishments in many sectors of the economy. By consolidating the performance of these activities of the enterprise at one establishment, economies of scale are achieved.

Government establishments primarily engaged in administering, overseeing, and managing governmental programs are classified in Sector 92, Public Administration. Establishments primarily engaged in providing a range of day-to-day office administrative services, such as financial planning, billing and recordkeeping, personnel, and physical distribution and logistics are classified in Industry 56111, Office Administrative Services.

For information on the subsectors of Management of Companies and Enterprises sector (NAICS 55), see www. census.gov/eos/www/naics/.

The **Administrative and Support and Waste Management and Remediation Services** sector (NAICS 56) comprises establishments performing routine support activities for the day-to-day operations of other organizations. These essential activities are often undertaken in-house by establishments in many sectors of the economy. The establishments in this sector specialize in one or more of these support activities and provide these services to clients in a variety of industries and, in some cases, to households. Activities performed include: office administration, hiring and placing of personnel, document preparation and similar clerical services, solicitation, collection, security and surveillance services, cleaning, and waste disposal services.

The administrative and management activities performed by establishments in this sector are typically on a contract or fee basis. These activities may also be performed by establishments that are part of the company or enterprise. However, establishments involved in administering, overseeing, and managing other establishments of the company or enterprise, are classified in Sector 55, Management of Companies and Enterprises. Establishments in Sector 55 normally undertake the strategic and organizational planning and decision-making role of the company or enterprise. Government establishments engaged in administering, overseeing, and managing governmental programs are classified in Sector 92, Public Administration.

For information on the subsectors of Administrative and Support and Waste Management and Remediation

Services sector (NAICS 56), see www.census.gov/eos/www/naics/.

The **Educational Services** sector (NAICS 61) comprises establishments that provide instruction and training in a wide variety of subjects. This instruction and training is provided by specialized establishments, such as schools, colleges, universities, and training centers. These establishments may be privately owned and operated for profit or not for profit, or they may be publicly owned and operated. They may also offer food and/or accommodation services to their students.

Educational services are usually delivered by teachers or instructors that explain, tell, demonstrate, supervise, and direct learning. Instruction is imparted in diverse settings, such as educational institutions, the workplace, or the home, and through diverse means, such as correspondence, television, the Internet, or other electronic and distance-learning methods. The training provided by these establishments may include the use of simulators and simulation methods. It can be adapted to the particular needs of the students, for example, sign language can replace verbal language for teaching students with hearing impairments. All industries in the sector share this commonality of process, namely, labor inputs of instructors with the requisite subject matter expertise and teaching ability.

For information on the subsectors of Educational Services sector (NAICS 61), see www.census.gov/eos/www/naics/.

The **Health Care and Social Assistance** sector (NAICS 62) comprises establishments providing health care and social assistance for individuals. The sector includes both health care and social assistance because it is sometimes difficult to distinguish between the boundaries of these two activities. The industries in this sector are arranged on a continuum starting with those establishments providing medical care exclusively, continuing with those providing health care and social assistance, and finally finishing with those providing only social assistance. The services provided by establishments in this sector are delivered by trained professionals. All industries in the sector share this commonality of process, namely, labor inputs of health practitioners or social workers with the requisite expertise. Many of the industries in the sector are defined based on the educational degree held by the practitioners included in the industry.

Excluded from this sector are aerobic classes in Subsector 713, Amusement, Gambling, and Recreation Industries and nonmedical diet and weight reducing centers in Subsector 812, Personal and Laundry Services. Although these can be viewed as health services, these services are not typically delivered by health practitioners.

For information on the subsectors of Health Care and Social Assistance sector (NAICS 62), see http://www.census.gov/eos/www/naics/.

The **Arts, Entertainment, and Recreation** sector (NAICS 71) includes a wide range of establishments that operate facilities or provide services to meet varied cultural, entertainment, and recreational interests of their patrons. This sector comprises (1) establishments that are involved in producing, promoting, or participating in live performances, events, or exhibits intended for public viewing; (2) establishments that preserve and exhibit objects and sites of historical, cultural, or educational interest; and (3) establishments that operate facilities or provide services that enable patrons to participate in recreational activities or pursue amusement, hobby, and leisure-time interests.

Some establishments that provide cultural, entertainment, or recreational facilities and services are classified in other sectors. Excluded from this sector are: (1) establishments that provide both accommodations and recreational facilities, such as hunting and fishing camps and resort and casino hotels are classified in Subsector 721, Accommodation; (2) restaurants and night clubs that provide live entertainment in addition to the sale of food and beverages are classified in Subsector 722, Food Services and Drinking Places; (3) motion picture theaters, libraries and archives, and publishers of newspapers, magazines, books, periodicals, and computer software are classified in Sector 51, Information; and (4) establishments using transportation equipment to provide recreational and entertainment services, such as those operating sightseeing buses, dinner cruises, or helicopter rides, are classified in Subsector 487, Scenic and Sightseeing Transportation.

For information on the subsectors of **Arts, Entertainment, and Recreation** sector (NAICS 71), see www.census.gov/eos/www/naics/.

The **Accommodation and Food Services** sector (NAICS 72) comprises establishments providing customers with lodging and/or preparing meals, snacks, and beverages for immediate consumption. The sector includes both accommodation and food services establishments because the two activities are often combined at the same establishment.

Excluded from this sector are civic and social organizations, amusement and recreation parks, theaters, and other recreation or entertainment facilities providing food and beverage services.

For information on the subsectors of Accommodation and Food Services sector (NAICS 72), see www.census.gov/eos/www/naics/.

The **Other Services** (except Public Administration) sector (NAICS 81) comprises establishments engaged in providing services not specifically provided for elsewhere in the classification system. Establishments in this sector are primarily engaged in activities, such as equipment and machinery repairing, promoting or administering religious activities, grantmaking, advocacy, and providing dry cleaning and laundry services, personal care services, death care services, pet care services, photofinishing services, temporary parking services, and dating services.

Private households that engage in employing workers on or about the premises in activities primarily concerned with the operation of the household are included in this sector.

Excluded from this sector are establishments primarily engaged in retailing new equipment and also performing repairs and general maintenance on equipment. These establishments are classified in Sector 44–45, Retail Trade.

For information on the subsectors of **Other Services** (except Public Administration) sector (NAICS 81), see www.census.gov/eos/www/naics/.

The **Public Administration** sector (NAICS 92) consists of establishments of federal, state, and local government agencies that administer, oversee, and manage public programs and have executive, legislative, or judicial authority over other institutions within a given area. These agencies also set policy, create laws, adjudicate civil and criminal legal cases, provide for public safety and for national defense. In general, government establishments in the Public Administration sector oversee governmental programs and activities that are not performed by private establishments. Establishments in this sector typically are engaged in the organization and financing of the production of public goods and services, most of which are provided for free or at prices that are not economically significant.

Government establishments also engage in a wide range of productive activities covering not only public goods and services but also individual goods and services similar to those produced in sectors typically identified with private-sector establishments. In general, ownership is not a criterion for classification in NAICS. Therefore, government establishments engaged in the production of private-sector-like goods and services should be classified in the same industry as private-sector establishments engaged in similar activities.

As a practical matter, it is difficult to identify separate establishment detail for many government agencies. To the extent that separate establishment records are available, the administration of governmental programs is classified in Sector 92, Public Administration, while the operation of that same governmental program is classified elsewhere in NAICS based on the activities performed. For example, the governmental administrative authority for an airport is classified in Industry 92612, Regulation and Administration of Transportation Programs, while operating the airport is classified in Industry 48811, Airport Operations. When separate records for multiestablishment companies are not available to distinguish between the administration of a governmental program and the operation of it, the establishment is classified in Sector 92, Public Administration.

Examples of government-provided goods and services that are classified in sectors other than Public Administration include: schools, classified in Sector 61, Educational Services; hospitals, classified in Subsector 622, Hospitals; establishments operating transportation facilities, classified in Sector 48–49, Transportation and Warehousing; the operation of utilities, classified in Sector 22, Utilities; and the Government Printing Office, classified in Subsector 323, Printing and Related Support Activities.

For information on the subsectors of Public Administration sector (NAICS 92), see http://www.census.gov/eos/www/naics/.

Census of Governments

A Census of Governments is taken at 5-year intervals as required by law under Title 13, U.S. Code, Section 161. The purpose of the Census of Governments is to provide periodic and comprehensive statistics about governments and governmental activities for all state and local governments in the U.S. Local governments include counties, cities, townships, special districts, and school districts. Data are obtained on government organizations, finances, and employment. Organization data include location, type, and characteristics of local governments and officials. Finances and employment data are the same as in comparable annual surveys and include revenue, expenditure, debt, assets, employees, payroll, and benefits. The U.S. Code, Title 13, requires this census and provides for voluntary responses. The 2012 census, similar to those taken since 1957, covers three major subject fields—government organization, public employment, and government finances.

The concept of local governments as defined by the Census Bureau covers three general-purpose governments (county, municipal, and township) and two limited-purpose governments (school district and special district). For information on the history, methodology, and concepts for the Census of Governments, see the *Governments Finance and Employment Classification Manual* at www.census.gov/govs/classification/.

The term "full-time equivalent employment" refers to a computed statistic representing the number of full-time employees that could have been employed if the reported number of hours worked by part-time employees had been worked by full-time employees. This statistic is calculated separately for each function of a government by dividing the "part-time hours paid" by the standard number of hours for full-time employees in the particular government and then adding the resulting quotient to the number of full-time employees.

Revenue includes all amounts of money received by a government from external sources during its fiscal year (i.e., those originating "outside the government"), net of refunds and other correcting transactions, other than issuance of debt, sale of investments, and agency or private trust transactions. Under this definition, revenue excludes amounts transferred from other funds or agencies of the same government. General revenue covers all government revenue except liquor stores revenue, insurance trust revenue, and utility revenue. Taxes are compulsory contributions exacted by a government for public purposes except employee and employer assessments for retirement and social insurance purposes, which are classified as insurance trust revenue. All tax revenue is classified as general revenue and comprises amounts received (including interest and penalties but excluding protested amounts and refunds) from all taxes imposed by a government. Local government tax revenue excludes any amounts from shares of state imposed and collected taxes, which are classified as intergovernmental revenue. Property taxes are taxes conditioned on ownership of property and measured by its value. This category includes general property taxes related to property as a whole, real and personal, tangible or intangible, whether taxed at a single rate or at classified rates, and taxes on selected types of property, such as motor vehicles or on certain or all intangibles. Direct expenditure includes payments to employees, suppliers, contractors, beneficiaries, and other final recipients of government payment; i.e., all expenditure other than intergovernmental expenditure, while general expenditure covers all government expenditure other than the specifically enumerated kinds of expenditure classified as utility expenditure, liquor stores expenditure, and employee retirement or other insurance trust expenditure.

Census of Agriculture

The Census Bureau took a census of agriculture every 10 years from 1840 to 1920; since 1925, this census has been taken roughly once every 5 years. The 1997 Census of Agriculture was the first one conducted by the National Agricultural Statistics Service of the U.S. Department of Agriculture. Over time, the definition of a farm has varied. For recent censuses (including the 2012 census), a farm has been defined as any place from which $1,000 or more of agricultural products were produced and sold or normally would have been sold during the census year. The census of agriculture is the leading source of facts and statistics about the Nation's agricultural production. It provides a detailed picture of U.S. farms and ranches every five years and is the only source of uniform, comprehensive agricultural data for every state and county or county equivalent in the U.S.

TABLE A—STATES

Table A, States, presents 82 tables with items of data for each state, the United States as a whole, and the District of Columbia. These tables are numbered A-1 through A-82.

A number of the statistics in Tables A-1 through A-82 are also presented for metropolitan areas in Tables B-1 through B-14, for metropolitan area component counties in Tables C-1 through C-4, and for micropolitan areas in Table D-1.

Table A-1. Area and Population

Sources: Area—U.S. Census Bureau, State Area Measurements and Internal Point Coordinates; https://www.census.gov/geo/reference/state-area.html; Population—U.S. Census Bureau, "Table 1: Annual Estimates of the Population for the United States, Regions, States, and Puerto Rico: April 1, 2010 to July 1, 2015," https://www.census.gov/data/tables/2015/demo/popest/state-total.html; Table 1. Intercensal Estimates of the Resident Population for the United States, Regions, States, and Puerto Rico: April 1, 2000 to July 1, 2010, https://www.census.gov/data/tables/time-series/demo/popest/intercensal-2000-2010-state.html; Population change—U.S. Census Bureau, "Table 4: Cumulative Estimates of the Components of Population Change for the United States, Regions and States: April 1, 2010 to July 1, 2015, https://www.census.gov/data/tables/2015/demo/popest/state-total.html.

Land area. The Census Bureau provides land area for the decennial censuses. Area was calculated from the specific set of boundaries recorded for the entity (in this case, states) in the Census Bureau's geographic database.

Land area measurements may disagree with the information displayed on census maps and in the TIGER® file because, for area measurement purposes, features identified as "intermittent water" and "glacier" are reported as land area. TIGER® is an acronym for the digital (computer-readable) geographic database that automates the mapping and related geographic activities required to support the Census Bureau's census and survey programs; TIGER® stands for Topologically Integrated Geographic Encoding and Referencing system.

The accuracy of any area measurement figure is limited by the inaccuracy inherent in (1) the location and shape of the various boundary features in the database and (2) rounding affecting the last digit in all operations that compute and/ or sum the area measurement. Identification of land and inland, coastal, and territorial is for statistical purposes and does not necessarily reflect legal definitions thereof.

Population data for 2015 and population estimates base data for 2010 and 2000 were used to calculate rates or describe various population characteristics in Tables A-2 through A-82.

Persons enumerated in the census were counted as inhabitants of their usual place of residence, which generally means the place where a person lives and sleeps the majority of the time. This place is not necessarily the same as the legal residence, voting residence, or domicile. In the vast majority of cases, however, the use of these different bases of classification would produce substantially the same statistics, although appreciable differences may exist for a few areas.

The implementation of this usual-residence practice has resulted in the establishment of residence rules for certain categories of persons whose usual place of residence is not immediately apparent (e.g., college students were counted at their college residence). As in the above example, persons were not always counted as residents of the place where they happened to be staying on census day. However, persons without a usual place of residence were counted where they were enumerated.

Rank numbers are assigned on the basis of area size for the rank of area and by population size for rank of population, with each state placed in descending order, largest to smallest. Where ties—two or more states with identical area or populations occur—the same rank is assigned to each of the tied states. In such cases, the following rank number(s) is omitted so that the lowest rank is usually equal to the number of states ranked.

Persons per square mile, also known as population density, is the average number of inhabitants per square mile of land area. These figures are derived by dividing the total number of residents by the number of square miles of land area in the specified geographic area. To determine population per square kilometer, multiply the population per square mile by .386103.

Net change represents the increase or decrease between the 2 years shown. **Percent change** represents the increase or decrease between the 2 years shown as a percentage of the beginning population.

Refer to the General Notes on population estimates for explanations of **international migration** and **internal migration**.

Table A-2. Population by Age Group and Sex

Sources: U.S. Census Bureau. Annual Estimates of the Resident Population for Selected Age Groups by Sex for the United States, States, Counties, and Puerto Rico Commonwealth and Municipios: April 1, 2010 to July 1, 2015 https://www.census.gov/programs-surveys/popest/data/tables.2015.html. U.S Census Bureau. Intercensal Estimates of the Resident Population by Sex and Age for States: April 1, 2000 to July 1, 2010 https://www.census.gov/data/tables/time-series/demo/popest/intercensal-2000-2010-state.html.

Refer to the General Notes on population estimates for explanations of **population by age and sex**.

Table A-3. Population by Race and Hispanic Origin

Sources: U.S. Census Bureau, Annual Estimates of the Resident Population by Sex, Age, Race, and Hispanic Origin for the United States and States: April 1, 2010 to July 1, 2015; https://www.census.gov/data/tables/2015/demo/popest/state-detail.html.

Race. The racial classifications used by the Census Bureau adhere to the October 30, 1997, *Federal Register Notice* entitled "Revisions to the Standards for the Classification of Federal Data on Race and Ethnicity" issued by the Office of Management and Budget (OMB); see Internet site https://obamawhitehouse.archives.gov/sites/default/files/omb/assets/omb/fedreg/ombdir15.pdf. These standards govern the categories used to collect and present federal data on race and ethnicity. The OMB requires federal agencies to use a minimum of five race categories: White, Black or African American, American Indian and Alaska Native, Asian, and Native Hawaiian and Other Pacific Islander. For respondents unable to identify with any of these five race categories, the OMB approved including a sixth category, "Some other race," beginning with the Census 2000 questionnaire.

The question on race for Census 2000 was different from past census in several ways. Most significant was that respondents were given the option of selecting one or more race categories to indicate their racial identities. Because of these changes, the Census 2000 data on race are not directly comparable with data from the 1990 census or earlier censuses. Caution is recommended when interpreting changes in the racial composition of the U.S. population over time.

Population estimates by race and Hispanic origin are calculated using a distributive cohort component method. Previously developed resident state population estimates by age and sex and residential national population estimates by age, sex, race, and Hispanic origin are used as a base. Estimated post-censal changes in the corresponding populations are applied with a cohort component model. These distributions are applied to the original state age-sex and national characteristics estimates. For further information, see Internet site https://www.census.gov/programs-surveys/popest/technical-documentation/methodology.html.

White refers to people having origins in any of the original peoples of Europe, the Middle East, or North Africa. It includes people who indicated their race or races as White or wrote in entries such as Irish, German, Italian, Lebanese, Near Easterner, Arab, or Polish.

Black or African American refers to people having origins in any of the Black racial groups of Africa. It includes people who indicated their race or races as Black, African American, or Negro or wrote in entries such as African American, Afro American, Nigerian, or Haitian.

American Indian and Alaska Native refers to people having origins in any of the original peoples of North and South America (including Central America) and who maintain tribal affiliation or community attachment. It includes people who indicated their race or races by marking this category or writing in their principal or enrolled tribe, such as Rosebud Sioux, Chippewa, or Navajo.

Asian refers to people having origins in any of the original peoples of the Far East, Southeast Asia, or the Indian subcontinent. It includes people who indicated their race or races as Asian Indian, Chinese, Filipino, Korean, Japanese, Vietnamese, or Other Asian or wrote in entries such as Burmese, Hmong, Pakistani, or Thai.

Native Hawaiian and Other Pacific Islander refers to people having origins in any of the original peoples of Hawaii, Guam, Samoa, or other Pacific Islands. It includes people who indicated their race or races as Native Hawaiian, Guamanian or Chamorro, Samoan, or Other Pacific Islander or wrote in entries such as Tahitian, Mariana Islander, or Chuukese.

Two or more races. People may have chosen to provide two or more races either by checking two or more race response check boxes, by providing multiple write-in responses, or by some combination of check boxes and write-in responses. The race response categories shown on the questionnaire were collapsed into the five minimum race groups by the OMB.

Hispanic or Latino. People who identify with the terms "Hispanic" or "Latino" are those who classify themselves in one of the specific Hispanic or Latino categories listed on the questionnaire, such as Mexican, Puerto Rican, or Cuban, as well as those who indicate that they are other Spanish, Hispanic, or Latino. Origin can be viewed as the heritage, nationality group, lineage, or country of birth of the person or the person's parents or ancestors before their arrival in the United States. People who identify their origin as Spanish, Hispanic, or Latino may be any race.

The concept of race, as used by the Census Bureau, reflects self-identification by people according to the race or races with which they most closely identify. These categories are sociopolitical constructs and should not be interpreted as being scientific or anthropological in nature. Furthermore, the race categories include both racial and national-origin groups.

Traditional and current data collection and classification treat race and Hispanic origin as two separate and distinct concepts in accordance with guidelines from the OMB. Race and Hispanic origin are two separate concepts in the federal statistical system. People who are Hispanic may be any race, and people in each race group may be either Hispanic or non-Hispanic. Also, each person has two attributes, their race (or races) and whether or not they are Hispanic. The overlap of race and Hispanic origin is the main comparability issue. For example, Black Hispanics (Hispanic Blacks) are included in both the number of Blacks and in the number of Hispanics. For further information, see https://factfinder.census.gov/help/en/index.htm#glossary.htm.

Table A-4. Population by Residence

Sources: Core-based statistical area population—U.S. Census Bureau, "Intercensal Estimates of the Resident Population for Counties: April 1, 2010 to July 1, 2015"; https://www.census.gov/data/tables/2015/demo/popest/counties-total.html.

Urban population—U.S. Census Bureau, 2010 Census of Population and Housing, Population and Housing Unit Counts CPH-2; and U.S. Census Bureau, Census 2000 Summary File 1 100% data; www.census.gov/prod/www/decennial.html; and factfinder.census.gov.

The U.S. Office of Management and Budget (OMB) defines Metropolitan and Micropolitan Statistical Areas according to published standards that are applied to the Census Bureau data. The general concept of a Metropolitan or Micropolitan Statistical Area (collectively referred to as Core Based Statistical Areas, or CBSAs) is that of an area containing a recognized population nucleus and adjacent communities that have a high degree of integration with that nucleus. A **Metropolitan Statistical Area** is defined by OMB as a CBSA associated with at least one urbanized area that has a population of at least 50,000. The Metropolitan Statistical Area comprises the central county or counties containing the core, plus adjacent outlying counties having a high degree of social and economic integration with the central county as measured through commuting. A **core** is a densely settled concentration of population, comprising either an urbanized area or urban cluster. A **Micropolitan Statistical Area** is defined as a CBSA associated with at least one urban cluster that has a population of at least 10,000, but less than 50,000. The micropolitan area comprises the central county or counties containing the core, plus adjacent outlying counties having a high degree of social and economic integration with the central county as a measure through commuting. For more information on metropolitan and micropolitan statistical areas, see https://www.census.gov/programs-surveys/metro-micro.html.

The metropolitan and micropolitan statistical area population estimates are based upon the county estimates. The county estimates methodology is available at: https://www.census.gov/programs-surveys/popest/technical-documentation/methodology.html.

The Census Bureau classifies as **urban** all territory, population, and housing units located within an urbanized area (UA) or an urban cluster (UC). An **urbanized area** consists of a central place and adjacent densely settled territory that together contain at least 50,000 people, generally with an overall population density of at least 1,000 people per square mile. An **urbanized cluster** consists of a central place and adjacent densely settled territory that together contain at least 2,500 people, generally with an overall population density of at least 1,000 people per square mile. Under certain conditions, the Census Bureau will consider less densely settled territories as part of an UA or UC. All territories located outside of UAs and UCs are classified as rural. Geographic entities such as metropolitan areas and counties often contain both urban and rural territory. For more information, see Internet site https://www.census.gov/geo/reference/urban-rural.html.

Table A-5. Households

Source: U.S. Census Bureau—2015 American Community Survey, Table DP02. Selected Social Characteristics in the United States; Table C11010. Nonfamily Households by Sex of Householder by Living Alone by Age of Householder; Table B11005. Households by Presence of People under 18 Years by Household Type; Table B11007.

Households by Presence of People 65 Years and over by Household Type. Census 2010 Summary File 1 (SF 1) 100 percent Data. Table DP-1. Profile of General Population and Housing Characteristics: 2010 http://factfinder.census.gov/).

A **household** consists of all the people who occupy a housing unit. A house, an apartment or other group of rooms, or a single room, is regarded as a housing unit when it is occupied or intended for occupancy as separate living quarters; that is, when the occupants do not live and eat with any other persons in the structure and there is direct access from the outside or through a common hall. A household includes the related family members and all the unrelated people, if any, such as lodgers, foster children, wards, or employees who share the housing unit. A person living alone in a housing unit, or a group of unrelated people sharing a housing unit such as partners or roomers, is also counted as a household. The count of households excludes group quarters. **People per household** (or average household size) is a measure obtained by dividing the number of people in households by the total number of households (or householder).

A **family household** is a household maintained by a householder who is in a family (as defined above) and includes any unrelated people (unrelated subfamily members and/or secondary individuals) who may be residing there. The number of family households is equal to the number of families. The count of family household members differs from the count of family members, however, in that the family household members include all people living in the household, whereas family members include only the householder and his/her relatives. The expression "**married-couple**" before the term "household," "family," or "subfamily" indicates that the household, family, or subfamily is maintained by a married couple. **Female householder, no husband present** includes a family with a female who maintains a household with no husband.

A **nonfamily household** consists of the householder who lives alone or with nonrelatives only.

Own child category is a never-married child under 18 years old who is a son or daughter of the householder by birth, marriage, or adoption.

For more information regarding household data, see https://www.census.gov/programs-surveys/acs/technical-documentation/code-lists.html.

Table A-6. Marital Status, 2015

Source: U.S. Census Bureau—American Community Survey 2015 1-year estimates, Table B12001. Sex by marital status for the population 15 years and over; factfinder.census.gov.

Marital status refers to how people responded when asked if they were now married, widowed, divorced, separated, or never married. Couples who live together (unmarried people, people in common-law marriages) were allowed to report the marital status they considered the most appropriate.

Never married includes all people who have never been married, including people whose only marriage(s) was annulled.

Now married, except separated includes people whose current marriage has not ended through widowhood, divorce, or separation (regardless of previous marital history). The category also includes couples who live together or people in common-law marriages if they consider this category the most appropriate.

Separated includes people legally separated or otherwise absent from their spouse because of marital discord. This category also includes people who have been deserted or who have parted because they no longer want to live together but who have not obtained a divorce.

Widowed includes widows and widowers who have not remarried.

Divorced includes people who are legally divorced and who have not remarried. Those without a final divorce decree are classified as "separated."

Table A-7. Residence 1 Year Ago, People Obtaining Legal Permanent Resident Status, and Language Spoken at Home

Sources: Residence 1 year ago—U.S. Census Bureau, 2015 American Community Survey; table B07001, "Geographical Mobility in the Past Year by age for Current Residence in the United States"; factfinder.census.gov.

People obtaining legal permanent resident status—U.S. Department of Homeland Security, Office of Immigration Statistics, 2015 and 2014 Yearbook of Immigration Statistics, table 4 and Supplemental table 1 www.dhs.gov/yearbook-immigration-statistics.

Language—U.S. Census Bureau, 2015 American Community Survey, table B06007, "Place of Birth by Language Spoken at Home and Ability to Speak English in the United States," factfinder.census.gov.

Residence 1 year ago. The American Community Survey asked those participants who had moved from another residence in the United States 1 year earlier to report the city, town, or post office, the name of the U.S. county, state,

and ZIP Code where they lived 1 year ago. People living outside of the United States were asked to report the name of the foreign country or U.S. Island Area where they were living 1 year ago. "Residence 1 year ago" is used in conjunction with location of current residence to determine the extent of residential mobility of the population and the resulting redistribution of the population across the various states, metropolitan areas, and regions of the country. When no information on previous residence was reported for a person, information for other family members, if available, was used to assign a location of residence 1 year ago. All cases of nonresponse or incomplete response that were not assigned a previous residence based on information from other family members were allocated to the previous residence of another person with similar characteristics who provided complete information.

ACS participants were also asked if they sometimes or always spoke a language other than English at home. **Language other than English** includes anyone responding yes to this question but does not include the speaking of a language only at school or if speaking is limited to a few expressions or slang. People reporting they did speak another language at home were asked to identify the language spoken.

People obtaining lawful permanent resident status refers to an alien admitted to the United States as a lawful permanent resident. Permanent residents are also commonly referred to as immigrants; however, the Immigration and Nationality Act (INA) broadly defines an immigrant as any alien in the United States, except one legally admitted under specific nonimmigrant categories (INA section 101(a) (15)). An illegal alien who entered the United States without inspection, for example, would be strictly defined as an immigrant under the INA but is not a permanent resident alien. Lawful permanent residents are legally accorded the privilege of residing permanently in the United States. They may be issued immigrant visas by the Department of State overseas or adjusted to permanent resident status by the Department of Homeland Security in the United States.

Table A-8. Place of Birth, 2015

Sources: U.S. Census Bureau, American Community Survey 2015; Table B05002. Place of birth by nativity and citizenship status; Table B05007. Place of birth by year of entry by citizenship status for the foreign born population; and table C05006. Place of Birth for the Foreign-Born Population, http://factfinder.census.gov.

Place of birth. Participants of the American Community Survey were asked where they were born and were asked to select from two categories: (1) in the United

States or (2) outside the United States. Respondents selecting category 1 were then asked to report the name of the state while respondents selecting category 2 were then asked to report the name of the foreign country, or Puerto Rico, Guam, etc. People not reporting a place of birth were assigned the state or country of birth of another family member, or were allocated the response of another individual with similar characteristics. People born outside the United States were asked to report their place of birth according to current international boundaries. Since numerous changes in boundaries of foreign countries have occurred in the last century, some people may have reported their place of birth in terms of boundaries that existed at the time of their birth or emigration, or in accordance with their own national preference.

The **foreign-born** population includes anyone who was not a U.S. citizen at birth. This includes respondents who indicated they were a U.S. citizen by naturalization or not a U.S. citizen. This excludes people born in the United States, Puerto Rico or a U.S. Island Area such as Guam or the U.S. Virgin Islands, or people born in a foreign country to a U.S. citizen parent(s).

Table A-9. Live Births and Birth Rates

Source: U.S. National Center for Health Statistics, National Vital Statistics Reports (NVSR), Births: Final Data 2015, Vol. 66, No. 1, January 5, 2017; Final Data 2010, Vol. 61, No. 1, August 28, 2012; Final Data 2000, Vol. 50, No. 5, Revised May 15, 2002 Vol. 61, No. 1, August 28, 2012 https://www.cdc.gov/nchs/products/nvsr.htm.

The National Vital Statistics System (NVSR) is an intergovernmental data system with the purpose of collecting and disseminating the nation's official vital statistics. These data are provided through contracts between NCHS and vital registration systems operated in the various jurisdictions legally responsible for the registration of vital events—births, deaths, marriages, divorces, and fetal deaths. In the United States, legal authority for the registration of these events resides individually with the 50 States, 2 cities (Washington, DC, and New York City), and 5 territories (Puerto Rico, the Virgin Islands, Guam, American Samoa, and the Commonwealth of the Northern Mariana Islands). These jurisdictions are responsible for maintaining registries of vital events and for issuing copies of birth, marriage, divorce, and death certificates.

Birth statistics are limited to events occurring during the year. The data are by place of residence and exclude events occurring to nonresidents of the United States. Births that occur outside the United States are excluded. Data for 2015 represent 99 percent of births in that year.

Birth rates represent the number of births per 1,000 resident population estimated as of July 1 for 2015 and enumerated as of April 1 for 2000 and 2010 (decennial census years).

Births to **unmarried women.** The mother's marital status is based on a question on the birth certificate. In most states, the question is: "Mother married? (At birth, conception, or any time between) (Yes or No)." If the question is answered "no," then the birth is considered nonmarital.

Teenage mothers are considered anyone under the age of 20.

Low birth weight is defined as less than 2,500 grams or 5 pounds, 8 ounces.

Table A-10. Births and Birth Rates by Race and Hispanic Origin and Fertility Rate: 2015

Source: U.S. National Center for Health Statistics, National Vital Statistics Reports (NVSR). Final Data 2015, Vol. 66, No. 1, January 5, 2017, https://www.cdc.gov/nchs/products/nvsr.htm.

Births by race. For information on how the National Vital Statistics System, the National Center for Health Statistics (NCHS) collects and publishes data see appendix entry for Table A-9.

Race and Hispanic origin are reported separately on the birth certificate. Beginning with the 1989 data year, NCHS started tabulating its birth data primarily by race of the mother. In 1988 and prior years, births were tabulated by the race of the child, which was determined from the race of the parents as entered on the birth certificate. Race categories are consistent with the 1997 Office of Management and Budget standards.

Table A-11. Deaths and Death Rates

Sources: Death for all races and infant deaths—U.S. National Center for Health Statistics and National Vital Statistics Reports (NVSR); www.cdc.gov/nchs/nvss.htm; Center for Disease Control and Prevention; CDC Wonder data base, Compressed Mortality; wonder.cdc.gov/.

Deaths. Mortality data for 2015 and 2010 are based on the continuous receipt and processing of statistical records by the National Center for Health Statistics (NCHS). NCHS received the data from states' vital registration systems through the Vital Statistics Cooperative Program.

Death statistics are limited to events occurring during the year. The data are by place of residence and exclude events occurring to nonresidents of the United States. Deaths that occur outside the United States are excluded. **Death rates** represent the number of deaths per 1,000 resident population estimated as of April 1 for 2010 (decennial census year) and July 1 for 2015.

Infant mortality rates are calculated by dividing the preliminary number of infant deaths that occurred during the year by the number of live births for the same period and are presented as rates per 1,000 live births.

Table A-12. Age-Adjusted Death Rates by Cause: 2015

Source: Centers for Disease Control and Prevention, National Center for Health Statistics. Compressed Mortality File 1999–2015 on CDC WONDER Online Database, released December 2016. Data are from the Compressed Mortality File 1999–2015 Series 20 No. 2U, 2016, as compiled from data provided by the 57 vital statistics jurisdictions through the Vital Statistics Cooperative Program.

Death rates by cause. Mortality statistics by cause of death are compiled in accordance with World Health Organization (WHO) regulations, which specify that member nations classify causes of death according to the current revision of the *International Statistical Classification of Diseases and Related Health Problems* (ICD). Effective with deaths occurring in 1999, the United States began using the Tenth Revision of this classification. Tabulations of cause-of-death statistics are based solely on the underlying cause of death. The underlying cause is defined by the WHO as "the disease or injury which initiated the train of events leading directly to death, or the circumstances of the accident or violence which produced the fatal injury." The underlying cause is selected from the conditions entered by the physician in the cause of death section of the death certificate. When more than one cause or condition is entered by the physician, the underlying cause is determined by the sequence of conditions on the certificate, provisions, of the ICD, and associated selection rules and modifications.

Age-adjusted rates are mortality rates adjusted for the different age distributions of separate populations. Certain causes of death can be more probable with a certain age group and will distort an area's risk of suffering from certain injuries or diseases. An age-adjusted rate will control the impact a particular age group will have on the death rate of an area and will allow the user to compare mortality risks between areas with different age groups or in a time series. Age-adjusted rates should be viewed as relative indexes rather than actual measures of mortality risk. The age-adjusted rates provided by the National Vital Statistics Reports (NVSR) were computed by the direct method of applying age-specific death rates to the U.S. standard population age distribution.

The rates of almost all causes of death vary by age. Age adjustment is a technique for "removing" the effects of age from crude rates, so as to allow meaningful comparisons across populations with different underlying age structures. For example, comparing the crude rate of heart disease in Florida to that of California is misleading, because the relatively older population in Florida will lead to a higher crude death rate, even if the age-specific rates of heart disease in Florida and California are the same. For such a comparison, age-adjusted rates are preferable. Age-adjusted rates should be viewed as relative indexes rather than as direct or actual measures of mortality risk.

Table A-13. Marriages and Divorces

Sources: Marriage and divorce rates—U.S. National Center for Health Statistics, National Vital Statistics System; https://www.cdc.gov/nchs/nvss/marriage-divorce.htm.

Marital history—U.S. Census Bureau, 2015 American Community Survey, Table B12007, Median age at first marriage; Table B12501, Marriages in the last year by sex by marital status for the population 15 years and over; Table B12503, Divorces in the last year by sex by marital status for the population 15 years and over; Table B12505, Number of times married by sex by marital status for the population 15 years and over, Factfinder.census.gov

Marriage and divorce. Information on the total rates of marriages and divorces at the national and state levels are published in the NCHS National Vital Statistics System. The collection of detailed data was suspended beginning in January 1996 (see Federal Register Notice, December 15, 1995). Beginning with the June 2003 data, detailed state tables of marriage and divorce levels have been included in the monthly reports of provisional data published in the NCHS National Vital Statistics Reports. Prior to this, these data were available in the "Detailed Statistical Tables" section of NCHS's Data Warehouse website.

Marriage and divorce rates (per 1000 people) provided by NVSS are based on all events occurring in the state that were received in the registration offices during a 1-month period. The yearly figures are derived from summing all 12 months. Divorce figures include reported annulments. There is considerable variability among the states in the procedures that are used to submit the counts of marriages and divorces to NCHS and in the extent to which the states update their counts of marriages and divorces as new information is received. Therefore, counts vary in their completeness.

Information on marital history is from the 2015 American Community Survey. Persons age 15 and older were asked about their marital status. Those who were "ever married" (including those now married, separated, widowed, or divorced) were asked if they had been married, widowed, or divorced in the past 12 months. They were asked how many times (once, two times, or three or more times) they have been married, and the year of their last marriage.

The median age at first marriage is calculated indirectly by estimating the proportion of young people who will marry during their lifetime, calculating one-half of this proportion, and determining the age (at the time of the survey) of people at this half-way mark by osculatory interpolation. It does not represent the actual median age of the population who married during the calendar year. It is shown to the nearest tenth of a year. Henry S. Shryock and Jacob S. Siegel outline the osculatory procedure in *Methods and Materials of Demography*, First Edition (May 1973), Volume 1, pages 291–96.

Table A-14. Health Care Services, Physicians, and Nurses

Sources: Health care services—U.S. Census Bureau, County Business Patterns, annual (related Internet site https://www.census.gov/programs-surveys/cbp.html).

Physicians and Nurses—Bureau of Labor Statistics, Occupational Employment Statistics, Occupational Employment and Wages; May 2016 Wage and Employment Statistics; https://www.bls.gov/oes/home.htm.

County Business Patterns (CBP) is an annual series that provides subnational economic data by industry. The series is useful for studying the economic activity of small areas, analyzing economic changes over time, and as a benchmark for statistical series, surveys, and databases between economic censuses. CBP covers most of the country's economic activity. The series excludes data on self-employed individuals, employees of private households, railroad employees, agricultural production employees, and most government employees.

CBP data are extracted from the Business Register, the Census Bureau's file of all known single- and multiestablishment companies. The Annual Company Organization Survey and quinquennial economic censuses provide individual establishment data for multilocation firms. Data for single-location firms are obtained from various programs conducted by the Census Bureau, such as the economic censuses, the Annual Survey of Manufactures, and Current Business Surveys, as well as from administrative records of the Internal Revenue Service (IRS), the

Social Security Administration (SSA), and the Bureau of Labor Statistics (BLS).

An **establishment** is a single physical location at which business is conducted or services or industrial operations are performed. It is not necessarily identical with a company or enterprise, which may consist of one or more establishments. When two or more activities are carried on at a single location under a single ownership, all activities generally are grouped together as a single establishment. The entire establishment is classified on the basis of its major activity and all data are included in that classification. Establishment counts represent the number of locations with paid employees any time during the year.

Paid **employment** consists of full- and part-time employees, including salaried officers and executives of corporations, who are on the payroll in the pay period including March 12. Included are employees on paid sick leave, holidays, and vacations; not included are proprietors and partners of unincorporated businesses.

Total **payroll** includes all forms of compensation, such as salaries, wages, reported tips, commissions, bonuses, vacation allowances, sick-leave pay, employee contributions to qualified pension plans, and the value of taxable fringe benefits. For corporations, it includes amounts paid to officers and executives; for unincorporated businesses, it does not include profit or other compensation of proprietors or partners. Payroll is reported before deductions for social security, income tax, insurance, union dues, etc.

Health Care and Social Assistance (NAICS 62) combines Ambulatory Health Care Services (NAICS 621), Hospitals (NAICS 622), Nursing and Residential Care Facilities (NAICS 623), and Social Assistance (NAICS 624.) Social Assistance is not presented separately in this table. For more information on health care services (2007, NAICS 62), see General Notes or Internet site https://www.census.gov/eos/www/naics/.

The numbers of **physicians** and **nurses** are from the Occupational Employment Statistics (OES) program, which produces employment and wage estimates annually for over 800 occupations. The OES survey is a semiannual mail survey of non-farm establishments. The BLS produces the survey materials and selects the establishments to be surveyed. The sampling frame (the list from which establishments to be surveyed are selected) is derived from the list of establishments maintained by State Workforce Agencies (SWAs) for unemployment insurance purposes. Establishments to be surveyed are selected in order to obtain data from every metropolitan and nonmetropolitan area in every state, across all surveyed industries, and from establishments of varying sizes. The SWAs mail the survey materials to the selected establishments and make follow-up calls to request data from nonrespondents or to clarify data. The collected data are used to produce occupational estimates at the National, State, and sub-State levels.

Table A-15. Health Care Employment and Type of Health Insurance

Source: U.S. Census Bureau, American Community Survey 2015. Employment in Health Care Occupations Table B24010. Sex by occupation for the civilian employed population 16 years and over. Health Insurance: B27002. Private health insurance status by sex by age; B27003. Public health insurance status by sex by age; B27004. Employer based health insurance by sex by age; B27005. Direct-purchase health insurance by sex by age; B27006. Medicare coverage by sex by age; B27007. Medicaid/means-tested public coverage by sex by age; B27008. TRICARE/military health coverage by sex by age; B27009. VA health care by sex by age. Factfinder.census.gov.

Health care employment is from the occupation data in the American Community Survey. Occupation describes the kind of work a person does on the job. Occupation data were derived from answers to two questions: "What kind of work was this person doing?" and "What were this person's most important activities or duties?" These questions were asked of all people 15 years old and over who had worked in the past 5 years. For employed people, the data refer to the person's job during the previous week. For those who worked two or more jobs, the data refer to the job where the person worked the greatest number of hours. For unemployed people and people who are not currently employed but report having a job within the last five years, the data refer to their last job. Table A-15 includes only employed persons aged 16 or older.

Occupation statistics are compiled from data that are coded based on the Standard Occupational Classification (SOC) Manual: 2010 (http://www.bls.gov/soc), published by the Executive Office of the President, Office of Management and Budget.

Census occupation codes, based on the 2010 SOC, provide 539 specific occupational categories, for employed people, including military, arranged into 23 major occupational groups. Respondents provided the data for the tabulations by writing on the questionnaires descriptions of the kind of work and activities they are doing. These write-ins are converted to a code category through automated coding. Cases not autocoded on both industry and occupation are sent to the clerical staff in the National Processing Center (NPC) in Jeffersonville, Indiana, who assign codes by comparing these descriptions to entries in the Alphabetical Index of Industries and Occupations

(http://www.census.gov/people/io/methodology/indexes.html).

The ACS combines some occupations.

- "Therapists" include occupational, physical, radiation, recreational, and respiratory therapists; speech-language pathologists; exercise physiologists; and all other therapists.

- "Other nurses" include nurse anesthetists, nurse midwives, and nurse practitioners.

- "Other health diagnosing and treating practitioners" include chiropractors, dentists, dietitians and nutritionists, optometrists, pharmacists, physician assistants, podiatrists, audiologists, veterinarians, and all other health diagnosing and treating practitioners.

- "Health technologists and technicians" include clinical laboratory technologists and technicians, dental hygienists, diagnostic related technologists and technicians, emergency medical technicians and paramedics, health practitioner support technologists and technicians, licensed practical and licensed vocational nurses, medical records and health information technicians, dispensing opticians, miscellaneous health technologists and technicians, and all other healthcare practitioners and technical occupations.

- "Other healthcare support occupations" include massage therapists, dental assistants, medical assistants, medical transcriptionists, pharmacy aides, veterinary assistants and laboratory animal caretakers, phlebotomists, and all other healthcare support workers, including medical equipment preparers.

Health Insurance Coverage. In the 2015 American Community Survey, respondents were instructed to report their current coverage and to mark "yes" or "no" for each of the eight types listed:

a. Insurance through a current or former employer or union (of this person or another family member)

b. Insurance purchased directly from an insurance company (by this person or another family member)

c. Medicare, for people 65 and older, or people with certain disabilities

d. Medicaid, Medical Assistance, or any kind of government-assistance plan for those with low incomes or a disability

e. TRICARE or other military health care

f. VA (including those who have ever used or enrolled for VA health care)

g. Indian Health Service

h. Any other type of health insurance or health coverage plan (Respondents who answered "yes" to question h were asked to provide their other type of coverage in a write-in field.)

Health insurance coverage in the ACS and other Census Bureau surveys define coverage to include plans and programs that provide comprehensive health coverage. Plans that provide insurance for specific conditions or situations such as cancer and long-term care policies are not considered coverage. Likewise, other types of insurance like dental, vision, life, and disability insurance are not considered health insurance coverage.

In defining types of coverage, write-in responses were reclassified into one of the first seven types of coverage or determined not to be a coverage type. Write-in responses that referenced the coverage of a family member were edited to assign coverage based on responses from other family members. As a result, only the first seven types of health coverage are included in the data. An eligibility edit was applied to give Medicaid, Medicare, and TRI-CARE coverage to individuals based on program eligibility rules. TRICARE or other military health care was given to active-duty military personnel and their spouses and children. Medicaid or other means-tested public coverage was given to foster children, certain individuals receiving Supplemental Security Income or Public Assistance, and the spouses and children of certain Medicaid beneficiaries. Medicare coverage was given to people 65 and older who received Social Security or Medicaid benefits. People were considered insured if they reported at least one "yes" to Questions a to f.

People who had no reported health coverage, or those whose only health coverage was Indian Health Service, were considered uninsured. For reporting purposes, the Census Bureau broadly classifies health insurance coverage as private health insurance or public coverage.

Private health insurance is a plan provided through an employer or union, a plan purchased by an individual from a private company, or TRICARE or other military health care. Respondents reporting a "yes" to the types listed in parts a, b, or e were considered to have private health insurance. Public health coverage includes the federal programs Medicare, Medicaid, and VA Health Care (provided through the Department of Veterans Affairs); the Children's Health Insurance Program (CHIP); and individual state health plans. Respondents reporting a "yes" to the types listed in c, d, or f were considered to have public coverage. The types of health insurance are not mutually exclusive; people may be covered by more than one at the same time.

Table A-16. Health Indicators: Health Risks

Source: U.S. Centers for Disease Control and Prevention, Atlanta, GA. Sortable Risk Factors and Health Indicators. https://sortablestats.cdc.gov/#/.

Health Indicators. The CDC's Sortable Risk Factors and Health Indicators website compiles data from various published CDC and federal sources into a format that allows users to view, sort, and analyze data at state/territory, regional, and national levels.

Table A-16 includes the following indicators for the United States and each state:

Adult Smoking (2014). The percent of adults (age 18+) who currently smoke cigarettes **(Source:** *Behavioral Risk Factor Surveillance System 2014.***)** Includes all 50 states, DC and territories (Guam, Puerto Rico, and the U.S. Virgin Islands). National data based on median state prevalence of these 54 areas (median %=21.1).

Youth Smoking (2015). The percent of High school students who smoked cigarettes on one or more days in the last 30 days. **(Source:** *Youth Risk Behavior Surveillance System (YRBSS), 2015)* National percentage is based on a separate, nationally representative survey. It is not based on results from individual state and territorial surveys. Data not available in MN, OR, and WA. 2015 Data not available in CO, GA, IA, KS, LA, NJ, OH, TX, UT, WI.

Adult Physical Activity (2013). The percent of adults that participated in 150 minutes or more of Aerobic Physical Activity per week. **(Source:** *Behavioral Risk Factors Surveillance System (BRFSS))* Includes all 50 states, DC and territories (Guam, Puerto Rico, and the U.S. Virgin Islands). National data based on median state prevalence of these 54 areas.

Youth Physical Activity (2015). The percent of high school students that are physically active at least 60 minutes per day on five or more days. **(Source:** *Youth Risk Behavior Surveillance System (YRBSS), 2015)* Physically active is defined as doing any kind of physical activity that increased the heart rate and made them breathe hard some of the time during the 7 days before the survey. National percentage is based on a separate, nationally representative survey. It is not based on results from individual state and territorial surveys. Data not available in MN, OR, and WA. 2015 Data not available in CO, GA, IA, KS, LA, NJ, OH, TX, UT, WI.

Adult Nutrition (2013). The percent of adults that consume vegetables less than one time per day. (**Source:** *Behavioral Risk Factors Surveillance System*) Includes all 50 states, DC and territories (Guam, Puerto Rico, and the U.S. Virgin Islands). National data based on median state prevalence of these 54 areas.

Youth Nutrition (2015). The percent of high school students that ate vegetables three or more times per day (**Source:** *Youth Risk Behavior Surveillance System (YRBSS), 2015)* National percentage is based on a separate, nationally representative survey. It is not based on results from individual state and territorial surveys. Data not available in MN, OR, and WA. 2015 Data not available in CO, GA, IA, KS, LA, NJ, OH, TX, UT, WI

Adult Binge Drinking (2014). The percent of adults (age over 18) who are binge drinkers: males having five or more drinks on one occasion, females having four or more drinks on one occasion. (**Source:** *Behavioral Risk Factor Surveillance System)* Includes all 50 states, DC and territories (Guam, Puerto Rico, and the U.S. Virgin Islands). National data based on median state prevalence of these 54 areas.

Youth Binge Drinking (2015). The percent of high school students reporting having five or more drinks of alcohol in a row within a couple of hours on at least 1 day in the last 30 days (**Source:** *Youth Risk Behavior Surveillance System (YRBSS), 2015)* National percentage is based on a separate, nationally representative survey. It is not based on results from individual state and territorial surveys. Data not available in MN, OR, and WA. 2015 Data not available in CO, GA, IA, KS, LA, NJ, OH, TX, UT, WI.

Observed Seat Belt Use (2014). The percent of observed seat belt use among front seat occupants based on probability samples in all 50 states (**Source:** *National Highway Traffic Safety Administration (NHTSA)).* NHTSA's National Occupant Protection Use Survey (NOPUS) is a national probability-based survey. National average of 85% includes 50 states, DC, and territories.

Youth Seat Belt Use (2015). Percent of high school students who wore a seat belt sometimes, most of the time, or always (**Source:** *Youth Risk Behavior Surveillance System (YRBSS), 2015)* National percentage is based on a separate, nationally representative survey. It is not based on results from individual state and territorial surveys. Data not available in MN, OR, and WA. 2015 Data not available in CO, GA, IA, KS, LA, NJ, OH, TX, UT, WI.

Youth Marijuana Use (2015). The percent of high school students who used marijuana on at least 1 or more days in the last 30 days (**Source:** *Youth Risk Behavior Surveillance*

System (YRBSS), 2015). National percentage is based on a separate, nationally representative survey. It is not based on results from individual state and territorial surveys. Data not available in MN, OR, and WA. 2015 Data not available in CO, GA, IA, KS, LA, NJ, OH, TX, UT, WI.

Table A-17. Health Indicators: Health Conditions and Preventive Measures

Source: U.S. Centers for Disease Control and Prevention, Atlanta, GA. Sortable Risk Factors and Health Indicators. https://sortablestats.cdc.gov/#/.

Health Indicators. The CDC's Sortable Risk Factors and Health Indicators website compiles data from various published CDC and federal sources into a format that allows users to view, sort, and analyze data at state/territory, regional, and national levels.

Table A-17 includes the following indicators:

HIV Diagnosis Rate (2014). The rate of persons diagnosed with HIV infection per 100,000 population (**Source:** *CDC HIV Surveillance Report)*. Diagnoses of HIV infection refers to laboratory-confirmatory evidence of HIV infection cases reported to CDC annually. The estimated rates of diagnoses of HIV infection are based on data from 46 states and 5 territories (American Samoa, Guam, the Northern Mariana Islands, Puerto Rico, and the U.S. Virgin Islands) that have had confidential name-based HIV infection reporting for a sufficient length of time (i.e., since at least January 2007, and reporting to CDC since at least June 2007). This figure does not include persons living with HIV who have NOT been diagnosed (20% of all persons living with HIV). Rates are per 100,000 population based on 2009 population estimates, and are statistical adjusted to account for reporting delays, but not for incomplete reporting.

Adult Obesity (2014). The percent of adults (age 18 and older) who are obese (Body Mass Index 30) (**Source:** *Behavioral Risk Factor Surveillance System 2012)*. Includes all 50 states, DC and territories (Guam, Puerto Rico, and the U.S. Virgin Islands). National data based on median state prevalence of these 54 areas (median %=27.8).

Youth Obesity (2015). **Indicator:** The percent of high school students who are obese (Body Mass Index=the 95th percentile for age/sex) (**Source:** *Youth Risk Behavior Surveillance System (YRBSS), 2015)*. National percentage is based on a separate, nationally representative survey. It is not based on results from individual state and territorial surveys. Data not available in MN, OR, and

WA. 2015 Data not available in CO, GA, IA, KS, LA, NJ, OH, TX, UT, WI.

Diagnosed Diabetes (2014). The percent of adults (age 18+) ever told by health professional that they have diabetes (**Source:** *Behavioral Risk Factor Surveillance System (BRFSS), 2014*). Women diagnosed only during pregnancy (gestational diabetes) and persons who reported they are pre-or borderline diabetic are excluded. Includes all 50 states, DC and territories (Guam, Puerto Rico, and the U.S. Virgin Islands). National data based on median state prevalence of these 54 areas (median %=9.5).

Diagnosed High Cholesterol (2013). The percent of adults who have had their blood cholesterol checked and have been told it was high (**Source:** *Behavioral Risk Factor Surveillance System (BRFSS)*). Includes all 50 states, DC and territories (Guam, Puerto Rico, and the U.S. Virgin Islands). National data based on median state prevalence of these 54 areas (median %=38.4).

Diagnosed Hypertension (2013). The percent of adults (age 18+) ever told by a health professional that they have high blood pressure. (**Source:** *Behavioral Risk Factor Surveillance System*). Includes all 50 states, DC and territories (Guam, Puerto Rico, and the U.S. Virgin Islands). National data based on median state prevalence of these 54 areas (median %=30.9).

Medicated Hypertension (2013). The percent of adults (age 18+) currently taking medicine for high blood pressure (hypertension) (**Source:** *Behavioral Risk Factor Surveillance System*). Percent is based on a subset of persons having been told by health professionals that they have high blood pressure. Data includes all 50 states, DC and territories (Guam, Puerto Rico, and the U.S. Virgin Islands). National data based on median state prevalence of these 54 areas.

Colorectal Cancer Screening (2014). The percent of persons age 50+ who have ever had a sigmoidoscopy or colonoscopy (**Source:** *Behavioral Risk Factor Surveillance System*). Includes all 50 states, DC and territories (Guam, Puerto Rico, and the U.S. Virgin Islands). National data based on median state prevalence of these 54 areas (median %=64.2).

Influenza Vaccination Coverage (2014). The percent of persons aged 6 months and older who received a seasonal influenza vaccination with the past year (**Source:** *Fluvaxview)* Combines estimates from the National Immunization Survey (NIS) and the Behavioral Risk Factor Surveillance System (BRFSS), from all 50 states and DC to estimate national and state level influenza vaccination coverage. National and regional rates exclude U.S. territories.

Child Vaccination Coverage (2014). The percent of children aged 19 to 35 months receiving the recommended doses of DTaP, polio, MMR, Hib, hepatitis B, Varicella and PCV. (**Source:** *National Immunization Survey (NIS))*. The Advisory Committee on Immunization Practices recommended series of vaccinations for children aged 19 to 35 months include at least four doses of diphtheria-tetanus-acellular pertussis (DTaP), at least three doses of polio, at least one dose of measles-mumps-rubella (MMR), at least three or four doses of Haemophilus influenzae B (Hib) depending on product type received, at least three doses of hepatitis B antigens, at least one dose of varicella, and at least four doses of PCV. In 2009, the full series was modified to include 3 or 4 doses of Hib vaccine (depending on product type received); which differs from the 2007 and 2008 full series included 3 doses of Hib vaccine.

Table A-18. People with and without Health Insurance Coverage

Source: U.S. Census Bureau, American Community Survey, Health Insurance Coverage in the United States, 2015, detailed tables and historical tables. https://www.census.gov/library/publications/2016/demo/p60-257.html.

Each year the Census Bureau issues a report on health insurance in the United States. This report presents statistics on health insurance coverage based on information collected in the Current Population Survey Annual Social and Economic Supplements (CPS ASEC) and the American Community Survey (ACS). Table A-18 is from the ACS data.

People who had no reported health coverage, or those whose only health coverage was Indian Health Service, were considered uninsured. For reporting purposes, the Census Bureau broadly classifies health insurance coverage as private health insurance or public coverage.

Private health insurance is a plan provided through an employer or union, a plan purchased by an individual from a private company, or TRICARE or other military health care. Public health coverage includes the federal programs Medicare, Medicaid, and VA Health Care (provided through the Department of Veterans Affairs); the Children's Health Insurance Program (CHIP); and individual state health plans. The types of health insurance are not mutually exclusive; people may be covered by more than one at the same time.

Table A-19. Public and Private School Fall Enrollment

Sources: Total enrollment—U.S. Census Bureau, *2015 American Community Survey*; table B14003, "Sex by school enrollment by type of school by age for the population 3 years and over"; using American FactFinder; factfinder.census.gov; Public enrollment—U.S. National Center for Education Statistics, Digest of Education Statistics, annual. See also http://www.nces.ed.gov/.

Total (public and private) enrollment data are provided by the American Community Survey. For information on the American Community Survey, see General Notes.

Total enrollment rate is the average percent of people aged 3–4 or 5–17 years who are enrolled in public or private school based on enumerated resident population for the ages of 3–4 or 5–17 as of July 1.

Public enrollment data are from the Common Core of Data (CCD), which is the National Center for Education Statistics' (NCES) primary database on elementary and secondary public education in the United States. The CCD, collected annually, is a comprehensive, national statistical database of all public elementary and secondary schools and school districts and contains data that are comparable across all states.

Data are collected for a particular school year via an online reporting system open to state education agencies during the school year. Beginning with the 2006–07 school year, nonfiscal CCD data are collected through the Department of Education's Education Data Exchange Network (EDEN). Since the CCD is a universe collection, CCD data are not subject to sampling errors. However, nonsampling errors could come from two sources: nonresponse and inaccurate reporting.

Table A-20. Public Elementary and Secondary Schools—Finances and Teachers

Source: U.S. Department of Education, National Center for Education Statistics, Common Core of Data (CCD), "National Public Education Financial Survey (State Fiscal)," 2013–2014 (FY 2014) v.1a; "State Nonfiscal Public Elementary/Secondary Education Survey Membership Data," 2014–2015 v.1a; "State Nonfiscal Public Elementary/Secondary Education Survey Staff Data," 2014–2015 v.1a.

Enrollment is the "Fall Membership," the total count of pupils that are enrolled on or about October 1st of the survey year.

Total Revenues is the sum of subtotals for Local Government, State Government, Intermediate Government Agencies, and Federal Government. Does not include other sources of revenue.

Local Revenues is the sum of Local Revenues and Revenues from Intermediate Agencies.

State Revenues are revenues received by the Local Education Agencies (LEAs) from the state and includes unrestricted and restricted grants-in-aid, revenue in lieu of taxes, and payments for, or on behalf of, LEAs.

Total Expenditures is the sum of Total Expenditures for Education, Direct State Support Expenditures for Private School Students, and Interest on long term debt.

Current expenditures are for public elementary and secondary education, grades prekindergarten through grade 12, including ungraded students. Expenditures for equipment, non-public education, school construction, debt financing and community services are excluded from this data item. Expenditures by state governments for and on behalf of LEAs are included in these expenditures, and all other expenditures here. This is the sum of expenditures for Instruction, Support Services, and Non-instructional Services (excluding Community Services) and Direct Program Support (excluding Support for Private school Students), and excludes Property expenditures.

Total Current Expenditures per pupil is the total current expenditures for public elementary and secondary education divided by the fall membership as reported in the state finance file. The Expenditures for equipment, non-public education, school construction, debt financing and community services are excluded from this data item.

A **teacher** is a professional school staff member who instructs students in prekindergarten, kindergarten, grades 1 through12, or ungraded classes, and who maintains daily student attendance records. The number of teachers represents full- time equivalent (FTE), computed by dividing the amount of time employed by the time normally required for a full-time position.

A kindergarten teacher is a teacher of a group or class that is part of a public school program and is taught during the year preceding first grade.

An elementary teacher is a teacher of a group or class that is within a general level of instruction classified by state and local practice as elementary, generally including grades 1 through 8.

A secondary school teacher is a teacher of a group or class that is within a general level of instruction classified by state and local practice as high school, generally including grades 9 through 12.

The **pupil/teacher ratio** includes teachers for students with disabilities and other special teachers, while these teachers are generally excluded from class size calculations. The student count for the pupil/teacher ratio includes all students enrolled in the fall of the school year.

Table A-21. Public High School Graduates and Educational Attainment

Sources: Public high school graduates—U.S. National Center for Education Statistics, *Projections of Education Statistics to 2024* (https://nces.ed.gov/pubsearch/pubsinfo.asp?pubid=2016013) Averaged high school graduation rates—*Trends in High School Dropout and Completion Rates in the United States: 2013* (https://nces.ed.gov/pubs2016/2016117rev.pdf); Attainment—U.S. Census Bureau, 2015 American Community Survey, Table C15003, "Educational Attainment for the Population 25 Years and Over" (factfinder.census.gov).

A **high school graduate** is defined as an individual who has received formal recognition from school authorities, by the granting of a diploma, for completing a prescribed course of study. This definition does not include other high school completers or high school equivalency recipients. Projections of graduates could be affected by changes in policies influencing graduation requirements.

The Averaged Freshman Graduation Rate (AFGR) provides an estimate of the percentage of high school students who graduate within 4 years of first starting 9th grade. The rate uses aggregate student enrollment data to estimate the size of an incoming freshman class and counts of the number of diplomas awarded 4 years later. The incoming freshman class size is estimated by summing the enrollment in 8th grade in year one, 9th grade for the next year, and 10th grade for the year after, and then dividing by three. The averaging has a smoothing effect that helps compensate for prior year retentions in the 8th-, 9th-, and 10th-grade enrollment counts.

Data on **educational attainment** are derived from questions asked of all respondents to the American Community Survey, and data presented here are tabulated for people 25 years old and over. Respondents are classified according to the highest degree or the highest level of school completed. Persons currently enrolled in school are asked to report the level of the previous grade attended or the highest degree received. **High school graduate** refers to respondents who received a high school diploma or the equivalent, such as passing the test of General Educational Development (G.E.D.), and did not attend college. **Some college, but no degree** refers to respondents who have attended college for some amount of time but have no degree. The category

associate's degree includes people whose highest degree is an associate's degree, which generally requires 2 years of college-level work and is either in an occupational program that prepares them for a specific occupation, or an academic program primarily in the arts and sciences. The course work may or may not be transferable to a **bachelor's degree**. **Advanced degree** refers to a graduate or professional degree.

Table A-22. Institutions of Higher Education

Source: Fall enrollment and degrees conferred—U.S. National Center for Education Statistics, *Digest of Education Statistics*, annual (https://nces.ed.gov/pubsearch/pubsinfo.asp?pubid=2016014).

Higher education is identified by the National Center for Education Statistics (NCES) as the study beyond secondary school at an institution that offers programs terminating in an associate, baccalaureate, or higher degrees. The data shown are based upon the Integrated Postsecondary Education Data System (IPEDS), established as the core postsecondary education data collection program for NCES. IPEDS is a system of surveys designed to collect data from all primary providers of postsecondary education in such areas as enrollment, program completions, faculty, staff, and finances. See the sources for methodological details.

Degrees conferred refer to awards conferred by a college, university, or other postsecondary educational institution as official recognition for the successful completion of a program of studies.

Table A-23. Violent Crimes and Crime Rates

Source: U.S. Federal Bureau of Investigation, *Crime in the United States*, annual. See https://ucr.fbi.gov/crime-in-the-u.s/2015/crime-in-the-u.s.-2015/home.

Data presented on crime are through the voluntary contribution of crime statistics by law enforcement agencies across the United States. The Uniform Crime Reporting (UCR) program provides periodic assessments of crime in the nation as measured by offenses coming to the attention of the law enforcement community. UCR program contributors compile and submit their crime data in one of two means: either directly to the FBI or through the state UCR programs.

Caution is advised when comparing data between areas based on these respective Crime Index figures. Assessing criminality and law enforcement's responses from area to area should encompass many elements (i.e., population density and urbanization, population composition, stability of population, modes of transportation, commuting patterns and highway systems, economic conditions, cultural conditions, family conditions, climate, effective strength and emphasis of law enforcement agencies, attitudes of citizenry toward crime, and crime reporting practices). These elements may have a significant impact on crime reporting. Also, not all law enforcement agencies provide data for all 12 months of the year and some agencies fail to report at all. Data in this publication are presented as reported to the FBI.

Data presented reflect the Hierarchy Rule, which requires that only the most serious offense in a multiple-offense criminal incident be counted. In descending order of severity, the violent crimes are murder and nonnegligent manslaughter, forcible rape, robbery, and aggravated assault, followed by the property crimes of burglary, larceny-theft, and motor vehicle theft. The Hierarchy Rule does not apply to the offense of arson.

Violent crimes include four crime categories: (1) Murder and nonnegligent manslaughter, as defined in the UCR program, is the willful (nonnegligent) killing of one human being by another. This offense excludes deaths caused by negligence, suicide, or accident; justifiable homicides; and attempts to murder or assaults to murder. (2) In 2013, the FBI UCR Program began collecting rape data under a revised definition, used in this book for the 2015 data. Previously, offense data for forcible rape were collected under the legacy UCR definition: the carnal knowledge of a female forcibly and against her will. Beginning with the 2013 data year, the term "forcible" was removed from the offense title, and the definition was changed. The revised UCR definition of rape is: penetration, no matter how slight, of the vagina or anus with any body part or object, or oral penetration by a sex organ of another person, without the consent of the victim. Attempts or assaults to commit rape are also included in the statistics presented here; however, statutory rape and incest are excluded. (3) Robbery is the taking or attempting to take anything of value from the care, custody, or control of a person or persons by force or threat of force or violence and/or by putting the victim in fear. (4) Aggravated assault is an unlawful attack by one person upon another for the purpose of inflicting severe or aggravated bodily injury. This type of assault is usually accompanied by the use of a weapon or by means likely to produce death or great bodily harm. Attempts are included since an injury does not necessarily have to result when a gun, knife, or other weapon is used, which could and probably would result in a serious personal injury if the crime were successfully completed.

Rates are based on Census Bureau resident population enumerated as of April 1 for decennial census years and estimated as of July 1 for other years.

Table A-24. Property Crimes and Crime Rates

Source: U.S. Federal Bureau of Investigation, *Crime in the United States*, annual. See https://ucr.fbi.gov/crime-in-the-u.s/2015/crime-in-the-u.s.-2015/home.

For information on the Uniform Crime Reporting (UCR) program and comparability of data, see appendix entry for Table A-23.

In general, property crimes include four crime categories: (1) Burglary is the unlawful entry of a structure to commit a felony or theft. (2) Larceny-theft is the unlawful taking, carrying, leading, or riding away of property from the possession or constructive possession of another. It includes crimes such as shoplifting, pocket picking, purse snatching, thefts from motor vehicles, thefts of motor vehicle parts and accessories, bicycle thefts, etc., in which no use of force, violence, or fraud occurs. This crime category does not include embezzlement, "con" games, forgery, worthless checks, and motor vehicle theft. (3) Motor vehicle theft is the theft or attempted theft of a motor vehicle. This definition excludes the taking of a motor vehicle for temporary use by those persons having lawful access. (4) Arson is any willful or malicious burning or attempt to burn, with or without intent to defraud, a dwelling house, public building, motor vehicle or aircraft, personal property of another, etc. Only fires determined through investigation to have been willfully or maliciously set are classified as arson. Fires of suspicious or unknown origins are excluded.

Table A-25. Juvenile Arrests, Child Abuse Cases, and Prisoners

Sources: Juvenile arrests—*Crime in the United States*, annual. See https://ucr.fbi.gov/crime-in-the-u.s/2015/crime-in-the-u.s.-2015/home; Child abuse and neglect—U.S. Department of Health and Human Services, Administration on Children, Youth and Families, *Child Maltreatment 2015*. https://www.acf.hhs.gov/cb/resource/child-maltreatment-2015; Estimated number and rate of persons supervised by adult correctional system—Bureau of Justice Statistics, *Correctional Populations in the United States, 2014*. https://www.bjs.gov/content/pub/pdf/cpus14.pdf.

Juvenile arrests. The FBI's Uniform Crime Reporting (UCR) Program counts one arrest for each separate instance in which a person is arrested, cited, or summoned for an offense. The UCR Program collects arrest data on 28 offenses, (https://ucr.fbi.gov/crime-in-the-u.s/2015/crime-in-the-u.s.-2015/resource-pages/offense-definitions) Because a person may be arrested multiple times during a year, the UCR arrest figures do not reflect the number of individuals who have been arrested; rather, the arrest data show the number of times that persons are arrested, as reported by law enforcement agencies to the UCR Program. Juveniles include all persons under 18. Traffic arrests are not included. The rape figures in this table are aggregate totals of the data submitted based on both the legacy and revised Uniform Crime Reporting definitions. Drunkenness is considered a crime in some states; therefore, the figures vary from state to state.

Data on **child abuse and neglect cases** are collected and analyzed through the National Child Abuse and Neglect Data System (NCANDS) by the Children's Bureau, Administration on Children, Youth, and Families in the Administration for Children and Families, U.S. Department of Health and Human Services. The number of investigations includes assessments and is based on the total number of investigations that received a disposition. The number of children subject of an investigation of assessment is based on the total number of children for whom an alleged maltreatment was substantiated, indicated, or assessed to have occurred or the child was at risk of occurrence. **Victims** are defined as children subject of a substantiated, indicated, or alternative response-victim maltreatment.

Each state has its own definitions of child abuse and neglect based on minimum standards set by federal law. Federal legislation provides a foundation for states by identifying a minimum set of acts or behaviors that define child abuse and neglect. The *Federal Child Abuse Prevention and Treatment Act* (CAPTA), (42 U.S.C.A. §5106g), as amended by the *Keeping Children and Families Safe Act of 2003*, defines child abuse and neglect as: Any recent act or failure to act on the part of a parent or caretaker which results in death, serious physical or emotional harm, sexual abuse or exploitation; or an act or failure to act which presents an imminent risk of serious harm.

Within the minimum standards set by CAPTA, each state is responsible for providing its own definitions of child abuse and neglect. Most states recognize four major types of maltreatment: neglect, physical abuse, sexual abuse, and psychological maltreatment.

Data for persons supervised by the U.S. adult correctional system were published in *Correctional Populations in the United States*, compiled from the Annual Probation Survey, Annual Parole Survey, Census of Jail Inmates, Deaths in Custody Reporting Program—Annual Summary on Inmates under Jail Jurisdiction, and National Prisoner Statistics program.

Table A-26. State and Local Justice Employment and Expenditures

Source: U.S. Bureau of Justice Statistics, Justice Expenditure and Employment Extracts, Preliminary 2012; and State

Prison Expenditures, Preliminary 2012, see Internet site https://www.bjs.gov/index.cfm?ty=pbdetail&iid=5239.

Justice expenditure and employment data are extracted from the Census Bureau's Annual Government Finance Survey and Annual Survey of Public Employment. **Employees** include both full-time and part-time employees. **Expenditure** refers to all amounts of money paid out other than for retirement of debt, investment in securities, extensions of loans, or agency transactions. It includes only external cash payments and excludes any intragovernmental transfers and noncash transactions. It also includes any payments financed from borrowing, fund balances, intergovernmental revenue, and other current revenue.

Police protection is the function of enforcing the law, and preserving order and traffic safety and apprehending those who violate the law, whether these activities are performed by a police department, a sheriff's department, or a special police force maintained by an agency whose primary responsibility is outside the justice system but that has a police force to perform these activities in its specialized area (geographic or functional). Data for police protection cover all activities concerned with the enforcement of law and order, including coroners' offices, police-training academies, investigation bureaus, and local jails, "lockup," or other detention facilities not intended to serve as correctional facilities. **Judicial and legal** services covers all civil and criminal activities associated with courts, including prosecution and public defense. Data for **corrections** cover all activities pertaining to the confinement and correction of adults and minors accused or convicted of criminal offenses. Any pardon, probation, and parole activities also are included here.

Table A-27. Civilian Labor Force and Employment

Source: U.S. Bureau of Labor Statistics, Local Area Unemployment Statistics program. https://www.bls.gov/lau/rdscnp16.htm.

The **civilian noninstitutionalized population** includes persons 16 years of age and older residing in the 50 states and the District of Columbia who are not inmates of institutions (for example, penal and mental facilities, homes for the aged), and who are not on active duty in the armed forces. The **civilian labor force** comprises all civilians 16 years old and over classified as employed or unemployed. Employed persons are all civilians who, during the survey week, did any work at all as paid employees, in their own business, profession, or on their own farm or who worked 15 hours or more as unpaid workers in an enterprise operated by a member of the family. It also includes all those who were not working but who had jobs or businesses from which they were temporarily absent because of illness, bad weather, vacation, labor-management disputes, job training, or personal reasons, whether they were paid for the time off or were seeking other jobs. Each employed person is counted only once regardless of how many jobs he or she may have.

Table A-28. Civilian Labor Force and Unemployment

Source: U.S. Bureau of Labor Statistics, Local Area Unemployment Statistics program. https://www.bls.gov/lau/rdscnp16.htm.

Unemployed persons are all civilians 16 years old and over who had no employment during the survey week, were available for work, except for temporary illness, and had actively pursued employment some time during the prior 4 weeks. Active efforts include sending out resumes, placing or answering advertisements, and contacting potential employers regarding employment opportunities. Those engaged in passive methods of job seeking are not classified as unemployed. Persons who were laid off or were waiting to report to a new job within 30 days did not need to be looking for work to be classified as unemployed. The **unemployment rate** for all civilian workers represents the number of unemployed as a percent of the civilian labor force.

Table A-29. Employed Civilians by Occupation

Source: U.S. Bureau of Labor Statistics, Occupational Employment Statistics program. https://www.bls.gov/oes/home.htm.

An **occupation** is a set of activities or tasks that employees are paid to perform. Employees who perform essentially the same tasks are in the same occupation, whether or not they work in the same industry. Some occupations are concentrated in a few particular industries; other occupations are found in many industries.

Table A-30. Private Industry Employment and Wages

Sources: U.S. Bureau of Labor Statistics, Quarterly Census of Employment and Wages https://data.bls.gov/cew/apps/table_maker/v4/table_maker.htm#type=0&year=2015&qtr=A&own=0&ind=10&supp=1.

Data from the Quarterly Census of Employment and Wages (QCEW) program (ES-202 program for employment and average annual pay) are the product of a federal-state cooperative program. The QCEW program derives its data from quarterly tax reports submitted to State Employment Security Agencies by over eight million employers subject to state unemployment insurance (UI) laws and from federal agencies subject to the Unemployment Compensation for Federal Employees (UCFE) program. This includes 99.7 percent of all wage and salary civilian employment. The summaries are a result of the administration of state unemployment insurance programs that require most employers to pay quarterly taxes based on the employment and wages of workers covered.

The QCEW program is an employer reported measure and therefore associated with filled jobs, whether full or part-time, and place of work. If a person holds two jobs, the person would be counted twice in QCEW data. Programs which measure full-time equivalent positions or vacant positions target a different concept, as do household reported measures, which more typically show number of people with jobs, regardless of how many, and keep track of them by place or residence. The QCEW program, by definition, measures employment covered by unemployment insurance laws. In excluding self-employed jobs, and others, it differs significantly from those programs that include that employment.

Average annual wages per employee for any given industry are computed by dividing total annual wages by annual average employment. A further division by 52 yields average weekly wages per employee. Annual pay data only approximate annual earnings, because an individual may not be employed by the same employer all year or may work for more than one employer at a time. Average weekly or annual pay is affected by the ratio of full-time to part-time workers, as well as by the numbers of individuals in high- and low-paying occupations. When comparing average pay levels among states and industries, data users should take these factors into consideration. For example, industries characterized by high proportions of part-time workers will show average weekly wage levels appreciably less than the weekly pay levels of regular full-time employees in these industries. The opposite is true of industries with low proportions of part-time workers and of industries that typically schedule heavy weekend and overtime work. Average wage data also may be influenced by work stoppages, labor turnover, retroactive payments, seasonal factors, and bonus payments.

Table A-31. Average Annual Employment by industry and Wages

Sources: U.S. Bureau of Labor Statistics, Quarterly Census of Employment and Wages: https://data.bls.gov/cew/apps/data_views/data_views.htm#tab=Tables.

See the text for Table A-30 for explanations of employment and annual pay data for the Quarterly Census of Employment and Wages program. Refer to General Notes to see information on different industries defined using the North American Industry Classification System (NAICS).

Table A-32. Union Membership

Sources: U.S. Bureau of Labor Statistics. BLS news release 16-0158 "Union Members—2015." https://www.bls.gov/news.release/pdf/union2.pdf.

The Bureau of Labor Statistics (BLS) provides information on union membership. The estimates from BLS are obtained from the Current Population Survey (CPS), which provides basic information on the labor force, employment, and unemployment. The survey is conducted monthly for the Bureau of Labor Statistics by the U.S. Census Bureau from a scientifically selected national sample of about 60,000 eligible households.

Table A-33. Median Income of Households in 2015 Inflation-Adjusted Dollars and Distribution by Income Level

Source: U.S. Census Bureau, American Community Survey, 2015. Table S1903. Median Income in the Past 12 Months (In 2015 Inflation-Adjusted Dollars); Table S1901. Income in the Past 12 Months (In 2015 Inflation-Adjusted Dollars). American Fact Finder https://factfinder.census.gov/.

Median income divides the income distribution into two equal parts: one-half of the cases falling below the median income and one-half above the median. For households and families, the median income is based on the distribution of the total number of households and families including those with no income. The median income for individuals is based on individuals 15 years old and over with income. Median income for households, families, and individuals is computed on the basis of a standard distribution. Median income is rounded to the nearest whole dollar. Median income figures are calculated using linear interpolation if the width of the interval containing the estimate is $2,500 or less. If the width of the interval containing the estimate is greater than $2,500, Pareto interpolation is used.

Income of households includes the income of the householder and all other individuals 15 years old and over in the household, whether they are related to the householder or not. Because many households consist of only one person, average household income is usually less than average family income. Although the household income statistics cover the past 12 months, the characteristics of individuals and the composition of households refer to the time of interview. Thus, the income of the household does not include amounts received by individuals who were members of the household during all or part of the past 12 months if these individuals no longer resided in the household at the time of interview. Similarly, income

amounts reported by individuals who did not reside in the household during the past 12 months but who were members of the household at the time of interview are included. However, the composition of most households was the same during the past 12 months as at the time of interview.

For the definition of a **household**, see appendix entry for Table A-5.

Table A-34. Family Income and Families and Individuals Below Poverty: 2015

Source: U.S. Census Bureau, Table B19101, Family Income in the Past 12 Months (In 2015 Inflation-Adjusted Dollars; B19113. Median Family Income in the Past 12 Months (In 2015 Inflation-Adjusted Dollars; Table S1701. Poverty Status in the Past 12 Months; Table S1702. Poverty Status in the Past 12 Months of Families. American FactFinder, https://factfinder.census.gov/.

In compiling statistics on family income, the incomes of all members 15 years old and over related to the householder are summed and treated as a single amount. Although the family income statistics cover the past 12 months, the characteristics of individuals and the composition of families refer to the time of enumeration. Thus, the income of the family does not include amounts received by individuals who were members of the family during all or part of the past 12 months if these individuals no longer resided with the family at the time of enumeration. Similarly, income amounts reported by individuals who did not reside with the family during the past 12 months but who were members of the family at the time of enumeration are included. However, the composition of most families was the same during the past 12 months as at the time of enumeration. See appendix entry for Table A-33 for information on **Median income**.

Poverty status is determined using thresholds arranged in a two-dimensional matrix. The matrix consists of family size cross-classified by presence and number of family members under age 18 years old. Unrelated individuals and two-person families are further differentiated by age of reference person. To determine a person's poverty status, one compares the person's total family income in the last 12 months with the poverty threshold appropriate for that person's family size and composition. If the total income of that person's family is less than the threshold appropriate for that family, then the person is considered poor or "below the poverty level," together with every member of his or her family. If a person is not living with anyone related by birth, marriage, or adoption, then the person's own income is compared with his or her poverty threshold. The total number of people below the poverty level was the sum of people in families and the number of unrelated individuals with incomes in the last 12 months below the poverty level.

https://www.census.gov/data/tables/time-series/demo/income-poverty/historical-poverty-thresholds.html.

Table A-35. Housing—Units and Characteristics

Source: U.S. Census Bureau, American Community Survey, 2015. Table DP04. Selected Housing Characteristics. American FactFinder, https://factfinder.census.gov/.

A **housing unit** is a house, apartment, mobile home or trailer, group of rooms, or single room occupied or, if vacant, intended for occupancy as separate living quarters. Separate living quarters are those in which the occupants do not live and eat with any other persons in the structure and that have direct access from the outside of the building through a common hall. For vacant units, the criteria of separateness and direct access are applied to the intended occupants whenever possible.

Units in structure. A structure is a separate building that either has open spaces on all sides or is separated from other structures by dividing walls that extend from ground to roof. In determining the number of units in a structure, all housing units, both occupied and vacant, are counted. Stores and office space are excluded. The statistics are presented for the number of housing units in structures of specified type and size, not for the number of residential buildings. **Mobile Homes** include both occupied and vacant mobile homes to which no permanent rooms have been added are counted in this category. Mobile homes used only for business purposes or for extra sleeping space and mobile homes for sale on a dealer's lot, at the factory, or in storage are not counted in the housing inventory. **1-Unit, Detached** are any 1-unit structure detached from any other house, that is, with open space on all four sides. Such structures are considered detached even if they have an adjoining shed or garage. A one-family house that contains a business is considered detached as long as the building has open space on all four sides. Mobile homes to which one or more permanent rooms have been added or built also are included. **1-Unit, Attached** include any 1-unit structure that has one or more walls extending from ground to roof separating it from adjoining structures. In row houses (sometimes called townhouses), double houses, or houses attached to nonresidential structures, each house is a separate, attached structure if the dividing or common wall goes from ground to roof.

Year structure built refers to when the building was first constructed, not when it was remodeled, added to, or converted. Housing units under construction are included as vacant housing if they meet the housing unit definition—that is, all exterior windows, doors, and final usable floors are in place. For mobile homes, houseboats, RVs, etc., the manufacturer's model year was assumed to be the year built. The data relate to the number of units built during the specified periods that were still in existence at the time of enumeration.

A housing unit is classified as **occupied** if it is the current place of residence of the person or group of people living in it at the time of enumeration, or if the occupants are only temporarily absent from the residence for 2 months or less; that is, away on vacation or a business trip. If all the people staying in the unit at the time of the interview are staying there for 2 months or less, the unit is considered to be temporarily occupied, and classified as "vacant." The occupants may be a single family, one person living alone, two or more families living together, or any other group of related or unrelated people who share living quarters. Occupied rooms or suites of rooms in hotel, motels, and similar places are classified as housing units only when occupied by permanent residents, that is, people who consider the hotel as their current place of residence or have no current place of residence elsewhere. If any of the occupants in rooming or boarding houses, congregate housing, or continuing care facilities live separately from others in the building and have direct access, their quarters are classified as separate housing units.

Data on **vehicles available** show the number of passenger cars, vans, and pickup or panel trucks of one-ton capacity or less kept at home and available for the use of household members. Vehicles rented or leased for 1 month or more, company vehicles, and police and government vehicles are included if kept at home and used for non-business purposes. Dismantled or immobile vehicles are excluded. Vehicles kept at home but used only for business purposes also are excluded.

House heating fuel data refer to occupied housing units. The data show the type of fuel used most to heat the house, apartment, or mobile home. Utility gas includes gas piped through underground pipes from a central system to serve the neighborhood. Electricity is generally supplied by means of above or underground electric power lines.

Table A-36. Owner- and Renter-Occupied Units—Value and Gross Rent

Source: U.S. Census Bureau, American Community Survey, 2015. Table DP04. Selected Housing Characteristics. American FactFinder, https://factfinder.census.gov/.

A housing unit is owner-occupied if the owner or co-owner lives in the unit even if it is mortgaged or not fully paid for. The owner or co-owner must live in the unit. The unit is owner-occupied if someone who lives in the household is purchasing the house with a mortgage or some other debt arrangement such as a deed of trust, trust deed, contract to purchase, land contract, or purchase agreement. The unit also is considered owned with a mortgage if it is built on leased land and there is a mortgage on the unit. Mobile homes occupied by owners with installment loan balances also are included in this category.

Value is the respondent's estimate of how much the property (house and lot, mobile home and lot, or condominium unit) would sell for if it were for sale. If the house or mobile home was owned or being bought, but the land on which it sits was not, the respondent was asked to estimate the combined value of the house or mobile home and the land. **Median value** divides the value distribution into two equal parts: one-half of the cases falling below the median value of the property and one-half above the median.

Renter Occupied includes all occupied housing units that are not owner occupied, whether they are rented for cash rent or occupied without payment of cash rent. "No cash rent" units are generally provided free by friends or relatives or in exchange for services such as resident manager, caretaker, minister, or tenant farmer. Housing units on military bases also are classified as "No cash rent." "Rented for cash rent" includes units in continuing care, sometimes called life care arrangements. These arrangements usually involve a contract between one or more individuals and a health services provider guaranteeing the individual shelter, usually a house or apartment, and services, such as meals or transportation to shopping or recreation.

Gross rent is the contract rent plus the estimated average monthly cost of utilities (electricity, gas, and water and sewer) and fuels (oil, coal, kerosene, wood, etc.) if these are being paid for by the renter (or paid for the renter by someone else). The **median rent** divides the rent distribution into two equal parts: one-half of the cases falling below the median contract rent and one-half above the median.

Table A-37. Home Ownership and Vacancy Rates

Sources: U.S. Census Bureau, Current Population Survey/ Housing Vacancy Survey https://www.census.gov/housing/hvs/index.html.

Vacancy rates and **homeownership rates** are based on data obtained from the Current Population Survey/Housing Vacancy Survey (CPS/HVS). Beginning in 2003, new weighting procedures based on the 2000 decennial census were implemented. The CPS/HVS includes the civilian

noninstitutionalized population. This universe includes civilians in households, people in noninstitutional group quarters (other than military barracks), and military in households living off post or with their families on post (as long as at least one household member is a civilian adult). The universe excludes other military in households and in group quarters (barracks) and people living in institutions. The weighting is controlled to independent counts of housing units for the month of the estimate. The sample size consists of approximately 71,000 addresses per month. A unit is in sample for 4 consecutive months, out for 8 months, back in sample for 4 months, and then retired from the sample. A housing unit is vacant if no one is living in it at the time of the interview, unless its occupants are only temporarily absent. In addition, a vacant unit may be one that is owned entirely by persons who have a usual residence elsewhere. **Rental vacancy rate** is the proportion of the rental inventory that is vacant for rent. The **homeowner vacancy rate** is the proportion of the homeowner inventory that is vacant for sale. The proportion of owner households to occupied households is termed the homeownership rate. It is computed by dividing the number of owner households by the number of occupied households.

Table A-38. Cost of Living Indicators— Housing, Public University, Hospital Stays, Energy Expenditures, and Utilities

Sources: Housing price index—Federal Housing Finance Agency, Annual House Price Indexes, https://www.fhfa.gov/ DataTools/Downloads/Pages/House-Price-Index.aspx; Average undergraduate tuition and fees—U.S. National Center for Education Statistics, Digest of Education Statistics 2015, and prior years; see http://nces.ed.gov/programs/ digest/; Energy expenditures, U.S. Department of Energy, Energy Price and Expenditure Estimates, https://www. eia.gov/state/seds/sep_prices/notes/pr_print.pdf; Gasoline state tax rates—U.S. Department of Transportation, Federal Highway Administration, https://www.fhwa.dot.gov/ policyinformation/statistics/2015/mf121t.cfm.

Data on **housing prices** are collected through the Federal Housing Finance Board's Monthly Interest Rate Survey (MIRS). This survey provides monthly information on interest rates, loan terms, and house prices by property type, by loan type, and by lender type, as well as information on 15- and 30-year fixed-rate loans. The sample consists of mortgage lenders who were asked to report the terms and conditions on all single-family, fully amortized, purchase-money, nonfarm loans that they close during the last 5 business days of the month. The survey excludes FHA-insured and VA-guaranteed loans, multifamily loans, mobile home loans, and loans created by refinancing another mortgage.

The indexes in this table are developmental annual state indexes. Indexes are calibrated using appraisal values and sales prices for mortgages bought or guaranteed by Fannie Mae and Freddie Mac. This table shows the index value with a base of 100 when first recorded (1975 in most cases).

Energy expenditure data refers to money directly spent by consumers to purchase energy. Expenditures equal the amount of energy used by the consumer times the price per unit paid by the consumer. In the calculation of the amount of energy used, process fuel and intermediate products are not included. Population estimates used to calculate per capita data are provided by the Census Bureau's population estimates.

This table shows **motor-fuel tax rates** that are levied as a dollar amount per volume of motor fuel. Taxes that apply to all petroleum products with distinguishing motor fuel are omitted. The gasohol rates shown are for gasoline blended with 10 percent ethanol. NOTE: The States which have exemptions are Hawaii (1 cent), Iowa (2 cents) Maine (6.5 cents), and Montana (4 cents). Tax rates include other miscellanous tax (enviromental, etc.).

Table A-39. Personal Income by State

Source: U.S. Bureau of Economic Analysis, Regional Economic Accounts https://www.bea.gov/regional/index.htm.

Personal income data are based on the Regional Economic Information System; see Appendix B for additional information. Personal Income is the income that is received by all persons from all sources. It is calculated as the sum of wage and salary disbursements, supplements to wages and salaries, proprietors' income with inventory valuation and capital consumption adjustments, rental income of persons with capital consumption adjustment, personal dividend income, personal interest income, and personal current transfer receipts, less contributions for government social insurance. The personal income of an area is the income that is received by, or on behalf of, all the individuals who live in the area; therefore, the estimates of personal income are presented by the place of residence of the income recipients.

Disposable income is total personal income minus personal current taxes. It is personal income that is available for spending or saving.

Estimates are in current dollars (not adjusted for inflation.) For explanations of current versus constant dollars, see appendix entry for Table A-42.

Table A-40. Personal Income per Capita

Source: U.S. Bureau of Economic Analysis, Regional Economic Accounts https://www.bea.gov/regional/index.htm.

Personal income data are based on the Regional Economic Information System; see Appendix B for additional information. Personal Income is the income that is received by all persons from all sources. It is calculated as the sum of wage and salary disbursements, supplements to wages and salaries, proprietors' income with inventory valuation and capital consumption adjustments, rental income of persons with capital consumption adjustment, personal dividend income, personal interest income, and personal current transfer receipts, less contributions for government social insurance. The personal income of an area is the income that is received by, or on behalf of, all the individuals who live in the area; therefore, the estimates of personal income are presented by the place of residence of the income recipients.

Disposable income is total personal income minus personal current taxes. It is personal income that is available for spending or saving.

Estimates are in current dollars (not adjusted for inflation.) For explanations of current versus constant dollars, see appendix entry for Table A-42.

Table A-41. Earnings by Industry

Source: U.S. Bureau of Economic Analysis, Regional Economic Accounts, https://www.bea.gov/regional/index.htm.

The components of **earnings** are wage and salary disbursements, other labor income, and proprietors' income. Wage and salary disbursements are defined as monetary remuneration of employees, including corporate officers; commissions, tips, and bonuses; and "pay-in-kind" that represents income to the recipient. They are measured before such deductions as social security contributions and union dues. All disbursements in the current period are covered. "Pay-in-kind" represents allowances for food, clothing, and lodging paid in kind to employees, which represent income to them, valued at the cost to the employer. Other labor income consists of employer contributions to privately administered pension and welfare funds and a few small items such as directors' fees, compensation of prison inmates, and miscellaneous judicial fees. Proprietors' income is the monetary income and income in-kind of proprietorships and partnerships, including the independent professions and of tax-exempt cooperatives. Refer to General Notes for information on specific industries.

Table A-42. Gross Domestic Product by State

Source: Bureau of Economic Analysis, Regional Economic Accounts https://www.bea.gov/regional/index.htm.

Total **Gross Domestic Product** (GDP) by state is the value added in production by the labor and capital located in a state. GDP for a state is derived as the sum of the gross state product originating in all industries in a state. In concept, an industry's GDP by state, referred to as its "value added," is equivalent to its gross output (sales or receipts and other operating income, commodity taxes, and inventory change) minus its intermediate inputs (consumption of goods and services purchased from other U.S. industries or imported). GDP by state is therefore the state counterpart of the nation's gross domestic product (GDP), BEA's featured measure of U.S. output.

GDP by state for the nation differs from GDP for the following reasons: GDP by state excludes and GDP includes the compensation of federal civilian and military personnel stationed abroad and government consumption of fixed capital for military structures located abroad and for military equipment, except office equipment and GDP by state and GDP have different revision schedules.

Current-dollar estimates are the market value of an item and reflect the prices of the period being measured.

Chained dollars are a measure used to express real prices, or prices that have been adjusted to account for inflation in order to represent a dollar's purchasing power. A chain-dollar estimate is a measure used to approximate the chained-typed index level and is calculated by taking the current-dollar level of a series in the base period and multiplying it by the change in the chained-type quantity index number for the series since the base period.

A chained-type index is an index based on the linking (chaining) of indexes to create a time series. Annual chained-type Fisher indices are used in BEA's national income and product accounts (NIPAs) whereby Fisher ideal price indices are calculated using the weights of adjacent years. Those annual changes are then multiplied (chained) together, forming the chained-type index time series. Chained-dollar estimates correctly show growth rates for a series, but are not additive in periods other than the base period.

Table A-43. Science and Engineering Indicators

Sources: Research and Development, and S&E doctorates awarded—National Science Foundation, Science and Engineering State Profiles: and previous editions https://www.nsf.gov/statistics/states/#ui-id-8.

The Division of Science Resources Statistics (SRS) of the National Science Foundation (NSF) compiles science and engineering (S&E) data that summarize state-specific data on personnel and finances. The SRS survey databases include doctoral scientists and engineers, S&E doctorates awarded, S&E graduate students and post-doctorates, federal research and development (R&D) obligations by agency and performer, total and industrial R&D expenditures, and academic R&D expenditures. See the source for further detailed information on these topics.

The indicator for engineers, life and physical scientist, and computer specialist represent the extent to which a state's workforce includes these scientists.

The indicator for **engineer** encompasses the standard occupational codes for engineering fields such as aerospace, agricultural biomedical, chemical, civil, computer hardware, electrical and electronics, environmental, industrial, marine and naval architectural, materials, mechanical, mining and geological, nuclear, and petroleum. Engineers design and operate production processes and create new products and services.

Life scientists are identified from standard occupational codes that include agricultural and food scientists, biological scientists, conservation scientists and foresters, and medical scientists.

Physical scientists are identified from standard occupational codes that include astronomers, physicists, atmospheric and space scientists, chemists, materials scientists, environmental scientists, and geoscientists, and postsecondary teachers in these subject areas.

Computer specialists are identified from 10 standard occupational codes that include computer and information scientists, programmers, software engineers, support specialist, systems analysts, database administrators, and network and computer system administrators.

As defined by the Organization for Economic Co-operation and Development, **research and development** comprises creative work "undertaken on a systematic basis to increase the stock of knowledge-including knowledge of man, culture, and society—and the use of this stock of knowledge to devise new applications."

The data source for **R&D expenditures** (or performance) was National Science Foundation/Division of Science Resources Statistics, *National Patterns of R&D Resources. National Patterns of R&D Resources.* Explanations of the methodology and technical issues involved in obtaining and compiling these R&D statistics can be found in *National Patterns of R&D Resources: 2006 Methodology Report.*

Table A-44. Employment Establishment Changes by Firm Size and State, 2010–2011

Source: U.S. Small Business Administration, www.sba.gov.

Firms are an aggregation of all establishments owned by a parent company with some annual payroll. Employer **firm births** represent an employing unit which is determined, for the first time, as meeting the definition of "employer" in the state unemployment compensation law or a previously terminated employing unit, which again is determined as meeting the definition of employer. Employer **firm deaths** refer to the voluntary or involuntary closure of a firm or establishment.

For information regarding establishments, employment, and annual payroll, see appendix entry for Table A-14.

Table A-45. Employer Firms and Nonemployer Establishments

Sources: Employer firms—U.S. Small Business Administration, Office of Advocacy, Research and Statistics, https://www.sba.gov/advocacy/firm-size-data. Nonemployer establishments—U.S. Census Bureau, "Nonemployer Statistics," https://www.census.gov/econ/nonemployer/.

The Census Bureau provides the Office of Advocacy of the U.S. Small Business Administration with data on employer firm size in the Statistics of U.S. Businesses (SUSB). A **firm** is defined as the aggregation of all establishments owned by a parent company (within a geographic location and/ or industry) that have some annual payroll. A firm may be located in one or more places. SUSBs employer data contain the number of firms, number of establishments, employment, and annual payroll for employment size of firm categories by location and industry. The employer data consist of static and dynamic data. Data are static or a "snapshot" of firms at a point in time. Industries are defined according to the North American Industry Classification System (NAICS) thereafter.

A **nonemployer** business is one that has no paid employees, has annual business receipts of $1,000 or more ($1 or more in the construction industries), and is subject to federal income taxes. Nonemployer businesses are generally small, such as real estate agents and independent contractors. Nonemployers constitute nearly three-quarters of all businesses, but they contribute only about 3 percent of overall sales and receipts data.

For information regarding establishments, employment, and annual payroll, see appendix entry for Table A-14.

Table A-46. Private Nonfarm Establishments, Employment, and Payroll

Source: U.S. Census Bureau, County Business Patterns, annual. https://www.census.gov/programs-surveys/cbp.html.

Data excludes governmental establishments except for wholesale liquor establishments, retail liquor stores, federally chartered savings institutions, federally chartered credit unions, and hospitals. Establishments without a fixed location or having an unknown county location within a state are included under a "state-wide" geography classification. For state data, a firm is defined as an aggregation of all establishments owned by a parent company within a state. Establishments are nonfarm locations with active payroll in any quarter.

For information regarding establishments, employment, and annual payroll, see appendix entry for Table A-14.

Table A-47. Foreign Direct Investment in the United States and U.S. Exports

Sources: U.S. affiliates—Bureau of Economic Analysis, International Economic Accounts, Foreign direct investment in the United States. https://www.bea.gov/international// and https://www.bea.gov/international/di1fdiop.htm. U.S. exports—U.S. Census Bureau, Foreign Trade Statistics, see Internet site https://www.census.gov/foreign-trade/index.html. U.S. agricultural exports—U.S. Department of Agriculture, Economic Research Service, U.S. Agricultural Trade database, https://www.ers.usda.gov/data-products/state-export-data/.

Foreign direct investment data in the United States are based on a survey of operations of nonbank U.S. affiliates that are majority-owned by foreign direct investors. A **U.S. affiliate** is a U.S. business enterprise in which there is foreign direct investment; that is, in which a single foreign person owns or controls, directly or indirectly, 10 percent or more of the voting securities of an incorporated U.S. business enterprise. "Person" is broadly defined to include any individual, corporation, branch, partnership, associated group, association, estate trust, or other organization and any government. A "foreign person" is any person that resides outside the United States; that is, outside the 50 states, the District of Columbia, the Commonwealth of Puerto Rico, and all U.S. territories and possessions.

Export statistics consist of goods valued at more than $2,500 per commodity shipped by individuals and organizations (including exporters, freight forwarders, and carriers) from the United States to other countries. Exports are valued at the F.A.S. (free alongside ship) value of merchandise at the

U.S. port of export, based on the transaction price including inland freight, insurance, and other charges incurred in placing the merchandise alongside the carrier at the U.S. port of exportation. Data on the value of U.S. agricultural exports by state of production are estimated by the Economic Research Service (ERS) using the customs district-level export data compiled by the Census Bureau and the state-level agricultural production data supplied by the National Agricultural Statistics Service (NASS). From these approximations a state that is the largest producer of an agricultural commodity will also account for the largest share of U.S. exports of that commodity.

U.S. agricultural commodity exports are often produced in inland states. From the farm, a commodity is sold to a local elevator, which in turn may sell it to a larger elevator located at a major transportation hub, which then moves the commodity to a port. As the commodity passes through several states before being exported, the state-of-origin often is lost or the product commingled with similar product from other states. Frequently, the state from which the commodity began its export journey, not necessarily the state in which the commodity was produced, is reported by the exporter. To more accurately reflect the situation for inland agricultural producing states, ERS calculates U.S. state agricultural exports based on a state's share of production of the exported commodity.

Table A-48. Farms and Farm Earnings

Sources: Farms—U.S. Department of Agriculture, National Agricultural Statistics Service, Farms and Land in Farms, 2016 Summary http://usda.mannlib.cornell.edu/usda/current/FarmLandIn/FarmLandIn-02-17-2017.pdf Earnings—U.S. Bureau of Economic Analysis, Regional Economic Accounts https://www.bea.gov/regional/index.htm.

A **farm** is any place from which $1,000 or more of agricultural products were produced and sold, or normally would have been sold, during the year. Government payments are included in sales. Ranches, institutional farms, experimental and research farms, and Indian Reservations are included as farms. Places with the entire acreage enrolled in the Conservation Reserve Program (CRP), Wetlands Reserve Program (WRP), or other government programs are counted as farms.

The acreage designated as "**land in farms**" consists primarily of agricultural land used for crops, pasture, or grazing. It also includes woodland and wasteland not actually under cultivation or used for pasture or grazing, provided it was part of the farm operator's total operation. Large acreages of woodland or wasteland held for nonagricultural purposes are not included. Land in farms includes Conservation Reserve, Wetlands Reserve Programs, or other government programs.

Average acreage per farm was calculated by dividing the total land in farms for an area by the number of farms in that area.

Farm earnings comprises the net income of sole proprietors, partners, and hired laborers arising directly from the current production of agricultural commodities, either livestock or crops. It includes net farm proprietors' income and the wages and salaries, pay-in-kind, and supplements to wages and salaries of hired farm laborers; but specifically excludes the income of nonfamily farm corporations.

Table A-49. Farm Finances and Income

Source: U.S. Department of Agriculture, Economic Research Service, Farm Income and Wealth Statistics, https://www.ers.usda.gov/data-products/farm-income-and-wealth-statistics/data-files-us-and-state-level-farm-income-and-wealth-statistics/.

The value of agricultural sector production is the sum of the value of crop production, the value of livestock production, and revenues from services and forestry in the value added table. The value of crop production and livestock production encompass cash receipts, home consumption, and inventory change. Revenues from services and forestry include machine hire and custom work income, sales of forestry products from farms, farm-related income, and gross imputed rental value of farm dwellings. The income and expenses associated with operators' dwellings are included in this account.

Net farm income is that portion of the net value added by agriculture to the national economy earned by farm operators. Farm operators typically benefit most from the increases and assimilate most of the declines arising from short-term, unanticipated weather and market conditions. Net farm income is a value of production measure indicating the farm operators' share of the net value added to the national economy within a calendar year, independent of whether it is received in cash or a non-cash form such as increases/decreases in inventories and imputed rental for the farm operator's dwelling.

Table A-50. Farm Income and Wealth Statistics

Sources: Government Payments—U.S. Department of Agriculture, Economic Research Service, Farm Income and Wealth Statistics, https://www.ers.usda.gov/data-products/farm-income-and-wealth-statistics.aspx.

Government payments consist of direct cash payments received by the farm operators. This includes disaster payments, loan deficiency payments from prior participation, payments from Conservation Reserve Programs (CRP), the Wetlands Reserve Programs (WRP), other conservation programs, and all other federal farm programs under which payments were made directly to farm operators. Commodity Credit Corporation (CCC) proceeds and federal crop insurance payments were not tabulated in this category.

Farm marketings represent quantities of agricultural products sold by farmers multiplied by prices received per unit of production at the local market. Information on prices received for farm products is generally obtained from surveys of firms (such as grain elevators, packers, and processors) purchasing agricultural commodities directly from producers. In some cases, the price information is obtained directly from the producers.

Table A-51. Natural Resource Industries and Minerals

Sources: Natural resource industries—U.S. Census Bureau, county Business Patterns, https://www.census.gov/programs-surveys/cbp.html; Nonfuel Mineral Production—National Geological Survey "Mineral Commodities Summaries—2017 Tables https://minerals.usgs.gov/minerals/pubs/mcs/; Mineral fuels—U.S. Energy Information Administration. https://www.eia.gov/petroleum/, https://www.eia.gov/naturalgas/, https://www.eia.gov/coal/.

Natural Resource Industries as presented here includes Agriculture, Forestry, Fishing, and Hunting (NAICS 11), Mining (NAICS 21), Wood Product Manufacturing (NAICS 321), and Paper Manufacturing (NAICS 322). For information on establishments, employment, and payroll, see the appendix entry for Table A-15. For detailed information on industry sectors and subsectors, see the General Notes of this appendix for the North American Industry Classification System (NAICS). Both Wood Product Manufacturing and Paper Manufacturing are subsectors of Manufacturing.

Nonfuel mineral production. The U.S. Geological Survey (USGS) collects information about the quantity and quality of all mineral resources. See the source listed for more detailed information on nonfuel mineral production.

The Energy Information Administration (EIA) collects production data on an ongoing basis for crude oil, natural gas, and coal.

Table A-52. Agriculture Census

Source: U.S. Department of Agriculture, National Agricultural Statistics Service, 2007 Census of Agriculture and 2012 Census of Agriculture

A **farm** is any place from which $1,000 or more of agricultural products were produced and sold, or normally would have been sold, during the year. Government payments are included in sales. Ranches, institutional farms, experimental and research farms, and Indian Reservations are included as farms. Places with the entire acreage enrolled in the Conservation Reserve Program (CRP), Wetlands Reserve Program (WRP), or other government programs are counted as farms.

The acreage designated as "**land in farms**" consists primarily of agricultural land used for crops, pasture, or grazing. It also includes woodland and wasteland not actually under cultivation or used for pasture or grazing, provided it was part of the farm operator's total operation. Large acreages of woodland or wasteland held for nonagricultural purposes are not included. Land in farms includes Conservation Reserve, Wetlands Reserve Programs, or other government programs.

Market value of agricultural products sold represents the gross market value before taxes and production expenses of all agricultural products sold or removed from the place in 2007 regardless of who received the payment. It is equivalent to total sales and it includes sales by the operators as well as the value of any shares received by partners, landlords, contractors, or others associated with the operation. It includes value of direct sales and the value of commodities placed in the Commodity Credit Corporation (CCC) loan program. Market value of agricultural products sold does not include payments received for participation in other federal farm programs. Also, it does not include income from farm-related sources such as custom work and other agricultural services or income from nonfarm sources. The value of crops sold in 2007 or 2002 does not necessarily represent the sales from crops harvested in 2007 or 2002. Data may include sales from crops produced in earlier years and may exclude some crops produced in the stated years but held in storage and not sold. Sales figures are expressed in current dollars.

Farms by combined government payments and market value of agricultural products sold represent the value of products sold plus government payments. Total value of products sold combines total sales not under production contract and total sales under production contract. Government payments consist of government payments received from the Conservation Reserve Program (CRP), Wetlands Reserve Program (WRP), Farmable Wetlands Program (FWP), or Conservation Reserve Enhancement Program (CREP) plus government payments received from federal, state, and local programs other than the CRP, WRP, FWP, and CREP, and Commodity Credit Corporation loans.

The term **operator** designates a person who operates a farm, either doing the work or making day-to-day decisions about such things as planting, harvesting, feeding, and marketing. The operator may be the owner, a member of the owner's household, a hired manager, a tenant, a renter, or a sharecropper. If a person rents land to others or has land worked on shares by others, he/she is considered the operator only of the land, which is retained for his/her own operation.

Table A-53. Utilities

Sources: Private utilities—U.S. Census Bureau, County Business Patterns, https://www.census.gov/programs-surveys/cbp.html. Water systems—Environmental Protection Agency https://www.epa.gov/ground-water-and-drinking-water/safe-drinking-water-information-system-sdwis-federal-reporting.

Private utilities. Refer to General Notes to see information on the private utilities industry defined using the North American Industry Classification System (NAICS). See the appendix entry for Table A-15 for information on establishments, employees, and annual payroll. For information on what constitutes residential, see appendix entry for Table A-54.

Data on **water systems** are obtained by the Environmental Protection Agency through the Safe Drinking Water Information System/Federal Version (SDWIS/FED), a database designed and implemented to meet the EPAs needs in the oversight and management of the Safe Drinking Water Act (SDWA). The database contains data submitted by states and EPA regions in conformance with reporting requirements established by statute, regulation, and guidance. Community systems include any public water system that supplies water to the same population year-round. Nontransient noncommunity systems include any public water system that regularly supplies water to at least 25 of the same people at least 6 months per year, but not year-round. Transient noncommunity systems include any public water system that provides water in a place such as a gas station or a campground where people do not remain for long periods of time.

Table A-54. Energy Consumption

Source: U.S. Energy Information Administration, State Energy Data System (SEDS), https://www.eia.gov/state/seds/.

Energy consumption is the use of energy as a source of heat or power or as an input in the manufacturing process. Data on energy consumption are from the State Energy Data System (SEDS), which is maintained and operated by the Energy Information Administration (EIA). SEDS has two principal objectives: (1) to provide state energy consumption, price, and expenditure estimates to members of Congress, federal and state agencies, and the general public and (2) to provide the historical series necessary for EIAs energy models.

An **end-use sector** is a firm or individual that purchases products for its own consumption and not for resale (i.e., an ultimate consumer).

The **residential sector** is the energy-consuming sector that consists of living quarters for private households. Common uses of energy associated with this sector include space heating, water heating, air conditioning, lighting, refrigeration, cooking, and running a variety of other appliances. The residential sector excludes institutional living quarters.

The **commercial sector** is the energy-consuming sector that consists of service-providing facilities and equipment of: businesses; federal, state, and local governments; and other private and public organizations, such as religious, social, or fraternal groups. The commercial sector includes institutional living quarters. It also includes sewage treatment facilities. Common uses of energy associated with this sector include space heating, water heating, air conditioning, lighting, refrigeration, cooking, and running a wide variety of other equipment. This sector includes generators that produce electricity and/or useful thermal output primarily to support the activities of the above-mentioned commercial establishments.

Industrial sector: An energy-consuming sector that consists of all facilities and equipment used for producing, processing, or assembling goods. The industrial sector encompasses the following types of activity: Manufacturing (NAICS codes 31–33); Agriculture, Forestry, Fishing, and Hunting (NAICS code 11); Mining, including oil and gas extraction (NAICS code 21); and Construction (NAICS code 23). Overall energy use in this sector is largely for process heat and cooling and powering machinery, with lesser amounts used for facility heating, air conditioning, and lighting. Fossil fuels are also used as raw material inputs to manufactured products. This sector includes generators that produce electricity and/or useful thermal output primarily to support the above-mentioned industrial activities.

Transportation sector: An energy-consuming sector that consists of all vehicles whose primary purpose is transporting people and/or goods from one physical location to another. Included are automobiles; trucks; buses; motorcycles; trains, subways, and other rail vehicles; aircraft; and ships, barges, and other waterborne vehicles. Vehicles whose primary purpose is not transportation (e.g., construction cranes and bulldozers, farming vehicles, and warehouse tractors and forklifts) are classified in the sector of their primary use. In this report, natural gas used in the operation of natural gas pipelines is included in the transportation sector.

Petroleum is a broadly defined class of liquid hydrocarbon mixtures. Included are crude oil, lease condensate, unfinished oils, refined products obtained from the processing of crude oil, and natural gas plant liquids. Volumes of finished petroleum products include nonhydrocarbon compounds, such as additives and detergents, after they have been blended into the products.

Hydroelectric Power is the production of electricity from the kinetic energy of falling water.

Nuclear electric power (nuclear power) is the electricity generated by the use of the thermal energy released from the fission of nuclear fuel in a reactor.

Table A-55. Energy Expenditures

Source: U.S. Energy Information Administration, https://www.eia.gov/state/seds/.

Energy expenditures refer to the money directly spent by consumers to purchase energy. Expenditures equal the amount of energy used by the consumer times the price per unit paid by the consumer. In the calculation of the amount of energy used, process fuel and intermediate products are not included.

Data on energy expenditures are from the State Energy Data System (SEDS), which is maintained and operated by the Energy Information Administration (EIA). For more information about the SEDS, end-use sector, or the various types of energy, see the appendix entry for Table A-54.

Table A-56. Construction

Sources: Employment—U.S. Bureau of Labor Statistics, Current Employment Statistics Program, https://www.bls.gov/sae/home.htm; Earnings—U.S. Bureau of Economic Analysis, Survey of Current Business https://www.bea.gov/regional/index.htm/; Establishments—U.S. Census Bureau, County Business Patterns, https://www.census.gov/programs-surveys/cbp.html; New housing units—U.S. Census Bureau, New Residential Construction, https://www.census.gov/construction/nrc/index.html.

Construction. Refer to General Notes of this appendix to see information on the Construction industry defined using the North American Industry Classification System (NAICS).

Data for nonfarm **employment** are based on the Current Employment Statistics (CES) survey of payroll records covering over 390,000 businesses on a monthly basis. Employment is defined as the total number of persons on establishment payrolls employed full- or part-time who received pay for any part of the pay period, which includes the 12th day of the month. Temporary and intermittent

employees are included, as are any workers who are on paid sick leave, on paid holiday, or who work during only part of the specified pay period. A striking worker who only works a small portion of the survey period, and is paid, would be included as employed under the CES definitions. Persons on the payroll of more than one establishment are counted in each establishment. Data exclude proprietors, self-employed, unpaid family or volunteer workers, farm workers, and domestic workers. Persons on layoff the entire pay period, on leave without pay, on strike for the entire period, or who have not yet reported for work are not counted as employed.

For information on **earnings**, see appendix entry for Table A-41.

Statistics on **housing units authorized by building permits** include housing units issued in local permit-issuing jurisdictions by a building or zoning permit. Not all areas of the country require a building or zoning permit. The statistics only represent those areas that do require a permit. Current surveys indicate that construction is undertaken for all but a very small percentage of housing units authorized by building permits. A major portion typically gets under way during the month of permit issuance and most of the remainder begin within the three following months. Because of this lag, the housing unit authorization statistics do not represent the number of units actually put into construction for the period shown, and should therefore not be directly interpreted as "housing starts."

Table A-57. Manufactures

Sources: Employment and average hourly earnings—U.S. Bureau of Labor Statistics, Current Employment Statistics Program, https://www.bls.gov/sae/home.htm; Earnings—U.S. Bureau of Economic Analysis, Survey of Current Business, https://www.bea.gov/regional/index.htm; Establishments—U.S. Census Bureau, County Business Patterns, https://www.census.gov/programs-surveys/cbp.html; Value of shipments—U.S. Census Bureau, https://www.census.gov/manufacturing/m3/index.html.

Manufactures. Refer to General Notes of this appendix to see information on the Manufacturing industry defined using the North American Industry Classification System (NAICS). See the notes and explanations for Table A-56 for information on employment. For information regarding earnings, see appendix entry for Table A-41. For information on establishments, see appendix entry for Table A-14.

Average hourly earnings are on a "gross" basis. They reflect not only changes in basic hourly and incentive wage rates, but also such variable factors as premium pay for overtime and late-shift work and changes in output of workers paid on an incentive plan. They also reflect shifts in the number of employees between relatively high-paid and low-paid work and changes in workers' earnings in individual establishments. Averages for groups and divisions further reflect changes in average hourly earnings for individual industries. Averages of hourly earnings differ from wage rates. Earnings are the actual return to the worker for a stated period; rates are the amount stipulated for a given unit of work or time. The earnings series do not measure the level of total labor costs on the part of the employer because the following are excluded: benefits, irregular bonuses, retroactive items, payroll taxes paid by employers, and earnings for those employees not covered under production worker, construction worker, or non-supervisory employee definitions.

Value of shipments includes the received or receivable net selling values, free on board plant (exclusive of freight and taxes), of all products shipped, both primary and secondary, as well as all miscellaneous receipts, such as receipts for contract work performed for others, installation and repair, sales of scrap, and sales of products bought and sold without further processing. Included are all items made by or for the establishments from material owned by it, whether sold, transferred to other plants of the same company, or shipped on consignment. The net selling value of products made in one plant on a contract basis from materials owned by another was reported by the plant providing the materials. In the case of multiunit companies, the manufacturer was requested to report the value of products transferred to other establishments of the same company at full economic or commercial value, including not only the direct cost of production but also a reasonable proportion of "all other costs" (including company overhead) and profit.

Table A-58. Manufactures Summary and Export-Related Shipments and Employment

Sources: Manufactures summary—U.S. Census Bureau, Annual Survey of Manufactures, Geographic Area Statistics https://www.census.gov/programs-surveys/asm.html, Export-related—U.S. Census Bureau, Exports from Manufacturing, https://www.census.gov/manufacturing/exports/

Employees includes all full-time and part-time employees on the payrolls of operating manufacturing establishments during any part of the pay period that included the 12th of the months specified on the report form. Included are employees on paid sick leave, paid holidays, and paid vacations; not included are proprietors and partners of unincorporated businesses. These individuals consist of all full-time and part-time employees who are on the payrolls of establishments who worked or received pay for any part of the pay period including the 12th of March, May, August, and November.

Payroll includes the gross earnings of all employees on the payrolls of operating manufacturing establishments

paid in the calendar year. Payroll includes all forms of compensation, such as salaries, wages, commissions, dismissal pay, bonuses, vacation and sick leave pay, and compensation in kind, prior to such deductions as employees' social security contributions, withholding taxes, group insurance, union dues, and savings bonds. The total includes salaries of officers of corporations. It excludes payments to proprietors or partners of unincorporated concerns. Also excluded are payments to members of Armed Forces and pensioners carried on the active payrolls of manufacturing establishments, and employers' social security contributions or other nonpayroll labor costs, such as employees' pension plans, group insurance premiums, and workers' compensation.

Production workers are the number of workers (up through the line-supervisor level) engaged in fabricating, processing, assembling, inspecting, receiving, storing, handling, packing, warehousing, shipping (but not delivering), maintenance, repair, janitorial and guard services, product development, auxiliary production for plant's own use (e.g., power plant), recordkeeping, and other services closely associated with these production operations at the establishment. Employees above the working-supervisor level are excluded from this item.

Production worker hours include all hours worked or paid for at the manufacturing plant, including actual overtime hours (not straight-time equivalent hours). It excludes hours paid for vacations, holidays, or sick leave when the employee is not at the establishment.

Value added by manufactures measures manufacturing activity derived by subtracting the cost of materials, supplies, containers, fuel, purchased electricity, and contract work from the value of shipments (products manufactured plus receipts for services rendered). The result of this calculation is adjusted by the addition of value added by merchandising operations (i.e., the difference between the sales value and the cost of merchandise sold without further manufacture, processing, or assembly) plus the net change in finished goods and work-in-process between the beginning- and end-of-year inventories. For those industries where value of production is collected instead of value of shipments, value added is adjusted only for the change in work-in-process inventories between the beginning and end of year. For those industries where value of work done is collected, the value added does not include an adjustment for the change in finished goods or work-in-process inventories. This item avoids the duplication in the figure for value of shipments that results from the use of products of some establishments as materials by others.

The estimates for **export-related** data are provided by the Census Bureau's 2006 Exports from Manufacturing Establishments report. The report relies upon 3 major information sources: (1) the Census Bureau's 2006 Annual Survey of Manufactures; (2) detailed data from the Census Bureau's 2006 edition of U.S. International Trade in Goods and Services; and (3) the Bureau of Economic Analysis' Input-Output (I/O) Accounts of the U.S. Economy for 2005. The data from each source is manipulated and converted so that they are comparable. The user should bear in mind that conversions and adjustments for such differences are imperfect, and a potential source of error in the figures presented in this report. These estimates are preliminary because I/O data for 2006 are not available when the estimates are calculated. Final estimates of export-related employment for 2006 will incorporate I/O data for 2006. A short description of the methodology is as follows: exports as reported by manufacturers on the 2006 Annual Survey of Manufactures (ASM) were allocated to the industry and state of that manufacturer. These export totals then were compared to the U.S. International Trade in Goods and Services, as reported by exporting firms. Because many manufacturers do not know whether or not their products are exported, the export data from the 2006 Annual Survey of Manufactures were adjusted to the totals from the U.S. International Trade in Goods and Services, with differences allocated to industries and states. These data then represented the "direct" exports of manufactured goods, by industry and by state. Refer to the source for further discussion of methodology.

Employment related to direct exports is not collected in the Annual Survey of Manufactures. However, the total value of shipments, as well as total employment, are estimated for each industry in each state. Using these data from the Annual Survey of Manufactures, employment related to direct exports was calculated by multiplying the total employment of each industry in each state by the ratio of the estimated total freight on board value of exports for that industry in that state to total shipments for that industry in that state. As with the estimates of exports, there are no measures available regarding the possible range of error associated with this estimating technique.

Table A-59. Major Manufacturing Sectors:

Sources: U.S. Census Bureau, Annual Survey of Manufactures, Geographic Area Statistics https://www.census.gov/programs-surveys/asm.html; factfinder.census.gov.

Refer to General Notes of this appendix to see information on the Manufacturing industry and major sectors defined using the North American Industry Classification System (NAICS). See appendix entry for Table A-14 for information on the County Business Patterns. See the notes and explanations for Table A-57 and A-58 for information on employment and value of shipments.

Table A-60. Information Industries

Sources: Employment—U.S. Bureau of Labor Statistics; State and Metro Area Employment, Hours, & Earnings; SAE Databases: Employment, Hours, and Earnings-State and Metro Area; www.bls.gov/sae/home.htm. Earnings—U.S. Bureau of Economic Analysis, Regional Economic Accounts, State Annual Personal Income and Employment; https://www.bea.gov/regional/index.htm. Establishments—U.S. Census Bureau, County Business Patterns, annual; https://www.census.gov/programs-surveys/cbp.html.

Refer to General Notes to see an explanation of the Information industry defined using the North American Industry Classification System (NAICS). See notes and explanations for Table A-56 for information on employment. For information on earnings, see appendix entry for Table A-41. For information on establishments, see appendix entry for Table A-14.

Table A-61. Wholesale and Retail Trade

Sources: Employment—U.S. Bureau of Labor Statistics; State and Metro Area Employment, Hours, & Earnings; SAE Databases: Employment, Hours, and Earnings-State and Metro Area; www.bls.gov/sae/home.htm\. Earnings—U.S. Bureau of Economic Analysis, Regional Economic Accounts, State Annual Personal Income and Employment; https://www.bea.gov/regional/index.htm. Establishments—U.S. Census Bureau, County Business Patterns, annual; https://www.census.gov/programs-surveys/cbp.html.

Refer to General Notes to see information on the Wholesale Trade and Retail Trade industries defined using the North American Industry Classification System (NAICS). See notes and explanations for Table A-56 for information on employment. For information on earnings, see appendix entry for Table A-41. For information on establishments, see appendix entry for Table A-14.

Table A-62. Retail Trade Earnings

Source: Earnings—U.S. Bureau of Economic Analysis, Regional Economic Accounts, State Annual Personal Income and Employment; https://www.bea.gov/regional/index.htm.

Refer to General Notes to see information on the Retail Trade industry defined using the North American Industry Classification System (NAICS). For information on earnings, see appendix entry for Table A-41.

Table A-63. Transportation and Commuting

Sources: Employment—U.S. Bureau of Labor Statistics, Current Employment Statistics Program, see Internet site https://www.bls.gov/sae/home.htm; Earnings—U.S. Bureau of Economic Analysis, Survey of Current Business, https://www.bea.gov/regional/index.htm; Establishments—U.S. Census Bureau, County Business Patterns, https://www.census.gov/programs-surveys/cbp.html; Workers 16 and over—U.S. Census Bureau, American Community Survey 2015, Table DP03. Selected Economic Characteristics, https://factfinder.census.gov; Vehicle miles of travel—U.S. Federal Highway Administration, Highway Statistics, annual, https://www.fhwa.dot.gov/policyinformation/statistics.cfm; Railroad and waterborne shipments—U.S. Bureau of Transportation Statistics, State Transportation Statistics https://www.rita.dot.gov/bts/publications/state_transportation_statistics.

Refer to General Notes to see information on the Transportation and Warehousing industry defined using the North American Industry Classification System (NAICS). See the notes and explanations for Table A-56 for information on employment and Table A-41 for information on earnings. For information on establishments, see appendix entry for Table A-14.

Vehicle miles of travel data are collected by the Federal Highway Administration (FHWA). Vehicle miles of travel are miles of travel by all types of motor vehicles as determined by the states on the basis of actual traffic counts and established estimating procedures.

Railroad shipment data are developed by the Association of American Railroads (AAR) from the Surface Transportation Board's Carload Waybill Sample. The sample contains detailed information on the origination and termination of carloads by commodity and carrier for virtually all U.S. freight railroads. Normal statistical variations and limited sampling of very small railroads may cause limited distortions.

Waterborne shipment data are compiled by the U.S. Army Corps of Engineers and include detailed data on the movements of vessels and commodities at the ports and harbors on the waterways and canals of the United States and its territories. Data on foreign commerce are supplied to the Corps of Engineers by the Census Bureau, U.S. Customs, and purchased from the Journal of Commerce, Port Import Export Reporting Service. The tonnage figures of shipments represent short tons (2,000 pounds).

Table A-64. Motor Vehicle and Motorcycle Registrations, Highway Mileage, Bridges, and Driver's Licenses

Sources: Registrations, highway mileage, and driver's licenses—U.S. Federal Highway Administration, Highway Statistics, annual, http://www.fhwa.dot.gov/policy/ohpi/hss/hsspubs.cfm.

Vehicle registration data are collected by the Federal Highway Administration (FHWA) from state motor vehicle registration agencies. Accordingly, registration practices and dates do vary. For uniformity, data have been adjusted to a calendar-year basis as registration years in states differ. Registration data include publicly, privately, and commercially owned vehicles.

Total **highway mileage** includes roads and streets in the functional systems, which are assigned to groups according to the character service they are intended to provide. The functional systems are (1) **arterial highways** that generally handle the long trips, (2) **collector facilities** that collect and disperse traffic between the arterials and the lower systems, and (3) **local roads and streets** that primarily serve direct access to residential areas. The **interstate system** connects, as directly as practicable, the nation's principal metropolitan areas, cities, and industrial centers.

Data on **bridges** are based on the National Bridge Inventory (NBI). The NBI is a compilation of data supplied by states as required by the National Bridge Inspection Standards for bridges located on public roads. The database is maintained in a format prescribed by the Recording and Coding Guide for the Structure Inventory and Appraisal of the Nation's Bridges. Bridges are structurally deficient if they have been restricted to light vehicles, require immediate rehabilitation to remain open, or are closed. Bridges are functionally obsolete if they have deck geometry, load-carrying capacity, clearance or approach roadway alignment that no longer meet the criteria for the system of which the bridge is carrying a part.

Driver's licenses. Each state and the District of Columbia administers its own driver licensing system. Since 1954, all states have required drivers to be licensed, and since 1959, all states have required examination prior to licensing. Tests of knowledge of state driving laws and practices, vision, and driving proficiency are now required for new licensees.

Table A-65. Traffic Fatalities and Seat Belt Use

Sources: Traffic fatalities—U.S. National Highway Traffic Safety Administration, Fatality Analysis Reporting System, https://www.nhtsa.gov/research-data/fatality-analysis-reporting-system-fars. Seat belts—U.S. Department of Transportation, National Highway Traffic Safety Administration, Seat Belt Use in 2014: Use Rates in the States and Territories.

Traffic fatalities. The National Highway Traffic Safety Administration (NHTSA) has a cooperative agreement with an agency in each state's government to provide information on all qualifying fatal crashes in the state. These agreements are managed by regional contracting

Officer's Technical Representatives located in the 10 NHTSA regional offices.

A fatal crash involves a motor vehicle in transport on a traffic way in which at least one person dies within 30 days of the crash. **Traffic fatality rate** is per 100 million vehicle miles traveled.

Traffic fatalities in alcohol-involved crashes include both drivers and occupants. Only the BAC of the operator is considered when classifying data as alcohol-involved.

Blood alcohol content (BAC) is measured as a percentage by weight of alcohol in the blood (grams/deciliter). A positive BAC level (0.01 g/dl and higher) indicates that alcohol was consumed by the person tested.

Seat belt use. Data for states are based on observational surveys conducted in accordance with Section 157, Title 23, U.S. Code. For national figures, data are based on the National Occupant Protection Use Survey (NOPUS). Motorists observed in the survey were counted as "belted" if they appeared to have a shoulder belt across the front of their body.

Table A-66. Communications

Sources: Mobile wireless subscribers—Federal Communications Commission, https://www.fcc.gov/general/iatd-data-statistical-reports; and https://apps.fcc.gov/edocs_public/attachmatch/DOC-329975A1.pdf; Number of payphones by state-Federal Communications Commission—Computer and internet Use in the United States, 2012—U.S. Census Bureau, https://www.census.gov/data/tables/2012/demo/computer-internet/computer-use-2012.html, End Use Revenue—Federal communications Commission "Universal Service Monitoring Report."

The Federal Communications Commission (FCC) provides data for households with telephones, computers, and **Internet access** based on the Current Population Survey (CPS) conducted by the Census Bureau. The CPS is a nationwide monthly survey of civilian noninstitutionalized population 15 years old and over that uses a sample of 50,000.

The FCC's local competition and broadband data gathering program collects data on **mobile wireless** telephone subscribership and high-speed connections from telecommunications carriers twice a year using FCC Form 477.

Table A-67. Financial Activities

Sources: Employment—U.S. Bureau of Labor Statistics, Current Employment and Statistics Program, https://www.bls.gov/sae/home.htm; Earnings—U.S. Bureau of

Economic Analysis, Survey of Current Business, https://www.bea.gov/regional/index.htm/; Establishments—U.S. Census Bureau, County Business Patterns, https://www.census.gov/programs-surveys/cbp.html; Financial Institutions—Federal Deposit Insurance Corporation, https://www5.fdic.gov/sod/sodSummary.asp?barItem.

Refer to General Notes to see information on Financial Activities defined using the North American Industry Classification System (NAICS). Financial Activities includes NAICS codes 52 (Finance and Insurance) and 53 (Real Estate and Rental and Leasing.) See notes and explanations for Table A-56 for information on employment. For information on earnings, see appendix entry for Table A-41. For information on establishments, see appendix entry for Table A-14.

FDIC-insured financial institutions includes both FDIC-insured commercial banks and FDIC-insured savings institutions. Also includes insured U.S. branches of foreign banks. The category of FDIC-insured commercial banks includes all commercial banks insured by the Federal Deposit Insurance Corporation (FDIC) either through the Bank Insurance Fund (BIF) or through the Savings Association Insurance Fund (SAIF). These institutions are regulated by and submit financial data to one of the three federal commercial bank regulators. The category of FDIC-insured savings institutions includes all institutions insured by either the FDIC Savings Association Insurance Fund (SAIF) operating under state or federal banking codes applicable to thrift institutions. These institutions are regulated by and submit financial data to the Office of Thrift Supervision or the FDIC.

The term "offices" includes both main offices and branches. Banking office is defined to include all offices and facilities that actually hold deposits, and does not include loan production offices, computer centers, and other nondeposit installations, such as automated teller machines (ATMs). Several institutions have designated home offices that do not accept deposits; these have been included to provide a more complete listing of all offices. The figures for each geographical area only include deposits of offices located within that area.

Table A-68. Professional and Business Services and Education and Health Services

Sources: Employment—U.S. Bureau of Labor Statistics, Current Employment Statistics Program, https://www.bls.gov/sae/home.htm; Earnings—U.S. Bureau of Economic Analysis, Survey of Current Business, https://www.bea.gov/regional/index.htm; Establishments—U.S. Census Bureau, County Business Patterns, https://www.census.gov/programs-surveys/cbp.html.

Professional and Business Services includes Professional, Scientific, and Technical Services; Management of Companies and Enterprises; and Administrative and Support and Waste Management and Remediation Services.

Education and Health Services includes Educational Services and Health Care and Social Assistance. Refer to General Notes to see information on the above industries defined using the North American Industry Classification System (NAICS).

For information on employment, see appendix entry for Table A-56. For information on earnings, see appendix entry for Table A-41. For information on establishments, see appendix entry for Table A-14.

Table A-69. Leisure and Hospitality Services

Sources: Employment—U.S. Bureau of Labor Statistics, Current Employment Statistics Program, https://www.bls. gov/sae/home.htm; Earnings—U.S. Bureau of Economic Analysis, Survey of Current Business, https://www.bea. gov/regional/index.htm; Establishments—U.S. Census Bureau, County Business Patterns, https://www.census. gov/programs-surveys/cbp.html.

Refer to General Notes to see information on **Arts, Entertainment, and Recreation Services** and **Accommodation and Food Services** industries defined using the North American Industry Classification System (NAICS). For information on employment, see appendix entry for Table A-56. For information on earnings, see appendix entry for Table A-41. For information on establishments, see appendix entry for Table A-14.

Table A-70. Travel and Tourism Indicators

Sources:; Travel and Tourism Indicators—U.S. Department of Homeland Security, Office of Immigration Statistics, 2015 Year Book of Immigration Statistics, see https:// www.dhs.gov/immigration-statistics/yearbook/2015; National parks—U.S. National Park Service, *ProQuest Statistical Abstract*.

Data on **domestic travel expenditures** represent U.S. spending on domestic overnight trips and day trips of 50 miles or more, one way, away from home. This excludes spending by foreign visitors and by U.S. residents in U.S. territories and abroad.

International visitors for pleasure: The Yearbook of Immigration Statistics is a compendium of tables that provides data on foreign nationals who, during a fiscal year, were granted lawful permanent residence (i.e., admitted as immigrants or became legal permanent residents), were

admitted into the United States on a temporary basis (e.g., tourists, students, or workers), applied for asylum or refugee status, or were naturalized. A nonimmigrant is defined by Section 101(a)(15) of the Immigration and Nationality Act (INA) as an alien who is not an immigrant and is admitted in one of the nonimmigrant alien classes of admission. Nonimmigrant admissions refer to number of events (i.e., entries into the United States) rather than persons. As such, one nonimmigrant may enter the United States more than once, and each entry would count as a separate admission record.

Visitors to national parks. A visit is defined as the entry of any person, except National Park Service (NPS) personnel, onto lands or waters administered by the NPS. A visit may occur as a recreation visit or a nonrecreation visit. A same-day reentry, negligible transit, and an entry to a detached portion of the same park on the same day are considered to be a single visit. Visits are reported separately for two contiguous parks.

Table A-71. Government

Sources: Employment—U.S. Bureau of Labor Statistics, Current Employment Statistics Program, (CES), https:// www.bls.gov/sae/data.htm; Earnings—U.S. Bureau of Economic Analysis, https://www.bea.gov/regional/index. htm/; Federal tax collections—Internal Revenue Service, Data Book 2015, previous years, https://www.irs.gov/uac/ tax-stats ; State tax collections—U.S. Census Bureau, Federal, state and local governments, Tax collections, State government tax collections, annual, see also, https://www. census.gov/govs/.

For information on **earnings**, refer to appendix entry for Table A-41. Government employment covers only civilian workers. Government enterprises are government agencies that cover a substantial portion of their operating costs by selling goods and services to the public and that maintain separate accounts. For addition information regarding employment, refer to the notes and explanations for Table A-56.

Data on **federal tax collections** are provided by the Internal Revenue Service (IRS) through the Statistics of Income (SOI) program. This program pulls data electronically from the master file and augments the data with items captured from the hard copies of taxpayers' returns. The IRS processes about 200 million tax returns each year, and SOI uses approximately half a million of these for statistics. Classification by state is based on the individual's address (or, in the case of businesses, the location of the principal office or place of business). However, some individuals may use the address of a tax attorney or accountant. Sole proprietors, partners in a partnership, or shareholders in an "S" corporation may use their business addresses. Such addresses could have been located in a state other than the state in which the individual resided. Similarly, taxes withheld reported by employers located near a state boundary might include substantial amounts withheld from salaries of employees who reside in a neighboring state. Also, while taxes of corporations may be paid from the principal office, the operations of these corporations may be located in one or more other state(s).

State tax collections data are collected by the Census Bureau through an Annual Survey of State Government Tax Collection. These statistics are of all 50 state governments in the United States and are for state governments only. They should not be interpreted as state area data (state plus local government tax collections combined). The state government tax data presented by the Census Bureau may differ from data published by state governments because the Census Bureau may be using a different definition of which organizations are covered under the term, "state government." For the purpose of State Government Tax Collections statistics, the term "state government" refers not only to the executive, legislative, and judicial branches of a given state, but it also includes agencies, institutions, commissions, and public authorities that operate separately or somewhat autonomously from the central state government but where the state government maintains administrative or fiscal control over their activities as defined by the Census Bureau. The tax revenue data pertain to state fiscal years that end on June 30, in all but four states (NY, TX, AL, MI). Amounts shown for these four states reflect the different timing of their respective fiscal years, which were the 12-month periods ending on March 31, for New York, August 31 for Texas, and September 30, for Alabama and Michigan.

Table A-72. State Government Employment and Finances

Sources: Employment—U.S. Census Bureau, State Government Employment and Payroll Data, U.S. Census Bureau, American FactFinder.

The Census Bureau collects data on **state government employment** by conducting an Annual Survey of Government Employment. Alternatively, every 5 years, in years ending in a "2" or "7," a Census of Governments, including an employment portion, is conducted. For both the census and the annual surveys, the employment detail is equivalent.

Employment refers to all persons gainfully employed by and performing services for a government. **Employees** include all persons paid for personal services performed, including persons paid from federally funded programs, paid elected or appointed officials, persons in a paid

leave status, and persons paid on a per-meeting, annual, semiannual, or quarterly basis. Unpaid officials, pensioners, persons whose work is performed on a fee basis, and contractors and their employees are excluded from the count of employees. **Full-time equivalent** employment refers to a computed statistic representing the number of full-time employees who could have been employed if the reported number of hours worked by part-time employees had been worked by full-time employees. This statistic is calculated separately for each function of a government by dividing the "part-time hours paid" by the standard number of hours for full-time employees in the particular government and then adding the resulting quotient to the number of full-time employees.

Finance data are collected by the Census Bureau through the Annual Survey of Government Finances, which covers all state and local governments in the United States. The survey content includes the entire range of government finance activities: revenue, expenditure, debt, and assets.

Revenue includes all amounts of money received by a government from external sources during its fiscal year net of refunds and other correcting transactions, other than issuance of debt, sale of investments, and agency or private trust transactions. Revenue excludes amounts transferred from other funds or agencies of the same government. Revenue comprises amounts received by all agencies, boards, commissions, or other organizations categorized as dependent on the government concerned. Stated in terms of the accounting procedures from which these data originate, revenue covers receipts from all accounting funds of a government, other than intragovernmental service (revolving), agency, and private trust funds.

General revenue comprises all revenue except that classified as liquor store, utility, or insurance trust revenue. Generally, the basis for this distinction is not the fund or administrative unit established to account for and control a particular activity, but rather the nature of the revenue source involved. Within general revenue are four main categories: taxes, intergovernmental revenue, current charges, and miscellaneous general revenue.

Intergovernmental revenue comprises monies from other governments, including grants, shared taxes, and contingent loans and advances for support of particular functions or for general financial support; any significant and identifiable amounts received as reimbursement for performance of governmental services for other governments; and any other form of revenue representing the sharing by other governments in the financing of activities administered by the receiving government. All intergovernmental revenue is reported in the general government sector, even if it is used to support activities in other sectors (such as utilities). Intergovernmental revenue excludes amounts received from the sale of property, commodities, and utility services to other governments (which are reported in different revenue categories). It also excludes amounts received from other governments as the employer share or for support of public employee retirement or other insurance trust funds of the recipient government, which are treated as insurance trust revenue.

Taxes are compulsory contributions exacted by a government for public purposes, other than for employee and employer assessments and contributions to finance retirement and social insurance trust systems and for special assessments to pay capital improvements. Tax revenue comprises gross amounts collected (including interest and penalties) minus amounts paid under protest and amounts refunded during the same period. It consists of all taxes imposed by a government whether the government collects the taxes itself or relies on another government to act as its collection agent.

Expenditure includes all amounts of money paid out by a government during its fiscal year—net of recoveries and other correcting transactions—other than for retirement of debt, purchase of investment securities, extension of loans, and agency or private trust transactions. Under this definition, expenditure relates to external payments of a government and excludes amounts Transferred to funds or agencies of the same government (other than payments to intragovernmental service funds).

Expenditure includes payments from all sources of funds, including not only current revenues but also proceeds from borrowing and prior year fund balances. Note, however, that the Census Bureau's finance statistics do not relate expenditure to their source of funding. Expenditure includes amounts spent by all agencies, boards, commissions, or other organizations categorized as dependent on the government concerned.

General expenditure comprises all expenditure except that classified as liquor store, utility, or insurance trust expenditure. As noted above, it includes all such payments regardless of the source of revenue from which they were financed. General government expenditures are classified by function and character and object.

Intergovernmental expenditure is defined as amounts paid to other governments for performance of specific functions or for general financial support. Includes grants, shared taxes, contingent loans and advances, and any significant and identifiable amounts or reimbursement paid to other governments for performance of general government services or activities. By definition, it excludes amounts paid to other governments for purchase of commodities, property, or utility services and for any tax levied as such on facilities of the government.

Direct expenditure comprises all final expenditures paid to current employees, former employees (retirees) and to private sector entities outside of the government itself (e.g., all expenditure other than intergovernmental expenditure).

Education expenditures cover the operation, maintenance, and construction of public schools and facilities for elementary and secondary education (kindergarten through high school), vocational-technical education, and other educational institutions except those for higher education. Covers operations by independent governments (school districts) as well as those operated as integral agencies of state, county, municipal, or township governments. Also covers financial support of public elementary and secondary schools.

Public welfare expenditures are those cash payments made directly to individuals contingent upon their need, other than those under federal categorical assistance programs.

Highway expenditures include maintenance, operation, repair, and construction of highways, streets, roads, alleys, sidewalks, bridges, tunnels, ferry boats, viaducts, and related nontoll structures.

Table A-73. State Government Tax Collections

Source: U.S. Census Bureau, Annual Survey of State Government Tax Collection, www.factfinder.census.gov.

Data on **state government tax collections** are collected by the Census Bureau by conducting an Annual Survey of State Government Tax Collection. The data are on the fiscal year tax collections of all 50 state governments in the United States and are for state governments only. They should not be interpreted as state area data (state plus local government tax collections combined). See appendix entry for Table A-71 for more information.

Property taxes include three types, all having in common the use of value as a basis for the tax. General property taxes, relating to property as a whole, taxed at a single rate or at classified rates according to the class of property. Property refers to real property (e.g., land and structures) as well as personal property; personal property can be either tangible (e.g., automobiles and boats) or intangible (e.g., bank accounts and stocks and bonds). Special property taxes, levied on selected types of property (e.g., oil and gas properties, house trailers, motor vehicles, and intangibles) and subject to rates not directly related to general property tax rates. Taxes based on income produced by property as a measure of its value on the assessment date. For more information on **Taxes**, see appendix entry for Table A-71 and A-72.

Sales and gross receipts taxes are taxes on goods and services, measured on the basis of the volume or value of their transfer, upon gross receipts or gross income there from, or as an amount per unit sold; and related taxes based upon use, storage, production, importation, or consumption of goods and service.

General sales and gross receipts taxes are applicable with only specified exceptions to sales of all types of goods and services or to all gross receipts, whether at a single rate or at classified rates, and sales use taxes.

Table A-74. Federal Government

Sources: U.S. Bureau of Economic Analysis, https://www. bea.gov/regional/index.htm; Federal funds and grants— U.S. Census Bureau, 2008 Consolidated Federal Funds Report, annual, see Internet site http://www.census.gov/ govs/cffr/.

Federal employment. Employment is a count of jobs, both full-time and part-time. It includes wage and salary jobs, sole proprietorships, and individual general partners, but not unpaid family workers nor volunteers. Federal civilian employment includes civilian employees of the federal government, including congressional staff and the U.S. Postal Service. The federal military category includes government establishments primarily engaged in national security and national affairs.

Earnings is the sum of three components of personal income—wages and salaries, supplements to wages and salaries, and proprietors' income. It can be used in the analyses of regional economies as a proxy for the income that is generated from participation in current production. Earnings estimates for 1929-47 are assumed to be on a place-of-residence basis; explicit adjustments were made for the principal interstate commuting flows.

Table A-75. Federal Individual Income Tax Returns

Sources: Tax returns—U.S. Internal Revenue Service, Internal Revenue Service Data Book; Property and land—U.S. General Services Administration, Federal Real Property Profile, annual, see Internet site https:// www.gsa.gov.

For information on **federal individual income tax returns**, see appendix entry for Table A-71 or consult the source.

Data on **federally owned property** and **federal lands** are collected through the General Services Administration's (GSA's) Federal Real Property Profile (FRPP) reporting system. Contributing agencies provide data annually based on their real property holdings as of September 30. Land acreage is divided into urban and rural categories. Leased land is usually not reported if it is included with a building lease. Buildings are roofed and walled structures built for permanent use. Buildings owned by the government, whether or not located on government-owned land, are included in the data. Buildings under construction are included only if they were available for use as of September 30 of the year shown.

Table A-76. Social Security, Supplemental Nutrition Assistance Programs, and School Lunch Programs

Sources: Social Security—U.S. Social Security Administration, Annual Statistical Supplement, https://www. ssa.gov/policy/docs/statcomps/supplement/; Federal food stamp and national school lunch programs—U.S. Department of Agriculture, Food and Nutrition Service, Supplemental Nutrition Assistance Program, Annual State Level Data, https://www.fns.usda.gov/pd/ supplemental-nutrition-assistance-program-snap.

Social security. The Old-Age, Survivors, and Disability Insurance Program (OASDI) provides monthly benefits for retired and disabled insured workers and their dependents and to survivors of insured workers. To be eligible for benefits, a worker must have had a specified period of employment in which OASDI taxes were paid. The data were derived from the Master Beneficiary Record (MBR), the principal administrative file of social security beneficiaries. Data for total recipients and retired workers include persons with special age-72 benefits. Special age-72 benefit represents the monthly benefit payable to men who attained age 72 before 1972 and for women who attained age 72 before 1970 and who do not have sufficient quarters to qualify for a retired-worker benefit under either the fully or the transitionally insured status provision.

As of October 1, 2008, **Supplemental Nutrition Assistance Program** (SNAP) was the new name for the federal Food Stamp Program. SNAP is the federal name for the program. State programs may have different names. SNAP provides low-income households with electronic benefits that can be used at most grocery stores. The U.S. Department of Agriculture administers SNAP at the federal level through its Food and Nutrition Service (FNS). State agencies administer the program at state and local levels, including determination of eligibility and allotments, and distribution of benefits. The average monthly benefit was about $101 per person and about $227 per household in Fiscal Year (FY) 2008. Consult source for more information on program.

The **National School Lunch Program** covers public and private elementary and secondary schools and residential child care institutions. Costs include federal cash reimbursements at rates set by law for each meal served and commodity costs. The Food and Nutrition Service administers the program at the federal level. At the state level, the National School Lunch Program is usually administered by state education agencies, which operate the program through agreements with school food authorities. Consult source for more information on program.

Table A-77. Social Insurance Programs and Workers' Compensation

Sources: U.S. Social Security Administration, Annual Statistical Supplement to the Social Security Bulletin; TANF—U.S. Administration for Children and Families, Temporary Assistance for Needy Families (TANF) Program, Administration for Children and families, https://www.acf.hhs.gov/sites/default/files/ofa/2015_recipient_tan.pdf; Unemployment insurance—U.S. Employment and Training Administration, https://workforcesecurity.doleta.gov/unemploy/.

The **Supplemental Security Income** (SSI) program provides cash payments in accordance with nationwide eligibility requirements to people with limited income and resources who are aged, blind, or disabled. An aged person is defined as an individual who is 65 years old or over. A blind person is anyone with vision of 20/200 or less with the use of correcting lens in the better eye or with tunnel vision of 20 degrees or less. The disabled classification refers to any person unable to engage in any substantial gainful activity by reason of any medically determinable physical or mental impairment expected to result in death or that has lasted or can be expected to last for a continuous period of at least 12 months. For a child under 18 years, eligibility is based on disability or severity comparable with that of an adult, since the criterion of "substantial gainful activity" is inapplicable for children.

The **Temporary Assistance for Needy Families** (TANF) program is a time-limited program that assists families with children when the parents or other responsible relatives cannot provide for the family's basic needs. The federal government provides grants to states to run the TANF program so that the states decide on the design of the program, the type and amount of assistance payments, the range of other services to be provided, and the rules for determining who is eligible for benefits. Prior to TANF, the cash assistance program to families was called Aid to Families with Dependent Children (1980–1996). Under the new welfare law (Personal Responsibility Reconciliation Act of 1996), the program became TANF.

Unemployment insurance is presently administered by the U.S. Employment and Training Administration and each state's employment security agency. The program provides unemployment benefits to eligible workers who are unemployed through no fault of their own (as determined under state law) and meet other eligibility requirements of state law. Unemployment insurance payments (benefits) are intended to provide temporary assistance to unemployed workers who meet the requirements of state law. Each state administers a separate unemployment insurance program within guidelines established by federal law. Eligibility for unemployment insurance, benefit amounts, and the length of time benefits are available are determined by the state law under which unemployment insurance claims are established. In the majority of states, benefit funding is based solely on a tax imposed on employers.

Workers' compensation provides protection to workers disabled from work-related injury or illness. The program includes protection under the laws of 50 states, the District of Columbia, and two federal programs (the Federal Employees Compensation Act and the Longshoremen's and Harbor Workers' Compensation Act). Payments represent compensation and medical benefits and include insurance losses paid by private insurance carriers, disbursements of state funds, and self-insurance payments.

Table A-78. Government Transfer Payments to Individuals

Source: U.S. Bureau of Economic Analysis, "Regional Accounts Data, Annual State Personal Income," https://www.bea.gov/regional/index.htm.

Personal current transfer receipts are personal income that are payments to persons for which no current services are performed. It consists of payments to individuals and to nonprofit institutions by federal, state, and local governments and by businesses. Government transfer payments to individuals consist of: retirement and disability insurance benefits, medical benefits, income maintenance benefits, unemployment insurance compensation, veteran's benefits, federal education and training assistance, and other transfer receipts of individuals from governments.

Retirement and disability insurance benefits consist of Old-Age, Survivors, and Disability (OASDI) benefits; railroad retirement and disability benefits; federal and state workers' compensation; temporary disability benefits; black lung benefits; and Pension Benefit Guaranty benefits.

Medical payments include medical benefits, public assistance medical care, and military medical insurance benefits. Medicare benefits are federal government payments made through intermediaries to beneficiaries for the care provided to individuals under the medicare program. Public assistance medical care benefits are received by low-income individuals. These payments consist mainly of the payments made through intermediaries to the vendors for care provided to individuals under the federally assisted, state-administered medicaid program and State Children's Health Insurance Program (SCHIP) and under the general assistance medical programs of state and local governments. Military medical insurance benefits are vendor payments made under the TriCare Management Program, formerly called the Civilian Health and Medical Plan of the Uniformed Services program, for the medical care of dependents of active duty military personnel and of retired military personnel and their dependents at nonmilitary medical facilities.

Income maintenance benefits consist largely of supplemental security income payments, family assistance, food stamp payments, and other assistance payments, including general assistance.

Unemployment insurance benefits are made up of state unemployment compensation; unemployment compensation of federal civilian employees, railroad employees, and veterans; and trade adjustment allowances. State unemployment compensation are benefits consisting mainly of the payments received by individuals under state-administered unemployment insurance (UI) programs, but they include the special benefits authorized by federal legislation for periods of high unemployment. The provisions that govern the eligibility, timing, and amount of benefit payments vary among the states, but the provisions that govern the coverage and financing are uniform nationally. Unemployment compensation of federal civilian employees are benefits received by former federal employees under a federal program administered by the state employment security agencies. Unemployment compensation of railroad employees are benefits received by railroad workers who are unemployed because of sickness or because work is unavailable in the railroad industry and in related industries, such as carrier affiliates. This UI program is administered by the Railroad Retirement Board (RRB) under a federal program that is applicable throughout the nation. Unemployment compensation of veterans are benefits that are received by unemployed veterans who have recently separated from military service and who are not eligible for military retirement benefits. The compensation is paid under a federal program that is administered by the state employment security agencies. Trade adjustment allowances are the payments received by workers who are unemployed because of the adverse economic effects of international trade arrangements.

Veterans' benefits include veterans' pension and disability benefits, veterans' readjustment benefits, veterans' life insurance benefits, and other assistance to veterans (federal government payments received by paraplegics and by certain other disabled veterans to purchase automobiles and other conveyances, state and local government payments of assistance to indigent veterans, and the state and local government payments of bonuses to veterans).

Federal education and training assistance consists of federal fellowships, higher education student assistance, Job Corps payments, and interest payments on guaranteed student loans. Federal fellowships consist of the payments to outstanding science students who receive National Science Foundation (NSF) grants, the subsistence payments to the cadets at the six state maritime academies, and the payments for all other federal fellowships. Higher education student assistance consists of the federal payments, called Pell Grants, for an undergraduate education for students with low incomes. Job Corps payments are primarily the allowances for living expenses received by economically disadvantaged individuals who are between the ages of 16 and 21 and who are enrolled in the designated vocational and educational training programs. These benefits also include the adjustment allowances received by trainees upon the successful completion of their training. Interest payments on guaranteed student loans are made by the Department of Education to commercial lending institutions on behalf of the individuals who receive low-interest, deferred-payment loans from these institutions in order to pay the expenses of higher education.

Other transfer receipts of individuals from governments consist largely of Bureau of Indian Affairs payments, education exchange payments, Alaska Permanent Fund dividend payments, compensation of survivors of public safety officers, compensation of victims of crime, disaster relief payments, compensation for Japanese internment, and other special payments to individuals.

Table A-79. Medicare, Medicaid, and Children's Health Insurance Program

Sources: Medicare enrollment—U.S. Centers for Medicare and Medicaid Services, Medicare State Enrollment, https://www.cms.hhs.gov/medicareEnrpts/; Number of Children Ever Enrolled in Medicaid and CHIP, https://www.medicaid.gov/chip/downloads/fy-2015-childrens-enrollment-report.pdf.

Medicare. Since July 1966, the federal medicare program has provided two coordinated plans for nearly all people age 65 and over: (1) a hospital insurance plan, which covers hospital and related services and (2) a voluntary supplementary medical insurance plan, financed partially by monthly premiums paid by participants, which partly covers physicians' and related medical services. Such insurance also applies, since July 1973, to disabled beneficiaries of any age after 24 months of entitlement to cash benefits under the social security or railroad retirement programs and to persons with end-state renal disease.

Medicaid is a health insurance program for certain low-income people. These include: certain low-income families with children; aged, blind, or disabled people on supplemental security income; certain low-income pregnant women and children; and people who have very high medical bills. Medicaid is funded and administered through a state-federal partnership. Although there are broad federal requirements for medicaid, states have a wide degree of flexibility to design their program. States have authority to establish eligibility standards, determine what benefits and services to cover, and set payment rates. All states, however, must cover these basic services: inpatient and outpatient hospital services; doctors' services, family planning, and periodic health checkups; and diagnosis and treatment for children.

Center for Medicare and Medicaid Service (CMS) administers the Children's Health Insurance Program (CHIP). Children began receiving insurance through CHIP in 1997 and the program helped states expand health care coverage to more than 5 million of the nation's uninsured children. The program was reauthorized on February 4, 2009, when the President signed into law the Children's Health Insurance Program Reauthorization Act of 2009 (CHIPRA or Public Law 111-3). CHIPRA finances the Children's Health Insurance Program (CHIP) through Fiscal Year (FY) 2013.

The Children's Health Insurance Program is jointly financed by the federal and state governments and is administered by the states. Within broad federal guidelines, each state determines the design of its program, eligibility groups, benefit packages, payment levels for coverage, and administrative and operating procedures. CHIP provides a capped amount of funds to states on a matching basis. Federal payments under title XXI to states are based on state expenditures under approved plans effective on or after October 1, 1997.

Table A-80. Department of Defense and Veterans

Sources: Department of Defense—U.S. Department of Defense, Atlas/Data Abstract for the United States and Selected Areas, annual, see http://siadapp.dmdc.osd.mil/ and https://www.dmdc.osd.mil/appj/dwp/searchResults.jsp?search=by+state and https://www.defense.gov/Portals/1/Documents/pubs/FY2014_Defense_Spending_by_State_Report.pdf. Veterans—U.S. Department of

Veterans Affairs, Office of Policy, Planning, and Preparedness, see http://www1.va.gov/vetdata/.

The **Department of Defense** (DoD) is responsible for providing the military forces of the United States. It includes the Office of the Secretary of Defense, the Joint Chiefs of Staff, the Army, the Navy, the Air Force, and the defense agencies. The President serves as Commander in Chief of the armed forces; from him, the authority flows to the Secretary of Defense and through the Joint Chiefs of Staff to the commanders of unified and specified commands (e.g., U.S. Strategic Command).

DoD personnel data include active duty military, civilian, and Reserve and National Guard. Expenditures include payroll outlays, contracts, and grants. Payroll outlays consist of active duty military pay, civilian pay, Reserve and National Guard pay, and retired military pay. Contracts include supply and equipment contracts, RDT&E contracts, service contracts, construction contracts, and civil function contracts. Consult the source for more information.

Veterans. The Office of Policy in the Department of Veterans Affairs (VA) is responsible for administering a range of programs and analyses concerning veteran surveys, demographics, and population estimates. Within the Office of Policy, the Office of the actuary (OACT) develops estimates and projections of the veteran population and their characteristics.

The Department of Veterans Affairs (VA) provides official estimates and projections of the veteran population using the Veteran Population Model (VetPop). The model is updated periodically for improved methodology, more recent data, and changing needs. For each year from April 1, 2000, to September 30, 2036, VetPop generates the number of veterans by selected characteristics: at the state and/or national levels—by age, gender, period of service, race/ethnicity, rank (Officer/Enlisted), and branch of service; at the county level—by age and gender. Veteran's data is derived from a combination of decennial census data, Defense Manpower Data Center (DMDC) losses, and GORGO, the projection model used by Department of Defense's Office of the Actuary.

A veteran is someone 18 years and older (there are a few 17-year-old veterans) who is not currently on active duty, but who once served on active duty in the U.S. Army, Navy, Air Force, Marine Corps, or Coast Guard, or who served in the Merchant Marine during World War II. There are many groups whose active service makes them veterans including: those who incurred a service-connected disability during active duty for training in the Reserves or National Guard, even though that service would not otherwise have counted for veteran status; members of a national guard or reserve component who have been ordered to active duty by order of the President or who have a full-time military job. The latter are called AGRs (Active Guard and Reserve). No one who has received a dishonorable discharge is a veteran.

Table A-81. Elections

Sources:; Voting-age population, 2016—U.S. Census Bureau, Population estimates, https://www.census.gov/data/tables/2016/demo/popest/state-detail.html; Electoral votes, 2012 percent of voting-age population voting for President, votes for President and votes for Senators—U.S. Congress, Clerk of the House, Statistics of the Presidential and Congressional Election, biennial, see Internet site history.house.gov/Institution/Election-Statistics/2016election/ and history.house.gov/Institution/Election-Statistics/2014election/.

The **voting-age population** relates to people 18 years old and over in all states and the District of Columbia. Data include armed forces stationed in each state, aliens, and the institutionalized population.

Votes cast for President. The Constitution specifies how the President and Vice President are selected. Each state elects, by popular vote, a group of electors equal in number to its total of members of Congress. The 23rd Amendment, adopted in 1961, grants the District of Columbia three presidential electors, a number equal to that of the least populous state. A majority vote of all electors is necessary to elect the President and Vice President. If no candidate receives a majority, the House of Representatives, with each state having one vote, is empowered to elect the President and Vice President, again, with a majority of votes required.

Votes cast for U.S. Senators. The U.S. Senate is composed of 100 members, two from each state, who are elected to serve for a term of 6 years. One-third of the Senate is elected every 2 years. Senators were originally chosen by the state legislatures. The 17th Amendment to the Constitution, adopted in 1913, prescribed that Senators be elected by popular vote.

Table A-82. Composition of Congress and Public Officials

Sources: U.S. Congress, Clerk of the House, Statistics of the Presidential and Congressional Election, biennial, see Internet site history.house.gov/Institution/Election-Statistics/2016election/ and history.house.gov/Institution/Election-Statistics/2014election/; Composition of Congress—Office of the Clerk, Official List of Members by State, annual, see also http://clerk.house.gov/.

In each state, totals for votes cast for Representatives represent the sum of votes cast in each Congressional District or votes cast for Representatives at Large in states where only one member is elected. In all years, there are numerous districts within the state where either the Republican or Democratic party had no candidate. In some states, the Republican and Democratic vote includes votes cast for the party candidate by endorsing parties. Refer to the notes and explanations for Table A-82 for information on Senators.

TABLE B. METROPOLITAN AREAS

Table B consists of 14 tables (B-1 through B-14) with 159 data items for 382 metropolitan statistical areas (MSAs), 11 metropolitan statistical areas with metropolitan divisions and 31 metropolitan divisions. They are presented alphabetically in each of the 14 tables.

All summaries, including historical data, are presented for the areas as currently defined. Where possible, the original figures have been retabulated to reflect the status of metropolitan area boundaries as of July 1, 2015. For more information on these areas, see Appendix C, Geographic Concepts and Codes.

Table B-1. Area and Population

Sources: Area—U.S. Census Bureau, 2016 U.S. Gazetteer Files, http://www.census.gov/geo/maps-data/data/gazetteer2016.html; Population—U.S. Census Bureau, Population Estimates Program, Population and Housing Unit Estimates Datasets for 2015, 2010, and 2000 www.census.gov/programs-surveys/popest/data/data-sets.html. For 1990, Population of States and Counties of the United States: 1790 to 1990, https://www.census.gov/population/www/censusdata/pop1790-1990.html.

Total area. Area measurement data provide the size, in square units, of geographic entities for which the Census Bureau tabulates and disseminates data. Area is calculated from the specific boundary recorded for each entity (in this case, counties which have been aggregated to metropolitan areas) in the Census Bureau's geographic database.

Area measurements may disagree with the information displayed on the Census Bureau maps and in the MAF. TIGER database because, for area measurement purposes, features identified as "intermittent water" and "glacier" are reported as land area. The accuracy of any area measurement data is limited by the accuracy inherent in (1) the location and shape of the various boundary information in the database, (2) the location and shapes of the shorelines of water bodies in that database, and

(3) rounding affecting the last digit in all operations that compute and/or sum the area measurements. Identification of land and inland, coastal, and territorial is for statistical purposes and does not necessarily reflect legal definitions thereof.

Population numbers for 2010, 2000, and 1990 are counts of the resident population on April 1 of those decennial census years. The April 1 estimates base populations for 2010 and 2000 may differ from the April 1 census count due to legal boundary updates, other geographic program changes, and Count Question Resolution actions. The 1990 census counts include corrections processed through August 1997, results of special censuses and test censuses, and do not include adjustments for census coverage errors.

Population estimates for 2015 measure the estimated population from the calculated number of people living in an area as of July 1. The Census Bureau develops county population estimates with a component of population change method in which they use administrative records and other data to estimate the household and group quarters population. For the household population, the components of population change are births, deaths, net domestic migration, and net international migration. They measure change in the nonhousehold, or group quarters, population by the net change in the population living in group quarters facilities.

A major assumption underlying this approach is that changes in selected administrative and other data sources closely approximate the components of population change. Therefore, Census Bureau demographers separately estimate each component of population change based on administrative records, including registered births and deaths, federal income tax returns, medicare enrollees, and military movement. They also separately estimate net international migration using information from the American Community Survey (ACS), the decennial census, and other data sources.

Most administrative record data sources lag the current estimate year by as much as 2 years, therefore, the Census Bureau projects the data for the current year based on past years' data. As updated data become available, they revise the projected input data so that each vintage's estimates are always based on the most recent data available.

For more information on the method used for these estimates, see Appendix B, Limitations and Methodology, and the website at http://www.census.gov/programs-surveys/popest/technical-documentation.html.

Rank numbers are assigned on the basis of population size, with each metropolitan area placed in descending order, largest to smallest. Where ties occur (two or more areas with identical populations) the same rank is assigned to each of the tied metropolitan areas. In such cases, the following rank number(s) is omitted so that the lowest rank is usually equal to the number of metropolitan areas ranked.

People per square mile of land area, also known as population density, is the average number of inhabitants per square mile of land area. These figures are derived by dividing the total number of residents by the number of square miles of land area in the specified geographic area.

Table B-2. Components of Population Change

Sources: U.S. Census Bureau, Population Estimates, Cumulative Estimates of the Components of Resident Population Change for Metropolitan Statistical Areas: April 1, 2010 to July 1, 2015; https://www.census.gov/programs-surveys/popest/data/data-sets.html.

The Census Bureau develops county population estimates with a component of population change method in which they use administrative records and other data to estimate the household and group quarters population. For the household population, the components of population change are births, deaths, net domestic migration, and net international migration. They measure change in the nonhousehold, or group quarters, population by the net change in the population living in group quarters facilities.

A major assumption underlying this approach is that changes in selected administrative and other data sources closely approximate the components of population change. Therefore, Census Bureau demographers separately estimate each component of population change based on administrative records, including registered births and deaths, federal income tax returns, medicare enrollees, and military movement. They also separately estimate net international migration using information from the American Community Survey (ACS), the decennial census, and other data sources.

Most administrative record data sources lag the current estimate year by as much as 2 years, therefore, the Census Bureau projects the data for the current year based on past years' data. As updated data become available, they revise the projected input data so that each vintage's estimates are always based on the most recent data available.

The Census Bureau produces the estimate of each county's population, starting with the base population from either the 2010 census (for the July 1, 2010, estimates) or the revised population estimate for the prior year (for the July 1, 2011, and later estimates). They then add or subtract the demographic components of population change calculated for that time period. Basically, they add the estimated number of births and subtract the estimated number of deaths for the time period. Next, they add the estimates of net domestic migration, net international migration, and the net change in the group quarters population. The definitions of these concepts follow.

The Census Bureau produces separate population estimates for the populations under age 65 and age 65 and over, mainly because different data are used to measure the domestic migration of these two populations. For the population under age 65, they use person-level data from individual federal tax returns to estimate net domestic migration. They use medicare enrollment data to calculate measures of migration for the population age 65 and over because this population is not always well represented on tax returns. County total population estimates are the sum of the estimates of the population under age 65 and age 65 years and over.

State and county estimates may also incorporate other changes due to corrections made since the 2010 census. The corrections occur outside the component estimation framework and are the result of successful local challenges or special censuses.

Natural increase. Births minus deaths. The rate of natural increase expresses natural increase during a time period as a percentage of an area's population at the midpoint of the time period.

Net international migration. Any change of residence across the borders of the United States (50 states and District of Columbia). The Census Bureau makes estimates of net international migration for the nation, states, and counties. They estimate net international migration in four parts: (1) net international migration of the foreign born, (2) net migration between the United States and Puerto Rico, (3) net migration of natives to and from the United States, and (4) net movement of the Armed Forces population between the United States and overseas. The largest component, net international migration of the foreign born, includes lawful permanent residents (immigrants), temporary migrants (such as students), humanitarian migrants (such as refugees), and people illegally present in the United States. Currently, they do not estimate these components individually.

Net Domestic Migration. The difference between domestic in-migration to an area and domestic out-migration from the same area during a time period. Domestic in- and out-migration consist of moves where both the origin and the destination are within the United States (excluding Puerto Rico).

Percentage population change is the difference between the population of an area at the beginning and end of a time period, expressed as a percentage of the beginning population.

Table B-3. Population by Age, Race, and Hispanic origin

Sources: U.S. Census Bureau, "*Annual County Resident Population Estimates by Age, Sex, Race and Hispanic Origin: April 1, 2010 to July 1, 20151*," see http://www.census.gov/data/datasets/2015/demo/popest/counties-detail.html.

Age, sex, and race estimates are based on the distributed cohort component method. For an overview, see http://www.census.gov/programs-surveys/popest/technical-documentation.html.

Age. The age classification is based on the age of the person in complete years as of July 1. The age of the person usually was derived from their date of birth information.

Race. The concept of race, as used by the Census Bureau, reflects self-identification by people according to the race or races with which they most closely identify. These categories are sociopolitical constructs and should not be interpreted as being scientific or anthropological in nature. Furthermore, the race categories include both racial and national-origin groups. Caution must be used when interpreting changes in the racial composition of the U.S. population over time. The racial classifications used by the Census Bureau adhere to the December 15, 2000 (revised from October 30, 1997), *Federal Register Notice* entitled, "Revisions to the Standards for the Classification of Federal Data on Race and Ethnicity" issued by the OMB, www.census.gov/population/race/. These standards govern the categories used to collect and present federal data on race and ethnicity. The OMB required federal agencies to use a minimum of five race categories: White, Black or African American, American Indian and Alaska Native, Asian, and Native Hawaiian and Other Pacific Islander. For respondents unable to identify with any of these five race categories, the OMB approved including a sixth category "Some other race."

The Census 2010 question on race included three areas where respondents could write in a more specific race group. The response categories and write-in answers can be combined to create the five minimum OMB race categories plus "Some other race." People who responded to the question on race by indicating only one race are referred to as the race alone population or the group that reported only one race category.

White. A person having origins in any of the original peoples of Europe, the Middle East, or North Africa. It includes people who indicate their race as "White" or report entries such as Irish, German, Italian, Lebanese, Near Easterner, Arab, or Polish.

Black or African American. A person having origins in any of the Black racial groups of Africa. It includes people who indicate their race as "Black, African American, or Negro," or who provide written entries such as African American, Afro American, Kenyan, Nigerian, or Haitian.

American Indian and Alaska Native. A person having origins in any of the original peoples of North and South America including Central America, and who maintain tribal affiliation or community attachment. It includes people who classify themselves as described below.

American Indian. Includes people who indicate their race as "American Indian," entered the name of an Indian tribe, or report such entries as Canadian Indian, French-American Indian, or Spanish-American Indian.

Alaska Native. Includes written responses of Eskimos, Aleuts, and Alaska Indians as well as entries such as Arctic Slope, Inupiat, Yupik, Alutiiq, Egeik, and Pribilovian. The Alaska tribes are the Alaskan Athabascan, Tlingit, and Haida.

Asian. A person having origins in any of the original peoples of the Far East, Southeast Asia, or the Indian subcontinent including Cambodia, China, India, Japan, Korea, Malaysia, Pakistan, the Philippine Islands, Thailand, and Vietnam. It includes "Asian Indian," "Chinese," "Filipino," "Korean," "Japanese," "Vietnamese," and "Other Asian."

Asian Indian includes people who indicate their race as "Asian Indian" or identify themselves as Bengalese, Bharat, Dravidian, East Indian, or Goanese. *Chinese* includes people who indicate their race as "Chinese" or who identify themselves as Cantonese or Chinese American. In some census tabulations, written entries of Taiwanese are included with Chinese while in others they are shown separately. *Filipino* includes people who indicate their race as "Filipino" or who report entries such as Philipano, Philipine, or Filipino American. *Japanese* includes people who indicate their race as "Japanese" or who report entries such as Nipponese or Japanese American. *Korean* includes people who indicate their race as "Korean" or who provide a response of Korean American. *Vietnamese* includes people who indicate their race as "Vietnamese" or who provide a response of Vietnamese American.

Native Hawaiian and Other Pacific Islander. A person having origins in any of the original peoples of Hawaii, Guam, Samoa, or other Pacific Islands. It includes people who indicate their race as "Native Hawaiian," "Guamanian or Chamorro," "Samoan," and "Other Pacific Islander."

Native Hawaiian includes people who indicate their race as "Native Hawaiian" or who identify themselves as "Part Hawaiian" or "Hawaiian." *Guamanian or Chamorro* includes people who indicate their race as such, including written entries of Chamorro or Guam. *Samoan* includes people who indicate their race as "Samoan" or who identified themselves as American Samoan or Western Samoan. *Other Pacific Islander* includes people who provided a write-in response of a Pacific Islander group such as Tahitian, Northern Mariana Islander, Palauan, Fijian, or a cultural group, such as Melanesian, Micronesian, or Polynesian.

Hispanic or Latino origin. People who identify with the terms "Hispanic" or "Latino" are those who classify themselves in one of the specific Hispanic or Latino categories listed on the questionnaire—"Mexican," "Puerto Rican," or "Cuban"—as well as those who indicate that they are "other Spanish, Hispanic, or Latino." Origin can be viewed as the heritage, nationality group, lineage, or country of birth of the person or the person's parents or ancestors before their arrival in the United States. People who identify their origin as Spanish, Hispanic, or Latino may be of any race.

Table B-4. Migration and Commuting, 2015

Source: U.S. Census Bureau, American Community Survey, "C07201: Geographical Mobility in the Past Year for Current Residence—Metropolitan Statistical Area Level in the United States, 2015"; "B08604: Worker Population for Workplace Geography, 2015"; "B08016: Place of Work for Workers 16 years Old and Over—Metropolitan Statistical Area Level, 2009-2011"; S2301: Employment Status"; " B08136: Aggregate Travel Time to Work (in minutes) of Workers by Means of Transportation to Work, 2015"; C08301: Means of Transportation to Work, 2015. //factfinder2.census.gov.

Residence one year ago. For the American Community Survey, people who had moved from another residence in the United States or Puerto Rico 1 year earlier were asked to report the exact address (number and street name); the name of the city, town, or post office; the name of the U.S. county or municipio in Puerto Rico; state or Puerto Rico; and the ZIP Code where they lived 1 year ago. People living outside the United States and Puerto Rico were asked to report the name of the foreign country or U.S. Island Area where they were living 1 year ago.

The tabulation category, "Same house," includes all people 1 year and over who did not move during the

1 year as well as those who had moved and returned to their residence 1 year ago. The category, "Different house in the United States" includes people who lived in the United States 1 year ago but in a different house or apartment from the one they occupied at the time of interview. These movers are then further subdivided according to the type of move. In most tabulations, movers within the U.S. are divided into three groups according to their previous residence: "Different house, same county," "Different county, same state," and "Different state." The last group may be further subdivided into region of residence 1 year ago. An additional category, "Abroad," includes those whose previous residence was in a foreign country, Puerto Rico, American Samoa, Guam, the Northern Marianas, or the U.S. Virgin Islands, including members of the Armed Forces and their dependents. Residence 1 year ago is used in conjunction with location of current residence to determine the extent of residential mobility of the population and the resulting redistribution of the population across the various states, metropolitan areas, and regions of the country. In Table B-4, the migration refers to the metropolitan areas.

Place of Work. Data were tabulated for workers 16 years old and over, that is, members of the Armed Forces and civilians who were at work during the reference week. Data on place of work refer to the geographic location at which workers carried out their occupational activities during the reference week.

In the American Community Survey, the exact address (number and street name) of the place of work was asked, as well as the place (city, town, or post office); whether the place of work was inside or outside the limits of that city or town; and the county, state or foreign country, and ZIP Code. If the respondent's employer operated in more than one location, the exact address of the location or branch where he or she worked was requested. When the number and street name were unknown, a description of the location, such as the building name or nearest street or intersection, was to be entered. People who worked at more than one location during the reference week were asked to report the location at which they worked the greatest number of hours. People who regularly worked in several locations each day during the reference week were requested to give the address at which they began work each day. For cases in which daily work did not begin at a central place each day, the respondent was asked to provide as much information as possible to describe the area in which he or she worked most during the reference week.

Employment/residence ratio. The employment/residence ratio is a measure of the total number of workers working in an area or place, relative to the total number of workers living in the area or place. It is often used as a rough indication of the jobs-workers balance in an area/place, although it does not take into account whether the resident workers possess the skills needed for the jobs available in their particular area/place. The employment/residence ratio is calculated by dividing the number of total workers working in an area/place by the number of total workers residing in the area/place. When the ratio is greater than 1.00, there are more workers coming into the metropolitan area. When the ratio is less than 1.00, more of the metropolitan area residents commute to jobs outside of the area.

Means of Transportation to Work. Means of transportation to work refers to the principal mode of travel or type of conveyance that the worker usually used to get from home to work during the reference week.

People who used different means of transportation on different days of the week were asked to specify the one they used most often, that is, the greatest number of days. People who used more than one means of transportation to get to work each day were asked to report the one used for the longest distance during the work trip. The category, "Car, truck, or van," includes workers using a car (including company cars but excluding taxicabs), a truck of one-ton capacity or less, or a van.

Private Vehicle Occupancy. Private vehicle occupancy refers to the number of people who usually rode to work in the vehicle during the reference week. The category, "Drove alone," includes people who usually drove alone to work as well as people who were driven to work by someone who then drove back home or to a non-work destination.

Mean Travel Time to Work (in Minutes). Mean travel time to work (in minutes) is the average travel time that workers usually took to get from home to work (one way) during the reference week. This measure is obtained by dividing the total number of minutes taken to get from home to work (the aggregate travel time) by the number of workers 16 years old and over who did not work at home. The travel time includes time spent waiting for public transportation, picking up passengers and carpools, and time spent in other activities related to getting to work. The aggregate travel time to work used to calculate mean travel time to work is rounded to the nearest tenth of a minute.

Table B-5. Population and Household Characteristics 2015

Source: U.S. Census Bureau, American Community Survey, "DP02. Selected Social Characteristics in the United States: 2015." //factfinder2.census.gov.

Household. A household includes all the people who occupy a housing unit as their usual place of residence.

Family household. A family includes a householder and one or more people living in the same household who are related to the householder by birth, marriage, or adoption. All people in a household who are related to the householder are regarded as members of his or her family. A family household may contain people not related to the householder, but those people are not included as part of the householder's family in census tabulations. Thus, the number of family households is equal to the number of families, but family households may include more members than do families. A household can contain only one family for purposes of census tabulations. Not all households contain families since a household may comprise a group of unrelated people or one person living alone.

Single-parent household. A family household with own children of the householder, with a male householder with no wife present or a female householder with no husband present.

Foreign-born population. The Census Bureau separates the U.S. resident population into two groups based on whether or not a person was a U.S. citizen at the time of birth. Anyone born in the United States or U.S. Island Area (such as Puerto Rico) or born abroad to a U.S. citizen parent is a U.S. citizen at the time of birth and consequently included in the *native population*. The term *foreign-born population* refers to anyone who is not a U.S. citizen at birth. This includes naturalized U.S. citizens, legal permanent resident aliens (immigrants), temporary migrants (such as students), humanitarian migrants (such as refugees), and people illegally present in the United States. Non-citizens are foreign-born individuals who have not become naturalized U.S. citizens.

Language Spoken at Home by the Respondent. The American community Survey asked about languages spoken at home in an effort to measure the current use of languages other than English. This category included persons 5 years old and over and excluded respondents who spoke a language other than English exclusively outside of the home.

Table B-6. Enrollment, Teachers, and Educational Attainment

Sources: Enrollment, number of teachers, and pupil/teacher ratio—National Center for Education Statistics, Common Core of Data, https://nces.ed.gov/ccd/elsi/; Educational attainment—U.S. Census Bureau, American Community Survey, "DP02. Selected Social Characteristics in the United States: 2009–2011." //factfinder2.census.gov.

Enrollment, teachers, and pupil/teacher ratio. The Common Core of Data (CCD) is the Department of Education's primary database on public elementary and secondary education in the United States. CCD is a comprehensive, annual, national statistical database of all public elementary and secondary schools and school districts, which contains data that are designed to be comparable across all states.

The objectives of the CCD are twofold: first, to provide an official listing of public elementary and secondary schools and school districts in the nation, which can be used to select samples for other NCES surveys. And second, to provide basic information and descriptive statistics on public elementary and secondary schools and schooling in general.

The CCD survey annually collects data about all public elementary and secondary schools, all local education agencies, and all state education agencies throughout the United States. CCD contains three categories of information: general descriptive information on schools and school districts; data on students and staff; and fiscal data. Much of the data are obtained from administrative records maintained by the state education agencies (SEAs) (the State survey), but there are also surveys of the School Districts and the individual schools.

The numbers of students enrolled in public schools and full-time equivalent teachers are provided by the schools in the school survey.

Educational Attainment. Educational attainment data in this table include persons who are 25 years old and over. In the American Community Survey, respondents are classified according to the highest degree or the highest level of school completed. The question included instructions for persons currently enrolled in school to report the level of the previous grade attended or the highest degree received. The category "High School Graduate or Less" includes people whose highest degree was a high school diploma or its equivalent, and people who had not graduated from high school. The category "Bachelor's degree or higher" includes those who received a bachelor's, master's, or professional or doctorate degree.

Table B-7. Median Income, Household Income Distribution, and Poverty Status: 2015

Source: U.S. Census Bureau, American Community Survey, "DP03. Selected Economic Characteristics in the United States: 2015"; factfinder2.census.gov.

Income. Total income is the sum of the amounts reported separately for wage or salary income; net self-employment income; interest, dividends, or net rental or royalty income or income from estates and trusts; Social Security or Railroad Retirement income; Supplemental Security Income (SSI); public assistance or welfare payments; retirement, survivor, or disability pensions; and all other income. Receipts from the following sources are not included as income: capital gains, money received from the sale of property (unless the recipient was engaged in the business of selling such property); the value of income "in kind" from food stamps, public housing subsidies, medical care, employer contributions for individuals, etc.; withdrawal of bank deposits; money borrowed; tax refunds; exchange of money between relatives living in the same household; gifts and lump-sum inheritances, insurance payments, and other types of lump-sum receipts.

Median income divides the income distribution into two equal parts: one-half of the cases falling below the median income and one-half above the median. For households and families, the median income is based on the distribution of the total number of households and families including those with no income. The median income for individuals is based on individuals 15 years old and over with income. Median income for households, families, and individuals is computed on the basis of a standard distribution. Median income is rounded to the nearest whole dollar. Median income figures are calculated using linear interpolation if the width of the interval containing the estimate is $2,500 or less. If the width of the interval containing the estimate is greater than $2,500, Pareto interpolation is used.

Income of households includes the income of the householder and all other individuals 15 years old and over. In compiling statistics on family and household income, the incomes of all persons 15 years old and over in the household (or family) are summed and treated as a single amount. Although the income statistics cover the past 12 months, the characteristics of individuals and the composition of families refer to the time of enumeration. Thus, the income of the family or household does not include amounts received by individuals who were members of the family or household during all or part of the past 12 months if these individuals no longer resided with the family at the time of enumeration. Similarly, income amounts reported by individuals who did not reside with the family or in the household during the past 12 months but who were members of the family or household at the time of enumeration are included. However, the composition of most families and most households was the same during the past 12 months as at the time of interview.

Poverty status is determined using thresholds arranged in a two-dimensional matrix. The matrix consists of family size cross-classified by presence and number of family members under age 18 years old. Unrelated individuals and two-person families are further differentiated by age of reference person. To determine a person's poverty status, one compares the person's total family income in the last 12 months with the poverty threshold appropriate for that person's family size and composition. If the total income of that person's family is less than the threshold appropriate for that family, then the person is considered poor or "below the poverty level," together with every member of his or her family. If a person is not living with anyone related by birth, marriage, or adoption, then the person's own income is compared with his or her poverty threshold. The total number of people below the poverty level was the sum of people in families and the number of unrelated individuals with incomes in the last 12 months below the poverty level. The average poverty threshold for a family of four in 2015 was $24,257. See https://www.census.gov/data/tables/time-series/demo/income-poverty/historical-poverty-thresholds.html for detailed poverty thresholds.

Table B-8. Health Insurance, Disability, Medicare, Social Security, and Supplemental Security Income

Sources: Persons with no health insurance—U.S. Census Bureau, American Community Survey, "DP03. Selected Economic Characteristics in the United States: 2015." Persons with a disability—U.S. Census Bureau, American Community Survey, "B18101. Sex by Age by Disablitiy Status: 2015." factfinder2.census.gov. Affordable Care Act Enrollment and Medicare program enrollment—Centers for Medicare and Medicaid Services, CMS Statistics: Marketplace Products, https://www.cms.gov/Research-Statistics-Data-and-Systems/Statistics-Trends-and-Reports/Marketplace-Products/Plan_Selections_County. html. Medicare Enrollment Dashboard, https://www.cms.gov/Research-Statistics-Data-and-Systems/Statistics-Trends-and-Reports/CMSProgramStatistics/Dashboard. html. Social Security—U.S. Social Security Administration, Office of Research and Statistics, OASDI Beneficiaries by State and County, www.ssa.gov/policy/docs/statcomps/oasdi_sc/2015/index.html. Supplemental security income—U.S. Social Security Administration, Office of Research, Evaluation, and Statistics, SSI Recipients by State and County, www.ssa.gov/policy/docs/statcomps/ssi_sc/2015/index.html.

Health Insurance. In the American Community Survey, respondents were instructed to report their current coverage for each of eight types of health insurance: Insurance through a current or former employer or union (of this person or another family member); Insurance purchased directly from an insurance company (by this person or another family member); Medicare, for people 65 and older, or people with certain disabilities; Medicaid,

Medical Assistance, or any kind of government-assistance plan for those with low incomes or a disability; TRICARE or other military health care; VA (including those who have ever used or enrolled for VA health care); Indian Health Service; or any other type of health insurance or health coverage plan.

Disability status. Disability is defined as the product of interactions among individuals' bodies; their physical, emotional, and mental health; and the physical and social environment in which they live, work, or play. Disability exists where this interaction results in limitations of activities and restrictions to full participation at school, at work, at home, or in the community. For example, disability may exist where a person is limited in their ability to work due to job discrimination against persons with specific health conditions; or, disability may exist where a child has difficulty learning because the school cannot accommodate the child's deafness. In an attempt to capture a variety of characteristics that encompass the definition of disability, the ACS identifies serious difficulty with four basic areas of functioning–hearing, vision, cognition, and ambulation.

Affordable Care Act enrollment. The number of persons enrolled through the Affordable Care Act includes the total number of unique individuals who have a non-cancelled plan selection with March 2016 coverage for the 38 states that used the HealthCare.gov platform, including the Federally-facilitated Marketplace, State Partnership Marketplaces and supported State-based Marketplaces. Plan selections occurred during the open enrollment period from November 1, 2015 through January 31, 2016, including additional special enrollment period activity reported through February 1, 2016.

The county numbers have been aggregated to metropolitan areas. Data are not available for metropolitan areas that are completely or primarily in states that have their own Healthcare marketplaces: California, Colorado, Connecticut, the District of Columbia, Hawaii, Idaho, Kentucky, Maryland, Massachusetts, Minnesota. Nevada, New Mexico, New York, Oregon, Rhode Island, Vermont, and Washington.

Medicare enrollment. When first implemented in 1966, Medicare covered only most persons age 65 and over. By the end of 1966, 3.7 million persons had received at least some health care services covered by Medicare. In 1973, other groups became eligible for Medicare benefits: persons who are entitled to social security or Railroad Retirement disability benefits for at least 24 months; persons with end stage renal disease (ESRD) requiring continuing dialysis or kidney transplant; and certain otherwise non-covered aged persons who elect to buy into Medicare.

Medicare consists of two primary parts: Hospital Insurance (HI), also known as Part A, and Supplementary Medical Insurance (SMI), also known as Part B. Health care services covered under Medicare's Hospital Insurance include inpatient hospital care, skilled nursing facility care, home health agency care, and hospice care. SMI coverage is optional and requires payment of a monthly premium.

The enrollment counts are determined using a person-year methodology, calculated by summing the total number of months that each person is enrolled and dividing by 12.

Social Security

The Old-Age, Survivors, and Disability Insurance Program (OASDI) provides monthly benefits for retired and disabled insured workers and their dependents and to survivors of insured workers. To be eligible for benefits, a worker must have had a specified period of employment in which OASDI taxes were paid. A worker becomes eligible for full retirement benefits at age 65 through 67 (depending on the year of birth), although reduced benefits may be obtained at age 62; the worker's spouse is under the same limitations. Survivor benefits are payable to dependents of deceased insured workers. Disability benefits are payable to an insured worker under age 65 with a prolonged disability and to that person's dependents on the same basis as dependents of a retired worker. Also, disability benefits are payable at age 50 to the disabled widow or widower of a deceased worker who was fully insured at the time of death. A lump-sum benefit is generally payable on the death of an insured worker to a spouse or minor children.

The data were derived from the Master Beneficiary Record (MBR), the principal administrative file of social security beneficiaries. Data for total recipients and retired workers include persons with special age-72 benefits. Special age-72 benefit represents the monthly benefit payable to men who attained age-72 before 1972 and for women who attained age 72 before 1970 and who do not have sufficient quarters to qualify for a retired-worker benefit under either the fully or the transitionally insured status provision.

Supplemental security income. The Supplemental Security Income (SSI) program provides cash payments in accordance with nationwide eligibility requirements to people with limited income and resources who are aged, blind, or disabled. Under the SSI program, each person living in his or her own household is provided a cash payment from the federal government that is sufficient, when added to the person's countable income (the total gross money income of an individual less certain exclusions), to bring the total monthly income up to a specified level (the federal benefit rate). If the individual or couple is living in another household, the guaranteed level is reduced by one-third.

An aged person is defined as an individual who is 65 years old or over. A blind person is anyone with vision of 20/200 or less with the use of correcting lens in the better eye or with tunnel vision of 20 degrees or less. The disabled classification refers to any person unable to engage in any substantial gainful activity by reason of any medically determinable physical or mental impairment expected to result in death or that has lasted or can be expected to last for a continuous period of at least 12 months. For a child under 18 years, eligibility is based on disability or severity comparable with that of an adult, since the criterion of "substantial gainful activity" is inapplicable for children.

Table B-9. Housing Units and Building Permits

Sources: Housing units—U.S. Census Bureau, "Annual Estimates of Housing Units for the United States, Regions, Divisions, States, and Counties: April 1, 2010 to July 1, 2015 "https://www.census.gov/data/tables/2015/demo/popest/total-housing-units.html; "Intercensal Estimates of Housing Units for Counties and States: April 1, 2000 to July 1, 2010"; https://www.census.gov/data/datasets/time-series/demo/popest/intercensal-2000-2010-housing-units.html. Building permits—U.S. Census Bureau, Annual New Privately-Owned Residential Building Permits: Permits by county or metropolitan area 2010 and 2015. www.census.gov/construction/bps/.

Housing unit estimates are developed by using building permits, mobile home shipments, and estimates of housing unit loss to measure housing unit change since the last census. For more information see www.census.gov/programs-surveys/popest.html.

Building permits data are based on reports submitted by local building permit officials in response to a Census Bureau mail survey. They are obtained using Form C-404, "Report of New Privately Owned Residential Building or Zoning Permits Issued." Data are collected from individual permit offices, most of which are municipalities; the remainder are counties, townships, or New England and Middle Atlantic-type towns. Currently, there are 20,000 permit-issuing places. When a report is not received, missing data are either (1) obtained from the Survey of Use of Permits, which is used to collect information on housing starts, or (2) imputed.

The data relate to new private housing units intended for occupancy on a housekeeping basis. They exclude mobile homes (trailers), hotels, motels, and group residential structures, such as nursing homes and college dormitories. They also exclude conversions of and alterations to existing buildings. A housing unit consists of a room or group of rooms intended for occupancy as separate living quarters by a family, by a group of unrelated persons living together, or by a person living alone.

Table B-10. Housing Units: 2015

Source: U.S. Census Bureau, American Community Survey, "DP04. Selected Housing Characteristics: 2015." factfinder.census.gov/.

A housing unit is a house, apartment, mobile home or trailer, group of rooms, or single room occupied or, if vacant, intended for occupancy as separate living quarters. Separate living quarters are those in which the occupants do not live and eat with any other persons in the structure and which have direct access from the outside of the building or through a common hall. A housing unit is classified as occupied if it is the usual place of residence of the person or group of people living in it at the time of census enumeration or if the occupants are only temporarily absent; that is, away on vacation or business. All occupied housing units are classified as either owner occupied or renter occupied. A housing unit is owner occupied if the owner or co-owner lives in the unit even if it is mortgaged or not fully paid for. All occupied housing units that are not owner occupied, whether they are rented for cash rent or occupied without payment of cash rent, are classified as renter occupied.

One-unit detached is a one-unit structure detached from any other house, that is, with open space on all four sides. Such structures are considered detached even if they have an adjoining shed or garage. A one-family house that contains a business is considered detached as long as the building has open space on all four sides. Mobile homes to which one or more permanent rooms have been added or built also are included.

Ownership rate is computed by dividing the number of owner-occupied housing units by the number of occupied housing units. A housing unit is **owner-occupied** if the owner or co-owner lives in the unit even if it is mortgaged or not fully paid for. The owner or co-owner must live in the unit. The unit is owner-occupied if someone who lives in the household is purchasing the house with a mortgage or some other debt arrangement such as a deed of trust, trust deed, contract to purchase, land contract, or purchase agreement. The unit also is considered owned with a mortgage if it is built on leased land and there is a mortgage on the unit. Mobile homes occupied by owners with installment loan balances also are included in this category.

Selected monthly owner costs were obtained for owner-occupied units. Selected monthly owner costs are the sum of payments for mortgages, deeds of trust, contracts to purchase, or similar debts on the property (including payments for the first mortgage, second mortgages, home equity loans, and other junior mortgages); real estate taxes; fire, hazard, and flood insurance on the property; utilities (electricity, gas, and water and sewer); and fuels (oil, coal, kerosene, wood, etc.). It also includes, where appropriate, the monthly condominium fee for condominiums and mobile home costs (installment loan payments, personal property taxes, site rent, registration fees, and license fees). Selected monthly owner costs were tabulated for all owner-occupied units, and usually are shown separately for units "with a mortgage" and for units "not mortgaged." Table B-10 includes only those units with a mortgage.

To inflate selected monthly owner costs from previous years, the dollar values are inflated to the latest year's dollar values by multiplying by a factor equal to the average annual Consumer Price Index (CPI-U-RS) factor for the current year, divided by the average annual CPI-U-RS factor for the earliest year.

Median Selected Monthly Owner Costs divides the selected monthly owner costs distribution into two equal parts: one-half of the cases falling below the median selected monthly owner costs and one-half above the median.

Monthly rent refers to the **gross rent** which is the contract rent plus the estimated average monthly cost of utilities (electricity, gas, and water and sewer) and fuels (oil, coal, kerosene, wood, etc.) if these are paid by the renter (or paid for the renter by someone else). Gross rent is intended to eliminate differentials that result from varying practices with respect to the inclusion of utilities and fuels as part of the rental payment. The estimated costs of water and sewer, and fuels are reported on a 12-month basis but are converted to monthly figures for the tabulations.

Vehicles available. The question on vehicles available was asked at occupied housing units. These data show the number of passenger cars, vans, and pickup or panel trucks of one-ton capacity or less kept at home and available for the use of household members. Vehicles rented or leased for one month or more, company vehicles, and police and government vehicles are included if kept at home and used for non-business purposes. Dismantled or immobile vehicles are excluded. Vehicles kept at home but used only for business purposes also are excluded.

Table B-11. Personal Income and Earnings by Place of Work

Sources: U.S. Bureau of Economic Analysis, Regional Economic Accounts, Local Area Personal Income and Employment, www.bea.gov/regional/index.htm.

Personal income is the income that is received by all persons from all sources. It is calculated as the sum of wage and salary disbursements, supplements to wages and salaries, proprietors' income with inventory valuation and capital consumption adjustments, rental income of people with capital consumption adjustment, personal dividend income, personal interest income, and personal current transfer receipts, less contributions for government social insurance.

The personal income of an area is the income that is received by, or on behalf of, all the individuals who live in the area; therefore, the estimates of personal income are presented by the place of residence of the income recipients.

Personal income differs by definition from money income, which is prepared by the Census Bureau, in that money income is measured before deduction of personal contributions for social insurance and does not include imputed income, lump-sum payments, and income received by quasi-individuals. Money income does include income from private pensions and annuities and from interpersonal transfer, such as child support; therefore it is not comparable to personal income. Total personal income is adjusted to place of residence.

About 90 percent of the state and county estimates of personal income are based on census data and on administrative-records data that are collected by other federal agencies. The data from censuses are mainly collected from the recipient of the income. The most important sources of census data for the state and county estimates are the census of agriculture and the census of population and housing that are conducted by the Census Bureau. The data from administrative records may originate either from the recipients of the income or from the source of the income. These data are a byproduct of the administration of various federal and state government programs. The most important sources of these data are as follows: the state unemployment insurance programs of the Employment and Training Administration, Department of Labor; the social insurance programs of the Social Security Administration and the Health Care Financing Administration, Department of Health and Human Services; the federal income tax program of the Internal Revenue Service, Department of the Treasury; the veterans benefit programs of the Department of Veterans Affairs; and the military payroll systems of the Department of Defense. The remaining 10 percent of the estimates are based on data from other sources. For example, the estimates of the components of farm proprietors' income, a component of personal income, are partly based on the state estimates of farm income and the county estimates of case receipts, crop production, and livestock inventory that are prepared by the

Department of Agriculture, which uses sample surveys, along with census data and administrative-records data, to derive its estimates.

Total **earnings** cover wage and salary disbursements, supplements to wages and salaries, and proprietor's income. Wage and salary disbursements consists of the monetary remuneration of employees, including corporate officers salaries and bonuses, commissions, pay-in-kind, incentive payments, and tips. It reflects the amount of payments disbursed, but not necessarily earned during the year. It is measured before deductions, such as social security contributions and union dues. Wage and salary disbursements includes stock options of nonqualified plans at the time that they have been exercised by the individual. Stock options are reported in wage and salary disbursements. The value that is included in wages is the difference between the exercise price and the price that the stock options were granted. Supplements to wages and salaries consists of employer contributions for employee pension and insurance funds and of employer contributions for government social insurance. Proprietor's income is the current-production income (including income in kind) of sole proprietorships and partnerships and of tax-exempt cooperatives. Corporate directors' fees are included in proprietors' income, but the imputed net rental income of owner-occupants of all dwellings is included in rental income of persons. Proprietors' income excludes dividends and monetary interest received by nonfinancial business and rental incomes received by persons not primarily engaged in the real estate business; these incomes are included in dividends, net interest, and rental income of persons, respectively.

Table B-12. Employees and Earnings by Selected Major Industries: 2015

Sources: U.S. Bureau of Economic Analysis, Regional Economic Accounts, Local Area Personal Income and Employment, www.bea.gov/regional/index.htm.

The estimates of employment and earnings from 2015 are based on the 2012 North American Industry Classification System (NAICS). For more information on NAICS please visit https://www.census.gov/eos/www/naics/.

The BEA employment series for states and local areas comprises estimates of the number of jobs, full-time plus part-time, by place of work. Full-time and part-time jobs are counted at equal weight. Employees, sole proprietors, and active partners are included, but unpaid family workers and volunteers are not included.

Earnings by place of work is the sum of Wage and Salary Disbursements, supplements to wages and salaries and proprietors' income.

Table B-13. Civilian Labor Force and Banking

Sources: Civilian labor force, U.S. Bureau of Labor Statistics (BLS), *Local Area Unemployment Statistics, Annual Averages,* www.bls.gov/lau/.

Civilian Labor Force

Civilian labor force data are the product of a federal-state cooperative program in which state employment security agencies prepare labor force and unemployment estimates under concepts, definitions, and technical procedures established by the BLS. These data for substate areas are produced by the BLS primarily for use in allocating funds under various federal legislative programs. Users of these data are cautioned that, because of the small size of many of the areas, as well as limitations of the data inputs, the estimates are subject to considerable, but nonquantifiable, error. An explanation of the technical procedures used to develop monthly and annual local area labor force estimates appears monthly in the Explanatory Note for state and area unemployment data in the BLS periodical, *Employment and Earnings.* Additional information may also be found at the BLS Web site at www.bls.gov/opub/hom/.

The civilian labor force comprises all persons in the civilian noninstitutional population classified as either employed or unemployed. Employed persons are persons 16 years and over in the civilian noninstitutional population who, during the reference week, (a) did any work at all (at least 1 hour) as paid employees; worked in their own business, profession, or on their own farm, or worked 15 hours or more as unpaid workers in an enterprise operated by a member of the family; and (b) all those who were not working but who had jobs or businesses from which they were temporarily absent because of vacation, illness, bad weather, childcare problems, maternity or paternity leave, labor-management dispute, job training, or other family or personal reasons, whether or not they were paid for the time off or were seeking other jobs. Each employed person is counted only once, even if he or she holds more than one job. Excluded are persons whose only activity consisted of work around their own house (painting, repairing, or own home housework) or volunteer work for religious, charitable, and other organizations.

Unemployed people are all civilians aged 16 years and older who had no employment during the reference week, were available for work, except for temporary illness, and had made specific efforts to find employment sometime during the 4-week period ending with the reference week. Persons who were waiting to be recalled to a job from which they had been laid off need not have been looking for work to be classified as unemployed.

The unemployment rate for all civilian workers represents the number of unemployed as a percent of the civilian labor force.

Table B-14. Banking, Government Employment, and Private Business Establishments and Employment

Sources: Banking—U.S. Federal Deposit Insurance Corporation (FDIC), www2.fdic.gov/sod/index.asp. Government Employment—U.S. Bureau of Economic Analysis—Regional Economic Accounts, http://www.bea.gov/regional/index.htm#state; Private nonfarm business—County Business Patterns, www.census.gov/econ/cbp/index.html.

Banking. The FDIC and OTS collect deposit data on each office of every FDIC-insured bank and saving association as of June 30 of each year in the Summary of Deposits (SOD) survey. The FDIC surveys all FDIC-insured commercial banks, savings banks, and U.S. branches of foreign banks, and the OTS surveys all savings associations. Data presented here exclude U.S. branch offices of foreign banks. For all counties, individual banking offices—not the combined totals of the bank—are the source of the data.

Insured **savings institutions** include all FDIC-insured (OTS-Regulated and FDIC-Regulated) financial institutions that operate under federal or state banking charters. The number of **banking offices** in any given area includes every location at which deposit business is transacted. Banking office is defined to include all offices and facilities that actually hold deposits, but to exclude loan production offices, computer centers, and other non-deposit installations, such as automated teller machines (ATMs). The term "offices" includes both main offices and branches. An institution with four branches operates a total of five offices.

Government Employment. Employment is measured as the average annual sum of full-time and part-time jobs. The estimates are on a place-of-work basis. State and local government employment includes person employed in all state and local government agencies and enterprises. Data for federal civilian employment include civilian employees of the federal government, including civilian employees of the Department of Defense. Military employment includes all persons on active duty status.

County Business Patterns (CBP) is an annual series that provides subnational economic data by industry. The series is useful for studying the economic activity of small areas; analyzing economic changes over time; and as a benchmark for statistical series, surveys, and databases between economic censuses. CBP covers most of the country's economic activity. The series excludes data on self-employed individuals, employees of private households, railroad employees, agricultural production employees, and most government employees. The County Business Patterns program has tabulated on a North American Industry Classification System (NAICS) basis since 1998. Data for 1997 and earlier years are based on the Standard Industrial Classification (SIC) system. For more information on the relationship between the two systems, see Concordances www.census.gov/eos/www/naics/concordances/concordances.html.

CBP data are extracted from the Business Register, the Census Bureau's file of all known single and multiestablishment companies. The Annual Company Organization Survey and quinquennial economic censuses provide individual establishment data for multilocation firms. Data for single-location firms are obtained from various programs censuses, the Annual Survey of Manufactures, and Current Business Surveys, as well as from administrative records of the Internal Revenue Service (IRS), the Social Security Administration (SSA), and the Bureau of Labor Statistics (BLS).

An **establishment** is a single physical location at which business is conducted or services or industrial operations are performed. It is not necessarily identical with a company or enterprise, which may consist of one or more establishments. When two or more activities are carried on at a single location under a single ownership, all activities generally are grouped together as a single establishment. The entire establishment is classified on the basis of its major activity and all data are included in that classification. Establishment-size designations are determined by paid employment in the mid-March pay period. The size group "1 to 4" includes establishments that did not report any paid employees in the mid-March pay period but paid wages to at least one employee at some time during the year.

Establishment counts represent the number of locations with paid employees any time during the year. This series excludes governmental establishments except for wholesale liquor establishments (NAICS 4248), retail liquor stores (NAICS 44531), federally-chartered savings institutions (NAICS 522120), federally-chartered credit unions (NAICS 522130), and hospitals (NAICS 622).

Total payroll includes all forms of compensation, such as salaries, wages, reported tips, commissions, bonuses, vacation allowances, sick-leave pay, employee contributions to qualified pension plans, and the value of taxable fringe benefits. For corporations, it includes amounts paid to officers and executives; for unincorporated businesses, it does not include profit or other compensation of proprietors or partners. Payroll is reported before deductions for social security, income tax, insurance, union dues, etc.

First-quarter payroll consists of payroll during the January-to-March quarter.

Paid employment consists of full- and part-time employees, including salaried officers and executives of corporations, who are on the payroll in the pay period including March 12. Included are employees on paid sick leave, holidays, and vacations; not included are proprietors and partners of unincorporated businesses.

TABLE C. METROPOLITAN AREAS WITH COMPONENT COUNTIES

Table C consists of 4 tables (C-1 through C-4) with 50 data items for 382 metropolitan statistical areas (MSAs), 31 metropolitan divisions (in 11 large metropolitan statistical areas), and 1,167 counties within the metropolitan areas. They are presented alphabetically in each of the 4 tables, with counties listed alphabetically within each metropolitan area.

All summaries, including historical data, are presented for the areas as currently defined. Where possible, the original figures have been retabulated to reflect the status of metropolitan area boundaries as of July 1, 2015. For more information on these areas, see Appendix C, Geographic Concepts and Codes.

Table C-1. Population and Population Characteristics

Sources: Population and change—U.S. Census Bureau, Population Estimates Program, Population and Housing Unit Estimates Datasets. www.census.gov/programs-surveys/popest/data/data-sets.html.

Population numbers for 2010 and 2000 are counts of the resident population on April 1 of those decennial census years. The April 1 estimates base population may differ from the April 1 census count due to legal boundary updates, other geographic program changes, and Count Question Resolution actions.

Population estimates for 2015 measure the estimated population from the calculated number of people living in an area as of July 1. The Census Bureau develops county population estimates with a component of population change method in which they use administrative records and other data to estimate the household and group quarters population. For the household population, the components of population change are births, deaths, net domestic migration, and net international migration. They measure change in the nonhousehold, or group quarters, population by the net change in the population living in group quarters facilities.

A major assumption underlying this approach is that changes in selected administrative and other data sources closely approximate the components of population change. Therefore, Census Bureau demographers separately estimate each component of population change based on administrative records, including registered births and deaths, federal income tax returns, medicare enrollees, and military movement. They also separately estimate net international migration using information from the American Community Survey (ACS), the decennial census, and other data sources.

Most administrative record data sources lag the current estimate year by as much as 2 years. Therefore, the Census Bureau projects the data for the current year based on past years' data. As updated data become available, they revise the projected input data so that each vintage's estimates are always based on the most recent data available.

For more information on the method used for these estimates, see Appendix B, Limitations and Methodology, and the website at http://www.census.gov/programs-surveys/popest/technical-documentation.html.

Age. The age classification is based on the age of the person in complete years as of July 1, 2015. The age of the person usually was derived from their date of birth information.

Table C-2. Population Characteristics and Housing Units

Sources: Population estimates by race and housing unit estimates—U.S. Census Bureau, Population Estimates Program, Population and Housing Unit Estimates Datasets www.census.gov/programs-surveys/popest/data/data-sets.html.

Race. The concept of race, as used by the Census Bureau, reflects self-identification by people according to the race or races with which they most closely identify. These categories are sociopolitical constructs and should not be interpreted as being scientific or anthropological in nature. Furthermore, the race categories include both racial and national-origin groups. Caution must be used when interpreting changes in the racial composition of the U.S. population over time. The racial classifications used by the Census Bureau adhere to the December 15, 2000 (revised from October 30, 1997), *Federal Register Notice* entitled, "Revisions to the Standards for the Classification of Federal Data on Race and Ethnicity" issued by the OMB. These standards govern the categories used to collect and present federal data on race and ethnicity. The OMB required federal agencies to use a minimum of five race categories: White, Black or African American, American Indian and Alaska Native, Asian, and Native

Hawaiian and Other Pacific Islander. For respondents unable to identify with any of these five race categories, the OMB approved including a sixth category "Some other race." See http://www.census.gov/topics/population/race.html.

The Census 2010 question on race included three areas where respondents could write in a more specific race group. The response categories and write-in answers can be combined to create the five minimum OMB race categories plus "Some other race."

People who responded to the question on race by indicating only one race are referred to as the "race alone" population or the group that reported only one race category. Table C-2 uses the "race alone or in combination" categories, which include all people who indicated a particular race, whether or not they indicated other races. Thus, the percentages of the individual groups may add up to more than 100 percent, because individuals can be in more than one group.

White. A person having origins in any of the original peoples of Europe, the Middle East, or North Africa. It includes people who indicate their race as "White" or report entries such as Irish, German, Italian, Lebanese, Near Easterner, Arab, or Polish.

Black or African American. A person having origins in any of the Black racial groups of Africa. It includes people who indicate their race as "Black, African American, or Negro," or who provide written entries such as African American, Afro American, Kenyan, Nigerian, or Haitian.

American Indian and Alaska Native. A person having origins in any of the original peoples of North and South America including Central America, and who maintain tribal affiliation or community attachment. It includes people who classify themselves as described below.

American Indian. Includes people who indicate their race as "American Indian," entered the name of an Indian tribe, or report such entries as Canadian Indian, French-American Indian, or Spanish-American Indian.

Alaska Native. Includes written responses of Eskimos, Aleuts, and Alaska Indians as well as entries such as Arctic Slope, Inupait, Yupik, Alutiiq, Egeik, and Pribilovian. The Alaska tribes are the Alaskan Athabascan, Tlingit, and Haida.

Asian. A person having origins in any of the original peoples of the Far East, Southeast Asia, or the Indian subcontinent including Cambodia, China, India, Japan, Korea, Malaysia, Pakistan, the Philippine Islands, Thailand, and Vietnam. It includes "Asian Indian," "Chinese," "Filipino," "Korean," "Japanese," "Vietnamese," and "Other Asian."

Asian Indian includes people who indicate their race as "Asian Indian" or identify themselves as Bengalese, Bharat, Dravidian, East Indian, or Goanese. *Chinese* includes people who indicate their race as "Chinese" or who identify themselves as Cantonese or Chinese American. In some census tabulations, written entries of Taiwanese are included with Chinese while in others they are shown separately. *Filipino* includes people who indicate their race as "Filipino" or who report entries such as Philipano, Philipine, or Filipino American. *Japanese* includes people who indicate their race as "Japanese" or who report entries such as Nipponese or Japanese American. *Korean* includes people who indicate their race as "Korean" or who provide a response of Korean American. *Vietnamese* includes people who indicate their race as "Vietnamese" or who provide a response of Vietnamese American.

Native Hawaiian and Other Pacific Islander. A person having origins in any of the original peoples of Hawaii, Guam, Samoa, or other Pacific Islands. It includes people who indicate their race as "Native Hawaiian," "Guamanian or Chamorro," "Samoan," and "Other Pacific Islander."

Native Hawaiian includes people who indicate their race as "Native Hawaiian" or who identify themselves as "Part Hawaiian" or "Hawaiian." *Guamanian or Chamorro* includes people who indicate their race as such, including written entries of Chamorro or Guam. *Samoan* includes people who indicate their race as "Samoan" or who identified themselves as American Samoan or Western Samoan. *Other Pacific Islander* includes people who provided a write-in response of a Pacific Islander group such as Tahitian, Northern Mariana Islander, Palauan, Fijian, or a cultural group, such as Melanesian, Micronesian, or Polynesian.

Hispanic or Latino origin. People who identify with the terms "Hispanic" or "Latino" are those who classify themselves in one of the specific Hispanic or Latino categories listed on the questionnaire—"Mexican," "Puerto Rican," or "Cuban"—as well as those who indicate that they are "other Spanish, Hispanic, or Latino." Origin can be viewed as the heritage, nationality group, lineage, or country of birth of the person or the person's parents or ancestors before their arrival in the United States. People who identify their origin as Spanish, Hispanic, or Latino may be of any race.

Housing unit estimates are developed by using building permits, mobile home shipments, and estimates of housing unit loss to measure housing unit change since the last census. For more information see http://www.census.gov/programs-surveys/popest/technical-documentation.html.

Table C-3. Personal Income and Earnings by Industry

Source: Personal income and earnings, U.S. Bureau of Economic Analysis, Regional Economic Accounts, State and Local Area Personal Income, https://bea.gov/regional/index.htm.

Personal income is the income that is received by all persons from all sources. It is calculated as the sum of wage and salary disbursements, supplements to wages and salaries, proprietors' income with inventory valuation and capital consumption adjustments, rental income of people with capital consumption adjustment, personal dividend income, personal interest income, and personal current transfer receipts, less contributions for government social insurance.

The personal income of an area is the income that is received by, or on behalf of, all the individuals who live in the area; therefore, the estimates of personal income are presented by the place of residence of the income recipients.

Personal income differs by definition from money income, which is prepared by the Census Bureau, in that money income is measured before deduction of personal contributions for social insurance and does not include imputed income, lump-sum payments, and income received by quasi-individuals. Money income does include income from private pensions and annuities and from interpersonal transfer, such as child support; therefore it is not comparable to personal income. Total personal income is adjusted to place of residence.

Per Capita personal income is the personal income of a given area divided by the resident population of the area, using the July 1 population estimate of the year shown.

About 90 percent of the state and county estimates of personal income are based on census data and on administrative-records data that are collected by other federal agencies. The data from censuses are mainly collected from the recipient of the income. The most important sources of census data for the state and county estimates are the census of agriculture and the census of population and housing that are conducted by the Census Bureau. The data from administrative records may originate either from the recipients of the income or from the source of the income. These data are a byproduct of the administration of various federal and state government programs. The most important sources of these data are as follows: the state unemployment insurance programs of the Employment and Training Administration,

Department of Labor; the social insurance programs of the Social Security Administration and the Health Care Financing Administration, Department of Health and Human Services; the federal income tax program of the Internal Revenue Service, Department of the Treasury; the veterans benefit programs of the Department of Veterans Affairs; and the military payroll systems of the Department of Defense. The remaining 10 percent of the estimates are based on data from other sources. For example, the estimates of the components of farm proprietors' income, a component of personal income, are partly based on the state estimates of farm income and the county estimates of case receipts, crop production, and livestock inventory that are prepared by the Department of Agriculture, which uses sample surveys, along with census data and administrative-records data, to derive its estimates.

Total **earnings** cover wage and salary disbursements, supplements to wages and salaries, and proprietor's income. Wage and salary disbursements consists of the monetary remuneration of employees, including corporate officers salaries and bonuses, commissions, pay-in-kind, incentive payments, and tips. It reflects the amount of payments disbursed, but not necessarily earned during the year. It is measured before deductions, such as social security contributions and union dues. Wage and salary disbursements includes stock options of nonqualified plans at the time that they have been exercised by the individual. Stock options are reported in wage and salary disbursements. The value that is included in wages is the difference between the exercise price and the price that the stock options were granted. Supplements to wages and salaries consists of employer contributions for employee pension and insurance funds and of employer contributions for government social insurance. Proprietor's income is the current-production income (including income in kind) of sole proprietorships and partnerships and of tax-exempt cooperatives. Corporate directors' fees are included in proprietors' income, but the imputed net rental income of owner-occupants of all dwellings is included in rental income of persons. Proprietors' income excludes dividends and monetary interest received by nonfinancial business and rental incomes received by persons not primarily engaged in the real estate business; these incomes are included in dividends, net interest, and rental income of persons, respectively.

The estimates of earnings from 2015 are based on the 2012 North American Industry Classification System (NAICS). For more information on NAICS please visit http://www.census.gov/eos/www/naics/.

Earnings by place of work is the sum of Wage and Salary Disbursements, supplements to wages and salaries and proprietors' income.

Table C-4. Labor Force and Private Business Establishments and Employment

Sources: Civilian labor force—U.S. Bureau of Labor Statistics, Local Area Unemployment, Annual Averages www.bls.gov/lau/. Private nonfarm businesses—U.S. Census Bureau, County Business Patterns http://www.census.gov/programs-surveys/cbp.html.

Civilian Labor Force

Civilian labor force data are the product of a federal-state cooperative program in which state employment security agencies prepare labor force and unemployment estimates under concepts, definitions, and technical procedures established by the BLS. These data for substate areas are produced by the BLS primarily for use in allocating funds under various federal legislative programs. Users of these data are cautioned that, because of the small size of many of the areas, as well as limitations of the data inputs, the estimates are subject to considerable, but nonquantifiable, error. An explanation of the technical procedures used to develop monthly and annual local area labor force estimates appears monthly in the Explanatory Note for state and area unemployment data in the BLS periodical, *Employment and Earnings*. Additional information may also be found at the BLS Web site at www.bls.gov/opub/hom/.

The civilian labor force comprises all persons in the civilian noninstitutional population classified as either employed or unemployed. Employed persons are persons 16 years and over in the civilian noninstitutional population who, during the reference week, (a) did any work at all (at least 1 hour) as paid employees; worked in their own business, profession, or on their own farm, or worked 15 hours or more as unpaid workers in an enterprise operated by a member of the family; and (b) all those who were not working but who had jobs or businesses from which they were temporarily absent because of vacation, illness, bad weather, childcare problems, maternity or paternity leave, labor-management dispute, job training, or other family or personal reasons, whether or not they were paid for the time off or were seeking other jobs. Each employed person is counted only once, even if he or she holds more than one job. Excluded are persons whose only activity consisted of work around their own house (painting, repairing, or own home housework) or volunteer work for religious, charitable, and other organizations.

Unemployed people are all civilians aged 16 years and older who had no employment during the reference week, were available for work, except for temporary illness, and had made specific efforts to find employment sometime during the 4-week period ending with the reference week.

Persons who were waiting to be recalled to a job from which they had been laid off need not have been looking for work to be classified as unemployed. The unemployment rate for all civilian workers represents the number of unemployed as a percent of the civilian labor force.

County Business Patterns (CBP) is an annual series that provides subnational economic data by industry. The series is useful for studying the economic activity of small areas; analyzing economic changes over time; and as a benchmark for statistical series, surveys, and databases between economic censuses. CBP covers most of the country's economic activity. The series excludes data on self-employed individuals, employees of private households, railroad employees, agricultural production employees, and most government employees. The County Business Patterns program has tabulated on a North American Industry Classification System (NAICS) basis since 1998. Data for 1997 and earlier years are based on the Standard Industrial Classification (SIC) system. For more information on the relationship between the two systems, see Concordances www.census.gov/eos/www/naics/concordances/concordances.html.

CBP data are extracted from the Business Register, the Census Bureau's file of all known single and multiestablishment companies. The Annual Company Organization Survey and quinquennial economic censuses provide individual establishment data for multilocation firms. Data for single-location firms are obtained from various programs censuses, the Annual Survey of Manufactures, and Current Business Surveys, as well as from administrative records of the Internal Revenue Service (IRS), the Social Security Administration (SSA), and the Bureau of Labor Statistics (BLS).

An **establishment** is a single physical location at which business is conducted or services or industrial operations are performed. It is not necessarily identical with a company or enterprise, which may consist of one or more establishments. When two or more activities are carried on at a single location under a single ownership, all activities generally are grouped together as a single establishment. The entire establishment is classified on the basis of its major activity and all data are included in that classification. Establishment-size designations are determined by paid employment in the mid-March pay period. The size group "1 to 4" includes establishments that did not report any paid employees in the mid-March pay period but paid wages to at least one employee at some time during the year.

Establishment counts represent the number of locations with paid employees any time during the year. This series excludes governmental establishments except for wholesale liquor establishments (NAICS 4248), retail liquor stores (NAICS 44531), federally-chartered savings institutions (NAICS 522120), federally-chartered credit unions (NAICS 522130), and hospitals (NAICS 622).

Total payroll includes all forms of compensation, such as salaries, wages, reported tips, commissions, bonuses, vacation allowances, sick-leave pay, employee contributions to qualified pension plans, and the value of taxable fringe benefits. For corporations, it includes amounts paid to officers and executives; for unincorporated businesses, it does not include profit or other compensation of proprietors or partners. Payroll is reported before deductions for social security, income tax, insurance, union dues, etc. First-quarter payroll consists of payroll during the January-to-March quarter.

Paid employment consists of full- and part-time employees, including salaried officers and executives of corporations, who are on the payroll in the pay period including March 12. Included are employees on paid sick leave, holidays, and vacations; not included are proprietors and partners of unincorporated businesses.

TABLE D. MICROPOLITAN AREAS WITH COMPONENT COUNTIES

Table D consists of 1 table (D-1) with 12 data items for 551 micropolitan statistical areas and 658 counties within the micropolitan areas. They are presented alphabetically, with counties listed alphabetically within each micropolitan area.

All summaries, including historical data, are presented for the areas as currently defined. Where possible, the original figures have been retabulated to reflect the status of micropolitan area boundaries as of July 1, 2015. For more information on these areas, see Appendix C, Geographic Concepts and Codes.

Table D-1. Population and Personal Income

Sources: Population—U.S. Census Bureau, Population Estimates Program, Population and Housing Unit Estimates Datasets www.census.gov/programs-surveys/popest/data/data-sets.html; Personal income—U.S. Bureau of Economic Analysis, Regional Economic Accounts, State and Local Area Personal Income https://bea.gov/regional/index.htm.

Population numbers for 2010 and 2000 are counts of the resident population on April 1 of those decennial census years. The April 1 estimates base population may differ from the April 1 census count due to legal boundary updates, other geographic program changes, and Count Question Resolution actions.

Population estimates for 2015 measure the estimated population from the calculated number of people living in an area as of July 1. The Census Bureau develops county population estimates with a component of population change method in which they use administrative records and other data to estimate the household and group quarters population. For the household population, the components of population change are births, deaths, net domestic migration, and net international migration. They measure change in the nonhousehold, or group quarters, population by the net change in the population living in group quarters facilities.

A major assumption underlying this approach is that changes in selected administrative and other data sources closely approximate the components of population change. Therefore, Census Bureau demographers separately estimate each component of population change based on administrative records, including registered births and deaths, federal income tax returns, medicare enrollees, and military movement. They also separately estimate net international migration using information from the American Community Survey (ACS), the decennial census, and other data sources.

Most administrative record data sources lag the current estimate year by as much as 2 years. Therefore, the Census Bureau projects the data for the current year based on past years' data. As updated data become available, they revise the projected input data so that each vintage's estimates are always based on the most recent data available.

For more information on the method used for these estimates, see Appendix B, Limitations and Methodology, and the website at http://www.census.gov/programs-surveys/popest/technical-documentation.html.

Personal income is the income that is received by all persons from all sources. It is calculated as the sum of wage and salary disbursements, supplements to wages and salaries, proprietors' income with inventory valuation and capital consumption adjustments, rental income of people with capital consumption adjustment, personal dividend income, personal interest income, and personal current transfer receipts, less contributions for government social insurance.

The personal income of an area is the income that is received by, or on behalf of, all the individuals who live in the area; therefore, the estimates of personal income are presented by the place of residence of the income recipients.

Per Capita personal income is the personal income of a given area divided by the resident population of the area, using the July 1 population estimate of the year shown. Personal income differs by definition from money income, which is prepared by the Census Bureau, in that money income is measured before deduction of personal contributions for social insurance and does not include imputed income, lump-sum payments, and income received by quasi-individuals. Money income does include income from private pensions and annuities and from interpersonal transfer, such as child support; therefore it is not comparable to personal income. Total personal income is adjusted to place of residence.

About 90 percent of the state and county estimates of personal income are based on census data and on administrative-records data that are collected by other federal agencies. The data from censuses are mainly collected from the recipient of the income. The most important sources of census data for the state and county estimates are the census of agriculture and the census of population and housing that are conducted by the Census Bureau. The data from administrative records may originate either from the recipients of the income or from the source of the income. These data are a byproduct of the administration of various federal and state government programs. The most important sources of these data are as follows: the state unemployment insurance programs of the Employment and Training Administration, Department of Labor; the social insurance programs of the Social Security Administration and the Health Care Financing Administration, Department of Health and Human Services; the federal income tax program of the Internal Revenue Service, Department of the Treasury; the veterans benefit programs of the Department of Veterans Affairs; and the military payroll systems of the Department of Defense. The remaining 10 percent of the estimates are based on data from other sources. For example, the estimates of the components of farm proprietors' income, a component of personal income, are partly based on the state estimates of farm income and the county estimates of case receipts, crop production, and livestock inventory that are prepared by the Department of Agriculture, which uses sample surveys, along with census data and administrative-records data, to derive its estimates.

APPENDIX B
LIMITATIONS OF THE DATA AND METHODOLOGY

INTRODUCTION

The data presented in this *State and Metropolitan Area Data Book* came from many sources. The sources include not only federal statistical bureaus and other organizations that collect and issue statistics as their principal activity, but also governmental administrative and regulatory agencies, private research bodies, trade associations, insurance companies, health associations, and private organizations such as the National Education Association and philanthropic foundations. Consequently, the data vary considerably as to reference periods, definitions of terms and, for ongoing series, the number and frequency of time periods for which data are available.

The statistics presented were obtained and tabulated by various means. Some statistics are based on complete enumerations or censuses while others are based on samples. Some information is extracted from records kept for administrative or regulatory purposes (school enrollment, hospital records, securities registration, financial accounts, social security records, income tax returns, and so on), while other information is obtained explicitly for statistical purposes through interviews or by mail. The estimation procedures used vary from highly sophisticated scientific techniques to crude "informed guesses."

Each set of data relates to a group of individuals or units of interest referred to as the *target universe* or *target population*, or simply as the *universe* or *population*. Prior to data collection the target universe should be clearly defined. For example, if data are to be collected for the universe of households in the United States, it is necessary to define a "household." The target universe may not be completely traceable. Cost and other considerations may restrict data collection to a survey universe based on some available list and that list may be inaccurate or out of date. This list is called a *survey frame* or *sampling frame*.

The data in many tables are based on data obtained for all population units, a census, or on data obtained for only a portion, or sample, of the population units. When the data presented are based on a sample, the sample is usually a scientifically selected probability sample. This is a sample selected from a list or sampling frame in such a way that every possible sample has a known chance of

selection and usually each unit selected can be assigned a number, greater than zero and less than or equal to one, representing its likelihood or probability of selection.

For large-scale sample surveys, the probability sample of units is often selected as a multistage sample. The first stage of a multistage sample is the selection of a probability sample of large groups of population members, referred to as primary sampling units (PSUs). For example, in a national multistage household sample, PSUs are often counties or groups of counties. The second stage of a multistage sample is the selection, within each PSU selected at the first stage, of smaller groups of population units, referred to as secondary sampling units. In subsequent stages of selection, smaller and smaller nested groups are chosen until the ultimate sample of population units is obtained. To qualify a multistage sample as a probability sample, all stages of sampling must be carried out using probability-sampling methods.

Prior to selection at each stage of a multistage (or a singlestage) sample, a list of the sampling units or sampling frame for that stage must be obtained. For example, for the first stage of selection of a national household sample, a list of the counties and county groups that form the PSUs must be obtained. For the final stage of selection, lists of households, and sometimes persons within the households, have to be compiled in the field. For surveys of economic entities and for the economic censuses the Census Bureau generally uses a frame constructed from the Census Bureau's Business Register. The Business Register contains all establishments with payroll in the United States including small single establishment firms as well as large multiestablishment firms.

Wherever the quantities in a table refer to an entire universe, but are constructed from data collected in a *sample survey*, the table quantities are referred to as sample estimates. In constructing a sample estimate, an attempt is made to come as close as is feasible to the corresponding universe quantity that would be obtained from a complete census of the universe. Estimates based on a sample will, however, generally differ from the hypothetical census figures. Two classifications of errors are associated with estimates based on sample surveys: (1) *sampling error*—the error arising from the use of a sample, rather than a census, to estimate population quantities and

(2) *nonsampling error*—those errors arising from nonsampling sources. As discussed below, the magnitude of the sampling error for an estimate can usually be estimated from the sample data. However, the magnitude of the nonsampling error for an estimate can rarely be estimated. Consequently, actual error in an estimate exceeds the error that can be estimated.

The particular sample used in a survey is only one of a large number of possible samples of the same size, which could have been selected using the same sampling procedure. Estimates derived from the different samples would, in general, differ from each other. The *standard error* (SE) is a measure of the variation among the estimates derived from all possible samples. The standard error is the most commonly used measure of the sampling error of an estimate. Valid estimates of the standard errors of survey estimates can usually be calculated from the data collected in a probability sample. For convenience, the standard error is sometimes expressed as a percent of the estimate and is called the relative standard error or *coefficient of variation* (CV). For example, an estimate of 200 units with an estimated standard error of 10 units has an estimated CV of 5 percent.

A sample estimate and an estimate of its standard error or CV can be used to construct interval estimates that have a prescribed confidence that the interval includes the average of the estimates derived from all possible samples with a known probability. To illustrate, if all possible samples were selected under essentially the same general conditions, and using the same sample design, and if an estimate and its estimated standard error were calculated from each sample, then: (1) approximately 68 percent of the intervals from one standard error below the estimate to one standard error above the estimate would include the average estimate derived from all possible samples; (2) approximately 90 percent of the intervals from 1.6 standard errors below the estimate to 1.6 standard errors above the estimate would include the average estimate derived from all possible samples; and (3) approximately 95 percent of the intervals from two standard errors below the estimate to two standard errors above the estimate would include the average estimate derived from all possible samples.

Thus, for a particular sample, one can say with the appropriate level of confidence (e.g., 90 percent or 95 percent) that the average of all possible samples is included in the constructed interval. Example of a confidence interval: an estimate is 200 units with a standard error of 10 units. An approximately 90 percent confidence interval (plus or minus 1.6 standard errors) is from 184 to 216.

All surveys and censuses are subject to nonsampling errors. Nonsampling errors are of two kinds *random and nonrandom*. Random nonsampling errors arise because of the varying interpretation of questions (by respondents or interviewers) and varying actions of coders, keyers, and other processors. Some randomness is also introduced when respondents must estimate. Nonrandom nonsampling errors result from total nonresponse (no usable data obtained for a sampled unit), partial or item nonresponse (only a portion of a response may be usable), inability or unwillingness on the part of respondents to provide correct information, difficulty interpreting questions, mistakes in recording or keying data, errors of collection or processing, and coverage problems (overcoverage and undercoverage of the target universe). Random nonresponse errors usually, but not always, result in an understatement of sampling errors and thus an overstatement of the precision of survey estimates. Estimating the magnitude of nonsampling errors would require special experiments or access to independent data and, consequently, the magnitudes are seldom available.

Nearly all types of nonsampling errors that affect surveys also occur in complete censuses. Since surveys can be conducted on a smaller scale than censuses, nonsampling errors can presumably be controlled more tightly. Relatively more funds and effort can perhaps be expended toward eliciting responses, detecting and correcting response error, and reducing processing errors. As a result, survey results can sometimes be more accurate than census results.

To compensate for suspected nonrandom errors, adjustments of the sample estimates are often made. For example, adjustments are frequently made for nonresponse, both total and partial. Adjustments made for either type of nonresponse are often referred to as *imputations*. Imputation for total nonresponse is usually made by substituting for the questionnaire responses of the nonrespondents the "average" questionnaire responses of the respondents. These imputations usually are made separately within various groups of sample members, formed by attempting to place respondents and nonrespondents together that have "similar" design or ancillary characteristics. Imputation for item nonresponse is usually made by substituting for a missing item the response to that item of a respondent having characteristics that are "similar" to those of the nonrespondent.

For an estimate calculated from a sample survey, the *total error* in the estimate is composed of the sampling error, which can usually be estimated from the sample, and the nonsampling error, which usually cannot be estimated from the sample. The total error present in a population quantity obtained from a complete census is composed of only nonsampling errors. Ideally, estimates of the total error associated with data given in these tables should be given. However, due to the unavailability of estimates of nonsampling errors, only estimates of the levels of sampling errors, in terms of estimated standard errors or coefficients of variation, are available. To obtain estimates of the estimated standard errors from the sample of interest, obtain a copy of the referenced report, which appears at the end of each table.

Source of Additional Material: The Federal Committee on Statistical Methodology (FCSM) is an interagency committee dedicated to improving the quality of federal statistics https://fcsm.sites.usa.gov/.

Principal databases: Beginning below are brief descriptions of 18 of the sample surveys, censuses, and administrative collections that provide a substantial portion of the data contained in this publication.

U.S. DEPARTMENT OF AGRICULTURE

National Agriculture Statistics Service (NASS)

Census of Agriculture

Universe, Frequency, and Types of Data: Complete count of U.S. farms and ranches conducted once every 5 years with data at the national, state, and county level. Data published on farm numbers and related items/characteristics.

Type of Data Collection Operation: Complete census for number of farms; land in farms; farm income; agriculture products sold; farms by type of organization; total cropland; irrigated land; farm operator characteristics; livestock and poultry inventory and sales; and selected crops harvested. Market value of land, buildings, and products sold, total farm production expenses, machinery and equipment, and fertilizer and chemicals.

Data Collection and Imputation Procedures: Data collection is by mailing questionnaires to all farmers and ranchers. Producers can return their forms by mail or online. Nonrespondents are contacted by telephone and correspondence follow-ups. Imputations were made for all nonresponse item/characteristics and coverage adjustments were made to account for missed farms and ranches.

Estimates of Sampling Error: Weight adjustments were made to account for the undercoverage and whole-unit nonresponse of farms on the Census Mail List (CML). These were treated as sampling errors.

Other (Nonsampling) Errors: Nonsampling errors are due to incompleteness of the census mailing list, duplications on the list, respondent reporting errors, errors in editing reported data, and in imputation for missing data. Evaluation studies are conducted to measure certain nonsampling errors such as list coverage and classification error. It is a reasonable assumption that the net effect of nonmeasurable errors is zero (the positive errors cancel the negative errors).

Sources of Additional Material: U.S. Department of Agriculture, National Agricultural Statistics Service (NASS), 2012 Census of Agriculture, Appendix A Census of Agriculture Methodology, Appendix B General Explanation and Census of Agriculture Report Form. https://www.agcensus.usda.gov/Publications/2012/.

Multiple Frame Surveys

Universe, Frequency, and Types of Data: Surveys of U.S. farm operators to obtain data on major livestock inventories, selected crop acreage and production, grain stocks, and farm labor characteristics, farm economic data, and chemical use data. Estimates are made quarterly, semiannually, or annually depending on the data series.

Type of Data Collection Operation: Primary frame is obtained from general or special purpose lists, supplemented by a probability sample of land areas used to estimate for list incompleteness.

Data Collection and Imputation Procedures: Mail, telephone, or personal interviews used for initial data collection. Mail nonrespondent follow-up by phone and personal interviews. Imputation based on average of respondents.

Estimates of Sampling Error: Estimated CVs range from 1 percent to 2 percent at the U.S. level for crop and livestock data series and 3 to 5 percent for economic data. Regional CVs range from 3 to 6 percent, while state estimate CVs run 5 to 10 percent.

Other (Nonsampling) Errors: In addition to above, replicated sampling procedures used to monitor effects of changes in survey procedures.

Sources of Additional Material: U.S. Department of Agriculture, National Agricultural Statistics Service (NASS), USDA's National Agricultural Statistics Service. https://www.agcensus.usda.gov/Publications/2012/.

U.S. BUREAU OF LABOR STATISTICS

Current Employment Statistics (CES) Program

Universe, Frequency, and Types of Data: Monthly survey drawn from a sampling frame of over 8 million unemployment insurance tax accounts in order to obtain data by industry on employment, hours, and earnings.

Type of Data Collection Operation: The CES sample included about 145,000 businesses and government agencies, which represent approximately 557,000 individual worksites.

Data Collection and Imputation Procedures: Each month, the state agencies cooperating with Bureau of Labor Statistics (BLS), as well as BLS Data Collection Centers, collect data through various automated collection modes and mail. BLS Washington staff prepares national estimates of employment, hours, and earnings while states use the data to develop state and area estimates.

Estimates of Sampling Errors: The relative standard error for total nonfarm employment is 0.1 percent. A birth/death model adjusts for the impact of business openings and closings. From April through December 2012, the cumulative birth/death model added 755,000 employees.

Other (nonsampling) Errors: Estimates of employment adjusted annually to reflect complete universe. Average adjustment is 0.2 percent over the last decade, with an absolute range from less than 0.1 percent to 0.6 percent.

Sources of Additional Material: U.S. Bureau of Labor Statistics, Employment & Earnings Online. See www.bls.gov/opub/ee/home.htm.

U.S. DEPARTMENT OF COMMERCE

U.S. BUREAU OF ECONOMIC ANALYSIS (BEA)

Regional Economic Accounts

Universe, Frequency, and Types of Data: The Regional Economic Accounts website contains estimates of personal income and its components and employment for local areas such as states, counties, metropolitan areas, and micropolitan areas.

Type of Data Collection Operation: The estimates of personal income are primarily based on administrative records data, census data, and survey data.

Data Collection and Imputation Procedures: The data are collected from administrative records, which may come from the recipients of the income or from the sources of the income. These data are a byproduct of the administration of various federal and state government programs. The most important sources of these data are—the state unemployment insurance programs of the Bureau of Labor Statistics (BLS), the social insurance programs of the Centers for Medicare and Medicaid Services, federal income tax program of the Internal Revenue Service, veterans benefit programs of the U.S.

Department of Veterans Affairs, and military payroll systems of the U.S. Department of Defense.

The data from censuses are mainly collected from the recipients of income. The most important sources for these data are the Census of Agriculture at the U.S. Department of Agriculture (USDA) and the Census of Population and Housing conducted by the U.S. Census Bureau. Other sources may include estimates of farm proprietors' income by the USDA, wages and salaries from County Business Patterns from the Census Bureau, and the Quarterly Census of Employment and Wages by the Department of Labor.

Estimates of Sampling Error: Not applicable, except component variables may be subject to error.

Other (Nonsampling) Errors: Nonsampling errors in the administrative data sets may affect personal income estimates.

Sources of Additional Material: Methodological information on other Bureau of Economic Analysis (BEA) datasets such as "State Personal Income" and "Gross State Product" may be found at www.bea.gov/regional/methods.cfm.

U.S. CENSUS BUREAU

American Community Survey (ACS)

Universe, Frequency, and Types of Data: Nationwide survey to obtain annual data about demographic, social, economic, and housing characteristics of housing units and the people residing in them. It covers the household population and, beginning in 2006, also includes the group quarters population living in prisons, nursing homes and college dormitories, and other group quarters.

Type of Data Collection Operation: Housing unit address sampling is performed twice a year in both August and January. First-phase of sampling defines the universe for the second stage of sampling through two steps. First, all addresses that were eligible for the second phase sampling within the past 4 years are excluded from eligibility. This ensures that no address is in sample more than once in any 5-year period. The second step is to select a 20 percent systematic sample of "new" units, i.e., those units that have never appeared on a previous Master Address File (MAF) extract. All new addresses are systematically assigned to either the current year or to one of four back-samples. This procedure maintains five equal partitions of the universe. The second-phase sampling is done on the current year's partition and results in approximately 3,000,000 housing unit addresses in the United States and 36,000 in Puerto Rico. Group quarter sampling is performed separately from the housing unit sampling. The sampling begins with separating the small (15 persons or fewer) and the large (more than 15 persons) group quarters. The target sampling rate for both groups is a 2.5 percent sample of the group quarters population. It results in approximately 200,000 group quarters residents being selected in the United States, and an additional 1,000 in Puerto Rico.

Data Collection and Imputation Procedures: The American Community Survey is conducted every month on independent samples. Each housing unit in the independent monthly samples is mailed a prenotice letter announcing the selection of the address to participate, a survey questionnaire package, and a reminder postcard. These sample units addresses receive a second (replacement) questionnaire package if the initial questionnaire has not been returned by mid-month. Sample addresses for which a questionnaire is not returned in the mail and a telephone number is not available are forwarded to telephone centers for follow-up. Interviewers attempt to contact and interview these mail nonresponse cases by telephone. Sample addresses that are still unresponsive after 2 months of attempts are forwarded for a possible personal visit. Unresponsive addresses are subsampled at rates between 1 in 3 and 2 in 3. Those addresses selected through this process are assigned to Field Representatives (FRs), who visit the addresses, verify their existence, determine their occupancy status, and conduct interviews. Collection of group quarters data is conducted by FRs only. Their methods include completing the questionnaire while speaking to the resident in person or over the telephone, or leaving paper questionnaires for residents to complete for themselves and then pick them up later. This last option is used for data collection in federal prisons. If needed, a personal interview can be conducted with a proxy, such as a relative or guardian. After data collection is completed, any remaining incomplete or inconsistent information on the questionnaire is imputed during the final automated edit of the collected data.

Estimates of Sampling Error: The data in the ACS products are estimates and can vary from the actual values that would have been obtained by conducting a census of the entire population. The estimates from the chosen sample addresses can also vary from those that would have been obtained from a different set of addresses. This variation causes uncertainty, which can be measured using statistics such as standard error, margin of error, and confidence interval. All ACS estimates are accompanied by margins of error to assist users.

Other (Nonsampling) Errors: Nonsampling Error—In addition to sampling error, data users should realize that other types of errors may be introduced during any of the various complex operations used to select, collect, and process survey data. An important goal of the ACS is to minimize the amount of nonsampling error introduced through coverage issues in the sample list, nonresponse from sample housing units, and transcribing or editing data. One way of accomplishing this is by finding additional sources of addresses, following up on nonrespondents, and maintaining quality control systems.

Sources of Additional Material: U.S. Census Bureau, American Community Survey Web site at www.census.gov/acs; U.S. Census Bureau, American Community Survey Accuracy of the Data documents at https://www.census.gov/programs-surveys/acs/technical-documentation/code-lists.html.

Annual Survey of Manufactures (ASM)

Universe, Frequency, and Types of Data: The Annual Survey of Manufactures is conducted annually, except for years ending in "2" and "7," for all manufacturing establishments having one or more paid employees. The purpose of the ASM is to provide key intercensal measures of manufacturing activity, products, and location for the public and private sectors. The ASM provides statistics on employment, payroll, worker hours, payroll supplements, cost of materials, value added by manufacturing, capital expenditures, inventories, and energy consumption. It also provides estimates of value of shipments for 1,800 classes of manufactured products.

Type of Data Collection Operation: The ASM includes approximately 50,000 establishments selected from the census universe of 328,500 manufacturing establishments. Approximately 15,400 large establishments are selected with certainty, and the remaining establishments are selected with probability proportional to a composite measure of establishment size. The survey is updated from two sources: Internal Revenue Service (IRS) administrative records are used to include new single-unit manufacturers and the Company Organization Survey identifies new establishments of multiunit forms.

Data Collection and Imputation Procedures: Survey is conducted by mail with phone and mail follow-ups of nonrespondents. Imputation (for all nonresponse items) is based on previous year reports, or for new establishments in survey, on industry averages.

Estimates of Sampling Error: Estimated relative standard errors for number of employees, new expenditures, and for value added totals are given in annual publications. For U.S.-level industry statistics, most estimated relative standard errors are 2 percent or less, but vary considerably for detailed characteristics.

Other (Nonsampling) Errors: The unit response rate is about 85 percent. Nonsampling errors include those due to collection, reporting, and transcription errors, many of which are corrected through computer and clerical checks.

Sources of Additional Material: U.S. Census Bureau, *Annual Survey of Manufactures*, https://www.census.gov/programs-surveys/asm.html.

State Government Tax Collections (STC)

Universe, Frequency, and Types of Data: The universe for the State Tax Collections Survey covers the 50 state governments only. No local governments are included in the universe for each state. The data have been collected annually since 1939. Statistics on the State Government Tax Collections Survey include measurement of tax by category: Property Tax, Sales and Gross Receipts Taxes, License Taxes, Income Taxes, and Other Taxes. Each tax category is broken down into subcategories (e.g., motor fuel sales, alcoholic beverage sales, motor vehicle licenses, alcoholic beverage licenses). There are currently 25 different tax codes that state tax revenue may fall into.

Type of Data Collection Operation: Most of the data in this report were gathered by a mail canvass of appropriate state government offices that are directly involved with state-administered taxes. There are approximately one hundred offices that are canvassed to collect data from all fifty states. Follow-up procedures include the use of mail, telephone, and email until data are received.

Data Editing and Imputation Procedures: Data are processed from several collection methods including direct response to survey forms from state government officials, as well as from the compilation of administrative records and supplemental sources. Regardless of the collection method, these data are edited using ratio edits of the current year's value to the prior year's value. The fifty state governments provide the Census Bureau with administrative records from their central accounting systems. These administrative records are unique to each state as each state is legally organized differently from every other state and, as such, each state has a unique organizational and accounting structure. It is the responsibility of the Census Bureau to classify the different accounting and organizational structures into uniform tax categories so that entities with different methods of government accounting can be presented on a comparable basis. The records represent the core, or central, state government and are limited to tax revenue. Data on state government tax revenues are compiled from state administrative records by Census Bureau employees, according to the Census Bureau's classification methodology. When state records do not include full tax revenue detail or reporting

units do not respond, supplemental data sources from external financial reports or the Census Bureau's *Annual Survey of State Government Finances and Quarterly Summary of State and Local Government Tax Revenue* are required to complete the datasets. This procedure is called imputation. Supplemental records are merged with data from the state governments. Although every effort is made to obtain financial information from all state government entities, financial statements may not be available at the time the Census Bureau closes the processing, or governmental entities may not respond to the Census Bureau's requests. Every year the data are subject to revisions as new data become available.

Estimates of Sampling Error: These data are not subject to sampling error because this is a complete enumeration of all 50 state governments.

Other (Nonsampling) Errors: Despite efforts made in all phases of collection, processing, and tabulation to minimize errors, the survey is subject to nonsampling errors such as the inability to obtain data for every variable for all units, inaccuracies in classification, mistakes in keying and coding, and coverage errors.

Sources of Additional Material: For further information, see the *Government Finance and Employment Classification Manual*, www.census.gov/govs/classification/ and the *2012 Census of Governments*, www.census.gov/govs/cog/.

Annual Survey of Public Employment and Payroll (ASPEP)

Universe, Frequency, and Types of Data: The population of interest for this survey includes the civilian employees of all federal government agencies (except the Central Intelligence Agency, the National Security Agency, and the Defense Intelligence Agency), all agencies of the 50 state governments, and 90,107 local governments (i.e., counties, municipalities, townships, special districts, and school districts) including the District of Columbia. Data have been collected annually since 1957. A census is conducted every 5 years (years ending in "2" and "7"). A sample of state and local governments is used to collect data in the intervening years. A new sample is selected every 5 years (in years ending in "4" and "9"). The survey provides data on full-time and part-time employment, part-time hours worked, full-time equivalent employment, and payroll statistics by governmental function (i.e., elementary and secondary education, higher education).

Type of Data Collection Operation: Data collected for the Annual Survey of Government Employment are public record and are not confidential, as authorized by Title 13, U.S. Code, Section 9. Census Bureau staff compiled federal government data from records of the U.S. Office of Personnel Management (OPM). These data are based on the Monthly Report of Federal Civilian Employment. Census Bureau staff collected some state government data through special arrangements, referred to as central collection agreements, wherein data for multiple state agencies or school districts are reported by a central respondent generally in an electronic file. Forty-five of the state governments provided data from central payroll records for all or most of their agencies/institutions. Data for agencies and institutions for the remaining state governments were obtained by mail canvass questionnaires. Local governments were also canvassed using a mail questionnaire. All respondents receiving the mail questionnaire had the option of responding electronically using the Web site developed for reporting data.

Data Editing and Imputation Procedures: Editing is a process that ensures survey data are accurate, complete, and consistent. Efforts are made at all phases of collection, processing, and tabulation to minimize errors. Although some edits are built into the Internet data collection instrument and the data entry programs, the majority of the edits are performed post collection. Edits consist primarily of two types: (1) *consistency edits* and (2) *historical ratio edits* of the current year's reported value to the prior year's value. The *consistency edits* check the logical relationships of data items reported on the form. For each function where employees are reported, the *historical ratio edits* compare data from two different time periods.

Not all respondents answer every item on the questionnaire. There are also questionnaires that are not returned despite efforts to gain a response. Imputation is the process of filling in missing or invalid data with reasonable values in order to have a complete data set for analytical purposes. For nonresponding governments, the imputations were based on recently reported historical data from either a prior year annual survey or the most recent Census of Governments. These data were adjusted by a growth rate that was determined by the growth of responding units that were similar (in size, geography, and type of government) to the nonrespondent. If there was no recent historical data available, the imputations were based on the data from a randomly selected responding donor that was similar to the nonrespondent. In cases where good secondary data sources exist, the data from those sources were used.

Estimates of Sampling Error: The intercensal data come from a sample rather than a census of all possible units. The particular sample that was selected is one of a larger number of possible samples of the same size and sample design that could have been selected. Each sample would have yielded different estimates. The estimated coefficients of variation, which are provided for each estimate

on www.census.gov/govs, are an estimate of this sampling variability.

Other (Nonsampling) Errors: Although every effort is made in all phases of collection, processing, and tabulation to minimize errors, the data are subject to nonsampling errors such as inability to obtain data for every variable from all units in the population of interest, inaccuracies in classification, response errors, misinterpretation of questions, mistakes in keying and coding, and coverage errors. The data processing section describes our efforts to mitigate errors due to nonresponse, keying, reporting errors, etc.

Sources of Additional Material: For further information, see the *Government Finance and Employment Classification Manual,* www.census.gov/govs/classification/ and the *2012 Census of Governments,* www.census.gov/govs/cog/.

Annual Finance Survey (AFS)

Universe, Frequency, and Types of Data: The population of interest for this survey contains the 50 state governments and 90,107 local governments (counties, municipalities, townships, special districts, and school districts) including the District of Columbia. In years ending in "2" and "7" the entire universe is canvassed. In intervening years, a sample of the population of interest is surveyed. The survey coverage includes all state and local governments in the United States.

The survey collects financial data. Revenue data include taxes (i.e., property, sales, tobacco, motor vehicle, licensing and permit), charges, interest, and other earnings. Expenditure data include total by function (i.e., education, highways, airports, water and sewerage, health, hospitals, corrections, fire and police protection), and by accounting category (i.e., current operations and capital outlays). Debt data include issuance, retirement, and amounts outstanding. Financial assets data include securities and other holdings, by type.

Type of Data Collection Operation: The data collection for the state and local finance survey (both census and sample survey) is made up of three modes to obtain data: mail canvass, internet collection, and central collection from state sources. Collection methods vary by state and type of government. Administrative data are compiled for most state government agencies and the 48 largest and most complex county and municipal governments. The survey melds several government finance surveys, including the Survey of Local Government Finances, Survey of Public-Employee Retirement Systems, Integrated Post-secondary Educational Data System (IPEDS) from the National Center for Education Statistics (NCES),

State Government Finances Survey, and the Survey of Public Elementary-Secondary Education Finances.

Data Editing and Imputation Procedures: Not all respondents answer every item on the questionnaire. There are also questionnaires that are not returned despite efforts to gain a response. Imputation is the process of filling in missing or invalid data with reasonable values in order to have a complete data set for analytical purposes. For nonresponding governments, imputations for missing units are based on recently reported historical data from either a prior year annual survey or the most recent census, adjusted by a growth rate. If no historical data are available, data from a randomly selected similar unit are used for the imputation.

Editing is a process that ensures data are accurate, complete, and consistent. Efforts are made at all phases of collection, processing, and tabulation to minimize errors. Although some edits are built into the internet data collection instrument and the data entry programs, the majority of the edits are performed post collection. Data are checked for internal consistency within the questionnaire and for historical accuracy.

Estimates of Sampling Error: In census years, all of the units in the population are surveyed, and there is no sampling error. In the intercensal years, the population is sampled, and the estimates are subject to sampling error. The coefficient of variation is a measure of sampling variability expressed as a percentage of the estimated total. Generally, the estimated coefficients of variation for state and local government revenues, expenditures, debt, or assets are under 3 percent in each state. Coefficients of variation for the estimates are given in the tables on the website www.census.gov/govs/estimate/index.html.

Other (Nonsampling) Errors: Although every effort is made in all phases of collection, processing, and tabulation to minimize errors, the data are subject to nonsampling errors such as inability to obtain data for every variable from all units in the population of interest, inaccuracies in classification, response errors, misinterpretation of questions, mistakes in keying and coding, and coverage errors.

Sources of Additional Material: For more information on the survey, see https://www.census.gov/govs/cog/. On that site, see the *Survey Methodology* and *Government Finance and Employment Classification Manual*.

2007 Economic Census

(Industry Series, Geographic Area Series, and Subject Series Reports) (for NAICS sectors 21 to 81).

Universe, Frequency, and Types of Data: Conducted every 5 years to obtain data on number of establishments, number of employees, payroll, total sales/receipts/revenue, and other industry- specific statistics. The universe is all establishments with paid employees excluding agriculture, forestry, fishing and hunting, and government. (Nonemployer Statistics, discussed separately, covers those establishments without paid employees.)

Type of Data Collection Operation: All large employer firms were surveyed (i.e., all employer firms above payroll-size cutoff s established to separate large from small employers) plus, in most sectors, a sample of the small employer firms.

Data Collection and Imputation Procedures: Mail questionnaires were used with both mail and telephone follow-ups for nonrespondents. Businesses also had the option to respond electronically. Data for nonrespondents and for small employer firms not mailed a questionnaire were obtained from administrative records of other federal agencies or imputed.

Estimates of Sampling Error: Not applicable for basic data such as sales, revenue, receipts, payroll, etc., for sectors other than Construction (NAICS 23). Estimates of sampling error for construction industries are included with the data as published on the Census Bureau Web site.

Other (Nonsampling) Errors: The overall response rate for the 2012 Economic Census was 84 percent. Nonsampling errors may occur during the collection, reporting, keying, and classification of the data.

Sources of Additional Material U.S. Census Bureau, see https://www.census.gov/programs-surveys/economic-census/technical-documentation/methodology.html.

Census of Population

Universe, Frequency, and Types of Data: Complete count of U.S. population conducted every 10 years since 1790. Data obtained on number and characteristics of people in the United States.

Type of Data Collection Operation: The 2010 census consisted of one form for 100 percent of the population. On this 2010 questionnaire and on the 100 percent questionnaire of the 1990 and 2000 censuses, the 100 percent items included: age, date of birth, sex, race, Hispanic origin, relationship to householder, homeownership and mortgage status. In 1980, approximately 19 percent of the housing units were included in the sample that received a longer questionnaire; in 1990 and 2000, approximately

17 percent were included in the sample. By 2010, the sample had been eliminated and replaced the ongoing American Community Survey.

Data Collection and Imputation Procedures: In 1980, 1990, 2000, and 2010 mail questionnaires were used extensively with personal interviews in the remainder. Extensive telephone and personal follow-up for nonrespondents was done in the censuses. Imputations were made for missing characteristics.

Estimates of Sampling Error. The 2010 census included no sampling. In prior censuses, sampling errors for data were estimated for all items collected by sample and varied by characteristic and geographic area. The coefficients of variation (CVs) for national and state estimates were generally very small.

Other (Nonsampling) Errors: Since 1950, evaluation programs have been conducted to provide information on the magnitude of some sources of nonsampling errors such as response bias and undercoverage in each census. Results from the evaluation program for the 1990 census indicated that the estimated net undercoverage amounted to about 1.5 percent of the total resident population. For the 2000 census, the evaluation program indicated a net overcount of 0.5 percent of the resident population.

Sources of Additional Material: U.S. Census Bureau, The Coverage of Population in the 1980 Census, PHC80-E4; *Content Reinterview Study: Accuracy of Data for Selected Population and Housing Characteristics as Measured by Reinterview*, PHC80-E2; *1980 Census of Population*, Vol. 1, (PC80-1), Appendixes B, C, and D. *Content Reinterview Survey: Accuracy of Data for Selected Population and Housing Characteristics as Measured by Reinterview*, 1990, CPH-E-1; Effectiveness of Quality Assurance, CPH-E-2; Programs to Improve Coverage in the 1990 Census, 1990, CPH-E-3. For 2000 census evaluations, see www.census.gov/pred/www. For 2010 census evaluations, see www.census.gov/2010census/about/cpex.php.

County Business Patterns

Universe, Frequency, and Types of Data: County Business Patterns is an annual tabulation of basic data items extracted from the Business Register, a file of all known single- and multi-location employer companies maintained and updated by the U.S. Census Bureau. Data include number of establishments, number of employees, first quarter and annual payrolls, and number of establishments by employment size class. Data are excluded for self-employed individuals, private households, railroad employees, agricultural production workers, and most government employees.

Type of Data Collection Operation: The annual Company Organization Survey provides individual establishment data for multi-location companies. Data for single establishment companies are obtained from various Census Bureau programs, such as the Annual Survey of Manufactures and Current Business Surveys, as well as from administrative records of the Internal Revenue Service, the Social Security Administration, and the Bureau of Labor Statistics.

Estimates of Sampling Error: Not applicable.

Other (Nonsampling) Error. The data are subject to nonsampling errors, such as inability to identify all cases in the universe; definition and classification difficulties; differences in interpretation of questions; errors in recording or coding the data obtained; and estimation of employers who reported too late to be included in the tabulations and for records with missing or misreported data.

Sources of Additional Materials: U.S. Census Bureau, County Business Patterns, https://www.census.gov/programs-surveys/cbp.html.

Current Population Survey (CPS)

Universe, Frequency, and Types of Data: Nationwide monthly sample designed primarily to produce national and state estimates of labor force characteristics of the civilian noninstitutionalized population 16 years of age and older.

Type of Data Collection Operation: Multistage probability sample that currently includes 72,000 households from 824 sample areas. Sample size increased in some states to improve data reliability for those areas on an annual average basis. A continual sample rotation system is used. Households are in sample 4 months, out for 8 months, and in for 4 more. Month-to-month overlap is 75 percent; year-to-year overlap is 50 percent.

Data Collection and Imputation Procedures: For first and fifth months that a household is in sample, personal interviews; other months, approximately 85 percent of the data collected by phone. Imputation is done for item nonresponse. Adjustment for total nonresponse is done by a predefined cluster of units, by state, metropolitan status and CBSA size; for item nonresponse imputation varies by subject matter.

Estimates of Sampling Error. The national total estimates of the civilian labor force and of employment have monthly CVs of about.2 percent and annual average CVs of about.1 percent. Unemployment is a much smaller characteristic and consequently has substantially larger CVs than the civilian labor force or employment. The national unemployment rate, the most important CPS statistic, has a monthly CV of about 2 percent and an annual average CV of about 1 percent. Assuming a 6 percent unemployment rate, states have annual average CVs of about 8 percent. The estimated CVs for family income and poverty rate for all persons in 2005 are .4 percent and 1.2 percent, respectively. CVs for subnational areas, such as states, tend to be larger and vary by area.

Other (Nonsampling) Errors: Estimates of response bias on unemployment are available. Estimates of the unemployment rate from reinterviews range from –2.4 percent to 1.0 percent of the basic CPS unemployment rate (over a 30-month span from January 2004 through June 2006). Eligible CPS households are approximately 82 percent of the assigned households, with a corresponding response rate of 92 percent.

Sources of Additional Material: U.S. Census Bureau and Bureau of Labor Statistics, Current Population Survey: Design and Methodology, (Technical Paper 66), available on the Internet www.census.gov/prod/2006pubs/tp-66.pdf and the Bureau of Labor Statistics, www.bls.gov/cps/ and the *BLS Handbook of Methods*, Chapter 1, available at www.bls.gov/opub/hom/homch1_a.htm.

Monthly Survey of Construction

Universe, Frequency, and Types of Data: Survey conducted monthly of newly constructed housing units (excluding mobile homes). Data are collected on the start, completion, and sale of housing. (Annual figures are aggregates of monthly estimates.)

Type of Data Collection Operation: A multistage probability sample of approximately 900 of the 20,000 permit- issuing jurisdictions in the United States was selected. Each month in each of these permit offices, field representatives list and select a sample of permits for which to collect data. to obtain data in areas where building permits are not required, a multistage probability sample of 80 land areas (census tracts or subsections of census tracts) was selected. All roads in these areas are canvassed and data are collected on all new residential construction found. Sampled buildings are followed up until they are completed (and sold, if for sale).

Data Collection and Imputation Procedures: Data are obtained by telephone inquiry and/or field visit. Nonresponse/ undercoverage adjustment factors are used to account for late reported data.

Estimates of Sampling Error: Estimated CV of 5 percent to 6 percent for estimates of national totals of units started, but may be higher than 20 percent for estimated totals of more detailed characteristics, such as housing units in multiunit structures.

Other (Nonsampling) Errors: Response rate is over 90 percent for most items. Nonsampling errors are attributed to definitional problems, differences in interpretation of questions, incorrect reporting, inability to obtain information about all cases in the sample, and processing errors.

Sources of Additional Material All data are available at https://www.census.gov/econ/overview/co0400.html. Further documentation of the survey is also available at that site.

Nonemployer Statistics

Universe, Frequency, and Types of Data: Nonemployer statistics are an annual tabulation of economic data by industry for active businesses without paid employees that are subject to federal income tax. Data showing the number of firms and receipts by industry are available for the United States, states, counties, and metropolitan areas. Most types of businesses covered by the Census Bureau's economic statistics programs are included in the nonemployer statistics. Tax-exempt and agricultural-production businesses are excluded from nonemployer statistics.

Type of Data Collection Operation: The universe of nonemployer firms is created annually as a byproduct of the Census Bureau's Business Register processing for employer establishments. If a business is active but without paid employees, then it becomes part of the potential nonemployer universe. Industry classification and receipts are available for each potential nonemployer business. These data are obtained primarily from the annual business income tax returns of the Internal Revenue Service (IRS). The potential nonemployer universe undergoes a series of complex processing, editing, and analytical review procedures at the Census Bureau to distinguish nonemployers from employers and to correct and complete data items used in creating the data tables.

Estimates of Sampling Error: Not applicable.

Other (Nonsampling) Errors: The data are subject to nonsampling errors, such as industry misclassification as well as errors of response, keying, nonreporting, and coverage.

Sources of Additional Material: U.S. Census Bureau, Nonemployer Statistics www.census.gov/econ/nonemployer/index.html.

Population Estimates

Universe, Frequency, and Types of Data: The U.S. Census Bureau annually produces estimates of total resident population for each state and county. County population estimates are produced with a component of population change method, while the state population estimates are solely the sum of the county populations.

Type of Data Collection Operation: The Census Bureau develops county population estimates with a demographic procedure called an "administrative records component of population change" method. A major assumption underlying this approach is that the components of population change are closely approximated by administrative data in a demographic change model. In order to apply the model, Census Bureau demographers estimate each component of population change separately. For the population residing in households the components of population change are births, deaths, and net migration, including net international migration. For the nonhousehold population, change is represented by the net change in the population living in group quarters facilities.

Estimates of Sampling Error: Not applicable.

Other (Nonsampling) Errors: Not available.

Sources of Additional Material: U.S. Census Bureau, "Methodology for the United States Resident Population Estimates by Age, Sex, Race, and Hispanic Origin and the State and County Total Resident Population Estimates" at https://www.census.gov/programs-surveys/popest/technical-documentation/methodology.html.

U.S. DEPARTMENT OF EDUCATION

National Center for Education Statistics Integrated Postsecondary Education Data Survey (IPEDS), Completions

Universe, Frequency, and Types of Data: Annual survey of all Title IV (federal financial aid) eligible postsecondary institutions to obtain data on earned degrees and other formal awards, conferred by field of study, level of degree, sex, and by racial/ethnic characteristics (every other year prior to 1989, then annually).

Type of Data Collection Operation: Complete census.

Data Collection and Imputation Procedures: Data are collected through a web-based survey in the fall of every year. Missing data are imputed by using data of similar institutions.

Estimates of Sampling Error: Not applicable.

Other (Nonsampling) Errors: For 2010-2011, the response rate for degree-granting institutions was 100.0 percent.

Sources of Additional Material: U.S. Department of Education, National Center for Education Statistics (NCES), *Postsecondary Institutions and Price of Attendance in 2011–2012; Degrees and Other Awards Conferred: 2010–2011; and 12-Month Enrollment: 2010–2011: First Look (Provisional Data)*. See https://nces.ed.gov/ipeds.

U.S. FEDERAL BUREAU OF INVESTIGATION

Uniform Crime Reporting (UCR) Program

Universe, Frequency, and Types of Data: Monthly reports on the number of criminal offenses that become known to law enforcement agencies. Data are also collected on crimes cleared by arrest or exceptional means; age, sex, and race of arrestees and for victims and offenders for homicides, number of law enforcement employees, on fatal and nonfatal assaults against law enforcement officers, and on hate crimes reported.

Type of Data Collection Operation: Crime statistics are based on reports of crime data submitted either directly to the FBI by contributing law enforcement agencies or through cooperating state UCR Programs.

Data Collection and Imputation Procedures: States with UCR programs collect data directly from individual law enforcement agencies and forward reports, prepared in accordance with UCR standards, to the FBI. Accuracy and consistency edits are performed by the FBI.

Estimates of Sampling Error: Not applicable.

Other (Nonsampling) Errors: During 2011, law enforcement agencies active in the UCR Program represented 97.8 percent of the total population. The coverage amounted to 98.8 percent of the U.S. population in metropolitan statistical areas, 92.3 percent of the population in cities outside metropolitan areas, and 93.1 percent in nonmetropolitan counties.

Sources of Additional Material: U.S. Department of Justice, Federal Bureau of Investigation, *Crime in the United States*, annual, *Hate Crime Statistics*, annual, *Law Enforcement Officers Killed and Assaulted*, annual, www.fbi.gov/about-us/cjis/ucr.

U.S. INTERNAL REVENUE SERVICE

Individual Income Tax Returns

Universe, Frequency, and Types of Data: Annual study of unaudited individual income tax returns, Forms 1040, 1040A, and 1040EZ, filed by U.S. citizens and residents.

Data provided on various financial characteristics by size of adjusted gross income, marital status, and by taxable and nontaxable returns. Data by state, based on the population of returns filed, also include returns from 1040NR, filed by nonresident aliens plus certain self-employment tax returns.

Type of Data Collection Operation: Stratified probability sample of 308,946 returns for tax year 2010. The sample is classified into sample strata based on the larger of total income or total loss amounts, the size of business plus farm receipts, and other criteria such as the potential usefulness of the return for tax policy modeling. Sampling rates for sample strata varied from 0.01 percent to 100 percent.

Data Collection and Imputation Procedures: Computer selection of sample of tax return records. Data adjusted during editing for incorrect, missing, or inconsistent entries to ensure consistency with other entries on return.

Estimates of Sampling Error: Estimated CVs for tax year 2010: adjusted gross income less deficit 0.09 percent; salaries and wages 0.17 percent; and tax-exempt interest received 1.25 percent. (State data not subject to sampling error.)

Other (Nonsampling) Errors: Processing errors and errors arising from the use of tolerance checks for the data.

Sources of Additional Material: U.S. Internal Revenue Service, Statistics of Income, Individual Income Tax Returns, annual, (Publication 1304). www.irs.gov/uac/SOI-Tax-Stats-Individual-Income-Tax-Returns-Publication-1304-%28Complete-Report%29.

NATIONAL CENTER FOR HEALTH STATISTICS (NCHS)

National Vital Statistics System

Universe, Frequency, and Types of Data: Annual data on births and deaths in the United States.

Type of Data Collection Operation: Mortality data based on complete file of death records, except 1972, based on 50 percent sample. Natality statistics 1951–1971, based on 50 percent sample of birth certificates, except a 20 percent to 50 percent sample in 1967, received by NCHS.

Data Collection and Imputation Procedures: Reports based on records from registration offices of all states, District of Columbia, New York City, Puerto Rico, Virgin Islands, Guam, American Samoa, and Northern Marianas.

Estimates of Sampling Error: For recent years, there is no sampling for these files; the files are based on 100 percent of events registered.

Other (Nonsampling) Errors: It is believed that more than 99 percent of the births and deaths occurring in this country are registered.

Sources of Additional Material U.S. National Center for Health Statistics, *Vital Statistics of the United States*, Vol. I and Vol. II annual, and the *National Vital Statistics Reports*. See the NCHS Web site at www.cdc.gov/nchs/nvss.htm.

NATIONAL HIGHWAY TRAFFIC SAFETY ADMINISTRATION (NHTSA)

Fatality Analysis Reporting System (FARS)

Universe, Frequency, and Types of Data: FARS is a census of all fatal motor vehicle traffic crashes that occur throughout the United States including the District of Columbia and Puerto Rico on roadways customarily open to the public. The crash must be reported to the state/jurisdiction and at least one directly related fatality must occur within 30 days of the crash.

Type of Data Collection Operation: One or more analysts, in each state, extract data from the official documents and enter the data into a standardized electronic database.

Data Collection and Imputation Procedures: Detailed data describing the characteristics of the fatal crash, the vehicles and persons involved are obtained from police crash reports, driver and vehicle registration records, autopsy reports, highway department, etc. Computerized edit checks monitor the accuracy and completeness of the data. The FARS incorporates a sophisticated mathematical multiple imputation procedure to develop a probability distribution of missing blood alcohol concentration (BAC) levels in the database for drivers, pedestrians, and cyclists.

Estimates of Sampling Error: Since this is census data, there are no sampling errors.

Other (Nonsampling) Errors: FARS represents a census of all police-reported crashes and captures all data reported at the state level. FARS data undergo a rigorous quality control process to prevent inaccurate reporting. However, these data are highly dependent on the accuracy of the police accident reports. Errors or omissions within police accident reports may not be detected.

Sources of Additional Material: The FARS Coding and Validation Manual, ANSI D16.1 Manual on Classification of Motor Vehicle Traffic Accidents (Sixth Edition). www.nhtsa.gov/FARS.

APPENDIX C
GEOGRAPHIC CONCEPTS

Geographic Concepts

STATES

States are the major political units of the United States. The District of Columbia is treated as a state equivalent in this publication. Tables A-1 through A-82 present data for the United States, the 50 states, and the District of Columbia. For census purposes, states are often grouped into geographic regions and divisions. However, Table A only uses an alphabetical state presentation.

METROPOLITAN AND MICROPOLITAN STATISTICAL AREAS

The U.S. Office of Management and Budget (OMB) defines metropolitan and micropolitan statistical areas according to published standards that are applied to U.S. Census Bureau data. The general concept of a metropolitan or micropolitan statistical area is that of a core area containing a substantial population nucleus, together with adjacent communities having a high degree of economic and social integration with that core. The term "core based statistical area" (CBSA) refers collectively to metropolitan and micropolitan statistical areas.

The major purpose of CBSAs is to enable all federal agencies to use the same geographic definitions in tabulating and publishing data for metropolitan and micropolitan areas. The definitions are designed to serve a wide variety of statistical and analytical purposes; adoption of the area for any specific purpose should be judged in terms of appropriateness for that purpose. While the definitions have been developed for statistical use by federal agencies, state and local governments as well as private business firms have often found the definitions helpful in presenting data for metropolitan and micropolitan areas.

The official 2010 Standards for Defining Metropolitan and Micropolitan Statistical Areas may be found on the OMB website at https://obamawhitehouse.archives.gov/sites/default/files/omb/assets/fedreg_2010/06282010_metro_standards.pdf and https://obamawhitehouse.archives.gov/sites/default/files/omb/assets/fedreg_2010/07072010_metro_standards-Correction.pdf. OMB Bulletin 15-01, which was issued on July 15, 2015, provides the listing of metropolitan and micropolitan statistical areas found in this publication; this document and related documents may be found at https://obamawhitehouse.archives.gov/sites/default/files/omb/bulletins/2015/15-01.pdf. Metropolitan areas presented in tables B-1 through B-14 and C-1 through C-4 and micropolitan areas presented in table D-1 of this publication are those county-based as defined on July 15, 2015. A series of maps showing these areas appears on pages 386 to 436.

Historical development. In 1910, the Census Bureau introduced "metropolitan districts" as an area classification. This marked the first use by the Census Bureau of a unit for reporting population data for large cities, together with their suburbs. Originally, only cities of at least 200,000 population were designated as the core of a metropolitan district. By 1940, the concept had been expanded to apply to a city of 50,000 or more inhabitants. The metropolitan district was generally defined to include contiguous minor civil divisions (MCDs) and incorporated places having a population density of at least 150 persons per square mile; therefore, the boundaries did not necessarily follow county lines.

A major limitation of the metropolitan district concept, from the standpoint of statistical presentation, was that not many data items beyond those available from the census of population and housing were available for MCDs and smaller places. The applicability of the metropolitan district concept also was limited because other generally similar area classifications were in use (e.g., the industrial areas of the census of manufactures and the labor market areas of the Labor Department's Employment and Training Administration), which were defined in different ways.

The standard metropolitan area (SMA) concept was developed in 1949 by the Bureau of the Budget (now OMB), with the advice of the newly established Federal Committee on Standard Metropolitan Areas, to overcome the above difficulties. It was designed so that a wide variety of statistical data on metropolitan areas might be presented for a uniform set of geographic areas. The SMAs consisted of one or more contiguous counties containing at least one city of 50,000 or more inhabitants. Additional counties had to meet certain criteria of metropolitan character and of social and economic integration with the central county in order to be included in an SMA.

Changes in the official criteria have been made at the time of each census since 1950. None of these changes have involved significant deviations from the basic metropolitan concept. Several modifications have been made in the rules for determining how large a city must be to have a metropolitan division defined. Criteria changes also have been made to reflect changing national conditions. For example, the 1949 rule specified that a county must have less than 25 percent of its workers engaged in agriculture. However, with a rapidly decreasing proportion of the population engaged in farming, this requirement has been eliminated because practically no counties are still affected by it. In 1959, the designation "standard metropolitan area" was changed to "standard metropolitan statistical area" (SMSA) to emphasize the nature and purpose of the areas. The SMSA designation was changed to the MSA/CMSA/PMSA designations in June 1983. The term "core based statistical area" (CBSA) was adopted in 2000 and refers collectively to metropolitan and micropolitan statistical areas.

The metropolitan and micropolitan statistical areas used in this book are based on application of 2010 standards that appeared in the Federal Register on June 28, 2010 (corrections issued July 7, 2010), to 2010 decennial census data. The lists of metropolitan and micropolitan statistical areas definitions may be found at https://www.census.gov/programs-surveys/metro-micro/about/delineation-files.html.

Defining metropolitan and micropolitan statistical areas. The 2010 standards provide that each CBSA must contain at least one urban area of 10,000 or more population. Each metropolitan statistical area must have at least one urbanized area of 50,000 or more inhabitants. Each micropolitan statistical area must have at least one urban cluster of at least 10,000 but less than 50,000 population.

Under the standards, the county (or counties) in which at least 50 percent of the population resides within urban areas of 10,000 or more population, or that contain at least 5,000 people residing within a single urban area of 10,000 or more population, is identified as a "central county" (counties). Additional outlying counties are included in the CBSA if they meet specified requirements of commuting to or from the central counties. Counties or equivalent entities form the geographic "building blocks" for metropolitan and micropolitan statistical areas throughout the United States and Puerto Rico.

If specified criteria are met, a metropolitan statistical area containing a single core with a population of 2.5 million or more may be subdivided to form smaller groupings of counties referred to as "metropolitan divisions."

Principal cities and metropolitan and micropolitan statistical area titles. The largest city in each metropolitan or micropolitan statistical area is designated a "principal city." Additional cities qualify if specified requirements are met concerning population size and employment. The title of each metropolitan or micropolitan statistical area consists of the names of up to three of its principal cities and the name of each state into which the metropolitan or micropolitan statistical area extends. Titles of metropolitan divisions also typically are based on principal city names but in certain cases consist of county names.

Defining New England city and town areas. In view of the importance of cities and towns in New England, the 2000 standards also provide for a set of geographic areas that are defined using cities and towns in the six New England states. The New England city and town areas (NECTAs) are defined using the same criteria as metropolitan and micropolitan statistical areas and are identified as either metropolitan or micropolitan, based, respectively, on the presence of either an urbanized area of 50,000 or more population or an urban cluster of at least 10,000 but less than 50,000 population. If the specified criteria are met, a NECTA containing a single core with a population of at least 2.5 million may be subdivided to form smaller groupings of cities and towns referred to as New England city and town area divisions. NECTAs are not included in this book.

Changes in definitions over time. Changes in the definitions of these statistical areas since the 1950 census have consisted chiefly of:

- The recognition of new areas as they reached the minimum required city or urbanized area population.

- The addition of counties (or cities and towns in New England) to existing areas as new decennial census data showed them to qualify.

- In some instances, formerly separate areas have been merged, components of an area have been transferred from one area to another, or components have been dropped from an area. The large majority of changes have taken place on the basis of decennial census data. However, Census Bureau data serve as the basis for intercensal updates in specified circumstances.

Because of these historical changes in geographic definitions, users must be cautious in comparing data for these statistical areas from different dates. For some purposes, comparisons of data for areas as defined at given dates may be appropriate; for other purposes, it may be preferable to maintain consistent area definitions. Historical metropolitan area definitions are available back to 1950 at https://www.census.gov/geographies/reference-files/time-series/demo/metro-micro/historical-delineation-files.html.

Special metropolitan area notes found in this publication. This report includes metropolitan and micropolitan statistical areas and metropolitan divisions defined by the Office of Management and Budget as of July 15, 2015. There are 382 metropolitan statistical areas and 551 micropolitan statistical areas in the United States. In addition, there are eight metropolitan statistical areas and five micropolitan statistical areas in Puerto Rico not covered in this publication. Within 11 of the largest metropolitan areas, there are 31 metropolitan divisions.

There are two metropolitan areas that we want to specially note for users. First, the Denver, CO, metropolitan had the special case involving the newly created county of Broomfield. Broomfield County, CO, was formed from parts of Adams, Boulder, Jefferson, and Weld Counties, CO, on November 15, 2001, and is coextensive with Broomfield city. For purposes of defining and presenting data for metropolitan statistical areas, Broomfield City is treated as if it were a county at the time of the 1990 and 2000 censuses. The other area is the St. Louis, MO-IL area. A portion of Sullivan city in Crawford County, MO, is legally part of the St. Louis, MO-IL MSA. Census 2000 tabulations and intercensal estimates for the St. Louis, MO-IL metropolitan statistical area do not include this small area.

COUNTIES

The primary political divisions of most states are termed "counties," which are the basic building blocks for metropolitan areas. In Louisiana, these divisions are known as "parishes." In Alaska, which has no counties, the county equivalents are the organized "boroughs" and the "census areas" that are delineated for statistical purposes by the State of Alaska and the Census Bureau. In four states (Maryland, Missouri, Nevada, and Virginia), there are one or more cities that are independent of any county organization and thus constitute primary divisions of their states. These cities are known as "independent cities" and are treated as equivalent to counties for statistical purposes. The District of Columbia has no primary divisions, and the entire area is considered equivalent to a county for statistical purposes.

Tables C-1 through C-4 present data for the 382 metropolitan statistical areas, 31 metropolitan divisions, and their 1,167 component counties defined as of July 2015. Table D-1 presents data for the 551 micropolitan statistical areas and their 658 counties likewise defined as of July 2015.

ALABAMA - Core Based Statistical Areas (CBSAs) and Counties

U.S. DEPARTMENT OF COMMERCE Economics and Statistics Administration U.S. Census Bureau

ALASKA - Core Based Statistical Areas (CBSAs) and Counties

ARIZONA - Core Based Statistical Areas (CBSAs) and Counties

LEGEND

Tucson-Nogales ——— Combined Statistical Area

YUMA ▨ Metropolitan Statistical Area

Payson ▨ Micropolitan Statistical Area

M E X I C O ——— International

UTAH ——— State or Statistical Equivalent

Apache ——— County or Statistical Equivalent

Pacific Ocean ——— Coastline

CBSA boundaries and names are as of February 2013. All
other boundaries and names are as of January 1, 2012.

COLORADO

NEVADA

UTAH

Las Vegas-Henderson

N

0 20 40 60 80 Kilometers

0 20 40 60 80 Miles

FLAGSTAFF

Coconino

LAKE HAVASU CITY-KINGMAN

Mohave

Show Low

Apache

NEW MEXICO

Navajo

CALIFORNIA

PRESCOTT

Yavapai

La Paz

Payson

PHOENIX-MESA-SCOTTSDALE

Gila

Greenlee

Maricopa

Tucson-Nogales

Pinal

Safford

Graham

YUMA

Yuma

Tucson-Nogales

SIERRA VISTA-DOUGLAS

TUCSON

Pima

Cochise

Pacific Ocean

Nogales

Santa Cruz

M E X I C O

Gulf of California

ARKANSAS - Core Based Statistical Areas (CBSAs) and Counties

CALIFORNIA - Core Based Statistical Areas (CBSAs) and Counties

KEY
1 VALLEJO-FAIRFIELD
2 Oakland-Hayward-Berkeley
3 SAN JOSE-SUNNYVALE-SANTA CLARA

LEGEND

Fresno-Madera	Combined Statistical Area
NAPA	Metropolitan Statistical Area
Ukiah	Micropolitan Statistical Area
San Rafael	Metropolitan Division
MEXICO	International
NEVADA	State or Statistical Equivalent
Alameda	County or Statistical Equivalent
Pacific Ocean	Coastline

CBSA boundaries and names are as of February 2013. All
other boundaries and names are as of January 1, 2012.

COLORADO - Core Based Statistical Areas (CBSAs) and Counties

U.S. DEPARTMENT OF COMMERCE Economics and Statistics Administration U.S. Census Bureau

CONNECTICUT - Core Based Statistical Areas (CBSAs) and Counties

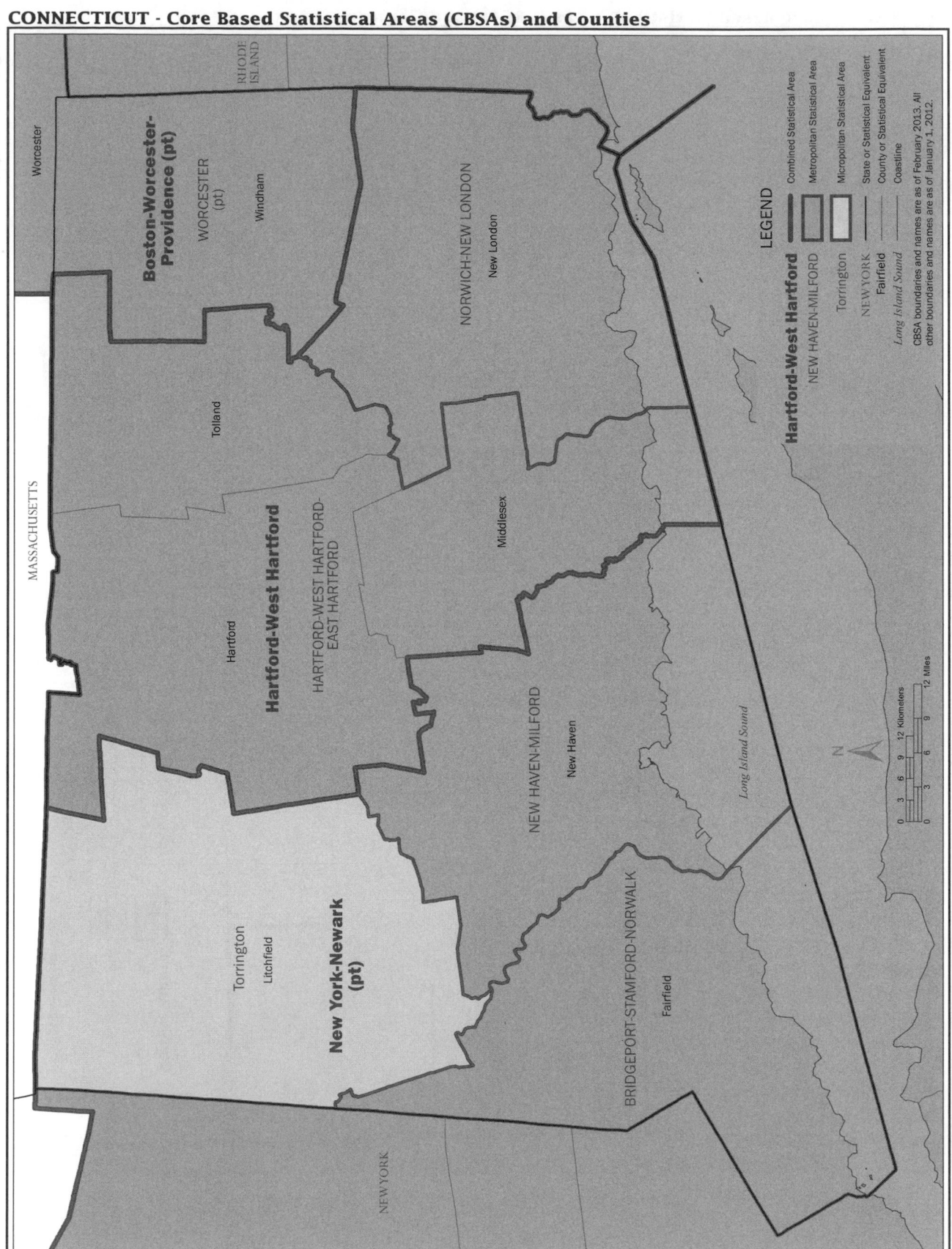

DELAWARE - Core Based Statistical Areas (CBSAs) and Counties

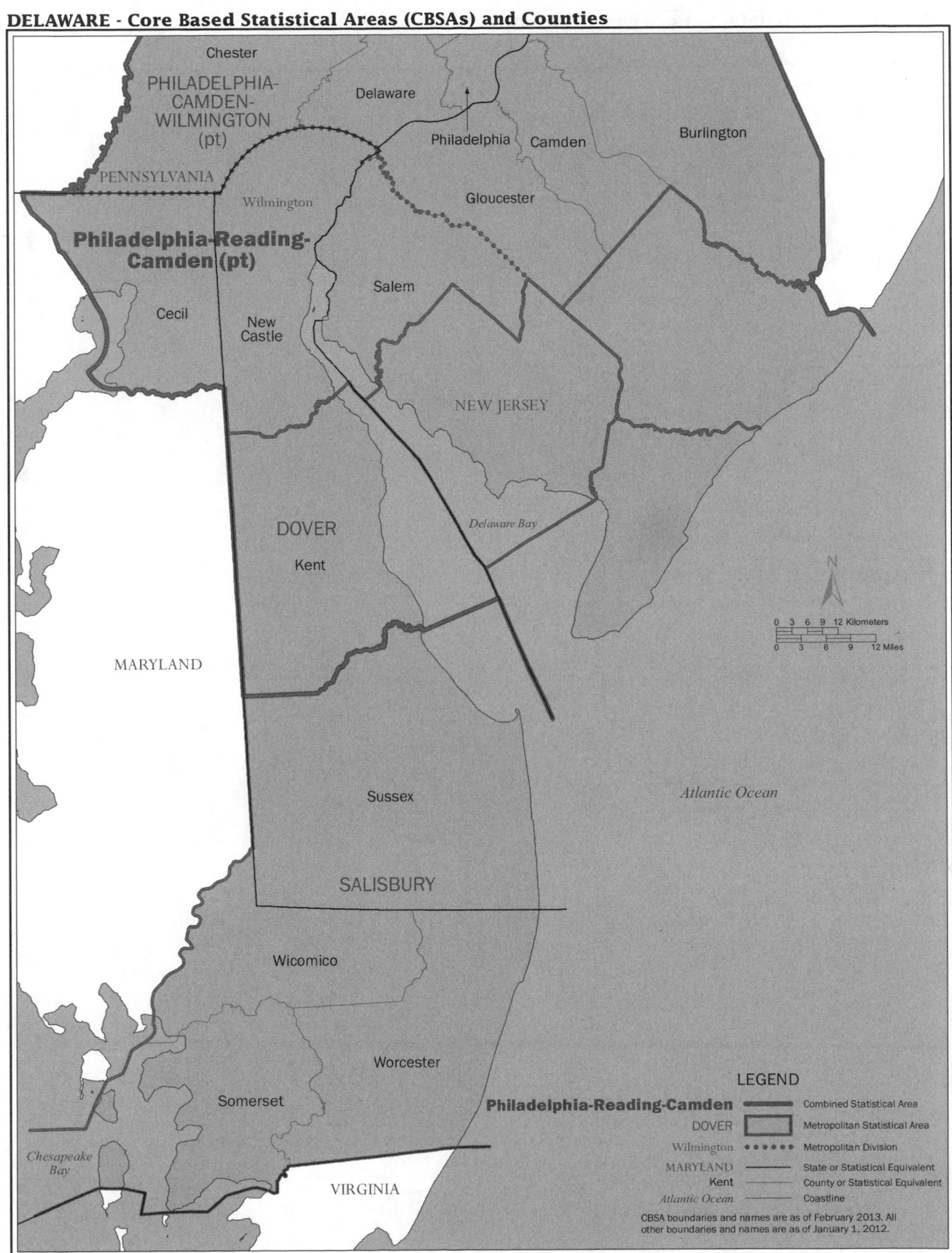

LEGEND

Philadelphia-Reading-Camden ▬▬▬ Combined Statistical Area

DOVER ▢ Metropolitan Statistical Area

Wilmington •••••• Metropolitan Division

MARYLAND ▬▬ State or Statistical Equivalent

Kent ▬ County or Statistical Equivalent

Atlantic Ocean ▬ Coastline

CBSA boundaries and names are as of February 2013. All
other boundaries and names are as of January 1, 2012.

U.S. DEPARTMENT OF COMMERCE Economics and Statistics Administration U.S. Census Bureau

DISTRICT OF COLUMBIA - Core Based Statistical Areas (CBSAs) and Counties

LEGEND

Washington-Baltimore-Arlington ———— Combined Statistical Area

WASHINGTON-BALTIMORE-ARLINGTON ▢ Metropolitan Statistical Area

Washington-Arlington-Alexandria ●●●●● Metropolitan Division

VIRGINIA ———— State or Statistical Equivalent

District of Columbia ———— County or Statistical Equivalent

Chesapeake Bay ———— Coastline

CBSA boundaries and names are as of February 2013. All
other boundaries and names are as of January 1, 2012.

FLORIDA - Core Based Statistical Areas (CBSAs) and Counties

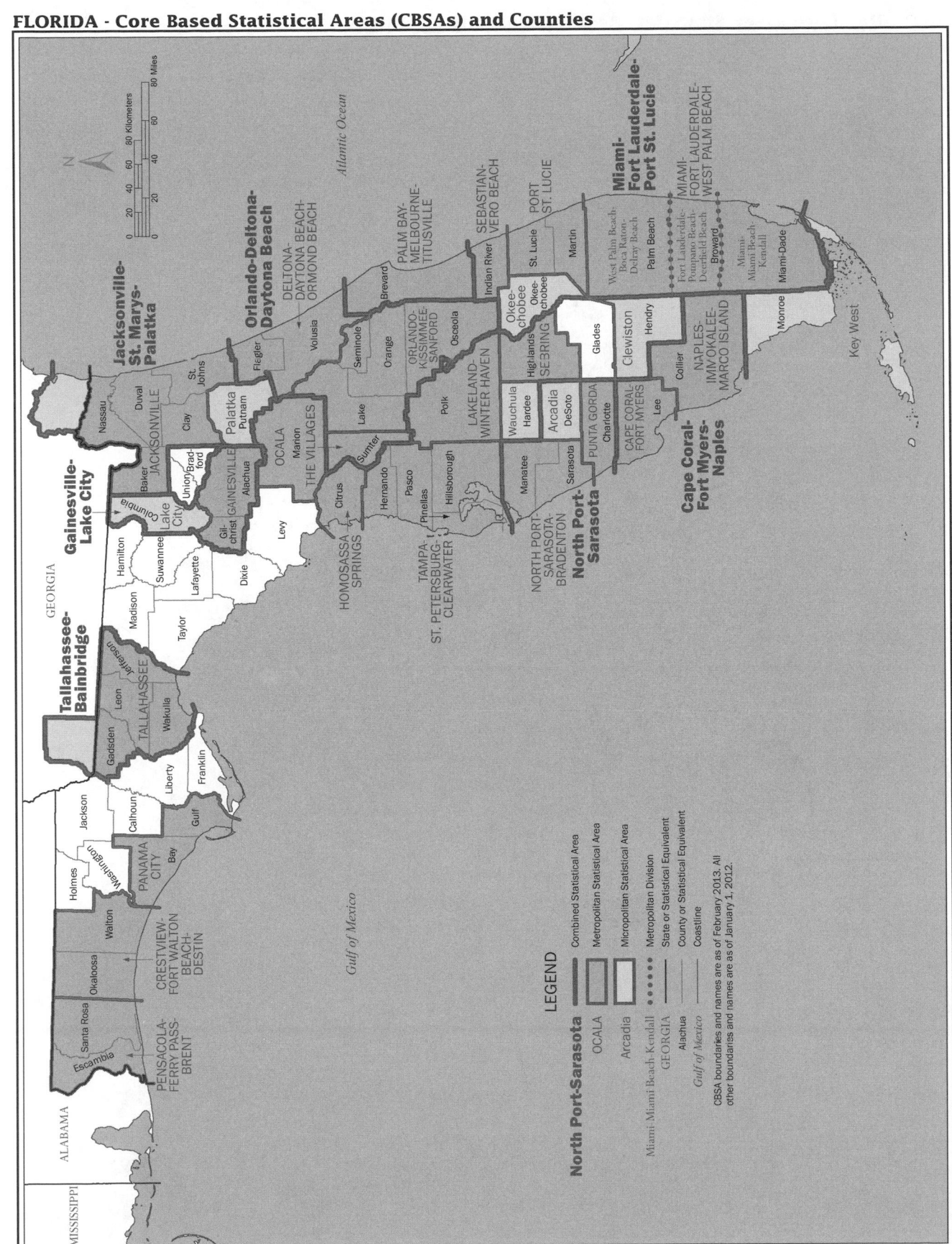

GEORGIA - Core Based Statistical Areas (CBSAs) and Counties

HAWAII - Core Based Statistical Areas (CBSAs) and Counties

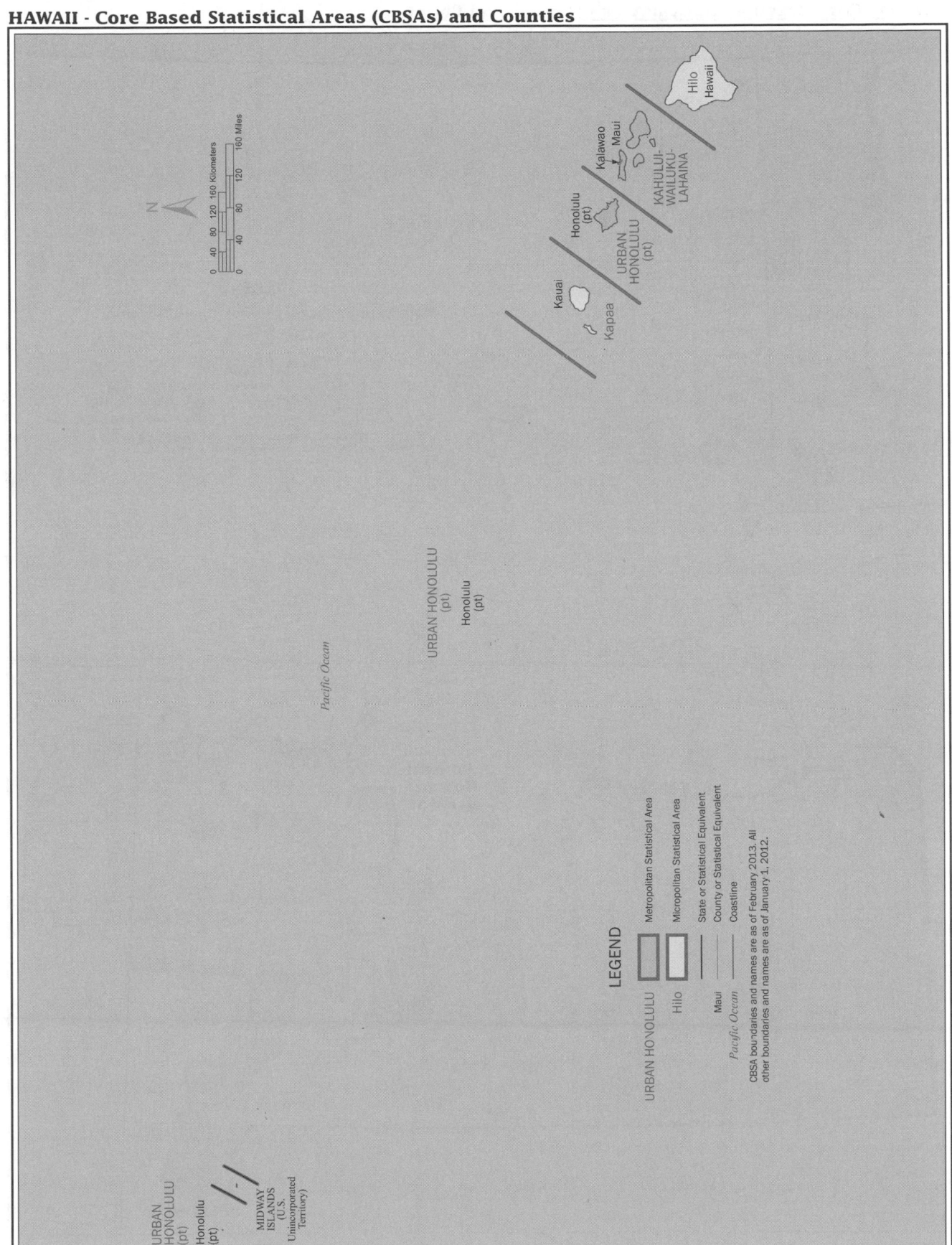

IDAHO - Core Based Statistical Areas (CBSAs) and Counties

LEGEND

Pullman-Moscow	Combined Statistical Area
LOGAN	Metropolitan Statistical Area
Burley	Micropolitan Statistical Area
CANADA	International
UTAH	State or Statistical Equivalent
Ada	County or Statistical Equivalent

CBSA boundaries and names are as of February 2013. All other boundaries and names are as of January 1, 2012.

ILLINOIS - Core Based Statistical Areas (CBSAs) and Counties

LEGEND

Peoria-Canton		Combined Statistical Area
PEORIA		Metropolitan Statistical Area
Dixon		Micropolitan Statistical Area
Elgin	• • • • •	Metropolitan Division
IOWA		State or Statistical Equivalent
Lee		County or Statistical Equivalent
Lake Michigan		Coastline

CBSA boundaries and names are as of February 2013. All
other boundaries and names are as of January 1, 2012.

INDIANA - Core Based Statistical Areas (CBSAs) and Counties

LEGEND

Kokomo-Peru — Combined Statistical Area

MUNCIE — Metropolitan Statistical Area

Peru — Micropolitan Statistical Area

Gary ••••• Metropolitan Division

OHIO — State or Statistical Equivalent

Jay — County or Statistical Equivalent

Lake Michigan — Coastline

CBSA boundaries and names are as of February 2013. All
other boundaries and names are as of January 1, 2012.

IOWA - Core Based Statistical Areas (CBSAs) and Counties

KANSAS - Core Based Statistical Areas (CBSAs) and Counties

KENTUCKY - Core Based Statistical Areas (CBSAs) and Counties

KEY
1 Frankfort
2 LEXINGTON-FAYETTE
3 Mount Sterling
4 Richmond-Berea
**5 Lexington-Fayette--
Richmond--Frankfort**

LEGEND

Combined Statistical Area

Metropolitan Statistical Area

Micropolitan Statistical Area

State or Statistical Equivalent

County or Statistical Equivalent

Martin-Union City
EVANSVILLE

London

OHIO

Adair

CBSA boundaries and names are as of February 2013. All
other boundaries and names are as of January 1, 2012.

LOUISIANA - Core Based Statistical Areas (CBSAs) and Counties

MAINE - Core Based Statistical Areas (CBSAs) and Counties

Aroostook

CANADA

Piscataquis

Somerset

BANGOR
Penobscot

Franklin

Washington

Oxford

Augusta-
Waterville

Kennebec

Waldo

Hancock

NEW
HAMPSHIRE

Andro-
scoggin

LEWISTON-
AUBURN

Knox

Lincoln

Sagadahoc

Cumberland

Atlantic Ocean

PORTLAND-
SOUTH
PORTLAND

York

**Portland-
Lewiston-
South Portland**

LEGEND

Portland-Lewiston-South Portland		Combined Statistical Area
BANGOR		Metropolitan Statistical Area
Augusta-Waterville		Micropolitan Statistical Area
CANADA		International
NEW HAMPSHIRE		State or Statistical Equivalent
Knox		County or Statistical Equivalent
Atlantic Ocean		Coastline

CBSA boundaries and names are as of February 2013. All
other boundaries and names are as of January 1, 2012.

MARYLAND - Core Based Statistical Areas (CBSAs) and Counties

MASSACHUSETTS - Core Based Statistical Areas (CBSAs) and Counties

U.S. DEPARTMENT OF COMMERCE Economics and Statistics Administration U.S. Census Bureau

MICHIGAN - Core Based Statistical Areas (CBSAs) and Counties

MINNESOTA - Core Based Statistical Areas (CBSAs) and Counties

MISSISSIPPI - Core Based Statistical Areas (CBSAs) and Counties

LEGEND

Cleveland-Indianola
JACKSON
Laurel
ALABAMA
Adams
Gulf of Mexico

━━━ Combined Statistical Area
▬ Metropolitan Statistical Area
▬ Micropolitan Statistical Area
─── State or Statistical Equivalent
········· County or Statistical Equivalent
─── Coastline

CBSA boundaries and names are as of February 2013. All
other boundaries and names are as of January 1, 2012.

MISSOURI - Core Based Statistical Areas (CBSAs) and Counties

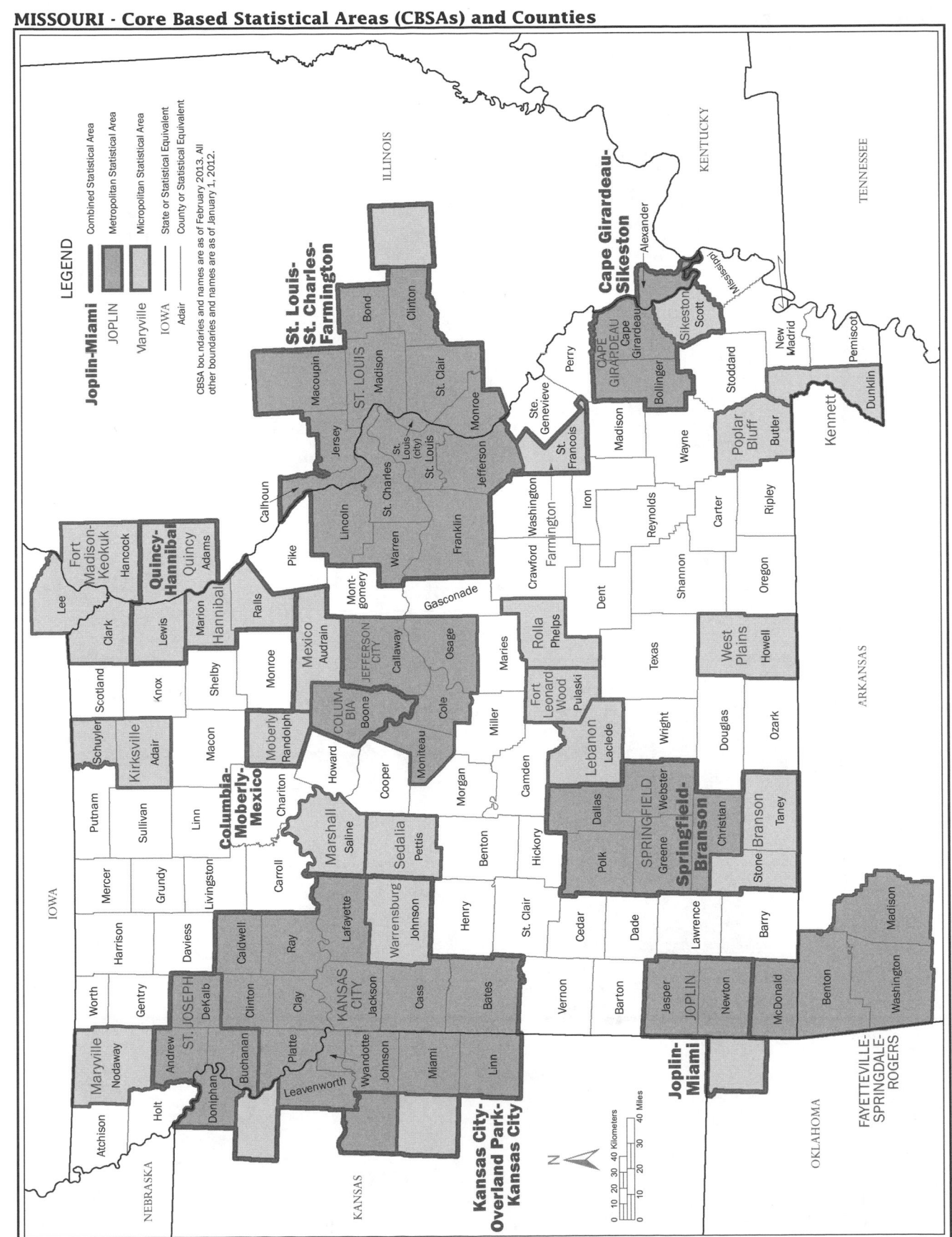

U.S. DEPARTMENT OF COMMERCE Economics and Statistics Administration U.S. Census Bureau

MONTANA - Core Based Statistical Areas (CBSAs) and Counties

NEBRASKA - Core Based Statistical Areas (CBSAs) and Counties

NEVADA - Core Based Statistical Areas (CBSAs) and Counties

NEW HAMPSHIRE - Core Based Statistical Areas (CBSAs) and Counties

LEGEND

Boston-Providence-Worcester	Combined Statistical Area
MANCHESTER-NASHUA	Metropolitan Statistical Area
Berlin	Micropolitan Statistical Area
Rockingham County-Strafford County	Metropolitan Division
CANADA	International
MAINE	State or Statistical Equivalent
Belknap	County or Statistical Equivalent
Atlantic Ocean	Coastline

CBSA boundaries and names are as of February 2013. All other boundaries and names are as of January 1, 2012.

CANADA

Essex

Berlin

Coos

MAINE

VERMONT

Orange

Grafton

Carroll

Claremont-Lebanon

Windsor

NEW YORK

Laconia

Belknap

Sullivan

Concord

Merrimack

Strafford

Boston-Worcester-Providence (pt)

Rockingham

BOSTON-CAMBRIDGE-NEWTON (pt)

Rockingham County-Strafford County

N

0 5 10 15 20 Kilometers
0 5 10 15 20 Miles

Keene

Cheshire

MANCHESTER-NASHUA

Hillsborough

Atlantic Ocean

Essex

MASSACHUSETTS

Middlesex

NEW JERSEY - Core Based Statistical Areas (CBSAs) and Counties

U.S. DEPARTMENT OF COMMERCE Economics and Statistics Administration U.S. Census Bureau

NEW MEXICO - Core Based Statistical Areas (CBSAs) and Counties

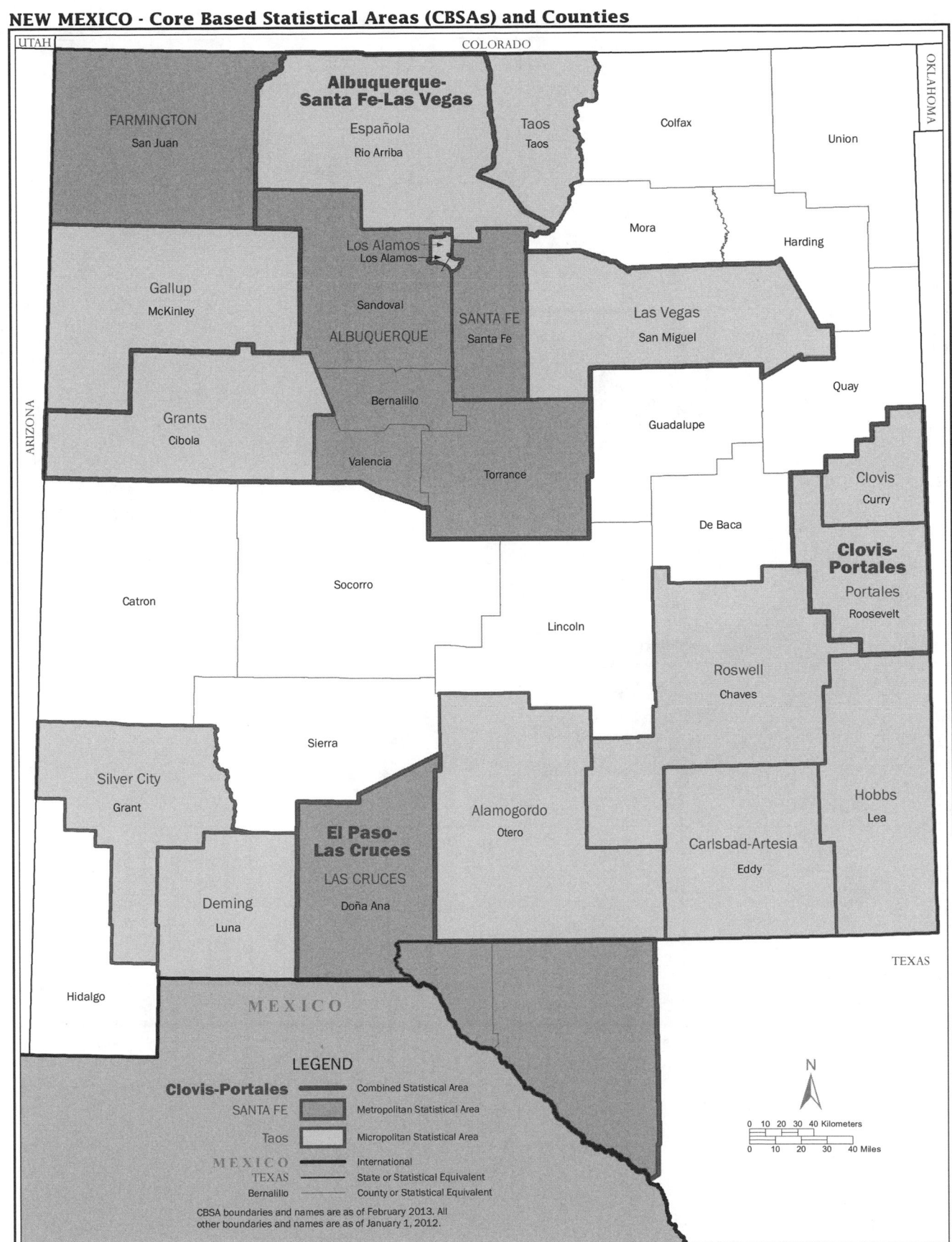

U.S. DEPARTMENT OF COMMERCE Economics and Statistics Administration U.S. Census Bureau

NEW YORK - Core Based Statistical Areas (CBSAs) and Counties

NORTH CAROLINA - Core Based Statistical Areas (CBSAs) and Counties

U.S. DEPARTMENT OF COMMERCE Economics and Statistics Administration U.S. Census Bureau

NORTH DAKOTA - Core Based Statistical Areas (CBSAs) and Counties

OHIO - Core Based Statistical Areas (CBSAs) and Counties

LEGEND

Findlay-Tiffin — Combined Statistical Area

AKRON — Metropolitan Statistical Area

Athens — Micropolitan Statistical Area

CANADA — International

INDIANA — State or Statistical Equivalent

Adams — County or Statistical Equivalent

Lake Erie — Coastline

CBSA boundaries and names are as of February 2013. All other boundaries and names are as of January 1, 2012.

OKLAHOMA - Core Based Statistical Areas (CBSAs) and Counties

OREGON - Core Based Statistical Areas (CBSAs) and Counties

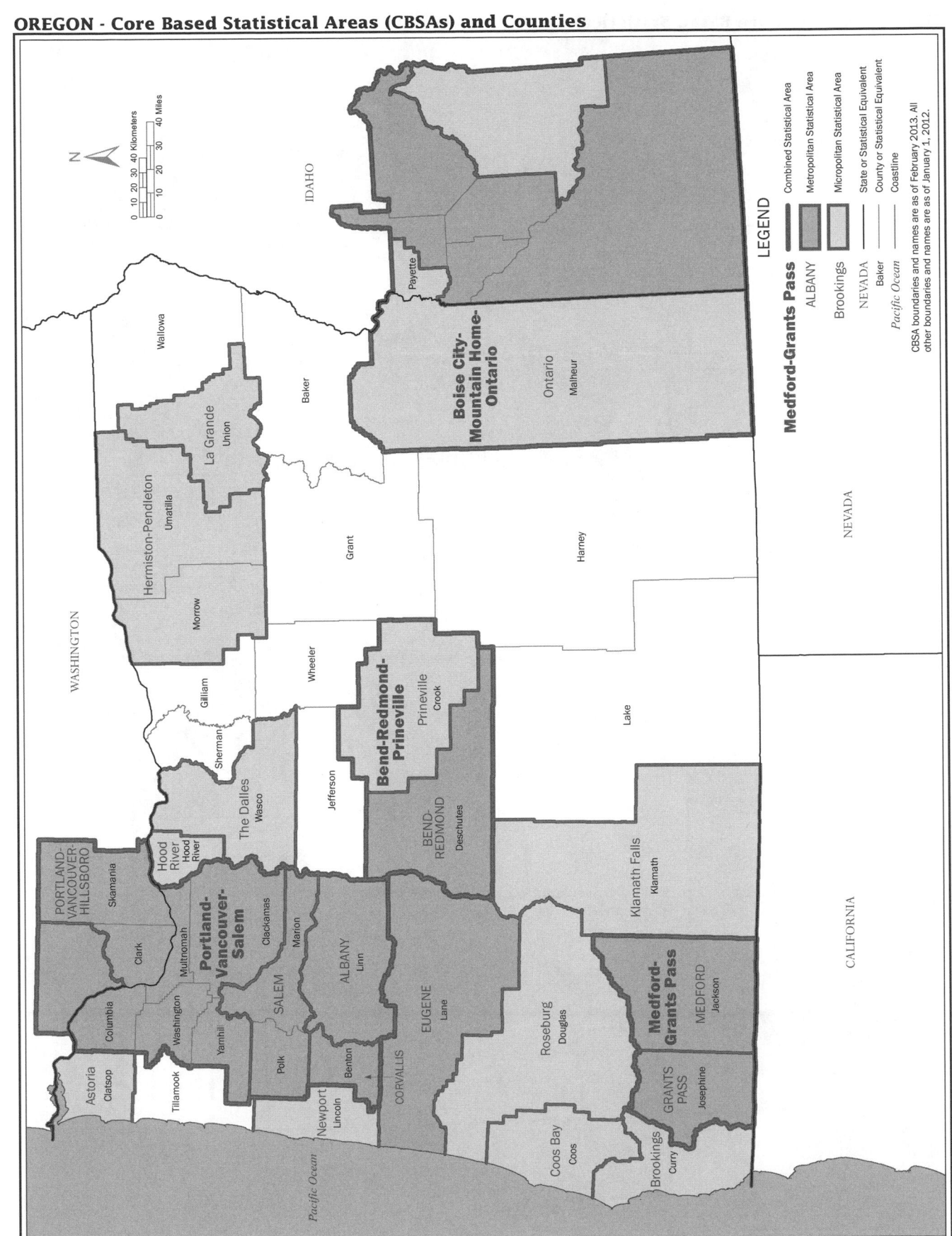

PENNSYLVANIA - Core Based Statistical Areas (CBSAs) and Counties

RHODE ISLAND - Core Based Statistical Areas (CBSAs) and Counties

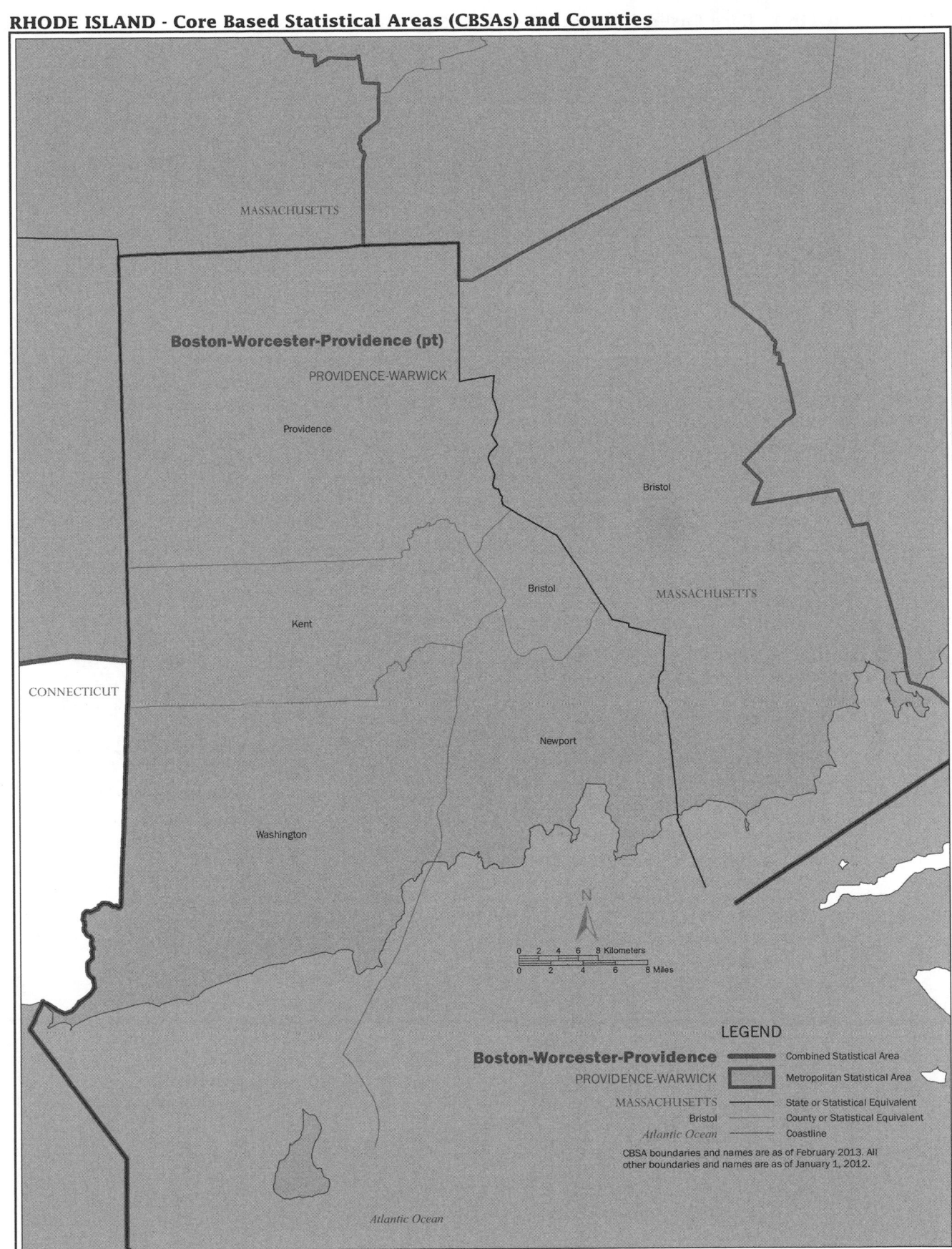

SOUTH CAROLINA - Core Based Statistical Areas (CBSAs) and Counties

SOUTH DAKOTA - Core Based Statistical Areas (CBSAs) and Counties

U.S. DEPARTMENT OF COMMERCE Economics and Statistics Administration U.S. Census Bureau

TENNESSEE - Core Based Statistical Areas (CBSAs) and Counties

LEGEND

Combined Statistical Area

Metropolitan Statistical Area

Micropolitan Statistical Area

GEORGIA   State or Statistical Equivalent

Bedford   County or Statistical Equivalent

CBSA boundaries and names are as of February 2013. All
other boundaries and names are as of January 1, 2012.

TEXAS - Core Based Statistical Areas (CBSAs) and Counties

UTAH - Core Based Statistical Areas (CBSAs) and Counties

VERMONT - Core Based Statistical Areas (CBSAs) and Counties

CANADA

Grand
Isle

Franklin

Orleans

BURLINGTON-
SOUTH BURLINGTON

Essex

Berlin

Coos

Lamoille

Chittenden

Caledonia

MAINE

Barre
Washington

Addison

Orange

Grafton

NEW YORK

Claremont-Lebanon

NEW HAMPSHIRE

Rutland
Rutland

Windsor

Sullivan

Bennington
Bennington

Windham

LEGEND

BURLINGTON-SOUTH BURLINGTON | Metropolitan Statistical Area

Barre | Micropolitan Statistical Area

CANADA | International

NEW HAMPSHIRE | State or Statistical Equivalent

Addison | County or Statistical Equivalent

CBSA boundaries and names are as of February 2013. All
other boundaries and names are as of January 1, 2012.

MASSACHUSETTS

U.S. DEPARTMENT OF COMMERCE Economics and Statistics Administration U.S. Census Bureau

VIRGINIA - Core Based Statistical Areas (CBSAs) and Counties

WASHINGTON - Core Based Statistical Areas (CBSAs) and Counties

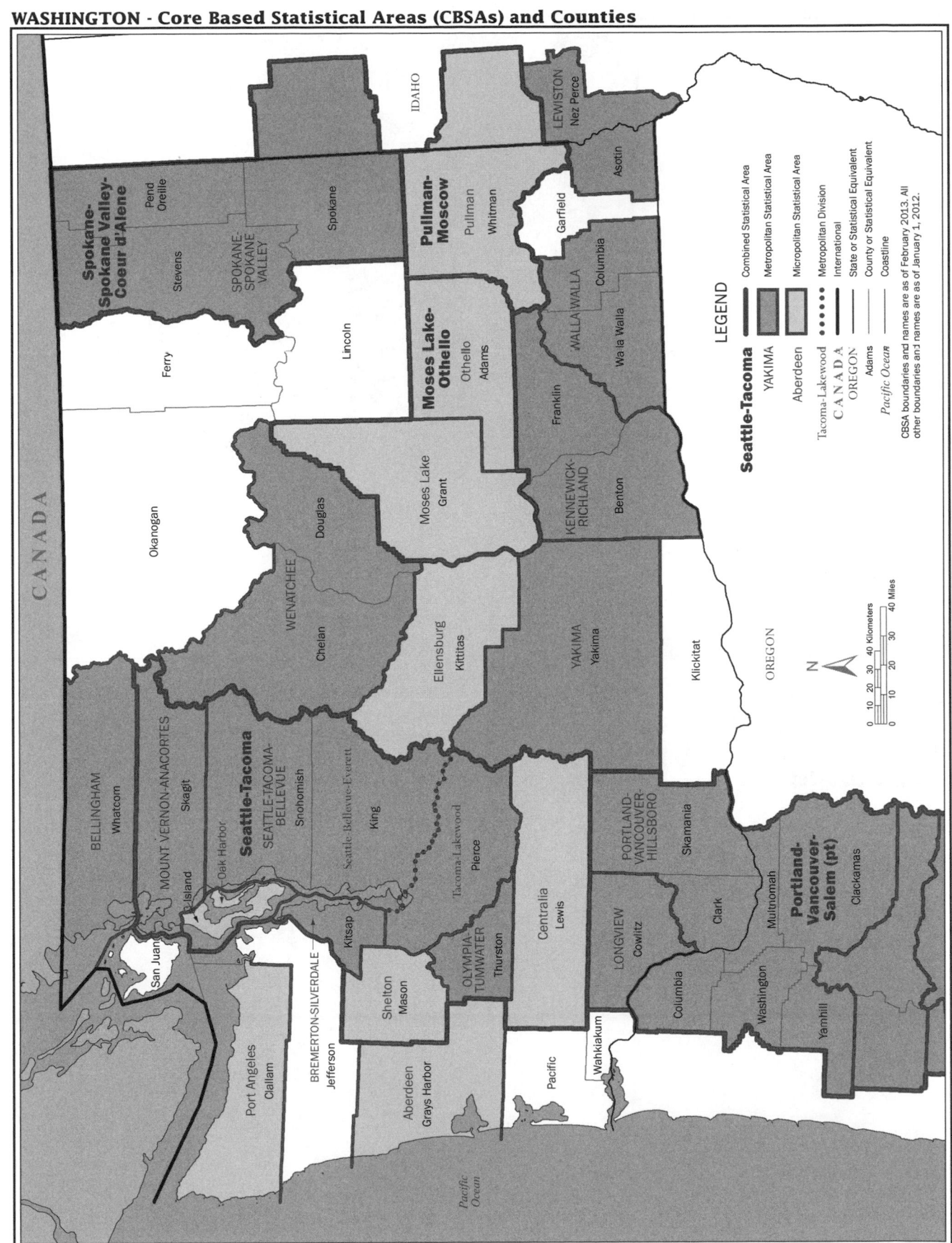

LEGEND

Seattle-Tacoma	Combined Statistical Area
YAKIMA	Metropolitan Statistical Area
Aberdeen	Micropolitan Statistical Area
Tacoma-Lakewood	Metropolitan Division
CANADA	International
OREGON	State or Statistical Equivalent
Adams	County or Statistical Equivalent
Pacific Ocean	Coastline

CBSA boundaries and names are as of February 2013. All other boundaries and names are as of January 1, 2012.

U.S. DEPARTMENT OF COMMERCE Economics and Statistics Administration U.S. Census Bureau

WEST VIRGINIA - Core Based Statistical Areas (CBSAs) and Counties

LEGEND

Combined Statistical Area

Metropolitan Statistical Area

Micropolitan Statistical Area

Metropolitan Division

State or Statistical Equivalent

County or Statistical Equivalent

Coastline

Morgantown-Fairmont

WHEELING

Elkins

Washington-Arlington-Alexandria

VIRGINIA

Barbour

CBSA boundaries and names are as of February 2013. All other boundaries and names are as of January 1, 2012.

WISCONSIN - Core Based Statistical Areas (CBSAs) and Counties

LEGEND

Green Bay-Shawano	Combined Statistical Area
APPLETON	Metropolitan Statistical Area
Baraboo	Micropolitan Statistical Area
Lake County-Kenosha County	Metropolitan Division
C A N A D A	International
ILLINOIS	State or Statistical Equivalent
Adams	County or Statistical Equivalent
Lake Michigan	Coastline

CBSA boundaries and names are as of February 2013. All other boundaries and names are as of January 1, 2012.

WYOMING - Core Based Statistical Areas (CBSAs) and Counties

The bibliography below includes the most recent statistical abstracts for states. For some states, a near equivalent has been listed in substitution for, or in addition to, a statistical abstract. All sources contain statistical tables on a variety of subjects for the state as a whole, its component parts, or both. Internet sites also contain statistical data.

Alabama
University of Alabama
Center for Business and Economic Research
P.O. Box 870221
Tuscaloosa, AL 35487-0221
Phone: 205-348-6191. Fax: 205-348-2951
http://cber.cba.ua.edu/

Alabama Economic Outlook, 2016. Revised annually
http://www.auber.org/pubs/CBER_Alabama_
    Outlook2016.pdf

Alaska
State of Alaska, Department of Commerce
Community and Economic Development
550 West 7th Avenue, Suite 1770
Anchorage, AK 99501-3569
Phone: 907-465-2500. Fax 907-269-8125
https://www.commerce.alaska.gov/web/

The Alaska Economic Performance Report, 2013. Online.
https://www.commerce.alaska.gov/web/Portals/6/
    pub/2013_Alaska_Economic_Performance_Report.
    pdf

Arizona
Arizona Commerce Authority
333 North Central Avenue
Suite 1900
Phoenix, AZ 85004
Phone: 800.542.5684
http://www.azcommerce.com/

University of Arizona, Economic and Business Research
    Center
1130 East Helen Street, McClelland Hall, Room 103
P.O. Box 210108
Tucson, AZ 85721-0108

Arizona— *Continued*
Phone: 520-621-2155.
https://ebr.eller.arizona.edu/

Arkansas
University of Arkansas at Little Rock, Institute for
    Economic Advancement
College of Business
2801 South University Avenue
Little Rock, AR 72204-1099
Phone: 501-569-8519. Fax: 501-569-8538.
http://iea.ualr.edu/

2016 Arkansas Economic Impact Report
http://www.arkansasedc.com/sites/default/files/content/
    file-nodes/aedc_2016_economic_impact_report.pdf

California
California Department of Finance
915 L Street
Sacramento, CA 95814
Phone: 916-445-3878
http://www.dof.ca.gov/

Colorado
University of Colorado at Boulder Government
    Publications
Library, 184 UCB
1720 Pleasant Street
Boulder, CO 80309-0184
Phone: 303-492-8705
http://www.colorado.edu/libraries/libraries/
    norlin-library/government-information-library

Colorado Office of Economic Development and
    International Trade
1625 Broadway, Suite 2700
Denver, CO 80202
Phone: 303-892-3840. Fax: 303-892-3848
http://choosecolorado.com/

Connecticut
Connecticut Department of Economic and Community
  Development
505 Hudson Street
Hartford, CT 06106-7106
Phone: 860-270-8000
http://www.ct.gov/ecd/site/default.asp

The Connecticut Economic Digest
http://www.ct.gov/ecd/cwp/view.
  asp?a=1106&q=303286&ecdNav=|

Connecticut Town Profiles, 2012
https://www.cerc.com/resources/town-profiles/

Delaware
Delaware Economic Development Office
99 Kings Highway, Dover, DE 1990.
Phone: 302-739-4271. Fax: 302-739-5749
http://dedo.delaware.gov/

2015 Delaware Data Book.
http://inde.delaware.gov/dedo_pdf/NewsEvents_pdf/
  publications/DE_DATA%20book_February%20
  2015.pdf

Florida
University of Florida, Bureau of Economic and
  Business Research,
P.O. Box 117145,
Gainesville, FL 32611-7145
Phone: 352-392-0171, ext. 219. Fax: 352-392-4739
https://www.bebr.ufl.edu/

Print versions of the *Florida Statistical Abstract*, the
  Florida County Perspective, and *the Florida County
  Rankings* were discontinued in 2011. However, most
  data from these publications are available online at:
  https://www.bebr.ufl.edu/data

Georgia
University of Georgia, Terry College of Business
Selig Center for Economic Growth
Athens, GA 30602-6269
Phone: 706-542-8100. Fax: 706-542-3835
http://www.terry.uga.edu/about/centers-institutes/selig

Hawaii
State of Hawaii, Department of Business, Economic
  Development and Tourism
P.O. Box 2359, Honolulu, HI 96804
Phone: 808-586-2480
http://dbedt.hawaii.gov/

Hawaii—*Continued*
The State of Hawaii Data Book 2015
http://dbedt.hawaii.gov/economic/databook/

Idaho
Idaho Department of Commerce
P.O. Box 83720
Boise, ID 83720-0093
Phone: 208-334-2470. Fax: 208-334-2631. Toll free:
  800-842-5858
http://commerce.idaho.gov/

Illinois
Illinois Department of Commerce and Economic
  Opportunity
100 W. Randolph
Chicago, IL 60601
Phone: 312-814-7179
https://www.illinois.gov/dceo/Pages/default.aspx

Indiana
Indiana University, Kelley School of Business
Indiana Business Research Center
100 South College Avenue, Suite 240
Bloomington, IN 47404
Phone: 812-855-5507
http://www.stats.indiana.edu/
STATS Indiana. Online only

Iowa
Iowa State University, University Extension
Regional Capacity Analysis Program
17 East Hall, Ames, IA 50011
Phone: 515-294-9903. Fax: 515-294-0592

State Library of Iowa, State Data Center of Iowa

Ola Babcock Miller Building
1112 East Grand
Des Moines, IA 50319-0233
Phone: 800-248-4483. Fax: 515-242-6543
http://www.iowadatacenter.org/

Kansas
University of Kansas, Institute for Policy and Social
  Research
1541 Lilac Lane, 607 Blake Hall
Lawrence, KS 66045-3129
Phone: 785-864-3701. Fax: 785-864-3683
www.ipsr.ku.edu/

Kansas Statistical Abstract, 2015. 50th ed.
http://ipsr.ku.edu/ksdata/ksah/

Kentucky
Kentucky Cabinet for Economic Development
Old Capitol Annex, 300 West Broadway
Frankfort, KY 40601-1975
Phone: 800-626-2930. Fax: 502-564-3256
http://www.thinkkentucky.com/

Kentucky Economic Development Guide
http://www.businessclimate.com/
    kentucky-economic-development-digital-magazine

Louisiana
Louisiana State Census Data Center
Division of Administration, Office of Information
    Technology
P.O. Box 94095
Baton Rouge, LA 70804
Phone: 225-219-9470. Fax: 225-219-9465
http://louisiana.gov/Explore/
    Demographics_and_Geography/

Maine
Maine State Planning Office
38 State House Station
Augusta, ME 04333-0038
Phone: 800-662-4545. Fax: 207-287-6489
http://www.maine.gov/portal/

Maryland
Maryland Department of Panning
301 West Preston Street, Room 702
Baltimore, MD 21201
Phone: 410-767-4450

Maryland State Data Center
http://www.mdp.state.md.us/msdc/

2014 Maryland Statistical Handbook
http://planning.maryland.gov/msdc/md_statistical_
    handbook14.pdf

Massachusetts
MassCHIP, Massachusetts Department of Public
    Health
Executive Office of Health and Human Services
One Ashburton Place
11th Floor
Boston, MA 02108
Phone: 617-573-1600
http://www.mass.gov/eohhs/researcher/
    community-health/masschip/

Michigan
Michigan Economic Development Corporation
300 North Washington Square
Lansing, MI 48913
Phone: 1-888-522-0103
http://www.michiganbusiness.org/#home-intro

Minnesota
Minnesota Department of Employment and Economic
    Development (DEED)
1st National Bank Building
332 Minnesota Street, Suite E200
Saint Paul, MN 55101-1351
Phone: 800-657-3858
https://mn.gov/deed/

Minnesota State Demographic Center
658 Cedar Street, Room 300
Saint Paul, MN 55155
Phone: 651-296-2557
https://mn.gov/admin/demography/

Mississippi
Mississippi State University Libraries
P.O. Box 5408
Mississippi State, MS 39762-5408
Phone: 662-325-7668
http://guides.library.msstate.edu/c.
    php?g=577981&p=3987516

Missouri
University of Missouri-Columbia
Economic and Policy Analysis Research Center
10 Professional Building, Columbia, MO 65211
Phone: 573-882-4805. Fax: 573-882-5563
http://eparc.missouri.edu/publications/archive/archive.
    html

Montana
Montana Department of Commerce
Census and Economic Information Center
301 South Park Avenue, P.O. Box 200500
Helena, MT 59620-0505
Phone: 406-841-2740. Fax: 406-841-2731
http://ceic.mt.gov/

Nebraska
Nebraska Department of Economic Development
301 Centennial Mall South, P. O. Box 94666
Lincoln, NE 68509-4666
Phone: 800-426-6505. Fax 402-471-3778
http://info.neded.org/

Nevada
Nevada Department of Administration
Division of Budget and Planning
209 East Musser Street, Room 200
Carson City, NV 89701-4298
Phone: 775-684-0222. Fax: 775-684-0260
www.budget.state.nv.us/

New Hampshire
New Hampshire Office of Energy and Planning
4 Chenell Drive
Concord, NH 03301-8501
Phone: 603-271-2155. Fax 603-271-2615
www.nh.gov/oep/index.htm

New Jersey
State of New Jersey Department of Labor and
    Workforce Development
1 John Fitch Plaza, P.O. Box 110
Trenton, NJ 08625-0110
Phone: 609-984-2595. Fax: 609-984-6833
http://lwd.dol.state.nj.us/labor/lpa/LMI_index.html

New Mexico
University of New Mexico
Bureau of Business and Economic Research, MSC06
    3510
1 University of New Mexico
Albuquerque, NM 87131-0001
Phone: 505-277-2216. Fax 505-277-7066.

New Mexico Business, Current Economic Report.
http://bber.unm.edu/

New York
Nelson A. Rockefeller Institute of Government,
411 State Street,
Albany, NY 12203-1003.
Phone: 518-443-5522. Fax: 518-443-5788.
http://www.rockinst.org/

New York State Statistical Yearbook, 2015. 39th ed.
http://www.rockinst.org/nys_statistics/

North Carolina
North Carolina Office of State Budget and
    Management
116 West Jones Street
Raleigh, NC 27603-8005
Phone: 919-807-4700. Fax: 919-733-0640
https://www.osbm.nc.gov/

How North Carolina Ranks, 2016.
https://www.osbm.nc.gov/document/
    how-north-carolina-ranks-2016

North Dakota
North Dakota Department of Commerce
Economic Development & Finance Division
P.O. Box 2057
Bismarck, North Dakota 58502-2057
Phone: 701-328-5300. Fax: 701-328-5320
https://www.business.nd.gov/

Ohio
Ohio Department of Development
Office of Policy Strategic Research and Strategic
    Planning
77 South High Street, P.O. Box 1001
Columbus, OH 43216-1001
Phone: 614-466-5017
https://development.ohio.gov/

Oklahoma
University of Oklahoma,
Michael F. Price College of Business
Center for Economic and Management Research
307 West Brooks, Room 3
Norman OK 73019-4004
Phone: 405-325-2931, Fax: 405-325-7688
http://www.ou.edu/price/centersresearch/cemr.html

Statistical Abstract of Oklahoma
http://www.ou.edu/price/centersresearch/cemr/cemr_
    publications.html

Oregon
Oregon State Archives
800 Summer Street, NE
Salem, OR 97310
Phone: 503-373-0701. Fax: 503-378-4118.
Oregon Blue Book. 2013–2014. Biennial
http://www.sos.state.or.us/bbook/

Pennsylvania
Penn State Harrisburg
Pennsylvania State Data Center
Institute of State and Regional Affairs
777 West Harrisburg Pike,
Middletown, PA 17057-4898
Phone: 717-948-6336. Fax: 717-948-6754
https://pasdc.hbg.psu.edu/Default.aspx

Pennsylvania Statistical Abstract, 2015. Also available on
    CD-ROM.
https://pasdc.hbg.psu.edu/Publications/
    PennsylvaniaAbstract/tabid/1018/Default.aspx

Pennsylvania State Facts, 2015
https://pasdc.hbg.psu.edu/sdc/pasdc_files/pastats/PA_
    Facts_2015.pdf

Rhode Island
Rhode Island Commerce Corporation
315 Iron Horse Way, Suite 101
Providence, RI 02908
Phone: 401-278-9100. Fax 401-273-8270
http://commerceri.com/

South Carolina
South Carolina Budget and Control Board
Office of Research and Statistics
1919 Blanding Street, Columbia, SC 29201
Phone: 803-898-9960

South Carolina Statistical Abstract
http://abstract.sc.gov/index.html

South Dakota
South Dakota Governor's Office on Economic
  Development
711 E. Wells Ave.
Pierre, South Dakota 57501
Phone: 605-367-4518
http://www.sdreadytowork.com/home.aspx

Tennessee
University of Tennessee
Center for Business and Economic Research
College of Business Administration
916 Volunteer Boulevard
Knoxville, TN 37996-0570
Phone: 865-974-5441. Fax: 865-974-3100.
http://cber.bus.utk.edu/Default.htm

Tennessee State Data Center
http://tndata.utk.edu/

Texas
Texas Almanac, University of North Texas
History Department
1155 Union Circle #310650, Denton, TX 76203-5017
Phone: 940-369-5200
Texas Almanac
http://texasalmanac.com/

Texas State Data Center and Office of the State
  Demographer
Institute for Demographic and Socioeconomic
  Research
University of Texas at San Antonio
One UTSA Circle
San Antonio, TX 78249-0704
Phone: 210-458-6543. Fax: 210-458-6541
http://txsdc.utsa.edu/

Utah
Governor's Office of Planning and Budget
Demographic and Economic Analysis, 150
P.O. Box 132210
Salt Lake City, UT 84114-2210
Phone 801-538-1027. Fax: 801-538-1547
https://gomb.utah.gov/

Vermont
Department of Labor
Economic and Labor Market Information
P.O. Box 488
Montpelier, VT 05601-0488
Phone: 802-828-4202. http://www.vtlmi.info/

Virginia
Weldon Cooper Center for Public Service
P.O. Box 400206
Charlottesville, VA 22904-4206
434-982-5522.
http://www.coopercenter.org/

Washington
Washington State Office of Financial Management
P.O. Box 43113
Olympia, WA 98504-3113
Phone: 360-902-0555
http://www.ofm.wa.gov/

Washington State Data Book, 2015.
http://www.ofm.wa.gov/databook/default.asp

West Virginia
West Virginia University
College of Business and Economics
Bureau of Business and Economic Research
P.O. Box 6025, Morgantown, WV 26506
Phone: 304-293-7831
http://business.wvu.edu/centers/
  bureau-of-business-and-economic-researchprofiles

Wisconsin
Wisconsin Legislative Reference Bureau
One East Main Street, Suite 200
Madison, WI 53703
608-266-0341. Fax: 608-266-5648
https://legis.wisconsin.gov/lrb

Wyoming
Department of Administration and Information
Economic Analysis Division
2800 Central Avenue, Suite 206
Cheyenne, WY 82002-0060
307-777-7504. Fax: 307-632-1819
http://eadiv.state.wy.us/

Wyoming 2016 – Just the Facts
http://eadiv.state.wy.us/Wy_facts/facts2016.pdf

KEY FEDERAL WEBSITES WITH STATE-LEVEL INFORMATION

Many federal government agencies publish state-level information. The sites listed below have large concentrations of state-level information on easy-to-locate websites.

U.S. BUREAU OF ECONOMIC ANALYSIS
Gross State Product and Personal income
https://www.bea.gov/regional/index.htm

U.S. BUREAU OF LABOR STATISTICS
Current Employment Statistics
https://www.bls.gov/sae/home.htm

Geographic Profile of Employment and Unemployment
https://www.bls.gov/gps/home.htm

State occupational injuries, illnesses, and fatalities
https://www.bls.gov/iif/oshstate.htm

U.S. CENSUS BUREAU
American Community Survey data
https://www.census.gov/programs-surveys/acs/

Annual Survey of Manufactures
https://www.census.gov/programs-surveys/asm.html

Building permits
https://www.census.gov/construction/bps/

County Business Patterns
https://www.census.gov/programs-surveys/cbp.html

Economic Census 2012 data
https://www.census.gov/econ/

Foreign trade
https://www.census.gov/foreign-trade/statistics/state/index.html

Population and Housing unit estimates
https://www.census.gov/programs-surveys/popest.html

State and County QuickFacts profiles

https://www.census.gov/quickfacts/table/PST045216/00
State government finances
https://www.census.gov/govs/state/

State government employment and payroll
https://www.census.gov/govs/apes/

U.S. DEPARTMENT OF AGRICULTURE
Economic Research Service
Agricultural Exports
https://www.ers.usda.gov/data-products/state-export-data/

Farm Income Wealth and Statistics
https://www.ers.usda.gov/data-products/farm-income-and-wealth-statistics/

State Fact Sheets
https://www.ers.usda.gov/StateFacts/ /

National Agricultural Statistics Service
Census of Agriculture
https://www.agcensus.usda.gov/ and

U.S. DEPARTMENT OF HEALTH AND HUMAN SERVICES
Centers for Disease Control and Prevention
Behavioral Risk Factor Surveillance System at
https://www.cdc.gov/brfss/

Fast Stats A to Z at
https://www.cdc.gov/nchs/fastats/

Substance Abuse and Mental Health Services Administration
State-level data at
https://www.samhsa.gov/

ENERGY INFORMATION ADMINISTRATION
Energy consumption
https://www.eia.gov/state/seds/

General state information
https://www.eia.gov/state/

State Electricity Profiles
https://www.eia.gov/state/

**NATIONAL CENTER OF EDUCATION
   STATISTICS**
State Education Data Profiles
https://nces.ed.gov/programs/stateprofiles/

NATIONAL SCIENCE FOUNDATION
Science and Engineering State Profiles
https://www.nsf.gov/statistics/states/

U.S. DEPARTMENT OF TRANSPORTATION
Federal Highway Administration

Highway statistics
https://www.fhwa.dot.gov/policyinformation/statistics.
   cfm

Federal Highway Administration
State traffic safety information
https://www.fhwa.dot.gov/publications/research/
   safety/06099/appendb.cfm

INDEX

ACCIDENTS
Age-adjusted death rates, by cause, 18
ACCOMMODATION AND FOOD SERVICES
States
earnings by industry, 54
employment figures, 86
ADMINISTRATIVE SERVICES
States
earnings by industry, 54
ADULT BINGE DRINKING
Figures by state, 23
ADULT NUTRITION
Figures by state, 23
ADULT OBESITY
Figures by state, 24
ADULT PHYSICAL ACTIVITY
Figures by state, 23
ADULT SMOKING
Figures by state, 23
AFRICAN AMERICANS
Generally
see **RACE**
AGE
Deaths and death rates
age-adjusted death rates, by cause, 18
Marriages and divorces
number and rate, 19
Metropolitan areas
population, by age, 117
Public and private school fall enrollment
figures by state, 26
States
death rates, by cause, 18
population, by age group and sex, 4
population, by households, 10
AGGRAVATED ASSAULT
States
violent crime and crime rates, 30
AGRICULTURE
States
agricultural census, 66
farm finances and income, 63
farm income and wealth statistics, 64
farms and farm earnings, 62
AIDS
States

figures by state, 24
ALABAMA
see **STATES**
ALASKA
see **STATES**
ALASKA NATIVE
Generally
see **RACE**
ALCOHOLIC BEVERAGES
Binge drinking figures by state, 23
AMBULATORY HEALTHCARE SERVICES
States
figures by state, 20
AMERICAN INDIANS
Generally
see **RACE**
AREA AND POPULATION
Metropolitan areas, 103
States, 3, 103
ARIZONA
see **STATES**
ARKANSAS
see **STATES**
ARTS, ENTERTAINMENT, AND RECREATION
States
earnings by industry, 54
employment figures, 86
ASIANS
Generally
see **RACE**

BANKING AND FINANCE
Counties
personal income and earnings by industry, 237
Metropolitan areas
employees and earnings, by selected industries, 175
private business establishments and employment, 187
States
earnings by industry, 54
financial activities, 84
BINGE DRINKING
Figures by state, 23
BIRTHPLACES
States
population, by place of birth, 13
BIRTH RATES

States
  figures by state, 14
  rates, by race and Hispanic origin, 15
BLACK RACE
Generally
    see **RACE**
BRIDGES
States
  number of bridges, 81
BUILDING PERMITS
Metropolitan areas
  housing units and building permits, 157
BURGLARY
States
  crime rates, 31
BUSINESSES
States
  establishment births and deaths, 58

CALIFORNIA
    see **STATES**
CELL PHONES
States
  wireless subscribers, 83
CHILD ABUSE CASES
States, 32
**CHILDREN'S HEALTH INSURANCE PROGRAM
       (CHIP)**
States
  enrollment figure by state, 96
CHILD VACCINATION COVERAGE
Rates by state, 24
CIGARETTE SMOKING
Figures by state, 23
CITIES
    see **METROPOLITAN AREAS**
CIVILIAN LABOR FORCE AND EMPLOYMENT
Metropolitan area figures, 181
State figures, 34, 35
COAL
States
  energy consumption, 69
  energy expenditures, 70
  production figures, 65
COLLEGES AND UNIVERSITIES
Metropolitan areas
  enrollment, teachers, and educational attainment, 138
States
  cost of living indicators, 48
  institutions of higher education, 29
  public high school graduates and educational
      attainment, 28
COLORADO
    see **STATES**
COLORECTAL CANCER SCREENING

Rates by state, 24
COMMUNICATIONS
States
  wireless subscribers, 83
COMMUNITY SUPERVISION
States
  figures by state, 32
COMMUTING
Metropolitan areas
  people living in metropolitan areas, 124
States
  transportation figures, 80
CONGRESS
Composition of Congress and public officials, 100
CONNECTICUT
    see **STATES**
CONSTRUCTION
States
  earnings by industry, 54, 71
  units and characteristics, 45
CORRECTIONS
States
  correctional populations, 32
  justice employment and expenditures, 33
COST OF LIVING INDICATORS
States
  housing, public university, energy expenditures, and
      motor fuels taxes, 48
COUNTIES
Banking and finance
  personal income and earnings by industry, 237
Changes in population characteristics, 195
Earnings
  personal income and earnings by industry, 237
  population and personal income, 283
Employment
  labor force and private establishments and
      employment, 260
Government
  personal income and earnings by industry, 237
Health care services
  personal income and earnings by industry, 237
Hispanic origin
  population characteristics and housing units, 216
Housing
  population characteristics and housing units, 216
Income
  personal income and earnings by industry, 237
  population and personal income, 283
Insurance
  personal income and earnings by industry, 237
Local government
  personal income and earnings by industry, 237
Manufacturing
  personal income and earnings by industry, 237

Population
    housing units and population characteristics, 216
    population and personal income, 283
    population and population characteristics, 195
Professional services
    personal income and earnings by industry, 237
Race
    population characteristics and housing units, 216
Retail trade
    personal income and earnings by industry, 237
Salaries
    personal income and earnings by industry, 237
    population and personal income, 283
Social services
    personal income and earnings by industry, 237
Unemployment
    labor force and private establishments and
        employment, 260
Wages
    personal income and earnings by industry, 237
    population and personal income, 283

CRIMES AND CRIME RATES
States, 30, 32
CROPS
Agriculture generally
    see **AGRICULTURE**
CRUDE OIL
States
    production figures, 65

DEATHS AND DEATH RATES
Age
    age-adjusted death rates, by cause, 18
Hispanic origin
    rates, by Hispanic origin, 16
Race
    rates, by race, 16
States
    age-adjusted death rates, by cause, 18
    by race and Hispanic origin, 16
DEFENSE DEPARTMENT
States
    employment by state, 97
    expenditures by state, 97
DELAWARE
    see **STATES**
DEMOCRATS
States
    composition of Congress and public officials, 100
    votes cast for President, 98
DIABETES
Diagnosis rates by state, 24
DIESEL FUEL
Energy expenditures
    cost of living indicators, 48

DISABILITY BENEFITS
States
    transfer payments to individuals, 95
DISEASE
Age-adjusted death rates, by cause, 18
DISTRICT OF COLUMBIA
    see **STATES**
DIVORCES
States
    number and rate, 19
DRINKING
Figures by state, 23
DRIVERS LICENSES
States
    number of licenses, 81
DRUG ABUSE
States
    youth marijuana use, 23

EARNINGS
Counties
    personal income and earnings by industry, 237
    population and personal income, 283
Federal government, 91
Metropolitan areas
    employees and earnings, by selected industries, 175
    personal income and earnings, by place of work, 169
    population and personal income, 283
States
    farms and farm earnings, 62
    government earnings, 88, 91
    industry earnings, 54
    population and personal income, 283
    wholesale and retail trade, 77, 78
EDUCATION
Metropolitan areas
    educational attainment, 138
    public and private school enrollment, 138
    teachers, number of, 138
States
    earnings by industry, 54
    employment figures, 85
    finances and teachers, 27
    institutions of higher education, 29
    public and private school enrollment, 26
    public high school graduates and educational
        attainment, 28
ELECTIONS
States
    number of voters and votes cast, 98
ELECTRICITY
States
    energy expenditures, 70
ELEMENTARY SCHOOLS
Metropolitan areas

enrollment, teachers, and educational attainment, 138

States

enrollment figures, 26

finances and teachers, 27

EMPLOYMENT

Counties

labor force and private establishments and
employment, 260

Federal government

Defense Department, 97

full-time and part-time employment, 91

Metropolitan areas

civilian labor force, 181

employees and earnings, by selected industries, 175

people living in metropolitan areas, 124

private business establishments and employment, 187

States

agricultural census, 66

arts and recreation, 86

business services, 85

civilian labor force and employment, 34, 35

Defense Department employment by state, 97

education, 85

employed civilians, by occupation, 36

employer firms and nonemployer establishments, 59

establishment births and deaths, 58

food services, 86

government employees, 88

government employees and finances, 89

health care employment, 21, 85

hotels and motels, 86

industry employment and wages, 39

information industries, 76

leisure and hospitality services, 86

manufactures summary and employment, 73

private industry employment and wages, 38

private nonfarm establishments, 60

professional services, 85

science and engineering indicators, 57

transportation figures, 80

union membership, 42

utilities, 68

wholesale and retail trade, 77

ENERGY CONSUMPTION

States, 69

ENERGY EXPENDITURES

Cost of living indicators, 48

State figures, 70

ENGINEERS

States

employment indicators, 57

EXERCISE

Adult and youth physical activity
figures by state, 23

EXPORTS

States

amount of exports by state, 61

manufactures summary and export-related shipments, 73

FACTORIES

States

earnings by industry, 54, 72

export-related shipments and employment, 73

major manufacturing sectors, 74

FAILED BUSINESSES

States

establishment births and deaths, 58

FAMILIES

Metropolitan areas

distribution by income level, 144

median income of households, 144

population characteristics, 131

poverty status, 144

States

income and individuals below poverty, 44

median income of households, 43

FARMS

see **AGRICULTURE**

**FEDERAL EDUCATION AND TRAINING
ASSISTANCE PAYMENTS**

States

transfer payments to individuals, 95

FEDERAL GOVERNMENT

Composition of Congress and public officials, 100

Earnings, 91

Elections

number of voters and votes cast, by state, 98

Employment

Defense Department, 97

full-time and part-time employment, 91

Food stamps, by state, 93

Income taxes

returns by state, 92

Metropolitan areas

government employment, 187

Social Security and SSI, 150

Real estate, 92

School lunch programs, by state, 93

Social Security, by metropolitan area, 150

Social Security, by state, 93

States

Defense Department employment by state, 97

earnings by industry, 54, 91

employment figures, 88

farm income and wealth statistics, 64

individual income tax returns, 92

Medicare, Medicaid, and Children's Health Insurance
Program, 96

tax collections, 88

transfer payments to individuals, 95

FERTILITY RATES
States
rates, by race and Hispanic origin, 15
FINANCIAL SERVICES
see **BANKING AND FINANCE**
FLORIDA
see **STATES**
FOOD SERVICES
States
earnings by industry, 54
employment figures, 86
FOOD STAMPS
States
recipients by state, 93
FOREIGN-BORN POPULATION
Metropolitan areas, 131
FOREIGN COUNTRIES
Place of birth
see **PLACE OF BIRTH**
FOREIGN DIRECT INVESTMENT
States
figures by state, 61

GAS AND OIL EXTRACTION
States
earnings by state, 54
GASOLINE
Energy expenditures
cost of living indicators, 48
state figures, 70
States
energy consumption, 69
energy expenditures, 70
GEORGIA
see **STATES**
GOVERNMENT
Counties
personal income and earnings by industry, 237
Metropolitan areas
employees and earnings, by selected industries, 175
government employment, 187
States
employees and finances, 89
state tax collections, 90
GRADUATE SCHOOLS
Metropolitan areas
enrollment, teachers, and educational attainment, 138
States
institutions of higher education, 29
public high school graduates and educational
attainment, 28
GROSS DOMESTIC PRODUCT
States, 56
GROSS RECEIPTS TAXES
State government tax collections, 90

HAWAII
see **STATES**
HEALTH CARE SERVICES
Counties
personal income and earnings by industry, 237
Metropolitan areas
employees and earnings, by selected industries, 175
States
earnings by industry, 54
employment figures, 85
figures by state, 20, 21
**HEALTH CONDITIONS AND PREVENTATIVE
MEASURES**
States
figures by state, 24
HEALTH INSURANCE
Metropolitan areas
figures by city, 150
States
Children's Health Insurance Program (CHIP), 96
figures by state, 21
people with and without health insurance coverage, 25
HEALTH RISKS
States
figures by state, 23
HEALTH TECHNOLOGISTS AND TECHNICIANS
States
figures by state, 21
HEATING OIL
Energy expenditures
cost of living indicators, 48
HIGH CHOLESTEROL
Diagnosis rates by state, 24
HIGH SCHOOLS
Metropolitan areas
enrollment, teachers, and educational attainment, 138
States
enrollment figures, 26
finances and teachers, 27
public high school graduates and educational
attainment, 28
HIGHWAYS
States
mileage figures, 81
traffic fatalities and seat belt use, 82
HISPANIC ORIGIN
Counties
population characteristics and housing units, 216
Metropolitan areas
population, by Hispanic origin, 117
States
births and birth rates, by Hispanic origin, 15
deaths and death rates, by Hispanic origin, 16
population, by race and Hispanic origin, 6
HIV DIAGNOSIS RATES

States
  figures by state, 24
HOMICIDE
States
  violent crime and crime rates, 30
HOSPITALS
States
  figures by state, 20
HOTELS AND MOTELS
States
  earnings by industry, 54
  employment figures, 86
HOUSEHOLDS
Metropolitan areas
  distribution by income level, 144
  median income of households, 144
  population characteristics, 131
  poverty status, 144
States
  distribution by income level, 43
  family income and individuals below poverty, 44
  median income of households, 43
  population, by households, 10
HOUSE OF REPRESENTATIVES
Composition of Congress and public officials, 100
HOUSING
Counties
  population characteristics and housing units, 216
Metropolitan areas
  housing units and building permits, 157
  mortgages, 163
  number of units, 163
  owner- and renter-occupied units, 163
  units and characteristics, 163
States
  cost of living indicators, 48
  earnings by industry, 54, 71
  home ownership and vacancy rates, 47
  mortgages, 46
  owner- and renter-occupied units, 46
  units and characteristics, 45
  values and gross rents, 46
HYDROELECTRIC POWER
States
  energy consumption, 69
HYPERTENSION
Diagnosis rates by state, 24

IDAHO
  see **STATES**
ILLINOIS
  see **STATES**
IMMUNIZATIONS
States

figures by state, 24
INCOME
Counties
  personal income and earnings by industry, 237
  population and personal income, 283
Metropolitan areas
  distribution of income, 144
  household income, 144
  personal income and earnings, by place of
      work, 169
  population and personal income, 283
  poverty status, 144
States
  adjusted gross incomes by state, 92
  family income and individuals below poverty, 44
  farm finances and income, 63
  farms and farm earnings, 62
  median income of households, 43
  personal income, 50
  personal income per capita, 52
  population and personal income, 283
INCOME MAINTENANCE BENEFITS
States
  transfer payments to individuals, 95
INCOME TAXES
Federal government
  returns by state, 92
INDIANA
  see **STATES**
INDUSTRY
States
  earnings by industry, 54
INFLUENZA VACCINATION COVERAGE
Rates by state, 24
INFORMATION INDUSTRIES
States
  earnings by industry, 54
  employment figures, 76
INSURANCE
Counties
  personal income and earnings by industry, 237
Metropolitan areas
  employees and earnings, by selected industries, 175
  health insurance, 150
States
  earnings by industry, 54
  financial activities, 84
  health insurance, 25
INTERNET
States
  access to Internet, 83
INVESTMENTS
States
  foreign direct investment by state, 61

IOWA
>*see* **STATES**

JAILS
States
>number of persons in local jails, 32

JUSTICE EMPLOYMENT AND EXPENDITURES
Local government, 33
States, 33

JUVENILE ARRESTS
States, 32

KANSAS
>*see* **STATES**

KENTUCKY
>*see* **STATES**

KINDERGARTENS
Metropolitan areas
>enrollment, teachers, and educational attainment, 138
States
>enrollment figures, 26
>finances and teachers, 27

LABOR UNIONS
States
>membership figures, 42

LANGUAGE SPOKEN AT HOME
Metropolitan areas
>population characteristics, 131
States
>population of states, by language spoken, 12

LARCENY
States
>crime rates, 31

LATINOS
>*see* **HISPANIC ORIGIN**

LEASING
States
>earnings by industry, 54

LEGAL PERMANENT RESIDENT STATUS
States
>population of states by, 12

LEISURE AND HOSPITALITY SERVICES
States
>employment figures, 86

LIVE BIRTHS
States
>rates, by race and Hispanic origin, 15
>rates by state, 14

LIVESTOCK
Agriculture generally
>*see* **AGRICULTURE**

LOCAL GOVERNMENT
Counties

>personal income and earnings by industry, 237
Justice employment and expenditures, 33
Metropolitan areas
>employees and earnings, by selected industries, 175
>government employment, 187
States
>earnings by industry, 54
>employment figures, 88
>government employees and finances, 89
>state government tax collections, 90

LOUISIANA
>*see* **STATES**

MAINE
>*see* **STATES**

MANUFACTURING
Counties
>personal income and earnings by industry, 237
Metropolitan areas
>employees and earnings, by selected industries, 175
States
>earnings by industry, 54, 72
>export-related shipments and employment, 73
>major manufacturing sectors, 74

MARIJUANA
Youth marijuana use, 23

MARITAL STATUS
States
>population, by marital status, 11

MARKETING
States
>farm income and wealth statistics, 64

MARRIAGES
States
>number and rate, 19

MARYLAND
>*see* **STATES**

MASSACHUSETTS
>*see* **STATES**

MEDICAID
States
>enrollment figure by state, 96
>figures by state, 21

MEDICAL PAYMENTS
States
>transfer payments to individuals, 95

MEDICARE
Metropolitan areas
>figures by city, 150
States
>enrollment figures by state, 96
>figures by state, 21

METROPOLITAN AREAS
Age

population, by age, 117
Area and population, 103
Banking and finance
    employees and earnings, by selected industries, 175
    private business establishments and employment, 187
Building permits
    housing units and building permits, 157
Civilian labor force, 181
Colleges and universities
    enrollment, teachers, and educational attainment, 138
Commuting
    people living in metropolitan areas, 124
Components of population change, 110
Counties
        see COUNTIES
Earnings
    employees and earnings, by selected industries, 175
    personal income and earnings, by place of work, 169
    population and personal income, 283
Education
    educational attainment, 138
    public and private school enrollment, 138
    teachers, number of, 138
Elementary schools
    enrollment, teachers, and educational attainment, 138
Employment
    civilian labor force, 181
    employees and earnings, by selected industries, 175
    people living in metropolitan areas, 124
    private business establishments and employment, 187
Families
    distribution by income level, 144
    median income of households, 144
    population characteristics, 131
    poverty status, 144
Federal government
    government employment, 187
    Social Security and SSI, 150
Foreign-born population, 131
Government
    employees and earnings, by selected industries, 175
    government employment, 187
Graduate schools
    enrollment, teachers, and educational attainment, 138
Health care services
    employees and earnings, by selected industries, 175
Health insurance
    figures by city, 150
High schools
    enrollment, teachers, and educational attainment, 138
Hispanic origin
    population, by Hispanic origin, 117
Households
    distribution by income level, 144

median income of households, 144
    population characteristics, 131
    poverty status, 144
Housing
    housing units and building permits, 157
    mortgages, 163
    number of units, 163
    owner- and renter-occupied units, 163
    units and characteristics, 163
Income
    distribution of income, 144
    household income, 144
    personal income and earnings, by place of work, 169
    population and personal income, 283
    poverty status, 144
Insurance
    employees and earnings, by selected industries, 175
    health insurance, 150
Kindergartens
    enrollment, teachers, and educational attainment, 138
Language spoken at home
    population characteristics, 131
Local government
    employees and earnings, by selected industries, 175
    government employment, 187
Manufacturing
    employees and earnings, by selected industries, 175
Medicare
    figures by city, 150
Migration
    people living in metropolitan areas, 124
Nursery schools
    enrollment, teachers, and educational attainment, 138
Personal income, 169
Personal income per capita, 169
Population
    components of population change, 110
Poverty
    median income and poverty status, 144
Private schools
    enrollment, teachers, and educational attainment, 138
Professional services
    employees and earnings, by selected industries, 175
Public schools
    enrollment, teachers, and educational attainment, 138
Race
    population, by race, 117
Salaries
    employees and earnings, by selected industries, 175
    household income distribution and poverty status, 144
    personal income and earnings, by place of work, 169
    population and personal income, 283
Secondary schools
    enrollment, teachers, and educational attainment, 138

Social Security
    figures by city, 150
Social services
    employees and earnings, by selected industries, 175
Supplemental Security Income (SSI)
    recipients by city, 150
Teachers
    enrollment, teachers, and educational attainment, 138
Unemployment
    civilian labor force, 181
Wages
    employees and earnings, by selected industries, 175
    household income distribution and poverty status, 144
    personal income and earnings, by place of work, 169
    population and personal income, 283
MICHIGAN
    see STATES
MIGRATION
Metropolitan areas
    people living in metropolitan areas, 124
MILITARY
States
    Defense Department employees by state, 97
    earnings by industry, 54
    expenditures by state, 91
MINING
States
    earnings by industry, 54
    natural resource industries and minerals, 65
MINNESOTA
    see STATES
MINORS
States
    juvenile arrests, 32
MISSISSIPPI
    see STATES
MISSOURI
    see STATES
MONTANA
    see STATES
MORTGAGES
Owner-occupied units, 46, 163
MOTORCYCLES
States
    registration figures, 81
MOTOR FUELS TAXES
Cost of living indicators, 48
MOTOR VEHICLES
States
    registration figures, 81
    traffic fatalities and seat belt use, 82
MOTOR VEHICLE THEFT
States
    crime rates, 31

MURDER
States
    violent crime and crime rates, 30

NATIONAL PARKS
States
    travel and tourism, 87
NATIVE HAWAIIANS
Generally
        see RACE
NATURAL GAS
States
    energy consumption, 69
    energy expenditures, 70
    production figures, 65
NATURAL RESOURCE INDUSTRIES
States, 65
NEBRASKA
    see STATES
NEVADA
    see STATES
NEW BUSINESSES
States
    establishment births and deaths, 58
NEW HAMPSHIRE
    see STATES
NEW JERSEY
    see STATES
NEW MEXICO
    see STATES
NEW YORK
    see STATES
NORTH CAROLINA
    see STATES
NORTH DAKOTA
    see STATES
NUCLEAR POWER
States
    energy consumption, 69
NURSERY SCHOOLS
Metropolitan areas
    enrollment, teachers, and educational attainment, 138
States
    enrollment figures, 26
    finances and teachers, 27
NURSES
States
    figures by state, 20, 21
NURSING CARE FACILITIES
States
    figures by state, 20
NUTRITION
Figures by state, 23

OBESITY
Adult obesity rates by state, 24
OCCUPATIONS
States
employed civilians, by occupation, 36
industry employment and wages, 39
private industry employment and wages, 38
OHIO
see **STATES**
OKLAHOMA
see **STATES**
OREGON
see **STATES**
OWNER-OCCUPIED UNITS
Mortgages, 46, 163
Values and gross rents, 46, 163

PACIFIC ISLANDERS
Generally
see **RACE**
PAYROLLS
States
employer firms and nonemployer establishments, 59
natural resource industries, 65
private nonfarm establishments, 60
utility companies, 68
PENNSYLVANIA
see **STATES**
PERMANENT RESIDENT STATUS
State populations by, 12
PERSONAL INCOME
Counties, 237
Metropolitan areas, 169
States, 50
PERSONAL INCOME PER CAPITA
Metropolitan areas, 169
States, 52
PETROLEUM
States
energy consumption, 69
energy expenditures, 70
PHYSICIANS AND SURGEONS
States
figures by state, 20, 21
PLACE OF BIRTH
States
population, by place of birth, 13
POLICE OFFICERS
States
justice employment and expenditures, 33
POPULATION
Age
death rates, by cause, 18
population of metropolitan areas by age, 117

population of states, by age group and sex, 4
Birthplaces
state population, by place of birth, 13
Birth rates
figures by state, 14
rates, by race and Hispanic origin, 15
Civilian labor force and employment, 34, 35, 181
Components of population change, 110
Counties
population and personal income, 283
population and population characteristics, 195
Deaths and death rates
age-adjusted death rates, by cause, 18
by race and Hispanic origin, 16
Divorces
number and rate, 19
Education
finances and teachers, 27
institutions of higher education, 29
public and private school fall enrollment, 26
public high school graduates and educational
attainment, 28
Employment
civilian labor force and employment, 34, 35
employed civilians, by occupation, 36
health care employment, 21
industry employment and wages, 39
private industry employment and wages, 38
union membership, 42
Foreign-born population, 131
Health care employment
figures by state, 21
Health care services
figures by state, 20, 21
Health insurance
figures by state, 21
people with and without health insurance coverage, 25
Health risks
figures by state, 23
Health technologists and technicians
figures by state, 21
Hispanic origin
births and birth rates, by Hispanic origin, 15
deaths and death rates, by Hispanic origin, 16
population of metropolitan areas by Hispanic origin,
117
population of states, by race and Hispanic origin, 6
Hospitals
figures by state, 20
Households
metropolitan area populations by households, 131
state population, by households, 10
Income
see **INCOME**

Insurance
  health insurance, 25
Juvenile arrests, child abuse cases, and prisoners, 32
Language spoken at home
  metropolitan areas by language spoken, 131
  state population, by language spoken, 12
Legal permanent resident status
  population of states by, 12
Live births
  rates, by race and Hispanic origin, 15
  rates by state, 14
Marital status
  state population, by marital status, 11
Marriages
  number and rate, 19
Metropolitan areas
      see **METROPOLITAN AREAS**
Nurses
  figures by state, 20, 21
Nursing care facilities
  figures by state, 20
Physicians
  figures by state, 20, 21
Place of birth
  state population, by place of birth, 13
Property crimes and crime rates, 31
Race
  births and birth rates, by race, 15
  deaths and death rates, by race, 16
  population of metropolitan areas by race, 117
  population of states, by race and Hispanic origin, 6
Registered nurses
  figures by state, 20, 21
Residence
  state population, by residence, 9, 12
Residential care facilities
  figures by state, 20
Sex
  population of states, by age group and sex, 4
Social services
  figures by state, 20
States
      see **STATES**
Unemployment
  civilian labor force and unemployment, 35
Violent crimes and crime rates, 30, 32
POVERTY
Metropolitan areas
  median income and poverty status, 144
States
  family income and individuals below poverty, 44
PRESIDENTIAL ELECTION
States
  number of voters and votes cast, 98

PRISONERS
States, 32
PRISONS
States
  number of persons in prison, 32
PRIVATE SCHOOLS
Metropolitan areas
  enrollment, teachers, and educational attainment, 138
States
  enrollment figures, 26
  finances and teachers, 27
PROBATION AND PAROLE
States
  figures by state, 32
PROFESSIONAL SERVICES
Counties
  personal income and earnings by industry, 237
Metropolitan areas
  employees and earnings, by selected industries, 175
States
  earnings by industry, 54
  employment figures, 85
PROFESSIONS
States
  employed civilians, by occupation, 36
PROPERTY CRIMES AND CRIME RATES
States, 31
PUBLIC SCHOOLS
Metropolitan areas
  enrollment, teachers, and educational attainment, 138
States
  enrollment figures, 26
  finances and teachers, 27
  high school graduates and educational attainment, 28
PUBLIC UTILITIES
      see **UTILITIES**

RACE
Counties
  population characteristics and housing units, 216
Metropolitan areas
  population, by race, 117
States
  births and birth rates, by race, 15
  deaths and death rates, by race, 16
  population, by race and Hispanic origin, 6
RAPE
States
  violent crimes and crime rates, 30
REAL ESTATE
Federal government, 92
States
  earnings by industry, 54
REGISTERED NURSES

States
   figures by state, 20, 21
REMEDIATION SERVICES
States
   earnings by industry, 54
RENTER-OCCUPIED UNITS
Vacancy rates, 47
Values and gross rents, 46, 163
REPUBLICANS
States
   composition of Congress and public officials, 100
   votes cast for President, 98
RESEARCH AND DEVELOPMENT
States
   science and engineering indicators, 57
RESIDENCE
States
   population, by residence, 9, 12
RESIDENTIAL CARE FACILITIES
States
   figures by state, 20
RETAIL TRADE
Counties
   personal income and earnings by industry, 237
States
   earnings by industry, 54
   employment and earnings, 77, 78
RETIREMENT BENEFITS
States
   transfer payments to individuals, 95
RHODE ISLAND
      see **STATES**
ROBBERY
States
   violent crime and crime rates, 30

SALARIES
Counties
   personal income and earnings by industry, 237
   population and personal income, 283
Metropolitan areas
   employees and earnings, by selected industries, 175
   household income distribution and poverty status, 144
   personal income and earnings, by place of work, 169
   population and personal income, 283
States
   family income and individuals below poverty, 44
   industry employment and wages, 39
   median income of households, 43
   population and personal income, 283
   private industry employment and wages, 38
SALES TAXES
State government tax collections, 90
SCHOOL LUNCH PROGRAMS

States
   recipients by state, 93
SCIENTISTS
States
   employment indicators, 57
SEAT BELT USE
Figures by state, 23, 82
SECONDARY SCHOOLS
Metropolitan areas
   enrollment, teachers, and educational attainment, 138
States
   enrollment figures, 26
   finances and teachers, 27
SENATE
Composition of Congress and public officials, 100
SEX
States
   population, by age group and sex, 4
SMOKING
Figures by state, 23
SOCIAL INSURANCE PROGRAMS
States
   recipients by state, 94
SOCIAL SECURITY
Metropolitan areas
   figures by city, 150
States
   recipients by state, 93
SOCIAL SERVICES
Counties
   personal income and earnings by industry, 237
Metropolitan areas
   employees and earnings, by selected industries, 175
States
   earnings by industry, 54
   figures by state, 20
SOUTH CAROLINA
      see **STATES**
SOUTH DAKOTA
      see **STATES**
STATE PARKS
States
   travel and tourism, 87
STATES
Accommodation and food services
   earnings by industry, 54
   employment figures, 86
Administrative services
   earnings by industry, 54
Age
   death rates, by cause, 18
   population, by age group and sex, 4
   population, by households, 10
Aggravated assault

violent crime and crime rates, 30
Agriculture
    agricultural census, 66
    farm finances and income, 63
    farm income and wealth statistics, 64
    farms and farm earnings, 62
AIDS
    figures by state, 24
Ambulatory healthcare services
    figures by state, 20
Area and population, 3, 103
Arts, entertainment, and recreation
    earnings by industry, 54
    employment figures, 86
Banking and finance
    earnings by industry, 54
    financial activities, 84
Birthplaces
    population, by place of birth, 13
Birth rates
    figures by state, 14
    rates, by race and Hispanic origin, 15
Bridges
    number of bridges, 81
Burglary
    crime rates, 31
Businesses
    employment figures, 85
    establishment births and deaths, 58
Cell phones
    wireless subscribers, 83
Child abuse cases, 32
Children's Health Insurance Program (CHIP)
    enrollment figure by state, 96
Civilian labor force and employment, 34, 35
Coal
    energy consumption, 69
    energy expenditures, 70
    production figures, 65
Colleges and universities
    cost of living indicators, 48
    institutions of higher education, 29
    public high school graduates and educational
        attainment, 28
Communications
    wireless subscribers, 83
Community supervision
    figures by state, 32
Commuting
    transportation figures, 80
Construction
    earnings by industry, 54, 71
    units and characteristics, 45
Corrections

correctional populations, 32
    justice employment and expenditures, 33
Cost of living indicators
    housing, public university, energy expenditures, and
        sales taxes, 48
Crimes and crime rates, 30, 31, 32
Crude oil
    production figures, 65
Deaths and death rates
    age-adjusted death rates, by cause, 18
    by race and Hispanic origin, 16
Defense Department
    employment by state, 97
    expenditures by state, 97
Democrats
    composition of Congress and public officials, 100
    votes cast for President, 98
Disability benefits
    transfer payments to individuals, 95
Divorces
    number and rate, 19
Drivers licenses
    number of licenses, 81
Earnings
    farms and farm earnings, 62
    government earnings, 88, 91
    industry earnings, 54
    population and personal income, 283
    wholesale and retail trade, 77, 78
Education
    earnings by industry, 54
    employment figures, 85
    finances and teachers, 27
    institutions of higher education, 29
    public and private school enrollment, 26
    public high school graduates and educational
        attainment, 28
Elections
    number of voters and votes cast, 98
Electricity
    energy expenditures, 70
Elementary schools
    enrollment figures, 26
    finances and teachers, 27
Employment
    agricultural census, 66
    arts and recreation, 86
    business services, 85
    civilian labor force and employment, 34, 35
    Defense Department employment by state, 97
    education, 85
    employed civilians, by occupation, 36
    employer firms and nonemployer establishments, 59
    establishment births and deaths, 58

food services, 86
government employees, 88
government employees and finances, 89
health care employment, 21, 85
hotels and motels, 86
industry employment and wages, 39
information industries, 76
leisure and hospitality services, 86
manufactures summary and employment, 73
private industry employment and wages, 38
private nonfarm establishments, 60
professional services, 85
science and engineering indicators, 57
transportation figures, 80
union membership, 42
utilities, 68
wholesale and retail trade, 77
Energy consumption, 69
Energy expenditures, 69
Engineers
employment indicators, 57
Exports
amount of exports by state, 61
manufactures summary and export-related shipments, 73
Factories
earnings by industry, 54, 72
export-related shipments and employment, 73
major manufacturing sectors, 74
Failed businesses
establishment births and deaths, 58
Families
income and individuals below poverty, 44
median income of households, 43
Farm finances and income, 63
Farms and farm earnings, 62
Federal education and training assistance payments
transfer payments to individuals, 95
Federal government
Defense Department employment by state, 97
earnings by industry, 54, 91
employment figures, 88
farm income and wealth statistics, 64
individual income tax returns, 92
Medicare, Medicaid, and Children's Health Insurance Program, 96
tax collections, 88
transfer payments to individuals, 95
Fertility rates
rates, by race and Hispanic origin, 15
Financial services
earnings by industry, 54
Food services
earnings by industry, 54

employment figures, 86
Food stamps
recipients by state, 93
Foreign direct investment
figures by state, 61
Gas and oil extraction
earnings by state, 54
Gasoline
energy consumption, 69
energy expenditures, 70
Government
employees and finances, 89
state tax collections, 90
Graduate schools
institutions of higher education, 29
public high school graduates and educational attainment, 28
Gross domestic product, 56
Gross receipts taxes
state government tax collections, 90
Health care employment
figures by state, 21
Health care services
earnings by industry, 54
figures by state, 20, 21
Health conditions and preventative measures
figures by state, 24
Health insurance
Children's Health Insurance Program (CHIP), 96
figures by state, 21
people with and without health insurance coverage, 25
Health risks
figures by state, 23
Health technologists and technicians
figures by state, 21
High schools
enrollment figures, 26
finances and teachers, 27
public high school graduates and educational attainment, 28
Highways
mileage figures, 81
traffic fatalities and seat belt use, 82
Hispanic origin
births and birth rates, by Hispanic origin, 15
deaths and death rates, by Hispanic origin, 16
population, by race and Hispanic origin, 6
HIV diagnosis rates
figures by state, 24
Homicide
violent crime and crime rates, 30
Hospitals
figures by state, 21
Hotels and motels

earnings by industry, 54
employment figures, 86

Households
distribution by income level, 43
family income and individuals below poverty, 44
median income of households, 43
population, by households, 10

Housing
cost of living indicators, 48
earnings by industry, 54, 71
home ownership and vacancy rates, 47
mortgages, 46
owner- and renter-occupied units, 46
units and characteristics, 45
values and gross rents, 46

Hydroelectric power
energy consumption, 69

Immunizations
figures by state, 24

Income
adjusted gross incomes by state, 92
farm finances and income, 63
farms and farm earnings, 62
median income of households, 43
personal income, 50
personal income per capita, 52
population and personal income, 283

Income maintenance benefits
transfer payments to individuals, 95

Income taxes
Federal individual income tax returns, 92

Industry
earnings by industry, 54

Information industries
earnings by industry, 54
employment figures, 76

Insurance
earnings by industry, 54
financial activities, 84
health insurance, 25

Internet
access to Internet, 83

Investments
foreign direct investment by state, 61

Jails
number of persons in local jails, 32

Justice employment and expenditures, 33

Juvenile arrests, 32

Kindergartens
enrollment figures, 26
finances and teachers, 27

Labor unions
membership figures, 42

Language spoken at home

population of states, by language spoken, 12

Larceny
crime rates, 31

Leasing
earnings by industry, 54

Legal permanent resident status
population of states by, 12

Leisure and hospitality services
employment figures, 86

Live births
rates, by race and Hispanic origin, 15
rates by state, 14

Local government
earnings by industry, 54
employment figures, 88
government employees and finances, 89
state government tax collections, 90

Manufacturing
earnings by industry, 54
export-related shipments and employment, 73
major manufacturing sectors, 74

Marital status
population, by marital status, 11

Marketing
farm income and wealth statistics, 64

Marriages
number and rate, 19

Medicaid
enrollment figure by state, 96
figures by state, 21

Medical payments
transfer payments to individuals, 95

Medicare
enrollment figures by state, 96
figures by state, 21

Metropolitan areas
see **METROPOLITAN AREAS**

Military
Defense Department employees by state, 97
earnings by industry, 54
expenditures by state, 91

Mining
earnings by industry, 54
natural resource industries and minerals, 65

Minors
juvenile arrests, 32

Motorcycles
registration figures, 81

Motor vehicles
registration figures, 81
traffic fatalities and seat belt use, 82

Motor vehicle theft
crime rates, 31

Murder

violent crime and crime rates, 30
National parks
   travel and tourism, 87
Natural gas
   energy consumption, 69
   energy expenditures, 70
   production figures, 65
Natural resource industries, 65
New businesses
   establishment births and deaths, 58
Nuclear power
   energy consumption, 69
Nursery schools
   enrollment figures, 26
   finances and teachers, 27
Nurses
   figures by state, 20, 21
Nursing homes
   figures by state, 21
Occupations
   employed civilians, by occupation, 36
   industry employment and wages, 39
   private industry employment and wages, 38
Personal income, 50
Personal income per capita, 52
Petroleum
   energy consumption, 69
   energy expenditures, 70
Physicians
   figures by state, 20, 21
Place of birth
   population, by place of birth, 13
Police officers
   justice employment and expenditures, 33
Population
   by age group and sex, 4
   by area, 3, 103
   by households, 10
   by marital status, 11
   by race and Hispanic origin, 6
   by residence, 9, 12
   previous year's population, 12
Poverty
   family income and individuals below poverty, 44
Presidential election
   number of voters and votes cast, 98
Prisoners, 32
Prisons
   number of persons in prison, 32
Private schools
   enrollment figures, 26
   finances and teachers, 27
Probation and parole
   figures by state, 32

Professional services
   earnings by industry, 54
   employment figures, 85
Professions
   employed civilians, by occupation, 36
Property crimes and crime rates, 31
Public schools
   enrollment figures, 26
   finances and teachers, 27
   high school graduates and educational attainment, 28
Race
   births and birth rates, by race, 15
   deaths and death rates, by race, 16
   population, by race and Hispanic origin, 6
Rape
   violent crimes and crime rates, 30
Real estate
   earnings by industry, 54
Registered nurses
   figures by state, 20, 21
Remediation services
   earnings by industry, 54
Republicans
   composition of Congress and public officials, 100
   votes cast for President, 98
Research and development
   science and engineering indicators, 57
Residence
   population, by residence, 9, 12
Residential care facilities
   figures by state, 20
Retail trade
   earnings by industry, 54
   employment and earnings, 77, 78
Retirement benefits
   transfer payments to individuals, 95
Robbery
   violent crime and crime rates, 30
Salaries
   family income and individuals below poverty, 44
   industry employment and wages, 39
   median income of households, 43
   population and personal income, 283
   private industry employment and wages, 38
School lunch programs
   recipients by state, 93
Scientists
   employment indicators, 57
Seat belt use, 82
Secondary schools
   enrollment figures, 26
   finances and teachers, 27
Sex
   population, by age group and sex, 4

Social insurance programs
    recipients by state, 94
Social Security
    recipients by state, 93
Social services
    earnings by industry, 54
    figures by state, 20
State parks
    travel and tourism, 87
Supplemental security income (SSI)
    recipients by state, 94
Taxation
    Federal individual income tax returns, 92
    tax collections, by state, 88, 90
Teachers
    finances and teachers, 27
Telecommunications
    revenue figures, 83
Temporary Assistance for Needy Families (TANF)
    recipients by state, 94
Traffic fatalities, 82
Transfer payments to individuals
    recipients by state, 95
Transportation
    earnings by industry, 54
    employment figures, 80
Travel and tourism
    indicators and figures, 87
TRICARE
    figures by state, 21
Trucks
    registration figures, 81
Unemployment
    civilian labor force and unemployment, 35
Unemployment benefits
    transfer payments to individuals, 95
Unemployment insurance
    recipients by state, 94
Unions
    membership figures, 42
Utilities
    earnings by industry, 54
    energy expenditures by state, 48
    payrolls and employment, 68
Vaccinations
    figures by state, 24
Veterans
    number of veterans by state, 97
Veterans benefits
    transfer payments to individuals, 95
Violent crimes and crime rates, 30, 32
Warehousing
    earnings by industry, 54
Waste services

    earnings by industry, 54
Wholesale trade
    earnings by industry, 54
    employment and earnings, 77, 78
Wireless communications
    wireless subscribers, 83
Workers' compensation
    recipients by state, 94
SUICIDE
    Age-adjusted death rates, by cause, 18
SUPPLEMENTAL SECURITY INCOME (SSI)
    Metropolitan areas
        recipients by city, 150
    States
        recipients by state, 94

TAXATION
    Federal tax collections, by state, 88
    Sales taxes
        cost of living indicators, 48
    States
        Federal individual income tax returns, 92
        tax collections, by state, 88, 90
TEACHERS
    Metropolitan areas
        enrollment, teachers, and educational attainment, 138
    States
        finances and teachers, 27
TELECOMMUNICATIONS
    States
        revenue figures, 83
TEMPORARY ASSISTANCE FOR NEEDY FAMILIES (TANF)
    States
        recipients by state, 94
TENNESSEE
        see STATES
TEXAS
        see STATES
TRAFFIC FATALITIES
    States, 82
TRANSFER PAYMENTS TO INDIVIDUALS
    States
        recipients by state, 95
TRANSPORTATION
    States
        earnings by industry, 54
        employment figures, 80
TRAVEL AND TOURISM
    States
        indicators and figures, 87
TRICARE
    States
        figures by state, 21

TRUCKS
States
registration figures, 81

UNEMPLOYMENT
Counties
labor force and private establishments and
employment, 260
Metropolitan areas
civilian labor force, 181
States
civilian labor force and unemployment, 35
UNEMPLOYMENT BENEFITS
States
transfer payments to individuals, 95
UNEMPLOYMENT INSURANCE
States
recipients by state, 94
UNIONS
States
membership figures, 42
UNIVERSITIES
see **COLLEGES AND UNIVERSITIES**
UTAH
see **STATES**
UTILITIES
States
earnings by industry, 54
energy expenditures by state, 48
payrolls and employment, 68

VACANCY RATES
Home ownership and vacancy rates, 47
VACCINATIONS
Coverage by state, 24
States
figures by state, 24
VERMONT
see **STATES**
VETERANS
States
number of veterans by state, 97
VETERANS BENEFITS
States
transfer payments to individuals, 95
VIOLENT CRIMES AND CRIME RATES
States, 30, 32
VIRGINIA
see **STATES**
VISA WAIVER
Travel and tourism, 87

WAGES
Counties
personal income and earnings by industry, 237

population and personal income, 283
Metropolitan areas
employees and earnings, by selected industries, 175
household income distribution and poverty status,
144
personal income and earnings, by place of work, 169
population and personal income, 283
States
family income and individuals below poverty, 44
industry employment and wages, 39
median income of households, 43
population and personal income, 283
private industry employment and wages, 38
WAREHOUSING
States
earnings by industry, 54
WASHINGTON
see **STATES**
WASTE SERVICES
States
earnings by industry, 54
WEIGHT
Overweight and obesity figures by state, 23
WEST VIRGINIA
see **STATES**
WHITE RACE
Generally
see **RACE**
WHOLESALE TRADE
States
earnings by industry, 54
employment and earnings, 77, 78
WIRELESS COMMUNICATIONS
States
wireless subscribers, 83
WISCONSIN
see **STATES**
WORKERS' COMPENSATION
States
recipients by state, 94
WYOMING
see **STATES**

YOUTH BINGE DRINKING
Figures by state, 23
YOUTH NUTRITION
Figures by state, 23
YOUTH OBESITY
Figures by state, 24
YOUTH PHYSICAL ACTIVITY
Figures by state, 23
YOUTH SEALT BELT USE
Figures by state, 23
YOUTH SMOKING
Figures by state, 23